CORPORATE FINANCE

CORPORATE FINANCE

FIFTH EUROPEAN EDITION

David Hillier,
Stephen Ross,
Randolph Westerfield,
Jeffrey Jaffe,
Bradford Jordan

Corporate Finance, 5th European Edition
David Hillier, Stephen Ross, Randolph Westerfield, Jeffrey Jaffe, Bradford Jordan
ISBN-13 9781526849915
ISBN-10 1526849917

Published by McGraw-Hill Education (UK) Limited
Unit 4, Foundation Park,
Roxborough Way,
Maidenhead SL6 3UD
T: +44 (0) 1628 502500
Website: www.mheducation.co.uk

British Library Cataloguing in Publication Data
A catalogue record for this book is available from the British Library

Portfolio Manager: Felicity Baines
Content Developer: Jo O'Neill
Content Product Manager: Ali Davis
Marketing Manager: Ros Letellier

Text design by Kamae Design
Cover design by Adam Renvoize

ISBN-13 9781526849915
ISBN-10 1526849917
eISBN-13 9781526849922

G11248 ACL 2025

Dedication

To Mary-Jo

Brief Table of Contents

Detailed Table of Contents

Preface

This is the fifth edition of *Corporate Finance: European Edition*, and the book has evolved significantly since it was first published in 2008. Each version has been deeply influenced by unexpected global occurrences. From the 2008 global financial crisis, through the advent of artificial intelligence, to the recent challenges posed by the global pandemic, war in Europe and climate change, *Corporate Finance* has continuously adapted. Financial managers today grapple with scenarios that would have seemed unimaginable when the first edition was released. We now witness Western countries with high inflation, climate change impacting all aspects of business operations, increasing complexities in international trade due to barriers, taxes and tariffs, and a surge in technology, cryptocurrencies, artificial intelligence and automation.

I began teaching finance courses in 1994, transitioning from a tutorial assistant in small-group classes for master's and undergraduate classes to lecturing in vast auditoriums accommodating several hundred attendees. In the last decade, my interactions with corporate executives and top-tier managers have intensified. Such experiences have been instrumental in refining the content of this book, ensuring its relevance to contemporary organizations and finance professionals. My collaborations with large multinationals, family-run businesses and social enterprises in the last few years have significantly influenced my perspective on finance and, in particular, sustainability. As a result, the practicality and applicability of the topics covered in *Corporate Finance* have been enhanced.

Now, the principles and applications of corporate finance are more crucial than ever, guiding organizations (both profit-driven and non-profit) through these unprecedented times. This edition features extensive updates across all chapters, new real-world examples for each topic and discussions updated with the latest research findings. The content has been validated for its relevance and applicability through my industry interactions. Moreover, the references for each section have been meticulously updated to include the latest research in the field.

I am profoundly grateful that both academics and industry professionals have found the previous editions of *Corporate Finance* valuable. Feedback from readers all over the world, received via email and my YouTube channel (professordavidhillier), has been instrumental in refining the book and rectifying occasional oversights. I deeply appreciate those who have reached out with insights and suggestions regarding the book. Writing this edition has been a fulfilling journey, and I genuinely hope you derive equal pleasure from reading it.

David Hillier
28 August 2023

Guided Tour

Understanding and Application

The best way to understand corporate finance is to explain it via situations and scenarios you can relate to.

- Each chapter opens with a set of **Learning Objectives** summarizing what skills, learning or understanding you will acquire from each chapter.
- **Example** boxes in every chapter provide hypothetical examples to illustrate theoretical concepts.
- **Opening chapter vignettes** illustrate topical discussions that will be covered in the chapter.
- **Real World Insight** boxes use real companies to show how they have applied corporate finance theories and concepts to their businesses and business decisions.
- **Sustainability in Action** boxes draw on issues relating to the environment, society, the economy and climate change to show how corporate finance is so important to the resolution of sustainability challenges.
- **Practical case studies, mini cases** and **additional reading** further aid your understanding of concepts and enable you to practise applying them.
- **Summary and Conclusions** sections briefly review and reinforce the main topics covered in each chapter, to ensure you have acquired a solid understanding of key concepts.

Real World Insight 15.1

The penultimate stage in venture capital finance is the initial public offering.[12] Venture capitalists are important participants in initial public offerings. Venture capitalists rarely sell all of the shares they own at the time of the initial public offering. Instead they usually sell out in subsequent public offerings.

What do Business Angels look for in an Investment?

(Excerpts taken from 'How to Find and Pitch your Business to an Angel Investor' from growthbusiness.co.uk)

Jenny Tooth, CEO of the UK Business Angels Association, explains what angel investors look for if they are thinking of investing in your growth business.

Where do I find an angel investor?

The best way to approach an angel investor is often through a warm introduction – one from a friend, contact, company or entrepreneur. Investors get a lot of inbound pitches, so it's hard to qualify what's a cold lead or not. There is a lack of infrastructure, which means that neither angels nor entrepreneurs are visible to one another.

What do angel investors want to know?

We want to know the challenge that you're addressing in the market or society, whether you have done your market research to show why your project meets a real need and can bring something new or disruptive to the market. We also want to know how you plan to make money and that your business model can be scaled. We will ask if you have tested it out on any potential customers – not necessarily having sold anything, but you have to prove interest and whether you have checked out your competitors. International scalability is growing ever more important, so to be able to think about how you would like your business to fit on an international stage is always a huge bonus.

Mini Case

West Coast Yachts Goes Public

Larissa Warren and Dan Ervin have been discussing the future of West Coast Yachts. The company has been experiencing fast growth and the future looks like clear sailing. However, the fast growth means that the company's growth can no longer be funded by internal sources, so Larissa and Dan have decided the time is right to take the company public. To this end, they have entered into discussions with the bank of Crowe & Mallard. The company has a working relationship with Robin Perry, the underwriter who assisted with the company's previous bond offering. Crowe & Mallard have helped numerous small companies in the IPO process, so Larissa and Dan feel confident with this choice.

Robin begins by telling Larissa and Dan about the process. Although Crowe & Mallard charged an underwriter fee of 4 per cent on the bond offering, the underwriter fee is 7 per cent on all initial equity offerings of the size of West Coast Yachts' initial offering. Robin tells Larissa and Dan that the company can expect to pay about £1,200,000 in legal fees and expenses, £12,000 in registration fees, and £15,000 in other filing fees. Additionally, to be listed on the London Stock Exchange, the company must pay £100,000. There are also transfer agent fees of £6,500 and engraving expenses of £450,000. The company should also expect to pay £75,000 for other expenses associated with the IPO.

Finally, Robin tells Larissa and Dan that, to file with the London Stock Exchange, the company must provide three years' worth of audited financial statements. She is unsure of the costs of the audit. Dan tells Robin that the company provides audited financial statements as part of its bond indenture, and the company pays £300,000 per year for the outside auditor.

1 At the end of the discussion Dan asks Robin about the Dutch auction IPO process. What are the differences in the expenses to West Coast Yachts if it uses a Dutch auction IPO versus a traditional IPO? Should the company go public with a Dutch auction or use a traditional underwritten offering?

Mastery of Mathematics

Many find the hardest part of learning finance is mastering the jargon, maths, data and standardized notation. *Corporate Finance* helps you by:

- Making extensive use of **figures and tables** that use real data throughout the text
- Listing in **key notation** boxes at the start of the chapter the variables and acronyms you will encounter as you read the chapter
- Numbering **maths equations** the first time they appear in full, for ease of reference and understanding.

Key Notations

#	Number of shares outstanding	σ^2	Variance (per year) of the continuous share price return
#w	Number of warrants	t	Time (in years) to expiration date
c_w	Value of a call option written on the equity of a firm *without* warrants	N(d)	Probability that a standardized, normally distributed, random variable will be less than or equal to d
S	Current share price		
E	Exercise price of option		
R	Annual risk-free rate of return, continuously compounded		$d_1 = [\ln(S/E) + (R + \sigma^2/2)t]/\sqrt{\sigma^2 t}$ $d_2 = d_1 - \sqrt{\sigma^2 t}$

Equation 23.1 $\underbrace{[0.45 \times (€2.10 - €2.74) \times 6 \text{ million} + 0.55 \times 0]/1.02}_{\text{Value of the call option}} + €1{,}000{,}000{,}000 = -€694{,}118$

As in the previous chapter, we are valuing an option using risk-neutral pricing. The cash flows of −€0.64 (= €2.10 − €2.74) and €0 per litre are multiplied by their risk-neutral probabilities. The entire first term in Equation 23.1 is then discounted at €1.02 because the cash flows in that term occur on 1 December. The €1,000,000 is not discounted because Mr Meyer receives it today, 1 September. Because the present value of the contract is negative, Mr Meyer would be wise to reject the contract.

As stated before, the distributor has sold a call option to CECO. The first term in the preceding equation, which equals −€1,694,118, can be viewed as the value of this call option. It is a negative number because the equation looks at the option from Mr Meyer's point of view. Therefore, the value of the call option would be +€1,694,118 to CECO. On a per-litre basis, the value of the option to CECO is:

Equation 23.2 $[0.45(€2.74 - €2.10) + 0.55 \times 0]/1.02 = €0.282$

Equation 23.2 shows that CECO will gain €0.64 (= €2.74 − €2.10) per litre in the up state because CECO can buy heating oil worth €2.74 for only €2.10 under the contract. By contrast, the contract is worth nothing to CECO in the down state because the utility will not pay €2.10 for oil selling for only €1.46 in the open market. Using risk-neutral pricing, the formula tells us that the value of the call option on one litre of heating oil is €0.282.

Guided Tour

PART 6

Options, Futures and Corporate Finance

23.1 Executive Share Options

Why Options?

Executive compensation (see **Chapter 2**, Section 2.2 for more on executive compensation) is usually made up of base salary plus some or all of the following elements:

- Base salary
- Annual bonuses
- Long-term incentives, such as retirement contributions, options and restricted stock units.

Chapter 2 Page 29

When stock markets are on an upward trajectory, the final component of compensation, options, is by far the most significant part of total compensation for many top executives. In many parts of Europe, full disclosure of executive pay is not yet standard practice. However, this has not stopped politicians and the media from criticizing the total compensation of executives, whose share options are a major component of their total remuneration. Figure 23.1 presents a breakdown of chief executive pay in Europe in 2015–2017. Bonuses represent any payments paid for performance during the year, and LTI is long-term incentives, which include executive share options.

Signposting and Navigation

To gain a full understanding of corporate finance it is important to understand how topics are linked together and how they relate to one another.

- **Part openers** provide a preface to the chapters that are to follow, linking the chapters, and explaining how and where topics are discussed within the chapters.
- **Chapter links** appear within the margin and are highlighted in the text; they provide a chapter and page reference for quick cross-referencing of information discussed in other chapters. They aid in the enhancement of your understanding and background to topics.

Practice and Proficiency

To obtain a solid understanding of finance it has been proven that practising questions is essential.

- At the end of every chapter there are **questions and problems;** these are presented by topic and level of difficulty. There are more than 1,000 in the book altogether!
- These end-of-chapter questions and problems are all integrated into **Connect.**
- **Algorithmic** versions of the questions appear in Connect to ensure equations and calculations are not learned by rote but by thorough understanding and practice.
- Also at the end of each the chapter are **exam questions** designed to take 45 minutes and test you in a more formal exam style.
- **SmartBook** is also available through **Connect** to help you learn; it adaptively assesses your skill and knowledge levels to track which topics you have mastered and which require further instruction and practice.

Questions and Problems connect

CONCEPT

1 **Executive Share Options** Why do companies issue options to executives if they cost the company more than they are worth to the executive? Why not just give cash and split the difference? Wouldn't that make both the company and the executive better off?

2 **Real Options** What are the two options that many businesses have? Why does a traditional NPV analysis tend to underestimate the value of an investment opportunity? Explain.

3 **Valuing a Start-up** Given that anything is possible in the future, why can't an entrepreneur who is seeking funding choose assumptions that make a start-up look good when it isn't? Is this more a danger with real option analysis than with normal capital budgeting analysis?

4 **The Binomial Model** Why is the binomial model more appropriate for real option analysis than Black-Scholes?

5 **Executive Stock Options** Do you think that executive stock options motivate executives to act in the best interests of the company? Explain.

Exam Question (45 minutes)

1 Your firm is considering a bid for a financially distressed football club that is in administration. The administrators have said you must pay an exclusivity fee of £500,000 to develop the bid further, show the seriousness of your bid and present your commitment to resolving the issue. There are three potential bidders and the exclusivity fee will guarantee you a period of one month in which you will be sole bidder. Since the club is in administration, your investment will be used to pay off all the outstanding creditors of the club, who are owed a total of £134 million. Your plan is to enter into a company voluntary agreement (CVA) with the creditors where they will receive £0.06 for every £1 of debt and you have estimated that there is a 50 per cent probability that they will accept. If this were to happen, you estimate the NPV of the bid is £3 million. However, if they do not accept the CVA, the bid will not go ahead and your exclusivity fee will be lost. Your company can borrow and lend at the risk-free rate of 6 per cent per annum. Is it worthwhile for you to pay the exclusivity fee? Explain. **(40 marks)**

2 What are the benefits of real option methodology over traditional methods? Why, in your opinion, do many firms not use real options to value investments? Explain. **(30 marks)**

3 In real options analysis, why is the binomial model preferred to Black-Scholes? Explain your answer, using a quantitative example. **(30 marks)**

Total: 100 Marks

Connect® for Finance

We have a wide selection of activities on hand to help students gain valuable practice during their course. By applying what they have learned to solve finance-related problems, these exercises help to test their knowledge and skills in preparation for the real world of finance.

Excel Simulations

Our Excel Simulation environment focuses on learning basic Excel skills, such as formulas and cell referencing, and requires students to enter answers as a formula. In addition to all basic cell referencing and mathematical operations, the following functions are featured:

Excel Features and Tools:

1. Absolute references
2. ActiveX control
3. Descriptive statistics
4. Goal seek
5. Loan amortization worksheet
6. Pivot tables
7. Scenario manager
8. Solver (add-in)
9. Trace dependents/ precedents
10. Two-way data tables

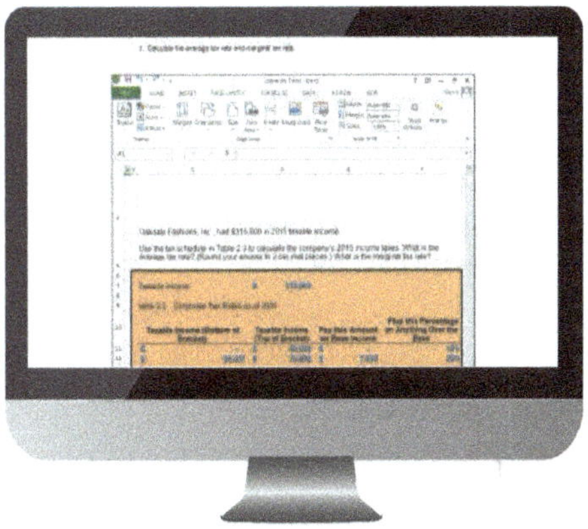

These questions feature animated, narrated Help and Show Me tutorials for students, when enabled, as well as automatic feedback and grading for both students and instructors.

Algorithmic Problem Sets

The problem sets help students to become more proficient in a topic by providing the opportunity to practice and master concepts with multiple versions of each problem. Algorithmic problems can also be used in class testing to provide each student with a different version than that seen by their peers.

Calculation Questions

Auto-graded calculation questions are available to test students' mathematical understanding

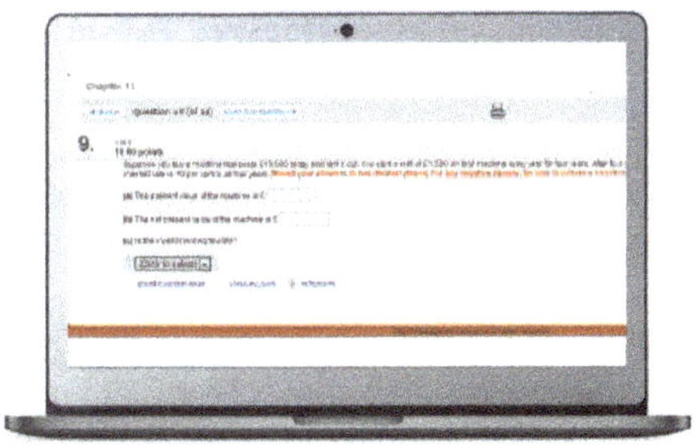

Case Studies

Ensure students develop strong analytical skills with case studies accompanied by questions which test their application on theory and concept.

Smarter studying with

McGraw Hill SMARTBOOK®

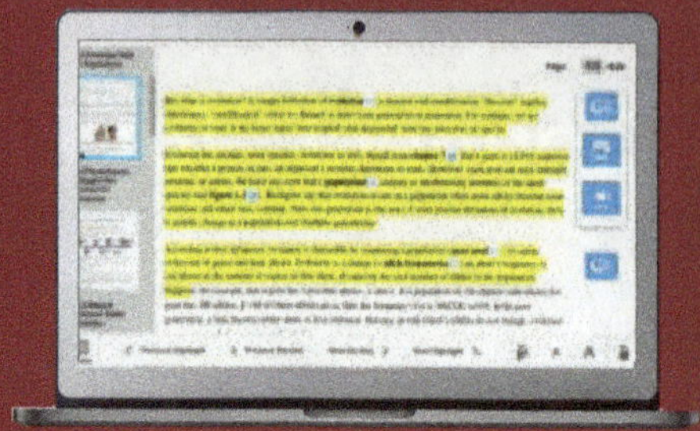

The **SmartBook® and Smartbook 2.0®** tool integrated within Connect® maximizes learning by helping students study more efficiently, highlighting the most important points in the chapter, asking verification questions and indicating additional resources.

More Personalised

SmartBook® and Smartbook 2.0® constantly adapts to students' needs, creating a personalised learning experience.

More Productive

SmartBook® and Smartbook 2.0® creates an extremely productive learning experience, focusing students' attention on the concepts they need to learn.

More Prepared

SmartBook® and Smartbook 2.0® helps students prepare for lessons, allowing you to use class time more dynamically

> "I liked the idea of continuous assessment online as it helped me to keep track of student performance while it freed up my time spent marking and meant I could focus on my research"
>
> **Alejandra Ramos, Trinity College Dublin, Ireland**

The ReadAnywhere App

To help you study anywhere, anytime! Gain mobile freedom to access your eBook anywhere, even offline, on your smartphone or tablet.

You can:

- Read offline and data-free by downloading the entire text or only the chapters you need
- Never lose an assignment, a note, or your place. ReadAnywhere includes the same functionality as the eBook offered in Connect® with auto-sync across both platforms
- Start studying anytime, anywhere

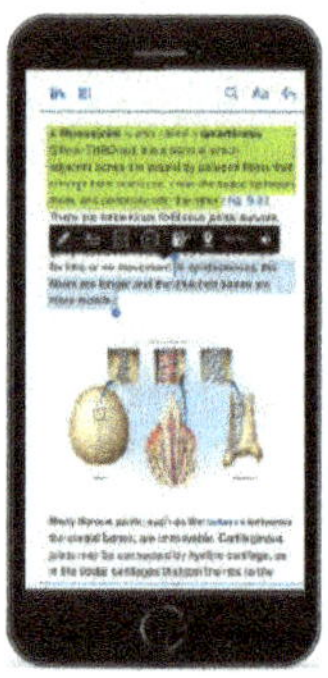

Available on:

App Store

Google Play

About the Author

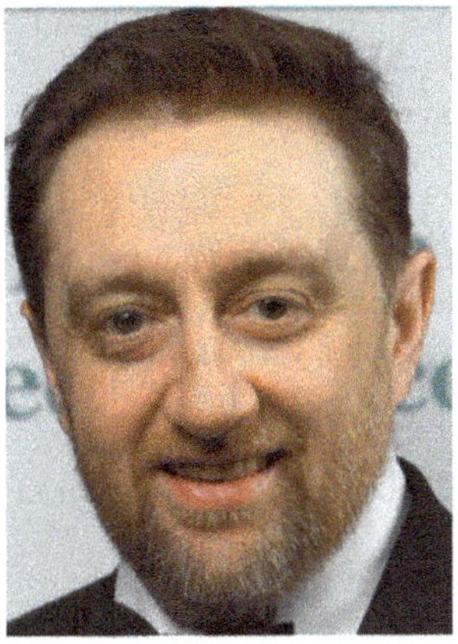

David Hillier is Associate Principal and Executive Dean of the University of Strathclyde Business School. A Professor of Finance, David was recognized as being in the top 3 per cent of the most prolific finance researchers in the world over the past 50 years (Heck and Cooley, 2009) and appears regularly in the media as a business commentator. His YouTube channel of finance lectures (professordavidhillier) has attracted nearly half a million views worldwide.

David has acted as a World Bank consultant, and provided consultancy advice to the NHS and several international stock exchanges. His executive clients include the Wise Group, Weir Group, Babcock, Wm Grant & Sons, Iberdrola and David Brown Gears. He has taught in many international environments, including China, Greece, Malaysia, the Netherlands, Oman, Bahrain, Switzerland, Tanzania and Romania. David is a non-executive director of Scotland's national skills agency, Skills Development Scotland, and sits on the CBI Scotland regional council and the MCR Pathways National Advisory Council. David has won a number of industry and academic awards, including the Institute of Directors Scotland Public Sector Director of the Year.

David publishes in the area of corporate finance. His PhD research is related to corporate insider trading and this is an area in which he is still very active. David's research has been funded by a number of international organizations, including the Italian and Spanish governments, the Thai Stock Exchange, Thai Securities and Exchange Commission, Thai Government Pension Fund, Australian Research Council, The Actuarial Profession, Rotman International Centre for Pension Management, and the Central Bank of Tanzania.

US Authors

Stephen A. Ross was the Franco Modigliani Professor of Finance and Economics at the Sloan School of Management, Massachusetts Institute of Technology.

Randolph W. Westerfield is Dean Emeritus of the University of Southern California's Marshall School of Business and is the Charles B. Thornton Professor of Finance.

Jeffrey F. Jaffe has been a frequent contributor to much finance and economics literature for a number of years.

Bradford D. Jordan is Professor of Finance and holder of the Richard W. and Janis H. Furst Endowed Chair in Finance at the University of Kentucky.

Acknowledgements

I would like to acknowledge the following individuals who have all contributed in one way or another to the book.

First mention must go to Felicity Bains and Jo O'Neill who worked with me tirelessly on this project from its inception. I am extremely grateful for their support.

The review process has been extensive and many individuals have provided advice and suggestions on how to make the text much more relevant and current to its intended readership. Every chapter has been scrutinized by several reviewers, leading to a substantial improvement in the quality of the text. In particular, I would like to recognize the efforts of:

Farooq Ahmad, SKEMA Business School
Mikael Bask, Uppsala University
Denita Cepiku, University of Rome Tor Vergata
Lawa Emmanuel, Durban University of Technology
Lorenzo Faccincani, University of Verona
Adam Golinski, University of York
Bertrand Groslambert, Skema Business School
Ronald Huisman, Erasmus School of Economics
Alberto Lanzavecchia, University of Padova
Joao Madeira, University of York
Susana Martinez Meyers, IE Business School
Barry McCarthy, University College London
Diogo Mendes, Stockholm School of Economics
Amir Moradi, HAN International School of Business
Fergal O'Brien, University of Limerick
Thiago de Oliveira Souza, University of Southern Denmark
Francesca Pampurini, Catholic University of the Sacred Heart of Milan
John Parker, Sheffield Hallam University
Lianfeng Quan, University of Greenwich
Alberto Rascon, Bern University of Applied Sciences
Sabrina Roszak, Skema Business School
Christoph Schneider, University of Münster
David Schroeder, Birkbeck College
Emanuela Sciubba, Birkbeck University of London
Alex Sclip, University of Udine
Cristina Tomàs, EAE Business School
Dennis Vossen, Saxion University
James Wright, University of Lincoln
Mo Yan, Queen Margaret University
Hai Zhang, Strathclyde Business School

A book of this type involves more than just writing the main text. The online learning materials have to be developed, checked and revised, and the drafts typeset and proofread. The marketing endeavour is also something that often gets ignored but it is an exceptionally important component of the book's production process. Finally, I am truly indebted to the sales representatives who are at the coalface in raising sales.

I'm very grateful to my family, who mean everything to me: Benjy, Danny, Con, Maria, Patrick, Saoirse and Thomas.

Finally, to Mary-Jo, my inspiration.

Improve your grades!
20% off any Study Skills Book!
The Ultimate Study Skills Handbook
Sarah Moore, Colin Neville, Maura Murphy and Cornelia Connolly
Open UP Study Skills
Study Skills for Business and Management Students
Barbara Allan
Open UP Study Skills
The Complete Guide to Referencing and Avoiding Plagiarism
Second Edition
Colin Neville
Our Study Skills books are packed with practical advice and tips that are easy to put into practice and will really improve the way you study.
Our books will help you:
✓ Improve your grades
✓ Avoid plagiarism
✓ Save time
✓ Develop new skills
✓ Write confidently
✓ Undertake research projects
✓ Sail through exams
✓ Find the perfect job
SPECIAL OFFER!
As a valued customer, buy online and receive 20% off any of our Study Skills books by entering the promo code BRILLIANT
www.openup.co.uk/studyskills
Permanent Marker

PART 1

Overview

You are at the beginning of an enriching journey. This book will help you to understand financial managers' decisions and how corporate finance is vital to all business aspects. Don't worry if you know absolutely nothing about finance. You will be provided with all the knowledge you need in terms of business terminology, accounting and finance. In addition, you will appreciate and become familiar with the international environment where companies raise funds and operate, understand the importance of aligning management incentives with company value maximization, and explore cultural variations in a global context. Finally, you will acquire the insight needed to be a key decision-maker and contribute to your company's growth.

Chapter 1
Introduction to Corporate Finance

Learning Objectives

After reading this chapter you should be able to:

LO1 Understand the fundamentals of corporate finance and its role in business decision-making.

LO2 Identify the primary goal of financial management and its implications for various stakeholders.

LO3 Evaluate the structure and functions of financial markets in relation to corporate finance.

LO4 Apply basic corporate finance concepts to analyse financial strategy.

Technology, the climate and geopolitics are in the process of revolutionizing corporate finance, and many established truths that existed prior to the global pandemic are now fiercely debated.

A common question is, 'Are financial markets rational?'

Classic corporate finance is based on the premise that all decisions are rational and those who make financial decisions are also rational. Once we drop this fundamental axiom, many financial theories become hard to prove. In fact, when we no longer expect decision-makers to be rational, many observed 'financial anomalies' make perfect sense.

There is now widespread recognition of the importance of ethics and sustainability in financial decision-making, and managers are expected to incorporate societal and environmental concerns in their business decisions. This has been accompanied by an increase in shareholder activism, especially from financial institutions that have become more vocal in their criticism of corporate management when bad decisions are made.

Another change is a greater understanding of the integrated nature of global supply chains and the bottlenecks that occur when systems face temporary halts or disruption due to natural disasters or military conflict. The international financial environment is now so central to business decision-making that any course on finance must give consideration to the dynamics of currency movements, geopolitical risk and economics. Financial risk management is an area that has consequently come to the fore as a result of these changes, and it will remain essential for years to come.

Source: imagesource/123RF.

In recent years, technological advancements have led to changes in business models, and corporate executives face an evolving economic environment where automation, artificial general intelligence and machine learning have become viable alternatives to skilled and unskilled human workforces. Technology also impacts corporate financing, and there are now more opportunities for companies to raise money for their operations than there were three years ago.

Finally, the role of the corporate executive has changed. Irrespective of background, today's leaders must be fully loaded with financial tools to cope with the rapidly changing business environment. The corporate executive must be an entrepreneur who not only understands risk but can also use it to their advantage. More than this, the executive must be willing and have the confidence to implement investment and financing decisions that fully incorporate risky outcomes in an ethical and sustainable way.

This text aims to bring these issues together and integrate them into a coherent framework for optimal financial decision-making. However, we first require an understanding of what is meant by the term 'corporate finance', why it is so essential to a successful business, the different financial environments in which companies operate, and the emerging trends in global business – all of which we discuss in **Chapter 1**.

1.1 What is Corporate Finance?

Suppose you decide to start a firm to make tennis balls. To do this you hire managers to buy raw materials, and you assemble a workforce that will produce and sell finished tennis balls. In the language of finance, you invest in assets such as inventory, machinery, land and labour, and you match the amount of cash you spend in assets with an equal amount of cash raised by financing. When you begin to sell tennis balls, your firm will generate cash, and this is the basis of value creation. The purpose of the firm is to create value for the owner, who may or may not be the manager of the firm. This concept of value is reflected in the framework of the simple balance sheet model of the firm.

The Balance Sheet Model of the Firm

Chapter 3 Page 60

Take a financial snapshot of the firm and its activities at a single point in time. Figure 1.1 shows a graphic conceptualization of a firm's **balance sheet**, and it will help introduce you to the field of corporate finance. (See **Chapter 3** for more information on the statement of financial position.)

Figure 1.1 The Balance Sheet Model of the Firm

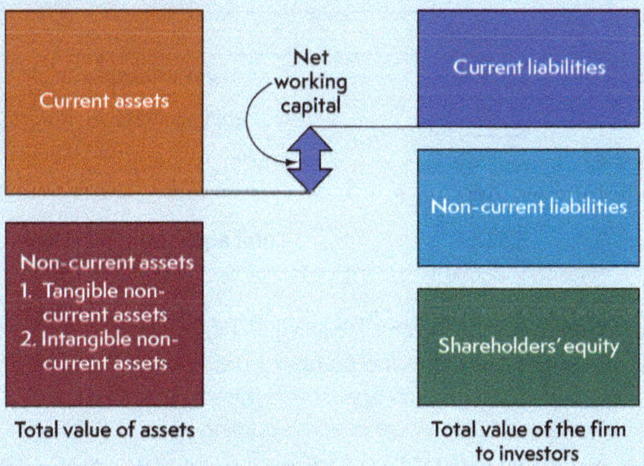

The assets of the firm are on the left side of the balance sheet. Think of these assets as short-term (current) and long-term (non-current). *Non-current assets* are those that will last a long time, such as buildings. Some non-current assets are tangible, such as machinery and equipment. Other non-current assets are intangible, such as patents and trademarks. The other category of assets, *current assets,* comprises those that have short lives, such as inventory. For example, tennis balls your firm has made but not yet sold are current assets. Unless you have overproduced, the tennis balls will leave the firm shortly and will not be in the company for a long time.

Before a company can invest in an asset, it must obtain financing, which means it must raise money to pay for the investment. The various forms of funding are represented on the right side of the balance sheet in Figure 1.1. A firm will issue (sell) pieces of paper called *bonds* (debt or loan agreements) or *shares* (certificates representing fractional ownership of the firm).

Just as we classify assets as long-lived or short-lived, so too are liabilities. Short-term debt is called a *current liability,* and represents loans and other obligations that must be repaid within one year. *Non-current liabilities* include debt that does not have to be repaid within one year. Shareholders' equity represents the difference between the value of the firm's assets and liabilities and, in this sense, it is a residual claim on the firm's assets.

From the balance sheet model of the firm, we can ask three questions:

1 In which long-lived assets should the firm invest? This question concerns the left side of the balance sheet. Of course, the types and proportions of assets the firm needs tend to be set by the nature of the business. We use the term **capital budgeting** to describe the process of making and managing expenditures on long-lived assets.

2 How can the firm raise cash for required capital expenditures? This question concerns the right side of the balance sheet. The answer to this question involves the firm's **capital structure**, which represents the proportions of the firm's financing from current and long-term debt and equity.

3 How should short-term operating cash flows be managed? This question concerns the upper portion of the balance sheet. There is often a mismatch between the timing of cash inflows and cash outflows during operating activities. Furthermore, financial managers do not know the amount and timing of operating cash flows with certainty and must manage the gaps in cash flow. From a balance sheet perspective, short-term management of cash flow is associated with a firm's **net working capital**. We define net working capital as current assets minus current liabilities. From a financial perspective, short-term cash flow problems come from the mismatching of cash inflows and outflows. This is the subject of short-term finance.

Real World Insight 1.1

Berkeley Group is a large British building company focusing on new housing estate developments. The assets of Berkeley Group include not only buildings and property (tangible assets) but also the value of its brand and skilled workforce (intangible assets). In 2022, the company had £357.4 million in tangible non-current assets and £17.2 million in intangible non-current assets. Current assets amounted to £6,213.1 million and current liabilities (liabilities due within one year) were £1,969.5 million. Berkeley Group had £1,482.1 million in non-current liabilities. A statement of financial position (balance sheet) for the company is presented below.

	£ million		**£ million**
Tangible assets	357.4	Non-current liabilities	1,482.1
Intangible assets	17.2	Current liabilities	1,969.5
Non-current assets	374.6	Equity	3,136.1
Current assets	6,213.1		
Total assets	**6,587.7**	**Total equity and liabilities**	**6,587.7**

Net working capital is (current assets − current liabilities) = £4,243.6 million. Typically, one would expect a positive net working capital figure to ensure that the company has enough liquid assets to pay off its short-term liabilities. Berkeley's net working capital is high in comparison to the size of the firm, and it would be considered cash rich. This will give the firm an excellent basis to invest over the coming year.

Capital Structure

Financing arrangements determine how the value of the firm is sliced up. The people or institutions that buy debt from (i.e. lend money to) the firm are called *creditors, bondholders* or *debtholders.* The holders of equity are called *shareholders.*

Sometimes it is useful to think of the firm as a pie. Initially, the size of the pie will depend on how well the firm has made its investment decisions. After a firm has invested, it determines the value of its assets (e.g. its buildings, land and inventories).

The firm can then determine its capital structure. It might initially have raised the cash to invest in its assets by issuing more debt than equity; now it can consider changing that mix by issuing more equity and using the proceeds to buy back (pay off) some of its debt. Financing decisions like this can be made independently of the original investment decisions. The decisions to issue debt and equity affect how the pie is sliced.

We depict the pie in Figure 1.2. The size of the pie is the value of the firm in the financial markets. We can write the value of the firm, V, as:

$$V = D + E$$

where D is the market value of the debt (bonds) and E is the market value of the equity (shares). The pie diagrams consider two ways of slicing the pie: 50 per cent debt and 50 per cent equity, and 25 per cent debt and 75 per cent equity. The way the pie is sliced could affect its value. If so, the goal of the financial manager will be to choose the ratio of debt to equity that makes the value of the pie – that is, the value of the firm, V – as large as it can be. (See **Chapter 15** for more information on capital structure.)

Figure 1.2 Two Pie Models of the Firm

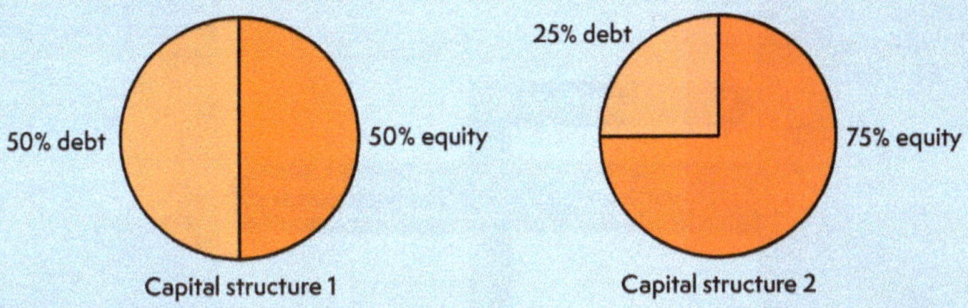

Real World Insight 1.2

Every company that needs cash must raise it from somewhere. In 2022, Volkswagen AG received a total of €9.4 billion by issuing new equity of its subsidiary Porsche AG on the German stock exchange, Deutsche Börse, as well as stock exchanges in Austria, Switzerland, France, Italy and Spain.

Why did Volkswagen choose to issue new equity? It based its decision on what would maximize the value of the company. In this case, equity was the most sensible option.

Volkswagen is an automobile company and does not have extensive experience of raising large amounts of external financing. This is where banks come in. Although banks are best known for lending funds to borrowers and taking deposits, they are also very experienced in marketing and raising money from other investors. We call this type of activity 'investment banking', and a number of banking institutions specialize in this area.

Many banks were involved in finding buyers for the €9.4 billion Volkswagen issue including Deutsche Bank, Goldman Sachs, J.P. Morgan, BNP Paribas, BofA Securities, Citi and Morgan Stanley.

The Financial Manager

In large firms, we usually associate finance activity with a top officer of the firm, such as the chief financial officer (CFO), and some lesser officers. Reporting to the CFO are the treasurer and the financial controller. The treasurer is responsible for handling cash flows, managing capital expenditure decisions and making financial plans. The financial controller handles the accounting function, which includes taxes, financial and management accounting, and information systems.

In smaller firms, a single employee covers many of the roles within an organization. Although each firm will be different, there will always be someone who is responsible for the duties of a financial manager. The most important role of a financial manager is to create value from the firm's capital budgeting, financing and net working capital activities. How do financial managers create value? The answer is that the firm should:

- Try to buy assets that generate more cash than they cost
- Sell bonds, shares and other financial instruments that raise more cash than they cost.

Thus, the firm must create more cash flow than it uses. The cash flows paid to bondholders and shareholders of the firm should be higher than the cash flows put in to the firm by the bondholders and shareholders. To see how this is done, we trace the cash flows from the firm to the financial markets and back again.

We illustrate the interplay of the firm's activities with the financial markets in Figure 1.3. The arrows in Figure 1.3 trace cash flow from the firm to the financial markets and back again. Suppose we begin with the firm's financing activities. The firm sells debt (bonds) and equity (shares) to investors in the financial markets to raise money, resulting in cash flowing from the financial markets to the firm (*A*). This cash is invested in the investment activities (assets) of the firm (*B*) by the firm's management. Shareholders and bondholders (*F*) are then paid with the cash generated by the firm (*C*). The shareholders receive cash in the form of dividends; the bondholders who lent funds to the firm receive interest and, when the initial loan is repaid, principal. Not all of the firm's cash is paid out: some is retained (*E*), and some is paid to the government as taxes (*D*).

Figure 1.3 Cash Flows Between the Firm and the Financial Markets

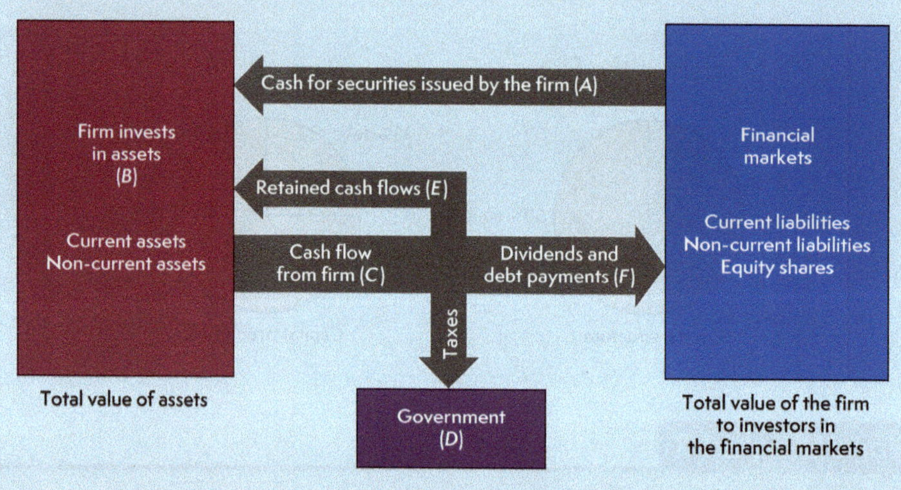

Over time, if the cash paid to shareholders and bondholders (*F*) is greater than the cash raised in the financial markets (*A*), value will be created.

Identification of Cash Flows

Unfortunately, it is not easy to observe cash flows directly. Much of the information we obtain is in the form of accounting statements, and much of the work of financial analysis is to extract cash flow information from accounting statements. Example 1.1 illustrates how this is done.

Example 1.1

Accounting Profit versus Cash Flows

Midland plc is an Irish firm that refines and trades gold. At the end of the year, it sold 2,500 ounces of gold for €1.67 million. The company had acquired the gold for €1 million at the beginning of the year by paying cash. Unfortunately, it has yet to collect from the customer. The following is a standard accounting of Midland's financial circumstances at year-end:

The Accounting View Midland plc Income Statement Year Ended 31 December	
	€
Sales	1,670,000
–Costs	1,000,000
Profit	670,000

Under International Financial Reporting Standards (IFRS), we record the sale even though the customer has yet to pay. We also assume the customer will pay soon. From the accounting perspective, Midland seems to be profitable. However, the perspective of corporate finance is different. It focuses on cash flows:

The Financial View Midland plc Income Statement Year Ended 31 December	
	€
Cash inflow	0
Cash outflow	−1,000,000
Net Cash Flow	−1,000,000

Corporate finance is interested in whether the gold trading operations of Midland create cash flow, because value creation depends on cash. For Midland, value creation depends on whether and when it receives the €1.67 million.

The Timing of Cash Flows

The value of an investment made by a firm depends on the timing of cash flows. One of the fundamental principles of finance is that individuals prefer to receive cash flows earlier rather than later. One euro received today is worth more than one euro received next year. See Example 1.2.

Example 1.2

Cash Flow Timing

The Italian firm Montana SpA is attempting to choose between two proposals for new products. Both projects will provide additional cash flows over four years and will initially cost €10,000. The cash flows from the proposals are as follows:

Year	New Product A (€)	New Product B (€)
1	0	4,000
2	0	4,000
3	0	4,000
4	20,000	4,000
Total	20,000	16,000

At first, it appears that Product A is better because it earns more money. However, the cash flows from Project B come earlier than those of A. Without more information, we cannot decide which set of cash flows would create the most value for the bondholders and shareholders. It depends on whether the benefit of getting cash from B up front outweighs the total extra cash from A. Bond and share prices reflect this preference for earlier cash, and we will see how to use them to decide between A and B.

Risk of Cash Flows

The firm must consider the risk of cash flows since their amount and timing are not usually known with certainty. Most investors have an aversion to risk.

Real World Insight 1.3

Risk

The Norwegian firm Fjell ASA is considering expanding operations overseas and is evaluating the Netherlands and South Africa as possible sites. The Netherlands is viewed as relatively safe, whereas operating in South Africa is seen as riskier. In both cases, the company would close down operations after one year.

After undertaking a complete financial analysis, Fjell has come up with the following cash flows for the alternative expansion plans under three scenarios – pessimistic, most likely and optimistic:

	Pessimistic (NKr)	Most likely (NKr)	Optimistic (NKr)
Netherlands	750,000	1,000,000	1,250,000
South Africa	0	1,500,000	2,000,000

If we ignore the pessimistic scenario, perhaps South Africa is the best alternative. When we take the pessimistic scenario into account, the choice is unclear. South Africa appears to be riskier, but it also offers a higher expected level of cash flow.

What Is Risk and How Can It Be Defined?

Financial managers cannot avoid facing risky decisions and much of our book is devoted to developing methods to help in these situations. We can measure risk in a number of ways and it isn't all about adverse outcomes. Companies can face upside risk as well as downside risk, and the financial manager's objective is to identify the risk, measure it, then optimally manage it.

In later chapters, we explore a number of quantitative risk measures and consider how these can be used to make good corporate decisions. Managers need not be afraid of risk and should see it as a friend, although one on which they keep a close eye!

There are two main ways a company can approach risk. It can speculate and attempt to benefit by leaving the company exposed to future fluctuations in prices or cash flows. This is risky and may lead to extremely good or bad outcomes. The alternative is to hedge against the risk and reduce its impact on the company's future cash flows. If a company hedges too much, it will not benefit from future price or cash flow fluctuations. However, if it hedges too little, it will be exposed to big shifts in cash flows or prices.

Striking a healthy balance is fundamental to the optimal running of companies and we discuss this in much more detail in later chapters.

1.2 The Goal of Financial Management

Assuming we restrict our discussion to for-profit businesses, the goal of financial management is to make money or add value for the owners. This goal is a little vague, of course, so we examine some different ways of formulating it to come up with a more precise definition. A clear definition is important because it leads to an objective basis for making and evaluating financial decisions.

Possible Goals

If we were to consider possible financial goals, we might come up with some ideas like the following:

- Survive
- Avoid financial distress and bankruptcy
- Beat the competition
- Maximize sales or market share
- Minimize costs
- Maximize profits
- Maintain steady earnings growth.

These are only a few of the goals we could list. Furthermore, each of these possibilities presents problems as a goal for the financial manager.

For example, it is easy to increase market share or unit sales – all we have to do is lower our prices or relax our credit terms. Similarly, we can always cut costs simply by doing away with things such as research and development. We can avoid bankruptcy by never borrowing any money or never taking any risks, and so on. It is not clear that any of these actions are in the shareholders' best interests.

Profit maximization would probably be the most commonly cited goal, but even this is not a precise objective. Do we mean profits this year? If so, then we should note that actions such as deferring maintenance, letting inventories run down and taking other short-run cost-cutting measures will tend to increase profits now, but these activities are not necessarily desirable.

The goal of maximizing profits may refer to some sort of 'long run' or 'average' profits, but it is still unclear exactly what this means. First, do we mean something like accounting net income or earnings per share? As we will see in more detail in **Chapter 4,** these accounting numbers may have little to do with what is good or bad for the firm. Second, what do we mean by the long run? As a famous economist once remarked, in the long run, we are all dead! More to the point, this goal does not tell us what the appropriate trade-off is between current and future profits.

The goals we have listed here are all different, but they tend to fall into two classes. The first of these relates to profitability. The goals involving sales, market share and cost control all relate, at least potentially, to different ways of earning or increasing profits. The goals in the second group, involving bankruptcy avoidance, stability and safety, relate in some way to controlling risk. Unfortunately, these two types of goals are somewhat contradictory. The pursuit of profit normally involves some element of risk, so it is not really possible to maximize both safety and profit. What we need, therefore, is a goal that encompasses both factors.

Chapter 4
Page 88

The Goal of Financial Management

The financial manager in a corporation makes decisions for the shareholders of the firm. So, instead of listing possible goals for the financial manager, we really need to answer a more fundamental question: from the shareholders' point of view, what is a good financial management decision?

If we assume that shareholders buy shares because they seek to gain financially, then the answer is obvious: good decisions increase the value of the company's shares, and poor decisions decrease the value of the shares.

From our observations, it follows that the financial manager acts in the shareholders' best interests by making decisions that increase the value of the company's shares. The appropriate goal for the financial manager can thus be stated quite easily:

The goal of financial management is to maximize the value of a company's equity shares.

The goal of maximizing share value avoids the problems associated with the different goals we listed earlier. There is no ambiguity in the criterion, and there is no short-run versus long-run issue. We explicitly mean that our goal is to maximize the *current* share price. (See **Chapter 4** for more information on value maximization.)

If this goal seems a little strong or one-dimensional to you, keep in mind that the shareholders in a firm are residual owners. By this we mean that they are entitled only to what is left after employees, suppliers and creditors (and everyone else with legitimate claims) are paid their due. If any of these groups go unpaid, the shareholders get nothing. So if the shareholders are winning in the sense that the leftover, residual portion is growing, it must be true that everyone else is winning also.

Because the goal of financial management is to maximize the value of the equity, we need to learn how to identify investments and financing arrangements that favourably impact share value. This is precisely what we will be studying. In fact, we could have defined *corporate finance* as the study of the relationship between business decisions and the value of the shares in the business.

A More General Goal

If our goal is as stated in the preceding section (to maximize the company's share price), an obvious question comes up: what is the appropriate goal when the firm has no traded shares? Corporations are certainly not the only type of business, and the shares in many corporations rarely change hands, so it is difficult to say what the value per share is at any particular time.

As long as we are considering for-profit businesses, only a slight modification is needed. The total value of the shares in a corporation is simply equal to the value of the owners' equity. Therefore, a more general way of stating our goal is as follows: maximize the market value of the existing owners' equity.

With this in mind, we do not care what the organizational form is, since good financial decisions increase the market value of the owners' equity, and poor financial decisions decrease it. In fact, although we choose to focus on corporations in the chapters ahead, the principles we develop apply to all forms of business. Many of them even apply to the not-for-profit sector.

Finally, our goal does not imply that the financial manager should take illegal or unethical actions in the hope of increasing the value of the equity in the firm. What we mean is that the financial manager best serves the owners of the business by identifying goods and services that add value to the firm because they are desired and valued in the free marketplace.

The Triple Bottom Line

In several quarters, shareholder value maximization (the profit objective) has attracted criticism because it appears to ignore other important factors, such as employees (the social objective) and sustainability (the environment objective).

Critics argue that, since companies consist of people and use the planet's resources, they have a responsibility not only to shareholders but to society as well. The triple bottom line is an attempt to bring sustainability to the centre of corporate decision-making by asking companies to maximize not just shareholder value, but also to measure their contribution to society and the environment.

One major difficulty with the triple bottom line is the difficulty in accurately measuring in monetary terms the effect a company has on society and the environment. For example, how would you measure the triple bottom line of a fracking company that extracts gas from underground shale formations? Fracking has been in existence since the 1990s but the long-term environmental effects are still unknown. To value the environmental and social costs of fracking would require assumptions, many of which are controversial and lack agreement.

Until we have designed a valuation paradigm that effectively incorporates all aspects of a company's operations, shareholder wealth maximization is the best option. In addition, assuming that shareholders value society and the environment in the same way as the general population, the goal of shareholder wealth maximization will necessarily capture societal and environmental objectives.

Consequently, the financial manager best serves shareholders (the business owners) by making decisions that are valued by shareholders, who in turn reflect the broader societal and environmental concerns of the general population. Therefore, shareholder wealth maximization is consistent with the triple bottom line approach (assuming shareholders have the same objectives and concerns as the general population).

Purpose-driven Businesses

Many firms proactively adopt a purpose or mission that transcends only financial concerns. These purpose-led businesses, also known as 'values driven' or 'mission driven' firms, regard social and environmental strategic objectives as equally important as financial performance. Examples of non-financial objectives include reducing carbon emissions and promoting sustainable agriculture.

According to Edmans and Kacperczyk (2022), companies choose to adopt a purpose-driven or sustainable approach for three main reasons. First, it is believed that pursuing sustainable objectives can enhance the overall value of the firm. Shareholders and owners of purpose-driven companies often invest with the intention of making a positive impact on society and the environment. This heightened demand for socially responsible companies can drive up their market value. Finally, a firm that prioritizes purpose and sustainability may experience improved employee morale, loyalty and productivity. Graham (2022) also finds that firms have increasingly focused their objectives around a broad community of stakeholders instead of just equity holders.

Take, for example, the British-based cosmetics firm, The Body Shop, which is strongly committed to the ethical and sustainable sourcing of ingredients, as well as fair-trade practices. The Body Shop actively campaigns on issues such as animal testing and human rights, and has a long-standing 'Trade Not Aid' programme, which helps support communities in the developing world.

Having a non-financial purpose shouldn't mean that financial performance is sacrificed. In fact, firms that integrate the triple bottom line in their financial decisions are regarded as pursuing sustainable financial management, or 'green finance'. While these types of companies often have more engaged and motivated employees, with higher levels of productivity and innovation, it is important to recognize those firms that cynically brand themselves as sustainable when they are anything but. This is a practice known as 'greenwashing', and investors should challenge management on the veracity of any claims it makes regarding a purpose-led or sustainable finance mission.

Sustainability in Action 1.1

The Triple Bottom Line at IKEA

One of the strongest supporters of the triple bottom line approach is IKEA, the Swedish furniture retail giant. The company's approach to sustainability is known as 'People & Planet Positive', and it is integrated into all aspects of its business.

A key aspect of IKEA's triple bottom line approach is its focus on environmental sustainability (planet), and the firm has ambitious targets to reduce its greenhouse gas emissions, energy consumption and waste. IKEA uses renewable energy sources such as wind and solar power to produce energy for its stores and factories, and is aiming to become completely climate positive by 2030.

IKEA places a strong emphasis on social sustainability (people) and is committed to fair employment practices, ensuring that workers in its supply chain are paid a fair wage and provided with safe working conditions. The company also focuses on promoting diversity and inclusion within its workforce and actively works to support communities where it operates, through initiatives such as education and community development programmes.

Finally, IKEA prioritizes financial sustainability (profit), which is evident in the company's strong financial performance. By setting specific and measurable goals, IKEA has been able to track its progress and make meaningful improvements in areas such as energy efficiency and waste reduction. Additionally, by integrating sustainability into all aspects of its business, the firm has been able to achieve strong financial performance while also making a positive impact on the environment and society.

1.3 Financial Markets

When firms require cash to invest in new projects, they have to choose the most efficient and cost-effective financing option from a range of appropriate alternatives. First, they must decide whether to borrow money (debt) or give up a fraction of ownership in their firm (equity). When borrowing, the company takes out a loan and agrees to later pay back the borrowed amount (principal) plus interest, to compensate the lender for giving the money to the borrower. If the firm decides to give up ownership, it sells a part of the company for a set cash amount. At the end of this process, the firm will end up with the cash it needs.

When a firm borrows, it can go to a bank for a loan, or it can issue *debt securities* in the financial markets. Debt securities are contractual obligations to repay corporate borrowing. If a firm gives up ownership, it can do this through private negotiation or a public sale. A public sale is undertaken through marketing and sale of *equity securities*. Equity securities are shares (known as ordinary shares or common stock) that represent non-contractual claims to the residual cash flow of the firm. Issues of debt and equity that are publicly sold by the firm are then traded in the financial markets, such as stock markets.

In many countries, the financial markets are not nearly as well developed as in Europe. For example, in Africa many stock exchanges are small, and only a handful of companies have publicly traded equity or debt securities. For these firms, it is usually cheaper to get funding from banks and strategic investors.

The financial markets are composed of the money markets and the capital markets. Money markets are for debt securities that will pay off in the short term (usually less than one year). Capital markets are for long-term debt (for longer than a year) and equities.

The term *money market* applies to a group of loosely connected markets, usually in the form of a dealer market. Dealers are firms that make continuous price quotations for which they stand ready to buy and sell short-term financial instruments for their inventory and at their own risk. Thus, the dealer is a principal in most transactions, which is different from a stockbroker acting as an agent for a customer in buying or selling shares on most stock exchanges. An agent will not acquire the securities.

Figure 1.4 illustrates the difference between dealer and agency markets. In both cases, Trader A wishes to sell to Trader B. Moreover, in each scenario, Trader A sells shares for £100 and Trader B buys shares for £110. So what is the difference between the market types? In the dealer market, the dealer bears the risk of holding the shares before he can find a counterparty to buy them. In Figure 1.4, the dealer finds someone to buy the shares at £110. However, if they are unable to locate a counterparty, they may end up with shares that are worth less than the value at which they were purchased (£100). This is known as inventory risk and constitutes a cost to the dealer. The difference between the dealer's buying and selling price is known as the *bid–ask spread,* which in this case is £10.

In an agency market, Trader A hires an agent or broker to find a counterparty. The broker, it is hoped, will find someone and then take a commission on the sale price, which in this case is £10. At no time does the broker own the shares that they are trying to sell and, as a result, they do not bear inventory risk.

At the core of the money markets are the money market banks (these tend to be large banks with headquarters in Frankfurt, London and New York), government securities dealers (some of which are the same large banks) and many money brokers. Money brokers specialize in finding short-term money for borrowers and placing money for lenders. The financial markets can be classified further as the *primary market* and the *secondary markets.*

Figure 1.4 Comparison of Dealer and Agency Markets

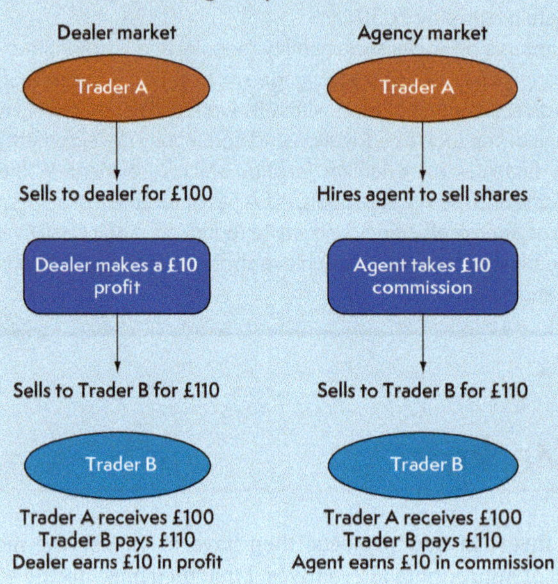

The Primary Market: New Issues

Governments and public corporations use the primary markets to sell securities. Corporations engage in two types of primary market sales of debt and equity: public offerings and private placements.

Most publicly offered corporate debt and equity come to the market underwritten by a syndicate of investment banking firms. The *underwriting* syndicate buys the new securities from the firm for the syndicate's own account and resells them at a higher price. Publicly issued debt and equity must be registered with the local regulatory authority. *Registration* requires the corporation to disclose all material information in a registration statement.

The legal, accounting and other costs of preparing the registration statement are not negligible. In part to avoid these costs, privately placed debt and equity are sold by private negotiation to large financial institutions, such as insurance companies and mutual funds, and other investors. Private placements tend not to be registered with regulatory authorities in the same way as public issues. (See **Chapters 14, 19** and **20** for more information on financing decisions.)

Chapter 14 Page 387
Chapter 19 Page 511
Chapter 20 Page 541

Every country has its own regulatory authority that deals with the registration of publicly traded securities. Corporations that wish to have traded securities in a country's securities exchange must register with the competent authority. Table 1.1 presents the names of regulators for a sample of countries.

Peer-to-peer Investing Platforms

A new type of trading platform has emerged giving companies, especially small and medium-sized enterprises, access to alternative sources of finance. Peer-to-peer trading platforms can be used by small companies to borrow without going through the normal stock exchange requirements for listing. Investors from all over the world lend to a company using an electronic platform without the need to go through a financial intermediary. Although there are lower transaction costs with these platforms, investors must undertake their own research into the company, which takes time and money. For borrowers, the cost of borrowing is likely to be lower because they don't need to pay fees to a bank. However, the amount they can borrow tends to be small (a maximum of £5 million) and the borrowing period is short (up to five years). Each platform is different and there is no consistency across platforms.

Given its recent emergence, peer-to-peer investing is not regulated in many countries and investors use this medium at their own risk. With the development of new financial technologies, such as blockchain, expect to see many more investing platforms in the future using not just standard currencies like euros and sterling, but cryptocurrencies, such as bitcoin and ethereum.

Table 1.1 Corporate and Financial Regulators

Country	Regulator
Australia	Australian Securities and Investment Commission
Austria	Financial Market Authority
Bahrain	Central Bank of Bahrain
Belgium	Financial Services and Markets Authority
China	China Securities Regulatory Commission
Denmark	Financial Supervisory Authority (Finanstilsynet)
Dubai	Dubai Financial Services Authority
Finland	Financial Supervision Authority
France	Autorité des Marchés Financiers (AMF)
Germany	Bundesanstalt für Finanzdienstleistungsaufsicht (BaFin)
Greece	Hellenic Capital Market Commission
India	Securities and Exchange Board of India
Ireland	Central Bank of Ireland
Israel	Israel Securities Authority
Italy	Commissione Nazionale per le Società e la Borsa
Malaysia	Securities Commission Malaysia
Netherlands	Netherlands Authority for the Financial Markets
Norway	Financial Supervisory Authority (Finanstilsynet)
Oman	Capital Market Authority (Oman)
Poland	Polish Financial Supervision Authority (KNF)
Portugal	Comissão do Mercado de Valores Mobiliários
Saudi Arabia	Capital Market Authority (Saudi Arabia)
Singapore	Money Authority of Singapore
South Africa	Financial Services Board (South Africa)
Spain	Comisión Nacional del Mercado de Valores
Sweden	Financial Supervisory Authority (Sweden) Finansinspektionen
Switzerland	Swiss Financial Market Supervisory Authority
Turkey	Capital Markets Board
UAE	Securities and Commodity Authority
UK	Financial Conduct Authority; Financial Policy Committee; Prudential Regulation Authority
USA	Securities and Exchange Commission

Secondary Markets

A secondary market transaction involves one owner or creditor selling to another. The secondary markets provide the means for transferring ownership of corporate securities. Although a corporation is only directly involved in a primary market transaction (when it sells securities to raise cash), the secondary markets are still critical to large corporations. The reason is that investors are more willing to purchase securities in a primary market transaction when they know that those securities can be resold later if desired. (See **Chapter 13** for more information on secondary markets.)

Chapter 13
Page 355

Dealer versus Auction Markets

There are two kinds of secondary market: *dealer* markets and *auction* markets. Generally speaking, dealers buy and sell for themselves, at their own risk. A car dealer, for example, buys and sells automobiles. In contrast, brokers and agents match buyers and sellers, but they do not own the commodity that is bought or sold. An estate agent, for example, does not normally buy and sell houses.

Dealer markets in equities and long-term debt are called *over-the-counter* (OTC) markets. Most trading in debt securities takes place over the counter. The expression *over the counter* refers to days of old when securities were bought and sold at counters in offices around the country. Today a significant fraction of the market for equities and almost all of the market for long-term debt has no central location and dealers are connected electronically.

Auction markets differ from dealer markets in two ways. First, an auction market or exchange has a physical location (such as Wall Street in New York). Second, in a dealer market, most of the buying and selling is done by the dealer. The primary purpose of an auction market, on the other hand, is to match those who wish to sell with those who want to buy. Dealers play only a limited role.

Trading in Corporate Securities

The equities of most large firms trade in organized auction markets. The largest such market is the New York Stock Exchange (NYSE). Other auction exchanges include Euronext, the Shanghai Stock Exchange and the London Stock Exchange Group.

In addition to the stock exchanges, there is a large OTC market for equities. The National Association of Securities Dealers Automated Quotation System (NASDAQ) in the United States and many equity securities traded on the London Stock Exchange are both examples of OTC markets. The fact that OTC markets have no physical location means national borders do not present a significant barrier, and there is now a huge international OTC debt market. Because of globalization, financial markets have reached the point where trading in many assets, commodities or securities never stops; it just travels around the world.

Stock market liquidity is essential to a listed company because the more accessible and cheaper it is to trade the firm's securities, the more demand there will be in the firm. Recent research has shown that companies have higher values when their shares are liquid and heavily traded, even after taking out all other factors that may drive valuation differences. Also, having numerous options on where to trade a company's shares does not harm the value, and in fact can make pricing of the shares more efficient (Fang et al., 2009; O'Hara and Ye, 2011).

Exchange Trading of Listed Companies

The London Stock Exchange is ideal for describing how shares are traded in a dealer system and auction system since both operate simultaneously on the exchange. In 2023, there were around 2,000 equities traded on the London Stock Exchange. Out of this number, the largest equities were traded on the main market and smaller companies were trading on the smaller market, the Alternative Investment Market (AIM).

On the main market, traders are allowed to submit orders to buy or sell at a stated price within a reasonable time (limit order) or to buy or sell a stated number of shares immediately at the best price (market order). If a limit order cannot execute immediately (i.e. there are not enough shares at the stated price to fulfil the order), it will stay in the limit order book, which lists all outstanding limit orders.

Smaller companies (around 850 firms listed on the AIM) are traded through a dealer system. Dealers compete with one another by posting buy and sell quotes for a maximum number of shares through an electronic system that lists every dealer's quotes. The dealer that quotes the highest buy price and the lowest sale price is most likely to trade.

Listing

Shares that trade on an organized exchange are said to be *listed* on that exchange or *publicly listed.* To be listed, firms must meet specific minimum criteria concerning, for example, asset size and number of shareholders. These criteria differ from one exchange to another. For instance, Euronext has three main requirements for listing. First, a company must have at least 25 per cent of its shares listed on the exchange and the value of these shares must be at least €5 million. The second requirement is that the listing firm has at least three years of financial accounts filed with the regulator. Finally, all of the company's financial statements must follow the recognized International Financial Reporting Standards, also known as IFRS.

Figure 1.5 gives a picture of the largest stock exchanges around the world as of October 2022. Although the US exchanges are the largest in the world, Asian stock exchanges have rapidly grown in size in recent years. The Saudi Stock Exchange is now larger than the London Stock Exchange, but this is because the largest company in the world, Saudi Aramco, is listed on the exchange (over $550 billion in equity value).

Figure 1.5 Largest Stock Exchanges in October 2022

Note: *The graph shows the largest stock exchanges by market capitalization of listed companies (in trillions of US$).*

Source: Statista.

Real World Insight 1.4

The London Stock Exchange

At more than 300 years of age, the London Stock Exchange is one of the world's oldest and largest exchanges. This stock exchange allows trading in equities, bonds and derivatives for UK companies as well as firms from all over the world. However, this isn't the end of the exchange's services – it is also involved in post-trade settlement and risk management for investors who use its products.

Data are a precious asset to any stock exchange, and a substantial part of the London Stock Exchange's revenues come from the sale of and subscription to real-time and reference data products that include stock quotes, orders and transaction prices. The exchange provides more than 200,000 international equity, bond and alternative asset class indices through its index provider, the FTSE.

To fully exploit the power of data, the London Stock Exchange provides high-performance trading platforms and capital markets software, as well as trading, surveillance and post-trade technology. Although the London Stock Exchange has its headquarters in London, it also has significant operations in Italy, France, North America and Sri Lanka, employing approximately 2,800 people.

1.4 Corporate Finance in Action: The Case of Alphabet

The verb 'to Google' is defined in *Webster's New Millennium™ Dictionary of English* as 'to search for information on the internet'. This integration into everyday language is just one signal of the exceptional success of the internet search engine that was started in 1996 by two Stanford PhD students, Sergey Brin and Larry Page. Google is now part of a much larger company called Alphabet, Inc., which is worth more than $709 billion. During its massive growth, the management of Google had to consider and deal with many issues, all of which we cover in this textbook over the next 29 chapters.

Early Days

The foundation of any new business is the product or service idea. Through their research, Brin and Page believed they had a more efficient model of searching through internet pages than the search engines that existed in 1996. Armed only with this idea and a few working algorithms, they approached several potential investors and successfully attracted $100,000 from one of the founders of Sun Microsystems to develop their business concept. Within a year, they had received a further $25 million from venture capitalists. To attract this financing, Brin and Page would have had to create a business plan and cash flow forecast that estimated their future costs and revenues. From business plans and cash flows, investors can arrive at a valuation of the potential company. We cover company valuation in Part 2 of this text.

Google and Corporate Governance

By 2004, Google had been so successful with its business model and grown so much that it needed significant injections of cash to capture the emerging business opportunities that were becoming available. To the two founders, Brin and Page, it was paramount that they retained control of the company, but they also knew that they would have to issue many shares to investors so the firm could receive adequate funding. As a solution, Google restructured its ownership to have two types of equity shares, A and B class. B-class shares, which were predominantly owned by Brin and Page, were awarded 10 votes at company meetings for every share certificate, while A-class shares received one vote for every share certificate. Even though the number of shares held by outside investors was much higher than the number held by the two founders combined, the number of votes available to outsiders was lower. Issues relating to ownership structure and corporate governance, in general, are covered in **Chapter 2**.

Chapter 2
Page 24

Google and Financing Decisions

When Google was thinking of raising capital, it had two choices. It could borrow the money (through a bank loan or public debt markets) or issue equity (through the equity markets). In the end, it chose to raise all the money in the form of equity financing. Google issued no long-term debt until 2011. There are several reasons for this, and there are many factors to take into consideration when a firm chooses its debt to equity mix, which is also known as its capital structure. Companies may even decide to use more complex instruments, such as options or warrants. We cover capital structure in Part 4 and complex funding securities in Part 6. For more information on financing decisions see **Chapter 15**.

Chapter 15
Page 404

Google and the Financing Process

Chapter 14 Page 387
Chapter 19 Page 511
Chapter 20 Page 541

The original Google share issue was highly unusual in that it was organized wholly over the internet. However, the management needed to address several fundamental issues. First, what should the value of the new shares be? Should A-class shares have a different value to B-class shares? How risky are the shares? These questions are of enormous importance to investors who wish to invest cash in new investments. We explore how to measure the risk of investments in Part 3 and review the process of issuing new securities in Part 5. (See **Chapters 14, 19** and **20** for more information on the financing process.)

Google Becomes Alphabet

By the time Google became Alphabet, it had acquired more than 160 companies. Most notably, it bought Motorola Mobility for $12.5 billion in 2011, YouTube ($1.65 billion) in 2006, DoubleClick ($3.1 billion) in 2007, and Nest Labs ($3.2 billion) in 2014. Google's operations spanned many countries, and with the range of businesses in its portfolio, it was concerned that the performance of its core internet search business was becoming difficult to analyse. It consequently created a new company, Alphabet, Inc., that would own all the acquired companies as well as Google. Creating this new structure allowed investors to see how well Google was doing, separately from the other businesses in its corporate family.

Alphabet, Inc. is one of the biggest companies in the world, and will continue to evolve and develop in the future. We explore the issues Google dealt with as it expanded in **Chapters 28–30**, where we cover topics like corporate restructuring, acquisitions and mergers, financial distress and international finance. These are extremely important to all companies, not just Alphabet. (See **Chapter 28** for more information on mergers and acquisitions.)

Chapter 28
Page 767

Alphabet as a Business

Although Alphabet is known as a technology firm, its success and size make it quite similar to other large firms in more capital-intensive industries. By 2022, Alphabet had more than $108 billion invested in property and equipment, and more than 186,000 workers. In fact, Alphabet's management was so concerned that the firm was losing its old values and culture that they appointed a chief cultural officer, whose remit was to develop and maintain the early Google working environment.

Alphabet and Short-term Financing

Chapter 26 Page 715
Chapter 27 Page 739

Like all other firms, Alphabet must ensure it has enough cash available to pay off its creditors. Short-term financial planning is therefore crucial to its continued existence. Unlike many companies, Alphabet is exceptionally cash rich. According to its 2022 Q3 accounts, the company had more than $116 billion in cash and highly marketable securities. Is this too much or too little? We cover short-term financing in Part 7 of the text. (See **Chapters 26** and **27** for more information on short-term financing.)

So What Is Corporate Finance?

Many people believe corporate finance is only about valuation and investment appraisal. It is to be hoped that this section shows that, for a business to be truly successful, the firm's leadership and its shareholders must have a solid understanding of all corporate finance areas and not just one or two topics. Alphabet, Inc. is a success not only because it had a fantastic business idea, but because it understands the fundamental basis of good business and corporate finance.

Summary and Conclusions

This chapter introduced you to some of the basic ideas in corporate finance:

1 Corporate finance has three main areas of concern:
   (a) *Capital budgeting:* What long-term investments should the firm take?
   (b) *Capital structure:* Where will the firm get the long-term financing to pay for its investments? Also, what mixture of debt and equity should it use to fund operations?
   (c) *Working capital management:* How should the firm manage its everyday financial activities?

2 The goal of financial management in a for-profit business is to make decisions that increase the value of the shares, or, more generally, the market value of the equity.

3 Sustainability: The triple bottom line focuses on maximizing shareholder value, societal contribution and environmental impact, while purpose-driven businesses emphasize social and environmental objectives alongside financial performance, potentially enhancing overall firm value, employee morale and market demand.

Throughout the text, we will be analysing many different financial decisions, but we will always ask the same question: How does the decision under consideration affect the value of the equity?

Questions and Problems

CONCEPT

1 **What is Corporate Finance?** What are the main elements of corporate finance? How might these elements relate to typical family life?

2 **Introduction to Corporate Finance** Which of the following is **not** a core element of corporate finance?
   (a) The investment decision
   (b) The equity decision
   (c) The financing decision
   (d) Short-term capital management

3 **Goal of Financial Management** Explain the assumption behind the statement: 'The goal of financial management is to maximize the current share price.' Why isn't the goal to maximize the future share price? Explain the concept of the triple bottom line and how it challenges the traditional focus on shareholder wealth maximization. Discuss its implications for businesses.

4 **Financial Markets** Why do you think there are so many different types of financial markets? Would it not make sense to have just one global stock exchange where every equity was traded? What are the reasons why this would and wouldn't happen in reality?

REGULAR

5 **Primary and Secondary Markets** Explain the difference between primary and secondary markets. Why should companies be interested in secondary markets if they don't raise money directly for transactions that take place on them?

6 **Corporate Finance in Action** The section highlighting Alphabet as a case study is special in many ways because of the firm's meteoric success. Extend the case study on Alphabet by looking at the title of each chapter in this book and then identifying a similar event or news story about the firm that captures the material in the book. Write your own case study on Alphabet.

7 **Balance Sheet Equation** Voyager plc has £850 million in assets that are easily convertible to cash, and a total of £2 billion worth of assets. The company also has £450 million in debts that are due within the next year and a total of £1.5 billion in liabilities. How much is Voyager plc's equity value? And how much does it have in long-term assets and long-term liabilities?

8 **Capital Structure** Continuing on from the previous question, Voyager plc announced that it plans to increase its non-current assets by €100 million. If the company wishes to maintain its ratio of total liabilities to equity, how much long-term debt should it issue?

9 **Accounting and Cash Flows** You work for a private airport that has just purchased a new radar system from the UK for £3.5 billion. You have paid £100 million up front, with the rest to be paid in three months. Explain how these figures would appear on an accounting statement and a statement of cash flows.

10 **Timing of Cash Flows** Your company has just entered into a 12-month contract to supply mobile telephones to all its staff. You have been given two payment options. The first is to pay £50,000 every month for 12 months. The second is to pay £600,000 at the end of the year. Which option should you choose? Why?

11 **Risk of Cash Flows** You are assessing the viability of two projects. Project A has a 25 per cent chance of losing €1,000,000, a 50 per cent chance of breaking even and a 25 per cent chance of making €1,000,000 profit. Project B has a 10 per cent chance of losing €2,000,000, an 80 per cent chance of breaking even and a 10 per cent chance of making €2,000,000 profit. Which project should you choose? Why?

12 **Corporate Goals** Explain what is meant by the triple bottom line. What are the main issues financial managers must consider when pursuing a triple bottom line perspective?

13 **Triple Bottom Line** Do you consider the triple bottom line to be important to a firm's management? Explain.

14 **Financing Goals** As a firm progresses throughout its life cycle it will typically move from seeking investment from private sources towards raising money on the capital markets. Explain why this is the case.

15 **Short-term Financing Goals** In 2019, it was reported that Apple had more than $250 billion in cash. This was more than the whole GDP of Finland, which is the market value of all goods and services produced by the country in a year. Is this a problem for Apple? Explain.

16 **Financial Management Goals** You have read the first chapter of this textbook and have taken over a company that you now discover is losing £100,000 a week. At the rate things are going, the company will not have any cash left in six months to pay its creditors. What are your goals as a financial manager? Is this consistent with what you have read in this chapter? Explain.

17 **Triple Bottom Line** Explain why shareholder wealth maximization is consistent with the triple bottom line concept. Are societal and environmental issues a necessary function of business? Explain.

18 **Ethical and Non-ethical Funds** You have just joined a graduate scheme in a fund management company, and your manager tells you that ethical funds do not significantly outperform non-ethical funds, according to the bulk of empirical evidence. How would you respond to your manager?

19 **Profit Maximization** Many 'experts' suggest that maximizing profit should be the main financial goal of a corporation. Is this a correct view? Explain.

20 Private Firm Financial Management Goals If you are in charge of a private firm and it doesn't have a share price, what should be your goal as a financial manager? Explain.

21 Different Financial Management Goals You have been manager of a small company for 20 years and have become great friends with your employees. In the last month, foreign owners have bought out the company's founding owner and have told you that they need to cut costs in order to maximize the value of the company. One of the things they suggest is to lay off 30 per cent of the workforce. However, you believe that the workforce is the company's greatest asset. On what basis do you argue against the new owners' opinions?

22 Purpose-driven Businesses Name three main reasons why companies in the UK or Europe might choose to adopt a purpose-driven or sustainable approach, according to Edmans and Kacperczyk (2022).

23 Sustainability Describe the practice of 'greenwashing' and explain its potential consequences for investors in developed markets.

CHALLENGE

24 Goals of the Firm Your company's new owners suggest the following changes to maximize the value of the firm. Write a brief report responding to each point in turn.

(a) Increase the pensions of retired employees by a cost-of-living adjustment of 2 per cent to account for inflation.

(b) With the recent surge in gold prices, revenues are expected to increase by 40 per cent.

(c) Increase exploration costs by 20 per cent and distribute the remaining profits to shareholders in the form of higher dividend payouts.

(d) Invest in cutting-edge, untested exploration methods through a new research and development initiative.

(e) Reduce the workforce by 20 per cent to minimize expenses.

25 Dealer versus Agency Markets Explain the difference between dealer and agency markets. Why do you think both types of market exist? Is there one type of market that is the best? Explain.

26 Statement of Financial Position If a firm is to cut costs as a result of falling revenues, how would this appear in the statement of financial position? Explain.

27 Dual-class Shares The multinational media company News Corporation has a dual-class share structure. Why might the company do this? Are there any drawbacks?

28 thyssenkrupp AG You have the following information for the German engineering firm, thyssenkrupp AG. All figures are in millions of euros (€).

	2023	2022
Non-current assets	14,118	14,501
Current assets	20,347	20,546
Total assets	**34,465**	**35,047**
Current liabilities	16,796	17,097
Non-current liabilities	14,334	14,546
Total liabilities	**31,130**	**31,643**
Total equity	3,335	3,404
Total liabilities plus equity	**34,465**	**35,047**

Give a brief interpretation of how you think thyssenkrupp AG did over the two-year period. Do you think its position improved or got worse? Explain.

29 Balance Sheet Assume that thyssenkrupp AG increased its non-current assets by €1 billion in 2024 and at the same time reduced its current assets by €500 million. Review the ways in which thyssenkrupp would be able to finance this expansion. What would the balance sheet look like under each strategy?

30 thyssenkrupp Statement of Financial Position Assume that, in 2024, thyssenkrupp purchased a new automation technology for €500 million. It paid this on credit and won't actually be due to pay for the automation technology until 2025. The managers of thyssenkrupp state that, in the future, any increase in assets will be wholly funded by debt. Using the data in Question 28, what would the statement of financial position look like at the end of 2024? At the end of 2025?

31 **Statement of Financial Position** Assume that, instead of fully financing the expansion with debt, the managers of thyssenkrupp say they wish to maintain the pre-transaction ratio of non-current liabilities to equity after the expansion. What would thyssenkrupp's statement of financial position look like in 2025?

32 **Financial Market Regulators** The UK's financial markets regulator states that its objectives are to promote efficient, orderly and fair markets, help retail consumers achieve a fair deal, and improve the country's business capacity and effectiveness. The German financial markets regulator, BaFin, states that, 'The objective of securities supervision is to ensure the transparency and integrity of the financial market and the protection of investors.' Are the British and German objectives consistent with each other? Explain.

33 **Balance Sheet Model of the Firm** The layout of financial accounts is rarely the same across companies and, sometimes, it can be difficult to establish a simple picture of a firm's balance sheet. The accounts below are for Rogik plc. Construct a simple balance sheet model of the firm in the same way as Real World Insight 1.1 for years 1 and 0. Provide a brief report on how you think the company has changed.

Current assets	Year 1	Year 0
Cash and cash equivalents	937.8	943.7
Marketable securities and financial assets	1,117.1	55.6
Trade accounts receivable	2,328.3	2,296.3
Inventories	1,691.1	1,673.5
Other current assets	250.2	564.7
Tax receivables	72.7	93.7
Assets held for sale	–	36.7
	6,397.2	**5,664.2**
Non-current assets		
Intangible assets	11,764.3	12,484.1
Property, plant and equipment	3,113.4	3,241.5
Investments at equity	–	5.0
Non-current financial assets	60.3	130.3
Financial assets covering pensions	–	216.9
Other non-current assets	54.9	52.9
Deferred tax assets	730.0	593.1
	15,722.9	**16,723.8**
Current liabilities		
Current financial liabilities	1,394.4	356.1
Trade accounts payable	1,100.8	1,200.1
Other current liabilities	1,102.1	1,054.6
Tax liabilities	399.4	368.4
Current provisions	365.5	374.5
Liabilities directly related to assets held for sale	–	5.9
	4,362.2	**3,359.6**
Non-current liabilities		
Non-current financial liabilities	4,144.9	5,127.4
Other non-current liabilities	43.6	42.9
Non-current provisions	619.5	524.2
Provisions for pensions and other post-employment benefits	1,136.9	1,581.6
Deferred tax liabilities	1,319.6	1,380.5
	7,264.5	**8,656.6**

Current assets	Year 1	Year 0
Net equity		
Equity capital	565.2	565.2
Reserves	8,671.7	8,484.2
Gains/losses recognized immediately in equity	1,210.2	1,280.4
Equity attributable to Rogik plc shareholders	10,447.1	10,329.8
Non-controlling interest	46.3	42.0
	10,493.4	**10,371.8**

34 **Goals of a Financial Manager** In 2012, the Argentinian government nationalized YPF, which is a subsidiary of Repsol, the Spanish oil giant. YPF was integral to the operations of Repsol. The firm was set up 10 years earlier and had received more than €20 billion of capital investment from Repsol. The benefits to Repsol's shareholders from YPF were large and, every year, more than €527 million of dividends were paid to the parent company. If you were the financial manager of YPF, how do you think your goals would change as a result of the change of owners (i.e. from Repsol to the Argentinian government)?

35 **Stock Exchanges** The UK has a hybrid stock exchange where the largest companies are traded on an electronic order book and the smallest firms are traded through a competitive dealer market. Do you think this is a sensible system? If you were a new firm, on which system would you prefer to have your shares listed? Explain.

36 **Life Cycle of Firms** Choose any company from your country and develop a chronology of its life cycle, from business start-up, through initial expansion, to stock exchange listing, and then (if applicable) death through merger, acquisition or insolvency. For each stage, explain the company's evolution through the eyes of a financial manager.

37 **Sustainable Business Models** Analyse the case of The Body Shop, a British-based cosmetics firm, and discuss how it integrates the triple bottom line into its financial decisions. Assess the challenges and benefits of its approach in the context of the business environment in which the firm operates.

Exam Question (45 minutes)

As a financial manager, you have been hired to help a well-known fashion designer, who is famous for creating clothing lines using eco-friendly materials. The designer wants to commercialize her brand and scale the business. The designer, who has never worked in industry since she left university, has been primarily funded by angel investors and grants. Unfortunately, the designer has very little understanding of how to develop a business that captures the true value of her brand while also staying true to her firm's mission of sustainability. The designer has a number of queries she feels are important to understand before going forward:

1 As a financial manager, what will be your main activities in the fashion company? **(10 marks)**

2 What will be your first priority when it comes to managing the financials of the firm? Explain. **(10 marks)**

3 Will the company need to invest money in order to grow and scale? Explain. **(10 marks)**

4 Will the company need financing in order to achieve its goals? Explain. **(10 marks)**

5 How will the company raise financing? Is it sensible to list the company on the stock market or issue debt? What about impact investing or crowdfunding? **(10 marks)**

6 What are the benefits of holding cash in the fashion company? **(10 marks)**

7 What should be the goal of the fashion company? Should it be solely focused on maximizing profit or is there room for a broader purpose? **(10 marks)**

8 The designer has said she does not wish to run a company that does not contribute to society or the environment. She asks if it is possible to have corporate objectives that are broader than just maximizing profit. Explain your view on purpose-driven companies and their potential impact on society and the environment. **(20 marks)**

Total Marks: 100

Practical Case Study

Choose three companies from your country that have been recognized as purpose-driven or socially responsible. These companies should have a clear mission or purpose that goes beyond maximizing profits.

Download their financial accounts for the most recent year. Look for their annual reports, financial statements and other relevant financial information on the companies' websites.

For each firm, construct the balance sheet and calculate the value of shareholders' equity. Use the following information to complete the balance sheet:

Non-current assets

Current assets

Current liabilities

Non-current liabilities

Analyse the financial performance of each company. Consider the following questions:

1 What do the figures say about each company's financial health?
2 What trends or patterns do you observe in the balance sheet?
3 How do the companies compare in terms of shareholders' equity?

Research the share price of each firm. Look for historical data on each company's stock performance. Analyse the data and consider the following questions:

1 What does the share price history tell you about each company's performance?
2 Are there any notable trends or patterns in the stock performance?
3 How does the stock performance compare to the overall market?

Read the news for each company. Look for articles, press releases and other relevant information about each company's social and environmental impact. Consider the following questions:

1 What does the news tell you about the company's mission and impact?
2 How does the company's purpose-driven approach affect its financial performance?
3 Are there any notable social or environmental initiatives that the company is undertaking?

Combining all the information, which company do you think is the best investment? Explain your reasoning using data and analysis from the previous steps. Consider the following questions:

1 How does the company's financial health and performance compare to the other companies you analysed?
2 How does the company's purpose-driven approach affect its financial performance?

Write a report that includes the following sections:

- Executive summary
- Company background and purpose
- Balance sheet and shareholders' equity analysis
- Share price analysis
- Social and environmental impact analysis
- Conclusion and investment recommendation

References

Edmans, A. and M. Kacperczyk (2022) 'Sustainable Finance', *Review of Finance*, Vol. 26, No. 6, 1309–1313.

Fang, V.W., T. Hoe and S. Tice (2009) 'Stock Market Liquidity and Firm Value', *Journal of Financial Economics*, Vol. 94, 150–169.

Graham, J.R. (2022) 'Presidential Address: Corporate Finance and Reality', *Journal of Finance*, Vol. 77, No. 4, 1975–2049.

O'Hara, M. and M. Ye (2011) 'Is Market Fragmentation Harming Market Quality?', *Journal of Financial Economics*, Vol. 100, 459–474.

Additional Reading

The field of corporate finance is enormous and evolves in conjunction with events in the global business environment. For readers who wish to delve further, details of several interesting papers are given below.

1 Bris, A., Y. Koskinen and M. Nilsson (2009) 'The Euro and Corporate Valuations', *Review of Financial Studies*, Vol. 22, No. 8, 3171–3209.

2 Graham, J.R., J. Grennan, C.R. Harvey and S. Rajgopal (2022) 'Corporate Culture: Evidence From the Field', *Journal of Financial Economics*, Vol. 146, No. 2, 552–593.

3 Rajan, R.G. (2012) 'Presidential Address: The Corporation in Finance', *Journal of Finance*, Vol. 67, 1173–1217.

4 Zingales, L. (2000) 'In Search of New Foundations', *Journal of Finance*, Vol. 55, No. 4, 1623–1653.

One question that has been approached in a very interesting way is 'Which is more important, the business plan or the managers who carry it out?' This is examined in the following paper:

5 Kaplan, S., B. Sensoy and P. Stromberg (2009) 'Should Investors Bet on the Jockey or the Horse? Evidence from the Evolution of Firms from Early Business Plans to Public Companies', *Journal of Finance*, Vol. 64, 75–115.

Some interesting papers on sustainable finance, purpose-driven firms and the triple bottom line are listed below:

6 Calvet, L., G. Gianfrate and R. Uppal (2022) 'The Finance of Climate Change', *Journal of Corporate Finance*, Vol. 73, No. 2, 102162.

7 Gillan, S.L., A. Koch and L.T. Starks (2021) 'Firms and Social Responsibility: A Review of ESG and CSR Research in Corporate Finance', *Journal of Corporate Finance*, Vol. 66, No. 3, 101889.

8 Glavas, A. and J. Mish (2015) 'Resources and Capabilities of Triple Bottom Line Firms: Going Over Old or Breaking New Ground?', *Journal of Business Ethics*, Vol. 127, No. 3, 623–642.

9 Hussain, N., U. Rigoni and R.P. Orij (2018) 'Corporate Governance and Sustainability Performance: Analysis of Triple Bottom Line Performance', *Journal of Business Ethics*, Vol. 149, No. 2, 411–432.

10 Slaper, T.F. and T.J. Hall (2011) 'The Triple Bottom Line: What Is It and How Does It Work?', *Indiana Business Review*, Vol. 86, No. 1, 4–8.

11 Tate, W.L. and L. Bals (2018) 'Achieving Shared Triple Bottom Line (TBL) Value Creation: Toward a Social Resource-based View (SRBV) of the Firm', *Journal of Business Ethics*, Vol. 152, No. 3, 803–826.

Finally, Luigi Zingales has written a very interesting paper criticizing the approach that finance academics sometimes take towards the subject. In the interests of humility, we present it here:

12 Zingales, L. (2015) 'DP10350, Does Finance Benefit Society?', CEPR Policy Paper.

Chapter 2
Corporate Governance

Learning Objectives

After reading this chapter you should be able to:

LO1 Comprehend the nature, purpose, components and advantages/disadvantages of corporate firms.

LO2 Investigate the agency problem, its implications, and methods for mitigating its effects within corporations.

LO3 Classify the elements, roles and responsibilities within corporate governance and ownership structures.

LO4 Recognise the importance, purpose and fundamental principles of effective corporate governance, emphasizing transparency, accountability and ethical conduct.

LO5 Analyse the global variations in corporate governance practices, the influence of culture, regulation and market forces, and the challenges in harmonizing international standards.

Does it matter how a company is structured for managers to make the best financial decisions? Does it matter who owns a company? Where do ethics come into the decision to invest a firm's resources, and does this have any relevance for the financial manager? Do managers always follow the wishes of shareholders? Are lenders equally important to owners of a firm? How should a company manage its relationships with diverse stakeholder groups, such as employees, customers and suppliers? Are some shareholders more important than others?

All of the above are significant in understanding the various pressures managers face when running a business. Unfortunately, many finance textbooks assume companies pursue firm value maximization without a discussion of other objectives. However, there is nothing to stop managers from pursuing their agendas over that of the firm or its owners.

The 2018 collapse of the multinational firm Carillion, with more than 40,000 redundancies, showed that poor corporate cultures could create existential risks for firms. However, despite concepts such as managerial accountability and transparency receiving much greater emphasis in recent times, there is still a long way to go to ensure that 'recklessness, hubris and greed' do not dominate managerial decision-making.

Source: perekotypole/123RF.

Financial institutions have become more involved in the strategic decisions of firms, and shareholder activism is common. Other changes have also affected the way companies are managed and run. For example, the influx of money from international investors in China, India, South America and the Middle East has influenced corporate cultures in ways we could not have imagined 10 years ago.

Unfortunately, even with improvements in corporate governance, scandals like the Carillion case occur with worrying frequency. What made Carillion so disturbing was a size of failure not seen since the 2008 financial crisis. The poor managerial behaviours were the same in 2018 as they had been 10 years earlier. An inquiry by the British government said that Carillion's failure was 'a story of recklessness, hubris and greed, its business model was a relentless dash for cash'. The inquiry also noted that Carillion directors misrepresented how well (or just how poorly) the company was performing.

Why did Carillion exhibit this behaviour, and did regulators and investors do anything to curtail it? When a firm reports healthy profits, investors react positively and increase their shareholdings. Stronger demand for the firm's shares would result in higher share prices and capital gains for investors. We must also ask questions about the power and effectiveness of independent monitors such as Carillion's non-executive directors and its auditor, KPMG. Why didn't they do anything?

In this chapter, we will cover the various issues involved with corporate governance, from the different organizational structures that can be created through the multiple ways investors put money into the firm and the powers of regulators in incentivizing positive management behaviour. The topic is necessarily broad, so our purpose is to provide a comprehensive introduction to corporate governance and how it affects financial decision-making. The interested reader is invited to review the articles in the reference list at the end of the chapter if they wish to investigate the area more deeply.

2.1 The Corporate Firm

A firm is a way of organizing the economic activity of many individuals. A basic problem faced by a firm is how to raise cash. The corporate form of business – that is, organizing the firm as a corporation – is the standard method for solving problems encountered in raising large amounts of cash. However, businesses can take other forms. In this section we consider the three basic legal forms of organizing firms, and we see how firms go about the task of raising large amounts of money under each form.

The Sole Proprietorship

A **sole proprietorship** is a business owned by one person. Suppose you decide to start a business to produce bagpipes. Going into business is simple: you announce to all who will listen, 'Today, I am going to build better bagpipes.'

A sole proprietorship is the most common form of business structure in the world. From London to Dar es Salaam, from Bangkok to Amsterdam, from Oman to Madrid, you will see people doing their business in the streets and at roadsides. These are all businesses owned by one person. Possibly, you, the reader, may come from a family that has a sole proprietorship business.

In many countries, you need a business licence to run a sole proprietorship, but it is also common for sole proprietorships to be set up without any paperwork. Once started, a sole proprietorship can hire as many people as needed and borrow whatever money is required. At year-end, all the profits and losses will belong to the owner and this becomes his or her annual income.

Here are some factors that are important in considering a sole proprietorship:

- The sole proprietorship is the cheapest business to form. No formal charter, articles or memoranda of association are required. Very few government regulations must be satisfied for most industries.
- A sole proprietorship pays no corporate income taxes. All profits of the business are taxed as individual income.
- The sole proprietorship has unlimited liability for business debts and obligations. No distinction is made between personal and business assets. This means that if a sole proprietorship owes money to creditors and cannot pay, the owner's own possessions must be used to pay off the firm's debts.
- The life of the sole proprietorship is limited by the life of the owner of the firm.
- Because the only money invested in the firm is the proprietor's, the cash that can be raised by the sole proprietor is limited to the proprietor's own personal wealth.

Example 2.1

JonMac Builders

JonMac Builders is a building contractor, owned as a sole proprietorship by John McAfee. Started in 1987 by a fresh-looking 24 year old with his own savings, John leased a small van for £200, used his own tools and began working on jobs garnered through word of mouth. The firm still exists as a sole proprietorship and now has four employees, all family members. All income from the company's activities is taxed at John's income tax rate and the firm's liabilities are secured by John's personal assets, such as his house.

The Partnership

Any two or more people can get together and form a **partnership**. Partnerships fall into two categories: (1) general partnerships and (2) limited partnerships.

In a *general partnership* all partners agree to provide some fraction of the work and cash, and share the profits and losses of the firm. Each partner is liable for the debts of the partnership. A partnership agreement specifies the nature of the arrangement. The partnership agreement may be an oral agreement or a formal document setting forth the understanding.

Limited partnerships permit the liability of some of the partners to be limited to the amount of cash each has contributed to the partnership. Limited partnerships usually require that (1) at least one partner be a general partner, and (2) the limited partners do not participate in managing the business. Here are some things that are important when considering a partnership:

- Partnerships are usually inexpensive and easy to form. Written documents are required in complicated arrangements, including general and limited partnerships. Business licences and filing fees may be necessary.
- General partners have unlimited liability for all debts. The liability of limited partners is usually limited to the contribution each has made to the partnership. If one general partner is unable to meet his or her commitment, the shortfall must be made up by the other general partners.
- The general partnership is terminated when a general partner dies or withdraws (but this is not so for a limited partner). It is difficult for a partnership to transfer ownership without dissolving. Usually all general partners must agree. However, limited partners may sell their interest in a business.
- It is difficult for a partnership to raise large amounts of cash. Equity contributions are usually limited to a partner's ability and desire to contribute to the partnership. Many companies start life as a sole proprietorship or partnership, but at some point they choose to convert to corporate form.
- Income from a partnership is taxed as personal income to the partners.
- Management control resides with the general partners. Usually a majority vote is required on important matters, such as the amount of profit to be retained in the business.

It is difficult for large business organizations to exist as sole proprietorships or partnerships. The main advantage to a sole proprietorship or partnership is the cost of getting started. Afterwards, the disadvantages, which may become severe, are (1) unlimited liability, (2) limited life of the enterprise, and (3) difficulty of transferring ownership. These three disadvantages lead to (4) difficulty in raising cash.

Example 2.2

NellaFola

NellaFola is a real estate broker consisting of 25 estate agents. Five of the estate agents are general partners who are responsible for the long-term strategy of the firm, in addition to managing their own clients. The other 20 estate agents have their own customers and earn commission for the partnership on real estate sales. Each estate agent will have a remuneration package that consists of a basic salary element plus a commission component. In addition to a basic salary and commission, the five general partners will also receive a component of the partnership's profits. Partnerships of this type are common in the law, medical and accounting professions.

The Corporation

Of the forms of business enterprise, the **corporation** is by far the most important. It is a distinct legal entity. This means that a corporation can have a name and enjoy many of the legal powers of natural persons. For example, corporations can acquire and exchange property. Corporations can enter contracts and may sue and be sued. For jurisdictional purposes the corporation is a citizen of its country of incorporation (it cannot vote, however).

The Articles of Incorporation and Memorandum of Association

Starting a corporation is more complicated than starting a sole proprietorship or partnership. The incorporators must prepare articles of incorporation and a memorandum of association (the terms differ from country to country, but the general requirements are the same). The articles of incorporation must include the following:

- Name of the corporation
- Intended life of the corporation (it may be for ever)
- Business purpose
- Number of shares that the corporation is authorized to issue, with a statement of limitations and rights of different classes of shares
- Nature of the rights granted to shareholders
- Number of members of the initial board of directors.

The memorandum of association contains the rules to be used by the corporation to regulate its own existence, and they concern its shareholders, directors and officers. The rules can range from the briefest possible statement of rules for the corporation's management to hundreds of pages of text.

Public versus Private Limited Corporations

A corporation will normally start off as a private limited corporation, in which the shares of the firm are not permitted to be traded or advertised in the public arena. The directors of the company will very likely also be the major shareholders. Private limited companies are usually very small, with the number of employees ranging from three to several thousand. Families are regularly the major shareholders in private limited companies.

In closely held corporations with few shareholders, there may be a large overlap among the shareholders, the directors and the top management. However, in larger corporations, the shareholders, directors and top management are likely to be separate groups. At this point, the corporation will comprise three sets of distinct interests: the shareholders (the owners), the directors and senior management, and the firm's stakeholders (e.g. lenders, employees, local community).

The senior executives of a corporation make up the board of directors. On the board, someone will have the chairperson's role and be responsible for ensuring that the interests of shareholders are actively considered in corporate decision-making. The chairperson is the most senior member of a corporation and leads all general meetings of the firm. The chief executive officer is the most senior manager of the corporation and is in ultimate charge of the day-to-day running of the firm. In many companies, the same person takes on the role of both chief executive and chairperson. The board also has other directors, and these are made up of two distinct categories. Executive directors are senior managers that work in the company on a day-to-day basis, while non-executive directors are independent and are not involved in management. Non-executives usually attend monthly board meetings, and will be individuals with significant business experience and possible political importance.

In countries with single-tier, or unitary, board structures (e.g. Belgium, Ireland, Italy, Portugal, Spain, Sweden, the UK and USA), the shareholders control the corporation's direction, policies and activities. The shareholders elect the board of directors, who in turn select top management. Members of top management serve as corporate officers and manage the operations of the corporation in the best interests of the shareholders.

In countries with two-tier board structures, a corporation's executive board (which is made up of directors and senior management) reports to, and is elected by, a supervisory board, which may consist of major shareholders, creditors, trade union representatives, major lenders and other important stakeholders. There are no non-executive directors on the executive board since the supervisory board has the responsibility of monitoring the actions of executive directors. Countries with two-tier boards include Austria, Denmark, Germany and the Netherlands. Countries where both unitary and two-tier boards can exist include Finland, France, Norway and Switzerland. However, things are never straightforward and there will always be country-specific differences. Belgium, for example, has a unitary board system but banks and insurance companies are allowed to have two-tier board structures.

Advantages of Corporations Over Partnerships and Sole Partnerships

The potential separation of ownership from management gives the corporation several advantages over sole proprietorships and partnerships:

- Because ownership in a corporation is represented by shares of equity, ownership can be readily transferred to new owners. Because the corporation exists independently of those who own its shares, there is no limit to the transferability of shares as there is in partnerships.
- The corporation has unlimited life. Because the corporation is separate from its owners, the death or withdrawal of an owner does not affect the corporation's legal existence. The corporation can continue on after the original owners have withdrawn.
- The shareholders' liability is limited to the amount invested in the ownership shares. For example, if a shareholder purchased €1,000 in shares of a corporation, the potential loss would be €1,000. In a partnership, a general partner with a €1,000 contribution could lose the €1,000 plus any other indebtedness of the partnership.

Limited liability, ease of ownership transfer and perpetual succession are the major advantages of the corporate form of business organization. These give the corporation an enhanced ability to raise cash.

There is, however, one great disadvantage to incorporation. Many countries tax corporate income in addition to the personal income tax that shareholders pay on dividend income they receive. Although there are normally tax rebates given to shareholders, this is, in effect, a double taxation when compared to taxation on sole proprietorships and partnerships.

Table 2.1 summarizes our discussion of partnerships and corporations.

Table 2.1 A Comparison of Sole Proprietorships, Partnerships and Corporations

	Corporation	Partnership	Sole Proprietorship
Liquidity and marketability	Shares can be exchanged without termination of the corporation. Shares can be listed on a stock exchange.	Shares are subject to substantial restrictions on transferability. There is usually no established trading market for partnership shares.	Shares are exceptionally illiquid and there is no established trading market for shares.
Voting rights	In single-tier board structures, usually each share of equity entitles the holder to one vote per share on matters requiring a vote and on the election of the directors. Directors determine top management.	Some voting rights by limited partners. However, general partners have exclusive control and management of operations.	The sole trader owns 100% of the firm, and has exclusive control and management of operations.
Taxation	Corporations may have double taxation: corporate income is taxable, and dividends to shareholders are also taxable. Each country has its own approach to how it deals with double taxation, and may give a full or partial rebate on the corporate tax payment.	Partnerships are not taxable. Partners pay personal taxes on partnership profits.	Sole traders pay personal taxes on company profits.
Reinvestment and dividend payout	Corporations have broad latitude on dividend payout decisions.	Partnerships are generally prohibited from reinvesting partnership profits. All profits are distributed to partners.	Sole proprietorships have a lot of freedom in reinvesting profits because they are treated as personal income.
Liability	Shareholders are not personally liable for obligations of the corporation.	Limited partners are not liable for obligations of partnerships. General partners may have unlimited liability.	Sole traders have unlimited liability for the obligations of the firm.
Continuity of existence	Corporations may have a perpetual life.	Partnerships have limited life.	Sole proprietorships have a limited life.

Real World Insight 2.1

Nokia Board Structure

Multinational technology and IT firm Nokia is one of the world's largest companies, with revenues above $23 billion. It is listed on two stock exchanges – NASDAQ Helsinki and the New York Stock Exchange – and has more than 100,000 employees. The company is managed by a board of directors.

Although the company does not have a policy regarding its chair and chief executive roles, these are currently held by two different people. The functions of chair and chief executive officer are held by Sari Baldauf and Pekka Lundmark, respectively. Nokia's policy is that the board of directors has a minimum of seven and maximum of 12 members.

Nokia has a policy on board diversity to ensure that candidates for board positions are considered with respect to gender, age, nationality, cultural and educational background, skills and experience. Its objective is to have 40 per cent of the board consisting of both genders by 2020. At the time of writing, the company has a 70:30 split between male and female board members.

The board has three subcommittees: the Audit Committee, Personnel Committee, and the Corporate Governance and Nomination Committee.

The Audit Committee is responsible for ensuring that the accounting and financial reporting processes are fit for purpose. The Personnel Committee oversees all personnel-related policies and practices at Nokia, including executive compensation. Finally the Corporate Governance and Nomination Committee leads on ensuring board composition is consistent with its policies, and monitors all issues related to corporate governance.

Source: www.nokia.com.

A Corporation by Another Name . . .

The corporate form of organization has many variations around the world. The exact laws and regulations differ from country to country, of course, but the essential features of public ownership and limited liability remain. These firms are often called *joint stock companies, public limited companies* or *limited liability companies,* depending on the specific nature of the firm and the country of origin.

Table 2.2 gives the names of a number of corporate abbreviations, their countries of origin, a translation of the abbreviation, and a description of its meaning.

Table 2.2 International Corporations

Type of Corporation	Country of Origin	In Original Language	Description
Pty Ltd.	Australia	Proprietary Limited	Private Limited
Limited	Australia	Limited	Publicly Listed
AG	Austria, Germany, Switzerland	Aktiengesellschaft	Publicly Listed
GmbH	Austria, Germany, Switzerland	Gesellschaft mit beschränkter Haftung	Private Limited
NV	Belgium, Netherlands	Naamloze Vennootschap	Publicly Listed
BV	Belgium, Netherlands	Besloten Vennootschap	Private Limited
SA	Belgium, France, Luxembourg, Portugal, Spain	Société Anonyme/Sociedade	Publicly Listed
AD	Bulgaria	акционерно дружество	Publicly Listed
OOD	Bulgaria	дружество с ограничена отговорност	Private Limited
股 有限公司	China Mainland	股 有限公司	Publicly Listed
有限公司	China Mainland	有限公司	Private Limited

Type of Corporation	Country of Origin	In Original Language	Description
ApS	Denmark	Anpartsselskab	Private Limited
A/S	Denmark	Aktieselskab	Publicly Listed
SE	European Union	Societas Europaea	Publicly Listed
Oy	Finland	Osakeyhtiö	Private Limited
Oyj	Finland	Julkinen Osakeyhtiö	Publicly Listed
AB	Finland, Sweden	Aktiebolag	Private Limited
Abp	Finland	Publikt Aktiebolag	Publicly Listed
SARL	France, Luxembourg	Société à Responsibilité Limitée	Private Limited
Ltd	Hong Kong	Limited	Private/Public
Pvt. Ltd	India	Private Limited Company	Private Limited
Plc	India, Ireland, Thailand, UK	Public Limited Company	Publicly Listed
Srl	Italy	Società a Responsabilità Limitata	Private Limited
SpA	Italy	Società per Azioni	Publicly Listed
AS	Norway	Aksjeselskap	Private Limited
ASA	Norway	Allmennaksjeselskap	Publicly Listed
OOO	Russia	Общество сограниченой ответственностью	Private Limited
AO	Russia	Акционерн общество	Publicly Listed
(Pty) Ltd	South Africa	Privaat Maatskappy	Private Limited
LTD	South Africa	Publieke Maatskappy	Publicly Listed
S.L.	Spain	Sociedad Limitada	Private Limited
Ltd	Ireland, UK, USA	Limited	Private Limited
Inc., Corp.	USA	Incorporated, Corporation	Publicly Listed

2.2 The Agency Problem and Control of the Corporation

We have seen that the financial manager acts in the best interests of the shareholders when they take actions that increase the value of the company's equity. However, in many large corporations, particularly in the UK, Ireland and the USA, ownership can be spread over a huge number of shareholders. This dispersion of ownership arguably means that no one shareholder will have enough power to influence management, suggesting that managers effectively control the firm. In this case, will management necessarily act in the best interests of the shareholders, and might not management pursue its own goals at the shareholders' expense?

A different type of problem exists in many European firms. Whereas large British and American firms have a dispersed ownership structure, many businesses in Europe have a dominant shareholder with a very large ownership stake. Primarily, these shareholders are family groups, banks or governments. In firms with a dominant shareholder it is possible that corporate objectives will be directed by only one individual or group at the expense of other smaller shareholders. In this case, managers will be acting in the interests of only a subset of the company's owners.

The issues we have discussed above are caused by what we call agency relationships. In the following pages, we briefly consider some of the arguments relating to this issue.

Type I Agency Relationships

The relationship between shareholders and management is called a Type I agency relationship. Such a relationship exists whenever someone (the principal) hires another (the agent) to represent his or her interests. For example, you might hire a company (the agent) to sell a car you own while you are away at university. In all such relationships, there is the possibility there may be a conflict of interest between the principal and the agent. Such a conflict is called a Type I agency problem.

Suppose you hire a company to sell your car and agree to pay a flat fee when the firm sells the car. The agent's incentive in this case is to make the sale, not necessarily to get you the best price. If you offer a commission of, say, 10 per cent of the sales price instead of a flat fee, then this problem might not exist. This example illustrates that the way in which an agent is compensated is one factor that affects agency problems.

Management Goals

To see how management and shareholder interests might differ, imagine that a firm is considering a new investment. The new investment is expected to favourably impact the share value, but it is also a relatively risky venture. The owners of the firm will wish to take the investment (because the share value will rise), but management may not because there is the possibility that things will turn out badly and management jobs will be lost. If management does not invest, then the shareholders may lose a valuable opportunity. This is one example of a Type I agency cost.

In general, an *agency cost* is the cost of a conflict of interest between shareholders and management (we will consider later another agency relationship between controlling and minority shareholders). These costs can be indirect or direct. An indirect agency cost is a lost opportunity, such as the one we have just described.

Direct agency costs come in two forms. The first type is a corporate expenditure that benefits management but costs the shareholders. Perhaps the purchase of a luxurious and unneeded corporate jet would fall under this heading. The second type of direct agency cost is an expense that comes from the need to monitor management actions. Paying outside auditors to assess the accuracy of financial statement information could be one example.

It is sometimes argued that, left to themselves, managers would tend to maximize the amount of resources over which they have control or, more generally, corporate power or wealth. This goal could lead to an overemphasis on corporate size or growth. For example, sometimes management is accused of overpaying to acquire another company just to increase the business size or to demonstrate corporate power. Obviously, if overpayment does take place, such a purchase does not benefit the shareholders of the purchasing company.

Our discussion indicates that management may tend to prioritize organizational survival to protect job security. Also, executives may dislike outside interference, so independence and corporate self-sufficiency could be important managerial goals.

Do Managers Act in the Shareholders' Interests?

Whether managers will, in fact, act in the best interests of shareholders depends on two factors. First, how closely are management goals aligned with shareholder goals? This question relates, at least in part, to the way managers are compensated. Second, can managers be replaced if they do not pursue shareholder goals? This issue relates to control of the firm. As we will discuss, there are a number of reasons to think that, even in the largest firms, The firm's management has a significant incentive to act in the interests of shareholders.

Managing Agency Costs in Sustainable Firms

Firms with clear sustainability objectives will emphasize environmental, social and governance (ESG) factors in their success criteria. However, while sustainability and green strategic goals can bring many benefits, they also create a new set of challenges, particularly with regard to agency costs.

In a traditional investment context, agency costs arise when managers make decisions that prioritize their own interests over those of shareholders. In the context of sustainable firms, the challenge is to ensure that managers are acting in a manner that is consistent with ESG principles.

One key area where agency costs arise is in the reporting of ESG metrics. Managers may have an incentive to overstate their ESG performance in order to attract investment or avoid criticism from stakeholders, which can lead to a lack of trust in ESG metrics. Another area is in the implementation of ESG policies. Managers may face conflicting interests when making decisions that affect ESG outcomes, such as reducing carbon emissions or increasing diversity and inclusion. For example, reducing carbon emissions may increase costs and reduce profits in the short term. In these situations, managers must balance the need to act in the best interests of the company with their commitment to ESG principles.

To mitigate the agency costs of sustainable firms, executives should implement strong governance structures to ensure that managers are accountable for their ESG performance. This can involve incorporating ESG metrics into performance evaluations, setting clear ESG targets, and engaging with stakeholders to understand their ESG concerns and priorities.

Managerial Compensation

Executives will frequently have a significant economic incentive to increase share value. First, managerial compensation, particularly at the top, is usually tied to financial performance and often specifically to share value. For example, managers are frequently given the option to buy equity at a bargain price. The more the equity is worth, the more valuable is this option. In fact, options are often used to motivate employees of all types, not just top managers. For example, Alphabet (the parent company of Google) has issued share options to all of its employees, thereby giving its workforce a significant stake in the company's share price, and better aligning employee and shareholder interests. Many other corporations, large and small, have similar policies.

The second incentive that managers have relates to job prospects. Better performers within the firm will tend to get promoted. More generally, managers who are successful in pursuing shareholder goals will be in greater demand in the labour market and thus command higher salaries.

In fact, managers who are successful in pursuing shareholder goals can reap enormous rewards. For example, the five best-paid (annual salary in brackets) executives for companies listed on the London Stock Exchange in 2021 were Sébastien de Montessus of mining company Endeavour (£16.9 million), Pascal Soriot of AstraZeneca (£13.9 million), Albert Manifold of construction company CRH (£11.7 million), Mark Cutifani formerly of Anglo American (£9.83 million) and Erik Engström of RELX (£9.83 million). Only one woman was in the top 10: Emma Walmsley of GSK (£8.2 million).

Annual remuneration comprises a number of different income streams. The executive will have a basic annual salary topped up with a variety of incentives. These are typically bonuses paid on the previous year's performance. A stock option grant is an award of executive share options. This is not actual cash but instead an offer (but not an obligation) to buy shares at some date in the future for a specified price. Executive share options are discussed in **Chapter 23**. A restricted stock grant is equity that is issued to the executive but not allowed to be traded before a stated date. Finally, there are other performance awards consisting of perquisites and personal benefits, tax benefits, discounted equity purchases, company contributions to a corporate pension plan or corporate payment of insurance premiums. (See **Chapter 23** for more information on managerial compensation.)

Chapter 23 Page 638

Executive Pay in Europe

The structure of executive pay differs markedly across the world. Figure 2.1 presents a breakdown of executive remuneration into five different components for European executives. Long-term incentives (LTI) represent stock- and option-based compensation. In Europe, the breakdown is roughly equal across all compensation categories, with

Figure 2.1 European Executive Pay Mix in 2018

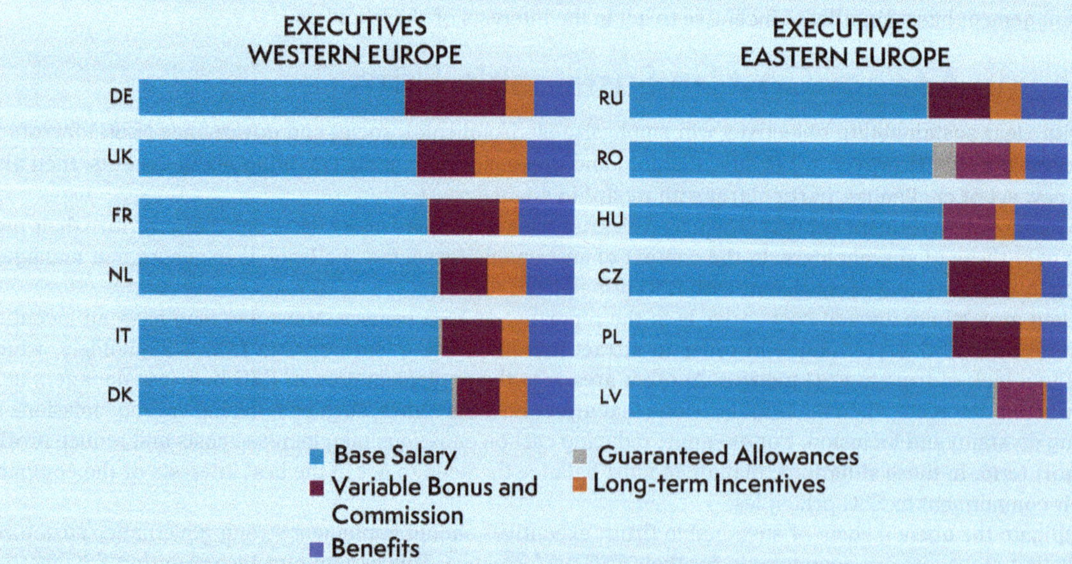

Source: Mercer European Executive Remuneration Trends, 2018 webcast.

Sustainability in Action 2.1

Elon Musk's Executive Pay at Tesla

The issue of executive compensation has been a topic of much debate in recent years. While some argue that executives deserve to be compensated for their hard work and contributions to a company's success, others believe that many executives are awarded obscene pay packages that lack sufficient performance-based criteria. One such case is Elon Musk's executive compensation at Tesla.

Tesla is one of the most successful electric vehicle firms in the world and is best known for its Tesla cars. In 2021, a major shareholder of Tesla, CtW Investment Group, mounted a rebellion against Elon Musk's pay package of $2.3 billion, claiming it was excessive and lacked sufficient performance-based criteria.

The pay package was divided into 12 tranches, each linked to specific targets that the company had to achieve. The first tranche was linked to Tesla's market capitalization reaching $100 billion and each subsequent tranche was linked to a further increase in market capitalization of $50 billion. The pay package was structured so that Elon Musk would receive the full $2.3 billion if all 12 tranches were achieved.

Despite the concerns raised by CtW Investment Group and other shareholders, Musk's annual remuneration was ultimately approved by a slim majority of shareholders.

base salary representing around 70 per cent of total pay. The UK has a stronger long-term incentive plan component than other countries, and Germany (DE) has a much higher percentage tied up in annual performance bonuses.

Control of the Firm

Control of the firm ultimately rests with shareholders. They elect the board of directors, which in turn hires and fires managers. The fact that shareholders control the corporation was made abundantly clear by the late Steve Jobs' experience at Apple. Even though he was a founder of the corporation, and largely responsible for its most successful products, there came a time when shareholders, through their elected directors, decided that Apple would be better off without him, so out he went. Of course, he was later rehired and helped turn Apple into the largest company in the world, with great new products such as the iPhone and iPad.

Shareholder Rights

The conceptual structure of the corporation assumes that shareholders elect directors who, in turn, hire managers to carry out their directives. Shareholders, therefore, control the corporation through the right to elect the directors. In countries with single-tier boards, only shareholders have this right, while in two-tier board countries, the supervisory board undertakes this task.

In two-tier board systems, the supervisory board (which consists of the main shareholder representatives, major creditors and employee representatives) chooses the executive board of directors. In companies with single-tier boards, directors are elected each year at an annual meeting. Although there are exceptions (discussed next), the general idea is 'one share, one vote' (not one shareholder, one vote). Directors are elected at an annual shareholders' meeting by a vote of the holders of a majority of shares who are present and entitled to vote. However, the exact mechanism for electing directors differs across companies. The most important difference is whether shares must be voted cumulatively or voted straight.

Example 2.3

Cumulative and Straight Voting

VanMore Ltd is considering two different voting procedures for four directors to be elected to the board. The firm has two shareholders: Smith with 20 shares and Jones with 80 shares. Each of them wants to be a director. There are also three applicants from within the firm who are not shareholders. The key issue facing the company is that Jones does not want Smith to be a director!

The company's first option is cumulative voting, which facilitates more minority shareholder participation. If cumulative voting is permitted, the total number of votes that each shareholder may cast is determined first. This is usually calculated as the number of shares (owned or controlled) multiplied by the number of directors to be elected. With cumulative voting, the directors are elected all at once. For VanMore Ltd, this means that the top four vote-getters will be the new directors. Each shareholder can distribute votes however he or she wishes.

Will Smith get a seat on the board? If we ignore the possibility of a five-way tie, then the answer is yes. Smith will cast 20 × 4 = 80 votes, and Jones will cast 80 × 4 = 320 votes. If Smith gives all his votes to himself, he is assured of a directorship. The reason is that Jones cannot divide 320 votes among four candidates in such a way as to give all of them more than 80 votes, so Smith will finish fourth at worst.

The second option is straight voting. With straight voting, the directors are elected one at a time. Each time, Smith can cast 20 votes and Jones can cast 80. As a consequence, Jones will elect all of the candidates.

In general, with cumulative voting, if there are N directors up for election, then $1/(N + 1)$ per cent of the shares plus one share will guarantee you a seat. In Example 2.3, this is $1/(4 + 1) = 20$ per cent. So the more seats that are up for election at one time, the easier (and cheaper) it is to win one. With straight voting, the only way to guarantee a seat is to own 50 per cent plus one share. This also guarantees that you will win every seat, so it is really all or nothing with this method.

Example 2.4

Buying the Election

Shares in Sole SpA sell for €20 each and feature cumulative voting. There are 10,000 shares outstanding. If three directors are up for election, how much does it cost to ensure yourself a seat on the board?

The question here is how many shares of equity it will take to get a seat. The answer is 2,501, so the cost is 2,501 × €20 = €50,020. Why 2,501? Because there is no way the remaining 7,499 votes can be divided among three people to give all of them more than 2,501 votes. For example, suppose two people receive 2,502 votes and the first two seats. A third person can receive at most 10,000 – 2,502 – 2,502 – 2,501 = 2,495, so the third seat is yours.

As we have illustrated, straight voting can 'freeze out' minority shareholders; that is why many companies have mandatory cumulative voting. In companies where cumulative voting is mandatory, devices have been worked out to minimize its impact.

One such device is to stagger the voting for the board of directors. With staggered elections, only a fraction of the directorships are up for election at a particular time. Thus if only two directors are up for election at any one time, it will take $1/(2 + 1) = 33.33$ per cent of the equity plus one share to guarantee a seat.

Overall, staggering has two basic effects:

1 Staggering makes it more difficult for a minority to elect a director when there is cumulative voting because there are fewer directors to be elected at any one time.

2 Staggering makes takeover attempts less likely to be successful because it makes it more difficult to vote in a majority of new directors.

We should note that staggering may serve a beneficial purpose. It provides 'institutional memory' – that is, continuity on the board of directors. This may be important for corporations with significant long-range plans and projects.

Proxy Voting

A proxy is the granting of authority by a shareholder to someone else to vote his or her shares. For convenience, much of the voting in large public corporations is actually done by proxy. As we have seen, with straight voting, each share of equity has one vote. The owner of 10,000 shares has 10,000 votes. Large companies have hundreds of thousands, or even millions, of shareholders. In single-tier board environments, shareholders can come to the annual meeting and vote in person, or they can transfer their right to vote to another party.

Obviously, management always tries to get as many proxies as possible transferred to it. However, if shareholders are not satisfied with management, an 'outside' group of shareholders can try to obtain votes via proxy. They can vote by proxy in an attempt to replace management by electing enough directors. The resulting battle is called a proxy fight.

Classes of Shares

Chapter 19
Page 511

Some firms have more than one class of ordinary equity (see **Chapter 19** for more information on equities). Often the classes are created with unequal voting rights. Google, for example, has two share classes. Its co-founders, Larry Page and Sergey Brin, own class-B shares, which represent 10 votes for each share. Other shareholders have class-A shares, which are entitled to one vote per share. So, although the founders own only 5.7 per cent of Google, they have 57 per cent of the voting power. Meta (formerly Facebook) is even more extreme: founder Mark Zuckerberg owns less than 1 per cent of the company's listed equity but controls 60 per cent of its votes. The prize, however, goes to Snapchat's owners, Snap Inc., which gave zero voting rights to investors in its £3.4 billion share issue in 2017!

Aggarwal et al. (2022) find that the increasing number of dual-class share issues is strongly linked to the presence of a controlling and dominant founder, like Mark Zuckerberg. The stronger the founder's bargaining power, the greater the wedge between the two share classes. A primary reason for creating dual or multiple classes of equity (such as with Meta and Mark Zuckerberg) has to do with control of the firm. If such shares exist, management can raise new equity capital by issuing non-voting or limited-voting shares while still maintaining control through voting power. The subject of unequal voting rights is controversial, and the idea of one share, one vote has a strong following and long history. Interestingly, however, shares with unequal voting rights are quite common in Europe.

Figure 2.2 presents the percentage of firms in each country (the sample is constituents of the MSCE Europe Index, which contains Europe's largest firms) that have only one class of shares with one vote per share. As can be seen, there is a lot of heterogeneity in firms around Europe. In the UK, Germany, Spain and Belgium, most firms have only one class of shares, which is substantially different to the situation in France and Sweden.

Clearly, there is a large proportion of European firms that do not have a one share, one vote system. Multiple-class shares can take a number of forms. For example, shares with *voting rate ceilings* restrict voting power for an investor to a specified percentage of shares irrespective of the actual shareholding. The actual ceiling percentage can vary but is usually between 5 and 20 per cent of total shares outstanding. *Ownership ceilings* forbid any shareholder from taking a holding of greater than a specified percentage of shares. *Priority shares* give the holders certain rights, such as being able to appoint a representative to the board of directors or veto a proposal at an annual general meeting. *Golden shares* are found in former state-owned enterprises and give the government beneficial powers, such as veto capability against new shareholders. Finally, *depositary receipts* are securities that have an equity ownership stake without the voting rights. Common in the Netherlands, a company's shares are held in a foundation which then issues depositary receipts to investors that mimic the cash flows of the underlying shares but have no voting rights. Frequently, the foundation's board of directors is linked to the underlying firm.

Figure 2.2 Percentage of Companies with a 'One Share, One Vote' Structure, by Country

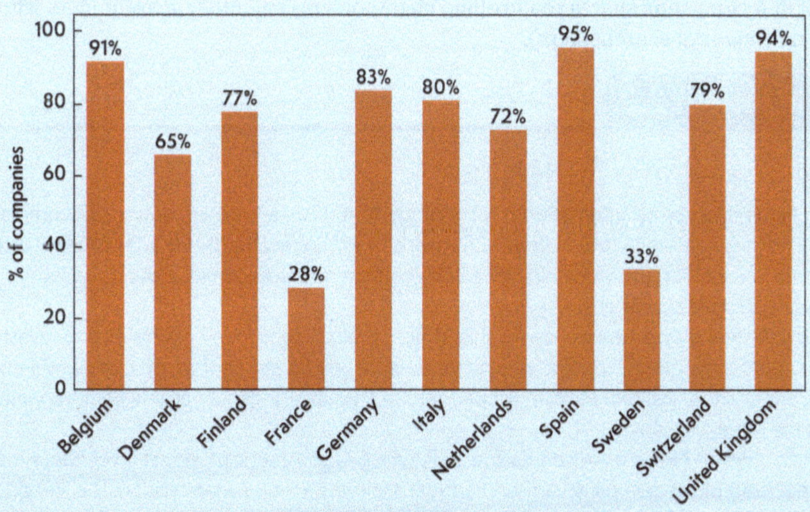

Source: OECD Corporate Governance Factbook 2019.

Other Rights

The value of a share of equity in a corporation is directly related to the general rights of shareholders. In addition to the right to vote for directors, shareholders usually have the following rights:

- The right to share proportionally in dividends paid
- The right to share proportionally in assets remaining after liabilities have been paid in a liquidation
- The right to vote on shareholder matters of great importance, such as a merger. Voting is usually done at the annual meeting or a special meeting.

Chapter 19 Page 511

In addition, shareholders sometimes have the right to share proportionally in any new equity sold. This is called the pre-emptive right (see **Chapter 19** for more information).

Essentially, a pre-emptive right means that a company that wishes to sell equity must first offer it to existing shareholders before marketing it to the general public. The purpose is to give shareholders the opportunity to protect their proportionate ownership in the firm.

Dividends

A distinctive feature of corporations is that they have shares of equity on which they are authorized by law to pay dividends to their shareholders. Dividends paid to shareholders represent a return on the capital directly or indirectly contributed to the corporation by the shareholders. The payment of dividends is at the discretion of the board of directors.

Some important characteristics of dividends include the following:

- Unless a dividend is declared by the board of directors of a corporation, it is not a liability of the corporation. A corporation cannot default on an undeclared dividend. As a consequence, corporations cannot become bankrupt because of non-payment of dividends. The amount of the dividend, and even whether it is paid, are decisions based on the business judgement of the board of directors.
- The payment of dividends by the corporation is not a business expense. Dividends are not deductible for corporate tax purposes. In short, dividends are paid out of the corporation's after-tax profits.
- Dividends received by individual shareholders are taxable.

There is a common belief that shareholders prefer companies to issue dividends because this imposes a form of discipline on incumbent managers. If a company has high levels of cash, managers may invest in projects that would not normally be chosen, simply because they can. By transferring the company's cash to shareholders through dividends, managers have less scope to squander resources.

The discussion so far has concerned the agency relationship between professional managers and outside shareholders. We will now discuss a different type of agency relationship, which is more subtle and complex, and is known as a Type II agency relationship. A Type II agency relationship exists between shareholders who own a significant amount of a company's shares (controlling shareholders) and other shareholders who own only a small proportional amount (minority shareholders).

Real World Insight 2.2

Nokia Oyj Ownership Structure

Consistent with its position as an international technology firm, Nokia is an exceptionally complex organization. The company is not a single entity but instead a network of different companies with product and geographical specialisms. In total, Nokia has an ownership stake in more than 550 companies around the world, spanning many industries in the firm's broad supply chain.

Given its international scope, Nokia's ownership structure also spans many countries and investors. The largest group of shareholders is the general public, which makes up nearly 55 per cent of the company's equity ownership. In second place are financial institutions, with 44 per cent of shareholdings. Other private companies and the firm's executives own the remaining shares.

A major shareholder of Nokia is Artisan Partners LP, which is an American global investment management firm and holds 1.46 per cent of the company. Artisan Partners itself has a major shareholder, The Vanguard Group, Inc., which owns 9.47 per cent of the company. Moving to The Vanguard Group, it has an unusual share structure. The Vanguard Group is owned by its funds, which in turn are owned by the investors in each fund.

Understanding who ultimately owns a company can be an almost impossible task and, in private companies, it is even more difficult to identify ultimate ownership. If an owner has a large enough stake in one company, it may influence the decisions of other companies in the ownership chain.

Source: www.nokia.com.

Type II Agency Relationships

The relationship between a dominant or controlling shareholder and other shareholders who have a small proportional ownership stake is known as a Type II agency relationship. Such a relationship exists whenever a company has a concentrated ownership structure, which is common in many countries. When investors own a large percentage of a company's shares, they have the ability to remove or install a board of directors through their voting power. This means that, indirectly, they can make the firm's objectives aligned to their own personal objectives, which may not be the same as those of other shareholders with a smaller proportionate stake.

It may seem strange that one set of shareholders can have a different objective to another set of shareholders in the same company. Surely all shareholders want to maximize the value of their firm? Agency theory recognizes that everyone has personal objectives and these may not be congruent with other groups in an organization. Thus, for example, a dominant shareholder may benefit more from having one of her firms trading at advantageous prices with another firm she owns. This is known as a related party transaction.

Alternatively, a controlling shareholder may need cash for an investment in, for example, Company A and wish to take the cash from Company B through an extraordinary dividend. This will obviously not be in the interests of Company B's other shareholders, but in aggregate the action may be more profitable for the controlling shareholder of Company B if it stands to make more money from an investment in Company A.

International Ownership Structure

Ownership structure varies considerably across the world. In the UK and USA, most large companies are widely held, which means that no single investor has a large ownership stake in a firm. In such environments, Type I agency relationships tend to dominate. The rest of the world is characterized by closely held firms, where governments, families and banks are the main shareholders in firms. Type II agency relationships are more important in closely held firms and their corporate governance structure should reflect this.

Table 2.3 presents a breakdown of the ownership structure of companies across the world. It is very clear from the table that no two countries are exactly the same. For example, the UK is characterized by a widely held ownership structure, whereas most of the large firms in Greece are run by families. Governments have a major role to play in many countries, with China, Oman and UAE among the countries with large state investors.

Table 2.3 Corporate Ownership Around the World

Country	State	Families/ Individuals	Private Firms	Closely Held	Widely Held Private Firms	Widely Held Public Firms	Widely Held Blockholder	Widely Held No Blockholder	Widely Held
Austria	8.3	19.8	39.6	**67.7**	7.3	7.3	17.7	0.0	**32.3**
Bahrain	19.5	12.2	9.8	**41.5**	4.9	7.3	41.5	4.9	**58.6**
Belgium	5.6	17.4	29.2	**52.2**	6.2	5.0	31.7	5.0	**47.9**
China	23.2	17.3	29.5	**70.0**	1.9	0.4	21.3	6.4	**30.0**
Denmark	0.6	7.1	17.3	**25.0**	5.8	5.1	55.8	8.3	**75.0**
Finland	7.1	8.8	15.0	**30.9**	0.9	4.4	53.1	10.6	**69.0**
France	2.9	29.2	24.9	**57.0**	5.8	5.2	29.9	2.2	**43.0**
Germany	3.6	26.2	25.3	**55.1**	6.4	7.2	28.5	2.8	**44.9**

Country	State	Families/ Individuals	Private Firms	Closely Held	Widely Held Private Firms	Widely Held Public Firms	Widely Held Blockholder	Widely Held No Blockholder	Widely Held
Greece	3.1	51.5	12.7	**67.3**	1.3	7.9	22.3	1.3	**32.8**
India	5.6	21.0	13.6	**40.2**	0.9	6.1	40.0	12.3	**76.8**
Ireland	1.5	7.7	13.8	**23.0**	1.5	1.5	61.5	12.3	**76.8**
Italy	3.8	36.1	22.9	**62.8**	2.3	4.5	25.6	4.9	**37.3**
Malaysia	5.9	16.1	26.7	**48.7**	0.8	5.3	40.2	5.1	**51.4**
Netherlands	2.3	10.5	21.1	**33.9**	6.0	6.8	51.9	1.5	**66.2**
Norway	5.0	13.4	16.9	**35.3**	4.0	2.0	54.2	4.5	**64.7**
Oman	24.4	22.0	12.2	**58.6**	2.4	4.9	31.7	2.4	**41.4**
Russia	26.6	16.7	25.9	**69.2**	5.3	3.9	20.2	1.4	**30.8**
Saudi Arabia	12.6	11.8	14.3	**38.7**	5.0	5.0	49.6	1.7	**61.3**
Singapore	5.9	19.0	17.2	**42.1**	1.4	5.1	34.8	16.6	**57.9**
South Africa	0.5	6.8	12.1	**19.4**	4.9	14.1	52.4	9.2	**80.6**
Spain	3.8	22.0	12.1	**37.9**	5.5	7.7	47.3	1.6	**62.1**
Sweden	1.2	13.4	19.3	**33.9**	3.6	5.3	47.8	9.5	**66.2**
Switzerland	6.9	19.9	14.5	**41.3**	5.4	4.7	42.4	6.2	**58.7**
UAE	37.2	19.1	7.4	**63.7**	2.1	2.1	31.9	0.0	**36.1**
UK	0.9	10.1	5.7	**16.7**	1.2	2.7	66.3	13.1	**83.3**
USA	0.9	10.1	5.7	**16.7**	1.2	2.7	66.3	13.1	**83.3**

Note: *This table reports the share of controlled firms by type (family-controlled, government-controlled, controlled by a private firm with an unmatched ultimate owner, controlled by a widely held private firm, controlled by a widely held public firm), the share of widely held firms with at least one block (stake >5 per cent), and the share of widely held corporations without any block. Identification of controlled corporations is based on the 20 per cent absolute voting rights cut-off.*

Source: Adapted from Table 1, Aminadav and Papaioannou, 2020.

The identity of controlling owners will influence managerial objectives and, whereas all shareholders wish to maximize the value of their investment, how value is assessed differs according to the individual. For example, if a firm is widely held in a market-based economy, such as the UK, corporate objectives are likely to be focused on maximizing share price performance. Family firms have slightly different objectives because not only do managers have to consider current shareholders but also the descendants of those shareholders. This would suggest that managers of family firms would have a longer-term perspective than other firms, which would influence the types of investments and funding they choose. Firms with the government as a major shareholder would have to consider political objectives in addition to maximizing share value.

The available theory and evidence are consistent with the view that shareholders control the firm and that shareholder wealth maximization is the relevant goal of the corporation. Even so, there will undoubtedly be times when management goals are pursued at the expense of some or all shareholders, at least temporarily.

Stakeholders

Our discussion thus far implies that management and shareholders are the only parties with an interest in the firm's decisions. This is an oversimplification, of course. Employees, customers, suppliers and even the government all have a financial interest in the firm.

Taken together, these various groups are called stakeholders. In general, a stakeholder is someone, other than a shareholder or creditor, who potentially has a claim on the cash flows of the firm. Such groups will also attempt to exert control over the firm, perhaps to the detriment of the owners. In countries with two-tier boards, such as the Netherlands and Germany, stakeholders are formally included in the decision-making activities of a firm, through its supervisory board, to which the executive board must report.

2.3 The Governance Structure of Corporations

In this section, we review in more detail the different ways in which corporations can be governed. Because of cultural and regulatory differences, a variety of governance structures can be seen operating successfully across companies in many different countries. Moreover, company size is very important. The largest companies may have more than 10 directors, a chairperson, a chief executive and other individuals on their executive board. Compare this with a private limited company, where the shareholders are also likely to be running the company, or, even more extreme, in a sole proprietorship where the manager is the owner. Some firms may be run by a family, with many family members involved in the firm's management, or may be state owned with executive appointments made through political decisions.

Real World Insight 2.3

Ownership Structure of HNA Group Co. Ltd

While the Nokia share ownership structure discussed in Real World Insight 2.2 may seem complex, it is nothing compared to what can be seen with large Asian firms. As trade tensions increase across the world, repeated questions with respect to large private foreign corporations are: Who owns the company? Where does the funding come from? Who is actually in control of the company? Is the company owned in an indirect way by a foreign government or individuals who are closely linked to a foreign government?

HNA Group Co. Ltd, is one of China's largest private businesses and has invested more than £30 billion in other international firms, including Deutsche Bank, Skybridge Capital and Hilton Hotels.

When requested by media outlets to provide its ownership structure, the company's external PR agency said that the firm had a 22.75 per cent ownership investment from HNA Group's own charity, Hainan Province Cihang Foundation, with the other 77.25 per cent ownership held by 18 anonymous individuals.

One week later, HNA Group released a formal statement with more information on its ownership structure. HNA Group's charity actually owned 52.25 per cent of the company. Of this amount, 22.75 per cent was held by the Chinese domiciled portion of the charitable foundation. The remaining (52.25 – 22.75 =) 29.50 per cent ownership was held by the New York-based portion of the charity. In addition to the Hainan Province Cihang Foundation investment of 52.25 per cent, HNA Group's two chairmen, Chen Fang and Wang Jian, each owned 14.98 per cent. The company's CEO, Adam Tan, owned 2.95 per cent and nine other directors held 14.63 per cent in total. Finally, Hainan Airlines Holding Company owned 0.25 per cent of the firm.

HNA Group stated that the charitable foundation was likely to increase its holdings over time because every individual shareholder had pledged to donate all their shares to the foundation upon their death or resignation from the company.

A question that comes to mind is: Who owns Hainan Province Cihang Foundation?

In all businesses, there are a number of duties or responsibilities that must be carried out by corporate executives. For example, a firm must know and form its long-term business strategy. It must be in control of its financial affairs, and actively seek out new and profitable investment opportunities. It should seek the most appropriate new financing when required and ensure it has complied with all relevant regulation.

As companies grow, these respective responsibilities become too large to be undertaken by only one individual and, consequently, must be delegated to a team or even a large department. Executives need to know what is happening in every sphere of their company's business activities and ensure that all aspects of business are operating at peak efficiency. Corporate governance is primarily concerned with ensuring that businesses are operating well, that business decisions are made rationally and that the appropriate individuals who make these decisions are held accountable when things go wrong.

Not all organizations are governed well. Just because a firm is listed on a stock exchange does not mean that correct business decisions are being made or that shareholder wealth is being maximized. In many companies, governance culture lags behind the growth of the firm. Small, successful companies are likely to have very different governance structures from large successful firms in the same industry. In many countries, individuals with political links are placed on corporate boards and their objectives are very different to those of shareholders.

While it is impossible to cover all the governance structures that exist in the business world, it is useful to see examples of the way in which different firms are governed.

The Sole Proprietorship

Let us return to JonMac Builders, the sole proprietorship that was introduced in Example 2.1. These types of firms are the easiest to understand since all the business activities are concentrated in one individual – the owner/manager. Business decisions, long-term strategy, short-term cash management and financing decisions are all made by John McAfee, the owner of JonMac Builders. John has no skill whatsoever in accounting, so he hires an accountant to draw up his financial accounts for the year. The main reason for hiring an accountant is to determine the amount of tax John has to pay based on the company's profits.

With the exception of the accounting function, everything in JonMac Builders is done informally and on a day-to-day basis. In these types of organizations, there is no real need for formal governance structures since there is nothing really to be governed. The only important formal aspect of the business, the financial accounting, has been outsourced to another company that specializes in the accounting function. It is hopefully clear that it is neither sensible nor cost-effective for JonMac builders to employ its own accountant or to introduce formal governance structures within the firm. This is the general position for most sole proprietorships.

Partnerships

A partnership is, in many ways, very similar to a sole proprietorship. Generally, partners will have unlimited liability, which means that they are personally liable for all of their firm's debts. Every partnership will have some form of formal agreement that governs the financial affairs of the firm, such as the apportioning of profits among partners. Senior partners may receive a higher proportion of the company's profits than junior partners and this will be enshrined within the partnership agreement. Rules on partners resigning, new partners joining and major corporate decisions may also be included.

Partnership agreements need not be complicated or filled with legal jargon. They can also be quite short. Example 2.5 shows an actual partnership agreement for Twiga Export Partners, a partnership that sources materials, automobiles and electrical appliances from around the world and exports them to Sub-Saharan Africa. There are five partners in the firm, all concerned with different aspects of the business. Three of the partners are based in East Africa and two are based in Europe.

Example 2.5

Partnership Agreement of Twiga Export Partners

This partnership agreement relates wholly, entirely and only to Twiga Export Partners, hereafter known as 'the business'. It does not convey rights or claim (partial, incidental or whole) towards any other activity or association to which any partner is involved.

This agreement applies as follows:

1. Each partner is due an equal share of all profits or losses accruing to the business. That is, each partner has claim to 20 per cent of profits or losses in any financial period.
2. Any injection of loan funds into the business will result in interest being paid, amounting to 8 per cent per annum compounded on an annual basis. Interest will be allocated against the partner's capital account.
3. Any withdrawal of funds from the business, not including any salary, will be charged interest at 8 per cent per annum compounded on an annual basis. Interest on drawings will be charged against the partner's capital account.
4. Any capital contributed by a partner must be agreed upon by all partners beforehand.
5. A partner will be paid a salary only on agreement by all partners. The level of salary must be agreed upon by all partners.
6. Before admission of any new partners, agreement and consent must be reached by all partners in business.
7. Upon leaving or retiring from the business, a partner will be paid in cash their total capital invested in the business as well as any goodwill owned by the partner. Goodwill will be calculated as 20 per cent of average net profit over the previous five years.
8. Changes in any of the points above must be agreed upon in writing by all partners.

Upon signing this document in the presence of two other partners, a partner will be deemed to accept the points in this document in full.

The partnership agreement deals only partially with the governance structure of a partnership. The firm must also have procedures in place for ensuring that all partners are carrying out their responsibilities fully. Normally, a partners' meeting will be held regularly to discuss business strategy and other long-term issues facing the business. They will also report on their own activity since the last partners' meeting. These meetings take place on a monthly basis or more frequently. In the case of Twiga Export Partners, the meetings take place every six months because of the geographical distance between partners. More regular meetings would not be cost-effective for Twiga, a trade-off that all companies must bear in mind when assessing the importance of better governance procedures.

Because the owners are also managers of the firm, partnerships do not normally require outside or independent individuals in the partners' meetings. In addition, they are also likely to appoint auditors and accountants to take care of the financial reporting of the firm.

Corporations

Because a corporation is a separate legal entity, the informality that is common in sole proprietorships and partnerships is substituted by formal corporate governance structures that are commonly seen in large organizations. Formal structures are necessary because the owners of the firm are less likely to be involved in management. As stated earlier, corporations must have articles of incorporation that govern the allocation and issuance of shares, the number of directors in the firm, as well as procedures for appointment and resignation from the board.

However, shareholders also require formal and explicit assurances that managers are running their company to maximize shareholder wealth. This is normally exhibited through the inclusion of external, non-executive and independent board members who attend all of the company's executive board meetings. In addition, there are usually a number of other governance structures ensuring that individuals do not have too much power within a firm, which could otherwise make them entrenched and less likely to pursue shareholders' objectives over their own.

Whereas regulatory requirements can force board structures into a two-tier or unitary board structure, there are a number of principles to which all corporations are recommended to adhere in order to minimize governance failures. Individual countries have their own specific approaches to corporate governance, but all follow the direction of the G20/OECD Principles of Corporate Governance, published by the Organisation for Economic Co-operation and Development. The principles themselves are not legally binding, but are recommendations on best governance practice within corporate organizations.

2.4 Corporate Governance Principles

Corporate governance principles vary from country to country. However, they all tend to be based around the G20/OECD Principles of Corporate Governance. These are centred on six major areas and concern all aspects of corporate governance. It is important to emphasize that there is no 'one size fits all' for corporate governance. Companies choose the level and type of structure that fits their environment, ownership structure and regulatory position. The G20/OECD principles are detailed in the sections that follow.

I. Ensuring the Basis for an Effective Corporate Governance Framework

The corporate governance framework should promote transparent and fair markets, and the efficient allocation of resources. It should be consistent with the rule of law and support effective supervision and enforcement.[1]

This principle emphasizes the need to recognize that corporations are fundamentally geared towards making money, and corporate governance structures must be designed to ensure this primary objective is not adversely affected. It also states that governance regulation should be consistent with the legal and regulatory environment in which the firm operates. Finally, the principle argues that there should be a strict and transparent delineation of responsibilities in setting, monitoring and managing the governance of corporations.

Real World Insight 2.4

Corruption

The Transparency International Corruption Perceptions Index is graded between 0 and 100 (see Figure 2.3), with a lower score indicating a country in which the public sector is perceived to be exceptionally corrupt. Scandinavian countries are perceived to have very little public-sector corruption, but this tends to get worse as one goes further south-east through Europe. Consistent with their lack of economic development, emerging markets tend to have more public-sector corruption than developed countries. Notably, the public sector in China and India is perceived to be exceptionally corrupt, even with these countries' incredible growth over the past 20 years.

Figure 2.3 2022 Corruption Perceptions Index

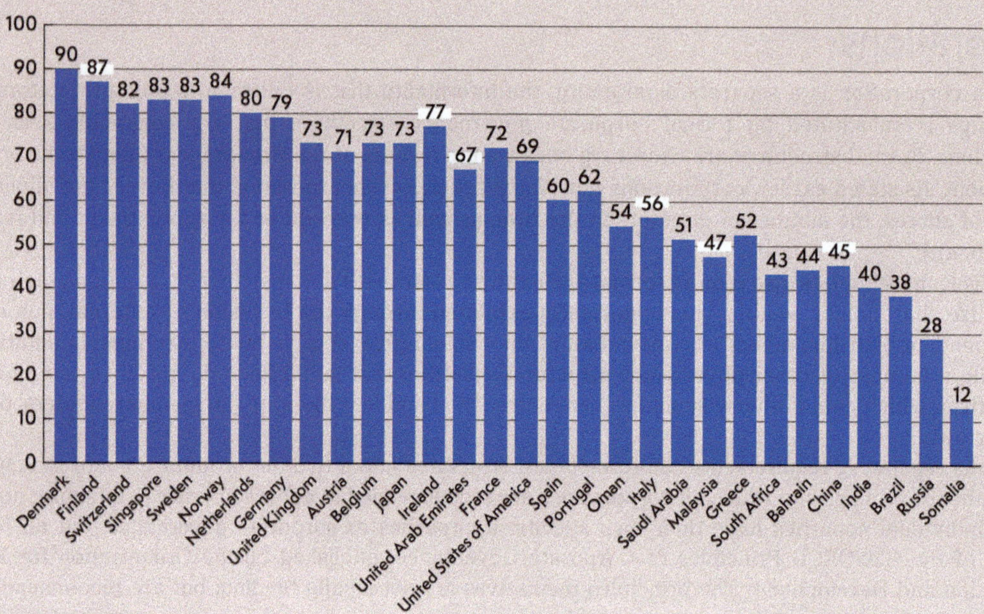

Note: *Transparency International's Corruption Perceptions Index measures the perceived level of public-sector corruption in countries and territories around the world on a scale of 0 (highly corrupt) to 100 (very clean).*

II. The Rights and Equitable Treatment of Shareholders and Key Ownership Functions

The corporate governance framework should protect and facilitate the exercise of shareholders' rights and ensure the equitable treatment of all shareholders, including minority and foreign shareholders. All shareholders should have the opportunity to obtain effective redress for violation of their rights.[1]

This second principle focuses on the most important stakeholder of corporations – the shareholder. As owner, the shareholder is entitled to basic rights such as being able to register ownership of their shares, selling their shares to other parties, having access to important information about the company, being able to participate at general shareholder meetings, being able to elect and remove members from the board of directors, and to share in the profits of the corporation.

Shareholders should also be notified of, and participate in, their company's major decisions, such as increasing the long-term financing of the company through debt or equity offerings, or when the company management decides to sell off a major proportion of the company's assets. Giving shareholders power to influence the direction of their company is the basic rationale underlying this principle and, as such, much of its discussion relates to creating a framework that allows shareholders to vote and participate at general meetings. The principle recommends that structures should be in place to allow shareholders to appoint the senior management and stop them from pursuing business objectives that are not consistent with maximizing shareholder wealth.

In many firms, there is one shareholder or a group of shareholders that owns a very large fraction of the outstanding shares. It is important that dominant, or controlling, shareholders do not run the company in their interests at the expense of minority shareholders. There are several ways in which this could be done. For example, the controlling shareholder may vote for personal friends or family to be on the corporate board. Given that minority shareholders are not strong enough to force their view at general meetings, majority shareholders will always get their way.

The second OECD governance principle recommends that firms ensure minority shareholders are protected and policies introduced by the company do not penalize them. Particularly important is that the voice of minority and foreign shareholders is heard at company general meetings.

Sustainability in Action 2.2

Shareholder Activism at Aberdeen Ethical World Fund

In recent years, there has been substantial growth in investment funds having a social, ethical, environmental or governance agenda. The funds have two main approaches: *voice* and *exit*. A *voice strategy* means that managers of funds that hold the equity of a firm will become directly and proactively involved in the management of the company. Managers with a voice strategy are called institutional shareholder activists. An *exit strategy* means that, if a fund manager is unhappy with a company's behaviour, it will exit from the investment.

An example of an activist fund is Aberdeen Ethical World Fund. The fund has positive and negative screening investment criteria regarding the companies in which it will invest, in addition to a proactive engagement policy. The following is an overview of the fund's voice strategy (*source:* Vigeo Eiris):

Engagement The fund visits all companies held within its ethical fund at least once every two years to discuss the socially responsible investment (SRI) issues covered by its SRI criteria. The fund maintains a dialogue on these topics with companies and follows up on issues to check to see if progress (if any) has been made.

Methods of engagement The fund communicates with company managers, investor relations representatives, and those responsible for policymaking and/or policy implementation regarding SRI/ethical issues, through visits, telephone conferences, letters and emails. The fund also collaborates with other shareholders on SRI issues and meets with other groups, such as non-government organizations, etc.

What further steps are taken when engagement is considered unsuccessful? The fund's stated policy is one of 'continued engagement with companies on important issues', with no cut-off period.

Voting The fund's voting policy seeks to support good corporate governance through quality management, transparency of corporate affairs and intentions, and fair and equal treatment of shareholders.

Are voting practices disclosed? No.

III. Institutional Investors, Stock Markets and Other Intermediaries

The corporate governance framework should provide sound incentives throughout the investment chain and provide for stock markets to function in a way that contributes to good corporate governance.[1]

The reality of the financial markets is that equity is not directly held by individuals. Instead, intermediaries like insurance companies, pension funds and collective investment schemes (mutual funds, investment trusts, etc.) are the main investors. Investors in these institutional intermediaries may be investment funds themselves and so the investment chain may be very long before it finally gets to individuals.

Principle III puts forward the recommendation that financial institutional investors should be transparent in their corporate governance and voting policies. This is because institutions must act as proxies for the individuals who invest in their funds, be they pensions, insurance policies or trusts.

The principle encourages shareholder activism, especially for those institutional shareholders who can exert significant pressure on the incumbent management of corporations because of the size of their shareholdings. The institutions themselves are recommended to publish their own governance structures and policies on voting in general meetings. They are also encouraged to consult with one another on issues concerning their basic shareholder rights.

Corporate executive behaviour is also addressed in Principle III, where it is recommended that company insiders be forbidden from trading when they have private specific and precise information, which could be used to personally benefit themselves at the expense of other shareholders. This is known as insider dealing, which is illegal in most countries. Board members should also disclose any conflicts of interest or material interests in corporate decisions to shareholders.

IV. The Role of Stakeholders in Corporate Governance

The corporate governance framework should recognize the rights of stakeholders established by law or through mutual agreements and encourage active co-operation between corporations and stakeholders in creating wealth, jobs, and the sustainability of financially sound enterprises.[1]

Principle IV considers the other stakeholders of the corporation, such as employees and local communities. All rights of stakeholders that are enshrined in law should be respected by the corporation and if a firm violates any stakeholder rights, there should be a process or structure to allow them to seek redress from the firm. The principle also encourages the development of employee share ownership schemes and other performance-enhancing schemes.

If a stakeholder group feels the company is not performing to its expectations or meeting its responsibilities to its stakeholders, it should be able to freely communicate its concerns to the company and expect the firm to proactively consider those concerns. Firms should also have a framework for dealing with insolvency procedures (to be used if needed) and effective enforcement of creditor rights.

Given that stakeholders are impacted by the operations of a firm, it is important to create a framework for ensuring the firm's operations are ethical and sustainable. One of the key elements of a sustainable corporate governance framework is effective risk management. This involves identifying and mitigating risks that could impact the company's operations, financial performance and reputation. An effective framework ensures firms operate in an ethical and responsible manner, while also maximizing shareholder value.

V. Disclosure and Transparency

The corporate governance framework should ensure that timely and accurate disclosure is made on all material matters regarding the corporation, including the financial situation, performance, ownership, and governance of the company.[1]

Prompt disclosure of new information relating to the activities of a corporation is an absolute necessity for investors. If little is known about a company, it is almost impossible for outside shareholders to form an accurate estimate of the value of a firm or evaluate the performance of its management. Principle V states the main types of information that companies should disclose to the market.

These include the following:

(a) The main financial results, namely the profit and loss over the year, a statement of the firm's assets and liabilities (the statement of financial position), and the cash flow position of the firm
(b) Corporate objectives
(c) The main shareholders and the various voting rights pertaining to different share classes
(d) Information on the individuals that comprise the board of directors, their salaries and annual bonuses, and a statement on whether a director is an independent or executive director should be published regularly
(e) Any trading of the company's shares undertaken by the firm's senior executives, their family, friends and other close associates
(f) The major risks facing the firm's operations
(g) Issues regarding employees and other stakeholders
(h) The main governance structures and policies of the firm.

The principle maintains that all information disclosed by the firm should be made as rigorous and informative as possible. This means that financial statements should be prepared by qualified accountants, and all the activities of a firm should be audited and assessed by an external professional firm, the auditor.

VI. The Responsibilities of the Board

The corporate governance framework should ensure the strategic guidance of the company, the effective monitoring of management by the board, and the board's accountability to the company and the shareholders.[1]

The final OECD principle of corporate governance focuses on the corporate board itself. Board members are expected to make decisions on an informed and ethical basis, and to always take the company and shareholder objectives into account. The board must take all shareholders into account and act in their best interests whether they are minority shareholders, foreign shareholders or other groups that have little combined power to influence management. All of the firm's major stakeholders (e.g. lenders, employees, local community, creditors) must also be taken into account when making corporate decisions.

The principle states that a corporate board must fulfil a set number of functions, including:

(a) Reviewing and guiding corporate strategy, major plans of action, risk policy, annual budgets and business plans; setting performance objectives; monitoring implementation and corporate performance; and overseeing major capital expenditures, acquisitions and divestitures
(b) Monitoring the effectiveness of the company's governance practices and making changes as needed
(c) Selecting, compensating, monitoring and, when necessary, replacing key executives and overseeing succession planning
(d) Aligning key executive and board remuneration with the longer-term interests of the company and its shareholders
(e) Ensuring a formal and transparent board nomination and election process
(f) Monitoring and managing potential conflicts of interest of management, board members and shareholders, including misuse of corporate assets and abuse in related party transactions
(g) Ensuring the integrity of the corporation's accounting and financial reporting systems, including the independent audit, and that appropriate systems of control are in place, in particular, systems for risk management, financial and operational control, and compliance with the law and relevant standards
(h) Overseeing the process of disclosure and communications.

It is expected that corporate boards approach the job of running a corporation in an objective and independent fashion. When there are conflicts of interest, non-executives should be used to manage potentially problematic situations. Subcommittees of the board, such as an audit committee, nomination committee and remuneration committee, should also be established to deal effectively with conflicts of interest.

Bringing It All Together

The basis of all good corporate finance decisions is a sound framework of corporate governance. This point cannot be emphasized too much because most of the problems that companies experience can usually be identified by failings in the way in which they are governed. When covering subjects in later chapters, the underlying assumption is that corporate executives are acting in the interests of shareholders and that the firm is well governed.

When a company does not have strong corporate governance, it may make decisions that do not maximize share value. For example, a firm may choose to invest in projects that maximize managerial wealth and not that of shareholders. They may also make financing decisions that minimize the risk of the firm for the management but not necessarily for the shareholders. This would lead them to make different investment and financing decisions to those recommended in later chapters.

Transparency and timely information disclosure are major aspects of good governance. Without this, investors would find it extremely difficult to value a firm or assess the risk of its operations. Part 3 of this textbook assumes that share prices efficiently incorporate information about a company. However, if the management of a firm does not see transparency and disclosure as an important part of its responsibilities, share prices will be uninformative and risk assessment would be meaningless.

The G20/OECD Principles of Corporate Governance set the basis by which individual countries set their own corporate governance codes. This has led to a proliferation of codes issued by regulators specific to individual countries. Table 2.4 lists the main corporate governance codes and their date of publication for different countries. All codes can be downloaded from the European Corporate Governance Institute website (www.ecgi.global).

Table 2.4 Country Codes of Corporate Governance

Country	
Australia	Corporate Governance Principles and Recommendations (2019)
Austria	Austrian Code of Corporate Governance (2021)
Bahrain	Corporate Governance Code Kingdom of Bahrain (2018)
Belgium	The 2009 Belgian Code on Corporate Governance (2020)

▷

Country	
China	Code of Corporate Governance for Listed Companies (2018)
Denmark	Recommendations for Corporate Governance (2017)
EU	EVCA Corporate Governance Guidelines (2005)
Finland	Finnish Corporate Governance Code (2020)
France	French Corporate Governance Code (2022)
Germany	German Corporate Governance Code (2022)
Greece	Hellenic Corporate Governance Code (2021)
India	Corporate Governance Voluntary Guidelines (2009)
Ireland	Follows the UK Corporate Governance Code (2019)
Italy	Italian Corporate Governance Code (2020)
Malaysia	Malaysian Code on Corporate Governance (2021)
Netherlands	Dutch Corporate Governance Code (2016)
Norway	Norwegian Code of Practice for Corporate Governance (2018)
OECD	G20/OECD Principles of Corporate Governance (2015)
Oman	Code of Corporate Governance for Public Listed Companies (2016)
Pakistan	Code of Corporate Governance (2012)
Poland	Code of Best Practice for WSE Companies (2012)
Portugal	Code of Corporate Governance (2020)
Saudi Arabia	Corporate Governance Regulations in the Kingdom of Saudi Arabia (2017)
Singapore	Code of Corporate Governance (2018)
South Africa	King Report on Corporate Governance for South Africa (2016)
Spain	Code of Good Governance of Listed Companies (2020)
Sweden	Swedish Code of Corporate Governance (2016)
Switzerland	Swiss Code of Best Practice for Corporate Governance (2014)
UAE	Corporate Governance Code for Small and Medium Enterprises Dubai (2011) Ministerial Resolution No. (518) of 2009 Concerning Governance Rules and Corporate Discipline Standards (2009)
UK	Principles for Purposeful Business (2019), UK Corporate Governance Code (2018)
US	Corporate Governance Principles for US Listed Companies (2017)

Real World Insight 2.5

The UK Corporate Governance Code

The UK Corporate Governance Code was introduced on 1 January 2019 and must be followed by all companies listed on the London Stock Exchange. It is centred on five areas that are crucial for a long-term sustainable business. The list below is taken direct from the Code.

1 **Board Leadership and Company Purpose**

- A successful company is led by an effective and entrepreneurial board, whose role is to promote the long-term sustainable success of the company, generating value for shareholders and contributing to wider society.
- The board should establish the company's purpose, values and strategy, and satisfy itself that these and its culture are aligned. All directors must act with integrity, lead by example and promote the desired culture.

- The board should ensure that the necessary resources are in place for the company to meet its objectives and measure performance against them. The board should also establish a framework of prudent and effective controls, which enable risk to be assessed and managed.
- In order for the company to meet its responsibilities to shareholders and stakeholders, the board should ensure effective engagement with, and encourage participation from, these parties.
- The board should ensure that workforce policies and practices are consistent with the company's values and support its long-term sustainable success. The workforce should be able to raise any matters of concern.

2 **Division of Responsibilities**

- The chair leads the board and is responsible for its overall effectiveness in directing the company. They should demonstrate objective judgement throughout their tenure and promote a culture of openness and debate. In addition, the chair facilitates constructive board relations and the effective contribution of all non-executive directors, and ensures that directors receive accurate, timely and clear information.
- The board should include an appropriate combination of executive and non-executive (and, in particular, independent non-executive) directors, such that no one individual or small group of individuals dominates the board's decision-making. There should be a clear division of responsibilities between the leadership of the board and the executive leadership of the company's business.
- Non-executive directors should have sufficient time to meet their board responsibilities. They should provide constructive challenge, strategic guidance, offer specialist advice and hold management to account.
- The board, supported by the company secretary, should ensure that it has the policies, processes, information, time and resources it needs in order to function effectively and efficiently.

3 **Composition, Succession and Evaluation**

- Appointments to the board should be subject to a formal, rigorous and transparent procedure, and an effective succession plan should be maintained for board and senior management. Both appointments and succession plans should be based on merit and objective criteria and, within this context, should promote diversity of gender, social and ethnic backgrounds, cognitive and personal strengths.
- The board and its committees should have a combination of skills, experience and knowledge. Consideration should be given to the length of service of the board as a whole and membership regularly refreshed.
- Annual evaluation of the board should consider its composition, diversity and how effectively members work together to achieve objectives. Individual evaluation should demonstrate whether each director continues to contribute effectively.

4 **Audit, Risk and Internal Control**

- The board should establish formal and transparent policies and procedures to ensure the independence and effectiveness of internal and external audit functions and satisfy itself on the integrity of financial and narrative statements.
- The board should present a fair, balanced and understandable assessment of the company's position and prospects.
- The board should establish procedures to manage risk, oversee the internal control framework, and determine the nature and extent of the principal risks the company is willing to take in order to achieve its long-term strategic objectives.

5 **Remuneration**

- Remuneration policies and practices should be designed to support strategy and promote long-term sustainable success. Executive remuneration should be aligned to company purpose and values, and be clearly linked to the successful delivery of the company's long-term strategy.
- A formal and transparent procedure for developing policy on executive remuneration and determining director and senior management remuneration should be established. No director should be involved in deciding their own remuneration outcome.
- Directors should exercise independent judgement and discretion when authorizing remuneration outcomes, taking account of company and individual performance, and wider circumstances.

Source: The UK Corporate Governance Code, July 2018. Financial Reporting Council.

2.5 International Corporate Governance

Why do countries have their own code of corporate governance and not just follow one generic code? The reason is that institutional differences exist across regions. Even in the European Union, there is a wide range of corporate governance practices and this, in turn, affects the way managers behave and make decisions. In this section, we will discuss some differences in corporate governance around the world and how they may impact upon the business decisions of corporations.

Investor Protection: The Legal Environment

The legal environment in which a corporation does business can have a big impact on its decisions. In a common law system, the law evolves as a result of the judgement decisions of courts, whereas in a civil law system, judges interpret the law, they cannot change it. With respect to commercial decisions, the UK and Ireland follow a common law system whereas the rest of Europe follows civil law.

The third form of legal system is based on religious principles: Canon Law for Christianity, Halakha for Judaism and Sharia for Islam. Under religious law, specific religious principles form the basis of legal decisions. This can have a considerable impact on business activity, especially when religion forbids specific activities. For example, Islam forbids the use of interest in any economic transaction and so financial loans are not allowed.

Figure 2.4 presents a snapshot of countries that follow different legal systems. Many countries do not follow one system alone, and the exact legal environment can be a hybrid of two systems. For example, India's legal system is based on common law, but personal laws are driven by religious law depending on an individual's religion. Scotland has a different legal system from the rest of the UK, with most laws based on continental or Roman civil law. Commercial law is an exception and it is similar to the rest of the UK in this regard.

Figure 2.4 Legal Systems Around the World

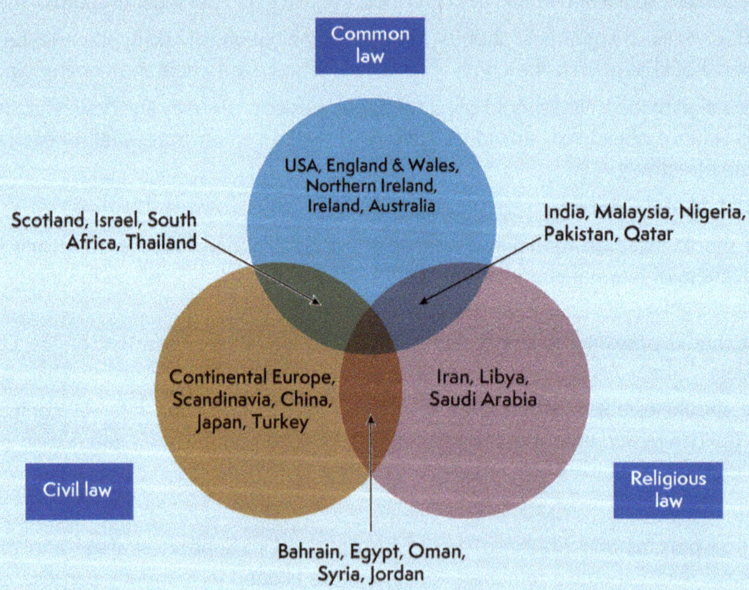

Because the corporate environment must respond quickly to different economic events, common law systems are able to adapt faster to these changes. For example, if a company can identify a loophole in the law that allows it to legally expropriate wealth from shareholders, a common law system can quickly close this loophole through the courts. In a civil law system, any changes in regulation must be enacted through government statute, which can take a much longer time to process.

The inherent flexibility of common law legal environments ensures that shareholders and outside stakeholders are better protected than in civil law countries. This constrains the activities of corporate managers and, as a result, they are held more accountable. In addition, because investor protection is better in common law environments, it would be expected that raising capital through the equity markets would be more popular in countries that follow this system.

The type of legal system is not the only factor that affects corporate investors. Adherence to the rule of law and efficiency of law enforcement can have a major impact on corporate decision-making and regulatory compliance. Clearly, a country can have very comprehensive laws, but if they are not enforced their effect is meaningless.

The Financial System: Bank and Market-based Countries

In a bank-based financial system, banks play a major role in facilitating the flow of money between investors with surplus cash and organizations that require funding. In market-based systems, financial markets take on the role of the main financial intermediary. Corporations in countries with very well-developed financial markets find it easier to raise money by issuing debt and equity to the public than through bank borrowing. Countries with bank-based systems have very strong banks that actively monitor corporations and are often involved in long-term strategic decisions.

It has been argued that corporations in market-based countries have a shorter-term focus than those in bank-based countries because of the emphasis on share price and market performance. When banks are the major source of funding to a company, managers may have longer investment horizons and be less willing to take risks. On the other hand, market-based systems have been argued to be more efficient at funding companies than bank systems. There are many ways in which a country's financial system can be classified as bank or market based. Table 2.5 shows, for a number of countries, the level of domestic deposits in banks divided by stock market size. A country with a high ratio would be regarded as having a strong banking sector.

Table 2.5 Bank versus Market-based Financial Systems

Country	Deposit Money Banks' Assets to GDP (%)	Stock Market Capitalization to GDP (%)	Deposit Money Banks' Assets/ Stock Market Capitalization
South Africa	77.91	245.42	0.32
USA	60.2	143.31	0.42
Switzerland	177.55	219.31	0.81
Saudi Arabia	66.27	70	0.95
India	69.3	71.5	0.97
Belgium	81.08	80.37	1.01
UK	134.69	112.11	1.20
Oman	72.12	56.38	1.28
Netherlands	128.26	92.92	1.38
France	112.68	79.24	1.42
Sweden	133.6	92.81	1.44
Bahrain	101.27	66.67	1.52
Australia	136.01	88.36	1.54
Ireland	100.47	61.5	1.63
Finland	101.88	57.22	1.78
UAE	102.65	54.09	1.90
Germany	96.6	47.12	2.05
Spain	154.51	67.26	2.30
Poland	68.15	29.3	2.33
China	153.41	64.14	2.39
Russian Federation	60.75	24.14	2.52
Norway	128.76	47.34	2.72

Country	Deposit Money Banks' Assets to GDP (%)	Stock Market Capitalization to GDP (%)	Deposit Money Banks' Assets/ Stock Market Capitalization
Denmark	184.59	61.18	3.02
Austria	104.09	23.42	4.44
Italy	130.17	28.02	4.65
Greece	128.45	22.59	5.69

Source: World Bank and author's own calculations.

Culture and Corporate Governance

Most of the discussion so far has related to Western governance environments where the principal–agent perspective is dominant. However, this is not fully accepted everywhere. For example, in the Middle East and parts of Asia and Africa, Islamic-based systems of governance are followed more closely. Furthermore, with governance scandals continuing to occur with regular frequency, Western commentators are questioning whether other approaches to governance may be more appropriate. One of the most important alternatives to Principal–Agent Theory is the Stewardship Theory of Corporate Governance, which regards the manager as a steward of the firm's assets rather than an agent of the firm's shareholders.

Agency Theory argues that managers are selfish agents who will pursue their own objectives at the expense of all other stakeholders, including shareholders. As a result, contractual obligations between the firm and management must exist that bring managerial objectives in line with shareholders. One way to do this is to construct a remuneration package that incentivizes (but not too much!) managers to do their job well and seek maximization of firm value. Another strategy is to reduce the power of the manager so they will be constrained in their behaviour. One typical governance innovation is to split the role of chair and chief executive into two different jobs. Since the chief executive, who is responsible for the day-to-day running of the company, must report to the chair there is less scope for non-value-maximizing activities to continue without getting queried.

When you think about it, to say a manager is selfish and only doing their own thing at the expense of everyone else is quite insulting! It also does not capture the vast majority of managers in business who are completely loyal to their firm and employees. Most companies in the world are run via families, founder-entrepreneurs or long-term investors. In such a situation, managerial tenures can be very long and people are employed at the same company for many years. Basically, Stewardship Theory argues that managers are motivated to do the very best for a company because they view themselves as stewards of the firm. The best way to do this is to have exceptionally strong relationships with the shareholders of a firm. In addition, Stewardship Theory would suggest that the role of chair and chief executive should be combined so that the manager has enough power and authority to make decisions and take a long-term strategic perspective.

The Stewardship Theory concept is relevant in the Middle East and in those countries where long-term investors such as families are common, such as southern Europe and most of Asia and Africa. Both theories argue that managers must be helped to make the best decisions for the firm, which will also be the best decisions for shareholders. How this happens and how a firm is structured contributes to the decision-making process and influences the financial choices made by managers.

Ethics and Corporate Governance

Many people confuse corporate governance with ethics and believe if a company has strong corporate governance it will necessarily be more ethical. This is not necessarily the case and many of the most significant corporate crises in recent times have been in companies with the highest level of observed corporate governance. Take the banking sector as an example. Although the industry is one of the most well governed in the global economy, it still followed fairly unethical practices that led to the financial crisis and subsequent sovereign debt bailouts across the world. Another example is Carillion, which was discussed at the beginning of this chapter. Arguably, Carillion had an absolutely top-quality governance structure, with non-executive directors, split chairman/chief executive position, a shareholder charter and a corporate social responsibility policy, among other things. However, the UK government inquiry presented 'a story of recklessness, hubris and greed, its business model was a relentless dash for cash'. Is this ethical?

The key to understanding corporate governance is that its objective is to facilitate the optimal allocation of resources in a firm. Resources do not only include physical assets like plant, property and equipment, but also human capital like employees. For the best financial decisions to be made, they must reflect both financial and social/ethical concerns. In sum, managers should optimize firm value conditional on an ethical framework of decision-making. Corporate governance can facilitate ethical decision-making, but it is not a necessary requisite nor does it lead to ethical decision-making. This is something that goes deeper than rules and regulations and cannot be mandated through simple corporate governance structures.

Many firms now explicitly consider their business and strategic model within the framework of the UN Sustainable Development Goals, and present these as part of their overall corporate governance framework. The goals span a range of socially optimal objectives, and contribute in a small way to the environment and society. Figure 2.5 presents these in a graphical format.

Figure 2.5 UN Sustainable Development Goals

Source: ALX1618/Shutterstock.

Since this book concerns financial decisions and how to maximize firm value, it is implicitly understood that corporate decisions will be ethical. When necessary, appropriate reference will be made to ethics, but it will not be emphasized in the text unless it clarifies aspects of a corporate decision.

2.6 Corporate Governance in Action: Starbucks

Starbucks, the international coffee retailer chain, is frequently under scrutiny regarding its corporate governance policies. This is because much of its raw materials (coffee beans) is created in very poor, developing countries. The scope for manipulation and exploitation of the coffee farmers is massive, and the company has to proactively ensure that one of its stakeholder groups (the farmers) is not adversely and unfairly treated by the board's strategic decisions.

To see how Starbucks adheres to the main corporate governance principles, it is useful to examine its corporate governance policy. This is available on its website and you can easily find it by searching for 'Starbucks corporate governance' on the internet.

The Starbucks corporate governance document states that the board is responsible for looking after the company's business and affairs, to ensure it meets the objectives and goals outlined by the company. The role of the board of directors is to uphold the company's goals and responsibilities. Directors must be appropriately qualified, and offer a wide variety of backgrounds and outlooks.

The board consists of the chairman and chief executive officer, executive directors and independent non-executive directors. The majority of board members must be independent non-executive directors.

Board Meetings

The board meets a minimum of five times per year and one of these meetings is solely concerned with long-term strategic planning. The chairman and chief executive officer are responsible for distributing the agenda of each meeting beforehand in a timely manner. All members of the board are expected to make every effort to attend the board meetings.

Authority and Responsibilities of the Board

Naturally, the company sees its shareholders as the main stakeholder group of the company. Starbucks states that the fundamental responsibility of the board is to promote the best interests of the company and its shareholders by overseeing the management of the company's business and affairs. This is the standard responsibility of a corporate board and translates itself into two basic legal obligations, namely (1) the duty of care, which imposes the obligation on the board to make appropriate decisions on behalf of the company and avoid unnecessary risk, and (2) the duty of loyalty, which requires that the board makes decisions that are in the interests of the company and its shareholders, without regard to any personal interest.

Policies and Practices

Starbucks is ahead of many other companies in that it has a corporate governance committee that reports directly to the board of directors. This places corporate governance at the same level of importance as the audit function, the remuneration of directors and their nomination to the board, which all have their separate committees.

The corporate governance document sets out detailed procedures for selecting new directorial candidates and their appointment to the board. It also describes the process by which agenda items are set for each board meeting.

Non-executive directors have time at each board meeting to meet on their own without any executive directors present. This is to ensure that a balanced discussion of the company's strategy can be carried out without the interference of the managers who are actually implementing the strategy.

Director Share Ownership

Starbucks insists that all its directors, whether they be executive or non-executive, hold shares in the company. This is important to the directors as it ensures some convergence of objectives of directors and shareholders. New directors have four years from the date of appointment to purchase these shares and must hold them for the period of appointment to the board.

Assessing Board Performance

Starbucks carries out an annual evaluation of the directors' performance, the effectiveness of the board of directors and all its subcommittees. An evaluation of the chairman and chief executive is also carried out. Both the chair and the chief executive of Starbucks are subjected to a formal evaluation each year based on a number of qualitative and quantitative benchmarks. The salaries of both chair and chief executive are consequently determined by this evaluation.

All the business and financing decisions of Starbucks are framed by the company's main corporate governance principles. By placing corporate governance at the very forefront of the Starbucks philosophy, shareholders and stakeholders know that their financial and human investment is governed in an appropriate manner.

Summary and Conclusions

All of the material in this textbook makes the assumption that firms are run properly, efficiently and ethically. Unfortunately, in practice, this may not be the case. Corporate governance is concerned with the way in which a firm is managed. There are a number of basic principles that should be followed to minimize the danger of firms getting into difficulty solely because of the way they are managed. The budding financial manager must be aware of and familiar with the basic principles underlying the way in which his or her company should be run. Without this knowledge, he or she will not be in a position to make the best financial decisions for the company's shareholders.

Questions and Problems

CONCEPT

1 **The Corporate Firm** Differentiate between sole proprietorships, partnerships and corporations. What are the advantages and weaknesses of each?

2 **Agency Problems** Is it ethical for a company's management to resist a hostile takeover offer that would result in a higher payout for shareholders, even if the management would lose their positions in the process? Explain.

3 **The Governance Structure of Corporations** Why do partnerships require formal agreements among the main shareholders when sole ownerships do not? Why are corporation articles and memoranda of understanding so complex compared to partnership agreements?

4 **Corporate Governance Principles** Review the G20/OECD Principles of Corporate Governance. Which principle relates to the ability of corporate executives to trade in the shares of their own company?

5 **Corporate Governance in Action** Give an overview of the UN Sustainable Development Goals and explain their importance to corporate finance.

REGULAR

6 **Private vs Public Companies** What are the main similarities and differences between private and public limited companies? Why are all firms not publicly listed?

7 **Macro Governance** Why do you think corporate behaviour in bank-based financial systems would be different from market-based financial systems? How do you think other differences in the macro environment can affect corporate objectives?

8 **Corporate Governance** Explain why you would (or would not) pay more for the shares of a well-governed company compared to a poorly governed one.

9 **Corporate Boards** Many regulators insist on public companies having board subcommittees such as the remuneration committee, audit committee and risk management committee. Why could this responsibility not simply be left to the board of directors? Explain.

10 **Corporate Governance Across the World** What are the key differences between the various models of corporate governance currently in use globally and how do these models impact the distribution of share ownership and decision-making power within a company? How does Chinese and Indian corporate governance compare with US, UK and European corporate governance?

11 **Sustainable Corporate Governance Across the World** How do models of corporate governance worldwide influence ecological responsibility? Compare the ecological and social implications of Chinese and Indian corporate governance with those in the United States, United Kingdom and Europe. Can one system learn anything from the other?

12 **Corporate Governance Around the World** In the Middle East, many companies have a Sharia Supervisory Board to which the board of directors reports. Evaluate the merits of such a governance structure and argue whether this approach to governance could be extended to other areas where the supervisory board guides on ethical, social or environmental matters.

13 **Partnerships** What are the differences between a general partnership and a limited partnership? Why do firms choose to be partnerships instead of limited liability corporations?

14 **Organizations** Is it possible for a firm to move from being a limited corporation to a partnership? Explain when this may happen.

15 **Comparing Corporate Governance Principles** Discuss the UK Corporate Governance Code. In what ways is it different to the G20/OECD Corporate Governance Principles?

16 **Corporate Governance Principles** Is it possible to improve one governance principle in a firm but weaken another at the same time? Use an illustration to explain your answer.

17 **Corporate Governance Policy** How do differences in the macro environment affect corporate governance?

18 **Principles of Good Governance** Discuss the G20/OECD Principles of Corporate Governance in detail, commenting on the major principles covered. In your opinion, what is the most important (if any) principle? Use practical examples to illustrate your answer.

19 **Sustainability in Governance** Incorporating sustainability into governance, explore the integration of environmental, social and economic factors in the G20/OECD Principles of Corporate Governance. Analyse how these principles address sustainable development, and identify which principle, in your perspective, carries the most significant impact on long-term global resilience and preservation.

20 **Regulatory Governance** What are the essential elements of a successful corporate governance framework for a developing country's manufacturing sector, and what specific measures would you propose to ensure the effective implementation of these governance structures?

21 **Audit Committees** The audit committee of a firm is an integral part of its corporate governance. Explain what an audit committee is, why it is important, its main responsibilities and how you can evaluate the audit process within a company. Your answer should refer to real-life examples where the audit process was ineffective or flawed.

22 **Agency Relationships** Who owns a corporation? How do owners control the firm's management? What is an agency relationship and what is the main reason an agency relationship exists?

23 **Agency Problems and Corporate Ownership** Corporate ownership varies around the world. Historically, individuals have owned the majority of shares in public corporations in the United States. In Germany and Japan, however, banks and other large financial institutions own most of the equity in public corporations. Do you think agency problems are likely to be more or less severe in Germany and Japan than in the United States? Why? In recent years, large financial institutions such as mutual funds and pension funds have been becoming the dominant owners of shares in the UK, and these institutions are becoming more active in corporate affairs. What are the implications of this trend for agency problems and corporate control?

24 **Government Ownership** After the 2008 financial crisis, some governments took control of banks through buying their shares. What impact does this have on the lending culture of banks? Is this consistent with shareholder maximization?

25 **Stakeholders** Discuss what is meant by a stakeholder. In what ways are stakeholders represented in two-tier board structures? How does this differ from companies with a unitary board structure? Use real-life examples to illustrate your answer.

26 **Institutional Shareholders** Regulators have developed a number of new policies with respect to institutional shareholder involvement in the running of firms. Review the reasons why regulators would prefer more or less involvement of institutions in the running of corporations. In addition, discuss the proposals that have been put forward by regulators in your own country and whether these are likely to be effective.

27 **Managerial Objectives** Why would we expect managers of a corporation to pursue the objectives of shareholders? What about bondholders?

CHALLENGE

28 **Codes of Corporate Governance** Choose a developed and an emerging market economy, and identify any differences and similarities between your chosen countries.

29 **Board of Directors** You have been hired as a consultant to evaluate the performance of a board of directors. What things would you look for? Why would shareholders want to hire a consultant to do such a job when the share price is supposed to give an accurate reflection of corporate performance?

30 **Managerial Ownership** How do agency costs in a firm change as managers build up their shareholdings? What does it mean when we say that managers are entrenched? Provide some examples of real-life cases where managers have acted in a selfish fashion even when they are shareholders in the firm.

31 **Executive Compensation** Critics have charged that compensation to top managers in the banking sector is simply too high and should be cut back. Look at the financial accounts of some banks in your region and determine the total pay of their chief executive officers. Are such amounts excessive? Explain.

32 **Managerial Objectives** In 2012, the Argentinian government nationalized YPF, which is a subsidiary of Repsol, the Spanish oil giant. YPF was integral to the operations of Repsol. The firm was set up 10 years earlier and had received more than €20 billion of capital investment from Repsol. The benefits to Repsol's shareholders from YPF were large and, every year, $600 million of dividends were paid to the parent company. How do you think the presence of a major state shareholder (the Argentinian government) changes the agency relationships within YPF? Explain.

Exam Question (45 minutes)

As the financial manager of a multinational technology company based in Berlin, you have been tasked with preparing the firm for a potential initial public offering (IPO). The company has a complex ownership structure, with multiple stakeholders including venture capital firms, angel investors and employee shareholders. Due to the company's rapid growth and diverse ownership, there has been limited attention paid to corporate governance issues in the past. The IPO will result in the dilution of the current shareholders' ownership and the influx of new, mainly institutional, shareholders. The board of directors has approached you with the following questions regarding corporate governance:

1 What measures should the company take to ensure effective communication and collaboration between the diverse group of shareholders post-IPO? **(20 marks)**

2 How should the company structure its board of directors to balance the interests of both current and new shareholders? **(20 marks)**

3 What processes should be put in place to address potential conflicts of interest among the various stakeholders? **(20 marks)**

4 What considerations should the company take into account when determining executive compensation post-IPO? **(20 marks)**

5 How should the company manage the expectations of its new institutional shareholders, who may have different priorities and decision-making processes than the current shareholders? **(20 marks)**

Total Marks: 100

Mini Case

Executive Remuneration

As a member of the remuneration committee of a sustainable energy firm, you have been tasked with creating a fair and effective pay package for the company's newly appointed CEO. The company has a strong commitment to sustainability and social responsibility and has been owned and operated by a group of socially conscious investors for the past decade.

The new CEO, an experienced professional from the traditional energy sector, has been brought in to lead the company's expansion and growth. However, the current shareholders are concerned about balancing the need for a competitive pay package that will attract and retain top talent with the company's commitment to sustainability and social responsibility.

After careful consideration, the proposed pay package for the CEO includes:

- A base salary that is competitive with industry standards and reflects the CEO's experience and qualifications.
- Performance-based bonuses linked to specific sustainability and social responsibility targets, such as reducing the company's carbon footprint and increasing community engagement initiatives.
- Stock options that align the CEO's financial incentives with the long-term success and sustainability of the company.
- An annual review process that allows for adjustments to the pay package based on the CEO's performance and the company's financial and sustainability goals.

1 Critically assess this renumeration package. Do you think it adequately recognizes the CEO's role?

2 Do you think it balances the company's desire for growth and success, while also taking into account the company's commitment to sustainability and social responsibility?

3 Develop a list of specific sustainability and social responsibility targets that could be used to measure the CEO's performance and link it to her bonus structure.

4 Draft a detailed report to the board of directors outlining the proposed pay package for the CEO, including a thorough explanation of the reasoning behind each component of the package and a discussion of its strengths and weaknesses.

Practical Case Study

In this case study, you will identify a publicly listed company, evaluate the existing corporate governance structure of the firm and provide recommendations for improvement.

1 Research the corporate governance code in the country in which your firm is headquartered.
2 Review the governance structure of your chosen firm, including its board of directors, committees and management. Evaluate how the organization's governance structure aligns with the principles outlined in the country's corporate governance code.
3 Research the OECD Principles of Corporate Governance and summarize the key principles. Evaluate your firm's performance in relation to each of the principles and provide specific examples to support your assessment.
4 Summarize your key findings and provide recommendations for improvement, including specific actions that should be taken within the next 12–24 months to enhance the quality of governance at the organization.

References

Aggarwal, D., O. Eldar, Y.V. Hochberg and L.P. Litov (2022) 'The Rise of Dual-class Stock IPOs', *Journal of Financial Economics*, Vol. 144, No. 1, 122–153.

Aminadav, G. and E. Papaioannou (2020) 'Corporate Control Around the World', *Journal of Finance*, Vol. 75, No. 3, 1191–1246.

Additional Reading

Corporate governance is one of the fastest-growing research areas in finance and the number of top-quality papers published over the last few years is enormous. The ownership structure and governance environment, as well as their impact on all aspects of financial decision-making, have rightly been recognized as crucial to understanding how corporations make decisions. Some good starting points for readers are listed below (country or region of study is given in bold):

1 Aguilera, R.V. and R. Crespi-Cladera (2016) 'Global Corporate Governance: On the Relevance of Firms' Ownership Structure', *Journal of World Business*, Vol. 51, No. 1, 50–57.
2 Anderson, R.C., D.M. Reeb and W. Zhao (2012) 'Family-controlled Firms and Informed Trading: Evidence from Short Sales', *Journal of Finance*, Vol. 67, No. 1, 351–386. **USA.**
3 Ansari, I.F., M. Goergen and S. Mira (2014) 'The Determinants of the CEO Successor Choice in Family Firms', *Journal of Corporate Finance*, Vol. 28, 6–25. **France, Germany and UK.**
4 Armstrong, C.S., J.E. Core and W.R. Guay (2014) 'Do Independent Directors Cause Improvements in Firm Transparency?', *Journal of Financial Economics*, Vol. 113, No. 3, 383–403.
5 Atanassov, J. (2013) 'Do Hostile Takeovers Stifle Innovation? Evidence from Antitakeover Legislation and Corporate Patenting', *Journal of Finance*, Vol. 68, No. 3, 1097–1131.
6 Bebchuk, L.A., A. Cohen and C.C. Wang (2013) 'Learning and the Disappearing Association Between Governance and Returns', *Journal of Financial Economics*, Vol. 108, No. 2, 323–348.
7 Belot, F., E. Ginglinger, M.B. Slovin and M.E. Sushka (2014) 'Freedom of Choice Between Unitary and Two-tier Boards: An Empirical Analysis', *Journal of Financial Economics*, Vol. 112, No. 3, 364–385. **France.**
8 Bena, J. and H. Ortiz-Molina (2013) 'Pyramidal Ownership and the Creation of New Firms', *Journal of Financial Economics*, Vol. 108, No. 3, 798–821. **Europe.**
9 Bodnaruk, A., M. Massa and A. Simonov (2013) 'Alliances and Corporate Governance', *Journal of Financial Economics*, Vol. 107, No. 3, 671–693. **USA.**
10 Boubakri, N., J.C. Cosset and W. Saffar (2013) 'The Role of State and Foreign Owners in Corporate Risk-taking: Evidence from Privatization', *Journal of Financial Economics*, Vol. 108, No. 3, 641–658. **International.**
11 Chhaochharia, V., A. Kumar and A. Niessen-Ruenzi (2012) 'Local Investors and Corporate Governance', *Journal of Accounting and Economics*, Vol. 54, No. 1, 42–67. **USA.**
12 Cohn, J.B. and U. Rajan (2013) 'Optimal Corporate Governance in the Presence of an Activist Investor', *Review of Financial Studies*, Vol. 26, No. 4, 985–1020.

13 Cornelli, F., Z. Kominek and A. Ljungqvist (2013) 'Monitoring Managers: Does it Matter?', *Journal of Finance,* Vol. 68, No. 2, 431–481. **Central and Eastern Europe.**

14 Cuñat, V., M. Gine and M. Guadalupe (2012) 'The Vote is Cast: The Effect of Corporate Governance on Shareholder Value', *Journal of Finance,* Vol. 67, No. 5, 1943–1977.

15 Cuomo, F., C. Mallin and A. Zattoni (2016) 'Corporate Governance Codes: A Review and Research Agenda', *Corporate Governance: An International Review,* Vol. 24, No. 3, 222–241.

16 Dhillon, A. and S. Rossetto (2015) 'Ownership Structure, Voting, and Risk', *Review of Financial Studies,* Vol. 28, No. 2. 521–560.

17 Erkens, D.H., M. Hung and P. Matos (2012) 'Corporate Governance in the 2007–2008 Financial Crisis: Evidence from Financial Institutions Worldwide', *Journal of Corporate Finance,* Vol. 18, No. 2, 389–411. **International.**

18 Falato, A., D. Kadyrzhanova and U. Lel (2014) 'Distracted Directors: Does Board Busyness Hurt Shareholder Value?', *Journal of Financial Economics,* Vol. 113, No. 3, 404–426.

19 Field, L., M. Lowry and A. Mkrtchyan (2013) 'Are Busy Boards Detrimental?', *Journal of Financial Economics,* Vol. 109, No. 1, 63–82.

20 Gantchev, N. (2013) 'The Costs of Shareholder Activism: Evidence from a Sequential Decision Model', *Journal of Financial Economics,* Vol. 107, No. 3, 610–631.

21 Ge, W., J.-B. Kim and B.Y. Song (2012) 'Internal Governance, Legal Institutions and Bank Loan Contracting around the World', *Journal of Corporate Finance,* Vol. 18, No. 3, 413–432. **International.**

22 Graham, J.R., J. Grennan, C.R. Harvey and S. Rajgopal (2022) 'Corporate Culture: Evidence From the Field', *Journal of Financial Economics,* Vol. 146, No. 2, 552–593.

23 Gugler, K., N. Ivanova and J. Zechner (2014) 'Ownership and Control in Central and Eastern Europe', *Journal of Corporate Finance,* Vol. 26, 145–163. **Central and Eastern Europe.**

24 Hafsi, T. and G. Turgut (2013) 'Boardroom Diversity and its Effect on Social Performance: Conceptualization and Empirical Evidence', *Journal of Business Ethics,* Vol. 112, No. 3, 463–479.

25 Hazarika, S., J.M. Karpoff and R. Nahata (2012) 'Internal Corporate Governance, CEO Turnover, and Earnings Management', *Journal of Financial Economics,* Vol. 104, No. 1, 44–69.

26 Hermalin, B.E. and M.S. Weisbach (2012) 'Information Disclosure and Corporate Governance', *Journal of Finance,* Vol. 67, No. 1, 195–234.

27 Hillier, D., V. Pereira de Queiroz, J. Pindado and C. De la Torre (2010) 'The Impact of Country-level Corporate Governance on Research and Development', *Journal of International Business Studies,* Vol. 42, No. 1, 76–98.

28 Hilscher, J. and E. S is li-Ciamarra (2013) 'Conflicts of Interest on Corporate Boards: The Effect of Creditor-directors on Acquisitions', *Journal of Corporate Finance,* Vol. 19, 140–158. **USA.**

29 Huang, J. and D.J. Kisgen (2013) 'Gender and Corporate Finance: Are Male Executives Overconfident Relative to Female Executives?', *Journal of Financial Economics,* Vol. 108, No. 3, 822–839.

30 Iliev, P., K.V. Lins, D.P. Miller and L. Roth (2015) 'Shareholder Voting and Corporate Governance Around the World', *Review of Financial Studies,* Vol. 28, No. 8, 2167–2202.

31 Kaplan, S.N., M.M. Klebanov and M. Sorensen (2012) 'Which CEO Characteristics and Abilities Matter?', *Journal of Finance,* Vol. 67, No. 3, 973–1007.

32 Kind, A. and M. Poltera (2013) 'The Value of Corporate Voting Rights Embedded in Option Prices', *Journal of Corporate Finance,* Vol. 22, 16–34. **Europe.**

33 Krüger, P. (2015) 'Corporate Goodness and Shareholder Wealth', *Journal of Financial Economics,* Vol. 115, No. 2, 304–329.

34 La Porta, L., F. Lopez-de-Silanes, A. Shleifer and R. Vishny (2000) 'Investor Protection and Corporate Governance', *Journal of Financial Economics,* Vol. 58, No. 1–2, 3–27.

35 Lel, U. (2012) 'Currency Hedging and Corporate Governance: A Cross-country Analysis', *Journal of Corporate Finance,* Vol. 18, No. 2, 221–237. **International.**

36 Lin, C., Y. Ma, P. Malatesta and Y. Xuan (2012) 'Corporate Ownership Structure and Bank Loan Syndicate Structure', *Journal of Financial Economics,* Vol. 104, No. 1, 1–22. **International.**

37 Masulis, R.W. and S. Mobbs (2014) 'Independent Director Incentives: Where Do Talented Directors Spend their Limited Time and Energy?', *Journal of Financial Economics,* Vol. 111, No. 2, 406–429. **USA.**

38 Masulis, R.W., C. Wang and F. Xie (2012) 'Globalizing the Boardroom: The Effects of Foreign Directors on Corporate Governance and Firm Performance', *Journal of Accounting and Economics,* Vol. 53, No. 3, 527–554. **USA.**

39 McCahery, J.A., Z. Sautner and L.T. Starks (2016) 'Behind the Scenes: The Corporate Governance Preferences of Institutional Investors', *Journal of Finance,* Vol. 71, No. 6, 2905–2932.

40 Mehrotra, V., R. Morck, J. Shim and Y. Wiwattanakantang (2013) 'Adoptive Expectations:

Rising Sons in Japanese Family Firms', *Journal of Financial Economics*, Vol. 108, No. 3, 840–854. **Japan.**

41 Mollah, S. and M. Zaman (2015) 'Shari'ah Supervision, Corporate Governance and Performance: Conventional vs. Islamic Banks', *Journal of Banking & Finance*, Vol. 58, 418–435.

42 Morellec, E., B. Nikolov and N. Schürhoff (2012) 'Corporate Governance and Capital Structure Dynamics', *Journal of Finance*, Vol. 67, No. 3, 803–848.

43 Noe, T.H. and M.J. Rebello (2012) 'Optimal Corporate Governance and Compensation in a Dynamic World', *Review of Financial Studies*, Vol. 25, No. 2, 480–521.

44 Norli, Ø., C. Ostergaard and I. Schindele (2015) 'Liquidity and Shareholder Activism', *Review of Financial Studies*, Vol. 28, No. 2, 486–520.

45 Schwartz-Ziv, M. and M.S. Weisbach (2013) 'What Do Boards Really Do? Evidence from Minutes of Board Meetings', *Journal of Financial Economics*, Vol. 108, No. 2, 349–366. **Israel.**

46 Yermack, D. (2017) 'Corporate Governance and Blockchains', *Review of Finance*, Vol. 21, No. 1, 7–31.

Endnote

1 OECD, Recommendation of the Council on Principles of Corporate Governance, OECD/LEGAL/0413.

PART 2

Value and Capital Budgeting

Part 2 delves into the investment decision process, exploring essential tools for financial decision-making. Focusing on cash flows and accounting data, we analyse financial performance in **Chapter 3** through ratio analysis and an in-depth case study. Introducing the time value of money, **Chapter 4** examines valuing diverse cash flow streams. Practical applications continue in **Chapter 5** with corporate bond and equity valuation, while **Chapters 6, 7** and **8** discuss methods for valuing strategic investments. By the end of Part 2, you'll be able to confidently assess investments and projects, determining their value to your firm.

Chapter 3
Financial Statement Analysis

Learning Objectives

After reading this chapter you should be able to:

LO1 Remember and define the key components of financial statements.

LO2 Understand the significance of financial statement analysis.

LO3 Apply ratio analysis to evaluate a company's financial performance.

LO4 Analyse the DuPont identity and be familiar with its implications for a company's return on equity.

LO5 Evaluate the practical use of financial statement information for decision-making.

In February 2023, shares in the world's largest brewer, Anheuser-Busch InBev (AB InBev), were trading for €55.25. At that price, AB InBev had a price–earnings (PE) ratio of 23.80, meaning that investors were willing to pay €23.80 for every euro in income earned by AB InBev. At the same time, investors were willing to pay €12.45 and €27.49 for each euro earned by Bayer Aktiengesellschaft and Schneider Electric, respectively. Although their PE ratios are different from AB InBev's, the share prices were similar (€60.80 and €153.08, respectively). Meanwhile, the average equity in the FTSE 100 Index, which contains 100 of the largest publicly traded companies in the United Kingdom, had a PE ratio of about 44.36. Table 3.1 presents the largest companies on the London Stock Exchange, with details of industry and price–earnings ratio.

Are the PE ratios of AB InBev, Bayer Aktiengesellschaft and Schneider Electric unnaturally high? What do PE ratios tell us and why are they important? To find out, this chapter explores a variety of ratios, and their use in financial analysis and planning. However, before examining PE ratios, we need to spend some time on the source of this ratio – the company's financial statements.

Source: Mykola Korolkov/123RF.

Key Notations

ROE	Return on equity	$CF(O)$	Cash flow from operations
ROA	Return on assets	$CF(I)$	Cash flow from investing activities
EPS	Earnings per share	$CF(F)$	Cash flow from financing activities
NCF	Net cash flow	PE	Price–earnings ratio

Table 3.1 Largest UK Listed Companies

Company	Industry	Market Value (£mn)	PE Ratio
HSBC Holdings	Financials	121,770	12.22
Shell	Energy	175,870	5.38
BP	Energy	100,110	-
AstraZeneca	Healthcare	175,900	65.35
GSK	Healthcare	60,910	13.62
Diageo	Consumer staples	80,050	22.65
BAT	Consumer staples	69,350	10.58
Unilever	Consumer staples	107,550	16.13
Rio Tinto	Basic materials	100,100	6.64
Vodafone Group	Telecommunications	25,450	14.56

Source: FT.Com, February 2023.

3.1 The Statement of Financial Position

Chapter 1
Page 3

The **statement of financial position** or **balance sheet** is an accountant's snapshot of a firm's accounting value on a particular date, as though the firm momentarily stood still (see **Chapter 1,** Section 1.1 for more information). The statement of financial position has two sides: on the left are the *assets* and on the right are the *liabilities* and *shareholders' equity*. The statement of financial position states what the firm owns and how it is financed. The accounting definition that underlies the statement of financial position and describes the relationship is:

$$\text{Assets} = \text{Liabilities} + \text{Shareholders' equity}$$

We have put a three-line equality in the balance equation to indicate that it must always hold, by definition. In fact, the shareholders' equity is *defined* to be the difference between the assets and the liabilities of the firm. In principle, equity is what the shareholders would have remaining after the firm discharged its obligations.

Table 3.2 gives the 2022 statement of financial position for the Swiss multinational commodities and energy trading company, Glencore plc. The assets in the statement of financial position are listed in order by the length of time it normally would take an ongoing firm to convert them into cash. The asset side depends on the nature of the business and how management chooses to conduct it. Management must make decisions about cash versus marketable securities, credit versus cash sales, whether to make or buy inventory, whether to lease or purchase items, the types of business in which to engage, and so on. The liabilities and the shareholders' equity are also listed in the order in which they would typically be paid over time.

The liabilities and equity side reflects the types and proportions of financing, which depend on management's choice of capital structure, as between debt and equity and between current debt and long-term debt.

When analysing a statement of financial position, the financial manager should be aware of three concerns: liquidity, debt versus equity and value versus cost.

Liquidity

Liquidity refers to the ease and speed with which assets can be converted to cash (without significant loss in value). *Current assets* are the most liquid, and include cash and assets that will be turned into cash within a year from the date of the statement of financial position. *Trade receivables* are amounts not yet collected from customers for goods or services sold to them (after adjustment for potential bad debts). *Inventories* are composed of raw materials to be used in production, work in progress and finished goods. *Non-current assets* are the least liquid kind of assets. Tangible non-current assets include property, plant and equipment. Non-current assets do not convert to cash from normal business activity, and they are not usually used to pay expenses such as payroll.

Table 3.2 2022 Statement of Financial Position (Balance Sheet) of Glencore plc

Non-current Assets	$m	Non-current Liabilities	$m
Property, Plant and Equipment	39,564	Borrowings	18,851
Intangible Assets	6,160	Other Financial Liabilities	16,834
Investments	12,334		**35,685**
Advances and Loans	2,654	Current Liabilities	
Other Non-current Assets	5,088	Borrowings	9,926
	65,800	Accounts Payable	29,726
Current Assets		Other Financial Liabilities	12,027
Inventories	33,460		**51,679**
Accounts Receivable	24,565	Total Liabilities	87,364
Other Current Assets	6,835	Total Shareholders Equity	**45,219**
Cash and Cash Equivalents	1,923		
	66,783		
Total Assets	**132,583**	**Total Assets**	**132,583**

Some non-current assets are intangible. Intangible assets have no physical existence but can be very valuable. Examples of intangible assets are the value of a trademark or the value of a patent. Goodwill is an accounting term that reflects the premium paid by companies when they acquire other companies. Note that Glencore's intangibles figure is $6,160 million because of past acquisitions made by the firm.

The more liquid a firm's assets, the less likely it is to experience problems meeting short-term obligations. Thus, the probability that a firm will avoid financial distress can be linked to its liquidity. Unfortunately, liquid assets frequently have lower rates of return than non-current assets; for example, cash generates no investment income. To the extent a firm invests in liquid assets, it sacrifices an opportunity to invest in more profitable investment vehicles.

Debt versus Equity

Liabilities are obligations of the firm that require a payout of cash within a stipulated period. Many liabilities involve contractual obligations to repay a stated amount and interest over a period. Thus, liabilities are debts and are frequently associated with nominally fixed cash burdens, called *debt service,* that put the firm in default of a contract if they are not paid. *Shareholders' equity* is a claim against the firm's assets that is residual and not fixed. In general terms, when the firm borrows, it gives the bondholders first claim on the firm's cash flow. Bondholders can sue the firm if the firm defaults on its bond contracts. This may lead the firm to declare itself bankrupt. Shareholders' equity is the residual difference between assets and liabilities:

$$\text{Assets} - \text{Liabilities} \equiv \text{Shareholders' equity}$$

This is the shareholders' ownership of the firm stated in accounting terms. The accounting value of shareholders' equity increases when retained earnings are added. This occurs when the firm retains part of its earnings instead of paying them out as dividends.

Value versus Cost

The accounting value of a firm's assets is frequently referred to as the *book value* of the assets. Firms in different countries use various accounting standards to report the value of their assets. All listed companies in the European Union are required to use **International Financial Reporting Standards (IFRS)**. IFRS value assets at theoretically true market or fair values. *Market or fair value* is the price at which willing buyers and sellers would trade the assets. Unfortunately, even with fair value accounting (IFRS), the tradable value of assets is likely to differ from their accounting value. This is because, in many cases, there is no liquid market that allows the calculation of an asset's accounting fair value. In these situations, the financial manager must estimate a fair value from a similar asset or a theoretical model.

The USA has a different set of accounting standards, called Generally Accepted Accounting Principles (GAAP). There are some differences between IFRS and GAAP, so the reader should be careful to ensure the accounting standards used by a firm are known. Fortunately, over the last few years, IFRS and GAAP have been converging, with several joint standards issued.

In this book, we will treat IFRS as the main accounting system because it is used for listed European and South African firms. However, if a company is private or a charity, there is much more flexibility and the level of detail expected by IFRS is not normally required. As long as there is consistency in approach from year to year, private firms can use as much of IFRS as required.

3.2 The Income Statement

The **income statement** or **statement of profit and loss** measures performance over a specific period – say, a year. The accounting definition of income is:

$$\text{Revenue} - \text{Expenses} = \text{Income}$$

If the statement of financial position is like a snapshot, the statement of profit and loss is like a video recording of what the people did between two snapshots. Table 3.3 gives the statement of profit and loss for Glencore for the year ending 2022.

Table 3.3 Glencore plc 2022 Statement of Profit and Loss

	$m
Revenue	255,984
Cost of Goods Sold	224,753
Depreciation	7,016
Profit Before Interest and Tax	**24,215**
Net Interest	1,336
Profit Before Tax	**22,879**
Tax	6,368
Profit After Tax	**16,511**
Number of Shares	12,414
EPS	1.33

$$\text{Earnings per share} = \frac{\text{Profit for the period attributable to equityholders}}{\text{Total shares outstanding}}$$

$$= \frac{\$16{,}511 \text{ million}}{12{,}414 \text{ million}}$$

$$= \$1.33 \text{ per share}$$

Source: Glencore plc accounts (2022).

The statement of profit and loss usually includes several sections. The operations section reports the firm's revenues and expenses from principal operations. Among other things, the non-operating part of the statement of profit and loss consists of all financing costs, such as interest expense. Usually, a second section reports as a separate item the amount of taxes levied on income. The last item on the statement of profit and loss is the bottom line, or net income. Net income is frequently expressed per share of equity – that is, earnings per share.

When analysing a statement of profit and loss, the financial manager should keep in mind non-cash items, time and costs.

Non-cash Items

The economic value of assets is naturally connected to their future incremental cash flows. However, cash flow does not appear on a statement of profit and loss. There are several **non-cash items** that are expenses against revenues but do not affect cash flow. The most important of these is *depreciation*. Depreciation reflects the accountant's estimate of the cost of equipment used up in the production process. For example, suppose an asset with a five-year life and no resale value is purchased for €1,000. According to accountants, the €1,000 cost must be expensed over the useful life of the asset. If straight-line depreciation is used, there will be five equal instalments, and €200 of depreciation expense will be incurred each year. From a finance perspective, the cost of the asset is the actual negative cash flow incurred when the asset is acquired (that is, €1,000, *not* the accountant's smoothed €200-per-year depreciation expense).

In practice, the difference between cash flows and accounting income can be quite dramatic, so it is essential to understand the difference. For example, while Glencore made a total profit of $16,511 million for the year ending 2022, its cash decreased by $1,310 million. We look at financial cash flow in more detail in Section 3.5.

Time and Costs

It is often useful to visualize all of future time as having two distinct parts: the *short run* and the *long run*. The short run is the period in which certain equipment, resources and commitments of the firm are fixed, but the time is long enough for the firm to vary its output by using more labour and raw materials. The short run is not a precise period that will be the same for all industries. However, all firms making decisions in the short run have some fixed costs – that is, costs that will not change because of fixed commitments. In real business activity, examples of fixed costs are bond interest, overhead and property taxes. Costs that are not fixed are variable. Variable costs change as the output of the firm changes; some examples are raw materials and wages for employees on the production line.

In the long run, all costs are variable. Accountants do not distinguish between variable costs and fixed costs. Instead, accounting costs usually fit into a classification that distinguishes product costs from period costs. Product costs are the total production costs incurred during a period – raw materials, direct labour and manufacturing overheads – and are reported on the statement of profit and loss as cost of goods sold. Both variable and fixed costs are included in product costs. Period costs are costs that are allocated to a time period; they are called *selling, general* and *administrative expenses*. One period cost would be the company chief executive's salary.

3.3 Taxes

Taxes can be one of the largest cash outflows a firm experiences. For example, for the year ending 2022, Glencore's profit before taxes was $22,879 million. Its tax bill for this period was $6,368 million, or about 27.8 per cent of its pretax earnings. The size of the tax bill is determined by the tax code of the region your firm operates in, an often amended set of rules, and any deferred taxes from an earlier year. In this section, we examine corporate tax rates and how taxes are calculated.

If the various taxation rules seem a little bizarre or convoluted to you, keep in mind that the tax code is the result of political, not economic, forces. As a result, there is no reason why it has to make economic sense.

Corporate Tax Rates

Chapter 15 Page 404
Chapter 16 Page 433

An overview of corporate tax rates that were in effect for 2023 for a sample of countries is shown in Table 3.4. Corporate taxes are not normally a simple arithmetic deduction from profit before taxes. Almost all countries in the world allow firms to carry forward losses they have made in previous years to offset their tax bill in the future. This is what happened to Glencore in 2022. Although the corporate tax rate in Switzerland is much lower than 27.8 per cent, Glencore would have had to pay tax in different jurisdictions, many of which would have been higher than Switzerland, as well as past taxes deferred from earlier years. (See **Chapter 15,** Section 15.5 and **Chapter 16,** Section 16.4 for more information on corporate tax.)

Table 3.4 Corporate Tax Rates Around the World

Country	Corporation Tax (%)	Country	Corporation Tax (%)
Australia	30	Netherlands	19/25.8
Austria	25	Norway	22
Bahrain	0	Oman	15
Belgium	25	Poland	19
China	25	Portugal	31.5
Denmark	22	Russia	20
Finland	20	Saudi Arabia	20
France	25.83	Singapore	17
Germany	29.83	South Africa	28
Greece	22	Spain	25
India	30	Sweden	20.6
Ireland	12.5	Switzerland	19.7
Italy	27.81	UAE	0
Japan	29.74	UK	19
Malaysia	24	USA	25.81

Source: Tax Foundation, www.taxfoundation.org, 2022.

The tax rates presented in Table 3.4 are average tax rates for the largest companies. Many countries apply differential taxation depending on how much a company earns in any given year. In the Netherlands, for example, there are two corporation tax bands. Firms that earn between €0 and €200,000 per annum have a tax rate of 19 per cent. Firms that earn above €200,000 must pay 25.8 per cent (as presented in Table 3.3).

Average versus Marginal Tax Rates

In making financial decisions, it is frequently important to distinguish between average and marginal tax rates. Your average tax rate is your tax bill divided by your taxable income – in other words, the percentage of your income that goes to pay taxes. Your marginal tax rate is the tax you would pay (in per cent) if you earned one more unit of currency. The percentage tax rates shown in Table 3.4 for the Netherlands are marginal rates. The first €200,000 earned by Dutch firms has a tax rate of 19 per cent. Any extra earnings are charged 25.8 per cent tax. Put another way, marginal tax rates apply to the part of income in the indicated range only, not all income.

The difference between average and marginal tax rates can best be illustrated with a simple example. Suppose our Dutch corporation has a taxable income of €400,000. What is the tax bill? Using Table 3.4, we can figure out the tax bill like this:

$$\begin{aligned} 0.19 \times €200{,}000 &= €38{,}000 \\ 0.258 \times (€400{,}000 - 200{,}000) &= \underline{€51{,}600} \\ & \underline{\underline{€89{,}600}} \end{aligned}$$

Our total tax is thus €89,600.

In our example, what is the average tax rate? We had a taxable income of €400,000 and a tax bill of €89,600, so the average tax rate is €89,600/400,000 = 22.4 per cent. What is the marginal tax rate? If we made one more euro, the tax on that euro would be 25.8 cents, so our marginal rate is 25.8 per cent.

Example 3.1

Deep in the Heart of Taxes

Assume that TomTom, the Dutch satellite navigation firm, has a taxable income of €850,000. What is its tax bill? What is its average tax rate? Its marginal tax rate?

From Table 3.4, we see that the tax rate applied to the first €200,000 is 19 per cent, and the rate applied to the next €650,000 is 25.8 per cent. So TomTom must pay 0.19 × €200,000 + 0.258 × 650,000 = €205,700. The average tax rate is thus €205,700/850,000 = 24.2 per cent. The marginal rate is 25.8 per cent because TomTom's taxes would rise by 25.8 cents if it had another euro in taxable income.

With a *flat-rate* tax, there is only one tax rate, so the rate is the same for all income levels. With such a tax, the marginal tax rate is always the same as the average tax rate. As it stands now, corporate taxation in the United Kingdom is based on a modified flat-rate tax.

Normally, the marginal tax rate will be relevant for financial decision-making. The reason is that any new cash flows will be taxed at that marginal rate. Because financial decisions usually involve new cash flows or changes in existing ones, this rate will tell us the marginal effect of a decision on our tax bill.

3.4 Net Working Capital

Net working capital is current assets minus current liabilities. Net working capital is positive when current assets are greater than current liabilities. This means the cash that will become available over the next 12 months will be more than the cash that must be paid out. The net working capital of Glencore plc in 2022 was $15,104 million:

	Current Assets ($m)	−	Current Liabilities ($m)	=	Net Working Capital ($m)
2022	66,783	−	51,679	=	15,104
2021	56,455	−	48,671	=	7,784

In addition to investing in non-current assets (i.e. capital expenditure), a firm can invest in net working capital. This is called the change in net working capital. The change in net working capital in 2022 is the difference between the net working capital in 2022 and 2021. In Glencore's case, this is $15,104 million – $7,784 million = $7,320 million. What is causing the increase in net working capital? Analysis of Glencore's statement of financial position shows that current assets jumped by more than $10 billion and current liabilities increased by only $3 billion in comparison. The increase in current assets was caused primarily by higher levels of debtors and inventories, whereas the change in liabilities was driven by $2 billion in borrowings.

3.5 Cash Flow

Chapter 4 Page 088

Perhaps the most important item to be extracted from financial statements is the actual cash flow of the firm. An official accounting statement, called the *statement of cash flows*, helps to explain the change in accounting cash and equivalents, which for Glencore was down $1.26 billion in 2022. (See **Chapter 4** for more information on cash flows.)

The first point we should mention is that cash flow is not the same as net working capital. For example, increasing inventory requires using cash. Because both inventories and cash are current assets, this does not affect net working capital. In this case, an increase in inventory is associated with decreasing cash flow.

A firm's cash flow comes from or goes to three main areas: operating activities, *CF*(O), investing activities, *CF*(I), and financing activities, *CF*(F). Just as we established that the value of a firm's assets is always equal to the combined value of the liabilities and the value of the equity, the net cash flow in a firm during a particular period is the sum of cash flows resulting from operating, investing and financing activities. A negative cash flow represents a movement of cash out of the firm.

$$NCF = CF(O) + CF(I) + CF(F)$$

The first step in determining the cash flows of the firm is to figure out the *operating cash flow* or, more formally, *net cash generated by operating activities*. As can be seen in Table 3.5, operating cash flow is the cash flow generated by business activities, including sales of goods and services. Operating cash flow reflects tax payments, but not financing, capital spending or changes in net working capital.

Table 3.5 Cash Flow of Glencore plc

	($m)
Cash Flow from Operating Activities	32,915
Changes in Working Capital	–13,269
Income Taxes Paid	–4,881
Net Interest Paid	–1,106
Net Cash Generated by Operating Activities	**13,659**
Purchase of Property, Plant and Equipment	–4,177
Dividends Received from Associates and Joint Ventures	1,691
Other Investments	767
Net Cash Generated by Investing Activities	**–1,719**
Repayment of Borrowings	–8,967
New Borrowings	3,306
Purchase of Own Shares	–2,503
Distributions to Equityholders (Dividends)	–5,036
Net Cash Generated by Financing Activities	**–13,200**
Net Change in Cash	**–1,260**

Another important component of cash flow involves *changes in cash flow from investing activities*. The net change in cash flow from investing activities equals the acquisition of non-current assets plus any security investments minus the sales of non-current assets. The result is the cash flow used for investment purposes. In Glencore's cash flow statement, this amounts to a net outflow of $1.719 billion in 2022.

Cash flows also come from financing purposes, such as the firm buying back its own shares, issuing new shares to the market, and increasing or decreasing borrowing. For Glencore in 2022, cash outflows from *financing activities* were $13.2 billion. This was largely because the company paid back a lot of borrowings ($8.97 billion), dividends ($5.04 billion) and bought back $2.5 billion of its equity.

Total net cash flows generated by the firm's assets in 2022 were then equal to:

	($ millions)
Net Cash Provided by Operating Activities	13,659
Net Cash Provided by Investing Activities	–1,719
Net Cash Provided by Financing Activities	–13,200
Net Cash Flow	–1,260

Some important observations can be drawn from our discussion of cash flow:

- Several types of cash flow are relevant to understanding the financial situation of the firm. Operating cash flow measures the cash generated from operations not counting cash flows arising from investment expenditure or financing. It is usually positive; a firm is in trouble if operating cash flow is negative for a long time because the firm is not generating enough cash to pay operating costs. The total cash flow of the firm includes adjustments for capital spending and new financing. It will frequently be negative. When a firm is growing at a rapid rate, spending on inventory and non-current assets can be higher than operating cash flow.

- Profit is not cash flow. The profit made by Glencore in 2022 was $16.5 billion, whereas cash flow was down $1.26 billion. The two numbers are not usually the same. In determining the economic and financial condition of a firm, cash flow is more revealing.

A firm's total cash flow sometimes goes by a different name: free cash flow. Of course, there is no such thing as 'free' cash. Instead, the name refers to cash that the firm is free to distribute to creditors and shareholders because it is not needed for working capital or investments. We will stick with 'total cash flow of the firm' as our label for this important concept because, in practice, there is some variation in exactly how free cash flow is computed. Nonetheless, whenever you hear the phrase 'free cash flow', you should understand that what is being discussed is cash flow from assets, or something quite similar.

Real World Insight 3.1

Glencore plc

Now that you have examined the three financial statements of Glencore plc, you have a lot of information with which to analyse the company's performance over the period. Download the most up-to-date accounts for Glencore from its website (www.glencore.com) and answer the following questions:

- Have revenues increased or decreased over time?
- How have costs changed over the same period?
- Is any component of the cost base changing in an unusual way?
- What is the overall operating income of the company and is it improving?
- Is the company making a profit or loss?
- Is the profit acceptable to the firm?
- How has the company's cash flow changed? Does the cash flow suggest the company is performing poorly or well?

Financial managers regularly ask these questions of their own company and those of their competitors to gain an insight into the comparative performance of their firm.

3.6 Financial Statement Analysis

Good working knowledge of financial statements is desirable simply because such statements, and numbers derived from these statements, are the primary means of communicating financial information both within the firm and outside the firm. In short, much of the language of business finance is rooted in the ideas we discuss in this chapter.

One important goal of the accountant is to report financial information to the user in a form useful for decision-making. Ironically, the information frequently does not come to the user in such a form. In other words, financial statements do not come with a user's guide. This chapter is the first step in filling this gap.

Standardizing Statements

One obvious thing we might want to do with a company's financial statements is to compare them to those of other, similar companies. We would immediately have a problem, however. It is almost impossible to directly compare the financial statements of two companies because of differences in size.

For example, Ryanair and Air France-KLM are obviously serious rivals in the European flights market, but Air France-KLM is much larger (in terms of assets), so it is difficult to compare them directly. For that matter, it is difficult even to compare financial statements from different points in time for the same company if the company's size has changed. The size problem is compounded if we try to compare Air France-KLM and, say, International

Airlines Group (IAG, formerly British Airways and Iberia). Since IAG's financial statements are denominated in British pounds, we have size *and* currency differences.

To start making comparisons, one obvious thing we might try to do is to somehow standardize the financial statements. One common and useful way of doing this is to work with percentages instead of total monetary amounts. The resulting financial statements are called common-size statements.

Common-size statements of financial position can be constructed by expressing each item as a percentage of total assets. In this form, financial statements are relatively easy to read and compare. For example, just looking at the statement of financial position for Glencore, we can see that current assets were 50.3 per cent of total assets in 2022. Current liabilities were 39.0 per cent of total assets over that same time. Similarly, shareholders' equity comprised 34.1 per cent of total asset value.

A useful way of standardizing the income statement shown in Table 3.3 is to express each item as a percentage of total revenues. A common-size income statement tells us what happens to each cash unit in revenues. For Glencore, 2022 taxes ate up $0.0249 of every cent made in revenues. When all is said and done, only $0.0645 of each dollar in revenues flows through to the bottom line (net income). These percentages are useful in comparisons. For example, a relevant figure is the cost percentage. For Glencore, $0.911 of each $1.00 in revenues goes in expenses. It would be interesting to compute the same percentage for Glencore's main competitors to see how the firm stacks up in terms of cost control.

3.7 Ratio Analysis

Another way of avoiding the problems involved in comparing companies of different sizes is to calculate and compare financial ratios. Such ratios are ways of comparing and investigating the relationships between different pieces of financial information. We cover some of the more common ratios next (there are many others we do not discuss here).

One problem with ratios is that different people and different sources frequently do not compute them in exactly the same way, and this leads to much confusion. The specific definitions we use here may or may not be the same as ones you have seen or will see elsewhere. If you are using ratios as tools for analysis, you should be careful to document how you calculate each one; and, if you are comparing your numbers to those of another source, be sure you know how their numbers are computed.

We will defer much of our discussion of how ratios are used and some problems that come up with using them until later in the chapter. For now, for each ratio we discuss, several questions come to mind:

- How is it computed?
- What is it intended to measure, and why might we be interested?
- What is the unit of measurement?
- What might a high or low value be telling us? How might such values be misleading?
- How could this measure be improved?

Financial ratios are traditionally grouped into the following categories:

- Short-term solvency, or liquidity, ratios
- Long-term solvency, or financial leverage, ratios
- Asset management, or turnover, ratios
- Profitability ratios
- Market value ratios.

We will consider each of these in turn. In calculating these numbers for Glencore we will use the ending statement of financial position (2022) figures unless we explicitly say otherwise.

Short-term Solvency or Liquidity Measures

As the name suggests, short-term solvency ratios as a group are intended to provide information about a firm's liquidity, and these ratios are sometimes called *liquidity measures*. The primary concern is the firm's ability to pay its bills over the short run without undue stress. Consequently, these ratios focus on current assets and current liabilities.

For obvious reasons, liquidity ratios are particularly interesting to short-term creditors. Because financial managers are constantly working with banks and other short-term lenders, an understanding of these ratios is essential.

One advantage of looking at current assets and liabilities is that their book values and market values are likely to be similar. Often (though not always), these assets and liabilities just do not live long enough for the two to get seriously out of step. On the other hand, like any type of near-cash, current assets and liabilities can and do change fairly rapidly, so today's amounts may not be a reliable guide to the future.

Current Ratio

One of the best-known and most widely used ratios is the *current ratio*. As you might guess, the current ratio is defined as:

Equation 3.1

$$\text{Current ratio} = \frac{\text{Current assets}}{\text{Current liabilities}}$$

For Glencore, the 2022 current ratio is:

$$\text{Current ratio} = \frac{\$66{,}783}{\$51{,}679} = 1.29 \text{ times}$$

Because current assets and liabilities are, in principle, converted to cash over the following 12 months, the current ratio is a measure of short-term liquidity. The unit of measurement is either in cash units (such as £s) or times. So, we could say Glencore has $1.29 in current assets for every $1 in current liabilities, or we could say Glencore has its current liabilities covered 1.29 times over.

To a creditor, particularly a short-term creditor such as a supplier, the higher the current ratio, the better. To the firm, a high current ratio indicates liquidity, but it also may indicate inefficient use of cash and other short-term assets. Absent some extraordinary circumstances, we would expect to see a current ratio of at least 1. A current ratio of less than 1 would mean that net working capital (current assets less current liabilities) is negative. This would be unusual in a healthy firm, at least for most types of businesses.

The current ratio, like any ratio, is affected by various types of transactions. For example, suppose the firm borrows over the long term to raise money. The short-run effect would be an increase in cash from the issue proceeds and an increase in long-term debt. Current liabilities would not be affected, so the current ratio would rise.

Example 3.2

Current Events

Suppose a firm were to pay off some of its suppliers and short-term creditors. What would happen to the current ratio? Suppose a firm buys some inventory. What happens in this case? What happens if a firm sells some merchandise?

The first case is a trick question. What happens is that the current ratio moves away from 1. If it is greater than 1 (the usual case), it will get bigger, but if it is less than 1, it will get smaller. To see this, suppose the firm has £4 in current assets and £2 in current liabilities for a current ratio of 2. If we use £1 in cash to reduce current liabilities, the new current ratio is (£4 – 1)/(£2 – 1) = 3. If we reverse the original situation to £2 in current assets and £4 in current liabilities, the change will cause the current ratio to fall to 1/3 from 1/2.

The second case is not quite as tricky. Nothing happens to the current ratio because cash goes down while inventory goes up – total current assets are unaffected.

In the third case, the current ratio would usually rise because inventory is normally shown at cost and the sale would normally be at something greater than cost (the difference is the markup). The increase in either cash or receivables is, therefore, greater than the decrease in inventory. This increases current assets, and the current ratio rises.

Finally, note that an apparently low current ratio may not be a bad sign for a company with a large reserve of untapped borrowing power.

Quick (or Acid-test) Ratio

Inventory is often the least liquid current asset. It is also the one for which the book values are least reliable as measures of market value because the quality of the inventory is not considered. Some of the inventory may later turn out to be damaged, obsolete or lost.

More to the point, relatively large inventories are often a sign of short-term trouble. The firm may have overestimated sales and overbought or overproduced as a result. In this case, the firm may have a substantial portion of its liquidity tied up in slow-moving inventory.

To further evaluate liquidity, the *quick,* or *acid-test, ratio* is computed just like the current ratio, except inventory is omitted:

Equation 3.2

$$\text{Quick ratio} = \frac{\text{Current assets} - \text{Inventory}}{\text{Current liabilities}}$$

Notice that using cash to buy inventory does not affect the current ratio, but it reduces the quick ratio. Again, the idea is that inventory is relatively illiquid compared to cash.

For Glencore, this ratio in 2022 was:

$$\text{Quick ratio} = \frac{\$66{,}783 - 33{,}460}{\$51{,}679} = 0.64 \text{ times}$$

The quick ratio for Glencore is lower because of the $33.5 billion of inventory in the company. Managers would need to keep an eye on this ratio to ensure inventory levels were not becoming too high, thereby reducing the quick ratio to unacceptably low levels.

Cash Ratio

A very short-term creditor might be interested in the *cash ratio:*

Equation 3.3

$$\text{Cash ratio} = \frac{\text{Cash and cash equivalents}}{\text{Current liabilities}}$$

You can verify that this works out to be 0.037 times for Glencore.

Long-term Solvency Measures

Long-term solvency ratios are intended to address the firm's long-run ability to meet its obligations or, more generally, its financial leverage. These ratios are sometimes called *financial leverage ratios* or just *leverage ratios.* We consider three commonly used measures and some variations.

Total Debt Ratio

The *total debt ratio* takes into account all debts of all maturities to all creditors. It can be defined in several ways, the easiest of which is this:

Equation 3.4

$$\begin{aligned}\text{Total debt ratio} &= \frac{\text{Total assets} - \text{Total equity}}{\text{Total assets}} \\ &= \frac{\$132{,}583 - 45{,}219}{\$132{,}583} = 0.6589 \text{ times}\end{aligned}$$

In this case, an analyst might say that Glencore uses 65.89 per cent debt. Whether this is high or low, or whether it even makes any difference, depends on whether capital structure matters, a subject we discuss in a later chapter.

Glencore has $0.6589 in debt for every $1 in assets. Therefore, there is $0.3411 in equity ($1 – 0.6589) for every $0.6589 in debt. With this in mind, we can define two useful variations on the total debt ratio, the *debt–equity ratio* and the *equity multiplier:*

Equation 3.5

$$\begin{aligned}\text{Debt} - \text{equity ratio} &= \text{Total debt/Total equity} \\ &= \$0.6589/\$0.3411 = 1.9320 \text{ times}\end{aligned}$$

The fact that the equity multiplier is 1 plus the debt–equity ratio is not a coincidence:

Equation 3.6

$$\begin{aligned}\text{Equity multiplier} &= \text{Total assets/Total equity} = \$1/\$0.3411 = 2.9320 \text{ times}\\ &= (\text{Total equity} + \text{Total debt})/\text{Total equity}\\ &= 1 + (\text{Debt/equity ratio}) = 2.9320 \text{ times}\end{aligned}$$

The thing to notice here is that, given any one of these three ratios, you can immediately calculate the other two, so they all say exactly the same thing.

Times Interest Earned

Another common measure of long-term solvency is the *times interest earned (TIE) ratio*. Once again, there are several possible (and common) definitions, but we will stick with the most traditional. The TIE formula for Glencore is:

Equation 3.7

$$\text{TIE ratio} = \frac{\text{Profit before interest and taxes}}{\text{Interest}} = \frac{\$24{,}215}{\$1{,}336} = 18.13 \text{ times}$$

Profit before interest and taxes is also known as earnings before interest and taxes, or EBIT. As the name suggests, this ratio measures how well a company has its interest obligations covered, and it is often called the *interest coverage ratio*. For Glencore, the interest bill is covered 18.13 times over.

Cash Coverage

A problem with the TIE ratio is that it is based on EBIT, which is not really a measure of cash available to pay interest. The reason is that depreciation, a non-cash expense, has been deducted out. Because interest is most definitely a cash outflow (to creditors), one way to define the *cash coverage ratio* is:

Equation 3.8

$$\begin{aligned}\text{Cash coverage ratio} &= \frac{\text{EBIT} + \text{Depreciation}}{\text{Interest}}\\ &= \frac{\$24{,}215 + 7{,}016}{\$1{,}336} = 23.38 \text{ times}\end{aligned}$$

The numerator here, EBIT plus depreciation, is often abbreviated to EBITD (earnings before interest, taxes and depreciation). It is a basic measure of the firm's ability to generate cash from operations, and it is frequently used as a measure of cash flow available to meet financial obligations.

Asset Management or Turnover Measures

We next turn our attention to the efficiency with which Glencore uses its assets. The measures in this section are sometimes called *asset management* or *utilization ratios*. The specific ratios we discuss can all be interpreted as measures of turnover. What they are intended to describe is how efficiently, or intensively, a firm uses its assets to generate sales. We first look at two important current assets: inventory and receivables.

Inventory Turnover and Days' Sales in Inventory

To calculate inventory turnover, one must first consider the cost of goods sold. This is the direct cost of earning the company's main revenues during the year. The costs should include materials used, labour costs, managerial salaries and other costs of earning the revenues. Depreciation is included in the figure if it is being charged on assets directly related to the main revenue stream. Otherwise, it is left out. In Glencore's case, we will assume that all depreciation concerns assets involved in the firm's core business.

Normally, *inventory turnover* is calculated as:

Equation 3.9

$$\text{Inventory turnover} = \frac{\text{Cost of goods sold}}{\text{Inventory}}$$

As long as your company is not running out of inventory and thereby forgoing sales, the higher is this ratio and the more efficient is your company at managing inventory. For Glencore, this is:

$$\text{Inventory turnover} = \frac{\text{Cost of goods sold}}{\text{Inventory}} = \frac{\$224{,}753}{\$33{,}460} = 6.7171$$

The inventory turnover figure of 6.7171 tells us that Glencore turned its inventory over 6.7171 times during the year. We can immediately figure out how long it took it to turn it over on average. The result is the average *days' sales in inventory:*

Equation 3.10

$$\text{Days' sales in inventory} = \frac{365 \text{ days}}{\text{Inventory turnover}} = \frac{365}{6.7171} = 54.34 \text{ days}$$

This tells us that, roughly speaking, inventory sits 54 days on average before it is sold. Alternatively, assuming we used the most recent inventory and cost figures, it will take about 54 days to work off our current inventory.

Receivables Turnover and Days' Sales in Receivables

Our inventory measures give some indication of how fast we can sell products. We now look at how fast we collect on those sales. The *receivables turnover* is defined in the same way as inventory turnover:

Equation 3.11

$$\text{Receivables turnover} = \frac{\text{Revenues}}{\text{Account receivables}} = \frac{\$225{,}984}{24{,}565} = 10.42 \text{ times}$$

Loosely speaking, Glencore collected its outstanding credit accounts and lent the money again 10.42 times during the year.

This ratio makes more sense if we convert it to days, so the *days' sales in receivables* is:

Equation 3.12

$$\text{Days' sales in receivable} = \frac{365 \text{ days}}{\text{Receivable turnover}} = \frac{365}{10.42} = 35.03 \text{ days}$$

Therefore, on average, Glencore collects on its credit sales in 35 days. For obvious reasons, this ratio is frequently called the *average collection period* (ACP). Also note that, if we are using the most recent figures, we can also say that Glencore has 35 days' worth of sales currently uncollected.

Unfortunately, this ratio illustrates the dangers of using financial ratios without really understanding their true meaning. The receivables turnover ratio and days' sales in receivables figure implicitly assumes that all sales in a firm are credit sales. When this is not true, only credit sales figures should be used – not total sales. For firms that take payment immediately, such as low-budget airlines, credit sales will make up only a small proportion of total sales. If we had the data, we should have used only credit sales in the numerator of Equation (3.11).

Example 3.3

Payables Turnover

Here is a variation on the receivables collection period. How long, on average, does it take for Glencore to *pay* its bills? To answer, we need to calculate the account (trade) payables turnover rate using cost of goods sold. We will assume that Glencore purchases everything on credit.

The operating expenses or cost of goods sold is \$224,753 million, and account payables are \$29,726 million. The turnover is therefore \$224,753/\$29,726 = 7.56 times. So, payables turned over about every 365/7.56 = 48.28 days. On average, then, Glencore takes 48 days to pay. As a potential creditor, we might take note of this fact.

Total Asset Turnover

Moving away from specific accounts like inventory or receivables, we can consider an important 'big picture' ratio, the *total asset turnover* ratio. As the name suggests, total asset turnover in 2022 for Glencore is:

Equation 3.13

$$\text{Total asset turnover} = \frac{\text{Revenues}}{\text{Total assets}} = \frac{\$255{,}984}{\$132{,}583} = 1.93 \text{ times}$$

In other words, for every dollar in assets, Glencore generated \$1.93 in sales.

Example 3.4

More Turnover

Suppose you find that a particular company generates £0.40 in annual sales for every pound in total assets. How often does this company turn over its total assets?

The total asset turnover here is 0.40 times per year. It takes 1/0.40 = 2.5 years to turn assets over completely.

Profitability Measures

The three measures we discuss in this section are probably the best known and most widely used of all financial ratios. In one form or another, they are intended to measure how efficiently the firm uses its assets and how efficiently the firm manages its operations. The focus in this group is on the bottom line – net income, also labelled as earnings after tax or profit after tax.

Profit Margin

Companies pay a great deal of attention to their *profit margin:*

Equation 3.14

$$\text{Profit margin} = \frac{\text{Net income}}{\text{Revenues}} = \frac{\$16{,}511}{\$255{,}984} = 6.45\%$$

This tells us that Glencore, in an accounting sense, generated \$0.065 in profit for every dollar in sales during the year ending 2022.

All other things being equal, a relatively high profit margin is obviously desirable. This situation corresponds to low expense ratios relative to sales. However, we hasten to add that other things are often not equal.

For example, lowering our sales price will usually increase unit volume but will normally cause profit margins to shrink. Total profit (or, more importantly, operating cash flow) may go up or down, so the fact that margins are smaller is not necessarily bad.

Profit margins are very different for different industries. Like regulated industries such as energy, grocery stores have a notoriously low profit margin, generally around 2 per cent. In contrast, the profit margin for the pharmaceutical industry is about 18 per cent.

Return on Assets

Return on assets (ROA) is a measure of profit per asset value. It can be defined several ways, but the most common is:

Equation 3.15

$$\text{Return on assets} = \frac{\text{Net income}}{\text{Total assets}} = \frac{\$16{,}511}{\$132{,}583} = 12.45\%$$

Return on Equity

Return on equity (ROE) is a measure of how the shareholders fared during the year. Because benefiting shareholders is our goal, ROE is, in an accounting sense, the true bottom-line measure of performance. ROE is usually measured as:

Equation 3.16

$$\text{Return on equity} = \frac{\text{Net income}}{\text{Total shareholders' equity}} = \frac{\$16{,}511}{\$45{,}219} = 36.51\%$$

Therefore, for every dollar in equity, Glencore generated approximately 36.5 cents in profit during 2022; but, again, this is correct only in accounting terms.

Because ROA and ROE are such commonly cited numbers, it is important to remember they are accounting rates of return. For this reason, these measures should properly be called *return on book assets* and *return on book equity*. Whatever it is called, it would be inappropriate to compare the result to, for example, an interest rate observed in the financial markets.

The fact that ROE exceeds ROA reflects Glencore's use of financial leverage. We will examine the relationship between these two measures in the next section.

Market Value Measures

Our final group of measures is based, in part, on information not necessarily contained in financial statements – the share price. Obviously, these measures can be calculated directly only for publicly traded companies.

At the beginning of 2023, Glencore had 12,414 million shares outstanding and its equity sold on the London Stock Exchange for £5.10 (or $6.11). If we recall that Glencore's net income was $16,511 million, then we can calculate that its earnings per share were:

Equation 3.17

$$\text{EPS} = \frac{\text{Net income}}{\text{Share outstanding}} = \frac{\$16{,}511}{12{,}414} = \$1.33$$

Price–earnings Ratio

The first of our market value measures, the *price–earnings* (or PE) *ratio* (or multiple), is defined as:

Equation 3.18

$$\begin{aligned}\text{PE ratio} &= \frac{\text{Price per share}}{\text{Earnings per share}}\\ &= \frac{\$6.11}{\$1.33} = 4.59 \text{ times}\end{aligned}$$

In the vernacular, we would say that Glencore equity sells for 4.59 times earnings, or we might say that Glencore shares have, or 'carry', a PE multiple of 4.59.

Because the PE ratio measures how much investors are willing to pay per unit of current earnings, higher PEs are often taken to mean that the firm has significant prospects for future growth. Of course, if a firm had no or almost no earnings, its PE would probably be quite large; so, as always, care is needed in interpreting this ratio.

Market-to-book Ratio

A second commonly quoted measure is the *market-to-book ratio:*

Equation 3.19

$$\begin{aligned}\text{Market-to-book ratio} &= \frac{\text{Market value per share}}{\text{Book value per share}}\\ &= \frac{\$6.11}{\$45{,}219/12{,}414} = 1.68 \text{ times}\end{aligned}$$

Notice also that book value per share is total equity (not just ordinary shares) divided by the total number of shares outstanding.

Book value per share is an accounting number that reflects historical costs. In a loose sense, the market-to-book ratio compares the market value of the firm's investments to their cost. A value less than 1 could mean that the firm has not been successful overall in creating value for its shareholders. Glencore plc's market-to-book ratio is 1.68, and reflects the value and growth prospects of the firm.

Many people get confused with financial ratios and worry about different versions of the same formulae covered in this section. It is important to remember that ratios are simply compound measures capturing some element of information of interest to an analyst. As long as you are consistent in using the same formula across companies and time, you won't get into too much bother.

This completes our definition of some common ratios. We could tell you about more of them, but these are enough for now. We will leave it here and go on to discuss some ways of using these ratios instead of just how to calculate them. Table 3.6 summarizes the ratios we have discussed.

Table 3.6 Common Financial Ratios

I. Short-term Solvency, or Liquidity, Ratios	
$\text{Current ratio} = \dfrac{\text{Current assets}}{\text{Current liabilities}}$	$\text{Days' sales in receivables} = \dfrac{\text{365 days}}{\text{Receivables turnover}}$
$\text{Quick ratio} = \dfrac{\text{Current assets} - \text{Inventory}}{\text{Current liabilities}}$	$\text{Total asset turnover} = \dfrac{\text{Sales}}{\text{Total assets}}$
$\text{Cash ratio} = \dfrac{\text{Cash}}{\text{Current liabilities}}$	$\text{Capital intensity} = \dfrac{\text{Total assets}}{\text{Sales}}$
II. Long-term Solvency, or Financial Leverage, Ratios	**IV. Profitability Ratios**
$\text{Total debt ratio} = \dfrac{\text{Total assets} - \text{Total equity}}{\text{Total assets}}$	$\text{Profit margin} = \dfrac{\text{Net income}}{\text{Sales}}$
Debt-equity ratio = Total debt/Total equity Equity multiplier = Total assets/Total equity	$\text{Return on assets (ROA)} = \dfrac{\text{Net income}}{\text{Total assets}}$
$\text{Times interest earned ratio} = \dfrac{\text{EBIT}}{\text{Interest}}$	$\text{Return on equity (ROA)} = \dfrac{\text{Net income}}{\text{Total equity}}$
$\text{Cash coverage ratio} = \dfrac{\text{EBIT} + \text{Depreciation}}{\text{Interest}}$	$\text{ROE} = \dfrac{\text{Net income}}{\text{Sales}} \times \dfrac{\text{Sales}}{\text{Assets}} \times \dfrac{\text{Assets}}{\text{Equity}}$
III. Asset Utilization, or Turnover, Ratios	**V. Market Value Ratios**
$\text{Inventory turnover} = \dfrac{\text{Cost of goods sold}}{\text{Inventory}}$	$\text{Price-earnings ratio} = \dfrac{\text{Price per share}}{\text{Earning per share}}$
$\text{Days' sales in inventory} = \dfrac{\text{365 days}}{\text{Inventory}}$	$\text{Marketing-to-book ratio} = \dfrac{\text{Market value per share}}{\text{Book value per share}}$
$\text{Receivables turnover} = \dfrac{\text{Sales}}{\text{Accounts receivable}}$	

3.8 The DuPont Identity

As we mentioned in discussing ROA and ROE, the difference between these two profitability measures reflects the use of debt financing or financial leverage. We illustrate the relationship between these measures in this section by investigating a famous way of decomposing ROE into its component parts.

A Closer Look at ROE

To begin, let us recall the definition of ROE:

$$\text{Return on equity} = \frac{\text{Net income}}{\text{Total equity}}$$

If we were so inclined, we could multiply this ratio by Assets/Assets without changing anything:

$$\begin{aligned}\text{Return on equity} &= \frac{\text{Net income}}{\text{Total equity}} = \frac{\text{Net income}}{\text{Total equity}} \times \frac{\text{Assets}}{\text{Assets}} \\ &= \frac{\text{Net income}}{\text{Assets}} \times \frac{\text{Assets}}{\text{Total equity}}\end{aligned}$$

Notice that we have expressed the ROE as the product of two other ratios – ROA and the equity multiplier:

$$\text{ROE} = \text{ROA} \times \text{Equity multiplier} = \text{ROA} \times (1 + \text{Debt} - \text{Equity ratio})$$

Looking back at Glencore, for example, we see that the debt–equity ratio was 1.93 and ROA was 0.125 per cent. Our work here implies that Glencore's ROE, as we previously calculated, is:

$$\text{ROE} = 12.45\% \times (1 + 1.932) = 36.51\%$$

The difference between ROE and ROA can be substantial, as you can see for Glencore plc. This is because of the amount of debt that the company has taken on.

We can further decompose ROE by multiplying the top and bottom by total sales:

$$\text{ROE} = \frac{\text{Sales}}{\text{Sales}} \times \frac{\text{Net income}}{\text{Assets}} \times \frac{\text{Assets}}{\text{Total equity}}$$

If we rearrange things a bit, ROE is:

Equation 3.20

$$\text{ROE} = \underbrace{\frac{\text{Net income}}{\text{Sales}} \times \frac{\text{Sales}}{\text{Assets}}}_{\text{Return on assets}} \times \frac{\text{Assets}}{\text{Total equity}}$$
$$= \text{Profit margin} \times \text{Total asset turnover} \times \text{Equity multiplier}$$

What we have now done is to partition ROA into its two component parts: profit margin and total asset turnover. The last expression of the preceding equation is called the DuPont identity after the DuPont Corporation, which popularized its use.

We can check this relationship for Glencore by noting that the profit margin was 6.45 per cent and the total asset turnover was 1.931. ROE should thus be:

$$\begin{aligned}\text{ROE} &= \text{Profit margin} \times \text{Total asset turnover} \times \text{Equity multiplier}\\ &= 6.45\% \times 1.931 \times 2.932\\ &= 36.51\%\end{aligned}$$

This 36.51 per cent ROE is exactly what we had before.

The DuPont identity tells us that ROE is affected by three things:

1 Operating efficiency (as measured by profit margin)
2 Asset use efficiency (as measured by total asset turnover)
3 Financial leverage (as measured by the equity multiplier).

Weakness in either operating or asset use efficiency (or both) will show up in a diminished return on assets, which will translate into a lower ROE.

Considering the DuPont identity, it appears that the ROE could be leveraged up by increasing the amount of debt in the firm. However, notice that increasing debt also increases interest expense, which reduces profit margins, and this acts to reduce ROE. More important, the use of debt financing has a number of other effects, and, as we discuss at some length in later chapters, the amount of leverage a firm uses is governed by its capital structure policy.

The decomposition of ROE we have discussed in this section is a convenient way of systematically approaching financial statement analysis. If ROE is unsatisfactory by some measure, then the DuPont identity tells you where to start looking for the reasons.

3.9 Using Financial Statement Information

Our next task is to discuss in more detail some practical aspects of financial statement analysis. In particular, we will look at reasons for doing financial statement analysis, how to go about getting benchmark information, and some of the problems that come up in the process.

Choosing a Benchmark

Given that we want to evaluate a division or a firm based on its financial statements, a fundamental problem immediately comes up. How do we choose a benchmark or a standard of comparison? In this section we describe some ways of getting started.

Time Trend Analysis

One standard we could use is history. Suppose we found that the current ratio for a particular firm is 2.4 based on the most recent financial statement information. Looking back over the last 10 years, we might find that this ratio had declined reasonably steadily over that period.

Based on this, we might wonder if the liquidity position of the firm has deteriorated. It could be, of course, that the firm has made changes that allow it to use its current assets more efficiently, that the nature of the firm's business has changed, or that business practices have changed. If we investigate, we might find any of these possible explanations behind the decline. This is an example of what we mean by management by exception – a deteriorating time trend may not be worrying, but it does merit investigation.

Peer Group Analysis

The second means of establishing a benchmark is to identify firms similar in the sense that they compete in the same markets, have similar assets and operate in similar ways. In other words, we need to identify a *peer group*. There are obvious problems with doing this: no two companies are identical. Ultimately, the choice of which companies to use as a basis for comparison is subjective.

A common way of identifying potential peers is based on Standard Industrial Classification (SIC) codes. In the UK, these are called UK Standard Industrial Classification (SIC) Codes, and in the European Union, they are called the Industrial Classification System, or 'Nomenclature Statistique des Activités Économiques dans la Communauté Européenne' (NACE). These are alphabetical categories subdivided by four-digit codes and used for statistical reporting purposes. Both SIC and NACE codes are virtually identical, and firms with the same SIC or NACE code are frequently assumed to be similar.

In total, there are 21 industry groups, categorized by alphabetical letter. The first SIC code digit establishes the general type of business. For example, firms engaged in finance, insurance and real estate have SIC codes beginning with 6. Each additional digit narrows the industry. Companies having SIC codes beginning with 64 are mostly banks and bank-like businesses; those with codes starting with 64.19 are generally commercial banks; and SIC code 64.11 is assigned to central banks. Table 3.7 lists selected two-digit codes (the first two digits of the four-digit SIC codes) and the industries they represent.

Table 3.7 Selected Two-digit SIC Codes

Code	Industry	Code	Industry
01–09	Agriculture, Forestry, Fishing	50–51	Wholesale Trade
10–14	Mining	52–59	Retail Trade
15–17	Construction	60–67	Finance, Insurance, Real Estate
20–39	Manufacturing	70–89	Services
40–49	Transportation and Public Utilities	91–99	Public Administration

Industry classification codes are far from perfect. For example, suppose you were examining financial statements for Tesco plc, one of the largest retailers in the world. However, Tesco is not involved only in supermarket retailing. It also has Tesco Telecom Services and Tesco Personal Finance, which includes credit cards and personal mortgages. Which industry code would Tesco plc have?

As this example illustrates, it is probably not appropriate to blindly use SIC code as the basis for carrying out a peer analysis. Instead, analysts often identify a set of primary competitors with similar activities and then compute a set of averages based on just this group. Also, we may be more concerned with a group of the top firms in an industry, not similar firms. Such a group is called an *aspirant group* because we aspire to be like its members. In this case, a financial statement analysis reveals how far we have to go.

There are many sources of financial information on the internet that an analyst can access. For example, www.ft.com, Reuters and Yahoo! Finance show a variety of ratios for publicly traded companies.

Sustainability in Action 3.1

Ørsted's Energy Transition

Consider Ørsted, a Danish renewable energy company. Ørsted transitioned from a fossil fuel-based company to a green energy leader, with a commitment to reduce its scope 1 and 2 emissions intensity by 98 per cent by 2025 (from 2006), have a 50 per cent absolute reduction in scope 3 emissions by 2032 (from 2018), and net-zero emissions in scopes 1, 2 and 3 and 90 per cent reduction in absolute emissions by 2040 (scope 3, from gas sales). This shift can be observed through the company's financial statements and climate KPIs, such as carbon intensity, renewable energy generation and green investments.

In 2021, Ørsted reported a reduction in carbon intensity of 89 per cent compared to 2006 levels. This achievement reflects the company's strategy to increase renewable energy generation, which reached 90 per cent of the total energy output in the same year. Analysing the firm's income statement, a substantial portion of the company's revenue was derived from green investments.

The balance sheet also reflects Ørsted's commitment to a low-carbon future, with significant investments in renewable energy assets such as offshore wind farms. The company's debt-to-equity ratio remained stable, showcasing a balanced approach to funding its green transition.

Furthermore, Ørsted's target reporting includes quantifiable goals and transparent progress updates, which allow investors to assess the company's commitment to sustainability. By incorporating climate KPIs into financial statement analysis, stakeholders can better evaluate Ørsted's performance and long-term strategy in the context of environmental responsibility and sustainable growth.

Source: www.orsted.com.

Problems with Financial Statement Analysis

We continue our chapter on financial statements by discussing some additional issues that can arise when using them. In one way or another, the primary problem with financial statement analysis is that there is no underlying theory to help us identify which quantities to guide us in establishing benchmarks.

As we discuss in other chapters, there are many cases in which financial theory and economic logic provide guidance in making judgements about value and risk. Little such help exists with financial statements. This is why we cannot say which ratios matter the most, or what a high or low value might be.

One particularly severe problem is that many firms are conglomerates, owning more or less unrelated lines of business. Anglo American plc is a well-known example. Anglo American was initially founded in South Africa as a mining firm, but is now involved in packaging, paper, coal and a variety of metal extraction activities. It is currently listed on the London Stock Exchange and regarded as a metals conglomerate. Similar to Tesco plc, the consolidated financial statements of Anglo American do not fit any neat industry category. More generally, the kind of peer group analysis we have been describing is going to work best when the firms are strictly in the same line of business, the industry is competitive and there is only one way of operating.

Another problem that is becoming increasingly common is that major competitors and natural peer group members in an industry may be scattered around the globe. The automobile industry is an obvious example. The problem here is that financial statements in many countries do not necessarily conform to IFRS (i.e. the accounting standards used in most countries). For example, US firms follow US GAAP, whereas European firms follow IFRS. The existence of different rules and procedures makes it difficult to compare financial statements across national borders.

Even companies that are clearly in the same line of business may not be comparable. For example, electric utilities engaged primarily in power generation are all classified in the same group. This group is often thought to be relatively homogeneous. However, most utilities operate as regulated monopolies, so they do not compete much with one another, at least not historically. Many have shareholders, and many are organized as cooperatives with no shareholders. There are several different ways of generating power, ranging from hydroelectric to nuclear, so the operating activities of these utilities can differ quite a bit. Finally, profitability is strongly affected by the regulatory environment, so utilities in different countries can be similar but show different profits.

Several other general problems frequently crop up. First, different firms use different accounting procedures, such as for inventories. This makes it difficult to compare statements. Second, firms end their fiscal years at different times. For firms in seasonal businesses (such as a retailer with a long Christmas season), this can lead to difficulties in comparing statements of financial position because of fluctuations in accounts during the year. Finally, for any particular firm, unusual or transient events, such as a one-time profit from an asset sale, may affect financial performance. Such events can give misleading signals as we compare firms.

Real World Insight 3.2

Inditex Comparative Financial Ratio Analysis

As stated above, one can look at the financial ratios of a firm over time or compare them to other companies in the same industry. The table below shows a comparative analysis of key financial ratios for Inditex (Industria de Diseño Textil, S.A.) and its peers.

There is a lot of information to take in. A simple comparison shows that Inditex has one of the highest valuations (P/E ratio), is of average liquidity (current ratio), performing better (return on equity) and has highest profitability among its peers (profit margin).

Company Name	PE Ratio	EPS	Current Ratio	Debt to Equity	Return on Equity	Profit Margin
Inditex	24.04	1.08	1.55	0.00	28.2%	13.3%
Gap	10.12	2.24	1.97	0.36	29.9%	5.8%
Nordstrom	15.57	2.87	1.12	2.23	49.0%	3.1%
Fast Retailing Company	38.43	1,517.71	3.24	0.63	19.4%	8.0%
H&M	17.19	9.78	0.44	0.30	23.2%	6.2%
Burberry Group	22.44	0.66	2.40	0.01	23.4%	11.9%

Source: Data from Investing.com.

Summary and Conclusions

This chapter focuses on working with information contained in financial statements. Specifically, we studied standardized financial statements and ratio analysis.

1 We explained that differences in firm size make it difficult to compare financial statements.
2 Evaluating ratios of accounting numbers is another way of comparing financial statement information. We defined a number of the most commonly used ratios, and we discussed the famous DuPont identity.

After you have studied this chapter, we hope that you have some perspective on the uses and abuses of financial statement information. You should also find that your vocabulary of business and financial terms has grown substantially.

In the online supplement to this chapter, we extend the discussion to include long-term financial planning and sustainable growth rates.

Questions and Problems

CONCEPT

1 **The Accounting Equation** Explain why the total value of the assets of a company should equal the sum of liabilities and equity.

2 **Book Values versus Market Values** Explain the difference between book value and market value. Under standard accounting rules, it is possible for a company's liabilities to exceed its assets. When this occurs, the owners' equity is negative. Can this happen with market values? Why, or why not?

3 **Operating Cash Flow** Identify two circumstances where negative operating cash flow might not necessarily be a sign of deteriorating financial health. When can negative operating cash flow become problematic for a company?

4 **Financial Ratio Analysis** A financial ratio by itself tells us little about a company because financial ratios vary a great deal across industries. There are two basic methods for analysing financial ratios for a company: time trend analysis and peer group analysis. Why might each of these analysis methods be useful? What does each tell you about the company's financial health?

5 **Depreciation** Explain what is meant by depreciation. Why is depreciation important to an accountant?

6 **The DuPont Identity** Both ROA and ROE measure profitability. What does each of them measure, and which one is more useful for comparing two companies? Why?

7 **Building a Statement of Financial Position** According to AEB Systems plc financial statements, the firm had current assets of £6.642 billion, non-current assets of £16.521 billion, current liabilities of £11.283 billion, and non-current liabilities of £6.589 billion. What is the value of the shareholders' equity for AEB Systems? How much is net working capital?

8 **Building an Income Statement** The UK insurance firm, Wheeler & Fox, had revenue of £38,440 million, total expenses of £37,133 million, tax of £487 million and zero depreciation. What is the net income for the firm? Wheeler & Fox paid out £238 million in cash dividends. What is the addition to retained earnings?

9 **Earnings per Share** Nordicbank has a price–earnings ratio of 6.35. If the firm's share price is SKr71.70, what is its earnings per share?

10 **Market Values and Book Values** Your company has just sealed a deal to sell a tract of land with accompanying warehouse for €3.2 million. This is significantly lower than the €7 million your firm paid when the plot was purchased at the height of the property boom. International Accounting Standards have been followed by your firm and so you will not make an accounting loss on the sale (why?). The company has non-current assets of €4 million, non-current liabilities of €2.2 million and net working capital (current assets less current liabilities) of €0.9 million. What impact does the sale have on your firm's statement of financial position?

11 **Calculating Taxes** The Dutch firm Herrera NV has €273,000 in taxable income. Using Table 3.4, what is the company's average tax rate? What is its marginal tax rate?

12 **Calculating NCF** A renewable energy firm has total revenues of £10 million and total expenses of £8 million, including £2 million in non-cash expenses. The firm spent £4 million on capital expenditures and had interest expenses of £500,000. The firm also paid a dividend of £1 million. What is the firm's net cash flow for the year?

13 **Calculating Net Capital Spending** Morena's Driving School's 2024 statement of financial position showed non-current assets of £4.2 million. One year later, the 2025 statement of financial position showed non-current assets of £4.7 million. The company's 2025 income statement showed a depreciation expense of £925,000. What was Morena's net capital spending for 2025?

14 **Tumbler SA Statement of Financial Position** The following table presents the long-term debt and shareholders' equity of Tumbler SA one year ago:

	(€m)
Long-term debt	60
Ordinary shares	25
Accumulated retained earnings	89

During the past year, Tumbler issued 20 million shares at a total price of €52 million, and issued €16 million in new long-term debt. The company generated €14 million in net income and paid €8 million in dividends. Construct the current statement of financial position reflecting the changes that occurred at Tumbler during the year.

REGULAR

15 **Calculating the DuPont Identity** Choose two companies from the same industry, gather their annual income statements and statement of financial positions for the most recent three years, and calculate the DuPont identity for each company. Analyse the changes in each component of the DuPont identity for each company over this period and compare the components between the two companies. Are the results what you expected? Why, or why not?

16 **Return on Equity** Firm A and Firm B have debt-to-total asset ratios of 40 per cent and 60 per cent, and returns on total assets of 15 per cent and 25 per cent, respectively. Calculate the return on equity for each firm, and determine which firm has a greater return on equity. Explain how the difference in debt-to-total asset ratios and returns on total assets affects the return on equity for each firm.

17 **Ratios and Foreign Companies** Midnight Bank made a profit of £3.47 billion on revenues of £18.197 billion. What is the company's profit margin? Does the fact that these figures are quoted in pounds sterling make any difference to a French investor. Why? In euros, revenues were €20.38 billion. What was the net income in euros?

18 **Cash Ratio** TJC plc has revenues of £1,027 million and total costs (excluding interest) of £817 million. Net interest expense was £29 million and depreciation was £12 million. What is the firm's cash coverage ratio?

19 **Days' Sales in Receivables** A company has net income of €173,000, a profit margin of 8.6 per cent and a trade receivables balance of €143,200. Assuming 75 per cent of sales are on credit, what is the company's days' sales in receivables?

20 **Ratios and Fixed Assets** Le Verd SA has a ratio of long-term debt to total assets of 0.70 and a current ratio of 1.20. Current liabilities are £850, revenues are £4,310, profit margin is 9.5 per cent and ROE is 21.5 per cent. What is the amount of the firm's non-current assets?

21 **Calculating the Cash Coverage Ratio** Titan SpA's net income for the most recent year was €4,850. The tax rate was 33 per cent. The firm paid €2,108 in total interest expense and deducted €1,687 in depreciation expense. What was Titan's cash coverage ratio for the year?

22 **Cost of Goods Sold** Guthrie plc has current liabilities of £340,000, a quick ratio of 1.8, inventory turnover of 4.2 and a current ratio of 3.3. What is the cost of goods sold for the company?

CHALLENGE

For questions 23 and 24, consider the summarized financial statements for Sement AG (in € millions):

Summarized Statement of Income	
Revenue	77,327
Cost of goods sold	56,284
Operating income	**21,043**
Less:	
Depreciation	2,130
Other expenses	16,039
Income from continuing operations before income taxes	**2,874**

Summarized Statement of Income	
Income taxes	1,015
Income from continuing operations	**1,859**
Income from discontinued operations, net of taxes	4,027
Net income	**5,886**

Summarized Statement of Financial Position			
Assets		Liabilities	
Current assets		Current liabilities	
Cash and cash equivalents	6,893	Trade payables	8,860
Trade and other receivables	15,785	Other current liabilities	33,591
Inventories	14,509	Total current liabilities	**42,451**
Other current assets	6,055	Long-term debt	14,260
Total current assets	**43,242**	Other non-current liabilities	10,372
Non-current assets	**51,221**	Total liabilities	**67,083**
		Equity	4,391
		Retained earnings	22,989
Total assets	**94,463**	Total liabilities and equity	**94,463**

23 Financial Ratios Calculate all relevant financial ratios for Sement AG.

24 Financial Statement Analysis What are the weaknesses in the Sement examples for interpreting its financial well-beinarg? Explain.

Questions 25–35 relate to Montgomery Organizations plc, whose annual accounts are given in the following tables. The firm has 14,685,856 shares and the share price is £2.78.

Fixed Assets (£ millions)	2024	2023	2022	2021
Tangible assets	164	167	180	188
Land and buildings	71	70	68	66
Freehold land	71	70		
Fixtures and fittings	78	81	93	103
Plant and vehicles	15	15	19	19
Plant	15	15		
Intangible assets	832	832	832	832
Investments	520	521	509	518
Fixed assets	1,517	1,520	1,521	1,538

Current Assets				
Stock and WIP				1
Stock				1
WIP				0
Finished goods				
Trade debtors	2	4		1
Bank and deposits	47	58	43	34
Other current assets	662	35	28	26
Group loans (asset)	618	0	0	0
Directors loans (asset)	0	0	0	0
Other debtors	12	5	28	26
Prepayments	32	30		
Current assets	711	97	72	61

Current Liabilities				
Trade creditors	−7	−10	−14	−18
Short-term loans and overdrafts	−1,924	−1,325	−1,260	−1,255
Bank overdrafts	0	0	0	0
Group loans (short t.)	−1,923	−1,324	−1,259	−1,255
Director loans (short t.)	0	0	0	0
Hire purch. and leas. (short t.)	0	−1	−1	0
Hire purchase (short t.)				
Leasing (short t.)			−1	
Other short-term loans	0	0	0	0
Total other current liabilities	−105	−78	−102	−102
Corporation tax	−29	−28	−36	−29
Dividends	0	0	0	0
Accruals and def. inc. (sh. t.)	−33	−21	−41	−37
Social securities and VAT	−19	−18	−20	−21
Other current liabilities	−25	−11	−5	−15
Current liabilities	−2,035	−1,413	−1,376	−1,374
Net current assets (liab.)	−1,324	−1,316	−1,304	−1,313
Net tangible assets (liab.)	−639	−628	−615	−607
Working capital	−1,324	−1,316	−1,304	−1,313
Total assets	2,228	1,617	1,593	1,599
Total assets less cur. liab.	193	204	217	225

Long-term Liabilities				
Provisions for other liab.	–12	–13	–31	–14
Deferred tax	–12	–13	–13	–12
Other provisions			–19	–2
Pension liabilities	–23	–31		
Long-term liabilities	–35	–44	–31	–14
Total assets less liabilities	158	160	186	210

Shareholders' Funds				
Issued capital	1	1	1	1
Ordinary shares	1	1		
Preference shares				
Other shares				
Total reserves	157	158	184	209
Share premium account	3	3	3	3
Profit (loss) account	159	162	180	205
Other reserves	–5	–6	1	1
Shareholders' funds	158	160	186	210
Turnover	14,569	13,480	13,337	7,127
Cost of sales	–13,932	–12,870	–12,708	–6,800
Gross profit	637	610	629	327
Administration expenses		–388	–369	–502
Other operating income pre OP	–377			
Exceptional items pre OP		–13		
Operating profit	260	210	260	–175
Other income	10	33	30	486
Total other income and int. received	22	43	30	486
Exceptional items			–16	–18
Profit (loss) before interest paid	282	253	274	293
Interest received	12	10		
Interest paid	–28	–37	–84	–92
Other interest paid	–28	–37		
Net interest	–16	–27	–84	–92
Profit (loss) before tax	254	216	190	201
Taxation	–53	–46	–49	–18
Profit (loss) after tax	201	170	141	183
Dividends	–210	–175	–150	–20
Retained profit (loss)	–9	–6	–9	163
Depreciation	26	27	30	26

25 **Earnings per share** What is the earnings per share for each year between 2021 and 2024 for Montgomery Organizations plc? What is your interpretation of these figures? Is EPS a reliable measure of performance?

26 **Tax Rate** What is the effective tax rate for Montgomery Organizations plc for each year?

27 **Net Working Capital** What is the net working capital of Montgomery Organizations plc in each year? What is the cause of the figures? Is this a healthy situation for the firm? Explain.

28 Liquidity How would you rate the liquidity position of Montgomery Organizations plc between 2021 and 2024? Provide a brief report on the company's liquidity over time.

29 Long-term Solvency How would you rate the long-term solvency position of Montgomery Organizations plc between 2021 and 2024? Provide a brief report on the company's long-term solvency over time.

30 Operations How efficient have Montgomery Organizations plc's operations been during 2024? Provide a brief report on the company's asset efficiency over time.

31 Profitability What is the profitability of Montgomery Organizations plc like over the period 2021 and 2024? Provide a brief report on the company's profitability over time. Do profitability ratios give a good insight into company performance?

32 Market Valuation Provide an overview of the company's relative market valuation over the period 2021–2024. What can be inferred from the company's relative market valuation?

33 The DuPont Identity and RoE Drivers Undertake a full DuPont identity analysis for the year 2024 to provide insights into the drivers of its return on equity.

34 Advantages and Disadvantages of Ratio Analysis Discuss the advantages and disadvantages of ratio analysis.

Exam Question (45 minutes)

You are tasked with analysing the last two years of accounts of a global mining firm. A simplified statement of financial position and statement of profit and loss are provided below.

Period Ending	Yr-0	Yr-1	Yr-2	Yr-3
Total Revenue	7,931	6,579	8,204	6,502
Cost of Revenue	5,787	5,136	5,318	3,840
Gross Profit	2,144	1,443	2,886	2,662
Depreciation	321	182	201	412
Other Expenses	100	134	115	247
EBIT	**1,723**	**1,127**	**2,570**	**2,003**
Interest	1,135	957	1,272	1,009
EBT	**588**	**170**	**1,298**	**994**
Tax	153	44	337	258
Net Income	**435**	**126**	**961**	**736**

Statement of Financial Position (£ millions)				
Period Ending	Yr-0	Yr-1	Yr-2	Yr-3
Assets				
Current Assets				
Cash and Cash Equivalents	390	381	458	1,585
Short-term Investments	6,849	4,547	4,608	578
Net Receivables	693	533	1,025	932
Inventory	1,261	909	1,299	880
Other Current Assets	200	250	86	74
Total Current Assets	**9,393**	**6,620**	**7,476**	**4,049**
Property, Plant and Equipment	10,201	10,920	10,300	10,350
Goodwill	21	23	28	40
Total Non-current Assets	**10,222**	**10,943**	**10,328**	**10,390**
Total Assets	**19,615**	**17,563**	**17,804**	**14,439**

Statement of Financial Position (£ millions)				
Period Ending	Yr-0	Yr-1	Yr-2	Yr-3
Liabilities				
Current Liabilities				
Accounts Payable	1,715	1,190	975	620
Short/Current Long-term Debt	8,945	5,836	3,656	1,727
Other Current Liabilities	111	169	303	655
Total Current Liabilities	**10,771**	**7,195**	**4,934**	**3,002**
Long-term Debt	7,161	3,816	1,557	1,478
Total Liabilities	**17,932**	**11,011**	**6,491**	**4,480**
Shareholders' Equity				
Total Shareholders' Equity	**1,683**	**6,552**	**11,313**	**9,959**
Equity Plus Liabilities	**19,615**	**17,563**	**17,804**	**14,439**

1 Using the information above, carry out a full financial statement analysis using a variety of financial ratios. **(60 marks)**

2 How do you think the company has been performing over the past five years? Has there been an improvement or deterioration in the firm's fortunes? What is driving the changing performance? Write a report, outlining your analysis and findings. **(40 marks)**

Total Marks: 100

Mini Case

Friday Quantum Solutions

Friday Quantum Solutions (FQS) develops and sells quantum technology solutions for the measurement of underwater sea-life diversity. It has only one product and, last year, FQS sold 10,000 units. This year, FQS reported sales of 16,000 units but net profit was lower than expected. You have been asked to prepare a report on the company's performance and financial position for the company's owners. Prior to the meeting, you have received the following information for the past two years:

	£000s This Year	£000s Last Year
Revenues	2,400	2,000
Cost of goods sold	1,440	900
Gross profit	**960**	**1,100**
Other expenses	600	400
Net profit before interest and tax	**360**	**700**
Interest expense for the year	170	100
Tax payable	57	180
Net income	**133**	**420**
Equity	3410.25641	3230.76923
Ratios		
Current ratio	4	3.7
Quick ratio	1.50	2.20
Debtor payment period	46	44
Creditor payment period	51	81
Debt/assets	0.27	0.2
Times interest earned	2.1	7

Write a short report on FQS's performance and financial position. Your report should identify possible causes for the changes in profitability, liquidity and financial position. You should also recommend a turnaround strategy to improve the company's performance and financial position. It is generally accepted that the selling price per unit cannot be increased without a major loss of market share. In addition, reductions in the cost of materials and labour are not possible.

Practical Case Study

Choose a listed company from your own country. Download the financial accounts from its website and carry out a full financial statement analysis. You should calculate financial ratios for not only the most recent year but past years as well. Write a brief report on your interpretation and the company's future well-being.

Relevant Accounting Standards

Given that this chapter is concerned with interpreting financial statements, all International Accounting Standards are relevant. However, the most important ones are IAS 1 *Presentation of Financial Statements*, IAS 7 *Statement of Cash Flows*, IAS 27 *Consolidated and Separate Financial Statements* and IAS 33 *Earnings per Share*. For an excellent summary of these and other International Accounting Standards, visit the IASPlus website.

Additional Reading

The interested reader can find a whole range of readings to peruse in accounting journals such as the *Journal of Accounting Research*, *The Accounting Review*, *Journal of Accounting and Economics*, *Journal of Business Finance and Accounting* and *Accounting and Business Research*. Insightful books are:

1 Engelhart, Y., H. Schilit and J. Perler (2018) *Financial Shenanigans: How to Detect Accounting Gimmicks and Fraud in Financial Reports*. New York: McGraw-Hill.

2 Fridson, M.S. and F. Alvarez (2011) *Financial Statement Analysis: A Practitioner's Guide*. Hoboken, NY: John Wiley & Sons.

3 Penman, S.H. (2012) *Financial Statement Analysis and Security Valuation*. New York: McGraw-Hill.

Chapter 4
Discounted Cash Flow Valuation

Learning Objectives

After reading this chapter you should be able to:

LO1 Define and understand the basic concepts of discounted cash flow valuation, including the one-period and multi-period case, compounding periods and simplifications.

LO2 Apply discounted cash flow valuation techniques to real-world financial scenarios.

LO3 Evaluate the impact of different assumptions and inputs on discounted cash flow valuation results.

Meta – the parent company of Facebook, WhatsApp and Instagram – makes money in a number of ways, but its most important revenue stream is advertising. Every time you go onto Facebook and read articles or friends' posts, the company's software records your activity and uses it for targeted advertising. The Meta business model is an approach that has been adopted by many technology companies. Essentially, you are Meta's product, not its customer. Meta gives you free access to its system so it can gather information on you to sell to advertisers. The more customers Meta can attract and the more often the company can get you to use its system, the more advertising revenue it can make.

Source: inkdrop/123RF.

To value Meta, you would forecast its future cash flows from advertisers. Advertising revenue is directly linked to Meta subscribers and their engagement on the various Meta platforms. As an analyst, you would forecast future subscribers and use this to calculate advertising revenues. As a Meta executive, you would seek ways to maximize user engagement and click-through on advertising.

This chapter gives you the 'basic tools of knowledge' to value companies such as Meta and assess whether their share prices are sensible. You will also be able to value real investment projects using the same tools. Finally, the material in this chapter will form the foundation of the majority of techniques developed in the rest of the book, so make sure you fully understand the chapter before progressing.

The theoretical foundation of discounted cash flow valuation is very rich and can enhance understanding, but some readers may feel that it is an unnecessary technical diversion at this stage. If you do wish to explore the theory underpinning this chapter, please refer to the online appendix. Although an appreciation of the theory is useful, it is not necessary to understand the intuition or practical application of the material in this chapter.

Key Notations

PV	Present value	FV	Future value
C_i	Cash flow at time i	m	Number of times that interest, r, is compounded in a year
r	Discount rate	APR	Annual percentage rate
NPV	Net present value	g	Growth rate

Real World Insight 4.1

Toshiba's Five-year Plan

Toshiba is one of the world's largest companies and is involved in the energy sector as well as electronics and digital solutions. Toshiba, like all companies, has a strategic plan to increase its value. Value has different drivers, and these will be found in the objectives a company sets for itself.

Consider Toshiba's strategic plan, below. Although many of the elements are strategic, there will be cash flow and risk considerations underlying each component:

1 Improve core earning power. Toshiba planned to withdraw from non-core sectors such as liquid natural gas and UK nuclear power plants. The company introduced more robust investment decision models and renewed its IT infrastructure. Finally, Toshiba invested approximately 810 billion yen in new projects, and approximately 930 billion yen in research and development (R&D).

2 Strengthen the business portfolio. Toshiba undertook a comprehensive review of the competitiveness of each of its businesses and their markets. Action plans were introduced to improve profit margins, and these were proactively monitored.

3 Improve shareholder return. Toshiba bought back shares of up to 700 billion yen and increased its total shareholder dividend.

4 Development of new growth fields. The big areas for growth were mega-trends and disruptive innovation. Examples are lithium-ion rechargeable batteries, semiconductor technology, and developing early cancer detection and individual treatment technologies.

5 Digital transformation. Toshiba adopted digitization as a policy for its internal business models.

6 A new organizational structure. Toshiba undertook a corporate reorganization to simplify its business structure. It took measures to develop internal talent while proactively seeking to hire new talent from outside. It strengthened its internal audit function and changed its executive officer compensation system so that the majority of performance-linked pay was restricted stock (**Chapter 23**).

All the actions set out in Toshiba's five-year plan required detailed time value of money calculations using the concepts covered in this chapter.

4.1 Valuation: The One-period Case

Chapter 3
Page 60

Keith Vaughan is trying to sell a piece of undeveloped land in Wales. Yesterday he was offered £10,000 for the property. He was about ready to accept the offer when another individual offered to pay him £11,424 a year from now for the same property. Keith has satisfied himself that both buyers are honest and financially solvent, so he has no fear that the offer he selects will fall through. We picture the two proposals as cash flows in Figure 4.1. Which offer should Keith choose? (See **Chapter 3,** Section 3.5 for more information on cash flows.)

Figure 4.1 Cash Flow for Keith Vaughan's Sale

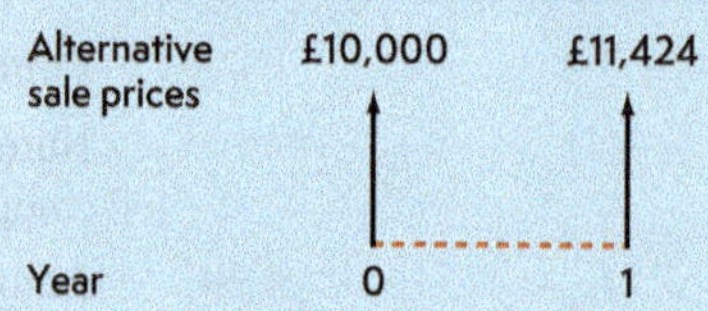

Mike Tuttle, Keith's financial adviser, points out that if Keith takes the first offer, he could invest the £10,000 in the bank at an insured rate of 12 per cent. At the end of one year, he would have:

$$\underbrace{£10{,}000}_{\text{Return of principal}} + \underbrace{(0.12 \times £10{,}000)}_{\text{Interest}} = £10{,}000 \times 1.12 = £11{,}200$$

Because this is less than the £11,424 Keith could receive from the second offer, Mike recommends that he take the latter. This analysis uses the concept of **future value (FV)** or **compound value**, which is the value of a sum after investing over one or more periods. The compound or future value of £10,000 at 12 per cent is £11,200.

An alternative method employs the concept of **present value (PV)**. One can determine present value by asking the following question: How much money must Keith put in the bank today so that he will have £11,424 next year? We can write this algebraically as:

$$PV \times 1.12 = £11{,}424$$

We want to solve for *PV*, the amount of money that yields £11,424 if invested at 12 per cent today. Solving for *PV*, we have:

$$PV = \frac{£11{,}424}{1.12} = £10{,}200$$

We write the formula for PV as follows:

Present value of investment:

Equation 4.1

$$PV = \frac{C_1}{1 + r}$$

where $C1$ is cash flow at date 1 and r is the rate of return that Keith Vaughan requires on his land sale. The variable, r, is sometimes referred to as the *discount rate*.

Present value analysis tells us that payment of £11,424 to be received next year has a present value of £10,200 today. In other words, at a 12 per cent interest rate, Keith is indifferent between £10,200 today or £11,424 next year. If you gave him £10,200 today, he could put it in the bank and receive £11,424 next year.

Because the second offer has a present value of £10,200, whereas the first offer is for only £10,000, present value analysis also indicates that Keith should take the second offer. In other words, both future value analysis and present value analysis lead to the same decision. As it turns out, present value analysis and future value analysis must always point to the same conclusion.

Example 4.1

Present Value

Lida Jennings, a financial analyst at Kaufman & Broad, a leading real estate firm, is thinking about recommending that Kaufman & Broad invest in a piece of land that costs €85,000. She is confident that next year the property will be worth €91,000, a sure €6,000 gain. Given that the guaranteed interest rate in the bank is 10 per cent, should Kaufman & Broad undertake the investment in land? We describe Ms Jennings' choice in Figure 4.2 with the cash flow time chart.

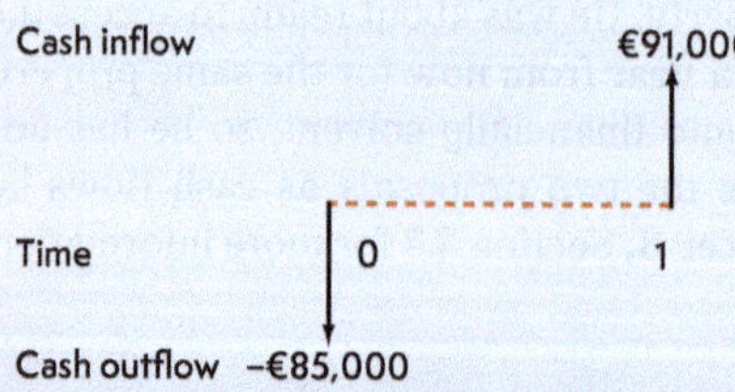

Figure 4.2 Cash Flows for Land Investment

A moment's thought should be all it takes to convince her that this is not an attractive business deal. By investing €85,000 in the land, she will have €91,000 available next year. Suppose, instead, that Kaufman & Broad puts the same €85,000 into the bank. At the interest rate of 10 per cent, this €85,000 would grow to:

$$(1 + 0.10) \times €85{,}000 = €93{,}500$$

next year.

It would be foolish to buy the land when investing the same €85,000 in the financial market would produce an extra €2,500 (that is, €93,500 from the bank minus €91,000 from the land investment). This is a future value calculation.

Alternatively, she could calculate the present value of the sale price next year as:

$$PV = \frac{€91{,}000}{1.10} = €82{,}727.27$$

Because the present value of next year's sales price is less than this year's purchase price of €85,000, present value analysis also indicates that she should not recommend purchasing the property.

As simple as this example is, it contains the basic principles that we will be working with over the next few chapters. We now use another example to develop the concept of **net present value (NPV)**.

Frequently, businesspeople want to determine the exact *cost* or *benefit* of a decision. In Example 4.1, we evaluate the decision to buy this year and sell next year as:

$$-€2{,}273 = \underbrace{-€85{,}000}_{\text{Cost of land today}} + \underbrace{\frac{€91{,}000}{1.10}}_{\text{Present value of next year's sales price}}$$

We write the formula for *NPV* as follows:

Net present value of investment:

Equation 4.2 $$NPV = -\text{Cost} + \text{PV}$$

Equation 4.2 says that the value of the investment is –€2,273, after stating all the benefits and all the costs as of date 0. The amount, –€2,273, is the net present value (NPV) of the investment. That is, NPV is the present value of future cash flows minus the present value of the cost of the investment. Because the net present value is negative, Lida Jennings should not recommend purchasing the land.

Both Vaughan and Jennings examples deal with perfect certainty. That is, Keith Vaughan knows with complete confidence he could sell his land for £11,424 next year. Similarly, Lida Jennings knows with absolute certainty that Kaufman & Broad could receive €91,000 for selling its property. Unfortunately, businesspeople frequently do not know future cash flows, and so we treat this uncertainty in the next example.

Example 4.2

Uncertainty and Valuation

Professional Artworks plc is a firm that speculates in modern paintings. The manager is thinking of buying an original Picasso for £400,000 with the intention of selling it at the end of one year. The manager expects that the painting will be worth £480,000 in one year. We depict the relevant cash flows in Figure 4.3.

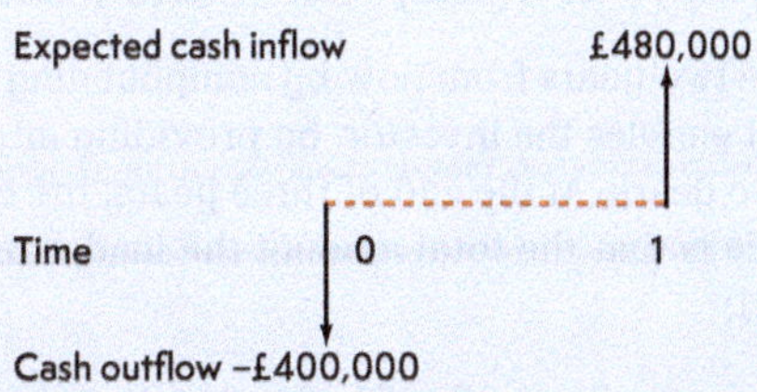

Figure 4.3 Cash Flows for Investment in Painting

Of course, this is only an expectation – the painting could be worth more or less than £480,000. Suppose the guaranteed interest rate granted by banks is 10 per cent. Should the firm purchase the piece of art?

Our first thought might be to discount at the interest rate, yielding:

$$\frac{£480,000}{1.10} = £436,364$$

Because £436,364 is more than £400,000, it looks at first glance as if Professional Artworks should purchase the painting. However, 10 per cent is the return one can earn on a riskless investment. Because the art investment is quite risky, a higher discount rate is required. The manager chooses a rate of 25 per cent to reflect this risk. In other words, he argues that a 25 per cent expected return is fair compensation for an investment project as risky as this painting.

The present value of the painting becomes:

$$\frac{£480,000}{1.25} = £384,000$$

Thus, the manager believes that the painting is currently overpriced at £400,000 and does not make the purchase.

The preceding analysis is typical of decision-making in today's corporations. Unfortunately, any example with risk poses a problem not presented by riskless cash flows. In a project with riskless cash flows, we can determine the appropriate interest by checking with a few banks. Choosing the discount rate for a risky investment, on the other hand, is quite a difficult task. We do not know at this point whether the discount rate on the painting in Example 4.2 should be 11 per cent, 25 per cent, 52 per cent, or some other percentage.

Choosing an appropriate discount rate is difficult, and we merely want to raise the issue here. We must wait until the specific material on risk and return is covered in later chapters before we show you how to calculate the discount rate for yourself.

4.2 Valuation: The Multi-period Case

The previous section presented future value and present value for one period only. We will now perform calculations for the multi-period case.

Future Value and Compounding

Suppose an individual were to make a loan of £1. At the end of the first year, the borrower would owe the lender the principal amount of £1 plus the interest on the loan at the interest rate of r. For the specific case where the interest rate is, say, 9 per cent, the borrower owes the lender:

$$£1 \times (1 + r) = £1 \times 1.09 = £1.09$$

At the end of the year, though, the lender has two choices. She can either take the £1.09 – or, more generally, $(1 + r)$ – out of the financial market, or she can leave it in and lend it again for a second year. The process of leaving the money in the financial market and lending it for another year is called **compounding**.

Suppose the lender decides to compound her loan for another year. She does this by taking the proceeds from her first one-year loan, £1.09, and lending this amount for the next year. At the end of next year, then, the borrower will owe her:

$$£1 \times (1 + r) \times (1 + r) = £1 \times (1 + r)^2 = 1 + 2r + r^2$$
$$£1 \times (1.09) \times (1.09) = £1 \times (1.09)^2 = £1 + £0.18 + £0.0081 = £1.1881$$

£1.1881 is the total she will receive two years from now by compounding the loan.

In other words, the capital market enables the investor, by providing an opportunity for lending, to transform £1 today into £1.1881 at the end of two years. At the end of three years, the cash will be $£1 \times (1.09)^3 = £1.2950$.

The most important point to notice is that the total amount the lender receives is not just the £1 that she lent plus two years' worth of interest on £1:

$$2 \times r = 2 \times £0.09 = £0.18$$

The lender also gets back an amount r^2, which is the interest in the second year on the interest that was earned in the first year. The term $2 \times r$ represents **simple interest** over the two years, and we refer to r^2 as *interest on interest*. In our example, this latter amount is:

$$r^2 = (£0.09)^2 = £0.0081$$

When we invest cash at **compound interest**, we reinvest each interest payment. With simple interest, the interest is not reinvested. We illustrate the difference between compound interest and simple interest in Figure 4.4. In this example, the difference does not amount to much because the loan is for €1. If the loan were for €1 million, the lender would receive €1,188,100 in two years. Of this amount, €8,100 is interest on interest. The lesson is that those small numbers beyond the decimal point can add up to a lot when the transactions are large. Also, the longer the loan lasts, the more important interest on interest becomes.

Figure 4.4 Simple and Compound Interest

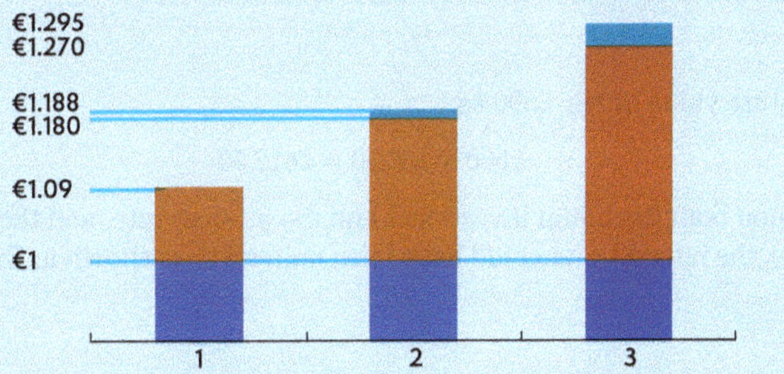

Note: *The light blue shaded area indicates the difference between compound and simple interest. The difference is substantial over a period of many years.*

We write the general formula for an investment over many periods as follows:

Future value of an investment:

Equation 4.3

$$FV = C_0 \times (1 + r)^T$$

where C_0 is the cash to be invested at date 0 (i.e. today), r is the interest rate per period, and T is the number of periods over which the cash is invested.

Example 4.3

Interest on Interest

Suh-Pyng Ku has put £500 in a savings account at Barclays, a major bank. The account earns 7 per cent, compounded annually. How much will Ms Ku have at the end of three years? The answer is:

$$£500 \times 1.07 \times 1.07 \times 1.07 = £500 \times (1.07)^3 = £612.52$$

Figure 4.5 illustrates the growth of Ms Ku's account.

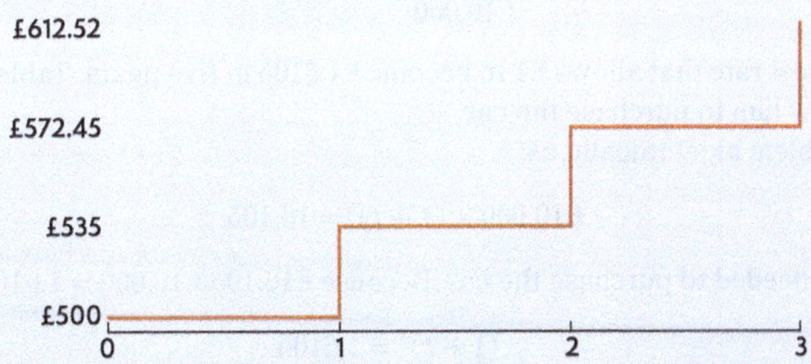

Figure 4.5 Suh-Pyng Ku's Savings Account

We can solve the previous example in a variety of ways. The computations could be done by hand, a calculator, spreadsheet, or with the help of a table. The appropriate table is Table A.3, which appears in the appendices on the Online Learning Centre. This table presents the *future value of £1 at the end of T periods*. We use the table by locating the appropriate interest rate on the horizontal and the appropriate number of periods on the vertical. For example, Suh-Pyng Ku would look at the following portion of Table A.3:

	Interest Rate		
Period	**6%**	**7%**	**8%**
1	1.0600	1.0700	1.0800
2	1.1236	1.1449	1.1664
3	1.1910	1.2250	1.2597
4	1.2625	1.3108	1.3605

She could calculate the future value of her £500 as

$$£500 \times 1.2250 = £612.50$$

In Example 4.3, we gave you both the initial investment and the interest rate, and then asked you to calculate the future value. Alternatively, the interest rate could have been unknown, as shown in Example 4.4.

Example 4.4

Finding the Rate

Carl Voigt, who recently won €10,000 in the lottery, wants to buy a car in five years. Carl estimates the vehicle will cost €16,105 at that time. We display his cash flows in Figure 4.6.

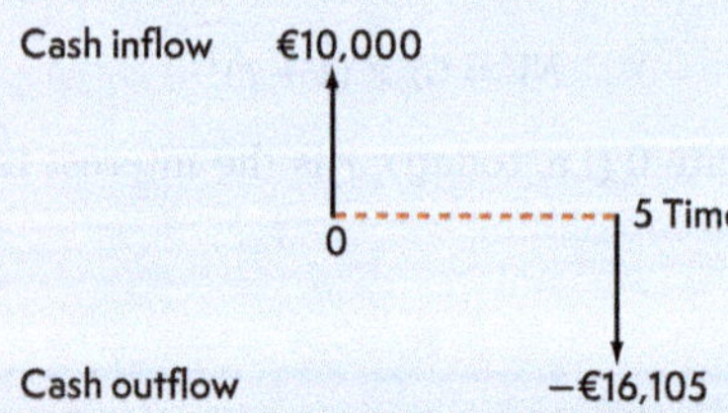

Figure 4.6 Cash Flows for Purchase of Carl Voigt's Car

What interest rate must Carl earn to be able to afford the car? The ratio of purchase price to initial cash is:

$$\frac{€16,105}{€10,000} = 1.6105$$

Thus, he must earn an interest rate that allows €1 to become €1.6105 in five years. Table A.3 tells us that an interest rate of 10 per cent will allow him to purchase the car.

We can express the problem algebraically as:

$$€10,000 \times (1 + r)^5 = 16,105$$

where r is the interest rate needed to purchase the car. Because €16,105/€10,000 = 1.6105, we have:

$$(1 + r)^5 = 1.6105$$
$$r = 10\%$$

Either the table or a calculator lets us solve for r.

The Power of Compounding: A Digression

Most people who have had any experience with compounding are impressed with its power over long periods. Take equities, for example. The average annual return on the 100 largest companies in the UK has been 8.47 per cent. Now assume that this is the average return on companies on the London Stock Exchange since it opened in 1801. If your great-great-grandmother invested £1 in the stock exchange on the very first day of trading, it would have been worth £74,825,522 in 2024! This is 8.47 per cent compounded annually for 223 years – that is, $(1.0847)^{223}$ = £74,825,522, ignoring a small rounding error.

The example illustrates the great difference between compound and simple interest. At 8.47 per cent, simple interest on £1 is 8.47 pence a year. Simple interest over 223 years is £18.89 (= 223 × £0.0847). That is, an individual withdrawing 8.47 pence every year would have withdrawn £18.89 (= 223 × £0.0847) over 223 years, which is quite a bit below the £74,825,522 obtained by reinvestment of all principal and interest.

Present Value and Discounting

We now know that an annual interest rate of 9 per cent enables the investor to transform £1 today into £1.1881 two years from now. Also, we would like to know the following:

How much would an investor need to lend today so that she could receive £1 two years from today?

Algebraically, we can write this as:

$$PV \times (1.09)^2 = £1$$

In the preceding equation, *PV* stands for present value, the amount of money we must lend today to receive £1 in two years.

Solving for *PV* in this equation, we have:

$$PV = \frac{£1}{1.1881} = £0.84$$

This process of calculating the present value of a future cash flow is called **discounting**. It is the opposite of compounding. To be certain that £0.84 is, in fact, the present value of £1 to be received in two years, we must check whether or not, if we lent £0.84 today and rolled over the loan for two years, we would get exactly £1 back. If this were the case, the capital markets would be saying that £1 received in two years is equivalent to having £0.84 today. Checking the exact numbers, we get:

$$£0.84168 \times 1.09 \times 1.09 = £1$$

In other words, when we have capital markets with a certain interest rate of 9 per cent, we are indifferent between receiving £0.84 today or £1 in two years. We have no reason to treat these two choices differently from each other because if we had £0.84 today and lent it out for two years, it would return £1 to us at the end of that time. The value 0.84 [= $1/(1.09)^2$] is called the present value factor. It is the factor used to calculate the present value of a future cash flow.

In the multi-period case, we write the formula for PV as follows:

The present value of an investment:

Equation 4.4

$$PV = \frac{C_T}{(1 + r)^T}$$

Here, C_T is the cash flow at date T and r is the appropriate discount rate.

Example 4.5

Multi-period Discounting

Allan Wolf will receive €10,000 three years from now. He can earn 8 per cent on his investments, so the appropriate discount rate is 8 per cent. What is the present value of his future cash flow? The answer is:

$$\begin{aligned} PV &= 10{,}000 \times \left(\frac{1}{1.08}\right)^3 \\ &= 10{,}000 \times 0.7938 \\ &= 7{,}938 \end{aligned}$$

Figure 4.7 illustrates the application of the present value factor to Allan's investment.

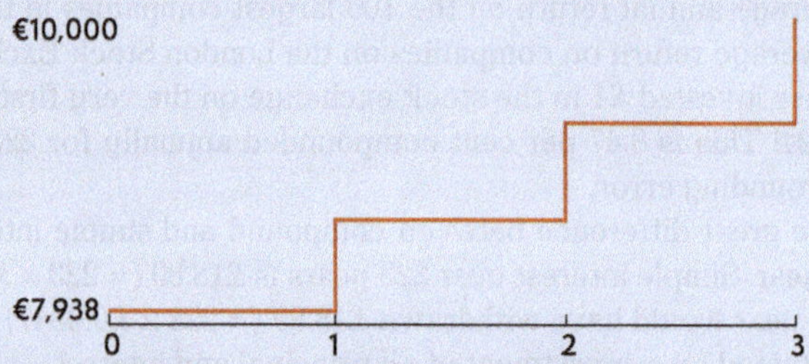

Figure 4.7 Discounting Allan's Opportunity

When his investments grow at an 8 per cent rate of interest, Allan is equally inclined towards receiving €7,938 now and receiving €10,000 in three years. After all, he could convert the €7,938 he receives today into €10,000 in three years by lending it at an interest rate of 8 per cent.

Allan could have reached his present value calculation in one of several ways. The computation could have been done by hand, by a calculator, with a spreadsheet, or with the help of Table A.1 in the appendices on the Online Learning Centre. This table presents the *present value of £1 or €1 to be received after T periods.* We use the table by locating the appropriate interest rate on the horizontal and the appropriate number of periods on the vertical.

The appropriate present value factor is 0.7938.

In the preceding example, we gave both the interest rate and the future cash flow. Alternatively, the interest rate could have been unknown.

Example 4.6

Finding the Rate

A customer of Chaffkin GmbH wants to buy a tugboat today. Rather than paying immediately, he will pay €50,000 in three years. It will cost Chaffkin GmbH €38,610 to build the boat today. We display the relevant cash flows to Chaffkin GmbH in Figure 4.8. At what interest rate would Chaffkin GmbH neither gain nor lose on the sale?

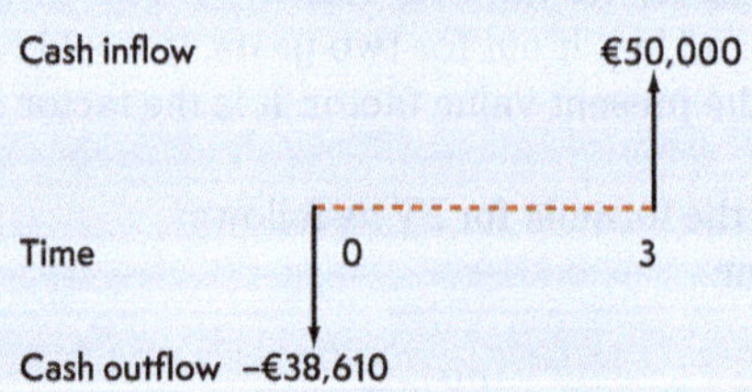

Figure 4.8 Cash Flows for Tugboat

The ratio of construction cost (present value) to the sale price (future value) is:

$$\frac{€38{,}610}{€50{,}000} = 0.7722$$

We must determine the interest rate that allows €1 to be received in three years to have a present value of €0.7722. Table A.1 tells us that 9 per cent is that interest rate.

Frequently, an investor or a business will receive more than one cash flow. The present value of the set of cash flows is merely the sum of the present values of the individual cash flows. We illustrate this in the following example.

Example 4.7

Cash Flow Valuation

Paul Wiggins has won a crossword competition and will receive the following set of cash flows over the next two years:

Year	Cash Flow
1	£2,000
2	£5,000

Paul can currently earn 6 per cent in his money market account, so the appropriate discount rate is 6 per cent. The present value of the cash flows is:

Year	Cash Flow × Present Value Factor = Present Value
1	$£2{,}000 \times \frac{1}{1.06} = £2{,}000 \times 0.943 = £1{,}887$
2	$£5{,}000 \times \left(\frac{1}{1.06}\right)^2 = £5{,}000 \times 0.890 = £4{,}450$
	Total £6,337

In other words, Paul is equally inclined towards receiving £6,337 today and receiving £2,000 and £5,000 over the next two years.

Example 4.8

NPV

Dratsel.com, an online broker based in Sweden, has an opportunity to invest in a new high-speed computer that costs SKr250,000. The computer will generate cash flows (from cost savings) of SKr125,000 one year from now, SKr100,000 two years from now and SKr75,000 three years from now. The computer will be worthless after three years, and no additional cash flows will occur. Dratsel.com has determined that the appropriate discount rate is 7 per cent for this investment. Should Dratsel.com make this investment in a new high-speed computer? What is the net present value of the investment?

The cash flows and present value factors of the proposed computer are as follows:

Year	Cash Flows (SKr)	Present Value Factor
0	−250,000	$1 = 1$
1	125,000	$\frac{1}{1.07} = 0.9346$
2	100,000	$\left(\frac{1}{1.07}\right)^2 = 0.8734$
3	75,000	$\left(\frac{1}{1.07}\right)^3 = 0.8163$

The present value of the cash flows is:

Year	Cash Flows (SKr) × Present Value Factor	=	Present Value (SKr)
0	−250,000 × 1	=	−250,000
1	125,000 × 0.9346	=	116,825
2	100,000 × 0.8734	=	87,340
3	75,000 × 0.8163	=	61,225.5
		Total:	15,387.5

Dratsel.com should invest in the new high-speed computer because the present value of its future cash flows is higher than its cost. The NPV is SKr15,387.5.

The Algebraic Formula

To derive an algebraic formula for the net present value of a cash flow, recall that the PV of receiving a cash flow one year from now is:

$$PV = \frac{C_1}{(1+r)}$$

and the PV of receiving a cash flow two years from now is:

$$PV = \frac{C_2}{(1+r)^2}$$

We can write the NPV of a T-period project as:

Equation 4.5

$$\begin{aligned} NPV &= -C_0 + \frac{C_1}{1+r} + \frac{C_2}{(1+r)^2} + \ldots + \frac{C_2}{(1+r)^T} \\ &= -C_0 + \sum_{t=1}^{T} \frac{C_t}{(1+r)^t} \end{aligned}$$

The initial flow, $-C_0$, is assumed to be negative because it represents an investment. The Σ is shorthand for the sum of the series.

4.3 Compounding Periods

So far, we have assumed that compounding and discounting occur yearly. Sometimes, compounding may occur more frequently than just once a year. For example, imagine a bank pays a 10 per cent interest rate 'compounded semi-annually'. This means that a £1,000 deposit in the bank would be worth £1,000 × 1.05 = £1,050 after six months, and £1,050 × 1.05 = £1,102.50 at the end of the year.

We write the end-of-year wealth as:

$$£1{,}000\left(1+\frac{0.10}{2}\right)^2 = £1{,}000 \times (1.05)^2 = £1{,}102.50$$

Of course, a £1,000 deposit would be worth £1,100 (£1,000 × 1.10) with yearly compounding. Note that the future value at the end of one year is greater with semi-annual compounding than with annual compounding. With annual compounding, the original £1,000 remains the investment base for the full year. The initial £1,000 is the investment base only for the first six months with semi-annual compounding. The base over the second six months is £1,050. Hence one gets *interest on interest* with semi-annual compounding.

Because £1,000 × 1.1025 = £1,102.50, 10 per cent compounded semi-annually is the same as 10.25 per cent compounded annually. In other words, a rational investor could not care less whether she is quoted a rate of 10 per cent compounded semi-annually or a rate of 10.25 per cent compounded annually.

Quarterly compounding at 10 per cent yields wealth at the end of one year of:

$$£1{,}000\left(1+\frac{0.10}{4}\right)^4 = £1{,}103.81$$

More generally, compounding an investment m times a year provides an end-of-year wealth of:

Equation 4.6

$$C_0\left(1+\frac{r}{m}\right)^m$$

where C_0 is the initial investment and r is the stated annual interest rate. The stated annual interest rate is the annual interest rate without consideration of compounding.

Example 4.9

The Effective Annual Rate

What is the end-of-year wealth if Marie Van Bommel receives a stated annual interest rate of 24 per cent compounded monthly on a €1 investment?

Using Equation 4.6, her wealth is:

$$£1\left(1+\frac{0.24}{12}\right)^{12} = £1 \times (1.02)^{12}$$
$$= £1.2682$$

The annual rate of return is 26.82 per cent. This annual rate of return is called either the **effective annual rate (EAR)** or the effective annual yield (EAY). Due to compounding, the effective annual interest rate is higher than the stated annual interest rate of 24 per cent. Algebraically, we can rewrite the effective annual interest rate as follows:

Effective annual rate:

Equation 4.7
$$\left(1+\frac{r}{m}\right)^m - 1$$

Students are often bothered by the subtraction of 1 in Equation 4.7. Note that end-of-year wealth is composed of both the interest earned over the year and the original principal. We remove the original principal by subtracting 1 in Equation 4.7.

Example 4.10

Compounding Frequencies

If the stated annual rate of interest, 8 per cent, is compounded quarterly, what is the effective annual rate?

Using Equation 4.7, we have:

$$\left(1+\frac{r}{m}\right)^m - 1 = \left(1+\frac{0.08}{4}\right)^4 - 1 = 0.0824 = 8.24\%$$

Referring back to our original example, where $C_0 = £1{,}000$ and $r = 10$ per cent, we can generate the following table:

C_0(£)	Compounding Frequency (m)	C_1(£)	Effective Annual Rate $= \left(1+\frac{r}{m}\right)^m - 1$
1,000	Yearly ($m = 1$)	1,100.00	0.10
1,000	Semi-annually ($m = 2$)	1,102.50	0.1025
1,000	Quarterly ($m = 4$)	1,103.81	0.10381
1,000	Daily ($m = 365$)	1,105.16	0.10516

Compounding Over Many Years

Equation 4.6 applies for an investment over one year. For an investment over one or more (T) years, the formula becomes:

Future value with compounding:

Equation 4.8
$$FV = C_0\left(1+\frac{r}{m}\right)^{mT}$$

Example 4.11

Multi-year Compounding

Harry DeAngelo is investing €5,000 at a stated annual interest rate of 12 per cent per year, compounded quarterly, for five years. What is his wealth at the end of five years?

Using Equation 4.8, his wealth is:

$$€5{,}000 \times \left(1+\frac{0.12}{4}\right)^{4\times 5} = €5{,}000 \times (1.03)^{20} = €5{,}000 \times 1.8061 = €9{,}030.50$$

The Annual Percentage Rate

Given the many different ways in which interest rates can be presented to the public, the European Union has a directive that harmonizes the way in which interest rates in any credit agreement for under €50,000 are presented. The UK extended the directive to all regulated loans, and the Netherlands uses it for mortgage loans. This harmonized interest rate is called the **annual percentage rate (APR)** and expresses the *total* cost of borrowing or investing as a percentage interest rate.

The reason for an APR is that a credit agreement may not just include interest payments, but also management fees, arrangement fees and other sundry costs that will affect the total charge for credit (TCC). Also, knowing the interest rate is still not enough to guarantee full comparability of different loans or investments. As shown above, the compounding frequency and the date when interest is charged will influence the effective annual rate of interest.

Under the EU directive, all providers of credit must prominently show the APR in any document or advertising material that promotes a particular type of loan or investment. To calculate APR, we use the standard present value formula. The main difference is in the cash flows included in the calculation:

Equation 4.9

$$PV = C_0 + \frac{C_1}{1+\text{APR}} + \frac{C_2}{(1+\text{APR})^2} + \cdots + \frac{C_T}{(1+\text{APR})^T}$$
$$= C_0 + \sum_{i=1}^{T} \frac{C_t}{(1+\text{APR})^i}$$

The definition used by the European Union for APR is very different from the formula used in the United States, and this can cause considerable confusion when Europeans read finance textbooks aimed at an American market. In the USA, the APR is simply the stated annual interest. Remember this if you ever plan to take out a loan overseas!

Example 4.12

APR

After much deliberation, Mary Ennis decides to buy a new Mercedes-Benz car for her family. The sale price of the car is £30,000. Mary arranges financing through the Mercedes dealer, who quotes a simple annual interest rate of 12 per cent on the original borrowed amount over three years, payable in 36 monthly instalments. This means that the lender will charge 12 per cent interest on the original loan of £30,000 every year for three years. Each year, the interest charge will be (12 per cent of £30,000) £3,600 making a total interest payment of £10,800 over three years.

The regular monthly instalments that Mary must pay are:

$$\text{Monthly instalment} = (£30{,}000 + £10{,}800)/36 = £1{,}133.33$$

In addition to the interest payments, the Mercedes dealer charges a £250 administration fee, which must be paid when the financing agreement is made. We now solve for APR in Equation 4.9:

$$£30{,}000 = £250 + \frac{£1{,}133.33}{(1+\text{APR})^{\frac{1}{12}}} + \frac{£1{,}133.33}{(1+\text{APR})^{\frac{2}{12}}} + \cdots + \frac{£1{,}133.33}{(1+\text{APR})^{\frac{36}{12}}}$$

This gives an APR of 24.13 per cent! The lender must also state the total amount paid at the end of the loan, which, in this case, is £41,049.88, so the full charge for credit is £11,049.88 (£41,049.88 − £30,000).

Continuous Compounding

The previous discussion shows that we can compound much more frequently than once a year. We could compound semi-annually, quarterly, monthly, daily, hourly, each minute, or even more often. The limiting case would be to compound every infinitesimal instant, which is commonly called continuous compounding. Surprisingly, banks and other financial institutions sometimes quote continuously compounded rates, which is why we study them.

Though the idea of compounding with such small intervals may boggle the mind, a simple formula is involved. With continuous compounding, we express the value at the end of T years as:

Equation 4.10

$$C_0 \times e^{rT}$$

where C_0 is the initial investment, r is the stated annual interest rate and T is the number of years over which the investment runs. The number e is a constant and is approximately equal to 2.718. It is not an unknown like C_0, r and T.

Example 4.13

Continuous Compounding

Belinda LeTissier invested £1,000 at a continuously compounded rate of 10 per cent for two years. What is the value of her wealth at the end of two years?

From Equation 4.10 we have:

$$£1{,}000 \times e^{0.10\times 2} = £1{,}000 \times 1.2214 = £1{,}221.40$$

This number can easily be read from Table A.5 in the appendices on the Online Learning Centre. We merely set r, the value on the horizontal dimension, to 10 per cent and T, the value on the vertical dimension, to 2. For this problem the relevant portion of the table is shown here:

	Continuously Compounded Rate (r)		
Period (T)	9%	10%	11%
1	1.0942	1.1052	1.1163
2	1.1972	1.2214	1.2461
3	1.3100	1.3499	1.3910

Figure 4.9 illustrates the relationship among annual, semi-annual and continuous compounding. Semi-annual compounding gives rise to both a smoother curve and a higher ending value than does annual compounding. Continuous compounding has both the smoothest curve and the highest ending value of all.

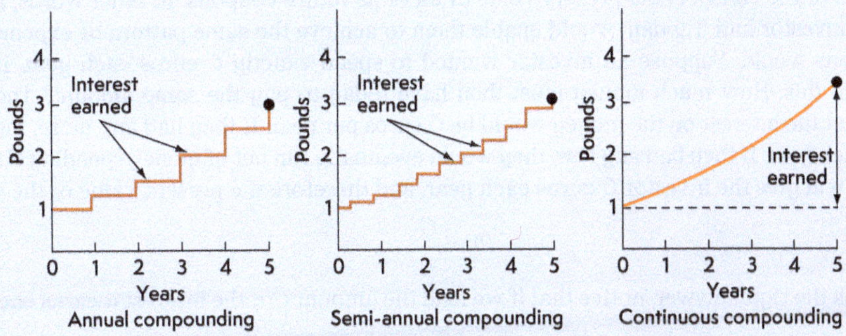

Figure 4.9 Annual, Semi-annual and Continuous Compounding

Example 4.14

Present Value with Continuous Compounding

A Twitch gaming competition is going to pay you €1,000 at the end of four years. If the annual continuously compounded rate of interest is 8 per cent, what is the present value of this payment?

$$€1{,}000 \times \frac{1}{e^{0.08 \times 4}} = €1{,}000 \times \frac{1}{1.3771} = €726.16$$

4.4 Simplifications

The previous sections of this chapter have examined the concepts of future value and present value. Although these concepts allow us to answer a host of problems concerning the time value of money, the human effort involved can be excessive. For example, consider calculating the present value of a 20-year monthly mortgage, which has 240 (= 20 × 12) payments. A lot of time is needed to perform such a conceptually simple task.

Because many basic finance problems are potentially time-consuming, we search for simplifications in this section. We provide simplifying formulae for four classes of cash flow streams:

1 Perpetuity
2 Growing perpetuity
3 Annuity
4 Growing annuity.

Perpetuity

A **perpetuity** is a constant stream of cash flows without end. If you think that perpetuities have no relevance to reality, it will surprise you that there is a well-known case of an unending cash flow stream: the British bonds called *consols*. An investor purchasing a consol is entitled to receive yearly interest from the British government for ever.

How can the price of a consol be determined? Consider a consol that pays a coupon of C each year and will do so for ever. Applying the PV formula gives us:

$$PV = \frac{C}{1+r} + \frac{C}{(1+r)^2} + \frac{C}{(1+r)^3} + \cdots$$

where the dots at the end of the formula stand for the infinite string of terms that continues the formula. A series like the preceding one is called a *geometric series*, and even though it has an infinite number of terms, the whole series has a finite sum because each term is only a fraction of the preceding term. Before turning to our calculus books, though, it is worth going back to our original principles to see if a bit of financial intuition can help us find the PV.

The present value of the consol is the present value of all of its future coupons. In other words, it is an amount of money that, if an investor had it today, would enable them to achieve the same pattern of expenditures that the consol and its coupons would. Suppose an investor wanted to spend exactly C euros each year. If they had the consol, they could do this. How much money must they have today to pay the same amount? They would need exactly enough so that the interest on the money would be C euros per year. If they had any more, they could spend more than C euros each year. If they had any less, they would eventually run out of money spending C euros per year.

The amount that will give the investor C euros each year, and therefore the present value of the consol, is:

Equation 4.11

$$PV = \frac{C}{r}$$

To confirm that this is the right answer, notice that if we lend the amount C/r, the interest it earns each year will be:

$$\text{Interest} = \frac{C}{r} \times r = C$$

which is the consol payment.

The formula for the present value of a perpetuity:

Equation 4.12

$$PV = \frac{C}{1+r} + \frac{C}{(1+r)^2} + \frac{C}{(1+r)^3} + \cdots$$
$$= \frac{C}{r}$$

It is comforting to know how easily we can use a bit of financial intuition to solve this mathematical problem.

Example 4.15

Perpetuities

Consider a perpetuity paying £100 a year. If the relevant interest rate is 8 per cent, what is the value of the consol?

Using Equation 4.11 we have:

$$PV = \frac{£100}{0.08} = £1{,}250$$

Now suppose that interest rates fall to 6 per cent. From Equation 4.11, the value of the perpetuity is:

$$PV = \frac{£100}{0.06} = £1{,}666.67$$

Note that the value of the perpetuity rises with a drop in the interest rate. Conversely, the value of the perpetuity falls with a rise in the interest rate.

Growing Perpetuity

Imagine an apartment building where cash flows to the landlord after expenses will be €100,000 next year. These cash flows are expected to rise at 5 per cent per year. If one assumes that this rise will continue indefinitely, the cash flow stream is termed a growing perpetuity. The relevant interest rate is 11 per cent. Therefore, the appropriate discount rate is 11 per cent, and the present value of the cash flows can be represented as:

$$PV = \frac{€100{,}000}{1.11} + \frac{€100{,}000(1.05)}{(1.11)^2} + \frac{€100{,}000\,(1.05)^2}{(1.11)^3} + \cdots + \frac{€100{,}000\,(1.05)^{N-1}}{(1.11)^N} + \cdots$$

Algebraically, we can write the formula as:

$$PV = \frac{C}{1+r} + \frac{C \times (1+g)}{(1+r)^2} + \frac{C \times (1+g)^2}{(1+r)^3} + \cdots + \frac{C \times (1+g)^{N-1}}{(1+r)^N} + \cdots$$

where C is the cash flow to be received one period hence, g is the rate of growth per period, expressed as a percentage, and r is the appropriate discount rate.

Fortunately, this formula reduces to the following simplification:

The formula for the present value of a growing perpetuity:

Equation 4.13

$$PV = \frac{C}{r-g}$$

From Equation 4.13 the present value of the cash flows from the apartment building is:

$$\frac{€100{,}000}{0.11 - 0.05} = €1{,}666{,}667$$

There are three important points concerning the growing perpetuity formula:

1 *The numerator:* The numerator in Equation 4.13 is the cash flow one period hence, not at date 0.

2 *The discount rate and the growth rate:* The discount rate r must be greater than the growth rate g for the growing perpetuity formula to work. Consider the case in which the growth rate approaches the interest rate

in magnitude. Then, the denominator in the growing perpetuity formula gets infinitesimally small, and the present value grows infinitely large. The present value is, in fact, undefined when r is less than g.

3 *The timing assumption:* Cash generally flows into and out of real-world firms both randomly and nearly continuously. However, Equation 4.13 assumes that cash flows are received and disbursed at regular and discrete points in time. In the example of the apartment, we assumed that the net cash flows of €100,000 occurred only once a year. In reality, rent is usually paid every month. Payments for maintenance and other expenses may happen at any time within the year.

We can apply the growing perpetuity formula of Equation 4.13 only by assuming a regular and discrete pattern of cash flows. Although this assumption is sensible because the formula saves so much time, the user should never forget that it is an *assumption*. This point will be mentioned again in the chapters ahead.

A few words should be said about terminology. Authors of financial textbooks generally use one of two conventions to refer to time. A minority of financial writers treat cash flows as being received on exact *dates* – for example date 0, date 1, and so forth. Under this convention, date 0 represents the present time. However, because a year is an interval, not a specific moment in time, the great majority of authors refer to cash flows that occur at the end of a year (or, alternatively, the end of a *period*). Under this *end-of-year* convention, the end of year 0 is the present, the end of year 1 occurs one period hence, and so on. (The beginning of year 0 has already passed and is not generally referred to.)[1]

The interchangeability of the two conventions can be seen from the following chart:

Date 0 = Now	Date 1	Date 2	Date 3	...
End of year 0 = Now	End of year 1	End of year 2	End of year 3	...

We strongly believe that the *dates convention* reduces ambiguity. However, we use both conventions because you are likely to see the *end-of-year convention* in later courses. In fact, both conventions may appear in the same example for the sake of practice.

Annuity

An **annuity** is a level stream of regular payments that lasts for a fixed number of periods. Not surprisingly, annuities are among the most common kinds of financial instruments. The pensions that people receive when they retire are often in the form of an annuity. Leases and mortgages are also often annuities.

To figure out the present value of an annuity we need to evaluate the following equation:

$$\frac{C}{1+r} + \frac{C}{(1+r)^2} + \frac{C}{(1+r)^3} + \cdots + \frac{C}{(1+r)^T}$$

The present value of receiving the coupons for only T periods must be less than the present value of a consol, but how much less? To answer this, we have to look at consols a bit more closely.

Consider the following time chart:

	Now						
Date (or end of year)	0	1	2	3	T	$(T+1)$	$(T+2)$
Consol 1		C	C	C...	C	C	C...
Consol 2						C	C...
Annuity		C	C	C...	C		

Consol 1 is a normal consol with its first payment at date 1. The first payment of consol 2 occurs at date $T+1$.

The present value of having a cash flow of C at each of T dates is equal to the present value of consol 1 minus the present value of consol 2. The present value of consol 1 is given by:

Equation 4.14 $$PV = \frac{C}{r}$$

Consol 2 is just a consol with its first payment at date $T + 1$. From the perpetuity formula, this consol will be worth C/r at date T.[2] However, we do not want the value at date T. We want the value now – in other words, the present value at date 0. We must discount C/r back by T periods. Therefore, the present value of consol 2 is:

Equation 4.15
$$PV = \frac{C}{r}\left[\frac{1}{(1+r)^T}\right]$$

The present value of having cash flows for T years is the present value of a consol with its first payment at date 1 minus the present value of a consol with its first payment at date $T + 1$. Thus the present value of an annuity is Equation 4.14 minus Equation 4.15. This can be written as:

$$\frac{C}{r} - \frac{C}{r}\left[\frac{1}{(1+r)^T}\right]$$

This simplifies to the following:

Formula for present value of annuity:

$$PV = C\left[\frac{1}{r} - \frac{1}{r(1+r)^T}\right]$$

This can also be written as:

Equation 4.16
$$PV = C\left[\frac{1 - \frac{1}{r(1+r)^T}}{r}\right]$$

Example 4.16

Lottery Valuation

Mark Lancaster has just won a competition paying £50,000 a year for 20 years. He is to receive his first payment a year from now. The competition organizers advertise this as the Million Pound Competition because £1,000,000 = £50,000 × 20. If the interest rate is 8 per cent, what is the true value of the prize?

Equation 4.16 yields:

$$\text{Present value of million pound competition} = £50{,}000 \times \left[1 - \frac{1}{(1.08)^{20}}\right]$$

$$\text{Periodic payment} \times \text{Annuity factor}$$
$$= £50{,}000 \times 9.8181$$
$$= £490{,}905$$

Rather than being overjoyed at winning, Mr Lancaster sues the company for misrepresentation and fraud. His legal brief states he was promised £1 million but received only £490,905.

The term we use to compute the present value of the stream of level payments, C, for T years is called an annuity factor. The annuity factor in the current example is 9.8181. Because the annuity factor is used so often in PV calculations, we have included it in Table A.2 in the appendices on the Online Learning Centre. The table gives the values of these factors for a range of interest rates, r, and maturity dates, T.

The annuity factor as expressed in the brackets of Equation 4.16 is a complicated formula. For simplification, we may from time to time refer to the annuity factor as:

$$A_r^T$$

This expression stands for the present value of £1 or €1 a year for T years at an interest rate of r.

We can also provide a formula for the future value of an annuity:

Equation 4.17
$$FV = C\left[\frac{(1+r)^T}{r} - \frac{1}{r}\right] = C\left[\frac{(1+r)^T - 1}{r}\right]$$

As with present value factors for annuities, we have compiled future value factors in Table A.4 in the appendices on the Online Learning Centre.

Example 4.17

Retirement Investing

Suppose you put £3,000 per year into a cash investment savings account. The account pays 6 per cent interest per year, tax free. How much will you have when you retire in 30 years?

This question asks for the future value of an annuity of £3,000 per year for 30 years at 6 per cent, which we can calculate as follows:

$$FV = C\left[\frac{(1+r)^T - 1}{r}\right] = £3{,}000 \times \left[\frac{1.06^{30} - 1}{0.06}\right]$$
$$= £3{,}000 \times 79.0582$$
$$= £237{,}174.56$$

So, you will have close to a quarter of a million pounds in the account.

Our experience is that annuity formulae are not hard, but awkward, for the beginning student. We present four tricks next.

Trick 1: A Delayed Annuity

One of the skills in working with annuities or perpetuities is getting the timing exactly right, and is particularly true when an annuity or perpetuity begins at a date many periods in the future. We have found that even the brightest beginning student can make errors here. Consider the following example.

Example 4.18

Delayed Annuities

Roberta Barontelli will receive a four-year annuity of €500 per year, beginning at date 6. If the interest rate is 10 per cent, what is the present value of her annuity? This situation can be graphed as follows:

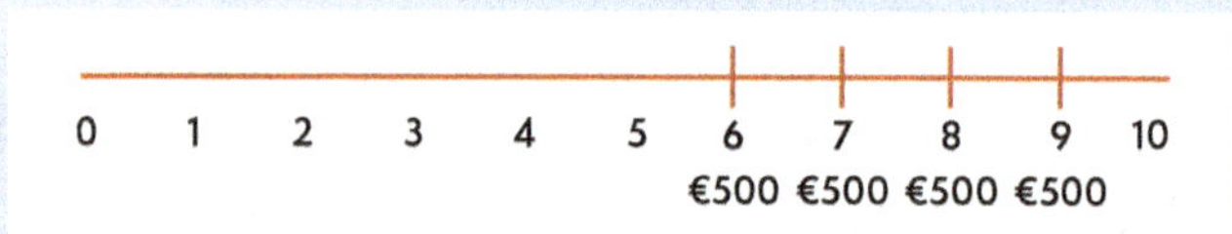

The analysis involves two steps:

1 Calculate the present value of the annuity using Equation 4.16:

Present value of annuity at date 5:

$$€500\left[\frac{1 - \frac{1}{(1.1)^4}}{0.1}\right] = €500 \times A^4_{0.10}$$
$$= €500 \times 3.1699$$
$$= €1{,}584.95$$

Note that €1,584.95 represents the present value at *date 5*.

Students frequently think that €1,584.95 is the present value at date 6 because the annuity begins at date 6. However, our formula values the annuity as of one period before the first payment, as is seen in the most typical case where the first payment occurs at date 1. The formula values the annuity as of date 0 in that case.

2 Discount the present value of the annuity back to date 0:
The present value at date 0:

$$\frac{€1{,}584.95}{(1.10)^5} = €984.13$$

Again, it is worthwhile mentioning that because the annuity formula brings Roberta's annuity back to date 5, the second calculation must discount over the remaining five periods.

Trick 2: Annuity Due

The annuity formula of Equation 4.16 assumes that the first annuity payment begins a full period hence. This type of annuity is sometimes called an *annuity in arrears* or an *ordinary annuity*. What happens if the annuity begins today – in other words, at date 0?

Example 4.19

Annuity Due

In a previous example, Mark Lancaster received £50,000 a year for 20 years from a competition. In that example, he was to receive the first payment a year from the winning date. Let us now assume that the first payment occurs immediately. The total number of payments remains 20.

Under this new assumption, we have a 19-date annuity with the first payment occurring at date 1 – plus an extra payment at date 0. The present value is:

$$\underset{\text{Payment at date 0}}{£50{,}000} + \underset{\text{19 – year annuity}}{£50{,}000 \times A^{19}_{0.08}}$$
$$= £50{,}000 + (£50{,}000 \times 9.6036)$$
$$= £530{,}180$$

£530,180, the present value in this example, is higher than £490,905, the present value in the earlier competition example, which is to be expected because the annuity of the current example begins earlier. An annuity with an immediate initial payment is called an *annuity in advance* or, more commonly, an *annuity due*. Always remember that Equation 4.16 and Table A.2 in the appendices on the Online Learning Centre refer to an *ordinary annuity*.

Trick 3: The Infrequent Annuity

The following example treats an annuity with payments occurring less frequently than once a year.

Example 4.20

Infrequent Annuities

Ann Chen receives an annuity of £450, payable once every two years. The annuity stretches out over 20 years. The first payment occurs at date two – that is, two years from today. The annual interest rate is 6 per cent.

The trick is to determine the interest rate over two years. The interest rate over two years is:

$$(1.06 \times 1.06) - 1 = 12.36\%$$

That is, £100 invested over two years will yield £112.36.

What we want is the present value of a £450 annuity over 10 periods, with an interest rate of 12.36 per cent per period:

$$£450\left[\frac{1-\frac{1}{(1+0.1236)^{10}}}{0.1236}\right] = £450 \times A^{10}_{0.1236} = £2{,}5050.57$$

Trick 4: Equating the Present Value of Two Annuities

The following example equates the present value of inflows with the present value of outflows.

Example 4.21

Working with Annuities

You are saving for the university education of your newborn daughter, Susan, and estimate that university expenses will be €30,000 per year when she reaches university in 18 years. The annual interest rate over the next few decades will be 14 per cent. How much money must you deposit in the bank each year so your daughter will be supported entirely through four years of university?

To simplify the calculations, we assume that your daughter is born today. You will make the first of four annual tuition payments on her 18th birthday. You will also make equal bank deposits on each of her first 17 birthdays, but no deposit at date 0, which we illustrate as follows:

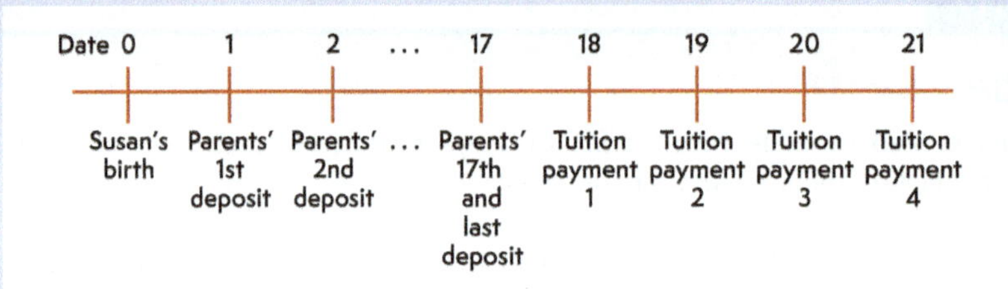

You will be making deposits to the bank over the next 17 years and will be withdrawing €30,000 per year over the following four years. We can be sure you will be able to withdraw fully €30,000 per year if the present value of the deposits is equal to the present value of the four €30,000 withdrawals.

This calculation requires three steps. The first two determine the present value of the withdrawals. The final step determines yearly deposits that will have a present value equal to that of the withdrawals.

1 We calculate the present value of the four years at university using the annuity formula:

$$€30{,}000\left[\frac{1-\dfrac{1}{(1.14)^4}}{0.14}\right] = €30{,}000 \times A^4_{0.14}$$

$$= €30{,}000 \times 2.9137 = €87{,}411$$

We assume that Susan enters university on her 18th birthday. Given our discussion in Trick 1, €87,411 represents the present value at date 17.

2 We calculate the present value of the university education at date 0 as:

$$\frac{€87{,}811}{(1.14)^{17}} = €9{,}422.91$$

3 Assuming you make deposits to the bank at the end of each of the 17 years, we calculate the annual deposit that will yield a present value of all deposits of €9,422.91. This is calculated as:

$$C \times A^{17}_{0.14} = €9{,}422.91$$

Because

$A^{17}_{0.14} = 6.3729$,

$$C = \frac{€9{,}422.91}{6.3729} = €1{,}478.59$$

Thus deposits of €1,478.59 made at the end of each of the first 17 years and invested at 14 per cent will provide enough money to make tuition payments of €30,000 over the following four years.

Growing Annuity

Cash flows in business are likely to increase over time, due either to real growth or to inflation. The growing perpetuity, which assumes an infinite number of cash flows, provides one formula to handle this growth. We now consider a growing annuity, which is a *finite* number of growing cash flows. Because perpetuities of any kind are rare, a formula for a growing annuity would be useful indeed. Here is the formula:

The formula for the present value of growing annuity:

Equation 4.18

$$PV = C\left[\frac{1}{r-g} - \frac{1}{r-g} \times \left(\frac{1+g}{1+r}\right)^T\right] = C\left[\frac{1-\left(\frac{1+g}{1+r}\right)^T}{r-g}\right]$$

As before, C is the payment to occur at the end of the first period, r is the interest rate, g is the rate of growth per period, expressed as a percentage, and T is the number of periods for the annuity.

Example 4.22

Growing Annuities

Stuart Gabriel, an MBA student, has just been offered a job at £80,000 a year. He anticipates his salary increasing by 9 per cent a year until his retirement in 40 years. Given an interest rate of 20 per cent, what is the present value of his lifetime salary?

We simplify by assuming he will be paid his £80,000 salary exactly one year from now, and that his salary will continue to be paid in annual instalments. The appropriate discount rate is 20 per cent. From Equation 4.18, the calculation is:

$$\text{Present value of Stuart's lifetime salary} = £80{,}000 \times \left[\frac{1-\left(\frac{1.09}{1.20}\right)^{40}}{0.20-0.09}\right] = £711{,}730.71$$

Example 4.23

More Growing Annuities

In Example 4.21, you planned to make 17 identical payments to fund the university education of your daughter, Susan. Alternatively, imagine that you planned to increase your payments at 4 per cent per year. What would your first payment be?

The first two steps of Example 4.21 showed that the present value of the college costs was €9,422.91. These two steps would be the same here. However, we must alter the third step and ask how much your first payment should be so that, if payments increase by 4 per cent per year, the present value of all payments will be €9,422.91.

We set the growing annuity formula equal to €9,422.91 and solve for C:

$$C\left[\frac{1-\left(\frac{1+g}{1+r}\right)^T}{r-g}\right] = C\left[\frac{1-\left(\frac{1.04}{1.14}\right)^T}{0.14-0.04}\right] = €9{,}422.91$$

Here, C = €1,192.78. Thus, the deposit on your daughter's first birthday is €1,192.78. The deposit on her second birthday is €1,240.49 (= 1.04 × €1,192.78), and so on.

Real World Insight 4.2

Research and Development in Drug Companies

How does a company value a new drug product? Research and development at large pharmaceutical firms is inherently risky because there is no guarantee that the drug will be accepted by regulatory authorities, be effective or have a receptive market wanting to buy it. Take Glybera, which reduces the likelihood of blood clotting. The drug costs nearly €800,000 per patient!

To justify such a high price, the costs are not only associated with very high research and development expense, but also the reduction in treatment costs related to taking the drug. Since one course of Glybera provides a permanent cure, not having ongoing treatment costs are equivalent to an increase in cash flow, which has value to the patient.

Thus, buying Glybera entails a very high initial cash outflow but also a long-term annuity of cash inflows to represent the reduction in future costs. Taken together, the initial cost of the drug may not seem so high after all.

Sustainability in Action 4.1

Calculating Present Value

A European investment firm, EcoInvest, has identified a potential opportunity to invest in a solar energy project in the UK. The project is estimated to have an initial cost of £10 million for the installation of solar panels, with a useful life of 30 years. The investment is expected to generate annual revenues of £1.5 million, with annual operating expenses of £0.5 million, resulting in net cash flows of £1 million per year. The firm's required rate of return for similar investments is 8 per cent.

To assess the viability of this project, EcoInvest will calculate the present value (PV) of the expected cash flows, taking into account the time value of money. Using the annuity formula, it can determine the PV of the cash flows over the 30-year period:

$$PV = C\left[\frac{1}{r} - \frac{1}{r(1+r)^T}\right] = 1\left[\frac{1}{.08} - \frac{1}{.08(1.08)^{30}}\right] = £11.26 \text{ million}$$

Since the PV of the cash flows (£11.26 million) is greater than the initial investment cost (£10 million), the project appears to be a sound investment.

By analysing the cash flows, the investment firm can determine whether the project aligns with its financial goals and overall sustainability objectives.

Summary and Conclusions

1. Two basic concepts, *future value* and *present value*, were introduced at the beginning of this chapter. With a 10 per cent interest rate, an investor with £1 today can generate a future value of £1.10 in a year, £1.21 [= £1 × $(1.10)^2$] in two years, and so on. Conversely, present value analysis places a current value on a future cash flow. With the same 10 per cent interest rate, £1 to be received in one year has a present value of £0.909 (= £1/1.10) in year 0. £1 to be received in two years has a present value of £0.826 [= £1/$(1.10)^2$].
2. We commonly express an interest rate as, say, 12 per cent per year. However, we can speak of the interest rate as 3 per cent per quarter. Although the stated annual interest rate remains 12 per cent (= 3 per cent × 4), the effective annual interest rate is 12.55 per cent [= $(1.03)^4$ × 1]. In other words, the compounding process increases the future value of an investment. The limiting case is continuous compounding, where we assume funds are reinvested every infinitesimal instant.
3. A basic quantitative technique for financial decision-making is net present value analysis. The net present value formula for an investment that generates cash flows (C_i) in future periods is:

$$NPV = -C_0 + \frac{C_1}{(1+r)} + \frac{C_2}{(1+r)^2} + \cdots + \frac{C_r}{(1+r)^T} = -C_0 + \sum_{i=1}^{T} \frac{C_i}{(1+r)^i}$$

The formula assumes that the cash flow at date 0 is the initial investment (a cash outflow).

4 Frequently, the actual calculation of present value is long and tedious. The computation of the present value of a long-term mortgage with monthly payments is an excellent example of this. We presented four simplifying formulae:

$$\text{Perpetuity: } PV = \frac{C}{r}$$

$$\text{Growing perpetuity: } PV = \frac{C}{r-g}$$

$$\text{Annuity: } PV = C\left[\frac{1-\frac{1}{(1+r)^T}}{r}\right]$$

$$\text{Growing annuity: } PV = C\left[\frac{1-\left(\frac{1+g}{1+r}\right)^T}{r-g}\right]$$

5 We stressed a few practical considerations in the application of these formulae:

(a) The numerator in each of the formulae, C, is the cash flow to be received *one full period hence.*
(b) Cash flows are generally irregular in practice. To avoid unwieldy problems, assumptions to create more regular cash flows are made both in this textbook and in the real world.
(c) Some present value problems involve annuities (or perpetuities) beginning a few periods hence. Students should practise combining the annuity (or perpetuity) formula with the discounting formula to solve these problems.
(d) Annuities and perpetuities may have periods of every two or every n years, rather than once a year. The annuity and perpetuity formulae can easily handle such circumstances.
(e) We frequently encounter problems where the present value of one annuity must be equated with the present value of another annuity.

Questions and Problems

CONCEPT

1 **Valuation: The One-period Case** Your friend tells you that it does not matter when you receive money since it is always worth the same. He tells you that £100 today is worth the same as £100 tomorrow. Is he correct? Would you be willing to pay £100 today in exchange for £150 in one year's time? What would be the key considerations in your decision?

2 **Valuation: The Multi-period Case** You have taken out a loan that requires annual payments of £110 for each of the next two years. You wish to pay back the loan over four years. Should the payment be £55 per year? Should it be more or less? Explain your answer.

3 **Compounding Periods** As you increase the length of time involved, what happens to future values? What happens to present values? What happens to the future value of an annuity if you increase the rate r? What happens to the present value?

4 **Simplifications** Can the simplified formulae provided in this chapter work for every valuation problem? Explain your answer with an illustration.

5 **What is a Firm Worth?** What is discounted cash flow (DCF) valuation? Can it be used to estimate the value of companies? What businesses could we value using DCF valuation? What are the advantages and disadvantages of such an approach?

REGULAR

6 **Interest** As a real estate agent, you have found a reliable property developer who is willing to sell you 50 acres of land for £300,000. You approach your two main investors, Mr Johnson and Ms Lee. Mr Johnson offers to buy the land from you in one year for £315,000, while Ms Lee says she will purchase the land in three years' time for £350,000. What is the annual percentage rate (APR) that Mr Johnson and Ms Lee are offering you? Based on the rates, which option would be the best for you as a real estate agent?

7 **Calculating Future Values** Calculate the future value of a £100 cash flow for the following combinations of rates and times:

(a) $r = 8\%; t = 10$ years

(b) $r = 8\%; t = 20$ years

(c) $r = 4\%; t = 10$ years

(d) $r = 4\%; t = 20$ years

8 **Double Your Money** If you invest £5,000 in a savings account that pays 3.5 per cent every year, how long would it take you to double your money?

9 **Calculating Present Values** Calculate the present value of a £100 cash flow for the following rates and times:

(a) $r = 8\%; t = 10$ years

(b) $r = 8\%; t = 20$ years

(c) $r = 4\%; t = 10$ years

(d) $r = 4\%; t = 20$ years

10 **Calculating Rates of Return** You own a property on the Isle of Arran, which you estimate will provide an annual income of £10,000 per year in perpetuity. If the property is valued at £250,000, what must be the discount rate?

11 **Annual Rates of Return** On 8 February 2009, John Madejski, chairman of Reading Football Club, sold the Edgar Degas bronze sculpture *Petite Danseuse de Quatorze Ans* at auction for a world-record price of £13.3 million. He bought the statue in 2004 for £5 million. What was his annual rate of return on this sculpture?

12 **Perpetuities** An investor purchasing a British consol is entitled to receive annual payments from the British government for ever. What is the price of a consol that pays £4 annually if the next payment occurs one year from today? The market interest rate is 4 per cent.

13 **Continuous Compounding** A zero coupon bond that will pay €1,000 in 10 years is selling today at €422.41. What is the continuously compounded annual interest rate on the bond?

14 **Net Present Value** Your company has the opportunity to invest in a new computer system that requires an initial outlay of €20,000 and will increase the firm's cash flows by €4,000 per year for the next eight years. The finance director has asked you to assess whether the system is worth installing if the required rate of return is (i) 9 per cent and (ii) 14 per cent. How high can the discount rate be before the project is rejected?

15 **Calculating Annuity Present Value** An investment offers €4,000 per year for 10 years, with the first payment occurring one year from now. If the required return is 9 per cent, what is the value of the investment? What would the value be if the payments occurred for 20 years? For 50 years? For ever?

16 **Calculating APR** Find the APR for the following five-year loan: a principal of £15,000 with a stated annual interest rate of 7 per cent on the original principal amount to be paid in 60 monthly instalments. The loan has a £250 arrangement fee to be paid as soon as the contract is signed.

17 **Present Value** A 25-year fixed-rate mortgage has monthly payments of €717 per month and a mortgage interest rate of 6.14 per cent per year compounded monthly. If a buyer purchases a home with the cash proceeds of the mortgage loan plus an additional 20 per cent deposit, what is the purchase price of the home?

18 **Future Value** What is the future value in four years of €1,000 invested in an account with a stated annual interest rate of 10 per cent,

(a) Compounded annually

(b) Compounded semi-annually

(c) Compounded monthly

(d) Compounded continuously?

Why does the future value increase as the compounding period shortens?

19 **Calculating Annuities** You are planning to save for retirement over the next 30 years. To do this, you will invest £500 a month in a share account and £500 a month in a bond account. The return of the share account is expected to be 7 per cent, and the bond account will pay 4 per cent. When you retire, you will combine your money into an account with a 6 per cent return. How much can you withdraw each month from your account assuming a 25-year withdrawal period?

20 **Compounding** What is the annualized interest rate, compounded daily, that is equivalent to 12 per cent interest compounded semi-annually? What is the daily compounded rate that is equivalent to 12 per cent compounded continuously?

21 **Growing Perpetuities** Oasis Healthtec has been working on a ring that measures blood pressure, heart rate variability and heart rate continuously when worn. It is charged through kinetic energy. The ring has been cleared for manufacture and development. Oasis Healthtec anticipates selling 2,000 units in the first year at a price of €200 per ring. Because of the licensing deal Oasis Healthtec has agreed with the manufacturers, the first cash flow will be received two years from today. Subsequent annual cash flows will grow at 5 per cent in perpetuity. What is the present value of the ring if the discount rate is 10 per cent?

22 **Unusual Perpetuities** You have invested in a project that will pay you £1,000 every two years. If the interest rate is 8 per cent, how much is the project worth today?

23 **Balloon Payments** Mario Guiglini has just sold his hotel and purchased a restaurant with the proceeds. The restaurant is on the Riccione seafront in northern Italy. The cost of the restaurant to Mario is €200,000 and the seller requires a 20 per cent up-front payment. Mario is able to pay the upfront payment from the proceeds of the hotel sale. He needs to take out a mortgage and has been able to arrange one with Unicredit Bank that charges a 12 per cent APR. Mario will make equal monthly payments over the next 20 years. His first payment will be due one month from now. However, the mortgage has a 10-year balloon payment option, meaning that the balance of the loan could be paid off at the end of year 10. There were no other transaction costs or finance charges. How much will Mario's balloon payment be in eight years?

24 **Calculating Interest Expense** You receive a credit card application from Shady Banks plc offering an introductory rate of 1.90 per cent per year, compounded monthly for the first six months, increasing thereafter to 16 per cent per year compounded monthly. Assuming you transfer the £4,000 balance from your existing credit card and make no subsequent payments, how much interest will you owe at the end of the first year?

25 **Growing Annuity** Your job pays you only once a year for all the work you did over the previous 12 months. Today, 31 December, you just received your salary of £100,000 and plan to spend all of it. However, you have also decided to join the company's employee pension scheme. Under the very generous scheme, your company contributes £2 for every £1 that you pay into the pension. You have decided that one year from today you will begin paying 2 per cent of your annual salary into the pension in which you are guaranteed to earn 8 per cent per year. Your salary will increase at 4 per cent per year throughout your career. How much money will you have on the date of your retirement 40 years from today?

26 **Quoted Rates and APR** A local finance company quotes a 14 per cent interest rate on one-year loans. So, if you borrow €20,000, the interest for the year will be €2,800. Because you must repay a total of €22,800 in one year, the finance company requires you to pay €22,800/12, or €1,900, per month over the next 12 months. Is this a 14 per cent loan? What rate would legally have to be quoted?

27 **Working with Annuities** A three-year annuity of six £5,000 semi-annual payments will begin 10 years from now, with the first payment coming 10.5 years from now. If the discount rate is 10 per cent compounded monthly, what is the value of this annuity five years from now? What is the value three years from now? What is the current value of the annuity?

28 **Calculating Annuities Due** You want to lease a set of golf clubs from Pings Ltd. The lease contract is in the form of 36 equal monthly payments at a 14 per cent stated annual interest rate, compounded monthly. Because the clubs cost £4,000 retail, Pings wants the PV of the lease payments to equal £4,000. Suppose that your first payment is due immediately. What will your monthly lease payments be?

CHALLENGE

29 **Annuities** A family plans to retire in 40 years and wants to have an annual retirement budget of £100,000 for 30 years. They anticipate earning 10 per cent interest on their retirement savings. If they decide to make annual payments into a savings plan, how much should they save each year to reach their goal? Additionally, if they also expect to spend £50,000 on their child's wedding in 15 years, how will this affect their retirement savings plan?

30 **Paying Loans Early** On 1 September 2018, Susan Chao bought a motorcycle for £15,000. She paid £1,000 down and financed the balance with a five-year loan at a stated annual interest rate of 9.6 per cent, compounded monthly. She started the monthly payments exactly one month after the purchase (i.e. 1 October 2018). Two years later, at the end of October 2020, Susan got a new job and decided to pay off the loan. If the bank charges her a 1 per cent prepayment penalty based on the loan balance, how much must she pay the bank on 1 November 2018?

31 **Calculating Annuity Values** You are serving on a jury. A plaintiff is suing the city for injuries sustained after a freak doggie poo accident. In the trial, doctors testified that it will be five years before the plaintiff is able to return to work. The jury has already decided in favour of the plaintiff. You are the foreperson of the jury and propose that the jury give the plaintiff an award to cover the following: (1) The present value of two years' back pay. The plaintiff's

annual salary for the last two years would have been €25,000 and €28,000, respectively. (2) The present value of five years' future salary. You assume the salary will be €28,000 per year. (3) €100,000 for pain, suffering and humiliation. (4) €20,000 for court costs. Assume that the salary payments are equal amounts paid at the end of each month. If the interest rate you choose is a 4 per cent APR, what is the size of the settlement? If you were the plaintiff, would you like to see a higher or lower interest rate?

32 **Choosing between Investments** You have just read a life-enhancing book that tells you that if you believe things will happen, they will! You decide that you want to become a millionaire by the time you are 65. You have just turned 22 and you decide to play the stock market. Your fantastic corporate finance textbook leads you to believe that you can earn 11.8 per cent per annum from investing in equities. How much must you invest each year in order to realize your dream? You have decided that investing each year will be boring and so you just want to invest an amount today and leave it in an account for 43 years. How much should you invest today?

33 **Ordinary Annuities and Annuities Due** As discussed in the text, an annuity due is identical to an ordinary annuity except that the periodic payments occur at the beginning of each period and not at the end of the period. Show that the relationship between the value of an ordinary annuity and the value of an otherwise equivalent annuity due is:

$$\text{Annuity due value} = \text{Ordinary annuity value} \times (1 + r)$$

Show this for both present and future values.

34 **Present Value of a Growing Perpetuity** What is the equation for the present value of a growing perpetuity with a payment of C one period from today if the payments grow by C each period?

35 **Rule of 72** A useful rule of thumb for the time it takes an investment to double with discrete compounding is the 'Rule of 72'. To use the Rule of 72, you simply divide 72 by the interest rate to determine the number of periods it takes for a value today to double. For example, if the interest rate is 6 per cent, the Rule of 72 says it will take 72/6 = 12 years to double. This is approximately equal to the actual answer of 11.90 years. The Rule of 72 can also be applied to determine what interest rate is needed to double money in a specified period. This is a useful approximation for many interest rates and periods. At what rate is the Rule of 72 exact? A corollary to the Rule of 72 is the Rule of 69.3. The Rule of 69.3 is exactly correct except for rounding when interest rates are compounded continuously. Prove the Rule of 69.3 for continuously compounded interest.

Exam Question (45 minutes)

1 Your new company, Rural Deliveries Inc., needs to purchase 30 small-sized trucks for its delivery service. Each truck costs £25,000 and requires a 25 per cent down payment. Your business plan forecasts the trucks being fully paid off in eight years and you wish to make monthly payments on the trucks starting one month from now. The APR of the loan is 8.5 per cent. What are the monthly payments? **(30 marks)**

2 You decide to pay off the truck loan in full after making 48 payments. The bank has indicated that early completion of your loan will incur a 2 per cent penalty. How much will you need to pay the bank today to cancel the loan? **(30 marks)**

3 Explain how you would modify the present value of an annuity shortcut formula to accommodate an equal payment stream that begins immediately. How would you change the present value of an annuity shortcut formula for an annuity that starts in year 3? How would you answer this question if the payment stream was a growing perpetuity? **(40 marks)**

Total Marks: 100

Mini Case

The MBA Decision

Suppose that Rachel Adams graduated from university three years ago with a degree in marketing. Her career goal is to become a brand manager for a major consumer goods company. She is considering two MBA programmes: at the Business School at Universidad de Negocios in Spain and the School of Business and Management at the University of Pisa in Italy.

The Universidad de Negocios is one of the top-ranked MBA programmes in Europe and requires two years of full-time enrolment. The annual tuition cost is €70,000, payable at the beginning of each school year. Books and other supplies are estimated to cost €3,000 per year. Rachel expects that, after graduation from Universidad de Negocios, she will receive a job offer for about €120,000 per year, with a €20,000 signing bonus. The salary at this job will increase at 3.5 per cent per year. Because she will be working in Spain, her average income tax rate will be 40 per cent.

The School of Business and Management at the University of Pisa offers a well-known MBA programme that requires one year of full-time enrolment. The tuition cost is €80,000, payable upon matriculation. Books and other supplies for the programme are expected to cost €4,000. Rachel thinks that she will receive an offer of €95,000 per year upon graduation, with a €15,000 signing bonus. The salary at this job will increase at 4 per cent per year. Because she will be working in the Italy, Rachel's average tax rate at this level of income will be 45 per cent.

Both schools offer a discounted health insurance plan that will cost €2,500 per year, payable at the beginning of the year. Rachel also estimates that room and board expenses will cost €18,000 per year at either school. The appropriate discount rate is 5 per cent.

1 How does Rachel's age affect her decision to get an MBA? What other, perhaps non-quantifiable, factors affect Rachel's decision to get an MBA?
2 Assuming all salaries are paid at the end of each year, what is the best option for Rachel – from a strictly financial standpoint?
3 Rachel believes that the appropriate analysis is to calculate the net present value of each option. How would you evaluate this statement?
4 What initial salary would Rachel need to receive to make her indifferent between attending Universidad de Negocios and staying in her current position?
5 Suppose, instead of being able to pay cash for her MBA, Rachel must borrow the money. The current borrowing rate is 4.8 per cent. How would this affect her decision?

Practical Case Study

1 In Yahoo! Finance, find the closing price for a company in your country. Find the price exactly four years before. What was your annual return over the last four years assuming you purchased the equity at the closing price four years ago? (Assume no dividends were paid.) Using this same return, what price will the company sell for five years from now? And 10 years from now? What if the stock price increases at 11 per cent per year? Are these figures realistic? Explain.
2 Find the share price for a company in your country by visiting Yahoo! Finance. You find an analyst who projects the share price will increase 12 per cent per year for the foreseeable future. Based on the most recent share price, if the projection holds true, when will the share price be 10 times higher? When will it be 20 times higher?

Additional Reading

Because this is an introductory chapter on discounted cash flow valuation, there are not many entry-level research papers that the reader would find of interest. However, if you are interested in a better understanding of the theoretical implications of discounted cash flow, the following paper is a worthwhile read:

Ruback, R.S. (2011) 'Downsides and DCF: Valuing Biased Cash Flow Forecasts', *Journal of Applied Corporate Finance*, Vol. 23, No. 2, 8–17.

Endnotes

1 Sometimes, financial writers merely speak of a cash flow in year x. Although this terminology is ambiguous, such writers generally mean the *end of year x*.

2 Students frequently think that C/r is the present value at date $T+1$ because the consol's first payment is at date $T+1$. However, the formula values the consol as of one period prior to the first payment.

Chapter 5
How to Value Bonds and Stocks

Learning Objectives

After reading this chapter you should be able to:

LO1 Define and describe the key elements of a bond and provide real-world examples.

LO2 Explain bond valuation methods and the factors that influence bond prices.

LO3 Apply the dividend growth model to estimate the present value of equity.

LO4 Analyse the differences and similarities between the dividend growth model and the NPVGO model.

LO5 Evaluate the accuracy and limitations of various firm valuation methods and stock market reporting practices.

When the London Stock Exchange closed for the holidays on 23 February 2023, the share price of the engineering company, Smiths Group plc, was £17.73. On the same day, the renewable energy firm, SSE plc, also closed at £17.73. Because the share prices were the same, you might expect both companies would offer the same level of dividends to shareholders, but you would be wrong. Smiths' dividend was £0.27 per share and SSE's was nearly three times that at £0.89 per share.

How would one go about estimating the value of a company's equity? Are the methods used to value debt the same? How would you value a firm? Although all the companies mentioned here have debt, finding information on their value can be difficult because companies can borrow privately (via bank loans) or publicly (via bonds). Even with public bond issues, getting bond prices is problematic because most bonds are not traded frequently.

As a financial manager, you may be asked to value firms. With the difficulties experienced in equity and bond valuation, this is no easy task. As we will see in this chapter, the dividends currently being paid are one of the primary factors we look at when attempting to value the shares of a company. We also need to consider how likely it is that earnings will grow in the future as well as the risk of a company's bonds. We begin our discussion with bond valuation and then consider equities. Finally, we look at ways in which you can value companies, even when equity and bond information is not available.

Source: phongphan/123RF.

Key Notations

C_i	Cash flow or coupon at time i	Div_i	Dividend at time i
F	Face value of a bond	g	Growth rate
R	Discount rate	EPS	Earnings per share
PV	Present value	NPVGO	Net present value of growth opportunities
T	Time period	$FCFF_i$	Free cash flow to the firm at time i

5.1 Definition and Example of a Bond

A *bond* is a certificate showing that a borrower owes a specified sum (see **Chapter 16** for more information on bonds). To repay the money, the borrower has agreed to make interest and principal payments on designated dates. For example, imagine that South African firm, Kreuger Enterprises, just issued 100,000 bonds for 10,000 rand each, where the bonds have a coupon rate of 5 per cent and a maturity of two years. Interest on the bonds is to be paid yearly, which means that:

1 R1 billion (= 100,000 × R100,000) has been borrowed by the firm

2 The firm must pay interest of R50 million (= 5% × R1 billion) at the end of one year

3 The firm must pay both R50 million of interest and R1 billion of principal at the end of two years.

Many types of bond exist in the capital markets, and issuers include corporations, private firms, banks and governments. In fact, the government bond market is one of the largest and most liquid markets in the world. Governments use bonds to manage their long- and short-term cash flow requirements and, as a result, almost every country will have government bonds. Corporate bonds are similar in structure to government bonds but, unlike governments, companies can issue both debt and equity. The corporate bond market is also smaller than the government bond market.

Table 5.1 presents a sample of bond issues. The bonds presented in Table 5.1 are all denominated in the currency of the country in which they were listed. Term to maturity is the life of the bond, and 'coupon %' is the coupon rate of the bond. For example, Table 5.1 shows that EBRD issued a one-year bond that pays interest of 7 per cent per year and each bond had a par value of R10,000. Par value is also known as face value, or principal.

The par value can be set to any amount, and you will see from Table 5.1 that the par value of the Barings bond is €1,000, whereas the United Kingdom government bond has a par value of only 1 pence. Knowing the amount borrowed and the par value allows you to calculate the number of bonds issued. So, for example, EBRD borrowed 750 million rand and since the par value was 10,000 rand this means that (750 million/10,000 =) 75,000 bonds were issued.

Table 5.1 A Sample of International Bond Issues

Borrower	Currency	Amount (millions)	Term to Maturity	Coupon (%)	Par Value
United Kingdom	Pounds	1,500	6 months	0%	£ 0.01
Goldman Sachs	Dollars	5	4 years	0%	$ 1,000
EBRD	Rand	750	1 year	7%	R 10,000
Barings	Euros	231.8	13 years	FRN	€ 1,000

Note: FRN denotes a bond with a floating coupon rate.

Bond prices are normally quoted as a percentage of the par value. So if the Barings bond was valued at €1,199 it would be quoted as 119.9. Quoting prices in percentage terms means bonds of all par values can be compared easily.

Bonds can have different types of coupons. In Table 5.1 we see that two of the bonds have a coupon of 0 per cent. This is called a zero coupon or pure discount bond. The EBRD bond has a coupon of 7 per cent, and this is known as a level or fixed coupon bond. The Barings bond has a floating rate, which ties the coupon to a benchmark rate that varies on a daily basis.

5.2 How to Value Bonds

Pure Discount Bonds

The pure discount bond is perhaps the simplest kind of bond. It promises a single payment, say £1, at a fixed future date. If the payment is one year from now, it is called a *one-year discount bond;* if it is two years from now, it is called a *two-year discount bond,* and so on.

The date when the issuer of the bond makes the last payment is called the **maturity date** of the bond, or just its *maturity* for short. The bond is said to mature or *expire* on the date of its final payment. The payment at maturity (£1 in this example) is termed the bond's **face value** or **par value**.

Pure discount bonds are often called *zero coupon bonds* to emphasize the fact that the holder receives no cash payments until maturity. We will use the terms *zero* and *discount* interchangeably to refer to bonds that pay no coupons.

The first row of Figure 5.1 shows the pattern of cash flows from a four-year pure discount bond. Note that the face value, F, is paid when the bond expires in the 48th month. There are no payments of either interest or principal prior to this date.

Figure 5.1 Different Types of Bonds

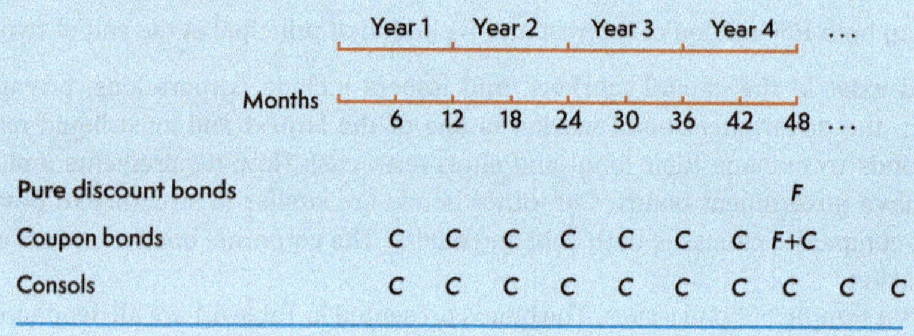

Note: C, coupon paid every six months; F, face value at year 4 (maturity for pure discount and coupon bonds).

In **Chapter 4**, we indicated that one discounts a future cash flow to determine its present value. The present value of a pure discount bond can easily be determined using the techniques covered in the previous chapter. For short, we sometimes speak of the *value* of a bond instead of its present value.

Consider a pure discount bond that pays a face value of F in T years, where the interest rate is R in each of the T years. (We also refer to this rate as the *market interest rate.*) Because the face value is the only cash flow that the bond pays, the present value of this face amount is calculated as follows:

Value of a pure discount bond:

$$PV = \frac{F}{(1+R)^T}$$

The present value formula can produce some surprising results. Suppose that the interest rate is 10 per cent. Consider a bond with a face value of €1 million that matures in 20 years.

Applying the formula to this bond, its PV is given by:

$$\begin{aligned} PV &= \frac{€1 \text{ million}}{(1.1)^{20}} \\ &= €148{,}644 \end{aligned}$$

or only about 15 per cent of the face value.

The United Kingdom government bond and Goldman Sachs corporate bond present in Table 5.1 are examples of pure discount bonds.

Level Coupon Bonds

Typical bonds issued by either governments or corporations offer cash payments not just at maturity but also at regular times in between. For example, payments on government issues and corporate bonds tend to be made every six months until the bonds mature. These payments are called the **coupons** of the bond. The middle row of Figure 5.1 illustrates the case of a four-year, *level coupon bond:* the coupon, C, is paid every six months in most countries (although annual and quarterly payments are also common) and is the same throughout the life of the bond. The EBRD bond in Table 5.1 is an example of a level coupon bond.

Note that the face value of the bond, F, is paid at maturity (end of year 4). F is sometimes called the *principal* or the *denomination*. Bonds issued in the United Kingdom typically have face values of £100,000 and, in the Eurozone, bonds tend to have face values of €1,000 or €10,000. However, this is not universally followed and, as seen in Table 5.1, can vary with the type of bond.

As we mentioned before, the value of a bond is simply the present value of its cash flows. Therefore, the value of a level coupon bond is merely the present value of its stream of coupon payments plus the present value of its repayment of principal. Because a level coupon bond is just an annuity of C each period, together with a payment at maturity of say, €1,000, the value of a level coupon bond is calculated as follows:

Value of a level coupon bond:

$$PV = \frac{C}{1+R} + \frac{C}{(1+R)^2} + \cdots + \frac{C}{(1+R)^T} + \frac{€1{,}000}{(1+R)^T}$$

where C is the coupon and the face value, F, is €1,000. The value of the bond can be rewritten like this:

Value of a level coupon bond:

$$PV = C \times A_R^T + \frac{€1{,}000}{(1+R)^T}$$

As mentioned in **Chapter 4**, $A^T{}_R$ is the present value of an annuity of €1 per period for T periods at an interest rate per period of R.

Example 5.1

Bond Prices

A five-year bond with an annual coupon of 1.375 per cent and face value of €10,000 has just been issued. The coupon is €137.5 (= 1.375% × €10,000). The face value is paid out five years from the issue date. By this we mean that the purchaser obtains claims to the following cash flows:

1	2	3	4	5
€137.5	€137.5	€137.5	€137.5	€137.5 + €10,000

If the annual interest rate is 1.48 per cent per year, what is the present value of the bond?

Our work on compounding in the previous chapter showed that the present value of the bond is:

$$PV = \frac{€137}{(1.0148)} + \frac{€137}{(1.0148)^2} + \frac{€137}{(1.0148)^3} + \frac{€137}{(1.0148)^4} + \frac{€10{,}000 + €137.5}{(1.0148)^5}$$
$$= €9950.1$$

Traders will generally quote the bond as 99.501, indicating that it is selling at 99.501 per cent of the face value of €10,000.

One final note concerning level coupon bonds: although Example 5.1 concerns corporate bonds, government bonds are identical in form. There is no difference in the pricing of government bonds and corporate bonds – the principles are exactly the same.

Consols

Not all bonds have a final maturity date. Bonds that never stop paying a coupon, have no final maturity date and therefore never mature are known as consol bonds, or consols. Thus, a consol is a perpetuity.

In the eighteenth century, the Bank of England issued 'English consols'. These were bonds the Bank of England guaranteed would pay the holder a cash flow for ever. Through wars and depressions, the Bank of England has continued to honour this commitment, and you can still buy these bonds on the London Stock Exchange today.

Consols can be valued using the perpetuity formula of the previous chapter. For example, if the market-wide interest rate is 10 per cent, a consol with a yearly interest payment of €50 is valued at:

$$\frac{€50}{0.10} = €500$$

5.3 Bond Concepts

We complete our discussion of bonds by considering two concepts concerning them. First, we examine the relationship between interest rates and bond prices. Then we define the concept of yield to maturity.

Interest Rates and Bond Prices

The discussion of level coupon bonds allows us to relate bond prices to interest rates. Consider Example 5.2:

Example 5.2

Bond Valuation

The interest rate is 10 per cent. A two-year bond with a 10 per cent coupon pays interest of £10 (= £100 × 10%). For simplicity, we assume interest is paid annually, and in this case we see that the bond is priced at its face value of £100:

$$\text{€}100 = +\frac{\text{€}10}{1.10}\frac{\text{€}100 + \text{€}10}{(1.10)^2}$$

If the interest rate unexpectedly rises to 12 per cent, the bond sells at:

$$\text{€}96.62 = +\frac{\text{€}10}{1.12}\frac{\text{€}100 + \text{€}10}{(1.12)^2}$$

Because £96.62 is less than £100, the bond is said to sell at a **discount**. This is a sensible result. Now that the interest rate is 12 per cent, a newly issued bond with a 12 per cent coupon rate will sell at £100. This newly issued bond will have coupon payments of £12 (= 0.12 × £100). Because our bond has interest payments of only £10, investors will pay less than £100 for it.

If interest rates fell to 8 per cent, the bond would sell at:

$$\text{€}103.567 = +\frac{\text{€}10}{1.08}\frac{\text{€}100 + \text{€}10}{(1.08)^2}$$

Because £103.567 is more than £100, the bond is said to sell at a premium.

Thus, we find that bond prices fall with a rise in interest rates and rise with a fall in interest rates. Furthermore, the general principle is that a level coupon bond sells in the following ways:

1 At its face value if the coupon rate is equal to the market-wide interest rate
2 At a discount if the coupon rate is below the market-wide interest rate
3 At a premium if the coupon rate is above the market-wide interest rate.

Yield to Maturity

Let us now consider the previous example *in reverse*. If our bond is selling at £103.567, what return is a bondholder receiving? We answer this by examining the following equation:

$$\text{€}103.567 = \frac{\text{€}10}{1+\gamma} + \frac{\text{€}100 + \text{€}10}{(1+\gamma)^2}$$

The unknown, γ, is the discount rate that equates the price of the bond with the discounted value of the coupons and face value. Our earlier work implies that $\gamma = 0.08$ or 8 per cent. Thus, traders state that the bond is yielding an 8 per cent return. Bond traders also say the bond has a **yield to maturity** of 8 per cent. The yield to maturity is frequently called the bond's *yield* for short. So, we would say the bond with its 10 per cent coupon is priced to yield 8 per cent at £103.567.

The Present Value Formulae for Bonds

Pure discount bonds

$$PV = \frac{F}{(1+R)^T}$$

Level coupon bonds

$$PV = C\left[\frac{1}{R} - \frac{1}{R\times(1+R)^T}\right] + \frac{F}{(1+R)^T}$$

where F is the face value.

Consols

$$PV = \frac{C}{R}$$

Real World Insight 5.1

Yield Curves and Bond Valuation

Governments regularly issue bonds to ensure their spending commitments over the short and long term are fully funded. For example, the United Kingdom government will, over the course of a year, issue bonds with terms ranging from one month to more than 50 years. Each bond will have a different yield to maturity to reflect the risk of the bond, and because risk is greater for longer-term investments, yields to maturity will tend to be higher for longer-maturity bonds.

We can plot the government yield to maturity on zero-coupon bonds against bond maturities to present this relationship succinctly. This is known as the yield curve. The UK yield curve is presented in Figure 5.2.

Bond yields have been increasing in all developed economies as inflation has returned. This has had significant implications for borrowers and lenders because it is more costly for companies to raise finance for new projects.

Figure 5.2 UK Yield Curve, February 2023

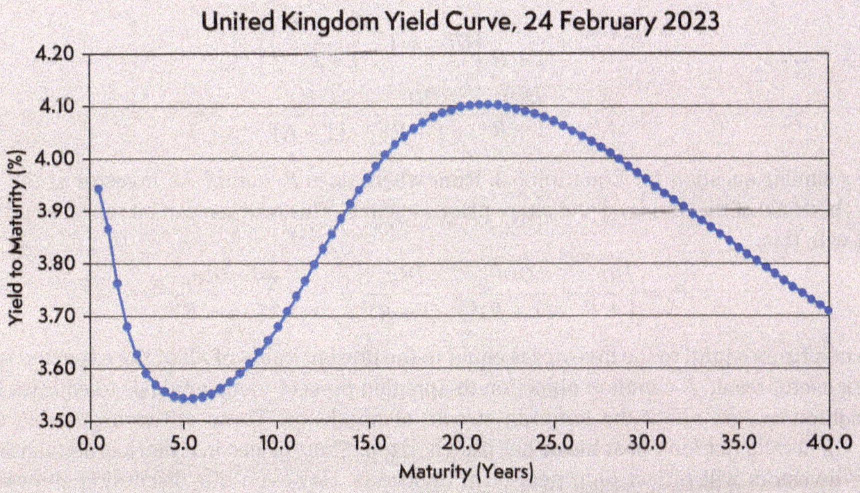

Source: Bank of England nominal government bond yield data, downloaded 24 February 2023, www.bankofengland.co.uk.

However, the bond market never stands still and it is possible that bond yields will decrease over the next few years as a result of changing economic dynamics and conditions.

If we wish to estimate the yield to maturity of a corporate bond, we would add a risk premium to the government bond yield of the same maturity to reflect the risk of the bond. We discuss corporate bond risk in much greater detail in **Chapter 16.**

5.4 The Present Value of Equity

Dividends versus Capital Gains

Our goal in this section is to value ordinary shares (see **Chapter 20** for more information). We learned in the previous chapter that an asset's value is determined by the present value of its future cash flows. Equities provide two kinds of cash flow. First, they may pay dividends on a regular basis. Second, the shareholder receives the sale price when they are sold. Thus, to value equity, we need to answer an interesting question. To which of the following is its value equal:

1 The discounted present value of the sum of next period's dividend plus next period's share price
2 The discounted present value of all future dividends?

This is the kind of question that students would love to see in a multiple-choice exam: both (1) and (2) are right.

To see that (1) and (2) are the same, let us start with an individual who will buy the equity and hold it for one year. In other words, she has a one-year *holding period.* Also, she is willing to pay P_0 for the share today. That is, she calculates:

Equation 5.1

$$P_0 = + \frac{Div}{1+R}\frac{P_1}{1+R}$$

Div_1 is the dividend paid at year's end, and P_1 is the price at year's end. P_0 is the PV of the equity investment. The term in the denominator, *R,* is the appropriate discount rate for the equity.

That seems easy enough, but from where does P_1 come? We don't pull P_1 out of thin air. Rather, there must be a buyer at the end of year 1 who is willing to purchase the equity for P_1. This buyer determines price as follows:

Equation 5.2

$$P_1 = \frac{Div_2}{1+R} + \frac{P_2}{1+R}$$

Substituting the value of P_1 from Equation 5.2 into Equation 5.1 yields:

Equation 5.3

$$P_0 = \frac{1}{1+R}\left[Div_1 + \left(\frac{Div_2 + P_2}{1+R}\right)\right]$$
$$= \frac{Div_1}{1+R} + \frac{Div_2}{(1+R)^2} + \frac{P_2}{(1+R)^2}$$

We can ask a similar question for Equation 5.3: from where does P_2 come? An investor at the end of year 2 is willing to pay P_2 because of the dividend and share price at year 3. This process can be repeated ad nauseam. In the end, we are left with this:

Equation 5.4

$$P_0 = \frac{Div_1}{1+R} + \frac{Div_1}{(1+R)^2} + \frac{Div_3}{(1+R)^3} + \cdots = \sum_{t=1}^{\infty} \frac{Div_t}{(1+R)^t}$$

Thus, the value of a firm's equity to the investor is equal to the present value of all of the expected future dividends.

This is a very useful result. A common objection to applying present value analysis to equities is that investors are too short-sighted to care about the long-run stream of dividends. These critics argue that an investor will generally not look past his or her time horizon. Thus, prices in a market dominated by short-term investors will reflect only near-term dividends. However, our discussion shows that a long-run dividend discount model holds even when investors have short investment horizons. Although an investor may want to cash out early, she must find another investor who is willing to buy. The price this second investor pays is dependent on dividends *after* his date of purchase.

Chapter 20
Page 541

Valuation of Different Types of Equities

The preceding discussion shows that the value of the firm is the present value of its future dividends. How do we apply this idea in practice? The above equation represents a very general model and is applicable regardless of whether the level of expected dividends is growing, fluctuating or constant. The general model can be simplified if the firm's dividends are expected to follow some basic patterns: (1) zero growth, (2) constant growth, and (3) differential growth. We illustrate these cases in Figure 5.3.

Figure 5.3 Zero Growth, Constant Growth and Differential Growth Patterns

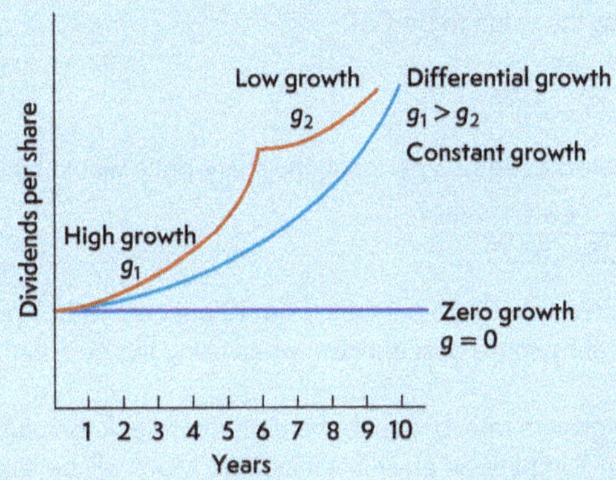

Dividend growth models:

Zero growth: $P_0 = \frac{Div_1}{R}$

Constant growth: $P_0 = \frac{Div_1}{R - g}$

Differential growth: $P_0 = \sum_{t=1}^{T} \frac{Div(1+g_1)^t}{(1+R)^t} + \frac{\frac{Div_{T+1}}{R-g_2}}{(1+R)^T}$

Case 1 (Zero Growth)

The value of an equity with a constant dividend is given by:

$$P_0 = \frac{Div_1}{1+R} + \frac{Div_2}{(1+R)^2} + \cdots = \frac{Div_1}{R}$$

Here it is assumed that $Div_1 = Div_2 = \ldots = Div$. This is just an application of the perpetuity formula from **Chapter 4**.

Case 2 (Constant Growth)

Dividends grow at rate g, as follows:

End of year dividend:

1	2	3	4	…
Div_1	$Div_1(1+g)$	$Div_1(1+g)^2$	$Div_1(1+g)^3$	

Note that Div_1 is the dividend at the end of the *first* period.

Example 5.3

Projected Dividends

Hampshire Products will pay a dividend of £4 per share a year from now. Financial analysts believe that dividends will rise at 6 per cent per year for the foreseeable future. What is the dividend per share at the end of each of the first five years? With 6 per cent growth we have this:

End of Year Dividend				
1	2	3	4	5
£4.00	£4 × (1.06) = £4.24	£4 × $(1.06)^2$ = £4.4944	£4 × $(1.06)^3$ = £4.7641	£4 × $(1.06)^4$ = £5.0499

The value of an equity security with dividends growing at a constant rate is:

$$P_0 = \frac{Div_1}{1+R} + \frac{Div_1(1+g)}{(1+R)^2} + \frac{Div_1(1+g)^2}{(1+R)^3} + \frac{Div_1(1+g)^3}{(1+R)^4} + \cdots = \frac{Div_1}{1-R}$$

where g is the growth rate. Div_1 is the dividend on the equity at the end of the first period. This is the formula for the present value of a growing perpetuity, which we derived in **Chapter 4**.

Example 5.4

Share Valuation

Suppose an investor is considering the purchase of a share of the Avila Mining Company. The equity will pay a €3 dividend a year from today. This dividend is expected to grow at 10 per cent per year ($g_1 = 15\%$) for the foreseeable future. The investor thinks that the required return (R) on this equity is 15 per cent, given her assessment of Avila Mining's risk. (We also refer to R as the discount rate for the equity.) What is the share price of Avila Mining Company?

Using the constant growth formula of case 2, we assess the value to be €60:

$$€60 = \frac{€3}{0.15 - 0.10}$$

P_0 is dependent on the value of g. If g had been estimated to be 12.5 per cent, the share price would have been:

$$€120 = \frac{€3}{0.15 - 0.125}$$

The share price doubles (from €60 to €120) when g increases only 25 per cent (from 10 per cent to 12.5 per cent). Because of P_0's dependence on g, one must maintain a healthy sense of scepticism when using this constant growth of dividends model.

Furthermore, note that P_0 is equal to infinity when the growth rate, g, equals the discount rate, R. Because share prices do not grow infinitely, an estimate of g greater than R implies an error in estimation. More will be said about this point later.

Case 3 (Differential Growth)

In this case, an algebraic formula would be too unwieldy. Instead, we present examples.

Example 5.5

Differential Growth

Consider the equity of Mint Drug Company, which has a new massage ointment and is enjoying rapid growth. The dividend per share a year from today will be €1.15. During the following four years, the dividend will grow at 15 per cent per year ($g_1 = 15\%$). After that, growth (g_2) will equal 10 per cent per year. Can you calculate the present value of the equity if the required return (R) is 15 per cent?

Figure 5.4 displays the growth in the dividends. We need to apply a two-step process to discount these dividends. We first calculate the net present value of the dividends growing at 15 per cent per annum. That is, we first calculate the present value of the dividends at the end of each of the first five years. Second, we estimate the present value of the dividends that begin at the end of year 6.

Calculate the present value of the first five dividends. The present value of dividend payments in years 1 through 5 is as follows:

Future Year	Growth Rate (g_1)	Expected Dividend (€)	Present Value (€)
1	0.15	1.15	1
2	0.15	1.3225	1
3	0.15	1.5209	1
4	0.15	1.7490	1
5	0.15	2.0114	1
Years 1–5 The present value of dividends = €5			

The growing annuity formula of **Chapter 4** could typically be used in this step. However, note that dividends grow at 15 per cent, which is also the discount rate. Because $g = R$, the growing annuity formula cannot be used in this example.

Figure 5.4 Zero Growth, Constant Growth and Differential Growth Patterns

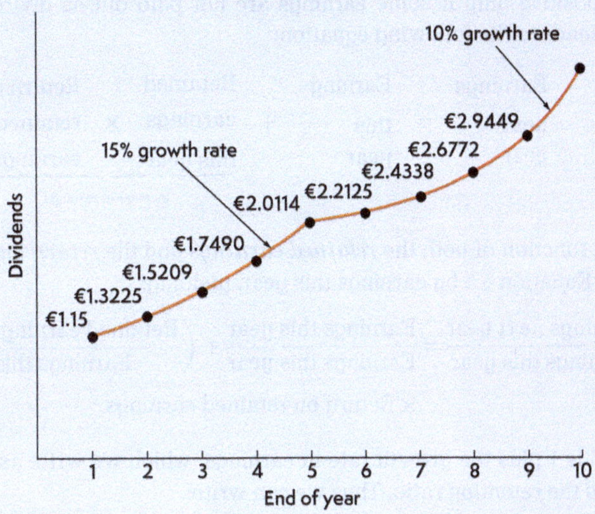

Calculate the present value of dividends beginning at the end of year 6. This is the procedure for deferred perpetuities and deferred annuities that we mentioned in **Chapter 4**. The dividends beginning at the end of year 6 are as follows:

End-of-year Dividend			
6	7	8	9
$Div_5 \times (1+g_2)$	$Div_5 \times (1+g_2)^2$	$Div_5 \times (1+g_2)^3$	$Div_5 \times (1+g_2)^4$
€2.0114 × (1.10) = €2.2125	€2.0114 × $(1.10)^2$ = €2.4338	€2.0114 × $(1.10)^3$ = €2.6772	€2.0114 × $(1.10)^4$ = €2.9449

As stated in **Chapter 4**, the growing perpetuity formula calculates the present value as of one year before the first payment. Because the payment begins at the end of year 6, the present value formula calculates the present value as of the end of year 5.

The price at the end of year 5 is given by:

$$P_5 = \frac{Div_6}{R - g_2} = \frac{€2.2125}{0.15 - 0.10}$$
$$= €44.25$$

The present value of P_5 today is:

$$\frac{P_5}{(1+R)^5} = \frac{€44.25}{(1.15)^5} = 22$$

The present value of *all* dividends today is €27 (= €22 + 5).

5.5 Estimates of Parameters in the Dividend Growth Model

The value of the firm is a function of its growth rate, g, and its discount rate, R. How do we estimate these variables?

Where Does g Come From?

The previous discussion of equities assumed that dividends grow at the rate g. We now want to estimate this rate of growth. This section extends the discussion of growth contained in **Chapter 3**. Consider a business whose earnings next year are expected to be the same as earnings this year unless a *net investment* is made. This situation is likely to occur because net investment is equal to gross, or total, investment less depreciation. A net investment of zero occurs when *total investment* equals depreciation. If the total investment is equal to depreciation, the firm's physical plant is maintained, consistent with no growth in earnings.

Net investment will be positive only if some earnings are not paid out as dividends – that is, only if some earnings are retained.[1] This leads to the following equation:

Equation 5.5

$$\text{Earnings next year} = \text{Earnings this year} + \underbrace{\text{Retained earnings this year} \times \text{Return on retained earnings}}_{\text{Increase in earnings}}$$

The increase in earnings is a function of both the *retained earnings* and the *return on the retained earnings.* We now divide both sides of Equation 5.5 by earnings this year, yielding:

Equation 5.6

$$\frac{\text{Earnings next year}}{\text{Earnings this year}} = \frac{\text{Earnings this year}}{\text{Earnings this year}} + \left(\frac{\text{Retained earnings this year}}{\text{Earnings this year}}\right) \times \text{Return on retained earnings}$$

The left side of Equation 5.6 is 1 plus the growth rate in earnings, which we write as $1 + g$. The ratio of retained earnings to earnings is called the retention ratio. Thus we can write:

Equation 5.7

$$1 + g = 1 + (\text{Retention ratio} \times \text{Return on retained earnings})$$

It is difficult for a financial analyst to determine the return to be earned on currently retained earnings: the details on forthcoming projects are not generally public information. However, it is frequently assumed that the projects selected in the current year have an anticipated return equal to returns from projects in other years. Here we can estimate the expected return on current retained earnings by the historical return on equity, or ROE. After all, ROE is merely the return on the firm's entire equity, which is the return on the accumulation of all the firm's past projects.

From Equation 5.7, we have a simple way to estimate growth:

The formula for a firm's growth rate:

Equation 5.8

$$g = \text{Retention ratio} \times \text{Return on retained earnings}$$

Previously, g referred to growth in dividends. However, the growth in earnings is equal to the growth rate in dividends in this context, because as we will presently see, the ratio of dividends to earnings is held constant.[2]

Example 5.6

Earnings Growth

Pagemaster plc just reported earnings of £2 million. It plans to retain 40 per cent of its earnings. The historical return on equity (ROE) has been 16 per cent, a figure that is expected to continue. How much will earnings grow over the coming year?

We first perform the calculation without reference to Equation 5.8. Then, we use Equation 5.8 as a check.

Calculation without reference to Equation 5.8. The firm will retain g = Retention ratio × Return on retained earnings. Assuming that historical ROE is an appropriate estimate for future returns, the anticipated increase in earnings is:

$$£800{,}000 \times 0.16 = £128{,}000$$

The percentage growth in earnings is:

$$\frac{\text{Change in earnings}}{\text{Total earnings}} = \frac{£\,128{,}000}{£\,2\text{ million}} = 0.064$$

This implies that earnings in one year will be £2,128,000 (= £2,000,000 × 1.064).

Check using Equation 5.8. We use g = Retention ratio × ROE. We have:

$$g = 0.4 \times 0.16 = 0.064$$

Where Does R Come From?

Thus far, we have taken the required return, or discount rate R, as given. We will have quite a bit to say about this subject in later chapters. For now, we want to examine the implications of the dividend growth model for this required return. Earlier we calculated P_0 as follows:

$$P_0 = Div_1/(R - g)$$

If we rearrange this to solve for R, we get:

Equation 5.9

$$R - g = Div_1/P_0$$
$$R = Div_1/P_0 + g$$

This tells us that the total return, R, has two components. The first of these, Div_1/P_0, is called the **dividend yield**. Because we calculate dividend yield as the expected cash dividend divided by the current price, it is conceptually similar to the current yield on a bond, which is the annual coupon divided by the bond's price.

The second part of the total return is the growth rate, g. As we will verify shortly, the dividend growth rate is also the rate at which the share price grows. Thus, we can interpret this growth rate as the **capital gains yield** – that is, the rate at which the value of the investment grows.

To illustrate the components of the required return, suppose we observe an equity selling for €20 per share. The next dividend will be €1 per share. You think that the dividend will grow by 10 per cent per year more or less indefinitely. What return does this equity offer you if this is correct?

The dividend growth model calculates total return as:

$$R = \text{Dividend yield} + \text{Capital gains yield}$$
$$R = Div_1/P_0 \quad + g$$

In this case, total return works out to be:

$$\begin{aligned} R &= €1/€20 + 10\% \\ &= 5\% + 10\% \\ &= 15\% \end{aligned}$$

This equity, therefore, has an expected return of 15 per cent.

We can verify this answer by calculating the price in one year, P_1, using 15 per cent as the required return. Based on the dividend growth model, this price is:

$$\begin{aligned} P_1 &= Div_1 \times (1 + g)/(R - g) \\ &= €1 \times 1.10/(0.15 - 0.10) \\ &= €1.10/0.05 \\ &= €22 \end{aligned}$$

Notice that this €22 is €20 × 1.1, so the share price has grown by 10 per cent as it should. If you pay €20 for the shares today, you will get a €1 dividend at the end of the year, and you will have a €22 – 20 = €2 gain. Your dividend yield is thus €1/20 = 5 per cent. Your capital gains yield is €2/20 = 10 per cent, so your total return would be 5 per cent + 10 per cent = 15 per cent.

To get a feel for actual numbers in this context, according to FT.com (which surveyed 24 analysts), the dividends of Siemens AG were expected to grow from €4.25 per share in 2022 to €4.40 in 2023. The share price at that time was €143.78 per share. What is the return investors required on Siemens? Here, the dividend yield is 3.06 per cent (= €4.40/€143.78), and the capital gains yield is 3.53 per cent (= [€4.40/€4.25] – 1), giving a total estimated required return of 6.59 per cent on Siemens shares.

Example 5.7

Calculating the Required Return

Pagemaster plc, the company examined in Example 5.6, has 1,000,000 shares outstanding. The equity is selling at £10. What is the required return on the shares?

Because the retention ratio is 40 per cent, the payout ratio is 60 per cent (= 1 – retention ratio). The payout ratio is the ratio of dividends/earnings. Because earnings one year from now will be £2,128,000 (= £2,000,000 × 1.064), dividends will be £1,276,800 (= 0.60 × £2,128,000). Dividends per share will be £1.28 (= £1,276,800/1,000,000). Given our previous result that $g = 0.064$, we calculate R from Equation 5.9 as follows:

$$0.192 = \frac{€1.28}{10.00} + 0.064$$

A Healthy Sense of Scepticism

Our approach merely *estimates g*; it does not *determine g* precisely. The one-year growth rate may not be the appropriate estimate of a long-term sustainable growth rate. For example, if one were to use the growth rate in Siemens dividends between 2018 (Div = €3.80) and 2019 (Div = €5.91) as the estimate of g, we would have recorded a growth rate for the company of 55.56 per cent, not 3.53 per cent. A possible solution is to consider growth rates over a longer period. So, in the case of Siemens, the dividend in 2018 was €3.80 and in 2022 it was €4.25. We could, for example, calculate an annual geometric growth rate of 2.84 per cent ($= (4.25/3.80)^{(1/4)} - 1$).

We base our estimate of g on a number of assumptions. For example, we assume the return on reinvestment of future retained earnings is equal to the firm's past ROE. We also assume the future retention ratio to be equal to the past retention ratio. Our estimate of g will be off if these assumptions prove to be wrong.

Unfortunately, the determination of R is highly dependent on g. For example, if g is estimated to be 0 in Example 5.6, R equals 12.8 per cent (= £1.28/£10.00). If g is 12 per cent, R equals 24.8 per cent (= £1.28/£10.00 + 12%). Thus, one should view estimates of R with a healthy sense of scepticism.

Because of the preceding, some financial economists generally argue that the estimation error for R on a single security is too large to be practical. Therefore, they suggest calculating the average R for an entire industry. This R would then be used to discount the dividends of a particular equity in the same industry.

One should be particularly sceptical of two extreme cases when estimating R for individual securities. First, consider a firm currently paying no dividend. The share price will be above zero because investors believe the firm may initiate a dividend or be acquired in the future. However, when a firm goes from no dividends to a positive number of dividends, the implied growth rate is *infinite*. Thus, Equation 5.9 must be used with extreme caution here, if at all – a point we emphasize later in this chapter.

Second, we mentioned earlier that the value of the firm is infinite when g is equal to R. Because share prices do not grow infinitely, an analyst whose estimate of g for a particular firm is equal to or above R will be wrong. Firms cannot maintain an abnormally high growth rate *for ever.*

Real World Insight 5.2

Estimating the Dividend Growth Rate of Apple Inc.

How do you value Apple? In recent years, Apple has seen sustained growth in its dividends, as shown below.

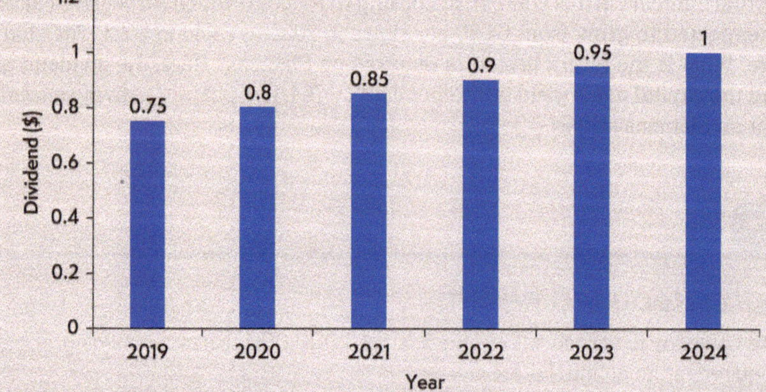

Figure 5.5 Apple Inc Dividend

At time of writing, the figures for 2023 and 2024 are estimates. To value Apple, we must estimate its growth in dividends. We have several options. We could use annual growth rate estimates as presented below:

Year	2020	2021	2022	2023	2024
Dividend	\$0.75	\$0.80	\$0.85	\$0.90	\$1.00
Annual Growth Rate	6.67%	6.25%	5.88%	5.56%	5.26%

Alternatively, we could calculate a long-term growth rate based on the five-year period between 2019 and the forecast 2024 dividend:

$$\text{Long-Term Growth Rate} = \left(\frac{\$0.75}{\$1.00}\right)^{\left(\frac{1}{5}\right)} - 1 = 5.92\%$$

For Apple, our growth estimates are between 5.26 and 6.67 per cent, and we would centre our initial analysis within this range. However, past performance may not reflect future performance and Apple will face a number of uncertainties over the coming years. As an analyst, you would start off with a baseline growth rate and adapt it to fit your expectations of the future.

5.6 Growth Opportunities

We previously spoke of the growth rate of dividends. We now want to address the related concept of growth opportunities. Imagine a company with a level stream of earnings per share in perpetuity. The company pays all of these earnings out to shareholders as dividends.

Hence we have:

$$\text{EPS} = Div$$

where *EPS* is *earnings per share* and *Div* is dividends per share. A company of this type is frequently called a *cash cow*.

The perpetuity formula of **Chapter 4** gives the value of a share of equity:

Value of a share of equity when a firm acts as a cash cow:

$$\frac{\text{EPS}}{R} = \frac{Div}{R}$$

where R is the discount rate on the firm's equity.

This policy of paying out all earnings as dividends may not be the optimal one. Many firms have *growth* opportunities: opportunities to invest in profitable projects. Because these projects can represent a significant fraction of the firm's value, it would be foolish to forgo them to pay out all earnings as dividends.

Although firms frequently think in terms of a *set* of growth opportunities, let us focus on only one opportunity – that is, the opportunity to invest in a single project. Suppose the firm retains the entire dividend at date 1 to invest in a particular capital budgeting project. The net present value *per share* of the project as of date 0 is *NPVGO*, which stands for the *net present value (per share) of the growth opportunity*.

What is the share price at date 0 if the firm decides to take on the project at date 1? Because we add the per share value of the project to the original share price, the share price must now be:

The share price after the firm commits to a new project:

Equation 5.10

$$\frac{\text{EPS}}{R} + NPVGO$$

Thus Equation 5.10 shows we can view the share price as the sum of two different items. The first term (*EPS/R*) is the value of the firm if it rested on its laurels – that is, if it distributed all earnings to the shareholders. The second term is the *additional* value if the firm retains earnings to fund new projects.

Example 5.8

Growth Opportunities

Sarro Shipping plc expects to earn £1 million per year in perpetuity if it undertakes no new investment opportunities. There are 100,000 shares of equity outstanding, so earnings per share equal £10 (=£1,000,000/100,000). The firm will have a chance at date 1 to spend £1,000,000 on a new marketing campaign. The new campaign will increase earnings in every subsequent period by £210,000 (or £2.10 per share), which is a 21 per cent return per year on the project. The firm's discount rate is 10 per cent. What is the share price before and after deciding to accept the marketing campaign?

The share price of Sarro Shipping before the campaign is:

The share price of Sarro when firm acts as a cash cow:

$$\frac{EPS}{R} = \frac{€10}{0.1} = €100$$

The value of the marketing campaign as of date 1 is:

Value of marketing campaign at date 1:

Equation 5.11

$$-€1{,}000{,}000 + \frac{€210{,}000}{0.1} = €1{,}100{,}000$$

Because the investment is made at date 1 and the first cash inflow occurs at date 2, Equation 5.11 represents the value of the marketing campaign as of date 1. We determine the value at date 0 by discounting back one period as follows:

Value of marketing campaign at date 0:

$$\frac{€1{,}100{,}000}{1.1} = €1{,}000{,}000$$

Thus NPVGO per share is £10 (= £1,000,000/100,000).

The share price is:

$$EPS/R + NPVGO = €100 + 10 = €110$$

The calculation in our example can also be made on a straight net present value basis. Because all the earnings at date 1 are spent on the marketing effort, no dividends are paid to shareholders on that date. Dividends in all subsequent periods are £1,210,000 (= £1,000,000 + £210,000). In this case, £1,000,000 is the annual dividend when Sarro is a cash cow. The additional contribution to the dividend from the marketing effort is £210,000. Dividends per share are £12.10 (= £1,210,000/100,000). Because these dividends start at date 2, the share price at date 1 is £121 (= £12.10/0.1). The share price at date 0 is £110 (= £121/1.1).

Note that value is created in this example because the project earned a 21 per cent rate of return when the discount rate was only 10 per cent. No value would have been created had the project earned a 10 per cent rate of return. The NPVGO would have been zero, and value would have been negative had the project earned a percentage return below 10 per cent. The NPVGO would be negative in that case.

Two conditions must be met to increase value:

1. Earnings must be retained so that projects can be funded[3]
2. The projects must have a positive net present value.

Surprisingly, some companies seem to invest in projects known to have *negative* net present values. For example, some firms may engage in corporate social responsibility initiatives that involve investments in environmental or social causes and may not generate a positive net present value. In such cases, the firm may justify the investment on the basis of its long-term benefits to the environment, society or the company's reputation.

Given that NPV analysis (such as that presented in **Chapter 4**) is common knowledge in business, why would managers choose projects with negative NPVs? One conjecture is that some managers enjoy controlling a large company. Because paying dividends in place of reinvesting earnings reduces the size of the firm, some managers find it emotionally challenging to pay high dividends.

Growth in Earnings and Dividends versus Growth Opportunities

As mentioned earlier, a firm's value increases when it invests in growth opportunities with positive NPVGOs. A firm's value falls when it selects opportunities with negative NPVGOs. However, dividends can grow whether projects with positive NPVs or negative NPVs are chosen. We explain this surprising result with the following example.

Example 5.9

NPV versus Dividends

Lane Supermarkets, a new firm, will earn €100,000 a year in perpetuity if it pays out all its earnings as dividends. However, the firm plans to invest 20 per cent of its earnings in projects that earn 10 per cent per year. The discount rate is 18 per cent. An earlier formula tells us that the growth rate of dividends is:

$$g = \text{Retention ratio} \times \text{Return on retained earnings} = 0.2 \times 0.10 = 2\%$$

For example, in this first year of the new policy, dividends are €80,000 [= (1 − 0.2) × €100,000]. Dividends next year are €81,600 (= €80,000 × 1.02). Dividends the following year are €83,232 [= €80,000 × $(1.02)^2$] and so on.[2] Because dividends represent a fixed percentage of earnings, earnings must grow at 2 per cent a year as well.

However, note that the policy reduces value because the rate of return on the projects of 10 per cent is less than the discount rate of 18 per cent. That is, the firm would have had a higher value at date 0 if it had a policy of paying all its earnings out as dividends. Thus, a strategy of investing in projects with negative NPVs rather than paying out earnings as dividends will lead to growth in dividends and earnings but will reduce value.

Dividends or Earnings: Which to Discount?

As mentioned earlier, this chapter applied the growing perpetuity formula to the valuation of equity. In our application, we discounted dividends, not earnings, and this is sensible because investors select shares for what they can get out of them. They get only two things out of shares: dividends and the ultimate sale price, which is determined by what future investors expect to receive in dividends.

The estimated share price would be too high were earnings to be discounted instead of dividends. As we saw in our estimation of a firm's growth rate, only a portion of earnings goes to the shareholders as dividends. The remainder is retained to generate future dividends. In our model, retained earnings are equal to the firm's investment. To discount earnings instead of dividends would be to ignore the investment a firm must make today to generate future returns.

The No-dividend Firm

Students frequently ask the following question: If the dividend discount model is correct, why aren't no dividend shares selling at zero? This is a good question and gets at the goals of the firm. A firm with many growth opportunities faces a dilemma. The firm can pay out dividends now, or it can forgo dividends now so that it can make investments that will generate even greater dividends in the future. This is often a painful choice because a strategy of dividend deferment may be optimal yet unpopular among certain shareholders.

Many firms choose to pay no dividends – and these firms sell at favourable prices. For example, most internet firms, such as Meta, Dropbox, Amazon, Alphabet and Netflix, pay no dividends. Rational shareholders believe that either they will receive dividends at some point or they will receive something just as good. That is, the firm will be acquired in a merger, with the shareholders receiving either cash or shares of equity at that time.

Of course, the actual application of the dividend discount model is difficult for firms of this type and the model for constant growth of dividends does not apply. Though the differential growth model can work in theory, the difficulties of estimating the date of the first dividend, the growth rate of dividends after that date and the ultimate merger price make application of the model quite tricky in reality.

Empirical evidence suggests that firms with high growth rates are likely to pay lower dividends, a result consistent with the analysis here. For example, consider Apple Inc. The company made its first dividend (ignoring the early years of the firm) in 2012, even though it was a billion-dollar company in both sales and market value of shareholders' equity before that date. Why did Apple wait so long to pay a dividend? It waited because it had excellent growth opportunities to exploit.

5.7 The Dividend Growth Model and the NPVGO Model

This chapter has revealed that the share price is the sum of its per-share value as a cash cow plus the per-share value of its growth opportunities. Example 5.8 illustrated this formula using only one growth opportunity. We also used the growing perpetuity formula to price an equity security with steady growth in dividends. When we apply the formula to shares, it is typically called the *dividend growth model*. A steady increase in dividends results from a continual investment in growth opportunities, not just investment in a single opportunity. Therefore, it is worthwhile to compare the dividend growth model with the *NPVGO model* when growth occurs through continual investing.

We can use an example to illustrate the main points. Suppose Manama Books has EPS of €10 at the end of the first year, a dividend payout ratio of 40 per cent, a discount rate of 16 per cent and a return on its retained earnings of 20 per cent. Because the firm retains some of its earnings each year, it is selecting growth opportunities each year. This is different from Sarro Shipping in Example 5.8, which had a growth opportunity in only one year. We wish to calculate the price per share using both the dividend growth model and the NPVGO model.

The Dividend Growth Model

The dividends at date 1 are 0.40 × €10 = €4 per share. The retention ratio is 0.60 (1 – 40), implying a growth rate in dividends of 0.12 (= 0.60 × 0.20).

From the dividend growth model, the price of a share today is:

$$\frac{Div_1}{R-g}=\frac{€4}{0.16-0.12}=€100$$

The NPVGO Model

Using the NPVGO model, it is more difficult to value a firm with growth opportunities each year (like Manama) than a firm with growth opportunities in only one year (like Sarro). To value according to the NPVGO model, we need to calculate on a per-share basis (1) the net present value of a single growth opportunity, (2) the net present value of all growth opportunities, and (3) the share price if the firm acts as a cash cow – that is, the value of the firm without these growth opportunities. The value of the firm is the sum of (2) + (3).

1 *Value per share of a single growth opportunity:* Out of the earnings per share of €10 at date 1, the firm retains €6 (= 0.6 × €10) at that date. The firm earns €1.20 (= €6 × 0.20) per year in perpetuity on that €6 investment.

We calculate the NPV from the investment as follows:

Per-share NPV generated from investment at date 1:

Equation 5.12

$$-€6=\frac{€1.20}{0.16}=€1.50$$

That is, the firm invests €6 to reap €1.20 per year on the investment. The earnings are discounted at 16 per cent, implying a value per share from the project of €1.50. Because the investment occurs at date 1 and the first cash flow occurs at date 2, €1.50 is the value of the investment at *date 1*. In other words, the NPV from the date 1 investment has *not* yet been brought back to date 0.

2 *Value per share of all opportunities:* As pointed out earlier, the growth rate of earnings and dividends is 12 per cent. Because retained earnings are a fixed percentage of total earnings, retained earnings must also grow at 12 per cent a year. That is, retained earnings at date 2 are €6.72 (= €6 × 1.12), retained earnings at date 3 are €7.5264 [= €6 × $(1.12)^2$], and so on.

Let us analyse the retained earnings at date 2 in more detail. Because projects will always earn 20 per cent per year, the firm earns €1.344 (= €6.72 × 0.20) in each future year on the €6.72 investment at date 2.

Here is the NPV from the investment:

NPV per share generated from investment at date 2:

Equation 5.13

$$-€6.72=\frac{€1.344}{€0.16}=€1.68$$

€1.68 is the NPV as of date 2 of the investment made at date 2. The NPV from the date 2 investment has *not* yet been brought back to date 0.

Now consider the retained earnings at date 3 in more detail. The firm earns €1.5053 (= €7.5264 × 0.20) per year on the investment of €7.5264 at date 3.

The NPV from the investment is thus:

NPV per share generated from investment at date 3:

Equation 5.14

$$-€7.5264 = \frac{€1.5053}{0.16} = €1.882$$

From Equations 5.12, 5.13 and 5.14, the NPV per share of all of the growth opportunities, discounted back to date 0, is:

Equation 5.15

$$\frac{€1.50}{1.16} + \frac{€1.68}{(1.16)^2} + \frac{€1.882}{(1.16)^3} + \cdots$$

Because it has an infinite number of terms, this expression looks quite difficult to compute. However, there is an easy simplification. Note that retained earnings are growing at 12 per cent per year. Because all projects earn the same rate of return per year, the NPVs in Equations 5.12, 5.13 and 5.14 are also growing at 12 per cent per year. Hence, we can write Equation 5.15 as:

$$\frac{€1.50}{1.16} + \frac{€1.50 \times 1.12}{(1.16)^2} + \frac{€1.50 \times (1.12)}{(1.16)^3} + \cdots$$

This is a growth perpetuity whose value is:

$$\text{NPVGO} = \frac{€1.50}{0.16 - 0.12} = €37.50$$

Because the first NPV of €1.50 occurs at date 1, the NPVGO is €37.50 as of date 0. In other words, the firm's policy of investing in new projects from retained earnings has an NPV of €37.50.

3 *Value per share if the firm is a cash cow:* We now assume that the firm pays out all of its earnings as dividends. The dividends would be €10 per year in this case. Because there would be no growth, the value per share would be evaluated by the perpetuity formula:

$$\frac{Div}{R} = \frac{€10}{0.16} = €62.50$$

Summation

Equation 5.10 states that share price is the value of a cash cow plus the value of the growth opportunities. This is:

$$€100 = €62.50 + €37.50$$

Hence, value is the same whether calculated by a discounted dividend approach or a growth opportunities approach. The share prices from the two approaches must be equal because they are different yet equivalent methods of applying concepts of present value.

5.8 Stock Market Reporting

If you visit Yahoo! Finance, Reuters or FT.com, you will find information about a large number of equities in several different markets. Figure 5.6 presents a typical report of the Antofagasta plc London Stock Exchange listing from 24 February 2023. Information on most listed equities is reported in the same way.

Notice that the currency is GBX, which is British pence (1,557.50). To convert into pounds you would divide the figure by 100 (£15.575). The table also shows that the price has fallen from the previous day's closing price of £15.825 but the price has varied between £13.84 and £18.375 over the previous 52 weeks. The average trading volume of Antofagasta is 1,849,641 shares traded a day. The beta of Antofagasta plc is a measure of risk, which will be discussed in much greater detail in **Chapter 10.**

Chapter 10
Page 260

The opening price of £15.805 is the price at which the equity started trading on 24 February 2023. The bid and ask prices are the prices for which an investor can sell and buy Antofagasta plc shares on the London Stock Exchange. Looking at the variation in prices over the previous six months illustrates the volatility of Antofagasta share prices.

Figure 5.6 Stock Market Listing for Antofagasta plc on 24 February 2023

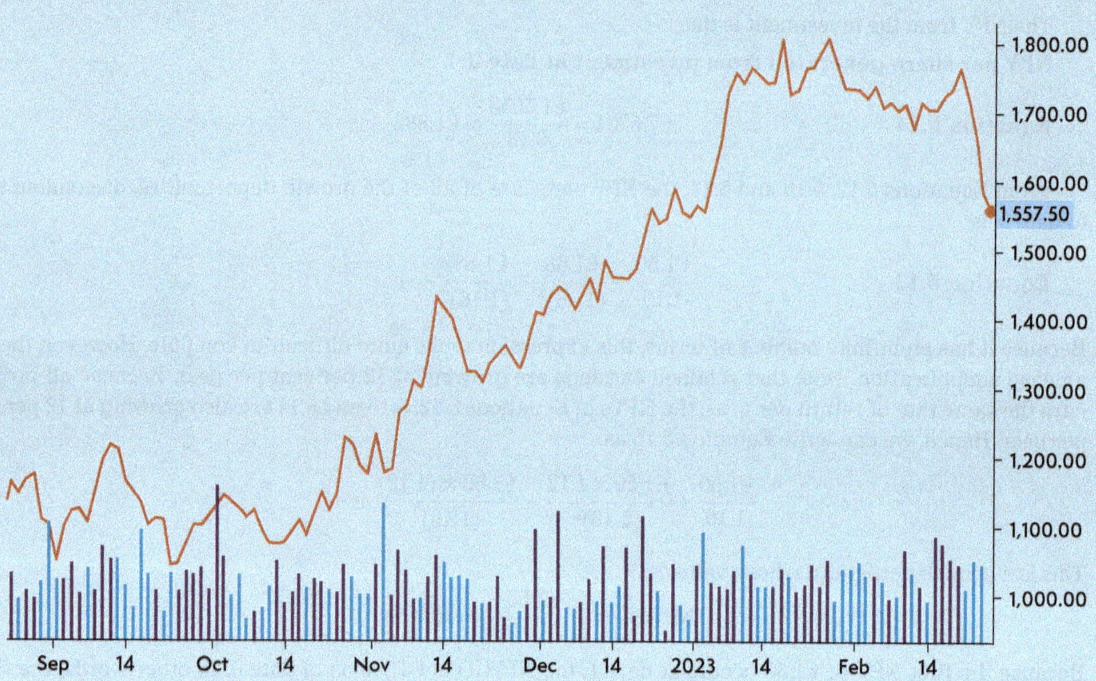

Previous close	1,582.50	Market cap	15.78B
Open	1,580.50	Beta (%Y monthly)	1.07
Bid	1,559.00 × 0	PE ratio (TTM)	12.19
Ask	1,561.00 × 0	EPS (TTM)	1.28
Day's range	1,552.50 – 1,600.00	Earnings date	Feb 21. 2023
52-week range	13.84 – 1,837.50	Forward dividend & yield	0.50 (2.98%)
Volume	427,679	Ex-dividend date	Apr 20, 2023
Avg. volume	1,849,641	1Y target est.	15.07

Source: Recreated from actual historical data, Yahoo! Finance.

Antofagasta plc is one of the largest companies in the UK, and the total value of Antofagasta's shares was £15.7 billion. The earnings per share of Antofagasta over the past 12 months (TTM stands for 'Trailing Twelve Months') were £1.28.

Sustainability in Action 5.1

Enel's Green Power Revolution

Enel, an Italian multinational energy company, has demonstrated its commitment to sustainability and the United Nations Sustainable Development Goals (SDGs) through its strategic focus on renewable energy. In 2015, Enel announced its plan to invest €18 billion in emerging markets such as Latin America and Africa, and to double capacity at its green power division, significantly reducing its dependence on fossil fuels.

By 2023, Enel had increased its renewable energy capacity to 51 GW, making it one of the world's largest renewable energy producers. The company's shift to clean energy not only lowered its carbon emissions but also generated value for shareholders, with a 43 per cent increase in its share price between 2015 and 2023, proving that sustainable business practices can create long-term value for investors.

5.9 Firm Valuation

A look back at **Chapter 1** shows that the assets of a firm are equal in value to the sum of a firm's liabilities and equity. Using the techniques in this chapter to value bonds and equities can assist you in the valuation process. However, firm valuation is a very imprecise science and the range of uncertainties the financial manager faces can make the task a very formidable one. In this section, we consider the most common approaches used in practice.

Valuation of a Firm's Cash Flows

Suppose you are a business appraiser trying to determine the value of small companies. How can you determine what a firm is worth? One way to think about the question of how much a firm is worth is to calculate the present value of its future cash flows.

Let us consider the example of a firm that is expected to generate net cash flows (cash inflows minus cash outflows) of £5,000 in the first year and £2,000 for each of the next five years. The firm can be sold for £10,000 in seven years. The owners of the firm would like to be able to make 10 per cent on their investment in the firm.

We find the value of the firm by multiplying the net cash flows by the appropriate present value factor. The value of the firm is the sum of the present values of the individual net cash flows.

The present value of the net cash flows is next.

The Present Value of the Firm			
End of Year	Net Cash Flow of the Firm (€)	Present Value Factor (10%)	Present Value of Net Cash Flows (€)
1	5,000	0.90909	4,545.45
2	2,000	0.82645	1,652.90
3	2,000	0.75131	1,502.62
4	2,000	0.68301	1,366.02
5	2,000	0.62092	1,241.84
6	2,000	0.56447	1,128.94
7	10,000	0.51316	5,131.58
		PV of firm	**16,569.35**

We can also use the simplifying formula for an annuity:

$$\frac{€5{,}000}{1.1} + \frac{(2{,}000 \times A_{0.10}^{5})}{1.1} + \frac{10{,}000}{(1.1)^7} = €16{,}569.35$$

Suppose you have the opportunity to acquire the firm for £12,000. Should you buy it? The answer is yes because the NPV is positive:

$$NPV = PV - \text{Cash}$$
$$€4{,}569.35 = €16{,}569.35 - €12{,}000$$

The incremental value (NPV) of acquiring the firm is £4,569.35.

Example 5.10

Firm Valuation

Del Piero's Pizza Company is contemplating investing €1 million in four new outlets in Italy. Mr Prandelli, the firm's chief financial officer (CFO), has estimated that the investments will pay out cash flows of €200,000 per year for nine years and nothing after that. (The cash flows will occur at the end of each year, and there will be no cash flow after year 9.) Mr Prandelli has determined that the relevant discount rate for this investment is 15 per cent. The discount rate of 15 per cent is the rate of return the firm can earn on comparable projects. Should Del Piero make the investments in the new outlets?

We evaluate the decision as follows:

$$\begin{aligned} NPV &= -€1{,}000{,}000 + \frac{€200{,}000}{1.15} + \frac{€200{,}000}{(1.15)^2} + \dots + \frac{€200{,}000}{(1.15)^9} \\ &= -€1{,}000{,}000 + €200{,}000 \times A_{0.15}^{9} \\ &= -€1{,}000{,}000 + €954{,}316.78 \\ &= -€45{,}683.22 \end{aligned}$$

The present value of the four new outlets is only €954,316.78. The outlets are worth less than they cost. Del Piero should not invest because the NPV is −€45,683.22. If Del Piero requires a 15 per cent rate of return, the new outlets are not a good investment.

Chapter 3
Page 60

When valuing another firm, the financial manager will not typically have estimates of future cash flows to hand. As a result, other sources of information must be used. **Chapter 3** illustrated the use of financial statements in assessing a firm's performance and growth rate. If the firm is listed on a stock exchange, past share price performance and volatility can also be used. Finally, comparative information on a firm's peers is necessary to calibrate your initial valuations.

The Price–Earnings Ratio

Chapter 3
Page 60

We argued earlier that one should not discount earnings to determine the share price. Nevertheless, financial analysts frequently relate earnings and share price, as made evident by their heavy reliance on the price–earnings, or PE, ratio (see **Chapter 3,** Section 3.7 for more information).

Our previous discussion stated that:

$$\text{Price per share} = \frac{EPS}{R} + NPVGO$$

Dividing by *EPS* yields the following:

$$\frac{\text{Price per share}}{\text{EPS}} = \frac{1}{R} + \frac{NPVGO}{\text{EPS}}$$

The left side is the formula for the price–earnings ratio. The equation shows that the PE ratio is related to the net present value of growth opportunities. As an example, consider two firms, each having just reported earnings per share of £1. However, one firm has many valuable growth opportunities, whereas the other firm has no growth opportunities at all. The firm with growth opportunities should sell at a higher price because an investor is buying both current income of £1 and growth opportunities. Suppose that the firm with growth opportunities sells for £16 and the other firm sells for £8. The £1 earnings per share number appears in the denominator of the PE ratio for both firms. Thus, the PE ratio is 16 for the firm with growth opportunities but only 8 for the firm without the opportunities.

This explanation seems to hold reasonably well in the real world. Electronic and other high-tech shares generally sell at very high PE ratios (or *multiples,* as they are often called) because they are perceived to have high growth rates. Some technology shares sell at high prices even though the companies have never earned a profit. Conversely, railroads, utilities and steel companies sell at lower multiples because of the prospects of lower growth. The average PE ratio for the FTSE 100 has been approximately 14, but this has historically varied from a high of 34.2 (September 2016) to a low of 7.4 (March 2009).

Of course, the market is merely pricing *perceptions* of the future, not the future itself. We will argue later in the text that the stock market generally has realistic perceptions of a firm's prospects. However, this is not always true. In the late 1960s, many electronics firms were selling at multiples of 200 times earnings. The high perceived growth rates did not materialize, causing a significant decline in share prices during the early 1970s. In earlier decades, fortunes were made in equities like IBM and Xerox because investors had not anticipated high growth rates. More recently, we experienced the dotcom collapse in 2001, when many internet stocks were trading at multiples of thousands of times annual earnings. In fact, most internet stocks had zero or negative earnings.

There is an additional factor that explains the PE ratio, and this is the discount rate, *R*. The previous formula shows that the PE ratio is *negatively* related to the firm's discount rate. We have already suggested that the discount rate is positively associated with the equity's risk or variability. Thus the PE ratio is negatively related to the equity's risk. To see that this is a sensible result, consider two firms, A and B, behaving as cash cows. The stock market *expects* both firms to have annual earnings of €1 per share for ever. However, the earnings of firm A are known with certainty, whereas the earnings of firm B are quite variable. A rational investor is likely to pay more for a share of firm A because of the absence of risk. If a share of equity in firm A sells at a higher price and both firms have the same EPS, the PE ratio of firm A must be higher.

Market Multiples Valuation

Many analysts use financial ratios like PE as a simple approach to valuing companies. The rationale is that if the financial markets are efficient, companies with similar characteristics will have similar values. Thus, two companies in the same industry with similar performance would be expected to have a similar PE ratio. There are a number of common valuation multiples in use and the most used are presented in Table 5.2.

Table 5.2 Common Valuation Multiples

Price Multiples	Enterprise Value (EV) Multiples	Other Ratios
Price/Earnings	EV/EBITDA	Dividend Yield
Price/Book Value of Equity	EV/Operating Profit	PEG (PE/Growth)
Price/Market Value of Equity		
Price/Cash Flow		
Price/Sales		

Note: Enterprise Value = Debt + Equity – Cash and Equivalents.

To value a firm using the multiples approach, you would first identify its peers in the industry. For each peer, calculate the valuation multiple and take an average of the multiple across the peers. This would become the benchmark valuation multiple for your target company, which allows you to value your firm. It is important to use forecasted figures in your valuations to reflect the future performance of the firm rather than the past.

Real World Insight 5.3

Valuing Eni Using PE Ratios

Eni SpA is an Italian gas firm and one of the largest in Europe. According to the Eni corporate website, its closest peers in terms of size (equity market capitalization) and industry are: Equinor ($79 billion), ConocoPhillips ($70 billion) and Anadarko ($31 billion). Eni has an equity market capitalization of $64 billion.

The PE ratios of Equinor, ConocoPhillips and Anadarko are 11.1, 12.8 and 17.4, giving an average PE ratio of 13.8 for Eni's peers.

Eni's net income was $6.845 billion, suggesting that its firm value should be ($6.845 billion × 13.8 =) $94.461 billion. Eni's equity market capitalization was $59.62 billion and its debt was $27.66 billion, giving a total estimated value of $87.28 billion.

On first reading, it looks like Eni is undervalued and represented a good investment.

Free Cash Flow to the Firm

In many countries, firms repurchase from shareholders as a substitute for paying dividends.[4] This makes the dividend valuation models presented in this chapter more challenging to implement because we must not only value dividends but also the present value of future share repurchases. An alternative solution is to value the cash flows that

Chapter 3 Page 60

accrue to the firm after removing the effect of financing. We do this through the statement of cash flows that is provided every year in the financial accounts (see **Chapter 3**). We can calculate free cash flow to the firm (FCFF) from either statement of profit and loss or statement of cash flows. Under International Accounting Standards, it is relatively straightforward to arrive at FCFF from the statement of cash flows, and this is what we will do in this section. The formula for FCFF (taking outflows as negative) is as follows:

Equation 5.16

$$\text{FCFF} = \text{Cash flow from operations} + \text{Cash flow from investing activities}$$

Under International Accounting Standards, firms will typically include interest expense under the heading *Cash Flow from Financing Activities*. However, firms have the option to include interest under *Cash Flow from Operations* if it is viewed to be part of a firm's operations. When this is the case, Equation 5.16 should be modified as follows:

Equation 5.17

$$\begin{aligned}\text{FCFF} = {} & \text{Cash flow from operations} + \text{Cash flow from investing activities} \\ & + \text{Net interest payment} \times (1 - \text{Tax rate})\end{aligned}$$

Example 5.11

Free Cash Flow to the Firm

Fresnillo plc is one of the world's largest mining firms, with particular strengths in silver and gold. It had the following statement of cash flows ($ millions) for 2017. What is the free cash flow to the firm?

Cash flow from operations	761
Cash flow from investing activities	–340
Cash flow from financing activities	–253

We calculate FCFF as follows:

$$\text{FCFF} = \$\,761 - \$\,340 = \$\,421 \text{ million}$$

Once we have calculated FCFF, it is a simple matter to discount the cash flows using the appropriate discount for the firm's operations. It is important to note that the discount rate used in the free cash flow valuation method will be different from the rate used for the dividend growth model. This is because the FCFF discount rate reflects the risk of the firm, whereas the discount rate used in the dividend growth model reflects the risk of the firm's equity. When a firm has no debt, the two discount rates will be the same.[5]

Example 5.12

FCFF Valuation

In Example 5.11, we estimated that Fresnillo plc had a FCFF of $421 million. If the appropriate discount rate for Fresnillo is 12 per cent and the company's cash flows are expected to grow at 7 per cent every year, what was the value of Fresnillo?

To estimate the value of Fresnillo we use the following valuation formula:

$$V_0 = \frac{\text{FCFF}_1}{r-g} = \frac{\text{FCFF}_0(1+g)}{r-g} = \frac{\$421\,(1.07)}{0.12-0.07}$$
$$= \$\,9{,}009.4 \text{ million}$$

If we compare the FCFF Fresnillo valuation to the actual market value, we are not far off in our estimate. In 2019, Fresnillo had a total equity market capitalization of $8.26 billion and total long-term debt of $1.02 billion, which is equal to a total firm value of $9.28 billion.

Although our calculation is not too far from the actual firm value, we still need to be careful about our assumptions regarding each of the formula's inputs.

Summary and Conclusions

In this chapter, we used general present value formulae from the previous chapter to price bonds and equities.

1 Pure discount bonds and perpetuities can be viewed as polar cases of bonds. The value of a pure discount bond (also called a zero coupon bond) is:

$$PV = \frac{F}{(1+R)^T}$$

The value of a perpetuity (also called a ***consol***) is:

$$PV = \frac{C}{R}$$

2 Level payment bonds can be viewed as an intermediate case. The coupon payments form an annuity, and the principal repayment is a lump sum. The value of this type of bond is the sum of the values of its two parts.

3 The yield to maturity on a bond is the single rate that discounts the payments on the bond to its purchase price.

4 An equity can be valued by discounting its dividends. We mentioned three types of situation:

(a) The case of zero growth of dividends

(b) The case of constant growth of dividends

(c) The case of differential growth.

5 An estimate of the growth rate of an equity is needed for the formulae for situations 4(b) or 4(c). A useful estimate of the growth rate is

$$g = \text{Retention ratio} \times \text{Return on retained earnings}$$

6 It is worthwhile to view a share as the sum of its worth if the company behaves like a cash cow (the company does no investing) and the value per share of its growth opportunities. We write the value of a share as:

$$\frac{EPS}{R} + NPVGO$$

We showed that, in theory, the share price must be the same whether the dividend growth model or the formula here is used.

7 From accounting, we know that earnings are divided into two parts: dividends and retained earnings. Most firms continually retain earnings to create future dividends. One should not discount earnings to obtain the share price because part of earnings must be reinvested. Only dividends reach the shareholders, and only they should be discounted to get the share price.

8 We suggested that a firm's price–earnings ratio is a function of three factors:

(a) The per-share amount of the firm's valuable growth opportunities

(b) The risk of the share price

(c) The type of accounting method used by the firm.

9 Valuation multiples can be used as a simple way to value a firm. The steps involved are: (1) identify similar peers in the same industry; (2) estimate key ratios for the target firm and its peers; (3) calculate benchmark ratios using the average of the peers' ratios; (4) use the benchmark ratios to value the target firm.

10 A firm can be valued via its free cash flow by estimating the amount of cash available to the company to either invest or pay out as dividends. The free cash flow to the firm (FCFF) formula is given below, where $FCFF_1$ is the free cash flow to the firm at time 1, r is the discount rate of the firm and g is the growth rate in the cash flows of the firm:

$$V_0 = \frac{FCFF_1}{r-g}$$

Questions and Problems

CONCEPT

1 **Definition of a Bond** What are the main characteristics of a bond? Provide examples of different types of bonds in terms of coupons, maturity and face value.

2 **Bond Valuation** Show how you would value a level coupon bond and a zero coupon bond. How would you value a bond with a changing coupon rate?

3 **Bond Concepts** Explain the difference between a coupon rate and a yield to maturity. Show, using examples, how changing the coupon rate and yield to maturity affect the bond price.

4 **The Present Value of Equity** Explain why the share price depends on dividends and capital gains.

5 **The Dividend Growth Model** Under what two assumptions can we use the dividend growth model to determine the share price? Comment on the reasonableness of these assumptions.

6 **Growth Opportunities** In the context of the dividend growth model, is it true that the growth rate in dividends and the growth rate in the share price are identical?

7 **Net Present Value of Growth Opportunities** Explain what is meant by NPVGO. In what circumstances is calculating the NPVGO better than other methods of share valuation?

8 **Price–Earnings Ratio** What are the three factors that determine a company's price–earnings ratio? Explain the possible reasons why the PE ratios vary between firms within the same sector, and between firms in different sectors.

9 **Stock Market Reporting** What information might a financial analyst need when valuing a company's prospects? Comment on the usefulness of this information.

10 **Firm Valuation** Explain how you would undertake a multiples valuation. Is this approach consistent with other valuation models that use discounted cash flow? Explain.

REGULAR

11 **Valuing Bonds** A 30-year gilt is issued with face value of £100, paying interest of £20 per year. If market yields increase shortly after the bond is issued, what happens to the:

(a) Coupon rate

(b) Price

(c) Yield to maturity

(d) Current yield?

12 **Share Values** Your manager has obtained the following information on comparable stocks A and B, both of which are estimated to have a discount rate of 15 per cent:

	Stock A	Stock B
Return on equity	15%	10%
Earnings per share	£2.00	£1.50
Dividends per share	£ 1.00	£1.00

Calculate the dividend payout ratios for each firm, the expected dividend growth rates for each firm and the 'true' stock price for each firm.

13 **Valuing A2A SpA** A2A SpA is an Italian utility firm. Its most recent dividend was €0.013 per share. In the past year, the company has experienced financial difficulties and the share price has dropped by more than 20 per cent. However, long-term growth in dividends is anticipated to be 7 per cent for ever. If A2A shares currently sell for €0.52, what is the required return? Does this make sense? Explain. What factors could cause A2A SpA's share price to have dropped by more than 20 per cent despite its expected long-term dividend growth rate of 7 per cent? What implications might this have for the company's cost of capital and required return, and how might investors factor in the company's financial difficulties when evaluating the risks and returns of investing in its shares? Additionally, how might changes in market conditions, investor sentiment or other factors affect the required return for A2A shares over time?

14 **Share Values and the Dividend Discount Model** ABC plc pays dividends that are expected to grow at 5 per cent each year. These will stop in year 5, at which point the company will pay out all its earnings as dividends. Next year's dividend is £0.87 and its EPS at the time will be £2.02. If the appropriate discount rate on ABC plc shares is 14 per cent, what is its share price today? How might the market's expectations for ABC plc's future earnings and dividend payouts affect its current share price, and how might this be reflected in the calculation of its present value using the dividend discount model? In addition, how might changes in market conditions, investor sentiment or other factors affect the appropriate discount rate for ABC plc shares over time, and what implications might this have for the company's valuation and the returns earned by its shareholders? Finally, what are the key assumptions and limitations of the dividend discount model, and how might these affect the accuracy and reliability of the estimated share price for ABC plc?

15 **Paying for Growth Opportunities** If your company were to distribute all its earnings, it could maintain a level dividend stream of £0.67 per share. How much is the market actually paying per share for growth opportunities?

16 **Equity Valuation** XYZ plc will pay a dividend next year of 40p per share, and it is estimated that XYZ's dividend will increase by 4 per cent per year for ever. Investors in XYZ require a rate of return of 10 per cent. What is the share price of XYZ plc?

17 **Bond Price Movements** Define each of the following terms:

(a) Treasury bill

(b) Pure discount bond

(c) Index-linked bond.

18 **Bond Returns** The UK government issues a five-year bond, which makes annual coupon payments of 5 per cent and offers a yield of 3 per cent annually compounded. Suppose that, one year later, the bond still yields 3 per cent. What return has the bondholder earned over the 12-month period? Now suppose that the bond yields 2 per cent at the end of the year. What return would the bondholder earn in this case?

19 **Non-constant Growth** Dylan Bearings is a young start-up company. No dividends will be paid on the shares over the next nine years because the firm needs to plough back its earnings to fuel growth. The company will pay an £8 per share dividend in 10 years and will increase the dividend by 6 per cent per year thereafter. If the required return is 13 per cent, what is the current share price?

20 **Valuing Preference Shares** Mark Bank has just issued some new preference shares. The issue will pay a £5 annual dividend in perpetuity, beginning four years from now. If the market requires an 8 per cent return on this investment, how much do preference shares cost today?

21 **Working with Non-constant Growth** The return on equity (ROE) of Child SA is 14 per cent and it has a payout ratio of €0.5. Current book value per share is €50 and the book value will grow as the firm reinvests earnings. Assume that the ROE and payout ratio stay constant for the next four years. After that, competition forces ROE down to 11.5 per cent and the payout ratio increases to 0.8. The appropriate discount rate is 11.5 per cent. What are Child's EPS and dividends next year? How will EPS and dividends grow in years 2, 3, 4, 5 and subsequent years? What is Child's share price? How does that value depend on the payout ratio and growth rate after year 4?

22 **Semi-annual Dividends** The Belgian food group Delhaize has just paid a dividend of €1.08. If the annual discount rate on Delhaize shares is 8 per cent and the dividend is expected to grow at 3 per cent per year, what is the current share price of Delhaize?

23 **Finding the Required Return** Regenboog NV earned €68 million for the fiscal year ending yesterday. The firm also paid out 25 per cent of its earnings as dividends yesterday. The firm will continue to pay out 25 per cent of its earnings as annual, end-of-year dividends. The remaining 75 per cent of earnings is retained by the company for use in projects. The company has 1.25 million shares of equity outstanding. The current share price is €272. The historical return on equity (ROE) of 12 per cent is expected to continue in the future. What is the required rate of return on the equity?

24 **Price–Earnings Ratio** The market consensus is that Pinto plc has an ROE of 9 per cent and plans to maintain its plowback ratio of 0.67. This year's earnings per share was €3. The discount rate on Pinto plc is 10 per cent. What is the current PE ratio for the company? What is the prospective PE ratio for the company?

25 **Pinto plc Growth Opportunities** For Pinto plc in Question 24 above, what is the present value of growth opportunities?

26 **Yorkshire Property Growth Opportunities** Yorkshire Property Ltd expects to earn £60 million per year in perpetuity if it does not undertake any new projects. The firm has an opportunity to invest £10 million today and £12 million in one year in real estate. The new investment will generate annual earnings of £15 million in perpetuity,

beginning two years from today. The firm has 10 million shares outstanding, and the required rate of return on the equity is 12 per cent. Land investments are not depreciable. Ignore taxes.

(a) What is the share price if the firm does not undertake the new investment?

(b) What is the value of the investment?

(c) What is the share price if the firm undertakes the investment?

27 **Firm Valuation using Cash Flow Statements** The ABC plc statement of cash flows for the latest financial year is given below. The appropriate discount and growth rates are 14 per cent and 4 per cent, respectively. Assume the marginal corporate tax rate is 23 per cent. What is the value of the firm?

Year Ended 31 March	£m
Net cash flows, from operating activities	
Cash generated from (used in) operations	611.6
Interest paid	(234.0)
Purchase of interest rate caps	-
Interest received	1.9
Corporate income tax (paid) refunded	(24.6)
Net cash generated from operating activities	354.9
Cash flows from investing activities	
Acquisition of subsidiary undertakings, net of cash acquired	(12.8)
Increased investment in subsidiary undertakings	–
Purchase of property, plant and equipment and software	(77.4)
Loans made to group companies	–
Net cash used in investing activities	(90.2)
Free cash flow	264.7
Cash flows from financing activities	
Net proceeds from share issues	0.8
Purchase of own shares	(0.2)
Treasury shares sold by trust	–
Repayment of borrowings	(216.5)
Net payments on revolving and short-term credit facilities	(6.6)
Financing fees paid	(0.4)
Net cash (used in) generated from financing activities	**(222.9)**
Net increase (decrease) in cash and cash equivalents	**41.8**
Cash and cash equivalents at beginning of the year	160.4
Exchange losses on cash and cash equivalents	(1.7)
Cash and cash equivalents at year end	**200.5**

28 **Dividends and Growth Opportunities** How might the valuation of a firm be affected by its dividend policy, potential for future investments and earnings growth, and other factors such as market conditions and investor sentiment? For example, if a firm pays out a dividend that is expected to grow at a rate of 6 per cent each year and then stops paying dividends in year 5, how might this affect its current share price given a discount rate of 14 per cent? If the firm instead plans to invest 25 per cent of its earnings in new sustainability projects starting in year 3, with each project earning 40 per cent at year-end in perpetuity, how might this investment plan affect the firm's share price today and over time?

CHALLENGE

29 **Firm Valuation** Your company's net income was €4.456 million, EPS was €73.56 and the dividend payout ratio was 23.7 per cent. The return on equity of the firm was 17.83 per cent and its debt to equity ratio is 1.31.

The appropriate discount rate is 18 per cent. What is the value of the firm's equity? What is the share price? What is the value of the firm's bonds? What is the value of the firm?

30 **Components of Bond Returns** Bond P is a premium bond with a 10 per cent coupon. Bond D is a 7 per cent coupon bond currently selling at a discount. Both bonds make annual payments, have a YTM of 9 per cent and have five years to maturity. What is the current yield for Bond P? For Bond D? If interest rates remain unchanged, what is the expected capital gains yield over the next year for Bond P? For Bond D? Explain your answers and the interrelationship among the various types of yield.

31 **Holding Period Yield** The YTM on a bond is the interest rate you earn on your investment if interest rates do not change. If you actually sell the bond before it matures, your realized return is known as the holding period yield (HPY).

(a) Suppose that today you buy an 8 per cent annual coupon bond for €1,150. The bond has 10 years to maturity. What rate of return do you expect to earn on your investment?

(b) Two years from now, the YTM on your bond has declined by 1 per cent and you decide to sell. What price will your bond sell for? What is the HPY on your investment? Compare this yield to the YTM when you first bought the bond. Why are they different?

32 **Discount Rate** Wonte is a German commercial vehicle manufacturer. Its DPS and EPS for last year were €2 and €4.62, respectively. The ROE of the firm was 11.85 per cent and the share price is €99.63. How would you calculate the appropriate discount rate for the firm's equity?

33 **Valuing Everest Ltd Bonds** Suppose a company called Everest Ltd has two bonds currently outstanding, Bond X and Bond Y. Bond X has a face value of £50,000 and a maturity of 15 years. The bond makes no payments for the first five years, then pays £2,500 every six months over the subsequent five years, and finally pays £3,500 every six months over the last five years. Bond Y also has a face value of £50,000 and a maturity of 15 years, but it makes no coupon payments over the life of the bond. If the required return on both bonds is 12 per cent compounded semi-annually, what is the current price of Bond X and Bond Y? How might changes in the required return, coupon payments or other factors affect the pricing and attractiveness of these bonds to investors? What are the key differences between Bond X and Bond Y, and how might investors evaluate the trade-offs between investing in these two bonds?

34 **Capital Gains versus Income** Consider four different equities, all of which have a required return of 15 per cent and a most recent dividend of £4.00 per share. Equities W, X and Y are expected to maintain constant growth rates in dividends for the foreseeable future of 10 per cent, 0 per cent and −5 per cent per year, respectively. Z is a growth stock that will increase its dividend by 20 per cent for the next two years and then maintain a constant 12 per cent growth rate thereafter. What is the dividend yield for each of these four equities? What is the expected capital gains yield? Discuss the relationship among the various returns that you find for each of these equities.

35 **Equity Valuation with Dividend Payment Frequency** Most corporations pay semi-annual rather than annual dividends on their equity. Barring any unusual circumstances during the year, the board raises, lowers or maintains the current dividend once a year and then pays this dividend out in equal biannual instalments to its shareholders.

(a) Suppose a company currently pays a €3.00 annual dividend on its equity in a single annual instalment, and management plans on raising this dividend by 6 per cent per year indefinitely. If the required return on this equity is 14 per cent, what is the current share price?

(b) Now suppose that the company in (a) actually pays its annual dividend in equal six-monthly instalments; thus this company has just paid a £1.50 dividend per share, as it has in the previous six months. What is the current share price now? (*Hint:* Find the equivalent annual end-of-year dividend for each year. Assume the dividends grew by 6 per cent every six months.) Comment on whether you think that this model of share valuation is appropriate.

36 **Nakamura Growth Opportunities** Nakamura has earnings of £10 million and is projected to grow at a constant rate of 5 per cent for ever because of the benefits gained from the learning curve. Currently all earnings are paid out as dividends. The company plans to launch a new project two years from now that would be completely internally funded and require 20 per cent of the earnings that year. The project would start generating revenues one year after the launch of the project, and the earnings from the new project in any year are estimated to be constant at £5 million. The company has 10 million shares outstanding. Estimate the value of Nakamura. The discount rate is 10 per cent.

37 **Equity Valuation and Discount Rates** Rando's share price is €56.99. You wish to value the company's equity and compare your valuation to the share price. The dividend that has just been paid is €1.78 and the earnings per share

is €7.96. The return on equity for the firm is 18.66 per cent. There are a number of estimated growth rates for the firm and these are given below:

Source	Growth Rate (%)
DPS growth (5 yr)	9.52
EPS growth (5 yr)	16.85
EPS growth (1 yr)	16.01
DPS growth (1 yr)	17.98

What is Rando's estimated discount rate for each growth rate? Which estimate makes most sense and why? Using your chosen discount rate, value the company based on your own growth rate calculation.

Exam Question (45 minutes)

Roxanne SA is a consumer goods company that is expected to grow at a rate of 5 per cent per year for the next five years. In year 6, the company will stop growing and pay out all its earnings as dividends. The current dividend is €15 and its EPS at the time will be €26.

1. If the appropriate discount rate on Roxanne SA shares is 7 per cent, what is the share price today? **(20 marks)**
2. Assume that Roxanne SA has two different growth opportunities, one with a net present value of €12 per share and another with a net present value of €8 per share. How much is the market paying per share for growth opportunities? **(20 marks)**
3. Suppose a 10-year government bond makes annual coupon payments of 2.5 per cent and offers a yield of 5 per cent annually compounded. One year later, the bond still yields 5 per cent. What return has the bondholder earned over the 12-month period? Now suppose that the bond yields 7 per cent at the end of the year. What return would the bondholder earn in this case? The face value of the bond is €3,000. **(20 marks)**
4. How would you value a firm that pays no dividends? Explain, using a quantitative example to illustrate your answer. Assume the firm has a net income of €120,000 per year and a cost of equity of 10 per cent. **(40 marks)**

Total Marks: 100

Mini Case

Equity Valuation at Ecorenewable Energy

Ecorenewable Energy is a renewable wave energy firm that was established in 2016 by two finance graduates. The company manufactures and installs wave energy converters through a point absorber buoy that floats on the surface of the water. Ecorenewable Energy has experienced rapid growth because of a proprietary technology that increases the energy efficiency of its systems. The company is owned equally by the two graduates, with each person holding 50,000 shares for a total of 100,000 shares in the company. In the event either wished to sell their shares, they first have to be offered to the other at a discounted price.

Both shareholders have decided they should value their holdings in the company for financial planning purposes. To accomplish this, they have gathered the following information about their main competitors:

Ecorenewable Energy plc Competitors					
	EPS (€)	DPS (€)	Share Price (€)	ROE (%)	R (%)
Surface Attenuator Systems	0.82	0.16	15.19	11	10
Wave Surge Oscillators plc	1.32	0.52	12.49	14	13
Water Column Oscillations SA	−0.47	0.54	48.60	14	12
Industry average	0.56	0.41	25.43	13	11.67

Water Column Oscillations SA's negative earnings per share (EPS) were the result of an accounting write-off last year. Without the write-off, EPS for the company would have been €2.34.

Last year, Ecorenewable Energy had an EPS of €4.32 and paid a total dividend of €108,000, shared equally between the two shareholders. The company had a return on equity of 25 per cent. This is more than the 20 per cent required return of the shareholders.

1 Assuming Ecorenewable Energy continues its current growth rate, what is the share price of the company's equity?

2 You have been hired to verify the share price valuation, and have been given information on Ecorenewable Energy and its three closest competitors. You believe that although Ecorenewable Energy has a technological advantage from the point absorber buoy, your research indicates that the firm's competitors are investigating a new technology that uses overtopping devices, which use wave velocity to power low-head turbines either on- or offshore. You expect Ecorenewable Energy's technological advantage will last for around five years, after which the company's growth rate will converge to the industry average growth rate. You also believe that the required return of 20 per cent is too high and that the industry average discount rate is more appropriate. With these assumptions, is your share price estimate higher or lower?

3 What is the industry average price–earnings ratio? What is Ecorenewable Energy's price–earnings ratio? Comment on any differences and explain why they may exist.

4 Assume the company's growth rate declines to the industry average after five years. What percentage of the equity's value is attributable to growth opportunities?

5 Assume the company's growth rate slows to the industry average in five years. What future return on equity does this imply?

6 Both shareholders of Ecorenewable Energy wish to increase the value of the company equity but want to retain control of the company. They will not sell shares to outside investors and believe the company's debt is at a manageable level. They also do not wish to borrow more money. What steps can Ecorenewable Energy take to increase the share price? Are there any conditions under which this strategy would not increase the share price?

Practical Case Study

For these problems, use any web service that provides financial information. Good examples are Yahoo! Finance, Hemscott, Reuters and FT.com. You can also go to the company's website and download financial accounts from there. Get used to accessing financial websites as this is a basic skill required by all financial managers.

1 **Dividend Discount Model** Choose any large company from your country and download its most recent statement of financial position and statement of profit and loss. Using the financial figures in the accounts, calculate the sustainable growth rate for your company. Now go to Yahoo! Finance or any other financial website and find the closing share price for the same month as the financial accounts you used. What is the implied required return on your company according to the dividend growth model? Does this number make sense? Why, or why not?

2 **Growth Opportunities** Assume that investors require an 8 per cent return on the company you studied for Question 1. Using this share price and the EPS for the most recent year, calculate the NPVGO for your company. What is the appropriate PE ratio for your company using these calculations? What is the PE ratio on Yahoo! Finance? Can you explain the difference, if any?

Relevant Accounting Standards

Accounting standards are very relevant for security valuation because you need to be able to interpret the correct growth rates from the accounting figures. Important standards relating to this chapter are IAS 33 *Earnings per Share* and IAS 39 *Financial Instruments: Recognition and Measurement*. IAS 39 provides definitions for different types of financial securities. This can sometimes be problematic for an accountant because many securities have equity and bond-like features. Visit the IASPlus website (www.iasplus.com) for more information.

Additional Reading

A major challenge in share and bond valuation is measuring growth rates. The following papers investigate this issue (country or region of study is given in bold):

1 Beck, T., A. Demirguc-Kunt and V. Maksimovic (2005) 'Financial and Legal Constraints to Growth: Does Firm Size Matter?', *Journal of Finance,* Vol. 60, No. 1, 137–177. **International.**

2 Chen, L. (2009) 'On the Reversal of Return and Dividend Growth Predictability: A Tale of Two Periods', *Journal of Financial Economics,* Vol. 92, No. 1, 128–151. **USA.**

3 Claessens, S. and L. Laeven (2003) 'Financial Development, Property Rights, and Growth', *Journal of Finance,* Vol. 58, No. 6, 2401–2436. **International.**

4 Penman, S. (2011) 'Accounting for Risk and Return in Valuation', *Journal of Applied Corporate Finance,* Vol. 23, No. 2, 50–58.

The following papers are also of interest:

5 Bansal, R., D. Wu and A. Yaron (2022) 'Socially Responsible Investing in Good and Bad Times', *The Review of Financial Studies,* Vol. 35, No. 4, 2067–2099.

6 Bris, A., Y. Koskinen and M. Nilsson (2009) 'The Euro and Corporate Valuations', *Review of Financial Studies,* Vol. 22, No. 8, 3171–3209. **Europe.**

7 Penman, S. (2006) 'Handling Valuation Models', *Journal of Applied Corporate Finance,* Vol. 18, No. 2, 48–55. **Theoretical.**

8 Pinto, J.E., T.R. Robinson and J.D. Stowe (2018) 'Equity Valuation: A Survey of Professional Practice', *Review of Financial Economics,* October.

Endnotes

1 We ignore the possibility of the issuance of equities or bonds to raise capital. These possibilities are considered in later chapters.

2 If you have read the online supplement to Chapter 3, you will have probably figured out that g is the sustainable growth rate.

3 Later in the text, we speak of issuing shares or debt to fund projects.

4 A full discussion of dividend policy, including share repurchases, is provided in Chapter 18.

5 The appropriate discount rate to use is discussed in detail in Chapter 12.

Chapter 6

Net Present Value and Other Investment Rules

Learning Objectives

After reading this chapter you should be able to:

LO1 Understand the net present value method and its role in investment decision-making.

LO2 Compare and contrast the payback period method and the discounted payback period method.

LO3 Apply the average accounting return method to evaluate the profitability of investment projects.

LO4 Calculate the internal rate of return and analyse its limitations as an investment appraisal method.

LO5 Use the profitability index to evaluate investment projects, and compare its advantages and disadvantages to those of other methods.

LO6 Identify other investment appraisal methods and understand their potential applications.

LO7 Analyse the practice of capital budgeting and the importance of effective investment decision-making in corporate finance.

Irrespective of the state of the economy, companies will invest to maintain existing operations or exploit new opportunities. Financial managers must decide whether the return from investing in a particular project, acquiring a new firm or expanding operations is enough to offset the costs of undertaking the investment. Investing is one of the financial manager's most important decisions and considerable time is spent assessing the viability of investment decisions.

Source: Lea Rae/Shutterstock.

Take, for example, the European business environment immediately after the Covid-19 pandemic. Supply chains across the world were severely disrupted, and the impact of Brexit on UK business was becoming

Key Notations

NPV	Net present value	PI	Profitability index
AAR	Average accounting return	R	Discount rate
IRR	Internal rate of return		

clearer. Climate change was also creating difficulties for firms because of extremes in weather (such as the 2023 shortage of staple groceries, when supermarket shelves were bare of tomatoes, cucumbers, peppers, mustard, olive oil and salads). One of the biggest uncertainties facing all companies is what trading conditions will look like in the future. The more uncertain the environment, the more difficult it is to predict future cash flows.

Investment decisions are as much about choosing new projects as they are about deciding to stop activities. For example, 2023 saw a number of firms announce structural reorganizations because of the uncertainty caused by the war in Ukraine, increased trade barriers in the USA and slowing demand across the world. For example, Twitter (now X) cut more than half of its 7,500 workforce to bring costs under control after experiencing falling revenues following its being bought by Elon Musk for $44 billion. Although Twitter was reducing staff, this is still an investment decision. The firm would have had to look at the benefits of such an action (lower salary bill) and the costs (reduced ability to run the business) before deciding if the action was worth it.

The change in branding from Twitter to X, and Facebook to Meta, for example, are also investment decisions. The cash outflows from rebranding will relate to legal costs and all the marketing and sales ramifications. The present value of cash inflows from higher sales and better market positioning are expected to more than offset the costs. In this chapter, we discuss the necessary tools used in making such decisions.

In Chapter 1, we saw that increasing the value of a company's equity is the goal of financial management. Thus, we need to know how a particular investment will achieve that. This chapter considers a variety of techniques that are used in practice for this purpose. More importantly, it shows how many of these techniques can be misleading when used on their own, and explains why, although the net present value approach may be the right approach in theory, it may not be the best approach in practice.

6.1 The Net Present Value Method

Chapter 4 Page 88

This chapter, as well as the next two, focuses on *capital budgeting,* the decision-making process for accepting or rejecting projects. We develop the basic capital budgeting methods, leaving much of the practical application to subsequent chapters. Fortunately, we do not have to develop these methods from scratch. In Chapter 4, we pointed out that one pound or euro received in the future is worth less than a pound or euro received today. The reason, of course, is that today's money can be reinvested, yielding a greater amount in the future. And we showed in Chapter 4 that the exact worth of a pound or euro to be received in the future is its present value. Furthermore, Section 4.1 suggested calculating the *net present value* of any project. That is, the section suggested calculating the difference between the sum of the present values of the project's future cash flows and the initial cost of the project.

The net present value (NPV) method is the first to be considered in this chapter. We begin by reviewing the approach with a simple example, then we ask why the method leads to good decisions.

Example 6.1

Net Present Value

Alpha Corporation is considering investing in a riskless project costing £100. The project receives £107 in one year and has no other cash flows. The discount rate is 6 per cent.

The NPV of the project can easily be calculated as:

Equation 6.1

$$£0.94 = -£100 + \frac{£100}{1.06}$$

From Chapter 4, we know that the project should be accepted because its NPV is positive. Had the NPV of the project been negative, as would have been the case with an interest rate greater than 7 per cent, the project should be rejected.

The basic investment rule can be generalized thus:

Accept a project if the NPV is greater than zero. Reject a project if the NPV is less than zero.

We refer to this as the NPV rule.

Why does the NPV rule lead to good decisions? Consider the following two strategies available to the managers of Alpha Corporation:

1 Use £100 of corporate cash to invest in the project. The £107 will be paid as a dividend in one year.

2 Forgo the project and pay the £100 of corporate cash as a dividend today.

If strategy 2 is employed, the shareholder might deposit the dividend in a bank for one year. With an interest rate of 6 per cent, strategy 2 would produce cash of £106 (= £100 × 1.06) at the end of the year. The shareholder would prefer strategy 1 because strategy 2 produces less than £107 at the end of the year.

Our basic point is this: accepting positive NPV projects benefits shareholders.

How do we interpret the exact NPV of £0.94? This is the increase in the value of the firm from the project. For example, imagine that the firm today has productive assets worth £V and has £100 of cash. If the firm forgoes the project, the value of the firm today would simply be:

$$\pounds V + \pounds 100$$

If the firm accepts the project, the firm will receive £107 in one year but will have no cash today. Thus, the firm's value today would be:

$$\pounds V + \frac{\pounds 107}{1.06}$$

The difference between these equations is just £0.94, the present value of Equation 6.1. Thus, the value of the firm rises by the NPV of the project.

Note that the value of the firm is merely the sum of the values of the different projects, divisions or other entities within the firm. This property, called value additivity, is quite important. It implies that the contribution of any project to a firm's value is simply the NPV of the project. As we will see later, alternative methods discussed in this chapter do not generally have this nice property.

One detail remains. We assumed that the project was riskless – a rather implausible assumption. Future cash flows of real-world projects are invariably risky. In other words, cash flows can only be estimated, rather than known. Imagine that the managers of Alpha *expect* the cash flow of the project to be £107 next year. That is, the cash flow could be higher, say £117, or lower, say £97. With this slight change, the project is risky. Suppose the project is about as risky as the stock market as a whole, where the expected return this year is perhaps 10 per cent. Then 10 per cent becomes the discount rate, implying that the NPV of the project would be:

$$-\pounds 2.73 = -\pounds 100 + \frac{\pounds 107}{1.10}$$

Because the NPV is negative, the project should be rejected. This makes sense. A shareholder of Alpha receiving a £100 dividend today could invest it in the stock market, expecting a 10 per cent return. Why accept a project with the same risk as the market but with an expected return of only 7 per cent?

Conceptually, the discount rate on a risky project is the return that one can expect to earn on a financial asset of comparable risk. This discount rate is often referred to as an *opportunity cost* because corporate investment in the project takes away the shareholder's opportunity to invest the dividend in a financial asset. If the actual calculation of the discount rate strikes you as extremely difficult in the real world, you are right. Although you can call a bank to find out the current interest rate, whom do you call to find the expected return on the market this year? And, if the risk of the project differs from that of the market, how do you make the adjustment? However, the calculation is by no means impossible. We forgo the calculation in this chapter, but we present it in later chapters.

Having shown that NPV is a sensible approach, how can we tell whether alternative methods are as good as NPV? The key to NPV is its three attributes:

1 *NPV uses cash flows.* Cash flows from a project can be used for other corporate purposes (such as dividend payments, other capital budgeting projects or payments of corporate interest). By contrast, earnings are an artificial construct. Although earnings are useful to accountants, they should not be used in capital budgeting because they do not represent cash.

2 *NPV uses all the cash flows of the project.* Other approaches ignore cash flows beyond a particular date; beware of these approaches.

3 *NPV discounts the cash flows properly.* Other approaches may ignore the time value of money when handling cash flows. Beware of these approaches as well.

Example 6.2

Using NPV to Evaluate a New Investment

Bannon Fodder SA makes ecologically friendly food products for agricultural purposes and is considering whether to invest in a new food manufacturing process that minimizes carbon emissions. The project will require an upfront investment of €2 million and will provide the following cash flows:

Year	1	2	3	4	5
Cash flow (€ millions)	0.25	0.50	0.75	1.00	1.25

The investment will attract a discount rate of 10 per cent. What is the NPV of the project?

$$NPV = -2 + \frac{0.25}{1.1} + \frac{0.50}{1.1^2} + \frac{0.75}{1.1^3} + \frac{1.00}{1.1^4} + \frac{1.25}{1.1^5} = €0.663 \text{ million}$$

Since the net present value is €663,000, Bannon Fodder should take the investment.

6.2 The Payback Period Method

Defining the Rule

One of the most popular alternatives to NPV is payback. Here is how payback works: consider a project with an initial investment of –€50,000. Cash flows are €30,000, €20,000 and €10,000 in the first three years, respectively. We illustrate these cash flows in Figure 6.1.

Figure 6.1 Cash Flows of an Investment Project

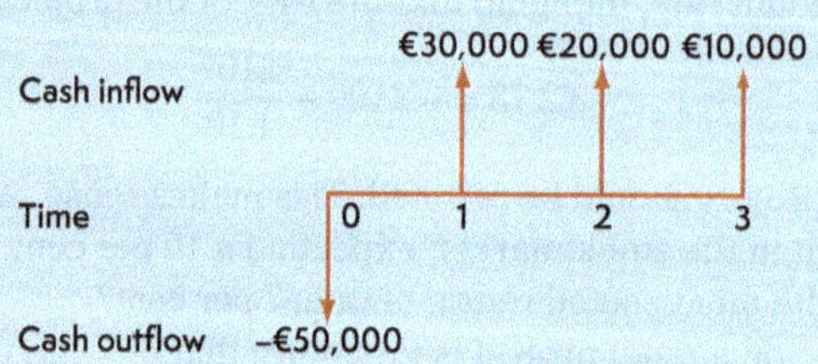

A useful way of writing down investments like the preceding is with the notation:

$$(-€50,000, €30,000, €20,000, €10,000)$$

The minus sign in front of the €50,000 reminds us that this is a cash outflow for the investor, and the commas between the different numbers indicate that they are received – or, if they are cash outflows, that they are paid out – at different times. In this example, we are assuming that the cash flows occur one year apart, with the first one occurring the moment we decide to take on the investment.

The firm receives cash flows of €30,000 and €20,000 in the first two years, which add up to the €50,000 original investment, meaning the firm has recovered its investment within two years. In this case, two years is the *payback period* of the investment.

The payback period rule for making investment decisions is simple. A particular cut-off date, say two years, is selected. All investment projects that have payback periods of two years or less are accepted, and all of those that pay off in more than two years – if at all – are rejected.

Problems with the Payback Method

There are at least three problems with payback. To illustrate the first two, we consider the three projects in Table 6.1. All three projects have the same three-year payback period, so they should all be equally attractive – right?

Table 6.1 Expected Cash Flows for Projects A–C

Year	A (£)	B (£)	C (£)
0	–100	–100	–100
1	20	50	50
2	30	30	30
3	50	20	20
4	60	60	60,000
Payback period (years)	3	3	3

Actually, they are not equally attractive, as can be seen by a comparison of different *pairs* of projects.

Problem 1: Timing of Cash Flows Within the Payback Period

Let us compare project A with project B. In years 1 through 3, the cash flows of project A rise from £20 to £50, while the cash flows of project B fall from £50 to £20. Because the cash flow of £50 comes earlier with project B, its net present value must be higher. Nevertheless, we just saw that the payback periods of the two projects are identical. Thus, a problem with the payback method is that it does not consider the timing of the cash flows within the payback period. This example shows that the payback method is inferior to NPV because, as we pointed out earlier, the NPV method *discounts the cash flows properly*.

Problem 2: Payments After the Payback Period

Now consider projects B and C, which have identical cash flows within the payback period. However, project C is preferred because it has a cash flow of £60,000 in the fourth year. Thus, another problem with the payback method is that it ignores all cash flows occurring after the payback period. Because of the short-term orientation of the payback method, some valuable long-term projects are likely to be rejected. The NPV method does not have this flaw because, as we pointed out earlier, this method *uses all the cash flows of the project.*

Problem 3: Arbitrary Standard for Payback Period

We do not need to refer to Table 6.1 when considering a third problem with the payback method. Capital markets help us estimate the discount rate used in the NPV method. The riskless rate, perhaps proxied by the yield on a Treasury instrument, would be the appropriate rate for a riskless investment. Later chapters of this textbook show how to use historical returns in the capital markets to estimate the discount rate for a risky project. However, there is no comparable guide for choosing the payback cut-off date, so the choice is somewhat arbitrary.

Managerial Perspective

The payback method is often used by large, sophisticated companies when making relatively small decisions. The decision to build a small warehouse, for example, or to pay for a tune-up for a truck is the sort of choice that is often made by lower-level management. Typically, a manager might reason that a tune-up would cost, say, £200, and if it saved £120 each year in reduced fuel costs, it would pay for itself in less than two years. On such a basis the decision would be made.

Although the treasurer of the company might not have decided in the same way, the company endorses such decision-making. Why would upper management condone or even encourage such retrograde activity in its employees? One answer would be that it is easy to make decisions using payback, and if we make 50 such decisions every month, the appeal of payback becomes clearer.

The payback method also has some desirable features for managerial control. Just as important as the investment decision is the company's ability to evaluate the manager's decision-making ability. Under the NPV method, a long time may pass before one decides whether a decision was correct. With the payback method, we will know in two years whether the manager's assessment of future cash flows was appropriate.

It has also been suggested that firms with good investment opportunities but no available cash may justifiably use payback. For example, the payback method could be used by small, privately held firms with good growth prospects but limited access to the capital markets. Quick cash recovery enhances the reinvestment possibilities for such firms. Payback period is also useful when firms invest in emerging markets. The uncertainty involved with such investments means that firms like to know they are getting their money back within a specified period. A short payback period equates roughly to a very high discount rate, where cash flows in the future have little present value.

Finally, practitioners often argue that standard academic criticisms of payback overstate real-world problems with the method. For example, textbooks typically make fun of payback by showing a project with low cash inflows in the early years but a massive cash inflow right after the payback cut-off date. This project would be rejected under the payback method, though its acceptance would, in truth, benefit the firm. Project C in Table 6.1 is an example of such a project.

Practitioners point out that the pattern of cash flows in these textbook examples is much too stylized to mirror the real world, and for the overwhelming majority of real-world projects, both payback and NPV lead to the same decision. These practitioners also indicate that if they were to encounter an investment like project C in practice, they would almost certainly make ad hoc adjustments to the payback rule so the project would be accepted.

Notwithstanding the previous discussion, it is not surprising to discover that when firms look at large investments, NPV becomes the preferred approach. For big-ticket decisions, such as buying a machine, building a factory or acquiring a company, the payback method is seldom used.

Summary of Payback

The payback method differs from NPV and is therefore conceptually wrong. With its arbitrary cut-off date and its blindness to cash flows after that date, it can lead to some flagrantly foolish decisions if it is used too literally. Nevertheless, because of its simplicity, as well as its other mentioned advantages, companies often use it as a screen for making the myriad minor investment decisions they continually face.

Although this means that you should be wary of trying to change approaches such as the payback method when you encounter them in companies, you should probably be careful not to accept the sloppy financial thinking they represent. After this course, you would do your company a disservice if you used payback instead of NPV when you had a choice.

Real World Insight 6.1

Replacing Workers with Automation

In many parts of the developed world, companies that require low-paid labour to undertake manual jobs have, in recent years, found it difficult to attract workers. This is because the wages offered by employers are too low for affluent domestic citizens, and nationalist government policies have focused on reducing unskilled immigration.

The agricultural sector has been particularly affected and farmers have explored automation to replace manual workers. Any activity that is repetitive, such as flattening land, planting seeds or picking fruit, is ripe (please excuse the pun!) for automation.

When using any investment appraisal approach, all cash flows arising from the project must be included. For a farmer considering the purchase of new automated equipment, there would be an initial cash outflow for the purchase, but there would then be future savings from not paying workers' wages.

Savings are treated as cash inflows because the farmer will have more cash in the future as a result of not paying workers (think about this). Treating savings as cash inflows allows you to undertake an investment appraisal of replacement decisions. We will discuss this in more detail in Section 7.5.

6.3 The Discounted Payback Period Method

Aware of the pitfalls of payback, some decision-makers use a variant called the discounted payback period method. Under this approach, we first discount the cash flows, then we ask how long it takes for the discounted cash flows to equal the initial investment. In other words, whereas payback period tells us how long it takes for an investment to make its money back, discounted payback period tells us how long it takes for an investment to create value for the investor.

For example, suppose that the discount rate is 10 per cent and the cash flows on a project are given by:

$$(-£100, £50, £50, £20)$$

This investment has a payback period of two years because the investment is paid back in that time.

To compute the project's discounted payback period, we first discount each of the cash flows at the 10 per cent rate. These discounted cash flows are:

$$\left[-£100, \frac{£50}{1.1}, \frac{£50}{1.1^2}, \frac{£20}{1.1^3}\right] = (-£100, £45.45, £41.32, £15.03)$$

The discounted payback period of the original investment is the payback period for these discounted cash flows. The payback period for the discounted cash flows is slightly less than three years because the discounted cash flows over the three years are £101.80 (= £45.45 + 41.32 + 15.03). As long as the cash flows and discount rate are positive, the discounted payback period will never be smaller than the payback period because discounting reduces the value of the cash flows.

At first glance discounted payback may seem like an attractive alternative, but on closer inspection we see that it has some of the same major flaws as payback. Like payback, discounted payback first requires us to make a somewhat magical choice of an arbitrary cut-off period, and then it ignores all cash flows after that date.

If we have already gone to the trouble of discounting the cash flows, we have lost any appeal to simplicity or managerial control that payback may have. We might just as well add up all the discounted cash flows and use NPV to make the decision. Although discounted payback looks a bit like NPV, it is just a poor compromise between the payback method and NPV.

Despite these concerns, the discounted payback period can be used effectively in regulated industries where projects last for many years (20-plus) and are funded through government investment. These types of investments tend to be capital-intensive and it takes many years for a firm to recoup its initial investment. Another reason discounted payback is used in large businesses is that it allows a comparison of payback across divisions of different risk. While NPV tells us how much value is eventually created for shareholders, discounted payback period gives an insight into how long it will take for a project to start generating that positive value.

6.4 The Average Accounting Return Method

Defining the Rule

Another attractive, but fatally flawed, approach to financial decision-making is the **average accounting return (AAR)**. The average accounting return is the average project earnings after taxes and depreciation, divided by the average book value of the investment during its life. In spite of its flaws, the average accounting return method is worth examining because it is used frequently in the real world.

It is worth scrutinizing Table 6.2. The first step in any project assessment is a careful look at projected cash flows. First-year sales for the store are estimated to be £433,333. Before-tax cash flow will be £233,333. Sales are expected to rise, and expenses are expected to fall in the second year, resulting in before-tax cash flow of £300,000. Competition from other stores and the loss in novelty will reduce before-tax cash flow to £166,667, £100,000 and £33,333, respectively, in the next three years.

Example 6.3

Average Accounting Return

Consider a company that is evaluating whether to buy a store in a new shopping centre. The purchase price is £500,000. We will assume that the store has an estimated life of five years and will need to be scrapped entirely or rebuilt at the end of that time. For simplicity's sake, the asset will be depreciated using straight-line depreciation (this does not occur in countries that use International Accounting Standards but serves to illustrate the method). We show the projected yearly sales and expense figures in Table 6.2.

Table 6.2 Projected Yearly Revenue and Costs for Average Accounting Return

	Year 1 (£)	Year 2 (£)	Year 3 (£)	Year 4 (£)	Year 5 (£)
Revenue	433,333	450,000	266,667	200,000	133,333
Expenses	200,000	150,000	100,000	100,000	100,000
Before-tax cash flow	233,333	300,000	166,667	100,000	33,333
Depreciation	100,000	100,000	100,000	100,000	100,000
Profit before taxes	133,333	200,000	66,667	0	−66,667
Taxes ($t_c = 25\%$)*	33,333	50,000	16,667	0	−16,667
Net income	100,000	150,000	50,000	0	−50,000

$$\text{Average net income} = \frac{£100{,}000 + 150{,}000 + 50{,}000 + 0 - 50{,}000}{5} = £50{,}000$$

$$\text{Average investment} = \frac{£500{,}000 + 0}{2} = £250{,}000$$

$$\text{AAR} = \frac{£50{,}000}{£250{,}000} = 20\%$$

** Corporate tax rate = t_c. The tax rebate in year 5 of −£16,667 occurs if the rest of the firm is profitable. Here the loss in the project reduces the taxes of the entire firm.*

To compute the average accounting return (AAR) on the project, we divide the average net income by the average amount invested. We do this in three steps.

Step 1: Determining Average Net Income

Net income in any year is net cash flow minus depreciation and taxes. Depreciation is *not* a cash outflow.[1] Instead, it is a charge reflecting the fact that the investment in the store becomes less valuable every year.

We assume the project has a useful life of five years, at which time it will be worthless. Because the initial investment is £500,000 and because it will be worthless in five years, we assume that it loses value at a rate of £100,000 each year. This steady loss in value of £100,000 is called *straight-line depreciation.* The method used in countries that employ International Accounting Standards is known as the *reducing balance method,* which will be discussed in detail in Section 7.2. We subtract both depreciation and taxes from before-tax cash flow to derive net income, as shown in Table 6.2. Net income is £100,000 in the first year, £150,000 in year 2, £50,000 in year 3, zero in year 4 and −£50,000 in the last year. The average net income over the life of the project is, therefore:

Average net income:

$$[£100{,}000 + 150{,}000 + 50{,}000 + 0 + (-50{,}000)]/5 = £50{,}000$$

Step 2: Determining Average Investment

We stated earlier that, due to depreciation, the investment in the store becomes less valuable every year. Because depreciation is £100,000 per year, the value at the end of year zero is £500,000, the value at the end of year 1 is £400,000, and so on. What is the average value of the investment over the life of the investment?

The mechanical calculation is:

Average investment:

Equation 6.2
$$(£500{,}000 + 400{,}000 + 300{,}000 + 200{,}000 + 100{,}000 + 0)/6 = £250{,}000$$

We divide by 6, not 5, because £500,000 is what the investment is worth at the beginning of the five years and £0 is what it is worth at the beginning of the sixth year. In other words, there are six terms in the parentheses of Equation 6.2.

Step 3: Determining AAR

The average return is:

$$AAR = \frac{£50,000}{£250,000} = 20\%$$

If the firm had a targeted accounting rate of return higher than 20 per cent, we would reject the project; if its targeted return were less than 20 per cent, we would accept it.

Analysing the Average Accounting Return Method

By now you should be able to see what is wrong with the AAR method.

The most important flaw with AAR is that it does not work with the right raw materials. It uses the net income and book value of the investment, both of which come from the accounting figures. Accounting numbers are somewhat arbitrary. For example, certain cash outflows, such as the cost of a building, are depreciated under specific accounting rules. Other flows, such as maintenance, are expensed. In real-world situations, the decision to depreciate or expense an item involves judgement. Thus, the primary inputs of the AAR method, income and average investment, are affected by the accountant's opinion. Conversely, the NPV method uses *cash flows*. Accounting judgements do not affect cash flow.

Second, AAR takes no account of timing. In the previous example, the AAR would have been the same if the £100,000 net income in the first year had occurred in the last year. However, delaying an inflow for five years would have lowered the NPV of the investment. As mentioned earlier in this chapter, in Section 6.1, the NPV approach *discounts correctly*.

Third, just as payback requires an arbitrary choice of cut-off date, the AAR method offers no guidance on what the right targeted rate of return should be. It could be the discount rate in the market. But then again, because the AAR method is not the same as the present value method, it is not evident this would be the right choice.

Given these problems, is the AAR method employed in practice? Like the payback method, the AAR (and variations on it) is frequently used as a 'backup' to discounted cash flow methods. Perhaps this is so because it is easy to calculate and uses accounting numbers readily available from the firm's accounting system. Also, both shareholders and the media pay a lot of attention to the overall profitability of a firm. Thus, some managers may feel pressured to select projects that are profitable in the near term, even if the projects come up short regarding NPV. These managers may focus on the AAR of individual projects more than they should.

6.5 The Internal Rate of Return

Now we come to the most important alternative to the NPV method: the internal rate of return, universally known as the IRR. The IRR is about as close as you can get to the NPV without actually being the NPV. The basic rationale behind the IRR method is that it provides a single number summarizing the merits of a project. That number does not depend on the interest rate prevailing in the capital market. That is why it is called the internal rate of return; the number is internal or intrinsic to the project and does not depend on anything except the cash flows of the project.

For example, consider the simple project (–£100, £110) in Figure 6.2.

Figure 6.2 Cash Flows for a Simple Project

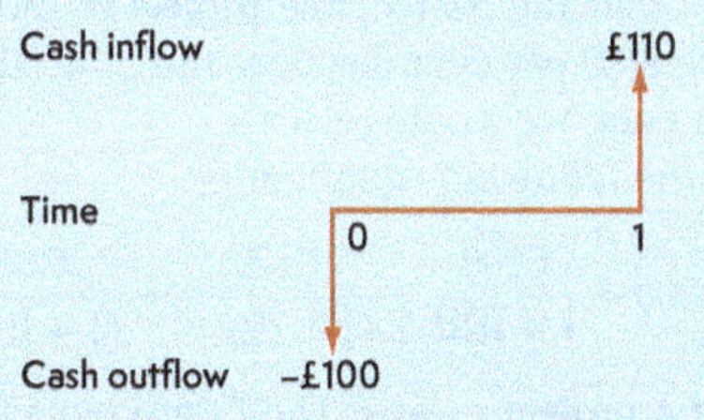

For a given rate, the net present value of this project can be described as:

$$NPV = -£100 + \frac{£110}{1+R}$$

where R is the discount rate. What must the discount rate be to make the NPV of the project equal to zero?

We begin by using an arbitrary discount rate of 0.08, which yields:

$$\text{£}1.85 = -\text{£}100 + \frac{\text{£}110}{1.08}$$

Because the NPV in this equation is positive, we now try a higher discount rate, such as 0.12. This yields:

$$\text{£}1.79 = -\text{£}100 + \frac{\text{£}110}{1.12}$$

Because the NPV in this equation is negative, we try lowering the discount rate to 0.10. This yields:

$$0 = -\text{£}100 + \frac{\text{£}110}{1.10}$$

This trial-and-error procedure tells us that the NPV of the project is zero when R equals 10 per cent.[2] Thus, we say that 10 per cent is the project's **internal rate of return (IRR)**. In general, the IRR is the rate that causes the NPV of the project to be zero. The implication of this exercise is very simple. The firm should be equally willing to accept or reject the project if the discount rate is 10 per cent. The firm should accept the project if the discount rate is below 10 per cent. The firm should reject the project if the discount rate is above 10 per cent.

The general investment rule is clear:

Accept the project if the IRR is greater than the discount rate. Reject the project if the IRR is less than the discount rate.

We refer to this as the basic IRR rule. Now we can try the more complicated example (–€200, €100, €100, €100) in Figure 6.3.

Figure 6.3 Cash Flows for a More Complex Project

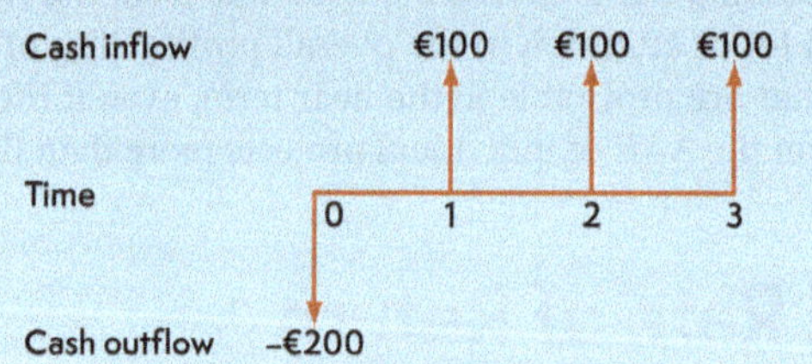

As we did previously, let us use trial and error to calculate the internal rate of return. We try 20 per cent and 30 per cent, yielding the following:

Discount Rate (%)	NPV (€)
20	10.65
30	–18.39

After much more trial and error, we find that the NPV of the project is zero when the discount rate is 23.37 per cent. Thus, the IRR is 23.37 per cent. With a 20 per cent discount rate, the NPV is positive and we would accept it. However, if the discount rate were 30 per cent, we would reject it.

Algebraically, IRR is the unknown in the following equation:[3]

$$0 = -\text{€}200 + \frac{\text{€}100}{1+\text{IRR}} + \frac{\text{€}100}{(1+\text{IRR})^2} + \frac{\text{€}100}{(1+\text{IRR})^3}$$

Figure 6.4 illustrates what the IRR of a project means. The figure plots the NPV as a function of the discount rate. The curve crosses the horizontal axis at the IRR of 23.37 per cent because this is where the NPV equals zero.

It should also be clear that the NPV is positive for discount rates below the IRR and negative for discount rates above the IRR. This means that if we accept projects like this one when the discount rate is less than the IRR, we will be accepting positive NPV projects. Thus, the IRR rule coincides exactly with the NPV rule.

Figure 6.4 Net Present Value (NPV) and Discount Rates for a More Complex Project

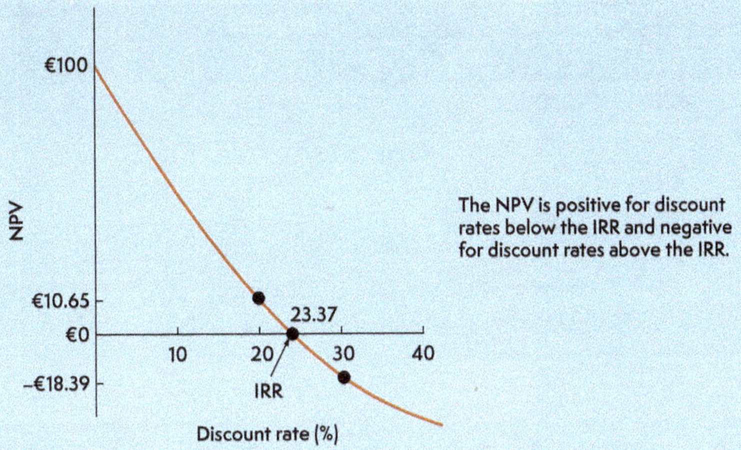

If this were all there were to it, the IRR rule would always coincide with the NPV rule. This would be a wonderful discovery because it would mean that just by computing the IRR for a project we would be able to tell where it ranks among all of the projects we are considering. For example, if the IRR rule really works, a project with an IRR of 20 per cent will always be at least as good as one with an IRR of 15 per cent.

Unfortunately, the world of finance is not so kind. The IRR rule and the NPV rule are the same only for examples like the one just discussed. Several problems with the IRR approach occur in more complicated situations.

6.6 Problems with the IRR Approach

Definition of Independent and Mutually Exclusive Projects

An independent project is one whose acceptance or rejection is independent of the acceptance or rejection of other projects. For example, imagine that Starbucks is considering putting a coffee outlet on a remote island off the north of Scotland. Acceptance or rejection of this outlet is likely to be unrelated to the acceptance or rejection of any other coffee outlet that Starbucks is thinking of opening. This is because the remoteness of the Scottish outlet ensures that it will not pull sales away from other outlets.

Now consider the other extreme, **mutually exclusive investments**. What does it mean for two projects, A and B, to be mutually exclusive? You can accept A or you can accept B or you can reject both of them, but you cannot accept both of them. For example, A might be a decision to build a house on a corner plot that you own, and B might be a decision to build a cinema on the same plot.

We now present two general problems with the IRR approach that affect both independent and mutually exclusive projects. Then we deal with two problems affecting mutually exclusive projects only.

Two General Problems Affecting Both Independent and Mutually Exclusive Projects

We begin our discussion with project A, which has the following cash flows:

$$(-£100, £130)$$

The IRR for project A is 30 per cent. Table 6.3 provides other relevant information about the project. The relationship between NPV and the discount rate is shown for this project in Figure 6.5. As you can see, the NPV declines as the discount rate rises.

Table 6.3 The Internal Rate of Return and Net Present Value

	Project A			Project B			Project C		
Dates:	0	1	2	0	1	2	0	1	2
Cash flows (£)	−100	130		100	−130		−100	230	−132
IRR (%)		30			30		10	and	20
NPV @10% (£)		18.2			−18.2			0	
Accept if market rate		<30%			>30%		>10%	but	<20%
Financing or investing		Investing			Financing			Mixture	

Figure 6.5 Net Present Value and Discount Rates for Projects A, B and C

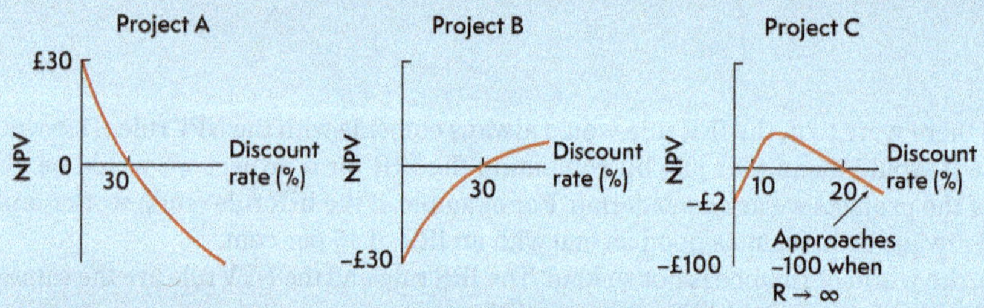

Project A has a cash outflow at date 0 followed by a cash inflow at date 1. Its NPV is negatively related to the discount rate.

Project B has a cash inflow at date 0 followed by a cash outflow at date 1. Its NPV is positively related to the discount rate.

Project C has two changes of sign in its cash flows. It has an outflow at date 0, an inflow at date 1, and an outflow at date 2.

Projects with more than one change of sign can have multiple rates of return.

Problem 1: Investing or Financing?

Now consider project B, with cash flows of:

$$(£100, -£130)$$

These cash flows are exactly the reverse of the flows for project A. In project B, the firm receives funds first and then pays out funds later. While unusual, projects of this type do exist. For example, consider a company conducting a seminar where the participants pay in advance. Because large expenses are frequently incurred at the seminar date, cash inflows precede cash outflows.

Consider our trial-and-error method to calculate IRR:

$$-£4 = +£100 - \frac{£130}{1.25}$$

$$£0 = +£100 - \frac{£130}{1.30}$$

$$£3.70 = +£100 - \frac{£130}{1.35}$$

As with project A, the internal rate of return is 30 per cent. However, notice that the net present value is *negative* when the discount rate is *below* 30 per cent. Conversely, the net present value is positive when the discount rate is above 30 per cent. The decision rule is exactly the opposite of our previous result. For this type of a project, the following rule applies:

Accept the project when the IRR is less than the discount rate. Reject the project when the IRR is greater than the discount rate.

This unusual decision rule follows from the graph of project B in Figure 6.5. The curve is upward sloping, implying that NPV is *positively* related to the discount rate.

The graph makes intuitive sense. Suppose the firm wants to obtain £100 immediately. It can either (1) accept project B, or (2) borrow £100 from a bank. Thus, the project is actually a substitute for borrowing. In fact, because the IRR is 30 per cent, taking on project B is tantamount to borrowing at 30 per cent. If the firm can borrow from a bank at, say, only 25 per cent, it should reject the project. However, if a firm can borrow from a bank only at, say, 35 per cent, it should accept the project. Thus project B will be accepted if and only if the discount rate is *above* the IRR.[4]

This should be contrasted with project A. If the firm has £100 of cash to invest, it can either (1) accept project A, or (2) lend £100 to the bank. The project is actually a substitute for lending. In fact, because the IRR is 30 per cent, taking on project A is tantamount to lending at 30 per cent. The firm should accept project A if the lending rate is below 30 per cent. Conversely, the firm should reject project A if the lending rate is above 30 per cent.

Because the firm initially pays out money with project A but initially receives money with project B, we refer to project A as an *investing type project* and project B as a *financing type project*. Investing type projects are the norm. Because the IRR rule is reversed for financing type projects, be careful when using it with this type of project.

Problem 2: Multiple Rates of Return

Suppose the cash flows from a project are:

$$(-\text{£}100, \text{£}230, -\text{£}132)$$

Because this project has a negative cash flow, a positive cash flow and another negative cash flow, we say that the project's cash flows exhibit two changes of sign, or 'flip-flops'. Although this pattern of cash flows might look a bit strange at first, many projects require outflows of cash after receiving some inflows. An example would be a strip-mining project. The first stage in such a project is the initial investment in excavating the mine. Profits from operating the mine are received in the second stage. The third stage involves a further investment to reclaim the land and satisfy the requirements of environmental protection legislation. Cash flows are negative at this stage.

It is easy to verify that this project has not one but two IRRs, 10 per cent and 20 per cent.[5] In a case like this, the IRR does not make any sense. What IRR are we to use – 10 per cent or 20 per cent? Because there is no good reason to use one over the other, IRR simply cannot be used here.

Why does this project have multiple rates of return? Project C generates multiple internal rates of return because both an inflow and an outflow occur after the initial investment. In general, these flip-flops, or changes, in sign produce multiple IRRs. In theory, a cash flow stream with K changes in sign can have up to K sensible internal rates of return (IRRs above –100 per cent). Therefore, because project C has two changes in sign, it can have as many as two IRRs. As we have pointed out, projects whose cash flows change sign repeatedly can occur in the real world.

NPV Rule

Of course, we should not be too worried about multiple rates of return. After all, we can always fall back on the NPV rule. Figure 6.5 plots the NPV of project C (–£100, £230, –£132) as a function of the discount rate. As the figure shows, the NPV is zero at both 10 per cent and 20 per cent, and negative outside the range. Thus, the NPV rule tells us to accept the project if the appropriate discount rate is between 10 per cent and 20 per cent. The project should be rejected if the discount rate lies outside this range.

The Guarantee Against Multiple IRRs

If the first cash flow of a project is negative (because it is the initial investment) and if all of the remaining flows are positive, there can only be a single, unique IRR, no matter how many periods the project lasts. This is easy to understand by using the concept of the time value of money. For example, it is simple to verify that project A in Table 6.3 has an IRR of 30 per cent because using a 30 per cent discount rate gives:

$$\begin{aligned} NPV &= -\text{£}100 + \frac{\text{£}130}{1.3} \\ &= 0 \end{aligned}$$

How do we know that this is the only IRR? Suppose we were to try a discount rate greater than 30 per cent. In computing the NPV, changing the discount rate does not change the value of the initial cash flow of −£100 because that cash flow is not discounted. But raising the discount rate can only lower the present value of the future cash flows. In other words, because the NPV is zero at 30 per cent, any increase in the rate will push the NPV into the negative range. Similarly, if we try a discount rate of less than 30 per cent, the overall NPV of the project will be positive. Though this example has only one positive flow, the above reasoning still implies a single, unique IRR if there are many inflows (but no outflows) after the initial investment.

If the initial cash flow is positive – and if all of the remaining flows are negative – there can only be a single, unique IRR. This result follows from similar reasoning. Both these cases have only one change of sign or flip-flop in the cash flows. Thus, we are safe from multiple IRRs whenever there is only one sign change in the cash flows.

General Rules

The following table summarizes our rules:

Flows	Number of IRRs	IRR Criterion	NPV Criterion
First cash flow is negative and all remaining cash flows are positive	1	Accept if IRR > *R* Reject if IRR < *R*	Accept if NPV < 0 Reject if NPV > 0
First cash flow is positive and all remaining cash flows are negative	1	Accept if IRR < *R* Reject if IRR > *R*	Accept if NPV > 0 Reject if NPV < 0
Some cash flows after first are positive and some cash flows after first are negative	May be more than 1	No valid IRR	Accept if NPV > 0 Reject if NPV < 0

Note that the NPV criterion is the same for each of the three cases. In other words, NPV analysis is always appropriate. Conversely, the IRR can be used only in certain cases.

Problems Specific to Mutually Exclusive Projects

As mentioned earlier, two or more projects are mutually exclusive if the firm can accept only one of them. We now present two problems dealing with the application of the IRR approach to mutually exclusive projects. These two problems are quite similar, though logically distinct.

The Scale Problem

A professor we know motivates class discussions of this topic with the statement: Students, I am prepared to let one of you choose between two mutually exclusive 'business' propositions: Opportunity 1 – You give me €1 now and I'll give you €1.50 back at the end of the class period. Opportunity 2 – You give me €10 and I'll give you €11 back at the end of the class period. You can choose only one of the two opportunities. And you cannot choose either opportunity more than once. I'll pick the first volunteer.

Which would you choose? The correct answer is opportunity 2. To see why, look at the following chart:

	Cash Flow at Beginning of Class	Cash Flow at End of Class (90 Minutes Later)	NPV[6]	IRR
Opportunity 1	−€1	+€1.50	€0.50	50%
Opportunity 2	−€10	+€11.00	€1.00	10%

As we have stressed earlier in the text, one should choose the opportunity with the highest NPV. This is opportunity 2 in the example.

This business proposition illustrates a defect with the internal rate of return criterion. The basic IRR rule indicates the selection of opportunity 1 because the IRR is 50 per cent. The IRR is only 10 per cent for opportunity 2.

Where does IRR go wrong? The problem with IRR is that it ignores issues of *scale*. Although opportunity 1 has a greater IRR, the investment is much smaller. In other words, the high percentage return on opportunity 1 is more than offset by the ability to earn at least a decent return on a much bigger investment under opportunity 2.

Because IRR seems to be misguided here, can we adjust or correct it? We illustrate how in Example 6.4.

Example 6.4

NPV versus IRR

Stanley Jaffe and Sherry Lansing have just purchased the rights to *Corporate Finance: The Motion Picture*. They will produce this major motion picture on either a small budget or a big budget. Here are the estimated cash flows:

	Cash Flow at Date 0 (€m)	Cash Flow at Date 1 (€m)	NPV @25% (€m)	IRR (%)
Small budget	−10	40	22	300
Large budget	−25	65	27	160

Because of high risk, a 25 per cent discount rate is considered appropriate. Sherry wants to adopt the large budget because the NPV is higher. Stanley wants to adopt the small budget because the IRR is higher. Who is right?

For the reasons espoused in the classroom example, NPV is correct. Hence Sherry is right. However, Stanley is very stubborn where IRR is concerned. How can Sherry justify the large budget to Stanley using the IRR approach?

This is where *incremental IRR* comes in. Sherry calculates the incremental cash flows from choosing the large budget instead of the small budget as follows:

	Cash Flow at Date 0 (€ millions)	Cash Flow at Date 1 (€ millions)
Incremental cash flows from choosing large budget instead of small budget	−25 − (−10) = −15	65 − 40 = 25

This chart shows that the incremental cash flows are −€15 million at date 0 and €25 million at date 1.

Sherry calculates incremental IRR as follows:

Formula for calculating incremental IRR:

$$0 = -€15\text{ million} + \frac{€25\text{ million}}{1 + \text{IRR}}$$

IRR equals 66.67 per cent in this equation, implying that the incremental IRR is 66.67 per cent. Incremental IRR is the IRR on the incremental investment from choosing the large project instead of the small project.

In addition, we can calculate the NPV of the incremental cash flows:

NPV of incremental cash flows:

$$-€15\text{ million} + \frac{€25\text{ million}}{1.25} = €5\text{ million}$$

We know the small-budget picture would be acceptable as an independent project because its NPV is positive. We want to know whether it is beneficial to invest an additional €15 million to make the large-budget picture instead of the small-budget picture. In other words, is it beneficial to invest an additional €15 million to receive an additional €25 million next year? First, our calculations show the NPV on the incremental investment to be positive. Second, the incremental IRR of 66.67 per cent is higher than the discount rate of 25 per cent. For both reasons, the incremental investment can be justified, so the large-budget movie should be made. The second reason is what Stanley needed to hear to be convinced.

In review, we can handle this example (or any mutually exclusive example) in one of three ways:

1. *Compare the NPVs of the two choices.* The NPV of the large-budget picture is greater than the NPV of the small-budget picture. That is, €27 million is greater than €22 million.
2. *Calculate the incremental NPV from making the large-budget picture instead of the small-budget picture.* Because the incremental NPV equals €5 million, we choose the large-budget picture.
3. *Compare the incremental IRR to the discount rate.* Because the incremental IRR is 66.67 per cent and the discount rate is 25 per cent, we take the large-budget picture.

All three approaches always give the same decision. However, we must *not* compare the IRRs of the two pictures. If we did, we would make the wrong choice. That is, we would accept the small-budget picture.

Although students frequently think that problems of scale are relatively unimportant, the truth is just the opposite. No real-world project comes in one clear-cut size. Rather, the firm has to *determine* the best size for the project. The movie budget of €25 million is not set in stone. Perhaps an extra €1 million to hire a bigger star or to film at a better location will increase the movie's gross revenues. Similarly, an industrial firm must decide whether it wants a warehouse of, say, 500,000 square metres or 600,000 square metres. Earlier in the chapter, we imagined Starbucks opening an outlet on a remote island. If it does this, it must decide how big the outlet should be. For almost any project, someone in the firm has to decide on its size, implying that problems of scale abound in the real world.

One final note here. Students often ask which project should be subtracted from the other in calculating incremental flows. Notice that we are subtracting the smaller project's cash flows from the bigger project's cash flows. This leaves an *outflow* at date 0. We then use the basic IRR rule on the incremental flows.[7]

The Timing Problem

Next we illustrate another, quite similar problem with the IRR approach to evaluating mutually exclusive projects.

Example 6.5

Mutually Exclusive Investments

Suppose that Kaufold plc has two alternative uses for a warehouse. It can store toxic waste containers (investment A) or electronic equipment (investment B). The cash flows are as follows:

	Cash Flow at Year				NPV			
Year:	**0 (£)**	**1 (£)**	**2 (£)**	**3 (£)**	**@0% (£)**	**@10% (£)**	**@15% (£)**	**IRR (%)**
Investment A	–10,000	10,000	1,000	1,000	2,000	669	109	16.04
Investment B	–10,000	1,000	1,000	12,000	4,000	751	–484	12.94

We find that the NPV of investment B is higher with low discount rates, and the NPV of investment A is higher with high discount rates. This is not surprising if you look closely at the cash flow patterns. The cash flows of A occur early, whereas the cash flows of B occur later. If we assume a high discount rate, we favour investment A because we are implicitly assuming that the early cash flow (for example, £10,000 in year 1) can be reinvested at that rate. Because most of investment B's cash flows occur in year 3, B's value is relatively high with low discount rates.

Project A has an NPV of £2,000 at a discount rate of zero. This is calculated by simply adding up the cash flows without discounting them. Project B has an NPV of £4,000 at the zero rate. However, the NPV of project B declines more rapidly as the discount rate increases than does the NPV of project A. As we mentioned, this occurs because the cash flows of B occur later. Both projects have the same NPV at a discount rate of 10.55 per cent. The IRR for a project is the rate at which the NPV equals zero. Because the NPV of B declines more rapidly, B actually has a lower IRR.

As with the movie example, we can select the better project with one of three different methods:

1 *Compare the NPVs of the two projects.* If the discount rate is below 10.55 per cent, we should choose project B because B has a higher NPV. If the rate is above 10.55 per cent, we should choose project A because A has a higher NPV.

2 *Compare incremental IRR to discount rate.* Method 1 employed NPV. Another way of determining that B is a better project is to subtract the cash flows of A from the cash flows of B and then to calculate the IRR. This is the incremental IRR approach we spoke of earlier.

Here are the incremental cash flows:

	NPV of Incremental Cash Flows							
Year:	**0 (£)**	**1 (£)**	**2 (£)**	**3 (£)**	**Incremental IRR (%)**	**@0% (£)**	**@10% (£)**	**@15% (£)**
B – A	0	-9,000	0	11,000	10.55	2,000	83	-593

The relevant discount rate is below 10.55 per cent, project B is preferred to project A. If the relevant discount rate is above 10.55 per cent, project A is preferred to project B.[8]

3 *Calculate NPV on incremental cash flows.* Finally, we could calculate the NPV on the incremental cash flows. The incremental NPV is positive when the discount rate is either 0 per cent or 10 per cent. The incremental NPV is negative if the discount rate is 15 per cent. If the NPV is positive on the incremental flows, we should choose B. If the NPV is negative, we should choose A.

In summary, the same decision is reached whether we (1) compare the NPVs of the two projects, (2) compare the incremental IRR to the relevant discount rate, or (3) examine the NPV of the incremental cash flows. However, as mentioned earlier, we should *not* compare the IRR of project A with the IRR of project B.

We suggested earlier that we should subtract the cash flows of the smaller project from the cash flows of the bigger project. What do we do here when the two projects have the same initial investment? Our suggestion in this case is to perform the subtraction so that the *first* non-zero cash flow is negative. In the Kaufold plc example we achieved this by subtracting A from B. In this way, we can still use the basic IRR rule for evaluating cash flows.

The preceding examples illustrate problems with the IRR approach in evaluating mutually exclusive projects. Both the professor–student example and the motion picture example illustrate the problem that arises when mutually exclusive projects have different initial investments. The Kaufold plc example illustrates the problem that arises when mutually exclusive projects have different cash flow timings. When working with mutually exclusive projects, it is not necessary to determine whether it is the scale problem or the timing problem that exists. Very likely both occur in any real-world situation. Instead, the practitioner should simply use either an incremental IRR or an NPV approach.

Redeeming Qualities of IRR

IRR probably survives because it fills a need that NPV does not. People seem to want a rule that summarizes the information about a project in a single rate of return. This single rate gives people a simple way of discussing projects. For example, one manager in a firm might say to another, 'Remodelling the north wing has a 20 per cent IRR.'

To their credit, however, companies that employ the IRR approach seem to understand its deficiencies. For example, companies frequently restrict managerial projections of cash flows to be negative at the beginning and strictly positive later. Perhaps, then, the ability of the IRR approach to capture a complex investment project in a single number and the ease of communicating that number explain the survival of the IRR.

A Test

To test your knowledge, consider the following two statements:

1 You must know the discount rate to compute the NPV of a project, but you compute the IRR without referring to the discount rate.

2 Hence, the IRR rule is easier to apply than the NPV rule because you do not use the discount rate when applying IRR.

The first statement is true. The discount rate is needed to *compute* NPV. The IRR is *computed* by solving for the rate where the NPV is zero. No mention is made of the discount rate in the mere computation. However, the second statement is false. To *apply* IRR, you must compare the internal rate of return with the discount rate. Thus the discount rate is needed for making a decision under either the NPV or IRR approach.

6.7 The Profitability Index

Another method used to evaluate projects is called the **profitability index (PI)**. This is the ratio of the present value of the future expected cash flows *after* the initial investment divided by the amount of the initial investment. We represent the profitability index like this:

$$\text{Profitability index (PI)} = \frac{\text{PV of cash flow } \textit{subsequent} \text{ to initial investment}}{\text{Initial investment}}$$

Example 6.6

Profitability Index

Hiram Finnegan Int. (HFI) applies a 12 per cent discount rate to two investment opportunities.

Project	Cash Flows (€000,000)			PV @ 12% of Cash Flows After Initial Investment (€000,000)	Profitability Index	NPV @ 12% (€000,000)
	C_0	C_1	C_2			
1	−20	70	10	70.5	3.53	50.5
2	−10	15	40	45.3	4.53	35.3

Calculation of the Profitability Index

The profitability index is calculated for project 1 as follows. The present value of the cash flows *after* the initial investment is:

$$€70.5 = \frac{€70}{1.12} + \frac{€10}{(1.12)^2}$$

We obtain the profitability index by dividing this result by the initial investment of €20. This yields:

$$3.53 = \frac{€70.5}{€20}$$

Application of the Profitability Index

How do we use the profitability index? We consider three situations:

1 *Independent projects:* Assume that HFI's two projects are independent. According to the NPV rule, we should accept both projects because NPV is positive in each case. The profitability index (PI) is greater than 1 whenever the NPV is positive. Thus, the PI *decision rule* is:

- Accept an independent project if PI >1.
- Reject it if PI <1.

2 *Mutually exclusive projects:* Let us now assume that HFI can accept only one of its two projects. NPV analysis says accept project 1 because this project has a higher NPV. Because project 2 has a bigger PI, the profitability index leads to the wrong selection.

The problem with the profitability index for mutually exclusive projects is the same as the scale problem with the IRR that we mentioned earlier. Project 2 is smaller than project 1. Because the PI is a ratio, this index misses the fact that project 1 has a bigger investment than project 2. Thus, like IRR, PI ignores differences of scale for mutually exclusive projects.

However, like IRR, the flaw with the PI approach can be corrected using incremental analysis. We write the incremental cash flows after subtracting project 2 from project 1 as follows:

Project	Cash Flows (€000,000)			PV @ 12% of Cash Flows After Initial Investment (€000,000)	Profitability Index	NPV @ 12% (€000,000)
	C_0	C_1	C_2			
1–2	−10	55	−30	25.2	2.52	15.2

Because the profitability index on the incremental cash flows is greater than 1.0, we should choose the bigger project – that is, project 1. This is the same decision we get with the NPV approach.

3 *Capital rationing:* The first two cases implicitly assumed that HFI could always attract enough capital to make any profitable investments. Now consider the case when the firm does not have enough money to fund all positive NPV projects. This is the case of **capital rationing**.

Imagine that the firm has a third project, as well as the first two. Project 3 has the following cash flows:

Project	Cash Flows (€000,000)			PV @ 12% of Cash Flows After Initial Investment (€000,000)	Profitability Index	NPV @ 12% (€000,000)
	C_0	C_1	C_2			
3	–10	–5	60	43.4	4.34	33.4

Further, imagine that (1) the projects of Hiram Finnegan Int. are independent, but (2) the firm has only €20 million to invest. Because project 1 has an initial investment of €20 million, the firm cannot select both this project and another one. Conversely, because projects 2 and 3 have initial investments of €10 million each, both these projects can be chosen. In other words, the cash constraint forces the firm to choose either project 1 or projects 2 and 3.

What should the firm do? Individually, projects 2 and 3 have lower NPVs than project 1. However, when we add the NPVs of projects 2 and 3 together, the sum is higher than the NPV of project 1. Thus, common sense dictates that projects 2 and 3 should be accepted.

What does our conclusion have to say about the NPV rule or the PI rule? In the case of limited funds, we cannot rank projects according to their NPVs. Instead, we should rank them according to the ratio of present value to initial investment. This is the PI rule. Both project 2 and project 3 have higher PI ratios than does project 1. Thus they should be ranked ahead of project 1 when capital is rationed.

The profitability index does not work if funds are limited beyond the initial period. For example, if massive cash outflows elsewhere in the firm were to occur at date 1, project 3, which also has a cash outflow at date 1, might need to be rejected. In other words, the profitability index cannot handle capital rationing over multiple periods.

Also, what economists term *indivisibilities* may reduce the effectiveness of the PI rule. Imagine that HFI has €30 million available for capital investment, not just €20 million. The firm now has enough cash for projects 1 and 2. Because the sum of the NPVs of these two projects is greater than the sum of the NPVs of projects 2 and 3, the firm would be better served by accepting projects 1 and 2. But because projects 2 and 3 still have the highest profitability indexes, the PI rule now leads to the wrong decision. Why does the PI rule lead us astray here? The key is that projects 1 and 2 use up all of the €30 million, whereas projects 2 and 3 have a combined initial investment of only €20 million (= €10 + 10). If projects 2 and 3 are accepted, the remaining €10 million must be left in the bank.

This situation points out that we should exercise care when using the profitability index in the real world. Nevertheless, while not perfect, the profitability index goes a long way towards handling capital rationing.

Real World Insight 6.2

Statoil

Even when market conditions are poor, there are still investment opportunities for sharp-eyed companies. Take Statoil, the international oil company, which invested $31 billion in a new North Sea oil field (the Johan Sverdrup field on the Norwegian side of the North Sea). With oil prices only $60 per barrel, and down from $110 just months before, it doesn't appear to make sense that an oil field investment would be worthwhile. Many oil firms had made significant redundancies and sold assets to stay afloat in this new regime of low oil prices and dwindling revenues.

So why did Statoil invest in the Johan Sverdrup field? It all comes down to investment appraisal. According to Statoil, investments of NOK120 billion are forecasted to be as much as NOK1,350 billion from total production revenues over 50 years. Production would be in the range of 315,000–380,000 barrels per day, so it would be easy to predict revenues based on different oil price forecasts. According to Wood Mackenzie, the energy consultancy firm, the IRR of this investment is about 23 per cent at an oil price of only $41 per barrel. At the cost of $60 per barrel, the IRR would be significantly higher.

6.8 Other Investment Appraisal Methods

This section considers three approaches that adapt standard investment appraisal models to specific situations.

The Modified Internal Rate of Return

Both the IRR and NPV methods assume that cash flows earned in the future are reinvested at the same rate as the internal rate of return. However, in many cases, this will not be true, and the firm may need to reinvest future investment cash flows in another part of the business or project with a different discount rate.

For example, consider a firm with a project generating the following cash flows. The company's discount rate is 10 per cent:

Year	0	1	2	3	4
Cash flow	-1,000	400	400	300	300

The IRR of this project is 16 per cent (check for yourself).

If the company were to reinvest the project cash flows elsewhere in the business, the reinvestment rate of the future cash flows would be the company's discount rate of 10 per cent. When the reinvestment rate differs from the IRR, we must calculate the modified internal rate of return (MIRR). Therefore, the first step is to calculate the terminal value of the project cash flows using the reinvestment rate. In this example, the reinvestment rate is 10 per cent, and the IRR is 16 per cent.

Year	0	1	2	3	4
Cash flow	-1,000	400	400	300	300
Year 1 cash flow of 400 compounded 3 years at 10 per cent					532.4
Year 2 cash flow of 400 compounded 2 years at 10 per cent					484
Year 3 cash flow of 300 compounded 1 year at 10 per cent					330
Cash flows	-1,000				1,646.4

We have converted the project to two cash flows: the initial outlay of 1,000 and the terminal value in year 4 of 1,646.4. We calculate the MIRR as follows:

$$MIRR = \frac{\sqrt[n]{\text{Terminal cash flow}}}{\text{Initial investment}} - 1$$

In the example above, the MIRR is:

$$MIRR = \sqrt[4]{\frac{1,646.4}{1,000}} - 1 = 0.1327 = 13.27\%$$

Note how the MIRR of 13.27 per cent is less than the IRR of 16 per cent. This is because the reinvestment rate of 10 per cent is lower than the IRR.

Many analysts argue that the MIRR method is more realistic than IRR because it assumes project cash flows will be reinvested elsewhere in the firm rather than in a similar project to the investment. That is, IRR and NPV assume project cash flows will be reinvested in the same project, which might not be possible.

Margin of Safety

The margin of safety is not so much a separate investment appraisal method as an additional step in using net present value. The rationale is you accept a project only if its present value is a certain percentage above the asking price or initial investment. In other words, the present value of future cash flows must be higher than the asking price by a target percentage rate (the margin of safety). The approach has well-known supporters, including Warren Buffett, the famous US investor.

Consider a project with a 10 per cent discount rate and the following cash flows:

Year	0	1	2	3
Cash flow	-€900	€200	€400	€600

Your company requires a margin of safety of 20 per cent on any investment to minimize the risk of losses. Therefore, the PV of future cash flows is:

$$\text{PV} = \frac{200}{1.1} + \frac{400}{1.1^2} + \frac{600}{1.1^3} = €963.19$$

The project thus has a positive NPV of €963.19. The margin of safety is presented below:

$$\text{Margin of safety} = 1 - \frac{\text{Initial investment}}{\text{Present value (Future cash flow)}} = 1 - \frac{€900}{€963.19} = 0.0656 = 6.56\%$$

Although the NPV is positive, the project would be rejected because the firm has a 20 per cent margin of safety.

The margin of safety has received a lot of criticism because it essentially adjusts for risk twice. The discount rate incorporates the risk of the project, and the margin of safety adds an additional arbitrary and subjective buffer.

Also, while the margin of safety minimizes the risk of loss, its recommendation is only as good as the project's cash flow and discount rate estimates. If either is biased or in error, the present value of the cash flows will be wrong, and the margin of safety may give an inappropriate sense of certainty in the decision.

Another criticism of the margin of safety is that the target percentage is arbitrary and subjective. This is the same criticism we made for the payback period – the margin of safety target percentage is dependent on the investor's risk tolerance, and perfectly good projects, like the one above, may be rejected. But on the other hand, ignoring too many positive NPV projects because they don't meet the margin of safety will reduce a company's growth opportunities and firm value.

Net Present Social Value

Many firms working in sustainability or large infrastructure projects will also wish to present the social benefits of an investment. This may be for the firm's shareholders or required by local government authorities to ensure large public works are not detrimental to society or the countryside.

Net present social value (NPSV) or net present public value (NPVV) is an investment appraisal method that considers the social benefits and costs associated with a project, in addition to the investment's financial costs and benefits. NPSV provides a way to assess the broader impact of a project on society, and is particularly useful for projects with significant social or environmental implications.

To calculate the NPSV of a project, the social benefits and costs must be quantified and valued and then discounted to their present value using a discount rate that reflects the time value of money and the risk associated with the project. If the present value of the social benefits exceeds the present value of the social costs, the project has a positive NPSV and is considered to have a positive impact on society.

To illustrate the calculation of NPSV, consider a hypothetical project to build a new community centre in a city. The project is expected to generate social benefits of £100,000 per year over the next five years, primarily from improved community cohesion and social well-being. However, the project is also expected to generate social costs of £50,000 per year over the same period, primarily from increased traffic and noise pollution.

To calculate the NPSV, we first need to discount the future social benefits and costs to their present value using a discount rate. For example, assume a discount rate of 5 per cent.

1 Calculate the net cash flows to society:

Year	1	2	3	4	5
Social Benefits	100,000	100,000	100,000	100,000	100,000
Social Costs	50,000	50,000	50,000	50,000	50,000
Net Cash Flows	**50,000**	**50,000**	**50,000**	**50,000**	**50,000**

1 Calculate the NPSV of the community centre:

$$\text{NPSV} = \frac{£50,000}{(1.05)^1} + \frac{£50,000}{(1.05)^2} + \frac{£50,000}{(1.05)^3} + \frac{£50,000}{(1.05)^4} + \frac{£50,000}{(1.05)^5} = £216,473.83$$

Since the NPSV is positive, the project positively impacts society. Clearly, the firm would also need to calculate the NPV to ensure the community centre added value to the shareholders.

Sustainability in Action 6.1

HS2 and NPSV

One example of using NPSV is the High Speed 2 (HS2) railway project in the United Kingdom. HS2 was a proposed high-speed rail link between London and the north of England to improve transport infrastructure and connectivity, promote economic growth and reduce carbon emissions. However, the project was criticized for its high cost and potential social and environmental impacts, such as noise pollution and loss of wildlife habitats.

There have been many studies into the impact of the proposed high-speed rail line. A cost–benefit analysis would need to be conducted to assess the NPSV of infrastructure projects like HS2, including financial and non-financial costs and benefits. For example, assume the present value of the project's social benefits is £55.7 billion, primarily from improved transport connectivity, economic growth and reduced carbon emissions. Assume the present value of the social costs is estimated to be £52.1 billion, primarily from the construction and operation of the railway and its potential impact on the environment.

The NPSV of the HS2 project would thus be estimated to be £3.6 billion. This positive NPSV suggests that the project has a net positive impact on society.

Source: https://assets.publishing.service.gov.uk/government/uploads/system/uploads/attachment_data/file/286611/hs2-economic-case.pdf

6.9 The Practice of Capital Budgeting

So far this chapter has asked 'Which capital budgeting methods should companies be using?' An equally important question is this: 'Which methods *are* companies using?' Table 6.4 helps answer this question. The figures in the table are the percentage of firms from the country sample that said they 'Always Used' or 'Almost Always Used' a method. As can be seen from the table, there is quite a substantial variation in the frequency with which different techniques are utilized. Most companies use the IRR and NPV methods, which is not surprising given the theoretical advantages of these approaches. The most interesting point is that, for a number of countries, the payback period is very popular.

Capital expenditures by individual corporations can add up to enormous sums for the economy as a whole. For example, for the financial year 2018, the energy firm Centrica showed an outflow of £491 million in investing activities. You may think this is a significant amount, but it is dwarfed by Shell, which spent more than £6 billion in capital expenditure over the same period.

The use of quantitative techniques in capital budgeting varies with the industry. As one would imagine, firms that are better able to estimate cash flows are more likely to use NPV. For example, estimation of cash flow in certain aspects of the oil business is entirely feasible. Because of this, energy-related firms were among the first to use NPV analysis. Conversely, the cash flows in the motion picture business are very hard to project. The grosses of great hits like *Titanic, Black Panther* and *Avengers* were far, far higher than anyone imagined. The substantial failures like *King Arthur: Legend of the Sword* and *Mortal Engines* were unexpected as well. Because of this, NPV analysis is frowned upon in the movie business.

Another insight from Table 6.4 is that companies use a combination of investment appraisal methods to make capital expenditure decisions. This is without a doubt the most sensible strategy, and combinations of the techniques introduced in this chapter can be the basis for hybrid decision rules for investment appraisal. For example, consider an energy firm that is capital rationed and experiences large winding-down costs for projects (such as dismantling oil rigs and clean-up costs at the end of an oil field's life). An appropriate combination would be NPV and payback period. NPV tells the financial manager whether the project will add value and includes all cash flows, while the payback period will say how long it takes to get the initial investment back. A decision rule that requires both a payback period less than four years and a positive NPV would be a typical decision rule. As can be seen, combining investment appraisal methods can open up a whole set of innovative decision rules to make financial decisions.

Table 6.4 Percentage of Firms in Selected Countries that Use Capital Budgeting Techniques

Country	NPV	IRR	Payback Period	AAR
Australia	96%	64%	59%	19%
China	84%	89%	84%	9%
Finland	62%	43%	51%	3%
France	70%	44%	51%	16%
Germany	78%	42%	50%	32%
India	50%	52%	38%	0%
Malaysia	91%	69%	71%	37%
Netherlands	89%	56%	65%	35%
Poland	76%	48%	87%	63%
Singapore	86%	71%	71%	47%
South Africa	99%	79%	54%	14%
Sweden	84%	30%	54%	24%
UK	80%	53%	69%	38%
USA	95%	76%	57%	20%

Source: Adapted from Table 10, Andor, G., S.K. Mohanty and T. Toth (2015) 'Capital Budgeting Practices: A Survey of Central and Eastern European Firms', *Emerging Markets Review*, Vol. 23, 148–172.

Summary and Conclusions

1. In this chapter, we covered different investment decision rules. We evaluated the most popular alternatives to the NPV: the payback period, the discounted payback period, the accounting rate of return, the internal rate of return and the profitability index. In doing so, we learned more about the NPV.
2. While we found that the alternatives have some redeeming qualities when all is said and done, they are not the NPV rule; for those of us in finance, that makes them decidedly second rate.
3. Of the competitors to NPV, IRR must be ranked above both payback and accounting rate of return. In fact, IRR always reaches the same decision as NPV in the typical case where the initial outflows of an independent investment project are followed only by a series of inflows.
4. We classified the flaws of IRR into two types. First, we considered the general case applying to both independent and mutually exclusive projects. There appeared to be two problems here:
   (a) Some projects have cash inflows followed by one or more outflows. The IRR rule is inverted here: one should accept when the IRR is *below* the discount rate.
   (b) Some projects have changes of sign in their cash flows. Here, there are likely to be multiple internal rates of return. The practitioner must use either NPV or modified internal rate of return here.
5. Next, we considered the specific problems with the NPV for mutually exclusive projects. We showed that, due to differences in either size or timing, the project with the highest IRR need not have the highest NPV. Hence, the IRR rule should not be applied. (Of course, NPV can still be used.)

   However, we then calculated incremental cash flows. For ease of calculation, we suggested subtracting the cash flows of the smaller project from the cash flows of the larger project. In that way the incremental initial cash flow is negative. One can always reach a correct decision by accepting the larger project if the incremental IRR is higher than the discount rate.
6. We described capital rationing as the case where funds are limited to a fixed monetary amount. With capital rationing, the profitability index is a useful method of adjusting the NPV.

Questions and Problems

CONCEPT

1 **Net Present Value** What is meant by a project's NPV, and what is the decision rule? List the main strengths of the net present value method. What do you think are the weaknesses of NPV in practical capital budgeting analysis?

2 **Payback Period** What is a project's payback period? Discuss the advantages and disadvantages of the payback period method. If a project has a payback period less than the lifetime of the project, can we know for sure whether the NPV will be positive or negative?

3 **Discounted Payback Period** Why would a manager use discounted payback period? Can the discounted payback ever be longer than the conventional payback? In what instances is discounted payback used?

4 **Average Accounting Return** Average accounting return is a popular method with accountants. Review the main strengths and weaknesses of the methodology for practical capital budgeting.

5 **Internal Rate of Return** In many countries, internal rate of return is the most popular capital budgeting technique, yet in almost all academic textbooks, NPV is put forward as the best method. Why do you think this is the case?

6 **Problems with IRR** Review the main problems that arise when one uses only IRR to evaluate potential projects. In spite of these pitfalls, why do many managers use IRR instead of NPV to evaluate projects?

7 **Profitability Index** What is the profitability index, and how is it calculated? Discuss the main applications of the profitability index in capital budgeting. When is it most useful and what are its weaknesses? What is its relationship with NPV?

8 **MIRR and NPSV** In which situations would you use MIRR instead of IRR? Explain your answer using a practical example. Why is the net present social value (NPSV) method considered useful for projects with significant social or environmental implications?

9 **Margin of Safety** Although margin of safety is used by many investors, explain the method's major criticisms. Do you agree with these? Explain.

10 **The Practice of Capital Budgeting** Why do you think certain capital budgeting techniques are used more often in some countries than in others? If NPV is theoretically the best methodology and most managers of large European corporations have studied corporate finance, why do not all companies use the method?

REGULAR

11 **Calculating Payback Period and NPV** Shire plc has the following mutually exclusive projects:

Year	Project A (£)	Project B (£)
0	−14,000	−6,000
1	4,000	4,500
2	5,500	2,200
3	8,000	200

(a) Suppose Shire's payback period cut-off is two years. Which of these two projects should be chosen?

(b) Suppose Shire uses the NPV rule to rank these two projects. Which project should be chosen if the appropriate discount rate is 12 per cent?

12 **Investment Criteria** Which of the following statements is correct?

(a) The NPV and the IRR always result in the same accept/reject decisions.

(b) The NPV cannot rank mutually exclusive projects.

(c) The IRR cannot rank mutually exclusive projects.

(d) The NPV cannot be used in cases of multiple IRRs.

13 **Discounted Payback and Discount Rates** A project has annual cash flows of −€45,000, €35,000, €15,000 and €5,000. What is the payback period for this project? What is the maximum discount rate that would result in a positive NPV? What is the discounted payback period with this discount rate? Does this surprise you? Explain.

14 Calculating Discounted Payback An investment project has annual cash inflows of £20,000, £35,400, £48,000 and £54,500, and a discount rate of 14 per cent. What is the discounted payback period for these cash flows if the initial cost is £100,000? What if the initial cost is £120,000? What if it is £170,000?

15 Average Accounting Return Your firm is considering purchasing a machine that requires an annual investment of €16,000. Depreciation is calculated using the straight-line method over the life of the machine. The machine generates, on average, €4,500 per year in additional net income. Assume that the estimated economic life is five years.

(a) What is the average accounting return for this machine?

(b) What three flaws are inherent in this decision rule?

16 Vedanta Resources AAR Vedanta Resources has invested £8 million in a new mining project lasting three years. Depreciation is charged on a straight-line basis to zero over the course of the project. The project generates pre-tax income of £2 million each year. The pre-tax income already includes the depreciation expense. If the tax rate is 23 per cent, what is the project's average accounting return (AAR)?

17 NPSV Consider a hypothetical project that generates social benefits of £40,000 per year over the next three years and social costs of £20,000 per year over the same period. Assume a discount rate of 8 per cent. Calculate the net present social value (NPSV) of the project.

18 Calculating NPV Calculate the NPV of the following project for discount rates of 5, 12 and 19 per cent:

Year	0	1	2
Cash flow	–£77,000	+£55,000	+£320,000

19 Calculating IRR and MIRR Marielle Machinery Works is considering a project that has an initial investment of £10,000 and expected cash flows of £0 in year 1, £7,500 in year 2 and £8,500 in year 3. The company uses the IRR rule to accept or reject projects, and has asked for your assessment on what to do if the required rate of return is 12 per cent. A colleague suggests that, since the firm can only reinvest the cash flows at the firm's discount rate of 12 per cent, you should use the MIRR method instead. What is the project's MIRR and how does it compare to the IRR? Which method should you use?

20 Calculating Profitability Index What is the profitability index for a project with an initial investment of €14,000, which has cash flows of €7,300 in year 1, €6,900 in year 2 and €5,700 in year 3? Should the project be accepted or rejected if the discount rate is 14 per cent?

21 Choosing between Projects with the Profitability Index Suppose the following two independent investment opportunities are available to Greenplain Ltd. The appropriate discount rate is 10 per cent.

Year	Project Alpha (€)	Project Beta (€)
0	-500	-2,000
1	300	300
2	700	1,800
3	600	1,700

(a) Compute the profitability index for each of the two projects.

(b) Which project(s) should Greenplain accept based on the profitability index rule?

22 Problems with IRR Suppose you are offered £5,000 today but must make the following payments:

Year	Cash Flows (£)
0	5,000
1	-2,500
2	-2,000
3	-1,000
4	-1,000

(a) What is the IRR of this offer?

(b) If the appropriate discount rate is 10 per cent, should you accept this offer?

(c) If the appropriate discount rate is 20 per cent, should you accept this offer?

(d) What is the NPV of the offer if the appropriate discount rate is 10 per cent? 20 per cent?

(e) Are the decisions under the NPV rule in part (d) consistent with those of the IRR rule?

23 NPV versus IRR Consider the following cash flows on two mutually exclusive projects for Tomatina Recreation SA. Both projects require an annual return of 15 per cent.

Year	Deepwater Fishing (€)	New Submarine Ride (€)
0	-600,000	-1,800,000
1	270,000	1,000,000
2	350,000	700,000
3	300,000	900,000

As a financial analyst for Tomatina, you are asked the following questions:

(a) If your decision rule is to accept the project with the greater IRR, which project should you choose?

(b) Because you are fully aware of the IRR rule's scale problem, you calculate the incremental IRR for the cash flows. Based on your computation, which project should you choose?

(c) To be prudent, you compute the NPV for both projects. Which project should you choose? Is it consistent with the incremental IRR rule?

24 Capital Budgeting Tools Consider the following cash flows:

Year	0	1	2	3	4	5
Cash flow	−£35,000	£14,000	£15,000	−£12,000	£17,000	£17,000

(a) What is the payback period for the above project? Assume the cash flows are received continuously throughout each year.

(b) If the discount rate is 10 per cent, what is the NPV of the project?

(c) If the discount rate is 10 per cent, what is the IRR of the project? How many IRRs does the project have? Explain how you would deal with this problem.

(d) If the discount rate is 10 per cent, what is the PI of the project?

25 Comparing Investment Criteria Software games company Avalanche Entertainment is considering expanding its highly successful online game franchise to the board game or trading card environment. The company has decided that it will invest in one project but not both. Consider the following cash flows of the two mutually exclusive projects. Assume the discount rate for Avalanche Entertainment is 10 per cent.

Year	Trading Cards (€)	Board Game (€)
0	-200	-2,000
1	300	2,200
2	100	900
3	100	500

(a) Based on the payback period rule, which project should be chosen?

(b) Based on the NPV, which project should be chosen?

(c) Based on the IRR, which project should be chosen?

(d) Based on the incremental IRR, which project should be chosen?

26 Capital Budgeting Sandy Grey Ltd is in the process of deciding whether or not to revise its line of mobile phones, which it manufactures and sells. Its sole market is large corporations and it has not as yet focused on the retail sector. It has estimated that the revision will cost £220,000. Cash flows from increased sales will be £80,000 in the first year. These cash flows will increase by 5 per cent per year. The firm estimates that the new line will be obsolete five years from now. Assume the initial cost is paid now and all revenues are received at the end of each year. If the company requires a 10 per cent return for such an investment, should it undertake the revision? Use three investment evaluation techniques to arrive at your answer. Would Sandy Grey go ahead if it invested only in projects with a margin of safety of 20 per cent?

27 Comparing Investment Criteria for Pinto plc Pinto plc is considering spending €10,000 on insulating its office, which will save it €1,000 per year in heating expenses in perpetuity.

(a) What is the NPV of the investment when the cost of capital is 8 per cent?

(b) What is the IRR of the investment?

(c) What is the payback period of the investment?

28 Comparing Investment Criteria for Amaro Canned Fruits The treasurer of Amaro Canned Fruits has projected the cash flows of projects A, B and C as follows:

Year	Project A (€)	Project B (€)	Project C (€)
0	−100,000	−200,000	−100,000
1	70,000	130,000	75,000
2	70,000	130,000	60,000

Suppose the relevant discount rate is 12 per cent a year.

(a) Compute the profitability index for each of the three projects.

(b) Compute the NPV for each of the three projects.

(c) Suppose these three projects are independent. Which project(s) should Amaro accept based on the profitability index rule?

(d) Suppose these three projects are mutually exclusive. Which project(s) should Amaro accept based on the profitability index rule?

(e) Suppose Amaro's budget for these projects is €300,000. The projects are not divisible. Which project(s) should Amaro accept?

(f) Suppose Amaro had a margin of safety of 10 per cent. Which project(s) should it accept?

29 Comparing Investment Criteria for Tadcaster Rubber Company Consider the following cash flows of two mutually exclusive projects for Tadcaster Rubber Company. Assume the discount rate for Tadcaster Rubber Company is 10 per cent.

Year	Dry Prepreg (€)	Solvent Prepreg (€)
0	−800,000	−600,000
1	500,000	400,000
2	300,000	600,000
3	900,000	200,000

(a) Based on the payback period, which project should be taken?

(b) Based on the NPV, which project should be taken?

(c) Based on the IRR, which project should be taken?

(d) Based on this analysis, is incremental IRR analysis necessary? If yes, please conduct the analysis.

CHALLENGE

30 Cash Flow Intuition A project has an initial cost of I, has a required return of R, and pays C annually for N years.

(a) Find C in terms of I and N such that the project has a payback period just equal to its life.

(b) Find C in terms of I, N and R such that this is a profitable project according to the NPV decision rule.

(c) Find C in terms of I, N and R such that the project has a benefit–cost ratio of 2.

31 Comparing Investments You are a senior manager at Airbus and have been authorized to spend up to €200,000 for projects. The three projects you are considering have the following characteristics:

Project A: Initial investment of €150,000. Cash flow of €50,000 at year 1 and €100,000 at year 2. This is a plant expansion project, where the required rate of return is 10 per cent.

Project B: Initial investment of €200,000. Cash flow of €200,000 at year 1 and €111,000 at year 2. This is a new product development project, where the required rate of return is 20 per cent.

Project C: Initial investment of €100,000. Cash flow of €100,000 at year 1 and €100,000 at year 2. This is a market expansion project, where the required rate of return is 20 per cent.

Assume the corporate discount rate is 10 per cent.

Please offer your recommendations, backed by your analysis:

	A	B	C	Implications
Payback period				
IRR				
Incremental IRR				
PI				
NPV				

32 **Project Valuation** The financial manager of Solsken is evaluating a proposal to purchase a new solar machine unit that has a lifetime of 10 years. The new machine would allow the company to make cost savings of SKr4 million per annum. The new fully solar machine would cost SKr9 million and have a resale value of SKr1 million at the end of the project. The required rate of return on such investments is 14 per cent. However, the firm can only reinvest future cash flows from the project at the company discount rate of 12 per cent. Use four methods to appraise the value of this investment.

33 **Payback and NPV** An investment under consideration has a payback of seven years and a cost of £483,000. If the required return is 12 per cent, what is the worst-case NPV? What is the best-case NPV? Explain. Assume the cash flows are conventional.

34 **Multiple IRRs** This problem is useful for testing the ability of financial calculators and computer software. Consider the following cash flows. How many different IRRs are there? (*Hint:* Search between 20 per cent and 70 per cent.) When should we take this project?

Year	Cash Flow (£)
0	−504
1	2,862
2	−6,070
3	5,700
4	−2,000

35 **NPV Valuation: Yuvhadit Ltd** Yuvhadit Ltd wants to set up a private cemetery business. According to the CFO, Barry M. Deep, business is 'looking up'. As a result, the cemetery project will provide a net cash inflow of €80,000 for the firm during the first year, and the cash flows are projected to grow at a rate of 6 per cent per year for ever. The project requires an initial investment of €800,000.

(a) If Yuvhadit requires a 12 per cent return on such undertakings, should the cemetery business be started?

(b) The company is somewhat unsure about the assumption of a 6 per cent growth rate in its cash flows. At what constant growth rate would the company just break even if it still required a 12 per cent return on investment?

36 **Calculating IRR: Moshi Mining** Moshi Mining is set to open a gold mine in northern Tanzania. The mine will cost 6 million rand to open and will have an economic life of 12 years. It will generate a cash inflow of 1 million rand at the end of the first year, and the cash inflows are projected to grow at 10 per cent per year for the next 11 years. After 12 years, the mine will be abandoned. Abandonment costs will be 500,000 rand at the end of year 12.

(a) What is the IRR for the gold mine?

(b) Moshi Mining requires a 10 per cent return on such undertakings. Should the mine be opened?

37 **Discussing IRR and NPV** You are out having dinner with your two colleagues who are also studying finance. John, who loves the IRR method, tells you that ranking projects by IRR is fine as long as each project's cash flows can be reinvested at the project's IRR. Your other friend, Beverley, is confused and asks whether NPV assumes that cash flows are always reinvested at the opportunity cost of capital. Take a deep breath and explain whether John and Beverley are correct. Explain to John and Beverley an appropriate method that addresses this issue.

38 **Investment Appraisal in Practice** Many companies have a set of appraisal methods that they recommend their managers use when considering new project investments. Assume that your company uses three methods: NPV (discount rate of 20 per cent on all new projects); payback period (two to three years maximum); and accounting rate of return (20 per cent on all new projects). Explain to your manager why the firm's investment policy may lead

to conflicting recommendations. Why do you think your firm has this policy? Is your manager correct to argue that you should focus mainly on the NPV method, using the other criteria as supplementary methodologies? What should the firm do if the project has an NPV of zero? The manager says that he is thinking of introducing a margin of safety on all new projects. What is your advice?

39 **Calculating Incremental Cash Flows** Darin Clay, the CFO of MakeMoney.com, has to decide between the following two projects:

Year	Project Million	Project Billion
0	−£1,500	$-£I_0$
1	$I_0 + 200$	$I_0 + 500$
2	1,200	1,500
3	1,500	2,000

The expected rate of return for either of the two projects is 12 per cent. What is the range of initial investment (I_0) for which Project Billion is more financially attractive than Project Million?

40 **Problems with IRR: Kimaheedin Ltd** Kimaheedin Ltd has a project with the following cash flows:

Year	Cash Flow (£)
0	20,000
1	-26,000
2	13,000

What is the IRR of the project? What is happening here?

41 **Limitations of NPSV** Discuss the limitations of using the net present social value (NPSV) method to evaluate investments in social and environmental projects. How can these limitations be addressed or overcome?

Exam Question (45 minutes)

1 Assume you are the new financial manager of the bed mattress firm Fairy Tale Lullaby Ltd. The firm has always used payback period and accounting rate of return to appraise new investments. With your trusty copy of *Corporate Finance* to hand, you believe that other methods may be more appropriate for the firm. Write a report to the owners of Fairy Tale Lullaby reviewing the different methods that can be used in investment appraisal, together with their strengths and weaknesses. Comment on any practical issues that Fairy Tale Lullaby may face in implementing these methods. **(50 marks)**

2 A solar panel production firm, Soleil SA, is considering an investment in new solar production technology. The new investment would require initial funding of €4 million today and further expenditure on manufacture of €1 million in each of years 6 and 7. The net cash inflow for years 1 to 4 is €2.34 million per year. Some equipment could be sold at the end of year 5 when the production ends and, together with the cash flows from operation, would produce a net cash flow of €4.85 million. Evaluate the investment using four investment appraisal criteria. The required rate of return of Soleil SA is 12 per cent and Soleil has been known to use a payback period of two years in the past. However, the firm's managers believe that this payback period may be too short. **(50 marks)**

Total Marks: 100

Mini Case

Davies Electronics

You have set up a new firm in Copenhagen to produce mobile face-recognition technology for all new smartphones. An opportunity has arisen that would result in a new contract with a major mobile phone manufacturer that would massively transform your firm's operations. The contract would require a significant upfront investment of €50 million and would last for eight years. The year after the contract has ended (that is, in year 9), your firm will bear all decommissioning costs, which are expected to be €8 million. The expected cash flows each year from the contract are shown in the table below. Davies Electronics has a 12 per cent required return on all of its technologies but can only reinvest future cash flows at a rate of 10 per cent.

Year	Cash Flow (€)
0	-50,000,000
1	6,000,000
2	9,000,000
3	17,000,000
4	23,000,000
5	20,500,000
6	14,000,000
7	11,000,000
8	7,000,000
9	-8,000,000

1 Construct a spreadsheet to calculate the payback period, internal rate of return, modified internal rate of return and net present value of the proposed new technology.
2 Based on your analysis, should the company produce the new face-recognition technology?
3 Bonus question: Most spreadsheets do not have a built-in formula to calculate the payback period. Write a macro that calculates the payback period for a project.

Practical Case Study

Climate change has been identified as one of the most significant challenges facing businesses worldwide. Many firms have been forced to undergo significant restructuring of their operations to adapt to the impacts of climate change, including supply chain disruptions. In this case study, you will examine the clothing firm, H&M.

H&M is a multinational clothing retailer headquartered in Sweden, with more than 5,000 stores in 74 countries worldwide. As a company that relies heavily on global supply chains, H&M has experienced significant disruptions to its operations in recent years due to the impacts of climate change. These disruptions have included extreme weather events, such as floods and wildfires, which have disrupted transportation and production facilities, as well as changes in temperature and rainfall patterns, which have affected crop yields and availability of raw materials.

1 What has been the impact of climate change on H&M's supply chain?
2 What has H&M done in response to climate change?
3 In your opinion, has H&M made enough of an effort to reduce its impact on the environment? Explain.

Additional Reading

The techniques presented in this chapter are used in all industries to assess the value of potential investments. The papers below give the reader some insight into their strengths and weaknesses:

1 Chiang, Y.H., E.W.L. Cheng and P.T.I. Lam (2010) 'Employing the Net Present Value – Consistent IRR Methods for PFI Contracts', *Journal of Construction Engineering and Management*, Vol. 136, No. 7, 811–814.

2 Johnson, N.H. and B.D. Solomon (2010) 'A Net Present Value Analysis for a Wind Turbine Purchase at a Small US College', *Energies*, Vol. 3, No. 5, 943–959.

3 Kahn, M.J. and E.F. Nelling (2010) 'Estimating the Value of Medical Education: A Net Present Value Approach', *Teaching and Learning in Medicine: An International Journal*, Vol. 22, No. 3, 205–208.

4 Marchioni, A. and C.A. Magni (2018) 'Investment Decisions and Sensitivity Analysis: NPV – Consistency of Rates of Return', *European Journal of Operational Research*, Vol. 268, No. 1, 361–372.

5 Patrick, M. and N. French (2016) 'The Internal Rate of Return (IRR): Projections, Benchmarks and Pitfalls', *Journal of Property Investment & Finance*, Vol. 34, No. 6, 664–669.

6 Zore, Ž., L. Čuček, D. Širovnik, Z.N. Pintarič and Z. Kravanja (2018) 'Maximizing the Sustainability Net Present Value of Renewable Energy Supply Networks', *Chemical Engineering Research and Design*, Vol. 131, 245–265.

Endnotes

1 Depreciation will be treated in more detail in the next chapter.

2 Of course, we could have directly solved for *R* in this example after setting NPV equal to zero. However, with long series of cash flows, one cannot generally directly solve for *R*. Instead, one is forced to use trial and error (or let a machine use trial and error).

3 One can derive the IRR directly for a problem with an initial outflow and up to four subsequent inflows. In the case of two subsequent inflows, for example, the quadratic formula is needed. In general, however, only trial and error will work for an outflow and five or more subsequent inflows.

4 This paragraph implicitly assumes that the cash flows of the project are risk free. In this way we can treat the borrowing rate as the discount rate for a firm needing £100. With risky cash flows, another discount rate would be chosen. However, the intuition behind the decision to accept when the IRR is less than the discount rate would still apply.

5 The calculations are

$$-£100 + \frac{£230}{1.1} - \frac{£132}{(1.1)^2}$$

$$-£10 + 209.09 - 109.09 = 0$$

and

$$-£100 + \frac{£230}{1.2} - \frac{£132}{(1.2)^2}$$

$$-£100 + 191.67 - 91.67 = 0$$

Thus, we have multiple rates of return.

6 We assume a zero rate of interest because his class lasted only 90 minutes. It just seemed like a lot longer.

7 Alternatively, we could have subtracted the larger project's cash flows from the smaller project's cash flows. This would have left an *inflow* at date 0, making it necessary to use the IRR rule for financing situations. This would work, but we find it more confusing.

8 In this example, we first showed that the NPVs of the two projects are equal when the discount rate is 10.55 per cent. We next showed that the incremental IRR is also 10.55 per cent. This is not a coincidence; this equality must *always* hold. The incremental IRR is the rate that causes the incremental cash flows to have zero NPV. The incremental cash flows have zero NPV when the two projects have the same NPV.

Chapter 7

Making Capital Investment Decisions

Learning Objectives

After reading this chapter you should be able to:

LO1 Explain the concept of incremental cash flows and their importance in capital investment decisions.

LO2 Analyse a real-world example to demonstrate the process of evaluating capital investment projects.

LO3 Evaluate the impact of inflation on capital budgeting and discuss appropriate methods for adjusting cash flows to account for inflation.

LO4 Compare and contrast alternative definitions of operating cash flow and their implications for capital investment analysis.

LO5 Apply the equivalent annual cost method to assess investments with unequal lives and determine the most cost-effective option.

Corporate financial managers have a responsibility to identify and exploit investment opportunities wherever they can. One such area relates to the rise of superbugs and dangerous antibiotic-resistant diseases. It may seem tasteless to think of financial gain from other people's misfortune, but investments in technology and medicine may result in the eradication of these microscopic killers and prevent the emergence of new and as yet unknown biological dangers.

For example, many pharmaceutical firms (e.g., Pfizer, BioNtech, Moderna, Johnson & Johnson and AstraZeneca) invested heavily in response to the global Covid-19 pandemic to create an effective vaccine. At the same time, almost all firms made new investments in digital technologies as working practices changed and the need for distributed workforces became urgent. All investment cases would have undergone a full financial analysis before an announcement was made.

This chapter follows up on Chapter 6 by delving more deeply into capital budgeting and the evaluation of investments similar to the examples presented above. We identify the relevant cash flows of a project, including initial investment, outlays, requirements for net working capital and operating cash flows. Further, we look at the effects of depreciation and taxes. We also examine the impact of inflation and show how to consistently evaluate the NPV analysis of a project.

Source: Jean-Marc Pierard/123RF.

Key Notations

NPV	Net present value	t_c	Corporate tax rate
EBIT	Earnings before interest and taxes	C_i	Cash flow at time i
OCF	Operating cash flows	PV	Present value

7.1 Incremental Cash Flows

Cash Flows, Not Accounting Income

Chapter 5 Page 137

You may not have thought about it, but there is a big difference between corporate finance courses and financial accounting courses. Techniques in corporate finance generally use cash flows, whereas financial accounting generally stresses income or earnings numbers. Certainly our text follows this tradition: our net present value techniques discount cash flows, not earnings. When considering a single project, we discount the cash flows that the firm receives from the project. When valuing the firm as a whole, we discount dividends – not earnings – because dividends are the cash flows that an investor receives. With the *free cash flow to the firm* method (see **Chapter 5**), we use cash flows themselves to value a firm.

Example 7.1

Relevant Cash Flows

Weber-Decker GmbH just paid €1 million in cash for a building as part of a new capital budgeting project. This entire €1 million is an immediate cash outflow. However, assuming 20 per cent reducing balance depreciation over 20 years, only €200,000 (= €1 million × 20 per cent) is considered an accounting expense in the current year. Current earnings are thereby reduced by only €200,000. The remaining €800,000 is expensed over the following 19 years. For capital budgeting purposes, the relevant cash outflow at date 0 is the full €1 million, not the reduction in earnings of only €200,000.

Always discount cash flows, not earnings, when performing a capital budgeting calculation. Earnings do not represent real money. You cannot spend out of earnings, you cannot eat out of earnings and you cannot pay dividends out of earnings. You can do these things only out of cash flow.

In addition, it is not enough to use cash flows. In calculating the NPV of a project, only cash flows that are *incremental* to the project should be used. These cash flows are the changes in the firm's cash flows that occur as a direct consequence of accepting the project. That is, we are interested in the difference between the cash flows of the firm with the project and the cash flows of the firm without the project.

The use of incremental cash flows sounds easy enough, but pitfalls abound in the real world. We describe how to avoid some of the pitfalls of determining incremental cash flows.

Sunk Costs

A **sunk cost** is a cost that has already occurred. Because sunk costs are in the past, they cannot be changed by the decision to accept or reject the project. Just as we 'let bygones be bygones', we should ignore such costs. Sunk costs are not incremental cash outflows.

Example 7.2

Sunk Costs

Hill Electronics Ltd is currently evaluating the NPV of establishing a line of 3D televisions. As part of the evaluation, the company had paid a consulting firm £100,000 to perform a test marketing analysis. The expenditure was made last year. Is this cost relevant for the capital budgeting decision now confronting the management of Hill Electronics Ltd?

The answer is no. The £100,000 is not recoverable, so the £100,000 expenditure is a sunk cost. Of course, the decision to spend £100,000 for a marketing analysis was a capital budgeting decision itself and was perfectly relevant *before* it was sunk. Our point is that once the company incurred the expense, the cost became irrelevant for any future decision.

Opportunity Costs

Your firm may have an asset that it is considering selling, leasing or employing elsewhere in the business. If the asset is used in a new project, potential revenues from alternative uses are lost. These lost revenues can meaningfully be viewed as costs. They are called **opportunity costs** because, by taking the project, the firm forgoes other opportunities for using the assets. Clearly, opportunity costs assume that another valuable opportunity will be forgone if the project is adopted. This, in itself, is a prediction of the future and estimated with a degree of uncertainty.

Example 7.3

Opportunity Costs

Suppose Martinez Trading has an empty warehouse in Salamanca that can be used to store a new line of e-readers. The company hopes to sell these e-readers to affluent European consumers. Should the warehouse be considered a cost in the decision to sell the machines?

The answer is yes. The company could sell the warehouse if the firm decides not to market the e-readers. Thus, the sales price of the warehouse is an opportunity cost in the e-reader decision.

Side Effects

Another difficulty in determining incremental cash flows comes from the side effects of the proposed project on other parts of the firm. A side effect is classified as either **erosion** (also cannibalization) or **synergy**. Erosion occurs when a new product reduces the sales and, hence, the cash flows of existing products. Synergy occurs when a new project increases the cash flows of existing projects. Because side effects predict the spending habits of customers, they are necessarily hypothetical and difficult to estimate.

Example 7.4

Synergies

Suppose Innovative Motors (IM) is determining the NPV of a new convertible sports car. Some of the customers who would purchase the car are owners of IM's SUVs. Are all sales and profits from the new convertible sports car incremental?

The answer is no because some of the cash flow represents transfers from other elements of IM's product line. This is erosion, which must be included in the NPV calculation. Without taking erosion into account, IM might erroneously calculate the NPV of the sports car to be, say, £100 million. If half the customers are transfers from the SUV and lost SUV sales have an NPV of –£150 million, the true NPV is –£50 million (= £100 million – £150 million).

IM is also contemplating the formation of a racing team. The team is forecast to lose money for the foreseeable future, with perhaps the best projection showing an NPV of –£35 million for the operation. However, IM's managers are aware that the team is likely to generate great publicity for all of IM's products. A consultant estimates that the increase in cash flows elsewhere in the firm has a present value of £65 million. Assuming that the consultant's estimates of synergy are trustworthy, the net present value of the team is £30 million (= £65 million – £35 million). The managers should form the team.

Allocated Costs

Frequently a particular expenditure benefits a number of projects. Accountants allocate this cost across the different projects when determining income. However, for capital budgeting purposes, this allocated cost should be viewed as a cash outflow of a project only if it is an incremental cost of the project.

Example 7.5

Allocated Costs

Voetmann Consulting NV devotes one wing of its suite of offices to a library requiring a cash outflow of €100,000 a year in upkeep. A proposed capital budgeting project is expected to generate revenue equal to 5 per cent of the overall firm's sales. An executive at the firm, H. Sears, argues that €5,000 (= 5 per cent × €100,000) should be viewed as the proposed project's share of the library's costs. Is this appropriate for capital budgeting?

The answer is no. One must ask what the difference is between the cash flows of the entire firm with the project and the cash flows of the entire firm without the project. The firm will spend €100,000 on library upkeep whether or not the proposed project is accepted. Because acceptance of the proposed project does not affect this cash flow, the cash flow should be ignored when calculating the NPV of the project.

7.2 Energy Renewables Ltd: An Example

We next consider the example of a proposed investment in an innovative renewable energy project. Our example involves the hypothetical firm, Energy Renewables Ltd, and the development of a new wind turbine technology.

In any capital budgeting analysis, the broad steps to follow are the same. These are:

1. Calculation of depreciation for each year
2. Generation of the statement of profit and loss (income statement) to identify the tax that is due to be paid
3. Construction of the cash flow forecast to generate cash flows
4. Investment appraisal analysis using the techniques introduced in Chapter 6.

In this example, we will take you through a detailed capital budgeting case, completing each step at a time. However, there is more than one way to arrive at the final decision so just try to understand the calculations and what is happening at each step.

History

Energy Renewables Ltd was originally established in 2001 to manufacture and research new solar power technology. However, in recent years, the company has moved away from its roots as a solar power expert to wind energy, as the market in this area has grown. Energy Renewables' management has sought opportunities in whatever businesses seem to have the potential for cash flow. Recently the firm identified a niche segment for small-scale wind turbines to provide low-cost energy to manufacturers that have an explicit environment policy relating to industrial waste. Although there are a number of options that environmentally friendly firms can pursue, Energy Renewables believes its wind technology will be very attractive to those firms that have an explicit policy towards environmental waste. It also believes that it would be difficult for competitors to take advantage of the opportunity because of the cost advantages from Energy Renewables' wind turbines and the firm's highly developed marketing skills in the sector.

Market Research

Market research has been carried out throughout Europe and the feedback was much better than expected. The company that Energy Renewables hired to undertake the analysis supported the conclusion that the new wind turbines could achieve a 10 to 15 per cent share of the market. Of course, some people at Energy Renewables complained about the £250,000 cost of the market research. (As we shall see later, this is a sunk cost and should not be included in project evaluation.)

The Proposal

As a result of the positive market research, Energy Renewables is considering an investment to build high-value manufacturing facilities to produce its wind turbines. The turbines would be manufactured in a large vacant lot owned by the firm. The vacant lot has been valued by an independent surveyor, who estimates that it could be sold now for £1,500,000 after taxes.

Your team has come up with the following estimates:

1 The technology underlying the wind turbines is expected to be obsolete after five years, at which point the project will be terminated.
2 The cost of the manufacturing facilities is £3,000,000. The facilities are expected to have an estimated market value at the end of five years of £1,000,000.
3 Production of wind turbines by year during the five-year life of the project is expected to be as follows: 8 units, 12 units, 24 units, 20 units and 12 units.
4 The price of turbines in the first year will be £200,000. The turbine market is uncertain, so you expect the price of turbines will increase at only 2 per cent per year, as compared to the anticipated general inflation rate of 5 per cent.
5 The rare metals used to produce wind turbines are rapidly becoming more expensive. Because of this, production cash outflows are expected to grow at 10 per cent per year. First-year production costs will be £100,000 per unit.
6 Net working capital (that is, investment in raw materials and inventory) will immediately (year 0) grow to £100,000. This will remain level until year 2, when it will grow to £160,000, then increase again to £250,000 in year 3. By year 4 the project will be winding down and net working capital will be £210,000. At the end of the project, net working capital will return to zero as all inventory and raw materials are sold off.
7 Based on Energy Renewables' taxable income, the appropriate incremental corporate tax rate in the wind turbine project is 20 per cent. The applicable discount rate for this type of investment is 12 per cent.

Step 1: Depreciation

In Europe, assets are depreciated for tax purposes using a system called capital allowances or tax depreciation. This effectively entails that assets are depreciated by a certain percentage each year. Assume the capital allowances rate on plant and machinery is 20 per cent per annum. That is, plant and machinery depreciate by 20 per cent per year. Depreciation of this kind is known as the reducing balance method, in contrast to straight-line depreciation, where asset values fall by the same amount each year.

The cost of the facilities is £3,000,000 and so depreciation in year 1 is £600,000 (20 per cent of £3,000,000). This leaves a residual value of £2,400,000 and, in year 2, the depreciation will be (20 per cent of £2,400,000 =) £480,000. The residual value at the end of year 2 will be (£2,400,000 – £480,000 =) £1,920,000. We calculate depreciation for the remaining life of the project in the same way. Table 7.1 provides a detailed breakdown of the depreciation calculation for the new project.

Table 7.1 Depreciation Calculation using Capital Allowances (20 per cent Reducing Balance, £s)

	1	2	3	4	5
Initial value	3,000,000	2,400,000	1,920,000	1,536,000	1,228,800
Depreciation	600,000	480,000	384,000	307,200	228,800
Residual value	2,400,000	1,920,000	1,536,000	1,228,800	1,000,000

Important note: In Table 7.1, we took the year 5 resale value of £1,000,000 and used this as the terminal value of the facilities. This resulted in a depreciation of £228,800 in the final year.

An alternative way of calculating the depreciation in the final year is to calculate depreciation as usual (that is, 20 per cent of £1,228,800 = £245,760), which gives a new terminal value of £1,228,800 – £245,760 = £983,040. There will then be a taxable gain of £16,960 on the sale of the facilities, which is the difference between the terminal value (£983,040) and the resale value (£1,000,000). The year 5 depreciation (£245,760) less the gain on the sale of the facilities (£16,960) is equal to £228,800, which is the same as the depreciation for year 5 in the approach taken in Table 7.1. Therefore, both methods end up with the same overall impact on net income and tax paid (check this for yourself).

In our alternative approach to depreciation, the market value of the facilities (£1,000,000) is greater than the book value (£983,040), giving a profit on the sale. Taxes must be paid on the profit because the difference between the market value and the book value is 'excess' depreciation, and it must be 'recaptured' when the asset is sold. In this case, Energy Renewables would have over-depreciated the asset by £16,960. Because the depreciation was too high, the company paid too little in taxes.

Notice this is not a tax on a long-term capital gain. Further, what is and what is not a capital gain is ultimately up to the taxing authorities, and the specific rules can be very complex. We will ignore capital gains taxes for the most part. Finally, if the book value exceeds the market value, then the difference is treated as a loss for tax purposes. For example, if Energy Renewables sold the facilities for £900,000, then the book value exceeds the market value by £83,040. In this case, Energy Renewables would make a tax saving.

Step 2: The Statement of Profit and Loss

In any capital budgeting analysis, an income statement must be prepared so that the firm's incremental tax costs can be calculated. Unlike depreciation, tax is a cash flow that must be estimated. Table 7.2 presents the operating revenues and costs of Energy Renewables; these follow from assumptions made by the corporate planning staff at the firm. In other words, the estimates critically depend on the fact that product prices are projected to increase at 2 per cent per year and costs per unit are projected to increase at 10 per cent per year.

Table 7.2 Operating Revenues and Costs of Energy Renewables (£s)

Year	1	2	3	4	5
Quantity produced	8	12	24	20	12
Price	200,000	204,000	208,080	212,242	216,486
Sales revenues	**1,600,000**	**2,448,000**	**4,993,920**	**4,244,832**	**2,597,837**
Cost per unit	100,000	110,000	121,000	133,100	146,410
Operating costs	**800,000**	**1,320,000**	**2,904,000**	**2,662,000**	**1,756,920**

Chapter 3 Page 63

The information in Table 7.2 is now used to prepare the project's income statement (see Chapter 3, Section 3.2 for more information on the income statement, or statement of profit and loss). The two main items are the sales revenues and operating costs. Table 7.3 gives the information that is used to calculate Energy Renewables' net income and tax payments. Remember that cash outflows are negative values and inflows are positive.

The key figure from Table 7.3 is the tax paid since this is a cash flow that needs to be included in step 3 of the capital budgeting analysis.

Table 7.3 Income Statement of Energy Renewables (£s)

Year	1	2	3	4	5
Sales	1,600,000	2,448,000	4,993,920	4,244,832	2,597,837
Operating costs	800,000	1,320,000	2,904,000	2,662,000	1,756,920
Depreciation	600,000	480,000	384,000	307,200	228,800
Income before taxes	200,000	648,000	1,705,920	1,275,632	612,117
Tax (at 20%)	40,000	129,600	341,184	255,126	122,423
Net income	160,000	518,400	1,364,736	1,020,506	489,694

Step 3: Cash Flow Forecast

In Step 3, we estimate the actual cash flows that will arise as a result of investing in the project. First, we need to calculate investment cash flows and then operating cash flows.

Investment Cash Flows

Chapter 26
Page 715

Investment cash flows arise from any expenditure on assets that are required to undertake the project. This includes inventory, property, machinery and other assets. We begin with net working capital.

Net working capital is defined as the difference between current assets and current liabilities (see **Chapter 26**, Section 26.1 for more information on managing net working capital). Like any other manufacturing firm, Energy Renewables finds that it must maintain an investment in working capital. It will purchase raw materials before production and sale, giving rise to an investment in inventory. It will maintain cash as a buffer against unforeseen expenditures. Its credit sales will generate trade receivables.

Management determines that an immediate (year 0) investment in the different items of working capital of £100,000 is required. Working capital is forecast to rise in the early years of the project as expansion occurs and then to fall to £0 by the project's end. In other words, the investment in working capital is to be completely recovered by the end of the project's life. This is a common assumption in capital budgeting and reflects the situation that all inventory is sold by the end, the cash balance maintained as a buffer is liquidated, and all outstanding credit sales (trade receivables) are collected.

Increases in working capital in the early years must be funded by cash generated elsewhere in the firm. Hence, these increases are viewed as cash *outflows*. To reiterate, it is the *increase* in working capital over a year that leads to a cash outflow in that year. Even if working capital is at a high level, there will be no cash outflow over a year if working capital stays constant over that year. Conversely, decreases in working capital in the later years are viewed as cash inflows. All of these cash flows are presented in Table 7.4. A more complete discussion of working capital is provided later in this section.

Table 7.4 Change in Net Working Capital (£s)

Year	0	1	2	3	4	5
Net working capital	100,000	100,000	160,000	250,000	210,000	
Change in net working capital	100,000		60,000	90,000	−40,000	−210,000
Cash flow	−100,000	0	−60,000	−90,000	40,000	210,000

Net working capital represents an investment of cash flows in the current assets and liabilities of the firm. These are short term in nature since they are used in the operationalization of the project. Long-term investment cash flows represent the investment in the manufacturing facilities themselves. We must also include any opportunity costs incurred as a result of undertaking the project.

The investment outlays for the project are summarized in Table 7.5 on the next page. They consist of four parts:

1. *The production facilities:* The purchase requires an immediate (year 0) cash outflow of £3,000,000. The firm realizes a cash inflow when the facilities are sold in year 5. These cash flows are shown in line 1 of Table 7.5.
2. *The opportunity cost of not selling the vacant lot:* If Energy Renewables accepts the wind turbine project, it will use a vacant lot and land that could otherwise be sold. The estimated sale price of the vacant lot and land is therefore included as an *opportunity cost* in year 0, as presented in line 2. Opportunity costs are treated as cash outflows for purposes of capital budgeting. However, note that if the project is accepted, management assumes that the vacant lot and land will be sold for £1,500,000 (after taxes) in year 5.
3. The market research cost of £250,000 is not included. The tests occurred in the past and should be viewed as a *sunk cost.*
4. *The investment in working capital:* To recap, there are three investments in this example: the manufacturing facilities, the opportunity cost of the vacant lot and land, and the changes in working capital. The total cash flow from these three investments is shown in line 4 of Table 7.5.

Operating Cash Flow

Chapter 3
Page 66

Operating cash flows arise from the investment itself (see **Chapter 3**, Section 3.5 for more information on cash flows). Clearly, these need to be positive for the project to be worthwhile. There are a number of ways to calculate operating cash flows and these are discussed in Section 7.4. For now, we will follow one approach by working from the net income figure in stage 2 of

Table 7.5 Investment Cash Flows (£s)*

Year	0	1	2	3	4	5
Manufacturing facilities	−3,000,000					1,000,000
Opportunity cost (vacant lot)	−1,500,000					1,500,000
Net working capital	−100,000	0	−60,000	−90,000	40,000	210,000
Investment cash flows	**−4,600,000**	**0**	**−60,000**	**−90,000**	**40,000**	**2,710,000**

* All cash flows occur at the end of the year.

the capital budgeting analysis and adding back all non-cash accounting items. In our example, the only non-cash item in the income statement is depreciation and so we simply add this to our net income figure to generate the operating cash flow for each year. Table 7.6 shows how the operating cash flow is calculated.

Table 7.6 Operating Cash Flows (£s)*

Year	1	2	3	4	5
Net income	160,000	518,400	1,364,736	1,020,506	489,694
Add depreciation	600,000	480,000	384,000	307,200	228,800
Operating cash flow	**760,000**	**998,400**	**1,748,736**	**1,327,706**	**718,494**

* All cash flows occur at the end of the year.

Net Cash Flow

Net cash flow is finally determined in Table 7.7 by adding together the investment cash flow and operating cash flow.

Table 7.7 Incremental Cash Flows for Energy Renewables (£s)

Year	0	1	2	3	4	5
Investment cash flow	−4,600,000	0	−60,000	−90,000	40,000	2,710,000
Operating cash flow		760,000	998,400	1,748,736	1,327,706	718,494
Net cash flow	−4,600,000	760,000	938,400	1,658,736	1,367,706	3,428,494

Step 4: Investment Appraisal

Net Present Value

The NPV of the Energy Renewables wind turbine project can be calculated from the net cash flows of Table 7.7. If the discount rate is 12 per cent, the NPV is as follows:

$$\text{NPV} = -\pounds 4{,}600{,}00 + \frac{\pounds 760{,}400}{1.12} + \frac{\pounds 938{,}400}{1.12^2} + \frac{\pounds 1{,}658{,}736}{1.12^3} + \frac{\pounds 1{,}367{,}706}{1.12^4} + \frac{\pounds 3{,}428{,}494}{1.12^5}$$

This gives an NPV of £821,934.75. If the discount rate is 17.48 per cent, the project will have a zero NPV. In other words, the project's internal rate of return is 17.48 per cent. If the discount rate of the Energy Renewables wind turbine project is above 17.48 per cent, it should not be accepted because its NPV would be negative.

A Note about Net Working Capital

The investment in net working capital is an important part of any capital budgeting analysis. While we explicitly considered net working capital in Table 7.4, readers may wonder where the numbers in these lines came from. An investment in net working capital arises whenever (1) inventory is purchased, (2) cash is kept in the project as a buffer against unexpected expenditures, and (3) credit sales are made, generating trade receivables rather than cash. (The investment in net working capital is reduced by credit purchases, which generate trade payables.) This investment in net working capital represents a cash outflow because cash generated elsewhere in the firm is tied up in the project.

To see how the investment in net working capital is built from its component parts, we focus on year 1. We see in Table 7.2 that Energy Renewables' managers predict sales in year 1 to be £1,600,000 and operating costs to be £800,000. If both the sales and costs were cash transactions, the firm would receive £800,000 (= £1,600,000 – £800,000). As stated earlier, this cash flow would occur at the *end* of year 1.

Now let us give you more information. The managers:

1. Forecast that there will be £1,490,000 of trade sales on credit but that £90,000 will still be owed at the end of year 1, implying accounts receivable of £90,000 will be collected at the end of year 2
2. Believe that they can defer payment on £30,000 of the £800,000 of costs until year 2
3. Decide that inventory of £25,000 should be left on hand at the end of year 1 to avoid *stockouts* (that is, running out of inventory)
4. Decide that cash of £15,000 should be earmarked for the project at the end of year 1 to avoid running out of cash.

Thus, net working capital at the end of year 1 is:

£90,000 Trade receivables	–	£30,000 Trade payables	+	£25,000 Inventory	+	£15,000 Cash	=	Net working capital

Because £100,000 of cash generated elsewhere in the firm must be used to offset this requirement for net working capital, Energy Renewables' managers correctly view the investment in net working capital as a cash outflow of the project. As the project grows over time, needs for the net working capital increase. *Changes* in net working capital from year to year represent further cash flows, as indicated by the negative numbers for the first few years on line 3 of Table 7.4. However, in the declining years of the project, net working capital is reduced – ultimately to zero. That is, trade receivables are finally collected, the project's cash buffer is returned to the rest of the corporation, and all remaining inventory is sold off. This frees up cash in the later years, as indicated by positive numbers in years 4 and 5 on line 3.

Typically corporate worksheets treat net working capital as a whole. The individual components of working capital (receivables, inventory and the like) do not generally appear in the worksheets. However, the reader should remember that the working capital numbers in the worksheets are not pulled out of thin air. Instead, they result from a meticulous forecast of the components, just as we illustrated for year 1.

A Note about Depreciation

The Energy Renewables case made some assumptions about depreciation. Where did these assumptions come from? Assets are depreciated according to the tax rules that apply in each country. In general, there are two main asset categories for depreciation: plant and machinery, and land/buildings. However, other countries may have more complex systems for estimating depreciation expenses and these should be considered before carrying out a capital budgeting analysis.

Depreciation rates change regularly and a financial manager must be up to date with the current applicable rates. For example, the rate is 18 per cent reducing balance on plant and machinery for the UK. Buildings and land tend not to be depreciated but should be revalued periodically to reflect value increases or decreases.

Currently, each country in the European Union has its own tax system and this is seen as one of the major obstacles for the full integration of European economies. However, in 2016, the European Commission launched the Common Consolidated Corporate Tax Base (CCCTB) for all countries. Although it will take several years for it to be enacted, the CCCTB is definitely a step in the right direction. The main recommendations of the working group are that all countries will work on a common tax basis so that European companies can easily operate in all countries within the EU.

Interest Expense

It may have bothered you that interest expense was ignored in the Energy Renewables example. After all, many projects are at least partially financed with debt, particularly wind turbine facilities that are likely to increase the debt capacity of the firm. As it turns out, our approach of assuming no debt financing is rather standard in the real world. Firms typically calculate a project's cash flows under the assumption that the project is financed only with equity. Any adjustments for debt financing are reflected in the discount rate, not the cash flows. The treatment of debt in capital budgeting will be covered in depth later in the text. Suffice it to say at this time that the full ramifications of debt financing are well beyond our current discussion.

Real World Insight 7.1

European Metals

European Metals is a mining firm with operations throughout the world. An important asset for the company's operations is the Cinovec lithium deposit near Prague, Czechia. Cinovec is the largest lithium deposit in Europe and the metal is of fundamental importance for the production of batteries.

European Metals purchased the Cinovec deposit and began geotechnical studies on the land as well as a feasibility study for opening a new mine. The study suggested the land had a probable ore reserve of 34.5 million tonnes, consisting of 0.65 per cent lithium oxide and 0.09 per cent tin. With an annual production of 22,800 tonnes of lithium carbonate lasting 20 years, the NPV of the deposit was calculated at $540 million.

In arriving at the NPV estimate, the firm would have forecasted mining performance, lithium price growth rates and an appropriate discount rate.

7.3 Inflation and Capital Budgeting

Chapter 30
Page 835

Inflation is an important fact of economic life, and it must be considered in capital budgeting. We begin our examination of inflation by considering the relationship between interest rates and inflation. (Inflation is discussed in more detail in **Chapter 30**, Section 30.4 in the context of international finance.)

Interest Rates and Inflation

Suppose a bank offers a one-year interest rate of 10 per cent. This means that an individual who deposits £1,000 will receive £1,100 (= £1,000 × 1.10) in one year. Although 10 per cent may seem like a handsome return, one can put it in perspective only after examining the rate of inflation.

Imagine that the rate of inflation is 6 per cent over the year and it affects all goods equally. For example, a restaurant that charges £1.00 for a hamburger today will charge £1.06 for the same hamburger at the end of the year. You can use your £1,000 to buy 1,000 hamburgers today (date 0). Alternatively, if you put your money in the bank, you can buy 1,038 (=£1,100/£1.06) hamburgers at date 1. Thus, lending increases your hamburger consumption by only 3.8 per cent.

Because the prices of all goods rise at this 6 per cent rate, lending lets you increase your consumption of any single good or any combination of goods by only 3.8 per cent. Thus, 3.8 per cent is what you are *really* earning through your savings account, after adjusting for inflation. Economists refer to the 3.8 per cent number as the *real interest rate*. Economists refer to the 10 per cent rate as the *nominal interest rate* or just the *interest rate*. We illustrated this discussion in Figure 7.1.

We have used an example with a specific nominal interest rate and inflation rate. In general, the formula between real and nominal interest rates can be written as follows:

$$1 + \text{Nominal interest rate} = (1 + \text{Real interest rate}) \times (1 + \text{Inflation rate})$$

Rearranging terms, we have:

Equation 7.1

$$\text{Real interest rate} = \frac{1 + \text{Nominal interest rate}}{1 + \text{Inflation rate}} - 1$$

Figure 7.1 Calculation of the Real Rate of Interest

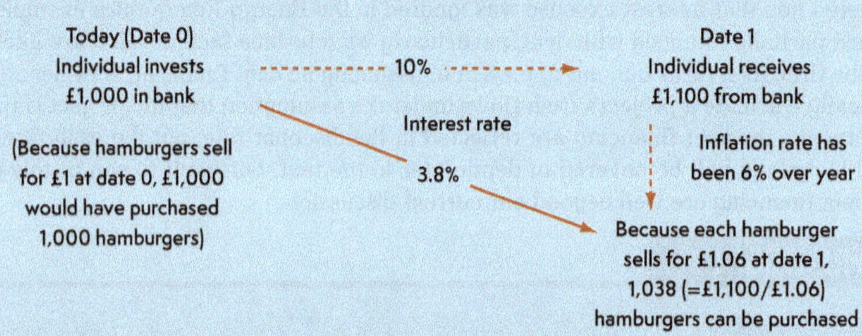

Hamburger is used as an illustrative good. 1,038 hamburgers can be purchased on date 1 instead of 1,000 hamburgers at date 0. Real interest rate = 1,038/1,000 – 1 = 3.8%.

The formula indicates that the real interest rate in our example is 3.8 per cent (= 1.10/1.06 – 1). Equation 7.1 determines the real interest rate precisely. The following formula is an approximation:

Equation 7.2 $$\text{Real interest rate} \cong \text{Nominal interest rate} - \text{Inflation rate}$$

The symbol $\cong$ indicates that the equation is approximately true. This latter formula calculates the real rate in our example like this:

$$4\% \cong 10\% - 6\%$$

The student should be aware that, although Equation 7.2 may seem more intuitive than Equation 7.1, 7.2 is only an approximation and should not be used in a formal analysis.

Cash Flow and Inflation

The previous analysis defines two types of interest rate – nominal rates and real rates – and relates them through Equation 7.1. Capital budgeting requires data on cash flows as well as on interest rates. Like interest rates, cash flows can be expressed in either nominal or real terms.

A nominal cash flow refers to the actual money in cash to be received (or paid out). A real cash flow refers to the cash flow's purchasing power. These definitions are best explained by an example.

Example 7.6

Nominal versus Real Cash Flow

Lioness Publishing has just purchased the rights for famed novelist Aria Patel's new book. Still unwritten, the book should be available to the public in four years. Currently, fictional novels sell for €10.00 in paperback. The publishers believe that inflation will be 6 per cent a year over the next four years. Because romantic novels are so popular, the publishers anticipate that their prices will rise about 2 per cent per year more than the inflation rate over the next four years. Lioness Publishing plans to sell the novel at €13.60 [= $(1.08)^4$ × €10.00] four years from now, anticipating sales of 100,000 copies.

The expected cash flow in the fourth year of €1.36 million (= €13.60 × 100,000) is a *nominal cash flow*. That is, the firm expects to receive €1.36 million at that time. In other words, a nominal cash flow refers to the actual cash flow in euros to be received in the future.

The purchasing power of €1.36 million in four years is:

$$€1.08\text{ million} = \frac{€1.36\text{ million}}{(1.06)^4}$$

The figure of €1.08 million is a *real cash flow* because it is expressed in terms of purchasing power.

Discounting: Nominal or Real?

Our previous discussion showed that we could express interest rates in either nominal or real terms. Similarly, we can present cash flows in either nominal or real terms. Given these choices, how should one use interest rates and cash flows when performing capital budgeting?

Financial practitioners correctly stress the need to maintain *consistency* between cash flows and discount rates. That is:

- *Nominal* cash flows must be discounted at the *nominal* rate.
- *Real* cash flows must be discounted at the *real* rate.

As long as one is consistent, either approach is correct. To minimize computational error, it is generally advisable in practice to choose the method that is easiest. We illustrate this idea in the following two examples.

Example 7.7

Real and Nominal Discounting

Shields Electric forecasts the following nominal cash flows on a particular project:

	0	1	2
Cash flow	−£1,000	£600	£650

The nominal discount rate is 14 per cent, and the inflation rate is forecast to be 5 per cent. What is the value of the project?

Using nominal quantities The NPV can be calculated as:

$$\text{£}26.47 = -\text{£}1{,}000 + \frac{\text{£}600}{1.14} + \frac{\text{£}650}{(1.14)^2}$$

The project should be accepted.

Using real quantities The real cash flows are these:

	0	1	2
Cash flow	**−£1,000**	**£571.43** $\left(\frac{\text{£}600}{1.05}\right)$	**£589.57** $\left(\frac{\text{£}650}{(1.05)^2}\right)$

As we have discussed, the real discount rate is 8.57143 per cent (= 1.14/1.05 − 1). We calculate the NPV as:

$$\text{£}26.47 = -\text{£}1{,}000 + \frac{\text{£}571.43}{1.0857143} + \frac{\text{£}589.57}{(1.0857143)^2}$$

The NPV is the same whether cash flows are expressed in nominal or in real quantities. It must always be the case that the NPV is the same under the two different approaches.

Because both approaches always yield the same result, which one should be used? Use the method that is simpler because the more straightforward approach generally leads to fewer computational errors. The Shields Electric example begins with nominal cash flows, so nominal quantities produce a simpler calculation here.

Example 7.8

Real and Nominal NPV

Bella SpA generated the following forecast for a capital budgeting project:

	Year		
	0 (€)	1 (€)	2 (€)
Capital expenditure	1,210		
Revenues (in real terms)		1,900	2,000
Cash expenses (in real terms)		950	1,000
Depreciation (straight-line)		605	605

The president, Mrs Bella, estimates inflation to be 10 per cent per year over the next two years. In addition, she believes that the cash flows of the project should be discounted at the nominal rate of 15.5 per cent. Her firm's tax rate is 40 per cent.

Mrs Bella forecasts all cash flows in *nominal* terms, leading to the following spreadsheet:

	Year		
	0 (€)	1 (€)	2 (€)
Capital expenditure	−1,210		
Revenues		2,090 (= 1,900 × 1.10)	2,420 [= 2,000 × (1.10)^2]
−Expenses		−1,045 (= 950 × 1.10)	−1,210 [= 1,000 × (1.10)^2]
−Depreciation		−605 (= 1,210/2)	−605
Taxable income		440	605
−Taxes (40%)		−176	−242
Income after taxes		264	363
+Depreciation		+605	+605
Cash flow		869	968

$$\text{NPV} = €\,-1{,}210 + \frac{€869}{1.155} + \frac{€968}{(1.155)^2} = 268$$

Mrs Bella's sidekick, Mr Barbi, prefers working in real terms. He first calculates the real rate to be 5 per cent (= 1.155/1.10 − 1). Next, he generates the following spreadsheet in *real* quantities:

	Year		
	0 (€)	1 (€)	2 (€)
Capital expenditure	−1,210		
Revenues		1,900	2,000
−Expenses		−950	−1,000
−Depreciation		−550 (= 605/1.1)	−500 [= 605/(1.1)^2]
Taxable income		400	500
−Taxes (40%)		−160	−200
Income after taxes		240	300
+Depreciation		+550	+500
Cash flow		790	800

$$\text{NPV} = €\,-1{,}210 + \frac{€790}{1.05} + \frac{€800}{(1.055)^2} = 268$$

In explaining his calculations to Mrs Bella, Mr Barbi points out these facts:

1. The capital expenditure occurs at date 0 (today), so its nominal value and its real value are equal.
2. Because yearly depreciation of €605 is a nominal quantity, one converts it to a real quantity by discounting at the inflation rate of 10 per cent.

It is no coincidence that both Mrs Bella and Mr Barbi arrive at the same NPV number. Both methods must always generate the same NPV.

7.4 Alternative Definitions of Operating Cash Flow

Chapter 3 Page 66

The analysis we went through in the previous section is quite general and can be adapted to just about any capital investment problem. In the next section, we illustrate a particularly useful variation. Before we do so, we need to discuss the fact that different definitions of project operating cash flow are commonly used, both in practice and in finance texts (see **Chapter 3**, Section 3.5, for more detail on statements of cash flow).

As we will see, the different approaches to operating cash flow all measure the same thing. If they are used correctly, they all produce the same answer, and one is not necessarily any better or more useful than another. Unfortunately, the fact that alternative definitions are used sometimes leads to confusion. For this reason, we examine several of these variations next to see how they are related.

In the discussion that follows, keep in mind that when we speak of cash flow, we mean *cash in less cash out*, which is our only concern. Different definitions of operating cash flow simply amount to different ways of manipulating basic accounting information about sales, costs, depreciation and taxes to get at cash flow.

For a particular project and year under consideration, suppose we have the following estimates:

$$\begin{aligned}\text{Sales} &= £1{,}500\\ \text{Costs} &= £700\\ \text{Depreciation} &= £600\end{aligned}$$

With these estimates, notice that earnings before interest and taxes (EBIT) is:

$$\begin{aligned}\text{EBIT} &= \text{Sales} - \text{Costs} - \text{Depreciation}\\ &= £1{,}500 - 700 - 600\\ &= £200\end{aligned}$$

Once again, we assume that no interest is paid, so the tax bill is:

$$\begin{aligned}\text{Taxes} &= \text{EBIT} \times t_c\\ &= £200 \times 028 = £56\end{aligned}$$

where t_c, the corporate tax rate, is 28 per cent.

When we put all of this together, we see that project operating cash flow (OCF) is:

$$\begin{aligned}\text{OCF} &= \text{EBIT} + \text{Depreciation} - \text{Taxes}\\ &= £200 + 600 - 56 = £744\end{aligned}$$

It turns out there are some other ways to determine OCF that could be (and are) used. We consider these next.

The Bottom-up Approach

Because we are ignoring any financing expenses, such as interest, in our calculations of project OCF, we can write project net income as:

$$\begin{aligned}\text{Project net income} &= \text{EBIT} - \text{Taxes}\\ &= £200 - 56\\ &= £144\end{aligned}$$

If we add the depreciation to both sides, we arrive at a slightly different and very common expression for OCF:

Equation 7.3

$$\begin{aligned} OCF &= \text{Net income} + \text{Depreciation} \\ &= £144 + 600 = £744 \end{aligned}$$

This is the *bottom-up* approach. Here, we start with the accountant's bottom line (net income) and add back any non-cash deductions such as depreciation. It is crucial to remember that this definition of operating cash flow as net income plus depreciation is correct only if there is no interest expense subtracted in the calculation of net income.

The Top-down Approach

Perhaps the most obvious way to calculate OCF is this:

Equation 7.4

$$\begin{aligned} OCF &= \text{Sales} - \text{Costs} - \text{Taxes} \\ &= £1{,}500 - 700 - 56 = £744 \end{aligned}$$

This is the *top-down* approach, the second variation on the basic OCF definition. Here we start at the top of the profit and loss statement with sales, and work our way down to net cash flow by subtracting costs, taxes and other expenses. Along the way, we leave out any strictly non-cash items such as depreciation.

The Tax Shield Approach

The third variation on our basic definition of OCF is the *tax shield* approach. This approach will be useful for some problems we consider in the Add next chapter. The tax shield definition of OCF is:

Equation 7.5

$$OCF = (\text{Sales} - \text{Costs}) \times (1 - t_c) + \text{Depreciation} \times t_c$$

where t_c is again the corporate tax rate. Assuming that t_c = 28 per cent, the OCF works out to be:

$$\begin{aligned} OCF &= (£1{,}500 - 700) \times 0.72 + 600 \times 0.28 \\ &= £576 + 168 \\ &= £744 \end{aligned}$$

This is just as we had before.

This approach views OCF as having two components. The first part is what the project's cash flow would be if there were no depreciation expense. In this case, this would-have-been cash flow is £576.

The second part of OCF in this approach is the depreciation deduction multiplied by the tax rate. This is called the **depreciation tax shield**. We know that depreciation is a non-cash expense. The only cash flow effect of deducting depreciation is to reduce our taxes, a benefit to us. At the current 28 per cent corporate tax rate, every pound in depreciation expense saves us 28 pence in taxes. So, in our example, the £600 depreciation deduction saves us £600 × 0.28 = £168 in taxes.

Conclusion

Now that we have seen that all of these approaches are the same, you are probably wondering why everybody does not just agree on one of them. One reason is that different methods are useful in different circumstances. The best one to use is whichever happens to be the most convenient for the problem at hand.

Sustainability in Action 7.1

Renewable Energy Systems (RES) Group

Renewable Energy Systems (RES) Group is a leading British company in the field of sustainability and renewable energy. Founded in 1981, RES has grown to become one of the world's largest independent renewable energy companies, with operations in Europe, North America and Asia-Pacific. The company's primary focus is on the development, construction and operation of onshore and offshore wind farms, solar farms and energy storage projects.

At the forefront of the industry for over 40 years, RES has delivered more than 23GW of renewable energy projects across the globe and supports an operational asset portfolio exceeding 12GW worldwide for a large client base. RES employs more than 2,500 people and is active in 14 countries working across onshore and offshore wind, solar, energy storage and transmission and distribution.

RES corporate website

In 2023, RES submitted a planning application for its 12-turbine Carnbuck Wind Farm, located in the townlands of Carnbuck, Magheraboy and Moneyneagh, near Corkey, Co. Antrim, Northern Ireland. Adjacent to the existing Gruig Wind Farm, Carnbuck would be capable of generating enough clean, low-cost renewable electricity for an additional 55,000 homes each year, if consented. The proposed scheme comprised 12 turbines with an overall installed capacity of around 50 MW, in addition to an energy storage facility, which would help maximize the generation capability and efficiency of the site.

David McVeigh, Development Project Manager at RES, commented:

The urgent need to reduce carbon emissions is ever pressing, and wind, as a free and inexhaustible resource, has a crucial role to play. Recent analysis has shown that Northern Ireland consumers saved £500m because wind farms produced 42 per cent of our electricity last year.

Before making the capital investment decision, RES would have conducted a thorough analysis of the project's incremental cash flows. The company will have taken into account various factors such as the initial capital outlay, ongoing operational costs, expected revenue from energy sales, and the potential value of any government incentives or subsidies. Inflation would also be considered, as it could have a significant impact on future cash flows and the overall financial viability of the project.

RES would have considered the project's alignment with its broader sustainability objectives and corporate social responsibility commitments. The company would assess the environmental and social impacts of the wind farm, including its potential to reduce greenhouse gas emissions, create local employment opportunities, and contribute to regional economic development.

After a comprehensive evaluation, RES will have decided to proceed with the capital investment, concluding that the wind farm project aligns with its strategic objectives, and would generate significant financial and sustainability benefits. The company's capital investment decision demonstrates its commitment to advancing renewable energy and promoting a more sustainable future for Europe and the world.

7.5 Investments of Unequal Lives: The Equivalent Annual Cost Method

Suppose a firm must choose between two machines of unequal lives. Both machines can do the same job, but they have different operating costs and will last for different time periods. A simple application of the NPV rule suggests taking the machine whose costs have the lower present value. This choice might be a mistake, however, because the lower-cost machine may need to be replaced before the other one.

Let us consider an example. The Downtown Athletic Club must choose between two mechanical tennis ball throwers. Machine A costs less than machine B but will not last as long. The cash *outflows* from the two machines are shown here:

	Date				
Machine	0 (€)	1 (€)	2 (€)	3 (€)	4 (€)
A	500	120	120	120	
B	600	100	100	100	100

Machine A costs €500 and lasts three years. There will be maintenance expenses of €120 to be paid at the end of each of the three years. Machine B costs €600 and lasts four years. There will be maintenance expenses of €100 to be paid at the end of each of the four years. We place all costs in real terms, an assumption greatly simplifying the analysis. Revenues per year are assumed to be the same, regardless of machine, so they are ignored in the analysis. Note that all numbers in the previous chart are *outflows*.

To get a handle on the decision, let us take the present value of the costs of each of the two machines. Assuming a discount rate of 10 per cent, we have:

$$\text{Machine A: €798.42} = \text{€500} + \frac{\text{€120}}{1.1} + \frac{\text{€120}}{(1.1)^2} + \frac{\text{€120}}{(1.1)^3}$$

$$\text{Machine B: €916.99} = \text{€600} + \frac{\text{€100}}{1.1} + \frac{\text{€100}}{(1.1)^2} + \frac{\text{€100}}{(1.1)^3} + \frac{\text{€100}}{(1.4)^4}$$

Machine B has a higher present value of outflows. A naive approach would be to select machine A because of its lower present value. However, machine B has a longer life, so perhaps its cost per year is actually lower.

Chapter 4 Page 102

How might one properly adjust for the difference in useful life when comparing the two machines? Perhaps the easiest approach involves calculating something called the *equivalent annual cost* of each machine (looking again at Chapter 4, Section 4.4, on annuities will help with this section). This approach puts costs on a per-year basis.

The previous equation showed that payments of (€500, €120, €120, €120) are equivalent to a single payment of €798.42 at date 0. We now wish to equate the single payment of €798.42 at date 0 with a three-year annuity. Using techniques of previous chapters, we have:

$$\text{€798.42} = C \times A^3_{0.10}$$

$A^3_{0.10}$ is an annuity of €1 a year for three years, discounted at 10 per cent. C is the unknown – the annuity payment per year such that the present value of all payments equals €798.42. Because $A^3_{0.10}$ equals 2.4869, C equals €321.05 (= €798.42/2.4869). Thus, a payment stream of (€500, €120, €120, €120) is equivalent to annuity payments of €321.05 made at the *end* of each year for three years. We refer to €321.05 as the *equivalent annual cost* of machine A.

This idea is summarized in the following chart:

	Date			
	0 (€)	**1 (€)**	**2 (€)**	**3 (€)**
Cash outflows of machine A	500.00	120.00	120.00	120.00
Equivalent annual cost of machine A		321.05	321.05	321.05

The Downtown Athletic Club should be indifferent between cash outflows of (€500, €120, €120, €120) and cash outflows of (€0, €321.05, €321.05, €321.05). Alternatively, one can say that the purchase of the machine is financially equivalent to a rental agreement calling for annual lease payments of €321.05.

Now let us turn to machine B. We calculate its equivalent annual cost from:

$$\text{€916.99} = C \times A^4_{0.10}$$

Because $A^4_{0.10}$ equals 3.1699, C equals €916.99/3.1699, or €289.28.

As we did for machine A, we can create the following chart for machine B:

	Date				
	0 (€)	**1 (€)**	**2 (€)**	**3 (€)**	**4 (€)**
Cash outflows of machine B	600.00	100.00	100.00	100.00	100.00
Equivalent annual cost of machine B		289.28	289.28	289.28	289.28

The decision is easy once the charts of the two machines are compared. Would you rather make annual lease payments of €321.05 or €289.28? Put this way, the problem becomes a no-brainer: a rational person would rather pay the lower amount. Thus, machine B is the preferred choice.

Two final remarks are in order. First, it is no accident that we specified the costs of the tennis ball machines in real terms. Although B would still have been the preferred machine had the costs been stated in nominal terms, the actual solution would have been much more difficult. As a general rule, always convert cash flows to real terms when working through problems of this type.

Second, such analysis applies only if one anticipates that both machines can be replaced. The analysis would differ if no replacement were possible. For example, imagine that the only company that manufactured tennis ball throwers just went out of business and no new producers are expected to enter the field. In this case, machine B would generate revenues in the fourth year whereas machine A would not. Here, simple net present value analysis for mutually exclusive projects including both revenues and costs would be appropriate.

The General Decision to Replace

The previous analysis concerned the choice between machine A and machine B, both of which were new acquisitions. More typically firms must decide when to replace an existing machine with a new one. This decision is actually quite straightforward. One should replace if the annual cost of the new machine is less than the annual cost of the old machine. As with much else in finance, an example clarifies this approach better than further explanation.

Example 7.9

Replacement Decisions

Consider the situation of BIKE, which must decide whether to replace an existing machine. BIKE currently pays no taxes. The replacement machine costs £9,000 now and requires maintenance of £1,000 at the end of every year for eight years. At the end of eight years, the machine would be sold for £2,000 after taxes.

The existing machine requires increasing amounts of maintenance each year, and its salvage value falls each year, as shown:

Year	Maintenance (£)	After-tax Salvage (£)
Present	0	4,000
1	1,000	2,500
2	2,000	1,500
3	3,000	1,500
4	4,000	0

This chart tells us that the existing machine can be sold for £4,000 now after taxes. If it is sold one year from now, the resale price will be £2,500 after taxes, and £1,000 must be spent on maintenance during the year to keep it running. For ease of calculation, we assume that this maintenance fee is paid at the end of the year. The machine will last for four more years before it falls apart. In other words, salvage value will be zero at the end of year 4. If BIKE faces an opportunity cost of capital of 15 per cent, when should it replace the machine?

Our approach is to compare the annual cost of the replacement machine with the annual cost of the old machine. The annual cost of the replacement machine is simply its *equivalent annual cost* (EAC). Let us calculate that first.

Equivalent annual cost of new machine The present value of the cost of the new replacement machine is as follows:

$$
\begin{aligned}
PV_{\text{costs}} &= £9{,}000 + £1{,}000 \times A_{0.15}^{8} - \frac{£2000}{(1.15)^8} \\
&= £9{,}000 + £1{,}000 \times (4.4873) - £2{,}000 \times (0.3269) \\
&= £12{,}833
\end{aligned}
$$

Notice that the £2,000 salvage value is an inflow. It is treated as a *negative* number in this equation because it *offsets* the cost of the machine.

The EAC of a new replacement machine equals:

$$
\text{PV/8-year annuity factor at 15\%} = \frac{\text{PV}}{A_{0.15}^{\ 8}} = \frac{£12{,}833}{4.4873} = £2{,}860
$$

This calculation implies that buying a replacement machine is financially equivalent to renting this machine for £2,860 per year.

Cost of old machine This calculation is a little trickier. If BIKE keeps the old machine for one year, the firm must pay maintenance costs of £1,000 a year from now. But this is not BIKE's only cost from keeping the machine for one year. BIKE will receive £2,500 at date 1 if the old machine is kept for one year but would receive £4,000 today if the old machine were sold immediately. This reduction in sales proceeds is clearly a cost as well.

Thus the PV of the costs of keeping the machine one more year before selling it equals:

$$
£4{,}000 + \frac{£1{,}000}{1.15} - \frac{£2{,}500}{1.15} = £2{,}696
$$

That is, if BIKE holds the old machine for one year, BIKE does *not* receive the £4,000 today. This £4,000 can be thought of as an opportunity cost. In addition, the firm must pay £1,000 a year from now. Finally, BIKE does receive £2,500 a year from now. This last item is treated as a negative number because it offsets the other two costs.

Although we normally express cash flows in terms of present value, the analysis to come is easier if we express the cash flow in terms of its future value one year from now. This future value is:

$$£2,696 \times 1.15 = £3,100$$

In other words, the cost of keeping the machine for one year is equivalent to paying £3,100 at the end of the year.

Making the comparison Now let us review the cash flows. If we replace the machine immediately, we can view our annual expense as £2,860, beginning at the end of the year. This annual expense occurs for ever if we replace the new machine every eight years. This cash flow stream can be written as follows:

	Year 1	Year 2	Year 3	Year 4	...
Expenses from replacing machine immediately	£2,860	£2,860	£2,860	£2,860	...

If we replace the old machine in one year, our expense from using the old machine for that final year can be viewed as £3,100, payable at the end of the year. After replacement, our annual expense is £2,860, beginning at the end of two years. This annual expense occurs for ever if we replace the new machine every eight years. This cash flow stream can be written like this:

	Year 1	Year 2	Year 3	Year 4	...
Expenses from using old machine for one year and then replacing it	£3,100	£2,860	£2,860	£2,860	...

Put this way, the choice is again a no-brainer. Anyone would rather pay £2,860 at the end of the year than £3,100 at the end of the year. Thus, BIKE should replace the old machine immediately to minimize the expense at year 1.[1]

Two final points should be made about the decision to replace. First, we have examined a situation where both the old machine and the replacement machine generate the same revenues. Because revenues are unaffected by the choice of machine, revenues do not enter our analysis. This situation is common in business. For example, the decision to replace either the heating system or the air-conditioning system in one's home office will probably not affect firm revenues. However, sometimes revenues will be greater with a new machine. The approach here can easily be amended to handle differential revenues.

Second, we want to stress the importance of the current approach. Applications of this approach are pervasive in business because *every* machine must be replaced at some point.

Summary and Conclusions

This chapter discussed a number of practical applications of capital budgeting.

1 Capital budgeting must be placed on an incremental basis. This means that sunk costs must be ignored, whereas both opportunity costs and side effects must be considered.

2 In the Energy Renewables case we computed NPV using the following two steps:

   (a) Calculate the net cash flow from all sources for each period.

   (b) Calculate the NPV using these cash flows.

3 Inflation must be handled consistently. One approach is to express both cash flows and the discount rate in nominal terms. The other approach is to express both cash flows and the discount rate in real terms. Because either approach yields the same NPV calculation, the simpler method should be used. The simpler method will generally depend on the type of capital budgeting problem.

4 A firm should use the equivalent annual cost approach when choosing between two machines of unequal lives.

Questions and Problems

CONCEPT

1 **Incremental Cash Flows** Why is it important for the financial analyst to focus on incremental cash flows? Which of the following should be treated as an incremental cash flow when computing the NPV of an investment?

(a) A reduction in the sales of a company's other products caused by the investment.

(b) An expenditure on plant and equipment that has not yet been made and will be made only if the project is accepted.

(c) Costs of developing a prototype of the product.

(d) Annual depreciation expense from the investment.

(e) Share buybacks by the firm.

(f) The resale value of plant and equipment at the end of the project's life.

(g) Salary and medical costs for production personnel who will be employed only if the project is accepted.

2 **Incremental Cash Flows and Capital Budgeting**

(a) In the context of capital budgeting, what is an opportunity cost? Why do we include this in a capital budgeting analysis? Give an example to support your answer.

(b) What is meant by operating cash flow? Review the different ways in which operating cash flow can be calculated.

3 **Inflation and Capital Budgeting** In a hyperinflationary environment, how would you incorporate inflation into a capital budgeting analysis? Explain your methodology in words to a manager who is worried about the power of capital budgeting when inflation is very high. How do increases in expected inflation affect the firm's accept/reject decision at the margin?

4 **Equivalent Annual Cost** Explain what is meant by the equivalent annual cost (EAC) method. When is EAC analysis appropriate for comparing two or more projects? Why is this method used? Are there any implicit assumptions required by this method that you find troubling? Explain.

5 **Depreciation** What is meant by the terms 'straight-line depreciation' and 'reducing balance depreciation'? What are the advantages and disadvantages of each? Explain.

REGULAR

6 **Calculating Project NPV** You have been appointed by a major automobile manufacturer as its new financial manager. The firm has opened new production facilities in France that are specifically targeted at developing safety-focused cars for the family sector. The firm has decided it will install new anti-skid technology in all its automobiles. The additional cost of installation is €3.2 million. The technology is licensed from a high-tech German firm and the company must pay a one-off fee of €1 million to use it in its cars. There will be a subsequent annual licence fee payment over the five-year life of the project of €200,000. The chief executive has asked you to deal with the transaction. The tax rate is 33.3 per cent and the relevant discount rate is 12 per cent. Assume that the anti-skid technology will be obsolete in five years. What is the present value of the cost of using the new technology?

7 **Calculating Project NPV: Wind Farm** You have been appointed as the financial manager of a renewable energy firm. The company is considering investing in a new wind farm in a remote location to increase its renewable energy portfolio. The project requires an initial investment of €8 million to set up the infrastructure and purchase the wind turbines. The wind farm has an expected life of 20 years and is estimated to generate an annual revenue of €2.4 million with an annual operating cost of €800,000. The company has also estimated that it will cost an additional €400,000 per year to maintain the wind turbines. The relevant discount rate is 8 per cent.

(a) What is the expected net present value (NPV) of the wind farm project?

(b) Calculate the internal rate of return (IRR) of the project and determine whether the investment is financially feasible.

(c) If the company decides to invest in the wind farm project, what are some potential risks and challenges that the company may face, and how can it mitigate them?

8 **Calculating Project NPV: Carlsberg** Carlsberg is considering a new retail lager investment in Copenhagen. Financial projections for the investment are tabulated below. The Danish corporate tax rate is 25 per cent and the investment is depreciated using 20 per cent reducing balances. Assume all sales revenue is received in cash, all operating costs and income taxes are paid in cash, and all cash flows occur at the end of the year. All net working capital is recovered at the end of the project and the investment is sold at its residual value after depreciation.

	Year 0 (€)	Year 1 (€)	Year 2 (€)	Year 3 (€)	Year 4 (€)
Investment	325,000	–	–	–	–
Sales revenue	–	105,000	105,000	105,000	105,000
Operating costs	–	20,000	20,000	20,000	20,000
Net working capital spending	10,000	2,000	3,000	4,000	?

(a) Compute the incremental net income of the investment for each year.

(b) Compute the incremental cash flows of the investment for each year.

(c) Suppose the appropriate discount rate is 12 per cent. What is the NPV of the project?

9 **Calculating Project Cash Flow from Assets** In the previous problem, suppose the project requires an initial investment in net working capital of €2,000 and the investment will have a market value of €1,000 at the end of the project. Assume the discounting rate to be 12 per cent. What is the project's year 0 net cash flow? Year 1? Year 2? Year 3? Year 4? What is the new NPV?

10 **NPV and Reducing Balance Depreciation** In the previous problem, suppose the investment is depreciated using the reducing balance method at 25 per cent per annum. All the other facts are the same. What is the project's year 1 net income now? Year 2? Year 3? Year 4? What is the new NPV?

11 **Project Evaluation** Your firm is contemplating the purchase of a new £925,000 computer-based order entry system. The system will be depreciated using reducing balance at 20 per cent per annum over its five-year life. It will be worth £90,000 at the end of that time. You will save £360,000 before taxes per year in order processing costs, and you will be able to reduce working capital by £125,000 (this is a one-time reduction). If the tax rate is 28 per cent, what is the IRR for this project?

12 **Project Evaluation: Dog Up! Franks** Dog Up! Franks is looking at a new sausage system with an installed cost of €390,000. This cost will be depreciated straight line to zero over the project's five-year life, at the end of which the sausage system can be scrapped for €60,000. The sausage system will save the firm €120,000 per year in pre-tax operating costs, and the system requires an initial investment in net working capital of €28,000. If the tax rate is 34 per cent and the discount rate is 10 per cent, what is the NPV of this project?

13 **Calculating Salvage Value** An asset used in a four-year project is depreciated at 20 per cent reducing balance for tax purposes. The asset has an acquisition cost of £9,300,000 and will be sold for £3,100,000 at the end of the project. If the tax rate is 28 per cent, what is the after-tax salvage value of the asset?

14 **Project Evaluation: Renewable Energy Ltd** Renewable Energy Ltd is considering investing in a new solar energy project. The initial cost of the project is £5 million, which includes purchasing land and equipment. If Renewable Energy Ltd proceeds with the project, it will receive £1.2 million per annum for the next five years, after which the contract will expire. The equipment will be depreciated using a straight-line method over five years, and will have a residual value of £500,000 at the end of the project. Operating expenses and cost of goods sold are expected to be 30 per cent of revenues combined. Renewable Energy Ltd needs to add net working capital of £200,000 immediately, which will be recovered at the end of the project's life. The corporate tax rate is 25 per cent. The required rate of return for this type of project is 12 per cent.

What is the net present value of the solar energy project? Should Renewable Energy Ltd proceed with the investment? What is the internal rate of return of the project? What is the payback period of the investment? What is the profitability index of the project?

15 **Calculating NPV** Edaw Construction is considering a bid for a new high-speed rail contract. The project complements its existing business of constructing high-value public-sector infrastructure projects. The contract would require the purchase of dedicated rail construction machinery, the cost of which is €2 billion. If Edaw wins the contract it will receive €800 million per annum for the next four years, after which the contract is ended. The new machinery would be depreciated using a 20 per cent reducing balance method. At the end of four years it will be sold at its residual value. Cost of goods sold and operating expenses related to the project are predicted to be 25 per cent of revenues. Edaw also needs to add net working capital of €20 million immediately. The additional net

working capital will be recovered in full at the end of the project's life. The corporate tax rate is 35 per cent. The required rate of return for this type of project is 14 per cent, but revenues from the project can be reinvested only at the firm's return of assets of 10 per cent. Should Edaw proceed with the project?

16 **Calculating EAC** Machine A costs £10,000 and costs £3,000 per year to maintain. It is expected to last three years. Machine B costs £8,000 and costs £5,000 per year to maintain. It is expected to last two years. Assume the discount rate is 7 per cent. Which machine should be purchased?

17 **Comparing Mutually Exclusive Projects** Hagar Industrial Systems Company (HISC) is trying to decide between two different conveyor belt systems. System A costs £600,000, has a four-year life and requires £120,000 in pre-tax annual operating costs. System B costs £500,000, has a six-year life and requires £100,000 in pre-tax annual operating costs. Both systems are to be depreciated using the reducing balance method of 20 per cent per annum and will have zero salvage value at the end of their life. Whichever system is chosen, it will *not* be replaced when it wears out. If the tax rate is 20 per cent and the discount rate is 15 per cent, which system should the firm choose?

18 **Comparing Mutually Exclusive Projects with Replacement** Suppose in the previous problem that HISC always needs a conveyor belt system; when one wears out, it must be replaced. Which system should the firm choose now?

19 **Inflation and Company Value** SA Mining has ongoing operations in Venezuela, where inflation is running at a staggering 450 per cent. SA Mining expects to mine 10,000 kilos of gold every year in perpetuity. This year, the gold is likely to sell for $41,000 per kilo in real terms. The total cost of extracting gold is $200 million per annum. Sales income and costs occur at year-end. Revenues and expenses will increase at a real rate of 5 per cent per annum. The real discount rate is 18 per cent. What is SA Mining worth today?

20 **Calculating Nominal Cash Flow** Etonic SA is considering an investment of €250,000 in an asset with an economic life of five years. The firm estimates that the nominal annual cash revenues and expenses at the end of the first year will be €200,000 and €50,000, respectively. Both revenues and expenses will grow thereafter at the annual inflation rate of 3 per cent. Etonic will use the 20 per cent reducing balance method to depreciate its asset over five years. The salvage value of the asset is estimated to be €30,000 in nominal terms at that time. The one-time net working capital investment of €10,000 is required immediately and will be recovered at the end of the project. All corporate cash flows are subject to a 34 per cent tax rate. What is the project's total nominal cash flow from assets for each year?

21 **Equivalent Annual Cost: Yell Group plc** Yell Group plc, the global advertising company, is evaluating the viability of a new machine to print telephone directories in emerging markets. The baseline machine costs £65,000, has a three-year life and costs £12,000 per year to operate. The relevant discount rate is 10 per cent. Assume that the reducing balance (20 per cent) depreciation method is used. Furthermore, assume the equipment has a salvage value of £20,000 at the end of the project's life. The relevant tax rate is 24 per cent. All cash flows occur at the end of the year. What is the equivalent annual cost (EAC) of this equipment?

22 **Calculating NPV and IRR for a Replacement** A firm is considering an investment in a new machine with a price of £32 million to replace its existing machine. The current machine has a book value of £8 million and a market value of £9 million. The new machine is expected to have a four-year life, and the old machine has four years left in which it can be used. If the firm replaces the old machine with the new machine, it expects to save £5 million in operating costs each year over the next four years. Both machines will have no salvage value in four years. If the firm purchases the new machine, it will also need an investment of £500,000 in net working capital. The required return on the investment is 10 per cent, and the tax rate is 39 per cent.

(a) What are the NPV and IRR of the decision to replace the old machine?

(b) The new machine saves £32 million over the next four years and has a cost of £32 million. When you consider the time value of money, how is it possible that the NPV of the decision to replace the old machine has a positive NPV?

23 **Calculating Project NPV: Start-Ups** With the growing popularity of casual surf-print clothing, two recent MBA graduates decided to broaden this casual surf concept to encompass 'surf lifestyle for the home'. With limited capital, they decided to focus on surf-print table and floor lamps to accent people's homes. They projected unit sales of these lamps to be 5,000 in the first year, with growth of 15 per cent each year for the next five years. Production of these lamps will require £28,000 in net working capital to start. Total fixed costs are £75,000 per year, variable production costs are £20 per unit, and the units are priced at £45 each. The equipment needed to begin production will cost £60,000. The equipment will be depreciated using the reducing balance (20 per cent) method and is not expected to have a salvage value. The effective tax rate is 28 per cent, and the required rate of return is 25 per cent. What is the NPV of this project?

24 **Calculating Project NPV: Machine Replacement** Industrial Hooks plc is deciding when to replace its old machine. The machine's current salvage value is £3 million. Its current book value is £4 million. If not sold, the old machine will require maintenance costs of £300,000 at the end of the year for the next five years. Depreciation on the old machine is calculated using 20 per cent reducing balances. At the end of five years, it will have a salvage value of £100,000. A replacement machine costs £5 million now and requires maintenance costs of £100,000 at the end of each year during its economic life of five years. At the end of the five years, the new machine will have a salvage value of £1,000,000. It will be depreciated by the reducing balance method (20 per cent). In five years a replacement machine will cost £6,000,000. Industrial Hooks will need to purchase this machine regardless of what choice it makes today. The corporate tax rate is 24 per cent and the appropriate discount rate is 12 per cent. The company is assumed to earn sufficient revenues to generate tax shields from depreciation. Should Industrial Hooks replace the old machine now or at the end of five years?

25 **Inflation** Your company manufactures non-stick frying pans. However, it outsources the production of the glass covers for the pans. Until now, this has been a good option. However, your supplier has become unreliable and doubled his prices. As a result, you feel that now might be the time to start producing your own glass covers. At the moment, your company produces 200,000 non-stick pans per year. The producer charges you €2 per cover and you estimate the costs of producing your own cover to be €1.50. A new machine will be required to produce the covers and this costs €150,000 in the market. The machine will last for 10 years, at which point it will have no value. The expansion will require an increase in working capital of €30,000. Your company pays 28 per cent tax and the appropriate discount rate is 15 per cent. Inflation is expected to be 4 per cent per year for the next 10 years. Assume you use the 20 per cent reducing balance method for depreciation. Should you undertake this investment? State clearly any additional assumptions you have made in your analysis.

26 **Project Analysis and Inflation** Dickinson Brothers is considering investing in a machine to produce computer keyboards. The price of the machine will be £400,000, and its economic life is five years. The machine will be depreciated by the reducing balance (20 per cent) method but will be worthless in five years. The machine will produce 10,000 keyboards each year. The price of each keyboard will be £40 in the first year and will increase by 5 per cent per year. The production cost per keyboard will be £20 in the first year and will increase by 10 per cent per year. The project will have an annual fixed cost of £50,000 and require an immediate investment of £25,000 in net working capital. The corporate tax rate for the company is 28 per cent. If the appropriate discount rate is 15 per cent, what is the NPV of the investment?

CHALLENGE

27 **Project Evaluation: Aguilera Acoustics** Aguilera Acoustics (AA) projects unit sales for a new seven-octave voice emulation implant as follows:

Year	Unit Sales
1	85,000
2	98,000
3	106,000
4	114,000
5	93,000

Production of the implants will require €1,500,000 in net working capital to start and additional net working capital investments each year equal to 15 per cent of the projected sales increase for the following year. Total fixed costs are €900,000 per year, variable production costs are €240 per unit, and the units are priced at €325 each. The equipment needed to begin production has an installed cost of €21,000,000. Because the implants are intended for professional singers, this equipment is considered industrial machinery and is thus depreciated by reducing balance method at 20 per cent per annum. In five years, this equipment can be sold for about 20 per cent of its acquisition cost. AA is in the 35 per cent marginal tax bracket and has a required return on all its projects of 18 per cent. Based on these preliminary project estimates, what is the NPV of the project? What is the IRR? If the firm can reinvest future cash flows only at a rate of 12 per cent, what is the MIRR?

28 **Calculating Required Savings** A proposed cost-saving device has an installed cost of £360,000. The device will be used in a five-year project and be depreciated using the reducing balance method at 20 per cent per annum. The required initial net working capital investment is £20,000, the marginal tax rate is 24 per cent and the project discount rate is 12 per cent. The device has an estimated year 5 salvage value of £60,000. What level of pre-tax cost savings do we require for this project to be profitable?

29 Calculating a Bid Price Another utilization of cash flow analysis is setting the bid price on a project. To calculate the bid price, we set the project NPV equal to zero and find the required price. Thus the bid price represents a financial break-even level for the project. Guthrie Enterprises needs someone to supply it with 150,000 cartons of machine screws per year to support its manufacturing needs over the next five years, and you have decided to bid on the contract. It will cost you €780,000 to install the equipment necessary to start production; you will depreciate this cost using 20 per cent reducing balances over the project's life. You estimate that in five years this equipment can be salvaged for €50,000. Your fixed production costs will be €240,000 per year, and your variable production costs should be €8.50 per carton. You also need an initial investment in net working capital of €75,000. If your tax rate is 35 per cent and you require a 16 per cent return on your investment, what bid price should you submit?

30 Financial Break-even Analysis The technique for calculating a bid price can be extended to many other types of problem. Answer the following questions using the same technique as setting a bid price; that is, set the project NPV to zero and solve for the variable in question.

(a) In the previous problem, assume that the price per carton is €13 and calculate the project NPV. What does your answer tell you about your bid price? What do you know about the number of cartons you can sell and still break even? How about your level of costs?

(b) Solve the previous problem again with the price still at €13 and calculate the quantity of cartons per year that you can supply and still break even.

(c) Repeat (b) with a price of €13 and the quantity at 150,000 cartons per year, then calculate the highest level of fixed costs you could afford and still break even.

31 Calculating a Bid Price for a New Contract Your company has been approached to bid on a contract to sell 10,000 new earbud voice translation units a year for four years. Due to technological improvements, beyond that time they will be outdated and no sales will be possible. The equipment necessary for production will cost £2.4 million and will be depreciated on a reducing balance (25 per cent) method. Production will require an investment in net working capital of £75,000 to be returned at the end of the project, and the equipment can be sold for £200,000 at the end of production. Fixed costs are £500,000 per year and variable costs are £165 per unit. In addition to the contract, you feel your company can sell 3,000, 6,000, 8,000 and 5,000 additional units to companies in other countries over the next four years, respectively, at a price of £275. This price is fixed. The tax rate is 24 per cent, and the required return is 13 per cent. Additionally, the managing director of the company will undertake the project only if it has an NPV of £100,000. What bid price should you set for the contract?

32 Project Analysis: Benson Enterprises Benson Enterprises is evaluating alternative uses for a three-storey manufacturing and warehousing building that it has purchased for £225,000. The company can continue to rent the building to the present occupants for £12,000 per year. The present occupants have indicated an interest in staying in the building for at least another 15 years. Alternatively, the company could modify the existing structure to use for its own manufacturing and warehousing needs. Benson's production engineer feels the building could be adapted to handle one of two new product lines. The cost and revenue data for the two product alternatives are as follows:

	Product A	Product B
Initial cash outlay for building modifications	£ 36,000	£ 54,000
Initial cash outlay for equipment	144,000	162,000
Annual pre-tax cash revenues (generated for 15 years)	105,000	127,500
Annual pre-tax expenditures (generated for 15 years)	60,000	75,000

The building will be used for only 15 years for either product A or product B. After 15 years the building will be too small for efficient production of either product line. At that time, Benson plans to rent the building to firms similar to the current occupants. To rent the building again, Benson will need to restore the building to its present layout. The estimated cash cost of restoring the building if product A has been undertaken is £3,750. If product B has been manufactured, the cash cost will be £28,125. These cash costs can be deducted for tax purposes in the year the expenditures occur.

Benson will depreciate the original building shell (purchased for £225,000) over a 30-year life to zero, regardless of which alternative it chooses. The building modifications and equipment purchases for either product are estimated to have a 15-year life. They will be depreciated by the 20 per cent reducing balance method. At the end of the project's life, the salvage value of the equipment will be equal to the residual value. The firm's tax rate is 28 per cent, and its required rate of return on such investments is 12 per cent.

For simplicity, assume all cash flows occur at the end of the year. The initial outlays for modifications and equipment will occur today (year 0), and the restoration outlays will occur at the end of year 15. Benson has other profitable ongoing operations that are sufficient to cover any losses. Which use of the building would you recommend to management? Assume the production of product A and B as project A and project B, respectively.

33 **Project Analysis and Inflation: Green Energy Corporation** Green Energy Corporation has purchased a wind farm with a capacity of 50 MW. The wind farm is located in a region with consistent wind patterns and is projected to generate annual revenues of £5 million for the next 20 years. Green Energy Corporation can either operate the wind farm for the next 20 years or sell it immediately for £50 million. If Green Energy Corporation decides to operate the wind farm, it will need to spend £10 million on maintenance and repairs over the next 20 years. The corporate tax rate is 30 per cent, and the required rate of return for the wind farm investment is 15 per cent.

Should Green Energy Corporation operate the wind farm or sell it immediately? What is the net present value of operating the wind farm over the next 20 years? What is the internal rate of return of the wind farm investment? What is the payback period for the wind farm investment? What is the profitability index of operating the wind farm over the next 20 years?

34 **Project Analysis and Inflation: GERS** Genetic Engineering Research Studies Ltd (GERS) has hired you as a consultant to evaluate the NPV of its proposed toad house. GERS plans to breed toads and sell them as ecologically desirable insect control mechanisms. It anticipates that the business will continue into perpetuity. Following the negligible start-up costs, GERS expects the following nominal cash flows at the end of the year:

Cash Flows	Amount
Revenues	£150,000
Labour costs	80,000
Other costs	40,000

The company will lease machinery for £20,000 per year. The lease payments start at the end of year 1 and are expressed in nominal terms. Revenues will increase by 5 per cent per year in real terms. Labour costs will increase by 3 per cent per year in real terms. Other costs will decrease by 1 per cent per year in real terms. The rate of inflation is expected to be 6 per cent per year. GERS's required rate of return is 10 per cent in real terms. The company has a 28 per cent tax rate. All cash flows occur at year-end. What is the NPV of GERS's proposed toad house today?

35 **Project Analysis and Inflation: Sony International** Sony International has an investment opportunity to produce a new 100-inch widescreen TV. The required investment on 1 January of this year is $32 million. The firm will depreciate the investment to zero using the straight-line method over four years. The investment has no resale value after completion of the project. The firm is in the 34 per cent tax bracket. The price of the product will be $400 per unit, in real terms, and will not change over the life of the project. Labour costs for year 1 will be $15.30 per hour, in real terms, and will increase at 2 per cent per year in real terms. Energy costs for year 1 will be $5.15 per physical unit, in real terms, and will increase at 3 per cent per year in real terms. The inflation rate is 5 per cent per year. Revenues are received and costs are paid at year-end. Refer to the following table for the production schedule:

	Year 1	Year 2	Year 3	Year 4
Physical production, in units	100,000	200,000	200,000	150,000
Labour input, in hours	2,000,000	2,000,000	2,000,000	2,000,000
Energy input, physical units	200,000	200,000	200,000	200,000

The real discount rate for Sony is 8 per cent. Calculate the NPV of this project.

36 **Project Analysis and Inflation: Pill plc** After extensive medical and marketing research, Pill plc believes it can penetrate the pain reliever market. It is considering two alternative products. The first is a medication for headache pain. The second is a pill for headache and arthritis pain. Both products would be introduced at a price of £4 per package in real terms. The headache-only medication is projected to sell 5 million packages a year, whereas the headache and arthritis remedy would sell 10 million packages a year. Cash costs of production in the first year are expected to be £1.50 per package in real terms for the headache-only brand. Production costs are expected to be £1.70 in real terms for the headache and arthritis pill. All prices and costs are expected to rise at the general inflation rate of 5 per cent.

Either product requires further investment. The headache-only pill could be produced using equipment costing £10.2 million. That equipment would last three years and have no resale value. The machinery required to produce the broader remedy would cost £12 million and last three years. The firm expects that equipment to have a £1 million resale value (in real terms) at the end of year 3.

Pill plc uses reducing balance (20 per cent) depreciation. The firm faces a corporate tax rate of 24 per cent and believes that the appropriate real discount rate is 13 per cent. Which pain reliever should the firm produce?

37 **Calculating Project NPV** Petracci SpA manufactures fine furniture. The company is deciding whether to introduce a new mahogany dining room table set. The set will sell for €5,600, including a set of eight chairs. The company feels that sales will be 1,300, 1,325, 1,375, 1,450 and 1,320 sets per year for the next five years, respectively. Variable costs will amount to 45 per cent of sales, and fixed costs are €1.7 million per year. The new tables will require inventory amounting to 10 per cent of sales, produced and stockpiled in the year prior to sales. It is believed that the addition of the new table will cause a loss of 200 tables per year of the oak tables the company produces. These tables sell for €4,500 and have variable costs of 40 per cent of sales. The inventory for this oak table is also 10 per cent. Petracci currently has excess production capacity. If the company buys the necessary equipment today, it will cost €10.5 million. However, the excess production capacity means the company can produce the new table without buying the new equipment. The company controller has said that the current excess capacity will end in two years with current production. This means that if the company uses the current excess capacity for the new table, it will be forced to spend the €10.5 million in two years to accommodate the increased sales of its current products. In five years, the new equipment will have a market value of €2.8 million if purchased today, and €6.1 million if purchased in two years. The equipment is depreciated using reducing balances at 20 per cent per annum. The company has a tax rate of 38 per cent, and the required return for the project is 14 per cent.

(a) Should Petracci undertake the new project?

(b) Can you perform an IRR analysis on this project? How many IRRs would you expect to find?

(c) How would you interpret the profitability index?

Exam Question (45 minutes)

Lothian Engineering Ltd has been offered a contract to supply one of its components to a company developing a new product. The contract would be for 400 units per annum for five years at a price of £600 per unit. Lothian does not have the capacity to fulfil the contract requirements and it would be necessary to invest in additional machinery. The company's management accountant believes that the estimates of the production costs can be based on those incurred in the manufacture of the product already being produced. The following estimates per unit are provided:

- Materials and components £180
- Labour £100
- Overheads (variable) £20
- Overheads (allocation of fixed general overheads) £40.

In addition, fixed costs of £25,000 per annum would be incurred. The investment in machinery required to produce the additional output would cost £160,000. This expenditure can be depreciated for tax purposes over the five-year life of the contract on a straight-line basis and it is anticipated that it could be sold for £50,000 at the end of the five-year period.

The company would also make use of some equipment it already owns. This is fully depreciated for tax purposes and could be sold today for £30,000. It is anticipated that after using it for another five years the equipment will have no second-hand value. The production would take place in the company's main factory. However, the company will have to relocate the production of another product to make space available. This will require renting some additional accommodation at a cost of £20,000 per annum. It will also be necessary to invest £15,000 in additional working capital. The tax rate is 30 per cent. The discount rate for this project is 14 per cent. Use four investment appraisal techniques to determine whether you should go ahead with the project.

Total Marks: 100

Mini Case

Revinci Airports

Revinci is a large multinational firm specializing in running regional airports. The firm currently owns 20 airports across Europe, the Middle East and Asia. Revinci's business model is to generate 60 per cent of its revenues from airlines leasing parking bays and using runways, with 40 per cent generated from passengers' expenditures.

The airport sector is extremely competitive as companies must generate enough passenger flow to persuade airlines to use the airport. Likewise, airport operators must attract airlines to the airport in order to attract passengers. It's a catch-22 situation and so airports managers must create value propositions to target two business segments: passengers and airlines.

Revinci has identified an opportunity in Finland to lease an airport for 10 years from the local regional government. The airport needs a lot of upgrade work to bring it up to international flying standards. The cost of the works will be €6 million but after these are complete the site will have an additional value of €4 million, which is unlikely to fall over the 10-year period.

Revinci will also need to outfit all the existing shopping space with current-technology automated counters and this will cost €3 million. The equipment will be depreciated using capital allowances (reducing balance) at 20 per cent per annum. After the 10-year project the equipment will be obsolete and worth nothing.

The airport is expected to receive 60,000 passengers per year, with each passenger paying an average of €30 per visit. Revinci feels that passenger numbers will grow by 5 per cent every year for the life of the contract. Target variable costs are 50 per cent per passenger, and fixed costs are €250,000 per year.

At the end of the 10-year contract, Revinci will return the airport to the regional government with a final one-off additional fee equivalent to 25 per cent of final-year revenue numbers. The company will also receive the land value arising from the initial improvement works at the beginning of the project. Revinci faces a 28 per cent tax rate and has a 12 per cent required return on new airport developments. Revinci can reinvest future cash flows at a rate of 10 per cent per annum. Assume that a loss in any year will result in a tax credit.

You have been approached by the chairman of the company with a request to analyse the project. Calculate the payback period, profitability index, average accounting return, net present value, internal rate of return and modified internal rate of return for the new airport. Should Revinci take the contract?

Practical Case Study

WindRise Energy, a leading player in the renewable energy sector, is considering investing in new machinery for the development of a wind farm project. The company has already invested £100,000 in research and development for the wind farm and is now evaluating the financial viability of an additional investment of £2,000,000 in the machinery.

It is your responsibility to evaluate the financial viability of this investment opportunity and present your findings to the management of WindRise Energy in the form of a brief report. Your report should provide context to the wind farm sector and clearly summarize the results of a comprehensive financial analysis of the investment.

Wind energy is one of the fastest-growing sources of renewable energy worldwide, with a growing demand for clean energy driving the development of wind farms globally. The wind farm sector is highly competitive, with many players looking to capitalize on this growth. In this context, it is crucial that WindRise Energy makes informed investment decisions to remain competitive and take advantage of the growth opportunities in the sector.

Given the following information, you are tasked with calculating the net present value (NPV), internal rate of return (IRR), payback period and profitability index (PI) of the investment in the machinery. In addition, you should conduct a sensitivity analysis and scenario analysis to identify the key drivers of the project's financial viability and assess the risk associated with the investment.

The wind farm is expected to operate for five years, after which it will be decommissioned, with a resale value of £1,000,000 at the end of the five-year period. Capital allowances will be calculated on a 20 per cent reducing balance basis over the five-year period for tax purposes.

It is expected that the wind farm will generate energy for 500,000 homes per annum for the years 1 to 5, with a selling price of £20 per unit of energy generated and variable costs of £10 per unit. In addition to these costs, fixed costs of £300,000 per annum are anticipated. The company will also incur overheads calculated as 4 per cent of revenues.

WindRise Energy already owns land suitable for the wind farm, but the management accounting system will charge £25,000 per annum for the use of the land, even though no other use is anticipated for this land over the next five years. The company requires a rate of return of 15 per cent per annum on this type of project, and the tax rate is 20 per cent. The company will also hold stocks of the necessary components to maintain the wind farm equivalent to 15 per cent of the expected energy generated.

You have been provided with a lot of information in this question, but you should use your own forecasts/figures based on industry trends/insight if you believe that you can improve the quality of your analysis. Some of the information may not even make sense when you undertake your analysis, and you must interrogate every assumption and justify it.

In your report, you should present the results of your financial analysis in a clear and concise manner, including tables, graphs and commentary. You should also present the results of the sensitivity analysis and scenario analysis, and provide recommendations to the management of WindRise Energy based on your findings.

The report should be no more than 10 pages in length, excluding appendices, and should provide a clear and detailed explanation of your findings and recommendations.

Relevant Accounting Standards

The main reason that accounting standards are important for capital budgeting is in the estimation of tax payments. Given that tax is derived from accounting statements and reduces cash flow, all the accounting standards are relevant. However, depreciation is possibly the most important issue and so IAS 16 *Property, Plant and Equipment,* IFRS 3 *Business Combinations* and IAS 38 *Intangible Assets* are particularly relevant. The analyst should also be aware of current practice in depreciating assets. This can be quite complex and more information will be found on each country's government tax site (for the UK, this is www.hmrc.gov.uk). Readers in the European Union should also be familiar with developments and harmonization towards a common tax base (http://ec.europa.eu).

Other important accounting standards include IAS 2 *Inventories,* IAS 17 *Leases,* IAS 21 *The Effects of Changes in Foreign Exchange Rates* and IAS 36 *Impairment of Assets.* Visit the IASPlus website (www.iasplus.com) for good summaries of each standard.

While it is easy to be overwhelmed by the number of accounting standards, everything that is needed to carry out a capital budgeting analysis is provided in this textbook, so do not worry. The accounting standards are for reference and should be consulted only when a real capital budgeting analysis is undertaken.

Additional Reading

An interesting paper that examines capital budgeting is as follows:

1 Durnev, A., R. Morck and B. Yeung (2004) 'Value-enhancing Capital Budgeting and Firm-specific Stock Return Variation', *Journal of Finance,* Vol. 59, No. 1, 65–105.

Some other interesting papers on capital budgeting methods include:

2 Andor, G., S.K. Mohanty and T. Toth (2015) 'Capital Budgeting Practices: A Survey of Central and Eastern European Firms', *Emerging Markets Review,* Vol. 23, 148–172.

3 Brunzell, T., E. Liljeblom and M. Vaikekoski (2013) 'Determinants of Capital Budgeting Methods and Hurdle Rates in Nordic Firms', *Accounting & Finance,* Vol. 53, No. 1, 85–110. **Nordic countries.**

4 Duchin, R. and D. Sosyura (2013) 'Divisional Managers and Internal Capital Markets', *Journal of Finance,* Vol. 68, No. 2, 387–429.

5 Holmén, M. and B. Pramborg (2009) 'Capital Budgeting and Political Risk: Empirical Evidence', *Journal of International Financial Management and Accounting,* Vol. 20, No. 2, 105–134. **Sweden.**

6 Rao, S., S. Koirala, C. Thapa and S. Neupane (2022) 'When Rain Matters! Investments and Value Relevance', *Journal of Corporate Finance,* Vol. 73, 101827.

7 Van Binsbergen, J.H., W.F. Diamond and M. Grotteria (2021) 'Risk-free Interest Rates', *Journal of Financial Economics,* Vol. 143, No. 1, 1–29.

Endnote

1 One caveat is in order. Perhaps the old machine's maintenance is high in the first year but drops after that. A decision to replace immediately might be premature in that case. Therefore, we need to check the cost of the old machine in future years.

The cost of keeping the existing machine a second year is:

$$\text{PV of costs at time 1} = £2{,}500 + \frac{£2{,}000}{1.15} - \frac{£1{,}500}{1.15} = £2{,}935$$

which has a future value of £3,375 (= £2,935 × 1.15).

The costs of keeping the existing machine for years 3 and 4 are also greater than the EAC of buying a new machine. Thus, BIKE's decision to replace the old machine immediately is still valid.

Chapter 8
Risk Analysis, Real Options and Capital Budgeting

Learning Objectives

After reading this chapter you should be able to:

LO1 Comprehend the principles and applications of sensitivity analysis, scenario analysis and break-even analysis in assessing project risk and decision-making.

LO2 Apply Monte Carlo simulation techniques to model the uncertainty of input variables and estimate project outcomes.

LO3 Analyse real options as a decision-making tool in the context of corporate finance and capital budgeting.

LO4 Construct decision trees to visualize and evaluate complex investment decisions under uncertainty.

LO5 Evaluate the strengths and limitations of each risk analysis method in various corporate finance situations.

For several years, companies have made strategic investment decisions in an exceptionally uncertain and harsh economic environment. Post-pandemic, all countries have experienced unprecedented upheaval, with supply chain disruptions, changing working practices and the global conflict affecting international trade. This has led to challenges in predicting future cash flows from investments. Reinvigorated populism, climate change, the cost of living crisis and high inflation worldwide are creating new risks in forecasting cash flows. The possibility of trade disputes and boycotts between countries has the potential to further affect companies, irrespective of where they operate.

Source: Andrii Yalanskyi/123RF.

Strategic decisions that reflect future uncertainty, such as potential new military conflicts or extreme economic conditions, need to be analysed in a way that incorporates all potential future events. Standard net present value valuation does not adequately capture alternative scenarios and so a modification of the methods must be developed. This chapter explores how firms can assess strategic investments in uncertain environments and what they can do to possibly mitigate the risk of their decisions.

Key Notations

NVP	Net present value
EAC	Equivalent annual cost
t_c	Corporate tax rate

8.1 Sensitivity Analysis, Scenario Analysis and Break-even Analysis

One main point of this book is that NPV analysis is a superior capital budgeting technique. Because the NPV approach uses cash flows rather than profits, includes all cash flows, and discounts cash flows correctly, it is hard to find any technical fault with it. However, in our conversations with businesspeople, we hear the phrase 'a false sense of security' frequently. These people point out that the documentation for capital budgeting proposals is often quite impressive. Cash flows are projected down to the last few pounds or euros for each year (or even each month). Opportunity costs and side effects are handled appropriately, and sunk costs are correctly ignored. When a high net present value appears at the bottom, one's temptation is to say 'yes' immediately. Nevertheless, the projected cash flow often goes unmet in practice, and the firm ends up with a money loser.

Sensitivity Analysis and Scenario Analysis

How can the firm get the net present value technique to live up to its potential? One approach is **sensitivity analysis**, which examines how sensitive a particular NPV calculation is to changes in underlying assumptions. Sensitivity analysis is also known as *what-if* analysis and *bop* (best, optimistic and pessimistic) analysis.

Consider the following example. Solar Electronics (SE) has recently developed a solar-powered jet engine and wants to go ahead with full-scale production. The initial (year 0) investment is £1,500 million, followed by manufacturing and sales over the next five years. The preliminary cash flow projection appears in Table 8.1.

Table 8.1 Cash Flow Forecasts for Solar Electronics' Jet Engine: Base Case (millions)*

	Year 0 (£)	Years 1–5 (£)
Revenues		6,000
Variable costs		3,000
Fixed costs		1,791
Depreciation		300
Pre-tax profit		909
Tax (t_c = 0.28)		255
Net profit		654
Initial investment costs	1,500	

* Assumptions: (1) Investment is depreciated in years 1 through 5 using the straight-line method for simplicity; (2) tax rate is 28 per cent; (3) the company receives no tax benefits for initial development costs.

If SE were to go ahead with investment in and production of the jet engine, the NPV at a discount rate of 15 per cent would be (in millions):

$$\begin{aligned} \text{NPV} &= -£1{,}500 + \sum_{t=1}^{5} \frac{£954}{(1.15)^t} \\ &= -£1{,}500 + £954 \times A_{0.15}^{5} \\ &= £1{,}700 \end{aligned}$$

Because NPV is positive, financial theory implies that SE should accept the project. However, is this all there is to say about the venture? Before actual funding, we ought to check out the project's underlying assumptions about revenues and costs.

Revenues

Let us assume that the marketing department has projected annual sales to be:

Number of jet engines sold per year	=	Market share	×	Size of jet engines market per year
3,000	=	0.30	×	10,000
Annual sales revenues	=	Number of jet engines sold	×	Price per engine
£6,000 million	=	33,000	×	£2 million

Thus, it turns out that the revenue estimates depend on three assumptions:

1. Market share
2. Size of the jet engine market
3. Price per engine.

Costs

Financial analysts frequently divide costs into two types: variable costs and fixed costs. **Variable costs** change as the output changes, and they are zero when production is zero. Costs of direct labour and raw materials are usually variable. It is common to assume that a variable cost is constant per unit of output, implying that total variable costs are proportional to the level of production. For example, if direct labour is variable and one unit of final output requires £10 of direct labour, then 100 units of final output should need £1,000 of direct labour.

Fixed costs are not dependent on the number of goods or services produced during the period. Fixed costs are usually measured as costs per unit of time, such as rent per month or salaries per year. Naturally, fixed costs are not fixed for ever. They are fixed only over a predetermined period.

The engineering department has estimated variable costs to be £1 million per engine. Fixed costs are £1,791 million per year. The cost breakdowns are:

Variable cost per year	=	Variable cost per unit	×	Number of jet engines sold per year
£3,000 million	=	£1 million	×	3,000
Total cost before taxes per year	=	Varible cost per year	+	Fixed per year
£4,791 million	=	£3,000 million	+	£2 million

These estimates for market size, market share, price, variable cost and fixed cost, as well as the initial investment, are presented in the middle column of Table 8.2. These figures represent the firm's expectations or best estimates of the different parameters. For comparison, the firm's analysts also prepared both optimistic and pessimistic forecasts for each of the different variables. These forecasts are provided in the table as well.

Table 8.2 Different Estimates for Solar Electronics' Solar Plane Engine

	Pessimistic	Expected or Best	Optimistic
Market size (per year)	5,000	10,000	20,000
Market share (%)	20	30	50
Price (£ million)	1.9	2	2.2
Variable cost (per engine) (£ million)	1.2	1	0.8
Fixed cost (per year) (£ million)	1,891	1,791	1,741
Investment (£ million)	1,900	1,500	1,000

Standard sensitivity analysis calls for an NPV calculation for all three possibilities of a single variable, along with the expected forecast for all other variables. We illustrate this procedure in Table 8.3. For example, consider the NPV calculation of £8,940 million provided in the upper right corner of this table. This NPV occurs when the optimistic forecast of 20,000 units per year is used for market size while all other variables are set at their expected forecasts from Table 8.2. Note that each row of the middle column of Table 8.3 shows a value of £1,700 million because the expected forecast is used for the variable that was singled out, as well as for all other variables.

Table 8.3 NPV Calculations for the Solar Plane Engine Using Sensitivity Analysis

	Pessimistic (£m)	Expected or Best (£m)	Optimistic (£m)
Market size	−1,921*	1,700	8,940
Market share	−714*	1,700	6,527
Price	976	1,700	3,148
Variable cost	251	1,700	3,148
Fixed cost	1,458	1,700	1,820
Investment	1,300	1,700	2,200

* We assume that the other divisions of the firm are profitable, implying that a loss on this project can offset income elsewhere in the firm, thereby reducing the overall taxes of the firm.

Under sensitivity analysis, one input is varied while all other inputs are assumed to meet their expectation. For example, an NPV of −£1,921 million occurs when the pessimistic forecast of 5,000 is used for market size, while all other variables are set at their expected forecasts from Table 8.2.

We can use Table 8.3 in several ways. First, taken as a whole, the table can indicate whether NPV analysis should be trusted. In other words, it reduces the false sense of security we spoke of earlier. Suppose that NPV is positive when the expected forecast for each variable is used. However, further suppose that every number in the pessimistic column is highly negative and every number in the optimistic column is highly positive. A change in a single forecast significantly alters the NPV estimate, making one wary of the net present value approach. A conservative manager might well scrap the entire NPV analysis in this situation. Fortunately, the solar plane engine does not exhibit this wide dispersion because all but two of the numbers in Table 8.3 are positive. Managers viewing the table are likely to consider NPV analysis to be useful for the solar-powered jet engine.

Second, sensitivity analysis shows where more information is needed. For example, an error in the estimate of investment appears to be relatively unimportant because, even under the pessimistic scenario, the NPV of £1,300 million is still highly positive. By contrast, the pessimistic forecast for market share leads to a negative NPV of −£714 million, and a pessimistic forecast for market size leads to a substantially negative NPV of −£1,921 million. Because the effect of incorrect estimates on revenues is so much greater than the effect of incorrect estimates on costs, more information about the factors determining revenues might be needed.

Unfortunately, sensitivity analysis also suffers from some drawbacks. For example, sensitivity analysis may unwittingly *increase* the false sense of security among managers. Suppose all pessimistic forecasts yield positive NPVs. A manager might feel that there is no way the project can lose money. Of course the forecasters may simply have an optimistic view of a pessimistic forecast. To combat this, some companies do not treat optimistic and pessimistic forecasts subjectively. Rather, their pessimistic forecasts are always, say, 20 per cent less than expected. Unfortunately, the cure in this case may be worse than the disease: a deviation of a fixed percentage ignores the fact that some variables are easier to forecast than others.

In addition, sensitivity analysis treats each variable in isolation when, in reality, the different variables are likely to be related. For example, if ineffective management allows costs to get out of control, it is likely that variable costs, fixed costs and investment will all rise above expectation at the same time. If the market is not receptive to a solar plane engine, both market share and price should decline together.

Managers frequently perform **scenario analysis**, a variant of sensitivity analysis, to minimize this problem. Simply put, this approach examines a number of different likely scenarios, where each scenario involves a confluence of factors. As a simple example, consider the effect of a few airline crashes. These crashes are likely to reduce flying in total, thereby limiting the demand for any new engines. Furthermore, even if the crashes do not involve solar-powered aircraft, the public could become more averse to any innovative and controversial technologies. Hence, SE's market share might fall as well. Perhaps the cash flow calculations would look like those in Table 8.4 under the scenario of a plane crash.

Given the calculations in the table, the NPV (in millions) would be:

$$-£2{,}162 = -£1{,}500 - £198 \times A^{5}_{0.15}$$

Table 8.4 Cash Flow Forecast under the Scenario of a Plane Crash*

	Year 1 (£m)	Years 1–5 (£m)
Revenues		2,800
Variable costs		1,400
Fixed costs		1,791
Depreciation		300
Pre-tax profit		−691
Tax ($t_c = 0.28$)†		193
Net profit		−498
Cash flow		−198
Initial investment cost	−1,500	

* Assumptions are: Market size 7,000 (70 per cent of expectation); Market share 20 per cent (⅔ of expectation); Forecasts for all other variables are the expected forecasts as given in Table 8.2.
† Tax loss offsets income elsewhere in firm.

A series of scenarios like this might illuminate issues concerning the project better than the standard application of sensitivity analysis would.

Sustainability in Action 8.1

The Impact of Oil Price Variability on Project Evaluation

What price will oil eventually stabilize at? The chart below presents the price of oil between 1971 and 2022. As you can see in Figure 8.1, prices have ranged from below $20 to over $140 in the time period.

Figure 8.1 Oil Prices between 1971 and 2022

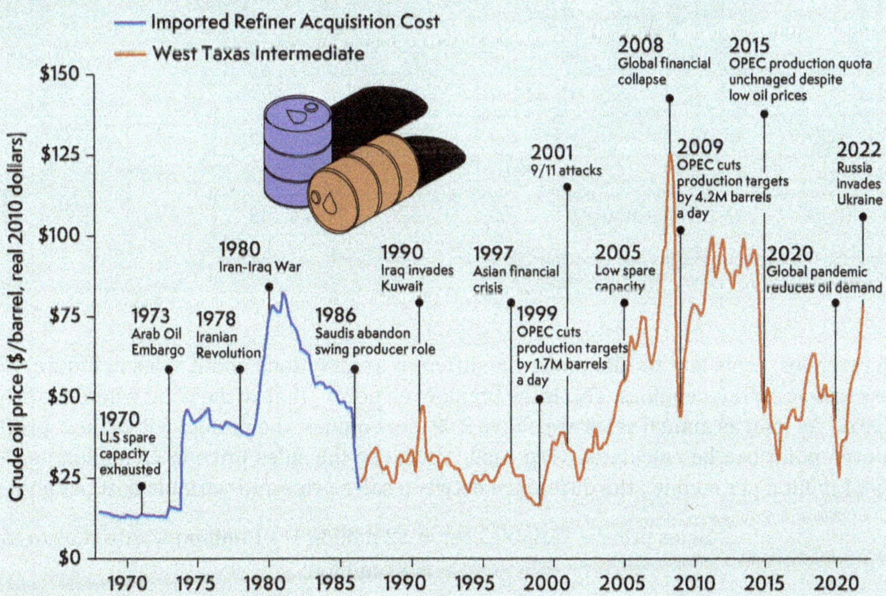

Source: https://advisor.visualcapitalist.com/historical-oil-prices/

Investment proposals that require the oil price as a revenue component or raw material cost must forecast oil prices for a number of years into the future. If you were undertaking a capital budgeting analysis in early 2020, it would be unlikely that you could ever have predicted oil prices to jump so high. As a result, your net present values will have probably misjudged the true net present value arising from a project. Sensitivity and scenario analysis allows you to consider such events and helps you to make better investment decisions in the presence of price volatility.

Break-even Analysis

Our discussion of sensitivity analysis and scenario analysis suggests that there are many ways to examine variability in forecasts. We now present another approach, break-even analysis. As its name implies, this approach determines the sales needed to break even. The approach is a useful complement to sensitivity analysis because it also sheds light on the severity of incorrect forecasts. We calculate the break-even point in terms of both accounting profit and present value.

Accounting Profit

Annual net profit under four different sales forecasts is as follows:

Annual Unit Sales	Net Profit (£m)
0	–1,506
1,000	–786
3,000	654
10,000	5,694

A more complete presentation of costs and revenues appears in Table 8.5.

Table 8.5 Revenues and Costs of Project under Different Sales Assumptions

Year 0	Years 1–5								
Initial Investment (£m)	Annual Unit Sales	Revenues (£m)	Variable Costs (£m)	Fixed Costs (£m)	Fixed Costs (£m)	Taxes* (t_c = 0.28) (£m)	Net Profit (£m)	Operating Cash Flows (£m)	NPV (Evaluated Date 0) (£m)
1,500	0	0	0	–1,791	–300	585	–1,506	–1,206	–5,541
1,500	1,000	2,000	–1,000	–1,791	–300	305	–786	–486	–3,128
1,500	3,000	6,000	–3,000	–1,791	–300	255	654	954	1,700
1,500	10,000	20,000	–10,000	–1,791	–300	–2,215	5,694	5,994	18,594

* Loss is incurred in the first two rows. For tax purposes, this loss offsets income elsewhere in the firm.

We plot the revenues, costs and profits under the different assumptions about sales in Figure 8.2. The revenue and cost curves cross at 2,091 jet engines. This is the break-even point – that is, the point where the project generates no profits or losses. As long as annual sales are above 2,091 jet engines, the project will make a profit.

This break-even point can be calculated very easily. Because the sales price is £2 million per engine and the variable cost is £1 million per engine,[1] the difference between sales price and variable cost per engine is:

$$\begin{aligned}\text{Sales price} - \text{Variable cost} &= £2\text{ million} - £1\text{ million}\\ &= £1\text{ million}\end{aligned}$$

This difference is called the pre-tax contribution margin because each additional engine contributes this amount to pre-tax profit. (Contribution margin can also be expressed on an after-tax basis.)

Figure 8.2 Break-even Point Using Accounting Numbers

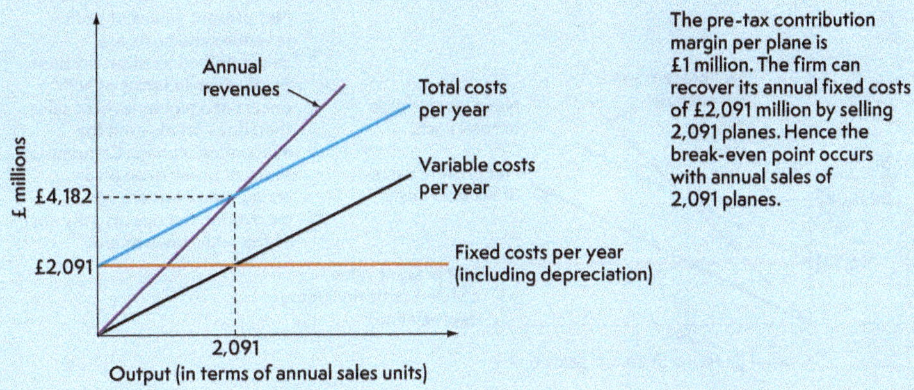

Fixed costs are £1,791 million and depreciation is £300 million, implying that the sum of these costs is:

$$\begin{aligned}\text{Fixed costs} + \text{Depreciation} &= £1{,}791 \text{ million} + £300 \text{ million}\\ &= £2{,}091 \text{ million}\end{aligned}$$

That is, the firm incurs costs of £2,091 million per year, regardless of the number of sales. Because each engine contributes £1 million, annual sales must reach the following level to offset the costs:

Accounting profit break-even point:

$$\frac{\text{Fixed costs} + \text{Depreciation}}{\text{Sales price} - \text{Variable costs}} = \frac{£2{,}091 \text{ million}}{£1 \text{ million}} = 2{,}091$$

Thus, 2,091 engines is the break-even point required for an accounting profit.

The astute reader might be wondering why taxes have been ignored in the calculation of break-even accounting profit. The reason is that a firm with a pre-tax profit of £0 will also have an after-tax profit of £0 because no taxes are paid if no pre-tax profit is reported. Thus, the number of units needed to break even on a pre-tax basis must be equal to the number of units needed to break even on an after-tax basis.

Present Value

As we have stated many times, we are more interested in present value than we are in profit. Therefore, we should calculate break-even in terms of present value. Given a discount rate of 15 per cent, the solar plane engine has the following net present values for different levels of annual sales:

Annual Unit Sales	NPV (£m)
0	−5,541
1,000	−3,128
3,000	1,700
10,000	18,594

These NPV calculations are reproduced from the last column of Table 8.5.

Figure 8.3 relates the net present value of both the revenues and the costs to output. There are at least two differences between Figure 8.3 and Figure 8.2, one of which is quite important while the other is much less so. First the less important point: the monetary amounts on the vertical dimension of Figure 8.3 are greater than those on the vertical dimension of Figure 8.2 because the net present values are calculated over five years. More important, accounting break-even occurs when 2,091 units are sold annually, whereas NPV break-even occurs when 2,296 units are sold annually.

Figure 8.3 Break-even Point Using Net Present Value

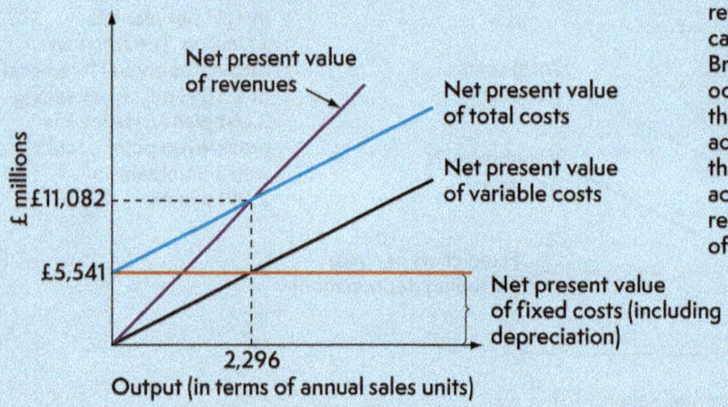

Net present values of both revenues and costs are calculated on an after-tax basis. Break-even in terms of NPV occurs at a higher level of sales than does break-even for accounting income. Companies that just break even on an accounting basis are not recovering the opportunity cost of the initial investment.

Of course the NPV break-even point can be calculated directly. The firm originally invested £1,500 million. This initial investment can be expressed as a five-year equivalent annual cost[2] (EAC), determined by dividing the initial investment by the appropriate five-year annuity factor:

$$\text{EAC} = \frac{\text{Initial investment}}{\text{5-year annuity factor at 15\%}} = \frac{\text{Initial investment}}{A^{5}_{0.15}}$$
$$= \frac{\text{£1,500 million}}{3.3522} = \text{£447.5 million}$$

Note that the EAC of £447.5 million is greater than the yearly depreciation of £300 million. This must occur because the calculation of EAC implicitly assumes that the £1,500 million investment could have been invested at 15 per cent.

After-tax costs, regardless of output, can be viewed like this:

$$\begin{array}{c}\text{£1,653}\\\text{million}\end{array} = \begin{array}{c}\text{£447.5}\\\text{million}\end{array} + \begin{array}{c}\text{£1,791}\\\text{million}\end{array} \times 0.72 - \begin{array}{c}\text{\$300}\\\text{million}\end{array} \times 0.28$$
$$= \text{EAC} + \text{Fixed costs} \times (1 - t_c) - \text{Depreciation} \times t_c$$

That is, in addition to the initial investment's equivalent annual cost of £447.5 million, the firm pays fixed costs each year and receives a depreciation tax shield each year. The depreciation tax shield is written as a negative number because it offsets the costs in the equation. Each plane contributes £0.72 million to after-tax profit, so it will take the following sales to offset the costs.

Present value break-even point:

$$\frac{\text{EAC} + \text{Fixed costs} \times (1 - t_c) - \text{Depreciation} \times t_c}{(\text{Sales price} - \text{Variable costs}) \times (1 - t_c)} = \frac{\text{£1.653 million}}{\text{£0.72 million}} = 2{,}296$$

Thus, 2,296 planes is the break-even point from the perspective of present value.

Why is the accounting break-even point different from the financial break-even point? When we use accounting profit as the basis for the break-even calculation, we subtract depreciation. Depreciation for the solar jet engines project is £300 million per year. If 2,091 solar jet engines are sold per year, SE will generate sufficient revenues to cover the £300 million depreciation expense plus other costs. Unfortunately, at this level of sales SE will not cover the economic opportunity costs of the £1,500 million laid out for the investment. If we take into account that the £1,500 million could have been invested at 15 per cent, the true annual cost of the investment is £447.5 million, not £300 million. Depreciation understates the true costs of recovering the initial investment. Thus companies that break even on an accounting basis are really losing money. They are losing the opportunity cost of the initial investment.

Is break-even analysis important? Very much so: all corporate executives fear losses. Break-even analysis determines how far sales can fall before the project is losing money, either in an accounting sense or an NPV sense.

8.2 Monte Carlo Simulation

Both sensitivity analysis and scenario analysis attempt to answer the question 'What if?' However, while we frequently use both analyses in the real world, each has its limitations. Sensitivity analysis allows only one variable to change at a time. By contrast, many variables are likely to move at the same time in the real world. Scenario analysis follows specific scenarios, such as changes in inflation, government regulation or the number of competitors. Although this methodology is often quite helpful, it cannot cover all sources of variability, and projects are likely to exhibit a lot of variability under just one economic scenario.

Monte Carlo simulation is a further attempt to model real-world uncertainty. This approach takes its name from the famous European gambling destination because it analyses projects the way one might investigate gambling strategies. Imagine a blackjack player who wonders if he should take a third card whenever his first two cards total 16. Most likely, a formal mathematical model would be too complex to be practical here. However, he could play thousands of hands in a casino, sometimes drawing a third card when his first two cards add to 16 and sometimes not drawing that third card. He could compare his winnings (or losings) under the two strategies to determine which were better. Of course, he would probably lose a lot of money performing this test in a real casino, so simulating the results from the two strategies on a computer might be cheaper. Monte Carlo simulation of capital budgeting projects is in this spirit.

Imagine that Backyard Barbeques (BB), a manufacturer of both charcoal and gas grills, has a blueprint for a new grill that cooks with compressed hydrogen. Its CFO, Edward H. Comiskey, being dissatisfied with simpler capital budgeting techniques, wants a Monte Carlo simulation for this new grill. A consultant specializing in the Monte Carlo approach, Lester Mauney, takes him through the five steps of the method.

Step 1: Specify the Basic Model

Les Mauney breaks up cash flow into three components: annual revenue, annual costs and initial investment.

The revenue in any year is viewed as:

Equation 8.1

$$\begin{matrix}\text{Number of grills sold} \\ \text{by entire industry}\end{matrix} \times \begin{matrix}\text{Market share of BB's} \\ \text{hydrogen grill (in per cent)}\end{matrix} \times \begin{matrix}\text{Price per} \\ \text{hydrogen grill}\end{matrix}$$

The cost in any year is:

$$\text{Fixed manufacturing costs} + \text{Variable manufacturing costs} + \text{Marketing costs} + \text{Selling costs}$$

Initial investment is viewed as:

$$\text{Cost of patent} + \text{Test marketing cost} + \text{Cost of production facility}$$

In step 1, you define the key inputs into your model. From above, revenues are a function of three components (the number of grills sold, market share and price per grill), annual costs are a function of four components (fixed costs, variable costs, marketing costs and selling costs), and the initial investment is a function of three components (patent, test marketing and cost of the facility).

As an analyst, you can make your Monte Carlo simulation as simple or as complex as you desire. You may, for example, decide to focus only on revenues and assume that costs are fixed. Alternatively, you may believe that every component is important and wish to simulate each separately.

Step 2: Specify a Distribution for Each Variable in the Model

Here comes the hard part. Let us start with revenue, which has three components in Equation 8.1. The consultant first models overall market size – that is, the number of grills sold by the entire industry. The trade publication *Outdoor Food (OF)* reported that 10 million grills of all types were sold in Europe last year, and it forecasts sales of 10.5 million next year. Mr Mauney, using *OF*'s forecast and his own intuition, creates the following distribution for next year's sales of grills by the entire industry:

Probability (%)	20	60	20
Next year's industry-wide unit sales	10 million	10.5 million	11 million

The tight distribution here reflects the slow but steady historical growth in the grill market. This probability distribution is graphed in Panel A of Figure 8.4.

Figure 8.4 Probability Distributions for Industry-wide Unit Sales, Market Share of BB's Hydrogen Grill, and Price of Hydrogen Grill

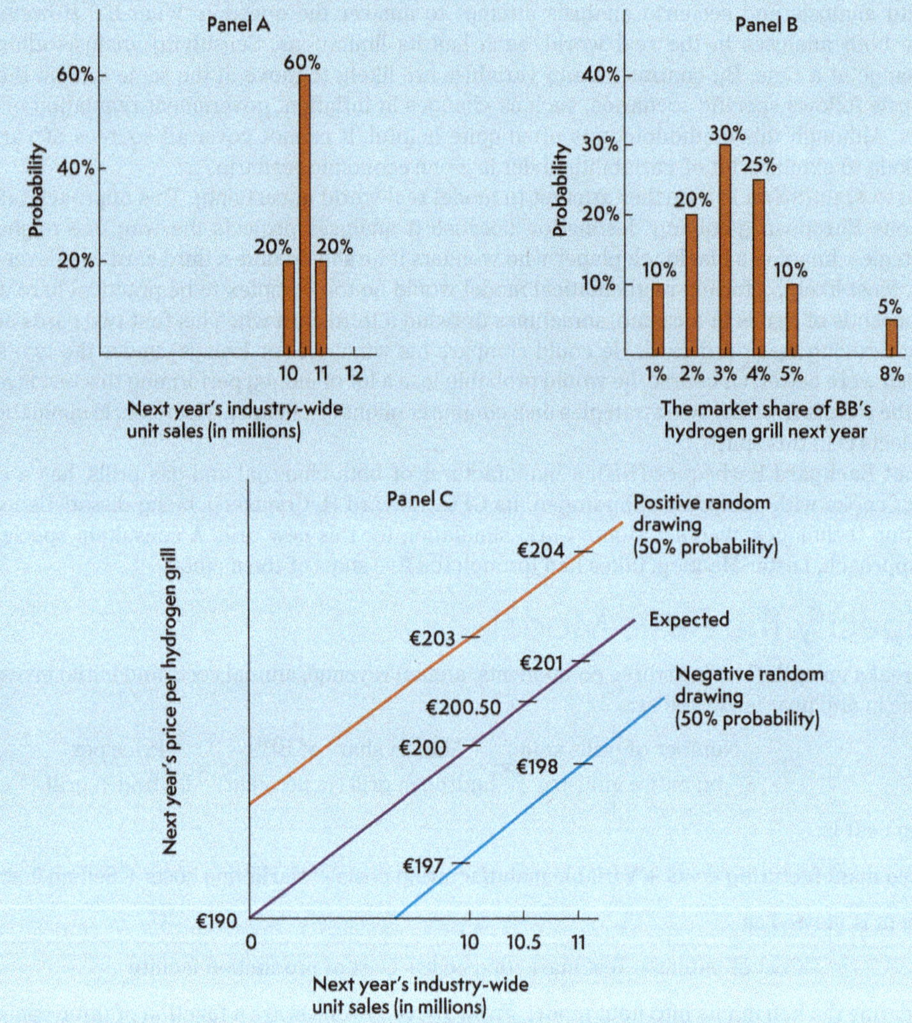

For each of the three variables, a drawing is generated by computer simulation. In addition, price per grill is dependent on industry-wide unit sales.

Lester Mauney realizes that estimating the market share of BB's hydrogen grill is more difficult. Nevertheless, after a great deal of analysis, he determines the distribution of next year's market share:

Probability (%)	10	20	30	25	10	5
Market share of BB's hydrogen grill next year (%)	1	2	3	4	5	8

Whereas the consultant assumed a symmetrical distribution for industry-wide unit sales, he believes a skewed distribution makes more sense for the project's market share. In his mind there is always the small possibility that sales of the hydrogen grill will really take off. This probability distribution is graphed in Panel B of Figure 8.4.

These forecasts assume that unit sales for the overall industry are unrelated to the project's market share. In other words, the two variables are *independent* of each other. Mr Mauney reasons that, although an economic boom might increase industry-wide grill sales and a recession might decrease them, the project's market share is unlikely to be related to economic conditions.

Now Mr Mauney must determine the distribution of price per grill. Mr Comiskey, the CFO, informs him that the price will be in the area of €200 per grill, given what other competitors are charging. However, the consultant believes that the price per hydrogen grill will almost certainly depend on the size of the overall market for grills. As in any business, you can usually charge more if demand is high.

After rejecting a number of complex models for price, Mr Mauney settles on the following specification:

Equation 8.2

$$\frac{\text{Next year's price}}{\text{per hydrogen grill}} = €190 + €11 \times \frac{\text{Industry-wide unit sales}}{\text{(in millions)} + /-€3}$$

The grill price in Equation 8.2 depends on the unit sales of the industry. In addition, random variation is modelled via the term '+/–€3', where a drawing of +€3 and a drawing of –€3 each occur 50 per cent of the time. For example, if industry-wide unit sales are 11 million, the price per unit would be either of the following:

$$€190 + €11 + €3 = €204 \text{ (50\% probability)}$$
$$€190 + €11 - €3 = €198 \text{ (50\% probability)}$$

The relationship between the price of a hydrogen grill and industry-wide unit sales is graphed in Panel C of Figure 8.4.

The consultant now has distributions for each of the three components of next year's revenue. However, he needs distributions for future years as well. Using forecasts from *Outdoor Food* and other publications, Mr Mauney forecasts the distribution of growth rates for the entire industry over the second year:

Probability (%)	20	60	20
Growth rate of industry-wide unit sales in second year (%)	1	3	5

Given both the distribution of next year's industry-wide unit sales and the distribution of growth rates for this variable over the second year, we can generate the distribution of industry-wide unit sales for the second year. A similar extension should give Mr Mauney a distribution for later years as well, though we will not go into the details here. And just as the consultant extended the first component of revenue (industry-wide unit sales) to later years, he would want to do the same thing for market share and unit price.

The preceding discussion shows how the three components of revenue can be modelled. Step 2 would be complete once the components of cost and investment are modelled in a similar way. Special attention must be paid to the interactions between variables here because ineffective management is likely to allow the different cost components to rise together. However, you are probably getting the idea now, so we will skip the rest of this step.

Step 3: The Computer Draws One Outcome

As we said, next year's revenue in our model is the product of three components. Step 3 requires you to randomly sample values for each component to generate a constructed random observation for each key input in the analysis. This can be done in a spreadsheet using dedicated functions for random number generation (for example, '=RAND$_{()}$' generates a random number between 0 and 1 in Excel) or with more sophisticated statistical software, such as Stata.

Imagine that the computer randomly picks industry-wide unit sales of 10 million, a market share for BB's hydrogen grill of 2 per cent, and a +€3 random price variation. Given these drawings, next year's price per hydrogen grill will be:

$$€190 + €10 + €3 = €203$$

and next year's revenue for BB's hydrogen grill will be:

$$10 \text{ million} \times 0.02 \times €203 = €40.6 \text{ million}$$

Of course, we are not done with the entire *outcome* yet. We would have to perform drawings for revenue and costs in each future year. Finally, a drawing for initial investment would have to be made as well. In this way, a single outcome, made up of a drawing for each variable in the model, would generate a cash flow from the project in each future year.

How likely is it that the specific outcome discussed would be drawn? We can answer this because we know the probability of each component. Because industry sales of €10 million has a 20 per cent probability, a market share of 2 per cent also has a 20 per cent probability and a random price variation of +€3 has a 50 per cent probability, the probability of these three drawings together in the same outcome is:

Equation 8.3

$$0.02 = 0.02 \times 0.20 \times 0.50$$

Of course the probability would get even smaller once drawings for future revenues, future costs and the initial investment are included in the outcome.

This step generates the cash flow for each year from a single outcome. What we are ultimately interested in is the *distribution* of cash flow each year across many outcomes. We ask the computer to randomly draw over and over again to give us this distribution, which is just what is done in the next step.

Step 4: Repeat the Procedure

The first three steps generate one outcome, but the essence of Monte Carlo simulation is repeated outcomes. Depending on the situation, the computer may be called on to generate thousands or even millions of outcomes. The result of all these drawings is a distribution of cash flow for each future year. This distribution is the basic output of Monte Carlo simulation.

Consider Figure 8.5. Here, repeated drawings have produced the simulated distribution of the third year's cash flow. There would be, of course, a distribution like the one in this figure for each future year. This leaves us with just one more step.

Figure 8.5 Simulated Distribution of the Third Year's Cash Flow for BB's New Hydrogen Grill

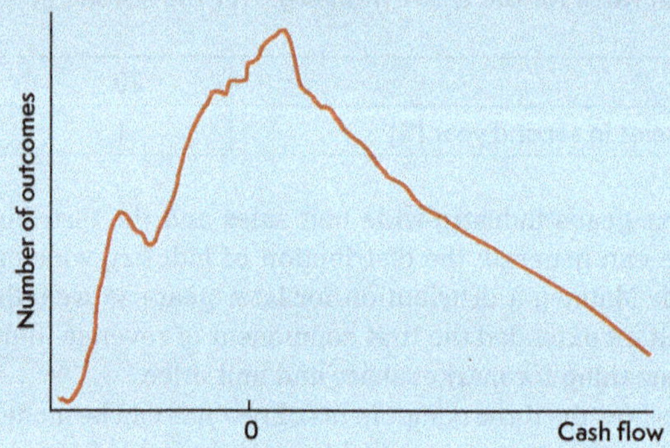

In Monte Carlo simulations, repeated sampling of all the variables from a specific model generates a statistical distribution.

Step 5: Calculate NPV

Given the distribution of cash flow for the third year in Figure 8.6, one can determine the expected cash flow for this year. In a similar manner, one can also determine the expected cash flow for each future year and then calculate the net present value of the project by discounting these expected cash flows at an appropriate rate.

Monte Carlo simulation is often viewed as a step beyond either sensitivity analysis or scenario analysis. Interactions between the variables are explicitly specified in Monte Carlo, so (at least in theory) this methodology provides a more complete analysis. And, as a by-product, having to build a precise model deepens the forecaster's understanding of the project.

One of the great benefits of Monte Carlo simulation is that the financial manager has a distribution of NPVs, instead of a single point estimate. This provides not only an insight into the scale of the NPV estimate (and any other investment appraisal method for that matter) but also the range of potential outcomes through the spread of simulated observations. These two pieces of information provide substantially more insight into the possible success of a proposed investment than a single value, which will considerably improve investment decisions.

Chapter 22 Page 602
Chapter 23 Page 638

8.3 Real Options

In Chapter 6, we stressed the superiority of net present value (NPV) analysis over other approaches when valuing capital budgeting projects. However, both scholars and practitioners have pointed out problems with NPV. The basic idea here is that NPV analysis, as well as all the other approaches in Chapter 6, ignores the adjustments that a firm can make after a project is accepted. These adjustments are called **real options**. In this respect, NPV underestimates the true value of a project. NPV's conservatism is best explained through a series of examples (Chapters 22 and 23 cover options and their valuation in a lot of detail).

The value of real options analysis comes from its ability to value managerial flexibility and corporate strategy. In almost all investments, managers continually assess and reassess ways in which costs can be reduced and revenues maximized. This activity requires identification of any possibility to expand, reduce, delay or even abandon production of an asset. Strategic flexibility provides an option to managers and, as with any option (see Chapters 22 and 23), it has value. Real options analysis is a methodology that allows you to value the strategic flexibility inherent in every project.

The Option to Expand

Farid Al-Malik, an entrepreneur, recently learned of a chemical treatment causing water to freeze at 20 degrees Celsius rather than 0 degrees. Of all the many practical applications for this treatment, Mr Al-Malik liked the idea of hotels made of ice more than anything else. He estimated the annual cash flows from a single ice hotel to be £2 million, based on an initial investment of £12 million. He felt that 20 per cent was an appropriate discount rate, given the risk of this new venture. Believing that the cash flows would be perpetual, Mr Al-Malik determined the NPV of the project to be:

$$-£12{,}000{,}000 + £2{,}000{,}000/0.20 = -£2 \text{ million}$$

Most entrepreneurs would have rejected this venture, given its negative NPV. But Farid was not your typical entrepreneur. He reasoned that NPV analysis missed a hidden source of value. While he was pretty sure that the initial investment would cost £12 million, there was some uncertainty concerning annual cash flows. His cash flow estimate of £2 million per year reflected his belief that there was a 50 per cent probability that yearly cash flows will be £3 million and a 50 per cent probability that they will be £1 million.

The NPV calculations for the two forecasts are as follows:

$$\text{Optimistic forecast: } -£12 \text{ million} + £3 \text{ million}/0.2 = -£3 \text{ million}$$

$$\text{Pessimistic forecast:} -£12 \text{ million} + £1 \text{ million}/0.20 = -£7 \text{ million}$$

On the surface, this new calculation does not seem to help Mr Al-Malik much. An average of the two forecasts yields an NPV for the project of:

$$50\% \times £3 \text{ million} + 50\%\,(-£7 \text{ million}) = -£2 \text{ million}$$

which is just the value he calculated in the first place.

However, if the optimistic forecast turns out to be correct, Mr Al-Malik would want to *expand*. If he believes that there are, say, 10 locations in the country that can support an ice hotel, the true NPV of the venture would be:

$$50\% \times £3 \text{ million} + 50\%\,(-£7 \text{ million}) = -£2 \text{ million}$$

Figure 8.6, which represents Mr Al-Malik's decision, is often called a decision tree. The idea expressed in Figure 8.6 is both basic and universal. The entrepreneur has the option to expand if the pilot location is successful. For example, think of all the people that start restaurants, most of them ultimately failing. These individuals are not necessarily overly optimistic. They may realize the likelihood of failure but go ahead anyway because of the small chance of starting the next McDonald's or Starbucks.

Figure 8.6 Decision Tree for Ice Hotel

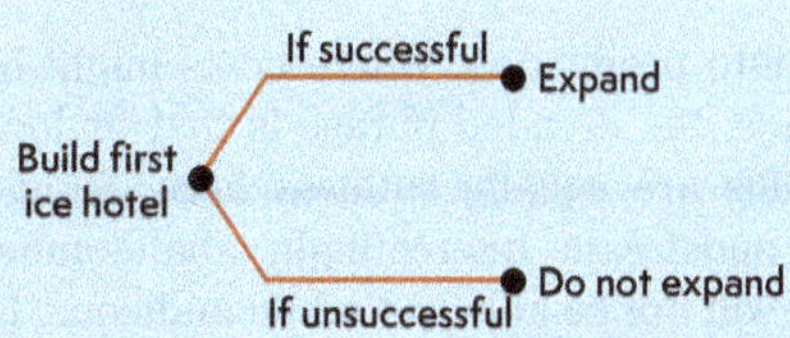

The Option to Abandon

Managers also have the option to abandon existing projects. Abandonment may seem cowardly, but it can often save companies a great deal of money. Because of this, the option to abandon increases the value of any potential project.

The example of ice hotels, which illustrated the option to expand, can also demonstrate the option to abandon. To see this, imagine that Mr Al-Malik now believes that there is a 50 per cent probability that annual cash flows will be £6 million and a 50 per cent probability that annual cash flows will be –£2 million. The NPV calculations under the two forecasts become:

$$\text{Optimistic forecast: } -\text{£}12\text{ million} + \text{£}6\text{ million}/0.2 = -\text{£}18\text{ million}$$

$$\text{Pessimistic forecast: } -\text{£}12\text{ million} + \text{£}2\text{ million}/0.2 = -\text{£}22\text{ million}$$

yielding an NPV for the project of:

Equation 8.4

$$50\% \times \text{£}18\text{ million} + 50\%\,(-\text{£}22\text{ million}) = \text{£}2\text{ million}$$

Furthermore, now imagine that Mr Al-Malik wants to own, at most, just one ice hotel, implying that there is no option to expand. Because the NPV in Equation 8.4 is negative, it looks as if he will not build the hotel.

But things change when we consider the abandonment option. As of date 1, the entrepreneur will know which forecast has come true. If cash flows equal those under the optimistic forecast, Farid will keep the project alive. If, however, cash flows equal those under the pessimistic forecast, he will abandon the hotel. If Mr Al-Malik knows these possibilities ahead of time, the NPV of the project becomes:

$$50\% \times \text{£}18\text{ million} + 50\%\,(-\text{£}22\text{ million} - \text{£}2\text{ million}/1.20) = \text{£}2.17\text{ million}$$

Because Mr Al-Malik quits after experiencing the cash flow of –£2 million at date 1, he does not have to endure this outflow in any of the later years. The NPV is now positive so that Farid will accept the project.

The example here is a stylized one. Whereas many years may pass before a project is abandoned in the real world, our ice hotel was discontinued after just one year. And, while salvage values generally accompany abandonment, we assumed no salvage value for the ice hotel. Nevertheless, abandonment options are pervasive in the real world.

For example, consider the film-making industry. As shown in Figure 8.7, films begin with either the purchase or the development of a script. A completed script might cost a film studio a few million pounds and potentially lead to actual production. However, the vast majority of scripts (perhaps well over 90 per cent) are abandoned. Why would studios abandon scripts that they commissioned in the first place? The studios know ahead of time that only a few scripts will be promising, but they do not know which ones. Thus, they cast a wide net, commissioning many scripts to get a few good ones. The studios must be ruthless with the bad scripts because the expenditure here pales in comparison to the enormous losses from producing a lousy film.

Figure 8.7 The Abandonment Option in the Film Industry

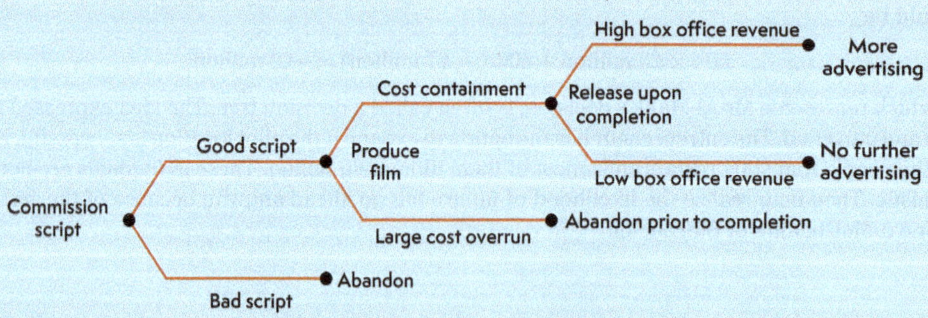

Film studios have abandonment options throughout the production of a film.

The few lucky scripts then move into production, where costs might be budgeted in the tens of millions of pounds, if not much more. At this stage, the dreaded phrase is that on-location production gets 'bogged down', creating cost overruns. But the studios are equally ruthless here. Should these overruns become excessive, production is likely to be abandoned midstream. Interestingly, abandonment almost always occurs due to high costs, not due to the fear that the film will not be able to find an audience. Little information on that score will be obtained until the film is released.

The release of a film is accompanied by significant advertising expenditures, perhaps in the range of £5 to £10 million, and sometimes even more. Advertising will continue following strong ticket sales, but it will probably be abandoned after a few weeks of poor box office performance.

Film-making is one of the riskiest businesses around, with studios receiving hundreds of millions of pounds or euros in a matter of weeks from a blockbuster while receiving practically nothing during this period from a flop. The abandonment options contain costs that might otherwise bankrupt the industry.

Timing Options

One often finds urban land that has been vacant for many years. Yet this land is bought and sold from time to time. Why would anyone pay a positive price for property that has no source of revenue? Indeed, one could not arrive at a positive price through NPV analysis. However, the paradox can easily be explained by using real options.

Suppose that the land's best use is as an office building. Total construction costs for the building are estimated to be €1 million. Currently, net rents (after all costs) are expected to be €90,000 per year in perpetuity, and the discount rate is 10 per cent. The NPV of this proposed building would be:

$$-€1 \text{ million} + €90{,}000/0.10 = -€100{,}000$$

Because this NPV is negative, one would not currently want to build. However, suppose that the government is planning various urban revitalization programmes for the city. Office rents are likely to increase if the programmes succeed. In this case, the property's owner might want to erect the office building after all. Conversely, office rents will remain the same, or even fall, if the programmes fail. The owner will not build in this case.

We say that the property owner has a *timing option*. Although she does not currently want to build, she will want to build in the future should rents in the area rise substantially. This timing option explains why vacant land often has value. There are costs, such as taxes, from holding raw land, but the value of an office building after a substantial rise in rents may more than offset these holding costs. Of course, the exact value of the vacant land depends on both the probability of success in the revitalization programme and the extent of the rent increase. Figure 8.8 illustrates this timing option.

Figure 8.8 Decision Tree for Vacant Land

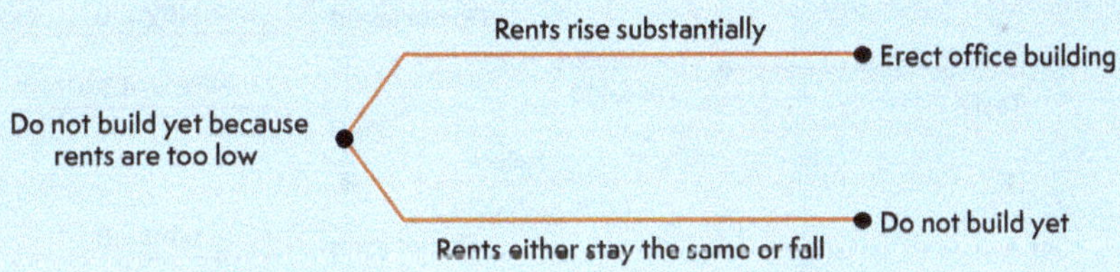

Vacant land may have value today because the owner can erect a profitable office building if rents rise.

Mining operations almost always provide timing options as well. Suppose you own a copper mine where the cost of mining each ton of copper exceeds the sales revenue. It is a no-brainer to say that you would not want to mine the copper currently. And because there are costs of ownership such as property taxes, insurance and security, you might want to pay someone to take the mine off your hands. However, we would caution you not to do so hastily. Copper prices in the future might increase enough so that production is profitable. Given that possibility, you could probably find someone to pay a positive price for the property today.

8.4 Decision Trees

As shown in the previous section, managers adjust their decisions because of new information. For example, a project may be expanded if an early experience is promising, whereas the same project might be abandoned in the wake of bad results. As we said earlier, the choices available to managers are called *real options* and an individual project can often be viewed as a series of real options, leading to valuation approaches beyond the basic present value methodology of earlier chapters.

Earlier in this chapter, we considered Solar Electronics' (SE's) solar-powered jet engine project, with cash flows as shown in Table 8.1. In that example, SE planned to invest £1,500 million at year 0 and expected to receive £954 million per year in each of the next five years. Our calculations showed an NPV of £1,700 million, so the firm would presumably want to go ahead with the project.

To illustrate decision trees in more detail, let us move back one year before year 0 when SE's decision was more complicated. At that time, the engineering group had developed the technology for a solar-powered plane engine, but test marketing had not begun. The marketing department proposed that SE develop some prototypes and conduct test marketing of the engine. A corporate planning group, including representatives from production, marketing and engineering, estimated that this preliminary phase would take a year and cost £100 million. Furthermore, the group believed there was a 75 per cent chance that the marketing tests would prove successful. After completion of the marketing tests, SE would decide whether to engage in full-scale production, necessitating the investment of £1,500 million.

The marketing tests add a layer of complexity to the analysis. Our previous work on the example assumed that the marketing tests had already proved successful. How do we analyse whether we want to go ahead with the marketing tests in the first place? This is where decision trees come in.

To recap, SE faces two decisions, both of which are represented in Figure 8.9. First, the firm must decide whether to go ahead with the marketing tests. And if the tests are performed, the firm must determine whether the results of the tests warrant full-scale production. The critical point here, as we will see, is that decision trees answer the two questions in *reverse* order. So let us work backwards, first considering what to do with the results of the tests, which can be either successful or unsuccessful.

Figure 8.9 Decision Tree for SE (£ millions)

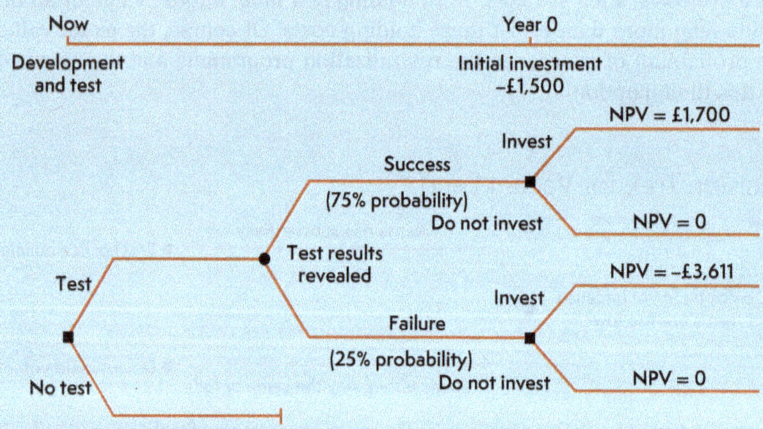

Squares represent decision points. Circle represents receipt of information.
SE must make two decisions:
1 Whether to develop and test the engine.
2 Whether to invest for full-scale production.
With decision trees, decisions are made in reverse order.

- *Assume tests have been successful (75 per cent probability).* Table 8.1 tells us that full-scale production will cost £1,500 million and will generate an annual cash flow of £954 million for five years, yielding an NPV of:

$$= -£1{,}500 + \sum_{t=1}^{5} \frac{£954}{(1.15)^t}$$

$$= -£1{,}500 + £954 \times A_{0.15}^{5}$$

$$= £1{,}700$$

Because the NPV is positive, successful marketing tests should lead to full-scale production. (Note that the NPV is calculated as of year 1, the time at which the investment of £1,500 million is made. Later we will discount this number back to year 0, when the decision on test marketing is to be made.)

- *Assume tests have not been successful (25 per cent probability).* Here, SE's £1,500 million investment would produce an NPV of –£3,611 million, calculated as of year 1. (To save space, we will not provide the raw numbers leading to this calculation.) Because the NPV here is negative, SE will not want full-scale production if the marketing tests are unsuccessful.

- *Decision on marketing tests.* Now we know what to do with the results of the marketing tests. Let us use these results to move back one year. That is, we now want to figure out whether SE should invest £100 million for the test marketing costs in the first place.

  The expected payoff evaluated at date 1 (in millions) is:

$$\text{Expected payoff} = \begin{pmatrix} \text{Probability} & & \text{Payoff} \\ \text{of} & \times & \text{if} \\ \text{success} & & \text{successful} \end{pmatrix} + \begin{pmatrix} \text{Probability} & & \text{Payoff} \\ \text{of} & \times & \text{if} \\ \text{failure} & & \text{failure} \end{pmatrix}$$

$$= (0.75 \times £1{,}700) + (0.25 \times £0) = £1{,}275$$

The NPV (in millions) of testing computed one year before year 0 is:

$$\text{NPV} = -£100 + \frac{£1{,}275}{1.15} = £1{,}008$$

Because the NPV is positive, the firm should test the market for solar-powered jet engines.

Warning

We have used a discount rate of 15 per cent for both the testing and the investment decisions. Perhaps a higher discount rate should have been used for the initial test marketing decision, which is likely to be riskier than the investment decision.

Recap

As mentioned above, the analysis is graphed in Figure 8.9. As can be seen from the figure, SE must make the following two decisions:

1. Whether to develop and test the solar-powered jet engine.
2. Whether to invest in full-scale production following the results of the test.

Using a decision tree, we answered the second question before we solved the first one.

Decision trees represent the best approach to solving SE's problem, given the information presented so far in the text. However, we will examine a more sophisticated approach to valuing options in a later chapter. Though this approach was first used to value financial options traded on organized option exchanges, it can be used to value real options as well.

Summary and Conclusions

This chapter discussed some practical applications of capital budgeting.

1. Though NPV is the best capital budgeting approach conceptually, it has been criticized in practice for giving managers a false sense of security. Sensitivity analysis shows NPV under varying assumptions, giving managers a better feel for the project's risks. Unfortunately, sensitivity analysis modifies only one variable at a time, but many variables are likely to vary together in the real world. Scenario analysis examines a project's performance under different scenarios (such as war breaking out or oil prices sky-rocketing). Finally, managers want to know how bad forecasts must be before a project loses money. Break-even analysis calculates the sales figure at which the project breaks even. Though break-even analysis is frequently performed on an accounting profit basis, we suggest that a net present value basis is more appropriate.
2. Monte Carlo simulation begins with a model of the firm's cash flows, based on both the interactions between different variables and the movement of each variable over time. Random sampling generates a distribution of these cash flows for each period, leading to a net present value calculation.
3. We analysed the hidden options in capital budgeting, such as the option to expand, the option to abandon and timing options.
4. Decision trees represent an approach for valuing projects with these hidden, or real, options.

Questions and Problems

CONCEPT

1 **NPV, Sensitivity Analysis, Break-even Analysis and Scenario Analysis** 'NPV is just a tool and as with any tool, it can be dangerous in the wrong hands.' Discuss this statement. In what way do sensitivity analysis, break-even analysis and scenario analysis improve things? Surely they are just tools as well?

2 **Monte Carlo Simulation** Explain the rationale underlying Monte Carlo simulation. How does it improve upon other forms of sensitivity analysis? Does it have any weaknesses? If so, what are they? How could you improve on the methodology?

3 **Real Options** When Apple launched its smartwatch, the NPV from the project was negative. However, the company proceeded with the project. Why do you think this was?

4 **Decision Trees** When should you stop decision tree analysis on a capital budgeting project? Explain using an example.

REGULAR

5 **Sensitivity Analysis and Break-even Point** A retail clothing firm is evaluating the development of a new range of all-weather coats. These coats contain an internal solar battery to provide heating whenever the garment is worn. The solar batteries cost £3.2 million to make and the expectation is that the project will last for five years. At the end of the project, the machinery to make the batteries will be worthless because of new technological developments. Assume that depreciation is 20 per cent using the reducing balance method. Sales are projected at 250,000 units per year. Price per battery is £10, variable cost per unit is £2.50 and fixed costs are £900,000 per year. The tax rate is 23 per cent, and we require a 13 per cent return on this project.

(a) Calculate the accounting break-even point.

(b) Calculate the base-case cash flow and NPV. What is the sensitivity of NPV to changes in the sales figure? Explain what your answer tells you about a 50,000-unit decrease in projected sales.

(c) What is the sensitivity of OCF to changes in the variable cost figure? Explain what your answer tells you about a £1 decrease in estimated variable costs.

6 **Scenario Analysis** A retail clothing firm is evaluating the development of a new range of all-weather coats. These coats contain an internal solar battery to provide heating whenever the garment is worn. The solar batteries cost £3.2 million to make and the expectation is that the project will last for five years. At the end of the project, the machinery to make the batteries will be worthless because of new technological developments. Assume that depreciation is 20 per cent using the reducing balance method. Sales are projected at 250,000 units per year. Price per battery is £10, variable cost per unit is £1.50, and fixed costs are £900,000 per year. The tax rate is 23 per cent, and we require a 13 per cent return on this project. Suppose the projections given for price, quantity, variable costs and fixed costs are all accurate to within ±10 per cent. Calculate the best-case and worst-case NPV figures.

7 **Financial Break-even** L.J.'s Toys has just purchased a £200,000 machine to produce toy cars. The machine will be fully depreciated using 20 per cent reducing balances over its five-year economic life. Each toy sells for £25. The variable cost per toy is £5, and the firm incurs fixed costs of £350,000 each year. The corporate tax rate for the company is 25 per cent. The appropriate discount rate is 12 per cent. What is the financial break-even point for the project?

8 **Option to Wait** Your company is deciding whether to invest in a new machine. The new machine will increase cash flow by €280,000 per year. You believe the technology used in the machine has a 10-year life; in other words, no matter when you purchase the machine, it will be obsolete 10 years from today. The machine is currently priced at €1,500,000 and should be depreciated using the 25 per cent reducing balance method. If your required return is 12 per cent, should you purchase the machine? If so, when should you purchase it?

9 **Decision Trees** Ang Electronics has developed a new wearable ring that continually checks blood pressure during the day. If the ring is successful, the present value of the payoff (when the product is brought to market) is £20 million. If the ring fails, the present value of the payoff is £5 million. If the product goes directly to market, there is a 50 per cent chance of success. Alternatively, Ang can delay the launch by one year and spend £2 million to test market the ring. Test marketing would allow the firm to improve the product and increase

the probability of success to 75 per cent. The appropriate discount rate is 15 per cent. Should the firm conduct test marketing?

10 **Option to Wait versus Immediate Investment** Global Investments has hired you as a financial consultant to advise it on whether to enter the shoe market – an investment opportunity that has an initial outlay of £35 million. During a board meeting, the CEO tells you that due to the upcoming summer season there is high demand in the shoe market, and he believes the time is right to open a shoe business today. However, with the country hosting a major sporting event next summer, the finance director of the company argues that waiting exactly one year from now would also be a good opportunity. He argues that in one year from now there should be even higher demand, and hence shoes can be sold at higher prices. After a further meeting with the company's management, you are given the following information:

- The value of a shoe company is estimated to be £40 million.
- Due to a high degree of market competition the flow of customers is uncertain, so the value of the company is volatile, and based on the standard deviation of the company's stock price you estimate this to be 25 per cent per year.
- 15 per cent of the value of the company is attributable to the value of the free cash flows expected in the first year.
- The one-year risk-free rate is 4 per cent.

The board cannot reach agreement, and so they ask for your opinion on when and if the company should go ahead with the project. What is your recommendation? Should they wait or invest?

11 **Decision Trees with New Products** B&B has a new baby powder ready to market. If the firm goes directly to the market with the product, there is only a 55 per cent chance of success. However, the firm can conduct customer segment research, which will take a year and cost €1 million. By going through research, B&B will be able to better target potential customers and will increase the probability of success to 70 per cent. If successful, the baby powder will bring a present value profit (at time of initial selling) of €30 million. If unsuccessful, the present value payoff is only €3 million. Should the firm conduct customer segment research or go directly to market? The appropriate discount rate is 15 per cent.

12 **Financial Break-even Analysis** You are considering investing in a company that cultivates truffles for sale to local restaurants. Use the following information:

Item	Amount
Sales price per truffle	£100.00
Variable costs per truffle	£72.00
Fixed costs per year	£340,000
Depreciation per year	£20,000
Tax rate	35%

The discount rate for the company is 15 per cent, the initial investment in truffle-detecting equipment is £140,000 and the project's economic life is seven years. Assume, for simplicity, that the equipment is depreciated on a straight-line basis over the project's life.

(a) What is the accounting break-even level for the project?

(b) What is the financial break-even level for the project?

13 **Scenario Analysis and Uncertainties** You have been given the following figures to assess the viability of a new portable hospital scanner. It is expected you will be able to capture 10 per cent of the total market of 1.1 million units. The market price will be €400,000 and the unit variable cost is 90 per cent of the market price. Fixed costs of running and manufacture amount to €2 billion per annum.

(a) What is the net income of the project?

(b) You have been approached by the management, who disagree on the figures that were originally used in the analysis. They want you to consider the following scenarios proposed by different directors in the company:

	Director A	Director B	Director C
Market size	0.8 million	1 million	1.2 million
Market share (%)	4	10	16
Unit price (€)	300,000	375,000	400,000
Variable cost (%)	116	80	70
Fixed cost (€)	5 billion	3 billion	1 billion

Carry out a sensitivity analysis of the project. What are the main uncertainties in the project?

14 **Break-even Intuition** Consider a project with a required return of *R* per cent that costs £*I* and will last for *N* years. The project uses straight-line depreciation to zero over the *N*-year life; there are neither salvage value nor net working capital requirements.

(a) At the accounting break-even level of output, what is the IRR of this project? The payback period? The NPV?

(b) At the cash break-even level of output, what is the IRR of this project? The payback period? The NPV?

(c) At the financial break-even level of output, what is the IRR of this project? The payback period? The NPV?

15 **Project Analysis** You are considering a new sustainability project launch that aims to reduce the company's carbon footprint. The project will cost £460,000, have a four-year life and have no salvage value; depreciation is 20 per cent reducing balance. Sales are projected at 150 units per year; price per unit will be £24,000; variable costs are 75 per cent of sales; and fixed costs will be £200,000 per year. The required return on the project is 15 per cent, and the relevant tax rate is 24 per cent.

(a) Based on your experience, you think the unit sales, variable cost and fixed cost projections given here are probably accurate to within ±10 per cent. What are the upper and lower bounds for these projections? What is the base-case NPV? What are the best-case and worst-case scenarios?

(b) Evaluate the sensitivity of your base-case NPV to changes in fixed costs.

(c) What is the accounting break-even level of output for this project?

16 **Project Analysis: McGilla Golf** McGilla Golf has decided to sell a new line of golf clubs. The clubs will sell for £700 per set and have a variable cost of £320 per set. The company has spent £150,000 for a marketing study that determined the company will sell 55,000 sets per year for seven years. The marketing study also determined that the company will lose sales of 13,000 sets of its high-priced clubs. The high-priced clubs sell at £1,100 and have variable costs of £600. The company will also increase sales of its cheap clubs by 10,000 sets. The cheap clubs sell for £400 and have variable costs of £180 per set. The fixed costs each year will be £7,500,000. The company has also spent £1,000,000 on research and development for the new clubs. The plant and equipment required will cost £18,200,000 and will be depreciated on a 20 per cent reducing balance basis. At the end of the seven years, the salvage value of the plant and equipment will be equal to the written down or residual value. The new clubs will also require an increase in net working capital of £950,000 that will be returned at the end of the project. The tax rate is 28 per cent, and the cost of capital is 14 per cent.

(a) Calculate the payback period, the NPV and the IRR for the base case.

(b) You feel that the values are accurate to within only ±10 per cent. What are the best-case and worst-case NPVs? (*Hint:* The price and variable costs for the two existing sets of clubs are known with certainty; only the sales gained or lost are uncertain.)

(c) McGilla would like to know the sensitivity of NPV to changes in the price of the new clubs and the quantity of new clubs sold. What is the sensitivity of the NPV to each of these variables?

17 **Abandonment Value** You are examining a new sustainability project. You expect to sell 7,000 units per year for the next 10 years, with a net cash flow of €60 per unit after accounting for the costs associated with reducing the company's carbon footprint. In other words, the annual operating cash flow is projected to be €60 × 7,000 = €420,000.

The relevant discount rate for this sustainability project is 16 per cent, and the initial investment required is €1,800,000.

(a) What is the base-case NPV?

(b) After the first year, the project can be dismantled and sold for €1,400,000. If expected sales are revised based on the first year's performance, when would it make sense to abandon the investment? In other words, at what level of expected sales would it make sense to abandon the project?

(c) Explain how the €1,400,000 abandonment value can be viewed as the opportunity cost of keeping the project in one year.

(d) Suppose you think it is likely that expected sales will be revised upward to 9,000 units if the first year is a success and revised downward to 4,000 units if the first year is not a success. If success and failure are equally likely, what is the NPV of the project? Consider the possibility of abandonment in answering. What is the value of the option to abandon?

18 **Abandonment and Expansion** In the previous problem, suppose the scale of the project can be doubled in one year in the sense that twice as many units can be produced and sold. Naturally, expansion would be desirable only if the project were a success. This implies that if the project is a success, projected sales after expansion will be 18,000. Again assuming that success and failure are equally likely, what is the NPV of the project? Note that abandonment is still an option if the project is a failure. What is the value of the option to expand?

19 **Decision Trees: Movies** Young screenwriter Carl Draper has just finished his first script. It has action, drama and humour, and he thinks it will be a blockbuster. He takes the script to every film studio in town and tries to sell it but to no avail. Finally, ACME studios offers to buy the script for either (a) $5,000 or (b) 1 per cent of the film's profits. There are two decisions the studio will have to make. The first is to decide if the script is good or bad, and second if the film is good or bad. First, there is a 90 per cent chance that the script is bad. If it is bad, the studio does nothing more and throws the script out. If the script is good, it will shoot the film. After the film is shot, the studio will review it, and there is a 70 per cent chance that the film is bad. If the film is bad, it will not be promoted and will not turn a profit. If the film is good, the studio will promote heavily; the average profit for this type of film is $10 million. Carl rejects the $5,000 and says he wants the 1 per cent of profits. Was this a good decision by Carl?

20 **Accounting Break-even: Samuelson GmbH** Samuelson GmbH has just purchased a €600,000 machine to produce calculators. The machine will be fully depreciated using the 20 per cent reducing balance method over its economic life of five years and will produce 20,000 calculators each year. The salvage value of the machine will be equal to its residual or written-down value. The variable production cost per calculator is €15, and total fixed costs are €900,000 per year. The corporate tax rate for the company is 30 per cent. For the firm to break even in terms of accounting profit, how much should it charge per calculator?

21 **Real Options: Petrofac Ltd** Petrofac Ltd, the international provider of oil and gas building facilities, has entered into an agreement with a number of Kenyan oil exploration firms to support development of oil wells in the Turkana region after a very large oil well was found there in 2012. The cost of setting up new facilities is £12 million and the well is expected to have a life of five years. Oil is currently fetching £84 per barrel in the international markets, and production and extraction costs stand at 85 per cent of the oil price. The appropriate discount rate for this project is 18 per cent. What is the break-even number of barrels that can be sold?

22 **Abandonment Decisions** Allied Products is considering a new product launch. The firm expects to have an annual operating cash flow of AED60 million for the next six years. Allied Products uses a discount rate of 14 per cent for new product launches. The initial investment is AED200 million. Assume that the project has no salvage value at the end of its economic life.

(a) What is the NPV of the new product?

(b) After the first year, the project can be dismantled and sold for AED50 million. If the estimates of remaining cash flows are revised based on the first year's experience, at what level of expected cash flows does it make sense to abandon the project?

23 **Expansion Decisions** Applied Nanotech is thinking about introducing a new surface cleaning machine. The marketing department has come up with the estimate that Applied Nanotech can sell 10 units per year at £0.3 million net cash flow per unit for the next five years. The engineering department has come up with the estimate that developing the machine will take a £10 million initial investment. The finance department has estimated that a 25 per cent discount rate should be used.

(a) What is the base-case NPV?

(b) If unsuccessful, after the first year the project can be dismantled and will have an after-tax salvage value of £5 million. Also, after the first year, expected cash flows will be revised up to 20 units per year or to 0 units, with equal probability. What is the revised NPV?

24 **Scenario Analysis for different Economic Forecasts** You are the financial analyst for a tennis racket manufacturer. The company is considering using a graphite-like material in its tennis rackets. The company has estimated the information in the following table about the market for a racket with the new material. The company

expects to sell the racket for five years. The equipment required for the project has no salvage value. The required return for projects of this type is 13 per cent, and the company has a 40 per cent tax rate. Should you recommend the project? Assume 20 per cent reducing balance depreciation.

	Pessimistic	Expected	Optimistic
Market size	110,000	120,000	130,000
Market share (%)	22	25	27
Selling price (€)	115	120	125
Variable costs per unit (€)	72	70	68
Fixed costs per year (€)	850,000	800,000	750,000
Initial investment (€)	1,500,000	1,500,000	1,500,000

CHALLENGE

25 The Capital Budgeting Process This question takes a step back from the quantitative analysis and makes you think about how you would manage a capital budgeting project in a firm with a focus on sustainability and combating climate change. You have just graduated from university and taken up your first job in a local distribution firm. The firm stores goods for various clients, including those in the food and beverage industry that may have a significant carbon footprint. The directors are considering expanding their business by building two new warehouses to increase capacity and reduce their carbon footprint by implementing sustainable practices in the construction and operation of the warehouses.

As a sustainability-focused corporate finance expert, you have been tasked with the job of managing the capital budgeting analysis from the initial idea to the start of operations. Prepare a flow chart or mind map for presentation to the directors that will deal with the following issues.

(a) Who will prepare the initial proposal, and how will they incorporate sustainability into the proposal?

(b) What information will the proposal contain, including metrics related to the project's expected carbon footprint reduction and the potential environmental benefits of the project?

(c) How will you evaluate the proposal from a financial and sustainability perspective, and who should be involved in the evaluation process?

(d) What approvals will be needed and who will give them, including any regulatory or environmental permits required for sustainable construction and operation of the warehouses?

(e) What happens if the expenditure is 25 per cent more than the original forecast?

(f) Finally, what will happen when the warehouses have been built, including the implementation of sustainable operating practices and ongoing monitoring of the project's sustainability performance?

26 Scenario Analysis and Forecast Error Consider a project to supply Italy with 40,000 tons of machine screws annually for automobile production. You will need an initial €1,500,000 investment in threading equipment to get the project started; the project will last for five years. The accounting department estimates that annual fixed costs will be €600,000 and that variable costs should be €210 per ton; accounting will depreciate the initial non-current asset investment using the 20 per cent reducing balance method over the five-year project life. It also estimates a salvage value of €800,000 after dismantling costs. The marketing department estimates that the auto makers will set the contract at a selling price of €230 per ton. The engineering department estimates you will need an initial net working capital investment of €450,000. You require a 13 per cent return and face a marginal tax rate of 32 per cent on this project.

(a) What is the estimated OCF for this project? The NPV? Should you pursue this project?

(b) Suppose you believe that the accounting department's initial cost and salvage value projections are accurate only to within ±15 per cent, the marketing department's price estimate is accurate only to within ±10 per cent and the engineering department's net working capital estimate is accurate only to within ±5 per cent. What is your worst-case scenario for this project? Your best-case scenario? Do you still want to pursue the project?

27 Sensitivity Analysis and Minimum Levels of Output In Problem 26, suppose you are confident about your own projections, but you are a little unsure about Italy's actual machine screw requirement. What is the sensitivity of the project OCF to changes in the quantity supplied? What about the sensitivity of NPV to changes in quantity supplied? Given the sensitivity number you calculated, is there some minimum level of output below which you would not want to operate? Why?

28 **Abandonment Decisions: Hand Clapper** Consider the following project for Hand Clapper. The company is considering a four-year project to manufacture clap-command garage door openers. This project requires an initial investment of €10 million that will be depreciated using the 20 per cent reducing balance method over the project's life. The salvage value at the end of the project's life is assumed to be equal to its residual or written-down value. An initial investment in net working capital of €3 million is required to support spare parts inventory; this cost is fully recoverable whenever the project ends. The company believes it can generate €8 million in pre-tax revenues with €2 million in total pre-tax operating costs. The tax rate is 34 per cent and the discount rate is 17 per cent. The market value of the equipment over the life of the project is as follows:

Year	Market Value (€ millions)
1	6.50
2	6.00
3	3.00
4	0.00

(a) Assuming Hand Clapper operates this project for four years, what is the NPV?

(b) Now compute the project NPVs assuming the project is abandoned after only one year, after two years and after three years. What economic life for this project maximizes its value to the firm? What does this problem tell you about not considering abandonment possibilities when evaluating projects?

29 **Abandonment Decisions: M.V.P. Games** M.V.P. Games has hired you to perform a feasibility study of a new video game that requires a $9 million initial investment. M.V.P. expects a total annual operating cash flow of $1,750,000 for the next 10 years. The relevant discount rate is 12 per cent. Cash flows occur at year-end.

(a) What is the NPV of the new video game?

(b) After one year, the estimate of remaining annual cash flows will be revised either upward to $2.5 million or downward to $520,000. Each revision has an equal probability of occurring. At that time, the video game project can be sold for $2,000,000. What is the revised NPV given that the firm can abandon the project after one year?

30 **Financial Break-even** The Wheatchopper Company is considering the purchase of a new harvester. Wheatchopper has hired you to determine the break-even purchase price in terms of present value of the harvester. This break-even purchase price is the price at which the project's NPV is zero. Base your analysis on the following facts:

- The new harvester is not expected to affect revenues, but pre-tax operating expenses will be reduced by €10,000 per year for 10 years.
- The old harvester is now five years old, with 10 years of its scheduled life remaining. It was originally purchased for €45,000 and has been depreciated using the 20 per cent reducing balance method.
- The old harvester can be sold for €20,000 today.
- The new harvester will be depreciated by the 20 per cent reducing balance method over its 10-year life.
- The corporate tax rate is 34 per cent.
- The firm's required rate of return is 15 per cent.
- The initial investment, the proceeds from selling the old harvester and any resulting tax effects occur immediately.
- All other cash flows occur at year-end.
- The market value of each harvester at the end of its economic life is equal to its residual or written-down value.

31 **Sensitivity Analysis of Replacement Decisions** Unmondo SpA is proposing to replace its manufacturing machinery with more modern equipment geared towards 3D printing. The new machinery costs €9 million (the existing machinery has no value). The attraction of the 3D printer is that it is expected to cut manufacturing costs from their current level of €8 per unit to €4 per unit. However, as the following table shows, there is some uncertainty about future sales and the performance of 3D printing technology.

	Pessimistic	Expected	Optimistic
Sales, millions of units	0.4	0.5	0.6
Manufacturing cost, €/unit	6	4	3
Life of new machine	7 years	10 years	13 years

(a) Carry out a sensitivity analysis of the replacement decision, assuming a discount rate of 12 per cent. Unmondo does not pay taxes.

(b) Unmondo SpA could commission engineering tests to determine the actual improvement in manufacturing costs generated by the proposed new 3D printer. The study would cost €450,000. Would you advise Unmondo to go ahead with the study?

32 **Option to Abandon** You own an unused gold mine that will cost $800,000 to reopen. If you open the mine, you expect to be able to extract 1,000 ounces of gold a year for each of three years. After that, the deposit will be exhausted. The gold price is currently $2,000 an ounce, and each year the price is equally likely to rise or fall by $100 from its level at the start of the year. The extraction cost is $920 an ounce and the discount rate is 14 per cent.

(a) Should you open the mine now or delay one year in the hope of a rise in the gold price?

(b) What difference would it make to your decision if you could costlessly (but irreversibly) shut down the mine at any stage?

33 **Options to Abandon and Expand** Grace and Danger plc is introducing a new product this year. If its luminous golf balls (with integrated beeper) are a success, the firm expects to be able to sell 50,000 units a year at a price of £60 each (they will not go missing so you will pay a lot for them!). If the new golf balls are not well received, only 30,000 units can be sold at a price of £55. The variable cost of each golf ball is £30 and the fixed costs are zero. The cost of the manufacturing equipment is £6 million, and the project life is estimated to be 10 years. The firm will use 20 per cent reducing balances as its method of depreciation and at the end of the project's life the machine will be worth nothing. Grace and Danger's tax rate is 28 per cent and the appropriate discount rate is 12 per cent.

(a) If each outcome is equally likely, what is the expected NPV? Will the firm accept the project?

(b) Suppose now that the firm can abandon the project and sell off the manufacturing equipment for £5.4 million if demand for the golf balls turns out to be weak. The firm will make the decision to continue or abandon after the first year of sales. Does the option to abandon change the firm's decision to accept the project?

(c) Now suppose Grace and Danger can expand production if the project is successful. By paying its workers overtime, it can increase production by 25,000 golf balls; the variable cost of each ball will be higher, however: equal to £35 per golf ball. By how much does this option to expand production increase the NPV of the project?

Exam Question (45 minutes)

1 You are the financial analyst for Weir Group plc, the global engineering firm. The company is considering the development of a new slurry pump in its existing products. The pump is expected to improve market share for the company if it is fully integrated into its existing product line-up. With the pace of new technological developments, you expect the slurry pump to be obsolete by the end of five years. The equipment required for the project has no salvage value. The required return for projects of this type is 20 per cent, and the company has a 24 per cent tax rate. Should you recommend the project? Assume 20 per cent reducing balance depreciation. **(75 marks)**

	Pessimistic	Expected	Optimistic
Market size	1,000	1,500	1,700
Market share (%)	15	20	25
Selling price (£)	10,000	15,000	20,000
Variable costs per unit (%)	72	70	68
Fixed costs per year (£)	400,000	450,000	550,000
Initial investment (£)	2,500,000	2,500,000	2,500,000

2 Explain the difference between sensitivity analysis, scenario analysis and break-even analysis. In the context of the problem in Part 1, what do you think is the most appropriate investment appraisal method? Explain your answer. **(25 marks)**

Total Marks: 100

Mini Case

Bunyan Lumber Ltd

Bunyan Lumber Ltd harvests timber and delivers logs to timber mills for sale. The company was founded 70 years ago by Pete Bunyan. The current CEO is Paula Bunyan, the granddaughter of the founder. The company is currently evaluating a 5,000-acre forest it owns in the Scottish Highlands. Paula has asked Steve Boles, the company's finance officer, to evaluate the project. Paula's concern is when the company should harvest the timber.

Lumber is sold by the company for its 'pond value'. Pond value is the amount a mill will pay for a log delivered to the mill location. The price paid for logs delivered to a mill is quoted in pounds per thousands of board feet (MBF), and the price depends on the grade of the logs. The forest Bunyan Lumber is evaluating was planted by the company 20 years ago and is made up entirely of Douglas fir trees. The table below shows the current price per MBF for the three grades of timber the company feels will come from the stand:

Timber Grade	Price Per MBF (£)
1P	1,050
2P	925
3P	770

Steve believes that the pond value of lumber will increase at the inflation rate. The company is planning to thin the forest today, and it expects to realize a positive cash flow of £1,000 per acre from thinning. The thinning is done to increase the growth rate of the remaining trees, and it is always done 20 years following a planting.

The major decision the company faces is when to log the forest. When the company logs the forest, it will immediately replant saplings, which will allow for a future harvest. The longer the forest is allowed to grow, the larger the harvest becomes per acre. Additionally, an older forest has a higher grade of timber. Steve has compiled the following table with the expected harvest per acre in thousands of board feet, along with the breakdown of the timber grades:

Years from Today to Begin Harvest	Harvest (MBF) Per Acre	Timber Grade		
		1P (%)	2P (%)	3P (%)
20	6	10	40	50
25	7.6	12	42	46
30	9	15	42	43
35	10	16	43	41

The company expects to lose 5 per cent of the timber it cuts due to defects and breakage.

The forest will be clear-cut when the company harvests the timber. This method of harvesting allows for faster growth of replanted trees. All of the harvesting, processing, replanting and transportation is to be handled by subcontractors hired by Bunyan Lumber. The cost of the logging is expected to be £140 per MBF. A road system has to be constructed and is expected to cost £50 per MBF on average. Sales preparation and administrative costs, excluding office overhead costs, are expected to be £18 per MBF.

As soon as the harvesting is complete, the company will reforest the land. Reforesting costs include the following:

	Per Acre Cost (£)
Excavator piling	150
Broadcast burning	300
Site preparation	145
Planting costs	225

All costs are expected to increase at the inflation rate.

Assume all cash flows occur at the year of harvest. For example, if the company begins harvesting the timber 20 years from today, the cash flow from the harvest will be received 20 years from today. When the company logs the land, it will immediately replant the land with new saplings. The harvest period chosen will be repeated for the foreseeable future. The company's nominal required return is 10 per cent, and the inflation rate is expected to be 3.7 per cent per year. Bunyan Lumber has a 35 per cent tax rate.

Clear-cutting is a controversial method of forest management. To obtain the necessary permits, Bunyan Lumber has agreed to contribute to a conservation fund every time it harvests the lumber. If the company harvested the forest today, the required contribution would be £100,000. The company has agreed that the required contribution will grow by 3.2 per cent per year. When should the company harvest the forest?

Practical Case Study

In many emerging market countries, concepts such as discount rates are significantly more cumbersome to estimate with any degree of accuracy. Furthermore, capital budgeting techniques can become significantly more difficult to use in practice. The following case is based on real experience, with identities and numbers changed for confidentiality. As part of a consultancy assignment in Dar es Salaam, Tanzania, you have been asked by a private cement manufacturing company to consider the viability of expanding its business operations into the north of the country.

The company has two main rivals in Tanzania: Tanga Cement Company Limited (SIMBA) (www.simbacement.co.tz) and Tanzania Portland Cement Company Limited (TWIGA) (www.twigacement.com). Both SIMBA and TWIGA are listed on the Dar es Salaam Stock Exchange (www.dse.co.tz). The company that has hired you as a consultant earns about one-quarter the revenues of SIMBA.

The new expansion requires an investment of 5 billion Tanzanian shillings (TSh) and as a result of the investment, you expect a permanent increase in total operating revenues for the firm of TSh800 million. While SIMBA is your closest rival in Dar es Salaam, TWIGA has more extensive operations in the north of Tanzania and so is more likely to be your rival in the new investment.

Growth in earnings is possible, but this depends on several factors. First, growth in the economy is uncertain. While Tanzania's economy has been fairly stable, analysts are uncertain as to how the country will fare in the future. This is largely because of uncertainty in international donor funding as a result of the recession affecting donor countries. Second, inflation appears to be higher on the streets than the government statistics suggest. Your estimates are that a more appropriate inflation figure is 3 per cent higher than existing government statistics present. Third, the demand for industrial expansion (and consequently cement) has in the past been vibrant in Tanzania but the future is less certain. Tanzanian economists are predicting that the country will continue to grow as in the past, less about 1.5 per cent. This is because they expect the global recession will largely bypass Tanzania given that the country's economy is not tightly integrated into other developed country economies. However, you are not too sure.

Later chapters explore the estimate of discount rates in more detail, but for now, we will approach the issue in a more basic way. Given that the financial markets in Tanzania are not well developed, you have decided to survey experts in each sector on the appropriate discount rates to use for your closest rivals, TWIGA and SIMBA. The survey responses have been surprising: Dar es Salaam Stock Exchange (12 per cent), pension funds (16 per cent), insurance companies (14 per cent), brokers and dealers (22 per cent), Bank of Tanzania (10 per cent).

A rule of thumb that you have been given is that you can approximate the growth rate in the economy as a whole by adding GDP growth to the rate of inflation. To then estimate the cost of capital for a private firm, you must add on a risk premium to reflect the increased risk.

The challenge facing you as a consultant is daunting but it reflects reality in many parts of the world. The company has asked you to prepare a report on how you plan to carry out your analysis. Specifically, you must consider the following:

Cash flows: What factors will affect the estimated cash flows? Carry out your own analysis on Tanzania, its economy, the cement industry and its rivals.

Growth rates: What factors will affect the growth rates of the firm? From your own analysis of the company and the project, report on the possible growth rates you may use.

Discount rates: Many of the models presented in later chapters do not work well in emerging markets because good-quality price data are not available. Carry out your own investigations into possible discount rates for the project.

Funding: We cover financing in detail in later chapters. However, carry out your own analysis into the different sources of funding that are available in Tanzania for a project of this type and size.

Capital budgeting methods: There are many methods available that you can use. Which ones will you focus on? Explain.

The executives of the cement company have decided to go ahead with the investment appraisal and have retained you for the more detailed analysis. In any capital budgeting investigation, you need an estimate of future net cash flows, future growth rates and appropriate discount rates. We will leave a detailed discussion of discount rates until later in the text.

Cash Flow In the first stage of the consultancy, you were informed that the investment will be TSh5 billion and operating revenues are expected to increase by TSh800 million per year. That was just an estimate and, after several interviews, you have come up with a more detailed cash flow forecast. First, the TSh5 billion investment is made up of three components. The cement company will need to purchase the land for TSh2 billion, and spend TSh2 billion on property, plant and machinery. The other TSh1 billion will be paid out in salaries, wages and other cash expenses every year.

You need to find out about taxation and depreciation in Tanzania. You know that the country follows International Accounting Standards and so all the material in this textbook is appropriate. However, you need the actual depreciation rules, which differ in every country. The first place you should look is the Tanzanian Ministry of Finance website (https://www.mof.go.tz). At this site you will find the appropriate corporate tax rate and all depreciation rates for your company.

Operating revenues are based on the expected total demand for cement and the current cement price of TSh90,000 per tonne. If the expansion goes ahead, the company expects to sell an additional 20,000 tonnes of cement at a constant gross profit margin of 44 per cent. However, these figures may change depending on economic conditions and changing costs. The company expects to run the new operations indefinitely.

Growth Rates In the previous chapter, you spent a lot of time thinking about the factors that drive growth rates. Now, with this information, you should consider several growth rate scenarios for your company. You should also be able to defend your assumptions.

Discount Rates Similarly, you should consider the information you have been given by the experts, as well as all other information available in the markets, to come up with several discount rate scenarios. You should be able to defend your choices here as well.

1 Carry out a full capital budgeting analysis on the above problem using one or more techniques you feel are appropriate here.

2 As with any real-life capital budgeting analysis, the leeway in assumptions can really make your analysis difficult. Carry out a full sensitivity analysis on the project based on your own private analysis.

3 Clearly state and explain all assumptions in your analysis.

4 Discuss some factors, costs, inputs or assumptions that have not appeared in the analysis, and suggest ways in which you can gather this information for an extension of the analysis.

5 Write a consultancy report on the analysis.

Many students will be put off by the complexity of this analysis but the practice of actually working with real and often poor data is one of the best skills you can develop. Corporate finance consultants get paid very handsomely for their work and this is primarily because the investment decision is one of the most important facing a firm. If managers get it right, a good investment can add millions to firm value. Get it wrong and the firm can go bankrupt!

Relevant Accounting Standards

This chapter is concerned with deepening the capital budgeting analysis and does not require specific accounting standards. See Chapter 7 for those standards that are relevant for capital budgeting.

Additional Reading

Real options is an emerging field of valuation and few accessible applied papers are written on the topic. Those listed below come from a variety of different fields that serve to present the variety of areas in which real options can be used. Two excellent review papers of real options theory are:

1 Lambrecht, B.M. (2017) 'Real Options in Finance', *Journal of Banking & Finance*, Vol. 81, 166–171.

2 Trigeorgis, L. and J.J. Reuer (2017) 'Real Options Theory in Strategic Management', *Strategic Management Journal*, Vol. 38, No. 1, 42–63.

Other interesting papers are presented below:

3 Aguerrevere, F.L. (2009) 'Real Options, Product Market Competition, and Asset Returns', *Journal of Finance*, Vol. 64, No. 2, 957–983.

4 Brouthers, K.B. and D. Dikova (2010) 'Acquisitions and Real Options: The Greenfield Alternative', *Journal of Management Studies*, Vol. 47, No. 6, 1048–1071. **Europe.**

5 Driouchi, T., M. Leseure and D. Bennett (2009) 'A Robustness Framework for Monitoring Real Options Under Uncertainty', *Omega*, Vol. 37, No. 3, 698–710.

6 Kitzing, L., N. Juul, M. Drud and T.K. Boomsma (2017) 'A Real Options Approach to Analyse Wind Energy Investments under Different Support Schemes', *Applied Energy*, Vol. 188, 83–96.

Endnotes

1 Though the previous discussion on this page considered both optimistic and pessimistic forecasts for sales price and variable cost, break-even analysis uses just the expected or best estimates of these variables.

2 Please refer to Chapter 7 for full details on how to calculate equivalent annual cost.

PART 3

Risk

In Chapter 4, you discovered that estimating the present value of a cash flow involves two key factors: its timing and risk. While forecasting timing is straightforward, quantifying risk is much more challenging, and there's no single approach. Techniques often rely on historical data, which may not predict the future. Chapters 9–11 of Part 3 cover different approaches to measuring risk, exploring the link between risk and expected return, portfolio theory and factor models. Chapter 12 applies these concepts to capital budgeting and corporate finance, introducing the cost of capital. Part 3 concludes with Chapter 13, where we examine market efficiency and behavioural finance.

Chapter 9
Risk and Return: Lessons from Market History

Learning Objectives

After reading this chapter you should be able to:

LO1 Define and understand key concepts of returns, holding period returns, risk-free returns and average equity returns.

LO2 Examine historical data to identify patterns and trends in stock market returns and risk statistics, and compare them to risk-free returns.

LO3 Calculate and interpret various return statistics, including holding period returns, average returns and risk statistics, for different investment scenarios.

LO4 Develop a comprehensive understanding of the relationship between risk and return in the context of market history.

On any single day, the stock market will see winners and losers. Take, for example, Friday 17 March 2023. The news for banks that week was fairly bleak, with Silicon Valley Bank and Credit Suisse requiring emergency funding. However, in contrast, much positive publicity surrounded technology firms when OpenAI released ChatGPT 4.0, and Google and Microsoft announced plans to incorporate AI into their office suites.

Could an investor have made money from buying shares in the morning and selling at night on 17 March 2023? The answer is yes. In the UK, Glencore plc, the global commodities production company, increased by 3.83 per cent. Another mining firm, Anglo American plc, saw its share price rise by 2.82 per cent. Could an investor have lost money following the same strategy? The answer is also a definite yes. BT Group shares were down by 3.14 per cent and United Utilities Group saw its share price fall by 2.39 per cent.

These examples show there are tremendous potential profits to be made, irrespective of whether markets are falling or growing. However, there is also the risk of losing money – lots of it. So what should you, as a stock market investor, expect when you invest your own money? In this chapter, we study decades of market history to find out.

Source: Kasper Nymann/123RF.

Key Notations

C_i	Cash flow at time i	R_i	Total return; discount rate
DIV_i	Dividend at time i	VaR	Value at risk
P_i	Price at time i		

9.1 Returns

Monetary Returns

Suppose the Video Concept Company has several thousand shares of equity outstanding, and you are a shareholder. Further, suppose you purchased some of the shares in the company at the beginning of the year; it is now year-end, and you want to figure out how well you have done on your investment. The return you get on an investment in shares, like that in bonds or any other investment, comes in two forms.

First, over the year most companies pay dividends to shareholders. As the owner of shares in the Video Concept Company, you are a part owner of the company. If the company is profitable, it will generally distribute some of its profits to the shareholders. Therefore, as the owner of shares, you will receive some cash, called a *dividend,* during the year. This cash is the *income component* of your return. In addition to the dividends, the other part of your return is the *capital gain* – or, if it is negative, the *capital loss* (negative capital gain) – on the investment.

For example, suppose we are considering the cash flows of the investment in Figure 9.1, showing that you purchased 100 shares at the beginning of the year at a price of £37 per share. Your total investment, then, was:

$$C_0 = £37 \times 100 = £3{,}700$$

Figure 9.1 Monetary Returns

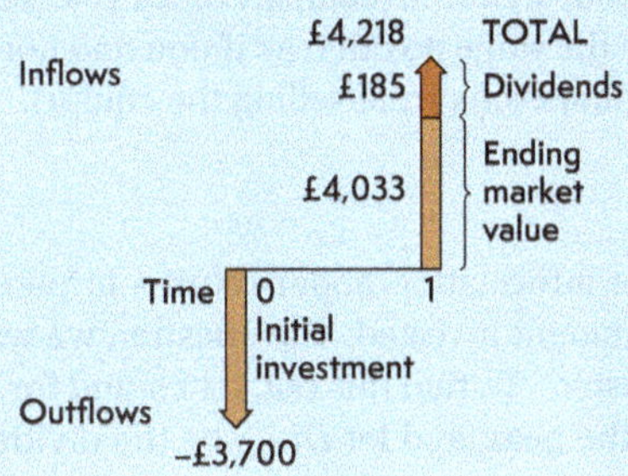

Suppose that over the year the shares paid a dividend of £1.85 per share. During the year, then, you received income of:

$$\text{Div} = £1.85 \times 100 = £185$$

Suppose, finally, that at the end of the year the market price of the equity is £40.33 per share. Because the shares increased in price, you had a capital gain of:

$$\text{Gain} = (£40.33 - £37) \times 100 = £333$$

The capital gain, like the dividend, is part of the return that shareholders require to maintain their investment in the Video Concept Company. Of course, if the price of Video Concept shares had dropped in value to, say, £34.78, you would have recorded this capital loss:

$$\text{Loss} = (£34.78 - £37) \times 100 = £222$$

The *total monetary return* on your investment is the sum of the dividend income and the capital gain or loss on the investment:

$$\text{Total monetary return} = \text{Dividend income} + \text{Capital gain (or loss)}$$

(From now on we will refer to *capital losses* as *negative capital gains* and not distinguish between them.) In our first example, the total monetary return is given by:

$$\text{Total monetary return} = £185 + £333 = £518$$

Notice that if you sold the shares at the end of the year, your total amount of cash would be the initial investment plus the total monetary return. In the preceding example you would have:

$$\begin{aligned}\text{Total cash if equity is sold} &= \text{Initial investment} + \text{Total monetary return}\\ &= £3{,}700 + £518\\ &= £4{,}218\end{aligned}$$

As a check, notice that this is the same as the proceeds from the sale of shares plus the dividends:

$$\begin{aligned}\text{Proceeds from equity sale} + \text{Dividends} &= £40.33 \times 100 + £185\\ &= £4{,}033 + £185\\ &= £4{,}218\end{aligned}$$

Suppose, however, that you hold your Video Concept shares and do not sell them at year-end. Should you still consider the capital gain as part of your return? Does this violate our previous present value rule that only cash matters?

The answer to the first question is a definite yes, and the answer to the second question is an equally firm no. The capital gain is every bit as much a part of your return as is the dividend, and you should certainly count it as part of your total return. That you have decided to hold on to the shares and not sell or *realize* the gain or the loss in no way changes the fact that, if you want to, you could get the cash value of the shares. After all, you could always sell the shares at year-end and immediately repurchase them. The total amount of cash you would have at year-end would be the £518 gain plus your initial investment of £3,700. You would not lose this return when you bought back 100 shares and would be in the same position as if you had not sold the shares (assuming there are no tax consequences and no brokerage commissions from selling the equity).

Percentage Returns

It is more convenient to summarize the information about returns in percentage terms than in monetary terms because the percentages apply to any amount invested. The question we want to answer is this: How much return do we get for each unit of currency invested? To find this out, let t stand for the year we are looking at, let P_t be the price of the equity at the beginning of the year, and let Div_{t+1} be the dividend paid on the equity during the year. Consider the cash flows in Figure 9.2.

Figure 9.2 Percentage Returns

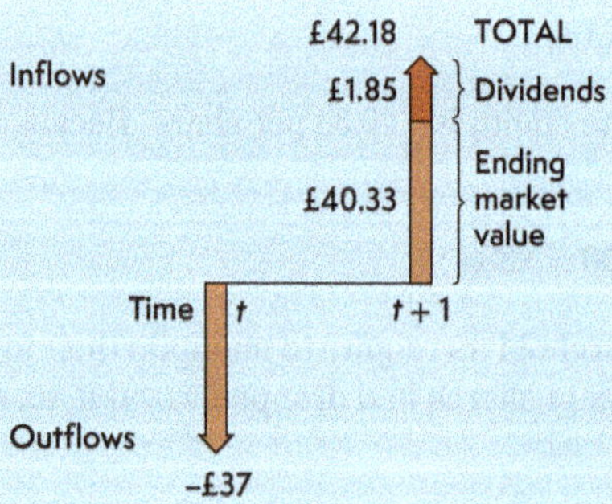

$$\text{Percentage return} = \frac{\text{Dividends paid at end of period} + \text{Change in market value over period}}{\text{Beginning market value}}$$

$$1 + \text{Percentage return} = \frac{\text{Dividends paid at end of period} + \text{Market value at end of period}}{\text{Beginning market value}}$$

In our example, the price at the beginning of the year was £37 per share and the dividend paid during the year on each share was £1.85. Hence the percentage income return, sometimes called the *dividend yield*, is:

$$\begin{aligned}\text{Dividend yield} &= Div_{t+1}/P_t\\ &= £1.85/£37\\ &= 0.05\\ &= 5\%\end{aligned}$$

The capital gain (or loss) is the change in the price of shares divided by the initial price. Letting P_{t+1} be the price of the equity at year-end, we can compute the capital gain as follows:

$$
\begin{aligned}
\text{Capital gain} &= (P_{t+1} - P_t)/P_t \\
&= (£40.33 - £37)/£37 \\
&= £3.37/£37 \\
&= 0.09 \\
&= 9\%
\end{aligned}
$$

Combining these two results, we find that the *total return* on the investment in Video Concept shares over the year, which we will label R_{t+1}, was:

$$
\begin{aligned}
R_{t+1} &= \frac{\text{Div}_{t+1}}{P_t} + \frac{(P_{t+1} - P_t)}{P_t} \\
&= 5\% + 9\% \\
&= 14\%
\end{aligned}
$$

From now on, we will refer to returns in percentage terms.

To give a more concrete example, shares in the sportswear firm Adidas began 2022 at €221.81 a share. Adidas paid a dividend of €0.70 during 2022, and the share price at the end of the year was €179.97. What was the annual return on Adidas? For practice, see if you agree that the answer is –18.5 per cent. Of course, positive returns can occur as well!

Example 9.1

Calculating Returns

Suppose an equity begins the year with a price of €25 per share and ends with a price of €35 per share. During the year it paid a €2 dividend per share. What are its dividend yield, its capital gain and its total return for the year? We can imagine the cash flows in Figure 9.3.

$$
\begin{aligned}
R_1 &= \frac{\text{Div}_1}{P_0} + \frac{P_1 + P_0}{P_0} \\
&= \frac{€2}{€25} + \frac{€35 - 25}{€25} = \frac{€12}{€25} \\
&= 8\% + 40\% = 48\%
\end{aligned}
$$

Figure 9.3 Cash Inflows and Outflows

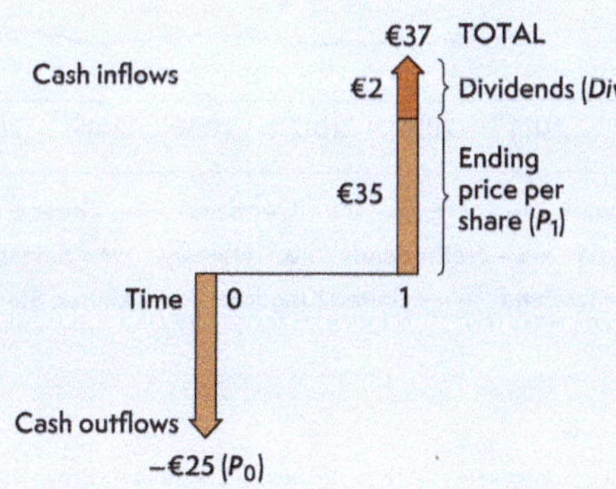

Thus, the equity's dividend yield, its capital gain yield and its total return are 8 per cent, 40 per cent and 48 per cent, respectively.

Suppose you had €5,000 invested. The total return you would have received on an investment in the shares is €5,000 × 0.48 = €2,400. If you know the total return on the equity, you do not need to know how many shares you would have had to purchase to figure out how much money you would have made on the €5,000 investment. You use the total return.

9.2 Holding Period Returns

In this section, we will discuss the rates of return on securities in different countries across Europe and the world. The countries we look at are China, Denmark, France, Germany, Greece, India, Italy, Malaysia, the Netherlands, Norway, Singapore, Spain, Sweden, Switzerland, the UK and the USA. The large company share portfolios are based on indices representing the largest companies in each country. In turn, these are the China Shanghai Composite Index (China), OMX Copenhagen 20 (Denmark), CAC40 (France), DAX30 (Germany), Athens Stock Exchange Index (Greece), BSE SENSEX (India), FTSE MIB (Italy), Kuala Lumpur Composite Index (Malaysia), Amsterdam SE All Shares (the Netherlands), Oslo Exchange All Shares (Norway), Straits Times Index (Singapore), IBEX35 (Spain), OMXS30 (Sweden), Swiss Market Index (Switzerland), FTSE 100 (UK) and S&P500 (USA).

Figure 9.4 shows the relative performance of different stock markets over the period 2011–2023. None of the returns is adjusted for taxes, transaction costs or inflation.[1] The time series starts during the European sovereign debt crisis, spans the global coronavirus pandemic and the energy crisis during 2021 and 2022. The best-performing market was Denmark, where the 2023 index was up 400 per cent on the starting value in 2011. At the other end of the performance spectrum, in 2023, Greece was just over 50 per cent of the 2011 index value.

Figure 9.4 Stock Market Index Levels for Various Countries, January 2011–January 2023

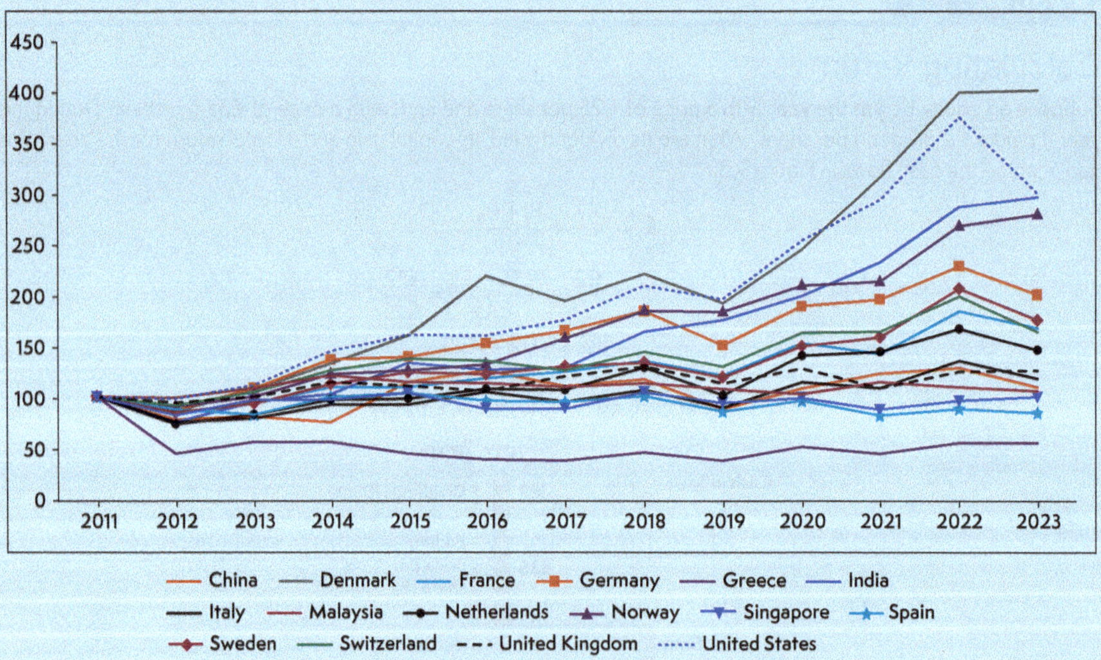

Source: Refinitiv.

Table 9.1 presents the index values for each stock market for every year between 2011 and 2023. Notice how many markets performed poorly in 2020 during the Covid-19 pandemic, In contrast, 2021 was an incredible year for the global stock market, which experienced sustained performance as the world recovered from the worldwide disruption in business activity. The central insight from Figure 9.4 is that most markets simultaneously tend to move (with some obvious exceptions) in the same direction. The correlation isn't perfect but when there are shocks, like in 2020 and 2021, stock markets move together. Of all the countries examined in Table 9.1, the clear loser is Greece, which was only 54.9 per cent of its 2011 value at the beginning of 2023.

Table 9.1 Year-by-year Stock Market Index Levels for Different Countries, 2011–2022

Year	China	Denmark	France	Germany	Greece	India	Italy	Malaysia	Netherlands	Norway	Singapore	Spain	Sweden	Switzerland	UK	USA
2011	100.00	100.00	100.00	100.00	100.00	100.00	100.00	100.00	100.00	100.00	100.00	100.00	100.00	100.00	100.00	100.00
2012	78.32	86.19	82.60	86.92	44.41	75.47	75.62	99.77	73.86	91.15	81.78	88.22	84.92	91.41	94.45	98.88
2013	80.81	107.42	93.34	108.91	56.22	95.23	79.63	109.40	82.87	100.07	97.88	82.60	93.87	105.06	99.96	112.13
2014	75.35	133.26	110.13	136.66	55.94	102.82	92.81	121.25	97.62	122.98	97.89	100.29	113.26	126.32	114.39	145.33
2015	115.19	161.17	109.53	140.28	44.17	133.78	93.03	114.58	98.75	126.44	104.00	103.96	124.45	138.34	111.29	161.88
2016	126.04	219.57	118.87	153.70	39.06	127.24	104.81	114.25	108.32	132.40	89.09	96.52	122.94	135.79	105.80	160.70
2017	110.53	194.84	125.16	165.93	37.93	129.35	95.74	109.60	107.59	157.69	89.03	95.25	129.74	126.58	121.07	176.03
2018	117.77	221.75	136.19	184.81	45.20	164.45	106.93	114.10	129.54	185.04	105.17	101.57	134.00	144.47	130.30	210.21
2019	88.81	193.02	121.27	151.06	37.54	176.33	89.66	108.05	102.04	184.08	94.84	86.36	119.70	129.80	114.04	197.10
2020	108.62	245.90	153.25	189.55	51.23	200.39	115.02	102.82	141.29	210.59	99.60	96.57	150.56	163.49	127.84	254.02
2021	123.68	317.21	142.31	196.27	44.55	232 81	108.79	114.76	145.03	213.71	87.89	81.65	159.30	164.82	109.50	295.32
2022	129.62	400.57	185.02	229.20	55.05	287.34	135.69	110.03	168.13	269.31	96.86	88.60	207.69	199.25	125.16	377.13
2023	110.01	402.31	169.05	201.28	54.90	297.49	118.21	106.34	146.65	280.20	100.48	84.64	176.38	165.22	126.30	301.88

Table 9.2 Year-by-year Stock Market Returns for Different Countries, 2011–2022

Year	China	Denmark	France	Germany	Greece	India	Italy	Malaysia	Netherlands	Norway	Singapore	Spain	Sweden	Switzerland	UK	USA
2011	−21.68%	−13.81%	−17.40%	−13.08%	−55.59%	−24.53%	−24.38%	−0.23%	−26.14%	−8.85%	−18.22%	−11.78%	−15.08%	−8.59%	−5.55%	−1.12%
2012	3.17%	24.63%	13.00%	25.30%	26.60%	26.18%	5.30%	9.65%	12.20%	9.79%	19.68%	−6.38%	10.54%	14.93%	5.84%	13.41%
2013	−6.75%	24.05%	17.99%	25.48%	−0.51%	7.97%	16.56%	10.82%	17.80%	22.89%	0.01%	21.42%	20.66%	20.24%	14.43%	29.60%
2014	52.87%	20.95%	−0.54%	2.65%	−21.03%	30.12%	0.23%	−5.50%	1.16%	2.81%	6.24%	3.66%	9.87%	9.51%	−2.71%	11.39%
2015	9.41%	36.23%	8.53%	9.56%	−11.57%	−4.90%	12.66%	−0.29%	9.69%	4.71%	−14.34%	−7.15%	−1.21%	−1.84%	−4.93%	−0.73%
2016	−12.31%	−11.26%	5.29%	7.96%	−2.89%	1.66%	−8.65%	−4.07%	−0.68%	19.10%	−0.07%	−1.31%	5.53%	−6.78%	14.43%	9.54%
2017	6.56%	13.81%	8.81%	11.37%	19.16%	27.14%	11.69%	4.11%	20.40%	17.35%	18.13%	6.64%	3.28%	14.14%	7.63%	19.42%
2018	−24.59%	−12.95%	−10.95%	−18.26%	−16.95%	7.22%	−16.15%	−5.30%	−21.23%	−0.52%	−9.82%	−14.97%	−10.67%	−10.15%	−12.48%	−6.24%
2019	22.30%	27.39%	26.37%	25.48%	36.48%	13.93%	28.28%	−4.84%	38.46%	14.40%	5.02%	11.82%	25.78%	25.95%	12.10%	28.88%
2020	13.87%	29.00%	−7.14%	3.55%	−13.03%	15.89%	−5.42%	11.61%	2.65%	1.48%	−11.76%	−15.45%	5.81%	0.82%	−14.34%	16.26%
2021	4.80%	26.28%	30.01%	16.78%	23.56%	23.64%	24.73%	−4.12%	15.93%	26.02%	10.21%	8.52%	30.37%	20.89%	14.30%	27.70%
2022	−15.13%	0.43%	−8.63%	−12.18%	−0.27%	3.35%	−12.88%	−3.35%	−12.78%	4.04%	3.74%	−4.47%	−15.07%	−17.08%	0.91%	−19.95%

The data in Table 9.1 show that an investor must be careful when reading information on company or stock market performance. For example, if one were to look at the holding period return for Denmark between January 2012 and January 2016, and compare this to the holding period return for the same country between January 2016 and January 2020, conflicting messages would be given. The holding period return for the years 2012–2016 is ((219.57/86.19) – 1) = 154.75 per cent, compared to the holding period return for the years 2016–2020 of ((245.90/219.57) – 1) = 11.99 per cent! Which is the correct performance measure? Unfortunately, both are correct from different perspectives.

Figure 9.4 gives the growth of an investment in various stock markets between January 2011 and January 2023. In other words, it shows what the worth of the investment would have been if the money that was initially invested had been left in the stock market and if each year the dividends from the previous year had been reinvested in more shares. If R_t is the return in year t (expressed in decimals), the value you would have at the end of year T is the product of 1 plus the return in each of the years:

$$(1 + R_1) \times (1 + R_2) \times \ldots (1 + R_t) \times \ldots \times (1 + R_T)$$

For example, in Table 9.2, the index values in Table 9.1 are presented as annual percentage returns.

Consider the returns for Italy in 2012 (5.30 per cent), 2013 (16.56 per cent) and 2014 (0.23 per cent). An investment of €1 at the beginning of 2012 would have been worth at the end of 2014:

$$(1 + R_1) \times (1 + R_2) \times (1 + R_3) = (€1 + .0530) \times (€1 + .1656) \times (€1 + .0023) = €1.2302$$

Notice that 0.2302 or 23.02 per cent is the total return and that it includes the return from reinvesting the first-year dividends in the stock market for two more years and reinvesting the second-year dividends for the final year. The 23.02 per cent is called a three-year holding period return.

9.3 Return Statistics

The history of capital market returns is too complicated to be handled in its undigested form. To use historical data, we must first find some manageable ways of describing it, dramatically condensing the detailed data into a few simple statements.

Two numbers are significant when summarizing stock market history. The first and most natural number is some single measure that best describes the past annual returns on the stock market. In other words, what is our best estimate of the return that an investor could have realized in a particular year over a period? This is called the *average return*.

Figure 9.5 plots the histogram of the yearly stock market returns for the UK FTSE All-Share Index of the UK's largest companies between 1926 and 2023. This plot is the frequency distribution of the returns. The height of the graph gives the percentage of sample observations in the range on the horizontal axis.

Figure 9.5 Histogram of Annual Returns on UK Equities, 1926–2023

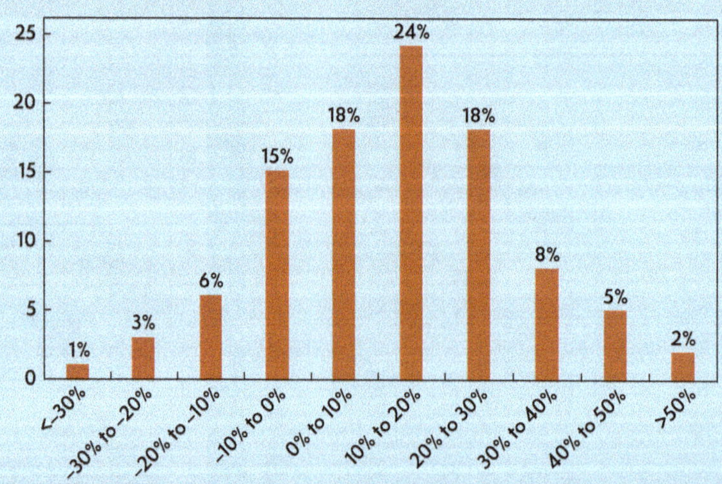

Source: FTSE All-Share Index.

Example 9.2

Calculating Average Returns

From Table 9.2, the returns on sizeable Danish company shares between 2012 and 2014 are 0.2463, 0.2405 and 0.2095, respectively. The average, or arithmetic mean, return over these three years is:

$$\overline{R} = \frac{0.2463 + 0.2405 + 0.2095}{3} = 0.2321$$

Given a frequency distribution like that in Figure 9.4, we can calculate the average, or mean, of the distribution. To compute the average of the distribution, we add up all of the values and divide by the total (T) number (93 in our case because we have 93 years of data). The bar over the R is used to represent the mean, and the formula is the usual formula for the average:

$$\text{Mean} = \overline{R} = \frac{(R_1 + \ldots + R_T)}{T}$$

The mean of the 93 annual large-company share price returns from 1926 to 2023 is approximately 12 per cent.

Sustainability in Action 9.1

Tesla Inc.

Tesla Inc. is one of the world's most iconic manufacturers of electric vehicles (EVs). The company has been at the forefront of the EV market, revolutionizing the automotive industry with its cutting-edge battery technology and innovative business model. It is listed on NASDAQ, and we present its share price performance between January 2018 and January 2023 in Figure 9.6.

Figure 9.6 Tesla Share Prices 2018–2023

Period of Uncertainty (2018–2019)

In 2018, Tesla's share price faced significant volatility. The company struggled with production bottlenecks, labour issues and concerns over profitability. In addition, the company's CEO, Elon Musk, made controversial comments on Twitter that led to an SEC (US Securities and Exchange Commission) investigation, adding to the uncertainty. Despite these challenges, Tesla managed to ramp up production of its automobile line.

Meteoritic Rise (2020)

The year 2020 marked a turning point for Tesla. The company opened its Shanghai Gigafactory, which increased production capacity and reduced supply chain risks. Additionally, Tesla reported positive net income for the first time, reinforcing investor confidence in its business model. The unveiling of its Cybertruck and growing sales of its automobiles further propelled the share price. Tesla's stock soared throughout 2020, culminating in a 5-for-1 stock split in August. By the end of the year, the share price had sky-rocketed a massive 960 per cent from the beginning of the year.

Volatility and Decline (2021–2022)

Tesla's share price continued to experience volatility in 2021 because of supply chain constraints due to the global semiconductor shortage resulting from the global pandemic restrictions. Nevertheless, Tesla achieved record vehicle deliveries. However, towards the end of 2021 and into 2022, investor confidence was rocked by Tesla's $1.5 billion investment in bitcoin and Elon Musk's $44 billion purchase of Twitter.

Conclusion

Tesla's share price journey from 2018 to 2021 made it a favourite among investors. However, increasing competition, target shortfalls and a seemingly distracted CEO have all contributed to a significant fall in firm value over the period to 2023. Using different periods to estimate average returns would give different estimates. For example, if you used the 2020 to 2021 figures for Tesla to calculate average returns, your estimate would be significantly higher than if you used data from 2021 to 2023. The financial manager should be aware of the impact of the sampling period on estimates when working with historical data.

Asset Class Performance

Figure 9.7 presents the annual performance for various asset classes from 2014 to 2023 according to BlackRock Investment Institute. Understanding the historical performance of different asset classes is essential for investors and financial managers. In this subsection, we will discuss the performance of the asset classes presented in Figure 9.7, specifically focusing on four major asset classes – equities, debt, property, and commodities – and drawing on key lessons from market history.

The first thing that jumps out from Figure 9.7 is volatility in different asset classes over time. Apart from 2021 and 2022, when commodities reported spectacular performance, a different asset class has headed the performance league. There is also a degree of mean reversion in the data. Consider, for example, Chinese equities, which reported their best year in 2020 and their worst year in 2021.

Equities: Over the long term, equities have been the most rewarding asset class in terms of returns, primarily due to their higher risk profile. The long-term annualized return of the FTSE 100 Index and other broad equity indices has been at least 10 per cent over the past 100 years. However, this high return has been accompanied by significant volatility, as demonstrated by events such as the 2008 global financial crisis and the global pandemic. These episodes highlight the importance of a long-term investment horizon and the need for diversification.

Debt: Publicly traded debt, particularly government bonds, is known for its lower risk and relatively stable returns compared to equities. While bonds generally offer lower returns than equities, they play a crucial role in portfolio diversification, as they tend to be less correlated with stock market movements.

Property: Property and real estate have long been considered a valuable asset class for both income generation and capital appreciation. The performance of property investments can be measured through indices like the MSCI Global Annual Property Index, which has shown an average annual return of approximately 8 per cent since the 1980s. Property investments, however, are subject to local market dynamics and may be vulnerable to economic downturns, as evidenced by Real Estate Investment Trusts' (REIT) performance in 2022 in the aftermath of the global pandemic.

Commodities: Commodities, including precious metals, agricultural products and energy resources, have served as a hedge against inflation and a source of diversification in investor portfolios. The performance of commodities can be tracked through indices such as the S&P GSCI, which has exhibited long-term average annual returns of around 5 per cent. Commodities, however, are prone to cyclical fluctuations and may be influenced by factors such as global economic growth, geopolitical events and technological advancements. The 2021 and 2022 coronavirus pandemic-induced market disruptions exemplify the potential volatility of commodity investments.

Figure 9.7 BlackRock Asset Return Map

2014	2015	2016	2017	2018	2019	2020	2021	2022	2023	Annualized
REITs 22.8%	Japan equities 9.9%	High yield 14.3%	China equities 54.3%	Cash 1.9%	US equities 31.6%	China equities 29.7%	Commodities 38.5%	Commodities 22%	Europe equities 8%	US equities 12.2%
US equities 13.4%	US equities 1.3%	Infrastructure 12.4%	EM equities 37.8%	DM gov. debt −0.4%	Infrastructure 27%	US equities 21.4%	REITs 32.5%	Cash 1.3%	REITs 4.6%	Infrastructure 6.4%
Infrastructure 13%	Emerging debt 1.2%	US equities 11.6%	Europe equities 26.2%	IG credit −3.5%	Europe equities 24.6%	EM equities 18.7%	US equities 27%	Infrastructure −0.2%	US equities 4%	Europe equities 5.7%
China equities 8.3%	REITs 0.6%	EM equities 11.6%	Japan equities 24.4%	High yield −4.1%	REITs 24.5%	Japan equities 14.9%	Europe equities 17%	High yield −12.7%	High yield 2.2%	Japan equities 5.5%
Emerging debt 5.5%	Cash 0.1%	Emerging debt 10.2%	US equities 21.9%	US equities −4.5%	China equities 23.7%	IG credit 10.1%	Infrastructure 11.9%	Europe equities −14.5%	Japan equities 2.1%	REITs 5%
IG credit 2.5%	Europe equities −2.3%	Commodities 9.7%	Infrastructure 20.1%	Emerging debt −4.6%	Japan equities 20.1%	DM gov. debt 9.5%	Japan equities 2%	IG credit −16.1%	Infrastructure 1.5%	High yield 3.1%
Cash 0.1%	High yield −2.7%	REITs 6.9%	High yield 10.4%	REITs −4.8%	EM equities 18.9%	High yield 7%	High yield 1%	Japan equities −16.3%	EM equities 0.9%	China equities 2.6%
High yield 0%	DM gov. debt −3.3%	IG credit 6%	Emerging debt 9.3%	Infrastructure −9.5%	Emerging debt 14.4%	Europe equities 5.9%	Cash 0%	Emerging debt −16.5%	IG credit 0.9%	EM equities 1.9%
DM gov. debt −0.8%	IG credit −3.8%	Japan equities 2.7%	IG credit 9.3%	Commodities −10.7%	High yield 12.6%	Emerging debt 5.9%	Emerging debt −1.5%	DM gov. debt −17.5%	Emerging debt 0.8%	Emerging debt 1.6%
EM equities −1.8%	China equities −7.6%	DM gov. debt 1.7%	REITs 8.6%	Japan equities −12.6%	IG credit 11.8%	Cash 0.7%	IG credit −2.1%	US equities −19.5%	Cash 0.7%	IG credit 1.4%
Japan equities −3.7%	Infrastructure −11.5%	China equities 1.1%	DM gov. debt 7.3%	EM equities −14.2%	Commodities 11.8%	Infrastructure −5.8%	EM equities −2.2%	EM equities −19.7%	China equities 0.2%	Cash 0.8%
Europe equities −5.7%	EM equities −14.6%	Cash 0.4%	Commodities 1.7%	Europe equities −14.3%	DM gov. debt 5.6%	REITs −8.1%	DM gov. debt −6.6%	China equities −21.8%	DM gov. debt −0.6%	Commodities 0.1%
Commodities −17.9%	Commodities −23.4%	Europe equities 0.2%	Cash 0.8%	China equities −18.7%	Cash 2.3%	Commodities −9.3%	China equities −21.6%	REITs −23.6%	Commodities −2.1%	DM gov. debt −1%

Key: Lowest return -------------------- Highest return

Notes: The table shows annual index total returns (income or dividends reinvested) in US dollars. Indices are unmanaged and, therefore not subject to fees. For example, 2022 shows year to 28 February 2023. Indexes or prices used are: US equities – MSCI USA Index, EM equities – MSCI Emerging Markets Index, Europe equities – MSCI Europe Index, Japan equities – MSCI Japan Index, China equities – MSCI China Index, DM gov. debt – Bloomberg Barclays Global Treasury Index, Emerging debt – J.P. Morgan Emerging Market Bond Index (EMBI) Global Composite, High yield – Bloomberg Barclays Global High Yield Index, IG credit – Barclays Global Corporate Credit Index, Commodities – Commodity Research Bureau (CRB) Index, Cash – Bloomberg Barclays US Treasury Bill Index, REITs – S&P Global Real Estate Investment Trust (REIT) Index, Infrastructure – S&P Global Infrastructure Index. Annualized column shows the annualized total return over the last 10 years from 28 February 2023.

Source: based on BlackRock Investment Institute, with data from Refinitiv Datastream, 1 March 2023. https://www.blackrock.com/corporate/insights/blackrock-investment-institute/interactive-charts/return-map

The asset classes in this section are a random selection and you could use other asset classes. An example is cryptocurrencies, which have become very popular among individual investors but not necessarily financial institutions. If you wish to read more about this asset class, check out the additional reading at the end of the chapter.

9.4 Average Stock Returns and Risk-free Returns

Now that we have computed the average return on the stock market, it seems sensible to compare it with the returns on other securities. The most obvious comparison is with the low-variability returns in the government bond market. These are free of most of the volatility we see in the stock market.

Governments borrow money by issuing bonds, which the investing public holds. As we discussed in Chapter 5, these bonds come in many forms, and the ones we will look at here are called *Treasury bills*, or *T-bills*. Once a week the government sells some bills at an auction. A typical bill is a pure discount bond that will mature in a year or less. Because governments can raise taxes to pay for the debt they incur – a trick that many of us would like to be able to perform – this debt is virtually free of the risk of default. Thus we will call this the *risk-free return* over a short time (one year or less).

An interesting comparison, then, is between the virtually risk-free return on T-bills and the very risky return on equity. This difference between risky returns and risk-free returns is often called the *excess return on the risky asset*. It is called *excess* because it is the additional return resulting from the riskiness of equities and is interpreted as an equity **risk premium**.

Table 9.3 shows the risk premium of equities in a number of countries in January 2023. The equity risk premium relates to two securities: long-term government bonds and short-term treasury bills. The table also presents the country risk premium, which is the difference between the individual country equity risk premium and a mature economy equity risk premium.

Table 9.3 Equity and Country Risk Premiums, January 2023

Country	Total Equity Risk Premium %	Country Risk Premium %	Country	Total Equity Risk Premium %	Country Risk Premium %
Abu Dhabi	6.79	0.85	Norway	5.94	0.00
Austria	6.63	0.69	Oman	12.15	6.21
Bahrain	15.43	9.49	Poland	7.40	1.46
Belgium	6.97	1.03	Portugal	9.23	3.29
China	7.16	1.22	Russia	18.88	12.94
Denmark	5.94	0.00	Rwanda	15.43	9.49
Finland	6.63	0.69	Saudi Arabia	7.16	1.22
France	6.79	0.85	Singapore	5.94	0.00
Germany	5.94	0.00	South Africa	11.13	5.19
Greece	12.15	6.21	Spain	8.70	2.76
India	9.73	3.79	Sweden	5.94	0.00
Ireland	7.16	1.22	Switzerland	5.94	0.00
Italy	9.73	3.79	Turkey	17.16	11.22
Malaysia	8.01	2.07	UAE	6.79	0.85
Netherlands	5.94	0.00	UK	6.97	1.03
Nigeria	17.16	11.22	USA	5.94	0.00

Source: Aswath Damodaran website, http://pages.stern.nyu.edu/~adamodar/New_Home_Page/datafile/ctryprem.html

Figure 9.8 presents a similar picture but for a much longer period of 109 years.

Figure 9.8 Worldwide Annualized Equity Risk Premium (%) Relative to Bills and Bonds, 1900–2010

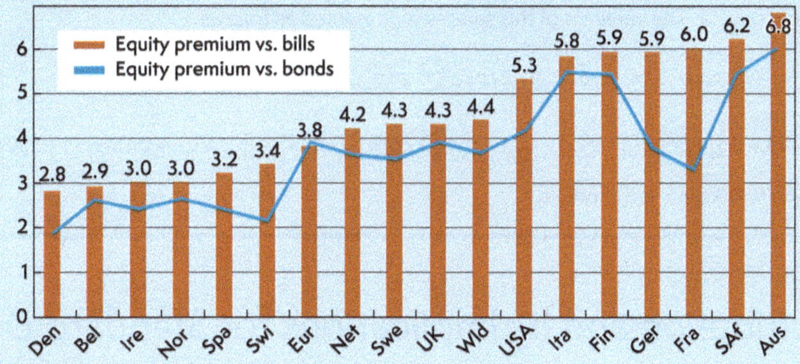

Note: Premiums for Germany are based on 109 years, excluding hyperinflationary 1922–23.
Data values are estimates

Source: Adapted from Dimson et al. (2002, 2011).

One of the most significant observations from Table 9.3 and Figure 9.8 is that the equity risk premium of every country was positive, both in 2023 and over the longer term. An investor was rewarded for investment in the stock market with an extra or excess return over what would have been achieved by simply investing in T-bills.

Why was there such a reward? Does this mean that it never pays to invest in T-bills and that someone who invested in them instead of in the stock market needs a course in finance? A complete answer to these questions lies at the heart of modern finance, and Chapter 10 is devoted entirely to this. However, part of the answer can be found in the variability of the various types of investment.

We see in Table 9.2 years when an investment in equities resulted in a loss of money (negative returns). The returns from an investment in equities are frequently negative (as shown for the UK in Figure 9.5), whereas an investment in T-bills never produces a negative return. So, we now turn our attention to measuring the variability of returns and an introductory discussion of risk.

9.5 Risk Statistics

The second number that we use to characterize the distribution of returns is a measure of the risk in returns. There is no universally agreed-upon definition of risk. One way to think about the risk of returns on company shares is in terms of the spread of returns over a period. The spread, or dispersion, of a distribution is a measure of how much a particular return can deviate from the mean return. If the distribution is very spread out, the returns that will occur are very uncertain. By contrast, a distribution whose returns are all within a few percentage points of one another is tight, and the returns are less uncertain. The measures of risk we will discuss are variance and standard deviation. It should be emphasized that the measures of risk used in this chapter are based on historical data. There are other approaches to measuring risk that use other characteristics of the price distribution but these are beyond the scope of the text.

Variance

The **variance** and its square root, the **standard deviation**, are the most common measures of variability or dispersion. We will use Var and σ^2 to denote the variance and SD and σ to represent the standard deviation. σ is, of course, the Greek letter sigma.

This formula tells us just what to do: take the T individual returns (R_1, R_2,. . .) and subtract the average return, $\overline{R}$, square the result, and add them up. Finally, this total must be divided by the number of returns less one ($T - 1$). The standard deviation is always just the square root of the variance.

Example 9.3

Volatility

Consider the returns on India's stock market between 2010 and 2014. These are, respectively, 0.1773, −0.2453, 0.2618, 0.0797 and 0.3012. The variance of this sample is computed as follows:

$$Var = \frac{1}{T-1}[(R_1 - \bar{R})^2 + (R_2 - \bar{R})^2 + (R_3 - \bar{R})^2 + (R_4 - \bar{R})^2 + (R_5 - \bar{R})^2]$$

$$0.04779 = \frac{1}{4}[(0.1773 - 0.1149)^2 + (-0.2453 - 0.1149)^2 + (0.2618 - 0.1149)^2 + (0.0797 - 0.1149)^2 + (0.3012 - 0.1149)^2]$$

$$SD = \sqrt{0.04779} = 0.2186 \text{ or } 21.86\%$$

Normal Distribution and Its Implications for Standard Deviation

A large enough sample drawn from a **normal distribution** looks like the bell-shaped curve illustrated in Figure 9.9. As you can see, this distribution is *symmetric* about its mean, not *skewed,* and has a much cleaner shape than the actual distribution of yearly returns drawn in Figure 9.5. Of course, if we had been able to observe stock market returns for 1,000 years, we might have filled in a lot of the jumps and jerks in Figure 9.5 and had a smoother curve.

Figure 9.9 The Normal Distribution

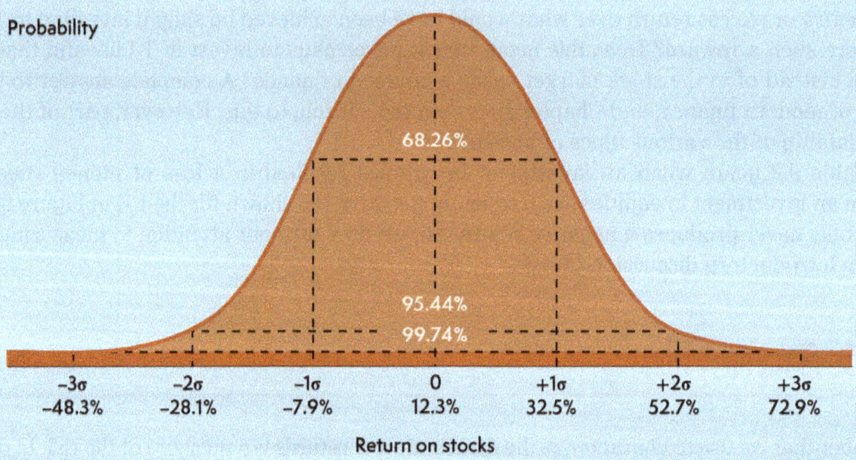

In the case of a normal distribution there is a 68.26 per cent probability that a return will be within one standard deviation of the mean. In this example there is a 68.26 per cent probability that a yearly return will be between −7.9 per cent and 32.5 per cent.

There is a 95.44 per cent probability that a return will be within two standard deviations of the mean. In this example, there is a 95.44 per cent probability that a yearly return will be between −28.1 per cent and 52.7 per cent.

Finally, there is a 99.74 per cent probability that a return will be within three standard deviations of the mean. In this example, there is a 99.74 per cent probability that a yearly return will be between −48.3 per cent and 72.9 per cent.

In classical statistics, the normal distribution plays a central role, and the standard deviation is the usual way to represent the spread of a normal distribution. For the normal distribution, the probability of having a return that is above or below the mean by a certain amount depends only on the standard deviation. For example, the likelihood of having a return that is within one standard deviation of the mean of the distribution is approximately 0.68, or 2/3, and the probability of having a return that is within two standard deviations of the mean is about 0.95.

We can also discuss the normal distribution in an alternative way. For example, we can say that there is only a 1 per cent probability that a return will be 2.33 standard deviations from the mean and only a 5 per cent probability that a return will be 1.645 standard deviations from the mean. Note that this way of discussing probabilities is just looking at one side of the normal distribution instead of both sides.

The 21.86 per cent standard deviation we found for the Indian stock market can now be interpreted in the following way: if equity returns are roughly normally distributed, the probability that a yearly return will fall within 21.86 per cent of the mean of 11.49 per cent will be approximately 2/3. That is, about 2/3 of the yearly returns will be between −10.37 per cent and 33.35 per cent. (Note that − 10.37 = 11.49 − 21.86 and 33.35 = 11.49 + 21.86.) The probability that the return in any year will fall within two standard deviations is about 0.95. That is, about 95 per cent of yearly returns will be between −32.22 per cent and 55.22 per cent.

Other Measures of Risk

Although variance and standard deviation are the most common risk measures, there are other approaches to assessing risk that are sometimes utilized by investors. One of the major drawbacks of variance and standard deviation is that they implicitly assume that increases in share prices are just as risky as price falls. However, many investors perceive a decrease in the value of their investment to be significantly more risky than when their investment grows in value. This asymmetry in personal perspectives is seen to be the major weakness of the variance and standard deviation measures.

Asymmetric measures of risk use only the downside variation in returns from some target return, which could be the mean historical return or some benchmark return set by the investor. The semi-variance is calculated as follows:

$$\text{Semi-variance} = \frac{1}{n-1}\left[\sum_{r_i<\text{target}}^{n} (\text{target} - r_i)^2\right]$$

where n is the number of observations below the target, r_i is the observed return and 'target' is the target return, which could be the historical mean return. The semi-variance has the advantage that only those deviations that are below the target or benchmark return are considered in the risk measure.

Another measure of risk that incorporates asymmetry in investment returns is that of skewness. Skewness refers to the extent to which a distribution is skewed to the left or right. In Figure 9.9, the normal distribution is symmetric, which means that downside and upside observations are equally likely. However, many return series have an asymmetric distribution, and skewness measures the degree to which observations are likely to be on the downside or upside. Consider Figure 9.10, which presents two skewed distributions. In the first diagram, negative returns are more likely, whereas in the second diagram positive returns are more likely. To measure the degree to which a return series is skewed, also known as skewness risk, divide the proportion of variation that is caused by upside deviations from the mean by the proportion of variation caused by downside deviations from the mean. Values of skewness risk above one correspond to positive skewness, where values of skewness risk below one correspond to negative skewness.

Figure 9.10 Skewed Distributions

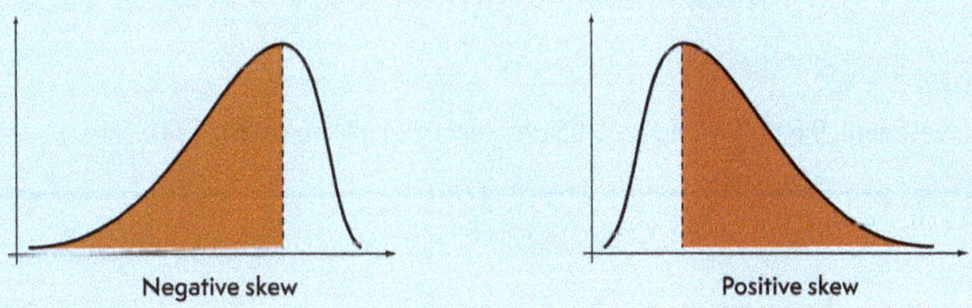

A second measure of risk that is related to the distribution of returns is kurtosis. Kurtosis is a measure of the frequency of very negative and very positive returns. The normal distribution predicts that approximately 4.56 per cent of all observed returns will be greater than two standard deviations away from the mean return. However, in many cases, share price returns have a much greater prevalence of extreme values, and this is reflected in the size of the kurtosis measure. The formula for kurtosis is quite complex but, fortunately, all statistical packages and spreadsheets calculate this for you. For example, in Microsoft Excel, the formula for kurtosis is KURT. Similarly, the formula for skewness is SKEW.

Value at Risk

A measure of risk that is commonly used for risk management purposes is called value at risk (or VaR). There are many ways to measure VaR, but for our purposes, we will focus on the approach that uses the normal distribution. VaR tells you how much you can potentially lose from an investment. More formally, it measures the potential loss in an asset's value within a specified period with a specified probability. For example, if the VaR on an equity portfolio is €100 million with a one-week holding period and a 5 per cent probability, you would say that there is a 5 per cent probability that you may lose more than €100 million in the value of your portfolio within the next week.

Measuring VaR is a relatively simple process, and we will show how to calculate it with an example. We start by stating the measurement period and probability for which we wish to measure VaR. Let us say we have a weekly holding period and a 1 per cent probability, which means we want to find the largest expected drop in value over the next week with a 99 per cent probability.

Example 9.4

Calculating VaR

Assume that we have invested £1 million in a fund that perfectly tracks the FTSE 100 Index for large UK company stocks. What is the biggest drop in value that we could expect over the next month with a 99 per cent probability?

Step 1: Find the Monthly Mean and Standard Deviation of the Fund's Returns

If data are available, you could calculate the mean and standard deviation using historical returns. A second approach is to use your forward-looking estimate. In this example, we will use the information in Table 9.2, which is annualized. To calculate monthly returns from annual data, we divide the annualized figure by 12. The average annual return for the FTSE 100 is the average return between 2011 and 2022, which is 2.47 per cent:

$$\bar{R}^{\text{Monthly}} = \frac{\bar{R}^{\text{Annual}}}{12} = \frac{2.47\%}{12} = 0.21\%$$

The conversion from annual standard deviation is slightly more complicated in that you divide the annualized standard deviation by the square root of 12. Assume the average annual standard deviation for the FTSE 100 is 10.5 per cent:

$$\bar{\sigma}^{\text{Monthly}} = \frac{\bar{\sigma}^{\text{Annual}}}{\sqrt{12}} = \frac{10.5\%}{\sqrt{12}} = 3.03\%$$

Step 2: Calculate the Negative Return That Will Occur 1 Per Cent of the Time

Since we assume that the FTSE 100 fund returns are normally distributed, we can say that a return that is 2.33 standard deviations below the mean will occur only 1 per cent of the time. In the FTSE 100 case, this return is:

$$R_{VaR}^{1\%\ \text{Monthly}} = 0.21\% - 2.33(3.03\%) = -6.85\%$$

Step 3: Calculate VaR

With a £1 million investment, the VaR would be 6.85 per cent of £1 million = £68,534.

9.6 More on Average Returns

Thus far in this chapter, we have looked closely at simple average returns. But there is another way of computing an average return. The fact that average returns are calculated in two different ways leads to some confusion, so our goal in this section is to explain the two approaches and the circumstances under which each is appropriate.

Arithmetic versus Geometric Averages

Let us start with a simple example. Suppose you buy a particular equity for £100. Unfortunately, the first year you own it, it falls to £50. The second year you own it, it rises back to £100, leaving you where you started (no dividends were paid).

What was your average return on this investment? Common sense seems to say that your average return must be zero because you started with £100 and ended with £100. But if we calculate the returns year by year, we see that you lost 50 per cent in the first year (you lost half of your money). The second year, you made 100 per cent (you doubled your money). Your average return over the two years was thus (– 50 per cent + 10 per cent) /2 = 25 per cent.

So which is correct, 0 per cent or 25 per cent? The answer is that both are correct; they answer different questions. The 0 per cent is called the **geometric average return**. The 25 per cent is called the **arithmetic average return**. The geometric average return answers the question, *'What was your average compound return per year over a particular period?' The arithmetic average return answers the question, 'What was your return in an average year over a particular period?'*

Notice that, in previous sections, the average returns we calculated were all arithmetic averages, so we already know how to calculate them. What we need to do now is (1) learn how to calculate geometric averages, and (2) learn the circumstances under which one average is more meaningful than the other.

Calculating Geometric Average Returns

First, to illustrate how we calculate a geometric average return, suppose a particular investment had annual returns of 10 per cent, 12 per cent, 3 per cent and –9 per cent over the last four years. The geometric average return over this four-year period is calculated as $(1.10 \times 1.12 \times 1.03 - 0.91)^{1/4} - 1 = 3.66$ per cent. In contrast, the average arithmetic return we have been calculating is $(0.10 + 0.12 + 0.03 - 0.09)/4 = 4.0$ per cent.

In general, if we have T years of returns, the geometric average return over these T years is calculated using this formula:

Equation 9.1 $$\text{Geometric average return} = [(1 + R_1) \times (1 + R_2) \times \ldots \times (1 + R_T)]^{1/T} - 1$$

This formula tells us that four steps are required:

1. Take each of the T annual returns R_1 $R_2, \ldots, R_T$ and add 1 to each (after converting them to decimals).
2. Multiply all the numbers from step 1 together.
3. Take the result from step 2 and raise it to the power of $1/T$.
4. Finally, subtract 1 from the result of step 3. The result is the geometric average return.

Example 9.5

Calculating the Geometric Average Return

Calculate the geometric average return for Norwegian stocks for 2010–2014 using the numbers given here. First, convert percentages to decimal returns, add 1, and then calculate their product:

Norwegian Returns	Product
16.68	1.1668
-8.85	× 0.9115
9.79	× 1.0979
22.89	× 1.2289
2.81	× 1.0281
	1.4753

Notice that the number 1.4753 is what our investment is worth after five years if we start with a 1 krone investment. The geometric average return is then calculated as follows:

$$\text{Geometric average return} = 1.4753^{1/5} - 1 = 0.0809, \text{ or } 8.09\%$$

Thus the geometric average return is about –8.09 per cent in this example. Here's a tip: using a financial calculator, you can put 1 in as the present value, 1.4753 as the future value and 5 as the number of periods. Then solve for the unknown rate. You should get the same answer we did.

Table 9.4 shows the arithmetic averages and standard deviations along with the geometric average returns and other data.

Table 9.4 Worldwide Risk Premiums Relative to Bonds, 1900–2010

Country	Geometric Mean (%)	Arithmetic Mean (%)	Standard Dev. (%)	Min. Return (%)	Max. Return (%)
Belgium	2.6	4.9	21.4	−60.3	84.4
Canada	3.7	5.3	18.2	−40.7	48.6
Denmark	2	3.4	17.2	−54.3	74.9
Finland	5.6	9.2	30.3	−56.3	173.1
France	3.2	5.6	22.9	−50.3	84.3
Germany	5.4	8.8	28.4	−50.8	116.6
Ireland	2.9	4.9	19.8	−66.6	83.2
Italy	3.7	7.2	29.6	−49.4	152.2
Netherlands	3.5	2.1	22.2	−55.6	107.6
Norway	2.5	5.5	28.0	−57.8	192.1
South Africa	5.5	1.9	19.6	−34.3	70.9
Spain	2.3	4.3	20.8	−42.7	69.1
Sweden	3.8	6.1	22.3	−48.1	87.5
Switzerland	2.1	3.6	17.6	−40.6	52.2
UK	3.9	1.6	17.0	−38.4	80.8
USA	4.4	1.9	20.5	−50.1	57.2
Europe	3.9	5.2	16.6	−47.6	67.9

Source: Adapted from Dimson et al. (2002, 2011).
Note: All statistics for Germany are based on 109 years, excluding hyperinflationary 1922–23.

Finally, we have to look at what is meant by arithmetic and geometric average returns, which we do in the next section.

Arithmetic Average Return or Geometric Average Return?

The difference between the geometric and arithmetic average returns is not hard to understand when we look at historical returns. To put it slightly differently, the geometric average tells you what you earned per year on average, compounded annually. The arithmetic average tells you what you earned in a typical year. You should use whichever one answers the question you want answered.

A somewhat trickier question concerns forecasting the future, and there is a lot of confusion about this point among analysts and financial planners. The problem is this: if we have *estimates* of both the arithmetic and geometric average returns, then the arithmetic average is probably too high for more extended periods, and the geometric average is probably too low for shorter periods.

The good news is that there is a simple way of combining the two averages, which we will call *Blume's formula.* Suppose we calculated geometric and arithmetic return averages from N years of data, and we wish to use these averages to form a T-year average return forecast, $R(T)$, where T is less than N. Here is how we do it:

Equation 9.2

$$R(T) = \frac{T-1}{N-1} \times \text{Geometric average} + \frac{N-T}{N-1} \times \text{Arithmetic average}$$

For example, suppose that, from 25 years of annual returns data, we calculate an arithmetic average return of 12 per cent and a geometric average return of 9 per cent. We wish to make 1-year, 5-year and 10-year average return forecasts from these averages. These three average return forecasts are calculated as follows:

$$R(1) = \frac{1-1}{24} \times 9\% + \frac{25-1}{24} \times 12\% = 12\%$$

$$R(5) = \frac{5-1}{24} \times 9\% + \frac{25-5}{24} \times 12\% = 11.5\%$$

$$R(10) = \frac{10-1}{24} \times 9\% + \frac{25-10}{24} \times 12\% = 10.875\%$$

Thus, 1-year, 5-year and 10-year forecasts are 12 per cent, 11.5 per cent and 10.875 per cent, respectively.

This concludes our discussion of geometric versus arithmetic averages. One last note: in subsequent chapters, when we say 'average return', we mean arithmetic average unless we explicitly say otherwise.

Real World Insight 9.1

Risk and Return of Volkswagen and Nestlé

In this Real World Insight, we consider the risk and equity return characteristics of two major European companies: Volkswagen AG, a leading German automobile manufacturer, and Nestlé SA, a Swiss multinational food and beverage company. We will explore the performance of these two companies in terms of holding period returns, average stock returns, risk statistics, and their relation to risk-free returns.

First, let's analyse the holding period returns for Volkswagen AG and Nestlé SA. Using the share price data for these two companies between 2003 and 2022, we can calculate the holding period return for different investment horizons. For example, if an investor had purchased Volkswagen AG shares at the beginning of 2003 and held them until the end of 2022, she would have experienced a holding period return of approximately 323 per cent. On the other hand, Nestlé SA's holding period return for the same period was around 258 per cent.

Next, we can calculate the average annual equity returns for both companies. Over the 20-year period, Volkswagen AG's average annual return was approximately 19.1 per cent, while Nestlé SA's was around 10.8 per cent. Comparing these average returns to the risk-free rate (e.g., the yield on 10-year German and Swiss government bonds) during the same period, which was about 2.0 per cent, we can observe that both companies provided a higher return than the risk-free rate.

Now, let's examine the risk statistics associated with these equities. By calculating the standard deviation of the annual returns, we can gauge the volatility of each equity. For example, the standard deviation of Volkswagen AG's returns was 40.3 per cent, whereas Nestlé SA's was 12.4 per cent. These data suggest that Volkswagen AG's equity was more volatile than Nestlé SA's and, therefore, riskier.

This Real World Insight demonstrates the importance of understanding the relationship between risk and return when making investment decisions. Although both Volkswagen AG and Nestlé SA provided higher returns than the risk-free rate, they also exhibited different levels of risk. Nestlé SA's lower volatility and average return suggest it may be a more suitable option for risk-averse investors. On the other hand, Volkswagen AG's higher volatility may appeal to those willing to take on more risk for potentially higher returns. Ultimately, the key is to balance risk and return based on individual investment objectives and risk tolerance.

Summary and Conclusions

1 This chapter presented returns for a number of different asset classes. The general conclusion is that equities have outperformed bonds over most of the past 100 years, though equities have also exhibited more risk.

2 The statistical measures in this chapter are necessary building blocks for the material of the next three chapters. In particular, standard deviation and variance measure the variability of the return on an individual security and on portfolios of securities. In the next chapter, we will argue that standard deviation and variance are appropriate measures of the risk of an individual security if an investor's portfolio is composed of that security only.

Questions and Problems

connect

CONCEPT

1 **Returns** What is meant by the term 'return'? What is the difference between monetary returns and percentage returns? Do monetary or percentage returns matter more to investors? Provide an example to explain your answer.

2 **Holding Period Returns** In what situations would you use a holding period return or a percentage return? Are the two measures the same?

3 **Return Statistics** Why would you wish to present return distributions? How do you think the distributions would change when you incorporated inflation into the return statistics?

4 **Risk Statistics** What do we mean by risk? In long-term investments, equities tend to give higher returns than bonds. Why, then, do all investors not invest in equities? Are such investors irrational?

5 **Other Return Measures** What is the difference between arithmetic and geometric returns? Suppose you have invested in a company's shares for the last 10 years. Which number is more important to you, the arithmetic or geometric return?

REGULAR

6 **Investment Selection: Ukraine** Given that the Ukraine Stock Exchange was up by over 80 per cent in 2018, why didn't all investors put their money in Ukraine?

7 **Investment Selection: Venezuala** Given that the Venezuela Stock Exchange was down 94.9 per cent in 2018, why did investors continue to hold shares in Venezuela? Why didn't they sell out before the market declined so sharply?

8 **Equities versus Gambling** Critically evaluate the following statement: 'Investing in the stock market is just like gambling. It has no social value and investors do it purely to give them a thrill.'

9 **Risk Premiums** Is it possible for the risk premium to be negative before an investment is undertaken? Can the risk premium be negative after the fact? Explain.

10 **Returns** Two years ago, General Materials' and Standard Fixtures' share prices were the same. During the first year, General Materials' share price increased by 10 per cent while Standard Fixtures' share price decreased by 10 per cent. During the second year, General Materials' share price decreased by 10 per cent and Standard Fixtures' share price increased by 10 per cent. Do these two equities have the same price today? Explain.

11 **Historical Returns** The historical returns presented in the chapter are not adjusted for inflation. What would happen to the estimated risk premium if we did account for inflation? The returns are also not adjusted for taxes. What would happen to the returns if we accounted for taxes? What would happen to the volatility?

12 **Calculating Returns** Suppose you bought an 8 per cent coupon bond one year ago for €1,200. The bond sells for €1,074 today.

(a) Assuming a €1,000 face value, what was your total euro return on this investment over the past year?

(b) What was your total nominal rate of return on this investment over the past year?

(c) If the inflation rate last year was 3 per cent, what was your total real rate of return on this investment?

13 **Calculating Returns and Variability** The returns of Lockhart Group plc and TJC plc are given below. Using the following returns, calculate the average returns, the variances and the standard deviations for Lockhart Group and TJC:

Year	Lockhart Group (%)	TJC (%)
2023	−60.7	−3.6
2022	24.1	37.5
2021	33.6	105.5
2020	−62.3	−61.8
2019	−21.8	−33.2

14 Risk Premiums: Returns and Standard Deviation Refer to Table 9.1 and look at the period 2011–2022.

(a) Calculate the arithmetic average returns for each country's stock market over this period.

(b) Calculate the standard deviation of the returns for each country over this period.

15 Calculating Returns and Variability You have observed the following prices for British Auto, the luxury car maker, for a number of years: Jan 2015: €26.87; Jan 2016: €35.19; Jan 2017: €32.17; Jan 2018: €37.23; Jan 2019: €46.84; Jan 2020: €36.80; Jan 2021: €18.61; Jan 2022: €30.96; Jan 2023: €56.08; Jan 2024: €65.39. The company paid the following dividends: 2015: €0.85; 2016: €0.52; 2017: €0.58; 2018: €0.62; 2019: €0.64; 2020: €0.70; 2021: nil; 2022: €0.30; 2023: €0.30; 2024: nil.

(a) What was the arithmetic average return on British Auto's shares over this period?

(b) What was the variance of British Auto's returns over this period? The standard deviation?

16 Calculating Real Returns and Risk Premiums In Problem 15, suppose the average inflation rate over this period was 4.2 per cent and the average T-bill rate over the period was 5.1 per cent.

(a) What was the average real return on British Auto's shares?

(b) What was the average nominal risk premium on British Auto's shares?

(c) What was the average real risk-free rate over this time period? What was the average real risk premium?

17 Holding Period Return A firm had the following share prices: Jan 2019: £1.12; Jan 2020: £1.34; Jan 2021: £1.68; Jan 2022: £1.8825; Jan 2023: £2.18; Jan 2024: £2.07. The equity paid no dividends. What was the holding period return?

18 Return Distributions Refer to Table 9.3. What range of risk premiums would you expect to see 68 per cent of the time for Europe? What about 95 per cent of the time?

19 Blume's Formula Over a 30-year period an asset had an arithmetic return of 12 per cent and a geometric return of 10 per cent. Using Blume's formula, what is your best estimate of the future annual returns over five years? 10 years? 20 years?

20 Arithmetic and Geometric Returns An equity has had returns of 10 per cent, 15 per cent, 20 per cent, –12 per cent, 2 per cent and –5 per cent over the past six years. What are its arithmetic and geometric returns?

21 Calculating Arithmetic and Geometric Returns An equity has had the following year-end prices and dividends:

Year	Price (£)	Dividend (£)
1	43.12	–
2	49.07	0.55
3	51.19	0.60
4	47.24	0.63
5	56.09	0.72
6	67.21	0.81

What are the arithmetic and geometric returns?

22 Calculating Investment Returns You bought one of Bergen Manufacturing's 8 per cent coupon bonds one year ago for NKr1,028.50. These bonds make annual payments and mature six years from now. Suppose you decide to sell your bonds today, when the required return on the bonds is 7 per cent. If the inflation rate was 4.8 per cent over the past year, what would be your total real return on the investment?

23 Using Return Distributions Suppose the returns on your company are normally distributed. The historical average share price return for your firm is 5.8 per cent, with a standard deviation of 9.3 per cent. What is the approximate probability that your return will be less than –3.5 per cent in a given year? What range of returns would you expect to see 95 per cent of the time? What range would you expect to see 99 per cent of the time?

24 Using Return Distributions to Estimate Probabilities Assume that the returns from holding French shares are normally distributed. From Table 9.2, what is the approximate normal distribution probability that your money will double in value in a single year? Triple in value?

25 **Distributions: Downside Risk** In the previous problem, what is the probability that the return is less than –100 per cent? (Think.) What are the implications for the distribution of returns?

26 **Using Return Distributions** Suppose the mean returns on long-term government bonds are 5.8 per cent, and are normally distributed with a standard deviation of 9.3 per cent. Based on the historical record, what is the approximate probability that your return on these bonds will be less than –3.5 per cent in a given year? What range of returns would you expect to see 95 per cent of the time? What range would you expect to see 99 per cent of the time?

27 **Distributions using Historical Data** Your investment portfolio has earned returns of 400 per cent once in the last 10 years, 0 per cent in eight out of the last 10 years and lost 90 per cent one year. What was the average arithmetic return and standard deviation of returns for this portfolio?

28 **Inflation** The inflation rates for the UK have been as follows: 2023: 9.2 per cent; 2022: 11.1 per cent; 2021: 2.52 per cent; 2020: 0.99 per cent; and in 2019: 1.74 per cent. Calculate the average real return of Lockhart Group and TJC from Question 13.

CHALLENGE

29 **Calculating Returns: Real Data** Go to the Yahoo! Finance website and look up any FTSE 100 company of your choice. Click on the Historical Prices link. Find its closing price yesterday and its closing price exactly one year earlier. From the historical prices on Yahoo! Finance you will see the total dividend paid out in the last year. What has been the annual return on the company? What was the dividend yield? The capital gains yield?

30 **Value at Risk** The monthly prices for Banco Ruida are as follows:

Date	Adj. Close
Mar 2024	514.2
Feb 2024	518
Jan 2024	493.35
Dec 2023	492.75
Nov 2023	473
Oct 2023	533
Sep 2023	539
Aug 2023	564
Jul 2023	640
Jun 2023	715
May 2023	720
Apr 2023	763
Mar 2023	714
Feb 2023	758
Jan 2023	764.5
Dec 2022	685.5
Nov 2022	610.5
Oct 2022	796.24

Assume you have €1 million invested in the bank. Calculate the analytical VaR for Banco Ruida using a monthly holding period and 1 per cent loss probability. What is the main limitation of the value-at-risk method?

Exam Question (45 minutes)

You have invested in the Mauritian stock market. Details on the performance of the market are given below:

Date	Mauritius
Jan-17	100
Jan-18	119.25
Jan-19	134.57
Jan-20	125.32
Jan-21	88.24
Jan-22	112.08
Jan-23	128.43
Jan-24	118.00

1 Calculate the average arithmetic returns, the variances and the standard deviations for Mauritius. **(30 marks)**

2 Calculate the geometric return on the Mauritius Stock Market and compare it to the arithmetic return. Comment on and explain the differences between the Mauritius arithmetic and geometric return. **(20 marks)**

3 What was the holding period return on Mauritius equities over the period? **(10 marks)**

4 Suppose the returns on Mauritius equities are normally distributed. Based on the data above, what is the approximate probability that your return on these will be less than –2 per cent in a given year? What range of returns would you expect to see 95 per cent of the time? What range would you expect to see 99 per cent of the time? **(20 marks)**

5 Review the difficulties in using historical data to measure expected returns on an investment. **(20 marks)**

Total Marks: 100

Mini Case

A Job at West Coast Yachts, Part 1

You recently graduated from university, and your job search led you to West Coast Yachts at Kip Marina. Because you felt the company's business was seaworthy, you accepted a job offer. The first day on the job, while you are finishing your employment paperwork, Dan Ervin, who works in Finance, stops by to inform you about the company's retirement plan.

Retirement plans are offered by many companies and are tax-deferred savings vehicles, meaning that any deposits you make into the plan are deducted from your current pretax income, so no current taxes are paid on the money. For example, assume your salary will be £50,000 per year. If you contribute £3,000 to the plan, you will pay taxes on only £47,000 in income. There are also no taxes paid on any capital gains or income while you are invested in the plan, but you do pay taxes when you withdraw money at retirement. As is fairly common, the company also has 5 per cent matched funding. This means that the company will match your contribution up to 5 per cent of your salary, but you must contribute to get the match.

The retirement plan has several options for investments, most of which are mutual funds. A mutual fund is a portfolio of assets. When you purchase shares in a mutual fund, you are actually purchasing partial ownership of the fund's assets. The return of the fund is the weighted average of the return of the assets owned by the fund, minus any expenses. The largest expense is typically the management fee, paid to the fund manager. The management fee is compensation for the manager, who makes all of the investment decisions for the fund.

West Coast Yachts uses Skandla Life Assurance Company Ltd as its retirement plan administrator. Here are the investment options offered for employees:

- **Company Shares** One option in the retirement plan is equity ownership of West Coast Yachts. The company is currently privately held. However, when you interviewed with the owner, Larissa Warren, she informed you the company shares were expected to go public in the next three to four years. Until then, a company share price is simply set each year by the board of directors.

- **Skandla Market Index Fund** This mutual fund tracks the FTSE 100 Index. Equities in the fund are weighted exactly the same as the FTSE 100. This means the fund return is approximately the return on the FTSE 100, minus expenses. Because an index fund purchases assets based on the composition of the index it is following, the fund manager is not required to research stocks and make investment decisions. The result is that the fund expenses are usually low. The Skandla Index Fund charges expenses of 0.15 per cent of assets per year.
- **Skandla Small-Cap Fund** This fund invests primarily in small-capitalization companies. As such, the returns of the fund are more volatile. The fund can also invest 10 per cent of its assets in companies based outside the United Kingdom. This fund charges 1.70 per cent in expenses.
- **Skandla Large-Company Equity Fund** This fund invests primarily in large-capitalization companies based in the United Kingdom. The fund is managed by Evan Skandla and has outperformed the market in six of the last eight years. The fund charges 1.50 per cent in expenses.
- **Skandla Bond Fund** This fund invests in long-term corporate bonds issued by UK-domiciled companies. The fund is restricted to investments in bonds with an investment-grade credit rating. This fund charges 1.40 per cent in expenses.
- **Skandla Money Market Fund** This fund invests in short-term, high-credit quality debt instruments, which include Treasury bills. As such, the return on the money market fund is only slightly higher than the return on Treasury bills. Because of the credit quality and short-term nature of the investments, there is only a very slight risk of negative return. The fund charges 0.60 per cent in expenses.

1 What advantages do the mutual funds offer compared to the company equity?

2 Assume that you invest 5 per cent of your salary and receive the full 5 per cent match from West Coast Yachts. What APR do you earn from the match? What conclusions do you draw about matching plans?

3 Assume you decide you should invest at least part of your money in large-capitalization companies based in the United Kingdom. What are the advantages and disadvantages of choosing the Skandla Large-Company Equity Fund compared to the Skandla Market Index Fund?

4 The returns on the Skandla Small-Cap Fund are the most volatile of all the mutual funds offered in the retirement plan. Why would you ever want to invest in this fund? When you examine the expenses of the mutual funds, you will notice that this fund also has the highest expenses. Does this affect your decision to invest in this fund?

5 A measure of risk-adjusted performance that is often used is the Sharpe ratio. The Sharpe ratio is calculated as the risk premium of an asset divided by its standard deviation. The standard deviation and return of the funds over the past 10 years are listed here. Calculate the Sharpe ratio for each of these funds. Assume that the expected return and standard deviation of the company equity will be 18 per cent and 70 per cent, respectively. Calculate the Sharpe ratio for the company shares. How appropriate is the Sharpe ratio for these assets? When would you use the Sharpe ratio?

	10-year Annual Return (%)	Standard Deviation (%)
Skandla Market Index Fund	11.48	15.82
Skandla Small-Cap Fund	16.68	19.64
Skandla Large-Company Equity Fund	11.85	15.41
Skandla Bond Fund	9.67	10.83

6 What portfolio allocation would you choose? Why? Explain your thinking carefully.

Practical Case Study

1 **Calculating Yields** Download the historical monthly share prices for a company of your choice from Yahoo! Finance. Find the closing share price for yesterday and for exactly two years ago. The dividends should also be listed in the monthly price series. What was the capital gains yield and dividend yield for your equity for each of these years? Now calculate the capital gains yield and dividend yield for another company from the same country. How do the returns for these two companies compare?

2 **Calculating Average Returns** Download the monthly adjusted share prices for a company of your choice. What is the return on the equity over the past 12 months? Now use the 1 month total return and calculate the average monthly return. Is this one-twelfth of the annual return you calculated? Why, or why not? What is the monthly standard deviation of your company's shares over the past year?

Relevant Accounting Standards

Now that we are moving into the realms of financial markets, accountancy standards take on less importance. However, one standard that has received a lot of attention in recent years is IAS 39 *Financial Instruments: Recognition and Measurement*. This standard guides the accountant on how all financial instruments should be presented in a company's financial statements. In addition, you should also be aware of IFRS 7 *Financial Instruments: Disclosure*. Visit the IASPlus website (www.iasplus.com) for more information.

References

Dimson, E., P. Marsh and M. Staunton (2002) *Triumph of the Optimists*. Princeton, NJ: Princeton University Press.

Dimson, E., P. Marsh and M. Staunton (2011) 'Equity Premia around the World', in P.B. Hammond, M.L. Leibowitz and L.B. Siegel (eds), *Rethinking the Equity Risk Premium* (CFA Institute).

Additional Reading

Although cryptocurrencies can be viewed as an alternative asset class, they are not yet established enough to be included at this time in many broad-based portfolios. However, that doesn't stop researchers from investigating cryptocurrencies. The following paper examines return distributions of this asset class.

Liu, Y. and A. Tsyvinski (2021) 'Risks and Returns of Cryptocurrency', *Review of Financial Studies*, Vol. 34, No. 6, 2689–2727.

Cochrane has proposed two conceptual frameworks for forming portfolios that improve on standard methods. The following is a fairly complex paper so read at your own risk!

Cochrane, J.H. (2022) 'Portfolios for Long-term Investors', *Review of Finance*, Vol. 26, No. 1, 1–42.

Other papers worth reading are:

1 Barrot, J.N., E. Loualiche and J. Sauvagnat (2019) 'The Globalization Risk Premium', *Journal of Finance*, Vol. 74, No. 5, 2391–2439.

2 Bartram, S.M., J.M. Griffin, T.H. Lim and D.T. Ng (2015) 'How Important are Foreign Ownership Linkages for International Stock Returns?', *Review of Financial Studies*, Vol. 28, No. 11, 3036–3072.

3 Bekaert, G., R.J. Hodrick and X. Zhang (2009) 'International Stock Return Comovements', *Journal of Finance*, Vol. 64, No. 6, 2591–2626.

4 Braione, M. and N.K. Scholtes (2016) 'Forecasting Value-at-risk under Different Distributional Assumptions', *Econometrics*, Vol. 4, No. 1, 3.

5 Diaz, E.M., J.C. Molero and F.P. de Gracia (2016) 'Oil Price Volatility and Stock Returns in the G7 Economies', *Energy Economics*, Vol. 54, 417–430.

6 Gay, R.D. (2016) 'Effect of Macroeconomic Variables on Stock Market Returns for Four Emerging Economies: Brazil, Russia, India, and China', *International Business & Economics Research Journal* (online), Vol. 15, No. 3, 119.

7 Lundblad, C. (2007) 'The Risk Return Tradeoff in the Long Run: 1836–2003', *Journal of Financial Economics*, Vol. 85, No. 1, 123–150.

8 Marimoutoi, V., B. Raggad and A. Tabelsi (2009) 'Extreme Value Theory and Value at Risk: Application to Oil Market', *Energy Economics*, Vol. 31, No. 4, 519–530.

9 Yuan, Y. (2015) 'Market-wide Attention, Trading, and Stock Returns', *Journal of Financial Economics*, Vol. 116, No. 3, 548–564.

Endnote

1 The data used in this chapter are available via the Online Learning Centre in Connect.

Chapter 10
Risk and Return: The Capital Asset Pricing Model

Learning Objectives

After reading this chapter you should be able to:

LO1 Explain the concepts of expected return, variance and covariance, and their significance in the context of individual securities and portfolio management.

LO2 Calculate the return and risk for portfolios, given the necessary information on individual securities, and construct the efficient set for two or more assets.

LO3 Analyse the effects of diversification on portfolio risk, and the implications of riskless borrowing and lending in the market.

LO4 Evaluate the assumptions and implications of market equilibrium and the capital asset pricing model (CAPM) in determining the relationship between risk and return.

LO5 Critique the CAPM by examining its limitations and explore alternative variations of the model that address these criticisms.

Expected returns on equities can vary quite a bit. One determinant is the industry in which a company operates. For example, in 2022, commodities grew by 22 per cent, whereas property (REITs) fell 23.6 per cent over the same period.

These estimates raise some obvious questions. First, why do industry returns differ so much, and how are these specific numbers calculated? Also, does the higher return offered by commodities mean that investors should prefer these to, say, the property sector? As we will see in this chapter, the answers to these questions form the basis of our modern understanding of risk and return.

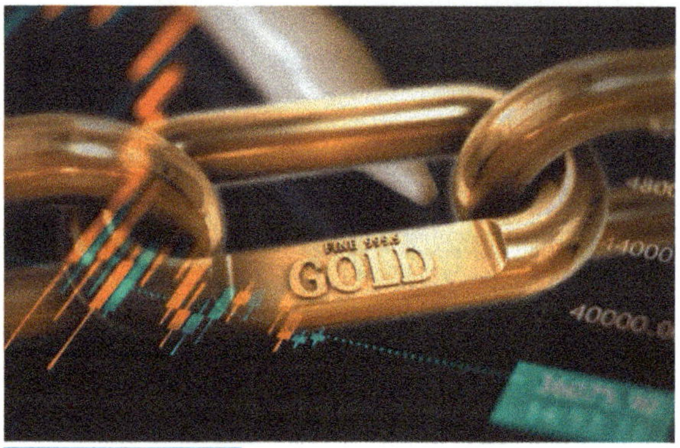

Source: pedrosek/123RF.

Key Notations

R_{it}	Return on security i at time t	R_F	The risk-free rate of return
Var or σ^2	Variance	R_M	The market rate of return
SD or σ	Standard deviation	β	Beta or systematic risk of a security
ρ_{AB}	Correlation between A and B	SML	Security market line
Cov(A, B)	Covariance between A and B	CAPM	Capital asset pricing model
X_A	The weight of an asset or security, A, in a portfolio	PE	Price–earnings ratio
N	Number of assets or securities in a portfolio	BM	Book value of equity to market value of equity ratio

10.1 Individual Securities

In the first part of this chapter, we will examine the characteristics of individual securities. In particular, we will discuss the following.

1 *Expected return:* This is the return that an individual expects a security to earn over the next period. Of course, because this is only an expectation, the actual return may be either higher or lower. An individual's expectation may simply be the average return per period a security has earned in the past. Alternatively, it may be based on a detailed analysis of a firm's prospects, on some computer-based model, or special (or inside) information. The expected return is usually calculated as a probability-weighted average of expected future returns in different economic states.

2 *Variance and standard deviation:* There are many ways to assess the volatility of a security's return. One of the most common is variance, which is a measure of the squared deviations of a security's return from its expected return. Standard deviation is the square root of the variance.

3 *Covariance and correlation:* Returns on individual securities are related to one another. Covariance is a statistic measuring the interrelationship between two securities. Alternatively, we can restate this relationship in terms of the correlation between the two securities. Covariance and correlation are building blocks to an understanding of the beta coefficient.

10.2 Expected Return, Variance and Covariance

Expected Return and Variance

Suppose financial analysts believe that there are four equally likely states of the economy: depression, recession, normal and boom. The returns on 'Supertech' are expected to follow the economy closely, while the returns on 'Slowburn' are not. The return predictions are as follows:

	Supertech Returns R_{At} (%)	Slowburn Returns R_{Bt} (%)
Depression	−20	5
Recession	10	20
Normal	30	−12
Boom	50	9

Variance can be calculated in four steps. An additional step is needed to calculate standard deviation. (The calculations are presented in Table 10.1.) The steps are as follows.

1 Calculate the expected return:

Supertech

$$\frac{-0.20 + 0.10 + 0.30 + 0.50}{4} = 0.175 = 17.5\% = \overline{R}_A$$

Table 10.1 Calculating Variance and Standard Deviation

(1) State of Economy	(2) Rate of Return Supertech*	(3) Deviation from Expected Return (Expected Return = 0.175)	(4) Squared Value of Deviation
	R_{At}	$(R_{At} - \overline{R}_A)$	$(R_{At} - \overline{R}_A)^2$
Depression	−0.20	−0.375	0.140625
		$(= -0.20 - 0.175)$	$[= (-0.375)^2]$
Recession	0.10	−0.075	0.005625
Normal	0.30	0.125	0.015625

(1) State of Economy	(2) Rate of Return Supertech*	(3) Deviation from Expected Return (Expected Return = 0.175)	(4) Squared Value of Deviation
Boom	0.50	0.325	0.105625
			0.267500
	Slowburn†	(Expected Return 0.055)	
	R_{Bt}	$(R_{Bt} - \overline{R}_B)$	$(R_{Bt} - \overline{R}_B)^2$
Depression	0.05	−0.005	0.000025
		(= 0.05 − 0.055)	[= (− 0.005)²]
Recession	0.20	0.145	0.021025
Normal	−0.12	−0.175	0.030625
Boom	0.09	0.035	0.001225
			0.052900

$$*\overline{R} = \frac{-0.20 + 0.10 + 0.30 + 0.50}{4} = 0.175 = 17.5\%$$

$$\text{Var}(R_A) = \sigma_A^2 = \frac{0.2675}{4} = 0.066875$$

$$\text{SD}(R_A) = \sigma_A = \sqrt{0.066875} = 0.2586 = 25.86\%$$

$$\dagger\overline{R}_B = \frac{0.05 + 0.20 - 0.12 + 0.09}{4} = 0.055 = 5.5\%$$

$$\text{Var}(R_B) = \sigma_B^2 = \frac{0.0529}{4} = 0.013225$$

$$\text{SD}(R_B) = \sigma_B = \sqrt{0.013225} = 0.1150 = 11.50\%$$

Slowburn

$$\frac{0.05 + 0.20 - 0.12 + 0.09}{4} = 0.055 = 5.5\% = \overline{R}_B$$

2 For each company, calculate the deviation of each possible return from the company's expected return given previously. This is presented in column 3 of Table 10.1.

3 The deviations we have calculated are indications of the dispersion of returns. However, because some are positive and some are negative, it is difficult to work with them in this form. For example, if we were to simply add up all the deviations for a single company, we would get zero as the sum.

To make the deviations more meaningful, we multiply each one by itself. Now all the numbers are positive, implying that their sum must be positive as well. The squared deviations are presented in column 4 of Table 10.1.

4 For each company, calculate the average squared deviation, which is the variance:[1]

Supertech

$$\frac{0.140625 + 0.005625 + 0.015625 + 0.105625}{4} = 0.066875$$

Slowburn

$$\frac{0.000025 + 0.021025 + 0.030625 + 0.001225}{4} = 0.013225$$

Thus, the variance of Supertech is 0.066875, and the variance of Slowburn is 0.013225.

5 Calculate standard deviation by taking the square root of the variance:

Supertech

$$\sqrt{0.066875} = 0.2586 = 25.86\%$$

Slowburn

$$\sqrt{0.013225} = 0.1150 = 11.50\%$$

Algebraically, the formula for variance can be expressed as:

$$\text{var}(R) = \textit{Expected value of}(R - \overline{R})^2$$

where $\overline{R}$ is the security's expected return and R is the actual return.

A look at the four-step calculation for variance makes it clear why it is a measure of the spread of the sample of returns. For each observation we square the difference between the actual return and the expected return. We then take an average of these squared differences. Squaring the differences makes them all positive. If we used the differences between each return and the expected return and then averaged these differences, we would get zero because the returns that were above the mean would cancel the ones below.

Chapter 9 Page 247

However, because the variance is still expressed in squared terms, it is difficult to interpret. Standard deviation has a much simpler interpretation, which was provided in Section 9.5. Standard deviation is simply the square root of the variance. The general formula for the standard deviation is:

$$\text{SD}(R) = \sqrt{\text{Var}(R)}$$

Covariance and Correlation

Variance and standard deviation measure the variability of individual securities. We now wish to measure the relationship between the return on one security and the return on another. This brings us to covariance and correlation.

Covariance and correlation measure how two random variables are related. We explain these terms by extending the Supertech and Slowburn example.

Example 10.1

Calculating Covariance and Correlation

We have already determined the expected returns and standard deviations for both Supertech and Slowburn. (The expected returns are 0.175 and 0.055 for Supertech and Slowburn, respectively. The standard deviations are 0.2586 and 0.1150, respectively.) In addition, we calculated the deviation of each possible return from the expected return for each firm. Using these data, we can calculate covariance in two steps. An extra step is needed to calculate correlation.

1 For each state of the economy, multiply Supertech's deviation from its expected return and Slowburn's deviation from its expected return together. For example, Supertech's rate of return in a depression is −0.20, which is −0.375(= −0.20 − 0.175) from its expected return. Slowburn's rate of return in a depression is 0.05, which is 0.005(= 0.05 − 0.055) from its expected return. Multiplying the two deviations together yields 0.001875[= (− 0.375) × (0.005)]. The actual calculations are given in the last column of Table 10.2. This procedure can be written algebraically as:

Equation 10.1

$$(R_{At} - \overline{R}_A) \times (R_{Bt} - \overline{R}_B)$$

where R_{At} and R_{Bt} are the returns on Supertech and Slowburn in state t. $\overline{R}_A$ and $\overline{R}_B$ are the expected returns on the two securities.

$$\sigma_{A,B} = \text{Cov}(R_A, R_B) = \frac{-0.0195}{4} = -0.004875$$

$$\rho_{A,B} = \text{Corr}(R_A, R_B) = \frac{\text{Cov}(R_A, R_B)}{\text{SD}(R_A) \times \text{SD}(R_B)} = \frac{-0.004875}{0.2586 \times 0.1150} = -0.1639$$

2 Calculate the average value of the four states in the last column. This average is the covariance. That is:[2]

$$\sigma_{A,B} = \text{Cov}(R_A, R_B) = \frac{-0.0195}{4} = -0.004875$$

Note that we represent the covariance between Supertech and Slowburn as either $\text{Cov}(R_A, R_B)$ or $\sigma_{A,B}$. Equation 10.1 illustrates the intuition of covariance. Suppose Supertech's return is generally above its average when Slowburn's return is above its average, and Supertech's return is generally below its average when Slowburn's return is below its average. This shows a positive dependency or a positive relationship between the two returns. Note that the term in Equation 10.1 will be *positive* in any state where both returns are *above* their averages. In addition, Equation 10.1 will still be *positive* in any state where both terms are *below* their averages. Thus a positive relationship between the two returns will give rise to a positive value for covariance.

Table 10.2 Calculating Covariance and Correlation

State of Economy	Rate of Return of Supertech R_{At}	Deviation from Expected Return $(R_{At}-\overline{R}_A)$	Rate of Return of Slowburn R_{Bt}	Deviation from Expected Return $(R_{Bt}-\overline{R}_B)$	Product of Deviations $(R_{At}-\overline{R}_A)(R_{Bt}-\overline{R}_B)$
		(Expected return = 0.175)		(Expected return = 0.055)	
Depression	−0.20	−0.375 (= −0.20 − 0.175)	0.05	−0.005 (= 0.05 − 0.055)	0.001875 (= −0.375 × −0.005)
Recession	0.10	−0.075	0.20	0.145	0.001875 (= −0.075 × −0.145)
Normal	0.30	0.125	−0.12	−0.175	−0.021875 (= 0.125 × −0.175)
Boom	0.50	0.325	0.09	0.035	0.011375 (= 0.325 × 0.035)
	0.70		0.22		−0.0195

Conversely, suppose Supertech's return is generally above its average when Slowburn's return is below its average, and Supertech's return is generally below its average when Slowburn's return is above its average. This demonstrates a negative dependency or a negative relationship between the two returns. Note that the term in Equation 10.1 will be *negative* in any state where one return is above its average and the other return is below its average. Thus a negative relationship between the two returns will give rise to a negative value for covariance.

Finally, suppose there is no relationship between the two returns. In this case, knowing whether the return on Supertech is above or below its expected return tells us nothing about the return on Slowburn. In the covariance formula, then, there will be no tendency for the deviations to be positive or negative together. On average, they will tend to offset each other and cancel out, making the covariance zero.

Of course, even if the two returns are unrelated to each other, the covariance formula will not equal zero exactly in any actual history. This is due to sampling error; randomness alone will make the calculation positive or negative. But for a historical sample that is long enough, if the two returns are not related to each other, we should expect the covariance to come close to zero.

The covariance formula seems to capture what we are looking for. If the two returns are positively related to each other, they will have a positive covariance, and if they are negatively related to each other, the covariance will be negative. Last, and very important, if they are unrelated, the covariance should be zero.

The formula for covariance can be written algebraically as:

$$\sigma_{A,B} = \text{Cov}(R_A, R_B) = \text{Expected value of } [(R_A - \overline{R}_A) \times (R_B - \overline{R}_B)]$$

where $\overline{R}_A$ and $\overline{R}_B$ are the expected returns for the two securities, and R_A and R_B are the actual returns. The ordering of the two variables is unimportant. That is, the covariance of A with B is equal to the covariance of B with A. This can be stated more formally as $\text{Cov}(R_A, R_B) = \text{Cov}(R_B, R_A)$ or $\sigma_{A,B} = \sigma_{B,A}$.

The covariance we calculated is −0.004875. A negative number like this implies that the return on one security is likely to be above its average when the return on the other security is below its average, and vice versa. However, the size of the number is difficult to interpret. Like the variance figure, the covariance is in squared deviation units. Until we can put it in perspective, we do not know what to make of it.

We solve the problem by computing the correlation.

3 To calculate the correlation, divide the covariance by the standard deviations of both of the two securities. For our example, we have:

Equation 10.2
$$\sigma_{A,B} = \text{Corr}(R_A, R_B) = \frac{\text{Cov}(R_A, R_B)}{\sigma_A \times \sigma_B} = \frac{-0.004875}{0.2586 \times 0.1150} = -0.1639$$

where σ_A and σ_B are the standard deviations of Supertech and Slowburn, respectively. Note that we represent the correlation between Supertech and Slowburn either as $\text{Corr}(R_A, R_B)$ or $\rho_{A,B}$. As with covariance, the ordering of the two variables is unimportant. That is, the correlation of A with B is equal to the correlation of B with A. More formally, $\text{Corr}(R_A, R_B) = \text{Corr}(R_A, R_B)$ or $\rho_{A,B} = \rho_{B,A}$.

Because the standard deviation is always positive, the sign of the correlation between two variables must be the same as that of the covariance between the two variables. If the correlation is positive, we say that the variables are *positively correlated;* if it is negative, we say that they are *negatively correlated;* and if it is zero, we say that they are *uncorrelated*. Furthermore, it can be proved that the correlation is always between −1 and +1. This is due to the standardizing procedure of dividing by the two standard deviations.

We can compare the correlation between different *pairs* of securities. For example, it turns out that the correlation between Persimmon and Bovis (both construction companies) is much higher than the correlation between Persimmon and AstraZeneca (a pharmaceutical firm). Hence, we can state that the first pair of securities is more interrelated than the second pair.

Figure 10.1 shows the three benchmark cases for two assets, A and B. The figure shows two assets with return correlations of +1, −1 and 0. This implies perfect positive correlation, perfect negative correlation, and no correlation, respectively. The graphs in the figure plot the separate returns on the two securities through time:

Figure 10.1 Examples of Different Correlation Coefficients – Graphs Plotting the Separate Returns on Two Securities through Time

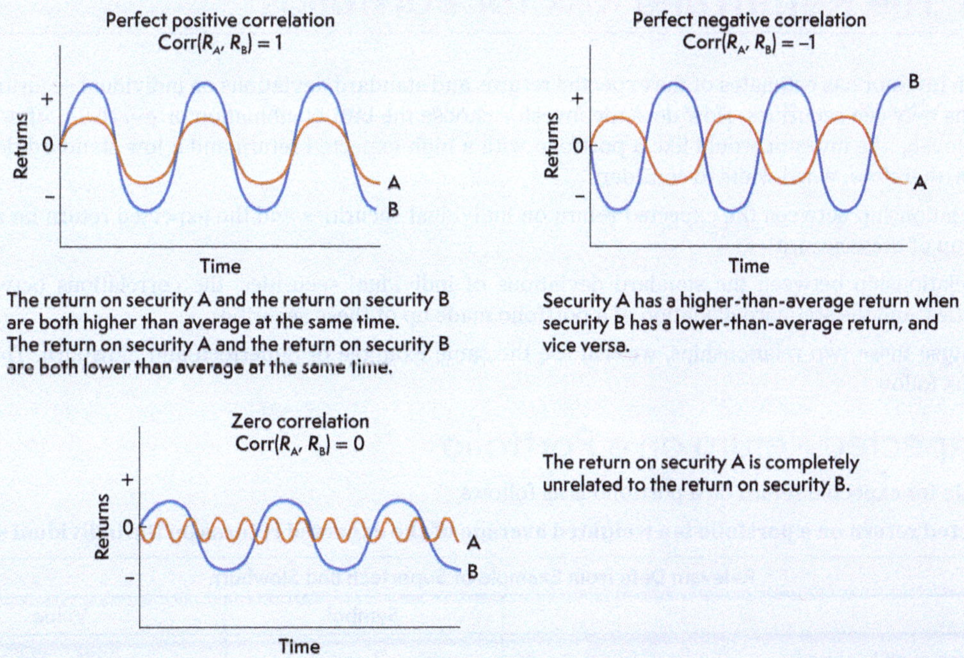

Real World Insight 10.1

Deutsche Bank and Deutsche Telekom

As their names suggest, both Deutsche Bank and Deutsche Telekom are German firms operating in the banking and telecommunications sectors. Given that they are large companies and come from the same country, it is likely that the returns on each company will be correlated with each other. This is the case with the correlation between both company's monthly returns equal to 0.40 using data between 2018 and 2023 (see Figure 10.2). A scatterplot of monthly returns is given in the figure. Although the correlation is quite high, there is still a lot of variation between the two companies.

Figure 10.2 Deutsche Telekom–Deutsche Bank Monthly Returns 2018–2023

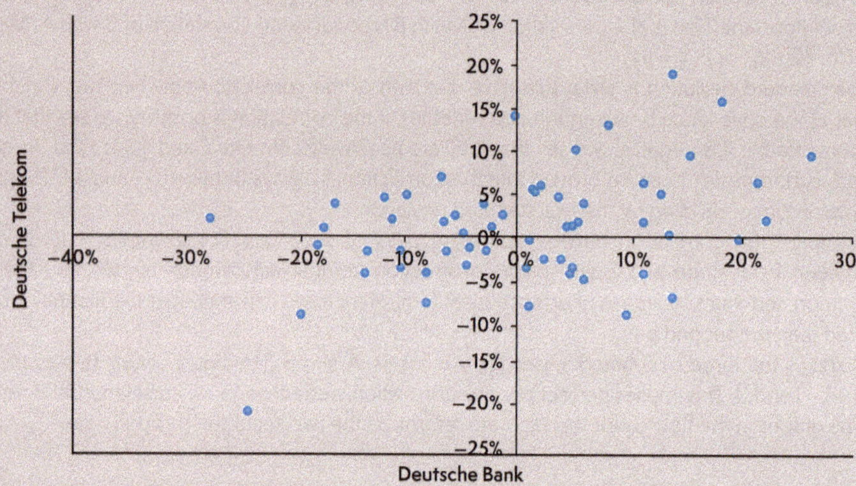

10.3 The Return and Risk for Portfolios

Suppose an investor has estimates of the expected returns and standard deviations on individual securities and the correlations between securities. How does the investor choose the best combination or **portfolio** of securities to hold? Obviously, the investor would like a portfolio with a high expected return and a low standard deviation of return. It is, therefore, worthwhile to consider:

1 The relationship between the expected return on individual securities and the expected return on a portfolio made up of these securities.

2 The relationship between the standard deviations of individual securities, the correlations between these securities, and the standard deviation of a portfolio made up of these securities.

To analyse these two relationships, we will use the same example of Supertech and Slowburn. The relevant calculations follow.

The Expected Return on a Portfolio

The formula for expected return on a portfolio is as follows:

The expected return on a portfolio is a weighted average of the expected returns on the individual securities.

Relevant Data from Example of Supertech and Slowburn		
Item	Symbol	Value
Expected return on Supertech	$\bar{R}_{Super}$	0.175 = 17.5%
Expected return on Slowburn	$\bar{R}_{Slow}$	0.055 = 5.5%

Relevant Data from Example of Supertech and Slowburn		
Item	**Symbol**	**Value**
Variance of Supertech	σ^2_{Super}	0.066875
Variance of Slowburn	σ^2_{Slow}	0.013225
The standard deviation of Supertech	σ_{Super}	0.2586 = 25.86%
The standard deviation of Slowburn	σ_{Slow}	0.1150 = 11.50%
Covariance between Supertech and Slowburn	$\sigma_{Super, Slow}$	−0.004875
Correlation between Supertech and Slowburn	$\rho_{Super, Slow}$	−0.1639

Example 10.2

Portfolio Expected Returns

Consider Supertech and Slowburn. From our earlier calculations, we find that the expected returns on these two securities are 17.5 per cent and 5.5 per cent, respectively.

The expected return on a portfolio of these two securities alone can be written as:

$$\text{Expected return on portfolio} = X_{Super}(17.5\%) + X_{Slow}(5.5\%) = \bar{R}_p$$

where X_{Super} is the percentage of the portfolio in Supertech and X_{Slow} is the percentage of the portfolio in Slowburn. If the investor with £100 invests £60 in Supertech and £40 in Slowburn, the expected return on the portfolio can be written as:

$$\text{Expected return on portfolio} = 0.6 \times 17.5\% + 0.4 \times 5.5\% = 12.7\%$$

Algebraically, we can write:

Equation 10.3

$$\text{Expected return on portfolio} = X_A\bar{R}_A + X_B\bar{R}_B = \bar{R}_p$$

where X_A and X_B are the proportions of the total portfolio in the assets A and B, respectively. (Because our investor can invest in only two securities, $X_A + X_B$ must equal 1 or 100 per cent.) $\bar{R}_A$ and $\bar{R}_B$ are the expected returns on the two securities.

Now consider two securities, each with an expected return of 10 per cent. The expected return on a portfolio composed of these two securities must be 10 per cent, regardless of the proportions of the two securities held. This result may seem obvious at this point, but it will become important later. The result implies that you do not reduce or *dissipate* your expected return by investing in several securities. Rather, the expected return on your portfolio is a weighted average of the expected returns on the individual assets in the portfolio.

Variance and Standard Deviation of a Portfolio

The formula for the variance of a portfolio composed of two securities, A and B, is:

The variance of the portfolio:

$$\text{Var (portfolio)} = X_A^2\sigma_A^2 + 2X_AX_B\sigma_{A,B} + X_B^2\sigma_B^2$$

Note that there are three terms on the right side of the equation. The first term involves the variance of A, (σ_A^2), the second term involves the covariance between the two securities, ($\sigma_{A,B}$), and the third term involves the variance of B, (σ_B^2). (As stated earlier in this chapter, $\sigma_{A,B} = \sigma_{B,A}$. That is, the ordering of the variables is not relevant when we are expressing the covariance between two securities.)

The formula indicates an important point. The variance of a portfolio depends on both the variances of the individual securities and the covariance between the two securities. The variance of a security measures the variability of an individual security's return. Covariance measures the relationship between the two securities. For given variances of the individual securities, a positive relationship or covariance between the two securities increases the variance of the entire portfolio. A negative relationship or covariance between the two securities decreases the variance of the entire portfolio. This important result seems to square with common sense. If one of your securities tends to go up when the other goes down, or vice versa, your two securities are offsetting each other. You are achieving what we call a *hedge* in finance, and the risk of your entire portfolio will be low. However, if both your securities rise and fall together, you are not hedging at all. Hence, the risk of your entire portfolio will be higher.

The variance formula for our two securities, Super and Slow, is:

Equation 10.4

$$\text{Var (portfolio)} = X^2_{\text{Super}}\sigma^2_{\text{Super}} + 2X_{\text{Super}}X_{\text{Super}}\sigma_{\text{Super, Slow}} + X^2_{\text{Super}}\sigma^2_{\text{Super}}$$

Given our earlier assumption that an individual with £100 invests £60 in Supertech and £40 in Slowburn, X Super = 0.6 and X Slow = 0.4. Using this assumption and the relevant data from our previous calculations, the variance of the portfolio is:

$$0.023851 = 0.36 \times 0.066875 + 2 \times [0.6 \times 0.4 \times (-0.004875)] + 0.16 \times 0.013225$$

The Matrix Approach

Alternatively, Equation 10.4 can be expressed in the following matrix format:

Supertech	$X^2_{\text{Super}}\sigma^2_{\text{Super}}$ 0.024075 = 0.36 × 0.0066875	$X_{\text{Super}}X_{\text{Slow}}\sigma_{\text{Super, Slow}}$ −0.00117 = 0.6 × 0.4 × (− 0.004875)
Slowburn	$X_{\text{Super}}X_{\text{Slow}}\sigma_{\text{Super, Slow}}$ −0.00117 = 0.6 × 0.4 × (− 0.004875)	$X^2_{\text{Super}}\sigma^2_{\text{Slow}}$ 0.002116 = 0.16 × 0.013225

There are four boxes in the matrix. We can add the terms in the boxes to obtain Equation 10.4, the variance of a portfolio composed of the two securities. The term in the upper left corner involves the variance of Supertech. The term in the lower right corner involves the variance of Slowburn. The other two boxes contain the term involving the covariance. These two boxes are identical, indicating why the covariance term is multiplied by 2 in Equation 10.4.

At this point, students often find the box approach to be more confusing than Equation 10.4. However, the box approach is easily generalized to more than two securities, a task we perform later in this chapter.

Standard Deviation of a Portfolio

Given Equation 10.4, we can now determine the standard deviation of the portfolio's return. This is:

Equation 10.5

$$\sigma_p = \text{SD(potfolio)} = \sqrt{\text{Var(portfolio)}} = \sqrt{0.023851}$$
$$= 0.1544 = 15.44\%$$

The interpretation of the standard deviation of the portfolio is the same as the interpretation of the standard deviation of an individual security. The expected return on our portfolio is 12.7 per cent. A return of −2.74 per cent (=12.7% − 15.44%) is one standard deviation below the mean, and a return of 28.14 per cent (=12.7% + 15.44%) is one standard deviation above the mean. If the return on the portfolio is normally distributed, a return between −2.74 per cent and +28.14 per cent and occurs about 68 per cent of the time.[3]

The Diversification Effect

It is instructive to compare the standard deviation of the portfolio with the standard deviation of the individual securities. The weighted average of the standard deviations of the individual securities is:

Equation 10.6

$$\text{Weighted average of standard deviations} = X_{\text{Super}}\sigma_{\text{Super}} + X_{\text{Slow}}\sigma_{\text{Slow}}$$
$$0.2012 = 0.\text{ss} \times 0.2586 + 0.4 \times 0.115$$

One of the most important results in this chapter concerns the difference between Equations 10.5 and 10.6. In our example, the standard deviation of the portfolio is *less* than a weighted average of the standard deviations of the individual securities.

We pointed out earlier that the expected return on the portfolio is a weighted average of the expected returns on the individual securities. Thus, we get a different type of result for the standard deviation of a portfolio than we do for the expected return on a portfolio.

It is generally argued that our result for the standard deviation of a portfolio is due to diversification. For example, Supertech and Slowburn are slightly negatively correlated ($\rho = -0.1639$). Supertech's return is likely to be a little below average if Slowburn's return is above average. Similarly, Supertech's return is likely to be a little above average if Slowburn's return is below average. Thus, the standard deviation of a portfolio composed of the two securities is less than a weighted average of the standard deviations of the two securities.

Our example has negative correlation. Clearly, there will be less benefit from diversification if the two securities exhibit positive correlation. How high must the positive correlation be before all diversification benefits vanish?

To answer this question, let us rewrite Equation 10.4 in terms of correlation rather than covariance. The covariance can be rewritten:[4]

Equation 10.7

$$S_{\text{Super, Slow}} = \rho_{\text{Super, Slow}}\sigma_{\text{Super}}\sigma_{\text{Slow}}$$

This formula states that the covariance between any two securities is the correlation between the two securities multiplied by the standard deviations of each. In other words, covariance incorporates both (1) the correlation between the two assets, and (2) the variability of each of the two securities as measured by standard deviation.

From our calculations earlier in this chapter we know that the correlation between the two securities is –0.1639. Given the variances used in Equation 10.4, the standard deviations are 0.2586 and 0.115 for Supertech and Slowburn, respectively. Thus, the variance of a portfolio can be expressed as follows:

The variance of the portfolio's return

Equation 10.8

$$= X^2_{\text{Super}}\sigma^2_{\text{Super}} + 2X_{\text{Super}}X_{\text{Slow}}\rho_{\text{Super, Slow}}\sigma_{\text{Super}}\sigma_{\text{Slow}} + X^2_{\text{Slow}}\sigma^2_{\text{Slow}}$$

$$0.023851 = 0.36 \times 0.066875 + 2 \times 0.6 \times 0.4 \times (-0.1639) \times 0.2586 \times 0.115 + 0.16 \times 0.013225$$

The middle term on the right side is now written in terms of correlation, ρ, not covariance.

Suppose $\rho_{\text{Super, Slow}} = 1$, the highest possible value for correlation. Assume all the other parameters in the example are the same. The variance of the portfolio is:

The variance of the portfolio's return

$$= 0.040466 = 0.36 \times 0.0066875 + 2 \times (0.6 \times 0.4 \times 1 \times 0.2586 \times 0.115) + 0.16 \times 0.013225$$

The standard deviation is:

Equation 10.9

$$\text{Standard deviation of portfolio's return} = \sqrt{0.040466} = 0.2012 = 20.12\%$$

Note that Equations 10.9 and 10.6 are equal. That is, the standard deviation of a portfolio's return is equal to the weighted average of the standard deviations of the individual returns when $\rho = 1$. Inspection of Equation 10.8 indicates that the variance and hence the standard deviation of the portfolio must fall as the correlation drops below 1. This leads to the following result:

> **As long as $\rho < 1$, the standard deviation of a portfolio of two securities is *less* than the weighted average of the standard deviations of the individual securities.**

In other words, the diversification effect applies as long as there is less than perfect correlation (as long as $\rho < 1$). Thus, our Supertech–Slowburn example is a case of overkill. We illustrated diversification by an example with negative correlation. We could have illustrated diversification by an example with positive correlation – as long as it was not *a perfect* positive correlation.

An Extension to Many Assets

The preceding insight can be extended to the case of many assets. That is, as long as correlations between pairs of securities are less than 1, the standard deviation of a portfolio of many assets is less than the weighted average of the standard deviations of the individual securities.

Now consider Table 10.3, which shows the standard deviation of the Dow Jones Euro Stoxx 50 (a portfolio of the 50 largest companies in the Eurozone) and the standard deviations of some of the individual securities listed in the index over a recent five-year period. Note that all of the individual securities in the table have higher standard deviations than that of the index. In general, the standard deviations of most of the individual securities in an index will be above the standard deviation of the index itself, though a few of the securities will have lower standard deviations than that of the index.

Table 10.3 Standard Deviations for Dow Jones Euro Stoxx 50 Index and for Selected Equities in the Index

Asset	Standard Deviation (%)
Euro Stoxx 50	19.11
Carrefour	12.02
Ageas (Ex-Fortis)	19.59
Vinci	23.79
Intesa Sanpaolo	26.77
Saint Gobain	42.00
Telecom Italia	30.69
Arcelormittal	32.84
Crédit Agricole	33.09
Adidas (XET)	39.97

Source: Yahoo! Finance, 2023.

As long as the correlations between pairs of securities are less than 1, the standard deviation of an index will always be less than the weighted average of the standard deviations of the individual securities within the index.

10.4 The Efficient Set for Two Assets

Our results for expected returns and standard deviations are graphed in Figure 10.3. The figure shows a dot labelled Slowburn and a dot marked Supertech. Each dot represents both the expected return and the standard deviation for an individual security. As can be seen, Supertech has both a higher expected return and a higher standard deviation.

Figure 10.3 Expected Returns and Standard Deviations for Supertech, Slowburn and a Portfolio Composed of 60 Per Cent in Supertech and 40 Per Cent in Slowburn

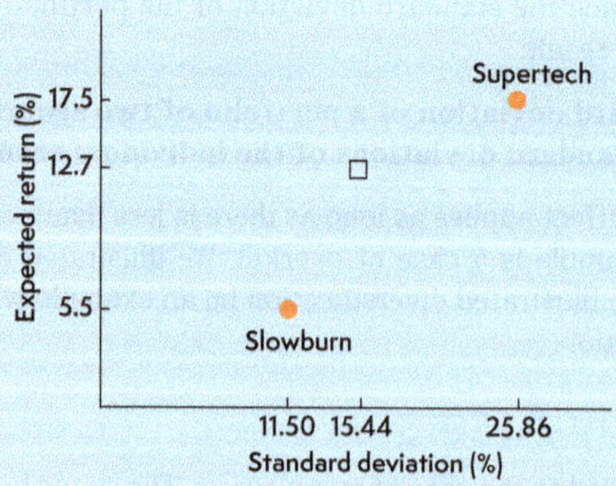

The box, '□', in the graph represents a portfolio with 60 per cent invested in Supertech and 40 per cent in Slowburn. You will recall that we previously calculated both the expected return and the standard deviation for this portfolio. The choice of 60 per cent in Supertech and 40 per cent in Slowburn is just one of an infinite number of portfolios that can be created. The set of portfolios is sketched by the curved line in Figure 10.4.

Consider portfolio 1, which is a portfolio composed of 90 per cent Slowburn and 10 per cent Supertech. Because it is weighted so heavily towards Slowburn, it appears close to the Slowburn point on the graph. Portfolio 2 is higher on the curve because it is composed of 50 per cent Slowburn and 50 per cent Supertech. Portfolio 3 is close to the Supertech point on the graph because it is formed of 90 per cent Supertech and 10 per cent Slowburn.

Figure 10.4 Frontier of Expected Returns and Standard Deviations for the Portfolio

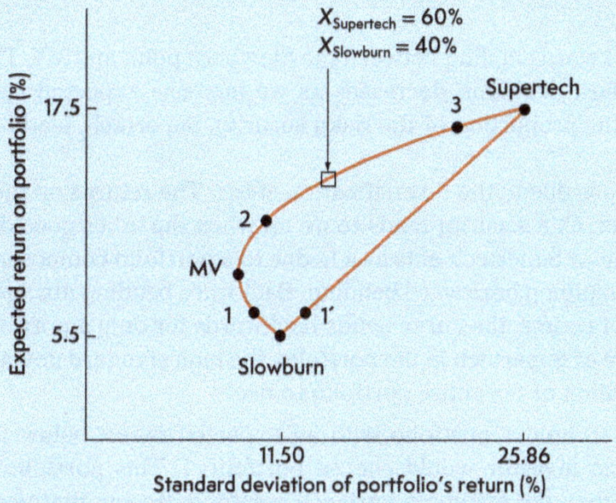

Portfolio 1 is composed of 90 per cent Slowburn and 10 per cent Supertech ($\rho = -0.1639$).
Portfolio 2 is composed of 50 per cent Slowburn and 50 per cent Supertech ($\rho = -0.1639$).
Portfolio 3 is composed of 10 per cent Slowburn and 90 per cent Supertech ($\rho = -0.1639$).
Portfolio 1′ is composed of 90 per cent Slowburn and 10 per cent Supertech ($\rho = 1$).
Point MV denotes the minimum variance portfolio. This is the portfolio with the lowest possible variance. By definition, the same portfolio must also have the lowest possible standard deviation.

There are a few important points concerning this graph:

1 We argued that the diversification effect occurs whenever the correlation between the two securities is below 1. The correlation between Supertech and Slowburn is –0.1639. The diversification effect can be illustrated by comparison with the straight line between the Supertech point and the Slowburn point. The straight line represents points that would have been generated had the correlation coefficient between the two securities been 1. The diversification effect is illustrated in the figure because the curved line is always to the left of the straight line. Consider point I'. This represents a portfolio composed of 90 per cent in Slowburn and 10 per cent in Supertech *if* the correlation between the two were exactly 1. We argue that there is no diversification effect if $\rho = 1$. However, the diversification effect applies to the curved line because point 1 has the same expected return as point 1' but has a lower standard deviation. (Points 2' and 3' are omitted to reduce the clutter of Figure 10.4.)

   Though the straight line and the curved line are both represented in Figure 10.4, they do not simultaneously exist in the same world. *Either* $\rho = -0.1639$ and the curve exists, *or* $\rho = 1$ and the straight line exists. In other words, though an investor can choose between different points on the curve if $\rho = -0.1639$, she cannot choose between points on the curve and points on the straight line.

2 The point MV represents the minimum variance portfolio. This is the portfolio with the lowest possible variance. By definition, this portfolio must also have the lowest possible standard deviation. (The term *minimum variance portfolio* is standard in the literature, and we will use that term. Perhaps minimum standard deviation would be better because standard deviation, not variance, is measured on the horizontal axis of Figure 10.4.)

3 An individual contemplating an investment in a portfolio of Slowburn and Supertech faces an opportunity set or feasible set represented by the curved line in Figure 10.4. That is, he can achieve any point on the curve by selecting the appropriate mix between the two securities. He cannot achieve any point above the curve because he cannot increase the return on the individual securities, decrease the standard deviations of the securities,

or reduce the correlation between the two securities. Neither can he achieve points below the curve because he cannot lower the returns on the individual securities, increase the standard deviations of the securities or increase the correlation. (Of course, he would not want to achieve points below the curve, even if he were able to do so.)

Were he relatively tolerant of risk, he might choose portfolio 3. (In fact, he could even choose the end point by investing all his money in Supertech.) An investor with less tolerance for risk might choose portfolio 2. An investor wanting as little risk as possible would choose MV, the portfolio with minimum variance or minimum standard deviation.

4 Note that the curve is backward bending between the Slowburn point and MV. This indicates that, for a portion of the feasible set, standard deviation decreases as we increase expected return. Students frequently ask, 'How can an increase in the proportion of the risky security, Supertech, lead to a reduction in the risk of the portfolio?'

This surprising finding is due to the diversification effect. The returns on the two securities are negatively correlated with each other. One security tends to go up when the other goes down, and vice versa. Thus, an addition of a small amount of Supertech acts as a hedge to a portfolio composed only of Slowburn. The risk of the portfolio is reduced, implying backward bending. Backward bending always occurs if $\rho < 0$. It may or may not happen when $\rho \geq 0$. Of course, the curve bends backwards for only a portion of its length. As we continue to increase the percentage of Supertech in the portfolio, the high standard deviation of this security eventually causes the standard deviation of the entire portfolio to rise.

5 No investor would want to hold a portfolio with an expected return below that of the minimum variance portfolio. For example, no investor would choose portfolio 1. This portfolio has less expected return but more standard deviation than the minimum variance portfolio. We say that portfolios such as portfolio 1 are *dominated* by the minimum variance portfolio. Though the entire curve from Slowburn to Supertech is called the *feasible set*, investors consider only the curve from MV to Supertech. Hence the curve from MV to Supertech is called the efficient set or the efficient frontier.

Figure 10.4 represents the opportunity set where $\rho = -0.1639$. It is worthwhile to examine Figure 10.5, which shows different curves for different correlations. As can be seen, the lower the correlation, the more bend there is in the curve. This indicates that the diversification effect rises as ρ declines. The strongest bend occurs in the limiting case where $\rho = -1$. This is perfect negative correlation. While this extreme case where $\rho = -1$ seems to fascinate students, it has little practical importance. Most pairs of securities exhibit a positive correlation. Strong negative correlations, let alone perfect negative correlation, are unlikely occurrences indeed.[5]

Figure 10.5 Opportunity Sets Composed of Holdings in Supertech and Slowburn

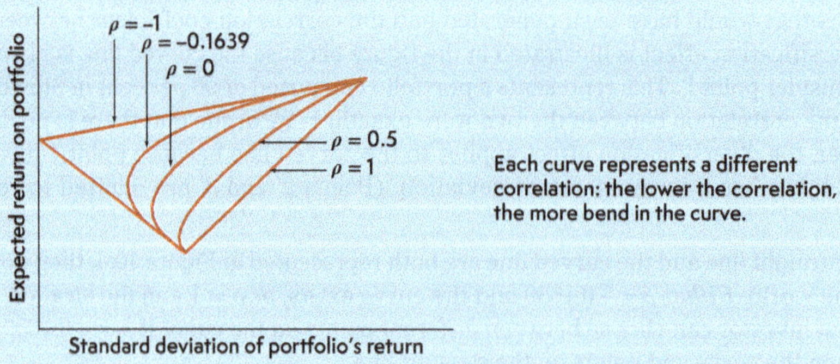

Note that there is only one correlation between a pair of securities. We stated earlier that the correlation between Slowburn and Supertech is –0.1639. Thus, the curve in Figure 10.5 representing this correlation is the correct one, and the other curves should be viewed as merely hypothetical.

The graphs we examined are not mere intellectual curiosities. Rather, efficient sets can easily be calculated in the real world. As mentioned earlier, data on returns, standard deviations and correlations are generally taken from past observations, though subjective notions can be used to determine the values of these parameters as well. Once the parameters have been determined, any one of a whole host of software packages can be purchased to generate an efficient set. However, the choice of the preferred portfolio within the efficient set is up to you. As with other important decisions like what job to choose, what house or car to buy, and how much time to allocate to this course, there is no computer program to select the preferred portfolio.

An efficient set can be generated where the two individual assets are portfolios themselves. For example, the two assets in Figure 10.6 are a diversified portfolio of US equities and a diversified portfolio of non-US equities. Expected returns, standard deviations and the correlation coefficient were calculated over the recent past. No subjectivity entered the analysis. The US equity portfolio with a standard deviation of about 0.173 is less risky than the non-US equity portfolio, which has a standard deviation of about 0.222. However, combining a small percentage of the non-US equity portfolio with the US portfolio reduces risk, as can be seen by the backwards-bending nature of the curve.

In other words, the diversification benefits from combining two different portfolios more than offset the introduction of a riskier set of equities into our holdings. The minimum variance portfolio occurs with about 80 per cent of our funds in US equities and about 20 per cent in non-US equities. The addition of non-US securities beyond this point increases the risk of the entire portfolio.

Figure 10.6 Return/Risk Trade-off for World Equities: Portfolio of US and non-US Equities

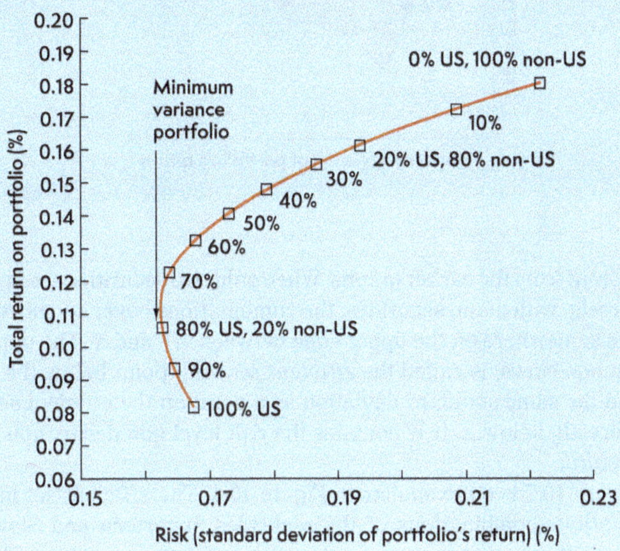

A point worth pondering concerns the potential pitfalls of using only past data to estimate future returns. For example, many asset classes have experienced phenomenal growth in the past few years. Thus, a graph like Figure 10.6 makes a substantial investment in these asset classes seem attractive. However, because abnormally high returns cannot be sustained for ever, some subjectivity must be used in forecasting future expected returns. A good example concerns property and real estate. At the beginning of 2021, if you used historical returns as an estimate of future returns, real estate would have had a heavy weighting in your investment portfolio. However, as it turned out, real estate was one of the world's worst-performing stock markets in 2021!

10.5 The Efficient Set for Many Securities

The previous discussion concerned two securities. We found that a simple curve sketched out all the possible portfolios. Because investors generally hold more than two securities, we should look at the same graph when more than two securities are held. The shaded area in Figure 10.7 represents the opportunity set or feasible set when many securities are considered. The shaded area represents all the possible combinations of expected return and standard deviation for a portfolio. For example, in a universe of 100 securities, point 1 might represent a portfolio of, say, 40 securities. Point 2 might represent a portfolio of 80 securities. Point 3 might represent a different set of 80 securities, or the same 80 securities held in different proportions, or something else. Obviously, the combinations are virtually endless. However, note that all possible combinations fit into a confined region. No security or combination of securities can fall outside the shaded region. That is, no one can choose a portfolio with an expected return above that given by the shaded region. Furthermore, no one can choose a portfolio with a standard deviation below that given in the shaded area. Perhaps more surprisingly, no one can choose an expected return below that given in the curve. In other words, the capital markets actually prevent a self-destructive person from taking on a guaranteed loss.[6]

Figure 10.7 The Feasible Set of Portfolios Constructed from Many Securities

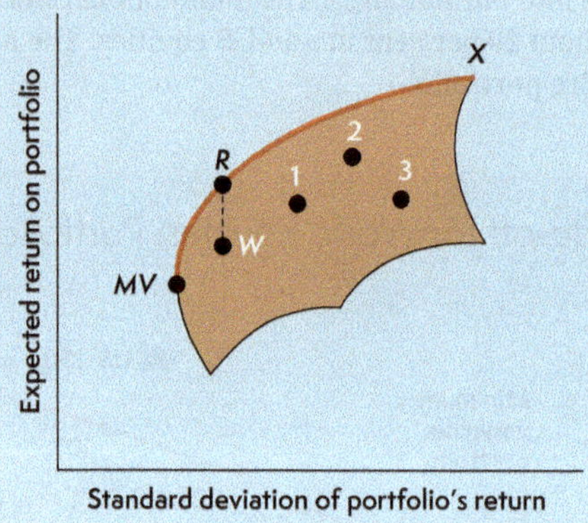

So far, Figure 10.7 is different from the earlier graphs. When only two securities are involved, all the combinations lie on a single curve. Conversely, with many securities, the combinations cover an entire area. However, notice that an individual will want to be somewhere on the upper edge between *MV* and *X*. The upper edge, which we indicate in Figure 10.7 by a thick orange curve, is called the *efficient set*. Any point below the efficient set would receive a lower expected return and the same standard deviation as a point on the efficient set. For example, consider *R* on the efficient set and *W* directly below it. If *W* contains the risk level you desire, you should choose *R* instead to receive a higher expected return.

In the final analysis, Figure 10.7 is quite similar to Figure 10.4. The efficient set in Figure 10.4 runs from *MV* to Supertech. It contains various combinations of the securities Supertech and Slowburn. The efficient set in Figure 10.7 runs from *MV* to *X*. It contains various combinations of many securities. The fact that a whole shaded area appears in Figure 10.7 but not in Figure 10.4 is just not an important difference; no investor would choose any point below the efficient set in Figure 10.7 anyway.

We mentioned before that an efficient set for two securities could be traced out easily in the real world. The task becomes more difficult when additional securities are included, because the number of observations grows. For example, using subjective analysis to estimate expected returns and standard deviations for, say, 100 or 500 securities may very well become overwhelming, and the difficulties with correlations may be greater still. There are almost 5,000 correlations between pairs of securities from a universe of 100 securities.

Though much of the mathematics of efficient set computation had been derived in the 1950s,[7] the high cost of computer time restricted application of the principles. In recent years this cost has been almost eliminated and an efficient frontier can now easily be computed with standard spreadsheet software.

Variance and Standard Deviation in a Portfolio of Many Assets

We earlier calculated the formulae for variance and standard deviation in the two-asset case. Because we considered a portfolio of many assets in Figure 10.7, it is worthwhile to calculate the formulae for variance and standard deviation in the many-asset case. The formula for the variance of a portfolio of many assets can be viewed as an extension of the formula for the variance of two assets.

To develop the formula, we employ the same type of matrix that we used in the two-asset case. This matrix is displayed in Table 10.4. Assuming that there are N assets, we write the numbers 1 through N on the horizontal axis and 1 through N on the vertical axis. This creates a matrix of $N \times N = N^2$ boxes. The variance of the portfolio is the sum of the terms in all the boxes.

Table 10.4 Matrix Used to Calculate the Variance of a Portfolio

Security	1	2	3	...	N
1	$X_1^2\sigma_1^2$	$X_1X_2\text{Cov}(R_1,R_2)$	$X_1X_3\text{Cov}(R_1,R_3)$		$X_1X_N\text{Cov}(R_1,R_N)$
2	$X_2X_1\text{Cov}(R_2,R_1)$	$X_2^2\sigma_2^2$	$X_2X_3\text{Cov}(R_2,R_3)$		$X_2X_N\text{Cov}(R_2,R_N)$
3	$X_3X_1\text{Cov}(R_3,R_1)$	$X_3X_2\text{Cov}(R_3,R_2)$	$X_3^2\sigma_3^2$		$X_3X_N\text{Cov}(R_3,R_N)$
⋮	⋮	⋮	⋮		⋮
N	$X_NX_1\text{Cov}(R_N,R_1)$	$X_NX_2\text{Cov}(R_N,R_2)$	$X_NX_3\text{Cov}(R_N,R_3)$		$X_N^2\sigma_N^2$

Notes: The variance of the portfolio is the sum of the terms in all the boxes.
σ_i is the standard deviation of security *i*.
$\text{Cov}(R_i,R_j)$ is the covariance between security i and security *j*.
Terms involving the standard deviation of a single security appear on the diagonal. Terms involving covariance between two securities appear off the diagonal.

Consider, for instance, the cell representing the second row and third column. The term in the cell is X_2X_3 Cov (R_2,R_3). X_2 and X_3 are the percentages of the entire portfolio that are invested in the second asset and the third asset, respectively. For example, if an individual with a portfolio of €1,000 invests €100 in the second asset, $X_2 = 10$ per cent (= €100/€1,000). $\text{Cov}(R_3,R_2)$ is the covariance between the returns on the third asset and the returns on the second asset. Next, consider the cell in the third row and the second column. The term in this box is X_3X_2 $\text{Cov}(R_3,R_2)$. Because $\text{Cov}(R_3,R_2) = \text{Cov}(R_2,R_3)$, both boxes have the same value. The second security and the third security make up one pair. In fact, every pair of securities appears twice in the table: once in the lower left side and once in the upper right side.

Now consider cells on the diagonal. For example, the term in the first cell on the diagonal is $X_1^2\sigma_1^2$. Here, σ_1^2 is the variance of the return on the first security.

Thus, the diagonal terms in the matrix contain the variances of the different securities. The off-diagonal terms contain the covariances. Table 10.5 relates the numbers of diagonal and off-diagonal elements to the size of the matrix. The number of diagonal terms (number of variance terms) is always the same as the number of securities in the portfolio. The number of off-diagonal terms (number of covariance terms) rises much faster than the number of diagonal terms. For example, a portfolio of 100 securities has 9,900 covariance terms. Because the variance of a portfolio's return is the sum of all the boxes, we have the following:

The variance of the return on a portfolio with many securities is more dependent on the covariances between the individual securities than on the variances of the individual securities.

Table 10.5 Number of Variance and Covariance Terms as a Function of the Number of Securities in the Portfolio

Number of Securities in Portfolio	Total Number of Terms	Number of Variance Terms (Number of Terms On Diagonal)	Number of Covariance Terms (Number of Terms Off Diagonal)
1	1	1	0
2	4	2	2
3	9	3	6
10	100	10	90
100	10,000	100	9,900
⋮	⋮	⋮	⋮
N	N^2	N	$N^2 - N$

Note: In a large portfolio, the number of terms involving covariance between two securities is much greater than the number of terms involving variance of a single security.

To give a recent example of the impact of diversification, consider an investment in large Chinese and Indian stocks. From Chapter 9, in 2018, China fell by a massive 24.59 per cent with India reporting growth in value of 7.22 per cent. A portfolio containing India and China would have partially offset the poor 2018 return performance in China with positive returns in India.

10.6 Diversification: An Example

The preceding point can be illustrated by altering the matrix in Table 10.4 slightly. Suppose we make the following three assumptions:

1 All securities possess the same variance, which we write as $\overline{\text{var}}$. In other words, $\sigma_1^2 = \overline{\text{var}}$ for every security.

2 All covariances in Table 10.4 are the same. We represent this uniform covariance as $\overline{\text{cov}}$. In other words. $\text{Cov}(R_i, R_j) = \overline{\text{cov}}$ for every pair of securities. It can easily be shown that $\overline{\text{var}} > \overline{\text{cov}}$.

3 All securities are equally weighted in the portfolio. Because there are N assets, the weight of each asset in the portfolio is $1/N$. In other words, $X_i = 1/N$ for each security i.

Table 10.6 is the matrix of variances and covariances under these three simplifying assumptions. Note that all of the diagonal terms are identical. Similarly, all of the off-diagonal terms are identical. As with Table 10.4, the variance of the portfolio is the sum of the terms in the boxes in Table 10.6. We know that there are N diagonal terms involving variance. Similarly, there are $N \times (N - 1)$ off-diagonal terms involving covariance. Summing across all the boxes in Table 10.6, we can express the variance of the portfolio as:

Equation 10.10

$$\text{Variance of portfolio} = \underset{\substack{\text{Number of}\\ \text{diagonal}\\ \text{terms}}}{N} \times \underset{\substack{\text{Each}\\ \text{diagonal}\\ \text{term}}}{\left[\frac{1}{N^2}\right]\overline{\text{var}}} + \underset{\substack{\text{Number of}\\ \text{off-diagonal}\\ \text{terms}}}{N(N-1)} \times \underset{\substack{\text{Each}\\ \text{off-diagonal}\\ \text{term}}}{\left[\frac{1}{N^2}\right]\overline{\text{cov}}}$$

$$= \left[\frac{1}{N}\right]\overline{\text{var}} + \left[\frac{N^2 - N}{N^{22}}\right]\overline{\text{cov}}$$

$$= \left[\frac{1}{N}\right]\overline{\text{var}} + \left[\frac{N^2 - N}{N^2}\right]\overline{\text{cov}}$$

Equation 10.10 expresses the variance of our special portfolio as a weighted sum of the average security variance and the average covariance.[8]

Table 10.6 Matrix Used to Calculate the Variance of a Portfolio*

Security	1	2	3	…	N
1	$(1/N^2)\,\overline{\text{var}}$	$(1/N^2)\,\overline{\text{cov}}$	$(1/N^2)\,\overline{\text{cov}}$	…	$(1/N^2)\,\overline{\text{cov}}$
2	$(1/N^2)\,\overline{\text{cov}}$	$(1/N^2)\,\overline{\text{var}}$	$(1/N^2)\,\overline{\text{cov}}$	…	$(1/N^2)\,\overline{\text{cov}}$
3	$(1/N^2)\,\overline{\text{cov}}$	$(1/N^2)\,\overline{\text{cov}}$	$(1/N^2)\,\overline{\text{var}}$	…	$(1/N^2)\,\overline{\text{cov}}$
⋮					
N	$(1/N^2)\,\overline{\text{cov}}$	$(1/N^2)\,\overline{\text{cov}}$	$(1/N^2)\,\overline{\text{cov}}$		$(1/N^2)\,\overline{\text{var}}$

* Matrix used to calculate the variance of a portfolio when (a) all securities possess the same variance, which we represent as $\overline{\text{var}}$, (b) all pairs of securities possess the same covariance, which we represent as $\overline{\text{cov}}$, (c) all securities are held in the same proportion, which is $1/N$.

Now, let us increase the number of securities in the portfolio without limit. The variance of the portfolio becomes:

Equation 10.11

$$\text{Variance of portfolio (when } N \rightarrow \infty) = \overline{\text{cov}}$$

This occurs because (1) the weight on the variance term, $1/N$, goes to 0 as N goes to infinity, and (2) the weight on the covariance term, $1 - 1/N$, goes to 1 as N goes to infinity.

Equation 10.10 provides an interesting and important result. In our special portfolio, the variances of the individual securities completely vanish as the number of securities becomes large. However, the covariance terms remain. In fact, the variance of the portfolio becomes the average covariance, $\overline{\text{cov}}$. We often hear that we should diversify. In other words, we should not put all our eggs in one basket. The effect of diversification on the risk of a portfolio can be illustrated in this example. The variances of the individual securities are diversified away, but the covariance terms cannot be diversified away.

The fact that part, but not all, of our risk can be diversified away should be explored. Consider Mr Smith, who brings £1,000 to the roulette table at a casino. It would be very risky if he put all his money on one spin of the wheel. For example, imagine that he put the full £1,000 on red at the table. If the wheel showed red, he would get £2,000; but if the wheel showed black, he would lose everything. Suppose instead he divided his money over 1,000 different spins by betting £1 at a time on red. Probability theory tells us that he could count on winning about 50 per cent of the time. This means he could count on pretty nearly getting all his original £1,000 back.[9] In other words, risk is essentially eliminated with 1,000 different spins.

Now, let us contrast this with our stock market example, which we illustrate in Figure 10.8. The variance of the portfolio with only one security is, of course $\overline{\text{var}}$ because the variance of a portfolio with one security is the variance of the security. The variance of the portfolio drops as more securities are added, which is evidence of the diversification effect. However, unlike Mr Smith's roulette example, the portfolio's variance can never drop to zero. Rather it reaches a floor of $\overline{\text{cov}}$, which is the covariance of each pair of securities.[10]

Figure 10.8 Relationship Between the Variance of a Portfolio's Return and the Number of Securities in the Portfolio

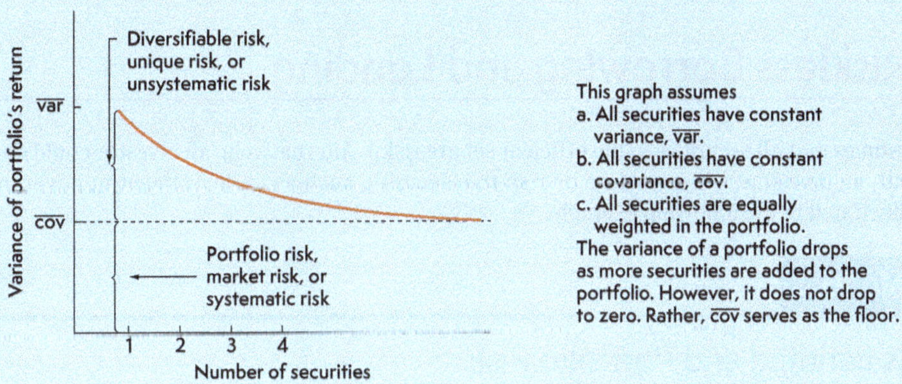

Because the variance of the portfolio asymptotically approaches $\overline{\text{cov}}$, each additional security continues to reduce risk. Thus, if there were neither commissions nor other transaction costs, it could be argued that we can never achieve too much diversification. However, there is a cost to diversification in the real world. Commissions per unit of money invested fall as we make larger purchases in a single security. Unfortunately, we must buy fewer shares of each security when buying more and more different securities. Comparing the costs and benefits of diversification, Meir Statman (1987) argues that a portfolio of about 30 equities is needed to achieve optimal diversification.

We mentioned earlier that $\overline{\text{var}}$ must be greater than $\overline{\text{cov}}$. Thus, the variance of a security's return can be broken down in the following way:

$$\underset{(\overline{\text{var}})}{\text{Total risk of individual security}} = \underset{(\overline{\text{cov}})}{\text{Portfolio risk}} + \underset{(\overline{\text{var}} - \overline{\text{cov}})}{\text{Unsystematic or diversifiable risk}}$$

Total risk, which is $\overline{\text{var}}$ in our example, is the risk we bear by holding onto one security only. *Portfolio risk* is the risk we still bear after achieving full diversification, which is $\overline{\text{cov}}$ in our example. Portfolio risk is often called **systematic** or **market risk** as well. **Diversifiable**, **unique** or **unsystematic risk** is the risk that can be diversified away in a large portfolio, which must be ($\overline{\text{var}} - \overline{\text{cov}}$) by definition.

To an individual who selects a diversified portfolio, the total risk of an individual security is not important. When considering adding a security to a diversified portfolio, the individual cares about only that portion of the risk of a security that cannot be diversified away. This risk can alternatively be viewed as the *contribution* of a security to the risk of an entire portfolio. We will talk later about the case where securities make different contributions to the risk of the entire portfolio.

Risk and the Sensible Investor

Having gone to all this trouble to show that unsystematic risk disappears in a well-diversified portfolio, how do we know that investors even want such portfolios? What if they like risk and do not want it to disappear?

We must admit that, theoretically at least, this is possible, but we will argue that it does not describe what we think of as the typical investor. Our typical investor is risk-averse. Risk-averse behaviour can be defined in many ways, but we prefer the following example: a fair gamble is one with zero expected return; a risk-averse investor would prefer to avoid fair gambles.

Why do investors choose well-diversified portfolios? Our answer is that they are risk-averse, and risk-averse people avoid unnecessary risk, such as the unsystematic risk on an equity. If you do not think this is much of an answer, consider whether you would take on such a risk. For example, suppose you had worked all summer and had saved €5,000, which you intended to use for your university expenses. Now, suppose someone came up to you and offered to flip a coin for the money: heads, you would double your money, tails you would lose it all.

Would you take such a bet? Perhaps you would, but most people would not. Leaving aside any moral question that might surround gambling, and recognizing that some people would take such a bet, it is our view that the average investor would not.

To induce the typical risk-averse investor to take a fair gamble, you must sweeten the pot. For example, you might need to raise the odds of winning from 50–50 to 70–30 or higher. The risk-averse investor can be induced to take fair gambles only if they are sweetened so that they become unfair to the investor's advantage.

10.7 Riskless Borrowing and Lending

Figure 10.7 assumes that all securities in the efficient set are risky. Alternatively, an investor could combine a risky investment with an investment in a riskless or *risk-free* security, such as an investment in government treasury bills. This is illustrated in the following example.

Example 10.3

Riskless Lending and Portfolio Risk

Ms Bagwell is considering investing in the equity of Merville Enterprises and will either borrow or lend at the risk-free rate. The relevant parameters are these:

	Equity of Merville (%)	Risk-free Asset (%)
Expected return	14	10
Standard deviation	20	0

Suppose Ms Bagwell chooses to invest a total of £1,000, £350 of which is to be invested in Merville Enterprises and £650 placed in the risk-free asset. The expected return on her total investment is a weighted average of the two returns:

Equation 10.12

$$\begin{array}{l}\text{Expected return on portfolio}\\ \text{composed of one riskless}\\ \text{and one risky asset}\end{array} = 0.114 = (0.35 \times 0.14) + (0.65 \times 0.10)$$

Because the expected return on the portfolio is a weighted average of the expected return on the risky asset (Merville Enterprises) and the risk-free return, the calculation is analogous to the way we treated two risky assets. In other words, Equation 10.3 applies here.

Using Equation 10.4, the formula for the variance of the portfolio can be written as:

$$X^2_{\text{Merville}}\ \sigma^2_{\text{Merville}} + 2X_{\text{Merville}}\ X_{\text{Risk-free}}\sigma_{\text{Merville, Risk-free}} + X^2_{\text{Merville}}\ \sigma^2_{\text{Risk-free}}$$

However, by definition, the risk-free asset has no variability. Thus both $\sigma_{\text{Merville, Risk-free}}$ and $\sigma^2_{\text{Risk-free}}$ are equal to zero, reducing the above expression to:

Equation 10.13

$$\text{Variance of portfolio composed of one riskless and one risky asset} = X^2_{\text{Merville}}\ \sigma^2_{\text{Merville}} = (0.35)^2 \times (0.20)^2 = 0.0049$$

The standard deviation of the portfolio is:

Equation 10.14

$$\text{Standard deviation of portfolio composed of one riskless and one risky asset} = X_{\text{Merville}}\ \sigma_{\text{Merville}} = 0.35 \times 0.20 = 0.07$$

The relationship between risk and expected return for one risky and one riskless asset can be seen in Figure 10.9. Ms Bagwell's split of 35–65 per cent between the two assets is represented on a *straight* line between the risk-free rate and a pure investment in Merville Enterprises. Note that, unlike the case of two risky assets, the opportunity set is straight, not curved.

Figure 10.9 Relationship Between Expected Return and Risk for a Portfolio of One Risky Asset and One Riskless Asset

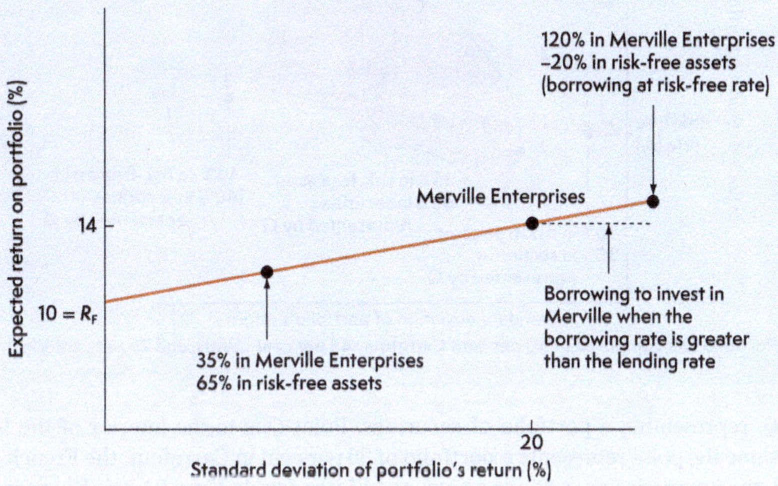

Suppose that, alternatively, Ms Bagwell borrows £200 at the risk-free rate. Combining this with her original sum of £1,000, she invests a total of £1,200 in Merville. Her expected return would be:

$$\begin{array}{l}\text{Expected return on portfolio}\\ \text{formed by borrowing} \\ \text{to invest in risky asset}\end{array} = 14.8\% = 1.20 \times 0.14 + (-0.2 \times 0.10)$$

Here, she invests 120 per cent of her original investment of £1,000 by borrowing 20 per cent of her original investment. Note that the return of 14.8 per cent is greater than the 14 per cent expected return on Merville Enterprises. This occurs because she is borrowing at 10 per cent to invest in a security with an expected return greater than 10 per cent.

The standard deviation is:

$$\begin{array}{l}\text{Standard deviation of portfolio}\\ \text{formed by borrowing to invest} \\ \text{in risky asset}\end{array} = 0.24 = 1.20 \times 0.2$$

The standard deviation of 0.24 is higher than 0.20, the standard deviation of the Merville investment, because borrowing increases the variability of the investment. This investment also appears in Figure 10.9.

So far, we have assumed that Ms Bagwell is able to borrow at the same rate at which she can lend.[11] Now let us consider the case where the borrowing rate is above the lending rate. The dotted line in Figure 10.9 illustrates the opportunity set for borrowing opportunities in this case. The dotted line is below the solid line because a higher borrowing rate lowers the expected return on the investment.

The Optimal Portfolio

The previous section concerned a portfolio formed between one riskless asset and one risky asset. In reality, an investor is likely to combine an investment in the riskless asset with a *portfolio* of risky assets. This is illustrated in Figure 10.10.

Figure 10.10 Relationship Between Expected Return and Standard Deviation for an Investment in a Combination of Risky Securities and the Riskless Asset

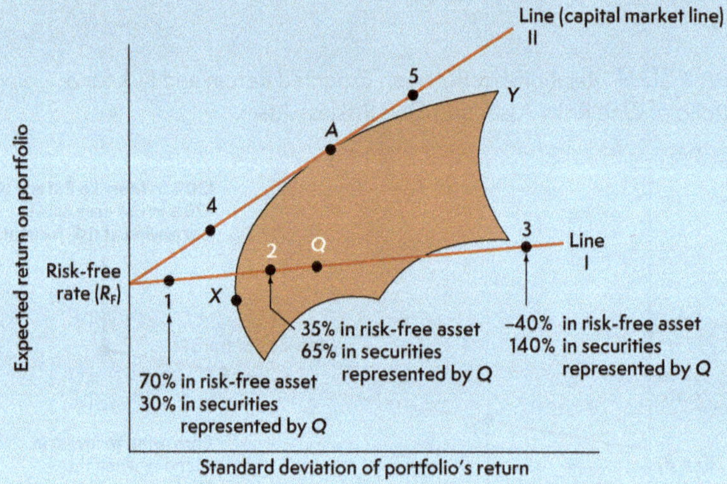

Portfolio Q is composed of 30 per cent Carrefour, 45 per cent LVMH, and 25 per cent Vinci.

Consider point Q, representing a portfolio of securities. Point Q is in the interior of the feasible set of risky securities. Let us assume the point represents a portfolio of 30 per cent in Carrefour, the French supermarket chain, 45 per cent in LVMH, the luxury designer goods group, and 25 per cent in Vinci SA, the European road builder.

Individuals combining investments in Q with investments in the riskless asset would achieve points along the straight line from R_F to Q. We refer to this as line I. For example, point 1 on the line represents a portfolio of 70 per cent in the riskless asset and 30 per cent in equities represented by Q. An investor with €100 choosing point 1 as his portfolio would put €70 in the risk-free asset and €30 in Q. This can be restated as €70 in the riskless asset, €9 (= 0.3 × €30) in Carrefour, €13.50 (= 0.45 × €30) in LVMH and €7.50 (= 0.25 × €30) in Vinci. Point 2 also represents a portfolio of the risk-free asset and Q, with more (65 per cent) being invested in Q.

Point 3 is obtained by borrowing to invest in Q. For example, an investor with €100 of her own would borrow €40 from the bank or broker to spend €140 on Q. So the investor would borrow €40 and contribute €100 of her money to invest €42 (= 0.3 × €140) in Carrefour, €63 (= 0.45 × €140) in LVMH, and €35 (= 0.25 × €140) in Vinci.

These investments can be summarized as follows:

	Point Q (€)	Point 1 (Lending €70) (€)	Point 3 (Borrowing €40) (€)
Carrefour	30.00	9.00	42.00
LVMH	45.00	13.50	63.00
Vinci	25.00	7.50	35.00
Risk-free	0	70.00	–40.00
Total investment	100.00	100.00	100.00

Though an investor can obtain any point on line I, no position on the line is optimal. To see this, consider line II, a line running from R_F through A. Point A represents a portfolio of risky securities. Line II represents portfolios formed by combinations of the risk-free asset and the securities in A. Points between R_F and A are portfolios in which some money is invested in the riskless asset, and the rest is placed in A. Points past A are achieved by borrowing at the riskless rate to buy more of A than we could with our original funds alone.

As drawn, line II is tangent to the efficient set of risky securities. Whatever point an individual can obtain on line I, he can obtain a point with the same standard deviation and a higher expected return on line II. In fact, because line II is tangent to the efficient set of risky assets, it provides the investor with the best possible opportunities. In other words, line II can be viewed as the efficient set of *all* assets, both risky and riskless. An investor with a fair degree of risk aversion might choose a point between R_F and A, perhaps point 4. An individual with less risk aversion might choose a point closer to A or even beyond A. For example, point 5 corresponds to an individual borrowing money to increase investment in A.

The graph illustrates an important point. With riskless borrowing and lending, the portfolio of *risky* assets held by any investor would always be point A. Regardless of the investor's tolerance for risk, she would never choose any other point on the efficient set of risky assets (represented by curve XAY) nor any point in the interior of the feasible region. Rather, she would combine the securities of A with the riskless assets if she had high aversion to risk. She would borrow the riskless asset to invest more funds in A had she low aversion to risk.

This result establishes what financial economists call the separation principle. That is, the investor's investment decision consists of two separate steps:

1. After estimating (a) the expected returns and variances of individual securities, and (b) the covariances between pairs of securities, the investor calculates the efficient set of risky assets, represented by curve XAY in Figure 10.10. He then determines point A, the tangency between the risk-free rate and the efficient set of risky assets (curve XAY). Point A represents the portfolio of risky assets that the investor will hold. This point is determined solely from his estimates of returns, variances and covariances. No personal characteristics, such as degree of risk aversion, are needed in this step.
2. The investor must now determine how he will combine point A, his portfolio of risky assets, with the riskless asset. He might invest some of his funds in the riskless asset and some in portfolio A. He would end up at a point on the line between R_F and A in this case. Alternatively, he might borrow at the risk-free rate and contribute some of his own funds as well, investing the sum in portfolio A. He would end up at a point on line II beyond A. His position in the riskless asset – that is, his choice of where on the line he wants to be – is determined by his internal characteristics, such as his ability to tolerate risk.

The separation principle is fundamentally important in corporate finance. We have shown that the optimal investment portfolio does not depend on an investor's risk preferences or personal characteristics. Investors will invest a fraction of their money in the risk-free asset and the rest in the optimal risky portfolio, A, to create the optimal portfolio specific to the investor's level of risk tolerance. Since the investment decision is separate from creation of the optimal risky portfolio, corporate managers can ignore individual investor preferences and focus only on maximizing firm value using the methods outlined in Chapter 6.

10.8 Market Equilibrium

Definition of the Market Equilibrium Portfolio

The preceding analysis concerns one investor. His estimates of the expected returns and variances for individual securities and the covariances between pairs of securities are his and his alone. Other investors would have different estimates of these variables. However, these might not vary much because all investors would be forming expectations from the same data about past price movements and other publicly available information.

Financial economists often imagine a world where all investors possess the *same* estimates of expected returns, variances and covariances. Though this can never be literally true, it can be a useful simplifying assumption in a world where investors have access to similar sources of information. This assumption is called homogeneous expectations.[12]

If all investors had homogeneous expectations, Figure 10.10 would be the same for all individuals. That is, all investors would sketch out the same efficient set of risky assets because they would be working with the same inputs. We represent the efficient set of risky assets by the curve XAY. Because the same risk-free rate would apply to everyone, all investors would regard point A as the portfolio of risky assets to be held.

This point A takes on great importance because all investors would purchase the risky securities that it represents. Investors with a high degree of risk aversion might combine A with an investment in the riskless asset, achieving point 4, for example. Others with a low aversion to risk might borrow to achieve, say, point 5. Because this is a significant conclusion, we restate it:

In a world with homogeneous expectations, all investors would hold the portfolio of risky assets represented by point *A*.

If all investors choose the same portfolio of risky assets, it is possible to determine what that portfolio is. Common sense tells us that it is a market value-weighted portfolio of all existing securities. It is the market portfolio.

In practice, economists use a broad-based index such as the FTSE 100, Dow Jones Euro Stoxx 50 or Standard & Poor's (S&P) 500 as a proxy for the market portfolio, depending on the country they analyse. Of course, all investors do not hold the same portfolio in practice. However, we know that many investors hold diversified portfolios, particularly when mutual funds or pension funds are included. A broad-based index is a good proxy for the highly diversified portfolios of many investors.

Definition of Risk When Investors Hold the Market Portfolio

The previous section states that many investors hold diversified portfolios similar to broad-based indexes. This result allows us to be more precise about the risk of a security in the context of a diversified portfolio.

Researchers have shown that the best measure of the risk of a security in a large portfolio is the *beta* of the security. We illustrate beta by an example.

Example 10.4

Beta

Consider the following possible returns both on the equity of Hicks plc and on the market:

State	Type of Economy	Return on Market (%)	Return on Hicks plc (%)
I	Bull	15	25
II	Bull	15	15
III	Bear	−5	−5
IV	Bear	−5	−15

Though the return on the market has only two possible outcomes (15 per cent and −5 per cent), the return on Hicks has four possible outcomes. It is helpful to consider the expected return on a security for a given return on the market. Assuming each state is equally likely, we have:

Type of Economy	Return on Market (%)	Expected Return on Hicks plc (%)
Bull	15	$20\% = 25\% \times \frac{1}{2} + 15\% \times \frac{1}{2}$
Bear	−5	$-10\% = (-5\%) \times \frac{1}{2} + (-15\%) \times \frac{1}{2}$

Hicks plc responds to market movements because its expected return is higher in bullish states than in bearish states. We now calculate how responsive the security is to market movements. The market's return in a bullish economy is 20 per cent $[= 15\% - (-5\%)]$ greater than the market's return in a bearish economy. However, the expected return on Hicks in a bullish economy is 30 per cent $[= 20\% - (-10\%)]$ greater than its expected return in a bearish state. Thus Hicks plc has a responsiveness coefficient of 1.5 $(= 30\% \div 20\%)$.

This relationship appears in Figure 10.11. The returns for both Hicks and the market in each state are plotted as four points. In addition, we plot the expected return on the security for each of the two possible returns on the market. These two points, each of which we designate by an X, are joined by a line called the characteristic line of the security. The slope of the line is 1.5, the number calculated in the previous paragraph. This responsiveness coefficient of 1.5 is the beta of Hicks.

Figure 10.11 Performance of Hicks plc and the Market Portfolio

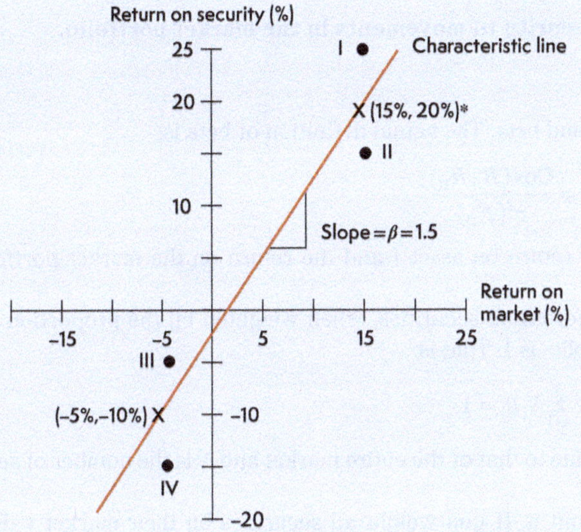

The two points marked X represent the expected return on Hicks for each possible outcome of the market portfolio. The expected return on Hicks is positively related to the return on the market. Because the slope is 1.5, we say that Hicks' beta is 1.5. Beta measures the responsiveness of the security's return to movement in the market.

*(15%, 20%) refers to the point where the return on the market is 15 per cent and the return on the security is 20 per cent.

The interpretation of beta from Figure 10.11 is intuitive. The graph tells us that the returns of Hicks are magnified 1.5 times over those of the market. When the market does well, Hicks' equity is expected to do even better. When the market does poorly, Hicks' equity is expected to do even worse. Now imagine an individual with a portfolio near that of the market who is considering the addition of Hicks to her portfolio. Because of Hicks' *magnification factor* of 1.5, she will view this security as contributing much to the risk of the portfolio. (We will show shortly that the beta of the average security in the market is 1.) Hicks contributes more to the risk of a large, diversified portfolio than does an average security because Hicks is more responsive to movements in the market.

We can get further insight by examining securities with negative betas. One should view these securities as either hedges or insurance policies. The security is expected to do well when the market does poorly, and vice versa. Because of this, adding a negative-beta security to a large, diversified portfolio actually reduces the risk of the portfolio.[13]

Table 10.7 presents empirical estimates of betas for individual securities. As can be seen, some securities are more responsive to the market than others. For example, Mercedes-Benz has a beta of 1.30, which means that for every 1 per cent movement in the market, Mercedes-Benz is expected to move 1.30 per cent in the same direction. Conversely, L'Oréal has a beta of 0.66, meaning that for every 1 per cent movement in the market, L'Oréal is expected to move only 0.66 per cent in the same direction.

Table 10.7 Estimates of Beta for Selected Individual Equities

Stock	Beta
Nokia	0.71
L'Oréal	0.66
SAP	1.00
Siemens	1.18
Mercedes-Benz	1.30
Koninklijke Philips	0.83
Renault	1.71
Volkswagen	1.30

Source: Yahoo! Finance © 2023 Yahoo! Inc.

The beta is defined as $\text{Cov}(R_i,R_M)/\text{Var}(R_M)$, where $\text{Cov}(R_i,R_M)$ is the covariance of the return on an individual equity, R_i, and the return on the market, R_M.$\text{Var}(R_M)$ is the variance of the return on the market, R_M.

We can summarize our discussion of beta by saying this:

Beta measures the responsiveness of a security to movements in the market portfolio.

The Formula for Beta

Our discussion so far has stressed the intuition behind beta. The actual definition of beta is:

Equation 10.15

$$\beta_i = \frac{\text{Cov}(R_i,R_M)}{\sigma^2(R_M)}$$

where $\text{Cov}(R_i,R_M)$ is the covariance between the return on asset i and the return on the market portfolio and $\sigma^2(R_M)$ is the variance of the market.

One useful property is that the average beta across all securities, when weighted by the proportion of each security's market value to that of the market portfolio, is 1. That is:

Equation 10.16

$$\sum_{i=1}^{N} X_i \beta_i = 1$$

where X_i is the proportion of security i's market value to that of the entire market and N is the number of securities in the market.

Equation 10.16 is intuitive, once you think about it. If you weight all securities by their market values, the resulting portfolio is the market. By definition, the beta of the market portfolio is 1. That is, for every 1 per cent movement in the market, the market must move 1 per cent – *by definition.*

A Test

We have put the following questions in past corporate finance examinations:

1 What sort of investor rationally views the variance (or standard deviation) of an individual security's return as the security's proper measure of risk?

2 What sort of investor rationally views the beta of a security as the security's proper measure of risk?

A good answer might be something like this:

> A rational, risk-averse investor views the variance (or standard deviation) of her portfolio's return as the proper measure of the risk of her portfolio. If for some reason the investor can hold only one security, the variance of that security's return becomes the variance of the portfolio's return. Hence, the variance of the security's return is the security's proper measure of risk.
>
> If an individual holds a diversified portfolio, she still views the variance (or standard deviation) of her portfolio's return as the proper measure of the risk of her portfolio. However, she is no longer interested in the variance of each security's return. Instead, she is interested in the contribution of an individual security to the variance of the portfolio.

Under the assumption of homogeneous expectations, all individuals hold the market portfolio. Thus, we measure risk as the contribution of an individual security to the variance of the market portfolio. This contribution, when standardized properly, is the beta of the security. Although few investors hold the market portfolio exactly, many hold reasonably diversified portfolios. These portfolios are close enough to the market portfolio so that the beta of a security is likely to be a reasonable measure of its risk.

10.9 The Capital Asset Pricing Model

It is commonplace to argue that the expected return on an asset should be positively related to its risk. That is, individuals will hold a risky asset only if its expected return compensates for its risk. In this section, we first estimate the expected return on the stock market as a whole. Next, we estimate expected returns on individual securities.

Expected Return on Market

Economists frequently argue that the expected return on the market can be represented as:

$$E[R_M] = R_F + \text{Risk premium}$$

In words, the expected return on the market is the sum of the risk-free rate plus some compensation for the risk inherent in the market portfolio. Note that the equation refers to the *expected* return on the market, not the actual return in a particular month or year. Because equities have risk, the actual return on the market over a specific period can, of course, be below R_F or can even be negative.

Because investors want compensation for risk, the risk premium is presumably positive. But exactly how positive is it? It is generally argued that the place to start looking for the risk premium in the future is the average risk premium in the past. As reported in Chapter 9, the average return on large UK companies was 6.35 per cent over 1900–2010. The average risk-free rate over the same interval was 4.96 per cent. Thus, the average difference between the two was 1.39 per cent (=6.35% – 4.96%). Financial economists find this to be a useful estimate of the difference to occur in the future.

For example, if the risk-free rate, estimated by the current yield on a one-year Treasury bill, is 1 per cent, the expected return on the market is:

$$2.39\% = 1\% + 1.39\%$$

Of course, the future equity risk premium could be higher or lower than the historical equity risk premium. This could be true if future risk is higher or lower than past risk or if individual risk aversions are higher or lower than those of the past.

Expected Return on an Individual Security

Now that we have estimated the expected return on the market as a whole, what is the expected return on an individual security? We have argued that the beta of a security is the appropriate measure of risk in a large, diversified portfolio. Because most investors are diversified, the expected return on a security should be positively related to its beta. We illustrate this in Figure 10.12.

Figure 10.12 Relationship Between Expected Return on an Individual Security and Beta of the Security

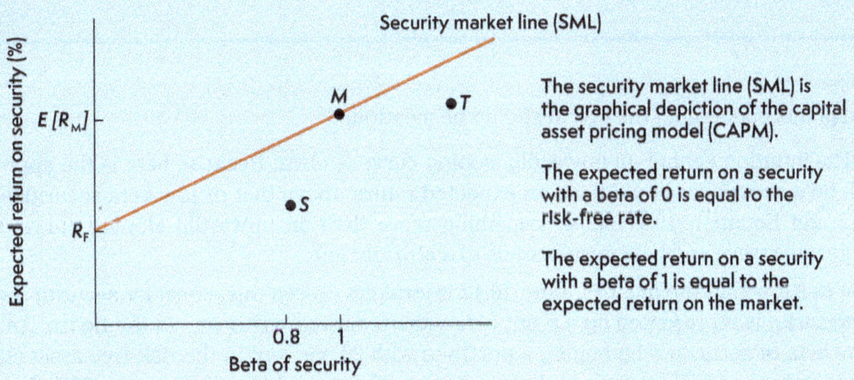

Economists can be more precise about the relationship between expected return and beta. They posit that under plausible conditions the relationship between expected return and beta can be represented by the following equation:[14]

The capital asset pricing model

Equation 10.17	$E[R_i]$	=	R_F	+	β	×	$(E[R_M] - R_F)$
	Expected return on a security		Risk-free rate		Beta of the security		Difference between expected return on market and risk-free rate

This formula, which is called the **capital asset pricing model** (or **CAPM** for short), implies that the expected return on a security is linearly related to its beta. Because the average return on the market has been higher than the average risk-free rate over long periods, $E[R_M] - R_F$ is presumably positive. Thus, the formula implies that the expected return on a security is *positively* related to its beta. We illustrate the formula by assuming a few special cases:

- *Assume that* $\beta = 0$. Here $E[R_i] = R_F$. That is, the expected return on the security is equal to the risk-free rate. Because a security with zero beta has no relevant risk, its expected return should equal the risk-free rate.
- *Assume that* $\beta = 1$. Equation 10.17 reduces to $E[R_i] = E[R_M]$. That is, the expected return on the security is equal to the expected return on the market. This makes sense because the beta of the market portfolio is also 1.

Equation 10.17 can be represented graphically by the upward-sloping line in Figure 10.12. Note that the line begins at R_F and rises to $R[R_M]$ when the beta is 1. This line is frequently called the **security market line (SML)**.

As with any line, the SML has both a slope and an intercept. R_F, the risk-free rate, is the intercept. Because the beta of a security is the horizontal axis, $E[R_M] - R_F$ is the slope. The line will be upward sloping as long as the expected return on the market is higher than the risk-free rate. Because the market portfolio is a risky asset, theory suggests that its expected return is above the risk-free rate. As mentioned, the empirical evidence of the previous chapter showed that the average return per year on the market portfolio (for large UK companies as an example) over the past 111 years was 1.39 per cent above the risk-free rate.

Example 10.5

The shares of Aardvark Enterprises and Zebra Enterprises have betas of 1.5 and 0.7, respectively. The risk-free rate is 3 per cent, and the difference between the expected return on the market and the risk-free rate is assumed to be 8.0 per cent. The expected returns on the two securities are:

The expected return for Aardvark

Equation 10.18a $$15.0\% = 3\% + 1.5 \times 8.0\%$$

The expected return for Zebra

Equation 10.18b $$8.6\% = 3\% + 0.7 \times 8.0\%$$

Three additional points concerning the CAPM should be mentioned:

1 *Linearity:* The intuition behind an upwardly sloping curve is clear. Because beta is the appropriate measure of risk, high-beta securities should have an expected return above that of low-beta securities. However, both Figure 10.12 and Equation 10.17 show something more than an upwardly sloping curve: the relationship between expected return and beta corresponds to a *straight* line.

It is easy to show that the line of Figure 10.12 is straight. To see this, consider security S with, say, a beta of 0.8. This security is represented by a point below the security market line in the figure. Any investor could duplicate the beta of security S by buying a portfolio with 20 per cent in the risk-free asset and 80 per cent in a security with a beta of 1. However, the homemade portfolio would itself lie on the SML. In other words, the portfolio dominates security S because the portfolio has a higher expected return and the same beta.

Now consider security T with, say, a beta greater than 1. This security is also below the SML in Figure 10.11. Any investor could duplicate the beta of security T by borrowing to invest in a security with a beta of 1. This portfolio must also lie on the SML, thereby dominating security T.

Because no one would hold either S or T, their prices would drop. This price adjustment would raise the expected returns on the two securities. The price adjustment would continue until the two securities lay on the security market line. The preceding example considered two overpriced equities and a straight SML. Securities lying above the SML are *underpriced*. Their prices must rise until their expected returns lie on the line. If the SML is itself curved, many equities would be mispriced. In equilibrium, all securities would be held only when prices change so that the SML became straight. In other words, linearity would be achieved.

2 *Portfolios as well as securities:* Our discussion of the CAPM considered individual securities. Does the relationship in Figure 10.12 and Equation 10.17 hold for portfolios as well?

Yes. To see this, consider a portfolio formed by investing equally in our two securities from Example 10.5, Aardvark and Zebra. The expected return on the portfolio is:

Expected return on a portfolio

Equation 10.19 $$11.8\% = 0.5 \times 15.0\% + 0.5 \times 8.6\%$$

The beta of the portfolio is simply a weighted average of the betas of the two securities. Thus, we have:

Beta of portfolio

$$1.1 = 0.5 \times 1.5 + 0.5 \times 0.7$$

Under the CAPM, the expected return on the portfolio is

Equation 10.20 $$11.8\% = 3\% + 1.1 \times 8.0\%$$

Because the expected return in Equation 10.19 is the same as the expected return in Equation 10.20, the example shows that the CAPM holds for portfolios as well as for individual securities.

3 *A potential confusion:* Students often confuse the SML in Figure 10.12 with line II in Figure 10.10, but the lines are entirely different. Line II traces the efficient set of portfolios formed from both risky assets and the riskless asset. Each point on the line represents an entire portfolio. Point *A* is a portfolio composed entirely of risky assets. Every other point on the line represents a portfolio of the securities in *A* combined with the riskless asset. The axes of Figure 10.10 are the expected return on a *portfolio* and the standard deviation of a *portfolio*. Individual securities do not lie along line II.

The SML in Figure 10.11 relates expected return to beta. Figure 10.12 differs from Figure 10.10 in at least two ways. First, beta appears in the horizontal axis of Figure 10.12, but standard deviation appears in the horizontal axis of Figure 10.9. Second, the SML in Figure 10.12 holds both for all individual securities and all possible portfolios, whereas line II in Figure 10.10 holds only for efficient portfolios.

We stated earlier that, under homogeneous expectations, point *A* in Figure 10.10 becomes the market portfolio. In this situation, line II is referred to as the capital market line (CML).

Sustainability in Action 10.1

Expected Return at Enel

Enel is Italy's largest renewable energy company and Europe's second-largest utility firm, with operations in more than 30 countries.

To find the expected return on Enel equity using the CAPM, you must collect three data items: the company's beta, the risk-free rate and the expected market risk premium.

Beta

Go to any financial website (examples include Yahoo! Finance, Google Finance, Reuters) and search for Enel. According to Yahoo! Finance, Enel's beta is 0.91.

Risk-free Rate

When using CAPM for corporate finance purposes, such as investment decisions, the rule of thumb is to use the 10-year government bond yield. This is because we are matching the term of the risk-free security with a typical life of an investment. A search of the markets data page on websites such as FT.com and Reuters shows that Italian 10-year government bond yields are 4.14 per cent.

Expected Market Risk Premium

There are many ways to forecast future market returns, but all methods suffer from the fact that you are trying to predict the future. For our purposes, we will use the information in Table 9.3 and go with the historical Italian market risk premium of 9.02 per cent.

Using this information, we can now estimate the expected return on Enel SpA shares:

$$E[R_{Enel}] = r_f + \beta(E[R_m] - r_f) = 4.14 + 0.91(9.02) = 12.35\%$$

In this section's discussion, we have talked of expectations, *E[R]*. The expected return on a security, *A*, is the return you expect security *A* to earn over the coming period. The expected return on the market is the return you expect the market to earn over the coming period. In contrast, an observed return (on either security *A* or the market) is the return that is actually earned over the period. The observed return may or may not be similar to the expected return. All we can say is that the expected return is the best estimate today of the return earned in the future.

Since nobody can tell the future, don't anticipate your expected return estimate to be the same. The more observant readers will ask why we are using historical data to estimate expected returns. This is because, in the absence of any other information, historical information is the best predictor of the future. Clearly if you have non-price information relating to a security (such as future sales contracts), you would adapt your estimates accordingly.

10.10 Criticisms of the CAPM

The capital asset pricing model represents one of the most significant advances in financial economics. It is useful for investment purposes because it shows how the expected return on an asset is related to its beta. Also, we will show in Chapter 12 that it is useful in corporate finance because the discount rate on a project is a function of the project's beta. However, never forget that, as with any other model, the CAPM is not revealed truth but, instead, a construct to be empirically tested and give some insights into what is reality. Nobody who works in finance will ever say that they believe the CAPM fully explains the returns on securities, investments or financial portfolios. All the CAPM does, as with any other theoretical model, is give insights into the truth.

Roll's (1977) Critique of the CAPM

Before we discuss empirical tests, it is necessary to understand whether we can test the CAPM at all. In 1977, Richard Roll, in the *Journal of Financial Economics*, argued that, because it is practically impossible to construct a portfolio that contains every single security (i.e., the true market portfolio), any test of the CAPM that uses a market proxy (e.g., FTSE 100, DAX, CAC 40) will be testing that specific portfolio and not the true market portfolio. This means that the CAPM is empirically untestable because the underlying market portfolio is unobservable. Any tests of the CAPM that use market proxies will be affected by this criticism.

Academics have spent a lot of time debating the merits of Roll's critique. However, use of the model in corporate finance and investment is widespread. Financial websites, such as Yahoo! Finance, Bloomberg and FT.com frequently provide estimates of the beta of listed firms. Given its massive popularity, and taking into account the weaknesses associated with any empirical tests, it is important to know whether the CAPM is successful in explaining at least some of the variation in security returns.

Empirical Tests of the CAPM

The first empirical tests of the CAPM occurred more than 30 years ago and were quite supportive of the model. Using data from the 1930s to the 1960s on US stock markets, researchers showed that the average return on a portfolio of stocks was positively related to the beta of the portfolio[15] – a finding consistent with the CAPM. Though some evidence in these studies was less consistent with the CAPM,[16] financial economists were quick to embrace the model following these empirical papers.

Although a large body of empirical work developed in the following decades, often with varying results, the CAPM was not seriously called into question until the 1990s. Two papers by Fama and French (1992, 1993) present evidence inconsistent with the model. Their work has received a great deal of attention, both in academic circles and in the popular press, with newspaper articles displaying headlines such as 'Beta is Dead!' These papers make two related points. First, they conclude that, for US firms, the relationship between average return and beta is weak over the period from 1941 to 1990, and virtually non-existent from 1963 to 1990. Second, they argue that the average return on a security is negatively related to both the firm's price–earnings (PE) ratio and the firm's market-to-book (MB) ratio. Other research has provided strong evidence against the CAPM by showing that securities that have performed well in the recent past tend to have higher returns in the near future (Carhart's (1997) momentum factor). Also, Ang et al. (2006) found that equities with a higher sensitivity to stock market volatility have lower returns than control firms with the same systematic risk. Finally, it is possible that these results are applicable only in the United States. However, the poor performance of beta has also been found in other countries by Fama and French (1998).

Fama and French (2015, 2016, 2017) extended their earlier analysis by adding two additional factors to the cross-sectional beta regression. The first variable (RMW) relates to profitability and is captured by the average return on the strongest operating profitability portfolios minus the average return on the weakest operating profitability portfolios. Profitability is measured as, *revenue minus the cost of goods sold, minus selling, general, and administrative expenses, minus interest expense, all divided by book equity.* The second variable is CMA, which captures the average return on the most conservative investment portfolios minus the average return on the most aggressive investment portfolios. Investment is measured as, *the change in total assets from the fiscal year ending in year t–2 to the fiscal year ending in t–1, divided by t–2 total assets.*

Fama and French (2016) provide additional damning evidence on the power of beta. Specifically, average returns are positively related to RMW and negatively related to CMA, virtually removing the explanatory power of beta in average US returns. Fama and French (2017) subsequently tested their model on European stock returns and found that the profitability factor (RMW) has explanatory power for average returns but the investment factor (CMA) adds little information.

These contentions, if confirmed by other research, would be quite damaging to the CAPM. After all, the CAPM states that the expected returns on equities should be related only to beta, and not to other factors such as PE, MB, momentum or market volatility.

Many researchers have criticized the research carried out by Fama and French. We avoid an in-depth discussion of the subtler points of the debate, but we mention a few issues. First, although Fama and French, Carhart, and Ang and colleagues cannot reject the hypothesis that average returns are unrelated to beta, they also cannot reject the hypothesis that average returns are related to beta exactly as specified by the CAPM. In other words, although 50 years of data seem like a lot, there may simply not be enough observations to test the CAPM properly. Second, the results may be due to a statistical fallacy called *hindsight bias.*[17] Third, PE, MB, momentum and market volatility are only four of an infinite number of possible factors. Thus, the relationship between average return and these variables may be spurious, being nothing more than the result of data mining. Fourth, average returns on US stocks are positively related to beta over the period from 1927 to the present. There appears to be no compelling reason for emphasizing a shorter period than this one. Fifth, average returns are positively related to beta over shorter periods when annual data, rather than monthly data, are used to estimate beta.[18] There appears to be no compelling reason for preferring either monthly data over annual data, or vice versa. Thus, we believe that although the results of Fama and French, Carhart, Ang et al., and others, are quite intriguing, we cannot view them as the final word.

10.11 Variations of the CAPM

The CAPM relates an individual security's expected return to the expected return on the market portfolio through its systematic risk, beta. Beta measures the sensitivity of an investor's wealth to movements in the underlying market portfolio. Many academics have argued that wealth, in itself, is not important in pricing securities. Instead, it is the effect of an investment on the consumption, or spending power, of an investor that is relevant. So, the more that investment makes consumption riskier, the higher should be its expected returns.

This view has led to a variation of the CAPM, known as the consumption capital asset pricing model, or CCAPM. Systematic risk, or beta, in the CAPM measures the covariance of security returns with market returns. However, in the CCAPM, beta is slightly more complicated. We express the CCAPM as follows:

Equation 10.21

$\overline{R}$	=	R_F	+	β_c	×	$(\overline{R}_M - R_F)$
Expected return on a security		Risk-free rate		Consumption beta of the security		Difference between expected return on market and risk-free rate

where the consumption beta, β_c, is equal to:

$$\beta_c = \frac{\text{Cov}(\overline{R}, \text{ consumption growth})}{\text{Cov}(\overline{R}_M, \text{ consumption growth})}$$

In the CCAPM, if a security has a higher expected return when consumption growth is higher, its consumption beta will be high. Similarly, a low covariance between security returns and consumption growth will lead to a lower CCAPM beta.

Another variation in the CAPM recognizes that not all of an individual's wealth comes from financial assets. In recent years, many people increased their wealth through investment in non-financial (human capital) assets such as housing and property. This has been particularly true in Europe (mainly the UK, Ireland and Eastern Europe), where property values have been growing at a high rate each year. The same high property growth rates have been observed in China, Hong Kong and India. The human capital CAPM, or HCAPM, incorporates both sources of wealth creation. According to the HCAPM, the return on the expected market portfolio is a linear combination (weighted by the relative investment of assets) of the expected return on the underlying financial portfolio and the underlying non-financial portfolio. If δ represents the fraction of total wealth that is invested in non-financial assets (or human capital), and $\overline{R}_{NF}$ and $\overline{R}_F$ represent the expected returns on non-financial and financial assets respectively, the expected return on the market is equal to:

$$\overline{R}_M = \delta\overline{R}_{NF} + (1 - \delta)\overline{R}_F$$

The expected return on financial assets is simply the market portfolio of the CAPM, whereas the expected return on non-financial assets is typically taken to be the growth in average earnings or labour income. The HCAPM has the same form as the standard CAPM. However, if the expected return on the market portfolio is disaggregated into its two components, the expected return on a security can be expressed as a linear function of its financial and non-financial betas. In this form, the expected return on a security is shown as follows:

$$\overline{R} = \beta_0 + \beta_F\overline{R}_F + \beta_{NF}\overline{R}_{NF}$$

Although both the CCAPM and HCAPM are theoretically sound, because of the difficulties in using the model with real data, the models do not tend to be used in practice. The CCAPM requires reliable data on total consumption growth, and the HCAPM utilizes data on non-financial wealth, both of which are rarely available on a continuing basis. For this reason, the standard CAPM is the most commonly used theoretical model in corporate finance.

In recent years, a variant of the CCAPM, known as the extrapolative capital asset pricing model, or X-CAPM, has emerged as an interesting model to explain aggregate stock returns. The basic premise of the model is that a subgroup of all investors form expectations of future stock returns based on past return information. When both groups of investors are combined in a CCAPM-type specification, the model captures many of the observed behaviours of stock returns.

To understand how the X-CAPM model works in practice, consider the dividend pricing model:

$$P_0 = \frac{Div_1}{r} \Rightarrow \frac{Div_1}{r} - P_0 = 0$$

If $\frac{Div_1}{r} > P_0$ we would expect prices to increase and stock returns to be positive. The converse is true for $\frac{Div_1}{r} < P_0$ and prices will fall, leading to negative returns. If there is a proportion of investors who extrapolate historical information to form expectations of future returns, then the difference $\frac{Div_1}{r} - P_0$ will be autocorrelated over time. Barberis et al. (2015) found that this difference measure was a good predictor of future share price returns. Barberis et al. (2018) found that the extrapolation concept can also be used to explain pricing bubbles in stock markets.

Summary and Conclusions

This chapter set forth the fundamentals of modern portfolio theory. Our basic points are these:

1 This chapter showed us how to calculate the expected return and variance for individual securities, and the covariance and correlation for pairs of securities. Given these statistics, we write the expected return and variance for a portfolio of two securities, A and B, as:

$$\text{Expected return on portfolio} = X_A\overline{R}_A + X_B\overline{R}_B$$
$$\text{Var (portfolio)} = X_A^2\sigma_A^2 + 2X_AX_B\sigma_{AB} + X_B^2\sigma_B^2$$

2 In our notation, X stands for the proportion of a security in a portfolio. By varying X we can trace out the efficient set of portfolios. We graphed the efficient set for the two-asset case as a curve, pointing out that the degree of curvature or bend in the graph reflects the diversification effect: the lower the correlation between the two securities, the sharper the bend. The same general shape of the efficient set holds in a world of many assets.

3 Just as the formula for variance in the two-asset case is computed from a 2 × 2 matrix, the variance formula is computed from an $N \times N$ matrix in the N-asset case. We showed that, with a large number of assets, there

are many more covariance terms than variance terms in the matrix. In fact the variance terms are effectively diversified away in a large portfolio, but the covariance terms are not. Thus, a diversified portfolio can eliminate some, but not all, of the risk of the individual securities.

4 The efficient set of risky assets can be combined with riskless borrowing and lending. In this case, a rational investor will always choose to hold the portfolio of risky securities represented by point *A* in Figure 10.10. Then he can either borrow or lend at the riskless rate to achieve any desired point on line II in the figure.

5 The contribution of a security to the risk of a large, well-diversified portfolio is proportional to the covariance of the security's return with the market's return. This contribution, when standardized, is called the beta. The beta of a security can also be interpreted as the responsiveness of a security's return to that of the market.

6 The CAPM states that:

$$\bar{R} = R_F + \beta(\bar{R}_M - R_F)$$

In other words, the expected return on a security is positively (and linearly) related to the security's beta.

7 The CAPM is a theoretical construct and gives only an insight into reality. Other theoretical models exist that do just as good a job at explaining variation in expected security returns, and sometimes an even better job.

Questions and Problems

connect

CONCEPT

1 **Individual Securities** What are the main characteristics of individual security returns? Provide a definition of each characteristic and say why it is important.

2 **Expected Return, Variance and Covariance** Explain what is meant by correlation and how it is used to measure the relationship between the returns on two securities. How is correlation related to variance and covariance? Use mathematical formulae to illustrate your answer. If a portfolio has a positive investment in every asset, can the expected return on the portfolio be greater or less than on every asset in the portfolio?

3 **Portfolio Risk and Return** Why does naive diversification reduce the risk of a portfolio? What benefits does naive diversification bring to international investment strategies?

4 **The Efficient Set for Two Assets** What is a minimum variance portfolio? In a world with only two assets, is it possible to have two portfolios with the same risk but different expected return? Explain your answer using a practical example. What is the two-fund spanning property of the efficient frontier?

5 **The Efficient Set for Many Securities** In a portfolio of many securities, all having positive correlation with one another, is it possible for the minimum variance portfolio to have zero risk? What happens to the efficient frontier when a risk-free asset exists?

6 **Diversification** Assume that every asset has the same expected return and variance. Furthermore, all assets have the same covariance with one another. As the number of assets in the portfolio grows, which becomes more important: variance or covariance? Clarify your answer using words, diagrams, formulae and a practical example.

7 **Riskless Borrowing and Lending** Explain what is meant by an optimal portfolio. What are the conditions that must exist for there to be only one optimal portfolio? Do you think these conditions are likely to persist in the real world? Explain.

8 **Market Equilibrium** Your company is following two stocks, ABC plc and XYZ plc, and your manager tells you the following:

'The shares of ABC plc have traded close to £15 for most of the past four years, and because of this lack of price movement the stock has a very low beta. XYZ plc, on the other hand, has traded as high as £90 and as low as its current £20. Since this stock has demonstrated a large amount of price movement, the stock has a very high beta.'

Do you agree with your manager's analysis?

9 **Relationship between Risk and Expected Return** Is it possible that a risky asset could have a beta of zero? Explain. Based on the CAPM, what is the expected return on such an asset? Is it possible that a risky asset could have a negative

beta? What does the CAPM predict about the expected return on such an asset? Can you give an explanation for your answer? Discuss the central predictions of the CAPM and give an overview of the empirical evidence.

10 **Criticisms of the CAPM** Define the market portfolio and provide a brief overview of Roll's (1977) critique. Do you agree or disagree with it? Why?

11 **Variations of the CAPM** Explain what is meant by the CCAPM, HCAPM and X-CAPM. Why do you think these models are not popular with practitioners? Give an overview of the empirical evidence concerning these models and their performance relative to the CAPM.

REGULAR

12 **Systematic versus Unsystematic Risk** Classify the following events as mostly systematic or mostly unsystematic:

- (a) The Bank of England's base rate increases unexpectedly.
- (b) A company renegotiates its bank debt after breaching a covenant agreement.
- (c) Oil prices unexpectedly decline.
- (d) No clear winner in the British general election.
- (e) A bank loses a multimillion-pound lawsuit for the mis-selling of derivative products.

13 **Short Selling** Explain what is meant by short selling. When is short selling profitable?

14 **Risk** A broker has advised you not to invest in technology stocks because they have high standard deviations. Is the broker's advice sound for a risk-averse investor like yourself? Why, or why not?

15 **Using the CAPM** An equity has a beta of 0.9 and an expected return of 9 per cent. A risk-free asset currently earns 2 per cent.

- (a) What is the expected return on a portfolio that is equally invested in the two assets?
- (b) If a portfolio of the two assets has a beta of 0.6, what are the portfolio weights?
- (c) If a portfolio of the two assets has an expected return of 6 per cent, what is its beta?
- (d) If a portfolio of the two assets has a beta of 1.50, what are the portfolio weights? How do you interpret the weights for the two assets in this case? Explain.

16 **Portfolio Risk** Assume the risk-free rate is 3 per cent and the expected return on the FTSE 100 index is 9 per cent. The standard deviation of the market index is 23 per cent. You are managing the pension fund of your company and would like to achieve an expected return of 5 per cent. How should your company's pension portfolio be structured so as to achieve this expected return? What is the risk of this portfolio?

17 **Using the SML** *W* has an expected return of 12 per cent and a beta of 1.2. If the risk-free rate is 3 per cent, complete the following table for portfolios of *W* and a risk-free asset. Illustrate the relationship between portfolio expected return and portfolio beta by plotting the expected returns against the betas. What is the slope of the line that results?

Percentage of Portfolio in *W*	Portfolio Expected Return	Portfolio Beta
0		
25		
50		
75		
100		
125		
150		

18 **Reward-to-risk Ratios** Y has a beta of 1.50 and an expected return of 17 per cent. Z has a beta of 0.80 and an expected return of 10.5 per cent. If the risk-free rate is 5.5 per cent and the market risk premium is 7.5 per cent, are these equities correctly priced? What would the risk-free rate have to be for the two equities to be correctly priced?

19 **Portfolio Returns and Deviations** Shares in Hellenic Telecom have an expected return of 15 per cent and the standard deviation of these returns is 30 per cent. National Bank of Greece's shares are expected to produce a return of 16 per cent with a standard deviation of 40 per cent. What would be the rate of return and risk of a portfolio made up of 40 per cent of Hellenic Telecom's shares and 60 per cent of National Bank of Greece's shares, if the returns on these shares have a correlation of 0.6?

20 Analysing a Portfolio You want to create a portfolio equally as risky as the market, and you have €1,000,000 to invest. Given this information, fill in the rest of the following table:

Asset	Investment (€)	Beta
Equity A	200,000	0.80
Equity B	250,000	1.30
Equity C		1.50
Risk-free asset		

21 Analysing a Portfolio: Risk-Return Trade-Offs and Diversification You have £24,000 to invest in a portfolio containing X, Y and a risk-free asset. You must invest all of your money. Your goal is to create a portfolio that has an expected return of 8.5 per cent and that has only 70 per cent of the risk of the overall market. If X has an expected return of 12 per cent and a beta of 1.5, Y has an expected return of 9 per cent and a beta of 1.2, and the risk-free rate is 3 per cent, how much money will you invest in X? How do you interpret your answer? Given the information provided, and considering that you aim to construct a portfolio with a target expected return of 8.5 per cent and only 70 per cent of the risk of the overall market, how can you determine the optimal weights of investments in assets X, Y and the risk-free asset in order to meet these objectives, and what insights can be drawn from these allocations in terms of the potential risk-return trade-offs and the diversification benefits within the portfolio?

22 Covariance and Correlation Based on the following information, calculate the expected return and standard deviation of each of the following equities. Assume each state of the economy is equally likely to happen. What are the covariance and correlation between the returns of the two equities?

State of Economy	Return on A	Return on B
Bear	0.063	−0.037
Normal	0.105	0.064
Bull	0.156	0.253

23 Covariance and Correlation: State Probabilities Based on the following information, calculate the expected return and standard deviation for each of the following equities. What are the covariance and correlation between the returns of the two equities?

State of Economy	Probability of State of Economy	Return on J	Return on K
Bear	0.25	−0.020	0.050
Normal	0.60	0.092	0.062
Bull	0.15	0.154	0.074

24 Portfolio Standard Deviation Suppose the expected returns and standard deviations of A and B are $E(R_A) = 0.15$, $E(R_B) = 0.25$, $\sigma_A = 0.40$, and $\sigma_B = 0.65$, respectively.

(a) Calculate the expected return and standard deviation of a portfolio that is composed of 40 per cent A and 60 per cent B when the correlation between the returns on A and B is 0.5.

(b) Calculate the standard deviation of a portfolio that is composed of 40 per cent A and 60 per cent B when the correlation coefficient between the returns on A and B is −0.5.

(c) How does the correlation between the returns on A and B affect the standard deviation of the portfolio?

25 Correlation and Beta You have been provided the following data about the equities of three firms, the market portfolio and the risk-free asset:

	Expected Return	Standard Deviation	Correlation*	Beta
Firm A	0.13	0.38	(i)	0.9
Firm B	0.16	(ii)	0.40	1.1
Firm C	0.25	0.65	0.35	(iii)

	Expected Return	Standard Deviation	Correlation*	Beta
The market portfolio	0.15	0.20	(iv)	(v)
The risk-free asset	0.05	(vi)	(vii)	(viii)

* With the market portfolio.

(a) Fill in the missing values (i)–(viii) in the table.

(b) Is the equity of Firm A correctly priced according to the capital asset pricing model (CAPM)? What about the equity of Firm B? Firm C? If these securities are not correctly priced, what is your investment recommendation for someone with a well-diversified portfolio?

26 CML The market portfolio has an expected return of 12 per cent and a standard deviation of 10 per cent. The risk-free rate is 5 per cent.

(a) What is the expected return on a well-diversified portfolio with a standard deviation of 7 per cent?

(b) What is the standard deviation of a well-diversified portfolio with an expected return of 20 per cent?

(c) How do these portfolios compare to the market portfolio in terms of risk-return trade-off?

27 CAPM The expected rates of return on the French firms, Publicis and Renault, the market portfolio (CAC 40) and the risk-free asset are given below, along with the standard deviations of these returns.

Asset	Expected Return (%)	Standard Deviation (%)
Publicis	17	40
Renault	10	20
CAC 40	14	17
Risk-free asset	3	0

(a) Assuming that returns are explained by the capital asset pricing model (CAPM), specify the betas for Publicis and Renault, and the risk of a portfolio of Publicis and Renault with an expected return the same as the CAC 40.

(b) Specify the composition of a portfolio consisting of the CAC 40 and the risk-free asset that will produce an expected return of 10 per cent. Contrast the risk on this portfolio with the risk of Renault.

28 Portfolios Below is given the standard deviation and correlation information on three South African companies, Afgri, Harmony Gold and SABMiller.

	Afgri	Harmony Gold	SABMiller	Standard Deviation (%)
Afgri	1	−0.2	0.5	29
Harmony Gold		1	0.4	21
SABMiller			1	23

(a) If a portfolio is made up of 30 per cent of Afgri, 40 per cent of Harmony Gold and 30 per cent of SABMiller, estimate the portfolio's standard deviation.

(b) If you were asked to design a portfolio using just Harmony Gold and Afgri, what percentage investment in each share would produce a zero standard deviation?

CHALLENGE

29 Systematic versus Unsystematic Risk Consider the following information about I and II:

State of Economy	Probability of State of Economy	Rate of Return if State Occurs	
		I	II
Recession	0.15	0.09	−0.30
Normal	0.70	0.42	0.12
Irrational exuberance	0.15	0.26	0.44

The market risk premium is 10 per cent, and the risk-free rate is 4 per cent. Which security has the most systematic risk? Which one has the most unsystematic risk? Which stock is 'riskier'? Explain.

30 CML and SML Explain in detail, using diagrams to illustrate your answer, what is meant by the terms 'capital market line' and 'security market line'.

31 SML Suppose you observe the following situation:

Security	Beta	Expected Return
Renewable Energy Corp	1.3	0.23
Statoil	0.6	0.13

Assume these securities are correctly priced. Based on the CAPM, what is the expected return on the market? What is the risk-free rate?

32 Portfolio Theory This question is designed to test your understanding of the mean standard deviation diagram.

(a) Draw a mean-standard deviation diagram to illustrate combinations of a risky asset and the risk-free asset.

(b) Extend this concept to a diagram of the risk-free asset and all possible risky portfolios.

(c) Why does one line, the capital market line, dominate all other possible portfolio combinations?

(d) Label the capital market line and that optimal portfolio.

(e) What condition must hold at the optimal portfolio?

33 Covariance and Portfolio Standard Deviation There are three securities in the market. The following chart shows their possible payoffs:

State	Probability of Outcome	Return on Security 1	Return on Security 2	Return on Security 3
1	0.10	0.25	0.25	0.10
2	0.40	0.20	0.15	0.15
3	0.40	0.15	0.20	0.20
4	0.10	0.10	0.10	0.25

(a) What are the expected return and standard deviation of each security?

(b) What are the covariances and correlations between the pairs of securities?

(c) What are the expected return and standard deviation of a portfolio with half of its funds invested in security 1 and half in security 2?

(d) What are the expected return and standard deviation of a portfolio with half of its funds invested in security 1 and half in security 3?

(e) What are the expected return and standard deviation of a portfolio with half of its funds invested in security 2 and half in security 3?

(f) What do your answers to parts (a), (c), (d) and (e) imply about diversification?

34 SML and Market Risk Premiums Suppose you observe the following situation:

State of Economy	Probability of State	Return if State Occurs	
		A	B
Bust	0.25	−0.10	−0.30
Normal	0.50	0.10	0.05
Boom	0.25	0.20	0.40

(a) Calculate the expected return on each equity.

(b) Assuming the capital asset pricing model holds and A's beta is greater than B's beta by 0.25, what is the expected market risk premium?

35 Standard Deviation and Beta There are two securities in the market, A and B. The price of A today is €50. The price of A next year will be €40 if the economy is in a recession, €55 if the economy is normal and €60 if the economy is expanding. The probabilities of recession, normal times and expansion are 0.1, 0.8 and 0.1, respectively. A pays no dividends and has a correlation of 0.8 with the market portfolio. B has an expected return of 9 per cent, a standard deviation of 12 per cent, a correlation with the market portfolio of 0.2, and a correlation with A of 0.6. The market portfolio has a standard deviation of 10 per cent. Assume the CAPM holds.

(a) If you are a typical, risk-averse investor with a well-diversified portfolio, which security would you prefer? Why?

(b) What are the expected return and standard deviation of a portfolio consisting of 70 per cent of A and 30 per cent of B?

(c) What is the beta of the portfolio in part (b)?

36 Company Beta Charles Ray plc has three main divisions: Oil & Gas, Minerals, and Power & Industrial. Oil & Gas accounts for 40 per cent of the company's assets and Minerals accounts for 35 per cent of the assets. It has been estimated that the asset betas for these divisions are 1.2, 0.8 and 0.6, respectively. Estimate the beta of Charles Ray's equity if the debt is risk-free.

37 Minimum Variance Portfolio Assume A and B have the following characteristics:

Equity	Expected Return (%)	Standard Deviation (%)
A	5	10
B	10	20

The covariance between the returns on the two equities is 0.001.

(a) Suppose an investor holds a portfolio consisting of only A and B. Find the portfolio weights, X_A and X_B, such that the variance of her portfolio is minimized. (*Hint:* Remember that the sum of the two weights must equal 1.)

(b) What is the expected return on the minimum variance portfolio?

(c) If the covariance between the returns on the two equities is −0.02, what are the minimum variance weights?

(d) What is the variance of the portfolio in part (c)?

38 CAPM: Expected Returns and Beta An investor holds a portfolio of three securities. She invests 30 per cent in A, 30 per cent in B and 40 per cent in C. The betas on A, B and C are 1.5, 0.6 and 1.1, respectively. If $E(R_M) = 12\%$ and $R_F = 4\%$, calculate the expected return and beta of the portfolio.

39 Minimum Variance Portfolio Consider the table below. Using either the historical return or expected return and Solver in Excel, compute the minimum variance portfolio for the universe of three Norwegian shares, Crew Gold, GGS and Marine Harvest, described below. Assume the risk-free return is 6 per cent. Which return measure did you use and why?

	Correlation with					
Stock	Crew Gold	GGS	Marine Harvest	Expected Return (%)	Historical Return (%)	Variance
Crew Gold	1	0.40	0.45	16	20.65	168
GGS	0.40	1	−0.09	10	−34.15	231
Marine Harvest	0.45	−0.09	1	30	68.6	433

40 Beta The following prices are for Rollway plc and the market index.

Date	Rollway plc	Market Index
Mar-23	1,187.00	5,768.50
Feb-23	1,077.00	5,871.50
Jan-23	941.00	5,681.60
Dec-22	852.00	5,572.30
Nov-22	922.50	5,505.40
Oct-22	1,179.00	5,544.20
Sep-22	1,263.00	5,128.50
Aug-22	1,365.00	5,394.50
Jul-22	1,549.00	5,815.20
Jun-22	1,661.00	5,945.70
May-22	1,723.00	5,990.00
Apr-22	1,692.00	6,069.90
Mar-22	1,554.00	5,908.80

Use a spreadsheet to calculate Rollway plc's beta for the full period. Now calculate the beta using data for March 2022 to September 2022. Calculate the beta for October 2022 to March 2023. What can you say about the different beta estimates? Is this evidence for or against the CAPM? Explain your answer.

Exam Question (45 minutes)

Below, you are given the expected returns and standard deviations of L'Oréal and Daimler AG, the Euro Stoxx 50 Index of largest Eurozone firms, and the risk-free asset.

Asset	Expected Return (%)	Standard Deviation (%)
L'Oréal	16	30
Daimler	12	25
Euro Stoxx 50	13	12
Risk-free asset	3	0

1 Assuming that the returns are explained by the capital asset pricing model, calculate the betas of L'Oréal and Daimler, and the risk of a portfolio holding L'Oréal and Daimler with an expected return the same as the Euro Stoxx 50 Index return. **(20 marks)**

2 Construct a portfolio consisting of the Euro Stoxx 50 Index and the risk-free asset that will produce an expected return of 12 per cent. Contrast the risk on this portfolio with the risk of Daimler. **(20 marks)**

3 Assuming that the expected return on an average security is 13 per cent with a standard deviation of 26 per cent, and the average covariance of returns between securities is +100, determine the expected risk of a portfolio with 28 securities and a portfolio with 1,000 securities. Comment briefly on your results. **(20 marks)**

4 Now assume that the returns on securities are independent. Continuing to assume that the expected return on an average security is 13 per cent with a standard deviation of 26 per cent, determine the risk of a portfolio with 28 securities and 1,000 securities. Comment on your results. **(20 marks)**

5 Explain what is meant by the separation principle. **(20 marks)**

Total Marks: 100

Mini Case

A Job at West Coast Yachts, Part 2

You are discussing your retirement plan with Dan Ervin when he mentions that Sarah Brown, a representative from Skandla Financial Services, is visiting West Coast Yachts today. You decide that you should meet with Sarah, so Dan sets up an appointment for you later in the day.

When you sit down with Sarah, she discusses the various investment options available in the company's retirement account. You mention to Sarah that you researched West Coast Yachts before you accepted your new job. You are confident in management's ability to lead the company. Analysis of the company has led to your belief that it is growing and will achieve a greater market share in the future. Given these considerations, you are leaning towards investing 100 per cent of your retirement account in West Coast Yachts.

Assume the risk-free rate is the return on a 30-day T-bill. The correlation between the Skandla bond fund and large-cap equity fund is 0.27.

1 Considering the effects of diversification, how should Sarah respond to the suggestion that you invest 100 per cent of your retirement account in West Coast Yachts?

2 Sarah's response to investing your retirement account entirely in West Coast Yachts has convinced you that this may not be the best alternative. You now consider that a 100 per cent investment in the bond fund may be the best alternative. Is it?

3 Using the returns for the Skandla Large-Company Equity Fund and the Skandla Bond Fund, graph the opportunity set of feasible portfolios.

4 After examining the opportunity set, you notice that you can invest in a portfolio consisting of the bond fund and the large-cap equity fund that will have exactly the same standard deviation as the bond fund. This portfolio will also have a greater expected return. What are the portfolio weights and expected return of this portfolio?

5 Examining the opportunity set, notice there is a portfolio that has the lowest standard deviation. This is the minimum variance portfolio. What are the portfolio weights, expected return and standard deviation of this portfolio? Why is the minimum variance portfolio important?

6 A measure of risk-adjusted performance that is often used is the Sharpe ratio. The Sharpe ratio is calculated as the risk premium of an asset divided by its standard deviation. The portfolio with the highest possible Sharpe ratio on the opportunity set is called the Sharpe optimal portfolio. What are the portfolio weights, expected return and standard deviation of the Sharpe optimal portfolio? How does the Sharpe ratio of this portfolio compare to the Sharpe ratios of the bond fund and the large-cap equity fund? Do you see a connection between the Sharpe optimal portfolio and the CAPM?

Practical Case Study

Using CAPM Find estimates of beta for two companies listed on your country's stock exchange. Using an estimate of the historical risk-free rate and market risk premium, calculate the expected return for each company based on the most recent beta. Is the expected return for each company what you would expect? Why, or why not?

References

Ang, A., R.J. Hodrick, Y. Xing and X. Zhang (2006) 'The Cross-section of Volatility and Expected Returns', *Journal of Finance*, Vol. 51, 259–299.

Barberis, N., R. Greenwood, L. Jin and A. Shleifer (2015) 'X-CAPM: An Extrapolative Capital Asset Pricing Model', *Journal of Financial Economics*, Vol. 115, No. 1, 1–24.

Barberis, N., R. Greenwood, L. Jin and A. Shleifer (2018) 'Extrapolation and Bubbles', *Journal of Financial Economics*, Vol. 129, No. 2, 203–227.

Black, F., M.C. Jensen and M.S. Scholes (1972) 'The Capital Asset Pricing Model: Some Empirical Tests', in M. Jensen (ed.), *Studies in the Theory of Capital Markets*. New York: Praeger.

Breen, W.J. and R.A. Koraczyk (1993) 'On Selection Biases in Book-to-market Based Tests of Asset Pricing Models', unpublished paper.

Carhart, M. (1997) 'On Persistence in Mutual Fund Performance', *Journal of Finance*, Vol. 52, 57–82.

Fama, E.F. and K.R. French (1992) 'The Cross-section of Expected Stock Returns', *Journal of Finance*, Vol. 47, 427–466.

Fama, E.F. and K.R. French (1993) 'Common Risk Factors in the Returns on Stocks and Bonds', *Journal of Financial Economics*, Vol. 17, 3–56.

Fama, E.F. and K.R. French (1998) 'Value versus Growth: The International Evidence', *Journal of Finance*, Vol. 53, 1975–1999.

Fama, E.F. and K.R. French (2015) 'A Five-factor Asset Pricing Model', *Journal of Financial Economics*, Vol. 116, No. 1, 1–22.

Fama, E.F. and K.R. French (2016) 'Dissecting Anomalies with a Five-factor Model', *Review of Financial Studies*, Vol. 29, No. 1, 69–103.

Fama, E.F. and K.R. French (2017) 'International Tests of a Five-factor Asset Pricing Model', *Journal of Financial Economics*, Vol. 123, No. 3, 441–463.

Fama, E.F. and J. MacBeth (1973) 'Risk, Return and Equilibrium: Some Empirical Tests', *Journal of Political Economy*, Vol. 8, 607–636.

Kothari, S.P., J. Shanken and R.G. Sloan (1995) 'Another Look at the Cross-section of Expected Stock Returns', *Journal of Finance*, Vol. 50, No. 1, 185–224.

Lintner, J. (1965) 'The Valuation of Risk Assets and the Selection of Risky Investments in Stock Portfolios and Capital Budgets', *Review of Economics and Statistics*, Vol. 47, No. 1, 13–37.

Markowitz, H. (1959) *Portfolio Selection*. New York: John Wiley & Sons.

Roll, R. (1977) 'A Critique of the Asset Pricing Theory's Tests', *Journal of Financial Economics*, Vol. 4, 129–176.

Sharpe, W.F. (1964) 'Capital Asset Prices: A Theory of Market Equilibrium Under Conditions of Risk', *Journal of Finance*, Vol. 19, No. 3, 425–442.

Statman, M. (1987) 'How Many Stocks Make a Diversified Portfolio?', *Journal of Financial Quantitative Analysis*, Vol. 22, No. 3, 353–363.

Additional Reading

Capital asset pricing theory is probably the most tested theory in modern investment finance. Given this, it is important that the interested reader is directed to the most relevant recent research in the area. A number of papers listed below directly test the power of the CAPM or market model beta under a variety of environments and with a number of other control variables. While it is easy to say that the range of CAPM anomalies suggests that the model is inferior to other, more complex models, it is still the most commonly used way to estimate the cost of equity (discount rate) of a listed firm. Most of the papers listed below study the US markets. The list does not follow any real theme, as is the case in other chapters. Moreover, the listing is a very small representation of recent research in the area. Those who wish to specialize should view the references as the tip of the iceberg and use them to build up their own reading list.

Good starting points for exploring the research on cross-sectional returns are:

Linnainmaa, J.T. and M.R. Roberts (2018) 'The History of the Cross-section of Stock Returns', *Review of Financial Studies*, Vol. 31, No. 7, 2606–2649.

McLean, R.D. and J. Pontiff (2016) 'Does Academic Research Destroy Stock Return Predictability?', *Journal of Finance*, Vol. 71, No. 1, 5–32.

Other more specialized papers are:

1 Bai, H., K. Hou, H. Kung, E.X. Li and L. Zhang (2019) 'The CAPM Strikes Back? An Equilibrium Model with Disasters', *Journal of Financial Economics*, Vol. 131, No. 2, 269–298.

2 Burlacu, R., P. Fontaine, S. Jimenez-Garcès and M.S. Seasholes (2012) 'Risk and the Cross Section of Stock Returns', *Journal of Financial Economics*, Vol. 105, No. 3, 511–522.

3 Dimson, E., P. Marsh and M. Staunton (2017) 'Factor-based Investing: The Long-term Evidence', *Journal of Portfolio Management*, Vol. 43, No. 5, 15.

4 Fama, E.F. and K.R. French (2012) 'Size, Value, and Momentum in International Stock Returns', *Journal of Financial Economics*, Vol. 105, No. 3, 457–472.

5 Fama, E.F. and K.R. French (2018) 'Choosing Factors', *Journal of Financial Economics*, Vol. 128, No. 2, 234–252.

6 Gârleanu, N., L. Kogan and S. Panageas (2012) 'Displacement Risk and Asset Returns', *Journal of Financial Economics*, Vol. 105, No. 3, 491–510.

7 Harvey, C.R., Y. Liu and H. Zhu, (2016) '. . . and the Cross-section of Expected Returns', *Review of Financial Studies*, Vol. 29, No. 1, 5–68.

8 Hou, K., C. Xue and L. Zhang (2015) 'Digesting Anomalies: An Investment Approach', *Review of Financial Studies*, Vol. 28, No. 3, 650–705.

9 Koijen, R.S., H. Lustig and S. Van Nieuwerburgh (2017) 'The Cross-section and Time Series of Stock and Bond Returns', *Journal of Monetary Economics*, Vol. 88, 50–69.

10 Medhat, M. and M. Schmeling (2022) 'Short-term Momentum', *Review of Financial Studies*, Vol. 35, No. 3, 1480–1526.

11 Novy-Marx, R. (2013) 'The Other Side of Value: The Gross Profitability Premium', *Journal of Financial Economics*, Vol. 108, No. 1, 1–28.

12 Trigeorgis, L. and N. Lambertides (2014) 'The Role of Growth Options in Explaining Stock Returns', *Journal of Financial and Quantitative Analysis*, Vol. 49, No. 3, 749–771.

Endnotes

1 In this example, the four states give rise to four *possible* outcomes for each security. Had we used past data, the outcomes would have actually occurred. In that case, statisticians argue that the correct divisor is $N - 1$, where N is the number of observations. Thus the denominator would be $3[= (4 - 1)]$ in the case of past data, not 4. Note that the example in Section 9.5 involved past data and we used a divisor of $N - 1$. While this difference causes grief to both students and textbook writers, it is a minor point in practice. In the real world, samples are generally so large that using N or $N - 1$ in the denominator has virtually no effect on the calculation of variance.

2 As with variance, we divided by N (4 in this example) because the four states give rise to four possible outcomes. However, had we used past data, the correct divisor would be $N - 1$ (3 in this example).

3 There are only four equally probable returns for Supertech and Slowburn, so neither security possesses a normal distribution. Thus, probabilities would be slightly different in our example.

4 As with covariance, the ordering of the two securities is not relevant when we express the correlation between the two securities. That is, $\rho_{\text{Super, Slow}} = \rho_{\text{Slow, Super}}$.

5 A major exception occurs with derivative securities. For example, the correlation between an equity share and a put on the equity is generally strongly negative. Puts will be treated later in the text.

6 Of course, someone dead set on parting with their money can do so. For example, one can trade frequently without purpose, so that commissions more than offset the positive expected returns on the portfolio.

7 The classic treatise is Harry Markowitz, *Portfolio Selection* (1959). Markowitz won the Nobel Prize in Economics in 1990 for his work on modern portfolio theory.

8 Equation 10.10 is actually a weighted *average* of the variance and covariance terms because the weights, $1/N$ and $1 - 1/N$, sum to 1.

9 This example ignores the casino's cut.

10 Though it is harder to show, this risk reduction effect also applies to the general case where variances and covariances are *not* equal.

11 Surprisingly, this appears to be a decent approximation because many investors can borrow from a stockbroker (called *going on margin*) when purchasing securities. The borrowing rate here is very near the riskless rate of interest, particularly for large investors.

12 The assumption of homogeneous expectations states that all investors have the same beliefs concerning returns, variances and covariances. It does not say that all investors have the same aversion to risk.

13 Unfortunately, empirical evidence shows that virtually no equities have negative betas.

14 This relationship was first proposed independently by John Lintner (1965) and William F. Sharpe (1964). The plausible conditions are as follows: (1) investors are interested only in the mean and variance of their investment returns; (2) markets are frictionless; (3) investors have homogeneous expectations.

15 Perhaps the two best-known papers were Black et al. (1972) and Fama and MacBeth (1973).

16 For example, the studies suggest that the average return on a zero-beta portfolio is above the risk-free rate, a finding inconsistent with the CAPM.

17 For example, see Breen and Koraczyk (1993) and Kothari et al. (1995).

18 Points 4 and 5 are addressed in Kothari et al. (1995).

Chapter 11

Factor Models, the Arbitrage Pricing Theory, and Other Alternatives to CAPM

Learning Objectives

After reading this chapter you should be able to:

LO1 Define the key concepts of factor models, announcements, surprises and expected returns.

LO2 Analyse the differences between systematic and unsystematic risk, and explain their significance in corporate finance.

LO3 Compare and contrast the capital asset pricing model (CAPM) and the arbitrage pricing theory (APT), evaluating their respective strengths and weaknesses.

To paint a picture of the exceptionally complex financial situation facing companies in recent years, one can look at the impact of oil and gas on operations and, ultimately, share prices. Without any doubt, oil and gas prices have been more volatile than they have been for many years. Given their centrality to almost every sector of the economy, oil and gas prices can have a significant impact on corporate profitability and the viability of existing or potential investments. If oil and gas form the basis of revenues (for example, in BP and Shell), increases in the oil and gas price will generally improve the share price performance of these firms. If oil and gas are significant costs (say, in manufacturing and airline travel), increases in these prices will increase the cost of doing business and hurt share prices. Although most Western countries have reduced their reliance on oil and gas because of net zero targets, their economies are still dependent on oil and gas. Many oil-exporting countries can balance their budgets only when the oil price exceeds $100 a barrel. When the oil price falls below this level, their budgets will be in deficit, and cuts will need to be made in public spending. This raises the question, should we consider changes in oil and gas prices when we forecast the share price returns of companies, or is the market return enough? Oil and gas are just two factors – what about the gold price or interest rates? This chapter explores the fundamental concepts of risk and return in detail, and considers advanced asset pricing models for the estimation of risk and return.

Source: Péter Gudella/123RF

Key Notations

R	Total return in a period
$E(R)$	Expected return, and
U	Unexpected return
β_F	Systematic risk with respect to factor, F
HML	High minus low Fama French factor
SMB	Small minus big Fama French factor
MOM	Carhart momentum factor
RMW	High minus low profitability Fama French factor
CMA	High minus low investment Fama French factor
X_i	The weight of asset i in the portfolio
N	Number of assets in the portfolio
R_M	Market return
R_F	The risk-free rate of return

11.1 Factor Models: Announcements, Surprises and Expected Returns

We learned in Chapter 10 how to construct portfolios and how to evaluate their returns. We now step back and examine the returns on individual securities more closely. By doing this, we will find that the portfolios inherit and alter the properties of the securities they comprise.

To be concrete, let us consider the return on the shares of the global technology firm, Apple. What will determine its share price return over, say, a monthly period?

Chapter 10 Page 261

The return on any equity traded in a financial market consists of two parts. First, the *normal* or *expected return* from the equity is the part of the return that shareholders in the market predict or expect (for more information on expected returns see Chapter 10, Section 10.2). It depends on all of the information shareholders have that bears on the company, and it uses all of our understanding of what will influence the share price in the next month.

The second part is the *uncertain* or *risky return* on the equity, which is the portion that comes from information that will be revealed within the month. The list of such information is endless, but here are some examples:

- News about Apple's research
- Government figures released for the gross national product (GNP)
- The results of patent policy enforcement in Asia
- The discovery that someone has tampered with a rival's product
- News that Apple's sales figures are higher than expected
- A sudden drop in interest rates
- The unexpected death of Apple's chief executive.

A way to write the return on Apple's shares in the coming month, then, is:

$$R = E(R) + U$$

where R is the actual total return in the month, $E(R)$ is the expected part of the return, and U stands for the unexpected part of the return.

We must exercise some care in studying the effect of these or other news items on the return. For example, the government might give us GNP or unemployment figures for this month, but how much of that is new information for shareholders? At the beginning of the month, shareholders will have some idea or forecast of what the monthly GNP will be. The expectations of shareholders should be factored in to the expected part of the return as of the beginning of the month, $E(R)$. On the other hand, insofar as the announcement by the government is a surprise and to the extent to which it influences share price returns, it will be part of U, the unanticipated component of the return.

As an example, suppose shareholders in the market had forecast that the GNP increase this month would be 0.5 per cent. If GNP influences our company's share price, this forecast will be part of the information shareholders use to form the expectation, $E(R)$, of the monthly return. If the actual announcement this month is exactly 0.5 per cent, the same as the forecast, then the shareholders learned nothing new and the information is not news. It is like hearing a rumour about a friend when you knew it all along.

On the other hand, suppose the government announced that the actual GNP increase during the year was 1.5 per cent. Now shareholders have learned something: that the GNP growth is one percentage point higher than they had forecast. This difference between the actual result and the forecast, one percentage point in this example, is sometimes called the *innovation* or *surprise*.

Any announcement can be broken into two parts – the anticipated or expected part, and the surprise or innovation:

$$\text{Announcement} = \text{Expected part} + \text{Surprise}$$

The expected part of any announcement is part of the information the market uses to form the expectation, $E(R)$, of the return on the equity. The surprise is the news that influences the unanticipated return on the equity, U.

Returning to the Apple example, consider historical iPad sales between 2011 and 2023 (see Figure 11.1). Note the cyclicality in sales by quarter. For almost every year since 2011, Q1 sales have always been higher than those in any of the other quarters in the year. This is because of Christmas and the many iPads given as gifts at this time. So, although sales are reported lower in Q2, this isn't necessarily taken as bad news by the market. It is the surprise component in the drop that leads to price changes. If the drop in unit sales from Q1 to Q2 is as expected, Apple's share price won't change. If the drop is smaller than expected, the Apple share price will probably increase, and if the sales drop is greater than expected we would anticipate a fall in Apple's share price.

Figure 11.1 Quarterly Global iPad Sales ($ millions), 2011–2023

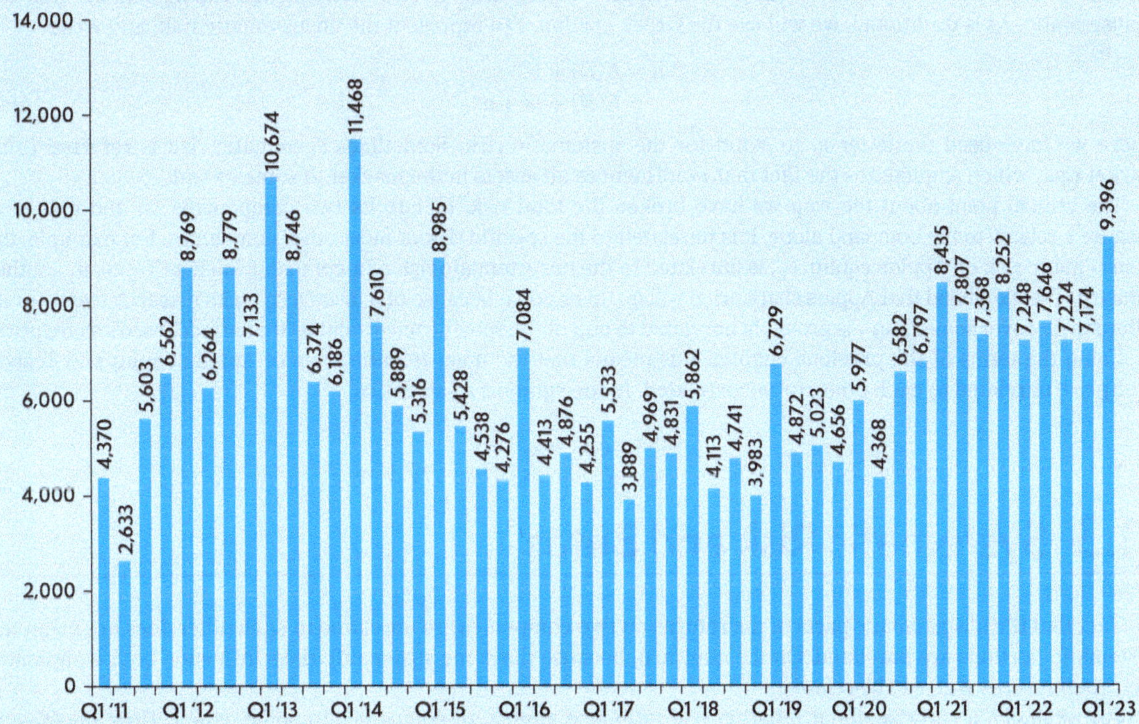

Source: www.statista.com

When we speak of news, then, we refer only to the surprise part of any announcement, and not any portion the market has expected and, therefore, already discounted.

11.2 Risk: Systematic and Unsystematic

The unanticipated part of the return – that portion resulting from surprises – is the actual risk of any investment. After all, if we got what we had expected, there would be no risk and no uncertainty.

There are differences, though, among sources of risk. Look at our previous list of news stories. Some of these stories explicitly concern Apple, while some are more about the economy. Which of the news items are of specific importance to Apple?

Chapter 10 Page 276

Announcements about interest rates or GNP are important for nearly all companies, whereas news about the Apple chief executive, its research, its sales or the affairs of a rival company are of specific interest to Apple's shareholders. We will divide these two types of announcements and the resulting risk, then, into two components: a systematic portion, called *systematic risk*, and the remainder, which we call *specific* or *unsystematic risk* (for more information on systematic and unsystematic risk, see Chapter 10, Section 10.6). The following definitions describe the difference:

- A *systematic risk* is any risk that affects a large number of assets, each to a greater or lesser degree.
- An *unsystematic risk* is a risk that affects a single asset or a small group of assets.[1]

Uncertainty about general economic conditions, such as GNP, interest rates or inflation, is an example of systematic risk. These conditions affect nearly all securities to some degree. An unanticipated or surprise increase in inflation affects wages and the costs of the supplies that companies buy, the value of the assets that companies own, and the prices at which companies sell their products. These forces to which all companies are susceptible are the essence of systematic risk.

In contrast, the announcement of a small technological innovation by Apple may affect that company alone, or a few other companies, but is unlikely to change global technology prices. To stress that such information is unsystematic and affects only some specific companies, we sometimes call it an *idiosyncratic risk*.

This permits us to break down the risk of Apple's equity into its two components: the systematic and the unsystematic. As is traditional, we will use the Greek epsilon, ε to represent the unsystematic risk, and write:

$$\begin{aligned} R &= E(R) + U \\ &= E(R) + m + \varepsilon \end{aligned}$$

where we have used the letter m to stand for the systematic risk. Sometimes systematic risk is referred to as market risk, which emphasizes the fact that m influences all assets in the market to some extent.

The critical point about the way we have broken the total risk, U, into its two components, m and ε, is that, because ε relates to the company alone, it is unrelated to the specific risk of most other companies. For example, the unsystematic risk on Apple's equity, ε_R, is unrelated to the unsystematic risk of a company, such as Tesco, in another industry. The likelihood that Apple's share price will go up or down because of a discovery by its research team – or its failure to discover something – is probably unrelated to any of the specific uncertainties that affect Tesco's share price.

Using the terms of the previous chapter, this means that the unsystematic risks of Apple's equity and Tesco's equity are unrelated to each other, or uncorrelated. In the symbols of statistics:

$$\text{Corr}(\varepsilon_{\text{Apple}}, \varepsilon_{\text{Tesco}}) = 0$$

11.3 Systematic Risk and Betas

The fact that the unsystematic parts of the returns on two companies are unrelated to each other does not mean the systematic portions are unrelated. On the contrary, because the same systematic risks influence both companies, their total returns will also be related.

For example, a surprise about inflation will influence almost all companies to some extent. How sensitive is Apple's share price return to unanticipated changes in inflation? If the Apple share price tends to go up on news that inflation is exceeding expectations, we would say it is positively related to inflation. If the share price goes down when inflation exceeds expectations and goes up when inflation falls short of expectations, it is negatively correlated. In the unusual case where an equity's return is uncorrelated with inflation surprises, inflation is irrelevant.

We capture the influence of a systematic risk by using the **beta coefficient**. The beta coefficient, β, tells us the response of the equity's return to a systematic risk. In Chapter 10, beta measured the responsiveness of a security's return to a specific risk factor, the return on the market portfolio. We used this type of responsiveness to develop the capital asset pricing model. Because we now consider many types of systematic risks, our current work is a generalization of our discussion in Chapter 10.

If a company's share price return is positively related to the risk of inflation, it has a positive inflation beta. If it is negatively related to inflation, its inflation beta is negative; and if it is uncorrelated with inflation, its inflation beta is zero.

It is not hard to imagine some equities with positive inflation betas and others with negative inflation betas. The equity of a company owning gold mines will probably have a positive inflation beta because gold prices tend to go up with an unanticipated rise in inflation. On the other hand, an automobile company facing stiff foreign competition might find an inflation increase leads to higher wages, but it cannot raise its prices to compensate. This profit squeeze, as the company's expenses rise faster than its revenues, would give its equity a negative inflation beta.

Some structure is useful at this point. Suppose we have identified three systematic risks on which we want to focus. We may believe that these three are sufficient to describe the systematic risks that influence share price returns. Three likely candidates are inflation, GNP and interest rates. Thus, every equity will have a beta associated with each of these systematic risks: an inflation beta, a GNP beta and an interest rate beta. We can write the return on the equity, then, in the following form:

$$\begin{aligned} R &= E(R) + U \\ &= E(R) + m + \varepsilon \\ &= E(R) + \beta_I F_I + \beta_{\text{GNP}} F_{\text{GNP}} + \beta_r F_r + \varepsilon \end{aligned}$$

where we have used the symbol β_I to denote the equity's inflation beta, β_{GNP} for its GNP beta, and β_r to stand for its interest rate beta. In the equation, F stands for a surprise, whether it be in inflation, GNP or interest rates.

Let us go through an example to see how the surprises and the expected return add up to produce the total return, R, on a given security. To make it more familiar, suppose that the return is over a horizon of a year and not just a month. Suppose that, at the beginning of the year, annual inflation is forecast to be 5 per cent, GNP is forecast to increase by 2 per cent and interest rates are not expected to change. Suppose the security we are looking at has the following betas:

$$\begin{aligned} \beta_I &= 2 \\ \beta_{\text{GNP}} &= 1 \\ \beta_r &= -1.8 \end{aligned}$$

The magnitude of the beta describes how great an impact a systematic risk has on a security's returns. A beta of +1 indicates that the security's return rises and falls one for one with the systematic factor. This means, in our example, that because the security has a GNP beta of 1, it experiences a 1 per cent increase in return for every 1 per cent surprise increase in GNP. If its GNP beta were –2, it would fall by 2 per cent when there was an unanticipated increase of 1 per cent in GNP, and it would rise by 2 per cent if GNP experienced a surprise 1 per cent decline.

Let us suppose that, during the year, the following events occur: inflation rises by 7 per cent, GNP rises by only 1 per cent, and interest rates fall by 2 per cent. Suppose we learn some good news about the company, perhaps that it is succeeding quickly with some new business strategy, and that this unanticipated development contributes 5 per cent to its return. In other words:

$$\varepsilon = 5\%$$

Let us assemble all of this information to find what return the security had during the year.

First, we must determine what news or surprises took place in the systematic factors. From our information we know that:

$$\begin{aligned} \text{Expected inflation} &= 5\% \\ \text{Expected GNP change} &= 2\% \end{aligned}$$

and:

$$\text{Expected change in interest rates} = 0\%$$

This means that the market had discounted these changes, and the surprises will be the difference between what actually takes place and these expectations:

$$\begin{aligned} F_I &= \text{Surprise in inflation} \\ &= \text{Actual inflation} - \text{Expected inflation} \\ &= 7\% - 5\% \\ &= 2\% \end{aligned}$$

Similarly:

$$\begin{aligned} F_{\text{GNP}} &= \text{Surprise in GNP} \\ &= \text{Actual GNP} - \text{Expected GNP} \\ &= 1\% - 2\% \\ &= -1\% \end{aligned}$$

and:
$$\begin{aligned} F_r &= \text{Surprise in change in interest rates} \\ &= \text{Actual change} - \text{Expected change} \\ &= -2\% - 0\% \\ &= -2\% \end{aligned}$$

The total effect of the systematic risks on the security return, then, is:

$$\begin{aligned} m &= \text{Systematic risk portion of return} \\ &= \beta_I F_I + \beta_{GNP} F_{GNP} + \beta_r F_r \\ &= [2 \times 2\%] + [1 \times (-1\%)] + [(-1.8) \times (-2\%)] \\ &= 6.6\% \end{aligned}$$

Combining this with the unsystematic risk portion, the total risky part of the return on the security is:

$$m + \varepsilon = 6.6\% + 5\% = 11.6\%$$

Last, if the expected return on the security for the year was, say, 4 per cent, the total return from all three components will be:

$$\begin{aligned} R &= E(R) + m + \varepsilon \\ &= 4\% + 6.6\% + 5\% \\ &= 15.6\% \end{aligned}$$

The model we have been looking at is called a factor model, and the systematic sources of risk, designated F, are called the *factors*. Formally, a *k-factor model* is a model where each security's return is generated by:

$$R = E(R) + \beta_1 F_1 + \beta_2 F_2 + \ldots + \beta_k F_k + \varepsilon$$

where ε is specific to a particular security and uncorrelated with the ε term for other securities. In our preceding example, we had a three-factor model. We used inflation, GNP and the change in interest rates as examples of systematic sources of risk, or factors. Researchers have not settled on what is the correct set of factors. Like so many other questions, this might be one of those matters that is never laid to rest.

In practice, researchers frequently use different models for returns. They do not use all of the economic factors we used previously as examples; instead, they use an index of stock market returns – like the FTSE 100 or DAX – in addition to returns on arbitrage portfolios representing factors that have been identified as being important from earlier research. Using the single-factor model, we can write returns like this:

$$R = E(R) + \beta\left[R_{FTSE100} - E(R_{FTSE100})\right] + \varepsilon$$

Where there is only one factor (such as the returns on the FTSE 100 or DAX index), we do not need to put a subscript on the beta. In this form (with minor modifications) the factor model is called a market model. This term is employed because the index that is used for the factor is an index of returns on the whole market. We write the market model as:

$$R = E(R) + \beta\left[R_M - E(R_M)\right] + \varepsilon$$

where R_M is the return on the market portfolio.[2] The single β is called the *beta coefficient*.

In the past 30 years, practice has changed significantly in the area of factor models because of two seminal research articles: one published by Eugene Fama and Kenneth French in 1993, and the other by Mark Carhart in 1997. Both papers recognized that the market index alone could not fully explain the variation in asset returns. Fama and French introduced the three-factor model using two new factors: HML and SMB. HML stands for high minus low book-to-market equity and represents the return on an arbitrage portfolio that is long (a positive investment) in high book-to-market equity companies and short (a negative investment or borrowing) in low book-to-market equity companies. An arbitrage portfolio has a zero net investment because the positive weights completely cancel out the negative weights on assets.

Similarly, SMB means small minus big companies and corresponds to an arbitrage portfolio that is long in small companies and short in big companies. Carhart added another factor that represented a momentum effect that is measured by the return on an arbitrage portfolio that is long in the best-performing equities of the previous year and short in the worst-performing equities of the previous year. Algebraically, we express the four-factor model as:

$$R - r_f = E(R) + \beta_1(R_M - r_f) + \beta_2 HML + \beta_3 SMB + \beta_4 MOM + \varepsilon$$

where there are four factors, representing the market risk premium, high minus low B/M, Small Minus Big, and momentum arbitrage portfolios, respectively. The Fama–French three-factor model is merely the four-factor model without the momentum factor. In 2016, Fama and French published new work on the three-factor model, and found that a five-factor model based on size, value, profitability and investment patterns performed better. We present the Fama–French five-factor model below:

$$R - r_f = E(R) + \beta_1(R_M - r_f) + \beta_2 HML + \beta_3 SMB + \beta_4 RMW + \beta_5 CMA + \varepsilon$$

where RMW is the difference between the returns on diversified equity portfolios of high and low profitability, CMA is the difference between the returns on diversified equity portfolios of low and high investment firms, and other variables are as defined earlier. A later paper by Fama and French (2017), looking at the international performance of their five-factor model, found that only RMW was significant in explaining the cross-section of European stock returns. Smith and Timmerman (2022) go even further and show, for US equities, that there is significant time variance in the relevance of additional factors. Since the financial crisis of 2008, the strength of many factors has fallen substantially, and different firms and industries have varying sensitivities to economic break-points.

Real World Insight 11.1

BP plc

BP is one of the world's largest oil and gas firms. With BP's international reach and reliance on oil, it could be argued that an additional risk factor related to oil will be important in explaining the company's equity returns. For this analysis, we will hypothesize that the market return and oil price returns explain the returns on BP. We will use monthly data between 2014 and 2023, and assume that expected returns on each of the two factors are zero. This is a common assumption in estimations of this type.

We specify the model as:

$$R - r_f = E(R) + \beta_1(R_M - r_f) + \beta_2 R_{oil} + \varepsilon$$

We will use the FTSE 100 as the market index, the 10-year government bond yield as the risk-free rate, and the historical oil and gold price returns for the commodity factors. A multiple regression model provides the following estimates (with *t*-statistics below):

$$\underset{(1.07)}{R - r_f = -0.007} \; \underset{(-0.61)}{-0.12\,(R_M - r_f)} + \underset{(3.56)}{0.21 R_{oil}} + \varepsilon$$

The *t*-statistics tell us which variables are important in the model, and in this case, only the oil factor is significant. This is unsurprising given that BP is an oil and gas company.

11.4 Portfolios and Factor Models

Chapter 10 Page 276

Now let us see what happens to portfolios of equities when each follows a one-factor model (we also discuss the properties of portfolios and diversification in Chapter 10, Section 10.6). For discussion purposes, we take the coming one-month period and examine returns. We could have used a day or a year or any other period. If the period represents the time between decisions, however, we would rather it be short than long, and a month is a reasonable time frame to use.

We will create portfolios from a list of N securities, and use a one-factor model to capture the systematic risk. The ith security in the list will, therefore, have returns:

Equation 11.1

$$R_i = E(R_i) + \beta_i F + \varepsilon_i$$

where we have subscripted the variables to indicate that they relate to the ith security. Notice that the factor F is not subscripted. The factor that represents systematic risk could be a surprise in GNP, or we could use the market model and let the difference between the market return and what we expect that return to be, $R_{market} - E(R_{market})$, be the factor. In either case, the factor applies to all of the securities in the portfolio.

The β_i is subscripted because it represents the unique way the factor influences the ith security. To recapitulate our discussion of factor models, if β_i is zero, the returns on the ith security are:

$$R_i = E(R_i) + \varepsilon_i$$

In words, the ith security's returns are unaffected by the factor, F, if β_i is zero. If β_i is positive, positive changes in the factor raise the ith security's returns, and negative changes lower them. Conversely, if β_i is negative, its returns and the factor move in opposite directions.

Figure 11.2 illustrates the relationship between a security's excess returns, $R_i - E(R_i)$, and the factor F for different betas, where $\beta_i > 0$. The lines in Figure 11.2 plot Equation 11.1 on the assumption that there has been no unsystematic risk. That is, $\varepsilon_i = 0$. Because we are assuming positive betas, the lines slope upwards, indicating that the return rises with F. Notice that, if the factor is zero ($F = 0$), the line passes through zero on the y-axis.

Figure 11.2 The One-factor Model

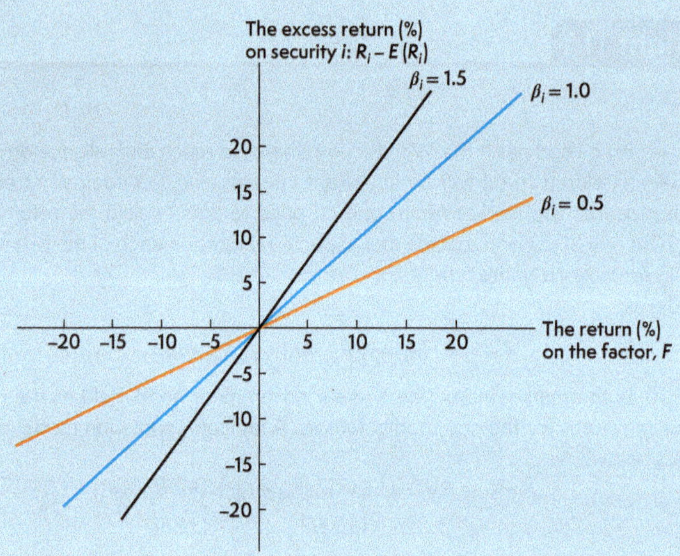

Each line represents a different security, where each security has a different beta.

Now let us see what happens when we create equity portfolios where each equity follows a one-factor model. Let X_i be the proportion of equity i in the portfolio. That is, if an individual with a portfolio of €100 wants €20 in AXA, we say $X_{\text{AXA}} = 20$ per cent. Because the Xs represent the proportions of wealth we are investing in each of the equities, we know that they must add up to 100 per cent or 1:

$$X_1 + X_2 + X_3 + \ldots + X_N = 1$$

We know that the portfolio return is the weighted average of the returns on the individual assets in the portfolio. Algebraically, we write this as follows:

Equation 11.2

$$R_P = X_1R_1 + X_2R_2 + X_3R_3 + \ldots + X_NR_N$$

We saw from Equation 11.1 that each asset, in turn, is determined by both the factor F and the unsystematic risk of ε_i. Thus by substituting Equation 11.1 for each R_i in Equation 11.2, we have:

Equation 11.3

$$R_p = \underbrace{X_1[E(R_1) + \beta_1F_1 + \varepsilon_1]}_{\text{(Return on equity 1)}} + \underbrace{X_2[E(R_2) + \beta_2F + \varepsilon_2]}_{\text{(Return on equity 2)}} + \underbrace{X_3[E(R_3) + \beta_3F + \varepsilon_3]}_{\text{(Return on equity 3)}} + \ldots + \underbrace{X_N[E(R_N) + \beta_NF + \varepsilon_N]}_{\text{(Return on equity N)}}$$

Equation 11.3 shows us that the return on a portfolio is determined by three sets of parameters:

1 The expected return on each security, $E(R_i)$.

2 The beta of each security multiplied by the factor, F.

3 The unsystematic risk of each security, ε_i.

We express Equation 11.3 in terms of these three sets of parameters like this:

The weighted average of expected returns

Equation 11.4 $$R_p = X_1E(R_1) + X_2E(R_2) + X_3E(R_3) + \ldots + X_NE(R_N)$$

The weighted average of betas × F

$$+(X_1\beta_1 + X_2\beta_2 + X_3\beta_3 + \ldots + X_N\beta_N)F$$

The weighted average of the unsystematic risk

$$+X_1\varepsilon_1 + X_2\varepsilon_2 + X_3\varepsilon_3 + \ldots + X_N\varepsilon_N$$

This rather imposing equation is actually straightforward. The first row is the weighted average of each security's expected return. The items in the parentheses of the second row represent the weighted average of each security's beta. This weighted average is, in turn, multiplied by the factor F. The third row represents a weighted average of the unsystematic risks of the individual securities.

Where does uncertainty appear in Equation 11.4? There is no uncertainty in the first row because only the expected value of each security's return appears there. Uncertainty in the second row is reflected by only one item, F. That is, while we know that the expected value of F is zero, we do not know what its value will be over a particular period. Uncertainty in the third row is reflected by each unsystematic risk, ε_i.

Portfolios and Diversification

In the previous sections of this chapter, we expressed the return on a single security in terms of our factor model. Portfolios were treated next. Because investors generally hold diversified portfolios, we now want to know what Equation 11.4 looks like in a *large* or diversified portfolio.[3]

As it turns out, something unusual occurs to Equation 11.4: the third row *disappears* in a large portfolio. To see this, consider a gambler who divides £1,000 by betting on red over many spins of the roulette wheel. For example, he may participate in 1,000 spins, betting £1 at a time. Though we do not know ahead of time whether a particular spin will yield red or black, we can be confident that red will win about 50 per cent of the time. Ignoring any casino fees, the investor can be expected to end up with just about his original £1,000.

Though we are concerned with securities, not roulette wheels, the same principle applies. Each security has its own unsystematic risk, where the surprise for one security is unrelated to the surprise of another security. By investing a small amount in each security, we bring the weighted average of the unsystematic risks close to zero in a large portfolio.[4]

Although the third row completely vanishes in a large portfolio, nothing unusual occurs in either row 1 or row 2. Row 1 remains a weighted average of the expected returns on the individual securities as securities are added to the portfolio. Because there is no uncertainty at all in the first row, there is no way for diversification to cause this row to vanish. The terms inside the parentheses of the second row remain a weighted average of the betas. They do not disappear, either, when securities are added. Because the factor F is unaffected when securities are added to the portfolios, the second row does not vanish.

Why does the third row vanish while the second row does not, though both rows reflect uncertainty? The key is that there are many unsystematic risks in row 3. Because these risks are independent of one another, the effect of diversification becomes stronger as we add more assets to the portfolio. The resulting portfolio grows less and less risky, and the return becomes more certain. However, the systematic risk, F, affects all securities because it is outside the parentheses in row 2. Because we cannot avoid this factor by investing in many securities, diversification does not occur in this row.

Example 11.1

Diversification and Unsystematic Risk

We explain the above material with the following example. We keep our one-factor model here but make three specific assumptions:

1 All securities have the same expected return of 10 per cent. This assumption implies that the first row of Equation 11.4 must also equal 10 per cent because this row is a weighted average of the expected returns of the individual securities.

2 All securities have a beta of 1. The sum of the terms inside the parentheses in the second row of Equation 11.4 must equal 1 because these terms are a weighted average of the individual betas. Because the terms inside the parentheses are multiplied by F, the value of the second row is $1 \times F = F$.

3 In this example, we focus on the behaviour of one individual, Walter V. Bagehot. Mr Bagehot decides to hold an equally weighted portfolio. That is, the proportion of each security in his portfolio is $1/N$.

We can express the return on Mr Bagehot's portfolio as follows:

Return on Walter V. Bagehot's portfolio

Equation 11.4′

$$R_P = \underset{\substack{\text{From}\\\text{row 1 of}\\\text{Equation 11.4}}}{10\%} + \underset{\substack{\text{From}\\\text{row 1 of}\\\text{Equation 11.4}}}{F} + \underbrace{\left(\frac{1}{N}\varepsilon_1 + \frac{1}{N}\varepsilon_2 + \frac{1}{N}\varepsilon_3 + \cdots + \frac{1}{N}\varepsilon_N\right)}_{\text{From row 3 of Equation 11.4}}$$

We mentioned before that as N increases without limit, row 3 of Equation 11.4 becomes equal to zero.[5] Thus, the return to Walter Bagehot's portfolio when the number of securities is very large is

Equation 11.4″

$$R_P = 10\% + F$$

The key to diversification is exhibited in Equation 11.4″. The unsystematic risk of row 3 vanishes, while the systematic risk of row 2 remains.

We illustrate this in Figure 11.3. Systematic risk, captured by variation in factor F, is not reduced through diversification. Conversely, unsystematic risk diminishes as securities are added, vanishing as the number of securities becomes infinite. Our result is analogous to the diversification example of Chapter 10. In that chapter, we said that undiversifiable or systematic risk arises from positive covariances between securities. In this chapter, we say that systematic risk stems from a common factor F. Because a common factor causes positive covariances, the arguments of the two chapters are parallel.

Figure 11.3 Diversification and the Portfolio Risk for an Equally Weighted Portfolio

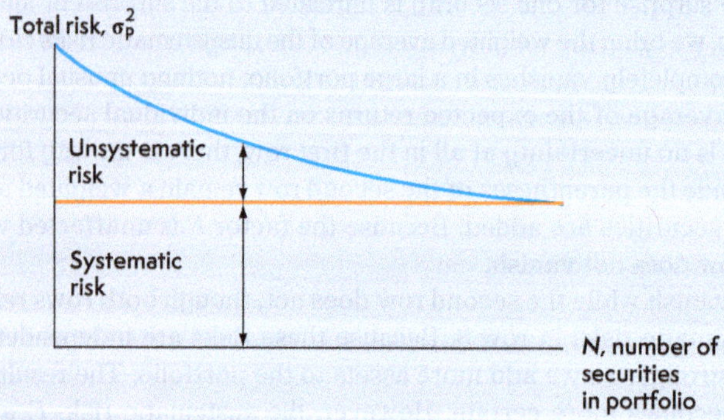

Total risk decreases as the number of securities in the portfolio rises. This drop occurs only in the unsystematic risk component. Systematic risk is unaffected by diversification.

11.5 Betas and Expected Returns

The Linear Relationship

We have argued many times that the expected return on a security compensates for its risk. In Chapter 10, we showed that market beta (the standardized covariance of the security's returns with those of the market) was the appropriate measure of risk under the assumptions of homogeneous expectations and riskless borrowing and lending. The capital asset pricing model (CAPM), which posited these assumptions, implied that the expected return on a security was positively (and linearly) related to its beta. We will find a similar relationship between risk and return in the one-factor model of this chapter.

We begin by noting that the relevant risk in large and well-diversified portfolios is all systematic because unsystematic risk is diversified away. An implication is that when a well-diversified shareholder considers changing her holdings of a particular security, she can ignore its unsystematic risk.

Notice that we are not claiming that equities, like portfolios, have no unsystematic risk. Nor are we saying that the unsystematic risk of an equity will not affect its returns. Shares do have unsystematic risk, and their actual returns do depend on the unsystematic risk. Because this risk washes out in a well-diversified portfolio, however, shareholders can ignore this unsystematic risk when they consider whether to add an equity to their portfolio. Therefore, if shareholders are ignoring the unsystematic risk, only the systematic risk of a security can be related to its *expected* return.

We illustrate this relationship in the security market line of Figure 11.4. Points *P*, *C*, *A* and *L* all lie on the line emanating from the risk-free rate of 10 per cent. The points representing each of these four assets can be created by combinations of the risk-free rate and any of the other three assets. For example, because *A* has a beta of 2.0 and *P* has a beta of 1.0, a portfolio with 50 per cent in asset *A* and 50 per cent in the riskless rate has the same beta as asset *P*. The risk-free rate is 10 per cent and the expected return on security *A* is 35 per cent, implying a portfolio return of 22.5 per cent [(10%+35%)/2], which is identical to security *P*'s expected return. Because security *P* has both the same beta and the same expected return as a combination of the riskless asset and security *A*, an individual is equally inclined to add a small amount of security *P* and to add a small amount of this combination to her portfolio. However, the unsystematic risk of security *P* need not be equal to the unsystematic risk of the combination of security *A* and the risk-free rate because unsystematic risk is diversified away in a large portfolio.

Figure 11.4 A Graph of Beta and Expected Return for Individual Securities under the One-factor Model

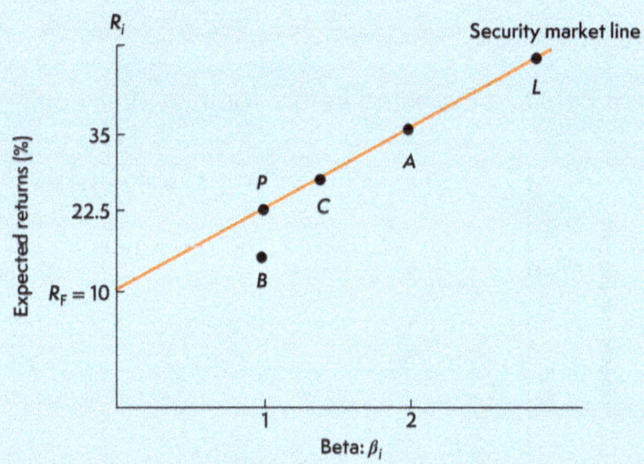

Of course, the potential combinations of points on the security market line are endless. We can duplicate *P* by combinations of the risk-free rate and either *C* or *L* (or both of them). We can duplicate *C* (or *A* or L) by borrowing at the risk-free rate to invest in *P*. The infinite number of points on the security market line that are not labelled can be used as well.

Now consider security *B*. Because its expected return is below the line, no investor would hold it. Instead, the investor would prefer security *P*, a combination of security *A* and the riskless asset, or some other combination. Thus, security *B*'s price is too high. Its price will fall in a competitive market, forcing its expected return back up to the line in equilibrium.

The preceding discussion allows us to provide an equation for the security market line of Figure 11.4. We know that a line can be described algebraically from two points. It is perhaps easiest to focus on the risk-free rate and asset *P* because the risk-free rate has a beta of 0 and *P* has a beta of 1.

Because we know the return on any zero-beta asset is R_F and the expected return on asset P is $E(R_p)$, we can show that:

Equation 11.5
$$E(R) = R_F + \beta[E(R_p) - R_F]$$

In Equation 11.5, we can think of $E(R)$ as the expected return on any security or portfolio lying on the security market line. β is the beta of that security or portfolio.

The Market Portfolio and the Single Factor

In the CAPM (see Chapter 10, Section 10.9), the beta of a security measures its responsiveness to movements in the market portfolio. In the one-factor model of the arbitrage pricing theory (APT), Chapter 10 the beta of a security measures its responsiveness to the factor. We now relate the market portfolio to the single factor.

Chapter 10 Page 284

A large, diversified portfolio has no unsystematic risk because the unsystematic risks of the individual securities are diversified away. Assuming enough securities so that the market portfolio is fully diversified, and assuming that no security has a disproportionate market share, this portfolio is fully diversified and contains no unsystematic risk.[6] In other words, the market portfolio is perfectly correlated with the single factor, implying that the market portfolio is really a scaled-up or scaled-down version of the factor. After scaling correctly, we can treat the market portfolio as the factor itself.

The market portfolio, like every security or portfolio, lies on the security market line. When the market portfolio is the factor, the beta of the market portfolio is 1 by definition, and this is shown in Figure 11.5. (We deleted the securities and the specific expected returns from Figure 11.4 for clarity: the two graphs are otherwise identical.) With the market portfolio as the factor, Equation 11.5 becomes:

$$E(R) = R_F + \beta[E(R_M) - R_F]$$

where $E(R_M)$ is the expected return on the market. This equation shows that the expected return on any asset, $E(R)$, is linearly related to the security's beta. The equation is identical to that of the CAPM, which we developed in Chapter 10.

Figure 11.5 A Graph of Beta and Expected Return for Individual Equities under the One-factor Model

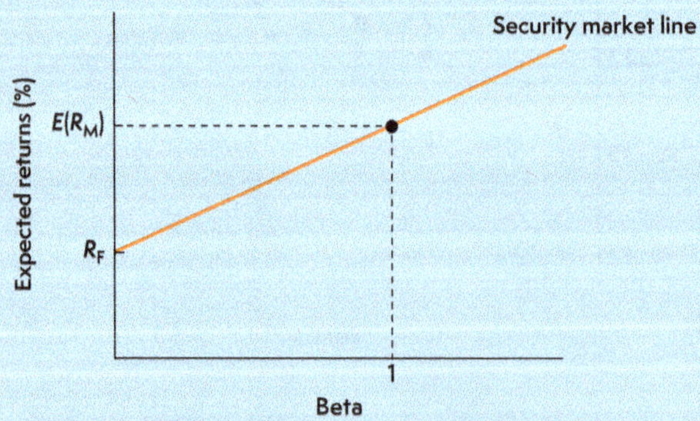

The factor is scaled so that it is identical to the market portfolio. The beta of the market portfolio is 1.

11.6 The Capital Asset Pricing Model and the Arbitrage Pricing Theory

The CAPM and the APT are alternative models of risk and return. It is worthwhile to consider the differences between the two models, both in terms of pedagogy and in terms of application.

Differences in Pedagogy

We feel that the CAPM has at least one strong advantage from the student's point of view. The derivation of the CAPM necessarily brings the reader through a discussion of efficient sets. This treatment – beginning with the case of two risky assets, moving to the case of many risky assets and finishing when a riskless asset is added to the many risky ones – is of great intuitive value. This sort of presentation is not as easily accomplished with the APT.

However, the APT has an offsetting advantage. The model adds factors until the unsystematic risk of any security is uncorrelated with the unsystematic risk of every other security. Under this formulation, it is easily shown that (1) unsystematic risk steadily falls (and ultimately vanishes) as the number of securities in the portfolio increases, but (2) the systematic risks do not decrease. This result was also shown in the CAPM, though the intuition was cloudier because the unsystematic risks could be correlated across securities.

Differences in Application

One advantage of the APT is that it can handle multiple factors while the CAPM ignores them. Although most of our presentation in this chapter has focused on the one-factor model, a multifactor model, like the Fama and French (2016) five-factor model, is probably more reflective of reality. That is, we must abstract from many market-wide and industry-wide factors before the unsystematic risk of one security becomes uncorrelated with the unsystematic risks of other securities. Under the five-factor model, the relationship between risk and return can be expressed as:

Equation 11.6 $$R - r_f = E(R) + \beta[E(R_M) - r_F] + \gamma HML + \delta SMB + \eta RMW + \theta CMA + \varepsilon$$

In this equation, β stands for the security's beta with respect to the first factor, γ stands for the security's beta with respect to the second factor, and so on. The equation states that the security's expected return is related to the security's factor betas. The intuition in Equation 11.6 is straightforward. Each factor represents a risk that cannot be diversified away. The higher a security's beta with regard to a particular factor, the higher the risk that the security bears. In a rational world, the expected return on the security should compensate for this risk. Equation 11.6 states that the expected return is a summation of the base expected return plus the compensation for each type of risk that the security bears.

As an example, consider the hypothetical coefficients for the four-factor model for British Land Company plc, the UK property developer. Assume that the expected monthly return on any equity, $E(R_S)$, can be described as:

$$E(R_s) = 0.0041 + 0.0136\beta - 0.0001\gamma - 0.0006\delta + 0.0072\mu + 0.0023\theta$$

Suppose British Land Company had the following betas: $\beta = 1.1, \gamma = 2, \delta = 3, \mu = 0.1$, and $\theta = 0.5$. The expected monthly return on that security would be:

$$\begin{aligned}\overline{R}_{BLC} &= 0.0041 + 0.0136 \times 1.1 - 0.0001 \times 2 - 0.0006 \times 3 + 0.0072 \times 0.1 + 0.0023 \times 0.5 \\ &= 0.0041 + 0.01496 - 0.0002 - 0.0018 + 0.0007 + .0012 \\ &= 0.01893\end{aligned}$$

Assuming that British Land Company is unlevered and that one of the firm's projects has risk equivalent to that of the firm, this value of 0.01893 (i.e. 1.89 per cent) can be used as the monthly discount rate for the project. (Because annual data are often supplied for capital budgeting purposes, the annual rate of $0.2524[=(1.01893)^{12} - 1]$ might be used instead.)

Because many factors appear on the right side of Equation 11.6, the four-factor formulation has the potential to measure expected returns more accurately than the CAPM. However, as mentioned earlier, we cannot easily determine whether these factors are appropriate. The factors in the preceding study were included because they were found to explain a significant proportion of returns for US companies. However, they were not derived from theory and may not be appropriate for European, Middle Eastern or African companies.

By contrast, the use of the market index in the CAPM formulation is implied by the theory of Chapter 10. We suggested in earlier chapters that market indices (such as the FTSE 100 and DJ Euro Stoxx 50) mirror stock market movements quite well.

Sustainability in Action 11.1

Vestas Wind Systems A/S and RWE AG

In the 2010s, two European companies, Vestas Wind Systems A/S (a green energy firm) and RWE AG (a diversified energy provider), faced different growth trajectories due to unexpected climate concerns. Vestas Wind Systems A/S, a Danish manufacturer of wind turbines, and RWE AG, a German energy company with coal-based energy operations, had been operating in the European energy market for years. Around 2010, unexpected news about climate concerns and stricter environmental regulations led to a surge in the demand for renewable energy sources. This sudden shift in public sentiment and government policy caught investors off guard and significantly impacted the stock prices of both companies.

Vestas Wind Systems' stock price experienced a substantial increase, and the company's realized returns during this period were higher than initially expected. On the other hand, RWE AG faced a decline in stock value due to the rise in environmental concerns and the push for greener energy solutions. This fall in price continued until RWE adopted a much strong renewable energy strategy around 2016, at which point the trend was reversed.

Pastor et al. (2022) have proposed a 'green minus brown' factor to represent the pricing of environmentally friendly green assets and environmentally unfriendly brown assets. To better understand the impact of green factors on asset pricing, they developed a two-factor model that incorporated the green factor, and this explained the historic underperformance of brown equities like RWE AG. However, the researchers found that the outperformance of green equities vanished after accounting for unexpected climate-related events, highlighting the importance of system-wide concerns about the state of the environment rather than any company-specific risk.

11.7 Other Alternatives to the CAPM

Practitioners have a number of criticisms about the CAPM, so let's review some of the issues they have raised:

- The CAPM is a theoretical model that provides a conceptual explanation for the risk–return relationship at the level of individual securities. It tends to perform poorly with real security data, particularly in less developed economies because quality of price information is poor.
- The CAPM uses only three inputs: the risk-free rate, beta and the expected market return. It would perform better if more information was included, such as additional variables relating to sectors or commodities. Using only past price information to predict future returns puts it at a disadvantage compared to other models.
- The CAPM treats risk symmetrically, whereas investors wish to maximize upside risk and minimize downside risk. Investors who set out to minimize the chances of losing money but maximize upside returns will find little value in a model that doesn't differentiate between downside and upside risk.

A potential solution to these weaknesses is to use factor models and the APT to increase the number of variables and sources of risk beyond the market portfolio. While these extensions improve the predictive power of the CAPM, they still use past price information and succumb to the same criticisms as before. In addition, the increased model complexity can put many investors off using factor models.

In the following sections we review other models that analysts use to estimate expected returns. We say nothing about their theoretical validity, only that they are useful practical proxies for the more formal models presented earlier in this chapter. They may also be useful in certain situations, such as emerging markets or private companies.

Price-based Models

The CAPM has three inputs and only one of these, beta, is specific to the individual security. Section 10.8 shows that beta can be expressed as:

$$\beta_i = \frac{\text{Cov}(R_i, R_M)}{\sigma^2(R_M)} = \frac{\sigma(R_i) \times \sigma(R_M) \times \rho(R_i, R_M)}{\sigma^2(R_M)} = \frac{\sigma(R_i) \times \rho(R_i, R_M)}{\sigma(R_M)}$$

As shown, the covariance term in the numerator can be decomposed into correlation and standard deviation terms. This simplifies further to a ratio of the standard deviation of security i returns to the standard deviation of the market return, all multiplied by the correlation between security i and the market, M.

Some analysts argue that observed instability in the CAPM comes from the correlation term because market movements make correlations volatile. They argue it is better to assume correlation is 1 for all security estimates and calculate a price-based beta that is calculated as follows:

$$\beta_i = \frac{\sigma(R_i) \times \rho(R_i, R_M)}{\sigma^2(R_M)} = \frac{\sigma(R_i) \times 1}{\sigma(R_M)} = \frac{\sigma(R_i)}{\sigma(R_M)}$$

While the assumption of correlation equal to 1 is clearly unrealistic, supporters argue that noise in actual beta estimations is such that the price-based model is just as good a proxy as the CAPM or the APT. In addition, standard deviations are much more stable than correlations, and this will help with forecasting returns.

One thing to note is that, because of the assumption that the correlation of returns between all assets and the market is equal to 1, the standard deviation of the market return is equal to the average of all the individual security standard deviations in the market.

The major weakness of the price-based model is its assumption that all securities have the same risk exposure to the market. It has no theoretical basis and so should be taken only as an empirical proxy. It also uses past price information, which has already been shown to be poor in predicting the future.

Real World Insight 11.2

Calculating Expected Returns of Volkswagen

According to Yahoo! Finance, Volkswagen has a beta of 0.83. Assume the 10-year German government bond yield is 0.09 per cent. Assume the mean annual standard deviation of all stocks on the Deutsche Börse is 40 per cent and the standard deviation of Volkswagen share price returns is 30.42 per cent. The expected market return is 9 per cent.

According to the CAPM:

$$E[R_{Volkswagen}] = r_f + \beta_{Volkswagen}[E(R_M) - r_f] = 0.0009 + 0.83[0.09 - 0.0009] = 0.0749 = 7.49\%$$

According to the price-based model:

$$E[R_{Volkswagen}] = r_f + \frac{\sigma(R_{Volkswagen})}{\sigma(R_{Market})}[E(R_M) - r_f] = 0.0009 + \frac{30.42}{40}[0.09 - 0.0009] = 0.0686 = 6.86\%$$

The expected return estimates are slightly different. According to the price-based model, the expected return of 6.86 per cent on Volkswagen should be slightly lower than the CAPM estimate of 7.49 per cent.

Accounting-based Pricing Models

In many countries (especially developing economies), stock markets are not particularly efficient and share prices may not be accurate. It could be prudent, therefore, to consider using accounting information to form an estimate of an equity's risk. While accounting data have their own issues (e.g. smoothing, accounting adjustments, historical data), the fact that a company's accounts are audited can provide some comfort to the analyst.

At this stage in the book (we cover risk in a lot more detail in Chapter 12), we know a few things about company risk. We know that the more debt a company has, the more likely it is to be risky, and companies with more cash are likely to be of lower risk. We would also expect, if earnings figures don't vary much from year to year, the company will not be very risky.

To calculate an accounting beta, we could use the following equation with EPS data:

$$\beta_i^{Acc} = \frac{\sigma(R_{EPS_i}) \times \rho(R_{EPS_i}, R_{EPS_M})}{\sigma(R_{EPS_M})}$$

where $\sigma(R_{EPS_i})$ is the standard deviation of changes in EPS for company i and $\sigma(R_{EPS_M})$ is the average standard deviation of changes in earnings for the whole market. This approach can also be used with private companies that don't have a share price but have historical earnings data.

To find the expected return of a company using an accounting beta, you would substitute the accounting beta for the standard market beta. All other inputs stay the same.

Real World Insight 11.3

Calculating Expected Returns of Volkswagen

We return to Volkswagen AG and this time we will use the firm's EPS to estimate beta. As before, the risk-free rate is 0.09 per cent and the expected return on the market is 9 per cent. The average standard deviation of EPS changes for the German stock market over a 10-year period is 11.78 per cent. The standard deviation of EPS changes for Volkswagen is much higher at 31.23 per cent. The correlation between Volkswagen and the German stock market EPS changes is 0.23. The accounting beta of Volkswagen is:

$$\beta^{Acc}\,Volkswagen = \frac{\sigma\left(R_{EPS_{Volkswagen}}\right) \times \rho\left(R_{EPS_{Volkswagen}}, R_{EPS_M}\right)}{\sigma\left(R_{EPS_M}\right)} = \frac{31.23 \times 0.33}{11.79} = 0.874$$

This means the expected return for Volkswagen is:

$$E\left[R_{Volkswagen}\right] = r_f + \beta^{Acc}{}_{Volkswagen}\left[E\left(R_M\right) - r_f\right] = 0.0009 + 0.874\left[0.09 - 0.0009\right] = 0.0798 = 7.98\%$$

Summary and Conclusions

Chapter 10 developed the capital asset pricing model (CAPM). As an alternative, this chapter developed the arbitrage pricing theory (APT) and introduced the Fama–French three-factor model and the Carhart four-factor model.

1 The APT assumes that security returns are generated according to factor models. For example, we might describe a stock's return as:

$$R = E(R) + \beta_I F_I + \beta_{GNP} F_{GNP} + \beta_r F_r + \varepsilon$$

where I, GNP and r stand for inflation, gross national product and the interest rate, respectively. The three factors F_I, F_{GNP} and F_r represent systematic risk because these factors affect many securities. The term ε is considered unsystematic risk because it is unique to each individual security.

2 For convenience, we frequently describe a security's return according to a one-factor model:

$$R = E(R) + \beta F + \varepsilon$$

3 The Fama–French and Carhart factor models are now frequently used by financial analysts. The Carhart four-factor model is expressed as follows:

$$R - r_f = E(R) + \beta[E(R_M) - r_f] + \gamma HML + \delta SMB + \eta MOM + \varepsilon$$

where $[E(R_M) - r_f]$ is the market risk premium, *HML* is the return on an arbitrage portfolio that is long in high B/M equities and short in low B/M stocks, *SMB* is the return on an arbitrage portfolio that is long in small market capitalization equities and short in large market capitalization equities, and *MOM* is the return on an arbitrage portfolio that is long in the best-performing equities and short in the worst-performing equities. The term ε is considered unsystematic risk because it is unique to each individual security. The Fama–French three-factor model is simply the Carhart model without the momentum factor.

4 The Fama–French five-factor model is presented below:

$$R - r_f = E(R) + \beta_1[E(R_M) - r_f] + \beta_2 HML + \beta_3 SMB + \beta_4 RMW + \beta_5 CMA + \varepsilon$$

where RMW is the difference between the returns on diversified equity portfolios of high and low profitability, CMA is the difference between the returns on diversified equity portfolios of low and high investment firms, and other variables are as defined earlier.

5 As securities are added to a portfolio, the unsystematic risks of the individual securities offset one another. A fully diversified portfolio has no unsystematic risk but still has systematic risk. This result indicates that diversification can eliminate some, but not all, of the risk of individual securities.

6 Because of this, the expected return on a security is related to its systematic risk. In a one-factor model, the systematic risk is simply the beta of the CAPM. Thus, the implications of the CAPM and the one-factor APT are identical. However, each security has many risks in a multifactor model such as the Carhart model. The expected return on a security is related to the beta of the security with each factor.

Questions and Problems

CONCEPT

1 **Announcements, Surprises and Expected Returns** What is the difference between an expected return and observed return? Is it possible to predict the surprise component of an observed return?

2 **Systematic versus Unsystematic Risk** You own equity in Lewis-Striden Drugs plc. Suppose you had expected the following events to occur last month:

(a) The government would announce that real GNP had grown 1.2 per cent during the previous quarter. The returns of Lewis-Striden are positively related to real GNP.

(b) The government would announce that inflation over the previous quarter was 3.7 per cent. The returns of Lewis-Striden are negatively related to inflation.

(c) Interest rates would rise 2.5 percentage points. The returns of Lewis-Striden are negatively related to interest rates.

(d) The chairman of the firm would announce his retirement. The retirement would be effective six months from the announcement day. The chairman is well liked: in general, he is considered an asset to the firm.

(e) Research data would conclusively prove the efficacy of an experimental drug. Completion of the efficacy testing means the drug will be on the market soon.

Suppose the following events actually occurred:

(a) The government announced that real GNP grew 2.3 per cent during the previous quarter.

(b) The government announced that inflation over the previous quarter was 3.7 per cent.

(c) Interest rates rose 2.1 percentage points.

(d) The chairman of the firm died suddenly of a heart attack.

(e) Research results in the efficacy testing were not as strong as expected. The drug must be tested for another six months, and the efficacy results must be resubmitted to the food regulation authority.

(f) Lab researchers had a breakthrough with another drug.

(g) A competitor announced that it will begin distribution and sale of a medicine that will compete directly with one of Lewis-Striden's top-selling products.

Discuss how each of the actual occurrences affects the returns on your Lewis-Striden shares. Which events represent systematic risk? Which events represent unsystematic risk?

3 **Systematic Risk and Betas** What is data mining? Is there anything wrong with measuring the performance of an Irish growth fund portfolio manager against a benchmark composed of Greek equities?

4 **Portfolios and Factor Models** You have recently been employed as a finance consultant to Bread plc. The CEO wants to use an APT model to estimate the required return on the company's stock, and the risk factors he plans to use in his model are the stock market risk premium, the inflation rate and the price of wheat (since wheat is one of the major costs his company faces). He has asked for your opinion on his choice of risk factors. Is there anything he has overlooked? Is there anything he has not included that should be? Explain.

5 **Betas and Expected Returns** Why does the market portfolio lie on the security market line? What does it mean if a security lies below the security market line? What would happen to the returns of the security if traders exploit any possible arbitrage opportunities?

6 **The APT** Your manager tells you that, for the APT to be useful, the number of systematic risk factors must be small. Is your manager right? Explain.

7 **Other Alternatives to the CAPM** You have been given an assignment to calculate the expected return on a listed firm in Malawi. What are the issues you would face and what are some possible solutions to this problem?

REGULAR

8 **The APT** As financial director of Renault SA, you have been tasked with estimating the required return on the company's equity. What risk factors should you use? Explain your choice.

9 **Market Model versus the Fama and French (2016) Model** What are the differences between the Fama and French (2016) model and the market model? Would you use the Fama and French (2016) model in Europe? Explain why, or why not.

10 **The APT vs the CAPM** What is the relationship between the one-factor model and the CAPM? In contrast to the CAPM, the APT does not indicate which factors are expected to determine the risk premium of an asset. How can we determine which factors should be included?

11 **Price-based Pricing Models** You are concerned about instability in the stock market, particularly with a company like Tesla Inc., and have decided to use a price-based model. Explain why you would choose this model and the weaknesses in such an approach. What other methods could you use to address market instability with respect to Tesla Inc.?

12 **Three Factor Model** You plan to purchase a company and wish to estimate the expected return on its equity using a three-factor model. You believe the appropriate factors are the market return, the percentage change in GNP and the oil price return. The market is expected to grow by 6 per cent, GNP is expected to grow by 2 per cent, and the oil price is expected to fall by 5 per cent. The company has betas of 0.8, 0.3 and –0.1 for the market, GNP and oil respectively. The expected rate of return on the equity is 15 per cent. What is the revised expected return if the market falls by 8 per cent, GNP contracts by 0.3 per cent and the oil price grows by 9 per cent?

13 **Factor Models** Suppose a factor model is appropriate to describe stock returns for a company, with information about these factors set out in the table below. The expected return on the stock is 13 per cent.

Factor	β	Expected Value	Actual Value
GNP growth	1.5	3%	0.5%
Inflation	–2	5.5%	10%

(a) What is the systematic risk of the stock return?

(b) The firm announced that its market share had unexpectedly increased from 23 per cent to 27 per cent. Investors know from past experience that the equity return will increase by 0.26 per cent for every 1 per cent increase in its market share. What is the unsystematic risk of the equity?

(c) What is the total return on this equity?

14 **Factor Models: Fama–French Five-factor Model** Suppose the Fama–French (2016) five-factor model is appropriate to describe the returns of an equity. Information about those five factors is presented in the following table:

Factor	β	Expected Value (%)	Actual Value (%)
$(R_m - r_f)$	0.75	8.4	12.1
HML	–0.90	2.1	3.8
SMB	–0.44	12.5	10.3
RMW	0.87	1.2	3.2
CMA	0.55	5.1	2.5

(a) What is the systematic risk of the equity return?

(b) Suppose unexpected bad news about the firm is announced that causes the share price to drop by 2.6 per cent. If the expected return is 9.5 per cent, what is the total return on this equity?

15 **Factor Models: Carhart Model** Suppose the Carhart (1997) factor model is appropriate to describe the returns on an equity. The current expected return on the equity is 10.5 per cent. Information about the factors is presented in the following table:

Factor	β	Expected Value	Actual Value
$(R_m - r_f)$	1.04	3.5	4.8
HML	–1.90	7.1	7.8
SMB	0.60	2.4	6.4
Momentum	0.44	0.23	–3.2

(a) What is the systematic risk of the equity return?

(b) The firm announced that its market share had unexpectedly increased from 23 per cent to 27 per cent. Investors know from past experience that the share price return will increase by 0.36 per cent for every 1 per cent increase in its market share. What is the equity's unsystematic risk?

(c) What is the equity's total return?

16 Factor Models: Fama–French Three-factor Model Suppose equity returns can be explained by the Fama–French three-factor model:

$$R = \overline{R} + \beta(R_M - r_f) + \gamma HML + \delta SMB + \varepsilon$$

Assume there is no firm-specific risk. The information for each equity is presented here:

	β	γ	δ
Equity A	1.20	0.90	0.20
Equity B	0.80	1.40	–0.30
Equity C	0.95	–0.05	1.50

The risk premiums for the three factors are 5.5 per cent, 4.2 per cent and 4.9 per cent, respectively. If you create a portfolio with 20 per cent invested in A, 20 per cent invested in B and the remainder in C, what is the expression for the return of your portfolio? Assuming that the base return for each equity is 5 per cent and the risk free rate is 5 per cent, what is the expected return of your portfolio?

17 Multifactor Models Suppose equity returns can be explained by the Fama–French three-factor model. The firm-specific risks for all equities are independent. The following table shows the information for three diversified portfolios:

	β	γ	δ	E[R](%)
Portfolio A	0.75	1.20	0.04	18
Portfolio B	1.60	–0.20	0.07	14
Portfolio C	0.85	1.20	0.65	22

Assuming that the base return on each portfolio is 6 per cent and the risk free rate is 5 per cent, what are the risk premiums for each factor in this model?

18 Market Model Assume that the market model is given by:

$$R_{i,t} = \alpha + \beta R_{M,t} + \varepsilon_{i,t}$$

In this equation, $R_{i,t}$ represents the return on asset i at time t; $R_{M,t}$ represents the return on a portfolio containing all risky assets in the same proportion at time t; and both $R_{M,t}$ and $\varepsilon_{i,t}$ are statistically independent variables. Short selling is allowed in the market. You are provided with the information set out in the table below:

Asset	β	Expected Return (%)	Var($\varepsilon_{i,t}$)
A	0.7	8.41	0.0100
B	1.2	12.06	0.0144
C	1.5	13.95	0.0225

The variance of the market is 0.0121. Assume that there are no transaction costs.

(a) Calculate the standard deviation of returns for each asset.

(b) Calculate the variance of return of three portfolios containing an infinite number of asset types *A*, *B* or *C*, respectively.

(c) Assume the risk-free rate is 3.3 per cent and the expected return on the market is 10.6 per cent. Which asset will not be held by rational investors?

(d) What equilibrium state will emerge such that no arbitrage opportunities exist? Why?

19 Portfolio Risk You are forming an equally weighted portfolio of equities. Many equities have the same beta of 0.84 for factor 1 and the same beta of 1.69 for factor 2. They also have the same expected return of 11 per cent. Assume a two-factor model describes the return on each of these equities.

(a) Write the equation of the returns on your portfolio if you place only five equities in it.

(b) Write the equation of the returns on your portfolio if you place in it a very large number of equities that all have the same expected returns and the same betas.

20 Arbitrage and the Arbitrage Pricing Theory The returns on three equities, A, B and C, are given by the following:

$$R_A = 2.4\% + 0.5F_1$$
$$R_B = 4.6\% + 1.2F_1 - 0.5F_2$$
$$R_C = 4.1\% - 0.4F_1 + 0.6F_2$$

(a) Are the returns correlated? Explain.

(b) Assume that you have another equity, D. This equity's returns are generated as:

$$R_D = \alpha + F_1 + F_2$$

If there are no arbitrage possibilities, what is the value of α?

21 Factor Models in the UK The UK is found to have two factors, GDP growth and the inflation rate, that generate the returns of all equities. The expected GDP growth rate in the next year is 2 per cent and the expected inflation rate is 1.5 per cent. Pinto plc has an expected return of 10 per cent, a GDP growth rate factor loading of 1.6 and an inflation rate factor loading of –0.5. If the actual GDP growth rate turns out to be 3 per cent and inflation is 2.3 per cent, what is your estimate of the expected return on Pinto plc?

CHALLENGE

22 APT and Correlations between Surprises There are two equity markets, each driven by the same common force F with an expected value of zero and standard deviation of 10 per cent. There are many securities in each market; thus you can invest in as many stocks as you wish. Due to restrictions, however, you can invest in only one of the two markets. The expected return on every security in both markets is 10 per cent.

The returns for each security i in the first market are generated by the relationship:

$$R_{1i} = 0.10 + 1.5F + \varepsilon_{1i}$$

where ε_{1i} is the term that measures the surprises in the returns of security i in the first market. These surprises are normally distributed; their mean is zero. The returns for security j in the second market are generated by the relationship

$$R_{2j} = 0.10 + 0.5F + \varepsilon_{2j}$$

where ε_{2j} is the term that measures the surprises in the returns of security j in market 2. These surprises are normally distributed; their mean is zero. The standard deviation of ε_{1i} and ε_{2j} for any two securities, i and j, is 20 per cent.

(a) If the correlation between the surprises in the returns of any two securities in the first market is zero, and if the correlation between the surprises in the returns of any two securities in the second market is zero, in which market would a risk-averse person prefer to invest? (*Note:* The correlation between ε_{1i} and ε_{1j} for any i and j is zero, and the correlation between ε_{2i} and ε_{2j} for any i and j is zero.)

(b) If the correlation between ε_{1i} and ε_{1j} in the first market is 0.9 and the correlation between ε_{2i} and ε_{2j} in the second market is zero, in which market would a risk-averse person prefer to invest?

(c) If the correlation between ε_{1i} and ε_{1j} in the first market is zero and the correlation between ε_{2i} and ε_{2j} in the second market is 0.5, in which market would a risk-averse person prefer to invest?

(d) In general, what is the relationship between the correlations of the disturbances in the two markets that would make a risk-averse person equally willing to invest in either of the two markets?

23 The APT and Portfolios Assume that the following market model adequately describes the return-generating behaviour of risky assets:

$$R_{it} = \alpha_i + \beta_i R_{Mt} + \varepsilon_{it}$$

Here:

R_{it} = the return for the ith asset at time t

R_{Mt} = the return on a portfolio containing all risky assets in some proportion at time t

R_{Mt} and ε_{it} are statistically independent.

Short selling (i.e., negative positions) is allowed in the market. You are given the following information:

Asset	β_i	$E(R_i)$ (%)	Var (ε_i)
A	0.7	8.41	0.0100
B	1.2	12.06	0.0144
C	1.5	13.95	0.0225

The variance of the market is 0.0121, and there are no transaction costs.

(a) Calculate the standard deviation of returns for each asset.

(b) Calculate the variance of return of three portfolios containing an infinite number of asset types A, B or C, respectively.

(c) Assume the risk-free rate is 3.3 per cent and the expected return on the market is 10.6 per cent. Which asset will not be held by rational investors?

(d) What equilibrium state will emerge such that no arbitrage opportunities exist? Why?

24 The APT and Arbitrage Opportunities Assume that the returns of individual securities are generated by the following two-factor model:

$$R_{it} = E(R_{it}) + \beta_{ij}F_{1t} + \beta_{i2}F_{2t}$$

Here:

R_{it} is the return for security i at time t

F_{1t} and F_{2t} are market factors with zero expectation and zero covariance.

In addition, assume that there is a capital market for four securities, and the capital market for these four assets is perfect in the sense that there are no transaction costs, and short sales (i.e., negative positions) are permitted. The characteristics of the four securities follow:

Security	β_1	β_2	$E(R)$(%)
1	1.0	1.50	20
2	0.5	2.00	20
3	1.0	0.50	10
4	1.5	0.75	10

(a) Construct a portfolio containing (long or short) securities 1 and 2, with a return that does not depend on the market factor, F_{1t}, in any way. (*Hint:* Such a portfolio will have $\beta_l = 0$.) Compute the expected return andβ_2 coefficient for this portfolio.

(b) Following the procedure in (a), construct a portfolio containing securities 3 and 4 with a return that does not depend on the market factor F_{1t}. Compute the expected return and β_2 coefficient for this portfolio.

(c) There is a risk-free asset with expected return equal to 5 per cent, $\beta_1 = 0$, and $\beta_2 = 0$. Describe a possible arbitrage opportunity in such detail that an investor could implement it.

(d) What effect would the existence of these kinds of arbitrage opportunities have on the capital markets for these securities in the short and long run? Graph your analysis.

25 Factor Models: Ericsson The returns on Ericsson, Electrolux and Swedbank are generated as follows:

$$R_{it} = \alpha_i + \beta_{i,SMB}R_{SMB} + \beta_{i,HML}R_{HML} + \varepsilon_{it}$$

Name	α(%)	β_{HML}	β_{SMB}
Ericsson	3	1.2	−0.3
Electrolux	5	0.9	−0.25
Swedbank	7	−0.5	1.3

How would you determine the return on an equally weighted portfolio of all three equities?

26 Factor Models: Theory Prove that the portfolio-weighted average of a security's sensitivity to a particular factor is the same as the covariance between the return of the portfolio and the factor divided by the variance of the factor if the factors are uncorrelated with each other.

27 Factor Models: Firm-specific Risk How can the return on a portfolio be expressed in terms of a factor model? What is the minimum number of factors needed to explain the expected returns of a group of five securities if the securities' returns have no firm-specific risk? Why?

28 **Factor Models: Variances and Covariances** Consider the following two-factor model for the returns of three securities. Assume that the factors and epsilons have means of zero. Also, assume the factors have variances of 0.1 and are uncorrelated with one another.

$$\tilde{r}_A = 0.13 + 0.6\tilde{F}_1 + 0.4\tilde{F}_2 + \tilde{\epsilon}_A$$
$$\tilde{r}_B = 0.15 + 0.2\tilde{F}_1 + 0.2\tilde{F}_2 + \tilde{\epsilon}_B$$
$$\tilde{r}_C = 0.07 + 0.5\tilde{F}_1 + 0.1\tilde{F}_2 + \tilde{\epsilon}_C$$

If

$$var(\tilde{\epsilon}_A) = 0.01 var(\tilde{\epsilon}_B) = 0.04 var(\tilde{\epsilon}_C) = 0.02$$

what are the variances of the returns of the three securities, as well as the covariances and correlations between them?

29 **Factor Models: Portfolio Sensitivity** A portfolio manager wants to create a simple portfolio from only two stocks, A and B. The returns for stocks A and B are given by the following equations:

$$R_A = 0.09 - 1F_{INF} + 1F_{GDP} + \varepsilon_A \text{ and } R_B = 0.12 - 2F_{INF} + 4F_{GDP} + \varepsilon_B$$

The manager forms a portfolio with market value weights of 40 per cent in stock A and 60 per cent in stock B. What is the sensitivity to the portfolio of a 1 per cent rise in inflation, in basis points?

Exam Question (45 minutes)

Assume a two-factor APT model is appropriate for asset returns, and there are an infinite number of assets in the economy. Three factors drive expected return: the percentage change in GDP, interest rates, and a green-minus-brown factor (Pastor et al., 2022). The cross-sectional relationship between expected return and factor betas indicates that GDP is expected to grow by 3.5 per cent, and interest rates will grow by 3 per cent. The expected return on a green-minus-brown portfolio is 2.1 per cent. You have estimated factor betas for equities X and Y as follows:

Equity	β_1	β_2	β_3
X	2.3	1.9	1.6
Y	0.6	−0.5	−0.6

1 The expected return on an asset having zero betas (with respect to all three factors) is 0.03. According to the APT, what are the approximate equilibrium returns on each of the two equities? **(25 marks)**

2 Discuss what the theoretical results in the APT say about the number of factors used in this question. **(25 marks)**

3 The APT expected return relationship looks very similar to the security market line that was derived in the capital asset pricing model (CAPM). Review the differences between the APT and CAPM. **(25 marks)**

4 You determine that there are two factors under the APT that affect the portfolios you have constructed for your limited clientele, who invest only in equities of firms that follow the UN Sustainable Development Goals: the rate of inflation and the growth rate of all green equities in relation to the growth rate of brown equities. You determine that the three factors will grow by 0.08, 0.20 and 0.8, respectively, with zero covariance between the three factors, and the zero beta portfolio's expected rate of return is 3 per cent. The beta for your portfolio is 1.2 with respect to all factors. Calculate the expected rate of return for your portfolio. **(25 marks)**

Total Marks: 100

Mini Case

The Fama–French (2016) Multifactor Model and Mutual Fund Returns

Dawn Browne, an investment broker, has been approached by client Jack Thomas about the risk of his investments. Dawn has recently read several articles concerning the risk factors that can potentially affect asset returns, and she has decided to examine Jack's mutual fund holdings. Jack is currently invested in the Fidelity Magellan Fund (FMAGX), the Fidelity Low-Priced Stock Fund (FLPSX), and the Baron Small Cap Fund (BSCFX).

Dawn would like to estimate the well-known multifactor model proposed by Fama and French (2016) to determine the risk of each mutual fund.

$$R_{it} - R_{Ft} = \alpha_i + \beta_1(R_{Mt} - R_{Ft}) + \beta_2(SMB_t) + \beta_3(HML_t) + \beta_4(RMW) + \beta_5(CMA) + \varepsilon_t$$

In models such as the one Dawn is considering, the alpha (α) term is of particular interest. It is the regression intercept; but, more important, it is also the excess return that the asset earned. In other words, if the alpha is positive, the asset earned a return greater than it should have given its level of risk; if the alpha is negative, the asset earned a return lower than it should have given its level of risk. This measure is called 'Jensen's alpha' and is a very widely used tool for mutual fund evaluation.

1 For a large-company equity mutual fund, would you expect the betas to be positive or negative for each of the factors in a Fama–French (2016) multifactor model?
2 The SMB, HML, RMW, CMA factors, and risk-free rates for the USA are available at Ken French's website: mba.tuck.dartmouth.edu/pages/faculty/ken.french/. Download the monthly factors and save the most recent 60 months for each factor. The historical prices for each of the mutual funds can be found on various websites, including finance.yahoo.com. Find the prices of each mutual fund for the same time as the Fama–French factors and calculate the returns for each month. Be sure to include dividends. For each mutual fund, estimate the multifactor regression equation using the Fama–French factors. How well do the regression estimates explain the variation in the return of each mutual fund?
3 What do you observe about the beta coefficients for the different mutual funds? Comment on any similarities or differences.
4 If the market is efficient, what value would you expect for alpha? Do your estimates support market efficiency?
5 Which fund has performed best considering its risk? Why?

Practical Case Study

The APT vs the CAPM

In this practical case study, you will apply the APT to a set of equities and compare it with the CAPM. Collect data from Yahoo! Finance (or another financial website) on the monthly returns of 10 equities from different industries in the same country for the past five years. You will also need to collect data on the following risk factors: the market return, the interest rate, the inflation rate and the consumer confidence index.

Perform the following steps:

(a) Calculate the excess returns of each equity by subtracting the risk-free rate from the actual returns.
(b) Estimate the factor loadings of each stock using a multiple regression model, where the dependent variable is the excess return of the equity, and the independent variables are the excess returns of the risk factors.
(c) Calculate the expected return of each stock using the APT formula.
(d) Compare the expected returns with the actual returns and calculate the average absolute error for each stock.
(e) Compare the results of the APT with those of the CAPM, which assumes only one risk factor (the market return).

1 Which equities have the highest and lowest factor loadings on each risk factor? How do you interpret these results?
2 Which equities have the highest and lowest expected returns according to the APT? How do they differ from the actual returns?
3 Which model (APT or CAPM) has a lower average absolute error for each equity? Which model do you prefer and why?
4 What are some of the advantages and disadvantages of using the APT over the CAPM?
5 What are some of the limitations and challenges of applying the APT in practice?

References

Carhart, M. (1997) 'On Persistence in Mutual Fund Performance', *Journal of Finance*, Vol. 52, 57–82.

Fama, E.F. and K.R. French (1993) 'Common Risk Factors in the Returns on Stocks and Bonds', *Journal of Financial Economics*, Vol. 17, 3–56.

Fama, E.F. and K.R. French (2016) 'Dissecting Anomalies with a Five-factor Model', *Review of Financial Studies*, Vol. 29, No. 1, 69–103.

Fama, E.F. and K.R. French (2017) 'International Tests of a Five-factor Asset Pricing Model', *Journal of Financial Economics*, Vol. 123, No. 3, 441–463.

Pástor, L., R.F. Stambaugh and L.A. Taylor (2022) 'Dissecting Green Returns', *Journal of Financial Economics*, Vol. 146, No. 2, 403–424.

Smith, S.C. and A. Timmermann (2022) 'Have Risk Premia Vanished?', *Journal of Financial Economics*, Vol. 145, No. 2, 553–576.

Additional Reading

Much of the research into asset pricing overlaps that of Chapter 10. The following articles have taken our understanding of asset pricing forward:

1 Avramov, D., S. Cheng, A. Lioui, and A. Tarelli (2022) 'Sustainable Investing with ESG Rating Uncertainty', *Journal of Financial Economics*, Vol. 145, No. 2, 642–664.

2 Bollerslev, T., A.J. Patton and R. Quaedvlieg (2022) 'Realized Semibetas: Disentangling "Good" and "Bad" Downside Risks', *Journal of Financial Economics*, Vol. 144, No. 1, 227–246.

3 Brogaard, J., T.H. Nguyen, T.J. Putnins and E. Wu (2022) 'What Moves Stock Prices? The Roles of News, Noise, and Information', *Review of Financial Studies*, Vol. 35, No. 9, 4341–4386.

4 Cohen, L., C. Malloy and Q. Nguyen (2020) 'Lazy Prices,' *Journal of Finance*, Vol. 75, No. 3, 1371–1415.

Fama and French are the lead researchers in this area and the interested reader is recommended to read their four most recent papers to get a good idea of current thinking:

5 Fama, E.F. and K.R. French (2015) 'A Five-factor Asset Pricing Model', *Journal of Financial Economics*, Vol. 116, No. 1, 1–22.

6 Fama, E.F. and K.R. French (2016) 'Dissecting Anomalies with a Five-factor Model', *Review of Financial Studies*, Vol. 29, No. 1, 69–103.

7 Fama, E.F. and K.R. French (2017) 'International Tests of a Five-factor Asset Pricing Model', *Journal of Financial Economics*, Vol. 123, No. 3, 441–463.

8 Fama, E.F. and K.R. French (2018) 'Choosing Factors', *Journal of Financial Economics*, Vol. 128, No. 2, 234–252.

9 Florackis, C., C. Louca, R. Michaely and M. Weber (2023) 'Cybersecurity Risk', *Review of Financial Studies*, Vol. 36, No. 1, 351–407.

10 Huang, S. (2022) 'The Momentum Gap and Return Predictability', *Review of Financial Studies*, Vol. 35, No. 7, 3303–3336.

11 Linnainmaa, J.T. and M.R. Roberts (2018) 'The History of the Cross-section of Stock Returns', *Review of Financial Studies*, Vol. 31, No. 7, 2606–2649.

12 Massa, M., J. O'Donovan and H. Zhang (2022) 'International Asset Pricing with Strategic Business Groups', *Journal of Financial Economics*, Vol. 145, No. 2, 339–361.

Endnotes

1 In Chapter 10, we briefly mentioned that unsystematic risk is risk that can be diversified away in a large portfolio. This result will also follow from the present analysis.

2 Alternatively, the market model could be written as:

$$R = \alpha + \beta R_M + \varepsilon$$

Here alpha (α) is an intercept term equal to:

$$\overline{R} - \beta \overline{R}_M$$

3 Technically, we can think of a large portfolio as one where an investor keeps increasing the number of securities without limit. In practice, *effective* diversification would occur if at least a few dozen securities were held.

4 More precisely, we say that the weighted average of the unsystematic risk approaches zero as the number of equally weighted securities in a portfolio approaches infinity.

5 Our presentation on this point has been non-rigorous. The student interested in more rigour should note that the variance of row 3 is:

$$\frac{1}{N^2}\sigma_\varepsilon^2 + \frac{1}{N^2}\sigma_\varepsilon^2 + \frac{1}{N^2}\sigma_\varepsilon^2 + \ldots + \frac{1}{N^2}\sigma_\varepsilon^2 = \frac{1}{N^2}\sigma_\varepsilon^2$$

where

$$\sigma_\varepsilon^2$$

is the variance of each ε This can be rewritten as

$$\sigma_\varepsilon^2/N,$$

which tends to 0 as N goes to infinity.

6 This assumption is plausible in the real world. For example, the market value of Royal Dutch Shell, which is the biggest company in the FTSE 100, is only 3 per cent to 4 per cent of the market value of the index.

Chapter 12
Risk, Cost of Capital and Capital Budgeting

Learning Objectives

After reading this chapter you should be able to:

LO1 Comprehend the concept of the cost of equity capital and its importance in corporate finance.

LO2 Estimate beta and its determinants.

LO3 Evaluate different extensions of cost of capital and their implications in various scenarios.

LO4 Synthesize knowledge on reducing the cost of capital and its practical estimation in practice.

LO5 Apply the concepts of economic value added (EVA) and sustainable value added (SVA) to measure corporate performance.

Risk is integral to every financial decision in business. Without understanding the risk of an investment or project, it is impossible to undertake a valuation appraisal. Risk is captured by the discount rate of a project, but what is meant by the discount rate? To an investor, it is the rate of return expected for undertaking the project, given its risk. To a corporate manager, it is the cost of raising capital to fund the company's investments. To arrive at a sensible value for discount rates, one must always keep in mind this duality in investor and management perspectives, and this is why the investor's rate of return is also called the cost of capital.

Source: Tyler Olson/123RF

In this chapter, we learn how to compute a firm's cost of capital, and find out what it means to the firm and its investors. We will also learn when to use the firm's cost of capital – and, perhaps more important, when not to use it.

Key Notations

R_E	Return on shares; the cost of equity capital
R_D	Return on debt; the cost of debt capital
α	Systematic risk; beta
R_M	Market return
R_F	The risk-free rate of return
$Cov(R_i, R_M)$; $\sigma_{i,M}$	Covariance between security i and the market, M
$Var(R_M)$; σ^2_M	The variance of the market return
S	The market value of equity
B	The market value of debt
R_{WACC}	The weighted average cost of capital
EVA	Economic value added
SVA	Sustainable value added

12.1 The Cost of Equity Capital

A firm can take one of two actions whenever it has extra cash. It can pay out the cash immediately as a dividend, or invest in a project, paying out the future cash flows as dividends. Which option would shareholders prefer? Whichever option provides the highest return to the shareholder.

If the dividend can be invested in another asset (physical or financial) that provides a higher expected return (given risk) than the company's proposed project, the dividend will be preferred. From the manager's perspective, the project should be undertaken only if its expected return is higher than that of a financial asset with comparable risk. This is illustrated in Figure 12.1.

Figure 12.1 Choices of a Firm with Extra Cash

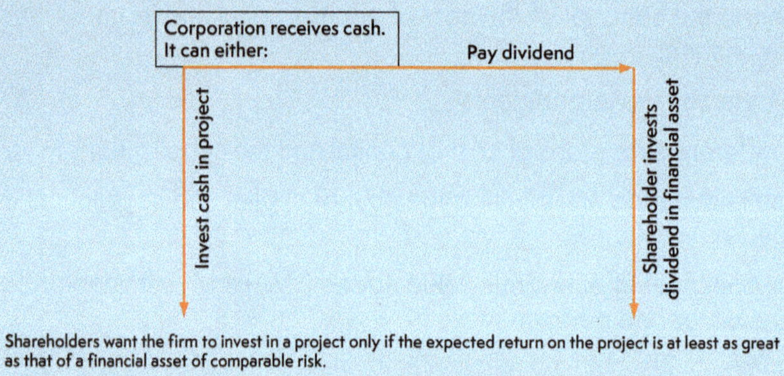

A project's discount rate should be the expected return on a financial asset of comparable risk.

From the firm's perspective, the expected return is the cost of equity capital. Under the CAPM, the expected return on a security is written as:

Equation 12.1
$$R_E = R_F + \beta \times (R_M - R_F)$$

where R_F is the risk-free rate and $R_M - R_F$ is the difference between the expected return on the market portfolio and the riskless rate. This difference is often called the expected *excess* market return or market risk premium. Note we have dropped the bar denoting expectations from our expression to simplify the notation, but remember that we are always thinking about expected returns with the CAPM.

We now have the tools to estimate a firm's cost of equity capital. To do this, we need to know three things:

1. The risk-free rate, R_F
2. The market risk premium, $R_M - R_F$
3. The company beta, β.

Example 12.1

Cost of Equity

According to Reuters, the beta of the French bank Société Générale SA is 2.29. Assume, for now, that the firm is 100 per cent equity financed – that is, it has no debt. Société Générale is considering some expansion projects that will double its size. Because these new projects are similar to the firm's existing ones, the average beta on the new projects is assumed to be equal to Société Générale's current beta. Assume that the risk-free rate is 1.5 per cent. What is the appropriate discount rate for these new projects, assuming a market risk premium of 7.2 per cent?

We estimate the cost of equity, R_E, for Société Générale as follows:

$$R_E = 1.5\% + (7.2\% \times 2.29)$$
$$= 1.5\% + 16.488\%$$
$$= 17.988\%$$

We made two key assumptions: (1) The beta risk of the new projects is the same as the risk of the firm, and (2) the firm is all equity financed. Given these assumptions, it follows that the cash flows of the new projects should be discounted at the 17.988 per cent rate.

Example 12.2

Project Evaluation and Beta

Rio Tinto is a diversified natural resource company listed on the London Stock Exchange. Suppose Rio Tinto is an all-equity firm with a beta of 1.24. Further, suppose the market risk premium is 7.5 per cent, and the risk-free rate is 2 per cent. We can determine the expected return on the Rio Tinto equity by using the SML of Equation 12.1. We find the expected return is:

$$2\% + (1.24 \times 7.5\%) = 11.3\%$$

Because this is the return shareholders can expect in the financial markets on equity with a β of 1.24, it is also the return they expect on Rio Tinto.

Further, suppose Rio Tinto is evaluating the following non-mutually exclusive projects in Greece:

Project	Project's Beta (β)	Project's Expected Cash Flows Next Year (£)	Project's Internal Rate of Return (%)	Project's NPV When Cash Flows are Discounted at 11.3% (£)	Accept or Reject
A	1.24	140	40	25.79	Accept
B	1.24	120	20	7.82	Accept
C	1.24	110	10	–1.17	Reject

Each project initially costs £100. All projects are assumed to have the same risk as the firm as a whole. Because the cost of equity capital is 11.3 per cent, projects in an all-equity firm are discounted at this rate. Projects A and B have positive NPVs, and C has a negative NPV. Thus, only A and B will be accepted, as illustrated in Figure 12.2.

Figure 12.2 Using the Security Market Line to Estimate the Risk-adjusted Discount Rate for Risky Projects

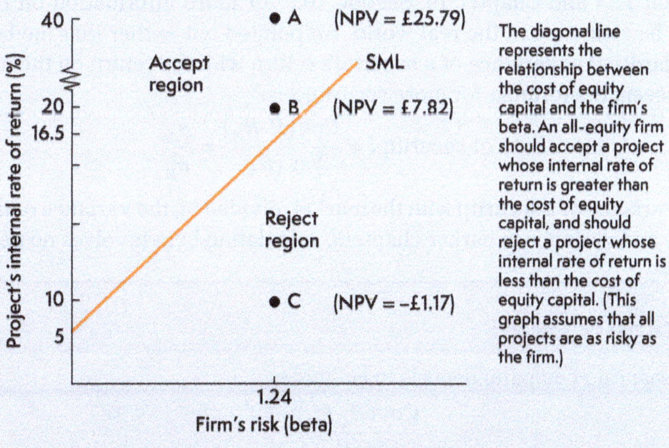

Sustainability in Action 12.1

Ørsted's Cost of Equity Capital

In this case study, we will examine the cost of equity for Ørsted. This Danish renewable energy firm has transitioned from being a fossil fuel-based firm to a leader in sustainable energy solutions. With a focus on offshore wind, onshore wind, solar energy and energy storage solutions, Ørsted has demonstrated a commitment to sustainability and a low-carbon future.

Ørsted, formerly known as DONG Energy, has been growing rapidly in the renewable energy market. As a result, the company (like any other firm) must attract external investment to finance its expansion and green initiatives. To do this, Ørsted must offer investors an appropriate return on their investment, and the cost of equity determines this. The cost of equity represents the return investors expect from investing in a company's equity.

To calculate Ørsted's cost of equity, we will use the capital asset pricing model (CAPM), a widely accepted method for estimating the required return on equity investments. The CAPM formula is as follows:

$$E[R_{Ørsted}] = r_f + \beta_{Ørsted}[R_{Market} - r_f]$$

The risk-free rate represents the return on a risk-free investment, such as government bonds. For instance, let's assume a risk-free rate of 2.5 per cent based on long-term Danish government bond yields in 2023.

Beta measures the equity's sensitivity to market movements and the risk associated with investing in the equity relative to the overall market. A higher beta indicates higher risk and a higher required return. Assume that Ørsted has a beta of 0.32 in 2023 (see Section 12.2 on how to calculate Ørsted's beta).

The market risk premium represents the additional return investors expect for taking on the risk of investing in the stock market instead of a risk-free investment. In this example, we assume a market risk premium of 6 per cent.

Using the CAPM formula, we can calculate Ørsted's cost of equity:

$$E[R_{Ørsted}] = r_f + \beta_{Ørsted}[R_{Market} - r_f] = 2.5\% + 0.32[6\%] = 4.42\%$$

Based on these figures, Ørsted's cost of equity should be 4.42 per cent. This means that investors require a 4.42 per cent return on their investment in Ørsted's equity to compensate for the risk associated with investing in the company.

The cost of equity can change over time due to changes in risk-free rates, market risk premiums or a company's beta. By maintaining a strong focus on sustainability and reducing exposure to volatile fossil fuel markets, Ørsted could lower its overall risk profile and, consequently, its cost of equity, making the company more attractive to potential investors.

12.2 Estimation of Beta

Chapter 10 Page 284
Chapter 11 Page 304

In Section 12.1, we assumed that the beta of the company was known (see Chapter 11, Section 11.3 and Chapter 10, Section 10.9 for more information on betas). Of course, beta must be estimated in the real world. We pointed out earlier that the beta of a security is the standardized covariance of a security's return with the return on the market portfolio. As we have seen, the formula for more security i is:

$$\text{Beta of security } i = \frac{\text{Cov}(R_i, R_M)}{\text{Var}(R_M)} = \frac{\sigma_{iM}}{\sigma_M^2}$$

In words, the beta is the covariance of a security with the market, divided by the variance of the market. Because we calculated both covariance and variance in earlier chapters, calculating beta involves no new material.

Measuring Company Betas

The basic method of measuring company betas is to estimate:

$$\frac{\text{Cov}(R_i, R_M)}{\text{Var}(R_M)}$$

using $t = 1, 2, \ldots, T$ observations.

Problems

1 Betas may vary over time.
2 The sample size may be inadequate.
3 Betas are influenced by changing financial leverage and business risk.

Solutions

- Problems 1 and 2 can be moderated by more sophisticated statistical techniques.
- Problem 3 can be lessened by adjusting for changes in business and financial risk.
- Look at average beta estimates of several comparable firms in the industry.

Real-world Betas

It is instructive to see how we calculate betas for real-world companies. Figure 12.3 plots monthly returns for Ørsted and LVMH Moët Hennessy against monthly returns on the Euro Stoxx 50 index. Using a standard regression technique, we fit a straight line through data points. The result is called the 'characteristic' line. The slope of the characteristic line is beta. Though we have not shown it in Table 12.1, we can also determine the intercept (commonly called alpha) of the characteristic line by regression.

Figure 12.3 Plots of Five Years of Monthly Returns (2018–2023) for Ørsted and LVMH Moët Hennessy against Five Years of Monthly Returns on the Euro Stoxx 50 Index

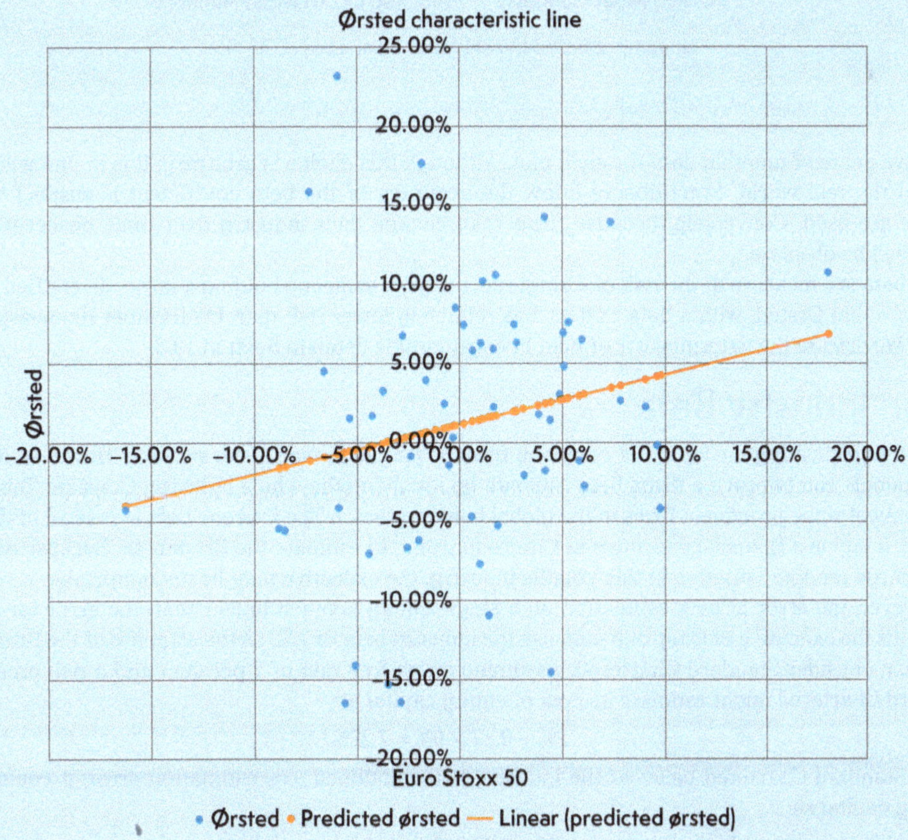

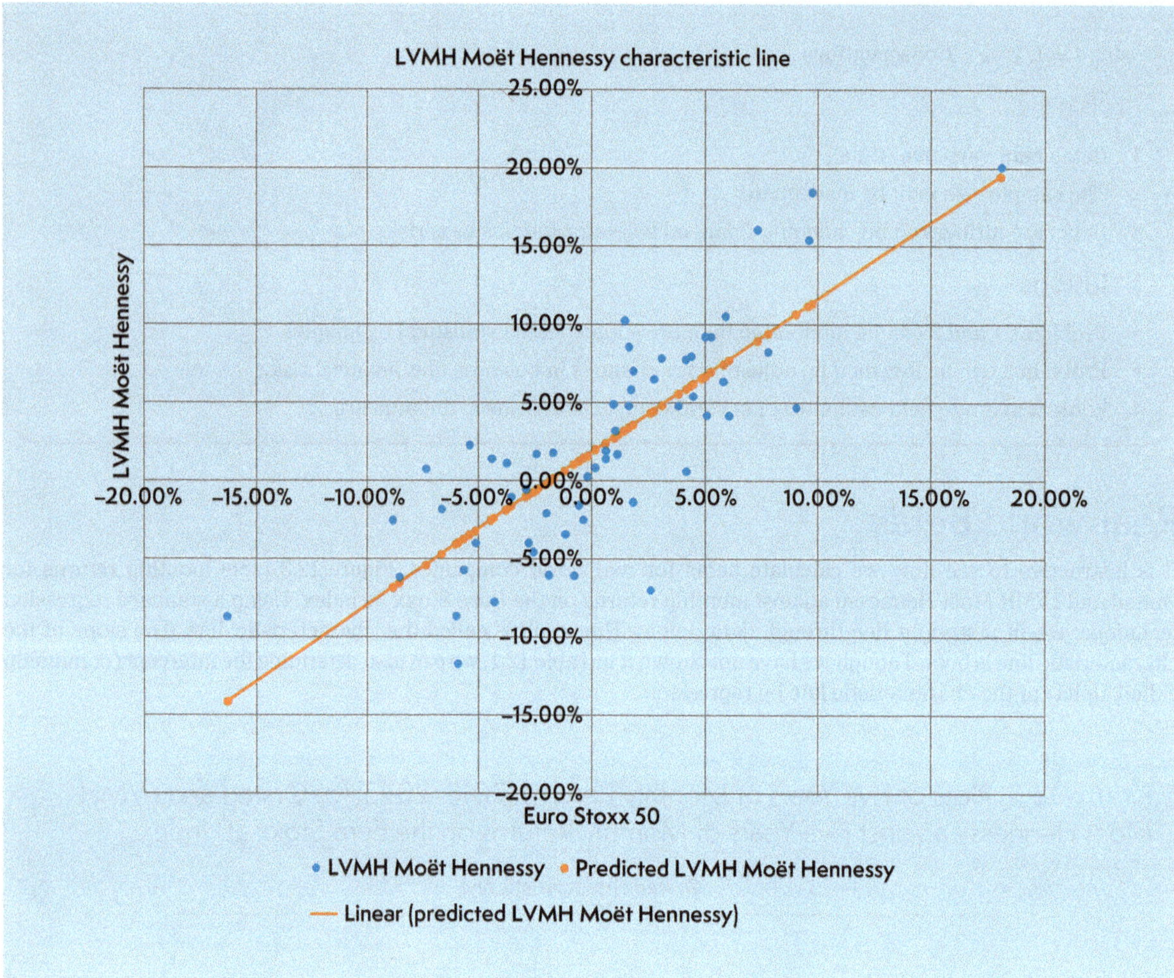

We use five years of monthly data for each plot. Although this choice is arbitrary, it is in line with calculations performed in the real world. Practitioners know the accuracy of the beta coefficient is suspect when too few observations are used. Conversely, because firms may change their industry over time, observations from the distant past will be obsolete.

Because beta is a measure of the risk of a single security for someone holding a large, diversified portfolio, our results indicate that Ørsted, with a beta of 0.32, has relatively lower risk than LVMH Moët Hennessy, which has a beta of 0.97. We discuss the determinants of beta in considerable detail in Section 12.3.

Using an Industry Beta

Our approach to estimating the beta of a company from its past data may seem sensible. However, it is frequently argued that people can improve a firm's beta estimate by involving the whole industry. Consider Table 12.1, which shows the betas of some prominent firms in the global banking sector. The average beta across all of the firms in the sector is 1.32. Imagine a financial executive at Citigroup trying to estimate the firm's beta. Because beta estimation is subject to large random variation in this volatile industry, the executive may be uncomfortable with the estimate of 1.56. However, the error in beta estimation on a single equity is much higher than the error for a portfolio of securities. Thus the executive of Citigroup may use the industry beta of 1.32 as the estimate of the firm's beta.

In contrast, consider Standard Chartered. Assuming a risk-free rate of 2 per cent and a risk premium of 6 per cent, Standard Chartered might estimate its cost of equity capital as:

$$2\% + 0.87 \times 6\% = 7.22\%$$

However, if Standard Chartered believed the industry beta contained less estimation error, it could calculate its cost of equity capital as:

$$2\% + 1.32 \times 6\% = 9.92\%$$

Table 12.1 Betas for Selected Banks, 2023

Name	Beta
Credit Agricole	1.68
Citigroup Inc.	1.56
Banco Santander	1.38
Deutsche Bank	1.37
Barclays	1.35
Bank of Ireland	1.34
Natwest Group	1.30
Lloyds Banking Group	1.22
J.P. Morgan Chase & Co	1.12
Wells Fargo & Co	1.09
Standard Chartered	0.87
Bank of the Ryukyus Ltd	0.26

The difference is substantial here, presenting a difficult choice for a financial executive at Standard Chartered.

While there is no formula for selecting the right beta, there is a very simple guideline. If you believe that the operations of a firm are similar to the operations of the rest of the industry, you should use the industry beta simply to reduce estimation error.[1] However, if an executive believes that the operations of the firm are fundamentally different from those in the rest of the industry, the firm's beta should be used.

When we discussed financial statement analysis in Chapter 3, we noted that a problem frequently comes up in practice – namely, what is the industry? For example, Tesco is normally regarded as a supermarket. However, the company is also involved in financial services. The risk of these different business operations can be quite different.

Chapter 3
Page 60

12.3 Determinants of Beta

The regression analysis approach in the previous section does not tell us from where beta comes. Of course, the beta of a security does not emerge from thin air. Instead, it is determined by the characteristics of the firm. We consider three factors: the cyclical nature of revenues, operating leverage and financial leverage.

Cyclicality of Revenues

The revenues of some firms are quite cyclical. That is, these firms do well in the expansion phase of the business cycle and poorly in the contraction phase. Empirical evidence suggests that high-tech firms, retailers and automotive firms fluctuate with the business cycle. Firms in industries such as utilities, railroads, food and airlines are less dependent on the cycle. Because beta is the standardized covariance of a security's return with the market's return, it is not surprising that highly cyclical securities have high betas.

It is worthwhile to point out that cyclicality is not the same as variability. For example, a film-making firm has highly variable revenues because it is not easy to predict hits and flops. However, because the revenues of a studio are more dependent on the quality of its releases than the phase of the business cycle, motion picture companies are not particularly cyclical. In other words, securities with high standard deviations need not have high betas – a point we have stressed before.

Operating Leverage

We distinguished fixed costs from variable costs in Chapter 3, Section 3.2. At that time, we mentioned that fixed costs do not change as quantity changes. Conversely, variable costs increase as the quantity of output rises. This difference between variable and fixed costs allows us to define operating leverage.

Example 12.3

Operating Leverage Illustrated

Consider a typical problem faced by Carlsberg, the Danish alcoholic drinks firm. As part of the brewing process, Carlsberg often needs to choose between two production technologies. Assume that Carlsberg can choose either technology A or technology B when making a particular drink. The relevant differences between the two technologies are displayed here:

Technology A	Technology B
Fixed cost: DKr1,000/year	Fixed cost: DKr2,000/year
Variable cost: DKr8/unit	Variable cost: DKr6/unit
Price: DKr10/unit	Price: DKr10/unit
Contribution margin: DKr2 (= DKr10 – DKr8)	Contribution margin: DKr4 (= DKr10 – DKr6)

Technology A has lower fixed costs and higher variable costs than technology B. Perhaps technology A involves less mechanization than B, or the equipment in A may be leased, whereas the equipment in B must be purchased. Alternatively, perhaps technology A involves a few employees but many subcontractors, whereas B has only highly skilled employees who it must retain in bad times. Because technology B has both lower variable costs and higher fixed costs, we say that it has higher operating leverage.

Figure 12.4 graphs the costs under both technologies. The slope of each total cost line represents variable costs under a single technology. The slope of A's line is steeper, indicating greater variable costs.

Figure 12.4 Illustration of Two Different Technologies

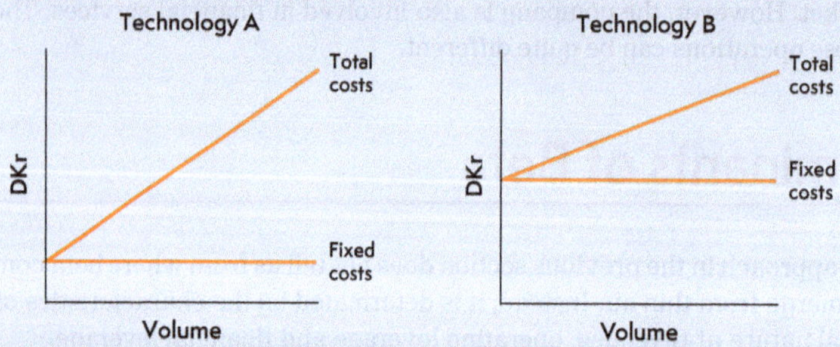

Technology A has higher variable costs and lower fixed costs than does technology B. Technology B has higher operating leverage.

Because the two technologies are used to produce the same drinks, a unit price of DKr10 applies for both cases. An unexpected sale increases profit by DKr2 under A but increases profit by DKr4 under B. Similarly, a sudden sale cancellation reduces profit by DKr2 under A but reduces profit by DKr4 under B. We illustrate this in Figure 12.5, which shows the change in earnings before interest and taxes for a given change in volume. Notice the slope of the right graph is steeper, and this indicates that technology B is riskier.

Figure 12.5 Illustration of the Effect of a Change in Volume on the Change in Earnings before Interest and Taxes (EBIT)

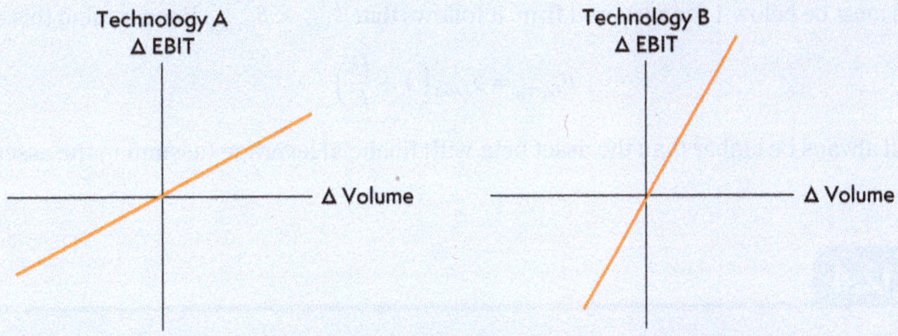

Technology B has lower variable costs than A, implying a higher contribution margin. The profits of the firm are more responsive to changes in volume under technology B than under A.

The cyclicality of a firm's revenues is a determinant of the firm's beta. Operating leverage magnifies the effect of cyclicality on beta. As mentioned earlier, business risk can generally be defined as the risk of a firm without financial leverage. Business risk depends both on the responsiveness of the firm's revenues to the business cycle and on the firm's operating leverage.

Although the above discussion concerns firms, it applies to projects as well. If we cannot estimate a project's beta in another way, we can examine the project's revenues and operating leverage. Projects whose revenues appear strongly cyclical and whose operating leverage appears high are likely to have high betas. Conversely, weak cyclicality and low operating leverage imply low betas. As mentioned earlier, this approach is unfortunately qualitative in nature. Because start-up projects have little data, quantitative estimates of beta generally are not feasible.

Financial Leverage and Beta

As suggested by their names, operating leverage and financial leverage are similar concepts. Operating leverage refers to the firm's fixed costs of *production*. Financial leverage is the extent to which a firm relies on debt, and a levered firm is a firm with some debt in its capital structure. Because a *levered* firm must make interest payments regardless of the firm's sales, financial leverage refers to the firm's fixed costs of *finance*.

Consider our discussion in Chapter 10 (Example 10.4) concerning the beta of Hicks plc. In that example, we estimated beta from the returns on Hicks' *equity*. Furthermore, the betas in Figure 12.3 from real-world firms were estimated from equity share price returns. Thus, in each case, we estimated the firm's equity beta. The beta of the assets of a levered firm is different from the beta of its equity. As the name suggests, the asset beta is the beta of the assets of the firm. We can also think of the asset beta as the beta of the firm's shares had the firm been financed only with equity.

Chapter 10 Page 282

Imagine an individual who owns all the firm's debt and all its equity. In other words, this individual owns the entire firm. What is the beta of her portfolio of the firm's debt and equity?

As with any portfolio, the beta of this portfolio is a weighted average of the betas of the individual items in the portfolio. Let D stand for the market value of the firm's debt and E stand for the market value of the firm's equity. We have:

Equation 12.2

$$\beta_{\text{Asset}} = \frac{E}{D+E} \times \beta_{\text{Equity}} + \frac{D}{D+E} \times \beta_{\text{Debt}}$$

where β_{Equity} is the beta of the equity of the *levered* firm. Notice that the beta of debt, β_{Debt}, is multiplied by $D/(D+E)$, the percentage of debt in the capital structure. Similarly, the equity beta is multiplied by the weighting of equity in the capital structure. Because the portfolio contains both the debt of the firm and the equity of the firm, the beta of the portfolio is the *asset beta*. As we have just said, the asset beta can also be viewed as the beta of the company's shares had the firm been all equity.

The beta of debt is very low in practice. If we make the common assumption that the beta of debt is zero, we have:

Equation 12.3

$$\beta_{\text{Asset}} = \frac{E}{D+E} \times \beta_{\text{Equity}}$$

Because $E/(D+E)$ must be below 1 for a levered firm, it follows that $\beta_{\text{Asset}} < \beta_{\text{Equity}}$. Rearranging this equation, we have:

$$\beta_{\text{Equity}} = \beta_{\text{Asset}}\left(1+\frac{D}{E}\right)$$

The equity beta will always be higher than the asset beta with financial leverage (assuming the asset beta is positive).[2]

Example 12.4

Asset versus Equity Betas

Consider a Swedish tree-growing company, Rapid Firs, which is currently all equity and has a beta of 0.8. The firm has decided to move to a capital structure of one part debt to two parts equity. Because the firm is staying in the same industry, its asset beta should remain at 0.8. However, assuming a zero beta for its debt, its equity beta would become:

$$\beta_{\text{Equity}} = \beta_{\text{Asset}}\left(1+\frac{D}{E}\right)$$

$$1.2 = 0.8\left(1+\frac{1}{2}\right)$$

If the firm had one part debt to one part equity in its capital structure, its equity beta would be:

$$1.6 = 0.8(1+1)$$

However, as long as it stayed in the same industry, its asset beta would remain at 0.8. The effect of leverage, then, is to increase the equity beta.

12.4 Extensions of the Basic Model

The Firm versus the Project

We now assume that the risk of a project differs from that of the firm while going back to the all-equity assumption. We began the chapter by pointing out that each project should be paired with a financial asset of comparable risk. If a project's beta differs from that of the firm, the project should be discounted at the rate that reflects project risk rather than firm risk. This is a very important point because firms frequently speak of a *corporate discount rate*. (*Hurdle rate, cut-off rate, benchmark* and *cost of capital* are used synonymously.) Unless all projects in the corporation are of the same risk, choosing the same discount rate for all projects is incorrect.

Example 12.5

Project Risk

D.D. Ronnelley, a publishing firm, may accept a project to adapt its existing textbooks into interactive textbook apps for the Apple and Android operating systems. Noting that computer software companies have high betas, the publishing firm views the software venture as riskier than the rest of its business. It should, therefore, discount the project at a rate commensurate with the risk of software companies. For example, it might use the average beta of a portfolio of publicly traded software firms. Instead, if all projects in D.D. Ronnelley were discounted at the same rate, a bias would result. The firm would accept too many high-risk projects (software ventures) and reject too many low-risk projects (books and magazines). We illustrate this point in Figure 12.6.

Figure 12.6 Relationship between the Firm's Cost of Capital and the Security Market Line

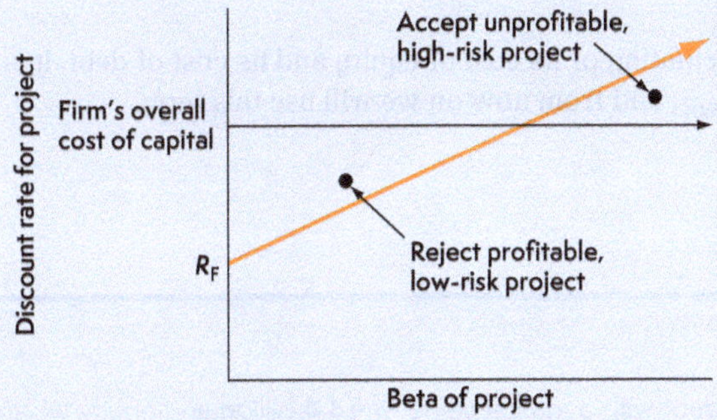

Use of a firm's cost of capital in calculations may lead to incorrect capital budgeting decisions.

Projects with high risk, such as the software venture for D.D. Ronnelley, should be discounted at a high rate. By using the firm's cost of capital, the firm is likely to accept too many high-risk projects.

Projects with low risk should be discounted at a low rate. By using the firm's cost of capital, the firm is likely to reject too many low-risk projects.

The D.D. Ronnelley example assumes that the proposed project has the same risk as the software industry, allowing the industry beta to be used. However, the beta of a new project may be higher than the beta of existing firms in the same industry because the very newness of the project is likely to increase its responsiveness to economy-wide movements. For example, a start-up computer venture may fail in a recession, whereas Apple will still be around. Conversely, in an economy-wide expansion, the enterprise may grow much faster than established technology firms.

Fortunately, a slight adjustment is all that is needed here. The new venture should be assigned a somewhat higher beta than that of the industry to reflect added risk. The adjustment is necessarily ad hoc, so no formula can be given. Our experience indicates that this approach is widespread in practice today.

The Cost of Capital with Debt

Section 12.1 showed how to choose the discount rate when a project is all equity financed. In this section, we discuss an adjustment when the project is funded with both debt and equity.

Suppose a firm uses both debt and equity to finance its investments. If the firm pays R_D for its debt financing and R_E for its equity, what is the overall or average cost of its capital? The cost of equity is R_E, as discussed in earlier sections. The cost of debt is the firm's borrowing rate, R_D, which we can often observe by looking at the yield to maturity on the firm's debt. If a firm uses both debt and equity, the cost of capital is a weighted average of the cost of each funding source:

$$\frac{E}{D+E} \times R_E + \frac{D}{D+E} \times R_D$$

The weights in the formula are, respectively, the proportion of total value represented by the equity:

$$\left(\frac{E}{D+E}\right)$$

and the proportion of total value represented by debt:

$$\left(\frac{D}{D+E}\right)$$

If the firm had issued no debt and was, therefore, an all-equity firm, its average cost of capital would equal its cost of equity, R_E. At the other extreme, if the firm had issued so much debt that its equity was valueless, it would be an all-debt firm, and its average cost of capital would be its cost of debt, R_D.

Of course, interest is tax deductible at the corporate level, a point to be treated in more detail in Chapter 19. The after-tax cost of debt is:

$$\text{Cost of debt (after corporate tax)} = R_D \times (1 - t_c)$$

where t_c is the corporation's tax rate.

Assembling these results, we get the average cost of capital (after tax) for the firm:

Equation 12.4

$$\text{Average cost of capital} = \left(\frac{E}{D+E}\right) \times R_E + \left(\frac{D}{D+E}\right) \times R_D \times (1 - t_c)$$

Because the average cost of capital is a weighting of its cost of equity and its cost of debt, it is usually referred to as the weighted average cost of capital, R_{WACC}, and from now on we will use this term.

Example 12.6

WACC

The European steelmaker, ArcelorMittal, has debt with a market value of €4.4 billion and equity worth €71.4 billion. ArcelorMittal has eight different types of bonds in issue, four of which were issued in Luxembourg (denominated in euros) and the other four denominated in dollars. For this example, assume that the bonds are all the same, denominated in dollars and pay interest of 6 per cent per annum. The company's shares have a beta of 1.81. Because of the range of countries and tax codes in regimes in which ArcelorMittal operates, the effective tax rate for the company is 13.1 per cent. Assume that the SML holds, that the risk premium on the market is 9.5 per cent (slightly higher than the historical equity risk premium), and that the current Treasury bill rate is 4.5 per cent. What is this firm's R_{WACC}?

To compute the R_{WACC} using Equation 12.4, we must know (1) the after-tax cost of debt, $R_D \times (1 - t_C)$, (2) the cost of equity, R_E, and (3) the proportions of debt and equity used by the firm. These three values are computed next:

1 The pre-tax cost of debt is 6 per cent, implying an after-tax cost of 5.214 per cent [6% × (1 − 0.131)].

2 We compute the cost of equity capital by using the SML:

$$\begin{aligned} R_E &= R_F + \beta(R_M - R_F) \\ &= 4.596 + 1.81 \times 9.5\% \\ &= 21.695\% \end{aligned}$$

3 We calculate the proportions of debt and equity from the market values of debt and equity. Because the market value of the firm is €75.8 billion (= €4.4 billion + €71.4 billion), the proportions of debt and equity are 5.8 and 94.2 per cent, respectively.

The cost of equity, R_E, is 21.695 per cent, and the after-tax cost of debt, $R_D \times (1 - t_C)$, is 5.214 per cent. D is €4.4 billion and E is €71.4 billion. Therefore:

$$\begin{aligned} R_{WACC} &= \frac{D}{D+E} \times R_D \times \left(1 - t_c\right) + \frac{E}{D+E} \times R_E \\ &= \frac{4.4}{75.8} \times 5.214\% + \frac{71.4}{75.8} \times 21.695\% \\ &= 20.738\% \end{aligned}$$

This procedure is presented in table form below:

(1) Financing Components	(2) Market Values (€)	(3) Weight	(4) Cost of Capital (After Corporate Tax)	(5) Weighted Cost of Capital (%)
Debt	4.4 billion	0.058	6% × (1 − 0.131) = 5.214%	0.302
Equity	71.4 billion	0.942	4.5% + 1.81 × 9.5% = 21.695%	20.436
	75.8 billion	1.000		20.738

The weights we used in Example 12.6 were market value weights. Market value weights are more appropriate than book value weights because the market values of the securities are closer to the actual money that would be received from their sale. It is usually useful to think in terms of 'target' market weights. These are the market weights expected to prevail over the life of the firm or project.

Example 12.7

Project Evaluation and the WACC

Suppose a firm has both a current and a target debt–equity ratio of 0.6, a cost of debt of 15.15 per cent and a cost of equity of 20 per cent. The corporate tax rate is 34 per cent.

Our first step calls for transforming the debt–equity (D/E) ratio to a debt–value ratio. A D/E ratio of 0.6 implies 6 parts debt for 10 parts equity. Because value is equal to the sum of the debt plus the equity, the debt–value ratio is $6/(6+10) = 0.375$. Similarly, the equity–value ratio is $10/(6+10) = 0.625$. The R_{WACC} will then be:

$$\begin{aligned} R_{WACC} &= \left(\frac{E}{D+E}\right) \times R_E + \left(\frac{D}{D+E}\right) \times R_D \times (1-t_c) \\ &= 0.625 \times 20\% + 0.375 \times 15.15\% \times 0.66 \\ &= 16.25\% \end{aligned}$$

Suppose the firm is considering taking on a warehouse renovation costing £50 million that is expected to yield cost savings of £12 million a year for six years. Using the NPV equation and discounting the six years of expected cash flows from the renovation at the R_{WACC}, we have:

$$\begin{aligned} NPV &= £50 + \frac{£12}{(1+R_{WACC})} + \ldots + \frac{£12}{(1+R_{WACC})^6} \\ &= -£50 + £12 \times £12 \times A^6_{0.1625} \\ &= -£50 + (12 \times 3.66) \\ &= -£6.07 \end{aligned}$$

Should the firm take on the warehouse renovation? The project has a negative NPV using the firm's R_{WACC}, which means that the financial markets offer superior projects in the same risk class (namely, the firm's risk class). The answer is clear: the firm should reject the project.

Real World Insight 12.1

Regulators and the WACC of Utilities

For all companies, WACC is a function of the risk of the company's operations. That is, the risk of the assets drives the risk of equity and debt. With utilities, the government decides what the WACC should be, meaning that the risk of operations is constrained by the regulators, which has a knock-on effect on the returns provided by utility companies' debt and equity securities.

In 2021, the Greek regulator stated that Greek energy WACCs should be no more than 7.05 per cent, meaning that the cost of debt would need to be below this level for Greek firms.

12.5 Estimating Carrefour Group's Cost of Capital

In Section 12.4, we calculated the cost of capital of ArcelorMittal and simplified a number of important inputs such as the annual interest payment. We will now calculate the cost of capital for Carrefour Group, the French supermarket chain, in the same way that a financial analyst would. Carrefour has stores in Europe, North and South America, and Asia, operating under the names Carrefour, Pryca, Stoc, Marché Plus, Optique and Comod.

Carrefour Group's Cost of Equity

Our first stop for Carrefour is www.reuters.com. Search for the company using its code (CARR.PA). As of May 2023, Carrefour had 730.61 million shares outstanding. The share price was €17.76 and the market value of the equity 730.61 × €17.76 = €12,975.63 million.

We assume a market risk premium of 7 per cent and a risk-free rate of 2.86 per cent (*source:* FT.com). A market risk premium of 7 per cent implies that the market is expected to go up by 9.86 per cent in the next year. From Reuters, Carrefour's beta is 0.53 and the industry average beta is 0.61. Using Carrefour's beta in the CAPM to estimate the cost of equity, we find:

$$R_E = 2.86 + 0.53(7.00) = 5.37\%$$

If we use the industry beta, we would find that the estimate for the cost of equity capital is:

$$R_E = 2.86 + 0.61(7.00) = 5.75\%$$

The decision as to which cost of equity estimate to use is up to the financial executive, based on knowledge and experience of both the company and the industry. In this case, we will choose to use the cost of equity using Carrefour's own estimated beta.

Carrefour's Cost of Debt

We must now find out about the different bonds that Carrefour has issued. To do this, download the Carrefour financial accounts from the company's website and read the information on bonds. Find the annual interest expense and divide it by the total borrowings to arrive at a noisy estimate of the cost of debt.

From the 2022 annual report (most recent at the time of writing), annual interest expense was €336 million and the total borrowings were €6,912 million, giving a cost of debt equal to 4.86 per cent.

Carrefour's WACC

We now have the various pieces necessary to calculate Carrefour's WACC. First, we need to calculate the capital structure weights. Carrefour's equity and debt are worth €12,975.63 million and (from the annual report) €43,365 million, respectively. The capital structure weight for equity is €12,975.63 million/€56,340.63 million = 0.230 and for debt it is €43,365 million/€56,340.63 million = 0.770, so the equity percentage is lower. According to Carrefour's 2022 annual report, the effective tax rate for Carrefour is 20.7 per cent.

With these weights, Carrefour's R_{WACC} is:

$$\begin{aligned} R_{\text{WACC}} &= 0.23 \times 5.37\% + 0.77 \times 4.86\% \times (1 - 0.207) \\ &= 4.20\% \end{aligned}$$

Thus, using market value weights, we get 4.20 per cent for Carrefour's R_{WACC}.

12.6 Reducing the Cost of Capital

Chapters 9–12 develop the idea that both the expected return on an equity and the cost of capital of the firm are positively related to risk. Recently, a number of academics have argued that expected return and cost of capital are also negatively related to liquidity.[3] In addition, these scholars make the interesting point that, although it is quite difficult to lower the risk of a firm, it is much easier to increase the liquidity of the firm's equity. Therefore they suggest that a firm can actually lower its cost of capital through liquidity enhancement. We develop this idea next.

What is Liquidity?

Anyone who owns a home probably thinks of liquidity in terms of the time it takes to buy or sell it. For example, apartments in city-centre areas are generally quite liquid. Particularly in good times, an apartment may sell within days of being placed on the market. By contrast, single-family homes in suburban areas may take weeks or months to sell. Special properties such as multimillion-pound mansions may take even longer.

The concept of liquidity is similar, but not identical, for equities. Here, we speak of the *cost* of buying and selling instead. That is, equities that are expensive to trade are considered less liquid than those that trade cheaply. What do we mean by the cost to trade? We generally think of three costs here: brokerage fees, the bid–ask spread, and market impact costs.

Brokerage fees are the easiest to understand because you must pay a broker to execute a trade. More difficult is the bid–ask spread. Consider the London Stock Exchange. If you want to trade 100 shares of XYZ plc, your broker will use a specialized trading terminal to get the best price that you can buy and sell. Suppose the broker provides a quote of 100.00–100.07. This means that you can buy at £100.07 per share and sell at £100 per share.

The spread of £0.07 is a cost to you because you are losing £0.07 per share over a round-trip transaction (over a purchase and a subsequent sale).

Finally, we have *market impact costs*. Suppose a trader wants to sell 10,000 shares instead of just 100 shares. Here, someone has to take on extra risk when buying. First, she has to pay out £1,000,000 (= 10,000 × £100), cash that may not be readily available. Second, the trader may be selling this large amount because she has special information that the share price will fall imminently. The counterparty bears the risk of losing a lot of money on that trade. Consequently, to compensate for these risks, the transaction price may not be £100 per share but a lower price. Similarly, a counterparty may be willing to sell a large block of equity only at a price above £100.07. The price drop associated with a large sale and the price rise associated with a large purchase are the market impact costs.

Liquidity, Expected Returns and the Cost of Capital

The cost of trading non-liquid shares reduces the total return that an investor receives. That is, if you buy a share for £100 and sell it later for £105, the gain before trading costs is £5. If you must pay £1 in commission when buying and another £1 when selling, the gain after trading costs is only £3. Both the bid–ask spread and market impact costs would reduce this gain still further.

As we will see later, trading costs vary across securities. In the previous four chapters we have stressed that investors demand a high expected return as compensation when investing in high-risk (e.g. high-beta) equities. Because the expected return to the investor is the cost of capital to the firm, the cost of capital is positively related to beta. Now we are saying the same thing for trading costs. Investors demand a high expected return when investing in equities with high trading costs – that is, with low liquidity. This high expected return implies a high cost of capital to the firm. This idea is illustrated in Figure 12.7.

Figure 12.7 Liquidity and the Cost of Capital

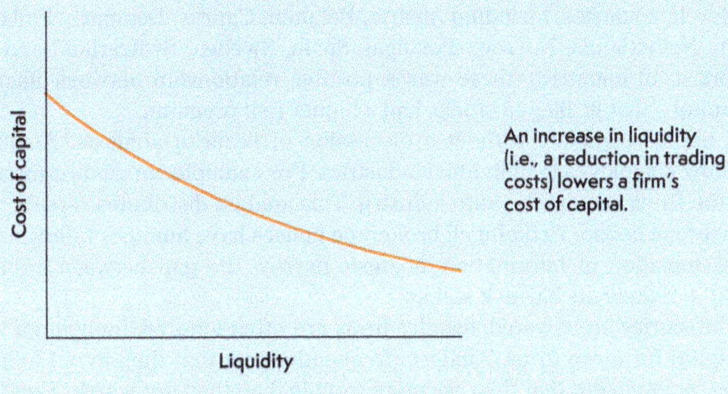

Liquidity and Adverse Selection

Although there are a number of factors that influence liquidity, we focus on just one: *adverse selection*. As mentioned before, a counterparty will lose money on a trade if the trader has information that the counterparty does not have. If you have special information that the share is worth £110 in the preceding example, you will want to buy shares at £100.07. Conversely, if you know that the equity is worth only £90 and you currently own 100 shares, you will be happy to sell these shares at £100. In either of these cases, we say that the counterparty has been *picked off*, or has been subject to adverse selection.

Traders in the market must protect themselves in some way here. Of course, they cannot forbid informed individuals from trading with them because they do not know ahead of time who these investors are. The next best alternative is to reduce the price at which you are willing to buy or increase the price at which you are willing to sell. The effect of this is that the bid–ask spread will widen, thereby increasing the costs of trading to *all* traders – both informed and uninformed. That is, if the spread is widened to, say, £99.98–£100.11, each trader pays a round-trip cost of £0.13 per share.

The key here is that the spread should be positively related to the ratio of informed to uninformed traders. That is, informed traders would pick off the market and uninformed traders will not. Thus, informed traders raise the required return on equity, thereby increasing the cost of capital.

What the Corporation Can Do

The corporation has an incentive to lower trading costs because (given the preceding discussion) a lower cost of capital should result. Amihud and Mendelson (2000) and Amihud et al. (2015a) identify two general strategies for corporations. First, they argue that firms should try to bring in more uninformed investors. Stock splits may be a useful tool here. Imagine that a company has 1 million shares outstanding with a share price of £100. Because investors generally buy in round lots of 100 shares, these investors would need £10,000 (= £100 × 100 shares) for a purchase. A number of small investors might be 'priced out' of the equity, although large investors would not be. Thus, the ratio of large investors to small investors would be high. Because large investors are generally more likely than small investors to be informed, the ratio of informed to uninformed investors is likely to be high.

A 2:1 stock split would give two shares of equity for every one share that the investor previously held. Because every investor would still keep the same proportional interest in the firm, each investor would be no better off than before. Thus, it is likely that the share price will fall to £50 from £100. Here, an individual with 100 shares worth £10,000 (= £100 × 100 shares) finds them still worth £10,000 (= £50 × 200 shares) after the split.

However, a round lot becomes more affordable, thereby bringing more small and uninformed investors into the firm. Consequently, the adverse selection costs are reduced, leading to lower bid–ask spreads. In turn, it is hoped the expected return on the equity and the cost of equity capital will fall as well. If this happens, the shares might trade at a price slightly above £50.

Another strategy to lower the cost of capital is to disclose more information, which narrows the gap between uninformed and informed investors, thereby decreasing the cost of capital. Suggestions include providing more financial data about corporate segments and more management forecasts. Amihud et al. (2015a) conclude that the bid–ask spread is reduced after the release of these forecasts. Amihud et al. (2015b) examined the liquidity–cost of capital relationship for 45 countries, including Austria, Belgium, Cyprus, Denmark, Finland, France, Germany, Greece, Israel, Italy, the Netherlands, Norway, Portugal, Spain, Sweden, Switzerland and the United Kingdom. They found that, in almost all countries, there was a positive relationship between illiquidity (the inverse of liquidity) and cost of capital – that is, illiquid stocks had a higher risk premium.

This section would not be complete without a discussion of security analysts. Analysts are employed by brokerage houses to follow companies in individual industries. For example, an analyst for a particular brokerage house might follow all the firms in, say, the auto industry. This analyst distributes reports and other information to the clients of the brokerage house. Virtually all brokerage houses have analysts following the major industries. Again, through the dissemination of information, analysts narrow the gap between informed and uninformed investors, which is likely to reduce the bid–ask spread.

Although all major industries are covered, smaller firms are often ignored, implying a higher bid–ask spread and a higher cost of capital for these firms. Analysts frequently state that they avoid following companies that release little information, pointing out that they are more trouble than they are worth. Thus, it behoves companies that are not followed to release as much information as possible to security analysts to attract their interest. Friendliness towards security analysts would be helpful as well. The argument here is not to get the analysts to make buy recommendations. Rather, it is simply to interest the analysts in following the company, thereby reducing the information asymmetry between informed and uninformed investors.

International Considerations

Thirty years ago, most companies raised funds in their own country. However, now there is a significantly greater choice as to where firms raise capital. Naturally, the costs of capital across countries have become an important issue for financial managers who wish to minimize the cost of raising funds.

A few years ago, the London Stock Exchange hired a financial consulting firm, Oxera, to compare the costs of capital in London with its regional competitors.[4] It decomposed the cost of raising capital into two main groups: the costs of going through an IPO and the ongoing costs of maintaining a public listing. Note that these costs are in addition to the return required by investors. Thus, if investors needed a 10 per cent return on an investment in a firm and the costs of raising funds was 3 per cent, the cost of capital for the company would be 13 per cent.

Taking IPOs first, we can decompose the costs into several components, including underwriting fees, professional fees, listing fees and price discounts. The costs of maintaining a listing include regulatory, corporate governance and professional fees, annual listing fees and trading costs. Table 12.2 presents an overview of the comparative costs of capital across Europe and the USA.

Table 12.2 Costs of Raising Capital across Europe and the USA

Costs	Evidence	Quantitative Impact on Cost of Capital
IPO costs		
Initial underwriting fees	Higher in USA than in UK, Germany and France	3–4% in Europe, 6.5–7% in USA
IPO price discounts	Differs across countries	10–15%
Initial listing fees	Deutsche Börse and LSE are lowest	< 0.1%
Professional fees	USA highest, then UK; France and Germany are lowest	3–6%
Ongoing costs		
Trading costs and liquidity: fees	Lowest on LSE, then NYSE; highest on Euronext, Deutsche Börse and Nasdaq	
Trading costs and liquidity: spreads	Lowest on NYSE; higher in Europe	
Annual exchange fees	For smaller firms, European exchanges are cheaper than the USA; for larger firms, Deutsche Börse and Euronext are cheaper	< 0.1%

Source: Partially reproduced from Oxera Consulting (2006).

Table 12.3 presents the upper and lower bounds WACCs for different industries in a number of countries as of March 2019. For a corporate manager, the weighted average cost of capital is most important for capital budgeting. A look at Table 12.3 shows very little difference across the UK and Europe for WACC. In contrast to the UK, debt markets are more efficient in Europe and so, overall, the weighted average cost of capital is quite stable for European industries.

Table 12.3 Weighted Average Cost of Capital by Country and Industry (March 2019)

(Min./Max.)	Automotive	Banks	Chemicals	Construction	Food & Beverage	Health Care	Industrial Goods & Services	Media	Oil & Gas	Household Goods	Retail	Technology	Telecoms	Travel	Utilities
Austria	(5.79/12.43)	(3.27/12.53)	(7.60/12/70)	(6.76/13.40)	(5.60/10.96)	(6.08/10.77)	(6.25/11.98)	(6.42/11.99)	(6.07/11.42)	(6.17/10.74)	(6.51/11.41)	(7.60/11.08)	(4.66/11.51)	(6.68/11.98)	3.76/11.03)
Belgium	(5.83/12.82)	(3.25/12.92)	(7.72/13.09)	(6.74/13.78)	(5.78/11.37)	(6.31/11.17)	(6.36/12.38)	(6.54/12.38)	(6.24/11.82)	(6.42/11.14)	(6.70/11.81)	(7.91/11.48)	(4.75/11.91)	(6.82/12.37)	3.87/11.43)
China	(6.52/12.15)	(4.06/11.17)	(8.24/12.93)	(7.49/13.24)	(6.22/11.08)	(6.64/11.15])	(6.91/12.01)	(7.07/12.07)	(6.66/11.68)	(6.73/11.14)	(7.09/11.71)	(8.08/11.81)	(5.39/10.98)	(7.34/12.08)	4.43/10.53)
Denmark	(5.74/12.28)	(3.25/12.39)	(7.53/12.56)	(6.70/13.24)	(5.54/10.84)	(6.01/10.64)	(6.19/11.84)	(6.36/11.85)	(6.01/11.28)	(6.11/10.61)	(6.44/11.27)	(7.51/10.95)	(4.62/11.38)	(6.62/11.84)	3.73/10.90)
Finland	(5.94/12.37)	(3.45/12.47)	(7.71/12.64)	(6.93/13.33)	(5.68/10.91)	(6.14/10.72)	(6.37/11.93)	(6.53/11.93)	(6.16/11.36)	(6.23/10.68)	(6.58/11.35)	(7.61/11.03)	(4.78/11.46)	(6.78/11.92)	3.88/10.98)
France	(5.52/12.39)	(2.99/12.50)	(7.37/12.67)	(6.42/13.35)	(5.44/10.95)	(5.95/10.75)	(6.03/11.96)	(6.21/11.96)	(5.89/11.39)	(6.05/10.72)	(6.34/11.38)	(7.52/11.06)	(4.43/11.49)	(6.48/11.95)	3.57/11.01)
Germany	(5.60/12.37)	(3.08/12.47)	(7.43/12.64)	(6.53/13.33)	(5.47/10.91)	(5.96/10.72)	(6.09/11.93)	(6.26/11.93)	(5.93/11.36)	(6.06/10.68)	(6.37/11.35)	(7.51/11.03)	(4.49/11.46)	(6.53/11.92)	3.62/10.98)
Greece	(11.23/18.62)	(8.15/18.72)	(13.32/18.89)	(12.16/19.65)	(11.34/17.19)	(11.95/17.01)	(11.88/18.19)	(12.08/18.19)	(11.79/17.64)	(12.07/16.97)	(12.31/17.63)	(13.68/17.31)	(10.08/17.73)	(12.39/18.18)	9.11/17.26)
India	(7.72/14.23)	(5.00/13.17)	(9.65/15.07)	(8.70/15.40)	(7.52/13.07)	(8.00/13.14)	(8.20/14.08)	(8.38/14/14)	(7.95/13.72)	(8.11/13/14)	(8.46/13.75)	(9.63/13.86)	(6.56/12.96)	(8.70/14.15)	5.50/12.48)
Ireland	(7.25/13.43)	(4.75/13.54)	(8.98/13.71)	(8.28/14.39)	(6.93/11.99)	(7.36/11.80)	(7.64/13.00)	(7.80/13.00)	(7.42/12.44)	(7.44/11.77)	(7.82/12.43)	(8.79/12.10)	(6.07/12.53)	(8.05/12.99)	5.14/12.06)
Italy	(6.60/13.63)	(3.93/13.73)	(8.52/13.90)	(7.52/14.59)	(6.56/12.18)	(7.09/11.98)	(7.14/13.19)	(7.33/13.19)	(7.02/12.63)	(7.20/11.95)	(7.49/12.61)	(8.71/12.29)	(5.49/12.72)	(7.61/13.18)	4.60/12.24)
Malaysia	(6.94/12.60)	(4.47/11.62)	(8.67/13.37)	(7.91/13.68)	(6.65/11.53)	(7.08/11.60)	(7.34/12.46)	(7.50/12.51)	(7.09/12.13)	(7.17/11.59)	(7.53/12.16)	(8.52/12.26)	(5.82/11.42)	(7.77/12.53)	4.85/10.98)
Netherlands	(5.82/12.49)	(3.29/12.60)	(7.64/12.77)	(6.79/13.46)	(5.63/11.02)	(6.11/10.82)	(6.28/12.04)	(6.45/12.05)	(6.10/11.47)	(6.20/10.79)	(6.54/11.46)	(7.64/11.13)	(4.68/11.57)	(6.72/12.04)	3.78/11.08)
Norway	(5.72/12.44)	(3.20/12.55)	(7.55/12.72)	(6.68/13.41)	(5.56/10.98)	(6.05/10.78)	(6.20/12.00)	(6.37/12.00)	(6.03/11.43)	(6.14/10.75)	(6.47/11.42)	(7.58/11.09)	(4.60/11.52)	(6.64/11.99)	3.71/11.04)
Oman	(6.89/12.09)	(4.46/11.12)	(8.55/12.85)	(7.92/13.16)	(6.48/11.03)	(6.87/11.10)	(7.23/11.95)	(7.38/12.01)	(6.95/11.62)	(6.95/11.09)	(7.35/11.65)	(8.24/11.75)	(5.70/10.93)	(7.62/12.02)	4.75/10.49)
Russia	(7.61/13.39)	(5.03/12.37)	(9.40/14.19)	(8.65/14.52)	(7.27/12.27)	(7.70/12.34)	(8.01/13.24)	(8.18/13.30)	(7.74/12.90)	(7.70/12.34)	(8.19/12.93)	(9.19/13.30)	(6.41/12.16)	(8.45/13.31)	5.40/11.70)
Saudi Arabia	(6.72/12.26)	(4.24/11.27)	(8.44/13.04)	(7.73/13.35)	(6.37/11.18)	(6.78/11.25)	(7.10/12.12)	(7.25/12.18)	(6.83/11.78)	(6.87/11.24)	(7.26/11.82)	(8.22/11.91)	(5.55/11.07)	(7.51/12.19)	4.58/10.62)
Singapore	(6.26/11.63)	(3.82/10.65)	(7.94/12.40)	(7.28/12.71)	(5.88/10.55)	(6.28/10.62)	(6.62/11.49)	(6.77/11.54)	(6.35/11.15)	(6.37/10.62)	(6.76/11.19)	(7.68/11.28)	(5.09/10.45)	(7.02/11.56)	4.13/10.01)
South Africa	(7.28/13.25)	(4.71/12.24)	(9.08/14.05)	(8.26/14.37)	(7.01/12.14)	(7.46/12.22)	(7.71/13.11)	(7.87/13.16)	(7.45/12.76)	(7.56/21.21)	(7.92/12.80)	(8.97/12.90)	(6.13/12.04)	(8.16/13.18)	5.13/11.58)
Spain	(6.67/13.65)	(4.01/13.76)	(8.58/13.93)	(7.60/14.62)	(6.61/12.20)	(7.14/12.01)	(7.21/13.21)	(7.39/13.22)	(7.07/12.65)	(7.25/11.97)	(7.54/12.64)	(8.74/12.31)	(5.56/12.74)	(7.67/13.21)	4.66/12.26)
Sweden	(5.78/12.19)	(3.32/12.29)	(7.54/12.46)	(6.75/13.13)	(5.55/10.75)	(6.01/10.56)	(6.21/11.75)	(6.38/11.75)	(6.02/11.19)	(6/10/10.53)	(6.44/11.18)	(7.48/10.86)	(4.65/11.29)	(6.63/11.75)	3.77/10.81)
Switzerland	(5.91/12.16)	(3.47/12.26)	(7.64/12.43)	(6.90/13.11)	(5.63/10.73)	(6.07/10.54)	(6.32/11.73)	(6.48/11.73)	(6.11/11.17)	(6.16/10.51)	(6.52/11.16)	(7.51/10.84)	(4.77/11.26)	(6.72/11.72)	3.87/10.79)
UAE	(5.43/11.78)	(3.05/10.81)	(7.21/12.54)	(6.22/12.84)	(5.38/10.72)	(5.85/10.79)	(5.92/11.64)	(6.09/11.69)	(5.73/11.31)	(5.96/10.78)	(6.22/11.34)	(7.37/11.44)	(4.48/10.62)	(6.40/11.71)	3.56/10.18)
UK	(6.06/12.60)	(3.53/12.71)	(7.85/12.88)	(7.05/13.58)	(5.82/11.13)	(6.27/10.94)	(6.50/12.16)	(6.66/12.16)	(6.30/11.59)	(6.37/10.90)	(6.73/11.58)	(7.78/11.25)	(4.89/11.68)	(6.92/12.15)	3.98/11.20)
USA	(5.23/12.37)	(2.69/12.47)	(7.14/12.64)	(6.10/13.33)	(5.24/10.91)	(5.77/10.72)	(5.79/11.93)	(5.97/11.93)	(5.68/11.36)	(5.88/10.68)	(6.15/11.35)	(7.40/11.03)	(4.18/11.46)	(6.25/11.93)	3.33/10.98)

Source: www.waccexpert.com

12.7 How Do Corporations Estimate Cost of Capital in Practice?

Chapter 5 Page 122
Chapter 9 Page 242
Chapter 10 Page 284
Chapter 11 Page 304

The material in this chapter is quite complex and the reader may be left wondering what firms actually do when they calculate the cost of capital in practice. Brounen, de Jong and Koedijk (2004) surveyed executives in France, Germany, the Netherlands and the UK on the methods they used to estimate the cost of capital for their firm, and the responses are presented in Table 12.4. Historical returns are covered in Chapter 9, Section 9.3, the CAPM is introduced in Chapter 10, Section 10.9, Chapter 11 discusses a wide range of multifactor models, and Chapter 5, Section 5.4, derives and explains the dividend growth model.

There are notable differences across countries, but the most commonly used method is the CAPM and beta. Historical returns on share prices are also frequently used and, in the Netherlands, a surprisingly large number of companies use a cost of capital estimate that is set by investors. Regulators play an important role in the UK and France, whereas in Germany they are not considered at all. It is interesting to note the popularity of historical returns across countries. This is essentially saying that the return investors received in the past is the best predictor of the return investors will receive in the future. Some argue that, with such volatility in financial markets, this is the most rational predictor!

Table 12.4 Of Firms that Estimate Cost of Capital, the Percentage that Use Specific Methods

	USA	UK	Netherlands	Germany	France
Capital asset pricing model	73.49	47.06	55.56	33.96	45.16
Historical returns	39.41	31.25	30.77	18.00	27.27
Multifactor models	34.29	27.27	15.38	16.07	30.30
Backed out from dividend growth model (i.e. $P = Div/r$)	15.74	10.00	10.71	10.42	10.34
Determined by investors	13.93	18.75	44.83	39.22	34.38
Determined by regulators	7.04	16.13	3.70	0.00	16.13

Source: Brounen et al. (2004), Table 2.

12.8 Economic and Sustainable Value Added

This chapter shows how to calculate the appropriate discount rate for capital budgeting and other valuation problems. We now consider the concepts of economic value added and sustainable value added, which use the same discount rate developed for capital budgeting. Consider the following simple example.

Many years ago, Henry Bodenheimer started Bodie's Blimps, one of the largest high-speed blimp manufacturers. Because growth was so rapid, Henry put most of his effort into capital budgeting. He forecasted cash flows for various projects and discounted them at the cost of capital appropriate to the beta of the blimp business. However, these projects have grown rapidly, in some cases becoming whole divisions. He now needs to evaluate the performance of these divisions to reward his division managers. How does he perform the appropriate analysis?

Henry is aware that capital budgeting and performance measurement are essentially mirror images of each other. Capital budgeting is forward looking because we must estimate future cash flows to value a project. By contrast, performance measurement is backward looking. Henry told a group of his executives, 'Capital budgeting is like looking through the windscreen while driving a car. You need to know what lies further down the road to calculate a net present value. Performance measurement is like looking into the rearview mirror. You find out where you have been.'

Chapter 3 Page 60

Henry first measured the performance of his various divisions by return on assets (ROA), an approach we treated in Chapter 3. For example, if a division had earnings after tax of €1,000 and had assets of €10,000, the ROA would be:

$$\frac{€1{,}000}{€10{,}000} = 10\%$$

He calculated the ROA ratio for each of his divisions, paying each of his division managers a bonus based on the size of that division's ROA. However, while ROA was generally effective in motivating his managers, there were some situations where it appeared that ROA was counterproductive.

For example, Henry always believed that Sharon Smith, head of the supersonic division, was his best manager. The ROA of Smith's division was generally in the high double digits, but the best estimate of the weighted average cost of capital for the division was only 20 per cent. Furthermore, the division had been growing rapidly. However, as soon as Henry paid bonuses based on ROA, the division stopped growing. At that time, Smith's division had after-tax earnings of €2,000,000 on an asset base of €2,000,000, for an ROA of 100 per cent (= €2 million/€2 million).

Henry discovered why the growth stopped when he suggested a project to Smith that would earn €1,000,000 per year on an investment of €2,000,000. This was an attractive project with an ROA of 50 per cent (= €1 million/€2 million). He thought that Smith would jump at the chance to place his project into her division because the ROA of the project was much higher than the cost of capital of 20 per cent. However, Smith did everything she could to kill the project. And, as Henry later figured out, Smith was rational to do so. Smith must have realized that if the project were accepted, the division's ROA would become:

$$\frac{€2{,}000{,}000 + €1{,}000{,}000}{€2{,}000{,}000 + €2{,}000{,}000} = 75\%$$

Thus the ROA of Smith's division would fall from 100 per cent to 75 per cent if the project were accepted, with Smith's bonus falling in tandem.

Henry was later exposed to the economic value added (EVA®) approach,[5] which seems to obviate this particular problem. The formula for EVA is:

$$(\text{ROA} - \text{Weighted average cost of capital}) \times \text{Total capital}$$

Without the new project, the EVA of Smith's division would be:

$$(100\% - 20\%) \times €2{,}000{,}000 = €1{,}600{,}000$$

This is an annual number. That is, the division would bring in €1.6 million above and beyond the cost of capital to the firm each year.

With the new project included, the EVA would jump to:

$$(75\% - 20\%) \times €4{,}000{,}000 = €2{,}200{,}000$$

If Sharon Smith knew that her bonus was based on EVA, she would now be incentivized to accept, not reject, the project. Although ROA appears in the EVA formula, EVA differs substantially from ROA. The big difference is that ROA is a percentage number while EVA is a monetary value. In the preceding example, EVA increased when the new project was added, even though the ROA actually decreased. In this situation, EVA correctly incorporates the fact that a high return on a large division may be better than a very high return on a smaller division. The concern here is similar to the scale problem in capital budgeting discussed in Section 6.6.

Further understanding of EVA can be achieved by rewriting the EVA formula. Because ROA × total capital is equal to earnings after tax, we can write the EVA formula as:

$$\text{Earnings after tax} - \text{Weighted average cost of capital} \times \text{Total capital}$$

Thus, EVA can be viewed as earnings after capital costs. Although accountants subtract many costs (including depreciation) to get the earnings number shown in financial reports, they do not subtract capital costs. We can see the logic of accountants because the cost of capital is very subjective. By contrast, COGS (cost of goods sold), SGA (sales, general and administration) and even depreciation can be measured more objectively. However, even if the cost of capital is difficult to estimate, it is hard to justify ignoring it altogether. After all, this textbook argues that the cost of capital is a necessary input to capital budgeting. So shouldn't it also be a necessary input to performance measurement?

The preceding example shows that EVA can increase investment for firms that are currently underinvesting. However, many firms are in the reverse situation: the managers are so focused on growing earnings that they take on projects for which the profits do not justify the capital outlays. These managers either are unaware of capital costs or, knowing these costs, choose to ignore them. Because the cost of capital is right in the middle of the EVA formula, managers will not easily ignore these costs when evaluated on an EVA system.

Another advantage of EVA is that it is so stark: the number is either positive or negative. Plenty of divisions have negative EVAs for years. Because these divisions are destroying more value than they are creating, a strong point can be made for liquidating these divisions. Although managers are generally emotionally opposed to this type of action, EVA analysis makes liquidation harder to ignore.

Criticisms of EVA

We now focus on two well-known problems with EVA. First, the preceding example uses EVA for performance measurement, where we believe it properly belongs. To us, EVA seems a clear improvement over ROA and other financial ratios. However, EVA has little to offer for capital budgeting because it focuses only on current earnings. By contrast, net present value analysis uses projections of all future cash flows, where the cash flows will generally differ from year to year. Thus, as far as capital budgeting is concerned, NPV analysis has a richness that EVA does not. Although supporters may argue that EVA correctly incorporates the weighted average cost of capital, remember that the discount rate in NPV analysis is the same as the weighted average cost of capital. Both approaches take the cost of equity capital based on beta and combine it with the cost of debt to get an estimate of this weighted average.

A second problem with EVA is that it may increase the short-sightedness of managers. Under EVA, a manager will be well rewarded today if earnings are high today. Future losses may not harm the manager because there is a good chance she will be promoted or leave the firm by then. Thus, the manager is incentivized to run a division with more regard for short-term than long-term value. The manager may increase current profits (and therefore current EVA) by raising prices or cutting quality. However, if customer satisfaction is reduced, future profits (and, therefore, future EVA) are likely to fall. But we should not be too harsh with EVA here because the same problem occurs with ROA. A manager who raises prices or cuts quality will increase current ROA at the expense of future ROA. The problem, then, is not with EVA per se but with the use of accounting numbers in general. Because shareholders want the discounted present value of all cash flows to be maximized, managers with bonuses based on some function of current profits or cash flows are likely to behave in a short-sighted way.

Sustainable Value Added

Sustainable value added (SVA) integrates sustainability principles into traditional financial performance measurements, such as economic value added (EVA). The purpose of SVA is to assess a company's ability to create value while considering its environmental, social and governance (ESG) performance. There has been a glut of evidence to suggest that companies that pursue sustainability goals have a lower cost of capital. For example, MSCI (reproduced in Figure 12.8 below) has shown that, between 2015 and 2019, higher ESG scores correlated directly with a lower cost of equity, cost of debt and WACC.

Figure 12.8 Relationship between Cost of Capital and MSCI Environmental, Social and Governance (ESG) Ratings

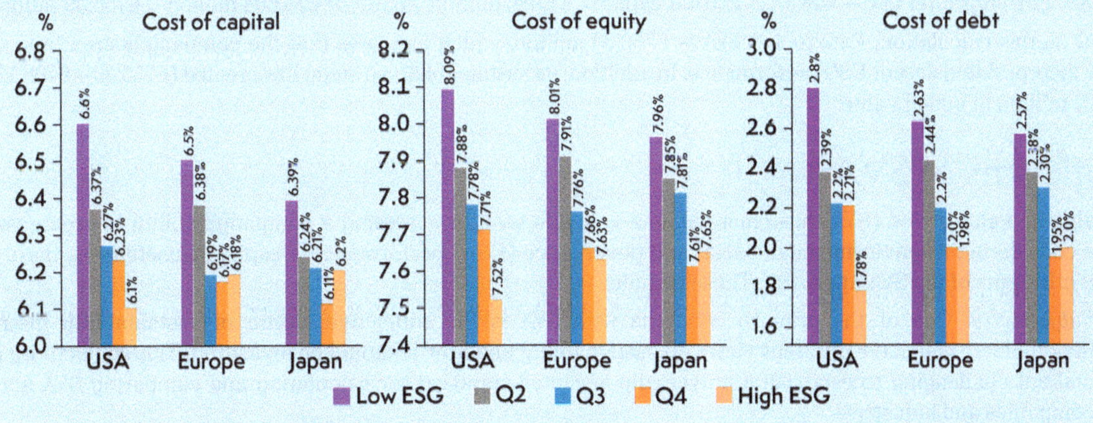

Note: Data values are estimates.

Source: https://www.msci.com/www/blog-posts/esg-and-the-cost-of-capital/01726513589

To illustrate the practical application of SVA, we will use a hypothetical example. Consider a manufacturing firm, Patagonia SA, that has significantly improved its sustainability practices and embraced corporate social responsibility. Patagonia's commitments span five key areas: (1) Biodiversity, (2) Climate, (3) Health, Quality and Education, (4) Business Ethics and Supply Chains, and (5) Employees. The company has taken significant steps to reduce its environmental footprint by investing in eco-friendly practices, such as reducing food waste, promoting sustainable farming, and increasing the use of renewable energy in its operations. These initiatives benefit the environment, contribute to local economies and support long-term growth. Second, Patagonia actively engages with local communities, striving to improve the quality of life of people in the areas where it operates. It also prioritizes employee well-being, and invests in training and development programmes to ensure a skilled, motivated workforce. Finally, the firm maintains high standards of transparency and accountability, regularly disclosing its ESG performance through sustainability reports and other communications.

To calculate the sustainable value added (SVA) for Patagonia, we first need to calculate the economic value added (EVA). Patagonia has reported earnings after tax of €1,986 million. The market value of its equity and debt is €13,716 million and €9,888 million, respectively. The company's tax rate is 28%, and its cost of equity is 7.5 per cent. Patagonia's cost of debt is 3.5 per cent.

Patagonia's weighted average cost of capital is:

$$\text{WACC} = \left(\frac{E}{D+E}\right) \times R_E + \left(\frac{D}{D+E}\right) \times R_D \times (1 - t_c) = \left(\frac{13{,}716}{23{,}604}\right) \times 7.5\% + \left(\frac{9{,}888}{23{,}604}\right) \times 3.5\% \times (1 - .28) = 5.41\%$$

This allows us to calculate Patagonia's EVA:

EVA = Earnings after tax − WACC × Total capital= €1,986 million – 5.41% × €23,604 million = €708.12 million

To calculate SVA, we will apply an ESG risk premium to a firm's WACC to reflect the higher or lower risk related to its pursuit of ESG strategic goals. This allows us to calculate an ESG-adjusted EVA, which we call sustainable value added (SVA).

Companies like MSCI (www.msci.com) and Sustainalytics (www.sustainalytics.com) provide ESG risk ratings on companies, and from these we can estimate the ESG risk premium. For example, assume that Patagonia has an ESG score of 28.4 on Sustainalytics, considered medium risk. We will assume an ESG equity risk premium of –0.3% and an ESG debt risk premium of –0.1% to reflect the lower risk associated with Patagonia's ESG performance:

$$\text{WACC} = \left(\frac{E}{D+E}\right) \times \left(R_E - R_{E,ESG}\right) + \left(\frac{D}{D+E}\right) \times \left(R_D - R_{D,ESG}\right) \times (1 - t_c) = \left(\frac{13{,}716}{23{,}604}\right) \times 7.2\% + \left(\frac{9{,}888}{23{,}604}\right) \times 3.4\% \times (1 - .28) = 5.21\%$$

Now, we can calculate the sustainable value added:

SVA = Earnings after tax − WACC_{ESG} × Total capital= €1,986 million – 5.21% × €23,604 million = €756.39 million

Based on this calculation, Patagonia's SVA is €756.39 million, which indicates that the company is creating value while incorporating decent ESG performance. In addition, its sustainability strategy has created (€756.39 – €708.12 =) €48.27 million in added value.

Criticisms of SVA

Sustainable value added (SVA) has emerged as a valuable tool for assessing a company's ability to create value while considering its environmental, social and governance (ESG) performance. Despite its usefulness, there are many criticisms of the SVA approach. These include:

- *Subjectivity:* One of the primary concerns with SVA is the subjective nature of sustainability metrics. Stakeholders may have different views on sustainability and how it should be measured. This subjectivity can make it challenging to establish a universally accepted standard for calculating and comparing SVA across companies and industries.
- *Lack of standardized metrics:* There is no widely accepted set of metrics or methodologies for evaluating SVA, which can lead to inconsistencies in measurement and reporting. This can make it difficult for investors and other stakeholders to compare the sustainability performance of different companies or even the same company over time.
- *Potential for greenwashing:* Companies might use SVA as a marketing tool to project a positive image of their sustainability efforts without actually making meaningful changes to their operations. This practice, known as

greenwashing, can mislead stakeholders and undermine the credibility of SVA as a performance measurement tool.

- *Limited scope:* SVA focuses primarily on the ESG aspects of a company's operations, which might not capture the full range of sustainability issues a company faces. For instance, it may not account for the indirect impacts a company's operations have on the environment, such as those resulting from its supply chain or the consumption of its products.
- *Complexity and resource intensiveness:* Calculating SVA can be complex and resource-intensive, as it requires gathering and analysing data on various ESG factors. Smaller companies, in particular, may lack the resources or expertise needed to implement and report on SVA effectively.

Despite the criticisms of sustainable value added, the method can provide valuable insights into a company's sustainability performance. Companies should use SVA in conjunction with other tools and frameworks to comprehensively understand their overall sustainability performance and potential areas for improvement. Finally, care must always be taken to ensure that the subjective nature of some of the assumptions of SVA don't lead to biases in estimates.

Summary and Conclusions

Earlier chapters about capital budgeting assumed that projects generate riskless cash flows. The appropriate discount rate, in that case, is the riskless interest rate. Of course, most cash flows from real-world capital budgeting projects are risky. This chapter discussed the discount rate when cash flows are risky.

1. A firm with excess cash can either pay a dividend or make a capital expenditure. Because shareholders can reinvest the dividend in risky financial assets, the expected return on a capital budgeting project should be at least as high as the expected return on a financial asset of comparable risk.
2. The expected return on any asset is dependent on its beta. Thus, we showed how to estimate the beta of an equity. The appropriate procedure employs regression analysis on historical returns.
3. We considered the case of a project whose beta risk was equal to that of the firm. If the firm is unlevered, the discount rate on the project is equal to:

$$R_F = \beta \times (R_M - R_F)$$

   where R_M is the expected return on the market portfolio, and R_F is the risk-free rate. In words, the discount rate on the project is equal to the CAPM's estimate of the expected return on the security.
4. If the project's beta differs from that of the firm, the discount rate should be based on the project's beta. We can generally estimate the project's beta by determining the average beta of the project's industry.
5. The beta of a company is a function of several factors. Perhaps the three most important are:
   - Cyclicality of revenues
   - Operating leverage
   - Financial leverage.
6. Sometimes we cannot use the average beta of the project's industry as an estimate of the beta of the project. For example, a new project may not fall neatly into any existing industry. In this case, we can estimate the project's beta by considering the project's cyclicality of revenues and its operating leverage. This approach is qualitative.
7. If a firm uses debt, the discount rate to use is the R_{WACC}. To calculate R_{WACC}, we must estimate the cost of equity and the cost of debt applicable to a project. If the project is similar to the firm, the cost of equity can be estimated using the SML for the firm's equity. Conceptually, a dividend growth model could be used as well, though it is likely to be far less accurate in practice.
8. Liquidity probably plays a role in determining a firm's cost of capital. A firm may be able to reduce its cost of capital by taking steps to improve liquidity.

Questions and Problems

CONCEPT

1 **The Cost of Equity Capital** Explain what is meant by the cost of equity capital. How is the cost of equity capital linked to the risk of the assets of a firm? How would you use cost of equity in a capital budget analysis? If a firm pursues sustainability goals, is this likely to impact the cost of equity?

2 **Determinants and Estimation of Beta** What factors determine the beta of a security? Define and describe each. Explain why an equity's beta is important in capital budgeting. How do you calculate beta and what are the pitfalls you may face in its calculation? Can you foresee any problems with using a historical beta for future capital budgeting projects? Explain.

3 **The Capital Budgeting Process** What are the six major steps involved in the capital budget process?

4 **Extensions of the Basic Model** How would you estimate the cost of capital for a project if its risk is different from the rest of the company? Similarly, how would you estimate the cost of capital for a project when the company has debt in its capital structure? When estimating the cost of debt, does it make a difference if the company's debt is privately or publicly held?

5 **Practical Concerns** What are the main issues you need to consider when estimating the cost of capital of a project in practice? State any potential problems or challenges you may face.

6 **Reducing the Cost of Capital** Why would a firm wish to reduce its cost of capital? Review different ways in which this can be done. Which way do you think is the most effective? Explain.

7 **Estimating the Cost of Capital in Practice** Corporations use many methods to estimate the cost of capital. Why do you think there is no consensus on the best method? If you were estimating the cost of capital in an emerging market, what method would you use? Explain.

8 **EVA and SVA** Explain what is meant by economic value added (EVA) and show how it can be used to evaluate the performance of a firm. How does sustainable value added (SVA) change the estimate of EVA? Do you think SVA is robust measure of performance? Explain.

REGULAR

9 **Project Risk** 'My company can borrow at 5 per cent so it means that its cost of capital for all new projects is 5 per cent.' Do you agree with this statement? Explain.

10 **Company Beta** The beta of Ericsson, the Swedish communications technology firm, is 0.38. What do you think is the main determinant of Ericsson's beta and why? Why do you think Ericsson's beta is so low?

11 **WACC and Taxes** 'If I use the after-tax cost of debt for my project analysis then I should use the after-tax cost of equity as well.' Do you agree with this statement? Explain.

12 **SML Cost of Equity Estimation** If you use the equity beta and the security market line to compute the discount rate for a project, what assumptions are you implicitly making? What are the advantages of using the SML approach to finding the cost of equity capital? What are the disadvantages? What are the specific pieces of information needed to use this method? Are all of these variables observable, or do they need to be estimated? What are some of the ways in which you could get these estimates?

13 **Industry Beta** What are the benefits of using an industry beta instead of a company beta when undertaking a capital budgeting analysis? Explain, using an example.

14 **Cost of Debt Estimation** How do you determine the appropriate cost of debt for a company? Does it make a difference if the company's debt is privately placed as opposed to being publicly traded? How would you estimate the cost of debt for a firm whose only debt issues are privately held by institutional investors?

15 **Reducing Cost of Capital** How would a manager of a new stock exchange-listed company reduce its cost of equity capital?

16 **Cost of Capital** As financial manager of Cosco Pacific Limited, you have been tasked with determining your firm's cost of debt and cost of equity capital.

(a) The shares currently sell for HK$10.40, and the dividend per share will probably be about HK$0.05736. Your assistant argues, 'It will cost us HK$0.05736 per share to use the shareholders' money this year, so the cost of equity is only equal to 0.55 per cent (HK$0.05736/HK$10.40).' What's wrong with this conclusion?

(b) Based on the most recent financial statements, Cosco Pacific Limited's total liabilities are HK$2.5 billion. Total interest expense for the coming year will be about HK$58 million. Your assistant therefore reasons, 'We owe HK$2.5 billion, and we will pay HK$58 million interest. Therefore, our cost of debt is obviously HK$58 million/HK$2.5 billion = 2.32 per cent.' What's wrong with this conclusion?

(c) Based on his own analysis, your assistant is recommending that the company increase its use of equity financing because 'debt costs 2.32 per cent, but equity only costs 0.55 per cent; thus equity is cheaper'. Ignoring all the other issues, what do you think about the conclusion that the cost of equity is less than the cost of debt?

17 **Company Risk versus Project Risk** Both AstraZeneca plc, a large pharmaceutical firm, and Takeda plc, a major prescription medicine manufacturer, are thinking of investing in an Indian generic drugs company. Assume that both AstraZeneca and Takeda have no debt and both firms are considering identical projects. They have analysed their respective investments, which would involve a negative cash flow now and positive expected cash flows in the future. These cash flows would be the same for both firms. No debt would be used to finance the projects. Both companies estimate that their projects would have a net present value of £10 million at a 12 per cent discount rate and a –£12 million NPV at a 15 per cent discount rate. AstraZeneca has a beta of 1.25, whereas Takeda has a beta of 0.75. The expected risk premium on the market is 8 per cent and risk-free bonds are yielding 3 per cent. Should either company proceed? Should both? Explain.

18 **Divisional Cost of Capital** Under what circumstances would it be appropriate for a firm to use different costs of capital for its different operating divisions? If the overall firm WACC were used as the hurdle rate for all divisions, would the riskier divisions or the more conservative divisions tend to get most of the investment projects? Why? If you were to try to estimate the appropriate cost of capital for different divisions, what problems might you encounter? What are two techniques you could use to develop a rough estimate for each division's cost of capital?

19 **SML and Cost of Capital** An all-equity firm is considering the following projects:

Project	Beta	Expected Return
A	0.6	11%
B	0.9	13%
C	1.2	14%
D	1.7	16%

The expected return on the market is 12 per cent, and the current rate on UK gilts is 5 per cent.

(a) Which projects have a higher expected return than the firm's 12 per cent cost of capital?

(b) Which projects should be accepted?

(c) Which projects would incorrectly be accepted or rejected if the firm's overall cost of capital were used as a hurdle rate?

20 **Calculating Cost of Equity** The Dybvig Corporation's equity has a beta of 1.3. If the risk-free rate is 4.5 per cent and the expected return on the market is 12 per cent, what is Dybvig's cost of equity capital?

21 **Calculating Cost of Debt** Advance plc is trying to determine its cost of debt. The firm has a debt issue outstanding with seven years to maturity that is quoted at 92 per cent of face value. The issue makes semi-annual payments and has a coupon rate of 4 per cent annually. What is Advance's pre-tax cost of debt? If the tax rate is 24 per cent, what is the after-tax cost of debt?

22 **Calculating Cost of Debt and Taxes** Shanken NV issued a 30-year, 10 per cent bond seven years ago. The bond currently sells for 108 per cent of its face value. The company's tax rate is 35 per cent.

(a) What is the pre-tax cost of debt?

(b) What is the after-tax cost of debt?

(c) Which is more relevant, the pre-tax or the after-tax cost of debt? Why?

23 **Calculating Cost of Debt and Debt Issues** For the firm in the previous problem, suppose the book value of the debt issue is €20 million. In addition, the company has a second debt issue on the market, a zero coupon bond with seven years left to maturity; the book value of this issue is €80 million and the bonds sell for 58 per cent of par. What is the company's total book value of debt? The total market value? What is your best estimate of the after-tax cost of debt now?

24 **Calculating WACC** Mullineaux Corporation has a target capital structure of 55 per cent equity and 45 per cent debt. Its cost of equity is 16 per cent, and the cost of debt is 9 per cent. The relevant tax rate is 35 per cent. What is Mullineaux's WACC?

25 **Calculating Beta** The returns of Siracha plc have a standard deviation of 40 per cent per annum and have a correlation with the FTSE 100 of 0.65. The standard deviation of the FTSE 100 is 20 per cent. What is Siracha's beta?

26 **Taxes and WACC** Miller Manufacturing has a target debt–equity ratio of 0.60. Its cost of equity is 18 per cent, and its cost of debt is 10 per cent. If the tax rate is 35 per cent, what is Miller's WACC?

27 **Leverage** Consider a levered firm's projects that have similar risks to the firm as a whole. Is the discount rate for the projects higher or lower than the rate computed using the security market line? Why/why not?

28 **Finding the Capital Structure** Fama's Llamas has a weighted average cost of capital of 11.5 per cent. The company's cost of equity is 16 per cent, and its cost of debt is 8.5 per cent. The tax rate is 35 per cent. What is Fama's debt–equity ratio?

29 **Book Value versus Market Value** Filer Manufacturing has 9.5 million shares of equity outstanding. The current share price is £53 and the book value per share is £5. Filer Manufacturing also has two bond issues outstanding. The first bond issue has a face value of £75 million and an 8 per cent coupon, and sells for 93 per cent of par. The second issue has a face value of £60 million and a 7.5 per cent coupon, and sells for 96.5 per cent of par. The first issue matures in 10 years, the second in six years.

(a) What are Filer's capital structure weights on a book value basis?

(b) What are Filer's capital structure weights on a market value basis?

(c) Which are more relevant, the book or market value weights? Why?

30 **Calculating the WACC** In the previous problem, suppose the company's equity has a beta of 1.2. The risk-free rate is 5.2 per cent and the market risk premium is 9 per cent. Assume that the overall cost of debt is the weighted average implied by the two outstanding debt issues. Both bonds make semi-annual payments. The tax rate is 35 per cent. What is the company's WACC?

31 **SVA** GreenLeaf is a medium-sized manufacturing company that is looking to improve its sustainability performance. The company has provided the following financial and ESG data for the last financial year: earnings after tax was £5 million, total capital was £25 million and WACC is 8 per cent. The impact of its sustainability initiatives are as follows: environmental impact reduction value is estimated to be £300,000, its social impact value was £200,000 and its governance value was £100,000. Calculate GreenLeaf's sustainable value added (SVA).

32 **WACC** Kose SA has a target debt–equity ratio of 0.80. Its WACC is 10.5 per cent and the tax rate is 35 per cent.

(a) If Kose's cost of equity is 15 per cent, what is its pre-tax cost of debt?

(b) If instead you know that the after-tax cost of debt is 6.4 per cent, what is the cost of equity?

33 **Finding the WACC** Given the following information for Huntington Power, find the WACC. Assume the company's tax rate is 28 per cent.

Debt: 40,000 7 per cent coupon bonds outstanding, £100 par value, 20 years to maturity, selling for 103 per cent of par; the bonds make semi-annual payments

Equity: 90,000 shares outstanding, selling for £57 per share; the beta is 1.10

Market: 8 per cent market risk premium and 6 per cent risk-free rate

34 **Finding the WACC: Raging Volts** The power systems firm, Raging Volts, has a market value of equity of £15.77 billion and total debt of £1.21 billion. The cost of equity capital is 19.96 per cent and the cost of debt is 5 per cent. If the company has a marginal tax rate of 24 per cent, what is its WACC?

35 **Finding the WACC: Titan Mining Corporation** Titan Mining Corporation has 9 million shares of equity outstanding and 1,200,000 8.5 per cent semi-annual bonds outstanding, par value £100 each. The equity currently sells for £34 per share and has a beta of 1.20, and the bonds have 15 years to maturity and sell for 93 per cent of par. The market risk premium is 10 per cent, T-bills are yielding 5 per cent and Titan Mining's tax rate is 28 per cent.

(a) What is the firm's market value capital structure?

(b) If Titan Mining is evaluating a new investment project that has the same risk as the firm's typical project, what rate should the firm use to discount the project's cash flows?

36 **SML and WACC** An all-equity firm is considering the following projects:

Project	Beta	Expected Return (%)
W	0.80	6
X	0.70	5
Y	1.15	9
Z	1.70	13

The T-bill rate is 3 per cent, and the expected return on the market is 7.5 per cent.

(a) Which projects have a higher expected return than the firm's 12 per cent cost of capital?

(b) Which projects should be accepted?

(c) Which projects would be incorrectly accepted or rejected if the firm's overall cost of capital were used as a hurdle rate?

37 WACC and NPV Och SpA is considering a project that will result in initial after-tax cash savings of €3.5 million at the end of the first year, and these savings will grow at a rate of 5 per cent per year indefinitely. The firm has a target debt–equity ratio of 0.65, a cost of equity of 15 per cent and an after-tax cost of debt of 5.5 per cent. The cost-saving proposal is somewhat riskier than the usual projects the firm undertakes; management uses the subjective approach and applies an adjustment factor of +2 per cent to the cost of capital for such risky projects. Under what circumstances should Och take on the project?

38 Preference Shares and WACC Bottled Water is a listed European company, which has a corporate finance structure as shown below. What is the company's WACC?

Debt:	50,000 bonds with a quoted price of 119.80, providing an 8 per cent coupon rate. The bonds have 25 years to maturity. There are also 150,000 zero-coupon bonds outstanding, with a quoted price of 13.85 and 30 years until maturity.
Preferred stock:	120,000 shares of 6.5 per cent preferred with a current price of €112 and a par value of €100.
Common stock:	2 million shares of common stock. The current share price is €65, and the beta of the stock is 1.1.
Market:	The corporate tax rate is 40 per cent, the market risk premium is 5 per cent and the risk-free rate is 4 per cent.

CHALLENGE

39 WACC and NPV: Financing Options Photochronograph Corporation (PC) manufactures time series photographic equipment. It is currently at its target debt–equity ratio of 1.3. It is considering building a new £45 million manufacturing facility. This new plant is expected to generate after-tax cash flows of £5.7 million in perpetuity. There are three financing options:

- A new issue of equity. The required return on the company's equity is 17 per cent.
- A new issue of 20-year bonds. If the company issues these new bonds at an annual coupon rate of 9 per cent, they will sell at par.
- Increased use of trade payables financing. Because this financing is part of the company's ongoing daily business, the company assigns it a cost that is the same as the overall firm WACC. Management has a target ratio of accounts payable to long-term debt of 0.20. (Assume there is no difference between the pre-tax and after-tax accounts payable cost.)

What is the NPV of the new plant? Assume that PC has a 28 per cent tax rate.

40 Advanced Project Evaluation This is a comprehensive project evaluation problem, bringing together much of what you have learned in this and previous chapters. Suppose you have been hired as a financial consultant to Defence Electronics International (DEI), a large, publicly traded firm that is the market share leader in radar detection systems (RDSs). The company is looking at setting up a manufacturing plant overseas to produce a new line of RDSs. This will be a five-year project. The company bought some land three years ago for £7 million in anticipation of using it as a toxic dump site for waste chemicals, but it built a piping system to safely discard the chemicals instead. If the company sold the land today, it would receive £6.5 million after taxes. In five years the land can be sold for £4.5 million after taxes and reclamation costs. The company wants to build its new manufacturing plant on this land; the plant will cost £15 million to build. The following market data on DEI's securities are current:

Debt:	150,000 7 per cent coupon bonds outstanding, 15 years to maturity, selling for 92 per cent of par; the bonds have a £100 par value each and make semi-annual payments.
Equity:	300,000 shares outstanding, selling for £75 per share; the beta is 1.3.
Preference shares:	20,000 shares with 5 per cent dividends outstanding, selling for £72 per share.
Market:	8 per cent expected market risk premium; 5 per cent risk-free rate.

DEI's tax rate is 28 per cent. The project requires £900,000 in initial net working capital investment to become operational.

(a) Calculate the project's initial time 0 cash flow, taking into account all side effects.

(b) The new RDS project is somewhat riskier than a typical project for DEI, primarily because the plant is being located overseas. Management has told you to use an adjustment factor of +2 per cent to account for this increased riskiness. Calculate the appropriate discount rate to use when evaluating DEI's project.

(c) The manufacturing plant has an eight-year tax life, and DEI uses 20 per cent reducing balance depreciation for the plant. At the end of the project (i.e. the end of year 5), the plant can be scrapped for £5 million. What is the after-tax salvage value of this manufacturing plant?

(d) The company will incur £400,000 in annual fixed costs. The plan is to manufacture 12,000 RDss per year and sell them at £10,000 per machine; the variable production costs are £9,000 per RDS. What is the annual operating cash flow (OCF) from this project?

(e) DEI's comptroller is primarily interested in the impact of DEI's investments on the bottom line of reported accounting statements. What will you tell her is the accounting break-even quantity of RDSs sold for this project?

(f) Finally, DEI's president wants you to throw all your calculations, assumptions and everything else into the report for the chief financial officer; all he wants to know is the RDS project's internal rate of return, IRR, and net present value, NPV. What will you report?

41 **SVA** Explain the process of calculating sustainable value added (SVA). Discuss the main components involved in the calculation and how a company's focus on environmental, social and governance (ESG) factors can impact its SVA.

42 **SVA: Carrefour** Analyse the relationship between a company's beta and its sustainability focus, using Carrefour as an example. How can a commitment to sustainability lead to a lower beta, and what implications does this have for the company's cost of equity and overall financial performance?

Exam Question (45 minutes)

1 Fresnillo plc explores and mines gold and silver in Mexico. The gold production accounts for 55 per cent of the activities of the firm, with the rest of the effort involved in silver mining. Other gold-mining firms have an average beta of 0.8 and a debt to equity ratio of 1/3. Silver mining is less risky and the average beta of silver-mining firms is 0.6. However, these companies tend to have more debt, with an average of 1/2. Fresnillo has an equity market capitalization of £11.93 billion and it has no debt. Determine the expected return on Fresnillo's shares if the expected return on the FTSE 100 is 12 per cent and the risk-free rate is 3 per cent. **(40 marks)**

2 Discuss the primary determinants of beta and how they can be measured. In Fresnillo's case, what do you think will be the most important determinant? Explain. **(30 marks)**

3 How could Fresnillo reduce its equity cost of capital? Explain, using examples to illustrate your answer. **(30 marks)**

Total Marks: 100

Mini Case

The Cost of Capital for Martyn Airlines

You have recently been hired by Martyn Airlines (MA), a budget airline based in and around the Eurozone region. MA was founded eight years ago by John Martyn and currently operates 74 flights in the Eurozone. MA is privately owned by John and his family, and had sales of £97 million last year.

MA sells primarily to online customers. Customers visit the MA website and choose the flight and fare combination appropriate to their requirements. All transactions are paid immediately via credit card.

MA's growth to date has been financed from its profits. Whenever the company had sufficient capital, it would open a new flight destination. Relatively little formal analysis has been used in the capital budgeting process. John has just read about capital budgeting techniques and has come to you for help. The company has never attempted to determine its cost of capital, and John would like you to perform the analysis. Because the company is privately owned, it is difficult to determine the cost of equity for the company. You have determined that, to estimate the cost of capital for MA, you will use Ryanair Holdings Ltd as a representative company.

The following steps will allow you to calculate this estimate:

1 Go to Ryanair's website and download its most recent financial accounts. Seek out the details on its borrowings and look for the coupon on its debt. If you cannot find it, you will need to go on to the internet to seek out similar budget airline debt issues. The objective is to find an indicative yield for MA bonds.
2 To estimate the cost of equity for MA, go to www.reuters.com and enter the ticker symbol 'RYA.L'. Follow the various links to find answers to the following questions: What is the most recent share price listed for Ryanair? What is the market value of equity, or market capitalization? How many shares of equity does Ryanair have outstanding? What is the beta for Ryanair? Now go to www.ft.com, follow the 'Markets Data' link and then the 'Bonds and Rates' link. What is the yield on three-month UK Treasury bills?
3 We now need to estimate the historical market risk premium. Go to Yahoo! Finance, download the monthly historical prices for the FTSE 100 Index for the last five years. Calculate the monthly returns, take the average and multiply this by 12 to get the annualized historical return on the FTSE 100. What is the historical market risk premium for the UK? Using the historical market risk premium, what is the cost of equity for Ryanair using the CAPM?
4 Go to www.reuters.com and find the list of competitors in the industry. Find the beta for each of these competitors and then calculate the industry average beta. Using the industry average beta, what is the cost of equity? Does it matter if you use the beta for Ryanair or the beta for the industry in this case?
5 You now need to calculate the cost of debt for Ryanair. Use the information on Ryanair bonds to find the weighted average cost of debt for Ryanair using the book value weights. Try to find bond prices for Ryanair debt. What should you do if no information is available? Does it make a difference in this case if you use book value weights or market value weights? Explain.
6 You now have all the necessary information to calculate the weighted average cost of capital for Ryanair. Calculate the weighted average cost of capital for Ryanair using book value weights and market value weights, assuming Ryanair has a 24 per cent tax rate. Which cost of capital number is more relevant?
7 You used Ryanair as a representative company to estimate the cost of capital for MA. What are some of the potential problems with this approach in this situation? What improvements might you suggest?

Practical Case Study

Cost of Equity and Capital Budgeting

In this practical case study, you will apply different methods for estimating the cost of equity and evaluating investment projects using NPV and IRR. Choose a company in an industry of your choice and collect data on the risk-free rate, the expected market return, and the dividend growth rate of the company, as well as its beta.

Assume the project you are considering is of the same risk as the company. You are considering an investment with the following series of cash flows:

Time	0	1	2	3	4	5
Net cash flow	−200	30	50	90	60	40

1 Calculate the cost of equity of your company using different methods, such as the dividend growth model or the CAPM.
2 Compare the results of different methods and explain the reasons for any discrepancies or similarities.
3 Calculate the NPV and IRR of your project using the cost of equity as the discount rate.
4 Analyse how different risk factors affect the cost of equity and the NPV and IRR of each project.
5 Which method for estimating cost of equity do you prefer and why?

References

Amihud, Y. and H. Mendelson (2000) 'The Liquidity Route to a Lower Cost of Capital', *Journal of Applied Corporate Finance,* Vol. 12, No. 4, 8–25.

Amihud, Y., A. Hameed, W. Kang and H. Zhang (2015a) 'Stock Liquidity and the Cost of Equity Capital in Global Markets', *Journal of Applied Corporate Finance,* Vol. 27, No. 4, 68–74.

Amihud, Y., A. Hameed, W. Kang and H. Zhang (2015b) 'The Illiquidity Premium: International Evidence', *Journal of Financial Economics,* Vol. 117, No. 2, 350–368.

Brennan, M.J. and C. Tamarowski (2000) 'Investor Relations, Liquidity, and Stock Prices', *Journal of Applied Corporate Finance*, Vol. 12, No. 4, 26–37.

Brounen, D., A. de Jong and K. Koedijk (2004) 'Corporate Finance in Europe: Confronting Theory with Practice', *Financial Management*, Vol. 33, No. 4, 71–101.

Oxera Consulting (2006) 'The Cost of Capital: An International Comparison', available at: www.oxera.com/wp-content/uploads/2018/07/The-cost-of-capital%E2%80%94an-international-comparison-1.pdf-1.pdf.

Additional Reading

The following papers are some of the more important studies in cost of capital that have been published in recent years, particularly for European firms.

1 Armitage, S. (2017) 'Discount Rates for Long-term Projects: The Cost of Capital and Social Discount Rate Compared', *European Journal of Finance*, Vol. 23, No. 1, 60–79.

2 Brav, O. (2009) 'Access to Capital, Capital Structure, and the Funding of the Firm', *Journal of Finance*, Vol. 64, No. 1, 263–308. **UK.**

3 Chen, K.C.W., Z. Chen and K.C.J. Wei (2009) 'Legal Protection of Investors, Corporate Governance, and the Cost of Equity Capital', *Journal of Corporate Finance*, Vol. 15, No. 3, 273–289. **International.**

4 Frank, M.Z. and T. Shen (2016) 'Investment and the Weighted Average Cost of Capital', *Journal of Financial Economics*, Vol. 119, No. 2, 300–315.

5 Hail, L. and C. Leuz (2009) 'Cost of Capital Effects and Changes in Growth Expectations around US Cross-listings', *Journal of Financial Economics*, Vol. 93, No. 3, 428–454. **International.**

6 Kisgen, D.J. and P.E. Strahan (2010) 'Do Regulations Based on Credit Ratings Affect a Firm's Cost of Capital?', *Review of Financial Studies*, Vol. 23, No. 12, 4324–4347.

7 Levi, Y. and I. Welch (2017) 'Best Practice for Cost-of-capital Estimates', *Journal of Financial and Quantitative Analysis*, Vol. 52, No. 2, 427–463.

8 Li, X. (2015) 'Accounting Conservatism and the Cost of Capital: An International Analysis', *Journal of Business Finance & Accounting*, Vol. 42, No. 5–6, 555–582.

Endnotes

1 As we will see later, an adjustment must be made when the debt level in the industry differs from that of the firm. However, we ignore this adjustment here for simplicity, to ensure the basic concept is clear.

2 It can be shown that the relationship between a firm's asset beta and its equity beta with corporate taxes is:

$$\beta_{\text{Equity}} = \beta_{\text{Asset}}\left[1 + (1 - t_c)\frac{B}{S}\right]$$

In this expression, t_c is the corporate tax rate. Tax effects are considered in more detail in a later chapter.

3 For example, see Amihud and Mendelson (2000), Brennan and Tamarowski (2000), and Amihud et al. (2015).

4 The full document, 'The Cost of Capital: An International Comparison' (2006), can be downloaded from Oxera's website: www.oxera.com/wp-content/uploads/2018/07/The-cost-of-capital%E2%80%94an-international-comparison-1.pdf-1.pdf.

5 EVA is a registered trademark of Stern Stewart & Company.

Chapter 13
Efficient Capital Markets and Behavioural Finance

Learning Objectives

After reading this chapter you should be able to:

LO1 Analyse the possibility of value creation in financing decisions and evaluate its implications for corporate finance strategies.

LO2 Explain the characteristics of efficient capital markets and discuss their importance for financial decision-making.

LO3 Differentiate between the types of efficiency in capital markets and examine their relevance for financial managers.

LO4 Assess the empirical evidence supporting efficient market hypotheses, and its implications for corporate financial management.

LO5 Identify common behavioural biases in corporate finance, and evaluate their impact on market efficiency and financial decision-making.

In 2021, the Dutch stock market experienced a return of more than 15 per cent. In 2022, the reverse occurred and the stock market fell by almost 13 per cent. The Netherlands wasn't unique in this regard and almost all other European markets experienced similar patterns of strong 2021 performance followed by dreadful returns in 2022 (see Chapter 9 for more information).

Chapter 9
Page 236

What caused the stock market growth in 2021 or the widespread falls in 2022? For the Netherlands, could it have been caused by the Covid pandemic restrictions? GDP growth in 2021 and 2022 was above 5 per cent. Could prices have been inflated in 2021 because of disruptions in the global supply chain and oil price increases being so high? It's possible. What made investors reverse their views so quickly? Did the Netherlands stock market experience a 'bubble' in prices, in which equity valuations are disproportionately high? Could other macroeconomic factors have been the root cause?

In this chapter, we discuss the competing ideas, present some evidence on both sides, and then examine the implications for financial managers.

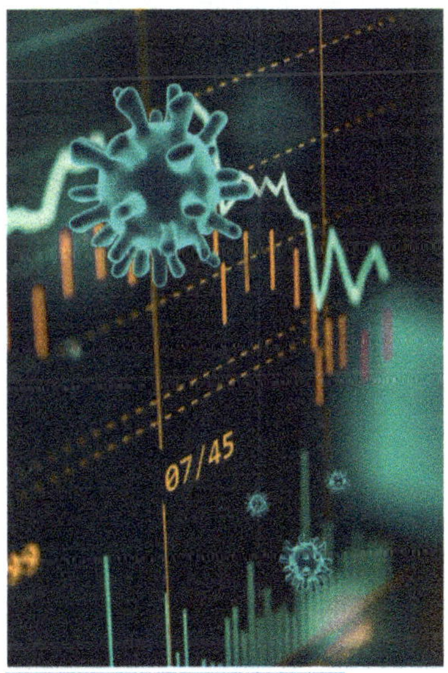

Source: OSORIOartist/Shutterstock

Key Notations

NPV	Net present value	R	Actual return
P_t	Price at time t	$E(R)$	Expected return
AR	Abnormal return	CAR	Cumulative abnormal return

13.1 Can Financing Decisions Create Value?

Earlier parts of the book showed how to evaluate projects according to the net present value criterion. The real world is a competitive one, where projects with positive net present value are not always easy to come by. However, through hard work or good fortune, a firm can identify winning projects. For example, to create value from capital budgeting decisions, the firm is likely to:

- Locate an unsatisfied demand for a particular product or service
- Create a barrier to make it more difficult for other firms to compete
- Produce products or services at a lower cost than the competition
- Be the first to develop a new product.

Typical financing decisions include how much debt and equity to sell, what types of debt and equity to sell, and when to sell them. Just as the net present value criterion was used to evaluate capital budgeting projects, we now want to use the same approach to assess financing decisions.

Though the procedure for evaluating financing decisions is identical to the method for evaluating projects, the results are different. It turns out the typical firm has many more capital expenditure opportunities with positive net present values than financing opportunities with positive net present values. In fact, we later show that some plausible financial models imply that no valuable financial opportunities exist at all.

Though this dearth of profitable financing opportunities will be examined in detail later, a few remarks are in order now. We maintain that there are three ways to create valuable financing opportunities:

1. *Investors lack an understanding of the risk and valuation of complex securities.* Assume that a firm can raise capital either by issuing equity or by issuing a more complex security – say, a combination of shares and warrants. Suppose that, in truth, 100 shares are worth the same as 50 units of our complex security. If investors have a misguided, overly optimistic view of the complex security, perhaps the 50 units can be sold for more than the 100 shares of equity can be sold. This complex security provides a valuable financing opportunity because the firm is getting more than fair value for it.

   Financial managers try to package securities to receive the highest value. Many have argued that the global credit crisis in 2007 and 2008 was caused by investors (including financial institutions) not understanding how to quantify the risk and value of the complex securities that banks issued on the back of subprime mortgage loans.

   The theory of efficient capital markets implies that investors cannot, in general, be easily fooled. It says that all securities are appropriately priced at all times. In our example, 50 units of the complex security would sell for the same price as 100 shares of equity. Thus, corporate managers cannot attempt to create value by fooling investors. Instead, managers must create value in other ways.

2. *Reduce costs or increase subsidies.* We show later that certain forms of financing have greater tax advantages than other types. For instance, a firm packaging securities to minimize taxes can increase firm value. Also, any financing technique involves other costs. For example, investment bankers, lawyers and accountants must be paid. A firm packaging securities to minimize these costs can also increase its value.

3. *Create a new security.* In recent decades there has been a massive surge in financial innovation. Though the advantage of each instrument is different, one general theme is that new complex securities cannot easily be duplicated by combinations of existing securities. Thus, a previously unsatisfied clientele may pay extra for a specialized security catering to its needs. Putable bonds, say, let the purchaser sell the bond at a fixed price back to the firm. This innovation creates a price floor, allowing the investor to reduce his or her downside risk. Perhaps risk-averse investors or those with little knowledge of the bond market would find this feature particularly attractive.

   Corporations gain by issuing these distinctive securities at high prices. However, the value captured by the innovator may well be small in the long run because the innovator usually cannot patent or copyright an idea. Soon many firms are issuing securities of the same kind, forcing prices down as a result.

Example 13.1

Valuing Financial Subsidies

Suppose Salamanca Electronics Company is thinking about relocating its plant to Mexico where labour costs are lower. In the hope that it can stay in Salamanca, the company has applied to the Castilla y León autonomous region to issue €2 million in five-year, tax-exempt industrial bonds. The coupon rate on industrial revenue bonds in

Castilla y León is currently 5 per cent. This is an attractive rate because the typical cost of debt capital for Salamanca Electronics Company is 10 per cent. What is the NPV of this potential financing transaction?

If the application is accepted and the industrial revenue bonds are issued by the Salamanca Electronics Company, the NPV (ignoring corporate taxes) is:

$$NPV = €2{,}000{,}000 - \left[\frac{€100{,}000}{1.1} + \frac{€100{,}000}{(1.1)^2} + \frac{€100{,}000}{(1.1)^3} + \frac{€100{,}000}{(1.1)^4} + \frac{€200{,}000}{(1.1)^5}\right]$$
$$= €2{,}000{,}000 - €1{,}620{,}921$$
$$= €379{,}079$$

This transaction has a positive NPV. The Salamanca Electronics Company obtains subsidized financing where the value of the subsidy is €379,079. Note that we used the normal cost of debt capital, 10 per cent, to discount the cash flows because this is the rate that accurately reflects the cost of debt for securities of similar risk in the markets.

This brief introduction sets the stage for the next several chapters of the book. The rest of this chapter examines the efficient capital markets hypothesis and an alternative involving behavioural finance. We show that if capital markets are efficient, corporate managers cannot create value by fooling investors. This is quite important because managers must create value in other, perhaps more difficult, ways. If markets are not efficient or are driven by irrationality, there will be opportunities for companies to create value. The following chapters concern the costs and subsidies of various forms of financing.

13.2 A Description of Efficient Capital Markets

An efficient capital market is one in which share prices fully reflect available information. To illustrate how an efficient market works, suppose F-stop Smartphone Cameras plc (FSC) is attempting to develop a new technology that utilizes AI to double the speed of the auto-focusing system now available in smartphones. FSC believes this research has a positive NPV.

Now consider a share of equity in FSC. What determines the willingness of investors to hold shares of FSC at a particular price? One factor is the probability that FSC will be the first company to develop the new auto-focusing system. In an efficient market, we would expect the share price of FSC to rise if this probability increases.

Suppose FSC hires a well-known technologist to develop the new auto-focusing system. In an efficient market, what will happen to FSC's share price when this is announced? If the technologist is paid a salary that fully reflects his or her contribution to the firm, the share price will not necessarily change. Suppose instead that hiring the technologist is a positive NPV transaction. In this case, the share price of FSC will increase because the firm can pay the technologist a salary below his or her true value to the company.

When will the increase in the share price of FSC occur? Assume the hiring announcement is made in a press release on Wednesday morning. In an efficient market, the FSC share price will *immediately* adjust to this new information. Investors should not be able to buy the shares on Wednesday afternoon and make a profit on Thursday. This would imply it took the equity market a day to realize the implication of the FSC press release. The efficient market hypothesis predicts that the FSC share price on Wednesday afternoon will already reflect the information contained in the Wednesday-morning press release.

The **efficient market hypothesis (EMH)** has implications for investors and firms:

- Because information is reflected in prices immediately, investors should expect to obtain only a normal rate of return. Awareness of information when it is released does an investor no good. The price adjusts before the investor has time to trade on it.
- Firms should expect to receive fair value for securities they sell. *Fair* means that the price they receive from issuing securities is the present value. Thus, valuable financing opportunities that arise from fooling investors are unavailable in efficient capital markets.

Figure 13.1 presents several possible adjustments in equity prices. The solid orange line represents the path taken by the security in an efficient market. In this case, the price adjusts immediately to the new information with no further price changes. The blue dotted line depicts a slow reaction. Here it takes the market 30 days to absorb the information fully. The solid orange line represents the path taken by the security in an efficient market. In this case, the price adjusts immediately to the new information with no further price changes. The black dotted line depicts a slow reaction. Here it takes the market 30 days to absorb the information fully. Finally, the blue dotted line illustrates an overreaction and subsequent correction back to the true price. The broken line and the dotted line show the paths that the share price might take in an inefficient market. If the share price takes several days to adjust, trading profits would be available to investors who timed their purchases and sales suitably.

Figure 13.1 Reaction of Share Price to New Information in Efficient and Inefficient Markets

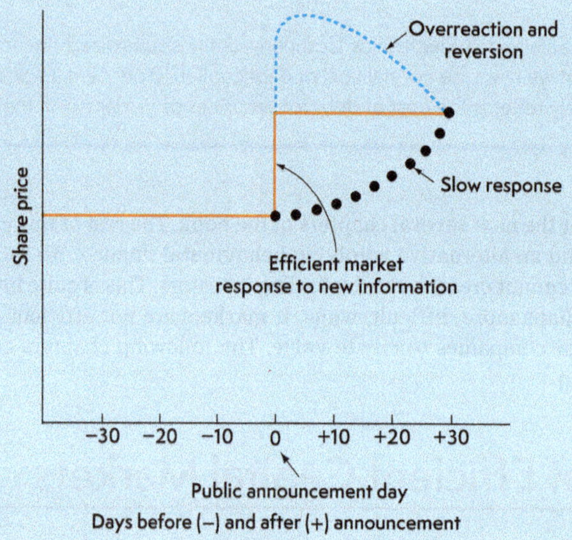

Efficient market response: The price instantaneously adjusts to and fully reflects new information; there is no tendency for subsequent increases and decreases.

Slow response: The price adjusts slowly to the new information; 30 days elapse before the price completely reflects the new information.

Overreaction: The price over-adjusts to the new information; there is a bubble in the price sequence.

Foundations of Market Efficiency

Figure 13.1 shows the consequences of market efficiency, but what are the conditions that *cause* market efficiency? Andrei Shleifer (2000) argues that there are three conditions, any one of which will lead to efficiency: (1) rationality, (2) independent deviations from rationality, and (3) arbitrage. A discussion of these conditions follows.

Rationality

Imagine all investors are rational. When new information is released in the marketplace, all investors rationally adjust their share price value estimates. In our example, investors will use the information in FSC's press release, in conjunction with existing information about the firm, to determine the NPV of FSC's new venture. If the information in the press release implies the NPV of the venture is £10 million, and there are 2 million shares, investors will calculate that the NPV is £5 per share. While FSC's old share price might be, say, £40, no one would now transact at that price. Anyone interested in selling would sell only at a price of at least £45 (= £40 + £5). Anyone interested in buying would now be willing to pay up to £45. In other words, the price would rise by £5. And the price would increase immediately because rational investors would see no reason to wait before trading at the new price.

Of course, we all know times when family members, friends, and yes, even we, seem to behave less than perfectly rationally. Thus, perhaps it is too much to ask that *all* investors behave rationally. But the market will still be efficient if the following scenario holds.

Independent Deviations from Rationality

Suppose FSC's press release is not all that clear. How many new camera units are likely to be sold? At what price? What is the expected cost per camera unit? Will other camera companies be able to develop competing products? How long is this likely to take? If these and other questions cannot be answered easily, it will be challenging to estimate NPV.

Now imagine that, with so many questions going unanswered, many investors do not think clearly. Some investors might get caught up in the romance of a new product, hoping for and ultimately believing in sales projections well above what is rational. They would overpay for new shares. And if they needed to sell shares (perhaps to finance current consumption), they would do so only at a high price. If these individuals dominate the market, the share price is likely to rise beyond what market efficiency would predict.

However, due to emotional resistance, investors could just as easily react to new information in a pessimistic manner. After all, business historians tell us that investors were initially quite sceptical about the benefits of the telephone, the copier, the automobile and the motion picture. Certainly, they could be overly cynical about this new AI camera technology. If investors were primarily of this type, the share price would be likely to rise less than market efficiency would predict.

Suppose as many individuals were irrationally optimistic as were irrationally pessimistic. Prices would be likely to rise in a manner consistent with market efficiency, even though most investors would be classified as less than fully rational. Thus market efficiency does not require rational individuals – only countervailing irrationalities.

However, this assumption of offsetting irrationalities at *all* times may be unrealistic. Perhaps, at certain times, most investors are swept away by excessive optimism and, at other times, are caught in the throes of extreme pessimism. But even here there is an assumption that will produce efficiency.

Arbitrage

Imagine a world with two types of individuals: irrational amateurs and rational professionals. The amateurs get caught up in their emotions, at times believing irrationally that an equity is undervalued and at other times thinking the opposite. If the passions of the different amateurs do not cancel one another out, these amateurs, by themselves, would tend to carry shares either above or below their efficient prices.

Now let us bring in the professionals. Suppose professionals go about their business methodically and rationally. They study companies thoroughly, evaluate the evidence objectively, estimate share prices coldly and clearly, and act accordingly. If an equity is underpriced, they would buy it. If it is overpriced, they would sell it. And their confidence is likely to be higher than that of the amateurs. Whereas an amateur might risk only a small sum, these professionals might risk large ones, *knowing* as they do that the security is mispriced.

Furthermore, they would be willing to rearrange their entire portfolio in search of a profit. *Arbitrage* is the word that comes to mind here because arbitrage generates profit from the simultaneous purchase and sale of different, but substitute, securities. If the arbitrage of professionals dominates the speculation of amateurs, markets would still be efficient.

13.3 The Different Types of Efficiency

In our previous discussion, we assumed that the market responds immediately to all available information. In actuality, information may affect share prices at different speeds. To handle differential response rates, researchers separate information into different types. The most common classification system identifies three types: information about past prices, publicly available information and all information. The effect of these three information sets on prices is examined next.

The Weak Form

Imagine a trading strategy that recommends buying a share after it has gone up three days in a row and recommends selling after it has gone down three days in a row. This strategy uses information based only on past prices. It does not use any other information, such as earnings, forecasts, merger announcements or money supply figures. A capital market is said to be *weakly efficient* or to satisfy weak form efficiency if it fully incorporates the information in past share prices. Thus, the strategy would not be able to generate profits if weak form efficiency holds.

Often weak form efficiency is represented mathematically as:

Equation 13.1

$$P_t = P_{t-1} + \textit{Expected return} + \textit{Random error}_t$$

Equation 13.1 states that the price today is equal to the sum of the last observed price plus the expected return on the equity (in currency) plus a random component occurring over the interval. The last observed price could have happened yesterday, last week or last month, depending on the sampling interval. The expected return is a function of a security's risk and would be based on the models of risk and return in previous chapters. The random component is due to new information about the company. It could be either positive or negative and has an expected value of zero. The random component in a period is unrelated to the random component in any past period. Hence this component is not predictable from past prices. If share prices follow Equation 13.1, they are said to follow a random walk.[1]

Weak form efficiency is the lowest type of efficiency we would expect a financial market to display because historical price information is the easiest kind of information to acquire. If it were possible to make extraordinary profits simply by finding patterns in share price movements, everyone would do it, and any profits would disappear in the scramble.

This effect of competition is seen in Figure 13.2. Suppose a company's share price displays a cyclical pattern, as indicated by the wavy curve. Shrewd investors would buy at the low points, forcing those prices up. Conversely, they would sell at the high points, forcing prices down. Via competition, cyclical regularities would be eliminated, leaving only random fluctuations.

Figure 13.2 Investor Behaviour Tends to Eliminate Cyclical Patterns

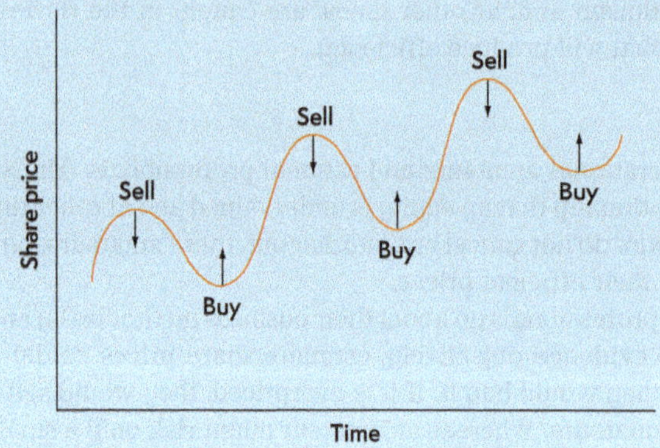

If an equity's price follows a cyclical pattern, the pattern will be quickly eliminated in an efficient market. A random pattern will emerge as investors buy at the trough and sell at the peak of a cycle.

The Semi-strong and Strong Forms

If weak form efficiency is controversial, even more contentious are the two stronger types of efficiency: semi-strong form efficiency and strong form efficiency. A market is semi-strong form efficient if prices reflect (incorporate) all publicly available information, including information such as published accounting statements for the firm as well as historical price information. A market is strong form efficient if prices reflect all information, public or private.

The information set of past prices is a subset of the information set of publicly available information, which in turn is a subset of all information. This is shown in Figure 13.3. Thus, strong form efficiency implies semi-strong form efficiency, and semi-strong form efficiency implies weak form efficiency. The distinction between semi-strong form efficiency and weak form efficiency is that semi-strong form efficiency requires not only that the market be efficient with respect to historical price information, but that *all* of the information available to the public be reflected in prices.

Figure 13.3 Relationship among Three Different Information Sets

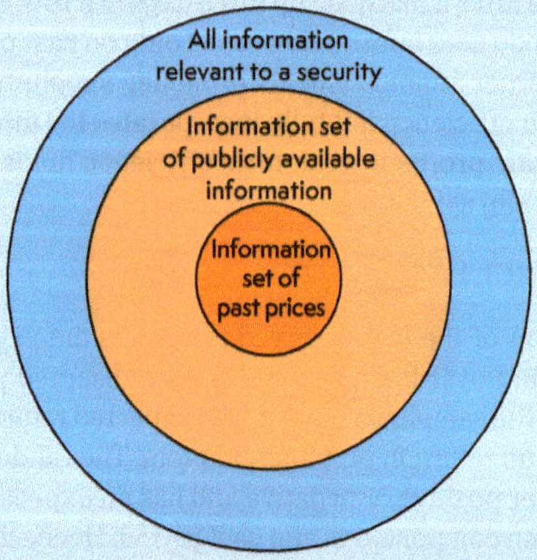

The information set of past prices is a subset of the set of all publicly available information, which in turn is a subset of all information. If today's price reflects only information about past prices, the market is weak form efficient. If today's price reflects all publicly available information, the market is semi-strong form efficient. If today's price reflects all information, both public and private, the market is strong form efficient.

Semi-strong form efficiency implies weak form efficiency, and strong form efficiency implies semi-strong form efficiency.

To illustrate the different forms of efficiency, imagine an investor who always sold a particular equity after its price had risen. A market that was only weak form efficient and not semi-strong form efficient would still prevent such a strategy from generating positive profits. According to weak form efficiency, a recent price rise does not imply that the equity is overvalued.

Now consider a firm reporting increased earnings. An individual might consider investing in the company's shares after reading the news release providing this information. However, if the market is semi-strong form efficient, the price should rise immediately upon the news release. Thus, the investor would end up paying the higher price, eliminating all chance for profit.

At the furthest end of the spectrum is strong form efficiency. This form says that anything that is pertinent to the value of the security and that is known to at least one investor is, in fact, fully incorporated into the share price. A strict believer in strong form efficiency would deny that an insider who knew whether a company mining operation had struck gold could profit from that information. Such a devotee of the strong form efficient market hypothesis might argue that, as soon as the insider tried to trade on his or her information, the market would recognize what was happening, and the price would shoot up before he or she could buy any of the shares. Alternatively, believers in strong form efficiency argue that there are no secrets, and as soon as the gold is discovered, the secret gets out.

One reason to expect that markets are weak-form efficient is that it is so cheap and easy to find patterns in share prices. Anyone who can program a computer and knows a little bit of statistics can search for such patterns. It stands to reason that, if there were patterns, people would find and exploit them, in the process causing them to disappear.

Semi-strong form efficiency, though, implies more sophisticated investors than does weak form efficiency. An investor must be skilled in accounting, finance and statistics, and steeped in the idiosyncrasies of individual industries and companies. Furthermore, to acquire and use such skills requires talent, ability and time. In the jargon of the economist, such an effort is costly, and the ability to be successful at it is probably in scarce supply.

As for strong form efficiency, this is just further down the road than semi-strong form efficiency. It is difficult to believe that the market is so efficient that someone with valuable inside information cannot prosper from it. And empirical evidence tends to be unfavourable to this form of market efficiency.

Some Common Misconceptions about the Efficient Market Hypothesis

No idea in finance has attracted as much attention as that of efficient markets, and not all of this has been flattering. To a certain extent, this is because much of the criticism has been based on a misunderstanding of what the hypothesis does and does not say. We illustrate three misconceptions next.

The Efficacy of Dart Throwing

When the notion of market efficiency was first publicized and debated in the popular financial press, it was often characterized by the following quote: 'throwing darts at the financial page will produce a portfolio that can be expected to do as well as any managed by professional security analysts' (Malkiel, 2003). This is almost, but not entirely, true.

All the efficient market hypothesis says is that, on average, the manager will not be able to achieve an abnormal or excess return. The excess return is defined with respect to some benchmark expected return, such as that from the security market line (SML) of Chapter 11. The investor must still decide how risky a portfolio he or she wants. Also, a random dart thrower might wind up with all of the darts sticking into one or two high-risk stocks that deal in genetic engineering. Would you really want all of your equity investments in two such stocks?

The failure to understand this has often led to confusion about market efficiency. For example, sometimes it is wrongly argued that market efficiency means that it does not matter what you do because the efficiency of the market will protect the unwary. However, someone once remarked, 'The efficient market protects the sheep from the wolves, but nothing can protect the sheep from themselves.'

What efficiency does say is that the price a firm obtains when it sells a share of its equity is a fair price in the sense that it reflects the value of that equity given the information that is available about it. Shareholders need not worry that they are paying too much for an equity with a low dividend or some other characteristic because the market has already incorporated it into the price. However, investors still have to worry about such things as their level of risk exposure and their degree of diversification.

Price Fluctuations

Much of the public is sceptical of efficiency because share prices fluctuate from day to day. However, daily price movement is in no way inconsistent with efficiency; an equity in an efficient market adjusts to new information by changing price. A great deal of new information comes into the stock market each day. In fact, the *absence* of daily price movements in a changing world might suggest an inefficiency.

Low Shareholder Interest

Many laypeople are sceptical that the market price can be efficient if only a fraction of the outstanding shares changes hands on any given day. However, the number of traders in a company's shares on a given day is generally far fewer than the number of people following the shares. This is true because an individual will trade only when his appraisal of the value of the equity differs enough from the market price to justify incurring brokerage commissions and other transaction costs. Furthermore, even if the number of traders following an equity is small relative to the number of outstanding shareholders, the company's shares can be expected to be efficiently priced as long as some interested traders use the publicly available information. That is, the share price can reflect the available information even if many shareholders never follow the company and are not considering trading in the near future.

13.4 The Evidence

The evidence on the efficient market hypothesis is extensive, with studies covering the broad categories of weak form, semi-strong form and strong form efficiency. In the first category, we investigate whether share price changes are random. We review both *event studies* and studies of the performance of mutual funds in the second category. In the third category, we look at the performance of corporate insiders.

The Weak Form

Weak form efficiency implies that a security's price movement in the past is unrelated to its price movement in the future. The work of Chapter 10 allows us to test this implication. In that chapter, we discussed the concept of correlation between the returns on two different securities. For example, the correlation between the return on HSBC and the return on Lloyds Banking Group is likely to be relatively high because both companies are in the banking industry. Conversely, the correlation between the return on HSBC and a Danish fast-food chain is likely to be low.

Financial economists frequently speak of serial correlation, which involves only one security. Serial correlation is the correlation between the current return on a security and the return on the same security over a later period. A positive serial correlation indicates a tendency towards *continuation*. That is, a higher-than-average return today is likely to be followed by higher-than-average returns in the future. Similarly, a lower-than-average return today is likely to be followed by lower-than-average returns in the future.

A negative serial correlation indicates a tendency towards *reversal*. A higher-than-average return today is likely to be followed by lower-than-average returns in the future. Similarly, a lower-than-average return today is likely to be followed by higher-than-average returns in the future. Both significantly positive and significantly negative serial correlation coefficients are indications of market inefficiencies; in either case, returns today can be used to predict future returns.

Serial correlation coefficients for share price returns near zero would be consistent with weak form efficiency. Thus, a share price return that is higher than average is equally likely to be followed by lower-than-average returns as by higher-than-average returns. Similarly, a return that is lower than average is equally likely to be followed by higher-than-average returns as by lower-than-average returns.

Table 13.1 shows the serial correlation for month returns on the main stock market index for selected countries. These coefficients indicate whether there are relationships between last month's return and this month's return. As can be seen, the majority of correlation coefficients are negative, which implies that a positive return today is likely to lead to a negative return tomorrow. Only one stock market index, China, has positive serial correlation, indicating the opposite relationship in that a positive return this month makes a positive return next month more likely.

Since correlation coefficients can, in principle, vary between –1 and 1, the reported coefficients in Table 13.1 are very small for most markets. However, for some countries (e.g. India, Singapore and the USA), the negative

Table 13.1 Serial Correlation Coefficients for Selected Stock Markets, 2011–2023

Country	Serial Correlation Coefficient
China	0.063897
Denmark	−0.01763
France	−0.08553
Germany	−0.05285
India	−0.17165
Italy	−0.08105
Malaysia	−0.08578
Netherlands	−0.07676
Norway	−0.02897
Singapore	−0.19804
Spain	−0.07666
Sweden	−0.13233
Switzerland	−0.08000
UK	−0.08425
USA	−0.19928

serial correlation is high for the period studied. Martin (2021) suggests that the negative serial correlation has existed only since the global financial crisis in 2008. For the markets studied in Table 13.1, the coefficients indicate that there is a pattern for some of the markets over the period studied, pointing to some evidence of weak form inefficiency.

This research raises an interesting thought: if price changes are genuinely random, why do so many believe prices follow patterns? The work of both psychologists and statisticians suggests that most people simply do not know what randomness looks like. For example, consider Figure 13.4. One line was generated by a computer using random numbers, and the other is the return index series for the Shanghai Stock Exchange. Do you see a pattern in either series? People can see different patterns and forecast different future price movements. However, in our experience, viewers are all quite confident about the patterns they see. Both lines may look quite non-random to some, suggesting weak form inefficiency. However, the Shanghai Stock Exchange Index series bears a close visual resemblance to the simulated price series in some years, and statistical tests indicate that it indeed behaves like a purely random series. Further, the correlation between the returns (not the prices) of Shanghai Stock Exchange and the simulated series is only −0.001! Thus, in our opinion, people claiming to see patterns in historical share price data may merely be seeing optical illusions.

The Semi-strong Form

The semi-strong form of the efficient market hypothesis implies that prices should reflect all publicly available information. We present two types of tests of this form.

Event Studies

The *abnormal return* (AR) on a given security for a particular day can be calculated by subtracting the market's return on the same day (R_m) – as measured by a broad-based index such as the FTSE All Share or Euro Stoxx 50 index – from the actual return (R) on the equity for that day.[2] We write this algebraically as:

$$AR = R - R_m$$

Figure 13.4 Simulated and Actual Shanghai Stock Exchange Return Index Movements, 2011–2023

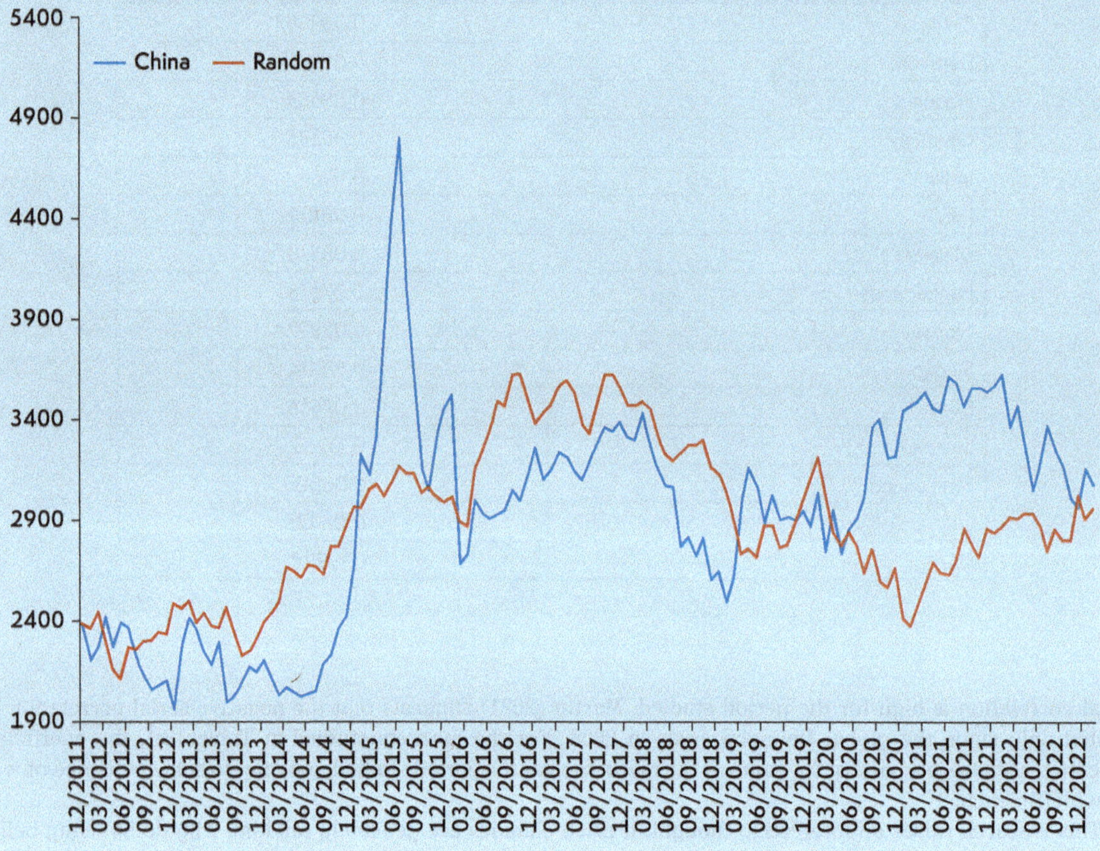

The following system will help us understand tests of the semi-strong form:

$$\text{Information released at time } t - 1 \rightarrow AR_{t-1}$$
$$\text{Information released at time } t \rightarrow AR_{t}$$
$$\text{Information released at time } t + 1 \rightarrow AR_{t+1}$$

The arrows indicate that the abnormal return in any time period is related only to the information released during that period.

According to the efficient market hypothesis, a company's abnormal return at time t, AR_t, should reflect the release of information at the same time, t. Any information released before then should not affect abnormal returns in this period because all of its influence should have been felt before. In other words, an efficient market would already have incorporated previous information into prices. Because a company's share price return today cannot depend on what the market does not yet know, information that will be known only in the future cannot influence the company's return either. Hence the arrows point in the direction that is shown, with information in any period affecting only that period's abnormal return. *Event studies* are statistical studies that examine whether the arrows are as shown or whether the release of information influences returns on other days.

These studies also speak of *cumulative abnormal returns* (CARs), as well as abnormal returns (ARs). As an example, consider a firm with ARs of 1 per cent, –3 per cent and 6 per cent for dates –1, 0 and 1, respectively, relative to a corporate announcement. The CARs for dates –1, 0 and 1 would be 1 per cent, –2 per cent [= 1 per cent + (–3 per cent)] and 4 per cent [= 1 per cent + (–3 per cent) + 6 per cent], respectively.

As an example, consider the cumulative abnormal returns around a major profit warning issued by Facebook Inc, (now Meta) on 26 July 2018. Figure 13.5 shows the plot of CARs and, because a profit warning is generally considered to be bad news, we would expect abnormal returns to be negative around the time of the announcement.

They are negative, as evidenced by the massive drop in CAR on the day of the announcement. The CARs get steadily worse over the next few days before recovering. This implies that there may have been a slight overreaction to the bad news over the immediate period following the announcement, at which point the share price recovered to stabilize at around –7 per cent.

Figure 13.5 Cumulative Abnormal Returns for Facebook around a Profit Warning in July 2018

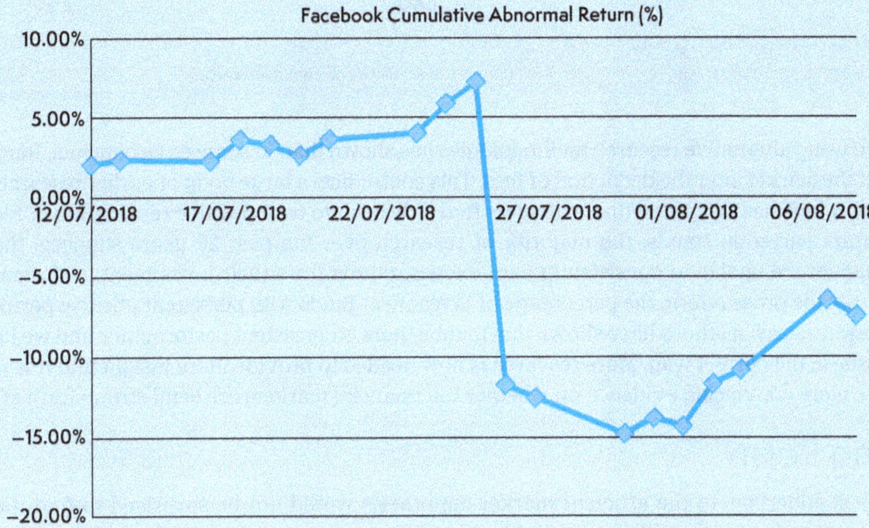

Does this provide evidence that the market is not semi-strong form efficient? More research on profit warnings is required to ascertain whether this is just confined to the Meta (Facebook) event or more generally.

Over the years, this type of event study methodology has been applied to many events. Announcements of dividends, earnings, mergers, capital expenditures and new issues of equity are a few examples of the vast literature in the area. The early event study tests generally supported the view that the market is semi-strong form (and therefore also weak form) efficient. However, some more recent studies present evidence that the market does not impound all relevant information immediately, and in some cases overreacts to news. Some conclude from this that the market is not efficient. Others argue that this conclusion is unwarranted, given statistical and methodological problems in the studies. This issue will be addressed in more detail later in the chapter (Section 13.5).

The Record of Investment Funds

If the market is efficient in the semi-strong form, then no matter what publicly available information fund managers rely on to pick equities, they will not be able to generate higher returns on average than a passive portfolio that replicates a benchmark index. We can test efficiency, then, by looking at the amount of excess cash generated by investment funds over and above what would be earned in a passive benchmark index investment minus fees.

Berk and van Binsbergen (2015) examined US mutual fund performance and found that, on average, funds generate in excess of $3 million per year (this is in excess of a passive benchmark and deduction of fees). Investors also recognize skill and this means better-performing funds receive more fees, with a positive correlation between current aggregate fees and future fund performance.

Korteweg and Sorensen (2017) carried out a similar type of analysis for private equity funds and reported persistence in fund performance of around 7 per cent per annum between the best- and worst-performing funds. However – and a major implication for the efficient market hypothesis – they found that the persistence in private equity performance was difficult to detect and so there was a low likelihood investors would be able to take advantage of the strong persistent private equity performance.

European evidence is conflicting. Whereas Otten and Bams (2002) reported positive performance for funds in four out of five European countries (see Table 13.2), Blake et al. (2017) found that no UK equity fund managers were able to consistently outperform the market after taking off fees.

Table 13.2 European Fund Performance After and Before Management Fees 1991–1998

Country	After Fees (%)	Before Fees (%)
France	0.80	**2.04**
Germany	**−2.17**	−1.32
Italy	0.43	**2.32**
Netherlands	**3.08**	**3.59**
UK	**1.40**	**2.59**

Source: Adapted from Otten and Bams (2002), Table 8.

Note: Figures are annualized alphas; bold text indicates the figure is statistically significant from zero.

New research using alternative research methodologies has shown that, in some environments, fund managers can consistently beat the market after the deduction of fees. This contradicts a large body of earlier research on investment fund performance which has suggested that managers find it difficult to earn positive returns, net of fees.

As the literature currently stands, the majority of research over the past 20 years suggests that professional investment managers are unable to consistently earn excess returns from their investment performance. Once fees are subtracted from the gross return, the percentage of investment funds with persistent positive performance is very low. However, new research methods have shown that maybe there is consistent performance and we just haven't been looking at the issue in the correct way. More research is now needed to provide more insight into this very interesting area and provide more convincing evidence on whether the financial markets are semi-strong form efficient.

The Strong Form

Even the strongest adherents to the efficient market hypothesis would not be surprised to find that markets are inefficient in the strong form. After all, if an individual has information that no one else has, it is likely that she can profit from it.

One group of studies of strong form efficiency investigates trading by senior executives in a company. Insiders, such as directors and chief executives, have access to information that is not generally available. But if the strong form of the efficient market hypothesis holds, insiders should not be able to profit by trading on their private information. Most government agencies require corporate insiders to reveal any trading they might do in their own company's stock. By examining the record of such trades, we can see whether they made abnormal returns.

Figure 13.6 shows the cumulative abnormal returns that UK directors earned from their trading between 1999 and 2013. It is clear there is a strong market reaction in the days after insider trading and that their trades were abnormally profitable. This view is supported using data in other countries. Given that it seems one can make abnormal profits from private information, strong form efficiency does not seem to be substantiated by the evidence.

Figure 13.6 Cumulative Abnormal Returns from UK Director Trading

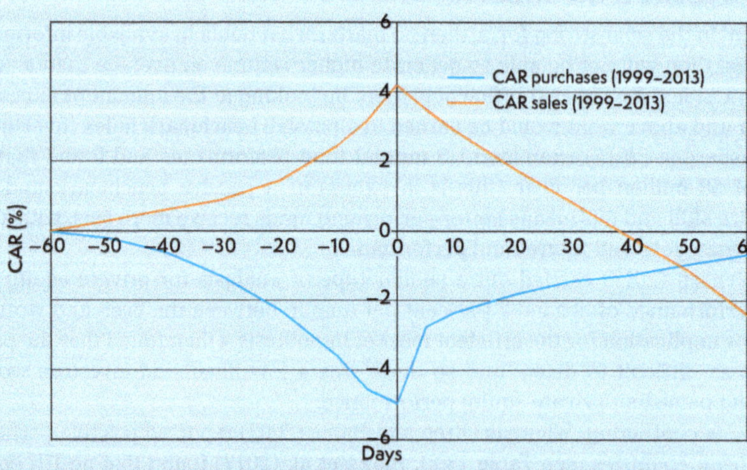

Source: The table is taken from the author's own calculations using data from Hemscott plc.

Taking all the results together, it is difficult to come to a view on whether markets are actually efficient. Interestingly, a recent study by Zaremba et al. (2020) examined 53 proven anomalies in 64 countries between 1973 and 2018, and found that their strength and profitability had fallen over the period, particularly in developed economies. This would suggest that, although there is evidence of market inefficiency in different contexts, the financial markets are becoming more efficient over time. Zaremba and colleagues' conclusions also highlight another issue with research in the financial markets: what may be true in a specific market at a specific time may not be true in the future. There will never be a time when research into financial markets will be exhausted!

Another issue is the number of possible anomalies one could consider. In an age of big data, where information is ubiquitous, a financial practitioner has far too much information available to hand to actually use it effectively. This was identified by Martin and Nagel (2022), who find that although variables may appear important, they may not be particularly useful in forecasts.

13.5 The Behavioural Challenge to Market Efficiency

In Section 13.2 we presented Professor Shleifer's three conditions, any one of which will lead to market efficiency. In that section, we made a case that at least one of the conditions is likely to hold in the real world. However, there is disagreement here. Many members of the academic community (including Professor Shleifer) argue that none of the three conditions is likely to hold in reality. This point of view is based on what is called *behavioural finance*. Let us examine the behavioural perspective of each of these three conditions.

Rationality

Are people really rational? Not always. Just travel to any casino to see people gambling, sometimes with large sums of money. The casino's take implies a negative expected return for the gambler. Because gambling is risky and has a negative expected return, it can never be on the efficient frontier. Also, gamblers will often bet on black at a roulette table after black has occurred a number of consecutive times, thinking that the run will continue. This strategy is faulty because roulette tables have no memory.

But, of course, gambling is only a sideshow as far as finance is concerned. Do we see irrationality in financial markets as well? The answer may well be yes. Many investors do not achieve the degree of diversification that they should. Others trade frequently, generating both commissions and taxes. In fact, taxes can be handled optimally by selling losers and holding onto winners. Although some individuals invest with tax minimization in mind, plenty of them do just the opposite. Many are more likely to sell their winners than their losers, a strategy leading to high tax payments.[3] The behavioural view is not that *all* investors are irrational but that some, perhaps many, investors are.

Independent Deviations from Rationality

Are deviations from rationality generally random, and thereby likely to cancel out in a whole population of investors? To the contrary, psychologists have long argued that people deviate from rationality in accordance with several basic principles. Not all of these principles have an application to finance and market efficiency, but at least two seem to do so.

The first principle, called *representativeness*, can be explained with the gambling example just used. The gambler believing a run of black will continue is in error because the probability of a black spin is still only about 50 per cent. Gamblers behaving in this way exhibit the psychological trait of representativeness. That is, they draw conclusions from insufficient data. In other words, the gambler believes the small sample he observed is more representative of the population than it really is.

How is this related to finance? Perhaps a market dominated by representativeness leads to bubbles. People see a sector of the market – for example, subprime mortgages – having a short history of high revenue growth, and extrapolate that it will continue for ever. When the growth inevitably stalls, prices have nowhere to go but down.

The second principle is *conservatism*, which means that people are too slow in adjusting their beliefs to new information. Suppose that your goal since childhood was to become a dentist. Perhaps you came from a family of dentists, maybe you liked the security and relatively high income that comes with that profession, or perhaps teeth always fascinated you. As things stand now, you could probably look forward to a long and productive career in that occupation. However, suppose a new drug was developed that would prevent tooth decay. That drug would undoubtedly reduce the demand for dentists. How quickly would you realize the implications as stated here? If you were emotionally attached to dentistry, you might adjust your beliefs slowly. Family and friends could tell you to switch out of dental courses at university, but you just might not be psychologically ready to do that. Instead, you might cling to your rosy view of dentistry's future.

Perhaps there is a relationship to finance here. For example, many studies report that prices seem to adjust slowly to the information contained in earnings announcements. Could it be that, because of conservatism, investors are slow in adapting their beliefs to new information? We will say more about this in the next section.

Arbitrage

In Section 13.2 we suggested that professional investors, knowing that securities are mispriced, could buy the underpriced ones while selling correctly priced (or even overpriced) substitutes. This might undo any mispricing caused by emotional amateurs.

Trading of this sort is likely to be riskier than it appears at first glance. Suppose professionals generally believed that the shares of the copper-mining firm Vedanta Resources plc were underpriced. They would buy them while selling their holdings in other mining firms, say Anglo American and Rio Tinto plc. However, if amateurs were taking opposite positions, prices would adjust to correct levels only if the positions of amateurs were small relative to those of the professionals. In a world of many amateurs, a few professionals would have to take large positions to bring prices into line, perhaps even engaging heavily in short selling. Buying large amounts of one company's shares and short selling large amounts of another company's shares is quite risky, even if the two shares are in the same industry. Here, unanticipated bad news about Vedanta Resources and unexpected good news about the other two companies would cause the professionals to register large losses.

Also, if amateurs mispriced Vedanta Resources today, what is to prevent Vedanta from being even *more* mispriced tomorrow? This risk of further mispricing, even in the presence of no new information, may also cause professionals to cut back their arbitrage positions. As an example, imagine a shrewd professional who believed technology stocks were underpriced in late 2018. Had he bet on technology equities rising at that time, he would have lost in the near term: prices fell towards the end of 2018. Yet, he would have eventually made money because prices later increased. The critical insight is that near-term risk may reduce the size of arbitrage strategies.

In conclusion, the arguments presented here suggest that the theoretical underpinnings of the efficient capital markets hypothesis, given in Section 13.2, might not hold in reality. That is, investors may be irrational, irrationality may be related across investors rather than cancelling out across investors, and arbitrage strategies may involve too much risk to eliminate market efficiencies.

13.6 Empirical Challenges to Market Efficiency

Section 13.4 presented empirical evidence supportive of market efficiency. We now present evidence challenging this hypothesis. (Adherents of market efficiency generally refer to results of this type as *anomalies.*)

Limits to Arbitrage

Royal Dutch Petroleum and Shell Transport merged their interests in 1907, with all subsequent cash flows being split on a 60–40 per cent basis between the two companies. However, both companies continued to be publicly traded separately until 2005. You might imagine that, before 2005, the market value of Royal Dutch would always have been 1.5 (= 60/40) times that of Shell. That is, if Royal Dutch ever became overpriced, rational investors would buy Shell instead of Royal Dutch. If Royal Dutch were underpriced, investors would buy Royal Dutch. In addition, arbitrageurs would go further by buying the underpriced security and selling the overpriced security short.

However, Figure 13.7 shows that Royal Dutch and Shell rarely traded at parity (i.e. 60/40) before their shares were combined in 2005. Why would these deviations have occurred? As stated in the previous section, behavioural finance suggests that there are limits to arbitrage. That is, an investor buying the overpriced asset and selling the underpriced asset does not have a sure thing. Deviations from parity could actually *increase* in the short run, implying losses for the arbitrageur. The well-known statement, 'Markets can stay irrational longer than you can stay solvent', attributed to John Maynard Keynes, applies here. Thus, risk considerations may force arbitrageurs to take positions that are too small to move prices back to parity.

Figure 13.7 Deviations of the Ratio of the Market Value of Royal Dutch to the Market Value of Shell from Parity

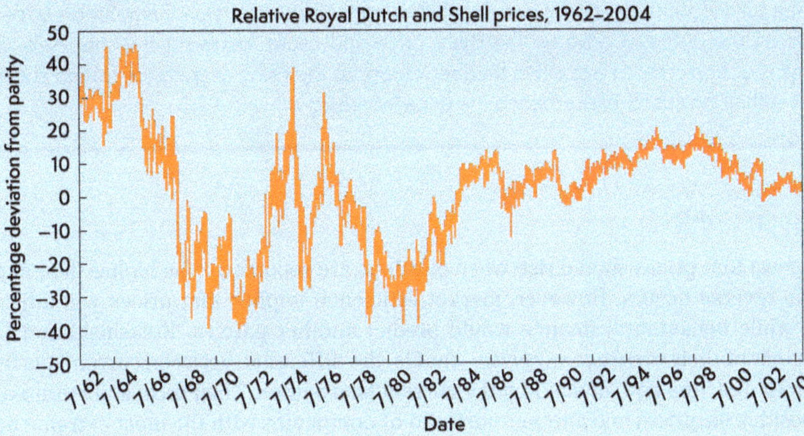

Academics have documented a number of these deviations from parity. Froot and Dabora (1999) show similar results for both the twin companies of Unilever NV and Unilever plc, and for two classes of SmithKline Beecham shares. Lamont and Thaler (2003) present similar findings for 3Com and its subsidiary Palm Inc. Other researchers find price behaviour in closed-end mutual funds suggestive of parity deviations.

Arbitrageurs will often short-sell securities they believe are overvalued. Short-selling means that a trader sells a security she does not own and buys the security in the market at a later date. If prices fall to the correct value between the short-selling date and the purchase date, the short-seller makes a profit. In the absence of transaction costs, short-selling can be an effective strategy in taking advantage of arbitrage opportunities.

However, short-selling is not free from constraints or transaction costs. Financial markets may have regulations banning short-selling activity, and margin requirements and account fees may limit arbitrage opportunities. Porras Prado, Saffi and Burgess (2016) have shown that a firm's ownership structure can strengthen limits to arbitrage. Specifically, companies that have active investors or shareholders with a high percentage ownership stake are less likely to present opportunities for arbitrage. This is because these firms have a lower supply of shares to trade, making it much more expensive to short-sell in the market.

Real World Insight 13.1

The Gamestop Short Squeeze

In January 2021, the share price of GameStop, a US-based video game retailer, experienced a meteoric rise, driven by a group of retail investors on the Reddit forum r/wallstreetbets. The retail investors targeted GameStop due to its heavily shorted position by institutional investors, primarily hedge funds. The share price surged from around $17 at the beginning of the year to a high of $483 on 28 January, a staggering 2,740 per cent increase.

The GameStop short squeeze is an excellent case study to illustrate limits to arbitrage. Arbitrage opportunities arise when assets are mispriced, and investors can profit from buying and selling these assets. In an efficient market, such opportunities should not persist for long, as arbitrageurs would exploit them, driving prices back to their fair values. However, the GameStop saga demonstrated that various factors can limit arbitrage, even in seemingly liquid markets.

Short-sale constraints played a significant role in the GameStop short squeeze. Shorting equity requires borrowing shares from a lender and selling them, with the expectation of repurchasing them at a lower price to return to the lender. In the case of GameStop, the demand for borrowing shares was extremely high, causing borrowing fees to sky-rocket. Additionally, some brokerages, due to risk management concerns, restricted trading in GameStop shares, further limiting the ability of investors to short the equity.

The short squeeze also highlighted the impact of noise traders and sentiment on market efficiency. The retail investors driving the buying frenzy were not necessarily basing their decisions on GameStop's underlying business model but instead on the desire to drive up the share price and cause losses for the short-selling hedge funds. This collective buying action created a positive feedback loop, as the rising share price forced short-sellers to buy back shares to cover their positions, exacerbating the price increase.

Earnings Surprises

Common sense suggests that prices should rise when earnings are reported to be higher than expected and prices should fall when the reverse occurs. However, market efficiency implies that prices will adjust immediately to the announcement, while behavioural finance would predict another pattern. Kolasinski and Li (2010) rank US companies by the extent of their *earnings surprise* – that is, the difference between current quarterly earnings and quarterly earnings four quarters ago, divided by the current share price. They form a portfolio of companies with the most extreme positive surprises and another portfolio of companies with the most extreme negative surprises. Figure 13.8 shows returns from buying the two portfolios, net of the return on the overall market. As can be seen, prices adjust slowly to the earnings announcements, with the portfolio with the positive surprises outperforming the portfolio with the negative surprises over both the next month and the next six months. Gerard (2012) extends this research to a large sample of European firms and finds the same post-earnings announcement drift.

Figure 13.8 Returns to Two Investment Strategies Based on Earnings Surprise

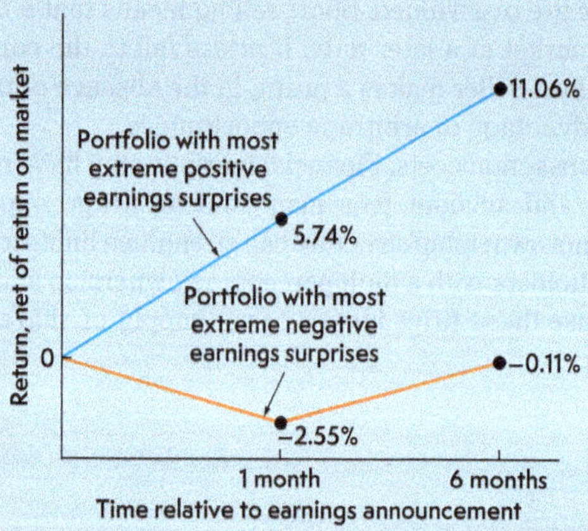

This figure shows returns net of the market return to a strategy of buying equities with extremely high positive earnings surprise (the difference between current quarterly earnings and quarterly earnings four quarters ago, divided by the current share price) and to a strategy of buying equities with extremely high negative earnings surprise. The graph shows a slow adjustment to the information in the earnings announcement.

Source: Adapted from Kolasinski and Li (2010), Table 1.

Dargenidou, Tonks and Tsoligkas (2018) examine the role of corporate insider trading on post-earnings announcement drift for UK companies and report that contrarian insider trading (bad news followed by insider purchases or good news followed by insider sales) can partially remove the drift, whereas confirmatory insider trades (that is, good news followed by insider buys or bad news followed by insider sales) strengthen the drift. Their interpretation of these results strongly suggests that the post-earnings announcement drift reflects slow price discovery because of market inefficiency. Corporate insider trading enhances the information content of prices, thereby making the market more informationally efficient.

Post-earnings announcement drift is one of the most durable of all financial market anomalies and continues to perplex finance academics to this day. Why do prices adjust slowly after earnings announcements? Behavioural finance suggests that investors may exhibit conservatism because they are slow to adjust to the information contained in the announcements. It is possible that investors are overconfident in their own beliefs and it takes time for them to change their views (Liang, 2003), or there are limits to arbitrage (Ng, Rusticus and Verdi, 2008).

Other views are that the drift is caused by investors not having the skill or not putting enough effort in to understanding the information presented by earnings announcements (Hirshleifer, Lim and Teoh, 2009). Other explanations are that the information provided by earnings announcements is inherently poor and so investors find it difficult to understand the significance of new earnings figures (Lee, 2012).

Value versus Growth

A number of papers have argued that equities with high book-value-to-share-price ratios and/or high earnings-to-price ratios (generally called *value stocks*) outperform equities with low ratios (*growth stocks*). For example, Fama and French (1998) find that, for 12 of 13 major international stock markets, the average return on equities with high book-value-to-share-price ratios is above the average return on equities with low book-value-to-share-price ratios.[4] Figure 13.9 shows the returns for a number of selected countries for the period 1991 to 2022. In every country – with the exception of Finland, Italy and Switzerland – value stocks outperformed growth stocks.

Figure 13.9 Annual Percentage Returns on Low Book-to-market Firms and High Book-to-market Firms in Selected Countries for the period 1991–2022

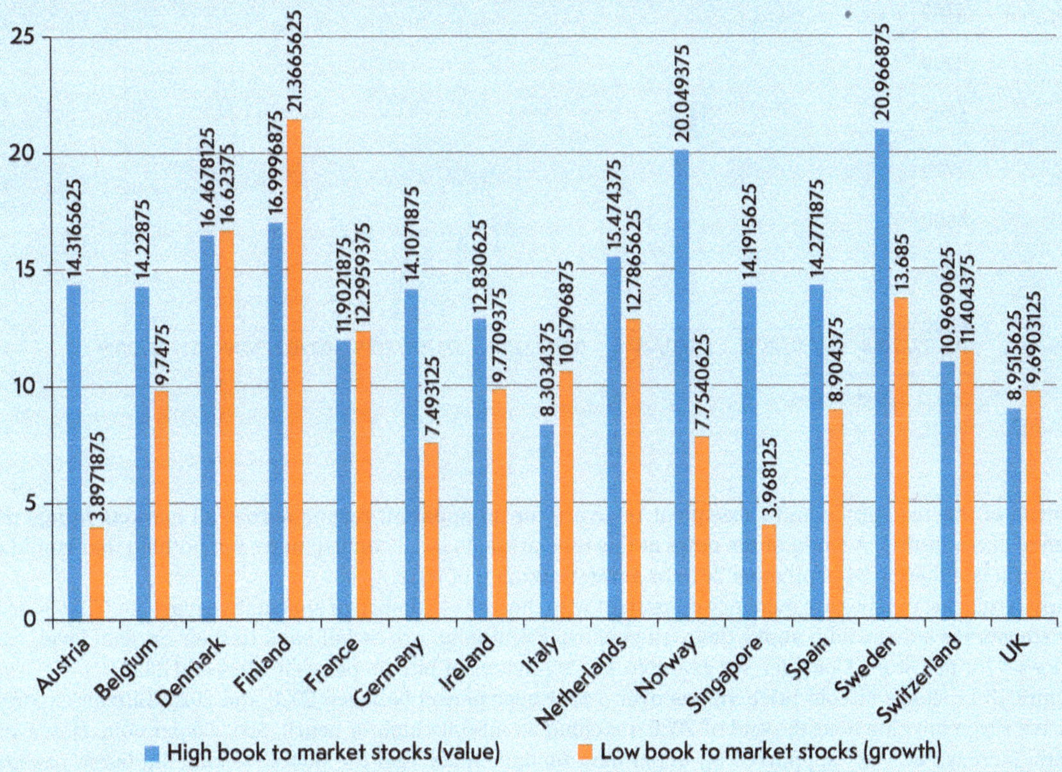

Source: The figures are the author's own calculations based on data taken from Kenneth French's website: http://mba.tuck.dartmouth.edu/pages/faculty/ken.french/index.html

Because the return difference is so large in many countries, and because these ratios can be obtained so easily for individual companies, the results may constitute strong evidence against market efficiency. However, a number of papers suggest the unusual returns are due to biases in commercial databases or to differences in risk, not to a true inefficiency.[5] Because the debate revolves around arcane statistical issues, we will not pursue the issue further. Notice, however, that in some markets (e.g. Denmark, France, Switzerland and the UK) there is very little difference between the two portfolios, which may imply that some markets are efficient with respect to these risk factors.

It is safe to say that no conclusion is warranted at this time. As with so many other topics in finance and economics, further research is needed.

Crashes and Bubbles

Between 28 September 2018 and 24 December 2018, most developed markets dropped in value by about 20 per cent. The first three months of 2019 saw a major recovery that wiped out most of the losses experienced over the previous three months. Figure 13.10 shows this strange collapse then reversal for the main French stock market index, CAC 40. Almost all other developed market indices exhibited a similar pattern over the same period.

Figure 13.10 CAC 40 Index between 3 September 2018 and 3 March 2019

Source: Yahoo! Finance.

A drop of this magnitude and subsequent recovery for no apparent reason across all markets brings market efficiency into question. A study of the news at this time presents local country news but nothing that would affect world markets either on 24 September 2018 or at the beginning of 2019.

Perhaps market crashes are evidence consistent with the **bubble** theory of speculative markets. That is, security prices sometimes move wildly above their true values. Eventually, prices fall back to their original level, causing great losses for investors. Consider, for example, the behaviour of bitcoin prices in 2021 and 2022.

Figure 13.11 shows bitcoin price values over a four-year period between 2020 and 2023. Bitcoin experienced a massive surge in value near the end of 2020, reaching an all-time high of nearly $65,000 per coin. However, this dramatic increase was not supported by underlying fundamentals, and the bubble eventually burst, causing the price to fall by 70 per cent.

Many commentators describe the rise and fall of bitcoin as a bubble. Is it correct to do so? Unfortunately, there is no fully agreed definition of the term. Some academics argue that the price movement in the figure is consistent with rationality. Prices rose initially, they say, because it appeared that bitcoin would soon capture a large chunk of international commerce as it was being adopted by companies like Paypal and Tesla. However, there is very little explanation for why the prices fell so much and you could argue that the initial rosy scenario was never supported by the facts. Rather, prices rose due to nothing more than 'irrational exuberance'.

Figure 13.11 Value of Index of Internet Stocks

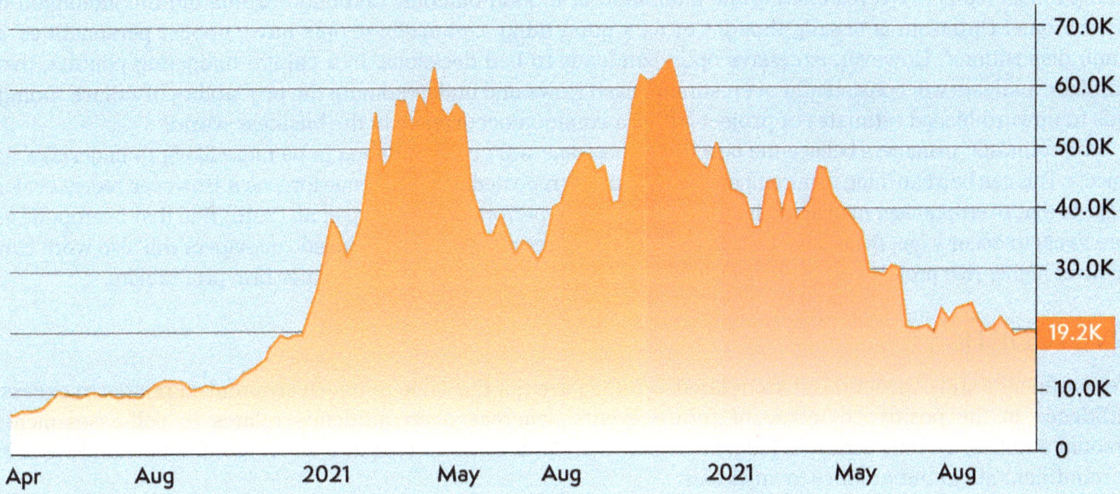

Real World Insight 13.2

Are Financial Markets Efficient?

It is fair to say that the financial markets have behaved very strangely in recent years. In 2019, several government bond yields were negative (for example, Japan and Switzerland) and stock markets had an excellent performance following a dreadful 2018. The 2019 rebound happened while trade wars were threatening to erupt between the USA and China. Europe faced its own issues with Brexit and a populist government in Italy that was picking economic quarrels with the European Central Bank. How can stock markets perform so well while economies are faring so poorly? What does all this mean for concepts like market efficiency?

Let's take negative government bond yields first. A negative bond yield means that the return you receive on this instrument is expected to be negative. On one level, you would argue this is definitely proof the market is inefficient since the positive risk–expected return relation is violated. However, it could also mean that investors are expecting deflation, where overall price levels are falling. In such a situation, if the positive return on bonds to compensate for risk (which is to be expected) is not larger than the drop in overall price levels, negative yields will result. Fortunately for finance practitioners, negative bond yields evaporated in 2022 with the return of inflation after the Covid pandemic.

13.7 Behavioural Biases in Corporate Finance

It is fair to say the controversy over efficient capital markets has not yet been resolved. Rather, people have sorted themselves into three camps, with some adhering to market efficiency, some believing in behavioural finance and others (perhaps the majority) not yet convinced that either side fully represents reality. This state of affairs is certainly different from, say, 30 years ago, when market efficiency went unchallenged. The efficient markets controversy is perhaps the most contentious of any area of corporate finance.

Because of the controversy, it is not likely our textbook, or any textbook, can easily resolve the differing points of view. In this section, we will review several behavioural biases you may experience in corporate finance and the financial markets. The Ancient Greek aphorism 'know thyself' is important here. As a finance practitioner, you should be aware of potential behavioural biases you and others may exhibit in financial decision-making. If you are lucky, you may be able to take advantage of these for your firm's benefit.

Overoptimism

Overoptimism leads to overestimating the likelihood of a good outcome and underestimating the likelihood of a bad outcome. Optimism is usually thought of as a good thing. Optimistic people have 'upbeat personalities' and 'sunny dispositions'. However, excessive optimism leads to bad decisions. In a capital budgeting context, overly optimistic analysts will consistently overestimate cash flows and underestimate the probability of failure. Doing so leads to upward-biased estimates of project NPVs, a common occurrence in the business world.

Overoptimistic managers believe the best future outcome will occur, and tend to be more likely to undertake risky projects. This can be a bad thing for a company if investments repeatedly miss revenue forecasts. However, recent evidence suggests that overoptimism may actually improve corporate performance. Hilary et al. (2016) find that overoptimism is more likely to occur when firms have been successful in the recent past. Overoptimistic managers will also work harder to deliver higher-risk projects to ensure success, and the increased effort leads to greater firm profitability.

Overconfidence

Overconfidence and overoptimism are related, but they are not the same thing. Overoptimism relates to excessive confidence in the positive outcome of future events, whereas overconfidence relates to self-assessment of personal abilities. Serious errors in judgement occur in the business world due to overconfidence, and we are all overconfident about our abilities to an extent.

For example, do you believe you are a better than average driver? It is highly probable more than 50 per cent of your friends believe they are better drivers than the average, and an even higher percentage of men believe they are better than average drivers!

In general, you are overconfident when you overestimate your ability to make the correct choice or decision. For example, most business decisions require judgements about the unknown future. The belief that you can forecast the future with precision is a common form of overconfidence.

An example of overconfidence in business is the opening of restaurants. We all know of specific locations where restaurant after restaurant opens without success. Each new owner believes that he or she will be successful where every previous owner has failed. Unfortunately, the probabilities are that the new owner will fare just as badly as previous owners. Overconfidence is very common in business.

Overconfident managers are more likely to make management forecasts predicting overoptimistic outcomes, then tend to underperform their forecasts (Hribar and Yang, 2016). Faccio, Marchica and Mura (2016) report results suggesting that higher risk-taking by male CEOs (which is indicative of overconfidence) leads to firms with higher debt ratios and earnings volatility. Firms with female CEOs were also found to have a higher likelihood of surviving than male-run firms.

Confirmation Bias

When you are evaluating a decision, you collect information and opinions. A common bias in this regard is to focus more on information that agrees with your opinion, and to downplay or ignore information that doesn't agree with or support your position. This phenomenon is known as confirmation bias, and people who suffer from it tend to spend too much time trying to prove themselves correct rather than searching for information that might prove them wrong.

Confirmation bias can lead managers to ignore negative information about potential investments and to focus only on that information which proves they are correct in their opinions. This can lead to a number of poor decisions that reduce firm value. This principle implies overweighting the results of small samples, as with the gambler who thinks a few consecutive spins of black on the roulette wheel make black a more likely outcome than red on the next spin.

Frame Dependence

In many business situations, the way an investment is presented can influence your decision. This is known as frame dependence and can be used against those who are not familiar with this bias. Consider the following example: your firm is dealing with a poor operating environment and 600 employees are at risk of redundancy. Looking at Scenario 1, you must choose between two strategies to turn the business around:

Scenario 1

Strategy A: The workforce will be reduced and 200 staff keep their jobs with certainty.

Strategy B: With this strategy, there is a 1/3 chance that everyone will keep their job but a 2/3 chance the company will fail and all 600 staff will be made redundant.

Which strategy would you choose? There is not necessarily a right answer, but most managers will choose Strategy A.

Now suppose your choices are as follows:

Scenario 2

Strategy C: The workforce will be reduced and 400 staff will be made redundant immediately, losing their jobs.

Strategy D: There is a 1/3 chance that strategy D will be a success and all 600 of your staff will keep their jobs. However, there is a 2/3 chance that the company will fail and everyone will be made redundant.

Now which do you pick?

Again, there is no right answer, but most managers will choose Strategy D. Although most managers will choose Strategies A and D in our hypothetical scenarios, you can probably see that doing so is inconsistent because Strategies A and C are identical, as are Strategies B and D.

Why do people make inconsistent choices? It's because the options are framed differently. The first scenario is positive because it emphasizes the number of jobs that will be saved. The second is negative because it focuses on losses, and people react differently to positive versus negative framing, which is a form of frame dependence.

Loss Aversion

Loss aversion occurs when managers dislike bad outcomes more than they like good outcomes. This leads to behaviour that is overly sensitive to downside risk in projects. Consider the following scenarios:

Scenario 1

Your firm is offering you a remuneration package. At the end of the year, you will be awarded €100,000. In addition to this base salary, you have the option to choose one of two additional components to your final remuneration.

Option A: You can receive another €50,000 for sure, to make a final remuneration of €150,000.

Option B: Your salary is tied to your company's share price and if the price increases (50 per cent probability) you will receive €200,000 in total. However, if the share price falls (50 per cent probability) you will receive nothing.

Scenario 2

Your basic salary is €200,000 and you have to choose one of two incentive plans.

Option C: Your salary will be reduced to €150,000.

Option D: Your salary is tied to your company's share price and if the price falls (50 per cent probability) you will lose €100,000 from your salary. However, if the share price increases (50 per cent probability) you lose nothing.

What were your answers? Did you choose option A in the first scenario and option D in the second? If that's what you did, you are guilty of just focusing on gains and losses, and not paying attention to what really matters, namely the impact on your wealth. However, you are not alone. About 85 per cent of the people who are presented with the first scenario choose option A, and about 70 per cent of the people who are presented with the second scenario choose option D.

If you look closely at the two scenarios, you will see they are actually identical. You end up with €150,000 for sure if you pick option A or C, or else you end up with a 50–50 chance of either €100,000 or €200,000 if you pick option B or D. So, you should pick the same option in both scenarios. Which option you prefer is up to you, but the point is that you should never pick option A in our first scenario and option D in our second one.

This example illustrates an important aspect of financial decision-making. Focusing on gains and losses instead of overall wealth is an example of narrow framing, and it leads to a phenomenon known as loss aversion. In fact, the reason that most people avoid option C in scenario 2 in our example is that it is expressed as a sure loss of €50,000. In general, researchers have found that individuals are reluctant to realize losses and will, for example, gamble at unfavourable odds to avoid doing so.

Loss aversion is also known as the break-even effect because it frequently shows up as companies hang on to bad investments and projects (and perhaps even invest more) hoping that something will happen that allows them to break even and thereby escape without a loss. For example, we discussed the irrelevance of sunk costs in the context of capital budgeting, and the idea of a sunk cost seems clear. Nonetheless, we constantly see companies throw good money after bad rather than just recognize a loss in the face of sunk costs.

In corporate finance, loss aversion can be quite damaging. We have already mentioned the pursuit of sunk costs. We also might see managers bypassing positive NPV projects because they have the possibility of large losses (perhaps with low probability). Another phenomenon that we see is debt avoidance. As we will discuss in our coverage of capital structure (Chapter 18), debt financing generates valuable tax shields for profitable companies.

Even so, there are hundreds of profitable companies listed on major stock exchanges that completely (or almost completely) avoid debt financing. Because debt financing increases the likelihood of losses, and even bankruptcy, this potentially costly behaviour could be due to loss aversion.

The Academic Viewpoints

The academic camps have different views of these results. The efficient market believers stress that behavioural finance can always find some behavioural bias to explain an anomaly. For example, Wikipedia lists more than 100 cognitive biases that managers may exhibit, on its page, 'List of cognitive biases'. Which bias should dominate in any particular situation? In other words, there is effectively no way to isolate the specific bias-causing behaviours and anomalies presented in this chapter.

Proponents of market efficiency say that, unless behaviourists can incontrovertibly isolate a specific behavioural bias as causing an anomaly in an experimental setting, the presentation of behavioural finance research is simply conjecture. In addition, even if a financial market has many investors exhibiting different behavioural biases, these will cancel out in the aggregate and markets will be efficient. If there is an observed market anomaly that is consistent with a behavioural bias, it is simply a chance event.

Adherents of behavioural finance see things a little differently. First, they point out that, as discussed in Section 13.5, the three theoretical foundations of market efficiency appear to be violated in the real world. Second, there are simply too many anomalies, with a number of them being replicated in out-of-sample tests. This argues against anomalies being mere chance events.

Sustainability in Action 13.1

Jimimac plc: Understanding Behavioural Biases in Practice

This case study refers to a hypothetical series of issues faced by a renewable energy company in the context of deciding and implementing a new solar investment. It illustrates the full gamut of behavioural finance concepts, such as overoptimism, overconfidence, confirmation bias, frame dependence and loss aversion (you should try to identify these in the text below).

Jimimac plc, a medium-sized company in the renewable energy sector, decided to invest in a new solar energy project to expand its sustainable energy portfolio. The project aimed to increase the company's revenue and contribute to a more environmentally friendly energy grid. Jimimac's management team, consisting of both optimists and pessimists, had been tasked with evaluating the project's feasibility and potential return on investment. The project was spearheaded by an overoptimistic and overconfident CEO, who believed that the project would not only be successful but would also revolutionize the renewable energy industry. This overoptimism led the CEO to consistently overestimate the project's future cash flows and underestimate the risks and challenges involved. This upward-biased estimation of the project's NPV persuaded Jimimac's management team to commit to the project without thoroughly considering its feasibility.

As the project progressed, Jimimac's management team began to encounter setbacks and cost overruns. However, rather than re-evaluating the project's feasibility, the CEO selectively focused on information that supported their original belief in the project's success. This led the management team to overlook critical issues and continue investing in the project.

The company's board of directors was presented with two options to address the project's challenges: (1) scale back the project and reduce costs, or (2) invest additional capital in the hope of turning the project around. The CEO was in charge of the presentation and forecasted a very positive future for the project. The way these options were framed influenced the board's decision, with the majority of members choosing to invest additional capital, despite the significant risks involved.

As the project continued to face setbacks, the company's management team and board of directors became increasingly focused on avoiding losses rather than considering the project's overall impact on the company's financial position. This led the company to continue investing in the struggling project, hoping that additional capital would enable it to break even.

Ultimately, Jimimac's decision to pursue the solar energy project resulted in significant financial losses and damaged the company's reputation. If the company management and board had understood the importance of behavioural biases in financial decision-making and how to mitigate against them, they could have ensured more rational, objective decisions that would have led to better outcomes for Jimimac and its stakeholders.

Summary and Conclusions

1 An efficient financial market processes the information available to investors and incorporates it into the prices of securities. Market efficiency has two general implications. First, in any given time period, an equity's abnormal return depends on information or news received by the market in that period. Second, an investor who uses the same information as the market cannot expect to earn abnormal returns. In other words, systems for playing the market are doomed to fail.

2 What information does the market use to determine prices? The weak form of the efficient market hypothesis says that the market uses the history of prices and is therefore efficient with respect to these past prices. This implies that security selection based on patterns of past share price movements is no better than random selection.

3 The semi-strong form states that the market uses all publicly available information in setting prices.

4 Strong form efficiency states that the market uses all of the information that anybody knows about equities, even inside information.

5 Much evidence from different financial markets supports weak form and semi-strong form efficiency but not strong form efficiency.

6 Behavioural finance states that the market is not efficient. Adherents argue that:

(a) Investors are not rational.

(b) Deviations from rationality are similar across investors.

(c) Arbitrage, being costly, will not eliminate inefficiencies.

7 Behaviourists point to many studies – including those showing that small company shares outperform large company shares, value stocks outperform growth stocks, and share prices adjust slowly to earnings surprises – as empirical confirmation of their beliefs.

Questions and Problems

CONCEPT

1 **Financing Decisions and Firm Value** What are the three ways a firm can create value from financing opportunities? Provide an example to illustrate each way.

2 **Efficient Capital Markets** What are the three conditions under which Fama (1970) argues markets may be efficient? Describe these in detail and provide a practical example illustrating each condition in practice. What are the three categories of market efficiency identified by Fama (1991)?

3 **Efficient Market Hypothesis** Can you describe the concept of the efficient market hypothesis and its implications for investors? Outline the three levels of market efficiency and discuss their characteristics in terms of profit-making opportunities. Show your response with an illustration.

4 **Efficient Market Hypothesis: The Evidence** Suppose XYZ plc announced this morning that it had missed all its company's net-zero targets. At the end of the day, the firm's share price is up 3 per cent from the opening price. Is this evidence against the efficient market hypothesis? Explain.

5 **Behavioural Finance** In recent years, a new interpretation of market behaviour has emerged. Explain this theory and review what it says about Shleifer's three conditions of market efficiency. Compare and contrast both theories. In your opinion, which is the most reflective of market behaviour? Explain.

6 **Empirical Challenges to Market Efficiency** Discuss some of the anomalies to market efficiency that have been detected in academic research. Taken together, do these anomalies provide concrete evidence that the market is inefficient? Why, or why not? Explain.

7 **Behavioural Biases in Corporate Finance** Review two cognitive biases corporate managers may exhibit. Use an example to illustrate their impact on firm value.

8 **Implications for Corporate Finance** What does efficient market theory and behavioural finance imply for corporate decision-making? Provide three examples of how each theory may affect managerial behaviour. In your opinion are the financial markets efficient? Explain.

REGULAR

9 **Efficient Market Hypothesis: What Does It Imply?** Which of the following statements are true about the efficient market hypothesis?

(a) It implies perfect forecasting ability.
(b) It implies that prices reflect all available information.
(c) It implies an irrational market.
(d) It implies that prices do not fluctuate.
(e) It results from keen competition among investors.

10 **Technical Trading** 'Every day I check the price patterns from the day before to identify the shares I wish to trade that day.' What do the efficient markets hypothesis and behavioural finance hypothesis say about this statement? Which explanation do you believe as being most valid?

11 **Investment Gurus** In every market crash, some investors can earn significantly positive returns. How can you explain this using the efficient markets hypothesis and behavioural finance theory?

12 **Competitive Product Markets** Assume that markets are efficient, and that investment firms have decided to retire all portfolio managers and financial analysts, letting random choice via a computer determine their security selection process. What mistake is implicit in this action?

13 **Corporate Insider Trading** The cumulative abnormal returns pattern for British insider trading (Figure 13.7) suggests that executives have private information that they exploit to their advantage. Is there a behavioural interpretation for the pattern? Does this violate any of the three forms of market efficiency? Explain.

14 **Investor Sentiment** Some people believe that, following the European Consumer Confidence Index (see chart below) allows you to predict future market movements. The index was consistently negative between 1985 and 2023. Look at the stock market indices of any European country for the same period. Do you think this is a good indicator? Explain.

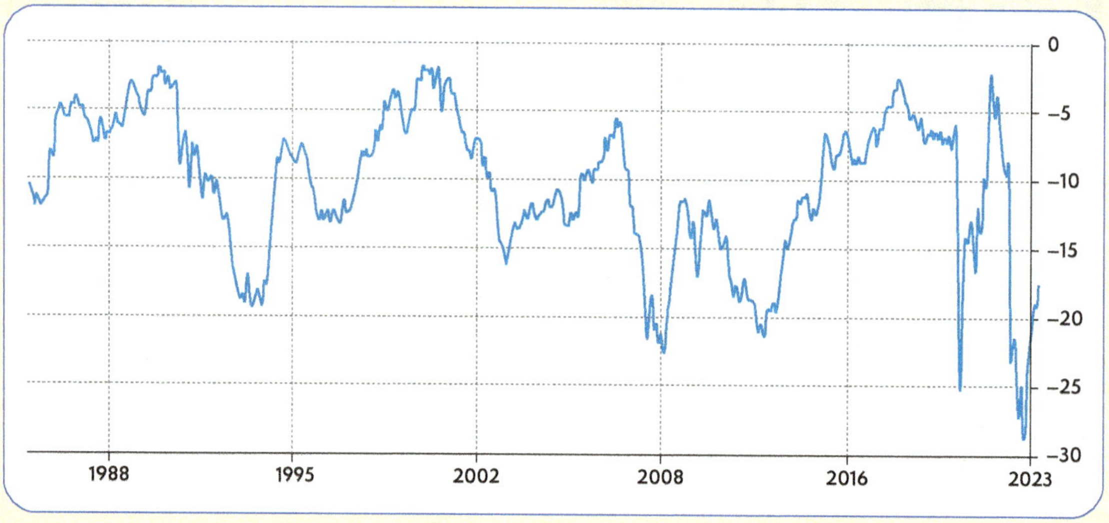

15 **Efficient Markets and Financial Statements** All publicly listed European companies follow International Accounting Standards. This means that financial statements are based largely on market values instead of historical cost measures. Assuming the market is semi-strong form efficient, does this mean financial statements can be used to make a profit from trading on information contained in them? Explain.

16 **Efficient Markets Hypothesis: New Information** Kasetsart Agriculture, a Thai agricultural technology research firm, announced this morning that it has hired the world's most knowledgeable and prolific agriculture researchers. Before today Kasetsart's equity had been selling for 100 baht. Assume that no other information is received over the next week and the Thai stock market as a whole does not move.

(a) What do you expect will happen to Kasetsart's share price?

(b) Consider the following scenarios:

(i) The share price jumps to 118 baht on the day of the announcement. In subsequent days it floats up to 123 baht, then falls back to 116 baht.

(ii) The share price jumps to 116 baht and remains at that level.

(iii) The share price gradually climbs to 116 baht over the next week.

Which scenario(s) indicate market efficiency? Which do not? Why? Provide a behavioural interpretation for each scenario.

17 **Behavioural Finance: Bitcoin** Do you think the bitcoin price will be more or less efficient than emerging market stock prices? Do you think it will be more or less sensitive to market sentiment? Explain.

18 **Efficient Markets Hypothesis: Founder Death** When the 56-year-old founder of Turkish firm Gulf Oil and Minerals died of a heart attack, its share price immediately jumped from 18.00 lira a share to 20.25 lira, a 12.5 per cent increase. This is evidence of market inefficiency because an efficient stock market would have anticipated his death and adjusted the price beforehand. Assume that no other information is received and the stock market as a whole does not move. Is this statement about market efficiency true or false? Explain.

19 **Efficient Markets Hypothesis: Insider Information** Newtech GmbH is going to adopt a new chip-testing device that can greatly improve its production efficiency. Do you think the lead engineer can profit from purchasing the firm's shares before the news release about the device? After reading the announcement in *Spiegel*, should you be able to earn an abnormal return from purchasing the equity if the market is efficient?

20 **Efficient Markets Hypothesis: Inventory Accounting** TransTrust NV has changed how it accounts for inventory. Taxes are unaffected, although the resulting earnings report released is 20 per cent higher than it would have been under the old accounting system. There is no other surprise in the earnings report, and the change in the accounting treatment was publicly announced. If the market is efficient, will the share price be higher when the market learns that the reported earnings are higher?

21 **Efficient Markets Hypothesis and Stock Picking Performance** The Durkin Investing Agency has been the best stock picker in the country for the past two years. Before this rise to fame occurred, the Durkin newsletter had 200 subscribers. Those subscribers beat the market consistently, earning substantially higher returns after adjustment for risk and transaction costs. Subscriptions have sky-rocketed to 10,000. Now, when the Durkin Investing Agency recommends an equity, the price instantly rises several points. The subscribers currently earn only a normal return when they buy recommended shares because the price rises before anybody can act on the information. Briefly explain this phenomenon. Is Durkin's ability to pick winners consistent with market efficiency?

22 **Efficient Markets Hypothesis and Firm Performance** Your broker commented that well-managed firms are better investments than poorly managed firms. As evidence he cited a recent study examining 100 small manufacturing firms that, eight years earlier, had been listed in an industry magazine as the best-managed small manufacturers in the country. In the ensuing eight years, the 100 firms listed have not earned more than the normal market return. Your broker continued to say that if the firms were well managed, they should have produced better than average returns. If the market is efficient, do you agree with him?

23 **Efficient Markets Hypothesis: Investment Gurus** A famous economist just announced in the *Financial Times* his findings that the recession is over and the economy is again entering an expansion. Assume market efficiency. Can you profit from investing in the stock market after you read this announcement? Assume behavioural finance is true. What do you think will happen in the stock market and why?

24 **Efficient Markets Hypothesis: Strong Form** Suppose the market is strong form efficient. Can you expect to earn excess returns if you make trades based on:

(a) An analyst's forecasts about future company earnings

(b) Rumours about the takeover of a firm

(c) A company's announcement of a successful prototype launch?

25 **Efficient Markets Hypothesis and Macroeconomic Variables** Imagine that a particular macroeconomic variable that influences your firm's net earnings is positively serially correlated. Assume market efficiency. Would you expect price changes in your shares to be serially correlated? Why, or why not?

26 **Behavioural Finance: Fund Performance** A global publication has identified a fund manager as consistently outperforming the market over the past five years. An analyst argues that the identification of this manager will lead investors to put more cash into the manager's fund and this money will be used to carry out more detailed analysis. This will in turn lead to further excess performance. Would such an argument be consistent with market efficiency or behavioural finance? Explain.

27 **Efficient Markets Hypothesis: Bad News** Assume markets are efficient. During a trading day, British Golf plc announces it has lost a contract for a large golfing project that, prior to the news, it was widely believed to have secured. If the market is efficient, how should the stock price react to this information if no additional information is released?

28 **Efficient Markets Hypothesis: Mining Discoveries** Prospectors plc is a publicly traded gold-prospecting company with operations in northern Tanzania. Although the firm's searches for gold usually fail, the prospectors occasionally find a rich vein of ore. What pattern would you expect to observe for Prospectors' cumulative abnormal returns if the market is efficient?

29 **Stock Market Movements** Some people argue that the efficient market hypothesis cannot explain the 2018 global stock market falls. Provide an explanation using the efficient market hypothesis and behavioural finance.

30 **Shareholder Activism** Many financial institutions use the media to drive shareholder activism strategies so that pressure is maximized on the target firm managers. Is this evidence that institutional shareholders believe in efficient markets, behavioural finance, or both? What would happen to market efficiency if all investors follow a passive buy-and-hold investment strategy? Explain.

31 **Initial Public Offerings** Research has shown that managers of newly listed firms rein in their capital expenditure plans if the market share price performance is not particularly strong around the IPO date. This is regularly put down to 'poor market sentiment'. Is this evidence that corporate managers believe in efficient markets, behavioural finance, or both? Explain.

32 **Insider Trading** When corporate executives trade the shares of their own company, the share price normally responds in a correlated way (i.e. share price increases after buy transactions and share price falls after sale transactions). Is this evidence of efficient markets, behavioural finance, or both? Explain.

CHALLENGE

33 **Cumulative Abnormal Returns** National Airlines Group, Air France-KLM and Lufthansa announced purchases of planes on 18 July (18/7), 12 February (12/2) and 7 October (7/10), respectively. Given the following information, calculate the cumulative abnormal return (CAR) for these equities as a group. Graph the result and provide an explanation. All of the stocks have a beta of 1 and no other announcements are made.

National Airlines Group			Air France-KLM			Lufthansa		
Date	Market Return	Company Return	Date	Market Return	Company Return	Date	Market Return	Company Return
12/7	−0.3	−0.5	8/2	−0.9	−1.1	1/10	0.5	0.3
13/7	0.0	0.2	9/2	−1.0	−1.1	2/10	0.4	0.6
16/7	0.5	0.7	10/2	0.4	0.2	3/10	1.1	1.1
17/7	−0.5	−0.3	11/2	0.6	0.8	6/10	0.1	−0.3
18/7	−2.2	1.1	12/2	−0.3	−0.1	7/10	−2.2	−0.3
19/7	−0.9	−0.7	15/2	1.1	1.2	8/10	0.5	0.5
20/7	−1.0	−1.1	16/2	0.5	0.5	9/10	−0.3	−0.2
23/7	0.7	0.5	17/2	−0.3	−0.2	10/10	0.3	0.1
24/7	0.2	0.1	18/2	0.3	0.2	13/10	0.0	−0.1

34 Cumulative Abnormal Returns and Market Efficiency The following diagram shows the cumulative abnormal returns (CAR) for 386 oil exploration companies announcing oil discoveries between 1950 and 1980. Month 0 in the diagram is the announcement month. Assume that no other information is received and the equity market as a whole does not move. Is the diagram consistent with market efficiency? Why, or why not?

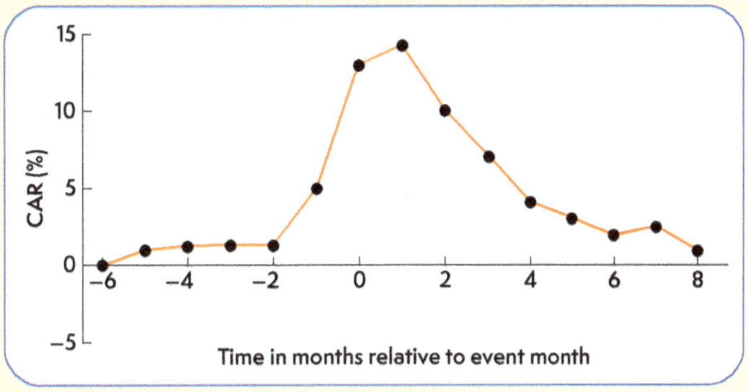

35 CAR Comparisons The diagrams below present the results of four cumulative abnormal returns (CAR) studies. Indicate whether the results of each study support, reject or are inconclusive about the semi-strong form of the efficient market hypothesis. In each figure time 0 is the date of an event.

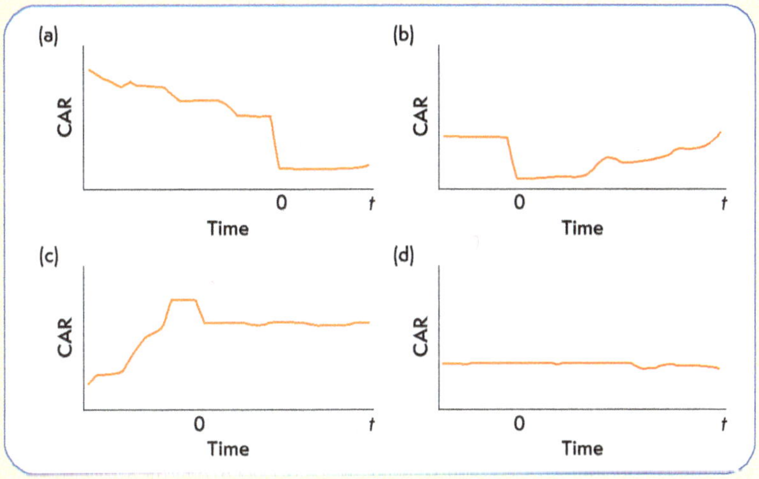

36 Negative Cumulative Abnormal Returns A study analysed the behaviour of the equity prices of firms that had lost monopoly cases. Included in the diagram below are all firms that lost the initial court decision, even if the decision was later overturned on appeal. The event at time 0 is the initial, pre-appeal court decision. Assume no other information was released, aside from that disclosed in the initial trial. The stock prices all have a beta of 1. Is the diagram consistent with market efficiency? Why, or why not?

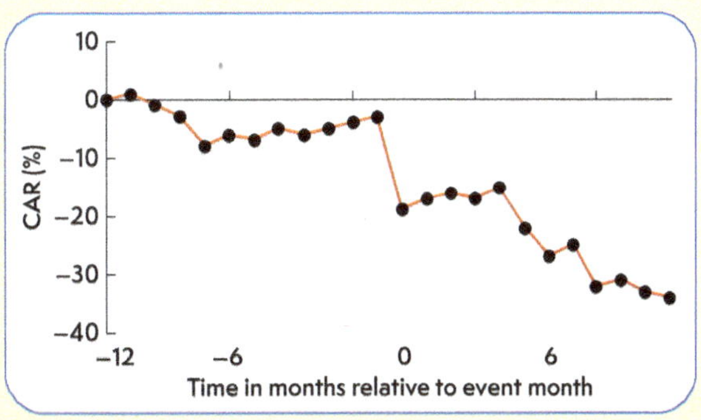

Exam Question (45 minutes)

1 Explain what is meant by efficient market theory and discuss some of its implications for corporate financial management. **(25 marks)**

2 *'Even in an efficient market it is still valid to seek out a "favourable" rate of return from an equity investment.'* Consider the argument that, in an efficient market, 'one security is as good as any other'. **(25 marks)**

3 Explain how behavioural finance can provide insights to corporate financial managers. **(25 marks)**

4 What strategies can financial managers follow if they believe behavioural finance is a valid hypothesis? **(25 marks)**

Total Marks: 100

Mini Case

Your Retirement Account at West Coast Yachts

You have been at your job for West Coast Yachts for a week now and have decided you need to sign up for the company's retirement plan. Even after your discussion with Sarah Brown, the Skandla Financial Services representative, you are still unsure which investment option you should choose. Recall that the options available to you are owning shares of West Coast Yachts, the Skandla Market Index Fund, the Skandla Large Company Equity Fund, the Skandla Small-Cap Fund, the Skandla Bond Fund and the Skandla Money Market Fund. You have decided that you should invest in a diversified portfolio, with 70 per cent of your investment in equity, 25 per cent in bonds and 5 per cent in the money market fund. You have also decided to focus your equity investment on large-cap company shares, but you are debating whether to select the Market Index Fund or the Large-Company Equity Fund.

In thinking it over, you understand the basic difference in the two funds. One is a purely passive fund that replicates a widely followed large-cap index, the FTSE 100, and has low fees. The other is actively managed with the intention that the skill of the portfolio manager will result in improved performance relative to an index. Fees are higher in the latter fund. You are just not certain which way to go, so you ask Dan Ervin, who works in the company's finance area, for advice.

After discussing your concerns, Dan gives you some information comparing the performance of equity mutual funds and the FTSE 100 Index Fund. The FTSE 100 Index Fund replicates the FTSE 100, and its return is only negligibly different from the Index itself. Fees are very low. As a result, the FTSE 100 Index Fund is essentially identical to the Skandla Market Index Fund offered in the retirement plan, but it has been in existence for much longer, so you can study its track record for over two decades. Dan tells you that 80 per cent of actively managed investment funds underperform a passive index fund, like the Skandla Market Index Fund.

1 What implications do you draw from Dan's information for mutual fund investors?

2 Is Dan's comment consistent or inconsistent with market efficiency? Explain carefully.

3 What investment decision would you make for the equity portion of your retirement account? Why?

Practical Case Study

In many countries, regulators have moved to ban an activity called equity short-selling. In order to sell equity short, a trader would open an account with a broker, borrow shares from existing shareholders for a fee and promise to give them back at some point in the future. Short-selling is normally used as an effective hedging tool. However, it can also be used to speculate against future falls in prices.

The practice of short selling came under intense scrutiny when it was blamed for the collapsing share prices of banks in 2008. Regulators argued that hedge funds were contributing to the collapse in share prices by irrationally forcing them down below their true level. As bank share prices imploded, there was clear evidence that many banks had very high levels of short-selling. As a result, the British government imposed a short-selling ban from 18 September 2008 until 16 January 2009. Other countries imposed similar bans.

If share prices were forced down by a small number of hedge funds (and their short-selling followers) purely because of speculative activity, it would be clear evidence against the efficient market hypothesis.

1 Visit Yahoo! Finance and download the share prices of five British banks for the dates 1 August 2008 to 31 January 2009. Also download the FTSE 100 Index for the same period.
2 Track each bank's share price before the ban, during the ban and after the ban. Do the share price movements support the view that the market was irrationally depressed because of speculative activity?
3 Carry out your own investigation of short-selling in Europe. How did other European governments deal with the short-selling controversy?
4 Write a report about the short-selling controversy in the context of the efficient markets hypothesis and behavioural finance. What does it say about the validity (if at all) of either theory?

Relevant Accounting Standards

If there is one area where International Financial Reporting Standards have faced a lot of criticism, it is with respect to their effect on market prices. Because financial assets and liabilities have to be reported at fair or market value, volatility in the stock markets inevitably leads to volatility in the accounting statements. The main standard is IAS 39 *Financial Instruments: Recognition and Measurement.* IAS 39 provides definitions for different types of financial securities and how to measure their value. Another is FRS 7 *Financial Instruments: Disclosure.* Given their hypothesized impact on accounting statements and the corresponding reinforced share price revisions, it is very likely that both standards will change over the next few years. Keep updated by visiting the IASPlus website: www.iasplus.com.

References

Barber, B. and T. Odean (1999) 'The Courage of Misguided Convictions', *Financial Analysts Journal,* Vol. 56, No. 6, 41–55.

Berk, J.B. and J.H. van Binsbergen (2015) 'Measuring Skill in the Mutual Fund Industry', *Journal of Financial Economics,* Vol. 118, No. 1, 1–20.

Blake, D., T. Caulfield, C. Ioannidis and I. Tonks (2017) 'New Evidence on Mutual Fund Performance: A Comparison of Alternative Bootstrap Methods', *Journal of Financial and Quantitative Analysis,* Vol. 52, No. 3, 1279–1299.

Dargenidou, C., I. Tonks and F. Tsoligkas (2018) 'Insider Trading and the Post-earnings Announcement Drift', *Journal of Business Finance & Accounting,* Vol. 45, No. 3–4, 482–508.

Faccio, M., M.I. Marchica and R. Mura (2016) 'CEO Gender, Corporate Risk-taking, and the Efficiency of Capital Allocation', *Journal of Corporate Finance,* Vol. 39, 193–209.

Fama, E.F. (1970) 'Efficient Capital Markets: A Review of Theory and Empirical Work', *Journal of Finance,* Vol. 25, No. 2, 383–417.

Fama, E.F. (1991) 'Efficient Capital Markets: II', *Journal of Finance,* Vol. 46, 1575–1617.

Fama, E.F. and K.R. French (1996) 'Multifactor Explanations of Asset Pricing Anomalies', *Journal of Finance,* Vol. 51, No. 1, 55–84.

Fama, E.F. and K.R. French (1998) 'Value versus Growth: The International Evidence', *Journal of Finance,* Vol. 53, 1975–1999.

Froot, K.A. and E.M. Dabora (1999) 'How Are Stock Prices Affected by the Location of Trade?', *Journal of Financial Economics,* Vol. 53, No. 2, 189–216.

Gerard, X. (2012) 'Information Uncertainty and the Post-earnings Announcement Drift in Europe', *Financial Analysts Journal,* Vol. 68, No. 2, 51–69.

Hilary, G., C. Hsu, B. Segal and R. Wang (2016) 'The Bright Side of Managerial Over-optimism', *Journal of Accounting and Economics,* Vol. 62, No. 1, 46–64.

Hirshleifer, D., S.S. Lim and S.H. Teoh (2009) 'Driven to Distraction: Extraneous Events and Underreaction to Earnings News', *Journal of Finance,* Vol. 64, 2289–2325.

Hribar, P. and H. Yang (2016) 'CEO Overconfidence and Management Forecasting', *Contemporary Accounting Research,* Vol. 33, No. 1, 204–227.

Kolasinski, A. and X. Li (2010) 'Are Corporate Managers Savvy about their Stock Price? Evidence from Insider Trading after Earnings Announcements', *Journal of Accounting and Public Policy,* Vol. 29, 27–44.

Korteweg, A. and M. Sorensen (2017) 'Skill and Luck in Private Equity Performance', *Journal of Financial Economics,* Vol. 124, No. 3, 535–562.

Kothari, P., J. Shanken and R.G. Sloan (1995) 'Another Look at the Cross-section of Stock Returns', *Journal of Finance*, Vol. 50, No. 1, 185–224.

Lamont, O. and R. Thaler (2003) 'Can the Market Add and Subtract? Mispricing in Tech Stock Carve-outs', *Journal of Political Economy*, Vol. 111, No. 2, 227–268.

Lee, Y.J. (2012) 'The Effect of Quarterly Report Readability on Information Efficiency of Stock Prices', *Contemporary Accounting Research*, Vol. 29, 1137–1170.

Liang, L. (2003) 'Post-earnings Announcement Drift and Market Participants' Information Processing Biases', *Review of Accounting Studies*, Vol. 8, 321–345.

Malkiel, B.G. (2003) *A Random Walk Down Wall Street*, 8th edn. New York: Norton.

Martin, I. (2021) 'On the Autocorrelation of the Stock Market', *Journal of Financial Econometrics*, Vol. 19, No. 1, 39–52.

Martin, I.W. and S. Nagel (2022) 'Market Efficiency in the Age of Big Data', *Journal of Financial Economics*, Vol. 145, No. 1, 154–177.

Ng, J., T.O. Rusticus and R.S. Verdi (2008) 'Implications of Transaction Costs for the Post-earnings Announcement Drift', *Journal of Accounting Research*, Vol. 46, 661–696.

Otten, R. and D. Bams (2002) 'European Mutual Fund Performance', *European Financial Management Journal*, Vol. 8, 75–101.

Porras Prado, M., P.A. Saffi and J. Sturgess (2016) 'Ownership Structure, Limits to Arbitrage, and Stock Returns: Evidence from Equity Lending Markets', *Review of Financial Studies*, Vol. 29, No. 12, 3211–3244.

Shleifer, A. (2000) *Inefficient Markets: An Introduction to Behavioural Finance*. Oxford: Oxford University Press.

Zaremba, A., M. Umutlu and A. Maydybura (2020) 'Where Have the Profits Gone? Market Efficiency and the Disappearing Equity Anomalies in Country and Industry Returns', *Journal of Banking & Finance*, Vol. 121, 105966.

Additional Reading

In recent years, the debate about market efficiency has exploded with the arrival of a new and very intuitive portfolio of research findings in the behavioural finance paradigm. If you are interested in understanding cognitive biases, the best starting point is *Thinking, Fast and Slow* by Daniel Kahneman. Kahneman won the Nobel Prize in Economics because of his research on cognitive biases.

Kahneman, D. (2011) *Thinking, Fast and Slow*. New York: Farrar, Straus and Giroux.

For a review of efficient markets research, check out the following papers:

1 Banz, R.W. (1981) 'The Relationship between Return and Market Value of Common Stocks', *Journal of Financial Economics*, Vol. 9, No. 1, 3–18.

2 Bennedsen, M., F. Pérez-González and D. Wolfenzon (2020) 'Do CEOs Matter? Evidence from Hospitalization Events', *Journal of Finance*, Vol. 75 No. 4, 1877–1911.

3 Borges, M.R. (2010) 'Efficient Market Hypothesis in European Stock Markets', *European Journal of Finance*, Vol. 16, No. 7, 711–726.

4 Degutis, A. and L. Novickyte. (2014) 'The Efficient Market Hypothesis: A Critical Review of Literature and Methodology', *Ekonomika*, Vol. 93, No. 2, 7–23.

5 Dong, X., Y. Li, D. Rapach and G. Zhou (2021) 'Anomalies and the Expected Market Return', Baruch College Zicklin School of Business Research Paper (2020–02), 02.

6 Easterday, K. (2005) 'The Declining January Effect? An Examination of Monthly Returns for Firms Trading on NYSE, AMEX, and NASDAQ', unpublished paper, University of Cincinnati.

7 Fama, E.F. and K.R. French (2021) 'Luck versus Skill in the Cross-section of Mutual Fund Returns', in J.H. Cochrane and T.J. Moskowitz (eds) *The Fama Portfolio*. Chicago, IL: University of Chicago Press.

8 Hartzmark, S.M. and D.H. Solomon (2022) 'Reconsidering Returns', *Review of Financial Studies*, Vol. 35, No. 1, 343–393.

9 Kirilenko, A., A.S. Kyle, M. Samadi and T. Tuzun (2017) 'The Flash Crash: High-frequency Trading in an Electronic Market', *Journal of Finance*, Vol. 72, No. 3, 967–998.

10 Reinganum, M.R. (1981) 'Misspecification of Capital Asset Pricing: Empirical Anomalies Based on Earnings Yields and Market Values', *Journal of Financial Economics*, Vol. 9, 19–46.

For a review of behavioural finance research, see the following:

11 Baker, M. and J. Wurgler (2011) 'Behavioral Corporate Finance: An Updated Survey', NBER Working Paper.

12 Baker, H.K., G. Filbeck and V. Ricciardi, V. (2017) 'How Behavioural Biases Affect Finance Professionals', *European Financial Review*, 2 January, 25–29.

13 Barberis, N. and R. Thaler (2003) 'A Survey of Behavioural Finance', in G. Constantinides, M. Harris and R. Stultz (eds), *The Handbook of the Economics of Finance*. Amsterdam: North Holland.

14 Forbes, W. (2009) *Behavioural Finance*. Chichester: John Wiley & Sons.

15 Muradoglu, G. and N. Harvey (2012) 'Behavioural Finance: The Role of Psychological Factors in Financial Decisions', *Review of Behavioural Finance*, Vol. 4, No. 2, 68–80.

16 Viale, R., S. Mousavi, B. Alemanni and U. Filotto (eds) (2018) *The Behavioural Finance Revolution: A New Approach to Financial Policies and Regulations*. Edward Elgar Publishing.

Endnotes

1 For the purposes of this text, the random walk can be considered synonymous with weak form efficiency. Technically, the random walk is a slightly more restrictive hypothesis because it assumes that share price returns are identically distributed through time. The random walk model is normally used to predict price movements, not explain them (as the CAPM does). Two main assumptions of investor behaviour are required for it to hold. First, investors are rational and their predictions of what will happen in the future are neither optimistic nor pessimistic – that is, they are unbiased. The other assumption is that price changes are caused by the arrival of new information only. Given that new information arrives randomly, prices must evolve randomly, hence the term random walk.

2 We can also measure the abnormal return by using the market model. In this case the abnormal return is:

$$AR = R - (\alpha + \beta R_M)$$

3 For example, see Barber and Odean (1999).

4 Taken from Table III of Fama and French (1998).

5 For example, see Kothari, Shanken and Sloan (1995), and Fama and French (1996).

PART 4

Long-term Financing

This book focuses primarily on applying theoretical foundations to practical valuation, investment and strategic financial decisions. However, when companies raise funds for operations, there is less consistency, theory or structure to how they do this. Financing methods vary across countries and regions due to different economic development and cultural norms, with participants ranging from large banks to informal family funding. Part 4 discusses commonalities in long-term financing over four chapters. Chapter 14 considers the types of securities used for long-term financing. Chapters 15 and 16 cover the challenges and characteristics of equity and debt financing. Finally, Chapter 17 explores leasing as an alternative financing vehicle that can substitute for debt in a company's capital structure.

Chapter 14
Long-term Financing: An Introduction

Learning Objectives

After reading this chapter you should be able to:

LO1 Be familiar with the fundamental concepts and characteristics of ordinary shares, corporate long-term debt and preference shares

LO2 Explain the different patterns of financing, and their implications for a company's capital structure.

LO3 Examine the hierarchies in long-term financing, and their impact on a company's financial flexibility and risk profile.

Companies that require cash to fund new investments have a variety of options to consider. They can take on more debt via bank loans or through the issue of bonds in the public markets. Alternatively, they can give up part ownership and issue new equity. Companies will not go through just one funding round, but many, and the choice of debt or equity-type instruments will change over time. Over the last few years, bank credit has become a lot more scarce, and this has led to a growth in public issues as well as alternative financing models such as crowdfunding (an informal source of financing for small start-up companies) and peer-to-peer lending platforms. In the first quarter of 2023, there were 299 global equity issues raising $21.5 billion, the biggest of which was Abu Dhabi energy company, ADNOC Gas, for $2.5 billion. In parallel, global debt markets raised $8.3 trillion (both corporate and government debt) in the whole of 2022.

What are the forms of long-term financing available to companies? This chapter introduces the basic sources of long-term financing: ordinary shares, preference shares and long-term debt. Subsequent chapters address the optimal mix of these sources. We will also discuss how companies have financed themselves in recent years.

Source: M4OS Photos/Alamy Stock Photo

14.1 Ordinary Shares: The Basics

Chapter 5
Page 122

Under International Financial Reporting Standards (IFRS), the term ordinary share has no precise meaning. It is usually applied to equity (see Chapter 5, Sections 5.4 – 5.8 on how to value equities) that has no special preference in either dividends or bankruptcy. Another name for ordinary shares is *common stock*, which is more common in the USA. Let us take a typical firm as an example.

Below is a description of the equity share capital of the energy firm ABB for the year ending 31 December 2022. ABB has equity listed on the SIX Swiss Exchange in Zurich, the NASDAQ OMX in Stockholm and the NYSE in New York.

Table 14.1 ABB Statement of Equity ($ million), Year End 31 December 2022

Stockholders' Equity:	$
Common stock, CHF 0.12 par value (1,965 million issued shares at 31 December 2022)	171
Additional paid-in capital	141
Retained earnings	20,082
Accumulated other comprehensive loss	(4,556)
Treasury stock, at cost (100 million shares at 31 December 2022)	(3,061)
Total ABB stockholders' equity	**12,777**

Source: ABB 2022 Financial Report.

Par and No-par Shares

Owners of ordinary shares are referred to as *shareholders* or *stockholders*. They receive share certificates for the *shares* they own. There is usually a stated value on each share certificate called the *par value, face value, stated value* or *nominal value*, which is similar in concept to the face value of a bond. Par value comes from a time when stock markets were not well regulated but is now no longer needed. Many shares have no par value, and from Table 14.1, ABB has a par value of 0.12 Swiss francs.

The total par value is the number of shares issued multiplied by the par value of each share, and is sometimes referred to as the *dedicated* or *called-up capital* of a corporation.

Authorized versus Outstanding Shares

Ordinary shares are the fundamental ownership units of the corporation. The articles of incorporation of a new company must state the number of ordinary shares the corporation is authorized to issue.

The board of directors of the corporation, after an agreement from the shareholders (in unitary board systems) or the supervisory board (in two-tier board systems), can amend the articles of incorporation to increase the number of shares authorized; there is no limit to the number of shares that can be authorized.[1] In 2022, ABB had issued 1,965 million shares. Although there are no legal limits to authorizing shares of equity, some practical considerations may exist:

- Some governments impose taxes based on the number of authorized shares.
- Authorizing a large number of shares may create concern on the part of investors because authorized shares can be issued later *with* the approval of the board of directors but *without* a vote of the shareholders or supervisory board.

Additional paid-in capital usually refers to amounts of directly contributed equity capital in excess of the par value.

Example 14.1

Par Value and Additional Paid-in Capital

Suppose 100 shares of equity have a par value of £2 each and are sold to shareholders for £10 per share. The additional paid-in capital would be (£10 – £2) × 100 = £8 × 100 = £800, and the total par value would be £2 × 100 = £200. What difference does it make if the total capital contribution is reported as par value or additional paid-in capital?

About the only difference is that the par value is locked in and cannot be distributed to shareholders except upon the liquidation of the corporation.

The additional paid-in capital of ABB is $56 million. This figure indicates that the price of new shares issued by ABB has exceeded the par value and the difference has been entered as *additional paid-in capital.*

Retained Earnings

In 2022, ABB paid out 58.76 per cent of its net income as dividends. The rest of the net income was retained in the business and is called retained earnings. Year on year, a company's retained earnings will accumulate, and if earnings in the past have been positive, this can be a substantial amount. For ABB, the cumulative retained earnings (since original incorporation) by the end of 2022 were $20,082 million.

The sum of the equity components, or the total equity, can be referred to as the firm's book value. The book value represents the amount contributed directly and indirectly to the corporation by equity investors.

Example 14.2

Equity Accounting

Suppose Louest Rouge plc was formed in 1910 and 10,000 shares of equity issued with each share valued at £1 par value. Because the shares were sold for £1, the first balance sheet showed a zero amount for capital surplus. By 2024, the company had become very profitable and retained profits of £100,000. The shareholders' equity of Louest Rouge in 2024 is as follows:

Louest Rouge plc Equity Accounts 1 January 2024	
Ordinary shares; par £1; 10,000 shares outstanding	£10,000
Additional paid-in capital	0
Retained earnings	100,000
Total shareholders' equity	£110,000

$$\text{Book value per share} = \frac{£110{,}000}{10{,}000} = £11$$

Suppose the company has profitable investment opportunities and decides to sell 10,000 shares of new equity. The current market price is £20 per share. The effect of the sale of shares on the balance sheet at the end of the year will be:

Louest Rouge plc Equity Accounts 31 December 2024	
Ordinary shares, £1 par, 20,000 shares outstanding	£20,000
Additional paid-in capital (£20 – £1) × 10,000 shares	190,000
Retained earnings	100,000
Total shareholders' equity	£310,000

$$\text{Book value per share} = \frac{£310{,}000}{20{,}000} = £15.5$$

What happened?

1. Because 10,000 shares of new equity were issued with a par value of £1, the par value rose £10,000.
2. The total amount raised by the new issue was £20 × 10,000 = £200,000 and £190,000 was entered into additional paid-in capital.
3. The book value per share increased because the market price of the new equity was higher than the book value of the old equity.

Market Value and Book Value

The book value of ABB for the year ending 31 December 2022 was $12,777 million. The company had repurchased approximately 100 million shares. The repurchased shares are called *treasury stock* or *treasury shares*. The book value per share was equal to:

$$\frac{\text{Total equity}}{\text{Shares outstanding}} = \frac{\$13,077,000,000}{(1,965,000,000 - 100,000,000)} = \$7.01$$

Since ABB is a large publicly owned company and listed in Zurich, Stockholm and New York, thousands of shares change hands every day throughout the world. In May 2023, the share price of ABB equity was $36.73 on the NYSE. Using the dollar valuation, the market price ($36.73) was substantially higher than the book value ($7.01). However, market valuations are volatile and over the previous 52 weeks, ABB's share price fluctuated between $24.16 and $36.98.

Shareholders' Rights

The value of a share of equity in a corporation is directly related to the general rights of shareholders. In addition to the right to vote for directors, shareholders usually have the following rights:

- The right to share proportionally in dividends paid.
- The right to share proportionally in assets remaining after liabilities have been paid in a liquidation.
- The right to vote on matters of great importance to shareholders, such as a merger, usually decided at the annual meeting or a special meeting.
- The right to share proportionally in any new equity sold. This is called the *pre-emptive right* and will be discussed in detail in later chapters.

Dividends

A distinctive feature of corporations is that they issue shares of equity and are authorized by law to pay dividends to the holders of those shares. **Dividends** paid to shareholders represent a return on the capital directly or indirectly contributed to the corporation by the shareholders. The payment of dividends occurs at the discretion of the board of directors.

Here are some important characteristics of dividends:

- Unless a dividend is declared by the board of directors of a corporation, it is not a liability of the corporation. A corporation cannot *default* on an undeclared dividend. As a consequence, corporations cannot become *bankrupt* because of non-payment of dividends. The amount of the dividend – and even whether or not it is paid – is a decision based on the business judgement of the board of directors.
- The payment of dividends by the corporation is not a business expense. Dividends are not deductible for corporate tax purposes. In short, dividends are paid out of the after-tax profits of the corporation.
- Dividends received by individual shareholders are for the most part considered ordinary income by the tax authorities, and are fully or partially taxable depending on the specific tax rules of the country in which the dividends are paid. Corporations that own shares in other corporations are generally permitted to exclude some component of the amounts they receive as dividends. In other words, they are taxed only on a certain percentage of the dividends.

Multiple Share Classes

Some firms issue more than one class of ordinary shares. The classes are usually created with unequal voting rights. All Chinese firms have two classes of equity, A and B class shares. A class shares can generally be owned only by Chinese nationals, whereas B class shares can be held by anyone. The number of A class shares is almost always more than the number of B class shares, ensuring that Chinese firms are ultimately controlled by Chinese nationals. An excellent example of an individual firm with dual-class shares is Alphabet, the holding company of Google. Alphabet has two classes of equity, A and B. Class A shares are held by the public, and each share has one vote. Class B shares are held by company insiders, and each class B share has 10 votes. As a result, Alphabet's founders and management control the company.

14.2 Corporate Long-term Debt: The Basics

Chapter 5
Page 117
Chapter 16
Page 433

Securities issued by corporations may be classified roughly as *equity* securities and *debt* securities. The distinction between equity and debt is fundamental to much of the modern theory and practice of corporate finance (see Chapter 16 for further discussion).

At its crudest level, debt represents something that must be repaid; it is the result of borrowing money (in Chapter 5, Sections 5.1 – 5.3 you are shown how to value bonds). When corporations borrow, they promise to make regularly scheduled interest payments and to repay the original amount borrowed (that is, the *principal*). The person or firm making the loan is called a *creditor* or *lender*.

Interest versus Dividends

The corporation borrowing the money is called a *debtor* or *borrower*. The amount owed to the creditor is a liability of the corporation; however, it is a liability of limited value. The corporation can legally default at any time on its debt, and this can be a valuable option. The creditors benefit if the assets have a value higher than the value of the liability, but this would happen only if management were foolish. On the other hand, the corporation and the equity investors benefit if the value of the assets is less than the value of the liabilities because equity investors can walk away from the liabilities and default on their payment.

From a financial point of view, the main differences between debt and equity are as follows:

- Debt is not an ownership interest in the firm. Creditors do not usually have voting power. The device used by creditors to protect themselves is the loan contract (that is, the *indenture*).
- The corporation's payment of interest on debt is considered a cost of doing business and is fully tax deductible. Thus interest expense is paid out to creditors before the corporate tax liability is computed. Dividends on ordinary and preference shares are paid to shareholders after the tax liability has been determined. Dividends are considered a return to shareholders on their contributed capital. Because interest expense can be used to reduce taxes, governments provide a direct tax subsidy on the use of debt when compared to equity. This point is discussed in detail in Chapters 15 and 16.
- Unpaid debt is a liability of the firm. If it is not paid, the creditors can legally claim the assets of the firm. This action may result in *liquidation* and *bankruptcy*. Thus, one of the costs of issuing debt is the possibility of *financial failure*, which does not arise when equity is issued.

Is It Debt or Equity?

Sometimes it is not clear whether a particular security is debt or equity. For example, suppose a 50-year bond is issued with interest payable solely from corporate income if, and only if, earned, and repayment is subordinate to all other debts of the business. Corporations are very adept at creating hybrid or compound securities that look like equity but are called *debt*. The distinction between debt and equity is important for tax purposes, and when corporations create a debt security that is really equity, they are trying to obtain the tax benefits of debt while eliminating its bankruptcy costs.

According to International Accounting Standard 32 (IAS 32), a debt instrument has a contractual obligation to deliver cash or another financial asset, whereas equity is a security that has a residual cash flow after all other liabilities have been paid. When accounting for hybrid or compound securities, the instrument should be disaggregated into its equity and debt components and recorded accordingly. So, for example, a debt instrument that can be converted into equity would have its value arising from the debt and equity components valued and recorded separately in the company's accounts.

Basic Features of Long-term Debt

Long-term corporate debt is usually denominated in multiples of 100 (e.g. £100,000 or €1,000), called the *principal* or *face value*. Long-term debt is a promise by the borrowing firm to repay the principal amount by a specific date, called the *maturity date*. Debt price is often expressed as a percentage of the par or face value. For instance, it might be said that Swedbank AB's debt is selling at 90, which means that a bond with a par value of SKr1,000 can be purchased for SKr900. In this case, the debt trades at a discount because the market price is less than the par value. Debt can also sell at a premium with respect to par value. The borrower using long-term debt generally pays interest at a rate expressed as a fraction of par value. Thus, at SKr1,000 par value, Swedbank's 7 per cent debt means that SKr70 of interest is paid to holders of the debt, usually in semi-annual instalments (for example, SKr35 on 30 June and 31 December). These payments are referred to as 'coupons', and the 7 per cent is called the *coupon rate.*

Different Types of Debt

Typical debt securities are called *bills, notes, debentures* or *bonds.* A debenture is an unsecured corporate debt, whereas a bond is secured by a mortgage on the corporate property. However, in common parlance, the word *bond* is used indiscriminately, and often refers to both secured and unsecured debt. A note usually refers to an unsecured debt with a maturity shorter than that of a debenture, perhaps under 10 years. A bill usually refers to a short-term debt instrument with a maturity less than a year. In the UK, government bonds are known as *gilts.*

Debentures and bonds are long-term debt or non-current liabilities. *Long-term debt* is any obligation that is payable more than one year from the date it was initially issued. Sometimes long-term debt is called *funded debt.* Debt that is due in less than one year is unfunded and is accounted for as a current liability. Some debt is perpetual and has no specific maturity. This type of debt is referred to as a *consol.*

Repayment

Long-term debt is typically repaid in regular amounts over the life of the debt. The payment of long-term debt by instalments is called *amortization.* At the end of the amortization, the entire indebtedness is said to be *extinguished.* Amortization is typically arranged by a *sinking fund.* Each year the corporation places money into a sinking fund, and the money is used to buy back the bonds.

Debt may be extinguished before maturity by a call. Historically, almost all publicly issued corporate long-term debt has been *callable.* These are debentures or bonds for which the firm has the right to pay a specific amount, the *call price,* to retire (extinguish) the debt before the stated maturity date. The call price is always higher than the par value of the debt. Debt that is callable at 105 is debt the firm can buy back from the holder at 105 per cent of the par value, such as £105 or €1,050 per debenture or bond. This will happen regardless of the actual market value of the debt. Call prices are always specified in the bond prospectus when the debt is initially issued.

Seniority

In general terms, seniority indicates preference in position over other lenders. Some debt is subordinated. In the event of default, holders of subordinated debt must give preference to other specified creditors. Usually, this means that the subordinated lenders will be paid off only after the specified creditors have been compensated. However, debt cannot be subordinated to equity, and this is discussed in more detail in Section 14.5.

Security

Security is a form of attachment to property; it provides that the property can be sold in the event of default to satisfy the debt for which security is given. A mortgage is used for security in tangible property – for instance, debt can be secured by mortgages on plant and equipment. Holders of such debt have a prior claim on the mortgaged assets in case of default. Debentures are not secured by a mortgage. Thus, if mortgaged property is sold in the event of default, debenture holders will obtain something only if the mortgage bondholders have been fully satisfied.

Indenture

The written agreement between the corporate debt issuer and the lender, setting forth maturity date, interest rate and all other terms, is called an *indenture.* We treat this in detail in later chapters. For now, we note that:

- The indenture completely describes the nature of the indebtedness.
- It lists all restrictions placed on the firm by the lenders. These restrictions are placed in *restrictive covenants.*

Some typical restrictive covenants are the following:

- Restrictions on further indebtedness
- A maximum on the dividends that can be paid
- A minimum level of working capital.

Real World Insight 14.1

Long-term Debt

The following table shows some of the many debt securities of Siemens AG in 2022 (in millions), listed in order of priority (highest first). LIBOR is the overnight rate British banks lend to one another.

Table 14.2 A Selection of Siemens AG Debt Securities

	30 September 2022	
(Interest/Issued/Maturity)	Currency Notional Amount (millions)	Carrying Amount (millions of €)
2.75%/2012/September 2025/GBP fixed-rate instruments	£ 350	355
3.75%/2012/September 2042/GBP fixed-rate instruments	£ 650	725
2.875%/2013/March 2028/EUR fixed-rate instruments	€ 1,000	998
3.5%/2013/March 2028/US $ fixed-rate instruments	US$ 100	101
0.375%/2018/September 2023/EUR fixed-rate instruments	€ 1,000	999
1.0%/2018/September 2027/EUR fixed-rate instruments	€ 750	676
1.375%/2018/September 2030/EUR fixed-rate instruments	€ 1,000	995
0.3%/2019/February 2024/EUR fixed-rate instruments	€ 750	724
0.9%/2019/February 2028/EUR fixed-rate instruments	€ 650	569
1.25%/2019/February 2031/EUR fixed-rate instruments	€ 800	665
1.75%/2019/February 2039/EUR fixed-rate instruments	€ 800	601
0.0%/2019/September 2024/EUR fixed-rate instruments	€ 500	47
0.125%/2019/September 2029/EUR fixed-rate instruments	€ 1,000	995
0.5%/2019/September 2034/EUR fixed-rate instruments	€ 1,000	992
3m EURIBOR + 0.7%/2019/December 2021/EUR floating-rate instrument	€ —	–
0.0%/2020/February 2023/EUR fixed-rate instruments	€ 1,250	1,251
0.0%/2020/February 2026/EUR fixed-rate instruments	€ 1,000	950
0.25%/2020/February 2029/EUR fixed-rate instruments	€ 1,000	997
0.5%/2020/February 2032/EUR fixed-rate instruments	€ 750	748
1.0%/2020/February 2025/GBP fixed-rate instruments	£ 850	878
0.125%/2020/June 2022/EUR fixed-rate instruments	€ —	–
0.25%/2020/June 2024/EUR fixed-rate instruments	€ 1,000	962
0.375%/2020/June 2026/EUR fixed-rate instruments	€ 1,000	921
0.875%/2020/June 2023/GBP fixed-rate instruments	£ 450	497
0.625%/2022/February 2027/EUR fixed-rate instruments	€ 500	454
1.00%/2022/February 2030/EUR fixed-rate instruments	€ 750	746
1.25%/2022/February 2035/EUR fixed-rate instruments	€ 750	738
2.25%/2022/March 2025/EUR fixed-rate instruments	€ 1,000	997
2.50%/2022/September 2027/EUR fixed-rate instruments	€ 500	499
2.75%/2022/September 2030/EUR fixed-rate instruments	€ 500	497
3.00%/2022/September 2033/EUR fixed-rate instruments	€ 1,000	997
Total Debt Issuance Programme		**22,006**

Siemens AG has bonds denominated in several currencies (dollars, euros and sterling). As can be seen, there are also different maturities and coupon rates (fixed and floating).

14.3 Preference Shares

Preference shares represent equity of a corporation, but they are different from ordinary shares because they are preferred in the payment of dividends and the assets of the corporation in the event of bankruptcy. *Preference* means only that the holder of the preference share must receive a dividend (in the case of an ongoing firm) before holders of ordinary shares are entitled to anything. Preference shares are the most common form of compound security and can be viewed as equity or debt depending on the exact characteristics of the security.

In some companies, a subsidiary will issue preference shares to raise funds, and lend these funds to the parent company to minimize tax payments for the firm as a whole. The loan will be tax-deductible from the perspective of the parent company. From the subsidiary's view, the dividend paid to the preference shareholders will be wholly offset by the interest paid by the parent company. This type of complex transaction is more likely to occur when the parent and the subsidiary operate in different tax locales.

Stated Value

Preference shares have a stated liquidating value, usually £100 or €100 per share. The dividend preference is described in terms of pounds or euros per share. For example, '£5 preferred' translates into a dividend yield of 5 per cent of stated value.

Cumulative and Non-cumulative Dividends

A preference share dividend is not like interest on a bond. The board of directors may decide not to pay the dividends on preference shares, and their decision may not have anything to do with the current net income of the corporation. Dividends payable on preference shares are either *cumulative* or *non-cumulative*. If preference share dividends are cumulative and are not paid in a particular year, they will be carried forward. Usually, both the cumulated (past) preference share dividends plus the current preference share dividends must be paid before the ordinary shareholders can receive anything. Unpaid preference share dividends are *not* debts of the firm. Directors elected by the ordinary shareholders can defer preference share dividends indefinitely. However, if so,

- Ordinary shareholders must forgo dividends.
- Though holders of preference shares do not always have voting rights, they will typically be granted these rights if preference share dividends have not been paid for some time.

Because preference shareholders receive no interest on the cumulated dividends, some have argued that firms have an incentive to delay paying preferred dividends.

Are Preference Shares Really Debt?

A good case can be made that preference shares are debt in disguise. Preference shareholders receive a stated dividend only, and if the corporation is liquidated they get a stated value. In recent years, many new issues of preference shares have had obligatory sinking funds.

The yields on preference shares are typically very low. For example, BP plc has an 8 per cent preference share with a stated £0.08 dividend. This dividend is perpetual – that is, it will be paid each year by BP plc for ever unless called. However, at a board meeting, holders of the 8 per cent preference shares have two votes for every five shares held, compared to one vote for every ordinary share held.

The IFRS, in the document IAS 32 *Financial Instruments – Presentation*, discusses in detail how preference shares should be regarded. The fundamental issue is whether the preference share has predominantly debt characteristics or equity characteristics. For example, the preference share would be viewed as debt if it contractually pays a fixed dividend and expires or is redeemed at a mandatory fixed future date. On the other hand, it will be regarded as equity if it is not obligated to pay a dividend or has a maturity date. When the preference share has clear debt and equity components, IFRS recommends that the equity and debt components are valued and reported separately in the financial accounts.

Equity versus Debt

Feature	Equity	Debt
Income	Dividends	Interest
Tax status	Dividends are taxed as personal income. Dividends are not a business expense.	Interest is taxed as personal income. Interest is a business expense, and corporations can deduct interest when computing corporate tax liability.
Control	Ordinary shares usually have voting rights.	Control is exercised with the loan agreement.
Default	Firms cannot be forced into bankruptcy for non-payment of dividends.	Unpaid debt is a liability of the firm. Non-payment results in bankruptcy.

Bottom line: tax status favours debt, but default favours equity. Control features of debt and equity are different, but one is not better than the other.

14.4 Patterns of Financing

Firms receive funding from several sources. First, they can reinvest their profits from existing operations. Second, they can borrow from the banking sector. Third, they can issue securities (debt and equity) to the public. (In Chapter 18, we look in detail at the capital structure decision, which is the amount of debt that is used to finance a firm's operations.)

Chapter 18 Page 478

Table 14.3 summarizes the patterns of funding for European companies from a survey of 12,500 companies carried out by the European Investment Bank in 2018.

Table 14.3 The Use of Financing Instruments by European Companies

Financing Instrument	% of Firms
Internal finance	87
Intra-group	6
Bank loans	39
Other bank finance	12
Bonds	2
Equity	1
Leasing/hire purchase	22
Factoring/invoicing	6
Family/friends	2
Grants	5
Other	1

Note: The table shows the weighted percentage of firms using different sources of finance. Survey carried out by the European Investment Bank on 12,500 European firms across all 28 member states.

Source: Ferrando and Lekpek (2018).

Corporations mostly rely on internal financing for their investment expenditure. Internal financing comes from internally generated cash flow and is defined as net income plus depreciation minus dividends. External financing is net new debt and new shares of equity net of buybacks.

Several features of long-term financing seem clear from Table 14.3:

- Internally generated cash flow dominates as a source of funding, with 87 per cent of firms using their own internally generated cash for investment.
- Bank loans constitute the largest source of external financing (39 per cent) followed by leasing and hire purchase (22 per cent).
- Notice how few companies issue public bonds (2 per cent) and equity (1 per cent). These are constrained to only the very largest firms in general, as evidenced by the low percentages.

The business cycle (the rise and fall of economic growth) may also impact the choice between debt and equity. For example, Begenau and Salomao (2019) report that when the economy is growing, large firms finance with debt, whereas small firms issue both equity and debt.

International Patterns in Capital Structure

Chapter 2 Page 24

Chapter 2 of this book established that there are many different corporate and ownership structures around the world. Firms that operate in China can look very different from similar firms doing business in the United Kingdom. State ownership is prevalent in many countries. There are even considerable differences in the ownership levels and board structures of firms that are incorporated in Europe. These differences suggest the question: are there differences in the capital structure of firms in different parts of the world?

Figure 14.1 presents the average leverage ratios (debt to market value of the firm) for many countries. While countries like Pakistan and Thailand have very high debt levels in general, most other countries use little debt. The figures are in market value terms and not book value terms. Given that the value of debt does not change very much, countries with vibrant and strongly performing equity markets would tend to have lower leverage ratios. Likewise, in markets where valuations are low, leverage ratios will be higher.

Figure 14.1 International Patterns of Capital Structure

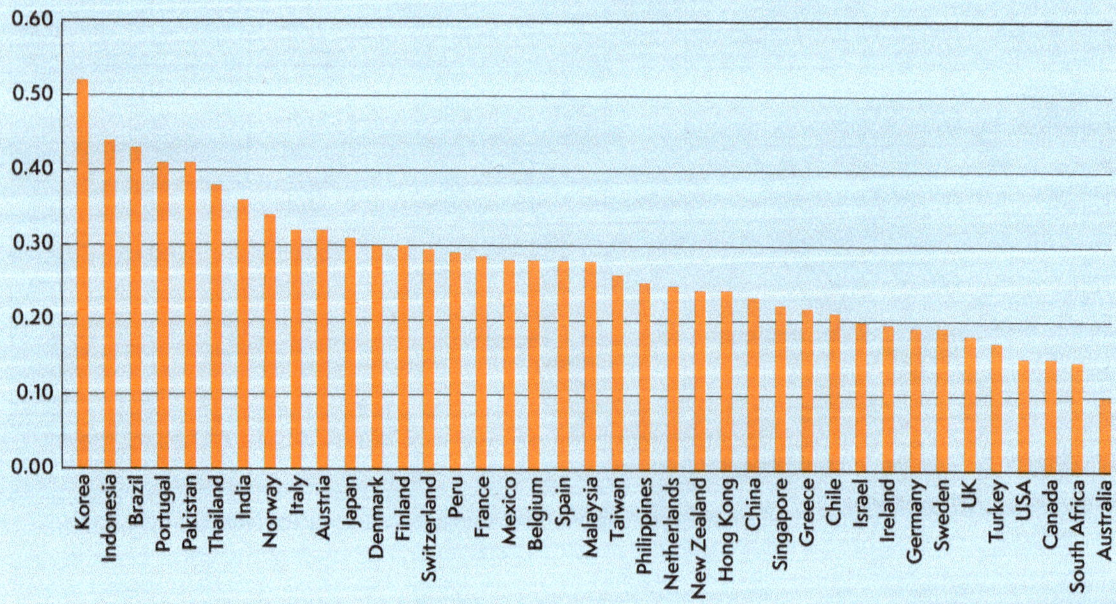

Note: Data values are estimated.

Source: Fan et al. (2012).

Which Are Best: Book or Market Values?

In general, financial economists prefer the use of market values when measuring debt ratios. This is true because market values reflect current rather than historical values. Most financial economists believe that current market values better reflect true intrinsic values than do historically based values. However, the use of market values contrasts with the perspective of many corporate practitioners.

Our conversations with corporate treasurers suggest to us that the use of book values is popular because of the volatility of the stock market, which has been a significant problem in recent times. It is frequently claimed that the inherent volatility of the stock market makes market-based debt ratios move around too much. It is also true that restrictions of debt in bond covenants are usually expressed in book values rather than market values. Moreover, firms such as Standard & Poor's and Moody's use debt ratios expressed in book values to measure creditworthiness.

A key fact is that, whether we use book or market values, debt ratios for most non-financial firms generally have been well below 100 per cent of total equity in recent years – that is, firms generally use less debt than equity.

Sustainability in Action 14.1

Tesla's Financing Decisions

In 2017, Tesla Inc., the electric vehicle and clean energy company, undertook a major financing decision to support its ambitious goals aligned with the United Nations' Sustainable Development Goal (SDG) 7: Affordable and Clean Energy. Tesla aimed to accelerate the world's transition to sustainable energy through its innovative electric vehicles, solar energy systems and energy storage products.

To finance the production of its new Model 3 electric vehicle and expand its charging network, Tesla raised approximately $1.2 billion in capital. The financing consisted of $250 million equity financing and $950 million convertible senior notes (debt financing).

Tesla's financing decision enabled the company to ramp up production, invest in its Supercharger network and improve its battery manufacturing capabilities at its Gigafactory. By the end of Q1 2023, Tesla had delivered 412,180 electric vehicles globally, making a significant impact on reducing carbon emissions and helping promote clean energy.

14.5 Hierarchies in Long-term Financing

In Real World Insight 14.1, it was shown that Siemens AG had many different types of debt. These were identified as senior and junior unsecured debt. If Siemens were to go bankrupt, the security holders would want as much of their initial investment back as possible. The hierarchy or priority of a company's securities determines who gets a claim on the assets of a bankrupt company first. In this section, we will review in more detail the different types of long-term financing and their priority in the list of corporate claims.

Senior Secured Debt

Senior secured debt is a debt instrument that is backed by a claim on the assets of the issuing company. This claim is known as collateral and may comprise buildings, manufacturing facilities, aeroplanes or any other non-current asset. Mortgaged debt is debt secured by property and buildings, and non-recourse debt is debt that is only partially secured by some assets in the company. Typically, the value of the collateral in non-recourse debt will be around 80 to 90 per cent of the total value of the debt. If the borrower defaults on the debt, the lender can only claim against the value of the collateral and no more. Senior secured debt has the first and highest claim on the assets of a defaulting company.

Second Lien Loans

Second lien loans are debt instruments that are typically secured to some form of collateral but are second in line for a claim of a company's assets behind senior secured debt.

Senior Unsecured Debt

The next financial security in the hierarchy is senior unsecured debt. Senior debt has a claim above other forms of debt, but in contrast to secured debt, the issue is not supported by any collateral.

Subordinated or Junior Debt

The ranking of debt below senior debt is commonly known as either subordinated or junior debt. Subordinated debt has a claim below all other senior debt instruments. Subordinated debt is relatively risky because, in the event of a corporate default, it is unlikely that the subordinated bondholders will receive any of their money back.

Shareholder Loans

Shareholder loans are very long-term low-interest loans given to a company by dominant shareholders. Because the loans are owned by the shareholders, they are commonly regarded as equity. For example, it would not make sense for the shareholder who gave a loan to make their firm bankrupt because this would directly hurt their shareholdings in the company. Given their unique nature, shareholder loans are the lowest ranking of all debt instruments.

Preference Shares

Preference shares have been discussed in Section 14.3. They fall below debt in the seniority of financial claims but sit above ordinary equity.

Ordinary Equity

Equity holders are at the very bottom of the financing hierarchy and are also known as residual claimants. This is because, in the event of a corporate bankruptcy, shareholders are the very last of all financial claimants to receive their money back. Usually, they would receive nothing at all.

Summary and Conclusions

The basic sources of long-term financing are long-term debt, preference shares and ordinary shares. This chapter described the essential features of each.

1 We emphasized that ordinary shareholders have:
   (a) Residual risk and return in a corporation
   (b) Voting rights
   (c) Limited liability if the corporation elects to default on its debt and must transfer some or all of its assets to the creditors.
2 Long-term debt involves contractual obligations set out in indentures. There are many kinds of debt, but the essential feature is that debt involves a stated amount that must be repaid. Interest payments on debt are considered a business expense and are tax deductible.
3 Preference shares have some of the features of debt and some of the features of ordinary equity. Holders of preference shares have preference in liquidation and in dividend payments compared to holders of ordinary equity.
4 Firms need financing for capital expenditures, working capital and other long-term uses. Most of the financing is provided from internally generated cash flow.

Questions and Problems

connect

CONCEPT

1 **Ordinary Shares** What is a proxy? What is the difference between voting rights and cash flow rights? Do you think this will have an impact on share values?

2 **Corporate Long-term Debt** Why do you think companies have issued bonds in different currencies, maturities and coupon rates? Shouldn't the coupon be the same on every bond? Explain.

3 **Preference Shares** Preference shares do not offer a corporate tax shield on the dividends paid. Why do we still observe some firms issuing preference shares?

4 **Patterns of Financing** Why do you think companies in certain countries prefer different forms of financing? Carry out your own research and comment on capital structure choice among firms in the G7 countries.

5 **Hierarchies** What is meant by hierarchies in long-term financing and why are bonds higher in priority than shares?

6 **Debt versus Equity Financing** Review the differences between debt and equity financing. Explain in detail how debt differs from equity. Are preference shares better than debt and equity because they have hybrid characteristics?

REGULAR

7 **Preference Shares and Bond Yields** The yields on non-convertible preference shares are lower than the yields on corporate bonds. Why is there a difference? Which investors are the primary holders of preference shares? Why?

8 **Corporate Financing** What are the main differences between corporate debt and equity? Why do some firms try to issue equity in the guise of debt? How would you categorize preference shares?

9 **Par Values** International Energy plc was formed in 1912 with 100,000 shares of equity with a £1 par value. Today, the company's share price is £9 and retained earnings are £213,000. International Energy has just decided that it wishes to issue 25,000 new shares. What will be the total par value, additional paid-in capital and book value per share after the issue?

10 **Corporate Financing Strategy** Prosperchain, a firm focusing on relieving poverty, has €6 million of positive NPV projects it would like to accept. If Prosperchain's managers follow the historical pattern of long-term financing for European firms, what will their financing strategy be?

11 **Preference Shares: Debt or Equity?** Do you think preference shares are more like debt or equity? Why?

12 **Book Value per Share** Consider the below shareholder equity statement for Toosoon plc. What is the book value per share?

Shareholders' Equity	£
Ordinary equity, 6,000,000 at £2 par value	12,000,000
Additional paid-in capital	48,000,000
Retained earnings	10,000,000
Treasury stock, at cost	−2,000,000
Shareholders' equity	68,000,000

13 **Long-term Financing** New equity issues are generally only a small portion of all new issues. At the same time, companies continue to issue new debt. Why do companies tend to issue little new equity but continue to issue new debt?

14 **Internal versus External Financing** What is the difference between internal financing and external financing? What factors influence a firm's choices of external versus internal equity financing? Do you think sustainable firms will be more likely to choose internal financing or external financing? Explain using a real case study.

15 **Security Priority** A company has €25 million in equity, €18 million in preference shares, €15 million in secured bonds and €34 million in unsecured bonds. Assume that, because of financial distress, the managers have decided to liquidate the firm's assets and pay off the funders. The asset sale (after legal expenses) resulted in €50 million being raised. Explain how much each funder gets from the asset sale.

16 **Shareholder Loans** In what situations would you consider using shareholder loans? What are the benefits from using shareholder loans and what are the drawbacks?

CHALLENGE

17 Equity Accounts: Dawn Technologies The equity accounts for Dawn Technologies are as follows:

Ordinary shares, £0.12 par value	120,000
Additional paid-in capital	4,526,123
Retained earnings	?
Total	6,421,830

(a) What are the retained earnings of Dawn Technologies?

(b) How many shares are outstanding?

(c) At what average price were the shares sold?

(d) What is the book value per share?

18 Equity Accounts: ABC plc The equity accounts for ABC plc are as follows:

Ordinary shares, £2 par value 500 shares outstanding	?
Capital surplus	250,000
Retained earnings	750,000
Total	?

(a) What are the ordinary share and total equity values for the equity account?

(b) The company has decided to issue 5,000 shares of equity at a price of £30 per share. Show the effects of the new issue on the equity accounts.

19 Equity Accounts: Ulrich plc Ulrich plc's articles of incorporation authorize the firm to issue 500,000 shares of £5 par value ordinary equity, of which 410,000 shares have been issued. Those shares were sold at an average of 30 per cent over par. In the quarter that ended last week, net income was £650,000; 30 per cent of that income was paid as a dividend. The previous balance sheet showed a retained earnings balance of £3,545,000.

(a) Create the equity statement for the company.

(b) Suppose the company sells 25,000 of the authorized but unissued shares at the price of £4 per share. What will the new equity statement look like?

20 Corporate Voting The shareholders of Unicorn plc need to elect seven new directors. There are 500,000 shares outstanding, currently trading at £34 per share. You would like to serve on the board of directors; unfortunately no one else will be voting for you. How much will it cost you to be certain that you can be elected if the company uses straight voting? How much will it cost you if the company uses cumulative voting?

21 Multiple Share Classes Meta founder Mark Zuckerberg owns 18 per cent of Meta's shares, with the other 82 per cent of shares owned by outside investors like financial institutions. Zuckerberg's shares are B class with 10 votes per share, while A class shares (held by institutions) have only 1 vote per share. What percentage of votes does Zuckerberg have in Meta? Who controls the company?

22 Multiple Share Classes: Institutional Investors What are the strengths of a dual-class share structure like that encountered in Meta? Answer from the perspective of an institutional investor and Mark Zuckerberg.

23 Hybrid Securities NourishEarth Global is a firm that is pursuing the reduction of global hunger (SDG2). It is considering the issue of a 'sustainable convertible bond', which can be converted into equity if the firm meets sustainability KPIs – that is, reducing greenhouse gas emissions, improving soil health and increasing crop yields. If NourishEarth Global achieves these KPIs, the bond will experience an adjustment in its conversion terms to be more attractive to investors. The sustainable convertible bond has seniority to ordinary bonds. Is this security equity or debt? How would you treat this in the company's balance sheet and income statement?

24 Share Capital The Akva Group ASA equity accounts for 2008 – 2010 are given below. Explain what each item is and how it changed over time.

	Note	2010	2009	2008
Equity				
Paid-in capital				
Share capital	15	17,223	17,223	17,223
Share premium reserve		256,178	256,178	256,178
Other paid-in capital		2,337	2,175	1,951
Total paid-in capital		275,738	275,576	275,352

25 Shareholdings In 2012, Rangers Football Club had a majority shareholder, Craig Whyte, who owned 83.5 per cent of the firm. The same individual also owned secured debt worth £18 million and was Rangers' largest secured creditor. Why would an individual choose to be a major lender at the same time as the main shareholder? Does this make sense? Explain.

26 Cumulative Voting An election is being held to fill three seats on the board of directors of a firm in which you are a shareholder. The company has 2,500 shares outstanding. If the election is conducted under cumulative voting and you own 300 shares, how many more shares must you buy to be assured of earning a seat on the board?

27 Family Firms and Long-term Financing Assume that you are the manager of a family firm and the company wishes to expand its operations into a new, unrelated business sector. The expansion requires funding. What type of financing (debt or equity) would you choose and why?

28 Financial Flexibility Your company plans to expand into a new business sector that requires higher levels of capital investment and fixed costs. Holding all else equal, what type of financing (debt or equity) would you choose to fund the expansion and why?

29 R&D-intensive Firms If you were the manager of a young research-intensive firm, which type of financing would you prefer and why? Carry out research on research-intensive firms in your country. What is the preferred financing choice of such firms in practice?

Exam Question (45 minutes)

1 Your company, Living Planet plc, was formed in 2021 to develop technologies that combat climate change. You started the firm with £80,000 financing, which consisted of 3,000 shares of equity amounting to £60,000 and a £20,000 bank loan. The company is listed on the small companies exchange and has accumulated earnings of £120,000. The share price is £7.50. You plan to expand the firm into solar technologies and have agreed to issue 1,000 new shares to a local investor. Construct the equity statement for your company before and after the share issue. The statement must include the total par value, additional paid-in capital, and book value per share. **(40 marks)**

2 You are concerned that other forms of financing may possibly be more appropriate and, in particular, you have heard about hybrid securities. Explain what these are and why companies use them. **(30 marks)**

3 If a company were to go into liquidation, which claims would have higher priority: bonds or equity? Why? How would you deal with hybrid securities in liquidation? **(30 marks)**

Total Marks: 100

Mini Case

Raising Capital

Two years ago, you launched a wearable technology firm with a single product. The product is a ring that measures heart rate, heart rate variability, skin temperature and blood pressure on a continuous basis. The firm has been extraordinarily successful and you plan to scale up operations across the world. You currently own 100 per cent of the firm and 1,000,000 shares with a share price of €6. The company needs to raise €36 million to have enough working capital and investment monies to successfully expand operations.

Your personal entrepreneurial and innovative reputation is exceptionally important to sell the firm and make it attractive to potential investors. Your financial adviser has recommended you provide a signal by creating a dual-class share structure that keeps you in the company. A class shares will be held by you and consist of your existing stakeholdings. B class shares will be sold to investors.

1 How would you structure the share classes so that you retain control over the firm?
2 What are the criticisms of this approach as a signal of keeping your influence on the firm?
3 How would you sell this dual-class share structure to potential investors?
4 Are there other ways you can guarantee your ongoing involvement in the firm?

Practical Case Study

Choose a company from your country. Download its financial accounts and find out how its long-term funding is structured. Does it have more debt than equity? Are there any securities that have debt and equity characteristics? Try to ascertain the funding hierarchy for the company.

Relevant Accounting Standards

As with all the chapters dealing with financial instruments, the main accounting standard is IAS 39 *Financial Instruments: Recognition and Measurement.* IAS 39 provides definitions for different types of financial securities and how these should be treated in the financial accounts. This can sometimes be problematic because many securities have equity and bond-like features. Visit the IASPlus website (www.iasplus.com) for more information.

References

Begenau, J. and J. Salomao (2019) 'Firm Financing Over the Business Cycle', *Review of Financial Studies,* Vol. 32, No. 4, 1235–1274.

Fan, J.P.H., S. Titman and G. Twite (2012) 'An International Comparison of Capital Structure and Debt Maturity Choices', *Journal of Financial and Quantitative Analysis,* Vol. 47, No. 1, 23.

Ferrando, A. and S. Lekpek (2018) *Access to Finance and Innovative Activity of EU Firms: A Cluster Analysis* (No. 2018/02). EIB Working Papers.

Additional Reading

The literature in this section investigates the factors that determine long-term financing decisions. References 5, 6 and 7 below are particularly relevant given their international focus. Dittmann and Ulbricht (2008) consider equity restructuring and should also be read for Chapter 15.

1 Brophy, D., P. Ouimet and C. Sialm (2009) 'Hedge Funds as Investors of Last Resort?', *Review of Financial Studies,* Vol. 22, No. 2, 541–574. **USA.**

2 Chang, X., S. Dasgupta and G. Hilary (2006) 'Analyst Coverage and Financing Decisions', *Journal of Finance,* Vol. 61, No. 6, 3009–3048. **USA.**

3 Dittmann, I. and N. Ulbricht (2008) 'Timing and Wealth Effects of German Dual Class Stock Unifications', *European Financial Management,* Vol. 14, No. 1, 163–196. **Germany.**

4 Dittmar, A.K. and R.F. Dittmar (2008) 'The Timing of Financing Decisions: An Examination of the Correlation in Financing Waves', *Journal of Financial Economics,* Vol. 90, No. 1, 59–83. **USA.**

5 Iannotta, G. and M. Navone (2008) 'Which Factors Affect Bond Underwriting Fees? The Role of Banking Relationships', *European Financial Management,* Vol. 14, No. 5, 944–961. **International.**

6 Martinsson, G. (2010) 'Equity Financing and Innovation: Is Europe Different from the United States?', *Journal of Banking and Finance,* Vol. 34, No. 6, 1215–1224. **International.**

7 Megginson, W.L., R.C. Nash, J.M. Netter and A.B. Poulsen (2004) 'The Choice of Private versus Public Capital Markets: Evidence from Privatizations', *Journal of Finance*, Vol. 59, No. 6, 2835–2870. **International.**

8 Mitton, T. (2008) 'Why Have Debt Ratios Increased for Firms in Emerging Markets?', *European Financial Management*, Vol. 14, No. 1, 127–151. **International.**

If you are interested in how financial technology can enhance access to financing, a short editorial by Bollaert et al. (2021) is very informative:

Bollaert, H., F.L. de Silanes and A. Schwienbacher (2021) 'Fintech and Access to Finance', *Journal of Corporate Finance*, Vol. 68, No. 2, 101941.

Endnotes

1 In the UK, regulation (Companies Act 2006) abolished the term 'authorized share capital' and now all British firms can issue capital without limit and when required.

Chapter 15
Equity Financing

Learning Objectives

After reading this chapter you should be able to:

LO1 Define and explain concepts related to equity financing, such as public issue, alternative issue methods, cash offer, shelf registration and private equity market.

LO2 Analyse and interpret the effects of announcing new equity on the value of a firm.

LO3 Calculate the cost of new issues.

LO4 Evaluate the advantages and disadvantages of different equity financing methods, including rights offerings and shelf registration, in various financial scenarios.

When a firm wishes to raise capital for new investment, it has two basic choices. One option is to issue new equity. Another is to borrow funds from financial institutions or through the public issue of debt. Every day in the financial press, you will read about companies that have gone to the markets to raise new equity.

Take the firm Florentaise SA, which was listed on Euronext on 13 April 2023. According to its press release:

> *Florentaise is France's leader and pioneer in low-carbon soils and eco-innovative growing mediums. The company sells close to one in five bags of all bags of potting soil that are sold to end consumers in France and serves 12% of the professional market. The Group markets patented wood fibres Hortifibre® and Turbofibre®, which allow users to avoid the use of peat, present in traditional potting soils and resulting in 20 to 50 times reduced greenhouse gas emissions.*

For it to scale in size, Florentaise needed at least €18 million to support its international expansion, innovation and sustainability projects. The issue price of the company was €9.44, which priced the firm at €78 million. Unfortunately, within a month of the issue, the share price had fallen 18 per cent to €7.71, which is equivalent to a market value of €63 million.

In this chapter, we examine the process by which companies such as Florentaise sell equity to the public, the costs of doing so and the role of intermediaries in the process. We pay particular attention to what is probably the most critical stage in a company's financial life cycle: the initial public offering. We look at how the issue price is set and what happens when the share price falls, such as in the case of Florentaise. We also look at alternatives to stock market listings and, in particular, the private equity market.

Source: elenathewise/123RF

15.1 The Public Issue

When considering the steps involved in the public issue of equity, it is important to recognize that each country has its own specific regulations and traditions, although the European Union has a comprehensive directive that covers all member countries. Table 15.1 illustrates the general process for European public equity issues.

Table 15.1 The Process of Raising Capital

Stages in Public Offering	Time Relative to Issue Date	Activities
1. Preparatory period	6 months before	Advisors appointed; listing eligibility established, due diligence starts, prospectus prepared
2. Prospectus draft	3 months before	Advisors submit first draft of prospectus to regulator
3. Listing announcement	2 months before	Company announces intention to list, draft prospectus published
4. Blackout period	1 month before	Research by connected brokers is published; no more connected research permitted after this period
5. Pathfinder prospectus	14 days before	Pathfinder prospectus issued with indicative issue price range, underwriters appointed and begin selling, pre-underwriting conferences held by company directors
6. Pricing date	3 days before	Issue price set and shares are allocated to subscribers, final prospectus published, price stabilization begins
7. Issue date	Day 0	Shares start trading

15.2 Alternative Issue Methods

When a company decides to issue a new security, it can have a public or a private issue. In a public issue, the shares are traded on a stock exchange and the firm is required to register the issue with the stock exchange on which it is listed. If the issue is sold to only a few institutions, it is called a *private placement* or *placing* and can be treated as a private issue. A registration statement is usually not required in this case.[1]

There are two kinds of public issue: the *general cash offer* and the *rights issue*. Cash offers are sold to all interested investors, and rights offers are sold to existing shareholders. Equity is sold by both the cash offer and the rights offer, though almost all debt is sold by a cash offer.

The first public equity issue that is made by a company is referred to as an **initial public offering (IPO)** or **unseasoned new issue.** All initial public offerings are cash offers because if the firm's existing shareholders wanted to buy the shares, the firm would not need to sell them publicly. IPO activity is positively related to the performance of stock markets, and this has been reflected in the slew of new issues in Europe and the USA over the past few years. A **seasoned issue** refers to a new issue of shares for a company that is already listed on a stock exchange. A seasoned issue of ordinary shares will typically be through a rights issue.

Methods of issuing new securities are shown in Table 15.2 and discussed in the next few sections.

Table 15.2 The Methods of Issuing New Securities

Method	Type	Definition
Public		
Traditional negotiated cash offer	Firm commitment cash offer	The company negotiates an agreement with a bank to underwrite and distribute the new shares. A specified number of shares are bought by underwriters and sold at a higher price.
	Best efforts cash offer	Company has underwriters sell as many of the new shares as possible at the agreed-upon price. There is no guarantee concerning how much cash will be raised. Some best efforts offerings do not use an underwriter.
	Dutch auction cash offer	Company has underwriters auction shares to determine the highest offer price obtainable for a given number of shares to be sold.
Privileged	Pre-emptive rights issue	Company offers the new equity direct to its existing shareholders.

Method	Type	Definition
Subscription	Standby rights issue	Like the pre-emptive rights issue, this contains a privileged subscription arrangement with existing shareholders. The net proceeds are guaranteed by the underwriters.
Non-traditional cash offer	Shelf cash offer	Qualifying companies can authorize all the shares they expect to sell over a specified period and sell them when needed.
	Competitive firm cash offer	Company can elect to award the underwriting contract through a public auction instead of negotiation.
Private		
	Direct placement	Securities are sold direct to the purchaser.

15.3 The Cash Offer

As just mentioned, equity is sold to all interested investors in a **cash offer**. If the cash offer is a public one, banks are usually involved. Banks are financial intermediaries that perform a wide variety of services. In addition to taking deposits and making loans, they also aid in the sale of securities, facilitate mergers and other corporate reorganizations, act as brokers to both individual and institutional clients, and trade for their own accounts. Much of this activity is undertaken by the investment arm of banks.

For corporate issuers, the investment banking function includes the following:

- Formulating the method used to issue new securities
- Pricing the new securities
- Selling the new securities.

There are three basic methods of issuing securities for cash:

1 *Firm commitment:* Under this method, the bank (or a group of banks) buys the securities for less than the offering price and accepts the risk of not being able to sell them. Because this function involves risk, we say that the banker *underwrites* the securities in a firm commitment. In other words, when participating in a firm commitment offering, the banker acts as an *underwriter.* (Because firm commitments are so prevalent, we will use the terms *banker* and *underwriter* interchangeably in this chapter.)

   To minimize the risks here, bankers combine to form an underwriting group (**underwriting syndicate**) to share the risk and to help sell the issue. In such a group, one or more managers arrange or co-manage the deal. The manager is designated as the lead manager or principal manager. The lead manager typically has responsibility for all aspects of the issue. The other investment bankers in the syndicate serve primarily to sell the issue to their clients.

   The difference between the underwriter's buying price and the offering price is called the *spread* or *discount.* It is the basic compensation received by the underwriter. Sometimes the underwriter will get non-cash compensation in the form of warrants or equity in addition to the spread.

   Firm commitment underwriting is really just a purchase–sale arrangement, and the syndicate's fee is the spread. The issuer receives the full amount of the proceeds less the spread, and all the risk is transferred to the underwriter. If the underwriter cannot sell all of the issue at the agreed-upon offering price, it may need to lower the price on the unsold shares. However, because the offering price usually is not set until the underwriters have investigated how receptive the market is to the issue, this risk is usually minimal. This is particularly true with seasoned new issues because the price of the new issue can be based on prior trades in the security.

2 *Best efforts:* The underwriter bears risk with a firm commitment because it buys the entire issue. Conversely, the syndicate avoids this risk under a best-efforts offering because it does not purchase the shares. Instead it merely acts as an agent, receiving a commission for each share sold. The syndicate is legally bound to use its best efforts to sell the securities at the agreed-upon offering price. If the issue cannot be sold at the offering price, it is usually withdrawn. This form of underwriting has become relatively rare.

3 *Dutch auction underwriting:* With **Dutch auction underwriting** the underwriter does not set a fixed price for the shares to be sold. Instead the underwriter invites investors to submit bids indicating the number of shares and price at which they wish to buy. When the auction is finished, shares are allocated in the order

of highest bid to lowest bid. This approach to selling securities to the public is relatively rare in the equity IPO market and has not been widely used there, but it is very common in the bond markets. For example, it is the sole procedure used by governments to sell enormous quantities of notes, bonds and bills to the public.

Dutch auctions are also becoming increasingly common in technology and issues where cryptocurrencies are used to buy shares. An example is Inveniam Capital Partners (ICP), which places new issues using cryptocurrencies as well as standard currencies through a Dutch auction. In February 2019, ICP raised $66 million in a share issue denominated in the world's 50 most active cryptocurrencies. The best way to understand how a Dutch auction works is to consider a simple example. Suppose the Rial Company wants to sell 400 shares to the public. The company receives five bids as follows:

Bidder	Quantity	Price (£)
A	100 shares	16
B	100 shares	14
C	100 shares	12
D	200 shares	12
E	200 shares	10

Thus, bidder A is willing to buy 100 shares at £16 each, bidder B is willing to buy 100 shares at £14, and so on. The Rial Company examines the bids to determine the highest price that will result in all 400 shares being sold. For example, at £14, A and B would buy only 200 shares, so that price is too high. Working our way down, all 400 shares will not be sold until we hit a price of £12, so £12 will be the offer price in the IPO. Bidders A to D will receive shares; bidder E will not.

There are two additional important points to observe in our example. First, all the winning bidders will pay £12 – even bidders A and B, who actually bid a higher price. The fact that all successful bidders pay the same price is the reason for the name 'uniform price auction'. The idea in such an auction is to encourage bidders to bid aggressively by providing some protection against bidding a price that is too high.

Second, notice that, at the £12 offer price, there are actually bids for 500 shares, which exceeds the 400 shares Rial wants to sell. Thus, there has to be some sort of allocation. How this is done varies a bit, but in the IPO market the approach has been to simply compute the ratio of shares offered to shares bid at the offer price or better, which in our example is 400/500 = 0.8, and allocate bidders that percentage of their bids. In other words, bidders A to D would each receive 80 per cent of the shares they bid at a price of £12 per share.

In most offerings, the principal underwriter is permitted to buy shares if the market price falls below the offering price. The purpose is to *support* the market and *stabilize* the price from temporary downward pressure. If the issue remains unsold after a time (for example, 30 days), members may leave the group and sell their shares at whatever price the market will allow.

Many underwriting contracts contain a **Green Shoe provision**, which gives the members of the underwriting group the option to purchase additional shares at the offering price.[2] The stated reason for the Green Shoe option is to cover excess demand and oversubscription. Green Shoe options usually last for about 30 days and involve no more than a percentage (usually less than 15 per cent) of the newly issued shares. The Green Shoe option is a benefit to the underwriting syndicate and a cost to the issuer. If the market price of the new issue goes above the offering price within 30 days, the underwriters can buy shares from the issuer and immediately resell the shares to the public. For example, Volkswagen raised €9.4 billion euros in 2022 for preference shares in Porsche, but it received only €9.1 billion euros because the green shoe option was exercised by the underwriters. That is over 3 per cent of the total cash raised.

The period after a new issue is initially sold to the public is called the *aftermarket*. During this period, the members of the underwriting syndicate generally do not sell shares of the new issue for less than the offer price.

Almost all underwriting agreements contain *lock-ups*. Such arrangements specify how long insiders must wait after an IPO before they can sell some of their shares. Typically, lock-up periods are set at 180 days, but can last for several years. Lock-ups are important because it is not unusual for the number of locked-up insider shares to be larger than the number of shares held by the public. Thus, there is the possibility that, when the lock-up period ends, a large number of shares will be sold by insiders, thereby depressing share prices.

Beginning well before an offering and extending for a period following an IPO, many countries require that a firm and its managing underwriters observe a 'quiet period'. This means that all communications with the public must be limited to ordinary announcements and other purely factual matters. The logic is that all relevant information should be contained in the prospectus. An important result of this requirement is that the underwriter's analysts are prohibited from making recommendations to investors. As soon as the quiet period ends, however, the managing underwriters typically publish research reports, usually accompanied by a favourable 'buy' recommendation.

Firms that do not stay quiet can have their IPOs delayed. For example, just before Google's IPO, an interview with co-founders Sergey Brin and Larry Page appeared in *Playboy*. The interview almost caused a postponement of the IPO, but Google was able to amend its prospectus in time (by including the article!).

Investment Banking

Investment banking is at the heart of new security issues. The investment banking arms of big banks provide advice, market the securities (after investigating the market's receptiveness to the issue) and underwrite the proceeds. They accept the risk that the market price may fall between the date the offering price is set and the time the issue is sold.

In addition, banks have the responsibility of pricing fairly. When a firm goes public, particularly for the first time, the buyers know relatively little about its operations. After all, it is not rational for a buyer of, say, only 1,000 shares of equity to study the company at length. Instead, the buyer must rely on the judgement of the bank, which has presumably examined the firm in detail. Given this asymmetry of information, what prevents the banker from pricing the issued securities too high? Although the underwriter has a short-term incentive to price high, it has a long-term incentive to make sure its customers do not pay too much; they might desert the underwriter in future deals if they lose money on this one. Thus, as long as banks plan to stay in business over time, it is in their own interest to price fairly.

In other words, financial economists argue that each bank has a reservoir of 'reputation capital'.[3] Mispricing of new issues or unethical dealings are likely to reduce this reputation capital.

Banks place great importance on their relative rankings and view downward movement in their placement with much distaste. While this jockeying for position may seem as unimportant as the currying of royal favour in the court of Louis XVI, it is explained by the preceding discussion. In any industry where reputation is so important, the firms in the industry must guard theirs with great vigilance.

There are two basic methods for selecting the syndicate. In a **competitive offer** the issuing firm can offer its securities to the underwriter bidding highest. In a negotiated offer the issuing firm works with one underwriter. Because the firm generally does not negotiate with many underwriters concurrently, negotiated deals may suffer from lack of competition.

In Their Own Words

Robert S. Hansen on the Economic Rationale for the Firm Commitment Offer

Underwriters provide four main functions: certification, monitoring, marketing and risk bearing.

Certification assures investors that the offer price is fair. Investors have concerns about whether the offer price is unfairly above the equity's intrinsic value. Certification increases issuer value by reducing investor doubt about fairness, making a better offer price possible.

Monitoring of issuing firm management and performance builds value because it adds to shareholders' ordinary monitoring. Underwriters provide collective monitoring on behalf of both capital suppliers and current shareholders. Individual shareholder monitoring is limited because the shareholder bears the entire cost, whereas all owners collectively share the benefit, pro rata. By contrast, in underwriter monitoring, all shareholders share both the costs and benefits, pro rata.

Due diligence and legal liability for the proceeds give investors assurance. However, what makes certification and monitoring credible is lead bank reputation in competitive capital markets, where they are disciplined over time. Evidence that disreputable behaviour is damaging to a bank's future abounds. Capital market participants punish poorly performing banks by refusing to hire them. The participants pay banks for certification and meaningful monitoring in 'quasi-rents' in the spread, which represent the fair cost of 'renting' the reputations.

Marketing is finding long-term investors who can be persuaded to buy the securities at the offer price. This would not be needed if demand for new shares were 'horizontal'. There is much evidence that issuers and syndicates repeatedly invest in costly marketing practices, such as expensive roadshows to identify and expand investor interest. Another is organizing members to avoid the redundant pursuit of the same customers. Lead banks provide trading support in the issuer's equity for several weeks after the offer.

Underwriting risk is like the risk of selling a put option. The syndicate agrees to buy all new shares at the offer price and resell them at that price or at the market price, whichever is lower. Thus, once the offer begins, the syndicate is exposed to potential losses on unsold inventory should the market price fall below the offer price. The risk is likely to be small, because offerings are typically well prepared for quick sale.

Robert S. Hansen is the Freeman Senior Research Professor of Finance at Tulane University.

Whereas competitive bidding occurs frequently in other areas of commerce, it may surprise you that negotiated deals in banking occur with all but the largest issuing firms. Investment bankers argue that they must expend much time and effort learning about the issuer before setting an issue price and a fee schedule. Except in the case of large issues, these underwriters could not expend the time and effort without the near certainty of receiving the contract.

Studies generally show that issuing costs are higher in negotiated deals than in competitive ones. However, many financial economists argue that issuing firms are not necessarily hurt by negotiated deals. They point out that the underwriter gains much information about the issuing firm through negotiation – information likely to increase the probability of a successful offering.[4]

Reputation is exceptionally important in underwriting, and investment banks compete with one another to get the very best-quality new issues. Similarly, the number of IPOs that an investment bank is able to undertake is a good proxy for underwriter quality. The better banks get more IPO business and, by implication, are better at generating new financing. Table 15.3 presents the top 10 underwriters in six major European markets for raising new financing. As can be seen, big players are active in more than one market, but there are also country-specific specialists. A comparison of the London Main Market and its smaller equivalent, AIM, shows that there are specialist firms working in each segment. Typically, larger investment banks will be underwriters for larger issues, whereas smaller firms will tend to focus on smaller issues. There is also a geographical home bias with, for example, more German underwriters in Frankfurt and more British/US underwriters in London.

Table 15.3 Ranking Underwriters of European IPOs

	Paris Euronext		Frankfurt		London Main Market		London Alternative Investment Market (AIM)	
	Name	No. IPOs	Name	No. IPOs	Name	No. IPOs	Name	No. IPOs
1	BNP Paribas	40	Landesbanken	75	UBS	38	Evolution Sec	123
2	Crédit Mutuel	39	Commerzbank	74	J.P. Morgan Chase	37	Dowgate CS	98
3	Crédit Agricole	37	DZ Bank	54	Evolution Sec	25	Collins Stewart	90
4	Oddo & Cie	37	Deutsche Bank	47	Investec	23	Peel Hunt	83
5	Société Générale	35	Unicredit	37	Crédit Suisse	23	Ambrian Capital	64
6	BFBP	33	Sal. Oppenheim	36	BoA Merrill Lynch	22	WH Ireland	62
7	Crédit du Nord	28	Gontard & Metallbank	23	Commerzbank	19	Landsbanki Sec	62
8	Crédit Lyonnais	27	VEM Aktienbank	23	Morgan Stanley	19	Grant Thornton	55
9	KBC	22	Concord Effekten	19	Goldman Sachs	19	Brewin Dolphin	53
10	Natixis	19	HSBC	16	Citigroup	15	Numis Sec	48

Source: Adapted from Migliorati and Vismara (2014), Table 4 (updated 2017).

The Offering Price

Determining the correct offering price is the most difficult thing the lead underwriter can do for an initial public offering. The issuing firm faces a potential cost if the offering price is set too high or too low. If the issue is priced too high, it may be unsuccessful and be withdrawn. If the issue is priced below the true market price, the issuer's existing shareholders will experience an opportunity loss.

Ljunqvist (2006) has found that unseasoned new equity issues are generally offered below their true market price in the vast majority of countries. Underpricing helps new shareholders earn a higher return on the shares they buy. However, the existing shareholders of the issuing firm are not necessarily helped by underpricing. To them it is an indirect cost of issuing new securities. Figure 15.1 shows the issue date average return on new IPOs for a variety of European countries, and Table 15.4 updates and extends Ljunqvist's analysis to many other countries and to 2019.

In Figure 15.1, underpricing is seen to be prevalent in all countries studied. The UAE, Saudi Arabia, China and Jordan have the biggest underpricing by a long distance. Many Western countries, including the UK and USA, have first-day underpricing around 16 per cent.

Figure 15.1 IPO Underpricing (%) Around the World (Average First-day Return)

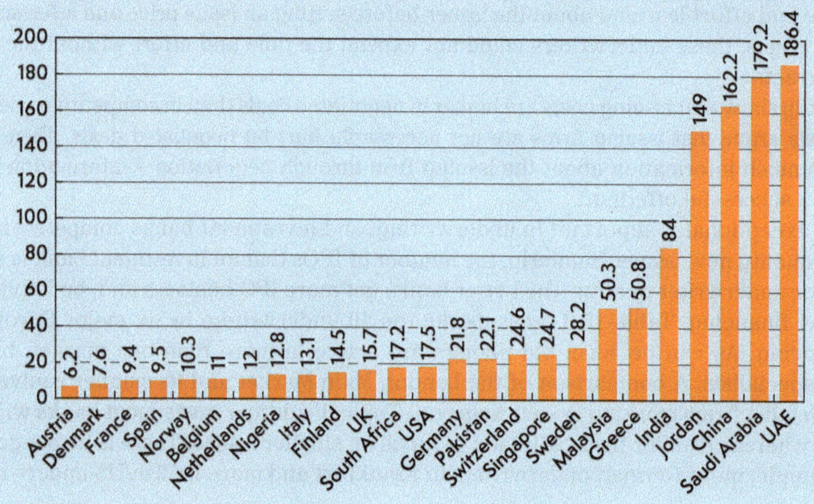

Source: Jay Ritter, University of Florida (2023)

Underpricing: A Possible Explanation

There are several possible explanations for underpricing, but so far there is little agreement among scholars as to which is correct. Table 15.4 shows that the greatest underpricing has been concentrated in medium-sized firms where sales are between \$50 million and \$200 million per year. Although companies of all sizes (in terms of sales) experienced positive average first-day returns, smaller firms and the very largest firms had lower underpricing. It used to be argued (see underpricing in Table 15.4 for earlier periods) that smaller firms, which tend to be young and have uncertain future prospects, had the most underpricing, but this hasn't been true since 2001.

Table 15.4 Average First-day Returns, Categorized by Sales, for IPOs: 1980–2022

	1980–1989 Return (%)	N	1990–1998 Return (%)	N	1999–2000 Return (%)	N	2001–2022 Return (%)	N
0 ≤ sales < \$10m	10.3	425	17.2	742	68.9	332	21.4	689
\$10m ≤ sales < \$20m	8.7	242	18.6	395	81.7	138	21.2	107
\$20m ≤ sales < \$50m	7.8	500	18.8	789	74.9	154	20.3	272
\$50m ≤ sales < \$100m	6.4	356	12.9	590	61.2	85	22.1	359
\$100m ≤ sales < \$200m	5.1	234	11.8	454	35.8	56	22.7	316
\$200m ≥ sales	3.4	290	8.7	646	25.2	91	13.9	865
All	7.2	2,047	14.8	3,616	64.5	856	19.0	2,608

Note: Sales, measured in millions, are for the 12 months prior to going public. All sales have been converted into dollars of 2003 purchasing power, using the Consumer Price Index. There are 9,127 IPOs, after excluding IPOs with an offer price of less than \$5.00 per share, units, REITs, ADRs, closed-end funds, banks and S&Ls, firms not listed on CRSP within six months of the offering, and natural resource related limited partnerships. Sales are from Thomson Financial's SDC, Dealogic, EDGAR and the Graeme Howard-Todd Huxster collection of pre-EDGAR prospectuses. The average first-day return is 19.0 per cent.

Source: Professor Jay R. Ritter, University of Florida.

Another explanation, proposed by Boulton, Smart and Zutter (2017), is that firms that voluntarily announce bad news when it happens and are conservative in their earnings figures, are more likely to experience less underpricing than other firms. Boulton and colleagues tested this hypothesis on more than 13,000 IPOs in 36 different countries and found strong evidence to support their views. Why would conservative accounting practices improve underpricing? The authors argue that because issuing firms tend to be high-growth and often with negative earnings, they are extremely difficult to value. With the timely provision of information on adverse events and restricting managers from inflating profits, outside investors will have more confidence in the IPO. Figure 15.2 presents the relationship between country-level conservatism and average IPO underpricing.

Figure 15.2 Country-level Conservatism and IPO Underpricing

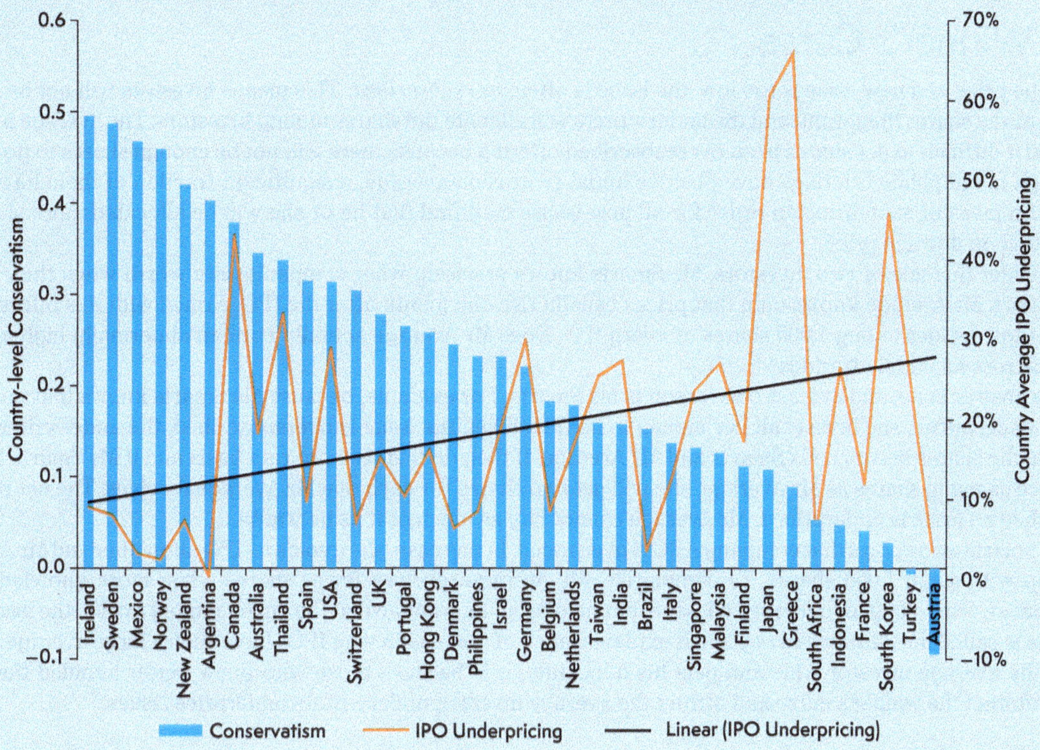

Source: Boulton et al. (2017).

Other factors explaining underpricing include positive media attention before the IPO date, local bias, recent market return, recent IPO activity, top-tier underwriters, VC-backed IPOs, an integer offer price, the IPO has a strong order flow, the underwriter has made a firm commitment to sell the issue, and the IPO is high-tech. Table 15.5 presents an overview of international evidence on the determinants of IPO underpricing across countries. A '+' entry means there is a positive relationship between the characteristic and IPO underpricing. A '–' entry means there is a negative relationship and '0' means there is no relationship. So, as an example, in all countries recent market performance is strongly associated with greater levels of underpricing.

Table 15.5 Determinants of Underpricing by Country

Country	Offer Size	Recent Market Return	Recent IPO Activity	Stock Market Turnover	Top-tier Underwriter	VC-backed IPO	Firm Commitment	High-tech Firm
United States	–	+	+	–	+	+	–	+
China	–	+	–	–	–	–	–	–
UK	–	+	+	+	–	–	–	+
France	0	+	+		0	–	0	+
Singapore	–	+	0	+	0	–	0	0
Germany	0	+	+	0	0	–	–	+
Malaysia	–	+	+	0	0	0	0	+
India	–	+	0	0	–	0	–	0

Source: Adapted from Boulton, Smart and Zutter (2018), Table 4.2.

There are other possible explanations for underpricing. According to Chen et al. (2022), societal secrecy is 'a preference for withholding information about a business from those who are not closely involved with its management and financing'. Chen and colleagues found that, in countries where societies are more secretive, there is pervasive underpricing in IPOs. Democratic countries have significantly lower underpricing (Duong et al., 2022), although underpricing is weaker when the issuing firm is audited by one of the Big Four auditing firms, backed by a venture capitalist, or is more specific about the use of the IPO funds.

The Winner's Curse

When the price of a new issue is too low, the issue is often *oversubscribed*. This means investors will not be able to buy all of the shares they want, and the underwriters will allocate the shares among investors. The average investor will find it difficult to get shares in an oversubscribed offering because there will not be enough shares to go round. Although initial public offerings have positive initial returns on average, a significant fraction of them have price drops. An investor submitting an order for all new issues may find that he or she will be allocated more shares in issues that go down in price.

Consider this tale of two investors. Ms Smarts knows precisely what companies are worth when their shares are offered. Mr Average knows only that prices usually rise one month after the IPO. Armed with this information, Mr Average decides to buy 1,000 shares of every IPO. Does Mr Average actually earn an abnormally high average return across all initial offerings?

The answer is no, and at least one reason is Ms Smarts. For example, because Ms Smarts knows that company XYZ is underpriced, she invests all her money in its IPO. When the issue is oversubscribed, the underwriters must allocate the shares between Ms Smarts and Mr Average. If they do this on a pro rata basis and if Ms Smarts has bid for twice as many shares as Mr Average, she will get two shares for each one Mr Average receives. The net result is that, when an issue is underpriced, Mr Average cannot buy as much of it as he wants.

Ms Smarts also knows that company ABC is overpriced. In this case, she avoids its IPO altogether and Mr Average ends up with a full 1,000 shares. To summarize, Mr Average receives fewer shares when more knowledgeable investors swarm to buy an underpriced issue, but he gets all he wants when the smart money avoids the issue.

This is called the *winner's curse*, and it explains much of the reason why IPOs have such a large average return. When the average investor wins and gets his allocation, it is because those who knew better avoided the issue. To counteract the winner's curse and attract the average investor, underwriters underprice issues.[5]

15.4 The Announcement of New Equity and the Value of the Firm

It seems reasonable to believe that firms arrange new long-term financing after positive net present value projects are put together. Consequently, when external funding is announced, the firm's market value should go up. As we mentioned in an earlier chapter, this is precisely the opposite of what happens in the case of new equity financing. Asquith and Mullins, Masulis and Korwar, and Mikkelson and Partch for the USA, Gajewski and Ginglinger for France, Martin-Ugedo for Spain, and Barnes and Walker for the UK have all found that the market value of existing equity drops on the announcement of a new public equity issue.[6] Plausible reasons for this strange result include the following:

- *Managerial information:* If managers have superior knowledge about the firm's market value, they may know when the firm is overvalued. If they do, they might attempt to issue new shares when the market value exceeds the correct value. This will benefit existing shareholders. However, potential new shareholders are not stupid. They will infer overvaluation from the new issue, thereby bidding down the share price on the announcement date.
- *Debt capacity:* The stereotypical firm chooses a debt–equity ratio that balances the tax shield from the debt with the cost of financial distress. When a firm's managers have exclusive information that the probability of financial distress has risen, the firm is more likely to raise capital through equity than through debt. If the market infers this chain of events, the share price should fall on the announcement date of an equity issue.
- *Falling earnings:*[7] When managers raise capital in amounts that are unexpectedly large (as most unanticipated financings will be) and if investors have a reasonable fix on the firm's upcoming investments and dividend payouts (as they do because capital expenditure announcements are often well known, as are future dividends), the unanticipated financings are roughly equal to unexpected shortfalls in earnings (this follows directly from the firm's sources and uses of funds identity). Therefore, announcing a new equity issue will also reveal a future earnings shortfall.

Sustainability in Action 15.1

Abundance Investment

Abundance Investment is a UK-based crowdfunding platform that funds renewable energy and ethical investment projects. The platform directly connects investors with projects focusing on sustainable development, addressing the United Nations' Sustainable Development Goals (SDGs), particularly Goal 7: Affordable and Clean Energy and Goal 13: Climate Action.

In 2015, Abundance Investment launched an equity crowdfunding campaign on the Seedrs platform, seeking to raise £1.2 million to expand its platform and connect more investors to sustainable projects.

The campaign aimed to raise capital for marketing initiatives, technological improvements and ongoing operations. In addition, Abundance wanted to accelerate the transition to clean energy by offering accessible investment opportunities to retail investors, allowing them to directly contribute to achieving the SDGs.

During the equity issue process, the firm faced the challenge of effectively communicating its unique sustainability value proposition and potential growth to prospective investors and, additionally, navigating the early regulatory environment for crowdfunding required diligence to ensure compliance with financial regulations.

Despite these challenges, Abundance Investment's equity crowdfunding campaign successfully raised financing from investors. This capital infusion enabled the company to expand its platform, support more sustainable projects and create a community of investors dedicated to positively impacting the environment.

15.5 The Cost of New Issues

Issuing securities to the public is not free, and the costs of different issuing methods are important determinants of which will be used. The costs fall into six categories:

1. *Spread or underwriting discount:* The spread is the difference between the price the issuer receives and the price offered to the public.
2. *Other direct expenses:* These are costs incurred by the issuer that are not part of the compensation to underwriters. They include filing fees, legal fees and taxes – all reported in the prospectus.
3. *Indirect expenses:* These costs are not reported in the prospectus and include management time spent on the new issue.
4. *Abnormal returns:* In a seasoned issue of equity, the price drops upon the announcement of the issue. The drop protects new shareholders against the firm selling overpriced equity to new shareholders.
5. *Underpricing:* For initial public offerings, the equity typically rises substantially after the issue date. This is a cost to the firm because the shares are sold for less than their efficient price in the aftermarket.[8]
6. *Green Shoe option:* The Green Shoe option gives the underwriters the right to buy additional shares at the offer price to cover over-allotments. This is a cost to the firm because the underwriter will purchase additional shares only when the offer price is below the price in the aftermarket.

An interesting study by Seth Armitage (2000) reports two of these six costs: underwriting discount and other non-underwriting direct expenses. Table 15.6, which is reproduced from Table 1 of Armitage's paper, provides three central insights:

1. The total issue costs decline as the gross proceeds of the offering increase for both US and UK companies. Thus, it appears that issuance costs are subject to substantial economies of scale.[9]
2. Issue costs in the USA are higher than in the UK for most levels of gross proceeds.
3. Last, and perhaps most important, the costs of issuing securities to the public are quite large. For example, total direct expenses are approximately 6 per cent in the UK and this rises to nearly 15 per cent for small issues. This implies that issuing equity is a weighty decision, especially for smaller companies. Although there are many benefits, such as raising needed capital and spreading ownership, the costs cannot be ignored.

Table 15.6 Cost of Issue by Issue Size

UK Rights Issues and Open Offers, Purged Sample		US SEOs	
Gross Proceeds (£m)	Total Costs (%)	Gross Proceeds ($ m)	Total Costs (%)
312.5+	2.17	500+	3.15
125.0–312.4	2.65	200–499.9	3.47
62.5–124.9	2.79	100–199.9	4.22
50.0–62.4	3.54	80–99.9	4.73
37.5–49.9	3.07	60–79.9	5.18
25.0–37.4	3.70	40–59.9	5.87
12.5–24.9	3.68	20–39.9	6.93
6.25–12.4	5.16	10–19.9	8.72
1.25–6.24	8.27	2–9.9	13.28
0.1–1.24	14.36		
Total	5.78		7.11
Median	4.28		

Source: Adapted from Armitage (2000), Table 1.

15.6 Rights

When new shares of equity are offered to the general public, the proportionate ownership of existing shareholders is likely to be reduced. However, if a pre-emptive right is contained in the firm's articles of incorporation, the firm must first offer any new issue of equity to existing shareholders. This assures each owner their proportionate owner's share.

An issue of equity to existing shareholders is called a *rights issue* or *rights offering.* Here each shareholder is issued an *option* to buy a specified number of new shares from the firm at a specified price within a specified time, after which the rights expire. For example, consider the £1.1 billion rights issue undertaken by Babcock International to partly fund a £1.6 billion acquisition of the helicopter firm Avincis. The firm's equity was selling at £13.66 on the announcement date, and current shareholders were able to buy a fixed number of shares at £7.90 per share within one month. The terms of the option are evidenced by certificates known as *share warrants* or *rights.* Such rights are often traded on securities exchanges or over the counter.

The Mechanics of a Rights Issue

The various considerations confronting a financial manager in a rights offering are illustrated by Babcock International. At the time, Babcock's equity was worth nearly £5 billion and it had 362 million shares outstanding.

The process of issuing rights differs from issuing shares of equity for cash. Existing shareholders are notified that they have been given a specific number of rights for each share of equity they own. Exercise occurs when a shareholder sends payment to the firm's subscription agent (usually a bank) and turns in the required number of rights. Shareholders of Babcock were given four choices:

1. Exercise some or all of your rights at £7.90 per right.
2. Sell all your rights.
3. Sell a proportion of your rights to generate sufficient funds to exercise the rest of your rights.
4. Do nothing and let the rights expire (this was the default option).

Babcock management had to answer the following questions:

- What price should the existing shareholders be allowed to pay for a share of new equity?
- How many rights will be required to purchase one share of equity?
- What effect will the rights offering have on the existing share price of the company?

Subscription Price

In a rights issue, the subscription price is the price that existing shareholders are allowed to pay for a share of equity. A rational shareholder will subscribe to the rights offering only if the subscription price is below the market price of the equity on the offer's expiration date. For example, if the share price at expiration is £5 and the subscription price is £7.90, no rational shareholder will subscribe. Why pay £7.90 for something worth only £5? Babcock International chose a price of £7.90, which was well below the existing market price of £13.66. As long as the market price did not fall below the subscription price of £7.90 before expiration, the rights offering would succeed.

Number of Rights Needed to Purchase a Share

Babcock International wanted to raise just over £1.1 billion in new equity. With a subscription price of £7.90, it needed to issue 139,259,204 new shares. This can be determined by dividing the total amount to be raised by the subscription price:

$$\text{Number of new shares} = \frac{\text{Funds to raise}}{\text{Subscription price}} = \frac{£1{,}100{,}147{,}712}{£7.90} = 139{,}259{,}204 \text{ shares}$$

To determine how many rights must be exercised to get one share of equity, we can divide the number of existing outstanding shares of equity by the number of new shares:

$$\text{Number of rights needed to buy a share of equity} = \frac{\text{'Old' shares}}{\text{'New' shares}} = \frac{362{,}073{,}930}{139{,}259{,}204} = 2.6 \text{ rights}$$

Clearly, it is impossible to own exactly 2.6 shares, and so in a rights issue one must construct terms so that the number of rights and shares are integers. In Babcock's case, the correct terms were 13 'old' shares for 5 'new' shares (13/5 = 2.6). In markets parlance, this would be called a '5 for 13 rights issue of 139,259,204 shares at £7.90 per share'. Thus each shareholder had to give up 13 rights plus £7.90 to receive 5 shares of new equity. If all the shareholders do this, Babcock will raise the required £1.1 billion.

It should be clear that the subscription price, the number of new shares and the number of rights needed to buy a new share of equity are interrelated. If Babcock International lowered the subscription price, it would have had to issue more new shares to raise £1.1 billion in new equity. Several alternatives appear here:

Subscription Price (£)	Number of New Shares	Number of Rights Needed to Buy a Share of Equity
9.00	122,238,635	2.962
7.90	139,259,204	2.600
5.00	220,029,542	1.646

Effect of Rights Offering on the Share Price

Rights clearly have value. In the case of Babcock International, the right to be able to buy a share of equity worth £13.66 for £7.90 was valuable.

Suppose a Babcock shareholder owns 13 shares of equity just before the rights offering. This situation is depicted in Table 15.7. Initially, the Babcock share price was £13.66, so the shareholder's total holding is worth 13 × £13.66 = £177.58. The shareholder who has 13 shares will receive 13 rights. The Babcock rights issue gave shareholders with 13 rights the opportunity to purchase 5 additional shares for £7.90. The holding of the shareholder who exercises these rights and buys the new shares would increase to 18 shares. The value of the new holding would be £177.58 + £39.50 = £217.08 (the £177.58 initial value plus the £39.50 paid to the company). Because the shareholder now holds 18 shares, the price per share would drop to £217.08/18 = £12.06 (rounded to two decimal places).

The difference between the old share price of £13.66 and the new share price of £12.06 reflects the fact that the old shares carried rights to subscribe to the new issue. The difference must be equal to the value of one right – that is, £13.66 – £12.06 = £1.60.

Just as we learned of an ex-dividend date in Chapter 14, there is an ex-rights date here. An individual buying the equity prior to the ex-rights date will receive the rights when they are distributed. An individual buying the equity on or after the ex-rights date will not receive the rights. In our example the price of the equity prior to the ex-rights date was £13.66. An individual buying on or after the ex-rights date is not entitled to the rights. The price on or after the ex-rights date will be £12.06.

Table 15.7 The Value to the Individual Shareholder of Babcock International's Rights

	The Shareholder
Initial position	
Number of shares	13
Share price	£13.66
Value of holding	£177.58
Terms of offer	
Subscription price	£7.90
Number of old shares for new shares	13 for 5
After offer	
Number of shares	18
Value of holding	£217.08
Share price	£12.06
Value of a right	
Old price – new price	£13.66 – £12.06 = £1.60
$\frac{\text{New price – Subscription price}}{\text{Number of rights for a share}}$	(£12.06 – £7.90)/2.6 = £1.60

Table 15.8 shows what happens to Babcock International. If all shareholders exercise their rights, the number of shares will increase to 501,333,134 and the value of the firm will increase to £6,046,077,601. After the rights offering the value of each share will drop to £12.06 (= £6,046,077,601/501,333,134).

Table 15.8 The Babcock International Rights Offering

Initial position	
Number of 'old' shares	362,073,930
Share price	£13.66
Value of firm	£4,945,929,889
Terms of offer	
Subscription price	£7.90
Number of 'new' shares	139,259,204
After offer	
Number of shares	501,333,134
Share price	£12.06
Value of firm	£6,046,077,601
Value of one right	£13.66 – £12.06 = £1.60 or (£12.06 – £7.90)/2.6 = £1.60

An investor holding no shares of Babcock International equity who wants to subscribe to the new issue can do so by buying rights. An outside investor buying 13 rights will pay £1.60 × 13 = £20.80 (to account for previous rounding). If the investor exercises the rights at a subscription cost of £7.90 to purchase five new shares, the total cost would be £20.80 + £39.50 = £60.30. In return for this expenditure, the investor will receive five shares of the new equity (worth £12.06 per share), totalling £60.30.

Of course, outside investors can also buy the Babcock International shares directly at £12.06 per share. In an efficient stock market it will make no difference whether new equity is obtained via rights or via direct purchase.

Effects on Shareholders

Shareholders can exercise their rights or sell them. In either case, the shareholder will neither win nor lose by the rights offering. The hypothetical holder of 13 Babcock International shares has a portfolio worth £177.58. On the one hand, if the shareholder exercises the rights, he or she ends up with five shares worth a total of £60.30. In other words, by spending £60.30, the investor increases the value of the holding by £60.30, which means that he or she is neither better nor worse off.

On the other hand, a shareholder who sells the 13 rights for £1.60 each obtains £1.60 × 13 = £20.80 in cash. Because the 13 shares are each worth £12.06, the holdings are valued at:

$$\begin{aligned} \text{Shares} &= 13 \times £12.06 = £156.78 \\ \text{Sold rights} &= 13 \times £1.60 = £\ 20.80 \\ \text{Total} &= \overline{£177.58} \end{aligned}$$

The new £156.78 market value plus £20.80 in cash is exactly the same as the original holding of £177.58. Thus, shareholders can neither lose nor gain from exercising or selling rights.

It is obvious that the new market price of the firm's equity will be lower after the rights offering than it was before the rights issue. The lower the subscription price, the greater the price decline of a rights issue. However, our analysis shows that the shareholders have suffered no loss because of the rights issue.

The Underwriting Arrangements

Undersubscription can occur if investors throw away rights or if bad news causes the market price of the equity to fall below the subscription price. To ensure against these possibilities, rights offerings are typically arranged by standby underwriting. Here the underwriter makes a firm commitment to purchase the unsubscribed portion of the issue at the subscription price less a take-up fee. The underwriter usually receives a standby fee as compensation for this risk-bearing function.

In practice the subscription price is usually set well below the current market price, making the probability of a rights failure quite small. Though a small percentage (less than 10 per cent) of shareholders fail to exercise valuable rights, shareholders are usually allowed to purchase unsubscribed shares at the subscription price. This oversubscription privilege makes it unlikely that the corporate issuer would need to turn to its underwriter for help.

Although the Babcock International rights issue was priced substantially lower than the market price, the issue was 96.62 per cent subscribed. This meant that the underwriter (also known as the bookrunner) had to purchase the 3.38 per cent unsubscribed portion of the issue. As the Babcock press release stated:

> *In accordance with their obligations as Joint Bookrunners in respect of the Rights Issue pursuant to the Underwriting Agreement, J.P. Morgan Securities plc, Jefferies International Limited, Barclays Bank PLC and HSBC Bank plc will endeavour to procure subscribers for the remaining 4,701,180 New Ordinary Shares not validly taken up in the Rights Issue and the 5,915 New Ordinary Shares representing fractional entitlements in respect of the Rights Issue, failing which J.P. Morgan Securities plc, Jefferies International Limited, Barclays Bank PLC and HSBC Bank plc have agreed to acquire, on a several basis, any remaining New Ordinary Shares.*

15.7 Shelf Registration

To simplify the procedures for issuing securities, many stock exchanges allow shelf registration. Shelf registration permits a corporation to register an offering that it reasonably expects to sell within a specified number of years. A master registration statement is filed at the time of registration. The company is permitted to sell the issue whenever it wants over the shelf registration period as long as it distributes a short-form statement.

Shelf registrations have been a lot more common over the past 10 years, particularly with seasoned equity offerings. Billet, Floros and Garfinkel (2018) report on the use of the *dribble* method of new equity issuance. A total of 63 per cent of all seasoned offerings were issued using this method. With dribbling, a company registers the issue and hires an underwriter to be its selling agent. The company sells shares in small amounts from time to time via a stock exchange.

Several arguments have been made for and against shelf registration:

- Companies exposed to potential short-selling will use shelf registrations. Traders can short-sell shares of companies that announce a seasoned equity offering to get a larger discount on the issue price. A shelf registration allows these firms to issue new equity without additional regulatory intervention and with very little advance warning (Dutordoir, Strong and Sun, 2019).
- The timeliness of disclosure is reduced with shelf registration because the master registration statement may have been prepared up to two years before the actual issue occurs.
- Some bankers have argued that shelf registration will cause a market overhang because registration informs the market of future issues. It has been suggested that this overhang will depress market prices. However, an empirical analysis by Bhagat, Marr and Thompson (1985) found that shelf registration is less costly than conventional underwriting, and found no evidence to suggest a market overhang effect.

15.8 The Private Equity Market

The previous sections of this chapter assumed that a company is big enough, successful enough and old enough to raise capital in the public equity market. Of course, many firms have not reached this stage and cannot use the public equity market. For start-up firms or firms in financial trouble, the public equity market is often not available. For these companies, the private equity market may be the best option.

Private Placement

Private placements avoid the costly procedures associated with the registration requirements that are part of public issues. Stock exchanges tend to restrict private placement issues to no more than a couple of dozen knowledgeable investors, including institutions such as insurance companies and pension funds. The biggest drawback of privately placed securities is that the securities cannot easily be resold. Most private placements involve debt securities, but equity securities can also be privately placed.

The Private Equity Firm

A large amount of private equity investment is undertaken by professional private equity managers representing large institutional investors such as mutual funds and pension funds. The limited partnership is the dominant form of intermediation in this market. Typically, the institutional investors act as limited partners, and the professional managers act as general partners. The general partners are firms that specialize in funding and managing equity investments in closely held private firms.

The private equity market has been important for both traditional start-up companies and established public firms. Thus, the private equity market can be divided into venture equity and non-venture equity markets. A large part of the non-venture market is made up of firms in financial distress. Firms in financial trouble are not likely to be able to issue public equity and typically cannot use traditional forms of debt such as bank loans or public debt. For these firms, the best alternative is to find a private equity firm. Outside the United States, the UK is the leading centre for private equity, and most private equity firms are based there. Table 15.9 lists the largest private equity firms in the world by total size of deals in 2022. The market is necessarily a global one and reflects the international nature of the sector.

Suppliers of Venture Capital

As we have pointed out, venture capital is an important part of the private equity market. There are at least four types of supplier of venture capital. First, a few old-line, wealthy families have traditionally provided start-up capital to promising businesses. These families have been involved in venture capital for at least a century. For example, over the years, the Rockefeller family has made the initial capital contribution to a number of successful businesses.

Second, a number of private partnerships and corporations have been formed to provide investment funds. The organizer behind the partnership might raise capital from institutional investors, such as insurance companies and pension funds. Alternatively, a group of individuals might provide the funds to be ultimately invested with budding entrepreneurs.

Table 15.9 Largest Private Equity Fundraisers in 2022

2022 Rank	Institution	Headquarters	Capital Raised ($m)
1	KKR	New York	126.508
2	Blackstone	New York	82.457
3	EQT	Stockholm	57.287
4	CVC Capital Partners	Luxembourg	55.414
5	Thoma Bravo	San Francisco	50.257
6	The Carlyle Group	Washington, DC	48.441
7	General Atlantic	New York	44.832
8	Clearlake Capital Group	Santa Monica	42.350
9	Hellman & Friedman	San Francisco	40.925
10	Insight Partners	New York	40.131

Source: www.privateequityinternational.com

Venture capital is a sub-activity of all private equity financing. The most common form of private equity financing in recent years is through buyouts. Examples of private equity buyout activity include EMI, Boots and Chrysler. Figure 15.3 provides a breakdown of European private equity funding in 2022.[10] The majority of venture capital funds are in growth and start-up investments, and much of this business is in the UK and Ireland, France and the Benelux countries.

Figure 15.3 Breakdown of Private Equity Funding by Stage, Focus and Region, 2022

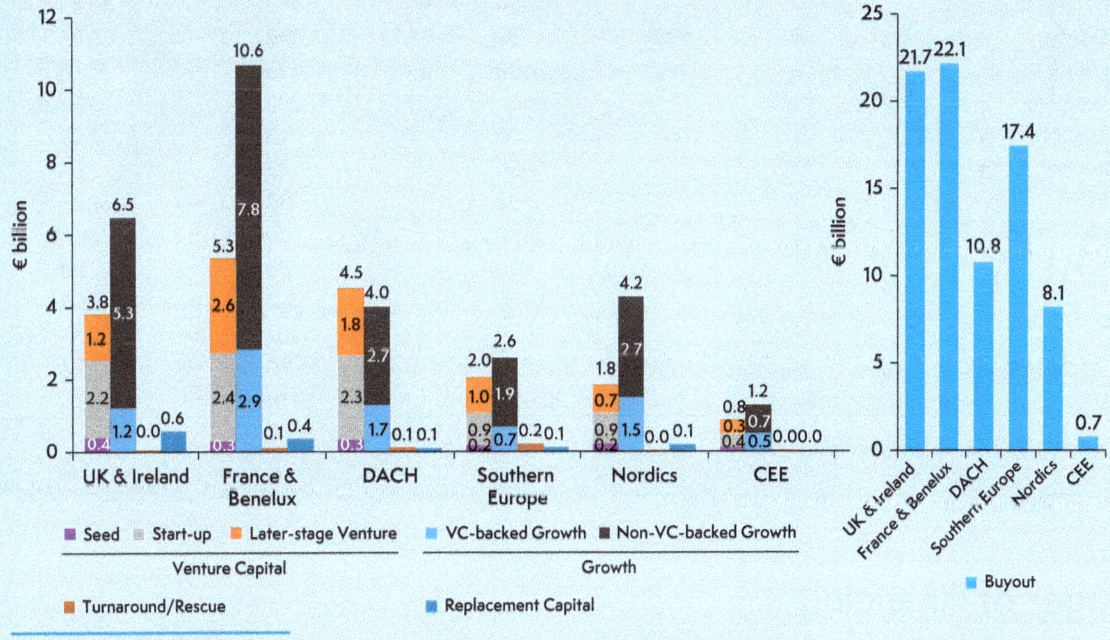

Source: Invest Europe/EDC (2023).

Stories used to abound about how easily an individual could obtain venture capital. Though that may have been the case in an earlier era, it is certainly not so today. Venture capital firms employ various screening procedures to prevent inappropriate funding. For example, because of the large demand for funds, many venture capitalists have at least one employee whose full-time job consists of reading business plans. Only the very best plans can expect to attract funds. Maier and Walker (1987) indicate that only about 2 per cent of requests actually receive financing.

Third, large industrial or financial corporations have established venture capital subsidiaries. Manufacturers Hanover Venture Capital Corp., Citicorp Venture Capital and Chemical Venture Capital Corporation of Chemical Bank are examples of this type. However, subsidiaries of this type appear to make up only a small portion of the venture capital market.

Fourth, there are also participants in an informal venture capital market.[11] Rather than belonging to any venture capital firm, these investors (often referred to as *angels*) act as individuals when providing financing. However, they should not, by any means, be viewed as isolated. Cipollone and Giordani (2019) and others indicate there is a rich network of angels across Europe continually relying on one another for advice. A number of researchers have stressed that, in any informal network, there is likely to be one knowledgeable and trustworthy individual who, when backing a venture, brings a few less experienced investors in with him.

The venture capital community has unfortunately chosen to refer to these individuals as 'dumb dentists'. Although a number indeed may be dentists, their intelligence should not be called into question. Wetzel asserts that the prototypical angel has income over $100,000, net worth over $1,000,000, and substantial business experience and knowledge. As we might expect, the informal venture capitalist is able to tolerate high risks. Table 15.10 presents data held by the European Business Angel Network on its business angel membership. The UK, Germany and France are the largest countries for business angels, and this reflects the overall size of each country's economy. However, business angels are in every country and form an important, if small, sector of the European financing sector. Though this informal market may seem small and unimportant, it is perhaps the largest of all sources of venture capital in Europe.

Table 15.10 International Business Angel Networks

Country	Number of Business Angel Networks	Number of Business Angels	Number of Investments	Total Investment Value (€m)
Austria	3	450	42	29.8
Belgium	7	500	44	30.2
Denmark	3	350	366	60.43
Finland	3	750	1,049	66.83
France	70	5,500	575	153.5
Germany	38	7,500	293	159.7
Greece	2	90	10	2.98
Ireland	13	950	47	25.4
Italy	11	600	138	67.28
Netherlands	10	1400	89	46.4
Norway	4	600	36	11.1
Spain	29	3,800	231	66.9
Sweden	4	900	107	34.55
Switzerland	9	850	70	55.4
UK	58	10,000	701	388.5

Source: European Business Angel Network, EBAN Statistics Compendium, European Early Stage Market Statistics (2021).

Stages of Financing

Bruno and Tyebjee (1985) identify six stages in venture capital financing:

1 *Seed money stage:* A small amount of financing needed to prove a concept or develop a product. Marketing is not included in this stage.

2 *Start-up:* Financing for firms that started within the past year. Funds are likely to pay for marketing and product development expenditures.

3 *First-round financing:* Additional money to begin sales and manufacturing after a firm has spent its start-up funds.

4 *Second-round financing:* Funds earmarked for working capital for a firm that is currently selling its product but still losing money.

5 *Third-round financing:* Financing for a company that is at least breaking even and is contemplating an expansion. This is also known as *mezzanine financing.*

6 *Fourth-round financing:* Money provided for firms that are likely to go public within half a year. This round is also known as *bridge financing.*

Although these categories may seem vague to the reader, we have found that the terms are well accepted within the industry. For example, the venture capital firms listed in *Pratt's Guide to Venture Capital Sources* indicate which of these stages they are interested in financing. Figure 15.2 also presents a breakdown of where private equity funding was made in Europe in 2017. The use of venture capital varied considerably across countries and, whereas in the UK and Ireland it was used to fund new growth, in continental Europe it was more associated with start-up funding.

Real World Insight 15.1

The penultimate stage in venture capital finance is the initial public offering.[12] Venture capitalists are important participants in initial public offerings. Venture capitalists rarely sell all of the shares they own at the time of the initial public offering. Instead they usually sell out in subsequent public offerings.

What do Business Angels look for in an Investment?

(Excerpts taken from 'How to Find and Pitch your Business to an Angel Investor' from growthbusiness.co.uk)

Jenny Tooth, CEO of the UK Business Angels Association, explains what angel investors look for if they are thinking of investing in your growth business.

Where do I find an angel investor?

The best way to approach an angel investor is often through a warm introduction – one from a friend, contact, company or entrepreneur. Investors get a lot of inbound pitches, so it's hard to qualify what's a cold lead or not. There is a lack of infrastructure, which means that neither angels nor entrepreneurs are visible to one another.

What do angel investors want to know?

We want to know the challenge that you're addressing in the market or society, whether you have done your market research to show why your project meets a real need and can bring something new or disruptive to the market. We also want to know how you plan to make money and that your business model can be scaled. We will ask if you have tested it out on any potential customers – not necessarily having sold anything, but you have to prove interest and whether you have checked out your competitors. International scalability is growing ever more important, so to be able to think about how you would like your business to fit on an international stage is always a huge bonus.

How much can a UK angel investor invest?

While business angels can invest on their own, more frequently angels invest alongside other angel investors through syndication. This enables you to pool your funds and share the risks, as well as share the due diligence and experience of other investors. The average individual angel investment is around £25,000, with syndicates providing – on average – around £190,000. How much an angel investor invests depends on the individual needs of both the business and the investor. Larger SMEs expanding internationally may require more funding than a small business looking to grow nationally. This is one of the ways in which angel investors can tailor their support in ways that may be unavailable from traditional bank lenders. It also benefits the investor with an increased flexibility to the amount invested, especially as part of a syndicate.

How long do angel investors stay on as investors?

Angel investing is generally regarded as 'patient capital' and you may not see an exit or a return for up to 8–10 years. Entrepreneurs often rely on the guidance of people who have experience in running and building a business. This guidance is of just as much importance as investment and funding. How long angels remain part of the business again varies on a case-by-case basis, depending on the amount of guidance needed in the life of the business. It is often beneficial to the business to retain the expertise and experience of angels, and what is good for the business is by extension good for the investors themselves.

How do angel investors make a profit?

Angel investors seek to share in the successful growth and have a return on their investment when the business exits successfully. There are five main routes of achieving an exit for angel investors, and the amount of profit or return on investment ultimately depends on the growth of the business.

1. *Trade sale:* The sale of the entire issued share capital to a third party as a trade sale. This is the most common exit, although occasionally by way of a 'buyout', where the investee company is acquired by an entity funded by a private equity investor, a bank and/or a management team.
2. *MBO:* The buy-back of the angel's shares by the company itself from its own resources, or by the entrepreneur. This is relatively unusual as an exit for angel investors.
3. *Purchase of shares:* Purchase of angel investors' shares by a VC, VCT, PE or corporate VC investor. The entry of a more significant investor party can enable the original angel investors to gain a partial or full exit.
4. *Secondary markets:* Some financial organizations are offering secondary markets to enable angel investors to exchange their shares for financial liquidity. This is a new area and further secondary markets may develop, including sector-specific opportunities.
5. *IPO:* You may also identify the opportunity to take the business to the next level of growth and raise more significant levels of risk capital by launching the business on to the public markets through AIM or IPO. This is not usually a direct exit for the angel investors but can enable some liquidity at the time of public market entry when other investors come on board.

Summary and Conclusions

This chapter looked closely at how equity is issued. The main points follow:

1. Large issues have proportionately much lower costs of issuing equity than small ones.
2. Firm commitment underwriting is far more prevalent for large issues than is best-efforts underwriting. Smaller issues probably primarily use best efforts because of the greater uncertainty of these issues. For an offering of a given size, the direct expenses of best-efforts underwriting and firm commitment underwriting are of the same magnitude.
3. Rights issues are cheaper than general cash offers and eliminate the problem of underpricing. Yet most new equity issues are underwritten general cash offers.
4. Shelf registration is a new method of issuing new debt and equity. The direct costs of shelf issues seem to be substantially lower than those of traditional issues.
5. Private equity is an increasingly important influence in start-up firms and subsequent financing.

Questions and Problems

CONCEPT

1 **The Public Issue** Review the steps involved in the public issue of equity. Do an online search for a public equity issue in your country, download all relevant news stories and track the issue process for the company. Is it similar to the one presented in this chapter? For IPOs, what do you think the main factors are that determine the stock exchange the company should list on?

2 **Alternative Issue Methods** What is the difference between a public offering and a private placement? What might explain a company's decision to favour one over the other? Your discussion should make reference to the advantages and disadvantages of each.

3 **Announcement Effects** Why do you think the share price tends to go down when an equity issue is announced?

4 **Shelf Registration** Explain the benefits of shelf registration. Why would shareholders not be keen on shelf registration?

REGULAR

5 **The Private Equity Market** Provide an overview of the private equity market. Why would firms wish to go private once they have listed on a stock exchange? In January 2023, the British budget airline Flybe delisted from the London Stock Exchange. Why do you think this was? Do you think this will be beneficial to the business?

6 **IPO Underpricing** What is meant by underpricing? Why are most IPOs underpriced? Drawing on the academic evidence, explain the main theories behind this phenomenon. Is this a sign of market inefficiency? Do you think firms that pursue sustainable development goals are likely to be underpriced? Explain.

7 **IPO Pricing** Adyen, a Dutch fintech company, had its IPO in June 2018 on the Euronext Amsterdam exchange. Assisted by a consortium of banks, including Morgan Stanley, J.P. Morgan and Goldman Sachs, Adyen sold shares at €240 each. At the end of the first day of trading, Adyen's shares soared 90 per cent to €455 per share. Based on the end-of-day numbers, Adyen shares were apparently underpriced by about 90 per cent, meaning that the company missed out on significant additional capital. Should Adyen be upset at Morgan Stanley, J.P. Morgan and Goldman Sachs over the underpricing?

8 **Costs and Benefits of IPOs** Outline the advantages and disadvantages for a company undertaking an IPO.

9 **IPO Underpricing around the World** IPO underpricing is a worldwide phenomenon. In the United Kingdom IPOs are underpriced by around 15.7 per cent, and most other advanced economies experience IPO underpricing of around 19 per cent. In the UAE, IPOs are underpriced by around 186 per cent, while for emerging markets it is around 60 per cent. What do you think explains these vast differences?

10 **Cash Offer versus Rights Offer** ThyssenKrup AG is an industrial component manufacturer based in Germany. Assume that it is considering opening a new plant in Poland. It has two choices to fund the investment: issue equity via a rights issue to its existing shareholders or have a full public underwritten cash offer. Give advice to the management of ThyssenKrup on the best issue method. What is your recommendation and why?

11 **IPO Underpricing: the Winner's Curse** Consider the following experiment: you submit a purchase order for every firm commitment initial public offering of oil and gas exploration companies. There are 22 of these offerings, and you submit a purchase order for approximately €1,000 in equity for each of the companies. However, for ten issues you are allocated no shares and for five issues you receive fewer than the requested number of shares. In only seven issues do you receive the number of shares you requested.

Assume that this was a very good year for oil and gas exploration company owners: on average, for the 22 companies that went public, the shares were selling for 80 per cent above the offering price a month after the initial offering date. However, you have looked at your own performance record and found that the €8,400 invested in the 12 companies had grown to €10,000, representing a return of only about 20 per cent (commissions were negligible). Did you have bad luck, or should you have expected to do worse than the average initial public offering investor? Explain.

12 **Investing in IPOs** The material below represents the cover page and summary of the prospectus for the initial public offering of the Pest Investigation Control Corporation SA (PICC), which is going public tomorrow with a firm commitment initial public offering managed by the investment banking firm of Bigelli and Pindado.

PICC PROSPECTUS

200,000 shares

PEST INVESTIGATION CONTROL CORPORATION

Of the shares being offered hereby, all 200,000 are being sold by the Pest Investigation Control Corporation SA ('the Company'). Before the offering there has been no public market for the shares of PICC, and no guarantee can be given that any such market will develop.

These securities have not been approved or disapproved by the Autorité des Marchés Financiers, nor has the Authority passed judgement upon the accuracy or adequacy of this prospectus. Any representation to the contrary is a criminal offence.

	Price to Public (€)	Underwriting Discount (€)	Proceeds to Company* (€)
Per share	11.00	1.10	9.90
Total	2,200,000	220,000	1,980,000

* Before deducting expenses estimated at €27,000 and payable by the company.

This is an initial public offering. The ordinary shares are being offered, subject to prior sale, when, as, and if delivered to and accepted by the Underwriters and subject to approval of certain legal matters by their Counsel and by Counsel for the Company. The Underwriters reserve the right to withdraw, cancel or modify such offers and to reject offers in whole or in part.

Bigelli and Pindado, Bankers 12 July 2024

Prospectus Summary

The Company	The Pest Investigation Control Corporation (PICC) breeds and markets toads and tree frogs as ecologically safe insect-control mechanisms.
The Offering	200,000 ordinary shares of equity, no par value.
Listing	The Company will seek listing on Euronext.
Shares Outstanding	As of 30 June 2024, 400,000 ordinary shares of equity were outstanding. After the offering, 600,000 ordinary shares of equity will be outstanding.
Use of Proceeds	To finance expansion of inventory and receivables and general working capital, and to pay for country club memberships for certain finance professors.

Selected Financial Information (amounts in thousands except per-share data)						
	Fiscal Year Ended 30 June				As of 30 June 2024	
	2022 (€)	2023 (€)	2024 (€)		Actual (€)	As Adjusted for this Offering (€)
Revenues	60.00	120.00	240.00	Working capital	0.8	1,961
Net earnings	3.80	15.90	36.10	Total assets	511	2,464
Earnings per share	0.01	0.04	0.09	Shareholders' equity	423	2,376

(a) Assume that you know nothing about PICC other than the information contained in the prospectus. Based on your knowledge of finance, what is your prediction for the price of PICC tomorrow? Provide a short explanation as to why you think this will occur.

(b) Assume that you have several thousand euros to invest. When you get home from class tonight, you find that your stockbroker, whom you have not talked to for weeks, has called. She has left a message that PICC is going public tomorrow and saying she can get you several hundred shares at the offering price if you call her back first thing in the morning. Discuss the merits of this opportunity.

13 **Competitive and Negotiated Offers** Assume you have been hired by the Spanish food exporter Distribuidora Internacional de Alimentacion SA to help progress a seasoned equity offering it plans to undertake in the autumn. You have been specifically asked to recommend either a competitive offer or a negotiated offer for the firm to undertake. What is your recommendation and why?

14 **Seasoned Equity Offers** For the firm in Question 13, you have been asked by a reporter why you are having a seasoned equity offering when typically share prices drop when they are announced. How would you explain the price drop?

15 **Raising Capital** For the firm in Question 13, you have been approached by a major shareholder who has asked you to consider either an underwritten cash offer or a rights issue (not underwritten) to current shareholders. The shareholder has insisted you maximize shareholder wealth. What is your decision? Explain.

16 **Shelf Registration** A sustainable energy company is planning to raise capital through multiple offerings over the next three years. The company wants to streamline the process, reduce costs, and retain flexibility in the timing and size of the offerings. How can the company leverage shelf registration to achieve these goals, and what are the potential benefits and drawbacks of using shelf registration specifically for sustainable firms?

17 **Commonalities in IPOs** Every IPO is unique, but what are the basic empirical regularities in IPOs?

18 **Rights Offerings: Balmorals plc** Balmorals plc is a well-established company that has run into difficulty in recent years. Its management has recently undertaken a review of its activities and has decided to proceed with a radical restructuring of the business. To restore the company's financial stability, it has been decided it will be necessary to raise £160 million through a rights issue. After consulting its investment bankers the company is planning to make the rights issue at a discount of 20 per cent to the current market price of £5. The company has 100 million shares outstanding.

(a) What is the value of a right?

(b) What are the current terms of the rights issue?

(c) How would an investor with 10,000 shares be affected if they:

(i) Exercised their rights
(ii) Sold their rights
(iii) Tail swallowed their rights?

19 **Rights Offering: Faff plc** Faff plc has announced a rights issue to raise £50 million for a new journal, the *Journal of Financial Excess*. This journal will review potential articles after the author pays a non-refundable reviewing fee of £5,000 per page. The equity currently sells for £40 per share and there are 5.2 million shares outstanding.

(a) What is the maximum possible subscription price? What is the minimum?

(b) If the subscription price is set at £35 per share, how many shares must be sold? How many rights will it take to buy one share?

(c) What is the ex-rights price? What is the value of a right?

(d) Show how a shareholder with 1,000 shares before the offering and no desire (or money) to buy additional shares is not harmed by the rights offer.

20 **Rights Offerings: Glasauge AB** Glasauge AB concluded that additional equity financing will be needed to expand operations and that the needed funds will best be obtained through a rights issue. It has correctly determined that, as a result of the rights issue, the share price will fall from €3.38 to €3.00 (€3.38 is the 'rights-on' price; €3.00 is the ex-rights price, also known as the *when-issued* price). The company is seeking €2 million in additional funds with a per-share subscription price equal to €2. How many shares are there currently, before the offering? (Assume that the increment to the market value of the equity equals the gross proceeds from the offering.)

21 **IPO Underpricing: Trading Strategy** Carlyle plc and Mullan plc have both announced IPOs at £40 per share. One of these is undervalued by £11, and the other is overvalued by £6, but you have no way of knowing which is which. You plan on buying 1,000 shares of each issue. If an issue is underpriced it will be rationed and only half your order will be filled. If you *could* get 1,000 shares in Carlyle and 1,000 shares in Mullan, what would your profit be? What profit do you actually expect? What principle have you illustrated?

22 **Calculating Flotation Costs** Groene Heuvels NV has just gone public. Under a firm commitment agreement, Groene Heuvels received €19.75 for each of the 5 million shares sold. The initial offering price was €21 per share, and the equity rose to €26 per share in the first few minutes of trading. Groene Heuvels paid €800,000 in direct legal and other costs, and €250,000 in indirect costs. What was the flotation cost as a percentage of funds raised?

23 **Price Dilution** Raggio SpA has 100,000 shares of equity outstanding. Each share is worth €90, so the company's market value of equity is €9,000,000. Suppose the firm issues 20,000 new shares at the following prices: €90, €85 and €70. What will the effect be of each of these alternative offering prices on the existing price per share?

24 **Stock Offerings** The Newton Company has 10,000 shares of equity, each of which sells for £40. Suppose the company issues 5,000 shares of the new equity at the following prices: £40, £20 and £10. What is the effect of each of the alternative offering prices on the existing price per share?

CHALLENGE

25 **Seasoned Equity Issue Methods** What are the different methods through which a company can raise seasoned equity? What might explain a company's decision to favour one over the other? Your discussion should define each and make reference to the advantages and disadvantages of each.

26 **Dilution: Larme SA** Larme SA wishes to expand its facilities. The company currently has 10 million shares outstanding and no debt. The equity sells for €50 per share, but the book value per share is €40. Net income for Larme is currently €15 million. The new facility will cost €35 million, and it will increase net income by €500,000.

(a) Assuming a constant price–earnings ratio, what will the effect be of issuing new equity to finance the investment? To answer, calculate the new book value per share, the new total earnings, the new EPS, the new share price and the new market-to-book ratio. What is going on here?

(b) What would the new net income for Larme have to be for the share price to remain unchanged?

27 **Dilution: EHMM plc** Elvis Heavy Metal Mining (EHMM) plc wants to diversify its operations. Some recent financial information for the company is shown here:

Share price (£)	98
Number of shares	14,000
Total assets (£)	6,000,000
Total liabilities (£)	2,400,000
Net income (£)	630,000

EHMM is considering an investment that has the same PE ratio as the firm. The cost of the investment is £1,100,000 and it will be financed with a new equity issue. The return on the investment will equal EHMM's current ROE. What will happen to the book value per share, the market value per share and the EPS? What is the NPV of this investment? Does dilution take place?

28 **Dilution: EHMM plc (continued)** In the previous problem, what would the ROE on the investment have to be if we wanted the price after the offering to be £98 per share? (Assume the PE ratio remains constant.) What is the NPV of this investment? Does any dilution take place?

29 **Rights: Manchicourt** Manchicourt's equity currently sells for £45 per share. Last week the firm issued rights to raise new equity. To purchase a new share, a shareholder must remit £10 and three rights.

(a) What is the ex-rights share price?

(b) What is the price of one right?

(c) When will the price drop occur? Why will it occur then?

30 **Rights: Gipfel** Gipfel equity is currently selling at €13 per share. There are 1 million shares outstanding. The firm is planning to raise €2 million to finance a new project. What are the ex-rights share price, the value of a right and the appropriate subscription prices under the following scenarios? How does the shareholders' wealth change from part (a) to part (b)?

(a) Two shares of outstanding equity are entitled to purchase one additional share of the new issue.

(b) Four shares of outstanding equity are entitled to purchase one additional share of the new issue.

31 **Rights: Hoobastink Mfg** Hoobastink Mfg is considering a rights offer. The company has determined that the ex-rights price would be €52. The current price is €55 per share and there are 5 million shares outstanding. The rights issue would raise a total of €60 million. What is the subscription price?

32 **Value of Right** Show that the value of a right can be written as

$$\text{Value of a right} = P_{RO} - P_X = (P_{RO} - P_S)/(N+1)$$

where P_{RO}, P_S and P_x stand for the 'rights-on' price, the subscription price and the ex-rights price, respectively, and N is the number of rights needed to buy one new share at the subscription price.

33 **Selling Rights** Wuttke plc wants to raise £3.65 million via a rights issue. The company currently has 490,000 ordinary shares outstanding that sell for £30 per share. Its underwriter has set a subscription price of £22 per share and will charge Wuttke a 6 per cent spread. If you currently own 6,000 shares of equity in the company and decide not to participate in the rights issue, how much money can you get by selling your rights?

34 Valuing a Right: Mitsi Inventory Systems Mitsi Inventory Systems has announced a rights offer. The company has announced that it will take four rights to buy a new share in the offering at a subscription price of €40. At the close of business the day before the ex-rights day, the company's shares sell for €80 per share. The next morning you notice that the equity sells for €72 per share and the rights sell for €6 each. Are the equity and/or the rights correctly priced on the ex-rights day? Describe a transaction in which you could use these prices to create an immediate profit.

Exam Question (45 minutes)

1 *'In a public share issue, the probability of receiving an allocation of an underpriced security is less than or equal to the probability of receiving an allocation of an overpriced issue.'* Discuss this statement in the context of initial public offerings. **(25 marks)**

Ai Due Fanali SA has decided to undertake a rights issue that will raise €288 million. The current share price is €4.50 and there are 160 million shares in circulation. They have to make a decision on whether to underwrite the rights issue. The underwriting fee will be 2 per cent of proceeds if the shares are offered at a 20 per cent discount. Ai Due Fanali's finance director believes that a discount of 40 per cent will avoid the need for underwriting altogether.

2 Set out the terms of the issue under each of the two alternatives referred to above. Calculate the theoretical ex-rights price and the value of a right. **(25 marks)**

3 Demonstrate that, in principle, a wealth-maximizing shareholder owning six shares will be indifferent between the two alternative methods of raising the funds. **(25 marks)**

4 Discuss the benefits of using an underwriter in a rights issue. Review the factors that determine an underwriter's fee. **(25 marks)**

Total Marks: 100

Mini Case

West Coast Yachts Goes Public

Larissa Warren and Dan Ervin have been discussing the future of West Coast Yachts. The company has been experiencing fast growth and the future looks like clear sailing. However, the fast growth means that the company's growth can no longer be funded by internal sources, so Larissa and Dan have decided the time is right to take the company public. To this end, they have entered into discussions with the bank of Crowe & Mallard. The company has a working relationship with Robin Perry, the underwriter who assisted with the company's previous bond offering. Crowe & Mallard have helped numerous small companies in the IPO process, so Larissa and Dan feel confident with this choice.

Robin begins by telling Larissa and Dan about the process. Although Crowe & Mallard charged an underwriter fee of 4 per cent on the bond offering, the underwriter fee is 7 per cent on all initial equity offerings of the size of West Coast Yachts' initial offering. Robin tells Larissa and Dan that the company can expect to pay about £1,200,000 in legal fees and expenses, £12,000 in registration fees, and £15,000 in other filing fees. Additionally, to be listed on the London Stock Exchange, the company must pay £100,000. There are also transfer agent fees of £6,500 and engraving expenses of £450,000. The company should also expect to pay £75,000 for other expenses associated with the IPO.

Finally, Robin tells Larissa and Dan that, to file with the London Stock Exchange, the company must provide three years' worth of audited financial statements. She is unsure of the costs of the audit. Dan tells Robin that the company provides audited financial statements as part of its bond indenture, and the company pays £300,000 per year for the outside auditor.

1 At the end of the discussion Dan asks Robin about the Dutch auction IPO process. What are the differences in the expenses to West Coast Yachts if it uses a Dutch auction IPO versus a traditional IPO? Should the company go public with a Dutch auction or use a traditional underwritten offering?

2 During the discussion of the potential IPO and West Coast Yachts' future, Dan states that he feels the company should raise £50 million. However, Larissa points out that, if the company needs more cash soon, a secondary offering close to the IPO would be potentially problematic. Instead she suggests that the company should raise £80 million in the IPO. How can we calculate the optimal size of the IPO? What are the advantages and disadvantage of increasing the size of the IPO to £80 million?

3 After deliberation, Larissa and Dan have decided that the company should use a firm commitment offering with Crowe & Mallard as the lead underwriter. The IPO will be for £60 million. Ignoring underpricing, how much will the IPO cost the company as a percentage of the funds received?

4 Many of the employees of West Coast Yachts have shares of equity in the company because of an existing employee stock purchase plan. To sell the equity, the employees can tender their shares to be sold in the IPO at the offering price, or they can retain their equity and sell it in the secondary market after West Coast Yachts goes public (once the 180-day lock-up expires). Larissa asks you to advise the employees about which option is best. What would you suggest to them?

Practical Case Study

Do a search on Google News for 10 announcements of new funding for companies in the past year. Look at the share price between the announcement date and five days later. Can you see any pattern between share price reaction and funding type? In what ways could you improve this very simplistic analysis?

Relevant Accounting Standards

The most important accounting standard for equities is IAS 39 *Financial Instruments: Recognition and Measurement.* Visit the IASPlus website (www.iasplus.com) for more information.

References

Altinkilic, O. and R.S. Hansen (2000) 'Are There Scale Economies in Underwriting Spreads? Evidence of Rising External Financing Costs', *Review of Financial Studies,* Vol. 13, 191–218.

Armitage, S. (2000) 'The Direct Costs of UK Rights Issues and Open Offers', *European Financial Management,* Vol. 6, No. 1, 57–68.

Asquith, P. and D. Mullins (1986) 'Equity Issues and Offering Dilution', *Journal of Financial Economics,* Vol. 15, No. 1–2, 61–89.

Barnes, E. and M. Walker (2006) 'The Seasoned-equity Issues of UK Firms: Market Reaction and Issuance Method', *Journal of Business Finance and Accounting,* Vol. 33, No. 1–2, 45–78.

Barry, C., C.J. Muscarella, J.W. Peavey III and M.R. Vetsuypens (1990) 'The Role of Venture Capital in the Creation of Public Companies: Evidence from the Going Public Process', *Journal of Financial Economics,* Vol. 27, No. 2, 447–471.

Beatty, R. and J. Ritter (1986) 'Investment Banking, Reputation, and the Underpricing of Initial Public Offerings', *Journal of Financial Economics,* Vol. 15, No. 1–2, 213–232.

Bhagat, S. (1986) 'The Effect of Management's Choice Between Negotiated and Competitive Equity Offerings on Shareholder Wealth', *Journal of Financial and Quantitative Analysis,* Vol. 21, No. 2, 181–196.

Bhagat, S., M.W. Marr and G.R. Thompson (1985) 'The Rule 415 Experiment: Equity Markets', *Journal of Finance,* Vol. 40, No. 5, 1385–1401.

Billett, M.T., I.V. Floros and J.A. Garfinkel (2018) 'At-the-market (ATM) Offerings', *Journal of Financial and Quantitative Analysis,* Vol. 44, 237–271.

Boulton, T.J., S.B. Smart and C.J. Zutter (2017) 'Conservatism and International IPO Underpricing', *Journal of International Business Studies,* Vol. 48, No. 6, 763–785.

Boulton, T.J., S.B. Smart and C.J. Zutter (2018) 'Determinants of Variation in IPO Underpricing', in D. Cumming (ed.), *The Oxford Handbook of IPOs,* 81. https://doi.org/10.1093/oxfordhb/9780190614577.013.10

Bruno, A.V. and T.T. Tyebjee (1985) 'The Entrepreneur's Search for Capital', *Journal of Business Venturing,* Vol. 1, 61–74.

Carter, R.B., F.H. Dark and T.A. Sapp (2011) 'Underwriter Reputation and IPO Issuer Alignment 1981–2005', *Quarterly Review of Economics and Finance,* Vol. 5, 443–455.

Carter, R. and S. Manaster (1990) 'Initial Public Offerings and Underwriter Reputation', *Journal of Finance,* Vol. 45, 1045–1067.

Chen, Y., A.C. Chui, A. Goyal and M. Veeraraghavan (2022) 'Societal Secrecy and IPO Underpricing', *Journal of Corporate Finance,* Vol. 76, 102257.

Cipollone, A. and P.E. Giordani (2019) 'Entrepreneurs Meet Financiers: Evidence from the Business Angel Market', *Journal of Business Venturing,* Vol. 34, No. 5, 105913.

Duong, H.N., A. Goyal, V. Kallinterakis and M. Veeraraghavan (2022) 'Democracy and the Pricing of Initial Public Offerings Around the World', *Journal of Financial Economics,* Vol. 145, No. 1, 322–341.

Dutordoir, M., N. Strong and P. Sun (2019) 'Shelf versus Traditional Seasoned Equity Offerings: The Impact of Potential Short Selling', *Journal of Financial and Quantitative Analysis,* Vol. 54, No. 3, 1285–1311.

Gajewski, J.-F. and E. Ginglinger (2002) 'Seasoned Equity Issues in a Closely Held Market: Evidence from France', *European Finance Review,* Vol. 6, No. 3, 291–319.

Hansen, R.S. and C. Crutchley (1990) 'Corporate Earnings and Financings: An Empirical Analysis', *Journal of Business,* Vol. 63, 347–372.

Hansen, R.S. and N. Khanna (1994) 'Why Negotiation with a Single Syndicate May Be Preferred to Making Syndicates Compete: The Problem of Trapped Bidders', *Journal of Business,* Vol. 67, No. 3, 423–457.

Ibbotson, R. (1975) 'Price Performance of Common Stock New Issues', *Journal of Financial Economics,* Vol. 2, 235–272.

Krigman, L., W. Shaw and K. Womack (2001) 'Why Do Firms Switch Underwriters?', *Journal of Financial Economics,* Vol. 60, No. 2–3, 245–284.

Ljunqvist, A. (2006) 'IPO Underpricing', in B. Espen Eckbo (ed.), *Handbook of Corporate Finance: Empirical Corporate Finance,* Vol. A, Ch. 7. Amsterdam: Elsevier/North Holland.

Logue, D. and R. Jarrow (1978) 'Negotiation vs. Competitive Bidding in the Sales of Securities by Public Utilities', *Financial Management,* Vol. 7, 31–39.

Logue, D. and S. Tiniç (1999) 'Optimal Choice of Contracting Methods: Negotiated versus Competitive Underwritings Revisited', *Journal of Financial Economics,* Vol. 51, No. 3, 451–471.

Maier, J.B. and D. Walker (1987) 'The Role of Venture Capital in Financing Small Business', *Journal of Business Venturing,* Vol. 2, No. 3, 207–214.

Martin-Ugedo, J. (2003) 'Equity Rights Issues in Spain: Flotation Costs and Wealth Effects', *Journal of Business Finance and Accounting,* Vol. 30, 1277–1304.

Masulis, R. and A.N. Korwar (1986) 'Seasoned Equity Offerings: An Empirical Investigation', *Journal of Financial Economics,* Vol. 15, No. 1–2, 91–118.

Migliorati, K. and S. Vismara (2014) 'Ranking Underwriters of European IPOs', *European Financial Management,* Vol. 20, 891–925.

Mikkelson, W.H. and M.M. Partch (1986) 'The Valuation Effects of Security Offerings and the Issuance Process', *Journal of Financial Economics,* Vol. 15, No. 1–2, 31–60.

Rock, K. (1986) 'Why New Issues are Underpriced', *Journal of Financial Economics,* Vol. 15, No. 1–2, 187–212.

Wetzel, W.E. (1987) 'The Informal Venture Capital Market: Aspects of Scale and Market Efficiency', *Journal of Business Venturing,* Vol. 2, No. 4, 299–313.

Additional Reading

Research in equity financing covers many areas and this is reflected in the number of papers recently published in the area. To aid understanding and targeted reading, the reference list below is categorized into separate but overlapping topics. As with every good academic paper, the implications can span several different areas. Equity financing research is no different in this regard.

Initial Public Offerings

1 Aghamolla, C. and R.T. Thakor (2022) 'IPO Peer Effects', *Journal of Financial Economics,* Vol. 144, No. 1, 206–226.

2 Bajo, E. and C. Raimondo (2017) 'Media Sentiment and IPO Underpricing', *Journal of Corporate Finance,* Vol. 46, 139–153.

3 Bancel, F. and U.R. Mittoo (2009) 'Why Do European Firms Go Public?', *European Financial Management,* Vol. 15, No. 4, 844–884. **Europe.**

4 Binay, M.M., V.A. Gatchev and C.A. Pirinsky (2007) 'The Role of Underwriter–investor Relationships in the IPO Process', *Journal of Financial and Quantitative Analysis,* Vol. 42, No. 3, 785–809. **USA.**

5 Bodnaruk, A., E. Kandel and M. Massa (2008) 'Shareholder Diversification and the Decision to Go

Public', *Review of Financial Studies*, Vol. 21, No. 6, 2779–2824. **Sweden.**

6 Brau, J.C. and S.E. Fawcett (2006) 'Initial Public Offerings: An Analysis of Theory and Practice', *Journal of Finance*, Vol. 61, No. 1, 399–436. **USA.**

7 Celikyurt, U., M. Sevilir and A. Shivdasani (2010) 'Going Public to Acquire? The Acquisition Motive in IPOs', *Journal of Financial Economics*, Vol. 96, No. 3, 345–363.

8 Chemmanur, T.J. and I. Paeglis (2005) 'Management Quality, Certification, and Initial Public Offerings', *Journal of Financial Economics*, Vol. 76, No. 2, 331–368. **USA.**

9 Chemmanur, T.J., S. He and D.K. Nandy (2010) 'The Going-public Decision and the Product Market', *Review of Financial Studies*, Vol. 23, No. 5, 1855–1908.

10 Chemmanur, T.J., G. Hu and J. Huang (2010) 'The Role of Institutional Investors in Initial Public Offerings', *Review of Financial Studies*, Vol. 23, No. 12, 4496–4540. **USA.**

11 Cook, D.O., R. Kieschnick and R.A. Van Ness (2006) 'On the Marketing of IPOs', *Journal of Financial Economics*, Vol. 82, No. 1, 35–61. **USA.**

12 Corwin, S.A. and P. Schultz (2005) 'The Role of IPO Underpricing Syndicates: Pricing, Information Production, and Underwriter Competition', *Journal of Finance*, Vol. 60, No. 1, 443–486. **USA.**

13 Deloof, M., W. De Maeseneire and K. Inghelbrecht (2009) 'How Do Investment Banks Value Initial Public Offerings (IPOs)?', *Journal of Business Finance and Accounting*, Vol. 36, Nos. 1 and 2, 130–160. **Belgium.**

14 Derrien, F. and A. Kecskes (2007) 'The Initial Public Offering of Listed Firms', *Journal of Finance*, Vol. 62, No. 1, 447–479. **UK.**

15 Edwards, A.K. and K. Weiss Hanley (2010) 'Short Selling in Initial Public Offerings', *Journal of Financial Economics*, Vol. 98, No. 1, 21–39. **USA.**

16 Ellul, A. and M. Pagano (2006) 'IPO Underpricing and After-market Liquidity', *Review of Financial Studies*, Vol. 19, No. 2, 381–421. **UK.**

17 Holmen, M. and P. Hogfeldt (2004) 'A Law and Finance Analysis of Initial Public Offerings', *Journal of Financial Intermediation*, Vol. 13, No. 3, 324–358. **Sweden.**

18 Jenkinson, T. and H. Jones (2009) 'IPO Pricing and Allocation: A Survey of the Views of Institutional Investors', *Review of Financial Studies*, Vol. 22, No. 4, 1477–1504. **International.**

19 Kaustia, M. and S. Knupfer (2008) 'Do Investors Overweight Personal Experience? Evidence from IPO Subscriptions', *Journal of Finance*, Vol. 63, No. 6, 2679–2702. **Finland.**

20 Kerins, F., K. Kutsuna and R. Smith (2007) 'Why are IPOs Underpriced? Evidence from Japan's Hybrid Auction-method Offerings', *Journal of Financial Economics*, Vol. 85, No. 3, 637–666. **Japan.**

21 Kutsuna, K., J. Kiholm Smith and R. Smith (2009) 'Public Information, IPO Price Formation, and Long-Run Returns: Japanese Evidence', *Journal of Finance*, Vol. 64, No. 1, 505–546. **Japan.**

22 Ljungqvist, A. and W.J. Wilhelm (2005) 'Does Prospect Theory Explain IPO Market Behavior?', *Journal of Finance*, Vol. 60, No. 4, 1759–1790. **USA.**

23 Loughran, T. and B. McDonald (2013) 'IPO First-day Returns, Offer Price Revisions, Volatility, and Form S-1 Language', *Journal of Financial Economics*, Vol. 109, No. 2, 307–326.

24 Lowry, M., M.S. Officer and G.W. Schwert (2010) 'The Variability of IPO Initial Returns', *Journal of Finance*, Vol. 65, No. 2, 425–465.

25 Nielsson, U. and D. Wójcik (2016) 'Proximity and IPO Underpricing', *Journal of Corporate Finance*, Vol. 38, 92–105.

26 Pastor, L. and P. Veronesi (2005) 'Rational IPO Waves', *Journal of Finance*, Vol. 60, No. 4, 1713–1757. **USA.**

27 Roosenboom, P. and W. Schramade (2006) 'The Price of Power: Valuing the Controlling Position of Owner-managers in French IPO Firms', *Journal of Corporate Finance*, Vol. 12, No. 2, 270–295. **France.**

Private Equity and Venture Capital

28 Acharya, V.V., O.F. Gottschalg, M. Hahn and C. Kehoe (2013) 'Corporate Governance and Value Creation: Evidence from Private Equity', *Review of Financial Studies*, Vol. 26, No. 2, 368–402.

29 Bharath, S.T. and A.K. Dittmar (2010) 'Why Do Firms Use Private Equity to Opt Out of Public Markets?', *Review of Financial Studies*, Vol. 23, No. 5, 1771–1818.

30 Botazzi, L., M. Da Rin and T. Hellmann (2008) 'Who Are the Active Investors? Evidence from Venture Capital', *Journal of Financial Economics*, Vol. 89, No. 3, 488–512, **Europe.**

31 Cochrane, J.H. (2005) 'The Risk and Return of Venture Capital', *Journal of Financial Economics*, Vol. 75, No. 1, 3–52. **USA.**

32 Cronqvist, H. and M. Nilsson (2005) 'The Choice between Rights Offerings and Private Equity Placements', *Journal of Financial Economics*, Vol. 78, No. 2, 375–407. **Sweden.**

33 Cumming, D. (2008) 'Contracts and Exits in Venture Capital Finance', *Review of Financial Studies,* Vol. 21, No. 5, 1947–1982. **Europe.**

34 Cumming, D. and U. Walz (2010) 'Private Equity Returns and Disclosure around the World', *Journal of International Business Studies,* Vol. 41, 727–754. **International.**

35 Cumming, D., D. Schmidt and U. Walz (2010) 'Legality and Venture Capital Governance around the World', *Journal of Business Venturing,* Vol. 25, No. 1, 54–72.

36 Diller, C. and C. Kaserer (2009) 'What Drives Private Equity Returns? Fund Inflows, Skilled GPs and/or Risk?', *European Financial Management,* Vol. 15, No. 3, 643–675.

37 Hochberg, Y.V., A. Ljungqvist and Y. Lu (2007) 'Whom You Know Matters: Venture Capital Networks and Investment Performance', *Journal of Finance,* Vol. 62, No. 1, 251–301. **USA.**

38 Ivashina, V. and A. Kovner (2011) 'The Private Equity Advantage: Leveraged Buyout Firms and Relationship Banking', *Review of Financial Studies,* Vol. 24, No. 7, 2462–2498.

39 Kaplan, S. and A. Schoar (2005) 'Private Equity Performance: Returns, Persistence, and Capital Flows', *Journal of Finance,* Vol. 60, No. 4, 1791–1823. **USA.**

40 Kaplan, S., S. Berk and P. Stromberg (2009) 'Should Investors Bet on the Jockey or the Horse? Evidence from the Evolution of Firms from Early Business Plans to Public Companies', *Journal of Finance,* Vol. 64, No. 1, 75–115. **USA.**

41 Kräussl, R. and S. Krause (2012) 'Has Europe Been Catching Up? An Industry Level Analysis of Venture Capital Success over 1985–2009', *European Financial Management,* Vol. 20, No. 1, 179–205. **Europe.**

42 Mettrick, A. and A. Yasuda (2010) 'The Economics of Private Equity Funds', *Review of Financial Studies,* Vol. 23, No. 6, 2303–2341. **International.**

43 Nahata, R. (2008) 'Venture Capital Reputation and Investment Performance', *Journal of Financial Economics,* Vol. 90, No. 2, 127–151. **USA.**

44 Phalippou, L. and O. Gottschalg (2009) 'The Performance of Private Equity Funds', *Review of Financial Studies,* Vol. 90, No. 4, 1747–1776. **USA.**

45 Renneboog, L., T. Simons and M. Wright (2007) 'Why Do Public Firms Go Private in the UK? The Impact of Private Equity Investors, Incentive Realignment and Undervaluation', *Journal of Corporate Finance,* Vol. 13, No. 4, 591–628. **UK.**

Seasoned Equity Offerings, Rights Issues and Reverse LBOs

46 Armitage, S. (2010) 'Block Buying and Choice of Issue Method in UK Seasoned Equity Offers', *Journal of Business Finance and Accounting,* Vol. 37, No. 3–4 (April/May), 422–448. **UK.**

47 Cao, J. and J. Lerner (2009) 'The Performance of Reverse Leveraged Buyouts', *Journal of Financial Economics,* Vol. 91, No. 2, 139–157. **USA.**

48 Coakley, J., A. Lazos and J.M. Liñares-Zegarra (2022) 'Seasoned Equity Crowdfunded Offerings', *Journal of Corporate Finance,* Vol. 77, 101880.

49 Cohen, D.A. and P. Zarowin (2010) 'Accrual-based and Real Earnings Management Activities around Seasoned Equity Offerings', *Journal of Accounting and Economics,* Vol. 50, No. 1, 2–19.

50 DeAngelo, H., L. DeAngelo and R.M. Stulz (2010) 'Seasoned Equity Offerings, Market Timing, and the Corporate Lifecycle', *Journal of Financial Economics,* Vol. 95, No. 3, 275–295. **USA.**

51 Gao, X. and J.R. Ritter (2010) 'The Marketing of Seasoned Equity Offerings', *Journal of Financial Economics,* Vol. 97, No. 1, 33–52.

52 Hillier, D. (2010) 'Discussion of Block Buying and Choice of Issue Method in UK Seasoned Equity Offers', *Journal of Business Finance and Accounting,* Vol. 37, No. 3–4, 449–455.

53 Iqbal, A. (2008) 'The Importance of the Sequence in UK Rights Issues', *Journal of Business Finance and Accounting,* Vol. 35, No. 1–2, 150–176. **UK.**

54 Lee, G. and R.W. Masulis (2009) 'Seasoned Equity Offerings: Quality of Accounting Information and Expected Flotation Costs', *Journal of Financial Economics,* Vol. 92, No. 3, 443–469. **USA.**

Other Relevant Research

55 Boubakri, N., J.-C. Cosset and O. Guedhami (2005) 'Postprivatization Corporate Governance: The Role of Ownership Structure and Investor Protection', *Journal of Financial Economics,* Vol. 76, No. 2, 369–399. **International.**

56 Hoberg, G. (2007) 'The Underwriter Persistence Phenomenon', *Journal of Finance,* Vol. 62, No. 3, 1169–1206. **USA.**

57 Sarkissian, S. and M. Schill (2009) 'Are there Permanent Valuation Gains to Overseas Listing?', *Review of Financial Studies,* Vol. 22, No. 1, 371–412. **International.**

Endnotes

1 As with the majority of the material covered in this chapter, the specific approach to placings is different in each country. Information on country regulations can usually be found in the listing rules of each stock exchange. These are normally downloadable from the exchange's website.

2 The Green Shoe Corp. in the USA was the first firm to allow this provision.

3 For example, see Beatty and Ritter (1986), Carter and Manaster (1990), Carter, Dark and Sapp (2011) and Krigman et al. (2001).

4 This choice has been studied by Logue and Jarrow (1978), Bhagat (1986), Hansen and Khanna (1994), and Logue and Tiniç (1999).

5 This explanation was first suggested in Rock (1986).

6 Asquith and Mullins (1986), Masulis and Korwar (1986), Mikkelson and Partch (1986), Gajewski and Ginglinger (2002), and Martin-Ugedo (2003). Barnes and Walker (2006) actually find that private placings elicit a positive response in contrast to a public listing, which is associated with significant negative returns.

7 Hansen and Crutchley (1990).

8 Some people have argued that the price in the aftermarket is not efficient after all. However, Ibbotson (1975) shows that, on average, new issues exhibit no abnormal price performance over the first five years following issuance. This result is generally viewed as being consistent with market efficiency. That is, the equity obtains an efficient price immediately following issuance and remains at an efficient price.

9 The notion of economies of scale has been contested by Altinkilic and Hansen (2000). They provide data and analysis showing that underwriter cost will be U-shaped.

10 The majority of information in this section comes from the European Private Equity and Venture Capital Association, a non-profit trade association of around 1,300 private equity firms (www.investeurope.eu).

11 See Wetzel (1987).

12 A very influential paper by Barry et al. (1990) shows that venture capitalists do not usually sell shares at the time of the initial public offering, but they usually have board seats and act as advisers to managers.

Chapter 16
Debt Financing

Learning Objectives

After reading this chapter you should be able to:

LO1 Define the concept of debt financing, explain its importance in corporate finance, and describe its different forms, including bank loans and bonds.

LO2 Analyse and evaluate the process and impact of public bond issues.

LO3 Interpret and discuss the implications of bond ratings.

LO4 Distinguish between different types of bonds, private placements and public issues.

In its basic form, a bond is a simple financial instrument. You lend a company some amount, say £10,000. The company periodically pays you interest, and it repays the original loan amount of £10,000 at a future date. Bank loans can be customized to the borrower, and the terms and conditions vary with each contract. Many bonds originating in the Middle East are Shariah-compliant and do not pay interest. In Britain and Europe, government bond issues have attracted intense scrutiny on the part of analysts looking for hints on the future direction of both economies.

One example of a bond is that issued by Co-operative Bank Finance in May 2023. The bond had a coupon rate of 9.5 per cent and a maturity of five years. In this chapter, we will discuss the various characteristics of debt financing and review the different possible debt instruments that corporations use to finance their operations (you may, at this point, want to reread Sections 5.1 to 5.3 in Chapter 5 to reacquaint yourself with bond valuation).

Chapter 5
Page 116

Key Notations

r	Yield to maturity; the cost of debt
C	Coupon

Source: Russell Kord/Alamy Stock Photo

16.1 Bank Loans

Bank loans form a significant part of debt financing for companies. Although the amount of credit available from banks has declined from pre-financial crisis levels, it still dominates other forms of funding in many countries. Figure 16.1 presents a time series of external financing data versus other financing types for the Eurozone area over the recent period. As can be seen, bank (MFI) loans have grown significantly since 2014. Private equity (shown as 'Unlisted shares and other equity' in Figure 16.1) is the largest source of external financing in the Eurozone.

Figure 16.1 Net Flows of External Financing to Non-financial Corporations in the Euro Area

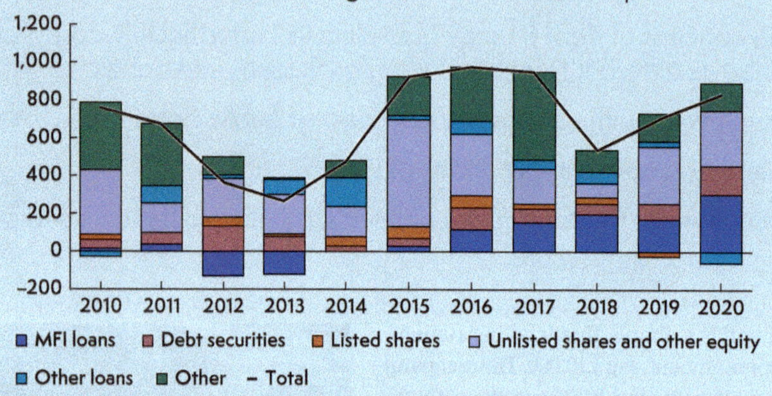

Notes: 'Other loans' includes loans from non-MFIs (other financial intermediaries, pension funds and insurance corporations) and from the rest of the world. 'MFI loans' and 'other loans' are corrected for loan sales and securitization. 'Other' is the difference between the total and the instruments included in the chart, and includes inter-company loans and trade credit. 'MFI' is a monetary financial institution (e.g. a bank). The latest observations are for the third quarter of 2020. Information available free of charge from the European Central Bank website.

Source: © European Central Bank, Frankfurt am Main, Germany.

Figure 16.2 presents data on the popularity of bank loans by country, clearly illustrating the importance of bank debt to European and UK firms. It is useful to compare the data in Figure 16.2 with that in Table 14.3. Although bank debt is the most common form of external financing, the pattern is quite varied across countries and reflects different financing cultures as well as liquidity in domestic financial markets.

Figure 16.2 Bank Loans as a Percentage of External Financing (2020)

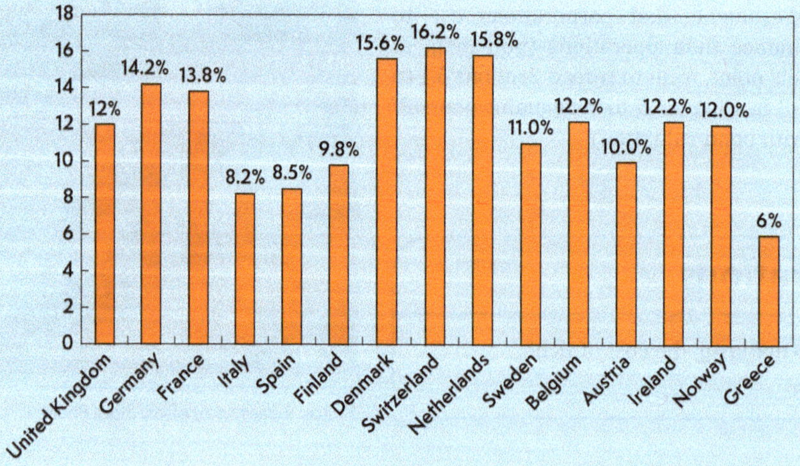

Note: *Bank loans to total external financing (%) is the ratio of bank loans to total external financing. It shows the share of bank loans in the total net financial flows to a country. A higher ratio means that a country relies more on bank loans to finance its development needs.*

Source: The World Bank.

Types of Bank Loan

Bank loans come in two types: lines of credit and loan commitments. A line of credit is an arrangement between a bank and a firm, typically for a short-term loan, whereby the bank authorizes the maximum loan amount but not the interest rate when setting up the line of credit. Lines of credit do not in a practical sense commit the bank to lend money because the bank is free to quote any interest rate it wishes at the time the borrowing firm requests funds. If the interest rate is too high, the firm will decline the available line of credit.

A loan commitment, on the other hand, is an arrangement that requires a bank to lend up to a maximum pre-specified loan amount at a pre-specified interest rate. The commitment is in place and available at the firm's request as long as the firm meets the requirements established when the contract was drawn up. There are two types of loan commitment. A revolver is a loan commitment in which funds flow back and forth between the bank and the firm without any predetermined schedule. Funds are drawn from the revolver whenever the company needs them, up to the maximum amount specified. Revolvers may also be subject to an annual clean-up in which the firm must retire all borrowings. A non-revolving loan commitment is one in which the firm cannot pay down the loan and then subsequently increase the amount of borrowing. Research has shown that firms with high levels of cash flow can obtain lines of credit, but less liquid firms tend to rely on cash for their short-term capital requirements.[1]

Sustainability in Action 16.1

COP26 and Its Impact on Global Financing

The COP26 UN Climate Change Conference catalysed a major shift in the finance industry, with more than 450 banks, including Citi, Morgan Stanley and Bank of America, making commitments to tie sustainability to their lending decisions. By reporting annually on the carbon emissions associated with their lending activities and committing trillions of dollars in green finance, these institutions have forced a new era in corporate decision-making. Businesses must now consider their carbon footprint when seeking financing, effectively tying environmental stewardship to corporate financial performance.

COP26 has had an impact on all dimensions of corporate finance. Asset managers, like BlackRock, have begun focusing on investing in companies with a sustainability emphasis, which is forcing management to reconsider their investment decision-making criteria. Some banks, like Wells Fargo and J.P. Morgan, have significantly reduced their fossil fuel lending, prompting businesses in carbon-intensive industries to reassess their operations and investment strategies to maintain access to capital. Other banks have committed funds to specific parts of the economy. For example, Goldman Sachs will deploy $750 billion by 2030 to accelerate climate transition and advance inclusive growth.

16.2 Debt Financing

Long-term debt securities are promises by the issuing firm to pay interest and principal on the unpaid balance. The *maturity* of a long-term debt instrument refers to the length of time the debt remains outstanding with some unpaid balance. Debt securities can be *short term* (maturities of one year or less) or *long term* (maturities of more than one year). Short-term debt is sometimes referred to as *unfunded debt* and long-term debt as *funded debt*.

The two major forms of long-term debt are publicly issued and privately placed debt. We discuss public-issue bonds first, and most of what we say about them holds true for privately placed long-term debt as well. The main difference between publicly issued and privately placed debt is that private debt is placed directly with a lending institution.

There are many other attributes to long-term debt, including security, call features, sinking funds, ratings and protective covenants. Table 16.1 illustrates the features of a fixed-rate bond recently issued by McDonald's, the world's largest fast-food company.

Table 16.1 Features of a Fixed-rate Bond Issued by McDonald's

	Term	Explanation
Amount of issue	€500 million	The company issued €500 million worth of bonds.
Date of issue	3 March 2023	The bonds were sold on 3 March 2023.
Maturity	7 March 2030	The bonds mature on 7 March 2030.
Face value	€100,000	The denomination of the bonds is €100,000.
Annual coupon	4.00%	Each bondholder will receive 4.00% per annum.
Offer price	99.384	The offer price was 99.384% of the face value of the bond. This is €99,384.
Coupon payment dates	7 March	Coupons of €4,000 will be paid on this date each year until maturity.
Security	Pari passu	Equal rank to other creditors.
Sinking fund	No	The bonds have no sinking fund.
Call provision	Yes	The bonds can be redeemed whole or in part prior to 7 January 2030.
Rating	BBB+	Adequate protection parameters.

16.3 The Public Issue of Bonds

The general procedures followed for a public issue of bonds are the same as those for equities, as described in Chapter 15. First, the offering must be approved by the board of directors. Sometimes a vote of shareholders (or supervisory board if the company operates in a country with a two-tier board system) is also required. Second, a registration statement is prepared for review by the relevant regulatory authority. Third, if accepted, the registration statement becomes effective at some point in the near future, and the securities are sold.

However, the registration statement for a public issue of bonds must include an indenture, a document not relevant for equities. An indenture is a written agreement between the corporation (the borrower) and a trust company. It is sometimes referred to as the deed of trust.[2] The trust company is appointed by the corporation to represent the bondholders. The trust company must (1) make sure the terms of the indenture are obeyed, (2) manage the sinking fund (if appropriate), and (3) represent bondholders if the company defaults on its payments.

The typical bond indenture can be a document of several hundred pages, and generally includes the following provisions:

1. The basic terms of the bonds
2. A description of property used as security
3. Details of the protective covenants
4. The sinking fund arrangements
5. The call provision.We discuss each of these in turn.

The Basic Terms

Bonds usually have a denomination (also known as face value or principal value) denominated in multiples of 100. For example, in the UK, government bonds tend to have a face value of £100 and corporate bonds, £100,000. In Europe, the denomination is often €1,000, €10,000 or €100,000. In the USA, it is usually $1,000. The denomination of the bond is always stated on the bond certificate. In addition, the par value (i.e. initial accounting value) of a bond is almost always the same as the face value.

Transactions between bond buyers and bond sellers determine the market value of the bond. Actual bond market values depend on the general level of interest rates, among other factors, and need not equal the face value. Bond prices are quoted as a percentage of the denomination, and we illustrate this in Example 16.1.

Example 16.1

Bond Prices

Suppose Nero SpA has issued 100 bonds. The amount stated on each bond certificate is £1,000. The total denomination, face value or principal value of the bonds is £100,000. Further, suppose the bonds are currently *priced* at 100, which means 100 per cent of £1,000. This means that buyers and sellers are holding bonds at a price per bond of £1,000. If interest rates rise, the price of the bond might fall to, say, 97, which means 97 per cent of £1,000, or £970.

Suppose the bonds have a stated interest rate of 12 per cent due on 1 January 2050. The bond indenture might read as follows:

> *The bond will mature on 1 January 2050 and will be limited in the aggregate denomination to £100,000. Each bond will bear interest at the rate of 12.0 per cent per annum from 1 January 2020, or from the most recent interest payment date to which interest has been paid. Interest is payable annually on 1 January of each year.*

As is typical of industrial bonds, the Nero bonds are registered. The indenture might read as follows:

> *Interest is payable annually on 1 January of each year to the person in whose name the bond is registered at close of business on 15 December prior.*

This means the company has a registrar who will record the ownership of each bond. The company will pay the interest and principal into the brokerage account of the registered owner on the stated date.

Some bonds are in bearer form, which means that ownership is not recorded in the company books. There are two drawbacks to bearer bonds. First, they can easily be lost or stolen. Second, because the company does not know who owns its bonds, it cannot notify bondholders of important events. However, bearer bonds have the advantage of secrecy because even the issuing company does not know who the bonds' owners are. This secrecy is particularly vexing to tax authorities because tax collection on interest is difficult if the holder is unknown.

A Note on Bond Price Quotes

If you buy a bond between coupon payment dates, the price you pay is usually more than the price you are quoted. The reason is that standard convention in the bond market is to quote prices net of 'accrued interest', meaning that accrued interest is deducted to arrive at the quoted price. This quoted price is called the clean price. The price you actually pay, however, includes the accrued interest. This price is the dirty price, also known as the 'full' or 'invoice' price.

An example is the easiest way to understand these issues. Suppose you buy a UK government bond with a 12 per cent annual coupon, payable semi-annually. You actually pay £108 for this bond, so £108 is the dirty, or invoice, price. Further, on the day you buy it, the next coupon is due in four months, so you are between coupon dates. Notice that the next coupon will be £6.

The accrued interest on a bond is calculated by taking the fraction of the coupon period that has passed – in this case, two months out of six – and multiplying this fraction by the next coupon, £6. So, the accrued interest in this example is 2/6 × £6 = £2. The bond's quoted price (i.e. its clean price) would be £108 – £2 = £106.

Security

Debt securities are also classified according to the collateral protecting the bondholder. Collateral is a general term for the assets that are pledged as security for payment of debt. For example, collateral trust bonds involve a pledge of equity held by the corporation.

Example 16.2

Collateral Trust Bonds

Suppose Railroad Holdings plc owns all of the ordinary shares of Track plc; that is, Track plc is a wholly owned subsidiary of Railroad Holdings plc. Railroad issues debt securities that pledge the equity of Track plc as collateral. The debts are collateral trust bonds; UK Sur Bank will hold them. If Railroad Holdings plc defaults on the debt, UK Sur Bank will be able to sell the equity of Track plc to satisfy Railroad's obligation.

Mortgage securities are secured by a mortgage on real estate or other long-term assets of the borrower. The legal document that describes the mortgage is called a mortgage trust indenture or trust deed. The mortgage can be closed-end so that there is a limit on the number of bonds that can be issued. More frequently it is open-end, without restriction to the number of bonds that may be issued.

Example 16.3

Mortgage Securities

Suppose Cuscin Bond Company has buildings and land worth £10 million and a £4 million mortgage on these properties. If the mortgage is closed-end, Cuscin Bond Company cannot issue more bonds on this property.

If the bond indenture contains no clause limiting the amount of additional bonds that can be issued, it is an open-end mortgage. In this case, Cuscin Bond Company can issue additional bonds on its property, making the existing bonds riskier. For example, if additional mortgage bonds of £2 million are issued, the property has been pledged for a total of £6 million of bonds. If Cuscin Bond Company must liquidate its property for £4 million, the original bondholders will receive 4/6, or 67 per cent, of their investment. If the mortgage had been closed-end, they would have received 100 per cent of the stated value.

The value of a mortgage depends on the market value of the underlying property. Because of this, mortgage bonds sometimes require the property to be adequately maintained and insured. Of course, a building and equipment bought in 1914 for manufacturing slide rules might not have much value no matter how well the company maintains it. The value of any property ultimately depends on its next best economic use. Bond indentures cannot easily insure against losses in economic value.

Sometimes mortgages are on specific property – for example, a single building. More often, blanket mortgages are used. A blanket mortgage pledges many assets owned by the company.

Some bonds represent unsecured obligations of the company. A debenture is an unsecured bond, where no specific pledge of property is made. Debenture holders have a claim on property not otherwise pledged: the property that remains after mortgages and collateral trusts are taken into account.

Protective Covenants

A protective covenant is that part of the indenture or loan agreement that limits specific actions of the borrowing company. Protective covenants can be classified into two types: negative covenants and positive covenants. A negative covenant limits or prohibits actions the company may take. Here are some typical examples:

- Limitations are placed on the amount of dividends a company may pay.
- The firm cannot pledge any of its assets to other lenders.
- The firm cannot merge with another firm.
- The firm may not sell or lease its major assets without approval by the lender.
- The firm cannot issue additional long-term debt.

A positive covenant specifies an action that the company agrees to take or a condition the company must abide by. Here are some examples:

- The company agrees to maintain its working capital at a minimum level.
- The company must furnish periodic financial statements to the lender.

The Sinking Fund

Bonds can be repaid entirely at maturity, at which time the bondholder will receive the stated value of the bond; or they can be repaid before maturity. Early repayment is more typical.

In a direct placement of debt, the repayment schedule is specified in the loan contract. For public issues, the repayment takes place through the use of a sinking fund and a call provision.

A sinking fund is an account managed by the bond trustee to repay the bonds. Typically, the company makes yearly payments to the trustee. The trustee can purchase bonds in the market or can select bonds randomly using a lottery and purchase them, generally at face value. There are many different kinds of sinking fund arrangements:

- Most sinking funds start between five and ten years after the initial issuance.
- Some sinking funds establish equal payments over the life of the bond.
- Most high-quality bond issues establish payments to the sinking fund that are not sufficient to redeem the entire issue. As a consequence, there is the possibility of a large *balloon* payment at maturity.

Sinking funds have two opposing effects on bondholders:

1. *Sinking funds provide extra protection to bondholders.* A firm experiencing financial difficulties would have trouble making sinking fund payments. Thus, sinking fund payments provide an early warning system to bondholders.
2. *Sinking funds give the firm an attractive option.* If bond prices fall below the face value, the firm will satisfy the sinking fund by buying bonds at the lower market prices. If bond prices rise above the face value, the firm will buy the bonds back at the lower face value (or other fixed price, depending on the specific terms).

The Call Provision

A *call provision* lets the company repurchase or *call* the entire bond issue at a predetermined price over a specified period.

Generally the call price is above the bond's face value. The difference between the call price and the face value is the **call premium**. For example, if the call price is 105 – that is, 105 per cent of, say, £1,000 – the call premium is £50. The amount of the call premium usually becomes smaller over time. One typical arrangement is to set the call premium initially equal to the annual coupon payment and then make it decline to zero over the life of the bond.

Call provisions are not usually operative during the first few years of a bond's life. For example, a company may be prohibited from calling its bonds for the first 10 years of issue. This is referred to as a deferred call. During this period the bond is said to be call-protected.

In just the last few years, a new type of call provision, a 'make-whole' call, has become widespread in the corporate bond market. With such a feature, bondholders receive approximately what the bonds are worth if they are called. Because bondholders do not suffer a loss in the event of a call, they are 'made whole'.

To determine the make-whole call price, we calculate the present value of the remaining interest and principal payments at a rate specified in the indenture. For example, assume that the McDonald's issue was callable and that the discount rate is 'Treasury rate plus 0.20 per cent'. What this means is that we determine the discount rate by first finding a British Treasury issue with the same maturity. We calculate the yield to maturity on the Treasury issue and then add on an additional 0.20 per cent to get the discount rate we use.

16.4 Bond Refunding

Replacing all or part of a bond issue is called bond refunding. Usually, the first step in a typical bond refunding is to call the entire issue of bonds at the call price. Bond refunding raises two questions:

1. Should firms issue callable bonds?
2. Given that callable bonds have been issued, when should the bonds be called?

We attempt to answer these questions in this section, focusing on traditional fixed-price call features.

Should Firms Issue Callable Bonds?

Common sense tells us that call provisions have value. First, many publicly issued bonds have call provisions. Second, it is obvious that a call works to the advantage of the issuer. If interest rates fall and bond prices go up, the option to buy back the bonds at the call price is valuable. In bond refunding, firms will typically replace the called bonds with a new bond issue. The new bonds will have a lower coupon rate than the called bonds.

However, bondholders will take the call provision into account when they buy the bond. For this reason we can expect that bondholders will demand higher interest rates on callable bonds than on non-callable bonds. In fact, financial economists view call provisions as being zero-sum in efficient capital markets.[3] Any expected gains to the issuer from being allowed to refund the bond at lower rates will be offset by higher initial interest rates. We illustrate the zero-sum aspect to callable bonds in Example 16.4.

Example 16.4

Scandinavian Intercable ASA

Suppose Scandinavian Intercable ASA intends to issue perpetual bonds of 1,000 Norwegian kroner (NKr) face value at a 10 per cent interest rate. Annual coupons have been set at NKr100. There is an equal chance that by the end of the year interest rates will do one of the following:

1. Fall to 6.67 per cent. If so, the bond price will increase to NKr1,500.
2. Increase to 20 per cent. If so, the bond price will fall to NKr500.

Non-callable Bond Suppose the market price of the non-callable bond is the expected price it will have next year plus the coupon, all discounted at the current 10 per cent interest rate.[4] The value of the non-callable bond is this:

Value of non-callable bond

$$\frac{\text{First-year coupon} + \text{Expected price at end of year}}{1+r}$$

$$= \frac{\text{NKr}100 + (0.5 \times \text{NKr}1,500) + (0.5 \times \text{NKr}500)}{1.10}$$

$$= \text{NKr}1,000$$

Callable Bond Now suppose Scandinavian Intercable ASA decides to issue callable bonds. The call premium is set at NKr100 over par value, and the bonds can be called *only* at the end of the first year.[5] In this case, the call provision will allow the company to buy back its bonds at NKr1,100 (NKr1,000 par value plus the NKr100 call premium). Should interest rates fall, the company will buy a bond for NKr1,100 that would be worth NKr1,500 in the absence of a call provision. Of course, if interest rates rise, Scandinavian Intercable would not want to call the bonds for NKr1,100 because they are worth only NKr500 on the market.

Suppose rates fall and Scandinavian Intercable calls the bonds by paying NKr1,100. If the firm simultaneously issues new bonds with a coupon of NKr100, it will bring in NKr1,500 (NKr100/0.0667) at the 6.67 per cent interest rate. This will allow Scandinavian Intercable to pay an extra dividend to shareholders of NKr400 (NKr1,500 – NKr1,100). In other words, if rates fall from 10 per cent to $6\frac{2}{3}$ per cent, exercise of the call will transfer NKr400 of potential bondholder gains to the shareholders.

When investors purchase callable bonds, they realize that they will forfeit their anticipated gains to shareholders if the bonds are called. As a consequence, they will not pay NKr1,000 for a callable bond with a coupon of NKr100.

How high must the coupon on the callable bond be so that it can be issued at the par value of NKr1,000? We can answer this in three steps.

Step 1: Determining End-of-year Value if Interest Rates Drop If the interest rate drops to $6\frac{2}{3}$ per cent by the end of the year, the bond will be called for NKr1,100. The bondholder will receive both this and the annual coupon payment. If we let *C* represent the coupon on the callable bond, the bondholder gets the following at the end of the year:

$$\text{NKr}1,100 + C$$

Step 2: Determining End-of-year Value if Interest Rates Rise If interest rates rise to 20 per cent, the value of the bondholder's position at the end of the year is:

$$\frac{C}{0.20} + C$$

That is, the perpetuity formula tells us that the bond will sell at $C/0.20$. In addition, the bondholder receives the coupon payment at the end of the year.

Step 3: Solving for C Because interest rates are equally likely to rise or to fall, the expected value of the bondholder's end-of-year position is:

$$(\text{NKr}1,100 + C) \times 0.5 + \left(\frac{C}{0.20} + C\right) \times 0.5$$

Using the current interest rate of 10 per cent, we set the present value of these payments equal to par:

$$\text{NKr}1,000 = \frac{(\text{NKr}1,100 + C) \times 0.5 + (C/0.20 + C) \times 0.5}{1.10}$$

C is the unknown in the equation. The equation holds if C = NKr157.14. In other words, callable bonds can sell at par only if their coupon rate is 15.714 per cent.

The Paradox Restated If Scandinavian Intercable issues a non-callable bond, it will need to pay only a 10 per cent interest rate. By contrast, Scandinavian Intercable must pay an interest rate of 15.7 per cent on a callable bond. The interest rate differential makes an investor indifferent to either bond in our example. Because the return to the investor is the same with either bond, the cost of debt capital is the same to Scandinavian Intercable with either bond. Thus, our example suggests that there is neither an advantage nor a disadvantage to issuing callable bonds.

Why, therefore, are callable bonds issued in the real world? This question has vexed financial economists for a long time. We now consider four specific reasons why a company might use a call provision:

1 Superior interest rate predictions
2 Taxes
3 Financial flexibility for future investment opportunities
4 Less interest rate risk.

Superior Interest Rate Forecasting

Company insiders may know more about interest rate changes on the company's bonds than does the investing public. For example, managers may be better informed about potential changes in the firm's credit rating. Thus, a company may prefer the call provision at a particular time because it believes that the expected fall in interest rates (the probability of a fall multiplied by the amount of the fall) is greater than the bondholders believe.

Although this is possible, there is a reason to doubt that inside information is the rationale for call provisions. Suppose firms really had superior ability to predict changes that would affect them. Bondholders would infer that a company expected an improvement in its credit rating whenever it issued callable bonds. Bondholders would require an increase in the coupon rate to protect them against a call if this occurred. As a result, we would expect that there would be no financial advantage to the firm from callable bonds over non-callable bonds.

Of course, there are many non-company-specific reasons why interest rates can fall. The interest rate level, for instance, is connected to the anticipated inflation rate. But it is difficult to see how companies could have more information about the general level of interest rates than other participants in the bond markets.

Taxes

Call provisions may have tax advantages if the bondholder is taxed at a lower rate than the company. We have seen that callable bonds have higher coupon rates than non-callable bonds. Because the coupons provide a deductible interest expense to the corporation and are taxable income to the bondholder, the corporation will gain more than a bondholder in a low tax bracket will lose. Presumably, some of the tax savings can be passed on to the bondholders in the form of a high coupon.

Future Investment Opportunities

As we have explained, bond indentures contain protective covenants that restrict a company's investment opportunities. For example, protective covenants may limit the company's ability to acquire another firm or to sell certain assets (such as a division of the company). If the covenants are sufficiently restrictive, the cost to the shareholders in lost net present value can be large. However, if bonds are callable, the company can buy back the bonds at the call price and take advantage of a superior investment opportunity.

Less Interest Rate Risk

The call provision will reduce the sensitivity of a bond's value to changes in the level of interest rates. As interest rates increase, the value of a non-callable bond will fall. Because the callable bond has a higher coupon rate, the value of a callable bond will fall less than the value of a non-callable bond. Kraus (1983) has argued that, by reducing the sensitivity of a bond's value to changes in interest rates, the call provision may reduce the risk of shareholders as well as bondholders.[6] He argues that, because the bond is a liability of the corporation, the shareholders bear risk as the bond changes value over time. Thus, it can be shown that, under certain conditions, reducing the risk of bonds through a call provision will also reduce the risk of equity.

Calling Bonds: When Does It Make Sense?

The value of the company is the value of the equity plus the value of the bonds. From the Modigliani–Miller theory and the pie model presented in earlier chapters, we know that firm value is unchanged by how it is divided between these two instruments. Therefore, maximizing shareholder wealth means minimizing the value of the callable bond. In a world with no transaction costs, it can be shown that the company should call its bonds whenever the callable bond value exceeds the call price. This policy minimizes the value of the callable bonds.

The preceding analysis is modified slightly by including the costs of issuing new bonds. These extra costs change the refunding rule to allow bonds to trade at prices above the call price. The objective of the company is to minimize the sum of the value of the callable bonds plus new issue costs. It has been observed that many real-world firms do not call their bonds when the market value of the bonds reaches the call price. Instead, they wait until the market value of the bonds exceeds the call price. Perhaps these issue costs are an explanation. Also, when a bond is called, the holder has about 30 days to surrender the bond and receive the call price in cash. In 30 days the market value of the bonds could fall below the call price. If so, the firm is giving away money. To forestall this possibility, it can be argued that firms should wait until the market value of the bond exceeds the call price before calling bonds.

16.5 Bond Ratings

Firms frequently pay to have their debt rated. The two leading bond-rating firms are Moody's Investors Service and Standard & Poor's (S&P). The debt ratings depend on (1) the likelihood that the firm will default, and (2) the protection afforded by the loan contract in the event of default. The ratings are constructed from information supplied by the corporation, primarily the financial statements of the firm. The rating classes are shown in Example 16.5.

The highest rating that debt can have is AAA or Aaa. Debt rated AAA or Aaa is judged to be the best quality and to have the lowest degree of risk. The lowest rating is D, which indicates that the firm is in default. In recent years, a growing part of corporate borrowing has taken the form of *low-grade bonds*. These bonds are also known as either *high-yield bonds* or *junk bonds*. Low-grade bonds are corporate bonds that are rated below *investment grade* by the major rating agencies (that is, below BBB for Standard & Poor's or Baa for Moody's).

Bond ratings are important because bonds with lower ratings tend to have higher interest costs. However, the most recent evidence is that bond ratings merely reflect bond risk. There is no conclusive evidence that bond ratings affect risk.[7] It is not surprising that the share prices and bond prices of firms do not show any unusual behaviour on the days around a rating change. Because the ratings are based on publicly available information, they probably do not, in themselves, supply new information to the market.[8]

Example 16.5

Bond Ratings

	Very High Quality	High Quality	Speculative	Very Poor
Standard & Poor's	AAA AA	A BBB	BB B	CCC CC C D
Moody's	Aaa Aa	A Baa	Ba B	Caa Ca C D

At times both Moody's and Standard & Poor's adjust these ratings. S&P uses plus and minus signs: A+ is the strongest A rating and A– the weakest. Moody's uses a 1, 2 or 3 designation, with 1 indicating the strongest. These increments are called notches.

Moody's	S&P	
Aaa	AAA	Debt rated Aaa and AAA has the highest rating. Capacity to pay interest and principal is extremely strong.
Aa	AA	Debt rated Aa and AA has a very strong capacity to pay interest and repay principal. Together with the highest rating, this group comprises the high-grade bond class.
A	A	Debt rated A has a strong capacity to pay interest and repay principal. However, it is somewhat more susceptible to adverse changes in circumstances and economic conditions.

Moody's	S&P	
Baa	BBB	Debt rated Baa and BBB is regarded as having an adequate capacity to pay interest and repay principal. Whereas it normally exhibits adequate protection parameters, adverse economic conditions or changing circumstances are more likely to lead to a weakened capacity to pay interest and repay principal for debt in this category than in higher-rated categories. These bonds are medium-grade obligations.
Ba B	BB B	Debt rated in these categories is regarded, on balance, as predominantly speculative. Ba and BB indicate the lowest degree of speculation, and Ca and CC the highest.
Caa Ca	CCC CC	Although such debt is likely to have some quality and protective characteristics, these are outweighed by large uncertainties or major risk exposure to adverse conditions.
C	C	This rating is reserved for income bonds on which no interest is being paid.
D	D	Debt rated D is in default, and payment of interest and/or repayment of principal is in arrears.

Source: Data from various editions of *Standard & Poor's Bond Guide* and *Moody's Bond Guide.*

Rating agencies do not always agree. For example, some bonds are known as 'crossover' or '5B' bonds. The reason is that they are rated triple-B (or Baa) by one rating agency and double-B (or Ba) by another: a 'split rating'.

Junk Bonds

The investment community has labelled bonds with a Standard & Poor's rating of BB and below or a Moody's rating of Ba and below as junk bonds. These bonds are also called *high-yield, speculative* or *low-grade;* we shall use all three terms interchangeably. Issuance has remained stable over the past few years, with an average €10 billion of junk bonds issued every year in Europe alone (*source:* Bloomberg).

During economic downturns, junk bonds are most likely to default because of their speculative nature. Figure 16.3 presents data by Standard & Poor's on junk bond defaults in the recent past. As can be seen, the default rate on junk bonds spiked during the Covid-19 pandemic in 2020 and the previous financial crisis in 2008.

Looking forward, Figure 16.4 shows that a large number of European high-yield bonds are due to expire between 2024 and 2029. This suggests that there may be a spike in defaults if economic conditions in Europe are poor and lower-grade borrowers struggle to refinance their debt.

Figure 16.3 Historical Default Rates: Global Junk Bonds, 1981–2022

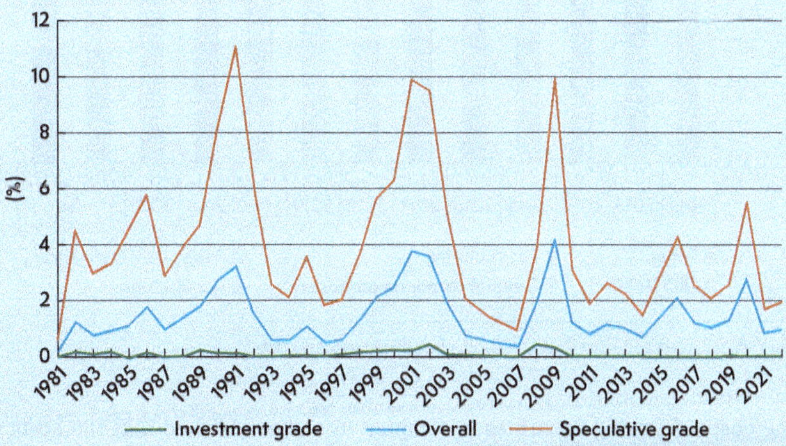

Source: 2022 Annual Global Corporate Default Study and Rating Transitions, 2023, S&P Global Ratings Newsletter.

Figure 16.4 European High-yield Bond Maturity Schedule for Issues Since 2023 (€ bn)

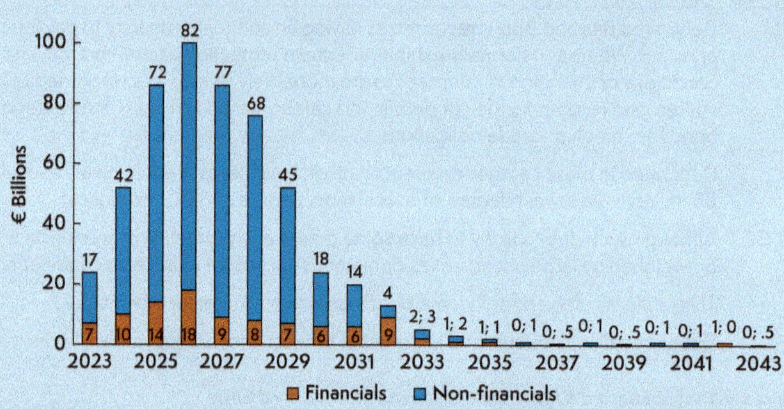

Source: European High Yield & Leveraged Loan Report (2022), afme, Finance for Europe.

Junk bonds can be used to finance mergers and other corporate restructurings. Whereas a firm can issue only a small amount of high-grade debt, the same firm can issue much more debt if low-grade financing is allowed as well. Therefore, the use of junk bonds lets acquirers effect takeovers that they could not do with only traditional bond financing techniques. Junk bonds can also be used to restructure a firm's debt or for working capital, and Figure 16.5 shows the different uses for which these bonds can be used. The greatest use of junk bonds is for general corporate purposes, followed by debt repayment and refinancing of existing debt. This is because the European economy has been dominated by a period of low interest rates, and so junk bond issuance is cheaper than would otherwise be the case.

Figure 16.5 Use of European High-yield Bond Proceeds

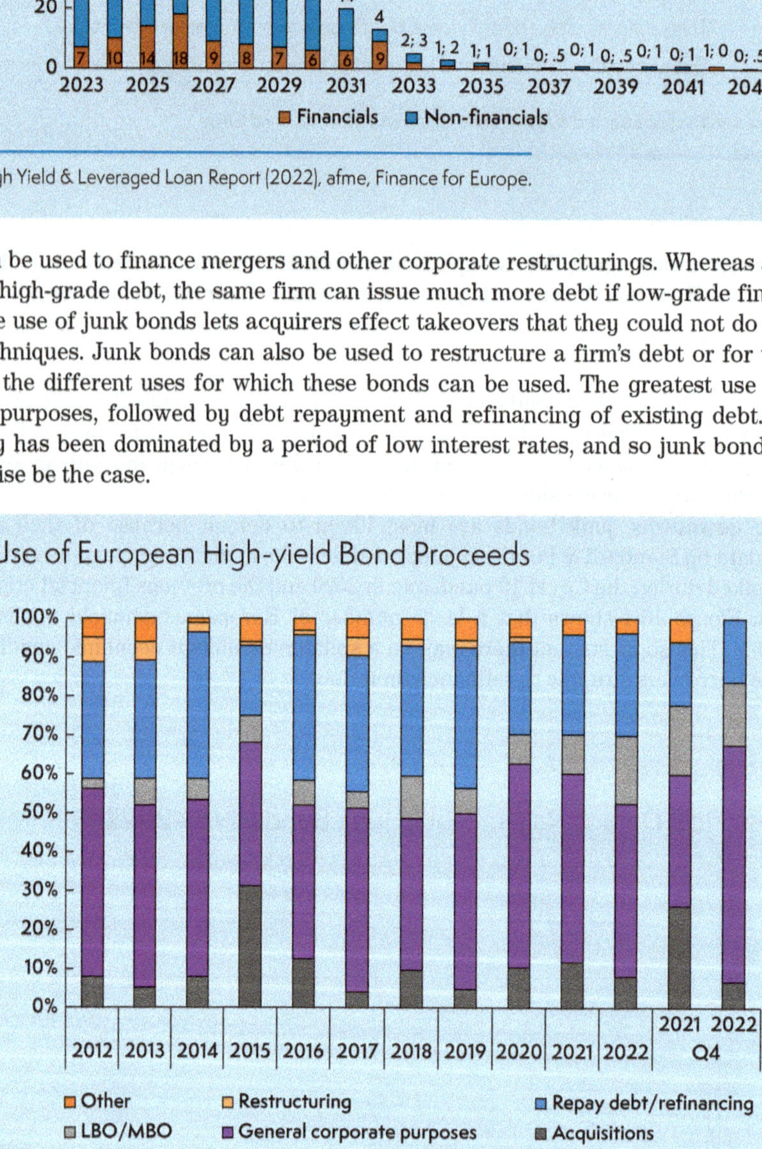

Source: European High Yield & Leveraged Loan Report (2022), afme, Finance for Europe.

We discussed the costs of issuing securities in Chapter 15 and established that the costs of issuing debt are substantially less than the costs of issuing equity. Table 16.2 clarifies several questions regarding the costs of issuing debt securities. It contains a breakdown of direct costs for bond issues after the investment and non-investment grades have been separated.

Table 16.2 Average Gross Spreads and Total Direct Costs for Domestic Debt Issues, 1990–2003

	Convertible Bonds				Straight Bonds I			
	Investment Grade		Non-investment Grade		Investment Grade		Non-investment Grade	
Proceeds ($ in millions)	Gross Spread (%)	Total Direct Cost (%)	Gross Spread (%)	Total Direct Cost (%)	Gross Spread (%)	Total Direct Cost (%)	Gross Spread (%)	Total Direct Cost (%)
2–9.99	–	–	–	–	0.62	1.90	–	–
10–19.99	–	–	4.00	5.67	0.50	1.35	2.74	4.80
20–39.99	–	–	3.47	5.02	0.58	1.21	3.06	4.36
40–59.99	1.92	2.43	3.33	4.48	0.39	0.86	3.01	3.93
60–79.99	1.65	2.09	2.78	3.40	0.57	0.97	2.99	4.07
80–99.99	0.89	1.16	2.54	3.19	0.66	0.94	2.74	3.66
100–199.99	2.22	2.55	2.57	3.00	0.55	0.80	2.71	3.39
200–499.99	1.99	2.18	2.62	2.85	0.50	0.81	2.49	2.90
500 and up	1.96	2.09	2.50	2.57	0.28	0.38	2.45	2.71
	1.99	2.26	2.81	3.47	0.51	0.85	2.68	3.35

Source: Adapted from Lee et al. (1996); updated by the authors.

First, there are substantial economies of scale here as well. Second, investment-grade issues have much lower direct costs, particularly for straight bonds. Finally, there are relatively few non-investment-grade issues in the smaller size categories, reflecting the fact that such issues are more commonly handled as private placements, which we discuss in Section 16.7.

Real World Insight 16.1

Oxford University 100-year Bond

Bonds are public equivalents to private financing such as bank loans. If an organization is large enough, it will be able to access the debt markets and this is true whether it is for-profit or a charity. In recent years, many universities have issued bonds to fund large-scale property investments.

For example, Oxford University has a £750 million 100-year bond with a 2.54 per cent interest rate, whose purpose is to improve the ancient institution's facilities. Oxford will need to pay interest of £19.05 million per annum until the year 2117. This bond issue was so attractive to investors that more than £2 billion of orders were offered by institutional investors for the issue.

16.6 Some Different Types of Bonds

Until now we have considered 'plain vanilla' bonds in our discussions. In this section, we look at some more unusual types: floating-rate bonds, deep-discount bonds and income bonds.

Floating-rate Bonds

The conventional bonds we have discussed in this chapter have *fixed monetary obligations.* That is, the coupon rate is set as a fixed percentage of the par value. With floating-rate bonds, the coupon payments are adjustable. The adjustments are tied to an *interest rate index* such as the Treasury bill interest rate, the London Interbank Offered Rate (LIBOR) or the European Interbank Offered Rate (EURIBOR).

In most cases, the coupon adjusts with a lag to some base rate. Suppose, say, a coupon rate adjustment is made on 1 June. The adjustment may be from a simple average of yields on six-month Treasury bills issued during March, April and May. In addition, the majority of these *floaters* have put provisions, and floor and ceiling provisions:

- With a *put provision,* the holder has the right to redeem his or her note at par on the coupon payment date. Frequently, the investor is prohibited from redeeming at par during the first few years of the bond's life.
- With floor and ceiling provisions the coupon rate is subject to a minimum and maximum. For example, the minimum coupon rate might be 8 per cent and the maximum rate might be 14 per cent.

The popularity of floating-rate bonds is connected to *inflation risk.* When inflation is higher than expected, issuers of fixed-rate bonds tend to make gains at the expense of lenders; and when inflation is less than expected, lenders make gains at the expense of borrowers. Because the inflation risk of long-term bonds is borne by both issuers and bondholders, it is in their interests to devise loan agreements that minimize inflation risk.[9]

Floaters reduce inflation risk because the coupon rate is tied to the current interest rate, which, in turn, is influenced by the rate of inflation. We can see this most clearly by considering the formula for the present value of a bond. As inflation increases the interest rate (the denominator of the formula), inflation increases a floater's coupon rate (the numerator of the formula). Hence, bond value is hardly affected by inflation. Conversely, the coupon rate of fixed-rate bonds cannot change, implying that the prices of these bonds are at the mercy of inflation.

As an alternative, an individual who is concerned about inflation risk can invest in short-term notes, such as Treasury bills, and *roll them over.* The investor can accomplish essentially the same objective by buying a floater that is adjusted to the Treasury bill rate. However, the purchaser of a floater can reduce transaction costs relative to rolling over short-term Treasury bills because floaters are long-term bonds. The same type of reduction in transaction costs makes floaters attractive to some corporations.[10] They benefit from issuing a floater instead of issuing a series of short-term notes.

In Section 16.4, we discussed callable bonds. Because the coupon on floaters varies with market-wide interest rates, floaters always sell at or near par. Therefore, it is not surprising that floaters do not generally have call features.

Deep-discount Bonds

A bond that pays no coupon must be offered at a price that is much lower than its face value. Such bonds are known as original-issue discount bonds, deep-discount bonds, pure discount bonds or zero coupon bonds. They are frequently called *zeros* for short.

Suppose DDB AG issues 1,000 Swiss francs (SFr) of five-year deep-discount bonds when the market-wide interest rate is 10 per cent. These bonds do not pay any coupons. The initial price is set at SFr621 because SFr621 = SFr1,000/(1.10^5).

Because these bonds have no intermediate coupon payments, they are attractive to certain investors and unattractive to others. Consider, for instance, an insurance company forecasting death benefit payments of SFr1,000,000 five years from today. The company would like to be sure that it will have the funds to pay off the liability in five years' time. The company could buy five-year zero coupon bonds with a face value of SFr1,000,000. The company is matching assets with liabilities here, a procedure that eliminates interest rate risk. That is, regardless of the movement of interest rates, the firm's set of zeros will always be able to pay off the SFr1,000,000 liability.

Conversely, the firm would be at risk if it bought coupon bonds instead. For example, if it bought five-year coupon bonds, it would need to reinvest the coupon payments through to the fifth year. Because interest rates in the future are not known with certainty today, we cannot be sure if these bonds will be worth more or less than SFr1,000,000 by the fifth year.

Now, consider a couple saving for their child's university education in 15 years. They *expect* that, with inflation, four years of university should cost SFr150,000 in 15 years. Thus they buy 15-year zero coupon bonds with a face value of SFr150,000.[11] If they have forecast inflation perfectly (and if university costs keep pace with inflation), their child's tuition will be fully funded. However, if inflation rises more than expected, the tuition will be more than SFr150,000. Because the zero coupon bonds produce a shortfall, the child might end up working his way through school. As an alternative, the parents might have considered rolling over Treasury bills. Because the yields on Treasury bills rise and fall with the inflation rate, this simple strategy is likely to cause less risk than the strategy with zeros.

The key to these examples concerns the distinction between nominal and real quantities. The insurance company's liability is SFr1,000,000 in *nominal* Swiss francs. Because the face value of a zero coupon bond is a nominal quantity, the purchase of zeros eliminates risk. However, it is easier to forecast university costs in real terms than in nominal terms. Thus, a zero coupon bond is a poor choice to reduce the financial risk of a child's university education.

Income Bonds

Income bonds are similar to conventional bonds, except that coupon payments depend on company income. Specifically, coupons are paid to bondholders only if the firm's income is sufficient.

Income bonds are a financial puzzle because, from the firm's standpoint, they appear to be a cheaper form of debt than conventional bonds. Income bonds provide the same tax advantage to corporations from interest deductions that conventional bonds do. However, a company that issues income bonds is less likely to experience financial distress. When a coupon payment is omitted because of insufficient corporate income, an income bond is not in default.

Why don't firms issue more income bonds? Two explanations have been offered:

1. *The 'smell of death' explanation:* Firms that issue income bonds signal the capital markets of their increased prospect of financial distress.
2. *The 'deadweight costs' explanation:* The calculation of corporate income is crucial to determining the status of bondholders' income, and shareholders and bondholders will not necessarily agree on how to calculate the income. This creates agency costs associated with the firm's accounting methods.

Although these are possibilities, there is still no truly satisfactory reason for the lack of more investor interest in income bonds.

Islamic Bonds

With the massive increase in the price of oil over the past few years, many Islamic investment funds and banks have been seeking ways to diversify their investment portfolios in ways that are consistent with their religious beliefs. One such instrument is a *sukuk,* otherwise known as an Islamic bond. An Islamic bond does not pay interest, to be compliant with Shariah law.

A *sukuk* is not a simple certificate like a bond that promises set periodic payments over the period of the bond. It is more akin to a financing company that is involved in profit sharing (*musharakah*), stated cost plus profit (*murabahah*), or sale and leasebacks (*ijarah*). Taking an *ijarah sukuk* as an example, a company wishes to raise funds just now in return for a set periodic payment in the future. To be compliant with Islamic law, the financing instrument cannot have any interest, or make money from money. An *ijarah sukuk* is structured as follows:

1. The company that wishes to raise funds creates a subsidiary specifically for the *ijarah sukuk.* This is generally known as a special purpose vehicle (SPV) or special investment vehicle (SIV).
2. The company sells its own assets (for instance, a manufacturing plant, technical machinery or property) to the SPV with a value equal to the amount of financing required.
3. The SPV issues securities or *sukuk* to the market. The *sukuk* pays periodic payments (fixed or floating depending on the underlying asset) from the cash flows generated by the assets. The money raised by the *sukuk* issue is used to pay for the assets in step 2.
4. The company immediately leases the assets back from the SPV, making periodic payments (fixed or floating depending on the asset) to the SPV. The payments are passed on to the *sukuk* holders.
5. At the end of the financing period, the company buys the assets back from the SPV and the SPV passes these on to the holders of the *sukuk.*

The cash flows from the *sukuk* to different parties are presented in Table 16.3. Notice how the cash flows from the *sukuk* are exactly the same as that of a bond, except that money is being generated from the underlying asset and not money in itself.

Table 16.3 Cash Flows from a *Sukuk,* or Islamic Bond

Step	Company	SPV	*Sukuk* Holders
1. Create SPV			
2. Company sells assets	+ Asset value	– Asset value	
3. SPV issues securities to market		+ Asset value	– Asset value
4. Company leases asset from SPV	– Periodic payment	+ Periodic payment – Periodic dicpayment	+ Periodic payment
5. Company buys assets back from SPV; SPV pays back *sukuk* holders	– Asset value	+ Asset value – Asset value	+ Asset value

Green Bonds

Green bonds are fixed-income securities designed to support specific climate-related or environmental projects. These bonds form part of the wider trend of environmental, social and governance investing, and often come with tax incentives like tax exemptions and tax credits. The green bond market has seen exponential growth over the years. In 2012, green bond issuance stood at only $2.6 billion. However, in 2020, the market had grown to almost $436 billion. Europe, including the United Kingdom, has been a leader in this sector alongside China and the United States.

The European Investment Bank is a major issuer of green bonds and has invested heavily in sustainable projects across Europe. These projects have ranged from renewable energy installations to sustainable transport initiatives. Green bonds can come in various forms, including *'use of proceeds' bonds*, *asset-backed securities*, *project bonds*, *securitization bonds*, *covered bonds* and *loans*. The specific characteristics of each bond are based on factors such as the issuer, the use of the proceeds, and the recourse of bondholders to the issuer's assets in the event of liquidation.

Investments in green bonds can be made by both institutional and retail investors. Retail investors wishing to align their portfolios with their environmental values can invest through various mutual funds and exchange traded funds that offer exposure to the green bond space.

Other Types of Bonds

Many bonds have unusual or exotic features and are really limited only by the imaginations of the parties involved. Unfortunately, there are far too many variations for us to cover in detail here. We, therefore, mention only a few of the more common types.

A *convertible bond* can be swapped for a fixed number of shares of equity any time before maturity at the holder's option. Convertibles are relatively common, but the number has been decreasing in recent years.

A *put bond* allows the *holder* to force the issuer to buy the bond back at a stated price. For example, Skyepharma plc, a UK speciality drug company, has bonds outstanding that allow the holder to force Skyepharma to buy the bonds back at 100 per cent of face value. The put feature is therefore just the reverse of the call provision.

A given bond may have many unusual features. Two of the most recent exotic bonds are CoCo bonds, which have a coupon payment, and NoNo bonds, which are zero coupon bonds. CoCo and NoNo bonds are contingent convertible, putable, callable, subordinated bonds. The contingent convertible clause is similar to the normal conversion feature, except the contingent feature must be met. For example, a contingent feature may require that the company equity trade at 110 per cent of the conversion price for 20 out of the most recent 30 days. Valuing a bond of this sort can be quite complex, and the yield to maturity calculation is often meaningless. In 2006, for instance, a NoNo issued by Merrill Lynch was selling at a price of $939.99, with a yield to maturity of negative 1.63 per cent. At the same time, a NoNo issued by Countrywide Financial was selling for $1,640, which implied a yield to maturity of negative 59 per cent!

16.7 Private Placement Compared to Public Issues

In Section 16.3, we described the mechanics of issuing debt to the public. However, more than 50 per cent of all debt is privately placed. There are two basic forms of direct private long-term financing: term loans and private placement.

Term loans are direct business loans with maturities of 1–15 years. The typical term loan is amortized over the life of the loan. That is, the loan is repaid by equal annual payments of interest and principal. The lenders are banks and insurance companies. A **private placement**, which also involves the sale of a bond or loan directly to a limited number of investors, is similar to a term loan except that the maturity is longer.

Here are some important differences between direct long-term financing and public issues:

- A direct long-term loan avoids the cost of registration with stock exchange authorities.
- Direct placement is likely to have more restrictive covenants.

- It is easier to renegotiate a term loan and a private placement in the event of a default. It is harder to renegotiate a public issue because hundreds of holders are usually involved.
- Life insurance companies and pension funds dominate the private placement segment of the bond market. Banks are significant participants in the term loan market.
- The costs of distributing bonds are lower in the private market.

The interest rates on term loans and private placements are usually higher than those on an equivalent public issue. Hayes et al. (1979) found that the yield to maturity on private placements was 0.46 per cent higher than on similar public issues. This finding reflects the trade-off between a higher interest rate and more flexible arrangements in the event of financial distress, as well as the lower transaction costs associated with private placements.

16.8 Long-term Syndicated Bank Loans

Most bank loans are for less than a year. They serve as a short-term 'bridge' for the acquisition of inventory and are typically self-liquidating – that is, when the firm sells the inventory, the cash is used to repay the bank loan. We talked about the need for short-term bank loans in Section 16.1. Now we focus on long-term bank loans.

First, we introduce the concept of commitment. Most bank loans are made with a commitment to a firm. That commitment establishes a line of credit and allows the firm to borrow up to a predetermined limit. Most commitments are in the form of a revolving credit commitment (i.e. a revolver) with a fixed term of up to three years or more. Revolving credit commitments are drawn or undrawn depending on whether the firm has a current need for the funds.

Now we turn to the concept of syndication. Very large banks such as Citigroup typically have a larger demand for loans than they can supply, and small regional banks frequently have more funds on hand than they can profitably lend to existing customers. Basically, they cannot generate enough good loans with the funds they have available. As a result, a very large bank may arrange a loan with a firm or country and then sell portions of it to a syndicate of other banks. With a syndicated loan, each bank has a separate loan agreement with the borrowers.

A syndicated loan is a corporate loan made by a group (or syndicate) of banks and other institutional investors. A syndicated loan may be publicly traded. It may be a line of credit and be 'undrawn', or it may be drawn and be used by a firm. Syndicated loans are always rated investment grade. However, a *leveraged* syndicated loan is rated speculative grade (i.e. it is 'junk'). In addition, syndicated loan prices are reported for a group of publicly traded loans. Altman and Suggitt (2000) report slightly higher default rates for syndicated loans than for comparable corporate bonds.

Syndicated Loans versus Corporate Bonds

How does the syndicated loan market interact with corporate bond issuance? Do firms treat each financing source as independent or is there a substitution effect where syndicated loans are more attractive in some periods than corporate bonds? What are the drivers of relative importance in each market?

Cortina-Lorente, Didier and Schmukler (2016) asked these questions for the World Bank using corporate borrowings between 1991 and 2014. They found that companies act to maintain their average debt maturity by proactively choosing the debt financing source (syndicated loans or corporate bonds) when debt market dynamics evolve.

Figure 16.6 shows a time series of financing (equity, debt, and syndicated loans) for 83,370 firms across the world, consisting of 282,751 corporate bond issues and 195,129 syndicated loan issues between 1991 and 2014.

While equity and corporate bond issues in developed economies have stayed relatively constant as a percentage of GDP since the mid-1990s, syndicated loans took on much more importance in the run-up to the financial crisis, before collapsing in line with the restriction in bank credit between 2009 and 2011. Syndicated bank loans have recovered their popularity in recent years. Emerging markets show a different pattern, which is consistent with China entering the WTO in 2001 and the gradual erosion of international trade barriers since then.

Figure 16.6 Security Issuance over Time

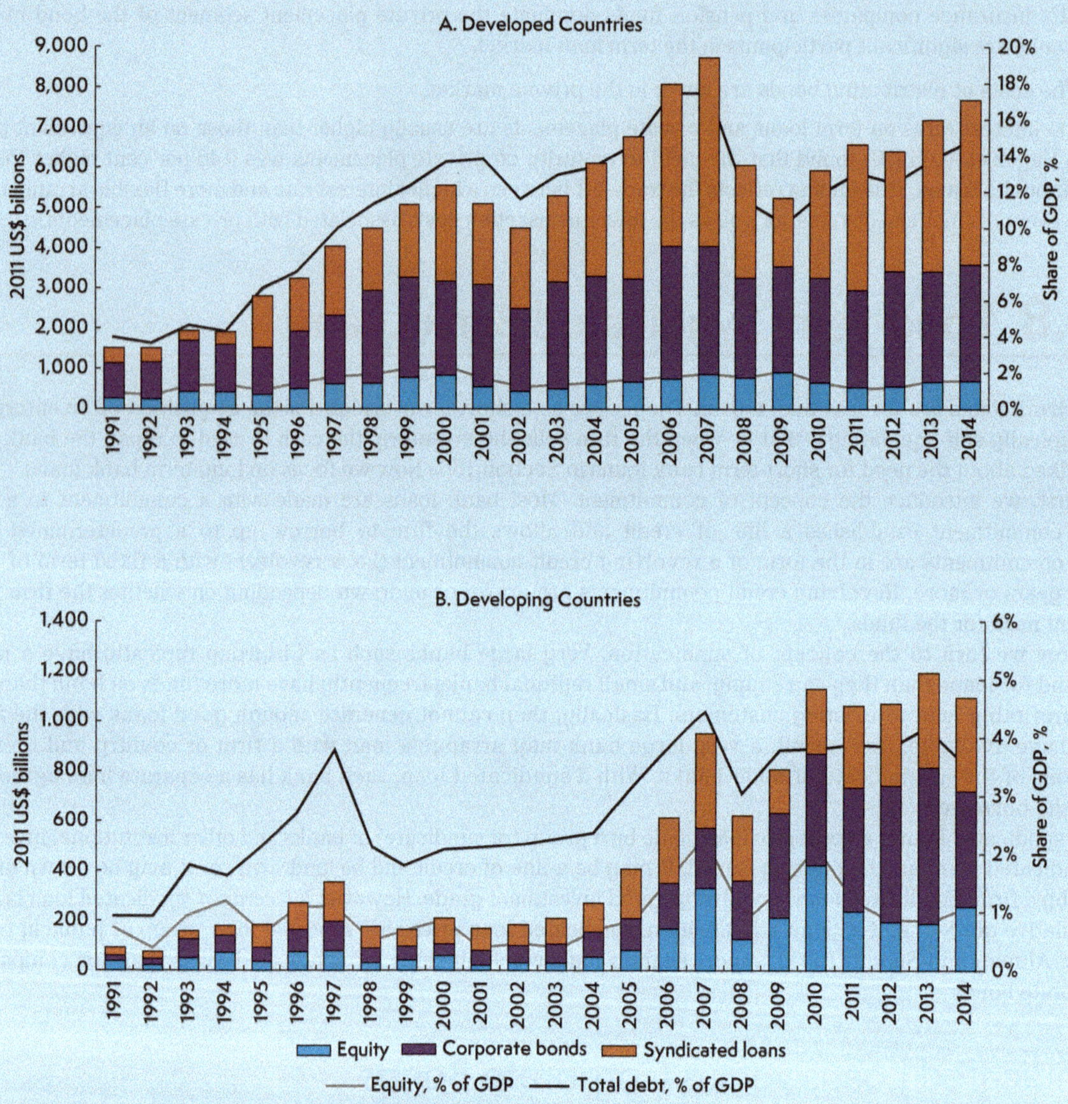

Source: Cortina-Lorente, J.J., T. Didier and S.L. Schmukler (2016) 'Corporate Borrowing and Debt Maturity: The Effects of Market Access and Crises', Policy Research Working Paper No. 7815. World Bank, Washington, DC. © World Bank. Available at: Open Knowledge Repository. Licence: CC BY 3.0 IGO (accessed 20 November 2019).

Summary and Conclusions

This chapter described some important aspects of long-term debt financing:

1 The written agreement describing the details of the long-term debt contract is called an *indenture*. Some of the main provisions are security, repayment, protective covenants and call provisions.

2 There are many ways that shareholders can take advantage of bondholders. Protective covenants are designed to protect bondholders from management decisions that favour equityholders at bondholders' expense.

3 Unsecured bonds are called *debentures* or *notes*. They are general claims on the company's value. Most public industrial bonds are unsecured. In contrast, utility bonds are usually secured. Mortgage bonds are secured by tangible property, and collateral trust bonds are secured by financial securities such as equities and bonds. If the company defaults on secured bonds, the trustee can repossess the assets. This makes secured bonds more valuable.

4 Long-term bonds usually provide for repayment of the principal before maturity. This is accomplished by a sinking fund. With a sinking fund, the company retires a certain number of bonds each year. A sinking fund protects bondholders because it reduces the average maturity of the bond, and its payment signals the financial condition of the company.

5 Most publicly issued bonds are callable. A callable bond is less attractive to bondholders than a non-callable bond. A callable bond can be bought back by the company at a call price that is less than the true value of the bond. As a consequence, callable bonds are priced to obtain higher stated interest rates for bondholders than non-callable bonds.

Generally, companies should exercise the call provision whenever the bond's value is greater than the call price.

There is no single reason for call provisions. Some sensible reasons include taxes, greater flexibility, management's ability to predict interest rates, and the fact that callable bonds are less sensitive to interest rate changes.

6 There are many different types of bonds, including floating-rate bonds, deep-discount bonds, green bonds and income bonds. This chapter also compared private placement with public issuance.

7 Islamic businesses can invest in special types of bonds, known as *sukuk*, that are designed to be consistent with Shariah law.

8 Long-term syndicated bank loans are an alternative source of debt finance that companies use to maintain their debt maturity profile when corporate bond markets become more attractive for shorter-term debt maturities.

Questions and Problems

McGraw Hill connect

CONCEPT

1 **Debt Financing** Review the characteristics of a bond. Why do you think short-term debt is known as unfunded debt and long-term debt as funded debt? Consider the increasing importance of environmental, social and governance (ESG) factors in corporate finance. How might these factors influence a company's decision to issue short-term or long-term debt?

2 **The Public Issue of Bonds** Explain what is meant by a bond covenant and provide examples of the different forms of covenant you may see in a bond indenture. What are the costs and benefits of bond covenants to the shareholders of the issuing firm?

3 **Bond Refunding** Why would a firm choose to issue callable bonds? Are there any disadvantages to issuing callable bonds? Explain.

4 **Different Types of Bonds** Explain what is meant by a *sukuk*. Why do you think it is called a bond? Global *sukuk* issuance has expanded rapidly over the last number of years. Why do you think this is? What is the unique nature of *sukuks* that makes them a suitable form of finance for infrastructure projects? Explain.

5 **Private Placement versus Public Issue** What are the benefits of a private placement over a public issue of bonds?

6 **Long-term Syndicated Bank Loans** What are the main agency issues involved in a syndicated loan? Do you think syndicated loans should be priced differently from public debt issues? Explain.

REGULAR

7 **Bank Loans** Bank loans are the major financing source for European companies. Why do you think bank loans continue to be important in some countries but less popular in others? Explain.

8 **Call Provisions** Assume you work for Veolia Environnement SA, a French company known for its work in water management and sanitation services. Your management has decided to have a long-term bond issue to fund investments in clean water and sanitation infrastructure projects in Africa. The company is considering whether to include a call provision in the bond issue.

What are the benefits to Veolia Environnement from including a call provision? What are the potential costs associated with it? How might these answers change for a put provision?

Given Veolia's sustainability focus, what other types of options could be embedded into the bond contracts that might help manage risks associated with large-scale infrastructure projects in regions with uncertain regulatory environments or unstable political conditions? Discuss how Veolia's commitment to sustainability and its alignment with SDG6 might affect investors' perceptions of the bond issue and the company's long-term financial stability.

9 **Coupon Rate** How would Veolia Environnement decide on an appropriate coupon rate to set on its bonds given that the investment is in Africa? Is the coupon rate the same as the required rate of return on the bond? Explain.

10 **Credit Ratings and Financial Markets** Empirically, share prices and bond prices have been shown to react only to a small degree to credit rating changes, if at all. Why do you think this is?

11 **Bond Ratings** Governments, as well as companies, have credit ratings. What impact do you think a government's credit rating has on a company that operates in that country?

12 **Crossover Bonds** Assume that Veolia Environnement had a bond issue and a credit rating from Moody's and S&P. However, Moody's has given a rating of Aaa and S&P has given a rating of BBB. What does this mean and why do you think it has happened? Explain.

13 **Borrowing Choices** Why might we expect firms with credit ratings in the middle of the spectrum to issue debt privately rather than publicly?

14 **Bond Indentures** Why do bonds have indentures? What, in your opinion, is the most important indenture for a bond? Are indentures more or less important for junk bond issues? Explain.

15 **Rating Agencies** A controversy erupted regarding bond rating agencies when some agencies began to provide unsolicited bond ratings. Why do you think this is controversial?

16 **Bonds as Equity** In 2018, Oxford University issued a 100-year bond. Critics charge that this issue is very similar to equity. Explain why critics would argue this is the case. Do you agree with the argument? What are the issues for Oxford to consider in this issue? Why would a for-profit company want to sell 'equity in disguise'?

17 **Callable Bonds** Do you agree or disagree with the following statement? 'In an efficient market, callable and non-callable bonds will be priced in such a way that there will be no advantage or disadvantage to the call provision.' Why?

18 **Bond Prices** If interest rates fall, will the price of non-callable bonds move up higher than that of callable bonds? Why, or why not?

19 **Junk Bonds** What is a 'junk bond'? What are some of the controversies created by junk bond financing? By looking at the time series of bond defaults in Figure 16.3, can you think of a profitable trading strategy for junk bonds? Explain.

20 **Sinking Funds** What is a sinking fund covenant? Sinking funds have both positive and negative characteristics for bondholders. Why?

21 **Mortgage Bonds** Which is riskier to a prospective creditor – an open-end mortgage or closed-end mortgage? Why?

22 **Public Issues versus Private Placements** Which of the following are characteristics of public issues, and which are characteristics of private placements?

(a) Stock exchange registration required

(b) Higher interest cost

(c) Higher fixed cost

(d) Quicker access to funds

(e) Active secondary market

(f) Easily renegotiated

(g) Lower flotation costs

(h) Regular amortization required

(i) Ease of repurchase at favourable prices

(j) High total cost to small borrowers

(k) Flexible terms

(l) Less intensive investigation required

23 **Bond Ratings and Price Movements** In general, why don't bond prices change when bond ratings change?

24 **Accrued Interest and Clean Prices** You purchase an Asian Paints Ltd bond on the Bombay Stock Exchange with an invoice price of R9,342. The bond has a coupon rate of 6.45 per cent, and there are five months to the next semi-annual coupon date. What is the clean price of the bond?

25 **Accrued Interest and Invoice Prices** You purchase a bond with a coupon rate of 5.2 per cent and a clean price of €865. If the next coupon payment is due in two months, what is the invoice price?

26 **Bond Refunding and Callability** Infineon AG plans to issue €500 million of bonds with a face value of €100,000, coupon rate of 3.5 per cent and 10 years to maturity. The current market interest rate on these bonds is 6 per cent. In one year, the interest rate on the bonds will be either 8 per cent or 5 per cent with equal probability. Assume investors are risk-neutral.

(a) If the bonds are non-callable, what is the price of the bonds today?

(b) If the bonds are callable one year from today at €120,000, will their price be greater than or less than the price you computed in (a)? Why?

27 **Bond Refunding: Parto SpA** Parto SpA has an outstanding perpetual bond with a 4 per cent coupon rate that can be called in one year. The bonds make annual coupon payments. The call premium is set at 120 per cent of par value. There is a 40 per cent chance that the interest rate in one year will be 8 per cent, and a 60 per cent chance that the interest rate will be 6 per cent. If the current interest rate is 7 per cent, what is the current market price of the bond?

28 **Bond Refunding: Mobistar** Mobistar intends to issue callable, perpetual bonds with annual coupon payments. The bonds are callable at €12,500. One-year interest rates are 6 per cent. There is a 60 per cent probability that long-term interest rates one year from today will be 9 per cent, and a 40 per cent probability that long-term interest rates will be 4 per cent. Assume that if interest rates fall the bonds will be called. What coupon rate should the bonds have in order to sell at par value?

29 **Bond Refunding: Heineken** Heineken NV has decided to borrow money by issuing perpetual bonds with a coupon rate of 6 per cent, payable annually. The one-year interest rate is 6 per cent. Next year, there is a 35 per cent probability that interest rates will increase to 7 per cent, and there is a 65 per cent probability that they will fall to 5 per cent.

(a) What will the market value of these bonds be if they are non-callable?

(b) If the company instead decides to make the bonds callable in one year, what coupon will be demanded by the bondholders for the bonds to sell at par? Assume that the bonds will be called if interest rates fall and that the call premium is equal to the annual coupon.

(c) What will be the value of the call provision to the company?

CHALLENGE

30 **Bond Refunding: Jeronimo Martins** An outstanding issue of Jeronimo Martins bonds has a call provision attached. The total principal value of the bonds is €120 million, and the bonds have an annual coupon rate of 6.6 per cent. The total cost of refunding would be 12 per cent of the principal amount raised. The appropriate tax rate for the company is 12.5 per cent. How low does the borrowing cost need to drop to justify refunding with a new bond issue?

31 **Bond Refunding: Charles River Associates** Charles River Associates is considering whether to refinance either of the two perpetual bond issues the company currently has outstanding. Here is information about the two bond issues:

	Bond A	Bond B
Coupon rate	8%	9%
Value outstanding	€75,000,000	€87,500,000
Call premium	8.5%	9.5%
Transaction cost of refunding	€10,000,000	€12,000,000
Current interest rate	7%	7.25%

The corporate tax rate is 12.5 per cent. What is the NPV of the refunding for each bond? Which bond should the company refinance?

32 **CoCo Bonds** Consider HSBC Holdings plc, which issued perpetual subordinated contingent convertible securities (CoCo bonds) totaling $2 billion on 9 March 2021. This issue was divided into two tranches, each worth $1 billion. The first tranche has a coupon of 4 per cent and is callable in 2026, while the second tranche has a 4.7 per cent coupon and is callable in 2031. A capital adequacy trigger event, which would cause automatic conversion of the bonds, will occur if, at any time, the non-transitional common equity Tier 1 ratio is less than 7.0 per cent. The conversion price is initially set at $3.7703 per share, and assuming no adjustment to the price, the maximum number of ordinary shares that may be issued upon an automatic conversion of the securities is approximately 530,464,581. Conduct research and identify the strengths and weaknesses of CoCo bonds from the perspectives of both HSBC as the issuer and the buyers of these bonds. How does the callable nature of these bonds affect their attractiveness to potential investors? What potential risks and benefits does the automatic conversion feature present to both parties?

33 **Valuing the Call Feature** Consider the prices in the following three Treasury issues as of 24 February 2020:

6.500	16 May	106:10	106:12	−13	5.28
8.250	16 May	103:14	103:16	.−3	5.24
12.000	16 May	134:25	134:31	−15	5.32

The bond in the middle is callable in February 2021. What is the implied value of the call feature? (*Hint:* Is there a way to combine the two non-callable issues to create an issue that has the same coupon as the callable bond?)

34 **Negative Yields** Over the past 10 years, some government bonds (for example, Switzerland and Japan) have traded at a negative yield to maturity. Why do you think investors are willing to buy bonds with a negative yield?

35 ***Sukuk*** Medhat International is a manufacturing firm operated along Islamic principles. It wishes to raise 20 billion Bahrain dinars and pay this back in equal instalments over six years. Comparable Western bonds have 8 per cent coupons. Construct a *sukuk* that is competitive with Western bonds.

Exam Question (45 minutes)

Stature Technologies plans to issue £100 million of bonds with a face value of £100,000, coupon rate of 4.125 per cent and 10 years to maturity. The current yield to maturity of these bonds is 4 per cent. In one year, the yield to maturity on the bonds will be either 6 per cent or 3.75 per cent with equal probability. Assume investors are risk-neutral.

1 If the bonds are non-callable, what is the price of the bonds today? **(30 marks)**

2 If the bonds are callable one year from today at 115 per cent of face value, will their price be greater than or less than the price you computed in (1)? Why? **(30 marks)**

3 If Stature Technologies wished to issue the bond (without call option) in Abu Dhabi as a *sukuk*, explain, using a diagram, how you would construct the Islamic bond. **(40 marks)**

Total Marks: 100

Mini Case

Financing West Coast Yachts' Expansion Plans with a Bond Issue

Larissa Warren, the owner of West Coast Yachts, has decided to expand her operations. She asked her newly hired financial analyst, Dan Ervin, to enlist an underwriter to help sell £30 million in new 20-year bonds to finance new construction. Dan has entered into discussions with Robyn Perry, an underwriter from the firm of Crowe & Mallard, about which bond features West Coast Yachts should consider and also what coupon rate the issue is likely to have. Although Dan is aware of bond features, he is uncertain of the costs and benefits of some features, so he is not sure how each feature would affect the coupon rate of the bond issue.

1 You are Robyn's assistant, and she has asked you to prepare a memo to Dan describing the effect of each of the following bond features on the coupon rate of the bond. She would also like you to list any advantages or disadvantages of each feature.

   (a) The security of the bond – that is, whether the bond has collateral
   (b) The seniority of the bond
   (c) The presence of a sinking fund
   (d) A call provision with specified call dates and call prices
   (e) A deferred call accompanying the call provision in (d)
   (f) A make-whole call provision
   (g) Any positive covenants; also, discuss several possible positive covenants West Coast Yachts might consider
   (h) Any negative covenants; also, discuss several possible negative covenants West Coast Yachts might consider
   (i) A conversion feature (note that West Coast Yachts is not a publicly traded company)
   (j) A floating-rate coupon

   Dan is also considering whether to issue coupon bearing bonds or zero coupon bonds. The YTM on either bond issue will be 8 per cent. The coupon bond would have an 8 per cent coupon rate. The company's tax rate is 28 per cent.

2 How many of the coupon bonds must West Coast Yachts issue to raise the £30 million? How many of the zeros must it issue?

3 In 20 years, what will be the principal repayment due if West Coast Yachts issues the coupon bonds? What if it issues the zeros?

4 What are the company's considerations in issuing a coupon bond compared to a zero coupon bond?

5 Suppose West Coast Yachts issues the coupon bonds with a make-whole call provision. The make-whole call rate is the Treasury rate plus 0.40 per cent. If West Coast calls the bonds in seven years when the Treasury rate is 5.6 per cent, what is the call price of the bond? What if it is 9.1 per cent?

6 Are investors really made whole with a make-whole call provision?

7 After considering all the relevant factors, would you recommend a zero coupon issue or a regular coupon issue? Why? Would you recommend an ordinary call feature or a make-whole call feature? Why?

Practical Case Study

Look up the websites and financial reports for Société Générale, Crédit Agricole, Enel SpA and ING Group, and find the credit rating for each firm. For some of these companies, you will need to search closely for the information. While it may seem a bit of a bore to do this, searching for data and reading through corporate financial websites gives fantastic experience in understanding corporate finance. Which companies (if any) have an investment-grade rating? Which companies are rated below investment grade? Are any unrated? Compare the change in share price over the last year and the rating for each company. Is there a relationship? What do credit ratings say about a firm's share price performance?

Relevant Accounting Standards

The most important accounting standard for bonds is IAS 39 *Financial Instruments: Recognition and Measurement.* However, you should also know IAS 23 *Borrowing Costs,* which deals with the way interest payments and other charges are presented in the financial accounts. Visit the IASPlus website (www.iasplus.com) for more information.

References

Altman, E.I. and H.J. Suggitt (2000) 'Default Rates in the Syndicated Bank Loan Market: A Mortality Analysis', *Journal of Banking and Finance,* Vol. 24, Nos. 1–2, 229–253.

Beck, T., A. Demirgüç-Kunt and V. Maksimovic (2008) 'Financing Patterns around the World: The Role of Institutions', *Journal of Financial Economics,* Vol. 89, 467–487.

Brooks, R., R. Faff, D. Hillier and J. Hillier (2004) 'The National Market Impact of Sovereign Rating Changes', *Journal of Banking and Finance,* Vol. 28, No. 1, 233–250.

Cornell, B. (1986) 'The Future of Floating-rate Bonds', in J.M. Stern and D.H. Chew, Jr (eds), *The Revolution in Corporate Finance.* New York: Basil Blackwell.

Cortina-Lorente, J.J., T. Didier and S.L. Schmukler (2016) 'Corporate Borrowing and Debt Maturity: The Effects of Market Access and Crises', Policy Research Working Paper No. 7815. World Bank.

Cox, J., J. Ingersoll and S.A. Ross (1980) 'An Analysis of Variable Rate Loan Contracts', *Journal of Finance,* Vol. 35, 389–403.

Gopal, M. and P. Schnabl (2022) 'The Rise of Finance Companies and Fintech Lenders in Small Business Lending', *Review of Financial Studies,* Vol. 35, No. 11, 4859–4901.

Hayes, P.A., M.D. Joehnk and R.W. Melicher (1979) 'Determinants of Risk Premiums in the Public and Private Bond Market', *Journal of Financial Research,* Vol. 2, 143–152.

Holthausen, R.W. and R.W. Leftwich (1986) 'The Effect of Bond Rating Changes on Common Stock Prices', *Journal of Financial Economics,* Vol. 17, No. 1, 57–89.

Kraus, A. (1983) 'An Analysis of Call Provisions and the Corporate Refunding Decision', *Midland Corporate Finance Journal,* Vol. 1, 46–60.

Lee, I., S. Lockhead, J. Ritter and Q. Zhao (1996) 'The Costs of Raising Capital', *Journal of Financial Research,* Vol. 19, No. 1, 59–74.

Ogden, J.P. (1987) 'Determinants of Relative Interest Rate Sensitivity of Corporate Bonds', *Financial Management,* Vol. 16, No. 1, 22–30.

Reilly, F. and M. Joehnk (1976) 'The Association between Market-based Risk Measures for Bonds and Bond Ratings', *Journal of Finance,* Vol. 31, No. 5, 1387–1403.

Sufi, A. (2009) 'Bank Lines of Credit in Corporate Finance: An Empirical Analysis', *Review of Financial Studies,* Vol. 22, 1057–1088.

Weinstein, M. (1977) 'The Effect of a Ratings Change Announcement on Bond Price', *Journal of Financial Economics,* Vol. 5, 29–44.

Weinstein, M. (1981) 'The Systematic Risk of Corporate Bonds', *Journal of Financial and Quantitative Analysis,* Vol. 16, No. 3, 257–78.

Additional Reading

The literature on debt financing can be conveniently separated into three areas: pricing, risk and structure. This is the approach we take in listing the relevant papers in the area.

Bond and Bank Loan Pricing

1 Cai, N., J. Helwege and A. Warga (2007) 'Underpricing in the Corporate Bond Market', *Review of Financial Studies,* Vol. 20, No. 6, 2021–2046. **USA.**

2 Carey, M. and G. Nini (2007) 'Is the Corporate Loan Market Globally Integrated? A Pricing Puzzle', *Journal of Finance,* Vol. 62, 2969–3007. **International.**

3 Chava, S., D. Livden and A. Purnanandam (2009) 'Do Shareholder Rights Affect the Cost of Bank Loans?', *Review of Financial Studies,* Vol. 22, 2973–3004.

4 Cremers, K.J.M., V.B. Nair and C. Wei (2007) 'Governance Mechanisms and Bond Prices', *Review of Financial Studies,* Vol. 20, No. 5, 1359–1388. **USA.**

5 Ross, D.G. (2010) 'The "Dominant Bank Effect": How High Lender Reputation Affects the Information Content and Terms of Bank Loans', *Review of Financial Studies*, Vol. 23, 2730–2756.

Bond Risk and Credit Ratings

6 Avramov, D., T. Chordia, G. Jostova and A. Philipov (2009) 'Dispersion in Analysts' Earnings Forecasts and Credit Rating', *Journal of Financial Economics*, Vol. 91, No. 1, 83–101. **USA.**

7 Behr, P. and A. Guttler (2008) 'The Informational Content of Unsolicited Ratings', *Journal of Banking and Finance*, Vol. 32, No. 5, 587–599. **USA.**

8 Brooks, R., R. Faff, D. Hillier and J. Hillier (2004) 'The National Market Impact of Sovereign Rating Changes', *Journal of Banking and Finance*, Vol. 28, No. 1, 233–250. **International.**

9 Butler, A. (2008) 'Distance Still Matters: Evidence from Municipal Bond Underwriting', *Review of Financial Studies*, Vol. 21, 763–784.

Bond Covenants and Structures

10 Billett, M.T., T. Dolly King and D.C. Mauer (2007) 'Growth Opportunities and the Choice of Leverage, Debt Maturity, and Covenants', *Journal of Finance*, Vol. 62, No. 2, 697–730. **USA.**

11 Chava, S. and M.R. Roberts (2008) 'How Does Financing Impact Investment? The Role of Debt Covenants', *Journal of Finance*, Vol. 63, No. 5, 2085–2121. **USA.**

12 Chen, Z., C.X. Mao and Y. Wang (2010) 'Why Firms Issue Callable Bonds: Hedging Investment Uncertainty', *Journal of Corporate Finance*, Vol. 16, 588–607.

13 Datta, S., M. Iskandar-Datta and K. Raman (2005) 'Managerial Stock Ownership and the Maturity Structure of Corporate Debt', *Journal of Finance*, Vol. 60, No. 5, 2333–2350. **USA.**

14 Jimenez, G., V. Salas and J. Saurina (2006) 'Determinants of Collateral', *Journal of Financial Economics*, Vol. 81, No. 1, 255–281. **Spain.**

15 Qian, J. and P.E. Strahan (2007) 'How Laws and Institutions Shape Financial Contracts: The Case of Bank Loans', *Journal of Finance*, Vol. 62, No. 6, 2803–2834. **International.**

16 Sufi, A. (2007) 'Information Asymmetry and Financing Arrangements: Evidence from Syndicated Loans', *Journal of Finance*, Vol. 62, No. 2, 629–668. **USA.**

Other Relevant Research

17 Agarwal, S. and R. Hauswald (2010) 'Distance and Private Information in Lending', *Review of Financial Studies*, Vol. 23, 2757–2788.

18 Begley, T.A. and K. Srinivasan (2022) 'Small Bank Lending in the Era of Fintech and Shadow Banks: A Sideshow?', *Review of Financial Studies*, Vol. 35, No. 11, 4948–4984.

19 Bonaccorsi Di Patti, E. and G. Gobbi (2007) 'Winners or Losers? The Effects of Banking Consolidation on Corporate Borrowers', *Journal of Finance*, Vol. 62, 669–695.

20 Carey, M. and G. Nini (2007) 'Is the Corporate Loan Market Globally Integrated? A Pricing Puzzle', *Journal of Finance*, Vol. 62, No. 6, 2969–3007. **International.**

21 Chernenko, S., I. Erel and R. Prilmeier (2022) 'Why Do Firms Borrow Directly from Nonbanks?', *Review of Financial Studies*, Vol. 35, No. 11, 4902–4947.

22 Cho, S.S., S. El Ghoul, O. Guedhami and J. Suh (2014) 'Creditor Rights and Capital Structure: Evidence from International Data', *Journal of Corporate Finance*, Vol. 25, 40–60.

23 Colla, P., F. Ippolito and K. Li (2013) 'Debt Specialization', *Journal of Finance*, Vol. 68, No. 5, 2117–2141.

24 Danielova, A., N. Smart, B. Scott and J. Boquist (2010) 'What Motivates Exchangeable Debt Offerings?', *Journal of Corporate Finance*, Vol. 16, 159–169.

25 Flammer, C. (2021) 'Corporate Green Bonds', *Journal of Financial Economics*, Vol. 22, 499–516.

26 Gillet, R. and H. de la Bruslerie (2010) 'The Consequences of Issuing Convertible Bonds: Dilution and/or Financial Restructuring?', *European Financial Management*, Vol. 16, 552–584.

27 Jang, W., L. Kai and P. Shao (2010) 'When Shareholders are Creditors: Effects of the Simultaneous Holding of Equity and Debt by Non-commercial Banking Institutions', *Review of Financial Studies*, Vol. 23, 3595–3637.

28 Lin, C., Y. Ma, P. Malatesta and Y. Xuan (2013) 'Corporate Ownership Structure and the Choice between Bank Debt and Public Debt', *Journal of Financial Economics*, Vol. 109, No. 2, 517–534.

29 McCahery, J. and A. Schweinbacher (2010) 'Bank Reputation in the Private Debt Market', *Journal of Corporate Finance*, Vol. 16, 498–515.

30 Roberts, M.R. and A. Sufi (2009) 'Control Rights and Capital Structure: An Empirical Investigation', *Journal of Finance*, Vol. 64, No. 4, 1657–1695. **USA.**

31 Tang, H. (2019) 'Peer-to-peer Lenders versus Banks: Substitutes or Complements?', *Review of Financial Studies*, Vol. 32, No. 5, 1900–1938.

Endnotes

1 Sufi (2009).

2 The term *loan agreement* or *loan contract* is usually used for privately placed debt and term loans.

3 See Kraus (1983)

4 We are assuming that the current price of the non-callable bonds is the expected value discounted at the risk-free rate of 10 per cent. This is equivalent to assuming that the risk is unsystematic and carries no risk premium.

5 Normally, bonds can be called over a period of many years. Our assumption that the bond can be called only at the end of the first year was introduced for simplicity.

6 Kraus (1983) points out that the call provision will not always reduce the equity's interest rate risk. If the firm as a whole bears interest rate risk, more of this risk may be shifted from shareholders to bondholders with non-callable debt. In this case, shareholders may actually bear more risk with callable debt.

7 Weinstein (1981); Ogden (1987); and Reilly and Joehnk (1976).

8 Weinstein (1977). However, Holthausen and Leftwich (1986) find that bond rating downgrades are associated with abnormal negative returns on the equity of the issuing firm. In addition, Brooks et al. (2004) show that stock market indices react negatively to downgrades of government credit rating.

9 See Cornell (1986).

10 Cox et al. (1980) developed a framework for pricing floating-rate notes.

11 A more precise strategy would be to buy zeros maturing in years 15, 16, 17 and 18, respectively. In this way the bonds might mature just in time to meet tuition payments.

Chapter 17
Leasing

Learning Objectives

After reading this chapter you should be able to:

LO1 Describe different types of lease financing and their characteristics.

LO2 Explain the accounting principles related to leasing.

LO3 Analyse the impact of discounting and debt capacity on the decision to lease or buy, considering corporate taxes.

LO4 Critically assess the circumstances in which leasing pays off and the reasons companies choose to lease.

Instead of incurring major capital expenditure through purchasing fixed assets, leasing allows a company to dispense with the need to raise capital for investment. For example, many airlines lease planes instead of owning them. Aercap, which is the world's largest airplane leasing company by fleet value, with annual revenues in excess of €5 billion, leases airplanes to airlines such as American Airlines, China Southern Airlines, Azul Brazilian Airlines, Air France-KLM and Ethiopian Airlines. The company currently owns more than 3,500 aircraft. So why is Aercap in the business of buying airplanes, only to lease them out? And why don't companies that lease from Aercap simply purchase the airplanes themselves? This chapter provides answers to these and other questions associated with leasing.

Chapter 7
Page 178

We discuss the different types of leases that companies can use. We then illustrate how you can assess the value of a lease in the same way as a standard capital budgeting problem (see Chapter 7). Unlike a standard NPV analysis, the identification of the appropriate discount rate is tricky and we show that the after-tax risk-free rate is the appropriate rate to use for lease decisions. The chapter closes by presenting reasons (good and bad) for why firms lease, followed by a general review of some areas that are still being investigated by researchers.

Source: Martin Bergsma/123RF

Key Notations

NPV	Net present value	L	Lease payment

17.1 Types of Lease Financing

A *lease* is a contractual agreement between a lessee and lessor. The agreement establishes that the lessee has the right to use an asset and in return must make periodic payments to the lessor, the owner of the asset. The lessor is either the asset's manufacturer or an independent leasing company. If the lessor is an independent leasing company, it must buy the asset from a manufacturer. Then the lessor delivers the asset to the lessee, and the lease goes into effect.

As far as the lessee is concerned, it is the use of the asset that is most important, not who owns the asset, and a lease contract allows the asset to be used without ownership. The alternative is for the user to buy the asset, and this will involve alternative financing arrangements.

The example in Figure 17.1 often happens in the computer industry. Firm U, the lessee, might be a hospital, a law firm or any other firm that uses computers. The lessor is an independent leasing company that purchased the equipment from a manufacturer such as Dell, HP or Apple. Leases of this type are called direct leases. In Figure 17.1, the lessor issued both debt and equity to finance the purchase.

Of course, a manufacturer like Apple could lease its *own* computers, though we do not show this situation in the example. Leases of this type are called sales-type leasing. In this case, Apple would compete with the independent computer leasing company.

Figure 17.1 Buying versus Leasing

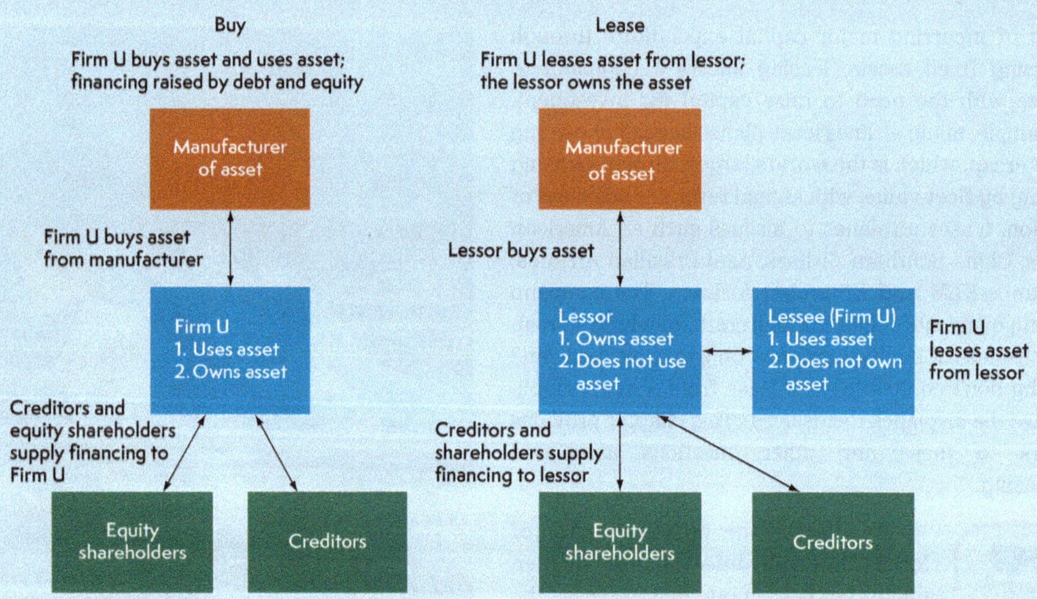

Operating Leases

Years ago, a lease where the lessee received an operator along with the equipment was called an operating lease. Though the operating lease defies an exact definition today, this form of leasing has several salient characteristics:

- Operating leases are usually not fully amortized. This means that the payments required under the terms of the lease are not enough to recover the full cost of the asset for the lessor. This occurs because the term or life of the operating lease is usually less than the economic life of the asset. Thus, the lessor must expect to recover the costs of the asset by renewing the lease or by selling the asset for its residual value.
- Operating leases usually require the lessor to maintain and insure the leased assets.
- Perhaps the most interesting feature of an operating lease is the cancellation option. This option gives the lessee the right to cancel the lease contract before the expiration date. If the option to cancel is exercised, the lessee must return the equipment to the lessor. The value of a cancellation clause depends on whether future technological or economic conditions are likely to make the value of the asset to the lessee less than the value of the future lease payments under the lease.

To leasing practitioners, these characteristics constitute an operating lease. However, accountants use the term in a slightly different way, as we will see shortly.

Financial Leases

Financial leases are the exact opposite of operating leases, as seen from their characteristics:

- Financial leases do not provide for maintenance or service by the lessor.
- Financial leases are fully amortized.
- The lessee usually has a right to renew the lease on expiration.
- Generally, financial leases cannot be cancelled. In other words, the lessee must make all payments or face the risk of bankruptcy.

Because of these characteristics, particularly the second, this lease provides an alternative method of financing to purchase. Hence, its name is a sensible one. Two particular types of financial lease are the sale and leaseback arrangement, and the leveraged lease.

Sale and Leaseback

A sale and leaseback occurs when a company sells an asset it owns to another firm and immediately leases it back. In a sale and leaseback two things happen:

1. The lessee receives cash from the sale of the asset.
2. The lessee makes periodic lease payments, thereby retaining use of the asset.

For example, in 2019, the British rail operator, Transport for London, had a £1 billion sale and leaseback initiative to raise capital to purchase new trains for the London Underground network. The contract will last until 2039 and Transport for London will pay a group of lessors, called the 345 Rail Leasing Consortium, lease payments over this period in return for the £1 billion.

Leveraged Leases

A leveraged lease is a three-sided arrangement among the lessee, the lessor and the lenders:

1. The lessee uses the assets and makes periodic lease payments.
2. The lessor purchases the assets, delivers them to the lessee and collects the lease payments. However, the lessor puts up no more than 40 to 50 per cent of the purchase price.
3. The lenders supply the remaining financing and receive interest payments from the lessor. Thus, the arrangement on the right side of Figure 17.1 would be a leveraged lease if creditors supplied the bulk of the financing.

Lenders in a leveraged lease typically use a non-recourse loan, which means the lessor is not obligated to the lender in a default. However, the lender is protected in two ways:

1. The lender has a first claim on the asset.
2. In the event of loan default, the lease payments are made directly to the lender.

The lessor puts up only part of the funds but gets the lease payments and all the tax benefits of ownership. These lease payments are used to pay the debt service of the non-recourse loan. The lessee benefits because, in a competitive market, the lease payment is lowered when the lessor saves taxes.

17.2 Accounting and Leasing

Twenty years ago, a firm could arrange to use an asset through a lease and not disclose the asset or the lease contract on the balance sheet. Lessees had to report information on leasing activity only in the footnotes of their financial statements, which led leasing to be known as off-balance-sheet financing. Things have changed significantly in recent years and leasing now has an accounting standard all to itself: IFRS 16 *Leases*.

Leases have different characteristics and this affects how they should be recorded in the financial statements of a firm. The major issue relates to the effective ownership of an asset, the risks and rewards of ownership, and to whom this should be attributed. Specifically, a lease is considered a finance lease if the lessee bears the majority of risks and reward of the asset, whereas it is viewed as an operating lease if the lessor bears the risk.

The IFRS accounting treatment of leases (applicable to most European and South African companies, IFRS 16) underwent a substantial evolution in 2019 and there were a number of major changes to the way leases impact the balance sheet of lessees (lessors were largely unimpacted by the changes). Older textbooks will treat leases differently and the reader must be very careful when drawing on these sources.

For the lessee, operating and finance leases are treated in the same way (this was not the situation in previous accounting standards), with the leased asset appearing on the statement of financial position and depreciated as a normal owned asset. The value to be recorded in the statement of financial position must be the fair or realizable value of the asset or, if lower, the present value of the lease payments. This means that, to all intents and purposes, assets funded by a lease are regarded in the exact same way as normal assets in a company. To offset the inclusion of an asset in the statement of financial position, a financial liability of equivalent value is also recorded. Each of these items (the leased asset and financial liability) must be treated separately in the financial statements. The leased asset will be depreciated each year and interest must be charged on the outstanding financial liability, with the principal paid off over time. This means the value of the leased asset and financial liability will diverge over the life of the lease. We examine this issue further in this chapter.

Short-term leases of less than 12 months, or low-value assets (such as tablets, laptops and mobile phones) are treated differently. Short-term and low-value leases treat the lease payments as simple expenses in the income statement, without the need to add the lease to the statement of financial position.

17.3 The Cash Flows of Leasing

In this section we identify the basic cash flows used in evaluating a lease. Consider the decision confronting Xomox Ltd, which manufactures long-distance gas pipes. Business has been expanding and Xomox currently has a five-year backlog of gas pipe orders for a trans-Scandinavian pipeline.

Global Boring Machines (GBM) makes a pipe-boring machine that can be purchased for €10,000. Xomox has determined that it needs a new machine, and the GBM model will save it €6,000 per year in reduced electricity bills for the next five years. These savings are known with certainty because Xomox has a long-term electricity purchase agreement with French Electric Utilities SA.

Xomox has an effective corporate tax rate of 28 per cent. We assume straight line depreciation over the life of the machine, and the machine has no value after five years.[1]

With a corporate tax rate of 28 per cent, the after-tax operating cost savings is €6,000 × (1 – 0.28) = €4,320.

Friendly Leasing Ltd has offered to lease the same pipe-boring machine to Xomox for €2,500 per year for five years. With the lease, Xomox would remain responsible for maintenance, insurance and operating expenses.

To assess the value of the lease opportunity, we must calculate the incremental cash flows from leasing the GBM machine in lieu of buying it. Table 17.1 shows the direct cash flow consequences of both buying and leasing the pipe-boring machine.

There are two parts to Table 17.1: the cash flows from the buy decision and the cash flows from the lease decision. Dealing with the buy decision first, if Xomox were to buy the asset, it would incur the purchase cost in year 0 and benefit from after-tax cost savings of €4,320 as well as the depreciation tax shield of €560 per annum. This results in an annual cash flow between years 1 and 5 of €4,880.

Turning to the lease cash flows in the lower half of Table 17.1, the direct costs as well as the tax benefits must be calculated. Unfortunately, the tax implications of a lease under IFRS 16 are fairly complex. The accounting standards require you to separately record the outstanding financial liability and leased asset value in the statement of financial position for each year. Both of these items (liability and asset) attract a tax benefit that will positively impact the company's cash flows.

Assume the appropriate pre-tax discount rate is 7.9308 per cent. This will be the lessee's *incremental borrowing rate*, which is the rate of interest the lessee would incur for a similar loan with the same life and risk as the leased asset. The discount rate that equates the present value of future lease payments to the market value of the underlying asset is known as the *interest rate implicit in the lease.* This is similar to the lease's internal rate of return and is equal in this example to 7.9308 per cent.

Table 17.1 Cash Flows to Xomox from Using the GBM Pipe-boring Machine: Buy versus Lease

Buy						
Year	**0**	**1**	**2**	**3**	**4**	**5**
Cost of machine	€(10,000)					
After-tax operating cost savings		€4,320	€4,320	€4,320	€4,320	€4,320
Depreciation tax benefit		€ 560	€ 560	€ 560	€ 560	€ 560
Cash flows	€(10,000)	€4,880	€4,880	€4,880	€4,880	€4,880
Lease						
Year	**0**	**1**	**2**	**3**	**4**	**5**
Payments		€(2,500)	€(2,500)	€(2,500)	€(2,500)	€(2,500)
After-tax operating cost savings		€ 4,320	€ 4,320	€ 4,320	€ 4,320	€ 4,320
Lease tax benefit (Table 17.2)		€ 782	€ 744	€ 703	€ 659	€ 611
Cash flows		€ 2,602	€ 2,564	€ 2,523	€ 2,529	€ 2,431

Note: In the buy decision, depreciation is calculated on a straight line basis over five years. With a machine cost of €10,000, the annual depreciation charge will be €2,000 and the tax benefit (tax rate = 28 per cent) from depreciation per year is 28% of €2,000 = €560. The tax benefit from the lease is calculated in Table 17.2.

There are a number of assumptions in the previous paragraph. First, we assume the lease is priced competitively, in line with the risk and life of the asset and risk of the borrower. Second, we assume there is no residual value at the end of the lease contract. In other words, the asset will be worthless at the end of the contract. This may not happen in practice since the lessee could opt for a lower annual lease payment with a balloon payment at the end of the contract. We discuss this advanced scenario in Section 17.7.

To a lessee, every lease has two components that will impact the tax paid by the firm. In the Xomox example, the leased asset must be recorded in the statement of financial position at the market value of €10,000 to be depreciated over five years to zero, giving an annual depreciation of €2,000. There is also the financial liability that is treated as a loan with an interest payment equal to the incremental borrowing rate of 7.9308 per cent. Both interest expense and annual depreciation will attract a tax benefit to the firm.

Table 17.2 shows the direct tax consequences of signing the lease agreement with Friendly Leasing Ltd. Note that the year 1 total expense of €2,793 recorded in the income statement is greater than the annual lease payment of €2,500. Over the life of the lease the total annual expense will fall below the annual lease payment. For example, in year 5 the total expense recorded in the income statement is €2,184 compared to the annual lease payment of €2,500.

Note also how the asset and liability values diverge over the course of the lease. This will impact the company's expenses in the income statement, which has a tax benefit as presented in the final column of Table 17.2. The annual interest payment is calculated as the incremental borrowing rate multiplied by the liability outstanding.

Table 17.2 Tax Benefit from Leasing

Year	Asset Initial Cost (€)	Depreciation (€)	Balance (€)	Outstanding Liability (€)	Interest (€)	Principal (€)	Balance (€)	Total Expense (€)	Tax Benefit (€)
1	10,000	**2,000**	8,000	10,000	**793**	1,707	8,293	**2,793**	**782**
2	8,000	**2,000**	6,000	8,293	**658**	1,842	6,451	**2,658**	**744**
3	6,000	**2,000**	4,000	6,451	**512**	1,988	4,462	**2,512**	**703**
4	4,000	**2,000**	2,000	4,462	**354**	2,146	2,316	**2,354**	**659**
5	2,000	**2,000**	0	2,316	**184**	2,316	0	**2,184**	**611**

For example, in year 1, the outstanding liability is €10,000. With an incremental borrowing rate of 7.9308 per cent, the interest payment will be €793.08 (rounded to €793 in Table 17.2). The principal paid (€1,707) is the difference between the annual lease payment (€2,500) and the interest paid (€793). The balance on the financial liability (€8,293) is the difference between the initial value (€10,000) and principal paid (€1,707). The total expense (€2,793) is the sum of the annual depreciation (€2,000) and interest (€793) expenses, and the tax benefit (€782) is the total expense (€2,793) multiplied by the tax rate (28 per cent).

Now that we have the tax benefit to the lessee, we can analyse the lease vs buy decision as presented in Table 17.3.

Table 17.3 Incremental Cash Flow Consequences for Xomox from Leasing Instead of Purchasing

Lease Minus Buy						
Year	0	1	2	3	4	5
Lease cash flows		€ 2,602	€ 2,564	€ 2,523	€ 2,479	€ 2,431
Buy cash flows	€(10,000)	€ 4,880	€ 4,880	€ 4,880	€ 4,880	€ 4,880
Lease minus buy cash flows	€ 10,000	€(2,278)	€ (2,316)	€ (2,357)	€ (2,401)	€(2,449)

Note: The bottom line presents the cash flows from leasing relative to the cash flows from purchase. The cash flows would be exactly the *opposite* if we considered the purchase relative to the lease.

Buy Minus Lease						
Year	0	1	2	3	4	5
Buy cash flows	€(10,000)	€4,880	€4,880	€4,880	€4,880	€4,880
Lease cash flows		€2,602	€2,564	€ 2,523	€ 2,479	€ 2,431
Buy minus lease cash flows	€(10,000)	€ 2,278	€ 2,316	€ 2,357	€ 2,401	€2,449

The net cash flows in Table 17.3 are presented in two ways. In the first part, the numbers represent the cash flows from *leasing* relative to the cash flows from the purchase. It is arbitrary that we express the flows in this way. We could have expressed the cash flows (the second part of Table 17.3) from the perspective of the *purchase* relative to the cash flows from leasing. Depending on our purpose, we may look at either the purchase relative to the lease, or vice versa. Thus, the student should become comfortable with either viewpoint.

Now that we have the cash flows, we can make our lease vs buy decision by discounting the flows properly. However, because the discount rate is tricky, we take a detour in the next section before moving back to the Xomox case. In the next section, we show that cash flows in the lease-versus-buy decision should be discounted at the *after-tax incremental borrowing rate* (i.e. the after-tax cost of debt capital).

17.4 A Detour for Discounting and Debt Capacity with Corporate Taxes

The analysis of leases can be difficult, and it is easy to make conceptual errors, particularly around tax calculations. We hope to avoid mistakes by beginning with the simplest type of example: a risk-free loan for one year. Though this example is unrelated to our lease-versus-buy situation in Section 17.3, principles developed here will apply directly to any lease–buy analysis.

Present Value of Riskless Cash Flows

Consider a corporation that lends €100 for a year. If the interest rate is 10 per cent, the firm will receive €110 at the end of the year. Of this amount, €10 is interest and the remaining €100 is the original principal. A corporate tax rate of 34 per cent implies taxes on the interest of €3.40 (0.34 × €10). Thus, the firm ends up with €106.60 (= €110 − €3.40) after taxes on a €100 investment.

Now, consider a company that borrows €100 for a year. With a 10 per cent interest rate, the firm must pay €110 to the bank at the end of the year. However, the borrowing firm can take the €10 of interest as a tax deduction. The corporation pays €3.40 (= €0.34 × €10) less in taxes than it would have paid had it not borrowed the money at all. Thus, considering this reduction in taxes, the firm must pay €106.60 (= €110 – €3.40) on a €100 loan. The cash flows from both lending and borrowing are displayed in Table 17.4.

Table 17.4 Lending and Borrowing in a World with Corporate Taxes (Interest Rate is 10% and Corporate Tax Rate is 34%)

Date 0		Date 1
Lending example		
Lend – €100		Receive + €100.00 of principal
		Receive + € 10.00 of interest
	6.6% lending rate →	Pay −€3.40 (= −0.34 × 10) in taxes
		+€106.60
After-tax lending rate is 6.6%.		
Borrowing example		
Borrow + €100		Pay – €100.00 of principal
		Pay −€ 10.00 of interest
	6.6% borrowing rate →	Receive +€3.40 (= −0.34 × 10) as a tax rebate
		−€106.60
After-tax borrowing rate is 6.6%.		

Note: *In a world with corporate taxes, riskless cash flows should be discounted at the after-tax interest rate.*

The previous two paragraphs show a very important result: the firm could not care less whether it received €100 today or €106.60 next year.[2] If it received €100 today, it could lend it out, thereby receiving €106.60 after corporate taxes at the end of the year. Conversely, if it knows today that it will receive €106.60 at the end of the year, it could borrow €100 today. The after-tax interest and principal payments on the loan would be paid with the €106.60 that the firm will receive at the end of the year. Because of this interchangeability, we say that a payment of €106.60 next year has a present value of €100. Because €100 = €106.60/1.066, a riskless cash flow should be discounted at the after-tax interest rate of 0.066 [= 0.10 × (1 – 0.34)].

Of course, the preceding discussion considers a specific example of a riskless cash flow. The general principle is this:

In a world with corporate taxes, the firm should discount riskless cash flows at the after-tax riskless rate of interest.

Optimal Debt Level and Riskless Cash Flows

Our simple example illustrates a related point concerning optimal debt level. Consider a firm that has just determined that the current level of debt in its capital structure is optimal. Immediately following that determination, it is surprised to learn that it will receive a guaranteed payment of €106.60 in one year from, say, a tax-exempt government lottery. This future windfall is an asset that, like any asset, should raise the firm's optimal debt level. How much does this payment raise the firm's optimal level?

Our analysis implies that the firm's optimal debt level must be €100 more than it previously was. That is, the firm could borrow €100 today, perhaps paying the entire amount out as a dividend. It would owe the bank €110 at the end of the year. However, because it receives a tax rebate of €3.40 (= 0.34 × €10), its net repayment will be €106.60. Thus, its borrowing of €100 today is fully offset by next year's government lottery proceeds of €106.60. In other words, the lottery proceeds act as an irrevocable trust that can service the increased debt. Note that we need not know the optimal debt level before the lottery was announced. We are merely saying that whatever this pre-lottery optimal level was, the optimal debt level is €100 more after the lottery announcement.

Of course, this is just one example. The general principle is this:[3]

In a world with corporate taxes, we determine the increase in the firm's optimal debt level by discounting a future guaranteed after-tax inflow at the after-tax riskless interest rate.

Conversely, suppose that a second, unrelated firm is surprised to learn that it must pay €106.60 next year to the government for back taxes. Clearly, this additional liability impinges on the second firm's debt capacity. By the previous reasoning, it follows that the second firm's optimal debt level must be lowered by exactly €100.

Appropriate Discount Rate for a Lease

It follows that the appropriate discount rate for a lease (which has risky cash flows) should be the lessee's after-tax incremental borrowing rate. From IFRS 16, this is the after-tax rate of interest a lessee would incur to borrow funds for an asset with the same life and risk as the lease. This is also known as the lessee's after-tax cost of debt.

In the Xomox example of Section 17.3, the firm's incremental borrowing rate is 7.9308 per cent and its corporate tax rate is 28 per cent. This means the appropriate discount rate for the lease is 5.7102 per cent [= 0.079308 × (1 – 0.28)].

17.5 NPV Analysis of the Lease-versus-buy Decision

Chapter 6 Page 147

Our detour leads to a simple method for evaluating leases: discount all cash flows at the after-tax incremental borrowing rate (this section also draws on the NPV discussion in Chapter 6, Section 6.1).

Let us assume Xomox can either borrow or lend at the interest rate of 7.9308 per cent. If the corporate tax rate is 28 per cent, the correct discount rate is the after-tax rate of 5.71 per cent [= 7.9308% × (1 – 0.28)]. When 5.7102 per cent is used to compute the NPV of the lease, we have the following cash flows and present values:

Lease minus buy						
Year	0	1	2	3	4	5
Lease cash flows		€2,602	€ 2,564	€ 2,523	€ 2,479	€ 2,431
Buy cash flows	€(10,000)	€4,880	€ 4,880	€4,880	€4,880	€ 4,880
Lease minus buy cash flows	€ 10,000	€(2,278)	€ (2,316)	€(2,357)	€(2,401)	€(2,449)
PV of cash flows	€ 10,000	€ (2,155)	€(2,072)	€ (1,995)	€ (1,923)	€ (1,855)

The NPV is the sum of the individual cash flow present values:

Equation 17.1

$$\begin{aligned} \text{NPV} &= €10{,}000 - €2{,}155 - €2{,}072 - €1{,}995 - €1{,}923 - €1{,}855 \\ &= €0 \end{aligned}$$

Because the net present value of the incremental cash flows from leasing relative to purchasing is approximately equal to zero, Xomox is indifferent between buying and leasing the machine.

Equation 17.1 is the correct approach to lease-versus-buy analysis. However, students are often bothered by two things. First, they question whether the cash flows in Table 17.3 should be discounted at the after-tax incremental borrowing rate if the leased asset is risky. Why shouldn't the lease be discounted at R_{WACC}, the weighted average cost of capital? We examine this issue next. Second, they feel that this approach lacks intuition. We address this concern a little later.

The Discount Rate

Because we discounted at the after-tax incremental borrowing rate, we have implicitly assumed that the cash flows in the Xomox example are less risky than the operations of the firm. Is this appropriate?

A lease payment is like the debt service on a secured bond issued by the lessee, and the discount rate should be approximately the same as the interest rate on such debt. In general, this rate will be lower than R_{WACC}, the weighted average cost of capital. In practice, the various tax shields could be somewhat riskier than the lease payments. First, the value of the depreciation tax benefits depends on the ability of Xomox to generate enough taxable income to use them. Second, the corporate tax rate may change in the future. For these two reasons, a firm might be justified in discounting the depreciation tax benefits at a rate higher than that used for the lease payments. However, our experience is that real-world companies discount both the depreciation shield and lease payments at the same rate. This implies that financial practitioners view these two risks as minor. We adopt the real-world convention of discounting the two flows at the same rate. This rate is the lessee's after-tax incremental borrowing rate.

17.6 Does Leasing Ever Pay?

The Base Case

We previously looked at the lease–buy decision from the point of view of the potential lessee, Xomox. Let us now look at the decision from the point of view of the lessor, Friendly Leasing Limited. This firm faces three cash flows, all of which are displayed in Table 17.5. First, Friendly purchases the machine for €10,000 at year 0. Second, because the asset is depreciated straight line over five years, the depreciation expense and depreciation tax shield at the end of each of the five years are as follows:

Initial Cost (€)	Depreciation (€)	Balance (€)	Tax Benefit (€)
10,000	2,000	8,000	560
	2,000	6,000	560
	2,000	4,000	560
	2,000	2,000	560
	2,000	0	560

Third, because the yearly lease payment is €2,500, the after-tax lease payments are as follows: €1,800 [= €2,500 × 1 − 0.28].

Table 17.5 Cash Flows to Friendly Leasing Limited as Lessor of GBM Pipe-boring Machine

Lessor						
Year	0	1	2	3	4	5
Cost of Machine	€(10,000)					
Depreciation Tax Benefit		€ 560	€ 560	€ 560	€ 560	€ 560
After-Tax Lease Payment		€1,800	€1,800	€1,800	€1,800	€1,800
Cash Flows	€(10,000)	€2,360	€2,360	€2,360	€2,360	€2,360
Present Value (Cash Flows)	€(10,000)	€2,233	€ 2,112	€1,998	€1,890	€ 1,788

Now examine the total cash flows to Friendly Leasing Limited, displayed in the bottom row of Table 17.5. The sum of the cash flows from year 0 to year 5 is €1,800. Compare this figure with the sum of Xomox's cash flows in the bottom line of the first panel of Table 17.3. It's the exact opposite. Those of you with a healthy sense of scepticism may be thinking something interesting: 'If the cash flows of the lessor are exactly the opposite of those of the lessee, the combined cash flow of the two parties must be zero each year. Thus, there does not seem to be any joint benefit to this lease.'

Time value of money (see Section 4.2) states that the net present value of leasing to the lessor and lessee will depend on the timing of the respective cash flows and risk. Since the risk of the two cash flow streams is the same, the issue of whether leasing ever pays becomes one of simple cash flow timing.

$$\begin{aligned} NPV &= -€10{,}000 + €2{,}233 + €2{,}112 + €1{,}998 + €1{,}890 + €1{,}788 \\ &\cong €20 \end{aligned}$$

The NPV of the lease to Friendly Leasing Limited is positive and so, in this example, it pays for Friendly to lease the asset.

It is important to investigate this further. Table 17.6 shows that while the sum of both lessee and lessor cash flows (€1,800) is the same, the timing is different. The net cash flow to the lessee and lessor is clearly equal, but the net present value of the lease is higher for the lessor than the lessee. Since Xomox is indifferent between buying and leasing (NPV = €0) and Friendly Leasing is positive about the lease (NPV = €20), the contract makes sense for both parties.

Table 17.6 Lessee versus Lessor Cash Flow Analysis

Year	0	1	2	3	4	5	Net Cash Flow	Net Present Value
Lessee (Table 17.3)	€10,000	(€ 2,278)	(€ 2,316)	(€ 2,357)	(€ 2,401)	(€2,449)	**(€1,800)**	**€ 0**
Lessor (Table 17.5)	(€10,000)	€2,360	€2,360	€2,360	€2,360	€2,360	**€1,800**	**€20**
Difference	€ 0	€ 82	€ 44	€ 3	(€ 41)	(€ 89)	**€ 0**	**€20**

We know a five-year lease contract of €2,500 per year for a €10,000 asset is acceptable to both Xomox and Friendly Leasing. However, Friendly Leasing will want to know the maximum acceptable lease payment to Xomox (the lessee), and Xomox will want to know the minimum acceptable lease payment to Friendly Leasing (the lessor). This provides both parties a window to negotiate a mutually beneficial contract.

Reservation Payment of Lessee

The maximum acceptable payment to a lessee is known as its *reservation payment*. This is the payment that sets the NPV of the contract to the lessee equal to zero. Since Xomox is indifferent between buying and leasing the asset (NPV = €0), we have already found the reservation payment. If the lease payment is higher than €2,500, the NPV of the lease vs buy decision will be negative and buying the asset will be more appropriate.

Reservation Payment of Lessor

The minimum acceptable payment to the lessor is also known as its *reservation payment*. This is the payment that sets the NPV of the contract to the lessor equal to zero. Since the NPV of the contract is positive to Friendly Leasing (NPV = €20), we must find the lease payment that sets the NPV of the lease to zero. We do this by solving for L_{MIN}, the payment that makes the value of the lease to the lessor zero. The cash flows to the lessor, in terms of L_{MIN}, are these:

Lease Minus Buy	Year 0	Year 1	Year 2	Year 3	Year 4	Year 5
Cost of Machine	(€10,000)					
Depreciation Tax Benefit		€560	€560	€560	€560	€560
Lease Payment		$L_{MIN} \times (1 - 0.28)$	$L_{MIN} \times (1 - 0.28)$	$L_{MIN} \times (1 - 0.28)$	$L_{MIN} \times (1 - 0.28)$	$L_{MIN} \times (1 - 0.28)$
Cash Flows	(€10,000)	€560 + $L_{MIN} \times (1 - 0.28)$	€560 + $L_{MIN} \times (1 - 0.28)$	€560 + $L_{MIN} \times (1 - 0.28)$	€560 + $L_{MIN} \times (1 - 0.28)$	€560 + $L_{MIN} \times (1 - 0.28)$

We will use a spreadsheet (for example, goal seek) to find the value of L_{MIN} that results in an NPV of zero for an after-tax discount rate of 5.7102 per cent. The value of L_{MIN} is €2,493, as shown in the table below:

Year	0	1	2	3	4	5
Cost of Machine	(€10,000)					
Depreciation Tax Benefit		€560	€560	€560	€560	€560
Lease Payment		€2,493 × (1 – 0.28) = €1,795	€2,493 × (1 – 0.28) = €1,795	€2,493 × (1 – 0.28) = €1,795	€2,493 × (1 – 0.28) = €1,795	€2,493 × (1 – 0.28) = €1,795
Cash Flows	(€10,000)	2355	2355	2355	2355	2355
Present Value (Cash Flows)	(€10,000)	2228	2108	1994	1886	1784

$$\text{NPV} = €10{,}000 - €2{,}228 - €2{,}108 - €1{,}994 - €1{,}886 - €1{,}784$$
$$= €0$$

After performing this calculation, the lessee knows that the lessor will never agree to a lease payment below €2,493.

Leases with Balloon Payments

In the Xomox–Friendly Leasing example, the financial liability is zero at the end of the contract. This means the lease is fully amortized and the asset will transfer ownership to the lessee at the end of the contract.

In many leases, the present value of the lease payments is less than the initial value of the asset and so a balloon payment is required in the final year. The evaluation of a lease is slightly more complex in this case, in that the residual value of the liability (the balloon payment) must be added to the final lease payment.

Assume the lease payment has been set at €2,400. This is less than the €2,500 payment required to pay off the financial liability over five years. The tax benefit of the lease in each year is now:

Year	Asset Initial Cost (€)	Depreciation (€)	Balance (€)	Liability Outstanding Value (€)	Lease Payment (€)	Interest (€)	Principal (€)	Balance (€)	Tax Benefit (€)
1	10000	2000	8000	10000	2400	793	1607	8393	782
2	8000	2000	6000	8393	2400	666	1734	6659	746
3	6000	2000	4000	6659	2400	528	1872	4787	708
4	4000	2000	2000	4787	2400	380	2020	2766	666
5	2000	2000	0	2766	2400	219	2181	**586**	621

The final financial liability balance of €586 must be paid back as a balloon payment in year 5 for a total lease payment of (€2,400 + €586 =) €2,986. The lease cash flows with the balloon payment in year 5 are as follows:

Year	1	2	3	4	5
Payments (€)	(2,400)	(2,400)	(2,400)	(2,400)	(2,986)
After-tax Operating Cost Savings (€)	4,320	4,320	4,320	4,320	4,320
Lease Tax Benefit (€)	782	746	708	666	621
Cash Flows (€)	2,702	2,666	2,628	2,586	1,956

Since the buy cash flows are unchanged, the lease vs buy analysis can be carried out in the same way as before:

Year	0	1	2	3	4	5
Lease Cash Flows (€)		2,702	2,666	2,628	2,586	1,956
Buy Cash Flows (€) (Table 17.1)	(10,000)	4,880	4,880	4,880	4,880	4,880
Lease Minus Buy (€)	10,000	(2,178)	(2,214)	(2,252)	(2,294)	(2,924)
Present Value (Cash Flows) (€)	10,000	(2,060)	(1,981)	(1,907)	(1,837)	(2,215)

Summing the present values shows that, with the balloon payment, the NPV is equal to 0 and Xomox is still indifferent between leasing and buying the asset. This result is to be expected because the lower lease payments in years 1 to 4 have been fully offset by the balloon payment in year 5.

17.7 Reasons for Leasing

Proponents of leasing make many claims about why firms should lease assets rather than buy them. Some of the reasons for supporting leasing are good, and some are not. We discuss the reasons for leasing that we think are good and some of the ones we think are not.

Good Reasons for Leasing

Leasing is a good choice if at least one of the following is true:

- The lease contract may reduce certain types of uncertainty.
- Transaction costs can be higher for buying an asset and financing it with debt or equity than for leasing the asset.

A Reduction of Uncertainty

We have noted that the lessee does not own the property when an operating lease expires. The value of the property at this time is called the *residual value,* and the lessor has a firm claim to it. When the lease contract is signed, there may be substantial uncertainty about what the residual value of the asset will be. Thus, under a lease contract, this residual risk is borne by the lessor. Conversely, the user bears this risk when purchasing.

It is common sense that the party best able to bear a particular risk should do so. If the user has little risk aversion, she will not suffer by purchasing. However, if the user is highly averse to risk, she should find a third-party lessor more capable of assuming this burden.

This latter situation frequently arises when the user is a small or newly formed firm. Because the risk of the entire firm is likely to be quite high, and because the principal shareholders are likely to be undiversified, the firm desires to minimize risk wherever possible. A potential lessor, such as a large, publicly held financial institution, is far more capable of bearing the risk. Conversely, this situation is not expected to happen when the user is a blue-chip corporation. That potential lessee is more able to bear risk.

Transaction Costs

The costs of changing an asset's ownership are generally greater than the costs of writing a lease agreement. Consider the choice that confronts a person who lives in Oslo but must do business in London for two days. It will clearly be cheaper to rent a hotel room for two nights than it would be to buy an apartment for two days and then to sell it.

Unfortunately, leases generate agency costs as well. For example, the lessee might misuse or overuse the asset because she has no interest in the asset's residual value. This cost will be implicitly paid by the lessee through a high lease payment. Although the lessor can reduce these agency costs through monitoring, monitoring itself is costly.

Thus, leasing is most beneficial when the transaction costs of purchase and resale are higher than the agency and monitoring costs of a lease.

Bad Reasons for Leasing

Taxes May Be Reduced by Leasing

Under previous accounting standards (IAS 17), it was possible to create value from leases if the lessee had a different corporate tax rate from the lessor. However, as we saw in Section 17.5, since the introduction of IFRS 16, the taxation benefits of leases to a lessee have effectively disappeared. This is because the lease now appears on the balance sheet instead of the income statement. With leased assets treated for tax considerations in the exact same way as bought assets, a firm cannot create value from choosing to lease instead of buying an asset.

Leasing and Accounting Income

Under IFRS changes introduced in 2019, the arguments for leasing improving a company's statement of financial position versus buying an asset were made obsolete. For most companies operating under IFRS (all publicly listed companies) there is now no difference between asset purchases and operating or financial leases in terms of the liabilities presented in the financial statements. However, prior to 2019, some managers believed that operating leases would improve the statement of financial position in comparison to financial leases because of different accounting treatments. Now that operating and financial leases are treated the same for the lessee, there is no accounting justification for differentiating between the two forms of leasing or outright purchase of an asset.

One Hundred Per Cent Financing

It is often claimed that leasing provides 100 per cent financing, whereas secured equipment loans require an initial down payment. However, if a firm has a target debt–equity ratio and follows International Accounting Standards, financial leases will displace debt elsewhere in the firm.

For example, a firm that purchases equipment will generally issue debt to finance the purchase. The debt becomes a liability of the firm. A lessee incurs a liability equal to the present value of all future lease payments.

Because of this, there is a strong argument that leases displace debt. The statements of financial position in Table 17.7 illustrate how leasing might affect debt.

Table 17.7 Debt Displacement Elsewhere in the Firm When a Lease is Instituted

Assets	(€)	Liabilities	(€)
Initial situation			
Current	50,000	Debt	60,000
Non-current	50,000	Equity	40,000
Total	100,000	Total	100,000
Buy with secured loan			
Current	50,000	Debt	66,000
Non-current	50,000	Equity	44,000
Machine	10,000	Total	110,000
Total	110,000		
Lease			
Current	50,000	Lease	10,000
Non-current	50,000	Debt	56,000
Machine	10,000	Equity	44,000
Total	110,000	Total	110,000

Note: This example shows that leases reduce the level of debt elsewhere in the firm. Though the example illustrates a point, it is not meant to show a precise method for calculating debt displacement.

Suppose a firm initially has €100,000 of assets and a 150 per cent target debt–equity ratio. The firm's debt is €60,000 and its equity is €40,000. As in the Xomox case, suppose the firm must use a new €10,000 machine. The firm has two alternatives:

1 *The firm can purchase the machine.* If it does, it will finance the purchase with a secured loan and with equity. The debt capacity of the machine is assumed to be the same as for the firm as a whole.

2 *The firm can lease the asset and get 100 per cent financing.* That is, the present value of the future lease payments will be €10,000.

If the firm finances the machine with both secured debt and new equity, its debt will increase by €6,000 and its equity by €4,000. Its target debt–equity ratio of 150 per cent will be maintained.

Conversely, consider the lease alternative. According to IFRS 16, the lease must appear in the statement of financial position. As just mentioned, the present value of the lease liability is €10,000. If the leasing firm is to maintain a debt–equity ratio of 150 per cent, debt elsewhere in the firm must fall by €4,000 when the lease is instituted. Because debt must be repurchased, net liabilities rise by only €6,000 (= €10,000 – €4,000) when €10,000 of assets are placed under lease.

Research by Eisfeldt and Rampini (2009) argues that the '100 per cent financing' argument is actually an important and good reason for leasing. They show that leasing makes repossession in the case of a default of an asset easier than borrowing, and that this increases the capacity of a firm to take on more debt via leases. They then provide evidence that small financially constrained firms use leases more than do unconstrained firms.

Debt displacement is a hidden cost of leasing. If a firm leases, it will not use as much regular debt as it would otherwise. The benefits of debt capacity will be lost – particularly the lower taxes associated with interest expense.

Other Reasons

There are, of course, many special reasons that some companies find advantages in leasing. In one celebrated case, the US Navy leased a fleet of tankers instead of asking Congress for appropriations. Thus, leasing may be used to circumvent capital expenditure control systems set up by bureaucratic firms.

Real World Insight 17.1

Property Leasing

Property leasing continues to be a viable strategy for many companies, offering flexibility and financial benefits over outright purchasing. In particular, property leasing allows companies to avoid significant upfront investments and the operational complexities of owning large estates. An example of this strategy is the European net lease property market.

In 2022, the European Central Bank reversed a long-standing policy of low-interest rates to control rampant inflation. This shift led to a new economic climate with higher financing costs, lower liquidity and slowing economic growth. In this environment, many businesses have pursued net lease or sale and leasebacks, which allow for stable, secure and inflation-linked cash flows in a volatile market environment.

Net lease properties tend to be perceived as most like bonds because of the significant portion of returns derived from contractually fixed income. In addition, the leases usually obligate the tenant to cover most or all property-related expenses. This insulates income from unexpected cost increases. Moreover, net lease investments can provide inflation protection through CPI-indexed leases, which is especially important during periods of high inflation growth.

One of the main ways net lease properties are sourced is through sale and leasebacks, a mechanism that has seen substantial growth in the European market. During 2021, EMEA corporate disposals reached €29.2 billion across 670 disposals, which was almost twice the amount in 2010. Sale and leasebacks offer companies several advantages, including the full realization of property value, elimination of refinancing risks and retention of operational control over the asset.

Going forward, it is expected that an increasing number of businesses will turn to sale and leasebacks as an alternative financing method, for several reasons. These include tighter credit standards, lower bond market liquidity, the European Central Bank's balance sheet reduction programme, and potential M&A opportunities.

Historically, net lease property has delivered attractive risk-adjusted returns relative to balanced commercial property portfolios. The benefits of net lease investments include less volatile, income-driven returns and inflation protection. European net lease cash flows are typically pegged to CPI, providing an effective inflation hedge in times of elevated inflation.

17.8 Some Unanswered Questions about Leasing

Our analysis suggests that the primary advantage of long-term leasing results from the differential tax rates of the lessor and the lessee. Other valid reasons for leasing are lower contracting costs and risk reduction. There are several questions our analysis has not specifically answered.

Are the Uses of Leases and Debt Complementary?

Ang and Peterson (1984) find that firms with high debt tend to lease frequently as well. This result should not be puzzling. The corporate attributes that provide high debt capacity may also make leasing advantageous. Thus, even though leasing displaces debt (that is, leasing and borrowing are substitutes) for an individual firm, high debt and high leasing can be positively associated when we look at a number of firms.

Why are Leases Offered by Both Manufacturers and Third-party Lessors?

The offsetting effects of taxes can explain why both manufacturers (for example, computer firms) and third-party lessors offer leases.

- For manufacturer lessors, the basis for determining depreciation is the manufacturer's cost. For third-party lessors, the basis is the sales price that the lessor paid to the manufacturer. Because the sales price is generally greater than the manufacturer's cost, this is an advantage to third-party lessors.
- However, the manufacturer must recognize a profit for tax purposes when selling the asset to the third-party lessor. The manufacturer's profit for some equipment can be deferred if the manufacturer becomes the lessor. This provides an incentive for manufacturers to lease.

Why are Some Assets Leased More than Others?

Certain assets appear to be leased more frequently than others. Smith and Wakeman (1985) have looked at non-tax incentives that affect leasing. Their analysis suggests many asset and firm characteristics that are important in the lease-or-buy decision. The following are among the things they mention:

- The more sensitive the value of an asset is to usage and maintenance decisions, the more likely it is that the asset will be purchased instead of leased. They argue that ownership provides a better incentive to minimize maintenance costs than does leasing.
- Price discrimination opportunities may be important. Leasing may be a way of circumventing laws against charging too *low* a price.

Are the Reasons for Leasing Different Across Firms?

At different stages in a company's life cycle, there are changing pressures and opportunities facing management. For example, small firms that are growing quickly find it difficult to regularly source new debt financing. In contrast, large established firms find it significantly easier to go to the debt markets or banks to arrange debt. Lasfer and Levis (1998) and Cosci et al. (2015), for Italian firms, show that smaller firms use leases because they are unable to get other forms of debt, whereas larger firms use debt and leasing interchangeably. They also find that large lessee firms are significantly more profitable than small lessee firms, suggesting that leases are used as a complement to debt in large firms, whereas they are a substitute for debt in small firms.

Lasfer and Levis's findings are supported by the work of Eisfeldt and Rampini (2009), who argue that leasing enhances debt capacity more than secured lending or debt. Because smaller firms are financially constrained, they value the debt capacity provided by leases and hence lease more than larger firms.

Sustainability in Action 17.1

Sale and Leasebacks for Sustainable Investments

According to Clarion Partners, a real estate investment group, there has been a significant increase in the use of net lease and sale and leasebacks as a strategy in the European commercial property market. This type of lease provides stable, secure and often inflation-linked cash flows, which can be attractive in volatile market conditions. They also enable investors to access potential long-term capital appreciation and diversification benefits.

One way that companies are using these leases to facilitate sustainability investments is through the sale and leaseback of energy-efficient buildings. This allows companies to raise capital, which can then be reinvested in other sustainability initiatives. For example, a company might use the proceeds from a sale-leaseback to invest in renewable energy technologies or other energy-efficient infrastructure.

Source: Clarion Partners (2023) 'The Case for Net Lease/Sale-Leasebacks in Europe'

Summary and Conclusions

A large fraction of the corporate world's equipment is leased rather than purchased. This chapter describes the institutional arrangements surrounding leases and explains how to evaluate leases financially.

1. Leases can be separated into two types. Operating leases allow the lessee to use the equipment, while ownership remains with the lessor. Although the lessor in a financial lease legally owns the equipment, the lessee maintains effective ownership because financial leases are fully amortized.
2. When a firm purchases an asset with debt, both the asset and the liability appear on the firm's balance sheet. New accounting rules mean that all leases must be treated in the same way as if the firm owned the asset, irrespective of its status as an operating or financial lease.
3. We showed that risk-free cash flows should be discounted at the after-tax risk-free rate. Because both lease payments and depreciation tax shields are nearly riskless, all relevant cash flows in the lease–buy decision should be discounted at the lessee firm's after-tax incremental borrowing rate.

4 If the lessor is in the same tax bracket as the lessee, the cash flows to the lessor are exactly the opposite of the cash flows to the lessee. However, because of differences in the timing of cash flows, the net present value of a lease contract to the lessee and lessor will be different. There are actually at least two good reasons for leasing:

(a) Shift of risk-bearing to the lessor

(b) Minimization of transaction costs.

We also documented a number of bad reasons for leasing.

Questions and Problems

connect

CONCEPT

1 **Types of Lease Financing** What is a lease, and what are the different types of lease financing available to firms?

2 **Accounting and Leasing** What is meant by 'off-balance-sheet financing'? Why has leasing historically been been viewed as off-balance-sheet funding when it appears in the financial statements? Is this term now a misnomer? Explain.

3 **The Cash Flows of Leasing** If you did not have the financing to purchase an asset, would you compare it to the buy decision in your leasing analysis? Explain.

4 **Discounting and Taxes** In a world with taxes, why is WACC not appropriate for discounting cash flows in a lease-versus-buy decision? What is the appropriate discount rate when evaluating a lease? Explain.

5 **Leasing** You have recently joined the finance department of a large retail company, and your manager tells you that the company's policy is to lease its assets, instead of buying them outright. He explains that because leasing reduces risk it will reduce the firm's cost of capital. Do you agree with him? Explain.

6 **Does Leasing Ever Pay?** Explain why the reservation payment of a lease is the amount that makes the lessee indifferent between buying an asset and leasing it.

7 **Reasons for Leasing** Review the reasons why firms undertake leasing. Explain why some of these reasons are not beneficial for shareholders.

8 **Unanswered Questions** Why do some firms lease and others do not? What are some of the reasons why firms may or may not lease?

REGULAR

9 **Accounting for Leases** Discuss how IFRS 16 treats finance and operating leases in the financial statements. In what ways does this impact the decision between debt financing and leasing?

10 **Accounting for Leases and Financial Statements** In 2019, IFRS 16 changed the way leases were treated in the financial statements. Carry out your own research on the new standard and discuss what progress has been made. What impact have the changes had on the lessee? Explain your answer.

11 **Sale and Leaseback** Why might a firm choose to engage in a sale and leaseback transaction? Give two reasons. Is a sale and leaseback good for firms in financial distress? How do sale and leasebacks help a firm pursue a sustainability agenda? What does the empirical evidence say? Explain.

12 **Lease or Buy** A company could purchase a machine for £100,000. The machine has annual maintenance costs of £10,000 and an anticipated useful life of five years, after which it will have zero salvage value. Tax depreciation can be claimed on a straight line basis. Assume all cash flows occur at the end of the financial year. The company pays a corporation tax rate of 18 per cent, and taxes are paid one year in arrears. The opportunity cost of capital for the machine is 10 per cent, based on the company's borrowing rate for the project. The asset would be purchased today at 1 January. The company's financial year end is 31 December. However, the company could alternatively lease the asset for five years. As this is an operating lease, maintenance costs will be borne by the lessor, and lease payments are due at the end of the year and are £20,873 per annum. Should the company buy or lease the machine?

13 **Leasing Cash Flows** You work for an airline that is contemplating leasing a new-design plane geo-navigational system. The system costs €22 million and will be depreciated using the straight line method. At the end of four years, the geo-navigational system will have zero value. You can lease it for €6.25 million per year for four years. If the appropriate pre-tax discount rate is 5 per cent, what is the value of the lease to the lessor? Assume a 23 per cent tax bracket.

14 Finding the Break-even Payment Using the information from Question 13, what would the lease payment have to be for the lessee to be indifferent buying or leasing the system? Assume that the tax rate is 23 per cent. The lessee can borrow at 5 per cent before taxes.

15 Taxes and Leasing Cash Flows Using the information in Question 13, assume your company does not contemplate paying taxes for the next several years. What are the annual cash flows to the lessee from leasing in this case?

16 Setting the Lease Payment In the previous question, over what range of lease payments will the lease be profitable for both parties? What are the minimum and maximum amounts?

17 Lease or Buy: Super Sonics Entertainment Super Sonics Entertainment is considering buying a machine that costs NKr3,500,000. The machine will be depreciated straight line to zero over four years. The company can lease the machine with year-end payments of NKr942,000 and a balloon payment of NKr500,000 at the end of the lease contract. The company can issue bonds at a 9 per cent interest rate. If the corporate tax rate is 28 per cent, should the company buy or lease?

Use the following information to solve problems 18–20.

The Progressive Tech Firm (PTF) is deliberating whether to lease or purchase a new AI-driven automation system for its software development operations. Management has decided that it must use the system to stay competitive; it will provide £700,000 in annual pre-tax cost savings. The system costs £6 million and will be depreciated using the straight line method. At the end of five years, it will have no value. PTF's tax rate is 18 per cent, and the firm can borrow at 9 per cent. Lambert Leasing Company has offered to lease the automation system to PTF for payments of £1,400,000 per year with a balloon payment of £700,000 in the final year of the contract.

18 Net Advantage to Leasing What is the net advantage to leasing (NAL) for PTF?

19 Maximum Reservation Payment What is the maximum lease payment that would be acceptable to PTF?

20 Minimum Reservation Payment What is the minimum lease payment that would be acceptable to Lambert Leasing Company?

21 Setting the Lease Price An asset costs £360,000 and will be depreciated using the straight line method. At the end of its three-year life it will be worthless. The corporate tax rate is 18 per cent and the appropriate pre-tax interest rate is 10 per cent. What set of lease payments will make the lessee and the lessor equally well off?

22 Lease or Buy with Bank Financing Wolfson plc has decided to purchase a new machine that costs £4.2 million. The machine will be depreciated on a straight line basis and will be worth nothing at the end of four years. The corporate tax rate is 18 per cent. The Sur Bank has offered Wolfson a four-year loan for £4.2 million. The repayment schedule is four-yearly principal repayments of £1.05 million and an interest charge of 9 per cent on the outstanding balance of the loan at the beginning of each year. Both principal repayments and interest are due at the end of each year. Cal Leasing Corporation offers to lease the same machine to Wolfson. Lease payments of £1.2 million per year are due at the end of each of the four years of the lease. Should Wolfson lease the machine or buy it with bank financing?

CHALLENGE

23 Lease or Buy: Advanced High electricity costs have made Farmer Corporation's chicken-plucking machine economically worthless. Only two machines are available to replace it. The International Plucking Machine (IPM) model is available only on a lease basis, but has a notional price of £8,000 for tax purposes. The lease payments will be £2,100 for five years, due at the beginning of the year. This machine will save Farmer £6,000 per year through reductions in electricity costs in every year. As an alternative, Farmer can purchase a more energy-efficient machine from Basic Machine Corporation (BMC) for £15,000. This machine will save £9,000 per year in electricity costs. A local bank has offered to finance the machine with a £15,000 loan. The interest rate on the loan will be 10 per cent on the remaining balance and five annual principal payments of £3,000. Farmer has a target debt-to-asset ratio of 67 per cent. Farmer has a corporation tax rate of 28 per cent. After five years, both machines will be worth nothing. The depreciation method is straight line over the life of the asset.

(a) Should Farmer lease the IPM machine or purchase the more efficient BMC machine?

(b) Does your answer depend on the form of financing for direct purchase?

24 Debt Capacity Many researchers are now coming to the conclusion that leasing has benefits from increasing the debt capacity of financially constrained firms. Explain why this is so and provide a review of the literature that proposes this idea. Present your own views on the purpose of leasing, and provide a counter-argument or confirmatory evidence on your position.

25 Moral Hazard Schneider (2010) argues that moral hazard in leasing is a major contributor to the level of accidents that New York taxi drivers experience. Explain what is meant by moral hazard and present a case for or against Schneider's findings.

26 **Asset Liquidity** Gavazza (2010) finds that 'more-liquid assets (1) make leasing, operating leasing in particular, more likely; (2) have shorter operating leases; (3) have longer capital leases; and (4) command lower markups of operating lease rates'. Explain Gavazza's findings in the context of the material covered in this chapter.

27 **Leasing and Accounting Quality** Beatty et al. (2010) argue that low accounting quality firms increase the likelihood that a firm will lease assets instead of buying them. Provide a critique of this view and explain why accounting quality would have an impact on the lease-versus-buy decision.

28 **Leasing and IFRS 16** The new leasing standard IFRS 16 made a number of fundamental changes in 2019 to the recording of leases in the financial statements. Review these changes. Do you think leasing will become more or less popular over the coming years as a result of these changes? Explain.

29 **Leasing and Sustainability** How can companies utilize leasing strategies to finance and achieve their sustainability objectives, particularly those aligned with the United Nations Sustainable Development Goals?

Exam Question (45 minutes)

1 Andrew and Gilstad (2005) write that 'business schools typically teach that leasing is a zero-sum game. However, the economic assumptions that lead to this belief often are not true. These incorrect assumptions have caused serious confusion and bias in lease evaluation for more than a generation.' Explain this statement. Do you believe the authors are correct? Provide examples to illustrate your answer. **(40 marks)**

2 Parklead Leasing is a successful leasing company, specializing in the highest-quality excavation equipment. It has a fleet of 300 vehicles, and a repair and maintenance section. It purchases a new machine for €80,000 that it plans to lease for six years, after which time it will be worthless. Parklead Leasing pays corporation tax of 23 per cent one year in arrears and the borrowing rate is 10 per cent on assets of this type. Straight line depreciation is charged on machinery. What are the cash flows to Parklead Leasing? **(30 marks)**

3 Ibro Tinmines plc requires the use of excavation machinery. It could lease the equipment for six years from Parklead Leasing for €22,000 per year, with a balloon payment at the end of the lease contract to offset any remaining financial liability. Evaluate the lease from the perspective of the lessee and the lessor. The tax rate is 23 per cent paid one year in arrears, and the discount rate for projects of this type is 10 per cent. Depreciation is straight line and it is expected that the equipment will be scrapped after six years. **(30 marks)**

Total Marks: 100

Mini Case

The Decision to Lease or Buy at Constructive Innovations

Constructive Innovations, a firm dedicated to developing sustainable infrastructure solutions, has decided to embark on the creation of an innovative, eco-friendly construction material. This new material is expected to revolutionize the construction industry and align with the company's commitment to improving sustainability in the sector. In order to begin production, the company needs to acquire specialized manufacturing equipment.

The only provider of such equipment, EarthTech Machinery, has proposed to sell the needed machinery to Constructive Innovations at a price of €6 million. The equipment will be depreciated using the straight-line method over a period of five years, at the end of which, it is expected to have a residual value of zero.

Alternatively, Constructive Innovations has the option to lease the equipment from GreenLease Providers. The lease contract requires five annual payments of €1.5 million at the beginning of each year, with a final balloon payment to eliminate any residual value.

Constructive Innovations is able to issue bonds at a yield of 10 per cent and operates within a tax bracket of 20 per cent. Should Constructive Innovations purchase the equipment outright or opt for the leasing option?

Practical Case Study

Download the financial accounts of five companies in your country. Look for information on operating leases, financial leases, and sale and leasebacks. In each case, decide whether the financing is long term or short term and how it affects the debt to equity ratio of each firm. Do you see evidence that leasing is used as a substitute for debt? Alternatively, is it used as a complement to debt? A reading of Yan (2006) may help for this case study. Write a brief report on your findings.

Relevant Accounting Standards

Because of its importance, leasing has an accounting standard all to itself, titled IFRS 16 *Leases*. This is a new standard as of 2019 and should be consulted when considering the use of any type of lease.

References

Andrew, G.M. and D.J. Gilstad (2005) 'A Generation of Bias against Leasing', *Journal of Equipment Lease Financing*, Vol. 23, No. 2, 1–14.

Ang, J. and P.P. Peterson (1984) 'The Leasing Puzzle', *Journal of Finance*, Vol. 39, 1055–1065.

Beatty, A., S. Liao and J. Weber (2010) 'Financial Reporting Quality, Private Information, Monitoring and the Lease-versus-buy Decision', *Accounting Review*, Vol. 85, 1215–1238.

Cosci, S., R. Guida and V. Meliciani (2015) 'Leasing Decisions and Credit Constraints: Empirical Analysis on a Sample of Italian Firms', *European Financial Management*, Vol. 21, No. 2, 377–398.

Eisfeldt, A.L. and A.A. Rampini (2009) 'Leasing, Ability to Repossess, and Debt Capacity', *Review of Financial Studies*, Vol. 22, No. 4, 1621–1657.

Gavazza, A. (2010) 'Asset Liquidity and Financial Contracts: Evidence from Aircraft Leases', *Journal of Financial Economics*, Vol. 95, No. 1, 62–84.

Lasfer, M. and M. Levis (1998) 'The Determinants of the Leasing Decision of Small and Large Companies', *European Financial Management*, Vol. 4, No. 2, 159–184.

Schneider, H. (2010) 'Moral Hazard in Leasing Contracts: Evidence from the New York City Taxi Industry', *Journal of Law and Economics*, Vol. 53, No. 4, 783–805.

Smith, C.W. Jr and L.M. Wakeman (1985) 'Determinants of Corporate Leasing Policy', *Journal of Finance*, Vol. 40, 895–908.

Yan, A. (2006) 'Leasing and Debt Financing: Substitutes or Complements?', *Journal of Financial and Quantitative Analysis*, Vol. 41, No. 3, 709–731.

Additional Reading

The following papers are of interest:

1 Beatty, A., S. Liao and J. Weber (2010) 'Financial Reporting Quality, Private Information, Monitoring and the Lease-versus-buy Decision', *Accounting Review*, Vol. 85, 1215–1238.

2 Eisfeldt, A.L. and A.A. Rampini (2009) 'Leasing, Ability to Repossess, and Debt Capacity', *Review of Financial Studies*, Vol. 22, No. 4, 1621–1657.

3 Gavazza, A. (2010) 'Asset Liquidity and Financial Contracts: Evidence from Aircraft Leases', *Journal of Financial Economics*, Vol. 95, No. 1, 62–84.

4 Gronlund, T., A. Louko and M. Vaihekoski (2008) 'Corporate Real Estate Sale and Leaseback Effect: Empirical Evidence from Europe', *European Financial Management*, Vol. 14, No. 4, 820–843. **Europe.**

5 Schneider, H. (2010) 'Moral Hazard in Leasing Contracts: Evidence from the New York City Taxi Industry', *Journal of Law and Economics*, Vol. 53, No. 4, 783–805.

6 Yan, A. (2006) 'Leasing and Debt Financing: Substitutes or Complements?', *Journal of Financial and Quantitative Analysis*, Vol. 41, No. 3, 709–731. **USA.**

Endnotes

1 For simplicity, we have assumed that lease payments are made at the end of each year. Actually, most leases require lease payments to be made at the beginning of the year.

2 For simplicity, assume that the firm received €100 or €106.60 *after* corporate taxes. Because 0.66 = 1 − 0.34, the pre-tax inflows would be €151.52 (€100/0.66) and €161.52 (€106.60/0.66), respectively.

3 This principle holds for riskless or guaranteed cash flows only. Unfortunately, there is no easy formula for determining the increase in optimal debt level from a *risky* cash flow.

PART 5

Capital Structure and Dividend Policy

The second pillar of corporate finance, capital structure, signifies the mix of debt and equity financing a company's operations. This pillar focuses on enhancing value through capital structure and dividend policy decisions. In Part 5, theoretical foundations, like the Modigliani–Miller Propositions, examine how capital structure affects firm value and equity risk. The impact of taxation on capital structure is also considered (Chapter 18). Further, practical issues and limitations of the theory are explored (Chapter 19) and new investment appraisal methods integrating capital structure decisions into valuation analysis are presented (Chapter 20). Finally, the role of dividend policy, different dividend decisions and their potential to increase firm value are investigated (Chapter 21).

Chapter 18
Capital Structure: Basic Concepts

Learning Objectives

After reading this chapter you should be able to:

LO1 Explain the concept of capital structure and articulate its relevance in corporate finance.

LO2 Distinguish between maximizing firm value and maximizing shareholder interests.

LO3 Critically evaluate the Modigliani and Miller Propositions (with and without taxes), and discuss their assumptions, implications and limitations.

LO4 Interpret the concepts of corporate and personal taxes in the context of the broader framework of capital structure.

In recent years, analysts of European soccer clubs have become seriously concerned about the level of indebtedness in their largest football institutions. In some countries, such as England, Germany and Spain, football has seen unparalleled injections of cash from global television deals. This additional spending power has inflated transfer fees, which in turn has required more funding. Several clubs, including Barcelona (€1.1 billion), Inter Milan (€306 million), Benfica (€336 million) and Manchester United (€536 million), have incredible levels of debt, which will expire at some point in the future. Several questions arise: Is the level of debt in European football too high? Will we see a debt crisis in the football sector, where clubs default on outstanding borrowings? How should a company choose a capital structure for itself and what are the important factors driving this? We will explore this and other issues in the following chapters.

Source: BRG.photography/Shutterstock

Key Notations

V	Market value of firm	MM	Modigliani–Miller Proposition I or II
E	Market value of equity	t_C	Corporate tax rate
D	Market value of bonds	NPV	Net present value
ROA	Return on assets	EBIT	Earnings before interest and taxes
ROE	Return on equity	V_U	Value of an unlevered firm
EBI	Earnings before interest	R_A	Cost of capital to an allequity firm
EPS	Earnings per share	V_L	Value of a levered firm
R_E	Return on equity; cost of equity capital	t_E	Personal tax rate on dividends
R_D	Return on debt; cost of debt capital	t_D	Personal tax rate on debt interest income
R_{WACC}	Weighted average cost of capital		

18.1 The Capital Structure Question and the Pie Theory

How should a firm choose its debt–equity ratio? We call our approach to the capital structure question the pie model. If you are wondering why we chose this name, take a look at Figure 18.1. The pie in question is the sum of the financial claims of the firm, debt and equity in this case. We *define* the value of the firm to be this sum. Hence the value of the firm, V, is:

Equation 18.1

$$V = D + E$$

where D is the market value of the debt and E is the market value of the equity. Figure 18.1 presents two possible ways of slicing this pie between equity and debt: 40 per cent–60 per cent and 60 per cent–40 per cent. If the goal of the management of the firm is to make the firm as valuable as possible, then the firm should pick the debt–equity ratio that makes the pie – the total value – as big as possible.

Figure 18.1 Two Pie Models of Capital Structure

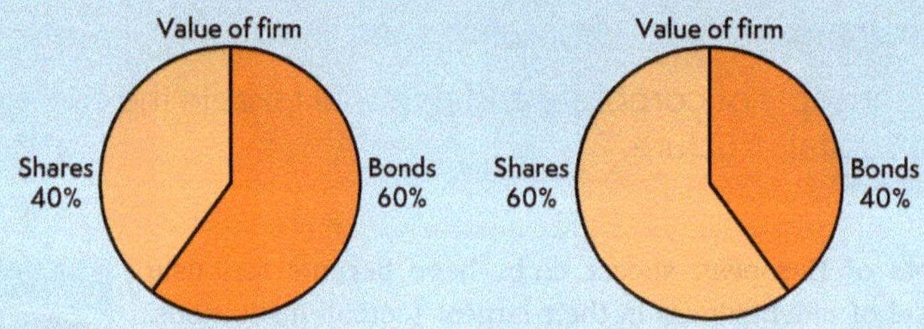

This discussion begs two important questions:

1 Why should the shareholders in the firm care about maximizing the value of the entire firm? After all, the value of the firm is, by definition, the sum of both the debt and the equity. Instead, why should the shareholders not prefer the strategy that maximizes their interests only?

2 What ratio of debt to equity maximizes the shareholders' interests?

Let us examine each of these two questions in turn.

Real World Insight18.1

Intercontinental Hotels Group plc

How much is too much leverage? Intercontinental Hotels Group plc (IHG) is a global hotel firm that owns nearly 5,000 hotels in more than 100 countries. Its brand names include Intercontinental Hotels, Crowne Plaza and Holiday Inn. IHG has reported increasing revenues and operating income every year since 2015 (with the exception of 2020 because of the coronavirus restrictions that closed down the tourism sector). The company's share price has also nearly doubled during this time.

A look at the capital structure of IHG can provide insights into how this growth has been funded. Total debt grew from \$1.67 billion to \$5.82 billion between 2015 and 2022, while the market value of its equity grew from around \$4.98 billion to \$11.44 billion. This gave a 2022 debt–assets (debt plus equity) ratio of 0.337, which means that 33.7 per cent (up from 25.1 per cent in 2015) of IHG's assets were funded by debt.

18.2 Maximizing Firm Value versus Maximizing Shareholder Interests

Example 18.1 illustrates that the capital structure that maximizes the value of the firm is the one that financial managers should choose for the shareholders.

Example 18.1

Debt and Firm Value

Suppose the market value of J.J. Sprint plc is £1,000. The company currently has no debt, and each of J.J. Sprint's 100 shares sells for £10. A company such as J.J. Sprint with no debt is called an *unlevered* company. Further suppose that J.J. Sprint plans to borrow £500 and pay the £500 proceeds to shareholders as an extra cash dividend of £5 per share. After the issuance of debt, the firm becomes *levered*. The investments of the firm will not change as a result of this transaction. What will the value of the firm be after the proposed restructuring?

Management recognizes that, by definition, only one of three outcomes can occur from restructuring. Firm value after restructuring can be (I) greater than the original firm value of £1,000, (II) equal to £1,000, or (III) less than £1,000. After consulting with investment bankers, management believes that restructuring will not change firm value more than £250 in either direction. Thus it views firm values of £1,250, £1,000 and £750 as the relevant range. The original capital structure and these three possibilities under the new capital structure are presented next:

	No Debt (Original Capital Structure) (£)	Value of Debt Plus Equity after Payment of Dividend (Three Possibilities)		
		I (£)	II (£)	III (£)
Debt	0	500	500	500
Equity	1,000	750	500	250
Firm value	1,000	1,250	1,000	750

Note that the value of equity is below £1,000 under all three possibilities. This can be explained in one of two ways. First, the table shows the value of the equity *after* the extra cash dividend is paid. Because cash is paid out, a dividend represents a partial liquidation of the firm. Consequently, there is less value in the firm for the equityholders after the dividend payment. Second, in the event of a future liquidation, shareholders will be paid only after bondholders have been paid in full. Thus the debt is an encumbrance of the firm, reducing the value of the equity.

Of course, management recognizes that there are infinite possible outcomes. These three are to be viewed as *representative* outcomes only. We can now determine the payoff to shareholders under the three possibilities:

	Payoff to Shareholders after Restructuring		
	I (£)	II (£)	III (£)
Capital gains	−250	−500	−750
Dividends	500	500	500
Net gain or loss to shareholders	250	0	−250

No one can be sure ahead of time which of the three outcomes will occur. However, imagine that managers believe that outcome I is most likely. They should definitely restructure the firm because the shareholders would gain £250. That is, although the price of the shares declines by £250 to £750, they receive £500 in dividends. Their net gain is £250 = −£250 + £500. Also, notice that the value of the firm would rise by £250 = £1,250 − £1,000.

Alternatively, imagine that managers believe that outcome III is most likely. In this case they should not restructure the firm because the shareholders would expect a £250 loss. That is, the equity falls by £750 to £250 and they receive £500 in dividends. Their net loss is −£250 = −£750 + £500. Also, notice that the value of the firm would change by −£250 = £750 − £1,000.

Finally, imagine that the managers believe that outcome II is most likely. A restructuring would not affect the shareholders' interest because the net gain to shareholders is zero. Also notice that the value of the firm is unchanged if outcome II occurs.

This example explains why managers should attempt to maximize the value of the firm. In other words, it answers question (1) in Section 18.1. We find in this example the following wisdom:

Changes in capital structure benefit the shareholders *if and only if* the value of the firm increases.

Conversely, these changes hurt the shareholders if and only if the value of the firm decreases. This result holds true for capital structure changes of many different types.[1] As a corollary, we can say the following:

Managers should choose the capital structure that they believe will have the highest firm value because this capital structure will be most beneficial to the firm's shareholders.

Note, however, that this example does not tell us which of the three outcomes is most likely to occur. Thus it does not tell us whether debt should be added to J.J. Sprint's capital structure. In other words, it does not answer question (2) in Section 18.1. This second question is treated in the next section.

18.3 Financial Leverage and Firm Value: An Example

Leverage and Returns to Shareholders

The previous section shows that the capital structure producing the highest firm value is the one that maximizes shareholder wealth. In this section, we wish to determine that optimal capital structure. We begin by illustrating the effect of capital structure on returns to shareholders. We will use a detailed example that we encourage students to study carefully. Once we fully understand this example, we will be ready to determine the optimal capital structure.

Autoveloce SpA currently has no debt in its capital structure. The firm is considering issuing debt to buy back some of its equity. Both its current and proposed capital structures are presented in Table 18.1. The firm's assets are €8,000. There are 400 shares of the all-equity firm, implying a market value per share of €20. The proposed debt issue is for €4,000, leaving €4,000 in equity. The interest rate is 10 per cent. Assume in all our examples that debt is issued at par.

Table 18.1 Financial Structure of Autoveloce SpA

	Current	Proposed
Assets (€)	8,000	8,000
Debt (€)	0	4,000
Equity (market and book) (€)	8,000	4,000
Interest rate (%)	10	10
Market value/share (€)	20	20
Shares outstanding	400	200

The proposed capital structure has leverage, whereas the current structure is all equity.

The effect of economic conditions on earnings per share is shown in Table 18.2 for the current capital structure (all-equity). Consider first the middle column where earnings are expected to be €1,200. Because assets are €8,000, the return on assets (ROA) is 15 per cent (= €1,200/€8,000). Assets equal equity for this all-equity firm, so return on equity (ROE) is also 15 per cent. Earnings per share (EPS) is €3.00 (= €1,200/400). Similar calculations yield EPS of €1.00 and €5.00 in the cases of recession and expansion, respectively.

Table 18.2 Autoveloce's Current Capital Structure: No Debt

	Recession	Expected	Expansion
Return on assets (%)	5	15	25
Earnings (€)	400	1,200	2,000
Return on equity = earnings/equity (%)	5	15	25
Earnings per share (€)	1.00	3.00	5.00

The case of leverage is presented in Table 18.3. ROA in the three economic states is identical in Tables 18.2 and 18.3 because this ratio is calculated before interest is considered. Debt is €4,000 here, so interest is €400 (= 0.10 × €4,000). Thus earnings after interest are €800 (= €1,200 – €400) in the middle (expected) case. Because equity is €4,000, ROE is 20 per cent (= €800/€4,000). Earnings per share are €4.00 (= €800/200). Similar calculations yield earnings of €0 and €8.00 for recession and expansion, respectively.

Table 18.3 Autoveloce's Proposed Capital Structure

	Recession	Expected	Expansion
Return on assets (%)	5	15	25
Earnings before interest (€)	400	1,200	2,000
Interest (€)	−400	−400	−400
Earnings after interest (€)	0	800	1,600
Return on equity = earnings after interest/equity (%)	0	20	40
Earnings per share (€)	0	4.00	8.00

Tables 18.2 and 18.3 show that the effect of financial leverage depends on the company's earnings before interest. If earnings before interest are equal to €1,200, the return on equity (ROE) is higher under the proposed structure. If earnings before interest are equal to €400, the ROE is higher under the current structure.

This idea is represented in Figure 18.2. The solid line represents the case of no leverage. The line begins at the origin, indicating that earnings per share (EPS) would be zero if earnings before interest (EBI) were zero. The EPS rise in tandem with a rise in EBI.

Figure 18.2 Financial Leverage: EPS and EBI for Autoveloce SpA

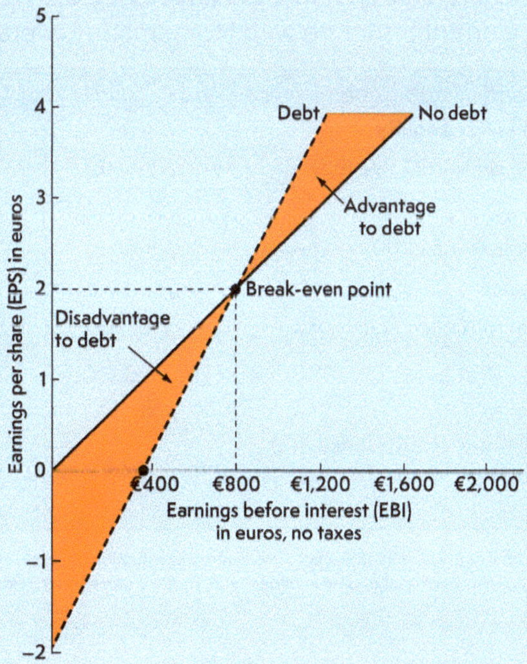

The dotted line represents the case of €4,000 of debt. Here EPS are negative if EBI are zero. This follows because €400 of interest must be paid regardless of the firm's profits.

Now consider the slopes of the two lines. The slope of the dotted line (the line with debt) is higher than the slope of the solid line. This occurs because the levered firm has *fewer* shares of equity outstanding than the unlevered firm. Therefore, any increase in EBI leads to a greater rise in EPS for the levered firm because the earnings increase is distributed over fewer shares of equity.

Because the dotted line has a lower intercept but a higher slope, the two lines must intersect. The *break-even* point occurs at €800 of EBI. Were earnings before interest to be €800, both firms would produce €2 of earnings per share (EPS). Because €800 is break-even, earnings above €800 lead to greater EPS for the levered firm. Earnings below €800 lead to greater EPS for the unlevered firm.

The Choice between Debt and Equity

Tables 18.2 and 18.3 and Figure 18.2 are important because they show the effect of leverage on earnings per share. Students should study the tables and figure until they feel comfortable with the calculation of each number in them. However, we have not yet presented the punchline. That is, we have not yet stated which capital structure is better for Autoveloce.

At this point many students believe that leverage is beneficial because EPS are expected to be €4.00 with leverage and only €3.00 without leverage. However, leverage also creates *risk*. Note that in a recession, EPS are higher (€1.00 versus €0) for the unlevered firm. Thus a risk-averse investor might prefer the all-equity firm, whereas a risk-neutral (or less risk-averse) investor might prefer leverage. Given this ambiguity, which capital structure *is* better?

Modigliani and Miller (MM) have a convincing argument that a firm cannot change the total value of its outstanding securities by changing the proportions of its capital structure. In other words, the value of the firm is always the same under different capital structures. In still other words, no capital structure is any better or worse than any other capital structure for the firm's shareholders. This rather pessimistic result is the famous **MM Proposition I.**[2]

Their argument compares a simple strategy, which we call strategy A, with a two-part strategy, which we call strategy B. Both of these strategies for shareholders of Autoveloce are illustrated in Table 18.4. Let us now examine the first strategy.

Table 18.4 Payoff and Cost to Shareholders of Autoveloce SpA Under the Proposed Structure and Under the Current Structure with Homemade Leverage

	Recession (€)	Expected (€)	Expansion (€)
Strategy A: Buy 100 shares of levered equity			
EPS of *levered* equity (taken from last line of Table 18.3)	0	4	8
Earnings per 100 shares	0	400	800
Initial cost = 100 shares @ €20/share = €2,000			
Strategy B: Homemade leverage			
Earnings per 200 shares in current *unlevered* Autoveloce	1 × 200 =	3 × 200 =	5 × 200 =
Interest at 10% on €2,000	−200	−200	−200
Net earnings	0	400	800
Initial cost = 200 shares @ €20/share (Cost of equity) − €2,000 (Amount borrowed) = €2,000			

Note: Investor receives the same payoff whether she (1) buys shares in a levered corporation or (2) buys shares in an unlevered firm and borrows on personal account. Her initial investment is the same in either case. Thus the firm neither helps nor hurts her by adding debt to capital structure.

Strategy A: Buy 100 shares of the levered equity

The first line in the top panel of Table 18.4 shows EPS for the proposed levered equity in the three economic states. The second line shows the earnings in the three states for an individual buying 100 shares. The next line shows that the cost of these 100 shares is €2,000.

Let us now consider the second strategy, which has two parts to it.

Strategy B: Homemade leverage

1 Borrow €2,000 from either a bank or, more likely, a brokerage house. (If the brokerage house is the lender, we say that this activity is *going on margin.*)

2 Use the borrowed proceeds plus your own investment of €2,000 (a total of €4,000) to buy 200 shares of the current unlevered equity at €20 per share.

The bottom panel of Table 18.4 shows payoffs under strategy B, which we call the *homemade leverage* strategy. First, observe the middle column, which indicates that 200 shares of the unlevered equity are expected to generate €600 of earnings. Assuming that the €2,000 is borrowed at a 10 per cent interest rate, the interest expense is €200 (= 0.10 × €2,000). Thus the net earnings are expected to be €400. A similar calculation generates net earnings of either €0 or €800 in recession or expansion, respectively.

Now let us compare these two strategies, both in terms of earnings per year and in terms of initial cost. The top panel of the table shows that strategy A generates earnings of €0, €400 and €800 in the three states. The bottom panel of the table shows that strategy B generates the *same* net earnings in the three states.

The top panel of the table shows that strategy A involves an initial cost of €2,000. Similarly, the bottom panel shows an *identical* net cost of €2,000 for strategy B.

This shows a very important result. Both the cost and the payoff from the two strategies are the same. Thus we must conclude that Autoveloce is neither helping nor hurting its shareholders by restructuring. In other words, an investor is not receiving anything from corporate leverage that she could not receive on her own.

Note that, as shown in Table 18.1, the equity of the unlevered firm is valued at €8,000. Because the equity of the levered firm is €4,000 and its debt is €4,000, the value of the levered firm is also €8,000. Now suppose that, for whatever reason, the value of the levered firm were actually greater than the value of the unlevered firm. Here strategy A would cost more than strategy B. In this case an investor would prefer to borrow on his own account and invest in the equity of the unlevered firm. He would get the same net earnings each year as if he had invested in the equity of the levered firm. However, his cost would be less. The strategy would not be unique to our investor. Given the higher value of the levered firm, no rational investor would invest in the shares of the levered firm. Anyone desiring shares in the levered firm would get the same euro return more cheaply by borrowing to finance a purchase of the unlevered firm's shares. The equilibrium result would be, of course, that the value of the levered firm would fall and the value of the unlevered firm would rise until they became equal. At this point individuals would be indifferent between strategy A and strategy B.

This example illustrates the basic result of Modigliani–Miller (MM) and is, as we have noted, commonly called their Proposition I. We restate this proposition as follows:

MM Proposition I (no taxes): The value of the levered firm is the same as the value of the unlevered firm.

This is perhaps the most important result in all of corporate finance. In fact, it is generally considered the beginning point of modern corporate finance. Before MM, the effect of leverage on the value of the firm was considered complex and convoluted. Modigliani and Miller showed a blindingly simple result: if levered firms are priced too high, rational investors will simply borrow on their personal accounts to buy shares in unlevered firms. This substitution is often called *homemade leverage*. As long as individuals borrow (and lend) on the same terms as the firms, they can duplicate the effects of corporate leverage on their own.

The example of Autoveloce SpA shows that leverage does not affect the value of the firm. Because we showed earlier that shareholders' welfare is directly related to the firm's value, the example also indicates that changes in capital structure cannot affect the shareholders' welfare.

A Key Assumption

The MM result hinges on the assumption that individuals can borrow as cheaply as corporations. If, alternatively, individuals can borrow only at a higher rate, we can easily show that corporations can increase firm value by borrowing.

Is this assumption of equal borrowing costs a good one? Individuals who want to buy shares and borrow can do so by establishing a margin account with a broker. Under this arrangement the broker lends the individual a portion of the purchase price. For example, the individual might buy €10,000 of equity by investing €6,000 of her own funds and borrowing €4,000 from the broker. Should the shares be worth €9,000 on the next day, the individual's net worth or equity in the account would be €5,000 = €9,000 – €4,000.[3]

The broker fears that a sudden price drop will cause the equity in the individual's account to be negative, implying that the broker may not get the loan repaid in full. To guard against this possibility, stock exchange rules require that the individual makes additional cash contributions (replenishes her margin account) as the share price falls. Because (1) the procedures for replenishing the account have developed over many years, and (2) the broker holds the equity as collateral, there is little default risk to the broker. In particular, if margin contributions are not made on time, the broker can sell the shares to satisfy the loan. Therefore, brokers generally charge low interest, with many rates being only slightly above the risk-free rate.

By contrast, corporations frequently borrow using illiquid assets (e.g. plant and equipment) as collateral. The costs to the lender of initial negotiation and ongoing supervision, as well as of working out arrangements in the event of financial distress, can be quite substantial. Thus it is difficult to argue that individuals must borrow at higher rates than corporations.

Sustainability in Action 18.1

The UN Sustainable Development Goals and Debt

While debt can create value from the tax shield it gives to companies, it can also have negative consequences, particularly in the pursuit of Sustainable Development Goals. Take, for example, SDG 10, which aims to reduce inequality by encouraging firms to adopt policies that promote greater equality, improve regulation and monitoring of financial markets, and encourage financial flows to countries in need.

One example of how financial leverage can impact SDG 10 is through the use of debt financing in developing countries. While debt can be an important source of funding for infrastructure projects and other development initiatives, it can also lead to unsustainable levels of debt that limit a company or country's ability to invest in social programmes and other initiatives to promote greater equality.

To address these challenges, SDG 10 recommends that countries adopt policies to promote the responsible use of financial leverage. This includes measures such as greater transparency and accountability in financial markets, as well as regulations that limit the use of leverage in ways that exacerbate inequality.

One example of a successful approach to promoting SDG 10 through the responsible use of financial leverage is the STOA Impact Fund. STOA was created in 2017 by the Caisse des Dépôts and the Agence Française de Développement (AFD) to finance infrastructure in emerging and developing countries. This private equity investor has developed a framework for assessing the impact of its investments on the SDGs, including SDG 10. By prioritizing investments that promote greater equality and social inclusion, STOA is helping to drive progress towards this important goal.

18.4 Modigliani and Miller: Proposition II (No Taxes)

Risk to Equityholders Rises with Leverage

At an Autoveloce board meeting, a director said, 'Well, maybe it does not matter whether the corporation or the individual levers – as long as some leverage takes place. Leverage benefits investors. After all, an investor's expected return rises with the amount of the leverage present.' He then pointed out that, as shown in Tables 18.2 and 18.3, the expected return on unlevered equity is 15 per cent whereas the expected return on levered equity is 20 per cent.

However, another director replied, 'Not necessarily. Though the expected return rises with leverage, the *risk* rises as well.' This point can be seen from an examination of Tables 18.2 and 18.3. With earnings before interest (EBI) varying between €400 and €2,000, earnings per share (EPS) for the shareholders of the unlevered firm vary between €1.00 and €5.00. EPS for the shareholders of the levered firm vary between €0 and €8.00. This greater range for the EPS of the levered firm implies greater risk for the levered firm's shareholders. In other words, levered shareholders have better returns in good times than do unlevered shareholders, but have worse returns in bad times. The two tables also show greater range for the ROE of the levered firm's shareholders. The earlier interpretation concerning risk applies here as well.

The same insight can be taken from Figure 18.2. The slope of the line for the levered firm is greater than the slope of the line for the unlevered firm. This means that the levered shareholders have better returns in good times than do unlevered shareholders but have worse returns in bad times, implying greater risk with leverage. In other words, the slope of the line measures the risk to shareholders because the slope indicates the responsiveness of ROE to changes in firm performance (earnings before interest).

Proposition II: Required Return to Equityholders Rises with Leverage

Because levered equity has greater risk, it should have a greater expected return as compensation. In our example, the market *requires* only a 15 per cent expected return for the unlevered equity, but it requires a 20 per cent expected return for the levered equity.

This type of reasoning allows us to develop **MM Proposition II**. Here MM argue that the expected return on equity is positively related to leverage because the risk to equityholders increases with leverage.

To develop this position, recall that the firm's weighted average cost of capital, R_{WACC}, can be written as:[4]

Equation 18.2

$$R_{WACC} = \frac{E}{D+E} \times R_E + \frac{D}{D+E} \times R_D$$

where R_D is the cost of debt; R_E is the expected return on equity, also called the *cost of equity* or the *required return on equity;* R_{WACC} is the firm's weighted average cost of capital; D is the market value of the firm's debt or bonds; and E is the market value of the firm's shares or equity.

Equation 18.2 is quite intuitive. It simply says that a firm's weighted average cost of capital is a weighted average of its cost of debt and its cost of equity. The weight applied to debt is the proportion of debt in the capital structure, and the weight applied to equity is the proportion of equity in the capital structure. Calculations of R_{WACC} from Equation 18.2 for both the unlevered and the levered firm are presented in Table 18.5.

Table 18.5 Cost of Capital Calculations for Autoveloce

	$R_{WACC} = \frac{E}{D+E} \times R_E + \frac{D}{D+E} \times R_D$
Unlevered firm:	$15\% = \frac{€0}{€8{,}000} \times 10\%^{*} + \frac{€8{,}000}{€8{,}000} \times 15\%^{\dagger}$
Levered firm:	$15\% = \frac{€4{,}000}{€8{,}000} \times 10\%^{*} + \frac{€4{,}000}{€8{,}000} \times 20^{\dagger\dagger}$

Notes: * 10% is the cost of debt.

† From the 'Expected' column in Table 18.2, we learn that expected earnings after interest for the unlevered firm are €1,200. From Table 18.1 we learn that equity for the unlevered firm is:

$$\frac{\text{Expected earnings after interest}}{\text{Equity}} = \frac{€1{,}200}{€8{,}000} = 15\%$$

†† From the 'Expected' column in Table 18.3, we learn that expected earnings after interest for the levered firm are €800. From Table 18.1 we learn that equity for the levered firm is €4,000. Thus R_E for the levered firm is:

$$\frac{\text{Expected earnings after interest}}{\text{Equity}} = \frac{€800}{€4{,}000} = 20\%$$

An implication of MM Proposition I is that R_{WACC} is a constant for a given firm, regardless of the capital structure.[5] For example, Table 18.5 shows that R_{WACC} for Autoveloce is 15 per cent, with or without leverage.

Let us now define R_A to be the *cost of capital for an all-equity firm*. For Autoveloce SpA, R_A is calculated as:

$$R_A = \frac{\text{Expected earnings to unlevered firm}}{\text{Unlevered equity}} = \frac{€1{,}200}{€8{,}000} = 15\%$$

As can be seen from Table 18.5, R_{WACC} is equal to R_A for Autoveloce. In fact, R_{WACC} must *always* equal R_A in a world without corporate taxes.[6]

Proposition II states the expected return on equity, R_E, in terms of leverage. The exact relationship, derived by setting $R_{WACC} = R_A$ and then rearranging Equation 18.2, is:[7]

MM Proposition II (no taxes)

Equation 18.3

$$R_E = R_A + \frac{D}{E}(R_A - R_D)$$

Equation 18.3 implies that the required return on equity is a linear function of the firm's debt–equity ratio. Examining Equation 18.3, we see that if R_A exceeds the cost of debt, R_D, then the cost of equity rises with increases in the debt–equity ratio, *D/E*. Normally R_A should exceed R_D. That is, because even unlevered equity is risky, it should have an expected return greater than that of riskless debt. Note that Equation 18.3 holds for Autoveloce in its levered state:

$$0.20 = 0.15 + \frac{€4{,}000}{€4{,}000}(0.15 - 0.10)$$

Figure 18.3 graphs Equation 18.3. As you can see, we have plotted the relation between the cost of equity, R_E, and the debt–equity ratio, *D/E*, as a straight line. What we witness in Equation 18.3 and illustrate in Figure 18.3 is the effect of leverage on the cost of equity. As the firm raises the debt–equity ratio, each euro of equity is levered with additional debt. This raises the risk of equity and therefore the required return, R_E, on the equity.

Figure 18.3 The Cost of Equity, the Cost of Debt, and the Weighted Average Cost of Capital: MM Proposition II with no Corporate Taxes

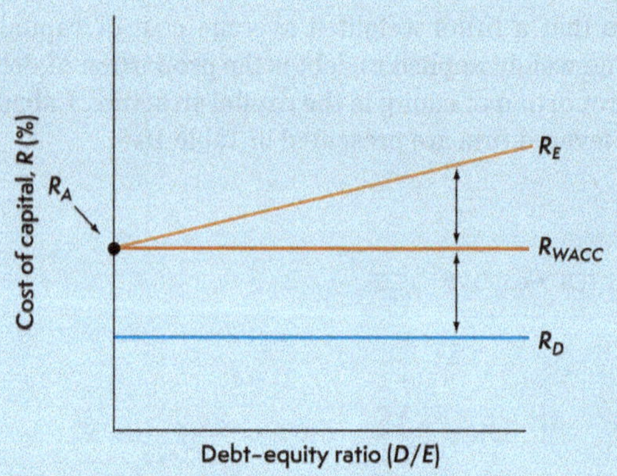

$R_E = R_A + (R_A - R_D)D/E$

R_E is the cost of equity.
R_D is the cost of debt.
R_A is the cost of capital for an all-equity firm.
R_{WACC} is a firm's weighted average cost of capital. In a world with no taxes, R_{WACC} for a levered firm is equal to R_A.
R_A is a single point whereas R_E, R_D and R_{WACC} are all entire lines.

The cost of equity capital, R_E, is positively related to the firm's debt-equity ratio. The firm's weighted average cost of capital, R_{WACC}, is invariant to the firm's debt-equity ratio.

Figure 18.3 also shows that R_{WACC} is unaffected by leverage, a point we have already made. (It is important for students to realize that R_A, the cost of capital for an all-equity firm, is represented by a single dot on the graph. By contrast, R_{WACC} is an entire line.)

Example 18.2

MM Propositions I and II

Canary Motors, an all-equity firm, has expected earnings of £10 million per year in perpetuity. The firm pays all of its earnings out as dividends, so the £10 million may also be viewed as the shareholders' expected cash flow. There are 10 million shares outstanding, implying expected annual cash flow of £1 per share. The cost of capital for this unlevered firm is 10 per cent. In addition, the firm will soon build a new plant for £4 million. The plant is expected to generate additional cash flow of £1 million per year. These figures can be described as follows:

Current Company	New Plant
Cash flow: £10 million	Initial outlay: £4 million
Number of outstanding shares: 10 million	Additional annual cash flow: £1 million

The project's net present value is

$$-£4 \text{ million} + \frac{£1 \text{ million}}{0.1} = £6 \text{ million}$$

assuming that the project is discounted at the same rate as the firm as a whole. Before the market knows of the project, the *market value* balance sheet of the firm is this:

CANARY MOTORS **Market Value Balance Sheet (all equity)**		
Old assets $\frac{£10 \text{ million}}{0.1} = £100$ million	Equity	£100 million (10 million shares)

The value of the firm is £100 million because the cash flow of £10 million per year is capitalized (discounted) at 10 per cent. A share of equity sells for £10 (= £100 million/10 million) because there are 10 million shares outstanding.

The firm will issue £4 million of either equity or debt. Let us consider the effect of equity and debt financing in turn.

Equity Financing

Imagine that the firm announces that in the near future it will raise £4 million in equity to build a new plant. The share price, and therefore the value of the firm, will rise to reflect the positive net present value of the plant. According to efficient markets, the increase occurs immediately. That is, the rise occurs on the day of the announcement, not on the date of either the onset of construction of the plant or the forthcoming equity offering. The market value balance sheet becomes this:

CANARY MOTORS
Market Value Balance Sheet
(upon announcement of debt issue to construct plant)

	(£)		(£)
Old assets	100 million	Equity	106 million (10 million shares)
NPV of plant $-£4\text{ million} + \frac{£1\text{ million}}{0.1}$	6 million		
Total assets	106 million		

Note that the NPV of the plant is included in the market value balance sheet. Because the new shares have not yet been issued, the number of outstanding shares remains 10 million. The price per share has now risen to £10.60 (= £106 million/10 million)) to reflect news concerning the plant.

Shortly thereafter, £4 million of equity is issued, or *floated*. Because the shares are selling at £10.60 per share, 377,358 (= £4 million/£10.60) shares are issued. Imagine that funds are put in the bank *temporarily* before being used to build the plant. The market value balance sheet becomes this:

CANARY MOTORS
Market Value Balance Sheet
(upon issuance of equity but before construction begins on plant)

	(£)		(£)
Old assets	100 million	Equity	110 million (10,377,358 shares)
NPV of plant	6 million		
Proceeds from new issue of equity (currently placed in bank)	4 million		
Total assets	110 million		

The number of shares outstanding is now 10,377,358 because 377,358 new shares were issued. The share price is £10.60 (= £110,000,000/10,377,358). Note that the price has not changed. This is consistent with efficient capital markets because the share price should move due only to new information.

Of course the funds are placed in the bank only temporarily. Shortly after the new issue, the £4 million is given to a contractor, who builds the plant. To avoid problems in discounting, we assume that the plant is built immediately. The market value balance sheet then looks like this:

CANARY MOTORS
Market Value Balance Sheet
(upon completion of the plant)

	(£)		(£)
Old assets	100 million	Equity	110 million (10,377,358 shares)
PV of plant $\frac{£1\text{ million}}{0.1} =$	10 million		
Total assets	110 million		

Though total assets do not change, the composition of the assets does. The bank account has been emptied to pay the contractor. The present value of cash flows of £1 million a year from the plant is reflected as an asset worth £10 million. Because the building expenditures of £4 million have already been paid, they no longer represent a future cost. Hence they no longer reduce the value of the plant. According to efficient capital markets, the share price remains £10.60.

Expected yearly cash flow from the firm is £11 million, £10 million of which comes from the old assets and £1 million from the new. The expected return to shareholders is:

$$R_E = \frac{£11 \text{ million}}{£110 \text{ million}} = 0.10$$

Because the firm is all equity, $R_E = R_A = 0.10$.

Debt Financing

Alternatively, imagine the firm announces that in the near future it will borrow £4 million at 6 per cent to build a new plant. This implies yearly interest payments of £240,000 (= £4,000,000 × 6%). Again the share price rises immediately to reflect the positive net present value of the plant. Thus we have the following:

CANARY MOTORS
Market Value Balance Sheet
(upon announcement of equity issue to construct plant)

	(£)		(£)
Old assets	100 million	Equity	106 million (10 million shares)
NPV of plant $-£4 \text{ million} + \frac{£1 \text{ million}}{0.1}$	6 million		
Total assets	106 million		

The value of the firm is the same as in the equity financing case because (1) the same plant is to be built, and (2) MM proved that debt financing is neither better nor worse than equity financing.

At some point £4 million of debt is issued. As before, the funds are placed in the bank temporarily. The market value balance sheet becomes this:

CANARY MOTORS
Market Value Balance Sheet
(upon debt issuance but before construction begins on plant)

	(£)		(£)
Old assets	100 million	Debt	4 million
NPV of plant	6 million	Equity	106 million (10 million shares)
Proceeds from debt issue (currently invested in bank)	4 million		
Total assets	110 million	Debt plus equity	110 million

Note that debt appears on the right side of the market value balance sheet. The share price is still £10.60, in accordance with our discussion of efficient capital markets.

Finally, the contractor receives £4 million and builds the plant. The market value balance sheet turns into this:

CANARY MOTORS
Market Value Balance Sheet
(upon completion of the plant)

	(£)		(£)	
Old assets	100 million	Debt	4 million	
PV of plant	10 million	Equity	106 million	(10 million shares)
Total assets	110 million	Debt plus equity	110 million	

The only change here is that the bank account has been depleted to pay the contractor. The shareholders expect yearly cash flow after interest of:

£10,000,000	+	£1,000,000	−	£240,000	=	£10,760,000
Cash flow on old assets		Cash flow on new assets		Interest: £4 million × 6%		

The shareholders expect to earn a return of:

$$\frac{£10,760,000}{£106,000,000} = 10.15\%$$

This return of 10.15 per cent for levered shareholders is higher than the 10 per cent return for the unlevered shareholders. This result is sensible because, as we argued earlier, levered equity is riskier. In fact, the return of 10.15 per cent should be exactly what MM Proposition II predicts. This prediction can be verified by plugging values into

$$R_E = R_A + \frac{D}{E}(R_A - R_D)$$

where we obtain:

$$10.15\% = 10\% + \frac{£4,000,000}{£106,000,000} \times (10\% - 6\%)$$

This example is useful for two reasons. First, we wanted to introduce the concept of market value balance sheets, a tool that will prove useful elsewhere in the text. Among other things, this technique allows us to calculate the share price of a new issue of shares. Second, the example illustrates three aspects of Modigliani and Miller:

1 The example is consistent with MM Proposition I because the value of the firm is £110 million after either equity or debt financing.
2 Students are often more interested in share price than in firm value. We show that the share price is always £10.60, regardless of whether debt or equity financing is used.
3 The example is consistent with MM Proposition II. The expected return to shareholders rises from 10 to 10.15 per cent, just as Equation 18.3 states. This rise occurs because the shareholders of a levered firm face more risk than do the shareholders of an unlevered firm.

MM: An Interpretation

The Modigliani–Miller results indicate that managers cannot change the value of a firm by repackaging the firm's securities. Though this idea was considered revolutionary when it was originally proposed in the late 1950s, the MM approach and proof have since met with wide acclaim.[8]

MM argue that the firm's overall cost of capital cannot be reduced as debt is substituted for equity, even though debt appears to be cheaper than equity. The reason for this is that, as the firm adds debt, the remaining equity becomes more risky. As this risk rises, the cost of equity capital rises as a result. The increase in the cost of the remaining equity capital offsets the higher proportion of the firm financed by low-cost debt. In fact, MM prove that the two effects exactly offset each other, so that both the value of the firm and the firm's overall cost of capital are invariant to leverage.

Food found its way into this chapter earlier when we viewed the firm as a pie. MM argue that the size of the pie does not change, no matter how shareholders and bondholders divide it. MM say that a firm's capital structure is irrelevant; it is what it is by some historical accident. The theory implies that firms' debt–equity ratios could be anything. They are what they are because of whimsical and random managerial decisions about how much to borrow and how much equity to issue.

Although scholars are always fascinated by far-reaching theories, students are perhaps more concerned with real-world applications. Do real-world managers follow MM by treating capital structure decisions with indifference? Unfortunately for the theory, virtually all companies in certain industries, such as banking, choose high debt–equity ratios. Conversely, companies in other industries, such as pharmaceuticals, choose low debt–equity ratios. In fact, almost any industry has a debt–equity ratio to which companies in that industry tend to adhere. Thus companies do not appear to be selecting their degree of leverage in a frivolous or random manner. Because of this, financial economists (including MM themselves) have argued that real-world factors may have been left out of the theory.

In Their Own Words

In Professor Miller's Words . . .

[The Modigliani–Miller results are not easy to understand fully. This point is related in a story told by Merton Miller.*]

How difficult it is to summarize briefly the contribution of the [Modigliani–Miller] papers was brought home to me very clearly last October after Franco Modigliani was awarded the Nobel Prize in Economics in part – but, of course, only in part – for the work in finance. The television camera crews from our local stations in Chicago immediately descended upon me. 'We understand,' they said, 'that you worked with Modigliani some years back in developing these M and M theorems and we wonder if you could explain them briefly to our television viewers.'

'How briefly?' I asked.

'Oh, take ten seconds,' was the reply.

Ten seconds to explain the work of a lifetime! Ten seconds to describe two carefully reasoned articles, each running to more than thirty printed pages and each with sixty or so long footnotes! When they saw the look of dismay on my face, they said, 'You don't have to go into details. Just give us the main points in simple, commonsense terms.'

The main point of the first or cost-of-capital article was, in principle at least, simple enough to make. It said that in an economist's ideal world of complete and perfect capital markets and with full and symmetric information among all market participants, the total market value of all the securities issued by a firm was governed by the earning power and risk of its underlying real assets and was independent of how the mix of securities issued to finance it was divided between debt instruments and equity capital . . .

Such a summary, however, uses too many shorthanded terms and concepts, like perfect capital markets, that are rich in connotations to economists but hardly so to the general public. So I thought, instead, of an analogy that we ourselves had invoked in the original paper . . .

'Think of the firm,' I said, 'as a gigantic tub of whole milk. The farmer can sell the whole milk as is. Or he can separate out the cream and sell it at a considerably higher price than the whole milk would bring. (That's the analogy of a firm selling low-yield and hence high-priced debt securities.) But, of course, what the farmer would have left would be skim milk with low butterfat content and that would sell for much less than whole milk. That corresponds to the levered equity. The M and M proposition says that if there were no costs of separation (and, of course, no government dairy support programme), the cream plus the skim milk would bring the same price as the whole milk.'

The television people conferred among themselves and came back to inform me that it was too long, too complicated, and too academic.

'Don't you have anything simpler?' they asked. I thought of another way that the M and M proposition is presented these days, which emphasizes the notion of market completeness and stresses the role of securities as devices for 'partitioning' a firm's payoffs in each possible state of the world among the group of its capital suppliers.

'Think of the firm,' I said, 'as a gigantic pizza, divided into quarters. If now you cut each quarter in half into eighths, the M and M proposition says that you will have more pieces but not more pizza.'

Again there was a whispered conference among the camera crew, and the director came back and said: 'Professor, we understand from the press releases that there were two M and M propositions. Can we try the other one?'

[Professor Miller tried valiantly to explain the second proposition, though this was apparently even more difficult to get across. After this attempt:]

Once again there was a whispered conversation. They shut the lights off. They folded up their equipment. They thanked me for giving them the time. They said that they'd get back to me. But I knew that I had somehow lost my chance to start a new career as a packager of economic wisdom for TV viewers in convenient ten-second bites. Some have the talent for it . . . and some just don't.

* Taken from *GSB Chicago*, University of Chicago (Autumn 1986).

Though many of our students have argued that individuals can borrow only at rates above the corporate borrowing rate, we disagreed with this argument earlier in the chapter. But when we look elsewhere for unrealistic assumptions in the theory, we find two:[9]

1 Taxes were ignored.
2 Bankruptcy costs and other agency costs were not considered.

We turn to taxes in the next section. Bankruptcy costs and other agency costs will be treated in the next chapter. A summary of the main Modigliani–Miller results without taxes is presented in the boxed section below.

Summary of Modigliani–Miller Propositions without Taxes

Assumptions

- No taxes.
- No transaction costs.
- Individuals and corporations borrow at the same rate.

Results

Proposition I: $V_L = V_U$ (Value of levered firm equals value of unlevered firm)

Proposition II: $R_E = R_A + \frac{D}{E}(R_A - R_D)$

Intuition

Proposition I: Through homemade leverage, individuals can either duplicate or undo the effects of corporate leverage.

Proposition II: The cost of equity rises with leverage because the risk to equity rises with leverage.

18.5 Corporate Taxes

The Basic Insight

Section 18.4 showed that firm value is unrelated to debt in a world without taxes. We now show that, in the presence of corporate taxes, the firm's value is positively related to its debt (taxes are introduced in **Chapter 3**, Section 3.3). The basic intuition can be seen from a pie chart, such as the one in Figure 18.4. Consider the all-equity firm on the left. Here both shareholders and tax authorities have claims on the firm. The value of the all-equity firm is, of course, that part of the pie owned by the shareholders. The proportion going to taxes is simply a cost.

Chapter 3 Page 64

Figure 18.4 Two Pie Models of Capital Structure Under Corporate Taxes

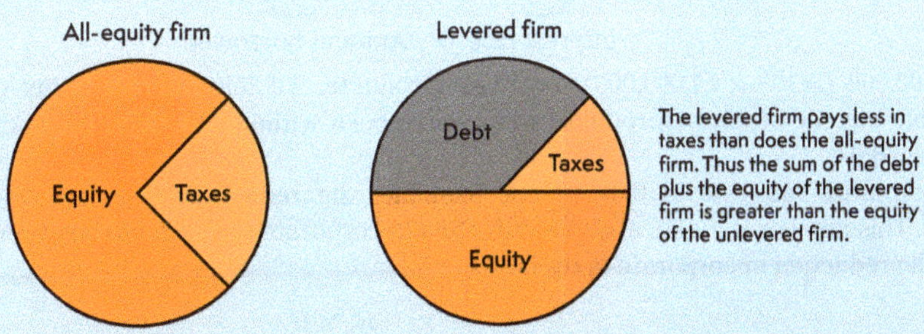

The pie on the right for the levered firm shows three claims: shareholders, debtholders and taxes. The value of the levered firm is the sum of the value of the debt and the value of the equity. In selecting between the two capital structures in the picture, a financial manager should select the one with the higher value. Assuming that the total area is the same for both pies,[10] value is maximized for the capital structure paying the least in taxes. In other words, the manager should choose the capital structure that the government hates the most.

We will show that, due to a quirk in corporate tax law, the proportion of the pie allocated to taxes is less for the levered firm than it is for the unlevered firm. Thus, managers should select high leverage.

Example 18.3

Taxes and Cash Flow

Wasserprodukte GmbH has a corporate tax rate, t_C, of 35 per cent and expected earnings before interest and taxes (EBIT) of €1 million each year. Its entire earnings after taxes are paid out as dividends.

The firm is considering two alternative capital structures. Under Plan I, Wasserprodukte would have no debt in its capital structure. Under Plan II, the company would have €4,000,000 of debt, D. The cost of debt, R_D, is 10 per cent.

The chief financial officer for Wasserprodukte makes the following calculations:

	Plan I (€)	Plan II (€)
Earnings before interest and corporate taxes (EBIT)	1,000,000	1,000,000
Interest ($R_D D$)	0	400,000
Earnings before taxes (EBT) = (EBT − $R_D D$)	1,000,000	600,000
Taxes ($t_C = 0.35$)	350,000	210,000
Earnings after corporate taxes (EAT) = [(EBIT − $R_D D$) × (1 − t_c)]	650,000	390,000
Total cash flow to both shareholders and bondholders [EBIT × (1 − t_c) + $t_c R_D D$	650,000	790,000

The most relevant numbers for our purposes are the two on the bottom line. Dividends, which are equal to earnings after taxes in this example, are the cash flow to shareholders, and interest is the cash flow to bondholders. Here we see that more cash flow reaches the owners of the firm (both shareholders and bondholders) under Plan II. The difference is €140,000 = €790,000 − €650,000. It does not take us long to realize the source of this difference. The government receives less tax under Plan II (€210,000) than it does under Plan I (€350,000). The difference here is €140,000 = €350,000 − €210,000.

This difference occurs because the way governments treat interest is different from the way they treat earnings going to shareholders.[11] Interest totally escapes corporate taxation, whereas earnings after interest but before corporate taxes (EBT) are taxed at the corporate tax rate.

Present Value of the Tax Shield

The previous discussion shows a tax advantage to debt or, equivalently, a tax disadvantage to equity. We now want to value this advantage. The interest in monetary terms is:

$$\text{Interest} = \underbrace{R_D}_{\text{Interest rate}} \times \underbrace{D}_{\text{Amount borrowed}}$$

This interest is €400,000 (= 10% × €4,000,000) for Wasserprodukte. All this interest is tax deductible. That is, whatever the taxable income of Wasserprodukte would have been without the debt, the taxable income is now €400,000 *less* with the debt.

Because the corporate tax rate is 0.35 in our example, the reduction in corporate taxes is €140,000 (= 0.35 × €400,000). This number is identical to the reduction in corporate taxes calculated previously.

Algebraically, the reduction in corporate taxes is:

Equation 18.4

$$\underbrace{t_C}_{\text{Corporate tax rate}} \times \underbrace{R_D \times D}_{\text{Interest paid}}$$

That is, whatever the taxes a firm would pay each year without debt, the firm will pay $t_C R_D D$ less with the debt of D. Equation 18.4 is often called the *tax shield from debt*. Note that it is an *annual* amount.

As long as the firm expects to be paying tax, we can assume that the cash flow in Equation 18.4 has the same risk as the interest on the debt. Thus its value can be determined by discounting at the cost of debt, R_D. Assuming that the cash flows are perpetual, the present value of the tax shield is:

$$\frac{t_C R_D D}{R_D} = t_c D$$

Value of the Levered Firm

We have just calculated the present value of the tax shield from debt. Our next step is to calculate the value of the levered firm. The annual after-tax cash flow of an unlevered firm is:

$$\text{EBIT} \times (1 - t_c)$$

where EBIT is earnings before interest and taxes. The value of an unlevered firm (that is, a firm with no debt) is the present value of EBIT $\times (1 - t_c)$

$$V_U = \frac{\text{EBIT} \times (1 - t_c)}{R_A}$$

Here V_U is the present value of an unlevered firm; EBIT $\times (1 - t_c)$ represents firm cash flows after corporate taxes; t_C is the corporate tax rate; R_A is the cost of capital to an all-equity firm. As can be seen from the formula, R_A now discounts *after-tax* cash flows.

As shown previously, leverage increases the value of the firm by the tax shield, which is $t_c D$ for perpetual debt. Thus we merely add this tax shield to the value of the unlevered firm to get the value of the levered firm.

We can write this algebraically as follows:[12]

MM Proposition I (Corporate Taxes)

Equation 18.5

$$V_L = \frac{\text{EBIT} \times (1 - t_c)}{R_A} + \frac{t_c R_D D}{R_D} = V_U + t_c D$$

Equation 18.5 is MM Proposition I under corporate taxes. The first term in Equation 18.5 is the value of the cash flows of the firm with no debt tax shield. In other words, this term is equal to V_U, the value of the all-equity firm. The value of the levered firm is the value of an all-equity firm plus $t_c D$, the tax rate times the value of the debt. $t_c D$ is the present value of the tax shield in the case of perpetual cash flows.[13] Because the tax shield increases with the amount of debt, the firm can raise its total cash flow and its value by substituting debt for equity.

Example 18.4

MM with Corporate Taxes

Divided Airlines is currently an unlevered firm. The company expects to generate €153.85 in earnings before interest and taxes (EBIT) in perpetuity. The corporate tax rate is 35 per cent, implying after-tax earnings of €100. All earnings after tax are paid out as dividends.

The firm is considering a capital restructuring to allow €200 of debt. Its cost of debt capital is 10 per cent. Unlevered firms in the same industry have a cost of equity capital of 20 per cent. What will the new value of Divided Airlines be?

The value of Divided Airlines will be equal to:

$$V_L = \frac{\text{EBIT} \times (1 - t_c)}{R_A} + \frac{t_c R_D D}{R_D} = V_U + t_c D$$

$$V_L = \frac{\text{EBIT} \times (1 - t_c)}{R_A} + t_c D$$

$$= \frac{€100}{0.20} + (0.35 \times €200)$$

$$= €500 + €70 = €570$$

The value of the levered firm is €570, which is greater than the unlevered value of €500. Because $V_L = D + E$, the value of levered equity, E, is equal to €570 − €200 = €370. The value of Divided Airlines as a function of leverage is illustrated in Figure 18.5.

Figure 18.5 The Effect of Financial Leverage on Firm Value: MM with Corporate Taxes in the Case of Divided Airlines

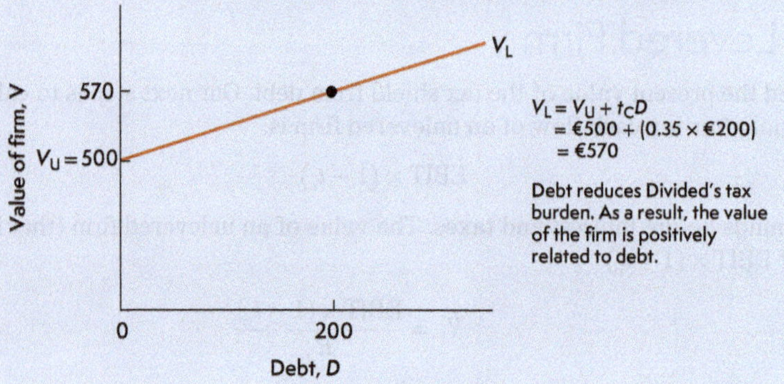

Expected Return and Leverage under Corporate Taxes

MM Proposition II under no taxes posits a positive relationship between the expected return on equity and leverage. This result occurs because the risk of equity increases with leverage. The same intuition also holds in a world of corporate taxes. The exact formula in a world of corporate taxes is this:[14]

MM Proposition II (Corporate Taxes)

Equation 18.6

$$R_E = R_A + \frac{D}{E} \times (1 - t_c) \times (R_A - R_D)$$

Applying the formula to Divided Airlines, we get:

$$R_E = 0.2351 = 0.20 + \frac{200}{370} \times (1 - 0.35) \times (0.20 - 0.10)$$

This calculation is illustrated in Figure 18.6.

Figure 18.6 The Effect of Financial Leverage on the Cost of Debt and Equity Capital

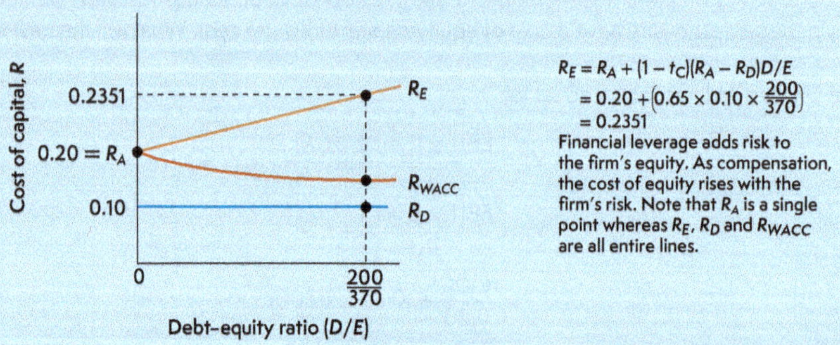

Whenever $R_A > R_D$, R_E increases with leverage, a result that we also found in the no-tax case. As stated earlier in this chapter, in Section 18.4, R_A should exceed R_D. That is, because equity (even unlevered equity) is risky, it should have an expected return greater than that on the less risky debt.

Let us check our calculations by determining the value of the levered equity in another way. The algebraic formula for the value of levered equity is:

$$E = \frac{(\text{EBIT} - R_D D) \times (1 - t_c)}{R_E}$$

The numerator is the expected cash flow to levered equity after interest and taxes. The denominator is the rate at which the cash flow to equity is discounted.

For Divided Airlines we get

$$\frac{(€153.85 - 0.10 \times €200)(1 - 0.35)}{0.2351} = €370$$

which is the same result we obtained earlier (ignoring a small rounding error).

The Weighted Average Cost of Capital, R_{WACC} and Corporate Taxes

Chapter 12 Page 325

In **Chapter 12** we defined the weighted average cost of capital (with corporate taxes) as follows (note that $V_L = D + E$):

$$R_{WACC} = \frac{E}{V_L} R_E + \frac{D}{V_L} R_D (1 - t_c)$$

Note that the cost of debt capital, R_D, is multiplied by $(1 - t_c)$ because interest is tax deductible at the corporate level. However, the cost of equity, R_E, is not multiplied by this factor because dividends are not deductible. In the no-tax case, R_{WACC} is not affected by leverage. This result is reflected in Figure 18.3, which we discussed earlier. However, because debt is tax advantaged relative to equity, it can be shown that R_{WACC} declines with leverage in a world with corporate taxes. This result can be seen in Figure 18.6.

For Divided Airlines, R_{WACC} is equal to:

$$\text{R}_{\text{WACC}} = \frac{370}{570} \times 0.2351 + \frac{200}{570} \times 0.1 \times (1 - 0.35) = 0.1754$$

Divided Airlines has reduced its R_{WACC} from 0.20 (with no debt) to 0.1754 with reliance on debt. This result is intuitively pleasing because it suggests that, when a firm lowers its R_{WACC}, the firm's value will increase. Using the R_{WACC} approach, we can confirm that the value of Divided Airlines is €570:

$$V_L = \frac{\text{EBIT} \times (1 - t_c)}{R_{\text{WACC}}} = \frac{€100}{0.1754} = €570$$

Share Prices and Leverage under Corporate Taxes

At this point students often believe the numbers – or at least are too intimidated to dispute them. However, they sometimes think we have asked the wrong question. 'Why are we choosing to maximize the value of the firm?' they will say. 'If managers are looking out for the shareholders' interests, why aren't they trying to maximize the share price?' If this question occurred to you, you have come to the right section.

Our response is twofold. First, we showed in Section 18.1 that the capital structure that maximizes firm value is also the one that most benefits the interests of the shareholders.

However, that general explanation is not always convincing to students. As a second procedure, we calculate the share price of Divided Airlines both before and after the exchange of debt for equity. We do this by presenting a set of market value balance sheets. The market value balance sheet for the company in its all-equity form can be represented as follows:

DIVIDED AIRLINES Market Value Balance Sheet (all-equity firm)			
Physical assets		Equity	€500 (100 shares)
$\frac{€153.85}{0.20} \times (1 - 0.35) =$	€500		

Assuming that there are 100 shares outstanding, each share is worth €5 = €500/100.

Next, imagine the company announces that in the near future it will issue €200 of debt to buy back €200 of equity. We know from our previous discussion that the value of the firm will rise to reflect the tax shield of debt. If we assume that capital markets efficiently price securities, the increase occurs immediately. That is, the rise occurs on the day of the announcement, not on the date of the debt-for-equity exchange. The market value balance sheet now becomes this:

DIVIDED AIRLINES
Market Value Balance Sheet
(upon announcement of debt issue)

	(€)		(€)
Physical assets	500	Equity	570 (100 shares)
Present value of tax shield:			
t_cD = 35% × €200 =	70		
Total assets	570		

Note that the debt has not yet been issued. Therefore, only equity appears on the right side of the balance sheet. Each share is now worth €570/100 = €5.70, implying that the shareholders have benefited by €70. The shareholders gain because they are the owners of a firm that has improved its financial policy.

The introduction of the tax shield to the balance sheet is perplexing to many students. Although physical assets are tangible, the ethereal nature of the tax shield bothers them. However, remember that an asset is any item with value. The tax shield has value because it reduces the stream of future taxes. The fact that one cannot touch the shield in the way that one can touch a physical asset is a philosophical, not financial, consideration.

At some point the exchange of debt for equity occurs. Debt of €200 is issued, and the proceeds are used to buy back shares. How many shares are repurchased? Because shares are now selling at €5.70 each, the number of shares that the firm acquires is €200/€5.70 = 35.09. This leaves 64.91 (= 100 − 35.09) shares outstanding. The market value balance sheet is now this:

DIVIDED AIRLINES
Market Value Balance Sheet
(after exchange has taken place)

	(€)		(€)
Physical assets	500	Equity	570 (100 shares)
Present value of tax shield	70		
t_CD = 35% × €200			
Total assets	570		

Each share is worth €370/64.91 = €5.70 after the exchange. Notice that the share price does not change on the exchange date. As we mentioned, the share price moves on the date of the announcement only. Because the shareholders participating in the exchange receive a price equal to the market price per share after the exchange, they do not care whether they exchange their equity.

This example was provided for two reasons. First, it shows that an increase in the value of the firm from debt financing leads to an increase in the price of the shares. In fact, the shareholders capture the entire €70 tax shield. Second, we wanted to provide more work with market value balance sheets.

A summary of the main results of Modigliani–Miller with corporate taxes is presented in the following box.

Summary of Modigliani–Miller Propositions with Corporate Taxes

Assumptions

- Corporations are taxed at the rate t_C, on earnings after interest.
- No transaction costs.
- Individuals and corporations borrow at the same rate.

Results

Proposition I: $V_L = V_U + t_c D$ (for a firm with perpetual debt)

Proposition II: $R_E = R_A + \frac{D}{E}(1 - t_c)(R_A - R_D)$

Intuition

Proposition I: Because corporations can deduct interest payments but not dividend payments, corporate leverage lowers tax payments.

Proposition II: The cost of equity rises with leverage because the risk to equity rises with leverage.

18.6 Personal Taxes

So far in this chapter, we have considered corporate taxes only. Because interest on debt is tax deductible whereas dividends on equity are not tax-deductible, we argued that the tax system gives firms an incentive to issue debt. But corporations are not the only ones paying taxes; individuals must pay taxes on both the dividends and the interest they receive. We cannot fully understand the effect of taxes on capital structure until all taxes, both corporate and personal, are considered.

The Basics of Personal Taxes

Let us begin by examining an all-equity firm that receives €1 of pre-tax earnings. If the corporate tax rate is t_c, the firm pays taxes t_c, leaving itself with earnings after taxes of $1 - t_c$. Let us assume that this entire amount is distributed to the shareholders as dividends. If the personal tax rate on share dividends is t_E, the shareholders pay taxes of $(1 - t_c) \times t_E$, leaving them with $(1 - t_c) \times (1 - t_E)$ after taxes.

Alternatively, imagine that the firm is financed with debt. Here, the entire €1 of earnings will be paid out as interest because interest is deductible at the corporate level. If the personal tax rate on interest is t_D, the bondholders pay taxes of t_D, leaving them with $1 - t_D$ after taxes.

The Effect of Personal Taxes on Capital Structure

To explore the effect of personal taxes on capital structure, let us consider three questions:

1 Ignoring costs of financial distress, what is the firm's optimal capital structure if dividends and interest are taxed at the same personal rate – that is, $t_E = t_D$?

The firm should select the capital structure that gets the most cash into the hands of its investors. This is tantamount to selecting a capital structure that minimizes the total amount of taxes at both the corporate and personal levels.

As we have said, beginning with €1 of pre-tax corporate earnings, shareholders receive $(1 - t_c) \times (1 - t_E)$, and bondholders receive $1 - t_D$. We can see that if $t_E = t_D$, bondholders receive more than shareholders. Thus, the firm should issue debt, not equity, in this situation. Intuitively, income is taxed twice – once at the corporate level and once at the personal level – if it is paid to shareholders. Conversely, income is taxed only at the personal level if it is paid to bondholders.

Note that the assumption of no personal taxes, which we used in the previous chapter, is a special case of the assumption that both interest and dividends are taxed at the same rate. Without personal taxes, the shareholders receive $1 - t_c$ while the bondholders receive £1. Thus, as we stated in a previous section, firms should issue debt in a world without personal taxes.

2 Under what conditions will the firm be indifferent between issuing equity or debt?

The firm will be indifferent if the cash flow to shareholders equals the cash flow to bondholders. That is, the firm is indifferent when:

Equation 18.7 $$(1 - t_c) \times (1 - t_E) = 1 - t_D$$

3 What should companies do in the real world?

Although this is clearly an important question, it is, unfortunately, a hard one – perhaps too hard to answer definitively. Nevertheless, let us begin by working with the highest tax rates for a specific country, the UK. As of 2020, the corporate tax rate was 18 per cent. For investors in the highest tax bracket, interest income was taxed at 45 per cent (46 per cent in Scotland). Investors in this highest bracket faced an effective 38.1 per cent tax rate on dividends (after the first tax-free £2,000 of dividend income).

At these rates, the left side of Equation 18.7 becomes (1 – 0.18) × (1 – 0.381), which equals 0.5076. The right side of the equation becomes 1 – 0.45, which equals 0.55. Because any rational firm would rather put £0.55 instead of £0.5076 into its investors' hands, it appears at first glance that firms should prefer debt over equity, just as we argued earlier. The relative differences between debt and equity in the UK have changed considerably in recent years with changes in tax rates. However, the debt advantage in the UK does not necessarily apply to other countries, where either debt or equity may have a distinct tax advantage.

Does anything else in the real world alter this conclusion? Perhaps. Our discussion on equity income is not yet complete. Firms can repurchase shares with excess cash instead of paying a dividend. Although capital gains on equities in the UK are taxed at 20 per cent (after a tax-free allowance of £11,700), the shareholder pays a capital gains tax only on the gain from sale, not on the entire proceeds from the repurchase. Thus, the *effective* tax rate on capital gains is actually lower than 20 per cent. Because firms both pay dividends and repurchase shares, the effective personal tax rate on *share distributions* must be below 38.1 per cent.

This lower effective tax rate makes equity issuance less burdensome. For example, suppose that the effective tax rate on share distributions is 30 per cent (to reflect a combination of share repurchases and dividends). From every pound of pre-tax corporate income, UK shareholders receive (1 – 0.18) × (1 – 0.3), which equals £0.574. This amount is now more than the £0.55 that bondholders receive.

Given that bonds appear to have the tax advantage in the UK against cash dividends but not against share repurchases, does this mean that companies should issue equities and have share repurchases instead of paying dividends? It looks as if many firms have actually followed this logic, with share repurchases now significantly more common than cash dividends.

There is also another reason for issuing equity instead of debt, and that is financial distress. We previously said that financial distress costs are an offset to debt's tax advantage, causing firms to employ less than 100 per cent leverage. The same point applies in the presence of personal taxes. And as long as the personal tax rate on equity income is below the personal tax rate on interest, the tax advantage to debt is smaller in a world with personal taxes than in a world without personal taxes. Thus, the optimal amount of debt will be lower in a world with personal taxes than in a world without them.

In a large-scale research study of US firms, Lin and Flannery (2013) examined the impact of new tax regulation, which led to a tax cut only for individual investors. They found that the tax cut reduced firm leverage by about 5 per cent, and this effect was stronger for firms with lower marginal corporate tax rates and for firms without financial constraints. This was perhaps the strongest evidence to date that personal tax does have an important impact on capital structure.

International Comparison of Tax Rates

Tax systems across the world are extremely varied, and the various combinations of corporation tax, income tax and capital gains tax make a lot of the discussion on tax and capital structure very country specific. The UK's tax system is complex. However, this has little relevance to an Italian financial manager whose shareholders are all from Italy. A sample of country tax rates is presented in Table 18.6. However, the reader should be mindful of these figures, for several reasons. First, every country's tax system is a complex set of rules that includes credits, discounts and exemptions for various taxpayer groups. The figures are effective tax rates for listed firms that will not correspond exactly to every individual's situation. Second, tax systems and tax rates change regularly. This means that some of the figures may become out of date over time (the figures are correct as of May 2023). In fact, the authors fully expect these rates to change as the governments respond to changes in the global economic landscape.

Table 18.6 Tax Rates Around the World, 2023

Country	Corporation Tax (%)	Income Tax (%)	Dividend Tax (%)	Capital Gains Tax (%)
Austria	25	55	25	25
Bahrain	0	0	0	0
Belgium	25	50	30	0
China	25	45	10	20
Denmark	22	55	27	42
Finland	20	56	34	34
France	26	45	30	30
Germany	30	45	25	28–29%
Greece	24	44	10	15
India	25	42	20.36	10
Ireland	12	48	20	33
Italy	24	43	26	26
Malaysia	23	28	15	0
Netherlands	25	49.5	15	0
Norway	22	38	25	27
Oman	15	0	10	10
Poland	19	32	19	19
Portugal	21	48	25	28
Qatar	10	0	10	10
Romania	16	10	5	16
Russia	20	13	13	13
Saudi Arabia	20	0	5	20
Singapore	17	22	0	0
Slovenia	19	50	15	19
South Africa	28	45	20	20
Spain	25	47	21	23
Sweden	20	52	30	30
Switzerland	14	40	35	0
Turkey	25	40	15	0
UAE	0	0	0	0
UK	18	40 (41 in Scotland)	33.75	18
USA	21	37	29	29

Summary and Conclusions

1 We began our discussion of the capital structure decision by arguing that the particular capital structure that maximizes the value of the firm is also the one that provides the most benefit to the shareholders.

2 In a world of no taxes, the famous Proposition I of Modigliani and Miller proves that the value of the firm is unaffected by the debt–equity ratio. In other words, a firm's capital structure is a matter of indifference in

that world. The authors obtain their results by showing that either a high or a low corporate ratio of debt to equity can be offset by homemade leverage. The result hinges on the assumption that individuals can borrow at the same rate as corporations, an assumption we believe to be quite plausible.

3 MM's Proposition II in a world without taxes states that:

$$R_E = R_A + \frac{D}{E}(R_A - R_D)$$

This implies that the expected rate of return on equity (also called the *cost of equity* or the *required return on equity*) is positively related to the firm's leverage. This makes intuitive sense because the risk of equity rises with leverage, a point illustrated by Figure 18.2.

4 Although the above work of MM is quite elegant, it does not explain the empirical findings on capital structure very well. MM imply that the capital structure decision is a matter of indifference, whereas the decision appears to be a weighty one in the real world. To achieve real-world applicability, we next considered corporate taxes.

5 In a world with corporate taxes but no bankruptcy costs, firm value is an increasing function of leverage. The formula for the value of the firm is:

$$V_L = V_U + t_C D$$

Expected return on levered equity can be expressed as:

$$R_E = R_A + (1 - t_c) \times (R_A - R_D) \times \frac{D}{E}$$

Here, value is positively related to leverage. This result implies that firms should have a capital structure almost entirely composed of debt. Because real-world firms select more moderate levels of debt, Chapter 19 considers modifications to the results of this chapter.

6 If distributions to shareholders are taxed at a lower effective personal tax rate than are interest payments, the tax advantage to debt at the corporate level is partially offset.

Questions and Problems

CONCEPT

1 **Capital Structure, the Pie Theory and MM** Use a pizza analogy to explain why capital structure should not influence firm value in a world with no taxes, transaction costs or financial distress costs. List three assumptions that lie behind the Modigliani–Miller theory in a world without taxes. Are these assumptions reasonable in the real world? How does the pursuit of sustainability objectives affect the validity of the Pie Theory of Capital Structure? Explain.

2 **Maximizing Firm Value versus Maximizing Shareholder Interests** Explain why, in a world with no taxes, transaction costs or financial distress costs, maximizing firm value is the same as maximizing share value. Are business risk and financial risk the same thing? If Firm A has greater business risk than Firm B, will it also have a higher cost of equity capital? Explain.

3 **Financial Leverage and Firm Value** In a world with no taxes, no transaction costs and no costs of financial distress, is the following statement true, false or uncertain? If a firm issues equity to repurchase some of its debt, the share price of the firm's equity will rise because the shares are less risky. Explain.

4 **Financial Leverage and Firm Value: An Example** In a world with no taxes, no transaction costs and no costs of financial distress, does moderate borrowing increase the required return on a firm's equity? Does it necessarily follow that increases in debt increase the riskiness of the firm? Explain.

5 **Corporate Taxes** How do corporate taxes affect the Modigliani–Miller theory of capital structure? Illustrate your answer with a practical example.

6 **Corporate Tax Incentives** In many countries, environmental taxes are used to incentivize companies to adopt sustainable practices and reduce their environmental impact. For example, a carbon tax encourages companies to reduce their greenhouse gas emissions by making it more expensive to emit carbon. How would these taxes affect the Modiglian–Miller theory of capital structure?

7 **Personal Taxes** Show the impact of personal taxes on the firm value in an MM universe. When would a firm be indifferent between issuing debt or equity? Illustrate your answer with a practical example.

REGULAR

8 **Return on Equity** Explain, using an example, how a change in the capital structure of a firm can affect the company's return on equity.

9 **Capital Structure** What is the basic goal of financial management with respect to capital structure? Is there an easily identifiable capital structure that will maximize the value of the firm? Why, or why not?

10 **Return on Equity: Mayou plc** Mayou plc currently has no debt in its capital structure but has decided to issue new debt to replace the equity so that the debt to equity ratio is 1:1. On the firm's accounting statements, the total asset value is £120,000. Equity book and market values are the same and there are currently 300 shares outstanding. The coupon on the bonds is 10 per cent and the bond issue will be at par. Assume that there are three possible economic states: recession, expected and boom time. The earnings in each state are £8,000, £10,000 and £12,000, respectively. Estimate the return on equity of Mayou plc in each state under the original capital structure and the capital structure including debt.

11 **EBIT and Gearing** Penybont plc is planning to raise funds to finance a major new development, and its management is considering borrowing on a long-term basis for the first time. It has been established that it is possible to borrow £600 million at an interest rate of 8 per cent to meet its funding requirements. Alternatively, it could issue 400 million shares at the prevailing market price of £1.50 through a private placement. The market has been kept informed of the company's investment plans and it is anticipated that such an issue will leave the share price unchanged. The company currently has 900 million shares outstanding, and its expected earnings before interest and tax have been estimated at £180 million.

(a) Assuming a corporate tax rate of 30 per cent, determine the expected earnings per share of the company under both forms of financing.

(b) Determine the level of earnings before interest and tax at which both plans will produce the same level of earnings per share.

12 **EBIT, Taxes and Leverage** Fresenius SE & Co has no debt outstanding and a total market value of €12.68 billion. Earnings before interest and taxes (EBIT) are projected to be €2.56 billion if economic conditions are normal. If there is strong expansion in the economy, then EBIT will be 30 per cent higher. If there is a recession, then EBIT will be 60 per cent lower. Fresenius is considering a €2 billion debt issue with a 5 per cent interest rate. The proceeds will be used to repurchase shares of equity. There are currently 1 billion shares outstanding. Fresenius has a tax rate of 15 per cent.

(a) Calculate earnings per share (EPS) under each of the three economic scenarios before any debt is issued.

(b) Calculate the percentage changes in EPS when the economy expands or enters a recession.

13 **ROE and Leverage** Using the information in the question above on Fresenius SE & Co, suppose Fresenius has a book value of €12.68 billion.

(a) Calculate return on equity, ROE, under each of the three economic scenarios before any debt is issued. Also calculate the percentage changes in ROE for economic expansion and recession, assuming no taxes.

(b) Repeat part (a) assuming the firm goes through with the proposed recapitalization.

(c) Repeat parts (a) and (b) of this problem assuming the firm has a tax rate of 20 per cent.

14 **Break-even EBIT** Hammerson plc is comparing two different capital structures: an all-equity plan (Plan I) and a levered plan (Plan II). Under Plan I, Hammerson would have 712 million shares of equity outstanding. Under Plan II, there would be 475 million shares of equity outstanding and £1 billion in debt outstanding. The interest rate on the debt is 5 per cent and there are no taxes.

(a) If EBIT is £459 million, which plan will result in the higher EPS?

(b) If EBIT is £80 million, which plan will result in the higher EPS?

(c) What is the break-even EBIT?

15 **MM and Share Value** In the previous problem, use MM Proposition I to find the share price under each of the two proposed plans. What is the value of the firm?

16 **Break-even EBIT and Leverage** Taiyuan Coal Gasification Ltd is comparing two different capital structures. Plan I would result in 1.62 billion shares of equity and 798 million yuan in debt. Plan II would result in 1 billion shares of equity and 2.1 billion yuan in debt. The interest rate on the debt is 11 per cent.

(a) Ignoring taxes, compare both of these plans to an all-equity plan assuming that EBIT will be 370 million yuan. The all-equity plan would result in 2 billion shares of equity outstanding. Which of the three plans has the highest EPS? The lowest?

(b) In part (a) what are the break-even levels of EBIT for each plan as compared to that for an all-equity plan? Is one higher than the other? Why?

(c) Ignoring taxes, when will EPS be identical for Plans I and II?

(d) Repeat parts (a), (b) and (c) assuming that the corporate tax rate is 25 per cent. Are the break-even levels of EBIT different from before? Why, or why not?

17 **Leverage and Share Value** ABC plc is comparing two different capital structures. Plan I would result in 1,100 shares of stock and €16,500 in debt. Plan II would result in 900 shares of stock and €27,500 in debt, on which it would pay interest of 8 per cent. What is the price per share of equity under Plan I? Plan II? What principle is illustrated by your answers?

18 **Homemade Leverage** Star plc, a prominent consumer products firm, is debating whether or not to convert its all-equity capital structure to one that is 40 per cent debt. Currently there are 2,000 shares outstanding and the share price is £70. EBIT is expected to remain at £16,000 per year for ever. The interest rate on new debt is 8 per cent, and there are no taxes.

(a) Ms Brown, a shareholder of the firm, owns 100 shares of equity. What is her cash flow under the current capital structure, assuming the firm has a dividend payout rate of 100 per cent?

(b) What will Ms Brown's cash flow be under the proposed capital structure of the firm? Assume that she keeps all 100 of her shares.

(c) Suppose Star does convert, but Ms Brown prefers the current all-equity capital structure. Show how she could unlever her shares to recreate the original capital structure.

(d) Using your answer to part (c), explain why Star's choice of capital structure is irrelevant.

19 **Homemade Leverage and WACC** ABC AG and XYZ AG are identical firms in all respects except for their capital structure. ABC is all equity financed, with NKr600,000 in equity shares. XYZ uses both shares and perpetual debt; its equity is worth NKr300,000 and the interest rate on its debt is 10 per cent. Both firms expect EBIT to be NKr73,000. Ignore taxes.

(a) Knut owns NKr30,000 worth of XYZ's shares. What rate of return is he expecting?

(b) Show how Knut could generate exactly the same cash flows and rate of return by investing in ABC and using homemade leverage.

(c) What is the cost of equity for ABC? What is it for XYZ?

(d) What is the WACC for ABC? For XYZ? What principle have you illustrated?

20 **MM** Nina plc uses no debt. The weighted average cost of capital is 13 per cent. If the current market value of the equity is £35 million and there are no taxes, what is EBIT?

21 **MM and Taxes** In the previous question, suppose the corporate tax rate is 28 per cent. What is EBIT in this case? What is the WACC? Assume that there is an addition carbon tax of 3 per cent levied on the firm. How does this affect the EBIT and WACC? Explain.

22 **Calculating WACC: Strade plc** Strade plc is an all equity financed company. The finance director suggested in a recent meeting with the board of directors a capital restructuring to introduce some debt in the company's financing to take advantage of the tax benefits of debt. With a corporate tax rate of 40 per cent, he argued that the advantages make the adjustment worthwhile. His proposal is to repurchase 30 million of the company's 100 million ordinary shares outstanding, which will be financed by an issue of debt at 8 per cent. The company's shares are currently trading at £0.75. While the company has no growth

prospects, it is anticipated that it can sustain its expected earnings for the next year of £200 million before tax indefinitely into the future. The proposal has been discussed with the company's investment bank and no problems are anticipated in its implementation.

(a) Determine the firm's weighted average cost of capital following the restructuring.

(b) Find the value of the geared firm.

23 **Calculating WACC: Shadow plc** Shadow plc has no debt but can borrow at 8 per cent. The firm's WACC is currently 12 per cent and the tax rate is 28 per cent.

(a) What is Shadow's cost of equity?

(b) If the firm converts to 25 per cent debt, what will its cost of equity be?

(c) If the firm converts to 50 per cent debt, what will its cost of equity be?

(d) What is Shadow's WACC in part (b)? In part (c)?

24 **MM and Taxes: Bruce & Co** Bruce & Co expects its EBIT to be £100,000 every year for ever. The firm can borrow at 10 per cent. Bruce currently has no debt, and its cost of equity is 20 per cent. If the tax rate is 21 per cent, what is the value of the firm? What will the value be if Bruce borrows £80,000 and uses the proceeds to repurchase shares?

25 **MM and Taxes: Bruce & Co (Continued)** In the previous problem, what is the cost of equity after recapitalization? What is the WACC? What are the implications for the firm's capital structure decision?

26 **MM Proposition** I Levered plc and Unlevered plc are identical in every way except their capital structures. Each company expects to earn £96 million before interest per year in perpetuity, with each company distributing all its earnings as dividends. Levered's perpetual debt has a market value of £275 million and costs 8 per cent per year. Levered has 4.5 million shares outstanding, currently worth £100 per share. Unlevered has no debt and 10 million shares outstanding, currently worth £80 per share. Neither firm pays taxes. Is Levered's equity a better buy than Unlevered's equity?

27 **MM and Debt–Equity Ratio** Tool Manufacturing has an expected EBIT of £35,000 in perpetuity and a tax rate of 28 per cent. The firm has £70,000 in outstanding debt at an interest rate of 9 per cent, and its unlevered cost of capital is 14 per cent. What is the value of the firm according to MM Proposition I with taxes? Should Tool change its debt–equity ratio if the goal is to maximize the value of the firm? Explain.

28 **Firm Value** Old School Corporation expects an EBIT of £9,000 every year for ever. Old School currently has no debt, and its cost of equity is 17 per cent. The firm can borrow at 10 per cent. If the corporate tax rate is 18 per cent, what is the value of the firm? What will the value be if Old School converts to 50 per cent debt? To 100 per cent debt?

29 **MM Proposition I with Taxes** Bigelli SpA is financed entirely with equity. The company is considering a loan of €1 million. The loan will be repaid in equal instalments over the next two years, and it has an 8 per cent interest rate. The company's tax rate is 35 per cent. According to MM Proposition I with taxes, what would be the increase in the value of the company after the loan?

30 **MM Proposition I without Taxes** Alpha NV and Beta NV are identical in every way except their capital structures. Alpha NV, an all-equity firm, has 5,000 shares of equity outstanding, currently worth €20 per share. Beta NV uses leverage in its capital structure. The market value of Beta's debt is €25,000, and its cost of debt is 12 per cent. Each firm is expected to have earnings before interest of €35,000 in perpetuity. Neither firm pays taxes. Assume that every investor can borrow at 12 per cent per year.

(a) What is the value of Alpha NV?

(b) What is the value of Beta NV?

(c) What is the market value of Beta NV's equity?

(d) How much will it cost to purchase 20 per cent of each firm's equity?

(e) Assuming each firm meets its earnings estimates, what will be the euro return to each position in part (d) over the next year?

(f) Construct an investment strategy in which an investor purchases 20 per cent of Alpha's equity and replicates both the cost and dollar return of purchasing 20 per cent of Beta's equity.

(g) Is Alpha's equity more or less risky than Beta's equity? Explain.

31 **Cost of Capital** Acetate SA has equity with a market value of €20 million and debt with a market value of €10 million. Treasury bills that mature in one year yield 8 per cent per year, and the expected return on the market portfolio over the next year is 18 per cent. The beta of Acetate's equity is 0.90. The firm pays no taxes.

(a) What is Acetate's debt–equity ratio?

(b) What is the firm's weighted average cost of capital?

(c) What is the cost of capital for an otherwise identical all-equity firm?

32 **Homemade Leverage** The Veblen Company and the Knight Company are identical in every respect except that Veblen is not levered. The market value of Knight Company's 6 per cent bonds is SKr1 million. Financial information for the two firms appears here. All earnings streams are perpetuities. Neither firm pays taxes. Both firms distribute all earnings available to ordinary shareholders immediately.

	Veblen (SKr)	Knight (SKr)
Projected operating income	300,000	300,000
Year-end interest on debt	–	60,000
Market value of stock	2,400,000	1,714,000
Market value of debt	–	1,000,000

(a) An investor who can borrow at 6 per cent per year wishes to purchase 5 per cent of Knight's equity. Can he increase his krona return by purchasing 5 per cent of Veblen's equity if he borrows so that the initial net costs of the two strategies are the same?

(b) Given the two investment strategies in (a), which will investors choose? When will this process cease?

33 **MM Propositions** Locomotive plc is planning to repurchase part of its ordinary share equity by issuing corporate debt. As a result, the firm's debt–equity ratio is expected to rise from 40 per cent to 50 per cent. The firm currently has £7.5 million worth of debt outstanding. The cost of this debt is 10 per cent per year. Locomotive expects to have an EBIT of £3.75 million per year in perpetuity. Locomotive pays no taxes.

(a) What is the market value of Locomotive plc before and after the repurchase announcement?

(b) What is the expected return on the firm's equity before the announcement of the share repurchase plan?

(c) What is the expected return on the equity of an otherwise identical all-equity firm?

(d) What is the expected return on the firm's equity after the announcement of the share repurchase plan?

34 **Share Value and Leverage** Renewable Manufacturing (RM) plc plans to announce that it will issue £2 million of perpetual green bonds and use the proceeds to repurchase equity. The bonds will sell at par with a 6 per cent annual coupon rate. RM is currently an all-equity firm worth £10 million with 500,000 shares of equity outstanding. After the sale of the bonds, RM will maintain the new capital structure indefinitely. RM currently generates annual pre-tax earnings of £1.5 million. This level of earnings is expected to remain constant in perpetuity. RM is subject to a corporate tax rate of 18 per cent.

(a) What is the expected return on RM's equity before the announcement of the debt issue?

(b) Construct RM's market value balance sheet before the announcement of the green bond issue. What is the price per share of the firm's equity?

(c) Construct RM's market value balance sheet immediately after the announcement of the green bond issue.

(d) What is RM's share price immediately after the repurchase announcement?

(e) How many shares will RM repurchase as a result of the green bond issue? How many shares of equity will remain after the repurchase?

(f) Construct the market value balance sheet after the restructuring.

(g) What is the required return on RM's equity after the restructuring?

35 **MM with Taxes** Williamsen GmbH has a debt–equity ratio of 2.5. The firm's weighted average cost of capital is 15 per cent and its pre-tax cost of debt is 10 per cent. Williamsen is subject to a corporate tax rate of 35 per cent.

(a) What is Williamsen's cost of equity capital?

(b) What is Williamsen's unlevered cost of equity capital?

(c) What would Williamsen's weighted average cost of capital be if the firm's debt–equity ratio were 0.75? What if it were 1.5?

CHALLENGE

36 Weighted Average Cost of Capital In a world of corporate taxes only, show that the R_{WACC} can be written as $R_{WACC} = R_A \times [1 - t_C(B/V)]$

37 Cost of Equity and Leverage Assuming a world of corporate taxes only, show that the cost of equity, R_S, is as given in the chapter by MM Proposition II with corporate taxes.

38 Business and Financial Risk Assume a firm's debt is risk-free, so that the cost of debt equals the risk-free rate, R_f. Define β_A as the firm's *asset* beta – that is, the systematic risk of the firm's assets. Define β_S to be the beta of the firm's equity. Use the capital asset pricing model, CAPM, along with MM Proposition II, to show that $\beta_E = \beta_A \times (1 + D/E)$, where D/E is the debt–equity ratio. Assume the tax rate is zero.

39 Shareholder Risk Suppose a firm's business operations mirror movements in the economy as a whole very closely – that is, the firm's asset beta is 1.0. Use the result of the previous problem to find the equity beta for this firm for debt–equity ratios of 0, 1, 5 and 20. What does this tell you about the relationship between capital structure and shareholder risk? How is the shareholders' required return on equity affected? Explain.

40 Unlevered Cost of Equity Beginning with the cost of capital equation – that is:

$$R_{WACC} = R_E + R_D \frac{E}{D+E} \frac{D}{D+E}$$

show that the cost of equity capital for a levered firm can be written as follows:

$$R_E = R_A + \frac{D}{E}(R_A - R_D)$$

Exam Question (45 minutes)

GreenSapphire is an all-equity financed company, which is valued at €250 million. The firm's shares are expected to produce a return of 15 per cent. The company has decided to modify its capital structure to capture the tax benefits of debt and to finance its sustainability initiatives. The plan is to have a target debt–equity ratio of 25 per cent and to invest the proceeds of the debt in renewable energy projects. The company has been told that any borrowings it makes will attract a rate of 7 per cent.

1 Calculate the return on equity of GreenSapphire before and after the restructuring. **(20 marks)**

2 Write a brief report to the management of GreenSapphire explaining why the return on equity has changed as a result of restructuring, and how it reflects the social and environmental impact of the firm's investments. (20 marks)

3 What is meant by green bonds? How do green bonds differ from conventional bonds in terms of their costs and benefits for the issuer and the investor? **(20 marks)**

4 Assume that the corporate tax rate is 20 per cent, capital gains tax is zero and the personal income tax rate is 47 per cent. What is the value of GreenSapphire before the restructuring? What is its value after? In what way do you think value creation depends on the expected returns and risks of the renewable energy projects? **(20 marks)**

5 What would the personal rate of tax on interest income have to be to push the tax advantage of debt to zero? **(20 marks)**

Total Marks: 100

Mini Case

Stephenson Real Estate Recapitalization

Stephenson Real Estate was founded 25 years ago by the current CEO, Robert Stephenson. The company purchases real estate, including land and buildings, and rents the property to tenants. The company has shown a profit every year for the past 18 years, and the shareholders are satisfied with the company's management. Prior to founding Stephenson Real Estate, Robert was the founder and CEO of a failed sheep farming operation. The resulting bankruptcy made him extremely averse to debt financing. As a result, the company is entirely equity financed, with 15 million shares outstanding. The shares currently trade at £32.50 per share.

Stephenson is evaluating a plan to purchase a huge tract of land in south-eastern England for £100 million. The land will subsequently be leased to tenant farmers. This purchase is expected to increase Stephenson's annual pre-tax earnings by £25 million in perpetuity. Kim Weyand, the company's new CFO, has been put in charge of the project. Kim has determined that the company's current cost of capital is 12.5 per cent. She feels that the company would be more valuable if it included debt in its capital structure, so she is evaluating whether the company should issue debt to entirely finance the project. Based on some conversations with investment banks, she thinks that the company can issue bonds at par value with an 8 per cent coupon rate. Based on her analysis, she also believes that a capital structure in the range of 70 per cent equity/30 per cent debt would be optimal. If the company goes beyond 30 per cent debt, its bonds would carry a lower rating and a much higher coupon because the possibility of financial distress, and the associated costs would rise sharply. Stephenson has an 18 per cent corporate tax rate.

1 If Stephenson wishes to maximize its total market value, would you recommend that it issue debt or equity to finance the land purchase? Explain.
2 Construct Stephenson's market value balance sheet before it announces the purchase.
3 Suppose Stephenson decides to issue equity to finance the purchase.
   (a) What is the net present value of the project?
   (b) Construct Stephenson's market value balance sheet after it announces that the firm will finance the purchase using equity. What would be the new price per share of the firm's equity? How many shares will Stephenson need to issue to finance the purchase?
   (c) Construct Stephenson's market value balance sheet after the equity issue but before the purchase has been made. How many shares of equity does Stephenson have outstanding? What is the price per share of the firm's equity?
   (d) Construct Stephenson's market value balance sheet after the purchase has been made.
4 Suppose Stephenson decides to issue debt to finance the purchase.
   (a) What will be the market value of the Stephenson company if the purchase is financed with debt?
   (b) Construct Stephenson's market value balance sheet after both the debt issue and the land purchase. What is the price per share of the firm's equity?
5 Which method of financing maximizes the per-share price of Stephenson's equity?

Practical Case Study

1 Locate the annual balance sheets for three firms from your country. For each company calculate the long-term debt–equity ratio for the prior two years. Why would these companies use such different capital structures?
2 Download the annual income statements for another company. For the most recent year, calculate the average tax rate and EBIT, and find the total interest expense. From the annual balance sheets calculate the total long-term debt (including the portion due within one year). Using the interest expense and total long-term debt, calculate the average cost of debt. Next, find the estimated beta for your company using real historical data or a financial website, such as Yahoo! Finance. Use the company's beta, an appropriate T-bill rate and the historical average market risk premium found in a previous chapter to calculate the levered cost of equity. Now calculate the unlevered cost of equity, then the unlevered EBIT. What is the unlevered value of your firm? What is the value of the interest tax shield and the value of the levered firm?

References

Lin, L. and M.J. Flannery (2013) 'Do Personal Taxes Affect Capital Structure? Evidence from the 2003 Tax Cut', *Journal of Financial Economics,* Vol. 109, No. 2, 549–565.

Miles, J.A. and J.R. Ezzel (1980) 'The Weighted Average Cost of Capital, Perfect Capital Markets and Project Life', *Journal of Financial and Quantitative Analysis,* Vol. 15, No. 3, 719–730.

Modigliani, F. and M. Miller (1958) 'The Cost of Capital, Corporation Finance and the Theory of Investment', *American Economic Review,* Vol. 48, 261–297.

Additional Reading

If you wish to delve deeper into the theory of capital structure and how it affects corporate strategy, you should read:

1 Hillier, D., M. Grinblatt and S. Titman (2023) *Financial Markets and Corporate Strategy: European Edition*, 3rd edn. Maidenhead: McGraw-Hill.

A couple of papers that look at the determinants of capital structure in a number of different countries are given below.

2 Antoniou, A., Y. Guney and K. Paudyal (2008) 'The Determinants of Capital Structure: Capital Market-oriented versus Bank-oriented Institutions', *Journal of Financial and Quantitative Analysis*, Vol. 43, No. 1, 59–92. **International.**

3 Öztekin, Ö. (2015) 'Capital Structure Decisions Around the World: Which Factors are Reliably Important?', *Journal of Financial and Quantitative Analysis*, Vol. 50, No. 3, 301–323.

Another paper of interest is:

4 De Jong, A., R. Kabir and T.T. Nguyen (2008) 'Capital Structure around the World: The Roles of Firm- and Country-specific Determinants', *Journal of Banking and Finance*, Vol. 32, No. 9, 1954–1969.

Endnotes

1 This result may not hold exactly in a more complex case where debt has a significant possibility of default. Issues of default are treated in the next chapter.

2 The original paper is Modigliani and Miller (1958).

3 We are ignoring the one-day interest charge on the loan.

4 Because we do not have taxes here, the cost of debt is R_D, not $R_D(1 - t_C)$ as it was in Chapter 12.

5 This statement holds in a world of no taxes. It does not hold in a world with taxes, a point to be brought out later in this chapter (see Figure 18.6).

6 This statement holds in a world of no taxes. It does not hold in a world with taxes, a point to be brought out later in this chapter (see Figure 18.6).

7 This can be derived from Equation 18.2 by setting $R_{WACC} = R_A$, yielding

$$\frac{D}{D+E}R_D + \frac{E}{D+E}R_E = R_A$$

Multiplying both sides by $(D+E)/E$ yields

$$\frac{D}{E}R_D + R_E = \frac{D+E}{E}R_A$$

We can rewrite the right side as

$$\frac{D}{E}R_D + R_E = \frac{D}{E}R_A + R_A$$

Moving $(D/E)R_D$ to the right side and rearranging yields

$$R_E = R_A + \frac{D}{E}(R_A - R_D)$$

8 Both Merton Miller and Franco Modigliani were awarded separate Nobel Prizes, in part for their work on capital structure.

9 MM were aware of both of these issues, as can be seen in their original paper (Modigliani and Miller, 1958).

10 Under the MM propositions developed earlier, the two pies should be of the same size.

11 Note that shareholders actually receive more under Plan I (£650,000) than under Plan II (£390,000). Students are often bothered by this because it seems to imply that they are better off without leverage. However, remember that there are more shares outstanding in Plan I than in Plan II. A full-blown model would show that earnings *per share* are higher with leverage.

12 This relationship holds when the debt level is assumed to be constant through time. A different formula would apply if the debt–equity ratio was assumed to be a non-constant over time. For a deeper treatment of this point, see Miles and Ezzel (1980).

13 The following example calculates the present value if we assume the debt has a finite life. Suppose Maxwell plc has £1 million in debt with an 8 per cent coupon rate. If the debt matures in two years and the cost of debt capital, *RD*, is 10 per cent, what is the present value of the tax shields if the corporate tax rate is 28 per cent? The debt is amortized in equal instalments over two years.

Year	Loan Balance (£)	Interest (£)	Tax Shield (£)	Present Value of Tax Shield (£)
0	1,000,000			
1	500,000	80,000	0.28 × 80,000	22,400
2	0	40,000	0.28 × 40,000	11,200
				33,600

The present value of the tax saving is

$$PV = \frac{0.28 \times €80{,}000}{1.10} + \frac{0.28 \times €80{,}000}{(1.10)^2} = €33{,}600$$

Maxwell plc's value is higher than that of a comparable unlevered firm by £33,600.

14 This relationship can be shown as follows. Given MM Proposition I under taxes, a levered firm's market value balance sheet can be written as:

V_U = Value of unlevered firm	D = Debt
$t_C D$ = Tax shield	E = Equity

The value of the unlevered firm is simply the value of the assets without benefit of leverage. The balance sheet indicates that the firm's value increases by t_C, D, when debt of D is added. The expected cash flow *from* the left side of the balance sheet can be written as

$$V_U R_A + t_C D R_D \qquad \text{(a)}$$

Because assets are risky, their expected rate of return is R_A. The tax shield has the same risk as the debt, so its expected rate of return is R_D.

The expected cash *to* bondholders and shareholders together is

$$E R_E + D R_D \qquad \text{(b)}$$

Expression (b) reflects the fact that equity earns an expected return of R_E and debt earns the interest rate R_D.

Because all cash flows are paid out as dividends in our no-growth perpetuity model, the cash flows going into the firm equal those going to shareholders. Hence (a) and (b) are equal:

$$E R_E + D R_E = V_U R_A + t_C D R_D \qquad \text{(c)}$$

Dividing both sides of (c) by E, subtracting DR_D from both sides, and rearranging yields

$$R_E = \frac{V_U}{E} \times R_A - (1 - t_C) \times \frac{D}{E} R_D \qquad \text{(d)}$$

Because the value of the levered firm, V_L, equals $V_U + t_C D = D + E$, it follows that $V_U = E + (1 - t_C) \times D$. Thus (d) can be rewritten as

$$R_E = \frac{E + (1 - t_C) \times D}{E} \times R_A - (1 - t_C) \times \frac{D}{E} R_D \qquad \text{(e)}$$

Bringing the terms involving $(1 - t_C) \times (D/E)$ together produces Equation 18.6.

The UK dividend tax rate is fairly complex and uses tax credits to augment payments. To summarize, for the year 2015, there are three basic dividend tax rates. If total taxable income is below £41,865, the tax rate on dividend income is 10 per cent. If taxable income is between £41,865 and £150,000, the tax rate on dividend income is 32.5 per cent. Higher earners have a tax rate on dividend income of 37.5 per cent. All taxpayers receive a dividend tax credit of 10 per cent on dividend income. Dividend income is the sum of the original dividend plus the tax credit. This means that the effective rate of dividend tax is significantly lower at 0 per cent, 25 per cent and 30.56 per cent for the three taxable income bands, respectively. An example will help to illustrate the calculation.

Three individuals, A, B and C, are paid a dividend of £100. A is in the lower tax bracket, B is in the middle tax bracket and C is in the upper tax bracket. Dividend calculations are given in the table below:

	A	B	C
Dividend	£100	£100	£100
Dividend income (£100/(1 – 10%))	£111.11	£111.11	£111.11
Tax credit	£11.11	£11.11	£11.11
Dividend tax rate	10%	32.5%	37.5%
Tax charged	£11.11	£36.11	£41.67
Tax paid (Tax charged – Tax credit)	£0	£25	£30.56
Effective tax rate (Tax paid/Dividend)	0%	25%	30.56%

Chapter 19
Capital Structure: Limits to the Use of Debt

Learning Objectives

After reading this chapter you should be able to:

LO1 Define key capital structure concepts, such as financial distress costs, signalling, shirking, agency costs of equity, pecking order theory and market timing theory.

LO2 Explain the implications of financial distress costs on a company's capital structure.

LO3 Assess the relative importance of pecking order theory and market timing theory in determining a firm's capital structure.

Although the use of debt brings benefits in the form of tax shields, there are dangers to having too much debt. Take Italy's flagship airline, Alitalia, which despite having government support, never made a profit in any year between 2009 and 2021. Basically, Alitalia's debt of €900 million meant that every year it was paying out a large portion of its revenues in the form of interest and, as a result, the debt and interest payments had severely damaged the airline, making it unsustainable. Despite all the support, Alitalia eventually collapsed in 2022, and its successor, ITA Airways, emerged as a much smaller firm with less than a quarter of the staff of Alitalia.

Source: JJs/Alamy Stock Photo

As the Alitalia situation suggests, financial leverage has a number of drawbacks, and there is a limit to the financial leverage a company can bear. The risk of too much leverage is bankruptcy. Chapter 29 covers bankruptcy law and the turnaround strategies that firms follow once they are in financial distress. In this chapter, we discuss the costs associated with bankruptcies and how companies attempt to avoid this process.

Key Notations

E	Market value of equity	V	Market value of firm
D	Market value of debt	EBIT	Earnings before interest and taxes

19.1 Costs of Financial Distress

Chapter 29
Page 789

Bankruptcy Risk or Bankruptcy Cost?

Debt puts pressure on the firm because interest and principal payments are obligations. If these obligations are not met, the firm may risk financial distress. The ultimate danger is *bankruptcy*, where ownership of the firm's assets is legally transferred from the shareholders to the bondholders (we cover financial distress in a lot more detail in Chapter 29). These debt obligations are fundamentally different from equity obligations. Although shareholders like and expect dividends, they are not legally entitled to them in the way bondholders are lawfully entitled to interest and principal payments.

We show next that bankruptcy costs or, more generally, financial distress costs tend to offset the advantages of debt. We begin by presenting a simple example of bankruptcy. All taxes are ignored to focus only on the costs of debt.

19.2 Description of Financial Distress Costs

Example 19.1 shows that bankruptcy costs can lower the value of the firm. In fact, the same general result holds even if a legal bankruptcy is prevented. Thus *financial distress costs* may be a better phrase than *bankruptcy costs*. It is worthwhile to describe these costs in more detail.

Example 19.1

Bankruptcy Costs

Knight NV plans to be in business for one more year. It forecasts a cash flow of either €100 or €50 in the coming year, each occurring with 50 per cent probability. The firm has no other assets. Previously issued debt requires payments of €49 of interest and principal. Day NV has identical cash flow prospects but has €60 of interest and principal obligations. The cash flows of these two firms can be represented as follows:

	Knight NV		Day NV	
	Boom Times (prob. 50%) (€)	Recession (prob. 50%) (€)	Boom Times (prob. 50%) (€)	Recession (prob. 50%) (€)
Cash flow	100	50	100	50
Payment of interest and principal on debt	49	49	60	50
Distribution to shareholders	51	1	40	0

For Knight NV in both boom times and recession, and for Day NV in boom times, cash flow exceeds interest and principal payments. In these situations the bondholders are paid in full, and the shareholders receive any residual. However, the most interesting of the four columns involves Day NV in a recession. Here the bondholders are owed €60, but the firm has only €50 in cash. Because we assumed that the firm has no other assets, the bondholders cannot be satisfied in full. If bankruptcy occurs, the bondholders will receive all of the firm's cash, and the shareholders will receive nothing. Importantly, the shareholders do not have to come up with the additional €10 (= €60 − €50). Corporations have limited liability in Europe and most other countries, implying that bondholders cannot sue the shareholders for the extra €10.[1]

We assume that (1) both bondholders and shareholders are risk-neutral, and (2) the interest rate is 10 per cent. Due to this risk neutrality, cash flows to both shareholders and bondholders are to be discounted at the 10 per cent rate.[2] We can evaluate the debt, the equity and the entire firm for both Knight and Day as follows:

$$E_{KNIGHT} = €23.64 = \frac{€51 \times \frac{1}{2} \times €1 \times \frac{1}{2}}{1.10} \qquad E_{DAY} = €18.18 = \frac{€40 \times \frac{1}{2} \times 0 \times \frac{1}{2}}{1.10}$$

$$D_{KNIGHT} = €44.54 = \frac{€49 \times \frac{1}{2} \times €49 \times \frac{1}{2}}{1.10} \qquad D_{DAY} = €50 = \frac{€60 \times \frac{1}{2} \times €50 \times \frac{1}{2}}{1.10}$$

$$V_{KNIGHT} = \overline{€68.18} \qquad V_{DAY} = \overline{€68.18}$$

Note that the two firms have the same value, even though Day runs the risk of bankruptcy. Furthermore, notice that Day's bondholders are valuing the bonds with 'their eyes open'. Though the promised payment of principal and interest is €60, the bondholders are willing to pay only €50. Hence their *promised* return or yield is:

$$\frac{€60}{€50} - 1 = 20\%$$

Day's debt can be viewed as a *junk bond* because the probability of default is so high. As with all junk bonds, Day's bondholders demand a high promised yield.

Day's example is not realistic because it ignores an important cash flow to be discussed next. A more realistic set of numbers might be these:

	Day NV		
	Boom Times (prob. 50%)	**Recession (prob. 50%) (€)**	
Earnings	100	50	$E_{DAY} = €18.18 = \frac{€40 \times \frac{1}{2} + 0 \times \frac{1}{2}}{1.10}$
Debt repayment	60	35	$E_{DAY} = €43.18 = \frac{€60 \times \frac{1}{2} + €35 \times \frac{1}{2}}{1.10}$
Distribution to stockholders	$\overline{40}$	$\overline{0}$	$V_{DAY} = \overline{€61.36}$

Why do the bondholders receive only €35 in a recession? If cash flow is only €50, bondholders will be informed that they will not be paid in full. These bondholders are likely to hire lawyers to negotiate or even to sue the company. Similarly, the firm is likely to hire lawyers to defend itself. Further costs will be incurred if the case gets to a bankruptcy court. These fees are always paid before the bondholders get paid. In this example, we are assuming that bankruptcy costs total €15 (= €50 − 35).

The value of the firm is now €61.36, an amount below the €68.18 figure calculated earlier. By comparing Day's value in a world with no bankruptcy costs to Day's value in a world with these costs, we conclude the following:

The possibility of bankruptcy has a negative effect on the value of the firm. However, it is not the *risk* of bankruptcy itself that lowers value. Rather it is the costs associated with bankruptcy that lower value.

The explanation follows from our pie example. In a world without bankruptcy costs, the bondholders and the shareholders share the entire pie. However, bankruptcy costs eat up some of the pie in the real world, leaving less for the shareholders and bondholders.

Because the bondholders are aware that they would receive little in a recession, they pay the low price of €43.18. In this case, their promised return is:

$$\frac{€60}{€43.18} - 1 = 39.0\%$$

The bondholders are paying a fair price if they are realistic about both the probability and the cost of bankruptcy. It is the *shareholders* who bear these future bankruptcy costs. To see this, imagine that Day NV was originally all equity. The shareholders want the firm to issue debt with a promised payment of €60 and use the proceeds to pay a dividend. If there had been no bankruptcy costs, our results show that bondholders would pay €50 to purchase debt with a promised payment of €60. Hence, a dividend of €50 could be paid to the shareholders. However, if bankruptcy costs exist, bondholders would only pay €43.18 for the debt. In that case, only a dividend of €43.18 could be paid to the shareholders. Because the dividend is smaller with bankruptcy costs, the shareholders are hurt by these costs.

Direct Costs of Financial Distress

As mentioned earlier, lawyers are involved throughout all the stages before and during bankruptcy. With fees often in the hundreds of pounds or euros an hour, these costs can add up quickly. Someone once remarked that bankruptcies are to lawyers what blood is to sharks. In addition, administrative and accounting fees can substantially add to the total bill. If a trial takes place, we must not forget expert witnesses. Each side may hire a number of these witnesses to testify about the fairness of a proposed settlement and their fees can easily rival those of lawyers or accountants.

Real World Insight 19.1

Lehman Brothers Bankruptcy

The largest ever bankruptcy concerned Lehman Brothers, at the time one of the biggest banks in the world. This bankruptcy followed large write-downs on subprime mortgage assets and a general collapse in interbank credit in September 2008. Estimates vary on the total cost of the bank's collapse but a conservative estimate is around \$2 billion, and it is very likely to be much higher. According to Lehman Brothers' official documentation, the total fees that were paid to administrators, lawyers and other parties amounted to \$1.05 billion within just two years of the bankruptcy. Given its enormous size, the bankruptcy affected nearly every country in Europe and the cost of winding up Lehman's European subsidiaries was almost as high at \$900 million. These are just the direct costs. The total (direct and indirect) costs of the bankruptcy will have been astronomical once the company's demise is considered more broadly in terms of impacting the local community and the wider financial sector.

Indirect Costs of Financial Distress

Bankruptcy hampers conduct with customers and suppliers. Sales are frequently lost because of both fear of impaired service and loss of trust. For example, when the UK airline Flybe announced in 2020 it was in financial distress, many potential customers refused to use the airline because of doubts that the firm would be able to service flights in the future. The same thing happened with other airlines, such as Thomas Cook and Level Europe, who were in a similar quandary.

A number of academic studies have measured the costs of financial distress. Davydenko et al. (2012) find that 30 per cent of a firm's value disappears in bankruptcy, and 14.7 per cent for debt renegotiations. Glover (2016) goes even further and argues that a firm will expect to lose up to 45 per cent of its value in the event of default.

Of course, few firms end up in bankruptcy. Thus, the preceding cost estimates must be multiplied by the probability of bankruptcy to yield the *expected* cost of bankruptcy. For example, consider a firm that has a 5 per cent probability of going into bankruptcy each year. If the firm declares bankruptcy, the direct costs it incurs amount to 30 per cent of the total value of the firm. The *expected* bankruptcy cost must be then 6 per cent $(= 0.05 \times 0.30)$.

Agency Costs

When a firm has debt, conflicts of interest arise between shareholders and bondholders. Because of this, shareholders are tempted to pursue selfish strategies. These conflicts of interest, which are magnified when financial distress is incurred, impose agency costs on the firm. We describe three kinds of selfish strategies that shareholders use to hurt the bondholders and help themselves. These strategies are costly because they will lower the market value of the whole firm.

Selfish Investment Strategy 1: Incentive to Take Large Risks

Firms near bankruptcy often take great chances because they believe that they are playing with someone else's money. To see this, imagine a levered firm considering two *mutually exclusive* projects: a low-risk one and a high-risk one. There are two equally likely outcomes: recession and boom. The firm is in such dire straits that, should a recession hit, it will come near to bankruptcy with one project and actually fall into bankruptcy with the other. The cash flows for the entire firm if the low-risk project is taken can be described as follows:

Value of Entire Firm if Low-risk Project is Chosen						
	Probability	Value of Firm (£)	=	Shares (£)	+	Bonds (£)
Recession	0.5	100	=	0	+	100
Boom	0.5	200	=	100	+	100

If recession occurs, the value of the firm will be £100; if a boom occurs, the value of the firm will be £200. The expected value of the firm is £150 (= 0.5 × £100 + 0.5 × £200)

The firm has promised to pay bondholders £100. Shareholders will obtain the difference between the total payoff and the amount paid to the bondholders. In other words, the bondholders have the prior claim on the payoffs, and the shareholders have the residual claim.

Now suppose that the riskier project can be substituted for the low-risk project. The payoffs and probabilities are as follows:

Value of Entire Firm if Low-risk Project is Chosen						
	Probability	Value of Firm (£)	=	Shares (£)	+	Bonds (£)
Recession	0.5	50	=	0	+	50
Boom	0.5	240	=	140	+	100

The expected value of the *firm* is £145 (= 0.5 × £50 + 0.5 × £240), which is lower than the expected value of the firm with the low-risk project. Thus the low-risk project would be accepted if the firm were all equity. However, note that the expected value of the *equity* is £70 (= 0.5 × 0 + 0.5 × £140) with the high-risk project, but only £50 (= 0.5 × 0 + 0.5 × £100) with the low-risk project. Given the firm's present levered state, shareholders will select the high-risk project, even though the high-risk project has a *lower* NPV.

The key is that, relative to the low-risk project, the high-risk project increases firm value in a boom and decreases firm value in a recession. The increase in value in a boom is captured by the shareholders because the bondholders are paid in full (they receive £100) regardless of which project is accepted. Conversely, the drop in value in a recession is lost by the bondholders because they are paid in full with the low-risk project but receive only £50 with the high-risk one. The shareholders will receive nothing in a recession anyway, whether the high-risk or low-risk project is selected. Thus, financial economists argue that shareholders expropriate value from the bondholders by selecting high-risk projects.

Selfish Investment Strategy 2: Incentive towards Underinvestment

Shareholders of a firm with a significant probability of bankruptcy often find that new investment helps the bondholders at the shareholders' expense. The simplest case might be a property owner facing imminent bankruptcy. If he took €100,000 out of his own pocket to refurbish the building, he could increase the building's value by, say, €150,000. Though this investment has a positive net present value, he will turn it down if the increase in value cannot prevent bankruptcy. 'Why,' he asks, 'should I use my own funds to improve the value of a building that the bank will soon repossess?'

This idea is formalized by the following simple example. Consider the firm in Table 19.1, which must decide whether to accept or reject a new project. The first two columns in the table show cash flows without the project. The firm receives cash inflows of £5,000 and £2,400 under a boom and a recession, respectively. Because the firm must pay principal and interest of £4,000, the firm will default in a recession.

Table 19.1 Example Illustrating Incentive to Underinvest

	Firm without Project		Firm with Project Costing £1,000	
	Boom (£)	Recession (£)	Boom (£)	Recession (£)
Firm cash flows	5,000	2,400	6,700	4,100
Bondholders' claim	4,000	2,400	4,000	4,000
Shareholders' claim	1,000	0	2,700	100

Note: The project has positive NPV. However, much of its value is captured by bondholders. Rational managers, acting in the shareholders' interest, will reject the project.

Alternatively, as indicated in the next two columns of the table, the firm could raise equity to invest in a new project. The project brings in £1,700 in either state, which is enough to prevent bankruptcy even in a recession. Because £1,700 is much greater than the project's cost of £1,000, the project has a positive NPV at any plausible interest rate. Clearly, an all-equity firm would accept the project.

However, the project hurts the shareholders of the levered firm. To see this, imagine the old shareholders contribute the £1,000 *themselves.*[3] Assuming that a boom and a recession are equally likely, the expected value of the shareholders' interest without the project is £500 (= 0.5 × £1,000 + 0.5 × 0). The expected value with the project is £1,400 (= 0.5 × £2,700 + 0.5 × £100). The shareholders' interest rises by only £900 (= £1,400 − £500) while costing £1,000.

Why does a project with a positive NPV hurt the shareholders? The key is that the shareholders contribute the full £1,000 investment, but the shareholders and bondholders *share* the benefits. The shareholders take the entire gain if boom times occur. Conversely, the bondholders reap most of the cash flow from the project in a recession.

The discussion of selfish strategy 1 is quite similar to the discussion of selfish strategy 2. In both cases, an investment strategy for the levered firm is different from the one for the unlevered firm. Thus, leverage results in distorted investment policy. Whereas the unlevered corporation always chooses projects with positive net present value, the levered firm may deviate from this policy.

Selfish Investment Strategy 3: Milking the Property

Another strategy is to pay out extra dividends or other distributions in times of financial distress, leaving less in the firm for the bondholders. This is known as *milking the property,* a phrase taken from real estate. Strategies 2 and 3 are very similar. In strategy 2, the firm chooses not to raise new equity. Strategy 3 goes one step further because equity is actually withdrawn through the dividend.

Summary of Selfish Strategies

The distortions just discussed occur only when there is a probability of bankruptcy or financial distress. Thus, these distortions *should not* affect, say, Vodafone because bankruptcy is not a realistic possibility for a diversified blue-chip firm such as this. In other words, Vodafone's debt will be virtually risk-free, regardless of the projects it accepts. By contrast, small firms in risky industries are more likely to experience financial distress and, in turn, to be affected by such distortions.

Who pays for the cost of selfish investment strategies? We argue that it is ultimately the shareholders. Rational bondholders know that, when financial distress is imminent, they cannot expect help from shareholders. Rather, shareholders are likely to choose investment strategies that reduce the value of the bonds. Bondholders protect themselves accordingly by raising the interest rate that they require on the bonds. Because the shareholders must pay these high rates, they ultimately bear the costs of selfish strategies. For firms that face these distortions, debt will be difficult and costly to obtain. These firms will have low leverage ratios.

The relationship between shareholders and bondholders is very similar to the relationship between Errol Flynn and David Niven, good friends and film stars in the 1930s. Niven reportedly said that the good thing about Flynn was that you knew exactly where you stood with him. When you needed his help, you could always count on him to let you down.

19.3 Can Costs of Debt Be Reduced?

Chapter 20 Page 541

Each of the costs of financial distress we have mentioned is substantial in its own right. The sum of them may well affect debt financing severely. Thus, managers have an incentive to reduce these costs. We now turn to some of their methods. However, it should be mentioned at the outset that the methods here can, at most, reduce the costs of debt. They cannot *eliminate* them entirely (check out Chapter 20 to find out more about the process of raising debt financing).

Protective Covenants

Because shareholders must pay higher interest rates as insurance against their own selfish strategies, they frequently make agreements with bondholders in the hope of lower rates. These agreements, called **protective covenants**, are incorporated as part of the loan document (or *indenture)* between shareholders and bondholders. The covenants must be taken seriously because a broken covenant can lead to default. Protective covenants can be classified into two types: negative covenants and positive covenants.

A negative covenant limits or prohibits actions that the company may take. Here are some typical negative covenants:

- Limitations are placed on the amount of dividends a company may pay.
- The firm may not pledge any of its assets to other lenders.
- The firm may not merge with another firm.
- The firm may not sell or lease its major assets without approval by the lender.
- The firm may not issue additional long-term debt.

A positive covenant specifies an action that the company agrees to take or a condition the company must abide by. Here are some examples:

- The company agrees to maintain its working capital at a minimum level.
- The company must furnish periodic financial statements to the lender.

These lists of covenants are not exhaustive. The authors have seen loan agreements with more than 30 covenants. Sustainability targets are also frequently included in bond covenants. Examples include:

- The firm must reduce its carbon emissions by a certain percentage.
- The firm must improve energy efficiency.
- The firm must invest in renewable energy.
- The firm must meet specific social or governance targets.

If a firm fails to meet these contractual obligations, it may trigger a default on the bond.

Smith and Warner (1979) examined public issues of debt and found that 91 per cent of the bond indentures included covenants that restricted the issuance of additional debt, 23 per cent restricted dividends, 39 per cent restricted mergers and 36 per cent limited the sale of assets. Qi et al. (2011) considered foreign bond issuance in the USA and provided evidence that highlights the importance of a country's creditor rights. Firms that come from countries with stronger creditor rights have fewer bond indentures. Hillier et al. (2018) looked at the difference in debt covenant strictness between family and non-family firms, and found that family firms are more likely to have less strict covenants, possibly because of their longer-term focus.

With this in mind, protective covenants should reduce the costs of bankruptcy, ultimately increasing the value of the firm. Thus, shareholders are likely to favour all reasonable covenants. To see this, consider three choices by shareholders to reduce bankruptcy costs:

1. *Issue no debt.* Because of the tax advantages to debt, this is a very costly way of avoiding conflicts.
2. *Issue debt with no restrictive and protective covenants.* In this case, bondholders will demand high interest rates to compensate for the unprotected status of their debt.
3. *Write protective and restrictive covenants into the loan contracts.* If the covenants are clearly written, the creditors may receive protection without large costs being imposed on the shareholders. The creditors will gladly accept a lower interest rate.

Thus, bond covenants, even if they reduce flexibility, can increase the value of the firm. They can be the lowest-cost solution to the shareholder–bondholder conflict. A list of typical bond covenants and their uses is presented in Table 19.2.

Table 19.2 Loan Covenants

Shareholder Action or Firm Circumstances	Covenant Type	Reason for Covenant
As firm approaches financial distress, shareholders may want firm to make high-risk investments.	Financial statement restrictions 1. Minimum working capital 2. Minimum interest coverage 3. Minimum net worth	High-risk investments transfer value from bondholders to shareholders when financial distress is a realistic possibility. Covenants reduce probability of financial distress.
Shareholders may attempt to transfer corporate assets to themselves.	Restrictions on asset disposition 1. Limit on dividends 2. Limit on sale of assets 3. Collateral and mortgages	Covenants limit the ability of shareholders to transfer assets to themselves and to underinvest.
Shareholders may attempt to increase risk of firm.	Restrictions on switching assets	Increased firm risk helps shareholders and hurts bondholders.
Shareholders may attempt to issue new debt of equal or greater priority.	Dilution restrictions 1. Limit on leasing 3. Limit on further borrowing	Covenants restrict dilution of the claim of existing bondholders.

Consolidation of Debt

One reason bankruptcy costs are so high is that different creditors (and their lawyers) contend with one another. This problem can be alleviated by proper arrangement of bondholders and shareholders. For example, perhaps one, or at most a few, lenders can shoulder the entire debt. Should financial distress occur, negotiating costs are minimized under this arrangement. In addition, bondholders can purchase equity as well. In this way, shareholders and debtholders are not pitted against one another because they are not separate entities. This appears to be the approach in Japan, where large banks generally take significant equity positions in the firms to which they lend money.[4]

19.4 Integration of Tax Effects and Financial Distress Costs

Chapter 18 Page 478

Modigliani and Miller argue that the firm's value rises with leverage in the presence of corporate taxes (the impact of taxation on capital structure was introduced in **Chapter 18,** Sections 18.5 and 18.6). Because this relationship implies that all firms should choose maximum debt, the theory does not predict the behaviour of firms in the real world. Other authors have suggested that bankruptcy and related costs reduce the value of the levered firm.

The integration of tax effects and distress costs appears in Figure 19.1. In the top graph of the figure, the diagonal straight line represents the value of the firm in a world without bankruptcy costs. The hump-shaped curve represents the value of the firm with these costs. This curve rises as the firm moves from all equity to a small amount of debt. Here, the present value of the distress costs is minimal because the probability of distress is so small. However, as more and more debt is added, the present value of these costs rises at an *increasing* rate. At some point, the increase in the present value of these costs from an additional unit of debt equals the increase in the present value of the tax shield. This is the debt level maximizing the value of the firm and is represented by D^* in Figure 19.1. In other words, D^* is the optimal amount of debt. Bankruptcy costs increase faster than the tax shield beyond this point, implying a reduction in firm value from further leverage.

In the bottom graph of Figure 19.1, the weighted average cost of capital (R_{WACC}) falls as debt is added to the capital structure. After reaching D^* the weighted average cost of capital rises. The optimal amount of debt produces the lowest weighted average cost of capital.

Our discussion implies that a firm's capital structure decision involves a trade-off between the tax benefits of debt and the costs of financial distress. In fact, this approach is frequently called the *trade-off* or the *static trade-off* theory of capital structure. The implication is that there is an optimal amount of debt for any individual firm. This amount of debt becomes the firm's target debt level. Because financial distress costs cannot be expressed in a precise way, no formula has yet been developed to determine a firm's optimal debt level exactly. However, the last section of this chapter offers some rules of thumb for selecting a debt–equity ratio in the real world.

Figure 19.1 The Optimal Amount of Debt and the Value of the Firm

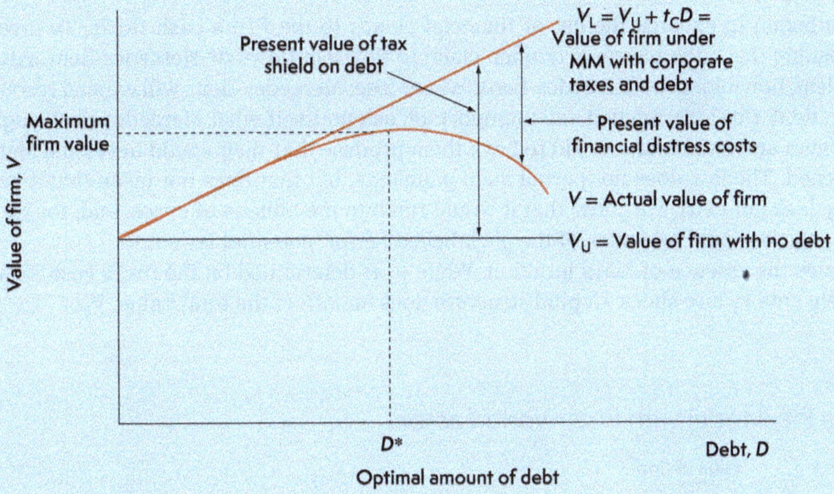

The tax shield increases the value of the levered firm. Financial distress costs lower the value of the levered firm. The two offsetting factors produce an optimal amount of debt at D^*.

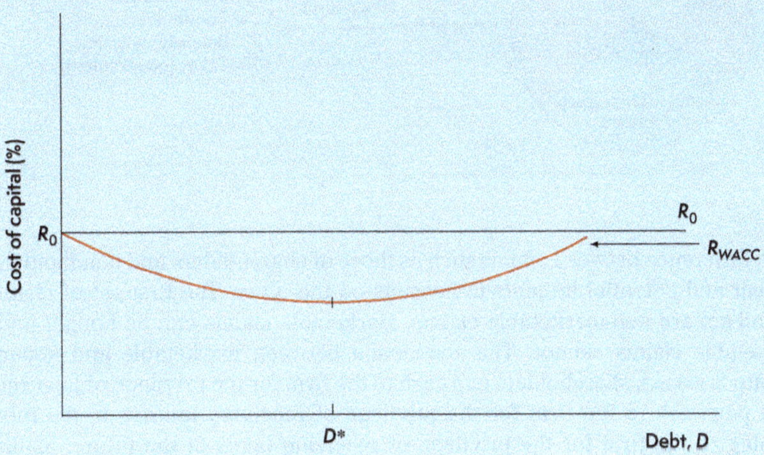

According to the static theory, the R_{WACC} falls initially, because of the tax advantage of debt. Beyond point D^* it begins to rise, because of financial distress costs.

Pie Again

Now that we have considered bankruptcy costs, let us return to the pie approach of Chapter 18. The cash flows of the firm go to four different claimants: shareholders, bondholders, the government (in the form of taxes) and, during the bankruptcy process, lawyers (and others). Algebraically, we must have:

$$\text{CF} = \text{Payments to shareholders} + \text{Payments to bondholders} + \text{Payments to the government} + \text{Payments to lawyers (and others)}$$

It follows that the total value of the firm, V_T, equals the sum of the following four components:

$$V_T = E + D + G + L$$

where E is the value of the equity, D is the value of the bonds, G is the value of the government claims from taxes, and L stands for the value that lawyers and others receive when the firm is under financial distress. This relationship is illustrated in Figure 19.2.

Nor have we even begun to exhaust the list of financial claims to the firm's cash flows. To give an unusual example, everyone reading this book has an economic claim to the cash flows of Mercedes-Benz. After all, if you are injured in an accident, you might sue Mercedes-Benz. Win or lose, Mercedes-Benz will expend resources dealing with the matter. If you think this is farfetched and unimportant, ask yourself what Mercedes-Benz might be willing to pay every man, woman and child in the world to have them promise that they would never sue Mercedes-Benz, no matter what happened. The law does not permit such payments, but that does not mean that a value to all of those potential claims does not exist. We guess that it would run into the billions of euros, and, for Mercedes-Benz or any other company, there should be a slice of the pie labelled *LS* for 'potential lawsuits'.

Figure 19.2 illustrates the essence of MM's intuition. While V_T is determined by the firm's cash flows, the firm's capital structure merely cuts V_T into slices. Capital structure does *not* affect the total value, V_T.

Figure 19.2 The Pie Model with Real-world Factors

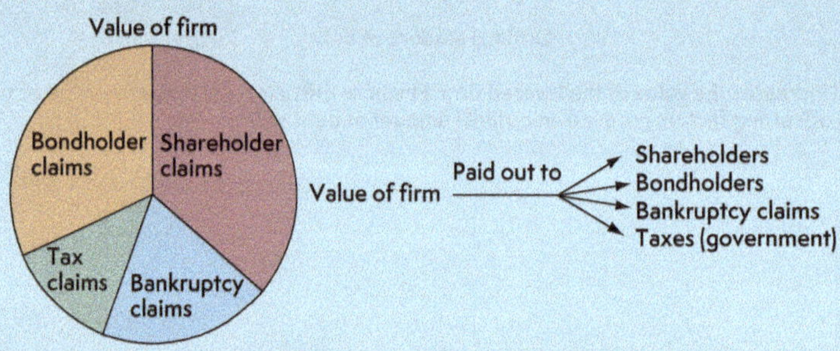

There is, however, a difference between claims such as those of shareholders and bondholders on the one hand, and those of government and potential litigants in lawsuits on the other. The first set of claims are marketable claims, while the second set are non-marketable claims. Marketable claims can be bought and sold in financial markets but non-marketable claims cannot. This distinction between marketable and non-marketable claims is important. When equity is issued, shareholders pay cash to the firm for the privilege of later receiving dividends. Similarly, bondholders pay cash to the firm for the privilege of receiving interest in the future. However, the government pays nothing to the firm for the privilege of receiving taxes in the future. Similarly, lawyers pay nothing to the firm for the privilege of receiving fees from the firm in the future.

When we speak of the *value of the firm*, we are referring just to the value of the marketable claims, V_M, and not the value of non-marketable claims, V_N. What we have shown is that capital structure does not affect the total value:

$$V_T = E + D + G + L$$
$$= V_M - V_N$$

But, as we saw, the value of the marketable claims, V_M, can change with changes in the capital structure.

By the pie theory, any increase in V_M must imply an identical decrease in V_N. Rational financial managers will choose a capital structure to maximize the value of the marketable claims, V_M. Equivalently, rational managers will work to minimize the value of the non-marketable claims, V_N. These are taxes and bankruptcy costs in the previous example, but they also include all the other non-marketable claims such as the potential lawsuits, *LS*, claim.

19.5 Signalling

Section 19.4 pointed out that the corporate leverage decision involves a trade-off between a tax subsidy and financial distress costs. This idea was graphed in Figure 19.1, where the marginal tax subsidy of debt exceeds the distress costs of debt for low levels of debt. The reverse holds for high levels of debt. The firm's capital structure is optimized where the marginal subsidy to debt equals the marginal cost.

Let us explore this idea a little more. What is the relationship between a company's profitability and its debt level? A firm with low anticipated profits is likely to take on a low level of debt. A small interest deduction is all that is needed to offset all of this firm's pre-tax profits. And too much debt would raise the firm's expected distress costs. A more successful firm would probably take on more debt. This firm could use the extra interest to reduce the taxes from its greater earnings. Being more financially secure, this firm would find its extra debt increasing the risk of bankruptcy only slightly. In other words, rational firms raise debt levels (and the concomitant interest payments) when profits are expected to increase.

How do investors react to an increase in debt? Rational investors are likely to infer a higher firm value from a higher debt level. Thus, these investors are likely to bid up a firm's share price after the firm has, say, issued debt in order to buy back equity. We say that investors view debt as a *signal* of firm value.

Now we get to the incentives of managers to fool the public. Consider a firm whose level of debt is optimal. That is, the marginal tax benefit of debt exactly equals the marginal distress costs of debt. However, imagine that the firm's manager desires to increase the firm's current share price, perhaps because he knows that many of his shareholders want to sell their equity soon. This manager might want to increase the level of debt just to make investors *think* that the firm is more valuable than it really is. If the strategy works, investors will push up the price of the shares.

This implies that firms can fool investors by taking on *some* additional leverage. Now let us ask the big question. Are there benefits to extra debt but no costs, implying that all firms will take on as much debt as possible? The answer, fortunately, is that there are costs as well. Imagine that a firm has issued extra debt just to fool the public. At some point, the market will learn that the company is not that valuable after all. At this time the share price should actually fall *below* what it would have been had the debt never been increased. Why? Because the firm's debt level is now above the optimal level. That is, the marginal tax benefit of debt is below the marginal cost of debt. Thus if the current shareholders plan to sell, say, half of their shares now and retain the other half, an increase in debt will help them on immediate sales but is likely to hurt them on later ones.

Now here is the important point. We said that, in a world where managers do not attempt to fool investors, valuable firms issue more debt than less valuable ones. It turns out that, even when managers attempt to fool investors, the more valuable firms will still want to issue more debt than the less valuable firms. That is, while all firms will increase debt levels somewhat to fool investors, the costs of extra debt prevent the less valuable firms from issuing more debt than the more valuable firms issue. Thus, investors can still treat debt level as a signal of firm value. In other words, investors can still view an announcement of debt as a positive sign for the firm.

The foregoing is a simplified example of debt signalling, and you might argue that it is too simplified. For example, perhaps the shareholders of some firms want to sell most of their equity immediately, whereas the shareholders of other firms want to sell only a little of theirs now. It is impossible to tell here whether the firms with the most debt are the most valuable or merely the ones with the most impatient shareholders. Because other objections can be brought up as well, signalling theory is best validated by empirical evidence. And, fortunately, the empirical evidence tends to support the theory.

For example, consider the evidence concerning exchange offers. Firms often change their debt levels through exchange offers, of which there are two types. The first type of offer allows shareholders to exchange some of their equity for debt, thereby increasing leverage. The second type allows bondholders to exchange some of their debt for equity, decreasing leverage. Figure 19.3 shows the share price behaviour of firms that change their proportions of debt and equity via exchange offers. The solid line in the figure indicates that share prices rise substantially on the date when an exchange offering increasing leverage is announced. (This date is referred to as date 0 in the figure.) Conversely, the dotted line in the figure indicates that the share price falls substantially when an offer decreasing leverage is announced.

The market infers from an increase in debt that the firm is better off, leading to a share price rise. Conversely, the market infers the reverse from a decrease in debt, implying a share price fall. Thus, we say that managers signal information when they change leverage.

Bank Debt

A subset of all debt issues is private bank loans. New bank debt not only offers assurance of strong firm prospects, but also a certification of borrowing quality. Banks continually monitor borrower creditworthiness and undertake advanced credit screening for potential loans. The stronger requirements of bank loans compound the general positive news associated with debt issues, and create a strong positive signal on the quality of the borrowing firm. Marshall et al. (2019) investigate the market reaction to UK bank debt announcements and confirm this signalling effect, but find evidence that the effect was weaker after the 2008 financial crisis.

Figure 19.3 Equity Returns at the Time of Announcements of Exchange Offers

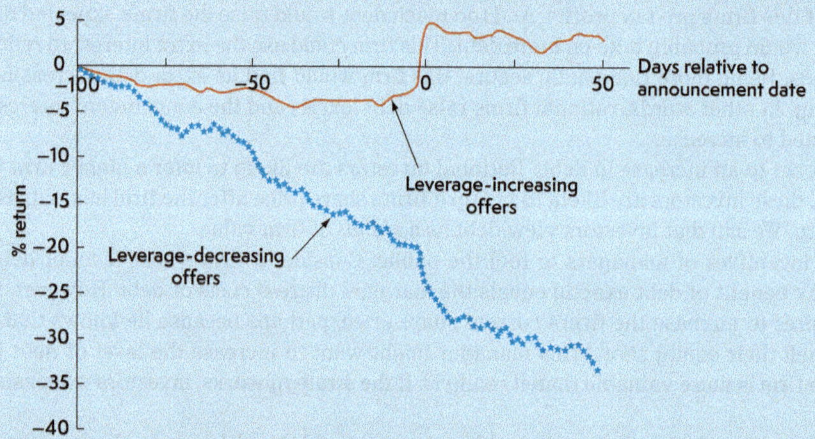

Exchange offers change the debt–equity ratios of firms. The graph shows that share prices increase for firms whose exchange offers increase leverage. Conversely, share prices decrease for firms whose offers decrease leverage.

Source: Shah (1994).

19.6 Shirking, Perquisites and Bad Investments: A Note on Agency Cost of Equity

Chapter 2 Page 24

Section 19.4 introduced the static trade-off model, where a rise in debt increases both the tax shield and the costs of distress. We now extend the trade-off model by considering an important agency cost of equity (agency costs are first introduced in Chapter 2, Section 2.2). A discussion of this cost of equity is contained in a well-known quote from Adam Smith:

> *The directors of such [joint-stock] companies, however, being the managers of other people's money than of their own, it cannot well be expected that they should watch over it with the same anxious vigilance with which the partners in a private copartnery frequently watch over their own. Like the stewards of a rich man, they are apt to consider attention to small matters as not for their master's honor, and very easily give themselves a dispensation from having it. Negligence and profusion, therefore, must always prevail, more or less, in the management of the affairs of such a company.*[5]

This elegant prose can be restated using more modern vocabulary. An individual will work harder for a firm if she is one of its owners than if she is just an employee. In addition, the individual will work harder if she owns a large percentage of the company than if she owns a small percentage. This idea has an important implication for capital structure, which we illustrate with the following example.

Example 19.2

Agency Costs

Ms Yildiz is an owner-entrepreneur running a computer services firm worth £1 million. She currently owns 100 per cent of the firm. Because of the need to expand, she must raise another £2 million. She can either issue £2 million of debt at 12 per cent interest or issue £2 million in equity. The cash flows under the two alternatives are presented here:

	Debt Issue				Equity Issue			
Work Intensity	Cash Flow (£)	Interest (£)	Cash Flow to Equity (£)	Cash Flow to Ms Yildiz (100% of Equity) (£)	Cash Flow (£)	Interest (£)	Cash Flow to Equity (£)	Cash Flow to Ms Yildiz (33⅓% of equity) (£)
6-hour days	300,000	240,000	60,000	60,000	300,000	0	300,000	100,000
10-hour days	400,000	240,000	160,000	160,000	400,000	0	400,000	133,333

Like any entrepreneur, Ms Yildiz can choose the degree of intensity with which she works. In our example, she can work either a 6- or a 10-hour day. With the debt issue, the extra work brings her £100,000 (= £160,000 – £60,000) more income. However, let us assume that with an equity issue she retains only a one-third interest in the equity. Here, the extra work brings her merely £33,333 (= £133,333 – £100,000). Being human, she is likely to work harder if she issues debt. In other words, she has more incentive to *shirk* if she issues equity.

In addition, she is likely to obtain more *perquisites* (a big office, a company car, more expense account meals) if she issues equity. If she is a one-third shareholder, two-thirds of these costs are paid for by the other shareholders. If she is the sole owner, any additional perquisites reduce her equity stake alone.

Finally, she is more likely to take on capital budgeting projects with negative net present values. It might seem surprising that a manager with any equity interest at all would take on negative NPV projects – the share price would clearly fall here. However, managerial salaries generally rise with firm size, providing managers with an incentive to accept some unprofitable projects after all the profitable ones have been taken on. That is, when an unprofitable project is accepted, the loss in share value to a manager with only a small equity interest may be less than the increase in salary. In fact, it is our opinion that losses from accepting bad projects are far greater than losses from either shirking or excessive perquisites. Hugely unprofitable projects have bankrupted whole firms, something that even the largest expense account is unlikely to do.

Thus, as the firm issues more equity, our entrepreneur is likely to increase leisure time, work-related perquisites and unprofitable investments. These three items are called *agency costs* because managers of the firm are agents of the shareholders.[6]

This example is quite applicable to a small company considering a large equity offering. Because a manager-owner will greatly dilute his or her share of the total equity in this case, a significant drop in work intensity or a significant increase in fringe benefits is possible. However, the example may be less applicable for a large corporation with many shareholders. For example, consider a large company such as ICI issuing shares for the umpteenth time. The typical manager there already has such a small percentage stake in the firm that any temptation for negligence has probably been experienced before. An additional offering cannot be expected to increase this temptation.

Who bears the burden of these agency costs? Shareholders do not bear these costs as long as they invest with their eyes open. Knowing that Ms Yildiz may work shorter hours, they will pay only a low price for the equity. Thus, it is the owner who is hurt by agency costs. However, Ms Yildiz can protect herself to some extent. Just as shareholders reduce bankruptcy costs through protective covenants, an owner may allow monitoring by new shareholders. However, though proper reporting and surveillance may reduce the agency costs of equity, these techniques are unlikely to eliminate them.

It is commonly suggested that leveraged buyouts (LBOs) significantly reduce these costs of equity. In an LBO, a purchaser (usually a team of existing management) buys out the shareholders at a price above the current market. In other words, the company goes private: the equity is placed in the hands of only a few people. Because the managers now own a substantial chunk of the business, they are likely to work harder than when they were simply hired hands.

Effect of Agency Costs of Equity on Debt–Equity Financing

The preceding discussion of the agency costs of equity should be viewed as an extension of the static trade-off model. That is, we stated in Section 19.4 that the change in the value of the firm when debt is substituted for equity is the difference between (1) the tax shield on debt and (2) the increase in the costs of financial distress (including the agency costs of debt). Now the change in the value of the firm is (1) the tax shield on debt, plus

(2) the reduction in the agency costs of equity, minus (3) the increase in the costs of financial distress (including the agency costs of debt). The optimal debt–equity ratio would be higher in a world with agency costs of equity than in a world without these costs. However, because costs of financial distress are so significant, the costs of equity do not imply 100 per cent debt financing.

Free Cash Flow

Any reader or viewer of murder mysteries knows that a criminal must have both motive and opportunity. The discussion thus far has been about motive. Managers with only a small ownership interest have an incentive for wasteful behaviour. For example, they bear only a small portion of the costs of, say, excessive expense accounts, but reap all of the benefits.

Now let us talk about opportunity. A manager can pad his expense account only if the firm has the cash flow to cover it. Thus, we might expect to see more wasteful activity in a firm with a capacity to generate large cash flows than in one with a capacity to generate only small cash flows. This simple idea, which is formally called the *free cash flow hypothesis,*[7] is backed by a fair amount of empirical research. One frequently cited paper found that firms with high free cash flow are more likely to make bad acquisitions than firms with low free cash flow (Lang et al., 1989).

The hypothesis has important implications for capital structure. Since dividends leave the firm, they reduce free cash flow. Thus, according to the free cash flow hypothesis, an increase in dividends should benefit the shareholders by reducing the ability of managers to pursue wasteful activities. Furthermore, since interest and principal also leave the firm, debt reduces free cash flow as well. In fact, interest and principal should have a greater effect than dividends have on the free-spending ways of managers, because bankruptcy will occur if the firm is unable to make future debt payments. By contrast, a future dividend reduction will cause fewer problems to the managers, since the firm has no legal obligation to pay dividends. Because of this, the free cash flow hypothesis argues that a shift from equity to debt will boost firm value.

In summary, the free cash flow hypothesis provides still another reason for firms to issue debt. We previously discussed the cost of equity; new equity dilutes the holdings of managers with equity interests, increasing their *motive* to waste corporate resources. We now state that debt reduces free cash flow, because the firm must make interest and principal payments. The free cash flow hypothesis implies that debt reduces the *opportunity* for managers to waste resources.

19.7 The Pecking Order Theory

Although the trade-off theory has dominated corporate finance circles for a long time, attention has also been paid to the *pecking order theory.*[8] To understand this view of the world, let us put ourselves in the position of a corporate finance manager whose firm needs new capital. The manager faces a choice between issuing debt and issuing equity. Previously, we evaluated the choice in terms of tax benefits, distress costs and agency costs. However, there is one consideration that we have so far neglected: timing.

Imagine the manager saying:

> *I want to issue equity in one situation only – when it is overvalued. If the equity of my firm is selling at £50 per share, but I think that it is actually worth £60, I will not issue equity. I would be giving new shareholders a gift because they would receive equity worth £60 but would only have to pay £50 for it. More important, my current shareholders would be upset because the firm would be receiving £50 in cash but giving away something worth £60. So if I believe that my equity is undervalued, I would issue bonds. Bonds, particularly those with little or no risk of default, are likely to be priced correctly. Their value is determined primarily by the market-wide interest rate, a variable that is publicly known.*
>
> *But suppose our equity is selling at £70. Now I'd like to issue equity. If I can get some fool to buy our shares for £70 while the equity is really worth only £60, I will be making £10 for our current shareholders.*

Although this may strike you as a cynical view, it seems to square well with reality. Managers, for example, seem more willing to issue equity after the price of their shares has risen than after their shares have fallen in price. So timing might be an important motive in equity issuance, perhaps even more important than the motives in the trade-off model. After all, the firm in the preceding example *immediately* makes £10 by properly timing the issuance of equity. £10 worth of agency costs and bankruptcy cost reduction might take many years to realize.

The key that makes the example work is *asymmetric information:* the manager must know more about his firm's prospects than does the typical investor. If the manager's estimate of the true worth of the company is no better than the estimate of a typical investor, any attempts by the manager to time the market will fail. This assumption of asymmetry is quite plausible. Managers should know more about their company than do outsiders because managers work at the company every day. (One caveat is that some managers are perpetually optimistic about their firm, blurring good judgement.)

But we are not done with this example yet; we must consider the investor. Imagine an investor saying:

> *I make investments carefully because they involve my hard-earned money. However, even with all the time I put into studying shares, I can't possibly know what the managers themselves know. After all, I've got a day job to be concerned with. So I watch what the managers do. If a firm issues equity, the firm was probably overvalued beforehand. If a firm issues debt, it was probably undervalued.*

When we look at both issuers and investors, we see a kind of poker game, with each side trying to outwit the other. What should the issuing firm do in this poker game? Clearly, the firm should issue debt if the equity is undervalued. But what if the equity is overvalued? Here it gets tricky because a first thought is that the firm should issue equity. However, if a firm issues equity, investors will infer the shares are overvalued. They will not buy them until the share price has fallen enough to eliminate any advantage from equity issuance. In fact, it can be shown that only the most overvalued firms have any incentive to issue equity. Should even a moderately overpriced firm issue equity, investors will infer that this firm is among the *most* overpriced, causing the shares to fall more than is deserved. Thus, the end result is that virtually no one will issue equity.[9]

This result that essentially all firms should issue debt is clearly an extreme one. It is as extreme as (1) the Modigliani–Miller (MM) result that, in a world without taxes, firms are indifferent to capital structure, and (2) the MM result that, in a world of corporate taxes but no financial distress costs, all firms should be 100 per cent debt-financed. Perhaps we in finance have a penchant for extreme models!

But just as we can temper MM's conclusions by combining financial distress costs with corporate taxes, we can temper those of the pure pecking order theory. This pure version assumes that timing is the financial manager's only consideration. In reality, a manager must consider taxes, financial distress costs and agency costs as well. Thus, a firm may issue debt only up to a point. If financial distress becomes a real possibility beyond that point, the firm may issue equity instead.

Rules of the Pecking Order

The previous discussion presented the basic ideas behind the pecking order theory. What are the practical implications of the theory for financial managers? The theory provides the following two rules for the real world.

Rule 1: Use Internal Financing

For expository purposes, we have oversimplified by comparing equity to *riskless* debt. Managers cannot use special knowledge of their firm to determine if this type of debt is mispriced because the price of riskless debt is determined solely by the marketwide interest rate. However, in reality, corporate debt has the possibility of default. Thus, just as managers tend to issue equity when they think it is overvalued, managers also tend to issue debt when they think it is overvalued.

When would managers view their debt as overvalued? Probably in the same situations when they think their equity is overvalued. For instance, if the public thinks that the firm's prospects are rosy but the managers see trouble ahead, these managers would view their debt – as well as their equity – as being overvalued. That is, the public might see the debt as nearly risk-free, whereas the managers see a strong possibility of default.

Thus, investors are likely to price a debt issue with the same scepticism that they have when pricing an equity issue. The way managers get out of this box is to finance projects out of retained earnings. You do not have to worry about investor scepticism if you can avoid going to investors in the first place. So the first rule of the pecking order is this:

Use internal financing.

Rule 2: Issue Safe Securities First

Although investors fear mispricing of both debt and equity, the fear is much greater for equity. Corporate debt still has relatively little risk compared to equity because, if financial distress is avoided, investors receive a fixed return. Thus, the pecking order theory implies that if outside financing is required, debt should be issued before equity. Only when the firm's debt capacity is reached should the firm consider equity.

Of course, there are many types of debt. For example, because convertible debt is more risky than straight debt, the pecking order theory implies that managers should issue straight debt before issuing convertibles. So, the second rule of pecking order theory is this:

Issue the safest securities first.

Implications

A number of implications associated with the pecking order theory are at odds with those of the trade-off theory.

- *There is no target amount of leverage.* According to the trade-off model, each firm balances the benefits of debt, such as the tax shield, with the costs of debt, such as distress costs. The optimal amount of leverage occurs where the marginal benefit of debt equals the marginal cost of debt.
  By contrast, the pecking order theory does not imply a target amount of leverage. Rather, each firm chooses its leverage ratio based on financing needs. Firms first fund projects out of retained earnings. This should lower the percentage of debt in the capital structure because profitable, internally funded projects raise both the book value and the market value of equity. Additional projects are funded with debt, clearly raising the debt level. However, at some point the debt capacity of the firm may be exhausted, giving way to equity issuance. Thus, the amount of leverage is determined by the happenstance of available projects. Firms do not pursue a target ratio of debt to equity.
- *Profitable firms use less debt.* Profitable firms generate cash internally, implying less need for outside financing. Because firms desiring outside capital turn to debt first, profitable firms end up relying on less debt. The trade-off model does not have this implication. Here the greater cash flow of more profitable firms creates greater debt capacity. These firms will use that debt capacity to capture the tax shield and the other benefits of leverage.
- *Companies like financial slack.* The pecking order theory is based on the difficulties of obtaining financing at a reasonable cost. A sceptical investing public thinks an equity is overvalued if the managers try to issue more of it, thereby leading to a share price decline. Because this happens with bonds only to a lesser extent, managers rely first on bond financing. However, firms can only issue so much debt before encountering the potential costs of financial distress.

Wouldn't it be easier to have the cash ahead of time? This is the idea behind *financial slack.* Because firms know that they will have to fund profitable projects at various times in the future, they accumulate cash today. They are then not forced to go to the capital markets when a project comes up. However, there is a limit to the amount of cash a firm will want to accumulate. As mentioned earlier in this chapter, in Section 19.6, too much free cash may tempt managers to pursue wasteful activities.

Example 19.3

Debt or Equity?

TBS Heets NV is a publicly listed Dutch firm looking to raise €100 million to fund new expansion into the UK. The company's share price is €2.47 and it must decide among three options:

1. Use its existing cash reserves.
2. Issue a five-year bond with a coupon rate of 7 per cent. The firm's management believes the appropriate yield to maturity of the bond should be 5 per cent.
3. Issue equity with the issue price discounted by 19 per cent.

We now examine the costs of each option.

1. *Existing cash reserves:* If the company has €100 million in cash and this is used for the project, the cost will be €100 million.
2. *Debt issue:* The present value of the cost of a €100 million five-year 7 per coupon bond with a yield to maturity is is €108.66 million (check this yourself). This is €8.66 million more costly than using cash.
3. *Equity issue:* The issue price is the existing price of €2.47 discounted by 19 per cent, which is equal to €2.00. The number of shares to be issued is (€100 million/€2.00=) 50 million. The total cost to TBS Heets of the equity issue is (50 million shares × €2.47=) €123.5 million. This is €23.5 million more costly than using cash.

The pecking order suggests the following ranking: internal funds, then debt and, finally, equity.

19.8 Growth and the Debt–Equity Ratio

Although the trade-off between the tax shield and bankruptcy costs (as illustrated in Figure 19.1) is often viewed as the 'standard model' of capital structure, it has its critics. For example, some point out that bankruptcy costs in the real world appear to be much smaller than the tax subsidy. Thus, the model implies that the optimal debt/value ratio should be near 100 per cent, an implication at odds with reality.[10]

Perhaps the pecking order theory is more consistent with the real world here. That is, firms are likely to have more equity in their capital structure than implied by the static trade-off theory because internal financing is preferred to external financing.

Chapter 5 Page 116

There is another approach that implies significant equity financing, even in a world with low bankruptcy costs. This idea, developed by Berens and Cuny (1995), argues that equity financing follows from growth (the effect of growth on equity valuation is discussed in Chapter 5, Section 5.5). To explain the idea, we first consider an example of a no-growth firm. Next, we examine the effect of growth on firm leverage.

No Growth

Imagine a world of perfect certainty[11] where a firm has annual earnings before interest and taxes (EBIT) of €100. In addition, the firm has issued €1,000 of debt at an interest rate of 10 per cent, implying interest payments of €100 per year. Here are the cash flows to the firm:

	Data			
	1 (€)	2 (€)	3 (€)	4 . . . (€)
Earnings before interest and taxes (EBIT)	100	100	100	100 . . .
Interest	−100	−100	−100	−100 . . .
Taxable income	0	0	0	0

The firm has issued just enough debt so that all EBIT are paid out as interest. Because interest is tax deductible, the firm pays no taxes. In this example, the equity is worthless because shareholders receive no cash flows. Since debt is worth €1,000, the firm is also valued at €1,000. Therefore the debt-to-value ratio is 100 per cent (= €1,000/€1,000).

Had the firm issued less than €1,000 of debt, the corporation would have positive taxable income and, consequently, would have ended up paying some taxes. Had the firm issued more than €1,000 of debt, interest would have exceeded EBIT, causing default. Consequently, the optimal debt-to-value ratio is 100 per cent.

Growth

Now imagine another firm where EBIT are also €100 at date 1 but are growing at 5 per cent per year.[12] To eliminate taxes, this firm also wants to issue enough debt so that interest equals EBIT. Because EBIT are growing at 5 per cent per year, interest must also grow at this rate. This is achieved by increasing debt by 5 per cent per year.[13] The debt, EBIT, interest and taxable income levels are these:

	Data				
	0 (€)	1 (€)	2 (€)	3 (€)	4 . . . (€)
Debt	1,000	1,050	1,102.50	1,157.63 . . .	
New debt issued		50	52.50	55.13 . . .	
EBIT		100	105	110.25	115.76 . . .
Interest		−100	−105	−110.25	−115.76 . . .
Taxable income		0	0	0	0

Note that interest on a particular date is always 10 per cent of the debt on the previous date. Debt is set so that interest is exactly equal to EBIT. As in the no-growth case, the levered firm has the maximum amount of debt at each date. Default would occur if interest payments were increased.

Because growth is 5 per cent per year, the value of the firm is:[14]

$$V_{\text{Firm}} = \frac{€100}{0.10 - 0.05} = €2{,}000$$

The equity at date 0 is the difference between the value of the firm at that time, €2,000 and the debt of €1,000. Hence, equity must be equal to €1,000,[15] implying a debt-to-value ratio of 50 per cent (= €1,000/€2,000). Note the important difference between the no-growth and the growth example. The no-growth example has no equity; the value of the firm is simply the value of the debt. With growth, there is equity as well as debt.

We can also value the equity in another way. It may appear at first glance that the shareholders receive nothing because the EBIT are paid out as interest each year. However, the new debt issued each year can be paid as a dividend to the shareholders. Because the new debt is €50 at date 1 and grows at 5 per cent per year, the value of the shareholders' interest is:

$$\frac{€50}{0.10 - 0.05} = €1{,}000$$

which is the same number that we obtained in the previous paragraph.

As we mentioned earlier, any further increase in debt above €1,000 at date 0 would lower the value of the firm in a world with bankruptcy costs. Thus, with growth, the optimal amount of debt is less than 100 per cent. Note, however, that bankruptcy costs need not be as large as the tax subsidy. In fact, even with infinitesimally small bankruptcy costs, firm value would decline if promised interest rose above €100 in the first year. The key to this example is that *today's* interest is set equal to *today's* income. Although the introduction of future growth opportunities increases firm value, it does not increase the current level of debt needed to shield today's income from today's taxes. Because equity is the difference between firm value and debt, growth increases the value of equity.

The preceding example captures an essential feature of the real world: growth. The same conclusion is reached in a world of inflation but with no growth opportunities. Thus, the result of this section, that 100 per cent debt financing is suboptimal, holds whether inflation or growth opportunities are present. Furthermore, high-growth firms should have lower debt ratios than low-growth firms. Most firms have growth opportunities and inflation has been with us for most of this and the previous centuries, so this section's example is based on realistic assumptions.[16]

19.9 Market Timing Theory

In recent years, a new view of capital structure has come to the fore that believes leverage ratios have nothing to do with a pecking order or optimal capital structure. The view, which was originally put forward by Baker and Wurgler (2002), suggests that differentials between market and book valuations drive capital structure levels in firms. For example, if a firm requires funding during a period when its market value to book value ratio is high, it is more likely to raise equity. Similarly, in low market to book value periods, debt is likely to be the funding vehicle of choice. This has a permanent effect on capital structures that have nothing to do with bankruptcy costs or pecking orders.

The pecking order theory also puts forward a timing motivation for funding choices. However, this theory argues that asymmetric information between managers and outside shareholders drives managers to always issue debt before equity, whenever it is possible to do so. Market timing theory disagrees and states that asymmetric information is irrelevant. Managers simply take advantage of market conditions when they decide to raise capital.

An analogous theoretical argument is made by Admati et al. (2018), who argue that firms with debt are reluctant to reduce leverage, even if this would increase the value of the firm. Similarly, firms will increase leverage, even if it reduces firm value. Admati and colleagues call this the *leverage ratchet effect*, and show that the decisions to adjust leverage are highly influenced by a firm's debt history rather than purely by considerations of efficiency or value maximization. Although this is not market timing, the main hypothesis of Admati et al. is that the only real driver of capital structure is past decisions rather than a trade-off or a pecking order.

Capital structure is one area (of many!) in which finance academics are divided, and there are supporters in each of the three camps (trade-off, pecking order and market timing). So how does the empirical evidence stack up? Fama and French (2002) showed that leverage ratios took too long to move back to mean levels after markets received a shock. This would indicate that, over the short term at least, there is no target capital structure. Similarly, Welch (2003) finds that companies tend to issue shares when market valuations are high. In contrast, Kayhan and Titman (2007) show that, over the longer term, capital structures do move towards a target level. Lemmon and Zender (2010) show that profitable and low leverage firms accumulate debt capacity for potential future investment needs. Finally, Mahajan and Tartaroglu (2008) consider market timing theory in the context of G7 countries and find that, although there is evidence of market timing, it is only a short-term phenomenon and washes out within five years of new equity issues.

19.10 How Firms Establish Capital Structure

The theories of capital structure are among the most elegant and sophisticated in the field of finance. Financial economists should (and do!) pat themselves on the back for contributions in this area. However, the practical applications of the theories are less than fully satisfying. Consider that our work on net present value produced an *exact* formula for evaluating projects. Prescriptions for capital structure under either the trade-off model, the pecking order theory or market timing are vague by comparison. No exact formula is available for evaluating the optimal debt–equity ratio. Because of this, we turn to evidence from the real world.

The following empirical regularities are worthwhile to consider when formulating capital structure policy.

- *Most corporations have low debt–asset ratios.* How much debt is used in the real world? The average debt ratio is never greater than 100 per cent. Figure 19.4 shows the average 2023 debt-to-asset ratios for European

Figure 19.4 Average 2023 Debt-to-asset Ratios for European Firms by Industry Sector

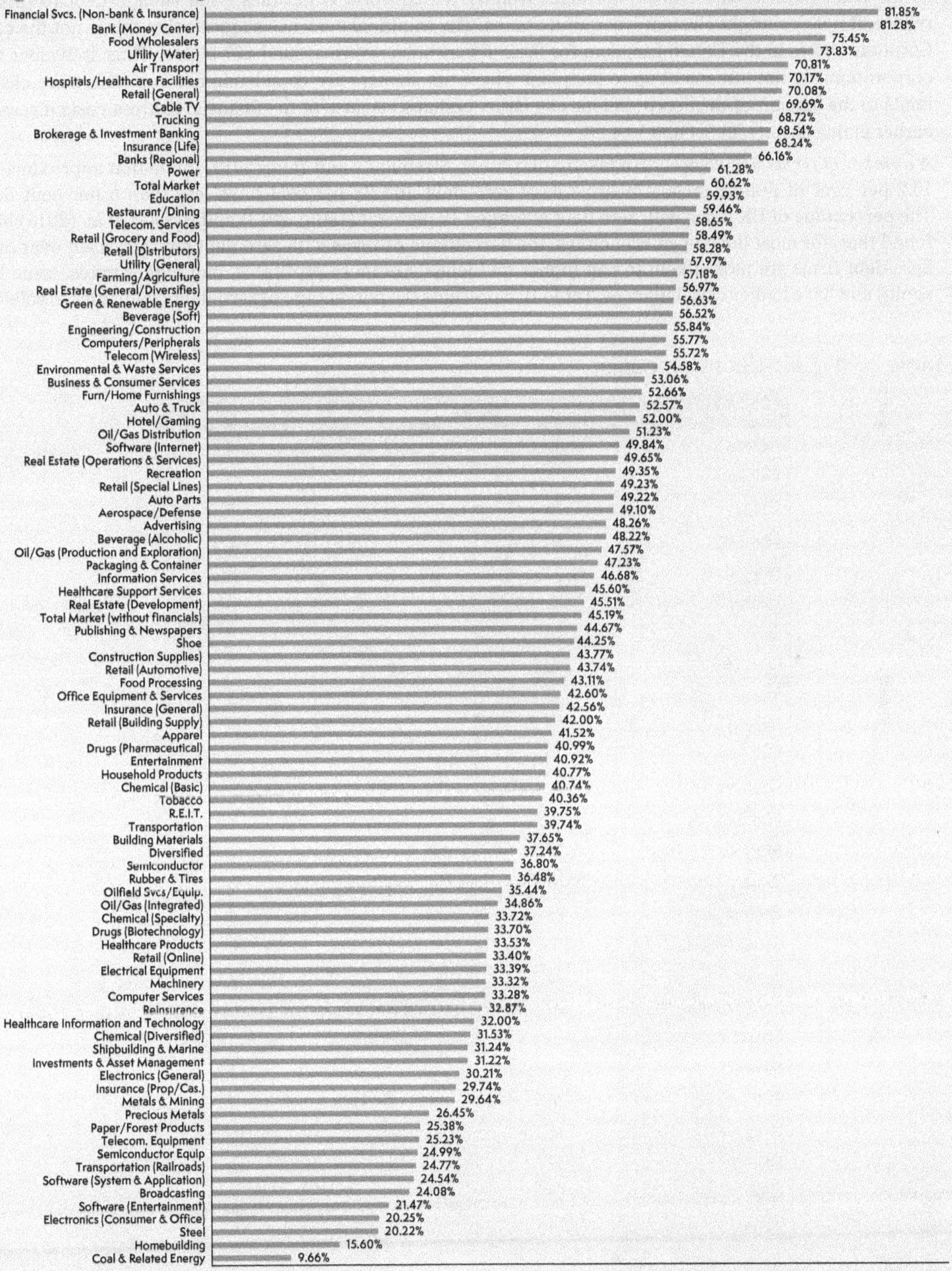

Source: Data taken from Damodaran Online

firms by industry sector. There are considerable inter-industry differences in debt ratios that persist over time. Debt–asset ratios tend to be quite low in high-growth industries with ample future investment opportunities, such as the software and electronics industries. This is true even when the need for external financing is great. Industries with large investments in tangible assets, such as utilities, tend to have high leverage.

Should we view these ratios as being high or low? Because academics generally see corporate tax reduction as the chief motivation for debt, we might wonder if real-world companies issue enough debt to greatly reduce, if not downright eliminate, corporate taxes. The empirical evidence suggests that this is not the case. Corporate taxes in the United Kingdom for 2022, for instance, were around £67 billion. Thus, it is clear that corporations do not issue debt up to the point where tax shelters are completely used up. There are clearly limits to the amount of debt corporations can issue, perhaps because of the financial distress costs discussed earlier in this chapter, in Section 19.4.

- *A number of firms use no debt.* In a fascinating study, Strebulaev and Yang (2013) found that approximately 10.2 per cent of non-financial US firms have zero debt and 22 per cent have less than 5 per cent debt. The percentage of UK firms with zero debt averaged 19 per cent (Dang, 2013) and Bessler et al. (2013) have found that, for most developed economies, the percentage of firms with zero debt has increased over time. Zero-debt firms are more likely to pay higher dividends, are more profitable, pay higher taxes, issue less equity and have higher cash balances. Table 19.3 presents the percentage of zero-debt companies in selected

Table 19.3 Zero-debt Companies

Country	Small Firms	Medium Firms	Large Firms
Austria	19	5	1
Belgium	7	5	0
China	16	8	5
Denmark	20	2	2
Finland	12	6	0
France	5	1	0
Germany	26	9	3
Greece	10	6	3
India	8	4	3
Ireland	33	10	2
Italy	12	3	0
Malaysia	12	10	4
Netherlands	20	14	4
Norway	27	11	2
Oman	20	19	0
Poland	25	11	4
Saudi Arabia	76	35	28
Singapore	13	7	2
South Africa	20	11	6
Spain	6	3	1
Sweden	34	11	3
Switzerland	24	7	2
UAE	36	27	16
UK	32	12	3
USA	21	18	7
Total	24	11	5

Source: Adapted from El Ghoul et al. (2017), Table 3.

countries as reported by El Ghoul et al. (2017), separated by size. Smaller firms are more likely to have no debt, primarily because of a lack of collateral. There is also variation across countries. Of particular note are Saudi Arabia, Oman and the UAE where there is a large population of Islamic firms, where debt is forbidden.

- *Many corporations employ target debt–equity ratios.* Brounen et al. (2006) asked 313 chief financial officers (CFOs) of European firms whether they use target debt–equity ratios. The great majority of firms across countries use targets, though the strictness of the targets varies across companies. A notable exception to this is France, where most firms do not pursue a target debt ratio. Even in the UK, nearly half of all firms do not consider a target debt ratio to be important.

How should companies establish target debt–equity ratios? While there is no mathematical formula for establishing a target ratio, we present three important factors affecting the ratio:

1 *Taxes:* As we pointed out earlier, firms can deduct interest for tax purposes only to the extent of their profits before interest. Thus, highly profitable firms are more likely to have larger target ratios than less profitable firms.[17]

2 *Types of assets:* Financial distress is costly, with or without formal bankruptcy proceedings. The costs of financial distress depend on the types of assets that the firm has. If a firm has a large investment in land, buildings and other tangible assets, say, it will have smaller costs of financial distress than a firm with a large investment in research and development. Research and development typically has less resale value than land. Thus, most of its value disappears in financial distress. Therefore, firms with large investments in tangible assets are likely to have higher target debt–equity ratios than firms with large investments in research and development.

3 *Uncertainty of operating income:* Firms with uncertain operating income have a high probability of experiencing financial distress, even without debt. Thus, these firms must finance mostly with equity. Pharmaceutical firms, for example, have uncertain operating income because no one can predict whether today's research will generate new, profitable drugs. Consequently, these firms issue little debt. By contrast, the operating income of firms in regulated industries, such as utilities, generally has low volatility. Relative to other industries, utilities use a great deal of debt.

4 *Peer firms influence capital structures.* Leary and Roberts (2014) and Grieser et al. (2022) found that peer firms play an important role in determining a company's capital structures. Peer effects dominated other factors, and smaller, less successful firms were very sensitive to larger, more successful peer capital structure choice. However, the opposite was not the case.

5 *Capital structures are unstable over time.* Average capital structures change markedly over time. Many firms have high and low leverage at different times, and only a very few consistently keep debt/asset ratios above 0.5. The only situation where capital structure appears stable is for low leverage firms. The graphs in Figure 19.5 show the time series of capital structures for a number of large multinational companies. As can be seen, they vary massively over time. Some of this variation may be driven by changes in share price because the total assets figure in the denominator of the ratios in Figure 19.5 uses market value, which is determined by the share price.

Figure 19.5 Capital Structures

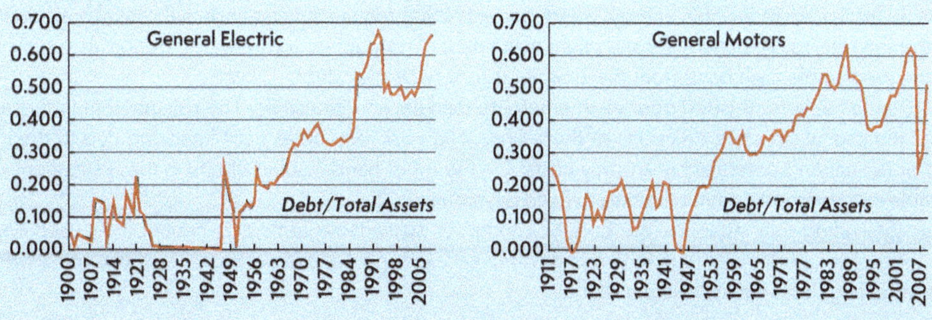

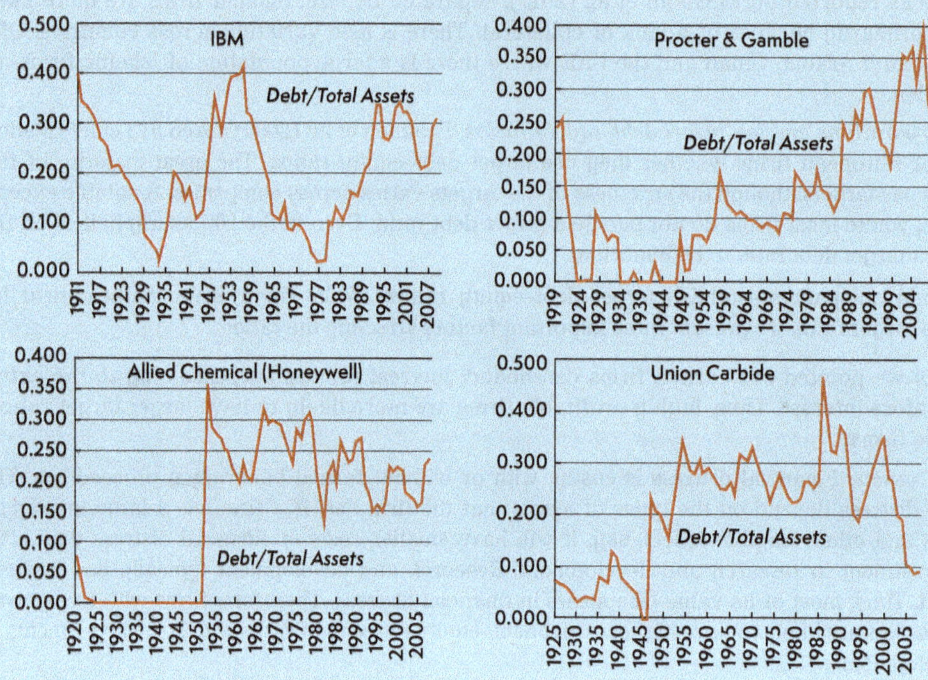

Source: DeAngelo and Roll (2015), Appendix A.

One final note is in order. Because no formula supports them, the preceding points may seem too nebulous to assist financial decision-making. Instead, many real-world firms simply base their capital structure decisions on industry averages. This may strike some as a cowardly approach, but it at least keeps firms from deviating far from accepted practice. After all, the existing firms in any industry are the survivors. Therefore we should pay at least some attention to their decisions.

Sustainability in Action 19.1

Sustainability and Capital Structure

Sustainable firms have unique issues to consider when it comes to deciding on their capital structure. As covered in this and the previous chapter, capital structure decisions influence the risk profile, cost of capital and, ultimately, the value of a firm. For sustainable firms, these decisions will also be influenced by a unique blend of factors, given their commitment to environmental, social and governance (ESG) principles.

First, the nature of the industry in which sustainable firms operate plays a crucial role. Many sustainable firms are involved in industries like renewable energy, where projects often require substantial initial capital outlay but provide stable long-term returns. This characteristic might make debt a more attractive financing option, as it allows firms to leverage the predictable cash flows from these projects to service their debt.

Second, sustainable firms often operate in emerging markets and industries. The risk inherent in these markets can impact the capital structure decisions of these firms. High risk may deter debt financing due to the increased likelihood of default and potential bankruptcy costs. On the other hand, issuing equity in these situations might be more suitable as it does not commit the firm to fixed payments.

Finally, ESG rating can influence the cost of capital for sustainable firms and hence, their capital structure. Research suggests that firms with high ESG ratings often access capital at a lower cost than those with lower ratings, potentially affecting debt–equity ratio decisions.

Summary and Conclusions

1 We mentioned in the previous chapter that, according to theory, firms should create all-debt capital structures under corporate taxation. Because firms generally employ moderate amounts of debt in the real world, the theory must have been missing something at that point. We stated in this chapter that costs of financial distress cause firms to restrain their issuance of debt. These costs are of two types: direct and indirect. Lawyers' and accountants' fees during the bankruptcy process are examples of direct costs. We mentioned four examples of indirect costs:

(a) Impaired ability to conduct business

(b) Incentive to take on risky projects

(c) Incentive towards underinvestment

(d) Distribution of funds to shareholders prior to bankruptcy.

2 Because financial distress costs are substantial and the shareholders ultimately bear them, firms have an incentive to reduce costs. Protective covenants and debt consolidation are two common cost-reduction techniques.

3 Because costs of financial distress can be reduced but not eliminated, firms will not finance entirely with debt. Figure 19.1 illustrates the relationship between firm value and debt. In the figure, firms select the debt–equity ratio at which firm value is maximized.

4 Signalling theory argues that profitable firms are likely to increase their leverage because the extra interest payments will offset some of the pre-tax profits. Rational shareholders will infer higher firm value from a higher debt level. Thus investors view debt as a signal of firm value.

5 Managers owning a small proportion of a firm's equity can be expected to work less, maintain more lavish expense accounts and accept more pet projects with negative NPVs than managers owning a large proportion of equity. Because new issues of equity dilute a manager's percentage interest in the firm, such agency costs are likely to increase when a firm's growth is financed through new equity rather than through new debt.

6 The pecking order theory implies that managers prefer internal to external financing. If external financing is required, managers tend to choose the safest securities, such as debt. Firms may accumulate slack to avoid external equity.

7 The market timing theory suggests that there is no pecking order or trade-off of capital structure choices. Observed debt ratios are simply a function of past market to book valuations and the timing of funding requirements. Firms will have more equity if they needed funding when market to book valuations were high. Conversely, if financing was required during low market to book periods, debt will tend to dominate.

8 Berens and Cuny (1995) argue that significant equity financing can be explained by real growth and inflation, even in a world of low bankruptcy costs.

9 Debt–equity ratios vary across industries. We present three factors determining the target debt–equity ratio:

(a) *Taxes:* Firms with high taxable income should rely more on debt than firms with low taxable income.

(b) *Types of assets:* Firms with a high percentage of intangible assets, such as research and development, should have low debt. Firms with primarily tangible assets should have higher debt.

(c) *Uncertainty of operating income:* Firms with high uncertainty of operating income should rely mostly on equity.

Questions and Problems

CONCEPT

1 **Costs of Financial Distress** What are the direct and indirect costs of bankruptcy? Briefly explain each and provide a practical example of these costs. Use a real-life example to illustrate the direct and indirect costs of bankruptcy.

2 **Description of Financial Distress Costs** Are managers liable to act differently when their firm is in financial distress? Explain your answer using practical examples.

3 **Rationale for the Tax Benefits of Debt** Despite the significant costs of high leverage, tax systems around the world have a built-in debt bias. Why do you think this is?

4 **Trade-off Theory** Explain what is meant by the trade-off theory of capital structure choice. Your answer should discuss the main costs and benefits of debt within this model and its empirical limitations.

5 **Signalling** Explain how managers can signal to the market the value of their firm through their capital structure decisions. Do you think this is an effective strategy?

6 **Agency Costs of Equity** What are the sources of agency costs of equity?

7 **Pecking Order Theory** Explain what is meant by the pecking order theory and how it relates to observed capital structures of companies. Where does a deeply discounted equity rights issue fit into the pecking order of financing choices? Explain your answer.

8 **Growth and the Debt–Equity Ratio** How does growth affect the desired debt to equity ratio of a company? Explain the impact of growth opportunities in the context of the static trade-off theory and pecking order theory of capital structure.

9 **Market Timing Theory** Is the market timing theory of financing choices consistent with the pecking order theory or trade-off theory? Explain your answer.

10 **Observed Capital Structures** In all countries, it appears that some firms have a target debt ratio while others do not have one. What does this say about the validity of the trade-off theory, pecking order theory and market timing theory? Explain.

REGULAR

11 **Theories of Capital Structure** Do you agree or disagree with the following statement? 'The shareholders of a firm that is pursuing the UN Sustainable Development Goals will always prefer debt over equity.' Which theory would best explain this? Why?

12 **Debt and Risk** You have been asked the following questions: 'If debt can reduce the weighted average cost of capital for project appraisal, why does it then increase the risk of a company? Is it possible for a financial manager to diversify bankruptcy risk away like other risks?' What are your answers?

13 **Capital Structure Decisions** During the past few years, many companies have suffered major trading losses because of the poor economic climate. Assume your firm has found itself in this situation and is considering a major redevelopment investment to exploit nascent growth opportunities. Due to the large losses incurred in recent years, your firm has significant tax loss carry-forwards, which means that it does not need to pay any tax for three years. Should you use debt or equity to finance the firm's redevelopment investment? Explain your choice.

14 **Observed Capital Structures** Refer to the observed capital structures given in Figure 19.4. What do you notice about the types of industries with respect to their average debt–asset ratios? Are certain types of industries more likely to be highly leveraged than others? What are some possible reasons for this observed segmentation? Do the operating results and tax history of the firms play a role? How about their future earnings prospects? What about the different institutional characteristics of each country? Explain.

15 **Costs of Bankruptcy** What is the average cost of bankruptcy? Why do bankruptcy costs differ both within a country and between countries? What type of costs are incurred in financial distress? Use an example to illustrate your answer.

16 **Bankruptcy and Corporate Ethics** Explain the ethical considerations of the following:

(a) Firms sometimes use the threat of a bankruptcy filing to force creditors to renegotiate terms. Critics argue that in such cases the firm is using bankruptcy laws 'as a sword rather than a shield'.

(b) A company files for bankruptcy as a means of reducing labour costs.

17 **Firm Value** Hoy plc has a profit before interest and taxes of £900,000 per year that is expected to continue in perpetuity. The unlevered cost of equity for the company is 17 per cent, and the corporate tax rate is 20 per cent. The company also has a perpetual bond issue outstanding with a market value of £2 million. What is the value of the company?

18 **Agency Costs** Nurvi Sharma is the owner, chairman and primary salesperson for Sharma Manufacturing. Because of this, the company's profits are driven by the amount of work Nurvi does. If they work 40 hours each week, the company's profit before interest and taxes will be £500,000 per year; if they work a 50-hour week, the company's profit before interest and taxes will be £600,000 per year. The company is currently worth £3 million. It needs a cash infusion of £2 million, and it can issue equity or issue debt with an interest rate of 9 per cent. Assume there are no corporate taxes.

(a) What are the cash flows to Nurvi under each scenario?

(b) Under which form of financing is Nurvi likely to work harder?

(c) What specific new costs will occur with each form of financing?

19 Capital Structure and Growth Transvaal Ltd currently has debt outstanding with a market value of R980,000 and a cost of 10 per cent. The company has an EBIT of R98,000 that is expected to continue in perpetuity. Assume there are no taxes.

(a) What is the value of the company's equity? What is the debt-to-value ratio?

(b) What are the equity value and debt-to-value ratio if the company's growth rate is 4 per cent?

(c) What are the equity value and debt-to-value ratio if the company's growth rate is 8 per cent?

20 Capital Structure and Non-marketed Claims Suppose the chief executive of the company in the previous problem stated that the company should increase the amount of debt in its capital structure because of the tax-advantaged status of its interest payments. His argument is that this action would increase the value of the company. How would you respond?

21 Costs of Financial Distress: Debt and Equity Steinberg plc and Dietrich plc are identical firms except that Dietrich is more levered. Both companies will remain in business for one more year. The companies' economists agree that the probability of the continuation of the current expansion is 80 per cent for the next year, and the probability of a recession is 20 per cent. If the expansion continues, each firm will generate profit before interest and taxes of £2 million. If a recession occurs, each firm will generate profit before interest and taxes of £800,000. Steinberg's debt obligation requires the firm to pay £750,000 at the end of the year. Dietrich's debt obligation requires the firm to pay £1 million at the end of the year. Neither firm pays taxes. Assume a discount rate of 15 per cent.

(a) What are the potential payoffs in one year to Steinberg's shareholders and bondholders? What about those for Dietrich's?

(b) Steinberg's CEO recently stated that Steinberg's value should be higher than Dietrich's because the firm has less debt and therefore less bankruptcy risk. Do you agree or disagree with this statement?'

22 Agency Costs Kasna Corporation's economists estimate that a good business environment and a bad business environment are equally likely for the coming year. The managers of Kasna must choose between two mutually exclusive projects. Assume that the project Kasna chooses will be the firm's only activity and that the firm will close one year from today. Kasna is obligated to make a CHK50,000 payment to bondholders at the end of the year. The projects have the same systematic risk but different volatilities. Consider the following information pertaining to the two projects:

Economy	Probability	Low-volatility Project Payoff (CHK)	High-volatility Project Payoff (CHK)
Bad	0.50	50,000	10,000
Good	0.50	70,000	80,000

(a) What is the expected value of the firm if the low-volatility project is undertaken? What if the high-volatility project is undertaken? Which of the two strategies maximizes the expected value of the firm?

(b) What is the expected value of the firm's equity if the low-volatility project is undertaken? What is it if the high-volatility project is undertaken?

(c) Which project would Kasna's shareholders prefer? Explain.

(d) Suppose bondholders are fully aware that shareholders might choose to maximize equity value rather than total firm value and opt for the high-volatility project. To minimize this agency cost, the firm's bondholders decide to use a bond covenant to stipulate that the bondholders can demand a higher payment if Kasna chooses to take on the high-volatility project. What payment to bondholders would make shareholders indifferent between the two projects?

23 Financial Distress and Debt Returns Good Time plc is a regional chain department store. It will remain in business for one more year. The probability of a boom year is 60 per cent and the probability of a recession is 40 per cent. It is projected that the company will generate a total cash flow of £250 million in a boom year and £100 million in a recession. The company's required debt payment at the end of the year is £150 million. The market value of the company's outstanding debt is £108.93 million. The company pays no taxes. Assume a discount rate of 12 per cent.

(a) What payoff do bondholders expect to receive in the event of a recession?

(b) What is the promised return on the company's debt?

(c) What is the expected return on the company's debt?

CHALLENGE

24 Personal Taxes, Bankruptcy Costs and Firm Value When personal taxes on interest income and bankruptcy costs are considered, the general expression for the value of a levered firm in a world in which the tax rate on equity distributions equals zero is:

$$V_L = V_U + \{1 - [(1 - t_c)(1 - t_B)]\} \times D - C(D)$$

where V_L is the value of a levered firm; V_U is the value of an unlevered firm; D is the value of the firm's debt; t_C is the tax rate on corporate income; t_B is the personal tax rate on interest income; $C(D)$ is the present value of the costs of financial distress.

(a) In their no-tax model, what do Modigliani and Miller assume about t_C, t_B and $C(D)$? What do these assumptions imply about a firm's optimal debt–equity ratio?

(b) In their model with corporate taxes, what do Modigliani and Miller assume about t_C, t_B and $C(D)$? What do these assumptions imply about a firm's optimal debt–equity ratio?

(c) Consider an all-equity Belgian firm that is certain to be able to use interest deductions to reduce its corporate tax bill. If the corporate tax rate is 33.99 per cent, the personal tax rate on interest income is 50 per cent and there are no costs of financial distress, by how much will the value of the firm change if it issues €1 million in debt and uses the proceeds to repurchase equity?

(d) Consider another all-equity Belgian firm that does not pay taxes due to large tax loss carry-forwards from previous years. The personal tax rate on interest income is 50 per cent, and there are no costs of financial distress. What would be the change in the value of this firm from adding €1 of perpetual debt rather than €1 of equity?

25 Personal Taxes, Bankruptcy Costs and Firm Value: Overnight Publishing Overnight Publishing SA (OP) has €2 million in excess cash. The firm plans to use this cash either to retire all of its outstanding debt or to repurchase equity. The firm's debt is held by one institution that is willing to sell it back to OP for €2 million. The institution will not charge OP any transaction costs. Once OP becomes an all-equity firm, it will remain unlevered for ever. If OP does not retire the debt, the company will use the €2 million in cash to buy back some of its equity on the open market. Repurchasing equity also has no transaction costs. The company will generate €1,100,000 of annual earnings before interest and taxes in perpetuity regardless of its capital structure. The firm immediately pays out all earnings as dividends at the end of each year. OP is subject to a corporate tax rate of 33.33 per cent, and the required rate of return on the firm's unlevered equity is 20 per cent. The personal tax rate on interest income is 40 per cent, and there are no taxes on equity distribution. Assume there are no bankruptcy costs.

(a) What is the value of OP if it chooses to retire all of its debt and become an unlevered firm?

(b) What is the value of OP if it decides to repurchase equity instead of retiring its debt? (*Hint:* Use the equation for the value of a levered firm with personal tax on interest income from the previous problem.)

(c) Assume that expected bankruptcy costs have a present value of €300,000. How does this influence OP's decision?

26 Islamic Financing Islamic financing forbids the use of interest in any financial security, and this will clearly have an impact on the capital structure decisions of firms that follow Shariah principles. At the same time, many Islamic securities have the same cash flow requirements as Western financial securities. Explain how the costs of financial distress are affected in the event a firm with Islamic securities finds itself near insolvency. Are Islamic securities better in this regard? Explain why, or why not.

27 Corporate Pension Plans Many firms have pension plans for their employees that are heavily in deficit (i.e., the asset value of the fund is less than the present value of its future pension payments). How does this affect the risk of firms? How would you incorporate the pension fund deficit or surplus into the Modigliani–Miller framework?

28 Guaranteed Debt Many companies in emerging markets use AAA-rated firms in the West to guarantee any debt issue that is made by the firm. A good example is the Bakrie family in Indonesia, who used Bumi plc in the UK to guarantee a loan of $473 million. In 2012, the Bakrie family's operations were not performing well and their firm was in financial distress. As a result, the share price of the guarantor, Bumi plc, fell 60 per cent on the possibility that the Bakrie family may default on its loan, thus engaging the guarantor, Bumi plc, to repay the full amount. How would you incorporate a guarantor contract in the Modigliani–Miller framework?

29 Debt Buybacks Companies in financial distress often bring their leverage ratios down to much lower levels until such periods as they are able to turn around operations and generate profit. A strategy for a recovered company is to repurchase its own debt. If debt brings tax benefits and gearing is not abnormally high, why would this be a sensible strategy?

30 Gearing Ratios and Market Timing Theory Look again at Figure 19.4. Can you provide a market timing interpretation to the distribution of gearing ratios in the diagram? Can you provide a more plausible or intuitive interpretation of the figures? Write a brief report, justifying your views.

Exam Question (45 minutes)

Biller Industries plc is a global haulage equipment and scaffolding manufacturer. The company has never borrowed before but feels that, in order to maximize growth and increase value, a debt issue is required. Currently the firm has 50 million shares outstanding, with a share price of £1.50. The profit before taxes is forecast to be £25 million. Biller Industries requires £30 million to fund its expansion plans. The firm feels that it could borrow £45 million and use the additional £15 million to also buy back shares in the company. The corporate tax rate is 18 per cent.

1 Determine the expected earnings per share for the company before and after the debt issue. **(20 marks)**

2 Using your answer to part (1), discuss the use of earnings per share as a basis for financial decision-taking. **(20 marks)**

3 Determine the value of Biller Industries plc after restructuring and the value of its equity using the Modigliani–Miller model with corporate taxes. **(15 marks)**

4 Determine the cost of equity for Biller Industries plc before and after the debt issue. **(15 marks)**

5 If the Miller (debt and taxes) model holds and capital gains tax is 28 per cent, corporation tax is 18 per cent and personal tax rate on interest income is 45 per cent, estimate the value of Biller Industries plc. **(15 marks)**

6 Determine the personal tax rate on interest income at which the tax advantage of debt is zero. **(15 marks)**

Total Marks: 100

Mini Case

McKenzie Restaurants plc's Capital Budgeting

Sam McKenzie is the founder and CEO of McKenzie Restaurants plc, a British company. Sam is considering opening several new restaurants. Taylor Thornton, the company's CFO, has been put in charge of the capital budgeting analysis. They have examined the potential for the company's expansion and determined that the success of the new restaurants will depend critically on the state of the economy over the next few years.

McKenzie currently has a bond issue outstanding with a face value of £25 million that is due in one year. Covenants associated with this bond issue prohibit the issuance of any additional debt. This restriction means that the expansion will be entirely financed with equity at a cost of £9 million. Taylor has summarized their analysis in the following table, which shows the value of the company in each state of the economy next year, both with and without expansion:

Economic Growth	Probability	Without Expansion (£)	With Expansion (£)
Low	0.30	20,000,000	24,000,000
Normal	0.50	34,000,000	45,000,000
High	0.20	41,000,000	53,000,000

1 What is the expected value of the company in one year, with and without expansion? Would the company's shareholders be better off with or without expansion? Why?

2 What is the expected value of the company's debt in one year, with and without the expansion?

3 One year from now, how much value creation is expected from the expansion? How much value is expected for shareholders? For bondholders?

4 If the company announces that it is not expanding, what do you think will happen to the price of its bonds? What will happen to the price of the bonds if the company does expand?

5 If the company opts not to expand, what are the implications for its future borrowing needs? What are the implications if the company does expand?

6 Because of the bond covenant, the expansion would have to be financed with equity. How would it affect your answer if the expansion were financed with cash on hand instead of new equity?

Practical Case Study

For this case study, you will need to access Yahoo! Finance. For your own country, choose an industry and find the debt to equity ratio of each company in the industry. Now choose another country and find the debt to equity ratios of all the companies in the same industry. Is the median leverage different between countries? If so, explain why you think this might be the case. If not, what does this tell you about the three theories (trade-off, pecking order, market timing) of capital structure? Write a brief report on your findings.

References

Admati, A.R., P.M. DeMarzo, M.F. Hellwig and P. Pfleiderer (2018) 'The Leverage Ratchet Effect', *Journal of Finance*, Vol. 73, No. 1, 145–198.

Baker, M. and J. Wurgler (2002) 'Market Timing and Capital Structure', *Journal of Finance*, Vol. 57, No. 1, 1–32.

Berens, J.L. and C.L. Cuny (1995) 'Inflation, Growth and Capital Structure', *Review of Financial Studies*, Vol. 8, 1185–1208.

Bessler, W., W. Drobetz, R. Haller and I. Meier (2013) 'The International Zero-leverage Phenomenon', *Journal of Corporate Finance*, Vol. 23, 196–221.

Brounen, D., A. de Jong and K. Koedijk (2006) 'Capital Structure Policies in Europe: Survey Evidence', *Journal of Banking and Finance*, Vol. 30, No. 5, 1409–1442.

Dang, V.A. (2013) 'An Empirical Analysis of Zero-leverage Firms: New Evidence from the UK', *International Review of Financial Analysis*, Vol. 30, 189–202.

Davydenko, S.A., I.A. Strebulaev and X. Zhao (2012) 'A Market-based Study of the Cost of Default', *Review of Financial Studies*, Vol. 25, No. 10, 2959–2999.

DeAngelo, H. and R. Roll (2015) 'How Stable are Corporate Capital Structures?', *Journal of Finance*, Vol. 70, No. 1, 373–418.

El Ghoul, S., O. Guedhami, C. Kwok and X. Zheng (2017) 'Zero-leverage Puzzle: An International Comparison', *Review of Finance*, Vol. 22, No. 3, 1063–1120.

Fama, E. and K. French (2002) 'Testing Trade-off and Pecking Order Predictions about Dividends and Debt', *Review of Financial Studies*, Vol. 15, No. 1, 1–33.

Glover, B. (2016) 'The Expected Cost of Default', *Journal of Financial Economics*, Vol. 119, No. 2, 284–299.

Grieser, W., C. Hadlock, J. LeSage and M. Zekhnini (2022) 'Network Effects in Corporate Financial Policies', *Journal of Financial Economics*, Vol. 144, No. 1, 247–272.

Hillier, D., B. Martinez, P.C. Patel, J. Pindado and I. Requejo (2018) 'Pound of Flesh? Debt Contract Strictness and Family Firms', *Entrepreneurship Theory and Practice*, Vol. 42, No. 2, 259–282.

Jensen, M.C. (1986) 'The Agency Costs of Free Cash Flow: Corporate Finance and Takeovers', *American Economic Review*, Vol. 76, No. 2, 323–339.

Jensen, M.C. and W. Meckling (1978) 'Theory of the Firm: Managerial Behavior, Agency Costs, and Ownership Structure', *Journal of Financial Economics*, Vol. 3, No. 4, 305–360.

Kayhan, A. and S. Titman (2007) 'Firms' Histories and their Capital Structures', *Journal of Financial Economics*, Vol. 83, No. 1, 1–32.

Lang, L., R. Stulz and R. Walkling (1989) 'Managerial Performance, Tobin's Q and the Gains in Tender Offers', *Journal of Financial Economics*, Vol. 24, 137–154.

Leary, M.T. and M.R. Roberts (2014) 'Do Peer Firms Affect Corporate Financial Policy?', *Journal of Finance*, Vol. 69, No. 1, 139–178.

Lemmon, M. and J. Zender (2010) 'Debt Capacity and Tests of Capital Structure Theories', *Journal of Financial and Quantitative Analysis*, Vol. 45, 1161–1187.

Mahajan, A. and S. Tartaroglu (2008) 'Equity Market Timing and Capital Structure: International Evidence', *Journal of Banking and Finance*, Vol. 32, No. 5, 754–766.

Marshall, A., L. McCann and P. McColgan (2019) 'The Market Reaction to Debt Announcements: UK Evidence Surrounding the Global Financial Crisis', *British Accounting Review*, Vol. 51, No. 1, 92–109.

Miller, M. (1977) 'Debt and Taxes', *Journal of Finance*, Vol. 32, 261–275.

Myers, S.C. (1984) 'The Capital Structure Puzzle', *Journal of Finance*, Vol. 39, No. 3, 574–592.

Qi, Y., L. Roth and J.K. Wald (2011) 'How Legal Environments Affect the Use of Bond Covenants', *Journal of International Business Studies*, Vol. 42, 235–262.

Shah, K. (1994) 'The Nature of Information Conveyed by Pure Capital Structure Changes', *Journal of Financial Economics*, Vol. 36, No. 1, 81–126.

Smith, A. (1937) *The Wealth of Nations* [1776], Cannon edition. New York: Modern Library.

Smith, C.W. and J.B. Warner (1979) 'On Financial Contracting: An Analysis of Bond Covenants', *Journal of Financial Economics*, Vol. 7, 117–161.

Strebulaev, I.A. and B. Yang (2013) 'The Mystery of Zero-leverage Firms', *Journal of Financial Economics*, Vol. 109, No. 1, 1–23.

Welch, I. (2003) 'Capital Structure and Stock Returns', *Journal of Political Economy*, Vol. 112, No. 1, 106–131.

Additional Reading

Since Baker and Wurgler's (2002) paper on market timing, the capital structure literature has taken on a completely new lease of life. For many years, researchers believed that pecking orders and static trade-offs were the only intuitive reasons why managers chose capital structures in practice. Now we have market timing and dynamic trade-offs to consider and things are uncertain again. The references to papers discussed in the main text are provided in the previous section. The following papers will add to your reading pleasure.

Trade-offs, Pecking Orders and Market Timing

1 Alti, A. (2006) 'How Persistent is the Impact of Market Timing on Capital Structure?', *Journal of Finance*, Vol. 61, No. 4, 1681–1710. **USA.**

2 Byoun, S. (2008) 'How and When Do Firms Adjust their Capital Structures toward Targets?', *Journal of Finance*, Vol. 63, No. 6, 3069–3096. **USA.**

3 Chang, X. and S. Dasgupta (2009) 'Target Behavior and Financing: How Conclusive is the Evidence?', *Journal of Finance*, Vol. 64, No. 4, 1767–1796. **USA.**

4 Elliott, W.B., J. Koeter-Kant and R.S. Warr (2007) 'A Valuation-based Test of Market Timing', *Journal of Corporate Finance*, Vol. 13, No. 1, 112–128. **USA.**

5 Elliott, W.B., J. Koeter-Kant and R.S. Warr (2008) 'Market Timing and the Debt–equity Choice', *Journal of Financial Intermediation*, Vol. 17, No. 2, 175–197. **USA.**

6 Graham, J.R. (2003) 'Taxes and Corporate Finance: A Review', *Review of Financial Studies*, Vol. 16, No. 4, 1075–1129. **Review paper.**

7 Graham, J.R. and A.L. Tucker (2006) 'Tax Shelters and Corporate Debt Policy', *Journal of Financial Economics*, Vol. 81, No. 3, 563–594. **USA.**

8 Hennessy, C. and T.M. Whited (2005) 'Debt Dynamics', *Journal of Finance*, Vol. 60, No. 3, 1129–1165. **USA.**

9 Hovakimian, A. (2006) 'Are Observed Capital Structures Determined by Equity Market Timing?', *Journal of Financial and Quantitative Analysis*, Vol. 41, No. 1, 221–243. **USA.**

10 Huang, R. and J.R. Ritter (2009) 'Testing Theories of Capital Structure and Estimating the Speed of Adjustment', *Journal of Financial and Quantitative Analysis*, Vol. 44, 237–271.

11 Kayhan, A. and S. Titman (2007) 'Firm's Histories and their Capital Structures', *Journal of Financial Economics*, Vol. 83, No. 1, 1–32. **USA.**

12 Leary, M.T. and M.R. Roberts (2005) 'Do Firms Rebalance their Capital Structures?', *Journal of Finance*, Vol. 60, No. 6, 2575–2619. **USA.**

13 Lemmon, M.L. and J.F. Zender (2010) 'Debt Capacity and Tests of Capital Structure Theories', *Journal of Financial and Quantitative Analysis*, Vol. 45, No. 5, 1161–1187.

14 Lemmon, M.L., M.R. Roberts and J.F. Zender (2008) 'Back to the Beginning: Persistence and the Cross-section of Corporate Capital Structure', *Journal of Finance*, Vol. 63, No. 4, 1575–1608. **USA.**

Other Papers on Capital Structure Choice

15 Almeida, H. and T. Philippon (2007) 'The Risk-adjusted Cost of Financial Distress', *Journal of Finance*, Vol. 62, No. 6, 2557–2586. **USA.**

16 Booth, L., V. Aivazian, A. Demirguc-Kunt and V. Maksimovic (2001) 'Capital Structures in Developing Countries', *Journal of Finance*, Vol. 56, No. 1, 87–130. **International.**

17 Bris, A., I. Welch and N. Zhu (2006) 'The Costs of Bankruptcy: Chapter 7 Liquidation versus Chapter 11 Reorganization', *Journal of Finance*, Vol. 61, No. 3, 1253–1303.

18 Danis, A., D.A. Rettl and T.M. Whited (2014) 'Refinancing, Profitability, and Capital Structure', *Journal of Financial Economics*, Vol. 114, No. 3, 424–443.

19 Desai, M.A., C.F. Foley and J.R. Hines (2004) 'A Multinational Perspective on Capital Structure Choice and Internal Capital Markets', *Journal of Finance*, Vol. 59, No. 6, 2451–2487. **International.**

20 Dittmar, A. and A. Thakor (2007) 'Why Do Firms Issue Equity?', *Journal of Finance*, Vol. 62, No. 1, 1–54. **USA.**

21 Fama, E.F. and K.R. French (2005) 'Financing Decisions: Who Issues Stock?', *Journal of Financial Economics*, Vol. 76, No. 3, 549–582. **USA.**

22 Fan, J.P.H., S. Titman and G. Twite (2012) 'An International Comparison of Capital Structure and Debt Maturity Choices', *Journal of Financial and Quantitative Analysis*, Vol. 47, No. 1, 23–56. **International.**

23 Faulkender, M. and M.A. Petersen (2006) 'Does the Source of Capital Affect Capital Structure?', *Review of Financial Studies*, Vol. 19, No. 1, 45–79. **USA.**

24 Frank, M.Z. and V.K. Goyal (2009) 'Capital Structure Decisions: Which Factors are Reliably Important?', *Financial Management*, Vol. 38, No. 1, 1–37.

25 Geelen, T., J. Hajda and E. Morellec (2022) 'Can Corporate Debt Foster Innovation and Growth?', *Review of Financial Studies*, Vol. 35, No. 9, 4152–4200.

26 Gonzalez, V.M. and F. Gonzalez (2008) 'Influence of Bank Concentration and Institutions on Capital Structure: New International Evidence', *Journal of Corporate Finance*, Vol. 14, No. 4, 363–375. **International.**

27 Kisgen, D.J. (2006) 'Credit Ratings and Capital Structure', *Journal of Finance*, Vol. 61, No. 3, 1035–1072. **USA.**

28 Klasa, S., H. Ortiz-Molina, M. Serfling and S. Srinivasan (2018) 'Protection of Trade Secrets and Capital Structure Decisions', *Journal of Financial Economics*, Vol. 128, No. 2, 266–286.

29 Molina, C.A. (2005) 'Are Firms Underleveraged? An Examination of the Effect of Leverage on Default Probabilities', *Journal of Finance*, Vol. 60, No. 3, 1427–1459. **USA.**

Endnotes

1 There are situations where the limited liability of corporations can be 'pierced'. Typically, fraud or misrepresentation must be present.

2 Normally, we assume that investors are *averse* to risk. In that case, the cost of debt capital, R_D, is less than the cost of equity capital, R_E, which rises with leverage, as shown in Chapter 18. In addition, R_D may rise when the increase in leverage allows the possibility of default.

For simplicity, we assume *risk neutrality* in this example. This means that investors are indifferent to the level of risk. Here, $R_E = R_D$ because risk-neutral investors do not demand compensation for bearing risk. In addition, neither R_E nor R_D rises with leverage. Because the interest rate is 10 per cent, our assumption of risk neutrality implies that $R_E = 10$ per cent as well.

Though financial economists believe that investors are risk-averse, they frequently develop examples based on risk neutrality to isolate a point unrelated to risk. This is our approach because we want to focus on bankruptcy costs, not bankruptcy risk. The same qualitative conclusions from this example can be drawn in a world of risk aversion, albeit with *much* more difficulty for the reader.

3 The same qualitative results will obtain if the £1,000 is raised from new shareholders. However, the arithmetic becomes much more difficult because we must determine how many new shares are issued.

4 Legal limitations may prevent this practice in other countries.

5 Smith (1937 [1776], p. 700), as quoted in Jensen and Meckling (1978).

6 As previously discussed, *agency costs* are generally defined as the costs from the conflicts of interest among shareholders, bondholders and managers. See Chapter 2 for more information.

7 The seminal theoretical article is Jensen (1986).

8 The pecking order theory is generally attributed to Myers (1984).

9 In the interest of simplicity, we have not presented our results in the form of a rigorous model. To the extent that a reader wants a deeper explanation, we refer them to Myers (1984).

10 See Merton Miller's Presidential Address to the American Finance Association, reprinted as 'Debt and Taxes' (1977).

11 The same qualitative results occur under uncertainty, though the mathematics is more troublesome.

12 For simplicity, assume that growth is achieved without earnings retention. The same conclusions would be reached with retained earnings, though the arithmetic would become more involved. Of course, growth without earnings retention is less realistic than growth with retention.

13 Because the firm makes no real investment, the new debt is used to buy back shares of equity.

14 The firm can also be valued by a variant of Equation 18.5:

$$V_L = V_U + PVTS$$
$$= \frac{€100\,(1 - t_C)}{0.10 - 0.05} + \frac{t_C \times €100}{0.10 - 0.05} = €2{,}000$$

Because of firm growth, both V_U and $PVTS$ are growing perpetuities.

15 Students are often surprised that equity has value when taxable income is zero. Actually, the equityholders are receiving cash flow each period. The proceeds from the new debt can be used either to pay dividends or to buy back shares.

16 Our example assumes a single perpetual bond with level coupon payments. Berens and Cuny (1995, p. 1201) point out that, with a number of different bonds, a firm might be able to construct an equally optimal capital structure with a greater debt-to-value (D/V) ratio. Because both capital structures are equally optimal, a firm might choose either one.

Although the analysis with many financing instruments is more complex, a firm can still choose a low D/V with no ill effect. Thus, Berens and Cuny's conclusion that firms *can* employ a significant amount of equity in a world with a low level of bankruptcy costs still holds.

17 By contrast, the pecking order theory argues that profitable firms will employ less debt because they can invest out of retained earnings. However, the pecking order theory argues against the use of target ratios in the first place.

Chapter 20
Valuation and Capital Budgeting for the Levered Firm

Learning Objectives

After reading this chapter you should be able to:

LO1 Explain the principles underlying the adjusted present value (APV), flow to equity (FTE), and weighted average cost of capital (WACC) approaches, and how they contribute to the understanding of capital structure and the limits to the use of debt.

LO2 Judge when to choose between APV, FTE and WACC for different types of capital budgeting decisions.

LO3 Compare and contrast the APV, FTE and WACC approaches with an understanding of their relative strengths and weaknesses.

The Private Finance Initiative (PFI) is a UK scheme that brings together the private and public sectors in major social infrastructure projects. Under PFI, a private consortium of firms will design, build, finance and operate an asset or service according to specifications imposed by the public sector. In return, the government will make periodic payments to the private consortium for this collaboration. The rationale underlying PFI is that private organizations are more efficient at running big investment projects, and this brings cost savings in addition to improved service and quality.

An example of the PFI is the building of the British Embassy in Berlin in 2000. Under this scheme, Arteos (a subsidiary of Bilfinger Berger, the German construction firm) financed and built the building. It was also contracted to operate it until 2030, after which ownership reverts to the British government. Why did Bilfinger Berger enter into the contract? One of the reasons was the attractive financial package offered to the company by the British government to undertake the collaboration.

Source: Josep Curto/123RF

Key Notations

APV	Adjusted present value	UCF	Unlevered cash flow
FTE	Flow to equity	LCF	Levered cash flow
NPV	Net present value	D	Value of debt
NPVF	Net present value of financing	E	Value of shares
t_C	Corporate tax rate	R_{WACC}	Weighted average cost of capital
R_0	Cost of capital for an all-equity firm	α	Beta of systematic risk
R_E	Cost of equity capital	R_F	Risk-free rate
R_D	Cost of debt capital		

Similarly, when a corporation opens a major plant or considers relocation, municipalities or regions often create a package loaded with subsidies, including tax credits, subsidized debt, educational training, road and infrastructure creation, and other incentives.

With subsidized debt, the government or region guarantees the debt, which allows the company to borrow at a much lower interest rate. If the interest rate on the debt is lower than the company's normal cost of debt, how does a company evaluate the financial benefits of this and other such subsidies? In this chapter, we illustrate how to assess projects using the adjusted present value and some flow to equity approaches in capital budgeting that allow us to answer this question. We also consider a variation of NPV, called net asset value, which should be used for mining projects.

20.1 Adjusted Present Value Approach

Chapter 7 Page 178

When financing issues are an important part of an investment proposal, a good methodology to use is the adjusted present value method (it is worthwhile reading over Chapter 7 again to refresh your mind on the more commonly used investment appraisal methods). The approach separates project cash flows from financing cash flows and values these separately. The project should be taken if the combined present values are positive. The adjusted present value (APV) method is described by the following formula:

$$APV = NPV + NPVF$$

In words, the value of a project to a levered firm (APV) is equal to the value of the project to an unlevered firm (NPV) plus the net present value of the financing side effects (NPVF). We can generally think of four side effects:

Chapter 8 Page 207

1 *The tax subsidy to debt:* This was discussed in Section 18.5, where we pointed out that, for perpetual debt, the value of the tax subsidy is t_C. (t_C is the corporate tax rate, and D is the value of the debt.) The material about valuation under corporate taxes in Section 18.5 is an application of the APV approach.

2 *The costs of issuing new securities:* As we discussed in detail in Section 15.5, bankers participate in the public issuance of corporate securities. These bankers must be compensated for their time and effort, a cost that lowers the value of the project.

Chapter 19 Page 511

3 *The costs of financial distress:* The possibility of financial distress, and bankruptcy in particular, arises with debt financing. As stated in Chapter 19, financial distress imposes costs, thereby lowering value.

4 *Subsidies to debt financing:* The interest on debt issued by state and local governments may not be taxable to the investor or the tax may be discounted. Because of this, the yield on government debt can be substantially below the yield on taxable debt. Frequently, corporations can obtain financing from a municipality at the tax-exempt rate because the municipality can borrow at that rate as well. As with any subsidy, this subsidy adds value.

Although each of the preceding four side effects is important, the tax deduction to debt almost certainly has the highest value in most actual situations. For this reason, the following example considers the tax subsidy but not the other three side effects. (A later example will deal with these three.)

Consider a project of P.B. Singer plc with the following characteristics.

- Cash inflows: £500,000 per year for the indefinite future.
- Cash costs: 72 per cent of sales.
- Initial investment: £520,000.
- $t_C = 28$ per cent.
- $R_A = 20$ per cent, where R_0 is the cost of capital for a project of an all-equity firm.

If both the project and the firm are financed with only equity, the project's cash flows are as follows:

	£
Cash inflows	500,000
Cash costs	–360,000
Profit before tax	140,000
Corporate tax (28% tax rate)	–39,200
Unlevered cash flow (UCF)	100,800

The distinction between present value and net present value is important for this example. The *present value* of a project is determined before the initial investment at date 0 is subtracted. The initial investment is subtracted for the calculation of *net* present value.

Given a discount rate of 20 per cent, the present value of the project is:

$$\frac{£100{,}800}{0.20} = £504{,}000$$

The net present value (NPV) of the project – that is, the value of the project to an all-equity firm – is:

$$£504{,}000 - £520{,}000 = -£16{,}000$$

Because the NPV is negative, the project would be rejected by an all-equity firm.

Now imagine that the firm finances the project with exactly £135,483.90 in debt, so that the remaining investment of £384,516.10 (= £520,000 – £135,483.90) is financed with equity. The net present value of the project under leverage, which we call the adjusted present value, or the APV, is:

$$APV = NPV + t_c \times D$$

$$£21{,}935 = -£16{,}000 + 0.28 \times £135{,}483.90$$

That is, the value of the project when financed with some leverage is equal to the value of the project when financed with all equity plus the tax shield from the debt. Because this number is positive, the project should be accepted.

You may be wondering why we chose such a precise amount of debt. Actually, we chose it so that the ratio of debt to the present value of the project under leverage is 0.25.[1]

In this example, debt is a fixed proportion of the present value of the project, not a fixed proportion of the initial investment of £520,000. This is consistent with the goal of a target debt-to-*market*-value ratio, which we find is followed by companies in many countries. For example, banks typically lend to property developers a fixed percentage of the appraised market value of a project, not a fixed percentage of the initial investment.

20.2 Flow to Equity Approach

Chapter 5 Page 116

The flow to equity (FTE) approach is an alternative capital budgeting approach and is similar to the free cash flow to the firm (FCFF) method that was used to value firms in Chapter 5. The formula simply calls for discounting the cash flow from the project to the shareholders of the levered firm at the cost of equity capital, R_E. For a perpetuity this becomes:

$$\frac{\text{Cash flow from project to equityholders of the levered firm}}{R_E}$$

There are three steps to the FTE approach.

Step 1: Calculating Levered Cash Flow (LCF)[2]

Assuming an interest rate of 10 per cent, the perpetual cash flow to shareholders in our P.B. Singer plc example is:

	£
Cash inflows	500,000
Cash costs	–360,000
Interest (10% x $135,483.90)	–13,548
Income after interest	126,452
Corporate tax (28% tax rate)	–35,407
Levered cash flow (LCF)	91,045

Alternatively, we can calculate levered cash flow (LCF) directly from unlevered cash flow (UCF). The key here is that the difference between the cash flow that shareholders receive in an unlevered firm and the cash flow that shareholders receive in a levered firm is the after-tax interest payment. (Repayment of principal does not appear in this example because the debt is perpetual.) We write this algebraically as:

$$UCF - LCF = (1 - t_C) \times R_D \times D$$

The term on the right side of this expression is the after-tax interest payment. Thus, because cash flow to the unlevered shareholders (UCF) is £100,800 and the after-tax interest payment is £9,754.84 [= 0.72 × 0.10 × £135,483.90], cash flow to the levered shareholders (LCF) is:

$$£100{,}800 - £9{,}755 = £91{,}045$$

which is exactly the number we calculated earlier.

Step 2: Calculating R_E

The next step is to calculate the discount rate, R_E. Note that we assumed that the discount rate on unlevered equity, R_A, is 0.20. As we saw in Section 18.5, the formula for R_E is:

$$R_E = R_A + \frac{D}{E}(1 - t_C)(R_A - R_D)$$

Note that our target debt-to-value ratio of 1/4 implies a target debt-to-equity ratio of 1/3. Applying the preceding formula to this example, we have:

$$\begin{aligned} R_E &= 0.02 + \frac{1}{3}(0.72)(0.20 - 0.10) \\ &= 0.224 \end{aligned}$$

Step 3: Valuation

The present value of the project's LCF is:

$$\frac{LCF}{R_E} = \frac{£91{,}045}{0.224} = £406{,}451$$

Because the initial investment is £520,000 and £135,483.90 is borrowed, the firm must advance the project £384,516.10 (= £520,000 – £135,483.90) out of its own cash reserves. The *net* present value of the project is simply the difference between the present value of the project's LCF and the investment not borrowed. Thus, the NPV is:

$$£406{,}451 - £384{,}516.10 = £21{,}935$$

which is identical to the result found with the APV approach.

20.3 Weighted Average Cost of Capital Method

Chapter 12 Page 325

Finally, we can value a project using the **weighted average cost of capital (WACC)** method. Although this method was discussed in earlier chapters (WACC is first discussed in Chapter 12, Section 12.5), it is worthwhile to review it here. The WACC approach begins with the insight that projects of levered firms are simultaneously financed with both debt and equity. The cost of capital is a weighted average of the cost of debt and cost of equity. The cost of equity is R_E. Ignoring taxes, the cost of debt is the borrowing rate, R_D. However, with corporate taxes, the appropriate cost of debt is $(1 - t_C)\,R_D$, the after-tax cost of debt.

The formula for determining the weighted average cost of capital, R_{WACC}, is:

$$R_{WACC} = \frac{E}{D+E}R_E + \frac{E}{D+E}R_D\,(1 - t_C)$$

The weight for equity, $E/(D + E)$, and the weight for debt, $D/(D + E)$, are target ratios. Target ratios are generally expressed in terms of market values, not accounting values. (Recall that another phrase for accounting value is *book value.*)

The formula calls for discounting the *unlevered* cash flow of the project (UCF) at the weighted average cost of capital, R_{WACC}. The net present value of the project can be written algebraically as:

$$\sum_{t=1}^{\infty} \frac{UCF_t}{(1 + R_{\text{WACC}})^t} - \text{Initial investment}$$

If the project is a perpetuity, the net present value is:

$$\frac{UCF}{R_{\text{WACC}}} - \text{Initial investment}$$

We previously stated that the target debt-to-value ratio of our project is 1/4 and the corporate tax rate is 0.28, implying that the weighted average cost of capital is:

$$R_{\text{WACC}} = \frac{3}{4} \times 0.224 + \frac{1}{4} \times 0.10 \times 0.72 = 0.186$$

Note that R_{WACC}, 0.186, is lower than the cost of equity capital for an all-equity firm, 0.20. This must always be the case because debt financing provides a tax subsidy that lowers the average cost of capital.

We previously determined the UCF of the project to be £100,800, implying that the present value of the project is:

$$\frac{£100{,}800}{0.186} = £541{,}935$$

This initial investment is £520,000, so the NPV of the project is:

$$£541{,}935 - £520{,}000 = £21{,}935$$

Note that all three approaches yield the same value.

20.4 A Comparison of the APV, FTE and WACC Approaches

Capital budgeting techniques in the early chapters of this text applied to all-equity firms. Capital budgeting for the levered firm could not be handled earlier in the book because the effects of debt on firm value were deferred until Chapters 18 and 19. There we learned that debt increases firm value through tax benefits but decreases value through bankruptcy and related costs.

In this chapter, we provide three approaches to capital budgeting for the levered firm. The adjusted present value (APV) approach first values the project on an all-equity basis. That is, the project's after-tax cash flows under all-equity financing (called unlevered cash flows, or UCF) are placed in the numerator of the capital budgeting equation. The discount rate, assuming all-equity financing, appears in the denominator. At this point, the calculation is identical to that performed in the early chapters of this book. We then add the net present value of the debt. We point out that the net present value of the debt is likely to be the sum of four parameters: tax effects, flotation costs, bankruptcy costs and interest subsidies.

Chapter 18
Page 478

The flow to equity (FTE) approach discounts the after-tax cash flow from a project going to the shareholders of a levered firm (LCF). LCF – which stands for levered cash flow – is the residual to shareholders after interest has been deducted. The discount rate is R_E, the cost of capital to the shareholders of a levered firm. For a firm with leverage, R_E must be higher than R_A, the cost of capital for an unlevered firm. This follows from our material in Section 18.4 showing that leverage raises the risk to the shareholders.

The final approach is the weighted average cost of capital (WACC) method. This technique calculates the project's after-tax cash flows assuming all-equity financing (UCF). The UCF is placed in the numerator of the capital budgeting equation. The denominator, R_{WACC}, is a weighted average of the cost of equity capital and the cost of debt capital. The tax advantage of debt is reflected in the denominator because the cost of debt capital is determined net of corporate tax. The numerator does not reflect debt at all.

Sustainability in Action 20.1

Hornsea One

Hornsea One is an offshore wind farm located off the Yorkshire coast in the UK, within the Hornsea Zone in the southern North Sea. The project is a 50:50 joint venture between renewable energy firm Ørsted and Global Infrastructure Partners. It became fully operational in 2022 and is the world's largest offshore wind farm, with a capacity of 1.2 GW and 174 7 MW turbines. It can generate enough green energy to power more than one million UK homes.

Projects like Hornsea One can be valued using the APV methodology. In this case study, we will use hypothetical values to illustrate the method. Assume the Hornsea One project cost £4 billion and was financed by an equal mix of equity and debt. Assume the project also received a contract for difference (CfD) from the UK government, which guarantees a fixed price of £140 per MWh for the electricity generated for ever. This provides a stable and predictable revenue stream for the Ørsted and Global Infrastructure Partners, equivalent to £20 million per year.

To value the Hornsea One project using adjusted present value (APV), we need to estimate the net present value (NPV) of the project if financed solely by equity and then add the present value (PV) of any financing benefits, such as subsidies and tax shields from interest payments. Assume a discount rate of 10 per cent, a tax rate of 19 per cent and an interest rate of 5 per cent. We also assume the project generates £700 million in cash flows per year, and these grow at a constant rate of 2 per cent per year.

To calculate the APV of the Hornsea One project, we would do the following:

1 Estimate the UCF of the project based on its expected revenues, costs and taxes. For simplicity, assume the costs are 40 per cent of the revenues and taxes are 19 per cent. All other inputs are zero. The UCF is, therefore, £340.2 million and grows at 2 per cent per year thereafter.

Cash inflows	£700 million
Costs	£280 million
EBIT	£420 million
Tax (19 per cent)	£79.8 million
Unlevered cash flow (UCF)	**£340.2 million**

2 Calculate the NPV of the UCF using the discount rate of 10 per cent and a growth rate of 2 per cent. The Hornsea project is assumed to last for ever, and so the cash flow is a perpetuity. PV = £340.2 million / (.1 – .02) = £4,252.50 million. Since the Hornsea project cost £4 billion as an investment, the NPV of the project is £4,252.50 million – £4,000 million = £252.50 million. This is the value of the unlevered project.

3 Calculate the present value of the tax shield. The project is funded 50 per cent by debt, which is £2 billion. The PV of the tax shield is, therefore, 19 per cent of £2 billion = £38 million.

4 Calculate the present value of the subsidy. The subsidy is £20 million per year, so the PV of the subsidy is £20/.1 = £200 million.

Using the hypothesized data, the APV of the Hornsea One project can be summarized as follows:

Item	Value (£m)
NPV of unlevered project	£252.50 million
Present value of tax shield	£38 million
Present value of subsidy	£200 million
Adjusted present value	**£490.50 million**

The APV shows that the Hornsea One project has a positive value of £490.50 million, which means that it is a profitable investment for its owners. The APV also shows that nearly half of the value comes from financing benefits, such as tax shields and subsidies, which reduce the cost and risk of debt, and increase the attractiveness of the investment.

Source: https://hornseaprojects.co.uk

Which Method is Best?

The net present value of our project is exactly the same under each of the three methods. In theory, this should always be the case.[3] However, one method usually provides an easier computation than another, and, in many cases, one or more of the methods are virtually impossible computationally. We first consider when it is best to use the WACC and FTE approaches.

If the risk of a project stays constant throughout its life, it is plausible to assume that R_A remains constant throughout the project's life. This assumption of constant risk appears to be reasonable for most real-world projects. In addition, if the debt-to-value ratio remains constant over the life of the project, both R_E and R_{WACC} will remain constant as well. Under this latter assumption, either the FTE or the WACC approach is easy to apply. However, if the debt-to-value ratio varies from year to year, both R_S and R_{WACC} vary from year to year as well. Using the FTE or the WACC approach when the denominator changes every year is computationally quite complex, and when computations become complex, the error rate rises. Thus, both the FTE and WACC approaches present difficulties when the debt-to-value *ratio* changes over time.

The APV approach is based on the *level* of debt in each future period. Consequently, when the debt level can be specified precisely for future periods, the APV approach is quite easy to use. However, when the debt level is uncertain, the APV approach becomes more problematic. For example, when the debt-to-value ratio is constant, the debt level varies with the value of the project. Because the value of the project in a future year cannot easily be forecast, the level of debt cannot easily be forecast either.

Thus, we suggest the following guideline:

Use WACC or FTE if the firm's target debt-to-value *ratio* applies to the project over its life. Use APV if the project's *level* of debt is known over the life of the project.

There are a number of situations where the APV approach is preferred. For example, in a leveraged buyout (LBO) the firm begins with a large amount of debt but rapidly pays down the debt over a number of years. Because the schedule of debt reduction in the future is known when the LBO is arranged, tax shields in every future year can easily be forecast. Thus, the APV approach is easy to use here. By contrast, the WACC and FTE approaches are virtually impossible to apply here because the debt-to-equity value cannot be expected to be constant over time. In addition, situations involving interest subsidies and flotation costs are much easier to handle with the APV approach. Finally, the APV approach handles the lease-versus-buy decision much more easily than does either the FTE or the WACC approach.

The preceding examples are special cases. Typical capital budgeting situations are more amenable to either the WACC or the FTE approach than to the APV approach. In many countries, financial managers think in terms of target debt-to-value *ratios*. If a project does better than expected, both its value and its debt capacity are likely to rise. The manager will increase debt correspondingly here. Conversely, the manager would be likely to reduce debt if the value of the project were to decline unexpectedly. Of course, because financing is a time-consuming task, the ratio cannot be adjusted daily or monthly. Rather, the adjustment can be expected to occur over the long run. As mentioned before, the WACC and FTE approaches are more appropriate than is the APV approach when a firm focuses on a target debt-to-value ratio.

Because of this, we recommend that the WACC and the FTE approaches, rather than the APV approach, be used in most real-world situations. In addition, frequent discussions with business executives have convinced us that the WACC is by far the most widely used method in the real world. Thus, practitioners seem to agree with us that, outside of the special situations mentioned, the APV approach is a less important method of capital budgeting.

The Three Methods of Capital Budgeting with Leverage

1. Adjusted present value (APV) method:

$$\sum_{t=1}^{\infty}\frac{UCF_t}{(1+R_A)^t} + \text{Additional effects of debt} - \text{Initial investment}$$

where UCF_t is the project's cash flow at date t to the equityholders of an unlevered firm and R_A is the cost of capital for a project in an unlevered firm.

2. Flow to equity (FTE) method:

$$\sum_{t=1}^{\infty}\frac{LCF_t}{(1+R_E)^t} - (\text{Initial investment} - \text{Amount borrowed})$$

where LCF_t is the project's cash flow at date t to the equityholders of a levered firm and R_E is the cost of equity capital with leverage.

3 Weighted average cost of capital (WACC) method:

$$\sum_{t=1}^{\infty} \frac{UCF_t}{(1+R_{WACC})^t} - \text{Initial investment}$$

where R_{WACC} is the weighted average cost of capital.

Notes

1 The middle term in the APV formula implies that the value of a project with leverage is greater than the value of the project without leverage. Because $R_{WACC} < R_A$, the WACC formula implies that the value of a project with leverage is greater than the value of the project without leverage.

2 In the FTE method, cash flow *after interest* (LCF) is used. Initial investment is reduced by *amount borrowed* as well.

Guidelines

1 Use WACC or FTE if the firm's target debt-to-value *ratio* applies to the project over its life.

2 Use APV if the project's *level* of debt is known over the life of the project.

20.5 Capital Budgeting When the Discount Rate Must Be Estimated

The previous sections of this chapter introduced APV, FTE and WACC – the three basic approaches to valuing a levered firm. However, one important detail remains. The example in Sections 20.1–20.3 *assumed* a discount rate. We now want to show how this rate is determined for real-world firms with leverage, with an application to the three preceding approaches. The example in this section brings together the work in Chapters 9–12 on the discount rate for unlevered firms with that in Chapter 19 on the effect of leverage on the cost of capital.

Example 20.1

Cost of Capital

World-Wide Enterprises (WWE) is a large conglomerate thinking of entering the widget business, where it plans to finance projects with a debt-to-value ratio of 25 per cent (or, alternatively, a debt-to-equity ratio of 1/3). There is currently one firm in the widget industry, Asian Widgets (AW). This firm is financed with 40 per cent debt and 60 per cent equity. The beta of AW's equity is 1.5. AW has a borrowing rate of 12 per cent and WWE expects to borrow for its widget venture at 10 per cent. The corporate tax rate for both firms is 0.40, the market risk premium is 8.5 per cent and the riskless interest rate is 8 per cent. What is the appropriate discount rate for WWE to use for its widget venture?

As shown in Sections 20.1–20.3, a corporation may use one of three capital budgeting approaches: APV, FTE or WACC. The appropriate discount rates for these three approaches are R_A, R_E and R_{WACC}, respectively. Because AW is WWE's only competitor in widgets, we look at AW's cost of capital to calculate R_A, R_E and R_{WACC} for WWE's widget venture. The following four-step procedure will allow us to calculate all three discount rates:

1 *Determining AW's cost of equity capital:* First, we determine AW's cost of equity capital using the security market line (SML):

AW's cost of equity capital

$$\begin{aligned} R_E &= R_F + \beta \times (\bar{R}_M - R_F) \\ &= 8\% + 1.5 \times 8.5\% \\ &= 20.75\% \end{aligned}$$

where $\bar{R}_M$ is the expected return on the market portfolio and R_F is the risk-free rate.

2 *Determining AW's hypothetical all-equity cost of capital:* We must standardize the preceding number in some way because AW and WWE's widget ventures have different target debt-to-value ratios. The easiest approach is to calculate the hypothetical cost of equity capital for AW, assuming all-equity financing. This can be determined from MM's Proposition II under taxes:

AW's cost of capital if all equity

$$R_E = R_A + \frac{D}{E}(1 - t_C)(R_A - R_D)$$

$$= R_A + \frac{0.4}{0.6}(0.60)(R_A - 12\%)$$

$$= 20.75\%$$

By solving the equation, we find that $R_A = 0.1825$. Of course, R_A is less than R_E because the cost of equity capital would be less when the firm employs no leverage.

At this point, firms in the real world generally make the assumption that the business risk of their venture is about equal to the business risk of the firms already in the business. Applying this assumption to our problem, we assert that the hypothetical discount rate of WWE's widget venture if all equity financed is also 0.1825.[4] This discount rate would be employed if WWE uses the APV approach because the APV approach calls for R_A, the project's cost of capital in a firm with no leverage.

3 *Determining R_E for WWE's widget venture:* Alternatively, WWE might use the FTE approach, where the discount rate for levered equity is determined like this:

Cost of equity capital for WWE's widget venture

$$R_E = R_A + \frac{D}{E}(1 - t_C)(R_A - R_D)$$

$$= 18.25\% + \frac{1}{3}(0.60)(18.25\% - 10\%)$$

$$= 19.9\%$$

Note that the cost of equity capital for WWE's widget venture, 0.199, is less than the cost of equity capital for AW, 0.2075. This occurs because AW has a higher debt-to-equity ratio. (As mentioned, both firms are assumed to have the same business risk.)

4 *Determining R_{wacc} for WWE's widget venture:* Finally, WWE might use the WACC approach. Here is the appropriate calculation:

R_{WACC} for WWE's widget venture

$$R_{WACC} = \frac{D}{D+E}R(1 - t_C) + \frac{E}{D+E}R_E$$

$$= \frac{1}{4}10\%(0.60) + \frac{3}{4}19.9\%$$

$$= 16.425\%$$

This example shows how the three discount rates, R_A, R_E and R_{WACC}, are determined in the real world. These are the appropriate rates for the APV, FTE and WACC approaches, respectively. Note that R_E for Asian Widgets is determined first because the cost of equity capital can be determined from the beta of the firm's equity. As discussed in an earlier chapter (Section 12.2), beta can easily be estimated for any publicly traded firm such as AW.

20.6 APV Example

As mentioned earlier in this chapter, firms generally set a target debt-to-equity ratio, allowing the use of WACC and FTE for capital budgeting. APV does not work as well here. However, as we also mentioned earlier, APV is the preferred approach when there are side benefits and side costs to debt. Because the analysis can be tricky, we now devote an entire section to an example where, in addition to the tax subsidy to debt, both flotation costs and interest subsidies come into play.

Example 20.2

APV

Bicksler Enterprises is considering a £10 million project that will last five years. The investment will be depreciated at 25 per cent reducing balance for tax purposes. At the end of the five years, the investment will be sold for its residual book value. The cash revenues less cash expenses per year are £3,500,000. The corporate tax bracket is 28 per cent. The risk-free rate is 10 per cent, and the cost of unlevered equity is 20 per cent.

First we will calculate the depreciation in each year:

	C_0	C_1	C_2	C_3	C_4	C_5
Initial outlay	−£10,000,000					
Depreciation		0.25 × (£2,500,000) = £700,000	0.25 × (£1,875,000) = £525,000	0.25 × (£1,406,250) = £393,750	0.25 × (£1,054,688) = £295,313	0.25 × £791,016 = £197,754
Residual value		£7,500,000	£5,625,000	£4,218,750	£3,164,063	£2,373,047

The cash flow projections each year are below. Because the investment is sold at its residual value, there are no tax implications for the final cash flow of £2,373,047. If, for example, Bicksler sold the investment for £3,000,000 it would be liable to pay tax on the profit of £626,953 (£3,000,000 − £2,373,047):

	C_0	C_1	C_2	C_3	C_4	C_5	C_6
Initial outlay	−£10,000,000						£2,373,047
Depreciation tax shield		0.28 × £2,500,000 = £700,000	0.28 × £1,875,000 = £525,000	0.28 × £1,406,250 = £393,750	0.28 × £1,054,688 = £295,313	0.28 × £791,0.16 = £197,754	
Revenue less expenses		(1 − 0.28) × £3,500,000 = £2,520,000	£2,520,000	£2,520,000	£2,520,000	£2,520,000	

We stated before that the APV of a project is the sum of its all-equity value plus the additional effects of debt. We examine each in turn.

All-equity Value

Assuming the project is financed with all equity, we will discount the revenues and initial outlay cash flows by the cost of unlevered equity. The depreciation tax shield should be discounted at the risk-free rate. The present value of each cash flow is given below:

	C_0	C_1	C_2	C_3	C_4	C_5	C_6
Initial outlay	−£10,000,000						£794,729
Depreciation tax shield		£636,364	£433,884	£295,830	£201,703	£122,790	
Revenue less expenses		£2,100,000	£1,750,000	£1,458,333	£1,215,278	£1,012,731	
Present value	−£10,000,000	£2,736,364	£2,183,884	£1,754,164	£1,416,981	£1,135,521	£794,729

The net present value is thus:

$$-£10,000,000 + £2,736,364 + £2,183,884 + £1,754,164 + £1,416,981 + £1,135,521 + £794,729 = £21,642$$

This calculation uses the techniques presented in the early chapters of this book. Notice again that the depreciation tax shield is discounted at the riskless rate of 10 per cent. The revenues and expenses are discounted at the higher rate of 20 per cent.

An all-equity firm would accept the project because the NPV is £21,642. However, equity flotation costs and economic volatility (not mentioned yet) would more than likely make the NPV negative. However, debt financing may add enough value to the project to justify acceptance. We consider the effects of debt next.

Additional Effects of Debt

Bicksler Enterprises can obtain a five-year, non-amortizing loan for £7,500,000 after flotation costs at the risk-free rate of 10 per cent. Flotation costs are fees paid when equity or debt is issued. These fees may go to printers, lawyers and bankers, among others. Bicksler Enterprises is informed that flotation costs will be 1 per cent of the gross proceeds of its loan. The previous chapter indicates that debt financing alters the NPV of a typical project.

Flotation Costs

Given that flotation costs are 1 per cent of the gross proceeds, we have:

$$£7{,}500{,}000 = (1 - 0.01) \times \text{Gross proceeds} = 0.99 \times \text{Gross proceeds}$$

Thus, the gross proceeds are:

$$\frac{£7{,}500{,}000}{1 - 0.01} = \frac{£7{,}500{,}000}{0.99} = £7{,}575{,}758$$

This implies flotation costs of £75,758(= 1% × £7,575,758). To check the calculation, note that net proceeds are £7,500,000(= £7,575,758 − £75,758). In other words, Bicksler Enterprises receives only £7,500,000. The flotation costs of £75,758 are received by intermediaries such as bankers.

Under International Financial Reporting Standards, flotation costs directly attributable to an investment in a particular asset should be depreciated using the same method as the asset itself. In our case, depreciation would be charged on the flotation costs using 25 per cent reducing balance. The tax shield can then be calculated accordingly. Flotation costs are paid immediately but are deducted from taxes by amortizing on a 25 per cent reducing balance basis over the life of the loan. The depreciation schedule on the flotation costs is presented below:

	C_0	C_1	C_2	C_3	C_4	C_5
Flotation costs	−£75,758					
Depreciation		0.25 × (£75,758) = £18,940	0.25 × (£56,818) = £14,205	0.25 × (£42,613) = £10,653	0.25 × (£31,960) = £7,990	0.25 × (£23,970) = £5,993
Residual value		£56,818	£42,613	£31,960	£23,970	£17,977

The cash flows from flotation costs are as follows:

	Date 0	Date 1	Date 2	Date 3	Date 4	Date 5	Date 6
Flotation costs	−£75,758						
Deduction		£18,940	£14,205	£10,653	£7,990	£5,993	£17,977
Tax shield from flotation costs		0.28(£18,940) = £5,303	0.28(£14,205) = £3,977	0.28(£10,653) = £2,983	0.28(£7,990) = £2,237	0.28(£5,993) = £1,678	0.28(£17,977) = £5,034
PV(Costs)	−£75,758	£4,821	£3,287	£2,241	£1,528	£1,042	£2,841

When we discount at 10 per cent, the net cost of flotation is:

$$-£75{,}758 + £4{,}821 + £3{,}287 + £2{,}241 + £1{,}528 + £1{,}042 + £2{,}841 = -£59{,}998$$

The net present value of the project after the flotation costs of debt but before the benefits of debt is:

$$£21{,}642 - £59{,}998 = -£38{,}356$$

Tax Subsidy

Interest must be paid on the gross proceeds of the loan, even though intermediaries receive the flotation costs. Because the gross proceeds of the loan are £7,575,578, annual interest is £757,576 (= £7,575,758 × 0.10).

The interest cost after taxes is £5545,455[£757,576 × (1 − 0.28)]. Because the loan is non-amortizing, the entire debt of £7,575,758 is repaid at date 5. These terms are indicated here:

	Date 0	Date 1	Date 2	Date 3	Date 4	Date 5
Loan (gross proceeds)	£7,575,758					
Interest paid		10% × £7,575,758 = 757,576	£757,576	£757,576	£757,576	£757,576
Interest cost after taxes		(1 − 0.28) × £757,576 = £545,455	£545,455	£545,455	£545,455	£545,455
Repayment of debt						£7,575,758

The relevant cash flows are listed in boldface in the preceding table. They are (1) loan received, (2) annual interest cost after taxes, and (3) repayment of debt. Note that we include the *gross* proceeds of the loan as an inflow because the flotation costs have previously been subtracted.

In Chapter 15 we mentioned that the financing decision can be evaluated in terms of net present value. The net present value of the loan is simply the sum of the net present values of each of the three cash flows. This can be represented as follows:

Equation 20.1

$$\text{NPV (loan)} = +\text{Amount borrowed} - \begin{matrix}\text{Present value}\\ \text{of after-tax}\\ \text{interest payments}\end{matrix} - \begin{matrix}\text{Present value}\\ \text{of loan}\\ \text{repayments}\end{matrix}$$

The calculations for this example are:

Equation 20.1′

$$£804{,}105 = +£7{,}575{,}758 - \frac{£545{,}455}{0.10} \times \left[1 - \left(\frac{1}{1.10}\right)^5\right] - \frac{£7{,}575{,}758}{(1.10)^5}$$

The NPV (loan) is positive, reflecting the interest tax shield.[5]

The adjusted present value of the project with this financing is:

Equation 20.2

$$\text{APV} = \text{All-equity value} - \text{Flotation cost of debt} + \text{NPV (loan)}$$

Equation 20.2′

$$£768{,}749 = £21{,}642 - £59{,}998 + £804{,}105$$

Though we previously saw that an all-equity firm would probably not accept the project (once equity flotation costs were taken into account), a firm would *accept* the project if a £7,500,000 (net) loan could be obtained.

Because the loan just discussed was at the market rate of 10 per cent, we have so far considered only two of the three additional effects of debt (flotation costs and tax subsidy). We now examine another loan where the third effect arises.

Non-market-rate Financing

A number of companies are fortunate enough to obtain subsidized financing from a governmental authority. Suppose that the project of Bicksler Enterprises is deemed socially beneficial and the UK government grants the firm a £7,500,000 loan at 8 per cent interest. In addition, all flotation costs are absorbed by the state. Clearly, the company will choose this loan over the one we previously calculated. Here are the cash flows from the loan:

	Date 0	Date 1	Date 2	Date 3	Date 4	Date 5
Loan received	£7,500,000					
Interest paid		8% × £7,500,000 = £600,000	£600,000	£600,000	£600,000	£600,000
After-tax interest		(1 − 0.28) £600,000 **= £432,000**	**£432,000**	**£432,000**	**£432,000**	**£432,000**
Repayment of debt						**£7,500,000**

The relevant cash flows are listed in boldface in the preceding table. Using Equation 20.1, the NPV (loan) is:

Equation 20.1″ $$£1{,}205{,}470 = +£7{,}500{,}000 - \times [1 - 11.10^5] - \frac{£432{,}000}{0.10}\,\frac{£7{,}500{,}000}{1.10^5}$$

Why do we discount the cash flows in Equation 20.1″ at 10 per cent when the firm is borrowing at 8 per cent? We discount at 10 per cent because that is the fair or market-wide rate. That is, 10 per cent is the rate at which the firm could borrow *without* benefit of subsidization. The net present value of the subsidized loan is larger than the net present value of the earlier loan because the firm is now borrowing at the below-market rate of 8 per cent. Note that the NPV (loan) calculation in Equation 20.1″ captures both the tax effect *and* the non-market-rate effect.

Equation 20.2 APV = All-equity value − Flotation costs of debt + NPV (loan)

Equation 20.2″ £1,227,112 = £21,642 − £0 + £1,205,470

This example illustrates the adjusted present value (APV) approach. The approach begins with the present value of a project for the all-equity firm. Next, the effects of debt are added in. The approach has much to recommend it. It is intuitively appealing because individual components are calculated separately and added together in a simple way. And, if the debt from the project can be specified precisely, the present value of the debt can be calculated precisely.

20.7 Beta and Leverage

Section 12.3 provides the formula for the relationship between the beta of the equity and leverage of the firm in a world without taxes. We reproduce this formula here:

The no-tax case

Equation 20.3 $$\beta_{\text{Equity}} = \beta_{\text{Asset}}\left(1 + \frac{\text{Debt}}{\text{Equity}}\right)$$

As pointed out earlier, this relationship holds under the assumption that the beta of debt is zero.

Because firms must pay corporate taxes in practice, it is worthwhile to provide the relationship in a world with corporate taxes. It can be shown that the relationship between the beta of the unlevered firm and the beta of the levered equity is this:[6]

The corporate tax case

Equation 20.4 $$\beta_{\text{Equity}} = \left[1 + \frac{(1 - t_C)\text{Debt}}{\text{Equity}}\right]\beta_{\text{Unlevered firm}}$$

when (1) the corporation is taxed at the rate of t_c, and (2) the debt has a zero beta.

Because $[1 + (1 - t_c)\text{Debt/Equity}]$ must be more than 1 for a levered firm, it follows that $\beta_{\text{Unlevered firm}} < \beta_{\text{Equity}}$. The corporate tax case of Equation 20.4 is quite similar to the no-tax case of Equation 20.3 because the beta of levered equity must be greater than the beta of the unlevered firm in either case. The intuition that leverage increases the risk of equity applies in both cases.

However, notice that the two equations are not equal. It can be shown that leverage increases the equity beta less rapidly under corporate taxes. This occurs because, under taxes, leverage creates a *riskless* tax shield, thereby lowering the risk of the entire firm.

Example 20.3

Unlevered Betas

Barajas SA is considering a scale-enhancing project. The market value of the firm's debt is €100 million, and the market value of the firm's equity is €200 million. The debt is considered riskless. The corporate tax rate is 28 per cent. Regression analysis indicates that the beta of the firm's equity is 2. The risk-free rate is 10 per cent, and the expected market premium is 8.5 per cent. What would the project's discount rate be in the hypothetical case that Barajas SA is all-equity?

We can answer this question in two steps.

1 *Determining beta of hypothetical all-equity firm:* Rearranging Equation 20.4, we have this:

Unlevered beta

Equation 20.5

$$\frac{\text{Equity}}{\text{Equity} + (1 - t_C) \times \text{Debt}} \times \beta_{\text{Equity}} = \beta_{\text{Unlevered firm}}$$

$$\frac{\text{€}200 \text{ million}}{\text{€}200 \text{ million} + (1 - 0.28) \times \text{€}100 \text{ million}} \times 2 = 1.47$$

2 *Determining discount rate:* We calculate the discount rate from the security market line (SML) as follows:

Discount rate

$$R_E = R_F + \beta \times (R_M - R_F)$$
$$= 10\% + 1.47 \times 8.5\%$$
$$= 22.5\%$$

The Project is Not Scale Enhancing

Because Example 20.3 assumed that the project is scale enhancing, we began with the beta of the firm's equity. If the project is not scale enhancing, we could begin with the equity betas of firms in the industry of the project. For each firm, we could calculate the hypothetical beta of the unlevered equity by Equation 20.5. The SML could then be used to determine the project's discount rate from the average of these betas.

Example 20.4

More Unlevered Betas

The Irish firm, J. Lowes plc, which currently manufactures staples, is considering a €1 million investment in a project in the aircraft adhesives industry. The corporation estimates unlevered after-tax cash flows (UCF) of €300,000 per year in perpetuity from the project. The firm will finance the project with a debt-to-value ratio of 0.5 (or, equivalently, a debt-to-equity ratio of 1:1).

The three competitors in this new industry are currently unlevered, with betas of 1.2, 1.3 and 1.4. Assuming a risk-free rate of 5 per cent, a market risk premium of 9 per cent and a corporate tax rate of 12.5 per cent, what is the net present value of the project?

We can answer this question in five steps.

1 *Calculating the average unlevered beta in the industry:* The average unlevered beta across all three existing competitors in the aircraft adhesives industry is:

$$\frac{1.2 + 1.3 + 1.4}{3} = 1.3$$

2 *Calculating the levered beta for J. Lowes' new project:* Assuming the same unlevered beta for this new project as for the existing competitors, we have, from Equation 20.4:

Levered beta

$$\beta_{\text{Equity}} = \left[1 + \frac{(1 - t_C)\text{Debt}}{\text{Equity}}\right]\beta_{\text{Unlevered firm}}$$
$$= \left(1 + \frac{0.875 \times 1}{1}\right) \times 1.3$$
$$= 2.4375$$

3 *Calculating the cost of levered equity for the new project:* We calculate the discount rate from the security market line (SML) as follows:

Discount rate

$$R_E = R_F + \beta \times (R_M - R_F)$$
$$= 0.05 + 2.4375 \times 0.09$$
$$= 0.269$$

4 *Calculating the WACC for the new project:* The formula for determining the weighted average cost of capital, R_{WACC}, is:

$$R_{WACC} = \frac{D}{D+E} R_D (1 - t_C) + \frac{E}{D+E} R_E$$

$$= \frac{1}{2} \times 0.05 \times 0.875 + \frac{1}{2} \times 0.269$$

$$= 0.156$$

5 *Determining the project's value:* Because the cash flows are perpetual, the NPV of the project is:

$$\frac{\text{Unlevered cash flows(UCF)}}{R_{WACC}} - \text{Initial investment}$$

$$\frac{€300{,}000}{0.156} - €1 \text{ million} = €923{,}077$$

Real World Insight 20.1

Investing in Student Apartments

A major growth area for investment in the UK is student accommodation. With more students than ever enrolling at UK universities, especially from overseas, incoming students are becoming increasingly choosy about the quality and affordability of their living arrangements. This has attracted a wave of investors who seek to leverage the excess demand for purpose-built student accommodation (PBSA). One such investor, US private equity firm Blackstone, has invested billions in UK student accommodation. Its first investment was the £4.7 billion purchase of iQ Student Accommodation, one of the UK's largest PBSA providers, in May 2020. This was followed by a £120 million acquisition of a portfolio of six student residences from Student Roost in December 2020. Finally, in March 2021, it agreed to buy GCP Student Living (a real estate investment trust that owns 11 student properties across London and Brighton) for £969 million. These deals contributed to a record-breaking year for investment in UK PBSA, with investors spending £5.77 billion in the sector in 2020, a 5.7 per cent increase on 2019.

Source: Savills (www.savills.co.uk)

20.8 Net Asset Value

In many real-life business situations, investment projects will last for as long as possible and will have no pre-set end date. As long as the product or service is useful to customers, there will be a business until a new model is introduced. To address the potential infinite life of a project, you would calculate a terminal value for the project at some point in the future, say year 5, as if you would be selling it at that date.

The analysis presented in Example 20.5 is not possible for projects that are dependent on a finite resource, such as a gold mine. In a gold mine, the project's cash flows will mainly be driven by two variables: gold price and the amount of gold in the mine. As gold is extracted, the gold resource will fall until there is no gold left.

Example 20.5

Calculating the NPV of a Project using Terminal Value

Mignonette SA is considering the creation of a new warehouse project to build hermetically sealed window frames. The project requires an initial investment of €2 million. The first-year cash flow from the warehouse will be €250,000 and this is likely to grow for the next four years at a rate of 20 per cent per annum. From year 5, the cash flows will cease to grow. Given the standardized technology, it is unlikely that demand will fall off or grow further after year 5. If the discount rate is 12 per cent, what is the NPV of the warehouse project?

The cash flows for the project are as follows:

Year	0	1	2	3	4	5	6+
Cash flow	–€2,000,000	€250,000	€300,000	€360,000	€432,000	€518,400	€518,400

From year 5 onwards, the project generates a perpetuity of €518,400 per annum. This is equal to a year 4 terminal value of V_4 = €518,400/.12 = €4,320,000. A revised cash flow table is presented below:

Year	0	1	2	3	4
Cash flow	–€2,000,000	€250,000	€300,000	€360,000	€432,000
Terminal value					€4,320,000
Net cash flow	–€2,000,000	€250,000	€300,000	€360,000	€4,752,000

The NPV of the warehouse project is €1,738,595.

For extractive industries such as mining, an alternative measure to NPV is used, called net asset value (NAV). Net asset value is simply the NPV of the mine but calculated from the two key value drivers. Terminal value is never used because there is no resource left to generate future revenues.

Example 20.6 is necessarily simplified so we can focus on the core concept of net asset value. As you will see, net asset value is effectively net present value for situations when the life of an asset is restricted because of resource constraints.

Example 20.6

Fairplay Mines

Fairplay plc has opened a new site for drilling gold at the northernmost tip of Finland. The mine has proven reserves of 1.5 million ounces of gold. It is anticipated that Fairplay can extract 100,000 ounces of gold per annum from the site. The current gold price per ounce is €1,500 and it is expected that this will grow by 5 per cent per annum for the foreseeable future. Initial set-up costs for the mine are €330 million. The variable cost of mining in year 1 is €900 per ounce of gold, but this is expected to grow at a rate of 9 per cent per annum to reflect the increasing difficulty to mine the ore over time as resources become depleted. The mine will be required to be decommissioned at the end of its life and this will cost €50 million in the year after it ceases production. Assume a zero tax rate due to government subsidies. If the appropriate discount rate for the gold mine is 6 per cent, what is its net asset value?

The cash flow forecast (with present value estimates) is given below:

	Gold Price	Units Mined	Revenues	Variable Costs	Total Variable Costs	Total Costs	Net Cash Flow	PV
0						330,000,000	(330,000,000)	(330,000,000)
1	1500	100,000	150,000,000	900	90,000,000	90,000,000	60,000,000	56,603,774
2	1575.00	100,000	157,500,000	981.00	98,100,000	98,100,000	59,400,000	52,865,789
3	1653.75	100,000	165,375,000	1,069.29	106,929,000	106,929,000	58,446,000	49,072,389
4	1736.44	100,000	173,643,750	1,165.53	116,552,610	116,552,610	57,091,140	45,221,530
5	1823.26	100,000	182,325,938	1,270.42	127,042,345	127,042,345	55,283,593	41,311,116
6	1914.42	100,000	191,442,234	1,384.76	138,476,156	138,476,156	52,966,078	37,338,995
7	2010.14	100,000	201,014,346	1,509.39	150,939,010	150,939,010	50,075,336	33,302,959
8	2110.65	100,000	211,065,063	1,645.24	164,523,521	164,523,521	46,541,543	29,200,740
9	2216.18	100,000	221,618,317	1,793.31	179,330,638	179,330,638	42,287,679	25,030,012
10	2326.99	100,000	232,699,232	1,954.70	195,470,395	195,470,395	37,228,837	20,788,388

	Gold Price	Units Mined	Revenues	Variable Costs	Total Variable Costs	Total Costs	Net Cash Flow	PV
11	2443.34	100,000	244,334,194	2,130.63	213,062,731	213,062,731	31,271,463	16,473,417
12	2565.51	100,000	256,550,904	2,322.38	232,238,376	232,238,376	24,312,527	12,082,581
13	2693.78	100,000	269,378,449	2,531.40	253,139,830	253,139,830	16,238,619	7,613,298
14	2828.47	100,000	282,847,371	2,759.22	275,922,415	275,922,415	6,924,956	3,062,915
15	2969.90	100,000	296,989,740	3,007.55	300,755,432	300,755,432	(3,765,693)	(1,571,292)
16						50,000,000	(50,000,000)	(19,682,314)

Summing the present values gives a net asset value of €78,714,269. The mine appears a good investment for Fairplay. However, the analysis is heavily dependent on the initial assumptions, which may or may not be realized. Particular concern would revolve around the forecasts for gold price and variable costs.

Summary and Conclusions

Earlier chapters of this text showed how to calculate net present value for projects of all-equity firms. We pointed out in Chapters 18 and 19 that the introduction of taxes and bankruptcy costs changes a firm's financing decisions. Rational corporations should employ some debt in a world of this type. Because of the benefits and costs associated with debt, the capital budgeting decision is different for levered firms than for unlevered firms. The present chapter has discussed three methods for capital budgeting by levered firms: the adjusted present value (APV), flows to equity (FTE) and weighted average cost of capital (WACC) approaches.

1 The APV formula can be written as:

$$\sum_{t=1}^{\infty} \frac{UCF_t}{(1+R_A)^t} + \text{Additional effects of debt} - \text{Initial investment}$$

There are four additional effects of debt:

(a) Tax shield from debt financing

(b) Flotation costs

(c) Bankruptcy costs

(d) Benefit of non-market-rate financing.

2 The FTE formula can be written as:

$$\sum_{t=1}^{\infty} + (\text{Initial investment} - \text{Amount borrowed}) \frac{LCF_t}{(1+R_E)^t}$$

3 The WACC formula can be written as:

$$\sum_{t=1}^{\infty} \frac{UCF_t}{(1+R_{WACC})^t} - \text{Initial investment}$$

4 Corporations frequently follow this guideline:

(a) Use WACC or FTE if the firm's target debt-to-value *ratio* applies to the project over its life.

(b) Use APV if the project's *level* of debt is known over the life of the project.

5 The APV method is used frequently for special situations like interest subsidies, LBOs and leases. The WACC and FTE methods are commonly used for more typical capital budgeting situations. The APV approach is a rather unimportant method for typical capital budgeting situations.

6 The beta of the equity of the firm is positively related to the leverage of the firm.

Questions and Problems

CONCEPT

1 **Adjusted Present Value** How is the APV of a project calculated? What about the FTE? What is the main difference between the APV, FTE and WACC?

2 **Net Asset Value** What is the main difference between net asset value and net present value? Why is net asset value important in mining investments?

3. **Weighted Average Cost of Capital** Is WACC consistent with a target debt–equity ratio? Explain.

4 **APV, FTE and WACC** Compare and contrast the three methods of capital budgeting. What are their strengths and weaknesses? When and why should you use each method instead of the other two? Are the three methods consistent when a firm does not have a target debt-to-equity ratio? Explain.

5. **Discount Rate in Capital Budgeting** Review the steps required in calculating the correct discount rate for capital budgeting when a firm has a high level of debt in its capital structure.

6 **Beta and Leverage** What are the two types of risk that are measured by a levered beta?

REGULAR

7 **Capital Budgeting** You are determining whether your company should undertake a new project, and have calculated the NPV of the project using the WACC method when the CFO, a former accountant, notices that you did not use the interest payments in calculating the cash flows of the project. What should you tell him? If he insists that you include the interest payments in calculating the cash flows, what method can you use? The former accountant also tells you to assume the opportunity cost of the company's idle asset is zero. Is he correct? Why, or why not?

8 **NPV and APV** Zoso is a rental car company that is considering whether to add 25 cars to its fleet. The company depreciates all its rental cars using 20 per cent reducing balance, and at the end of five years assumes that the cars will be sold at residual value. The new cars are expected to generate £120,000 per year in earnings before taxes and depreciation for five years. The company is financed entirely by equity and has a 18 per cent tax rate. The required return on the company's unlevered equity is 10 per cent, and the new fleet will not change the risk of the company.

(a) What is the maximum price that the company should be willing to pay for the new fleet of cars if it remains an all-equity company?

(b) Suppose the company can purchase the fleet of cars for £375,000. Additionally, assume the company can issue £250,000 of five-year, 8 per cent debt to finance the project. All principal will be repaid in one balloon payment at the end of the fifth year. What is the adjusted present value (APV) of the project?

9 **NPV Capital Budgeting** Culdesac NV has developed a design for new wireless noise-reducing earphones and is considering whether it should replace its existing wired earphones, whose popularity has decreased in the last year. The company publishes its financial accounts at 31 December and today is 1 January. As the financial manager of the business you have been provided with the following information:

- The machinery required to produce the earphones will cost €100 million today. The project is likely to become obsolete after five years, at which time the machinery will have an expected resale value of €30 million.
- The company has already spent €20 million on market research and development of the prototype for the product.
- Production will take place on premises currently owned but rented out by the company for €35 million per annum.
- The annual sales volume over the life of the project is expected to be 100,000, 100,000, 200,000, 300,000 and 200,000 in years 1–5, respectively. The selling price per unit will be €300 throughout the life of the project.
- The variable costs per unit produced are expected to be as follows:

Materials	€90 per item
Wages	€30 per item
Others	€30 per item

- The firm's fixed costs are currently €50 million, and are expected to increase to €55 million as a direct result of this project.
- The project's working capital requirements for the project are as follows:

Raw materials	one-tenth of annual material requirements
Finished goods	one-tenth of annual total costs of production
Debtors	one-fifth of annual sales
Creditors	one-fifth of annual material requirements

- Tax depreciation on the purchase of the machinery is allowed at 25 per cent on a reducing balance basis.
- The company pays corporation tax at 35 per cent, which is payable one year in arrears.
- The opportunity cost of capital for the project is 10 per cent.

Produce a working capital schedule and tax depreciation schedule for the project. Also prepare a change in income statement and show the change in cash flows. Calculate the project's NPV. Should the project be accepted?

10 **APV** Gemini Green Solutions Ltd, a firm with a zero-debt capital structure, is dedicated to promoting responsible consumption and production. The firm is contemplating a €2.4 million investment in an innovative recycling plant featuring advanced technologies to increase the rate of recycling and reduce waste. The investment will be depreciated using a 25 per cent reducing balance method over a four-year period, after which the plant is expected to be sold for its residual value.

The recycling project is projected to contribute earnings before taxes and depreciation of €850,000 annually for the four years of its operation. Importantly, this project won't alter the risk profile of the firm. To fund this project, Gemini Green Solutions has the opportunity to secure a four-year, 9.5 per cent loan from a green finance initiative at a local bank. The principal of the loan will be paid as one lump sum at the end of the fourth year, and the bank will charge €24,000 in fees related to the loan issuance, which can be spread out and paid over the four-year loan period.

On the other hand, if Gemini Green Solutions decided to finance the project solely through equity, it would have a cost of capital of 13 per cent. The company operates in a jurisdiction where the corporate tax rate is 12.5 per cent.

Using the adjusted present value (APV) approach, evaluate whether Gemini Green Solutions should proceed with the proposed recycling plant project.

11 **Flow to Equity** Milano Pizza owns three identical restaurants popular for their speciality pizzas. Each restaurant has a debt–equity ratio of 40 per cent and makes interest payments of €29,500 at the end of each year. The cost of the firm's levered equity is 19 per cent. Each store estimates that annual sales will be €1 million, annual cost of goods sold will be €450,000, and annual general and administrative costs will be €325,000. These cash flows are expected to remain the same for ever. The corporate tax rate is 37.2 per cent.

(a) Use the flow to equity approach to determine the value of the company's equity.

(b) What is the total value of the company?

12 **WACC** Cryo NV is a carbon-neutral firm engaged in property and casualty insurance. In an effort to fund its green initiatives, Cryo is about to issue a 10-year green bond at par with an 8 per cent coupon. Prior to the green bond issue, the firm has a beta of 0.8 but anticipates this will shift as the firm transitions to its new target debt–equity ratio of 0.25, intending to leverage this debt to finance its climate action strategies. The expected return on the Euro Stoxx 50 index is 13 per cent and Treasury bills currently yield 3.4 per cent. What will be Cryo NV's cost of debt, cost of equity and WACC once the green bond is issued, considering the potential climate risk-adjusted returns? The corporate tax rate stands at 23 per cent.

13 **WACC: Wild Widgets** If Wild Widgets were an all-equity company, it would have a beta of 1.1. The company has a target debt–equity ratio of 0.40. The expected return on the market portfolio is 13 per cent and Treasury bills currently yield 7 per cent. The company has one bond issue outstanding that matures in 20 years and has a 9 per cent coupon rate. The bond currently sells for £97.50. The corporate tax rate is 28 per cent.

(a) What is the company's cost of debt?

(b) What is the company's cost of equity?

(c) What is the company's weighted average cost of capital?

14 **Beta and Leverage** Maersk A/S and Lundberg A/S would have identical equity betas of 0.9 if both were all equity financed. The market value information for each company is shown here:

	Maersk A/S (DKr)	Lundberg A/S (DKr)
Debt	11,400,000	25,600,000
Equity	25,600,000	11,400,000

The expected return on the market portfolio is 9 per cent, and the risk-free rate is 2.3 per cent. Both companies are subject to a corporate tax rate of 25 per cent. Assume the beta of debt is zero.

(a) What is the equity beta of each of the two companies?

(b) What is the required rate of return on each of the two companies' equity?

15 **NPV of Loans** Daniel Kaffe, CFO of Kendrick Enterprises, is evaluating a six-year, 13 per cent loan with gross proceeds of €9,000,000. The interest payments on the loan will be made annually. Flotation costs are estimated to be 1 per cent of gross proceeds and will be amortized using a 25 per cent reducing balance method over the six-year life of the loan. The company has a tax rate of 35 per cent, and the loan will not increase the risk of financial distress for the company.

(a) Calculate the net present value of the loan excluding flotation costs.

(b) Calculate the net present value of the loan including flotation costs.

16 **NPV: Station GmbH** Station GmbH is a German all-equity firm that is about to issue a new 10-year, 17 per cent bond with interest paid annually. The debt issue of €10 million is to fund an expansion of the firm's activities into Switzerland. Flotation costs are 0.8 per cent of gross proceeds, amortized over the life of the bond using 20 per cent reducing balances. Station's tax rate is 33 per cent and the bond will not increase the risk of financial distress. You believe that the company may be better off issuing the bond in Switzerland (rather than Germany) to raise visibility of the company among its new customer base. You estimate that a Swiss bond issue will increase cash flows by €200,000 per annum over 10 years from additional Swiss revenues. However, flotation costs are 1.2 per cent in Switzerland. What is the net present value of the loan if it is made in Germany? Is a Swiss bond issue a better decision? Explain.

17 **NPV for an All-equity Company** Shattered Glass plc is an all-equity firm. The cost of the company's equity is currently 22 per cent and the risk-free rate is 3 per cent. The company is currently considering a project that will cost £8 million and last five years. The project will generate revenues minus expenses each year (excluding depreciation) in the amount of £2.3 million. If the company has a tax rate of 18 per cent, should it accept the project? The initial investment is depreciated using 20 per cent reducing balance and will have zero salvage value at the end of its life.

18 **Calculating WACC** XYZ plc is considering purchasing new equipment that would cost £40 million. The expected unlevered cash flows from this investment are £13 million per annum for the next five years. The company's stock returns have a covariance with the market portfolio of 0.048. The standard deviation of the returns on the market portfolio is 20 per cent, and the expected market risk premium is 7.5 per cent. XYZ currently has bonds outstanding with a market value of £30 million and a yield to maturity of 8 per cent. The company also has 5 million ordinary shares outstanding, currently selling at £20 per share. The company's CEO considers the current debt–equity ratio as optimal. Government debt is currently selling at a yield of 6 per cent, and the company pays a corporation tax rate of 21 per cent.

(a) Use the WACC approach to determine whether XYZ plc should purchase the equipment.

(b) If the company decides to buy the equipment financed solely with debt, what is the cost of capital for the project?

19 **WACC: Bolero plc** Bolero plc has compiled the following information on its financing costs:

Type of Financing	Book Value (£)	Market Value (£)	Cost (%)
Long-term debt	2,000,000	2,000,000	3.5
Short-term debt	9,000,000	8,000,000	6.8
Ordinary shares	6,000,000	22,000,000	14.5
Total	17,000,000	32,000,000	

The company is in the 28 per cent tax bracket and has a target debt–equity ratio of 60 per cent. The target short-term debt/long-term debt ratio is 20 per cent.

(a) What is the company's weighted average cost of capital using book value weights?

(b) What is the company's weighted average cost of capital using market value weights?

(c) What is the company's weighted average cost of capital using target capital structure weights?

(d) What is the difference between WACCs? Which is the correct WACC to use for project evaluation?

20 **NAV: Letlago plc** Letlago plc has established a joint venture with a Kenyan firm, Wannako Ltd, to build a new gold mine in Kenya. The initial investment in paving equipment is £12 million. The equipment will be depreciated using the 20 per cent reducing balance method over its economic life of five years, at the end of which it will be sold for its residual value. Earnings before interest, taxes and depreciation collected from the gold mine are projected to be £0.8 million per annum for 20 years starting from the end of the first year. The corporate tax rate is 23 per cent. The required rate of return for the project under all-equity financing is 19 per cent. The pre-tax cost of debt for the joint partnership is 8.5 per cent. To encourage investment in the country's infrastructure, the Kenyan government will subsidize the project with a £10 million, 15-year loan at an interest rate of 7 per cent per year. All principal will be repaid in one balloon payment at the end of year 15. What is the net asset value of this project?

21 **NAV and Subsidized Debt** For the company in the previous problem, what is the value of being able to issue subsidized debt instead of having to issue debt at the terms it would normally receive? Assume the face amount and maturity of the debt issue are the same.

22 **APV and Expansion Decisions** MVP GmbH has produced football supplies for more than 20 years. The company currently has a debt–equity ratio of 50 per cent and is in the 29.8 per cent tax bracket. The required return on the firm's levered equity is 16 per cent. MVP is planning to expand its production capacity. The equipment to be purchased is expected to generate the following unlevered cash flows:

Year	Cash Flow (€)
0	−24,000,000
1	8,000,000
2	13,000,000
3	10,000,000

The company has arranged a €12 million debt issue to partially finance the expansion. Under the loan, the company would pay interest of 9 per cent at the end of each year on the outstanding balance at the beginning of the year. The company would also make year-end principal payments of €4 million per year, completely retiring the issue by the end of the third year. Using the adjusted present value method, should the company proceed with the expansion?

23 **WACC: Neon Corporation** Neon Corporation's share price returns have a covariance with the market portfolio of 0.048. The standard deviation of the returns on the market portfolio is 20 per cent and the expected market risk premium is 7.5 per cent. The company has bonds outstanding with a total market value of £30 million and a yield to maturity of 8 per cent. The company also has 5 million ordinary shares outstanding, each selling for £20. The company's CEO considers the firm's current debt–equity ratio optimal. The corporate tax rate is 28 per cent, and Treasury bills currently yield 6 per cent. The company is considering the purchase of additional equipment that would cost £40 million. The expected unlevered cash flows from the equipment are £13 million per year for five years. Purchasing the equipment will not change the risk level of the firm.

(a) Use the weighted average cost of capital approach to determine whether Neon should purchase the equipment.

(b) Suppose the company decides to fund the purchase of the equipment entirely with debt. What is the cost of capital for the project now? Explain.

CHALLENGE

24 **APV, FTE and WACC: Seger plc** Seger plc is an unlevered firm with expected annual earnings before taxes of £35 million in perpetuity. The current required return on the firm's equity is 20 per cent, and the firm distributes all of its earnings as dividends at the end of each year. The company has 1.5 million ordinary shares outstanding

and is subject to a corporate tax rate of 28 per cent. The firm is planning a recapitalization under which it will issue £40 million of perpetual 9 per cent debt and use the proceeds to buy back shares.

(a) Calculate the value of the company before the recapitalization plan is announced. What is the value of equity before the announcement? What is the price per share?

(b) Use the APV method to calculate the company value after the recapitalization plan is announced. What is the value of equity after the announcement? What is the price per share?

(c) How many shares will be repurchased? What is the value of equity after the repurchase has been completed? What is the price per share?

(d) Use the flow to equity method to calculate the value of the company's equity after the recapitalization.

25 **APV, FTE and WACC: Mojito Mint Company** Mojito Mint Company has a debt–equity ratio of 0.45. The required return on the company's unlevered equity is 17 per cent, and the pre-tax cost of the firm's debt is 9 per cent. Sales revenue for the company is expected to remain stable indefinitely at last year's level of £23,500,000. Variable costs amount to 60 per cent of sales. The tax rate is 28 per cent, and the company distributes all its earnings as dividends at the end of each year.

(a) If the company were financed entirely by equity, how much would it be worth?

(b) What is the required return on the firm's levered equity?

(c) Use the weighted average cost of capital method to calculate the value of the company. What is the value of the company's equity? What is the value of the company's debt?

(d) Use the flow to equity method to calculate the value of the company's equity.

26 **APV, FTE and WACC: Lone Star Industries** Lone Star Industries has just issued £160,000 of perpetual 10 per cent debt and used the proceeds to repurchase equity. The company expects to generate £75,000 of earnings before interest and taxes in perpetuity. The company distributes all its earnings as dividends at the end of each year. The firm's unlevered cost of capital is 18 per cent, and the corporate tax rate is 28 per cent.

(a) What is the value of the company as an unlevered firm?

(b) Use the adjusted present value method to calculate the value of the company with leverage.

(c) What is the required return on the firm's levered equity?

(d) Use the flow to equity method to calculate the value of the company's equity.

27 **Projects that Are Not Scale Enhancing** Blue Angel Ltd, a private firm in the holiday gift industry, is considering a new project. The company currently has a target debt–equity ratio of 0.40, but the industry target debt–equity ratio is 0.35. The industry average beta is 1.2. The market risk premium is 8 per cent and the risk-free rate is 7 per cent. Assume all companies in this industry can issue debt at the risk-free rate. The corporate tax rate is 28 per cent. The project requires an initial outlay of £450,000 and is expected to result in a £75,000 cash inflow at the end of the first year. The project will be financed at Blue Angel's target debt–equity ratio. Annual cash flows from the project will grow at a constant rate of 5 per cent until the end of the fifth year and remain constant for ever thereafter. Should Blue Angel invest in the project?

28 **APV and Infrastructure Projects** The Great Barrier Reef Restoration project is an initiative in Australia, with the goal of revitalizing and preserving the biodiversity of the Great Barrier Reef. The project is a collaborative effort between the renewable energy company, EcoPower, and the Global Environmental Trust. It was launched in 2023 and is touted as one of the most ambitious marine conservation initiatives in the world. It involves the creation of artificial reefs and the use of renewable energy sources to power all on-site operations.

Suppose the Great Barrier Reef Restoration project requires an investment of AUD5 billion, financed by a 60:40 mix of equity and debt. Assume further that the project receives a green bond from the Australian government, ensuring a fixed return of AUD120 per MWh for the renewable energy generated by the project in perpetuity and equivalent to AUD25 million per annum.

The project has a discount rate of 8 per cent and a tax rate of 30 per cent. The interest rate on the debt is 4 per cent. The project will generate AUD800 million in cash flows annually, and these cash flows will grow at a steady rate of 3 per cent per year. Calculate the APV of the project.

29 Equivalence of WACC and APV Select a range of empirical studies on capital budgeting and discuss their findings. What, in your opinion, are the most interesting findings?

30 NPV as an Investment Appraisal Tool After graduating from university you get a job for a non-dividend-paying company which has recently listed on the stock exchange. Your manager tells you that the company does not favour the NPV approach to capital budgeting. Do you think this is a good decision by the company's management?

Exam Question (45 minutes)

Electrolar AB is planning to set up new operations in northern Sweden. Having established that the investment has a positive net present value, it now has to consider its financing decision. The underwriters to the company state that the total funding required amounts to SKr0.5 billion and that this can be raised through a debt issue or an equity issue.

1. Its first option concerns the use of debt financing. The underwriters suggest that a 10-year bond issue with a 7 per cent coupon may be a sensible route to raising these funds. If interest payments are tax deductible and the tax rate is 26.33 per cent, estimate the required rate of return for debt financing to the nearest half per cent. **(25 marks)**
2. The second option relates to equity financing. The underwriters believe that, if the company were to issue shares to fund the proposed project, they would have to be sold at a discount of 20 per cent. Issue expenses will be 1 per cent of the funding requirement. Estimate the return required by investors when investing in Electrolar plc's new share issue. **(25 marks)**
3. Review the ways in which positive net present value opportunities may arise when a company wishes to raise funds in the financial markets. Use an example to illustrate your answer. **(25 marks)**
4. Compare and contrast the strengths and weaknesses of the adjusted present value, weighted average cost of capital and flow to equity approaches to investment appraisal. Which method, in your opinion, is the best? Explain. **(25 marks)**

Total Marks: 100

Mini Case

The Leveraged Buyout of Cheek Products Ltd

Cheek Products Ltd was founded 53 years ago by Joe Cheek, and originally sold snack foods such as crisps and biscuits. Through acquisitions, the company has grown into a conglomerate with major divisions in the snack food industry, home security systems, cosmetics and plastics. Additionally, the company has several smaller divisions. In recent years the company has been underperforming, but its management does not seem to be aggressively pursuing opportunities to improve operations (and the share price).

Meg Sato is a financial analyst specializing in identifying potential buyout targets. They believe that two major changes are needed at Cheek Products. First, they think that the company would be better off if it sold several divisions and concentrated on its core competencies in snack foods and home security systems. Second, the company is financed entirely with equity. Because the cash flows of the company are relatively steady, Meg thinks the company's debt–equity ratio should be at least 0.25. They believe these changes would significantly enhance shareholder wealth, but they also believe that the existing board and company management are unlikely to take the necessary actions. As a result, Meg thinks the company is a good candidate for a leveraged buyout.

A leveraged buyout (LBO) is the acquisition by a small group of equity investors of a public or private company. Generally, an LBO is financed primarily with debt. The new shareholders service the heavy interest and principal payments with cash from operations and/or asset sales. Shareholders generally hope to reverse the LBO within three to seven years by way of a public offering or sale of the company to another firm. A buyout is therefore likely to be successful only if the firm generates enough cash to serve the debt in the early years and if the company is attractive to other buyers a few years down the road.

Meg has suggested the potential LBO to their partners, Jacob Lapinska and Lina Ott. Jacob and Lina have asked Meg to provide projections of the cash flows for the company. Meg has provided the following estimates (in millions):

	2021 (£)	2022 (£)	2023 (£)	2024 (£)	2025 (£)
Sales	1,627	1,824	1,965	2,012	2,106
Costs	432	568	597	645	680
Depreciation	287	305	318	334	340
EBT	908	951	1,050	1,033	1,086
Capital expenditures	165	143	180	182	195
Change in net working capital	(72)	(110)	60	56	64
Asset sales	840	610			

At the end of five years, Meg estimates that the growth rate in cash flows will be 3.5 per cent per year. The capital expenditures are for new projects and the replacement of equipment that wears out. Additionally, the company would realize cash flow from the sale of several divisions. Even though the company will sell these divisions, overall sales should increase because of a more concentrated effort by the remaining divisions.

After ploughing through the company's financials and various pro forma scenarios, Jacob and Lina feel that, in five years, they will be able to sell the company to another party or take it public again. They are also aware that they will have to borrow a considerable amount of the purchase price. The interest payments on the debt for each of the next five years if the LBO is undertaken will be these (in millions):

	2021	2022	2023	2024	2025
Interest payments (£)	1,140	1,100	1,180	1,150	1,190

The company currently has a required return on assets of 14 per cent. Because of the high debt level, the debt will carry a yield to maturity of 12.5 per cent for the next five years. When the debt is refinanced in five years, they believe the new yield to maturity will be 8 per cent.

Cheek Products Ltd currently has 104 million shares of equity outstanding that sell for £53 per share. The corporate tax rate is 28 per cent. If Meg, Jacob and Lina decide to undertake the LBO, what is the most they should offer per share?

Practical Case Study

We now return to our Practical Case Study in Chapter 8. So far, we have gone with a consensus discount rate and assumed away any complications from leverage. The cement company for which you are carrying out consultancy has no debt funding. However, it wishes to borrow from a multinational bank in Tanzania the total amount required for the loan. If it does this, its debt–equity ratio will increase to 50 per cent. Assuming that the surveyed discount rates (see the Practical Case Study in Chapter 8) are for the firm prior to any debt increase, how would you now alter the analysis to take into account the increased debt? Use all information available to you, including the financial statements of other relevant companies.

Reference

Inselbag, I. and H. Kaufold (1997) 'Two Approaches for Valuing Companies under Alternative Financial Strategies (and How to Choose between Them)', *Journal of Applied Corporate Finance*, Vol. 10, No. 1, 114–122.

Additional Reading

For recent developments, see:

1 Bernstein, A., M.T. Gustafson and R. Lewis (2019) 'Disaster on the Horizon: The Price Effect of Sea Level Rise', *Journal of Financial Economics*, Vol. 134, No. 2, 253–272.

2 Booth, L. (2002) 'Finding Value Where None Exists: Pitfalls in Using Adjusted Present Value', *Journal of Applied Corporate Finance*, Vol. 15, No. 1, 8–17.

3 Booth, L. (2007) 'Capital Cash Flows, APV and Valuation', *European Financial Management*, Vol. 13, No. 1, 29–48.

4 Cooper, I.A. and K.G. Nyborg (2018) 'Consistent Valuation of Project Finance and LBOs using the Flows-to-equity Method', *European Financial Management*, Vol. 24, No. 1, 34–52.

5 Dempsey, M. (2013) 'Consistent Cash Flow Valuation with Tax-deductible Debt: A Clarification', *European Financial Management*, Vol. 19, No. 4, 830–836.

6 Dessaint, O., J. Olivier, C.A. Otto and D. Thesmar (2021) 'CAPM-based Company (Mis)valuations', *Review of Financial Studies*, Vol. 34, No. 1, 1–66.

7 Krüger, P., A. Landier and D. Thesmar (2015) 'The WACC Fallacy: The Real Effects of Using a Unique Discount Rate', *Journal of Finance*, Vol. 70, No. 3, 1253–1285.

8 Massari, M., F. Roncaglio and L. Zanetti (2008) 'On the Equivalence between the APV and WACC Approach in a Growing Leveraged Firm', *European Financial Management*, Vol. 14, No. 1, 152–162.

Endnotes

1 That is, the present value of the project after the initial investment has been made is £541,935.49 (= £21,935.49 + £520,000). Thus, the debt-to-value ratio of the project is 0.25 (£135,483.90/£541,935.49).

This level of debt can be calculated directly. Note that:

Present value of levered project = Present value of unlevered project project + $t_C \times D$

$$V_{\text{With debt}} = £504{,}000 + 0.28 \times 0.25 \times V_{\text{With debt}}$$

Rearranging the last line, we have:

$$V_{\text{With debt}} \times (1 - 0.28 \times 0.25) = £504{,}000$$
$$V_{\text{With debt}} = £541{,}935.50$$

Debt is 0.25 of value:
£135,483.90(= 0.25 × £541,935.50).

2 We use the term *levered cash flow* (LCF) for simplicity. A more complete term would be *cash flow from the project to the shareholders of a levered firm*. Similarly, a more complete term for *unlevered cash flow* (UCF) would be *cash flow from the project to the shareholders of an unlevered firm*.

3 See Inselbag and Kaufold (1997).

4 Alternatively, a firm might assume that its venture would be somewhat riskier because it is a new entrant. Thus, the firm might select a discount rate slightly higher than 0.1825. Of course, no exact formula exists for adjusting the discount rate upwards.

5 The NPV (loan) must be zero in a no-tax world because interest provides no tax shield there. To check this intuition, we calculate:

$$0 = +£7{,}575{,}758 - \frac{£757{,}576}{0.10} \times \left[1 - \left(\frac{1}{1.10}\right)^5\right] - \frac{£7{,}575{,}758}{(1.10)^5}$$

6 This result holds only if the beta of debt equals zero. To see this, note that:

$$V_U + t_C D = V_L = D + E \qquad \text{(a)}$$

where: V_U is the value of unlevered firm; V_L is the value of levered firm; D is the market value of debt in a levered firm; and E is the market value of equity in a levered firm.

As we stated in the text, the beta of the levered firm is a weighted average of the debt beta and the equity beta:

$$\frac{D}{D+E} \times \beta_D + \frac{E}{D+E} \times \beta_E$$

where β_D and β_E are the betas of the debt and the equity of the levered firm, respectively. Because $V_L = D + E$, we have:

$$\frac{D}{V_L} \times \beta_D + \frac{E}{V_L} \times \beta_E \qquad \text{(b)}$$

The beta of the levered firm can *also* be expressed as a weighted average of the beta of the unlevered firm and the beta of the tax shield:

$$\frac{V_U}{V_U + t_C D} \times \beta_U + \frac{t_C D}{V_U + t_C D} \times \beta_D$$

where β_U is the beta of the unlevered firm. This follows from Equation (a). Because $V_L = V_U + t_C D$, we have:

$$\frac{V_U}{V_L} \times \beta_U + \frac{t_C D}{V_L} \times \beta_D \qquad \text{(c)}$$

We can equate (b) and (c) because both represent the beta of a levered firm. Equation (a) tells us that $_U = S + (1 - t_C) \times D$. Under the assumption that $\beta_D = 0$, equating (b) and (c) and using Equation (a) yields Equation 20.4.

The generalized formula for the levered beta (where β_D is not zero) is:

$$\beta_E = \beta_U + (1 - t_C)(\beta_U - \beta_D)\frac{D}{E}$$

and

$$\beta_E = \frac{E}{D(1 - t_C) + E}\beta_E + \frac{D(1 - t_C)}{D(1 - t_C) + E}\beta_D$$

Chapter 21
Dividends and Other Payouts

Learning Objectives

After reading this chapter you should be able to:

LO1 Recall the different types of dividends and the standard method of cash dividend payment.

LO2 Appreciate the irrelevance of dividend policy and the impact of personal taxes on dividends.

LO3 Analysye the factors that might favour a high-dividend policy in the real world, as well as the clientele effect and the catering theory of dividends.

During uncertain economic periods, many companies maintain or raise their dividends even though simultaneously providing cautious statements about future operations and the economy. The combination of positive news (dividend increases) with negative information (caution about the future) often leaves investors uncertain of the sustainability of the dividend increases. In an interview with Reuters, Stuart Reeve (BlackRock Global Equity) summed up the feeling with the following words:

> *There are two things that threaten dividends – the first is that you pay out too much cash in a cyclical business and the second is that you're just too leveraged. We want to know what investment stream we can expect delivered and the capital growth we can reasonably hope for. We don't plan for what might come our way in buybacks. We want to know what the sustainable underlying dividend is.*

Why are dividends so important? What is meant by buybacks? This chapter explores the importance of dividends to corporate managers and the reasons why firms like to pay them. We also consider other forms of payouts to investors and why they are becoming more relevant.

Source: pedrosala/123RF

Key Notations

V_i	Value at time i
Div_i	Dividend at time i
R_E	Cost of equity capital; discount rate

21.1 Different Types of Dividends

The term *dividend* usually refers to a cash distribution of earnings. If a distribution is made from sources other than current or accumulated retained earnings, the term *distribution* rather than dividend is used. However, it is acceptable to refer to a distribution from earnings as a *dividend* and a distribution from capital as a *liquidating dividend*. More generally, any direct payment by the corporation to shareholders may be considered part of dividend policy.

The most common type of dividend is in the form of cash. Public companies usually pay **regular cash dividends** up to four times a year. Sometimes firms will pay a regular cash dividend and an *extra cash dividend*. Paying a cash dividend reduces corporate cash and retained earnings – except in the case of a liquidating dividend (where paid-in capital may be reduced).

Another type of dividend is paid out in shares of equity. This dividend is referred to as a **stock dividend**. It is not a true dividend because no cash leaves the firm. Rather, a stock dividend increases the number of shares outstanding, thereby reducing the value of each share. A stock dividend is commonly expressed as a ratio; for example, with a 2 per cent stock dividend a shareholder receives 1 new share for every 50 currently owned.

When a firm declares a **stock split**, it increases the number of shares outstanding. Because each share is now entitled to a smaller percentage of the firm's cash flow, the share price should fall. For example, if the managers of a firm whose equity is selling at €90 declare a 3:1 stock split, the price of a share of equity should fall to about €30. A stock split strongly resembles a stock dividend except that it is usually much larger.

Real World Insight 21.1

Centrica plc

Prior to the global pandemic of 2020 and 2021, the owner of British Gas, Centrica plc, experienced a near continuous fall in share price from £2.87 to £1.10.

Figure 21.1 Centrica Share Prices, 2013–2019

At the same time, Centrica's dividend changed very little while its earnings/share has fallen significantly.

Year	Dividend/share	EPS
2013	17p	27.6p
2014	13.5p	21.3p
2015	12p	22.9p
2016	12p	16.4p
2017	12p	25.4p
2018	12p	15.1p

Despite worsening earnings and market valuations, Centrica's management was exceptionally hesitant to reduce the company's dividend. Why had the dividend not changed between 2015 and 2018?

There are several reasons: maybe Centrica's management felt it was able to turn the business around. It's also possible the company didn't want to signal that it couldn't continue paying the level of dividends it had committed to investors. There are many explanations for Centrica's behaviour and we discuss these in this chapter.

The dividends followed a very different path in the years afterwards. In 2019, Centrica paid an interim dividend only of 1.5 pence with no final dividend. No dividends were paid at all in 2020 and 2021, but in 2022 Centrica paid an annual dividend of 3 pence. Why do you think there was such a big change in dividend policy? Was it really because of Covid or do you think it could be another reason?

Four reasons are plausible:

1 The impact of the energy price cap introduced by the UK government in 2019 reduced the revenues and margins of Centrica's retail business.
2 The decline in oil and gas prices due to oversupply and weak demand affected Centrica's upstream and trading segments.
3 The disruption caused by the Covid-19 pandemic reduced energy consumption and increased customer arrears, as well as delayed some asset sales and restructuring plans.
4 The strategic shift to focus on low-carbon energy and customer solutions required significant investments and divestments, as well as impairments and write-downs of some legacy assets.

21.2 Standard Method of Cash Dividend Payment

The decision to pay a dividend rests in the hands of the board of directors of the corporation. A dividend is distributable to shareholders of record on a specific date. When a dividend has been declared, it becomes a liability of the firm and cannot easily be rescinded by the corporation. The amount of dividend is expressed as pounds/euros/currency per share (*dividend per share*), as a percentage of the market price (*dividend yield*) or as a percentage of earnings per share (*dividend payout*).

The mechanics of a dividend payment can be illustrated by the example in Figure 21.2 and the following chronology:

1 *Declaration date:* On 15 January (the declaration date), the board of directors passes a resolution to pay a dividend of £1 per share on 16 February to all holders of record on 30 January.
2 *Record date:* The corporation prepares a list on 30 January of all individuals believed to be shareholders as of this date. The word *believed* is important here: the dividend will not be paid to individuals whose notification of purchase is received by the company after 30 January.
3 *Ex-dividend date:* The procedure for the date of record would be unfair if efficient brokerage houses could notify the corporation by 30 January of a trade occurring on 29 January, whereas the same trade might not reach the corporation until 2 February if executed by a less efficient house. To eliminate this problem, all brokerage firms entitle shareholders to receive the dividend if they purchased the equity three business days before the date of record. The second day before the date of record, which in our example is Wednesday, 28 January, is called the *ex-dividend date*. Before this date the shares are said to trade *cum dividend*.
4 *Date of payment:* The dividend cheques are mailed to the shareholders on 16 February.

Figure 21.2 Example of Procedure for Dividend Payment

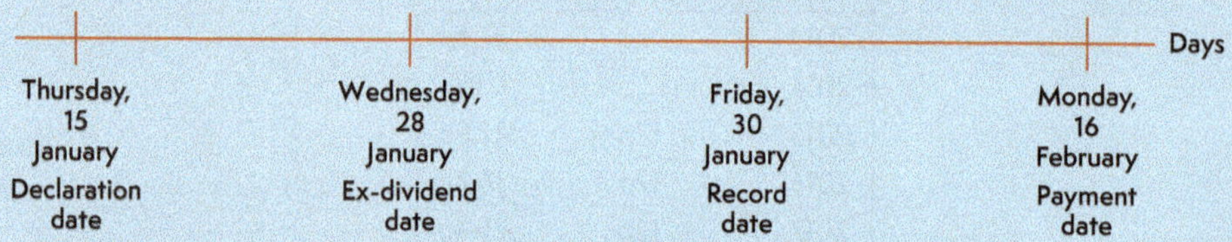

1 *Declaration date*: The board of directors declares a payment of dividends.
2 *Record date*: The declared dividends are distributable to shareholders of record on a specific date.
3 *Ex-dividend date*: A share of equity becomes ex dividend on the date the seller is entitled to keep the dividend; under stock exchange rules, shares are traded ex dividend on and after the second business day before the record date.
4 *Payment date*: The dividend cheques are mailed to shareholders of record.

Obviously, the ex-dividend date is important because an individual purchasing the security before the ex-dividend date will receive the current dividend, whereas another individual purchasing the security on or after this date will not receive the dividend. The share price will therefore fall on the ex-dividend date (assuming no other events occur). It is worthwhile to note that this drop is an indication of efficiency, not inefficiency, because the market rationally attaches value to a cash dividend. In a world with neither taxes nor transaction costs, the share price would be expected to fall by the amount of the dividend (illustrated in Figure 21.3).

Figure 21.3 Price Behaviour around the Ex-dividend Date for a £1 Cash Dividend

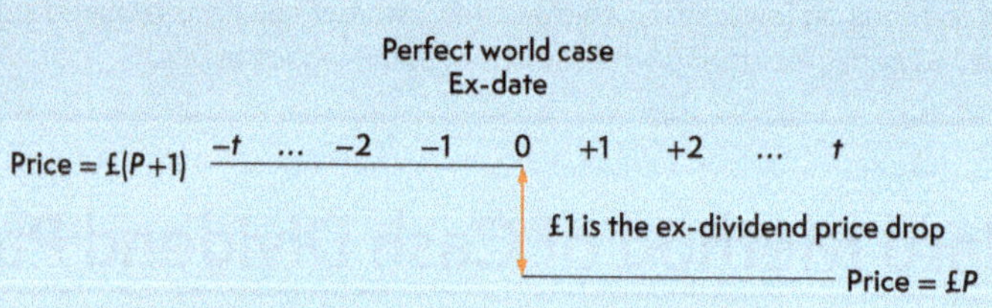

In a world without taxes, the share price will fall by the amount of the dividend on the ex-date (time 0). If the dividend is £1 per share, the price will be equal to *P* on the ex-date.

Before ex-date (−1)	Price = £(*P*+1)
Ex-date (0)	Price = £*P*

The amount of the price drop may depend on tax rates. For example, consider the case with no capital gains taxes. On the day before an equity goes ex dividend, a purchaser must decide either (1) to buy the shares immediately and pay tax on the forthcoming dividend, or (2) to buy the shares tomorrow, thereby missing the dividend. If all investors are in the 25 per cent bracket and the dividend is £1, the share price should fall by £0.75 on the ex-dividend date. That is, if the share price falls by this amount on the ex-dividend date, purchasers will receive the same return from either strategy.

As an example of the price drop on the ex-dividend date, consider a dividend paid by French bank, BNP Paribas, in 2018. The shares went ex-dividend on 25 May 2018 with a total dividend of €1.75819 per share (see Figure 21.4). The share price chart in Figure 21.4 shows the price of BNP Paribas shares in the event window before and after the ex-dividend date.

The shares closed at €36.31 on 24 May and fell by €2.26 to €34.05 on 25 May (a Friday). The price fell further over the weekend by €2.65. The overall drop was much higher than the dividend itself and so there must have been an additional factor at play to cause such a large change in price. We consider possible reasons later in the chapter (Sections 21.6–21.8).

Figure 21.4 BNP Paribas Share Price

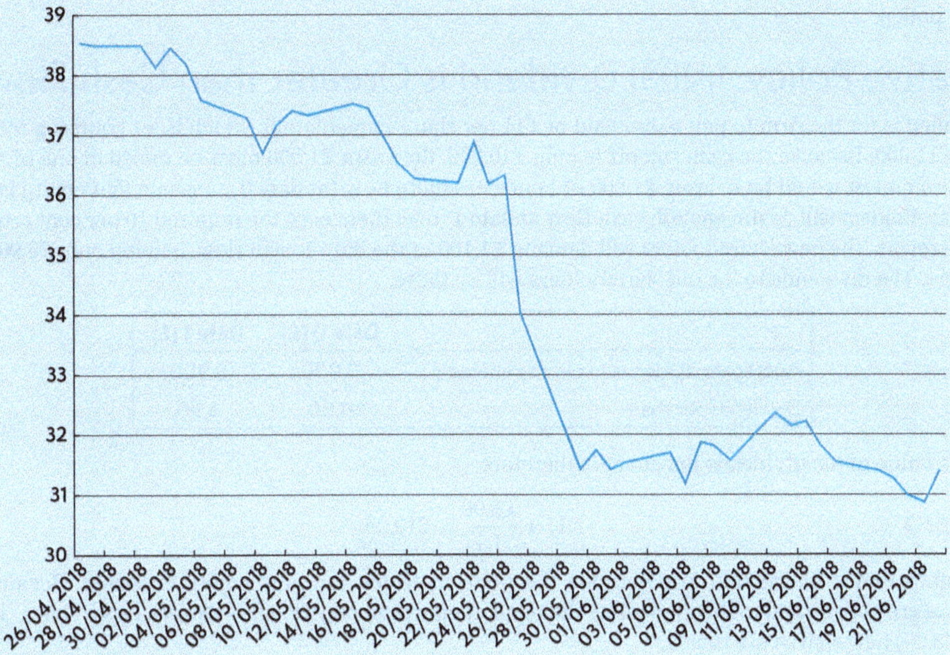

Source: Data drawn from Yahoo! Finance.

21.3 The Benchmark Case: An Illustration of the Irrelevance of Dividend Policy

A powerful argument can be made that dividend policy does not matter. This will be illustrated with the Bristol Corporation. Bristol is an all-equity firm started 10 years ago. The current financial managers know at the present time (date 0) that the firm will dissolve in one year (date 1). At date 0 the managers are able to forecast cash flows with perfect certainty. The managers know that the firm will receive a cash flow of £10,000 immediately and another £10,000 next year. Bristol has no additional positive NPV projects.

Current Policy: Dividends Set Equal to Cash Flow

At the present time, dividends (Div) at each date are set equal to the cash flow of £10,000. The value of the firm can be calculated by discounting these dividends. This value is expressed as:

$$V_0 = Div_0 + \frac{Div_1}{1 + R_E}$$

where Div_0 and Div_1 are the cash flows paid out in dividends, and R_E is the discount rate. The first dividend is not discounted because it will be paid immediately.

Assuming $R_E = 10$ per cent, the value of the firm is:

$$£10{,}000 + \frac{£10{,}000}{1.1} = £19{,}090.91$$

If 1,000 shares are outstanding, the value of each share is:

Equation 21.1

$$£10 + \frac{£10}{1.1} = £19.09$$

To simplify the example, we assume that the ex-dividend date is the same as the date of payment. After the imminent dividend is paid, the share price will immediately fall to £9.09(= £19.09 – £10). Several members of Bristol's board have expressed dissatisfaction with the current dividend policy and have asked you to analyse an alternative policy.

Alternative Policy: Initial Dividend is Greater than Cash Flow

Another policy is for the firm to pay a dividend of £11 per share immediately, which is, of course, a total dividend payout of £11,000. Because the cash run-off is only £10,000, the extra £1,000 must be raised in one of a few ways. Perhaps the simplest would be to issue £1,000 of bonds or equity now (at date 0). Assume that equity is issued and the new shareholders will desire enough cash flow at date 1 to let them earn the required 10 per cent return on their date 0 investment. The new shareholders will demand £1,100 of the date 1 cash flow, leaving only £8,900 to the old shareholders. The dividends to the old shareholders will be these:

	Date 0 (£)	Date 1 (£)
Aggregate dividends to old shareholders	11,000	8,900
Dividends per share	11.00	8.90

The present value of the dividends per share is therefore:

Equation 21.2
$$£11 + \frac{£8.90}{1.1} = £19.09$$

Students often find it instructive to determine the price at which the new equity is issued. Because the new shareholders are not entitled to the immediate dividend, they would pay £8.09 (= £8.90/1.1) per share. Thus, 123.61 (=£1,000/£8.09) new shares are issued.

The Indifference Proposition

Note that Equations 21.1 and 21.2 are equal. This leads to the initially surprising conclusion that the change in dividend policy did not affect the value of a share of equity. However, on reflection, the result seems sensible. The new shareholders are parting with their money at date 0 and receiving it back with the appropriate return at date 1. In other words, they are taking on a zero NPV investment. As illustrated in Figure 21.5, old shareholders are receiving additional funds at date 0 but must pay the new shareholders their money with the appropriate return at date 1. Because the old shareholders must pay back principal plus the appropriate return, the act of issuing new equity at date 0 will not increase or decrease the value of the old shareholders' holdings. That is, they are giving up a zero NPV investment to the new shareholders. An increase in dividends at date 0 leads to the necessary reduction of dividends at date 1, so the value of the old shareholders' holdings remains unchanged.

This illustration is based on the pioneering work of Miller and Modigliani (MM). Although our presentation is in the form of a numerical example, the MM paper proves that investors are indifferent to dividend policy in a more general setting.

Homemade Dividends

To illustrate the indifference investors have towards dividend policy in our example, we used present value equations. An alternative and perhaps more intuitively appealing explanation avoids the mathematics of discounted cash flows.

Suppose individual investor X prefers dividends per share of £10 at both dates 0 and 1. Would she be disappointed when informed that the firm's management is adopting the alternative dividend policy (dividends of £11 and £8.90 on the two dates, respectively)? Not necessarily: she could easily reinvest the £1 of unneeded funds received on date 0, yielding an incremental return of £1.10 at date 1. Thus, she would receive her desired net cash flow of £11 – £1 = £10 at date 0 and £8.90 + £1.10 = £10 at date 1.

Conversely, imagine investor Z preferring £11 of cash flow at date 0 and £8.90 of cash flow at date 1, who finds that management will pay dividends of £10 at both dates 0 and 1. He can sell off shares of equity at date 0 to receive the desired amount of cash flow. That is, if he sells off shares (or fractions of shares) at date 0 totalling £1, his cash flow at date 0 becomes £10 + £1 = £11. Because a £1 sale of shares at date 0 will reduce his dividends by £1.10 at date 1, his net cash flow at date 1 would be £10 – £1.10 = £8.90.

Figure 21.5 Current and Alternative Dividend Policies

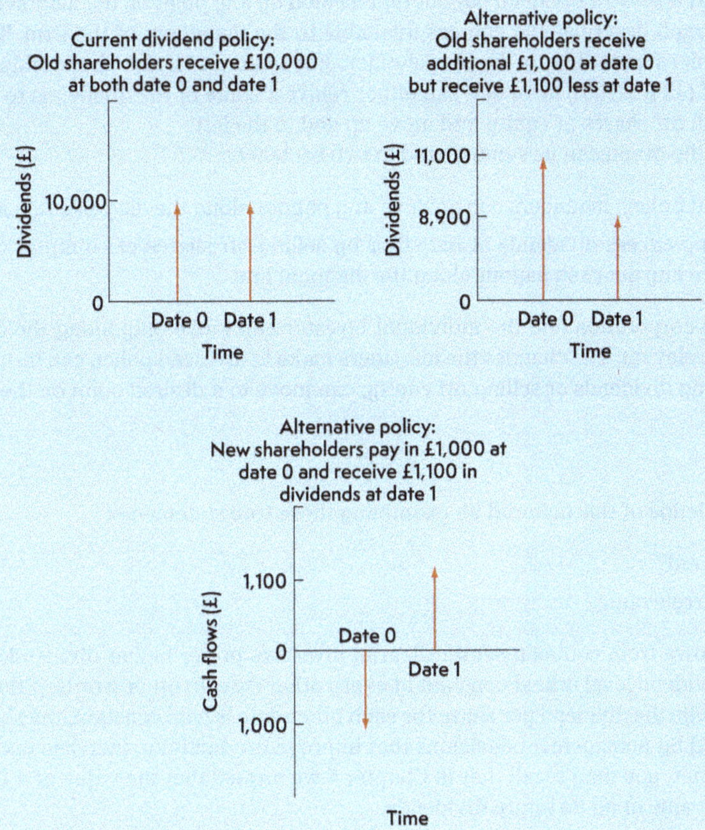

Figure 21.6 Homemade Dividends: A Trade-off between Dividends per Share at Date 0 and Dividends per Share at Date 1

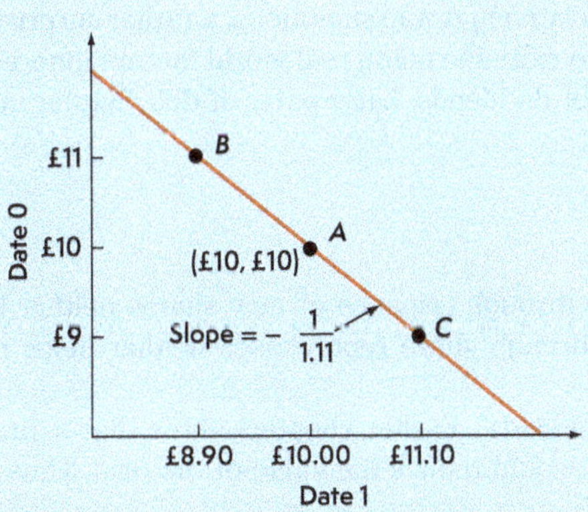

The graph illustrates both (a) how managers can vary dividend policy, and (b) how individuals can undo the firm's dividend policy.

Managers varying dividend policy: A firm paying out all cash flows immediately is at point *A* on the graph. The firm could achieve point *B* by issuing equity to pay extra dividends or achieve point *C* by buying back old equity with some of its cash.

Individuals undoing the firm's dividend policy: Suppose the firm adopts the dividend policy represented by point *B*: dividends per share of £11 at date 0 and £8.90 at date 1. An investor can reinvest £1 of the dividends at 10 per cent, which will place her at point *A*. Suppose, alternatively, the firm adopts the dividend policy represented by point *A*. An investor can sell off £1 of equity at date 0, placing him at point *B*. No matter what dividend policy the firm establishes, a shareholder can undo it.

The example illustrates how investors can make **homemade dividends**. In this instance, corporate dividend policy is being undone by a potentially dissatisfied shareholder. This homemade dividend is illustrated by Figure 21.6. Here the firm's cash flows of £10 per share at both dates 0 and 1 are represented by point *A*. This point also represents the initial dividend payout. However, as we just saw, the firm could alternatively pay out £11 per share at date 0 and £8.90 per share at date 1, a strategy represented by point *B*. Similarly, by either issuing new equity or buying back old equity, the firm could achieve a dividend payout represented by any point on the diagonal line.

The previous paragraph describes the choices available to the managers of the firm. The same diagonal line also represents the choices available to the shareholder. For example, if the shareholder receives a per-share dividend distribution of (£11, £8.90), he or she can either reinvest some of the dividends to move down and to the right on the graph or sell off shares of equity and move up and to the left.

The implications of the graph can be summarized in two sentences:

1 By varying dividend policy, managers can achieve any payout along the diagonal line in Figure 21.6.

2 Either by reinvesting excess dividends at date 0 or by selling off shares of equity at this date, an individual investor can achieve any net cash payout along the diagonal line.

Thus, because both the corporation and the individual investor can move only along the diagonal line, dividend policy in this model is irrelevant. The changes the managers make in dividend policy can be undone by an individual who, either by reinvesting dividends or selling off equity, can move to a desired point on the diagonal line.

A Test

You can test your knowledge of this material by examining these true statements:

1 Dividends are relevant.

2 Dividend policy is irrelevant.

The first statement follows from common sense. Clearly, investors prefer higher dividends to lower dividends at any single date if the dividend level is held constant at every other date. In other words, if the dividend per share at a given date is raised while the dividend per share for each other date is held constant, the share price will rise. This act can be accomplished by management decisions that improve productivity, increase tax savings or strengthen product marketing. In fact, you may recall that in Chapter 5 we argued that the value of a firm's equity is equal to the discounted present value of all its future dividends.

The second statement is understandable once we realize that dividend policy cannot raise the dividend per share at one date while holding the dividend level per share constant at all other dates. Rather, dividend policy merely establishes the trade-off between dividends at one date and dividends at another date. As we saw in Figure 21.6, an increase in date 0 dividends can be accomplished only by a decrease in date 1 dividends. The extent of the decrease is such that the present value of all dividends is not affected.

Thus, in this simple world, dividend policy does not matter. That is, managers choosing either to raise or to lower the current dividend do not affect the current value of their firm. This theory is powerful, and the work of MM is generally considered a classic in modern finance. With relatively few assumptions, a rather surprising result is shown to be perfectly true. Nevertheless, because we want to examine many real-world factors ignored by MM, their work is only a starting point in this chapter's discussion of dividends. Later parts of this chapter investigate these real-world considerations.

Dividends and Investment Policy

The preceding argument shows that an increase in dividends through issuance of new shares neither helps nor hurts the shareholders. Similarly, a reduction in dividends through share repurchases neither helps nor hurts shareholders.

What about reducing capital expenditures to increase dividends? Earlier chapters show that a firm should accept all positive net present value projects. To do otherwise would reduce the value of the firm. Thus, we have an important point:

Firms should never give up a positive NPV project to increase a dividend (or to pay a dividend for the first time).

This idea was implicitly considered by Miller and Modigliani. One of the assumptions underlying their dividend irrelevance proposition was this: 'The investment policy of the firm is set ahead of time and is not altered by changes in dividend policy.'

As later sections will show, there is always more to real life than theory predicts.

21.4 Share Repurchases

Instead of paying dividends, a firm may use cash to repurchase shares of its own equity. Share repurchases have taken on increased importance in recent years. According to UK government research (BEIS, 2019), UK firms pay out an average of 36 per cent of their net earnings in dividends compared to only 11 per cent in share repurchases. Data for US companies show a different distribution, with share repurchases being much more important relative to dividends. Table 21.1 shows the trend in dividends and share repurchases as a ratio of capital expenditure for US firms over the period 1992–2018. Between 1992 and 2000, share repurchases were only 32 per cent of capital expenditure. This ratio was much higher by 2018, where share repurchases were equivalent to 85 per cent of annual capital expenditures. This was substantially higher than dividends, which were 55 per cent of capital expenditures.

Table 21.1 Trends in Dividends and Share Repurchases for US firms between 1992 and 2018

	1992–2000	2002–2007	2010–2017	2018
Dividends/capital expenditure	0.34	0.42	0.49	0.55
Share repurchases/capital expenditure	0.32	0.68	0.64	0.85

Source: Adapted from Barua, A. and P. Buckley (2019) 'Share Buybacks and Dividends Outshine Capital Expenditure', *Deloitte Economics Spotlight*, Figure 2.

There are several possible reasons why share repurchases are more common in the USA than in Europe and the UK:

- *Taxation:* In the USA, dividends are taxed at a higher rate than capital gains, which are realized when shareholders sell their shares after a repurchase. This creates an incentive for companies to return cash to shareholders through share repurchases rather than dividends. In contrast, in many European countries, dividends and capital gains are taxed at the same rate or dividends are taxed at a lower rate, which reduces the tax advantage of share repurchases.
- *Regulation:* In the USA, share repurchases are subject to fewer legal restrictions and disclosure requirements than in Europe or the UK. For example, in the USA, companies can repurchase their shares on the open market without prior shareholder approval or public announcement as long as they comply with certain stock exchange rules. In contrast, in Europe or the UK, companies have to obtain shareholder authorization and disclose their repurchase plans and transactions in advance.

Share repurchases are typically accomplished in one of three ways. First, companies may simply purchase their own equity, just as anyone would buy shares of a particular company. In these *open market purchases*, the firm does not reveal itself as the buyer. Thus, the seller does not know whether the shares were sold back to the firm or to just another investor.

Second, the firm could institute a *tender offer*. Here, the firm announces to all of its shareholders that it is willing to buy a fixed number of shares at a specific price. Suppose, for instance, Arts and Crafts (A&C) has 1 million shares outstanding, with a share price of €50. The firm makes a tender offer to buy back 300,000 shares at €60 per share. A&C chooses a price above €50 to induce shareholders to sell – that is, tender – their shares. In fact, if the tender price is set high enough, shareholders may want to sell more than the 300,000 shares. In the extreme case where all outstanding shares are tendered, A&C will buy back three out of every 10 shares that a shareholder has.

Finally, firms may repurchase shares from specific individual shareholders, a procedure called a *targeted repurchase*. Say International Biotechnology AB purchased approximately 10 per cent of the outstanding shares of Prime Robotics Ltd (P-R Ltd) in April at around SKr38 per share. At that time, International Biotechnology announced to the Stockholm Stock Exchange that it might eventually try to take control of P-R Ltd. In May, P-R Ltd repurchased International Biotechnology holdings at SKr48 per share, well above the market price at that time. This offer was not extended to other shareholders.

Companies engage in targeted repurchases for a variety of reasons. In some rare cases, a single large shareholder can be bought out at a price lower than that in a tender offer. The legal fees in a targeted repurchase may also be lower than those in a more typical buyback. In addition, the shares of large shareholders are often repurchased to avoid a takeover unfavourable to management.

We now consider an example of a repurchase presented in the theoretical world of a perfect capital market. We next discuss real-world factors involved in the repurchase decision.

Real World Insight 21.2

Eni Share Repurchase Plan

After a successful reorganization in 2018, Eni, the Italian oil giant, presented a new 2019–2022 strategic plan to invest €3.5 billion in oil and gas exploration. The firm's total capital expenditure for all investments is estimated to be €33 billion over the three-year period and the company's focus was on high-NPV projects with short payback periods.

The firm also initiated a four-year share repurchase programme, initially worth €400 million. Between 2020 and 2022, Eni repurchased between €400 and €800 million of shares every year, depending on global oil prices.

Dividend versus Repurchase: Conceptual Example

Imagine that Telephonic Industries has excess cash of £300,000 (or £3 per share) and is considering an immediate payment of this amount as an extra dividend. The firm forecasts that, after the dividend, earnings will be £450,000 per year, or £4.50 for each of the 100,000 shares outstanding. Because the price-earnings ratio is 6 for comparable companies, the shares of the firm should sell for £27 (=£4.50 × 6) after the dividend is paid. These figures are presented in the top half of Table 21.2. Because the dividend is £3 per share, the equity would have sold for £30 a share *before* payment of the dividend.

Table 21.2 Dividend versus Repurchase Example for Telephonic Industries

	For Entire Firm (£)	Per Share (£)
Extra dividend		**(100,000 shares outstanding)**
Proposed dividend	300,000	3.00
Forecast annual earnings after dividend	450,000	4.50
Market value of equity after dividend	2,700,000	27.00
Repurchase		**(90,000 shares outstanding)**
Forecast annual earnings after repurchase	450,000	5.00
Market value of equity after repurchase	2,700,000	30.00

Alternatively, the firm could use the excess cash to repurchase some of its own equity. Imagine that a tender offer of £30 a share is made. Here, 10,000 shares are repurchased so that the total number of shares remaining is 90,000. With fewer shares outstanding, the earnings per share will rise to £5 (=£450,000/90,000). The price-earnings ratio remains at 6 because both the business and financial risks of the firm are the same in the repurchase case as they were in the dividend case. Thus, the price of a share after the repurchase is £30 (=£5 × 6). These results are presented in the bottom half of Table 21.2.

If commissions, taxes and other imperfections are ignored in our example, the shareholders are indifferent between a dividend and a repurchase. With dividends each shareholder owns a share worth £27 and receives £3 in dividends, so that the total value is £30. This figure is the same as both the amount received by the selling shareholders and the value of the equity for the remaining shareholders in the repurchase case.

This example illustrates the important point that, in a perfect market, the firm is indifferent between a dividend payment and a share repurchase. This result is quite similar to the indifference propositions established by MM for debt versus equity financing and for dividends versus capital gains.

You may often read in the popular financial press that a repurchase agreement is beneficial because earnings per share increase. Earnings per share do rise for Telephonic Industries if a repurchase is substituted for a cash dividend: the EPS is £4.50 after a dividend and £5 after the repurchase. This result holds because the drop in shares after a repurchase implies a reduction in the denominator of the EPS ratio.

However, the financial press frequently places undue emphasis on EPS figures in a repurchase agreement. Given the irrelevance propositions we have discussed, the increase in EPS here is not beneficial. Table 21.2 shows that, in a perfect capital market, the total value to the shareholder is the same under the dividend payment strategy as under the repurchase strategy.

Dividends versus Repurchases: Real-world Considerations

Why do some firms choose repurchases over dividends? Here are five of the perhaps most common reasons.

1 Flexibility

Firms often view dividends as a commitment to their shareholders and are quite hesitant to reduce an existing dividend. Repurchases do not represent a similar commitment. Thus, a firm with a permanent increase in cash flow is likely to increase its dividend. Conversely, a firm whose cash flow increase is only temporary is likely to repurchase shares of equity.

2 Executive Compensation

Executives are frequently given share options as part of their overall compensation. Let us revisit the Telephonic Industries example of Table 21.2, where the firm's equity was selling at £30 when the firm was considering either a dividend or a repurchase. Further imagine that Telephonic had granted 1,000 share options to its CEO, Ralph Taylor, two years earlier. At that time, the share price was, say, only £20. This means that Mr Taylor can buy 1,000 shares for £20 a share at any time between the grant of the options and their expiration, a procedure called *exercising* the options. His gain from exercising is directly proportional to the rise in the share price above £20. As we saw in the example, the price of the equity would fall to £27 following a dividend but would remain at £30 following a repurchase. The CEO would clearly prefer a repurchase to a dividend because the difference between the share price and the exercise price of £20 would be £10 (=£30 – £20) following the repurchase but only £7 (=£27 – £20) following the dividend. Existing share options will always have greater value when the firm repurchases shares instead of paying a dividend because the share price will be greater after a repurchase than after a dividend.

3 Offset to Dilution

In addition, the exercise of share options increases the number of shares outstanding. In other words, exercise causes dilution of the shares. Firms frequently buy back shares of equity to offset this dilution. However, it is hard to argue that this is a valid reason for repurchase. As we showed in Table 21.2, repurchase is neither better nor worse for the shareholders than a dividend. Our argument holds whether or not share options have been exercised previously.

4 Undervaluation

Many companies buy back shares because they believe that a repurchase is their best investment. This occurs more frequently when managers believe that the share price is temporarily depressed.

The fact that some companies repurchase their equity when they believe it is undervalued does not imply that the management of the company must be correct; only empirical studies can make this determination. The immediate market reaction to the announcement of a share repurchase is usually quite favourable. In addition, some empirical work has shown that the long-term share price performance of securities after a buyback is better than the share price performance of comparable companies that do not repurchase.

5 Taxes

Because taxes for both dividends and share repurchases are treated in depth in the next section, suffice it to say at this point that repurchases provide a tax advantage over dividends.

21.5 Personal Taxes and Dividends

Chapter 18 Page 478

Section 18.3 asserted that, in a world without taxes and other frictions, dividend policy is irrelevant. Similarly, Section 18.4 concluded that the choice between a share repurchase and a dividend is irrelevant in a world of this type. This section examines the effect of taxes on both dividends and repurchases (see also Chapter 18, Section 18.6 for the effect of personal taxes on capital structure). Our discussion is facilitated by classifying firms into two types: those without sufficient cash to pay a dividend and those with sufficient cash to do so.

Firms without Sufficient Cash to Pay a Dividend

It is simplest to begin with a firm without cash and owned by a single entrepreneur. If this firm should decide to pay a dividend of £100, it must raise capital. The firm might choose among a number of different equity and bond issues to pay the dividend. However, for simplicity, we assume that the entrepreneur contributes cash to the firm by issuing shares to himself. This transaction, diagrammed in the left side of Figure 21.7, would clearly be a *wash* in a world of no taxes. The £100 cash goes into the firm when equity is issued and is immediately paid out as a dividend. Thus, the entrepreneur neither benefits nor loses when the dividend is paid, a result consistent with Miller-Modigliani.

Figure 21.7 Firm Issues Equity to Pay a Dividend

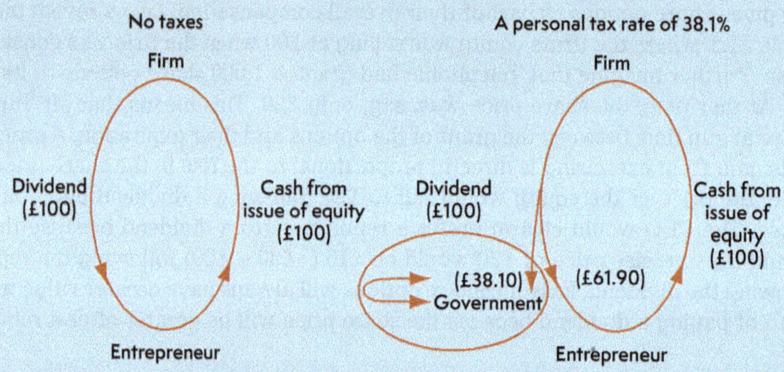

In the no-tax case, the entrepreneur receives the £100 in dividends that he gave to the firm when purchasing equity. The entire operation is called a *wash*; in other words, it has no economic effect. With taxes, the entrepreneur still receives £100 in dividends. However, he must pay £38.10 in taxes to the government. The entrepreneur loses and the government wins when a firm issues equity to pay a dividend.

Now assume that dividends are taxed at the owner's personal tax rate of 38.1 per cent (in the UK, this is the effective tax rate on dividend income for individuals in the higher tax bracket). The firm still receives £100 upon issuance of equity. However, the entrepreneur does not get to keep the full £100 dividend. Instead the dividend payment is taxed, implying that the owner receives only £61.90 net after tax. Thus, the entrepreneur loses £38.10.

Though the example is clearly contrived and unrealistic, similar results can be reached for more plausible situations. Thus, financial economists generally agree that, in a world of personal taxes, firms should not issue equity to pay dividends.

The direct costs of issuance will add to this effect. Bankers must be paid when new capital is raised. Thus, the net receipts due to the firm from a new issue are less than 100 per cent of total capital raised. Because the size of new issues can be lowered by a reduction in dividends, we have another argument in favour of a low-dividend policy.

Of course, our advice not to finance dividends through new equity issues might need to be modified somewhat in the real world. A company with a large and steady cash flow for many years in the past might be paying a regular dividend. If the cash flow unexpectedly dried up for a single year, should new equity be issued so that dividends could be continued? Although our previous discussion would imply that new equity should not be issued, many managers might issue the equity anyway for practical reasons. In particular, shareholders appear to prefer dividend stability. Thus, managers might be forced to issue equity to achieve this stability, knowing full well the adverse tax consequences.

Firms with Sufficient Cash to Pay a Dividend

The previous discussion argued that, in a world with personal taxes, a firm should not issue equity to pay a dividend. Does the tax disadvantage of dividends imply the stronger policy, 'Never, under any circumstances, pay dividends in a world with personal taxes'?

We argue next that this prescription does not necessarily apply to firms with excess cash. To see this, imagine a firm with £1 million in extra cash after selecting all positive NPV projects and determining the level of prudent cash balances. The firm might consider the following alternatives to a dividend:

1 *Select additional capital budgeting projects:* Because the firm has taken all the available positive NPV projects already, it must invest its excess cash in negative NPV projects. This is clearly a policy at variance with the principles of corporate finance.

In spite of our distaste for this policy, researchers have suggested that many managers purposely take on negative NPV projects in lieu of paying dividends.[1] The idea here is that managers would rather keep the funds in the firm because their prestige, pay and perquisites are often tied to the firm's size. Although managers may help themselves here, they are hurting shareholders. We broached this subject in the section titled 'Free Cash Flow' in Section 19.6, and we will have more to say about it later in this chapter, in Section 21.9.

Chapter 19 Page 511

2 *Acquire other companies:* To avoid the payment of dividends, a firm might use excess cash to acquire another company. This strategy has the advantage of acquiring profitable assets. However, a firm often incurs heavy costs when it embarks upon an acquisition programme. In addition, acquisitions are invariably made above the market price. Premiums of 20 to 80 per cent are not uncommon. Because of this, a number of researchers have argued that mergers are not generally profitable to the acquiring company, even when firms are merged for a valid business purpose. Therefore, a company making an acquisition merely to avoid a dividend is unlikely to succeed.

3 *Purchase financial assets:* The strategy of purchasing financial assets in lieu of a dividend payment can be illustrated by Example 21.1.

Example 21.1

Dividends and Taxes

Regional Electric NV has €1,000 of extra cash. It can retain the cash and invest it in Treasury bills yielding 10 per cent, or it can pay the cash to shareholders as a dividend. Shareholders can also invest in Treasury bills with the same yield. Assume the effective corporate tax rate is 30 per cent, the dividend tax rate is 15 per cent and the personal tax rate for shareholders is 28 per cent. How much cash will investors have after five years under each policy?

If dividends are paid now, shareholders will receive:

$$£1,000 \times (1 - 0.15) = £850$$

today after taxes. Because their return after personal tax on Treasury bills is 7.2 [= 10 × (1 − 0.28)] per cent, shareholders will have:

Equation 21.3 $$£850 \times (1.072)^5 = £1,203.35$$

in five years. Note that interest income is taxed at the personal tax rate (28 per cent in this example), but dividends are taxed at the lower rate of 15 per cent.

If Regional Electric NV retains the cash to invest in Treasury bills, its after-tax interest rate will be 0.07 [= 0.10 × (1 − 0.3)]. At the end of five years, the firm will have:

$$£1,000 \times (1.07)^5 = £1,402.55$$

If these proceeds are then paid as a dividend, the shareholders will receive:

Equation 21.4 $$£1,402.55 \times (1 - 0.15) = £1,192.17$$

after personal taxes at date 5. The value in Equation 21.3 is greater than that in Equation 21.4, implying that cash to shareholders will be greater if the firm pays the dividend now.

This example shows that, for a firm with extra cash, the dividend payout decision will depend on personal and corporate tax rates. If personal tax rates are higher than corporate tax rates, a firm will have an incentive to reduce dividend payouts. However, if personal tax rates are lower than corporate tax rates, a firm will have an incentive to pay out any excess cash as dividends.

Table 18.6 shows quite clearly that tax systems differ considerably across countries. In some countries, many investors face marginal tax rates that are above the corporate tax rate. However, at the same time, many investors face marginal tax rates well below the maximum. The interaction between personal and corporate tax rates within a country will mean that the environment faced by investors will be unique and a function of where they stay. As a result, firms may or may not have an incentive not to hoard cash.

4 *Repurchase shares:* The example we described in the previous section showed that investors are indifferent between share repurchase and dividends in a world without taxes and transaction costs. However, under current international tax laws, shareholders will generally prefer a repurchase to a dividend.

As an example, consider an individual receiving a dividend of €1 on each of 100 shares of an equity. With a 15 per cent tax rate, that individual would pay taxes of €15 on the dividend. Selling shareholders would pay lower taxes if the firm repurchased €100 of existing shares. This occurs because taxes are paid only on the *profit* from a sale. The individual's gain on a sale would be only €40 if the shares sold for €100 were originally purchased for, say, €60. The capital gains tax would be €6(=0.15 × €40), a number below the tax on dividends of €15. Note that the tax from a repurchase is less than the tax on a dividend even though the same 15 per cent tax rate applies to both the repurchase and the dividend.

Of all the alternatives to dividends mentioned in this section, the strongest case can be made for repurchases. In fact, academics have long wondered why firms *ever* pay a dividend instead of repurchasing shares. There have been at least two possible reasons for avoiding repurchases. First, in many countries, including the UK, there is the fear that share repurchase programmes can lead to illegal price manipulation. Second, tax authorities can penalize firms repurchasing their own shares if the only reason is to avoid the taxes that would be levied on dividends. However, this threat has not materialized with the growth in corporate repurchases.

Summary of Personal Taxes

This section suggests that, because of personal taxes, firms have an incentive to reduce dividends. For example, they might increase capital expenditures, acquire other companies or purchase financial assets. However, due to financial considerations and legal constraints, rational firms with large cash flows are likely to exhaust these activities, with plenty of cash left over for dividends. Isakov et al. (2021) show for Swiss firms that, after a tax cut, companies increased their dividend payout by 30 per cent.

It is harder to explain why firms pay dividends instead of repurchasing shares. The tax savings from buybacks are significant, and fear of either the stock exchange or tax authorities seems overblown. Academics are of two minds here. Some argue that corporations were simply slow to grasp the benefits from repurchases. However, since the idea has now firmly caught on, the trend towards replacement of dividends with buybacks will continue. We might even conjecture that dividends will be as unimportant in the future as repurchases were in the past. Conversely, others argue that companies have paid dividends all along for good reason. Perhaps the legal hassles, particularly from tax authorities, are significant after all. Or there may be other, more subtle benefits from dividends. We consider potential benefits of dividends in the next section.

21.6 Real-world Factors Favouring a High-dividend Policy

The previous section pointed out that, because individuals pay taxes on dividends, financial managers might seek ways to reduce dividends. While we discussed the problems with taking on more capital budgeting projects, acquiring other firms and hoarding cash, we stated that share repurchase has many of the benefits of a dividend with less of a tax disadvantage. This section considers reasons why a firm might pay its shareholders high dividends even in the presence of personal taxes on these dividends.

Desire for Current Income

It has been argued that many individuals desire current income. The classic example is the group of retired people and others living on a fixed income. The argument further states that these individuals would bid up the share price should dividends rise and bid down the share price should dividends fall.

This argument does not hold in Miller and Modigliani's theoretical model. An individual preferring high current cash flow but holding low-dividend securities could easily sell off shares to provide the necessary funds. Thus, in a world of no transaction costs, a high current dividend policy would be of no value to the shareholder.

However, the current income argument is relevant in the real world. Equity sales involve brokerage fees and other transaction costs – direct cash expenses that could be avoided by an investment in high-dividend securities. In addition, equity sales are time-consuming, further leading investors to buy high-dividend securities.

To put this argument in perspective, remember that financial intermediaries such as mutual funds can perform repackaging transactions at low cost. Such intermediaries could buy low-dividend equities and, by a controlled policy of realizing gains, pay their investors at a higher rate.

Behavioural Finance

Suppose it turned out that the transaction costs in selling no-dividend securities could not account for the preference of investors for dividends. Would there still be a reason for high dividends? We introduced the topic of behavioural finance in Chapter 13, pointing out that the ideas of behaviourists represent a strong challenge to the theory of efficient capital markets. It turns out that behavioural finance also has an argument for high dividends.

The basic idea here concerns *self-control,* a concept that, though quite important in psychology, has received virtually no emphasis in finance. Although we cannot review all that psychology has to say about self-control, let us focus on one example – losing weight. Suppose Mateo Martinez, a university student, just got back from the Christmas break more than a few pounds heavier than he would like. Mateo wishes to lose weight through doing yoga. Each day Mateo would balance the costs and the benefits of doing yoga. Perhaps he would choose to exercise on most days because losing the weight is important to him. However, when he is too busy with exams, he might rationally choose not to exercise because he cannot afford the time. So he may rationally choose to avoid doing yoga on days when other social commitments become too time-consuming.

Unfortunately, Mateo must make a proactive choice to do yoga every day, and there may be too many days when his lack of self-control gets the better of him. He may tell himself that he does not have the time to exercise on a particular day, simply because he is starting to find yoga boring, not because he really does not have the time. Before long, he is avoiding yoga on most days – and overeating in reaction to the guilt from not exercising!

Is there an alternative? One way would be to set rigid rules. Perhaps Mateo may decide to do yoga every day *no matter what.* This is not necessarily the best approach for everyone, but there is no question that many of us (perhaps most of us) live by a set of rules.

What does this have to do with dividends? Investors must also deal with self-control. Suppose a retiree wants to consume £20,000 a year from savings, in addition to her pension. On one hand, she could buy shares with a dividend yield high enough to generate £20,000 in dividends. On the other hand, she could place her savings in no-dividend shares, selling off £20,000 each year for consumption. Though these two approaches seem equivalent financially, the second one may allow for too much leeway. If lack of self-control gets the better of her, she might sell off too much, leaving little for her later years. Better, perhaps, to short-circuit this possibility by investing in dividend-paying equities with a firm personal rule of *never* 'dipping into principal'. Although behaviourists do not claim that this approach is for everyone, they argue that enough people think this way to explain why firms pay dividends – even though, as we said earlier, dividends are tax disadvantaged.

Does behavioural finance argue for increased share repurchases as well as increased dividends? The answer is no because investors will sell the shares that firms repurchase. As we have said, selling shares involves too much leeway. Investors might sell too many shares, leaving little for later years. Thus, the behaviourist argument may explain why companies pay dividends in a world with personal taxes.

Agency Costs

Although shareholders, bondholders and management form firms for mutually beneficial reasons, one party may later gain at the other's expense. Take the potential conflict between bondholders and shareholders: bondholders would like shareholders to leave as much cash as possible in the firm so that this cash would be available to pay the bondholders during times of financial distress; conversely, shareholders would like to keep this extra cash for themselves. That is where dividends come in. Managers, acting on behalf of the shareholders, may pay dividends simply to keep the cash away from the bondholders. In other words, a dividend can be viewed as a wealth transfer from bondholders to shareholders. There is empirical evidence for this view of things. DeAngelo and DeAngelo (1990), for instance, find that firms in financial distress are reluctant to cut dividends.[2] Of course, bondholders know about the propensity of shareholders to transfer money out of the firm. To protect themselves, bondholders frequently create loan agreements stating that dividends can be paid only if the firm has earnings, cash flow and working capital above specified levels.

Although managers may be looking out for shareholders in any conflict with bondholders, managers may pursue selfish goals at the expense of shareholders in other situations. For example, as discussed in Chapter 2, Section 2.2, managers might pad expense accounts, take on pet projects with negative NPVs, or simply not work hard. Managers find it easier to pursue these selfish goals when the firm has plenty of free cash flow. After all, one cannot squander funds if the funds are not available in the first place. And that is where dividends come in.

Several scholars have suggested that the board of directors can use dividends to reduce agency costs.[3] By paying dividends equal to the amount of 'surplus' cash flow, a firm can reduce management's ability to squander the firm's resources.

This discussion suggests a reason for increased dividends, but the same argument applies to share repurchases. Managers, acting on behalf of shareholders, can just as easily keep cash from bondholders through repurchases as through dividends. And the board of directors, also acting on behalf of shareholders, can reduce the cash available to spendthrift managers just as easily through repurchases as through dividends. Thus, the presence of agency costs is not an argument for dividends over repurchases. Rather, agency costs imply firms may increase either dividends or share repurchases rather than hoard large amounts of cash.

Information Content of Dividends and Dividend Signalling

Information Content

While there are many things researchers do not know about dividends, we know one thing for sure: the share price of a firm generally rises when the firm announces a dividend increase and generally falls when a dividend reduction is announced. For example, Lee and Mauck (2016) estimate that share prices rise about 2.66 per cent following announcements of dividend initiations. Henry et al. (2017) find that share prices fall about 7 per cent following announcements of dividend omissions.

The question is how we should *interpret* this empirical evidence. Consider the following three positions on dividends:

1 From the homemade dividend argument of MM, dividend policy is irrelevant, given that future earnings (and cash flows) are held constant.

2 Because of tax effects, a firm's share price is negatively related to the current dividend when future earnings (or cash flows) are held constant.

3 Because of shareholders' desire for current income, a firm's share price is positively related to its current dividend, even when future earnings (or cash flows) are held constant.

At first glance, the empirical evidence that share prices rise when dividend increases are announced may seem consistent with position 3 and inconsistent with positions 1 and 2. In fact, many writers have said this. However, other authors have countered that the observation itself is consistent with all three positions. They point out that companies do not like to cut a dividend. Thus, firms will raise the dividend only when future earnings, cash flow and so on are expected to rise enough so that the dividend is not likely to be reduced later to its original level. A dividend increase is management's *signal* to the market that the firm is expected to do well.

It is the expectation of good times, and not only the shareholders' affinity for current income, that raises a share price. The rise in the share price following the dividend signal is called the **information content effect** of the dividend. To recapitulate, imagine that the share price is unaffected or even negatively affected by the level of dividends, given that future earnings (or cash flows) are held constant. Nevertheless, the information content effect implies that share prices may rise when dividends are raised – if dividends simultaneously cause shareholders to *increase* their expectations of future earnings and cash flows.

Dividend Signalling

We just argued that the market infers a rise in earnings and cash flows from a dividend increase, leading to a higher share price. Conversely, the market infers a decrease in cash flows from a dividend reduction, leading to a drop in share price. This raises an interesting corporate strategy: could management increase dividends just to make the market *think* that cash flows will be higher, even when management knows that cash flows will not rise?

While this strategy may seem dishonest, academics take the position that managers frequently attempt it. Academics begin with the following accounting identity for an all-equity firm:[4]

Equation 21.5
$$\text{Cash flow} = \text{Capital expenditures} + \text{Dividends}$$

Equation 21.5 must hold if a firm is neither issuing nor repurchasing equity. That is, the cash flow from the firm must go somewhere. If it is not paid out in dividends, it must be used in some expenditure. Whether the expenditure involves a capital budgeting project or a purchase of Treasury bills, it is still an expenditure.

Imagine that we are in the middle of the year and investors are trying to make some forecast of cash flow over the entire year. These investors may use Equation 21.5 to estimate cash flow. For example, suppose the firm announces that current dividends will be £50 million and the market believes that capital expenditures are £80 million. The market would then determine cash flow to be:

$$£130 \text{ million}(=£50 + 80).$$

Now, suppose that the firm had, alternatively, announced a dividend of £70 million. The market might assume that cash flow remains at £130 million, implying capital expenditures of £60 million(=£130 – 70). Here, the increase in dividends would hurt the share price because the market anticipates valuable capital expenditures will be crowded out. Alternatively, the market might assume that capital expenditures remain at £80 million, implying the estimate of cash flow to be £150 million (=£70 + 80). The share price would probably rise here because share prices usually increase with cash flow. In general, academics believe that models where investors assume capital expenditures remain the same are more realistic. Thus, an increase in dividends raises the share price.

Now we come to the incentives of managers to fool the public. Suppose you are a manager who wants to boost the share price, perhaps because you are planning to sell some of your personal holdings of the company's equity immediately. You might increase dividends so that the market would raise its estimate of the firm's cash flow, thereby also boosting the current share price.

If this strategy is appealing, would anything prevent you from raising dividends without limit? The answer is yes because there is also a *cost* to raising dividends. That is, the firm will have to forgo some of its profitable projects. Remember that cash flow in Equation 21.5 is a constant, so an increase in dividends is obtained only by a reduction in capital expenditures. At some point the market will learn that cash flow has not increased, but instead profitable capital expenditures have been cut. Once the market absorbs this information, the share price should fall below what it would have been had dividends never been raised. Thus, if you plan to sell, say, half of your shares and retain the other half, an increase in dividends should help you on the immediate sale but hurt you when you sell your remaining shares years later. So your decision on the level of dividends will be based, among other things, on the timing of your personal equity sales.

This is a simplified example of dividend signalling, where the manager sets dividend policy based on maximum benefit for himself.[5] Alternatively, a given manager may have no desire to sell his shares immediately but knows that, at any one time, plenty of ordinary shareholders will want to do so. Thus, for the benefit of shareholders in general, a manager will always be aware of the trade-off between current and future share price. This, then, is the essence of signalling with dividends. It is not enough for a manager to set dividend policy to maximize the true (or intrinsic) value of the firm. He must also consider the effect of dividend policy on the current share price, even if the current share price does not reflect true value.

There is another way that managers can signal to financial markets. The level of power a manager holds within a company can greatly impact their ability to make decisions about dividend payouts. If a manager has a lot of power, they may act in their own interests by reducing dividends, overestimating returns and making excessive investments, ultimately leading to a decrease in shareholder wealth. However, if these powerful managers anticipate needing external funding, they may choose to pay out dividends to improve their image and secure more favourable financing terms. Because investors may view a powerful CEO as a risk, this could lead to higher demands for returns and increased external financing costs. Therefore, powerful CEOs may choose to pay dividends to mitigate their reputation risk and increase their chances of attracting external funding, similar to managers in poorly governed or entrenched firms (Sheikh, 2022).

Does a motive to signal imply that managers will increase dividends rather than share repurchases? The answer is likely to be no: most academic models imply that dividends and share repurchases are perfect substitutes.[6] Rather, these models indicate that managers will consider reducing capital spending (even on projects with positive NPVs) to increase either dividends or share repurchases.

Managerial Characteristics

Hossain et al. (2023) have shown that CEO marital status is related to dividend policy. This may seem strange at first, but Hossain and colleagues find that married CEOs are more likely to pay dividends. Firms run by single CEOs are less likely to pay dividends, and this is even more of an issue when the CEO is less risk-averse and less engaged in CSR activities. These findings are consistent with other research in this area on CEO personal attributes and marital status (see, for example, Bertrand and Schoar, 2003; Roussanov and Savor, 2014; Serfling, 2014; Faccio et al., 2016; Cronqvist and Yu, 2017; Hilary et al., 2017; Hegde and Mishra, 2019).

21.7 The Clientele Effect

In the previous two sections, we pointed out that the existence of personal taxes favours a low-dividend policy, whereas other factors favour high dividends. The finance profession had hoped that it would be easy to determine which of these sets of factors dominates. Unfortunately, after years of research, no one has been able to conclude which of the two is more important. This is surprising: we might be sceptical that the two sets of factors would cancel each other out so perfectly.

However, one particular idea – known as the *clientele effect* – implies that the two sets of factors are likely to cancel each other out after all. To understand this idea, let us separate investors in high tax brackets from those in low tax brackets. Individuals in high tax brackets are likely to prefer either no or low dividends. Low tax bracket investors generally fall into two categories. First, there are individual investors in low brackets. They are likely to prefer some dividends if they desire current income. Second, in many countries, pension funds pay no taxes on either dividends or capital gains. Because they face no tax consequences, pension funds will also prefer dividends if they have a preference for current income. Suppose that 40 per cent of all investors prefer high dividends and 60 per cent prefer low dividends, yet only 20 per cent of firms pay high dividends, while 80 per cent pay low dividends. Here, the high-dividend firms will be in short supply, implying that their equity should be bid up while the shares of low-dividend firms should be bid down.

However, the dividend policies of all firms need not be fixed in the long run. In this example, we would expect enough low-dividend firms to increase their payout so that 40 per cent of the firms pay high dividends and 60 per cent of the firms pay low dividends. After this adjustment, no firm will gain from changing its dividend policy. Once payouts of corporations conform to the desires of shareholders, no single firm can affect its market value by switching from one dividend strategy to another.

Clienteles are likely to form in the following way:

Group	Equities
Individuals in high tax brackets	Zero- to low-payout shares
Individuals in low tax brackets	Low- to medium-payout shares
Tax-free institutions	Medium- to high-payout shares

To see if you understand the clientele effect, consider the following statement: 'In a world where many investors like high dividends, a firm can boost its share price by increasing its dividend payout ratio.' True or false?

The statement is likely to be false. As long as there are already enough high-dividend firms to satisfy dividend-loving investors, a firm will not be able to boost its share price by paying high dividends. A firm can boost its share price only if an *unsatisfied* clientele exists.

Our discussion of clienteles followed from the fact that tax brackets vary across investors. If shareholders care about taxes, equities should attract clienteles based on dividend yield. Is there any evidence that this is the case?

Consider Figure 21.8. Here, John Graham and Alok Kumar (2006) rank equities by their dividend yields (the ratio of dividend to share price) and place them into five portfolios, called quintiles. The bottom quintile contains the 20 per cent of shares with the lowest dividend yields; the next quintile contains the 20 per cent of shares with the next lowest dividend yields; and so on. The figure shows the weight of each quintile in the portfolios of low-, medium- and high-income investors. As can be seen, relative to low-income investors, high-income investors put a greater percentage of their assets into low-dividend securities. Conversely, again relative to low-income investors, high-income investors put a smaller percentage of their assets into high-dividend securities.

Figure 21.8 Preferences of Investors for Dividend Yield

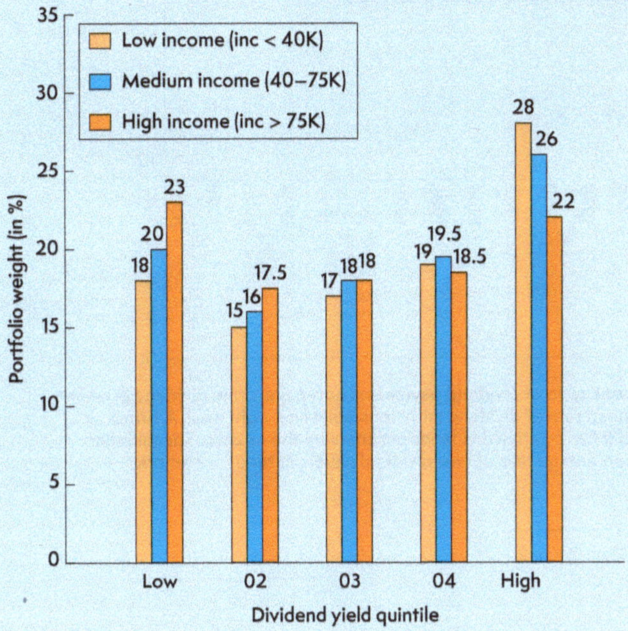

All shares are ranked on their dividend yields and placed into five quintile portfolios. The figure shows the weight of each quintile in the portfolios of low-, medium- and high-income investors. Relative to those with lower income, high-income investors place a greater percentage of their assets in low-dividend shares and a smaller percentage in high-dividend shares.

Source: Adapted from Graham and Kumar (2006), Figure 2.

21.8 A Catering Theory of Dividends

A perspective on why companies pay dividends has been proposed by Malcolm Baker and Jeffrey Wurgler (2004). The basic premise is that there are times when companies are mispriced in the stock market or when there are changes in the demand for dividend-paying equities. This may be because of the clientele effect, which predicts that if the proportion of dividend-paying companies in a market increases or decreases, the demand for dividend-paying shares will shift to a new equilibrium, temporarily imparting a premium or discount on shares of companies that pay dividends.

Instead of focusing on investor decisions, the catering theory of dividends predicts that managers will rationally respond to time variation in investor demand for dividends by modifying their company's dividend policy. In effect, the theory makes less of a statement about market efficiency or behavioural finance than it does about the logical business decisions by corporate management. Baker and Wurgler (2004) show that management behaviour in the USA is consistent with this theory. They consider dividend initiation and omission decisions, and relate them to share price premiums for dividend-paying shares. For initiations, in particular, the relationship with a price premium for dividends is exceptionally strong. This is clearly shown by Figure 21.9, where the link between dividend premium (market to book value) and dividend initiation is presented.

Kumar et al. (2022) found a similar result during the Covid pandemic, where firms initiated or increased dividends at the same time as the volume of internet searches for dividends increased. They argue that dividends are more likely to be paid when dividend sentiment is stronger.

So, according to the catering theory, will dividend increases lead to a positive price reaction? Not necessarily. If the time-varying demand for dividend-paying shares is low, an announcement by a company that it is increasing its dividend is not likely to be met with a positive reaction. In this situation, a dividend omission may elicit a more positive market response.

Figure 21.9 The Dividend Premium and the Rate of Dividend Initiation, 1962 to 2000

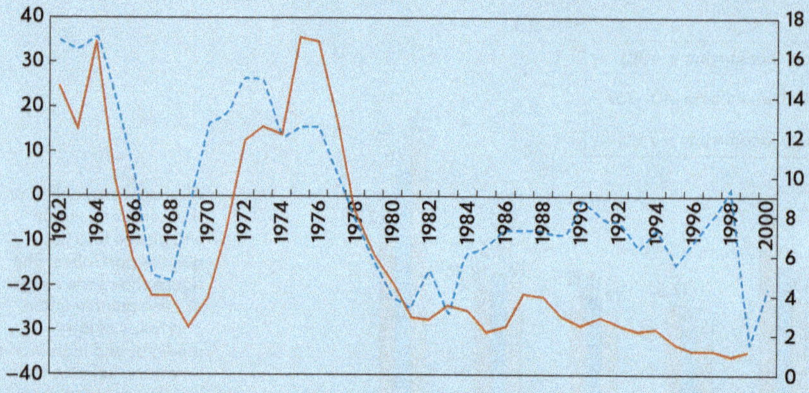

The log difference in the market-to-book ratio of dividend payers and non-payers (the dividend premium, dashed line–left axis) and one-year-ahead rate of dividend initiations (solid line–right axis). A firm is defined as a dividend payer at time *t* if it has positive dividends per share by the ex date. The initiation rate Initiate in $t + 1$ is defined as the percentage rate of new dividend payers at time $t + 1$ among surviving non-payers from *t*.

Source: Based on Baker and Wurgler (2004), Figure 2.

21.9 What We Know and Do Not Know about Dividend Policy

Corporate Dividends are Substantial

We pointed out earlier in the chapter that dividends are tax disadvantaged relative to capital gains because dividends are taxed upon payment whereas taxes on capital gains are deferred until sale. Nevertheless, the total monetary value of dividends paid by companies is substantial. As presented in Table 21.1, total real dividends (share repurchases and cash dividends) have increased significantly since 1992, in line with corporate profits and payout rates (Kahle and Stulz, 2021).

We could argue that the taxation on dividends is actually minimal, perhaps because dividends are paid primarily to individuals in low tax brackets or because institutions such as pension funds, which normally pay no taxes, are the primary recipients. However, Peterson et al. (1985) found that about two-thirds of dividends went to individuals and that the average marginal tax bracket for these individuals was about 40 per cent. Thus, we must conclude that large amounts of dividends are paid, even in the presence of substantial taxation.

Fewer Companies Pay Dividends

Although dividends are substantial, von Eije and Megginson (2008) point out that the percentage of European companies paying cash dividends has fallen over the last few decades. They show that these have largely been replaced by share repurchases. Fama and French (2001) argue that the decline was caused primarily by an explosion of small, currently unprofitable companies that have recently listed on various stock exchanges. For the most part, firms of this type do not pay dividends.

DeAngelo et al. (2004) point out that, while small firms have shied away from dividends, the largest firms have substantially increased their dividends over recent decades. In fact, by the end of 2017, global dividends had grown to $1.25 trillion. Table 21.3 presents annual dividends by region for the period 2020–2022. Dividends have increased in all regions (apart from Japan), mostly as a result of the recovery from the global pandemic.

Table 21.3 Annual Dividends by Region, 2020–2022 ($ billions)

Region	2020	2021	2022
Emerging markets	103.7	135.2	150.1
Europe ex. UK	168.8	230.4	255.6
Japan	80.5	81.8	73.6
North America	551.0	572.6	631.6
Asia Pacific	128.3	172.5	184.9
UK	63.1	87.5	89.2
Total	1,095.3	1,279.9	1,385.0
Divs outside top 1,200	139.0	162.4	175.7
Grand total	**1,234.3**	**1,442.3**	**1,560.8**

Source: Data from Janus Henderson Global Dividend Index (2023), Edition 38.

Corporations Smooth Dividends

In 1956, John Lintner made two important observations concerning dividend policy. First, real-world companies typically set long-term target ratios of dividends to earnings. A firm is likely to set a low target ratio if it has many positive NPV projects relative to available cash flow and a high ratio if it has few positive NPV projects. Second, managers know that only part of any change in earnings is likely to be permanent. Because managers need time to assess the permanence of any earnings rise, dividend changes appear to lag earnings changes by a number of periods.

Taken together, Lintner's observations suggest that two parameters describe dividend policy: the target payout ratio (t) and the speed of adjustment of current dividends to the target (s). Dividend changes will tend to conform to the following model:

Equation 21.6

$$0.5 \times (£6 - £3) = £1.50$$

where Div_1 and Div_0 are dividends in the next year and dividends in the current year, respectively; s is the speed of adjustment coefficient; and EPS_1 is earnings per share in the next year.

Example 21.2

Dividend Smoothing

Calculator Graphics International (CGI) has a target payout ratio of 0.30. Last year's earnings per share were £10, and in accordance with the target, CGI paid cash dividends of £3 per share. However, earnings have jumped to £20 this year. Because the managers do not believe that this increase is permanent, they do *not* plan to raise dividends all the way to £6(= 0.30 × £20). Rather, their speed of adjustment coefficient, *s*, is 0.5, implying that the *increase* in dividends from last year to this year will be:

$$0.5 \times (£6 - £4.50) = £0.75$$

That is, the increase in dividends is the product of the speed of adjustment coefficient, 0.50, times the difference between what dividends would be with full adjustment [£6(= 0.30 × £20)] and last year's dividends. Dividends will increase by £1.50, so dividends this year will be £4.50(= £3 + £1.50).

Now, suppose that earnings stay at £20 next year. The increase in dividends next year will be:

$$0.5 \times (£6 - £4.50) = £0.75$$

In words, the increase in dividends from this year to next year will be the speed of adjustment coefficient (0.50) times the difference between what dividends would have been next year with full adjustment (£6) and this year's dividends (£4.50). Because dividends will increase by £0.75, dividends next year will be:

$$£5.25(= £4.50 + £0.75)$$

In this way, dividends will slowly rise every year if earnings in all future years remain at £20. However, dividends will reach £6 only at infinity.

The limiting cases in Equation 21.6 occur when $s = 1$ and $s = 0$. If $s = 1$, the actual change in dividends will be equal to the target change in dividends. Here, full adjustment occurs immediately. If $s = 0$, $Div_1 = Div_0$. In other words, there is no change in dividends at all. Real-world companies can be expected to set s between 0 and 1.

An implication of Lintner's model is that the dividends-to-earnings ratio rises when a company begins a period of bad times, and the ratio falls when a company starts a period of good times. Thus, dividends display less variability than do earnings. In other words, firms *smooth* dividends.

Payouts Provide Information to the Market

We previously observed that the price of a firm's shares frequently rises when either its current dividend is increased or a share repurchase is announced. Conversely, the price of a firm's shares can fall significantly when its dividend is cut. This is a very strong signal that companies have less cash to pay out to shareholders and the accompanying price falls may suggest that investors are looking at current dividends for clues concerning the level of future earnings and dividends.

A Sensible Payout Policy

The knowledge of the finance profession varies across topic areas. For example, capital budgeting techniques are both powerful and precise. A single net present value equation can accurately determine whether a multimillion-pound or euro project should be accepted or rejected. The capital asset pricing model and the arbitrage pricing model provide empirically validated relationships between expected return and risk.

However, the profession has less knowledge of capital structure policy. Though a number of elegant theories relate firm value to the level of debt, no formula can be used to calculate the firm's optimal debt-equity ratio. Academics and practitioners are forced too frequently to employ rules of thumb, such as treating the industry's average ratio as the optimal one for the firm. The field's knowledge of dividend policy is, perhaps, similar to its knowledge of capital structure policy.

We do know the following:

- The intrinsic value of a firm is reduced when positive NPV projects are rejected to pay a dividend.
- Firms should avoid issuing shares to pay a dividend in a world with personal taxes.
- Share repurchases represent a sensible alternative to dividends.

However, there is no formula for calculating the optimal dividend-to-earnings ratio. In addition, there is no formula for determining the optimal mix between share repurchases and dividends. It can be argued that, for tax reasons, firms should always substitute share repurchases for dividends. But while the volume of repurchases has greatly increased over time, Figure 21.7 does not suggest that dividends are on the way out.

The Pros and Cons of Paying Dividends

Pros	Cons
1. Dividends may appeal to investors who desire stable cash flow but do not want to incur the transaction costs from periodically selling shares of equity. 2. Behavioural finance argues that investors with limited self-control can meet current consumption needs with high-dividend shares while adhering to the policy of never dipping into principal. 3. Managers, acting on behalf of shareholders, can pay dividends in order to keep cash from bondholders. 4. The board of directors, acting on behalf of shareholders, can use dividends to reduce the cash available to spendthrift managers. 5. Managers may increase dividends to signal their optimism concerning future cash flow.	1. Dividends are taxed as ordinary income. 2. Dividends can reduce internal sources of financing. Dividends may force the firm to forgo positive NPV projects or to rely on costly external equity financing. 3. Once established, dividend cuts are hard to make without adversely affecting a firm's share price.

Some Survey Evidence about Dividends

In a study surveying a large number of financial executives regarding dividend policy, one of the questions asked was this: 'Do these statements describe factors that affect your company's dividend decisions?' Table 21.4 shows some of the results.

Table 21.4 Survey Responses on Dividend Decisions

Policy Statements		Percentage Who Agree or Strongly Agree
1	We try to avoid reducing dividends per share.	93.8
2	We try to maintain a smooth dividend from year to year.	89.6
3	We consider the level of dividends per share that we have paid in recent quarters.	88.2
4	We are reluctant to make dividend changes that might have to be reversed in the future.	77.9
5	We consider the change or growth in dividends per share.	66.7
6	We consider the cost of raising external capital to be smaller than the cost of cutting dividends.	42.8
7	We pay dividends to attract investors subject to 'prudent man' investment restrictions.	41.7

Source: Adapted from Brav et al. (2005), Table 4.
Note: Survey respondents were asked the question, 'Do these statements describe factors that affect your company's dividend decisions?'

As shown in Table 21.4, financial managers are very disinclined to cut dividends. Moreover, they are very conscious of their previous dividends and desire to maintain a relatively steady dividend. In contrast, the cost of external capital and the desire to attract 'prudent man' investors (those with fiduciary duties) are less important.

Table 21.5 is drawn from the same survey, but here the responses are to the question, 'How important are the following factors to your company's dividend decisions?' Not surprisingly given the responses in Table 21.4 and our earlier discussion, the highest priority is maintaining a consistent dividend policy. The next several items are also consistent with our previous analysis. Financial managers are very concerned about earnings stability and future earnings levels in making dividend decisions, and they consider the availability of good investment opportunities. Survey respondents also believed that attracting both institutional and individual (retail) investors was relatively important.

Table 21.5 Survey Responses on Dividend Decisions

Policy Statements		Percentage Who Think This is Important or Very Important
1	Maintaining consistency with our historic dividend policy.	84.1
2	Stability of future earnings.	71.9
3	A sustainable change in earnings.	67.1
4	Attracting institutional investors to purchase our stock.	52.5
5	The availability of good investment opportunities for our firm to pursue.	47.6
6	Attracting retail investors to purchase our stock.	44.5
7	Personal taxes our stockholders pay when receiving dividends.	21.1
8	Flotation costs to issuing new equity.	9.3

Source: Adapted from Brav et al. (2005), Table 4.
Note: Survey respondents were asked the question, 'How important are the following factors to your company's dividend decisions?'

In contrast to our discussion of taxes and flotation costs earlier in this chapter (Section 21.4), the financial managers in this survey did not think that personal taxes paid on dividends by shareholders are very important. And even fewer thought that equity flotation costs are relevant.

Sustainability in Action 21.1

Unilever

Unilever, a leading UK-based multinational consumer goods company, has successfully linked sustainability to its dividend policy. Sustainability forms a core part of Unilever's operational strategy. The company has set a target to halve its environmental impact by 2030, demonstrating its commitment to sustainable practices. This dedication to ESG principles has positioned Unilever as a market leader in reducing exposure to materials such as unrecyclable packaging and palm oil. Furthermore, Unilever has managed to grow its sales by 10.5 per cent in 2023, with turnover increasing 7.0 per cent to €14.8 billion. This growth was driven by strategic priorities, which include a strong focus on sustainability.

Unilever's ability to integrate dividend policy with its sustainability goals illustrates a financial strategy that aligns with environmental responsibility. The combination of economic success and environmental commitment demonstrates how Unilever is putting sustainability into action, creating value for both shareholders and the planet.

21.10 Stock Dividends and Stock Splits

Another type of dividend is paid out in shares of equity. This type of dividend is called a stock or share dividend. A stock dividend is not a true dividend because it is not paid in cash. The effect of a stock dividend is to increase the number of shares that each owner holds. Because there are more shares outstanding, each is worth less.

A stock dividend is commonly expressed as a percentage; for example, a 20 per cent stock dividend means that a shareholder receives one new share for every five currently owned (a 20 per cent increase). Because every shareholder receives 20 per cent more shares, the total number of shares outstanding rises by 20 per cent. As we will see in a moment, the result is that each share of equity is worth about 20 per cent less.

A **stock split** is essentially the same thing as a stock dividend, except that a split is expressed as a ratio instead of a percentage. When a split is declared, each share is split up to create additional shares. In a three-for-one stock split, for instance, each old share is split into three new shares.

Some Details about Stock Splits and Stock Dividends

Stock splits and stock dividends have essentially the same impact on the corporation and the shareholder: they increase the number of shares outstanding and reduce the value per share. For European firms, there is no distinction between a cash dividend and a stock dividend, and International Financial Reporting Standards (IFRS) considers a stock dividend to be a cash dividend to shareholders with a simultaneous purchase of shares by the same shareholders.

Value of Stock Splits and Stock Dividends

The laws of logic tell us that stock splits and stock dividends can (1) leave the value of the firm unaffected, (2) increase its value or (3) decrease its value. Unfortunately, the issues are complex enough that we cannot easily determine which of the three relationships holds.

The Benchmark Case

A strong case can be made that stock dividends and splits do not change either the wealth of any shareholder or the wealth of the firm as a whole. Consider an all-equity firm with a total market value of €660,000 and 10,000 shares. With the 10 per cent stock dividend, the number of shares increases to 11,000, so it seems that each would be worth €660,000/11,000 = €60.

For example, a shareholder who had 100 shares worth €66 each before the dividend would have 110 shares worth €60 each afterwards. The total value of the equity is €6,600 either way, so the stock dividend does not really have any economic effect.

Now consider a two-for-one stock split. After the stock split, there are 20,000 shares outstanding, so each should be worth €660,000/20,000 = €33. In other words, the number of shares doubles and the price halves. From these calculations, it appears that stock dividends and splits are just paper transactions. This is the view taken by the International Accounting Standards Board in its International Financial Reporting Standards (IFRS).

Although these results are relatively obvious, there are reasons that are often given to suggest that there may be some benefits to these actions. The typical financial manager is aware of many real-world complexities and, for that reason, the stock split or stock dividend decision is not treated lightly in practice.

Popular Trading Range

Proponents of stock dividends and stock splits frequently argue that a security has a proper trading range. When the security is priced above this level, many investors do not have the funds to buy the common trading unit of 100 shares, called a *round lot.* Although securities can be purchased in *odd-lot* form (fewer than 100 shares), the commissions are greater. Thus, firms will split the shares to keep the price in this trading range.

In June 2014, for example, Apple announced a seven-for-one stock split. This was the fourth split for Apple since the company went public in 1980. The stock had split two-for-two on each of the three previous occasions (in 2005, 2000 and 1987). So for every share of Apple you owned in 1980 when the company first went public, you would own 56 shares as of the most recent stock split in 2014.

Although this argument of a trading range is a popular one, its validity is questionable for a number of reasons. Mutual funds, pension funds and other institutions have steadily increased their trading activity since World War II and now handle a sizeable percentage of total trading volume. Because these institutions buy and sell in huge amounts, the individual share price is of little concern.

Furthermore, we sometimes observe share prices that are quite large that do not appear to cause problems. To take an extreme case, consider the Swiss chocolatier Lindt. In April 2019, Lindt shares were selling for around 78,000 Swiss francs each. This is fairly expensive, but also consider Berkshire Hathaway, the company run by legendary investor Warren Buffet. In the same month as Lindt, each share in the company sold for about $306,666!

Finally, there is evidence that stock splits may actually decrease the liquidity of the company's shares. Following a two-for-one split, the number of shares traded should more than double if liquidity is increased by the split. This does not appear to happen, and the reverse is sometimes observed.

Reverse Splits

A less frequently encountered financial manoeuvre is the reverse split. For example, in 2019, TheStreet, an internet business news portal, underwent a one-for-ten reverse stock split. In a one-for-ten reverse split, each investor exchanges ten old shares for one new share. As with stock splits and stock dividends, a case can be made that a reverse split has no real effect.

Given real-world imperfections, three related reasons are cited for reverse splits. First, transaction costs to shareholders may be less after the reverse split. Second, the liquidity and marketability of a company's equity might be improved when its price is raised to the popular trading range. Third, shares selling at prices below a certain level are not considered respectable, meaning that investors underestimate these firms' earnings, cash flow, growth and stability. Some financial analysts argue that a reverse split can achieve instant respectability. As was the case with stock splits, none of these reasons is particularly compelling, especially not the third one.

There are two other reasons for reverse splits. First, stock exchanges have minimum price per share requirements. A reverse split may bring the share price up to such a minimum. The most common reason for these reverse splits is that some exchanges can delist companies whose share price drops below an acceptable value per share. Second, companies sometimes perform reverse splits and, at the same time, buy out any shareholders who end up with less than a certain number of shares.

Summary and Conclusions

1 The dividend policy of a firm is irrelevant in a perfect capital market because the shareholder can effectively undo the firm's dividend strategy. If a shareholder receives a greater dividend than desired, he or she can reinvest the excess. Conversely, if the shareholder receives a smaller dividend than desired, he or she can sell off extra shares of equity. This argument is due to MM and is similar to their homemade leverage concept, discussed in Section 18.3.

2 Shareholders will be indifferent between dividends and share repurchases in a perfect capital market.

3 Because dividends are taxed, companies should not issue equity to pay out a dividend.

4 Also because of taxes, firms have an incentive to reduce dividends. For example, they might consider increasing capital expenditures, acquiring other companies or purchasing financial assets. However, due to financial considerations and legal constraints, rational firms with large cash flows are likely to exhaust these activities, with plenty of cash left over for dividends.

5 In a world with personal taxes, a strong case can be made for repurchasing shares instead of paying dividends.

6 Nevertheless, there are a number of justifications for dividends even in a world with personal taxes:

(a) Investors in no-dividend equities incur transaction costs when selling off shares for current consumption.

(b) Behavioural finance argues that investors with limited self-control can meet current consumption needs via high-dividend equities while adhering to a policy of 'never dipping into principal'.

(c) Managers, acting on behalf of shareholders, can pay dividends to keep cash from bondholders. The board of directors, also acting on behalf of shareholders, can use dividends to reduce the cash available to spendthrift managers.

7 The stock market reacts positively to increases in dividends (or an initial payment) and negatively to decreases in dividends. This suggests that there is information content in dividend payments.

8 High (low) dividend firms should arise to meet the demands of dividend-preferring (capital gains preferring) investors. Because of these clienteles, it is not clear that a firm can create value by changing its dividend policy.

9 Time-varying demand for dividends means that, in some periods, companies that pay dividends are traded at a premium and in other cases they are not. Managers will time their dividend policies to take advantage of this premium.

Questions and Problems

CONCEPT

1 **Different Types of Dividends** Explain the difference between a cash dividend, a stock dividend, a special dividend and a stock buyback.

2 **The Dividend Payment Process** How is it possible that dividends are so important but at the same time dividend policy is irrelevant? When a dividend is paid, give some reasons why the share price decline may not be the same as the actual dividend payment.

3 **Disappearing Dividends** Explain what is meant by the disappearing dividend phenomenon. What are the competing explanations for the phenomenon?

4 **Share Repurchases** Stock buybacks are happening in rapid succession among companies all over the world. Is this good or bad news for shareholders? Explain.

5 **Dividends, Taxes and other Real-world Factors** Explain the importance of taxes in dividend policy. What are the real-world factors that would encourage firms to follow a high dividend policy?

6 **Agency Theory and Payout Policy** Explain how corporate payout policy can be used to align the interests of managers, shareholders and bondholders with the goals of sustainability.

7 **Clienteles** What is meant by dividend clienteles? If dividend clienteles exist, what does that imply for firms that adopt a new dividend policy in order to increase firm value?

8 **Catering Theory** How does the catering theory of dividends suggest that managers can respond to the preferences of socially responsible investors for dividend-paying firms? How does this affect the firm's value and sustainability performance? What does the empirical evidence say about the impact of catering dividends on social and environmental outcomes?

9 **Dividend Policy in Practice** Under the assumptions set out by Modigliani and Miller, is a firm with a low payout dividend stream that uses retentions to finance investment more or less viable than a high payout firm that issues

new issues to finance investment? Do you think dividend policy is important in practice? Justify your answer using information you have read in this chapter.

10 **Stock Dividends and Stock Splits** Why would firms have a reverse split? Should a reverse split have any impact on the value of the firm?

REGULAR

11 **Dividend Policy** It is sometimes suggested that firms should follow a 'residual' dividend policy. With such a policy, the main idea is that a firm should focus on meeting its investment needs and maintaining its desired debt-equity ratio. Having done so, a firm pays out any leftover, or residual, income as dividends. What do you think would be the chief drawback to a residual dividend policy?

12 **Dividends and Clientele** Bodyswerve plc has experienced significant performance gains over previous years and there is no reason to expect any different in the future. The firm has engaged with a potential investor to purchase its shares in the open market. However, the investor has argued that a Bodyswerve investment is not good value for money because the firm has never paid a dividend and their preference is to choose equities that only pay dividends.

(a) Does the investor's argument make sense? Explain.

(b) What argument should be used to convince the investor that Bodyswerve equity is the investment for them?

(c) What counterarguments could be made?

13 **Dividends and Taxes** You are approaching retirement and considering ways to minimize the tax bill from your investment portfolio. Assuming that you are investing only in equities within your own country, what is the best way to maximize your after-tax investment return? Explain.

14 **Dividends versus Capital Gains** It is clear in many countries that investors prefer dividend-paying stocks to those that pay no dividends. How do you explain this if dividend policy is irrelevant?

15 **Dividend Irrelevancy** 'We must ensure that dividends do not fall from one year to the next, even if our company makes a loss. However, if we make a profit then we should increase the dividend.' Does this statement make sense? Explain.

16 **Share Repurchases** SEA Company is a marine conservation firm that has a market capitalization of £500 million and 50 million shares outstanding. It is committed to protecting and restoring the oceans and their biodiversity. Its board has decided to distribute £50 million to shareholders through a repurchase programme. How many shares will be repurchased?

17 **Ex-dividend Price** Thesepe plc has declared a £2 per share dividend and sells for £8.40 per share. Assuming that the tax rate on capital gains and dividends is zero, what do you think the ex-dividend price will be? Explain.

18 **Stock Dividends** The shareholder equity accounts for Hexagon International are shown here:

	£
Ordinary shares (£1 par value)	10,000
Capital surplus	180,000
Retained earnings	586,500
Total owners' equity	776,500

(a) If Hexagon shares currently sell for £25 per share and a 10 per cent stock dividend is declared, how many new shares will be distributed? Show how the equity accounts would change.

(b) If Hexagon declared a 25 per cent stock dividend, how would the accounts change?

19 **Stock Splits** For the company in the previous problem, show how the equity accounts will change if:

(a) Hexagon declares a four-for-one stock split. How many shares are outstanding now? What is the new par value per share?

(b) Hexagon declares a one-for-five reverse stock split. How many shares are outstanding now? What is the new par value per share?

20 **Stock Splits and Stock Dividends** Eurasion Natural Resources Corporation currently has 2.4 million shares outstanding that sell for £5.16 per share. Assuming no market imperfections or tax effects exist, what will the share price be after:

(a) A three-for-two stock split?

(b) An 8 per cent stock dividend?

(c) A 20 per cent stock dividend?

(d) A two-for-three reverse stock split?

Determine the new number of shares outstanding in parts (a) to (d).

21 **Regular Dividends** The balance sheet for Severn Trent plc is shown below in market value terms. There are 2.4 billion shares outstanding.

Market Value Balance Sheet (£m)			
Cash	5,045	Equity	4,022
Non-current assets	5,526	Liabilities	6,549
Total	10,571	Total	10,571

The company has declared a dividend of £0.40 per share. The equity goes ex dividend tomorrow. Ignoring any tax effects, what are the shares selling for today? What will they sell for tomorrow? What will the market value balance sheet look like after the dividends are paid?

22 **Share Repurchases and Cash Dividends** In the previous problem, suppose Severn Trent plc has announced it is going to repurchase £1 billion worth of equity. What effect will this transaction have on the equity of the firm? How many shares will be outstanding? What will the price per share be after the repurchase? Ignoring tax effects, show how the share repurchase is effectively the same as a cash dividend.

23 **Stock Dividends: KL Air** The market value balance sheet for KL Air is shown below. KL Air has declared a 20 per cent stock dividend. The equity goes ex dividend tomorrow (the chronology for a stock dividend is similar to that for a cash dividend). There are 15,000 shares of equity outstanding. What will the ex-dividend price be?

Market Value Balance Sheet (£m)			
Cash	1,290,000	Debt	1,682,500
Non-current assets	5,440,000	Equity	5,047,500
Total	6,730,000	Total	6,730,000

24 **Stock Dividends** The company with the equity accounts shown in the table below has declared a 12 per cent stock dividend when the market value of its equity is €20 per share. What effects on the equity accounts will the distribution of the stock dividend have?

	(€)
Ordinary shares (€1 par value)	350,000
Capital surplus	1,650,000
Retained earnings	3,000,000
Total owners' equity	5,000,000

25 **Stock Splits** In the previous problem, suppose the company instead decides on a five-for-one stock split. The firm's 70 cents per share cash dividend on the new (post-split) shares represents an increase of 10 per cent over last year's dividend on the pre-split equity. What effect does this have on the equity accounts? What was last year's dividend per share?

26 **Residual Dividend Policy** Hillshire plc uses a residual dividend policy (see Problem 11). A debt-equity ratio of 0.60 is considered optimal. Earnings for the period just ended were £524,292 and a dividend of £50,000 was declared. How much in new debt was borrowed? What were total capital outlays?

27 **Residual Dividend Policy: Worthington AG** Worthington AG has declared an annual dividend of 1.50 Swiss francs (SFr) per share. For the year just ended, earnings were SFr14 per share.

(a) What is Worthington's payout ratio?

(b) Suppose Worthington has 12 million shares outstanding. Borrowing for the coming year is planned at SFr25 million. What are planned investment outlays assuming a residual dividend policy (see Problem 11)? What target capital structure is implicit in these calculations?

28 **Residual Dividend Policy: Red Zeppelin plc** Red Zeppelin plc follows a strict residual dividend policy (see Problem 11). Its debt-equity ratio is 3.

(a) If earnings for the year are £180,000, what is the maximum amount of capital spending possible with no new equity?

(b) If planned investment outlays for the coming year are £760,000, will Red Zeppelin pay a dividend? If so, how much?

(c) Does Red Zeppelin maintain a constant dividend payout? Why, or why not?

29 **Residual Dividend Policy: Preti Rock SA** Preti Rock (PR) predicts that earnings in the coming year will be €56 million. There are 12 million shares, and PR maintains a debt-equity ratio of 2.

(a) Calculate the maximum investment funds available without issuing new equity, and the increase in borrowing that goes along with it.

(b) Suppose the firm uses a residual dividend policy (see Problem 11). Planned capital expenditures total €72 million. Based on this information, what will the dividend per share be?

(c) In part (b), how much borrowing will take place? What is the addition to retained earnings?

(d) Suppose PR plans no capital outlays for the coming year. What will the dividend be under a residual policy? What will new borrowing be?

30 **Dividends and Share Price** Mann Company belongs to a risk class for which the appropriate discount rate is 10 per cent. Mann currently has 100,000 outstanding shares selling at £100 each. The firm is contemplating the declaration of a £5 dividend at the end of the fiscal year just begun. Assume there are no taxes on dividends. Answer the following questions based on the Miller and Modigliani model discussed in the text.

(a) What will be the price of the shares on the ex-dividend date if the dividend is declared?

(b) What will be the price of the shares at the end of the year if the dividend is not declared?

(c) If Mann makes £2 million of new investments at the beginning of the period, earns net income of £1 million and pays the dividend at the end of the year, how many shares of new equity must the firm issue to meet its funding needs?

(d) Is it realistic to use the MM model in the real world to value equity? Why, or why not?

31 **Homemade Dividends: Avondale Property plc** You own 2,000 shares of equity in Avondale Property plc. You will receive a £0.25 per share dividend in one year. In two years, Avondale will pay a liquidating dividend of £0.75 per share. The required return on Avondale shares is 18 per cent. What is the current share price of your equity (ignoring taxes)? If you would rather have equal dividends in each of the next two years, show how you can accomplish this by creating homemade dividends. (*Hint:* Dividends will be in the form of an annuity.)

32 **Homemade Dividends: Avondale Property plc** In the previous problem, suppose you want only £400 total in dividends the first year. What will your homemade dividend be in two years?

33 **Share Repurchase: Flychucker SA** Flychucker SA is evaluating an extra dividend versus a share repurchase. In either case €5,000 would be spent. Current earnings are €0.95 per share and the equity currently sells for €40 per share. There are 200 shares outstanding. Ignore taxes and other imperfections in answering parts (a) and (b).

(a) Evaluate the two alternatives in terms of the effect on the price per share of the equity and shareholder wealth.

(b) What will be the effect on Flychucker's EPS and PE ratio under the two different scenarios?

(c) In the real world, which of these actions would you recommend? Why?

34 **Dividends and Firm Value** The net income of Novis AS is 32,000 kroner (DKr). The company has 10,000 outstanding shares and a 100 per cent payout policy. The expected value of the firm one year from now is DKr1,545,600. The appropriate discount rate for Novis is 12 per cent, and the dividend tax rate is zero.

(a) What is the current value of firm assuming the current dividend has not yet been paid?

(b) What is the ex-dividend price of Novis's equity if the board follows its current policy?

(c) At the dividend declaration meeting, several board members claimed that the dividend is too meagre and is probably depressing Novis's price. They proposed that Novis sell enough new shares to finance a DKr4.25 dividend.

(i) Comment on the claim that the low dividend is depressing the share price. Support your argument with calculations.

(ii) If the proposal is adopted, at what price will the new shares sell? How many will be sold?

35 **Dividend Policy: Newcastle Autos plc** Newcastle Autos plc has a current period cash flow of £4.2 million and pays no dividends. The present value of the company's future cash flows is £72 million. The company is entirely financed with equity and has 1 million shares outstanding. Assume the dividend tax rate is zero.

(a) What is the share price of Newcastle Autos' equity?

(b) Suppose the board of directors of Newcastle Autos announces its plan to pay out 40 per cent of its current cash flow as cash dividends to its shareholders. How could you achieve a zero payout policy on your own, if you own 1,000 shares of Newcastle Autos' equity?

36 **Dividend Smoothing** Sharpe SA has just paid a dividend of €1.25 per share of equity. Its target payout ratio is 40 per cent. The company expects to have an earnings per share of €4.50 one year from now.

(a) If the adjustment rate is 0.3 as defined in the Lintner model, what is the dividend one year from now?

(b) If the adjustment rate is 0.6 instead, what is the dividend one year from now?

(c) Which adjustment rate is more conservative? Why?

CHALLENGE

37 **Expected Return, Dividends and Taxes** Gecko Company and Gordon Company are two firms whose business risk is the same but that have different dividend policies. Gecko pays no dividend, whereas Gordon has an expected dividend yield of 6 per cent. Suppose the capital gains tax rate is zero, whereas the dividend tax rate is 12.5 per cent. Gecko has an expected earnings growth rate of 15 per cent annually, and its share price is expected to grow at this same rate. If the after-tax expected returns on the two equities are equal (because they are in the same risk class), what is the pre-tax required return on Gordon's shares?

38 **Dividends and Real-World Tax Considerations** As discussed in the text, in the absence of market imperfections and tax effects, we would expect the share price to decline by the amount of the dividend payment when the equity goes ex dividend. Once we consider the role of taxes, however, this is not necessarily true. One model has been proposed that incorporates tax effects into determining the ex-dividend price (Elton and Gruber, 1970):

$$(P_0 - P_X)/D = (1 - t_P)/(1 - t_G)$$

Here P_0 is the price just before the share goes ex, P_x is the ex-dividend share price, D is the amount of the dividend per share, t_P is the relevant marginal personal tax rate on dividends, and t_G is the effective marginal tax rate on capital gains.

(a) If $t_P = t_G = 0$, how much will the share price fall when the equity goes ex?

(b) If $t_P = 36.1$ per cent and $t_G = 0$ per cent, how much will the share price fall?

(c) If $t_P = 36.1$ per cent and $t_G = 28$ per cent, how much will the share price fall?

(d) What does this problem tell you about real-world tax considerations and the dividend policy of the firm?

39 **Signalling through Corporate Payout Policy** Miller and Rock (1985) put forward a signalling model of corporate payout policy. Critically evaluate this model, with specific reference to the theoretical and empirical literature that supports or contradicts the model.

40 **Dividends versus Reinvestment** After completing its capital spending for the year, Carlson Manufacturing has £1,000 extra cash. Carlson's managers must choose between investing the cash in Treasury bonds that yield 8 per cent or paying the cash out to investors who would invest in the bonds themselves.

(a) If the corporate tax rate is 23 per cent, what personal tax rate would make the investors equally willing to receive the dividend or to let Carlson invest the money?

(b) Is the answer to (a) reasonable? Why, or why not?

Exam Question (45 minutes)

1 You have been asked by a client to forecast the dividend per share of Clouds plc over the next three years. From initial investigation, you find out that the company paid a dividend of £1.00 per share last year. An examination of analysts' earnings forecasts points to an expected earnings per share of £3 next year, which is an increase from the current earnings per share of £2.75. The earnings per share two years from now are expected to be £3.50. Using Lintner's model, you estimate that the company has a long-term payout rate of 60 per cent and an adjustment factor of 50 per cent. **(40 marks)**

2 Review the reasons why corporations issue dividends when it appears from a tax perspective suboptimal to do so. **(30 marks)**

3 In recent years, share repurchases have become more common than cash dividends. Explain why you think this is so, using research you have read to support your answer. **(30 marks)**

Total: 100 Marks

Mini Case

Forest Future Foundation (FFF)

Forest Future Foundation (FFF) is an environmental company that was launched 15 years ago by ecologists Juliette Grégoire and Luc Lefèvre. FFF focuses on sustainable forest management practices and has recently ventured into the market of carbon offsetting services. These services involve the calculation, reduction and offsetting of carbon footprints, which are essential for sustainable environmental management. Their carbon offsetting tools were initially utilized in the local community management sector, but the market subsequently grew to encompass large-scale infrastructure projects, household applications and other environmentally conscious consumer platforms such as sustainable tourism and green technology devices. FFF also develops and markets custom sustainability-specific solutions (SSS) for corporate clients. These SSS designs combine data analytics and environmental science or mixed-discipline technology. Besides Juliette and Luc, Emmanuelle Bourdin, who provided funding for the company, is the third primary stakeholder. Each holds 25 per cent of the 1 million shares outstanding. Numerous other individuals, including current employees, own the remaining company shares.

Recently, the company devised a new carbon offset algorithm. The algorithm is not only more efficient but also less costly to implement, and the FFF algorithm is anticipated to become standard in many environmental management systems. However, after evaluating the potential of building an in-house platform to implement the algorithm, FFF concluded that the associated costs would be too high. The stakeholders also decided they were not prepared to invite another major outside stakeholder. Instead, FFF sold the algorithm to an external company. The sale of the carbon offset algorithm resulted in a post-tax payment of €30 million.

1 Juliette proposes that the company should use the extra funds to pay a unique one-time dividend. What would be the repercussions of this proposal on the stock price? How would it affect the company's value?

2 Luc contends that the company should use the extra funds to pay off debt and further enhance and expand its existing forestry management practices. How would Luc's proposals influence the company?

3 Emmanuelle supports a stock buyback, arguing that a buyback will improve the company's P/E ratio, return on assets and return on equity. Are her arguments valid? How will a share repurchase impact the company's value?

4 Another suggestion discussed by Juliette, Luc and Emmanuelle would be to initiate a regular dividend payment to shareholders. How would you assess this proposal?

5 One way to value a share of equity is the dividend growth, or growing perpetuity, model. Consider the following: The dividend payout ratio is 1 minus *b*, where *b* is the 'retention' or 'ploughback' ratio. So, the dividend next year will be the earnings next year, E_1, times 1 minus the retention ratio. The most commonly used equation to calculate the sustainable growth rate is the return on equity times the retention ratio. Substituting these relationships into the dividend growth model, we get the following equation to calculate the price of a share of equity today:

$$P_0 = \frac{E_1(1-b)}{R_s - ROE \times b}$$

What does this result imply in terms of whether the company should pay a dividend or enhance and expand its forestry management practices? Explain.

6 Does the question of whether the company should pay a dividend depend on whether it is organized as a corporation or partnership?

Practical Case Study

Use the annual financial statements for three companies in your country to find the dividend payout ratio for each firm for the past three years. Why would these companies pay out a different percentage of income as dividends?

Relevant Accounting Standards

Dividend policy in itself is not affected by accounting standards, however the presentation of dividends is affected by IAS 1 *Presentation of Financial Statements,* IAS 27 *Consolidated and Separate Financial Statements* and IAS 33 *Earnings per Share.* Visit the IASPlus website (www.iasplus.com) for more information.

References

Allen, F., A. Bernardo and I. Welch (2002) 'A Theory of Dividends Based on Tax Clienteles', *Journal of Finance,* Vol. 55, No. 6, 2499–2536.

Baker, M. and J. Wurgler (2004) 'A Catering Theory of Dividends', *Journal of Finance,* Vol. 59, No. 3, 1125–1165.

BEIS, Department for Business, Energy and Industrial Strategy (2019) 'Share Repurchases, Executive Pay and Investment', UK Government.

Bertrand, M. and A. Schoar (2003) 'Managing with Style: The Effect of Managers on Firm Policies', *Quarterly Journal of Economics,* Vol. 118, No. 4, 1169–1208.

Bhattacharya, S. (1979) 'Imperfect Information, Dividend Policy, and "the Bird in the Hand" Fallacy', *Bell Journal of Economics,* Vol. 10, No. 1, 259–270.

Bhattacharya, S. (1980) 'Non-dissipative Signaling Structure and Dividend Policy', *Quarterly Journal of Economics,* Vol. 95, No. 1, 1–24.

Brav, A., J.R. Graham, C.R. Harvey and R. Michaely (2005) 'Payout Policy in the 21st Century', *Journal of Financial Economics,* Vol. 77, No. 3, 487–527.

Cronqvist, H. and F. Yu (2017) 'Shaped by Their Daughters: Executives, Female Socialization, and Corporate Social Responsibility', *Journal of Financial Economics,* Vol. 126, No. 3, 543–562.

DeAngelo, H. and L. DeAngelo (1990) 'Dividend Policy and Financial Distress: An Empirical Investigation of Troubled NYSE Firms', *Journal of Finance,* Vol. 45, No. 5, 1415–1431.

DeAngelo, H., L. DeAngelo and D. Skinner (2004) 'Are Dividends Disappearing? Dividend Concentration and the Consolidation of Earnings', *Journal of Financial Economics,* Vol. 72, No. 3, 425–456.

Elton, N. and M. Gruber (1970) 'Marginal Stockholder Tax Rates and the Clientele Effect', *Review of Economics and Statistics,* Vol. 52, No. 1, 68–74.

Faccio, M., M.T. Marchica and R. Mura (2016) 'CEO Gender, Corporate Risk-taking, and the Efficiency of Capital Allocation', *Journal of Corporate Finance,* Vol. 39, 193–209.

Fama, E.F. and K.R. French (2001) 'Disappearing Dividends: Changing Firm Characteristics or Lower Propensity to Pay?', *Journal of Financial Economics,* Vol. 60, 3–43.

Graham, J.R. and A. Kumar (2006) 'Do Dividend Clienteles Exist? Evidence on Dividend Preferences of Retail Investors', *Journal of Finance,* Vol. 61, No. 3, 1305–1336.

Hansen, R.S., R. Kumar and D.K. Shome (1994) 'Dividend Policy and Corporate Monitoring: Evidence from the Regulated Electric Utility Industry', *Financial Management,* Vol. 23, No. 1, 16–22.

Hegde, S.P. and D.R. Mishra (2019) 'Married CEOs and Corporate Social Responsibility', *Journal of Corporate Finance,* 58, 226–246.

Henry, D., L. Nguyen and V.H. Pham (2017) 'Institutional Trading before Dividend Reduction Announcements', *Journal of Financial Markets,* Vol. 36, 40–55.

Hilary, G., S. Huang and Y. Xu (2017) 'Marital Status and Earnings Management', *European Accounting Review,* Vol. 26, No. 1, 153–158.

Hossain, M.N., M.K. Rabarison, B. Ater and C.K. Sobngwi (2023) 'CEO Marital Status and Dividend Policy', *Journal of Corporate Finance,* Vol. 78, 102342.

Isakov, D., C. Pérignon and J.P. Weisskopf (2021) 'What if Dividends were Tax-exempt? Evidence from a Natural Experiment', *Review of Financial Studies,* Vol. 34, No. 12, 5756–5795.

Jensen, M.C. (1986) 'Agency Costs of Free Cash Flows, Corporate Finance, and Takeovers', *American Economic Review*, Vol. 76, No. 2, 323–329.

Kahle, K. and R.M. Stulz (2021) 'Why Are Corporate Payouts So High in the 2000s?', *Journal of Financial Economics*, Vol. 142, No. 3, 1359–1380.

Kose, J. and J. Williams (1985) 'Dividends, Dilution and Taxes: A Signaling Equilibrium', *Journal of Finance*, Vol. 40, No. 4, 1053–1070.

Kumar, A., Z. Lei and C. Zhang (2022) 'Dividend Sentiment, Catering Incentives, and Return Predictability', *Journal of Corporate Finance*, Vol. 72, 102128.

Lee, B.S. and N. Mauck (2016) 'Dividend Initiations, Increases and Idiosyncratic Volatility', *Journal of CorporateFinance*, Vol. 40, 47–60.

Lintner, J. (1956) 'Distribution and Incomes of Corporations among Dividends, Retained Earnings, and Taxes', *American Economic Review*, Vol. 46, No. 2, 97–113.

Michaely, R. and A. Moin (2022) 'Disappearing and Reappearing Dividends', *Journal of Financial Economics*, Vol. 143, No. 1, 207–226.

Miller, M. and K. Rock (1985) 'Dividend Policy under Asymmetric Information', *Journal of Finance*, Vol. 40, No. 4, 1031–1051.

Peterson, P., D. Peterson and J. Ang (1985) 'Direct Evidence on the Marginal Rate of Taxation on Dividend Income', *Journal of Financial Economics*, Vol. 14, 267–282.

Rangvid, J., M. Schmeling and A. Schrimpf (2014) 'Dividend Predictability around the World', *Journal of Financial and Quantitative Analysis*, Vol. 49, 1–46.

Ross, S. (1977) 'The Determination of Financial Structure: The Incentive Signaling Approach', *Bell Journal of Economics*, Vol. 8, No. 1, 23–40.

Roussanov, N. and P. Savor (2014) 'Marriage and Managers' Attitudes to Risk', *Management Science*, Vol. 60, No. 10, 2496–2508.

Rozeff, M. (1986) 'How Companies Set their Dividend Payout Ratios', in J.M. Stern and D.H. Chew (eds), *The Revolution in Corporate Finance*. New York: Basil Blackwell.

Serfling, M.A. (2014) 'CEO Age and the Riskiness of Corporate Policies', *Journal of Corporate Finance*, Vol. 25, 251–273.

Sheikh, S. (2022) 'CEO Power and the Likelihood of Paying Dividends: Effect of Profitability and Cash Flow Volatility', *Journal of Corporate Finance*, Vol. 73, 102186.

von Eije, H. and W. Megginson (2008) 'Dividends and Share Repurchases in the European Union', *Journal of Financial Economics*, Vol. 89, 347–374.

Additional Reading

Dividend policy, the reasons why firms issue dividends, the factors affecting dividend policy, and their importance to investors are issues that have been bothering academics since Modigliani and Miller published their original dividend irrelevance theorem. The papers that are referenced below consider dividends in detail.

Theoretical Developments

1 Allen, F., A.E. Bernardo and I. Welch (2000) 'A Theory of Dividends Based on Tax Clienteles', *Journal of Finance*, Vol. 55, No. 6, 2499–2536.

2 DeAngelo, H. and L. DeAngelo (2006) 'The Irrelevance of the MM Dividend Irrelevance Theorem', *Journal of Financial Economics*, Vol. 80, No. 2, 299–315.

3 Lambrecht, B.M. and S.C. Myers (2012) 'A Lintner Model of Payout and Managerial Rents', *Journal of Finance*, Vol. 67, No. 5, 1761–1810.

4 Ohlson, J.A., A.J. Ostaszewski and Z. Gao (2011) 'Dividend Policy Irrelevancy and the Construct of Earnings', Working Paper.

Dividend Policy, Share Repurchases and Stock Splits

5 Andres, C., A. Betzer, M. Goergen and L. Renneboog (2009) 'Dividend Policy of German Firms: A Panel Data Analysis of Partial Adjustment Models', *Journal of Empirical Finance*, Vol. 16, No. 2, 175–187. **Germany.**

6 Atmaz, A. and S. Basak (2022) 'Stock Market and No-dividend Stocks,' *Journal of Finance*, Vol. 77, No. 1, 545–599.

7 Bargeron, L., M. Kulchania and S. Thomas (2011) 'Accelerated Share Repurchases', *Journal of Financial Economics*, Vol. 101, No. 1, 69–89.

8 Bell, L. and T. Jenkinson (2002) 'New Evidence of the Impact of Dividend Taxation and on the Identity of the Marginal Investor', *Journal of Finance*, Vol. 57, No. 3, 1321–1346. **UK.**

9 Brav, A., J.R. Graham, C.R. Harvey and R. Michaely (2005) 'Payout Policy in the 21st Century', *Journal of Financial Economics*, Vol. 77, No. 3, 483–527. **USA.**

10 Brockman, P. and E. Unlu (2009) 'Dividend Policy, Creditor Rights, and the Agency Costs of Debt', *Journal of Financial Economics*, Vol. 92, No. 2, 276–299. **International.**

11 Chan, K., D.L. Ikenberry, I. Lee and Y. Wang (2010) 'Share Repurchases as a Potential Tool to Mislead Investors', *Journal of Corporate Finance*, Vol. 16, No. 2, 137–158. **USA.**

12 DeAngelo, H., L. DeAngelo and R.M. Stulz (2006) 'Dividend Policy and the Earned/Contributed Capital

Mix: A Test of the Life-cycle Theory', *Journal of Financial Economics,* Vol. 81, No. 1, 227–254. **USA.**

13 De Cesari, A., S. Espenlaub, A. Khurshed and M. Simkovi (2012) 'The Effects of Ownership and Stock Liquidity on the Timing of Repurchase Transactions', *Journal of Corporate Finance,* Vol. 18, No. 5, 1023–1050.

14 Ferris, S.P., N. Jayaraman and S. Sabherwal (2009) 'Catering Effects in Corporate Dividend Policy: The International Evidence', *Journal of Banking and Finance,* Vol. 33, No. 9, 1730–1738.

15 Graham, J.R. and A. Kumar (2006) 'Do Dividend Clienteles Exist? Evidence on Dividend Preferences of Retail Investors', *Journal of Finance,* Vol. 61, No. 3, 1305–1336. **USA.**

16 Grinstein, Y. and R. Michaely (2005) 'Institutional Holdings and Payout Policy', *Journal of Finance,* Vol. 60, No. 3, 1389–1426. **USA.**

17 Hartzmark, S.M. and D.H. Solomon (2019) 'The Dividend Disconnect', *Journal of Finance,* Vol. 74, No. 5, 2153–2199.

18 Henock, L. and H. White (2007) 'Do Managers Intentionally Use Repurchase Tender Offers to Signal Private Information? Evidence from Firm Financial Reporting Behavior', *Journal of Financial Economics,* Vol. 85, No. 1, 205–233. **USA.**

19 Hoberg, G. and N. Prabhala (2009) 'Disappearing Dividends, Catering, and Risk', *Review of Financial Studies,* Vol. 22, No. 1, 79–116. **USA.**

20 Holmen, M., J.D. Knopf and S. Peterson (2008) 'Inside Shareholders' Effective Tax Rates and Dividends', *Journal of Banking and Finance,* Vol. 32, No. 9, 1860–1869. **Sweden.**

21 Jiang, Z., K.A. Kim, E. Lie and S. Yang (2013) 'Share Repurchases, Catering, and Dividend Substitution', *Journal of Corporate Finance,* Vol. 21, 36–50.

22 Kinkki, S. (2008) 'Minority Protection and Dividend Policy in Finland', *European Financial Management,* Vol. 14, No. 3, 470–502. **Finland.**

23 Kunz, R.M. and S. Rosa-Majhensek (2008) 'Stock Splits in Switzerland: To Signal or Not to Signal', *Financial Management,* Vol. 37, No. 2, 193–226. **Switzerland.**

24 La Porta, L., F. Lopez-de-Silanes, A. Shliefer and R. Vishney (2000) 'Agency Problems and Dividend Policy around the World', *Journal of Finance,* Vol. 55, No. 1, 1–33. **International.**

25 Li, W. and E. Lie (2006) 'Dividend Changes and Catering Incentives', *Journal of Financial Economics,* Vol. 80, No. 2, 293–308. **USA.**

26 Lin, J.-C., A.K. Singh and W. Yu (2009) 'Stock Splits, Trading Continuity, and the Cost of Equity Capital', *Journal of Financial Economics,* Vol. 93, No. 3, 474–489.

27 Massa, M., Z. Rehman and T. Vermaelen (2007) 'Mimicking Repurchases', *Journal of Financial Economics,* Vol. 84, No. 3, 624–666. **USA.**

28 Moder, W.J. (2007) 'The Effect of Shareholder Taxes on Corporate Payout Choice', *Journal of Financial and Quantitative Analysis,* Vol. 42, No. 4, 991–1019. **USA.**

29 Oswald, D. and S. Young (2008) 'Share Reacquisitions, Surplus Cash, and Agency Problems', *Journal of Banking and Finance,* Vol. 32, No. 5, 795–806. **UK.**

30 Renneboog, L. and G. Trojanowski (2011) 'Patterns in Payout Policy and Payout Channel Choice', *Journal of Banking and Finance,* Vol. 35, No. 6, 1477–1490. **UK.**

31 Rommens, A., L. Cuyvers and M. Deloof (2012) 'Dividend Policies of Privately Held Companies: Stand-alone and Group Companies in Belgium', *European Financial Management,* Vol. 18, No. 5, 816–835.

32 Schultz, P. (2000) 'Stock Splits, Tick Size, and Sponsorship', *Journal of Finance,* Vol. 55, No. 1, 429–450. **USA.**

Other Relevant Research

33 Alzahrani, M. and M. Lasfer (2012) 'Investor Protection, Taxation, and Dividends', *Journal of Corporate Finance,* Vol. 18, No. 4, 745–762.

34 Asquith, P. and D. Mullins, Jr (1983) 'The Impact of Initiating Dividend Payments on Shareholder Wealth', *Journal of Business,* Vol. 56, 77–96.

35 Berkman, H. and P.D. Koch (2017) 'Drips and the Dividend Pay Date Effect', *Journal of Financial and Quantitative Analysis,* Vol. 52, No. 4, 1765–1795.

36 Bonaimé, A.A., K.W. Hankins and J. Harford (2014) 'Financial Flexibility, Risk Management, and Payout Choice', *Review of Financial Studies,* Vol. 27, No. 4, 1074–1101.

37 Bremberger, F., C. Cambini, K. Gugler and L. Rondi (2016) 'Dividend Policy in Regulated Network Industries: Evidence from the EU', *Economic Inquiry,* Vol. 54, No. 1, 408–432.

38 Chen, J., W.S. Leung and M. Goergen (2017) 'The Impact of Board Gender Composition on Dividend Payouts', *Journal of Corporate Finance,* Vol. 43, 86–105.

39 Del Brio, E.B. and A. De Miguel (2010) 'Dividends and Market Signalling: An Analysis of Corporate Insider Trading', *European Financial Management,* Vol. 16, No. 3, 480–497. **Spain.**

40 Dong, M., C. Robinson and C. Veld (2005) 'Why Individual Investors Want Dividends', *Journal of Corporate Finance,* Vol. 12, No. 1, 121–158. **The Netherlands.**

41 Grennan, J. (2019) 'Dividend Payments as a Response to Peer Influence', *Journal of Financial Economics,* Vol. 131, No. 3, 549–570.

42 He, W., L. Ng, N. Zaiats and B. Zhang (2017) 'Dividend Policy and Earnings Management across Countries', *Journal of Corporate Finance,* Vol. 42, 267–286.

43 Jacob, M. and R. Michaely (2017) 'Taxation and Dividend Policy: The Muting Effect of Agency Issues and Shareholder Conflicts', *Review of Financial Studies,* Vol. 30, No. 9, 3176–3222.

44 Julio, B. and D. Ikenberry (2004) 'Reappearing Dividends', *Journal of Applied Corporate Finance,* Vol. 16, 89–100.

45 Koo, D.S., S. Ramalingegowda and Y. Yu (2017) 'The Effect of Financial Reporting Quality on Corporate Dividend Policy', *Review of Accounting Studies,* Vol. 22, No. 2, 753–790.

46 Larkin, Y., M.T. Leary and R. Michaely (2016) 'Do Investors Value Dividend-smoothing Stocks Differently?', *Management Science,* Vol. 63, No. 12, 4114–4136.

47 Liu, Y., S.H. Szewczyck and Z. Zantout (2008) 'Underreaction to Dividend Reductions and Omissions?', *Journal of Finance,* Vol. 62, No. 2, 987–1020. **USA.**

48 Michaely, R., R.H. Thaler and K. Womack (1995) 'Price Reactions to Dividend Initiations and Omissions: Overreactions to Drift', *Journal of Finance,* Vol. 50, No. 2, 573–608.

49 Pinkowitz, L., R. Stulz and R. Williamson (2006) 'Does the Contribution of Corporate Cash Holdings and Dividends to Firm Value Depend on Governance? A Cross-country Analysis', *Journal of Finance,* Vol. 61, No. 6, 2725–2751. **International.**

Endnotes

1 See, for example, Jensen (1986).

2 See also Brav et al. (2005).

3 Rozeff (1986). See also Hansen et al. (1994).

4 The correct representation of Equation 21.5 involves cash flow, not earnings. However, with little loss of understanding, we could discuss dividend signalling in terms of earnings, not cash flow.

5 Papers examining fully developed models of signalling include Bhattacharya (1979), Bhattacharya (1980), Ross (1977), and Miller and Rock (1985).

6 Signalling models where dividends and repurchases are not perfect substitutes are contained in Allen et al. (2002), Kose and Williams (1985), and Rangvid et al. (2014).

PART 6

Options, Futures and Corporate Finance

Derivative securities are essential tools for firms to manage risk. Derivatives like forward contracts, futures, options and warrants can be innovatively combined to meet investor and company requirements. In Part 6, we'll delve into derivatives, exploring their traits, their use in risk optimization and valuation. We'll also examine hybrid securities with derivative features and risk management, a crucial emerging finance field.

Specifically, Part 6 begins in Chapter 22 with a study of options and their use in corporate finance. We then extend the conceptual material in Chapter 23 to look at real-world applications of options and how they can be used to make better financial decisions. Warrants and convertible bonds are investigated in Chapter 24, and Chapter 25 ends Part 6 with a very detailed look at financial risk management.

Chapter 22
Options and Corporate Finance

Learning Objectives

After reading this chapter you should be able to:

LO1 Define and describe the characteristics of call options and put options.

LO2 Understand the process of writing options and combining different options to create strategic positions.

LO3 Evaluate different methodologies for valuing options, including the application of an option pricing formula.

On 26 May 2023 the closing share prices for DCC plc and Ashtead Group plc were £49.76 and £49.78, respectively. Each company had several option contracts to buy and sell the securities at some future date. You may think the price of the options would be similar if the agreed future price, date and amount are the same. However, this is highly unlikely to be the case because one must forecast today what the future DCC plc and Ashtead Group plc share prices will be. If you think the DCC price will increase and the Ashtead Group price will fall, the option values will be very different.

Even if the expectation is that both securities will grow in value, the option prices may still differ because the volatility of both company's share prices may be different. Share price volatility is an important determinant of an option's underlying value, and, in this chapter, we explore this issue – and many others – in much greater depth using the Noble Prize-winning Black-Scholes option pricing model.

Source: BEST-BACKGROUNDS/Shutterstock

Key Notations

C	Value of a call option
P	Value of a put option
S	Current share price
E	Exercise price of option
R	Annual risk-free rate of return, continuously compounded
σ^2	Variance (per year) of the continuous share price return
t	Time (in years) to expiration date
$N(d)$	Probability that a standardized, normally distributed, random variable will be less than or equal to d

$d_1 = [\text{In}(S/E) + (R + \sigma^2/2)t]/\sqrt{\sigma^2}$

$d_2 = d_1 - \sqrt{\sigma^{2t}}$

22.1 Options

An **option** is a contract giving its owner the right to buy or sell an asset at a fixed price on or before a given date. For example, an option on a building might give the buyer the right to buy the building for €1 million on or any time before the Saturday prior to the third Wednesday in January 2026. Options are a unique type of financial contract because they give the buyer the right, but not the *obligation*, to do something. The buyer uses the option only if it is advantageous to do so; otherwise, the option can be thrown away.

There is a special vocabulary associated with options. Here are some important definitions:

- *Exercising the option:* The act of buying or selling the underlying asset via the option contract.
- *Strike or exercise price:* The fixed price in the option contract at which the holder can buy or sell the underlying asset.
- *Expiration date:* The maturity date of the option; after this date, the option is dead.
- *American and European options:* An American option may be exercised any time up to the expiration date. A European option differs from an American option in that it can be exercised only on the expiration date.

22.2 Call Options

The most common type of option is a **call option**. A call option gives the owner the right to buy an asset at a fixed price during a particular period. There is no restriction on the kind of asset, but the most common ones traded on exchanges are options on shares and bonds.

Call options on Associated British Foods plc shares, for example, can be purchased on the Intercontinental Exchange, ICE. Associated British Foods does not issue (that is, sell) call options on its equity. Instead, individual investors are the original buyers and sellers of call options on Associated British Foods equity. A representative call option on Associated British Foods enables an investor to buy 100 shares of Associated British Foods on or before 15 July at an exercise price of £7.00. This is a valuable option if there is some probability that the price of Associated British Foods equity will exceed £7.00 on or before 15 July.

The Value of a Call Option at Expiration

What is the value of a call option contract on equity at expiration? The answer depends on the value of the underlying shares at expiration.

Let us continue with the Associated British Foods example. Suppose the share price is £8.00 at expiration. The buyer[1] of the call option has the right to buy the underlying shares at the exercise price of £7.00. In other words, he has the right to exercise the call. Having the right to buy something for £7.00 when it is worth £8.00 is obviously a good thing. The value of this right is £1.00 (= £8.00 – £7.00) on the expiration day.[2]

The call would be worth even more if the share price were higher on expiration day. If, say, Associated British Foods were selling for £8.50 on the date of expiration, the call would be worth £1.50 (= £8.50 – £7.00) at that time. In fact, the call's value increases £1 for every £1 rise in the share price.

If the share price is greater than the exercise price, we say that the call is *in the money*. Of course, it is also possible that the value of the equity will turn out to be less than the exercise price, in which case we say that the call is *out of the money*. The holder will not exercise in this case. For instance, if the share price at the expiration date is £6.00, no rational investor would exercise. Why pay £7.00 for shares worth only £6.00? Because the option holder has no obligation to exercise the call, they can *walk away* from the option. As a consequence, if Associated British Food's share price is less than £7.00 on the expiration date, the value of the call option will be £0. In this case, the value of the call option is not the difference between Associated British Food's share price and £7.00, as it would be if the holder of the call option had the *obligation* to exercise the call.

Here is the payoff of this call option at expiration:

	Payoff on the Expiration Date	
	If Share Price is Less than £7.00	**If Share Price is Greater than £7.00**
Call option value	£0	Share price – £7.00

Example 22.1

Call Option Payoffs

Suppose Mr Optimist holds a one-year call option on equity of the Belgian imaging and IT company, Agfa Gevaert. It is a European call option and can be exercised at €1.80. Assume that the expiration date has arrived. What is the value of the Agfa Gevaert call option on the expiration date? If Agfa Gevaert is selling for €2.00 per share, Mr Optimist can exercise the option – purchase Agfa Gevaert at £1.80 – and then immediately sell the share at €2.00. Mr Optimist will have made €0.20 (= €2.00 – €1.80). Thus, the price of this call option must be €0.20 at expiration.

Instead, assume that Agfa Gevaert is selling for €1.00 per share on the expiration date. If Mr Optimist still holds the call option, he will throw it out. The value of the Agfa Gevaert call on the expiration date will be zero in this case.

Figure 22.1 plots the value of the call at expiration against the value of Associated British Foods' equity. This is referred to as the *hockey stick diagram* of call option values. If the share price is less than £7.00, the call is out of the money and worthless. If the share price is greater than £7.00, the call is in the money and its value rises one-for-one with increases in the share price. Notice that the call can never have a negative value. It is a *limited liability instrument*, which means that all the holder can lose is the initial amount they paid for it.

Figure 22.1 The Value of a Call Option on the Expiration Date

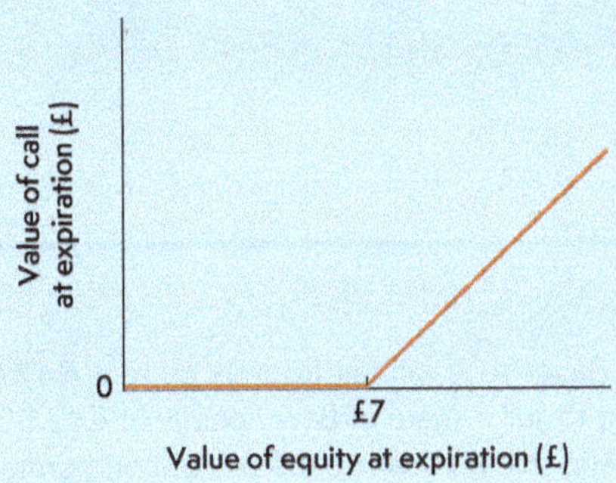

A call option gives the owner the right to buy an asset at a fixed price during a particular time period. If, at the expiration date, Associated British Foods' share price is greater than the exercise price of £100, the call's value is

Share price – £7

If Associated British Foods' share price is less than £7 at this time, the value of the call is zero.

22.3 Put Options

A **put option** can be viewed as the opposite of a call option. Just as a call gives the holder the right to buy the share at a fixed price, a put gives the holder the right to *sell* the share for a fixed exercise price.

The Value of a Put Option at Expiration

The circumstances that determine the value of the put are the opposite of those for a call option because a put option gives the holder the right to sell shares. Let us assume that the exercise price of the put is £50 and the share price at expiration is £40. The owner of this put option has the right to sell the share for *more* than it is worth, something that is clearly profitable. That is, he can buy the share at the market price of £40 and immediately sell it at the exercise price of £50, generating a profit of £10 (= £50 – £40). Thus, the value of the option at expiration must be £10.

The profit would be greater still if the share price were lower. For example, if the share price were only £30, the value of the option would be £20 (= £50 – £30). In fact, for every £1 that the share price declines at expiration, the value of the put rises by £1.

However, suppose that the equity at expiration is trading at £60 – or any price above the exercise price of £50. The owner of the put would not want to exercise here. It is a losing proposition to sell shares for £50 when they trade in the open market at £60. Instead, the owner of the put will walk away from the option. That is, he will let the put option expire.

Here is the payoff of this put option:

	Payoff on the Expiration Date	
	If Share Price is Less than £50.00	**If Share Price is Greater than £50.00**
Put option value	£50 – Share price	£0

Figure 22.2 plots the values of a put option for all possible values of the underlying share. It is instructive to compare Figure 22.2 with Figure 22.1 for the call option. The call option is valuable when the share price is above the exercise price, and the put is valuable when the share price is below the exercise price.

Figure 22.2 The Value of a Put Option on the Expiration Date

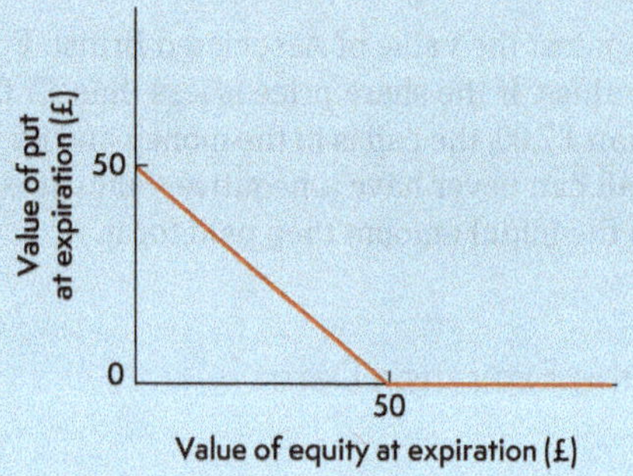

A put option gives the owner the right to sell an asset at a fixed price during a particular period. If the share price is greater than the exercise price of £50, the put value is zero. If the share price is less than £50, the put value is:

£50 – Share price

Example 22.2

Put Option Payoffs

Ms Pessimist believes that the German healthcare firm, Bayer AG, will fall from its current €42.00 share price. She buys a put. Her put option contract gives her the right to sell a share of Bayer equity at €42.00 one year from now. If the price of Bayer is €44.00 on the expiration date, she will tear up the put option contract because it is worthless. That is, she will not want to sell shares worth €44.00 for the exercise price of €42.00.

On the other hand, if Bayer is selling for €40.00 on the expiration date, she will exercise the option. In this case, she can buy a share of Bayer in the market for €40.00 and turn around and sell the share at the exercise price of €42.00. Her profit will be €2.00 (= €42.00 – €40.00). The value of the put option on the expiration date, therefore, will be €2.00.

22.4 Writing Options

An investor who sells (or *writes*) a call on equity must deliver shares of the equity if required to do so by the call option holder. Notice that the seller is *obligated* to do so.

If at the expiration date the price of the equity is higher than the exercise price, the holder will exercise the call and the seller must give the holder shares of equity in exchange for the exercise price. The seller loses the difference between the share price and the exercise price. Assume, for example, that the share price is £60 and the exercise price is £50. Knowing that exercise is imminent, the option seller buys equity in the open market at £60. Because she is obligated to sell at £50, she loses £10 (= £50 – £60). Conversely, if at the expiration date the price of the equity is below the exercise price, the call option will not be exercised, and the seller's liability is zero.

Why would the seller of a call place herself in such a precarious position? After all, the seller loses money if the share price ends up above the exercise price, and she merely avoids losing money if the share price ends up below the exercise price. The answer is that the seller is paid to take this risk. On the day that the option transaction takes place, the seller receives the price that the buyer pays.

Now let us look at the seller of puts. An investor who sells a put on equity agrees to purchase shares of equity if the put holder should so request. The seller loses on this deal if the share price falls below the exercise price. Assume, for instance, that the share price is £40 and the exercise price is £50. The holder of the put will exercise in this case. In other words, she will sell the underlying share at the exercise price of £50. This means that the seller of the put must buy the underlying equity at the exercise price of £50. Because each share is worth only £40, the loss here is £10 (= £40 − £50).

The values of the 'sell-a-call' and 'sell-a-put' positions are depicted in Figure 22.3. The graph on the left side of the figure shows that the seller of a call loses nothing when the share price at expiration date is below £50. However, the seller loses a pound for every pound that the share price rises above £50. The graph in the centre of the figure shows that the seller of a put loses nothing when the share price at expiration date is above £50. However, the seller loses a pound for every pound that the share price falls below £50.

Figure 22.3 The Payoffs to Sellers of Calls and Puts and Buyers of Equity

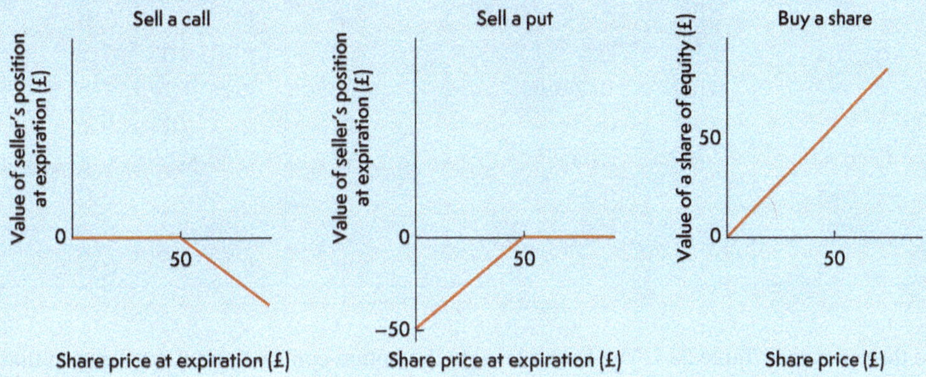

It is worthwhile to spend a few minutes comparing the graphs in Figure 22.3 to those in Figures 22.1 and 22.2. The diagram of selling a call (the graph on the left side) is the mirror image of the graph of buying a call (Figure 22.1).[3] This occurs because options are a zero-sum game. The seller of a call loses what the buyer makes. Similarly, the graph of selling a put (the middle graph in Figure 22.3) is the mirror image of the graph of buying a put (Figure 22.2). Again, the seller of a put loses what the buyer makes.

Figure 22.3 also shows the value at expiration of buying equity. Notice that buying the share is the same as buying a call option on the share with an exercise price of zero. This is not surprising. If the exercise price is zero, the call holder can buy the share for nothing, which is the same as owning it.

22.5 Option Quotes

Now that we understand the definitions for calls and puts, let us see how these options are quoted. Table 22.1 presents information, obtained from the NYSE Euronext website (www.euronext.com), about Air France-KLM options expiring in June 2023. At the time of these quotes, Air France-KLM was selling for €1.64.

Table 22.1 Information about the Options of Air France-KLM Corporation

Codes and Classification						
Code	AF2	**Market**	Euronext Paris	**Vol.**	49	26 May 2023
Exercise type	European	**Currency**	€	**O.I.**	83,825	26 May 2023

Underlying					
Name	Air France-KLM	ISIN	FR0000031122	Market	Euronext Paris
Currency	€	Best bid	1.64 26 May 23 10:52	Best ask	1.64 09 26 May 23 10:52
Time	CET	Last	1.64 26 May 23 10:52	Last Change %	-0.27%
Volume	1,695,923	High	1.67	Low	1.64

JUNE 2023 PRICE – 26/05/23										
SETTL.	LAST	BID	ASK		STRIKE		BID	ASK	LAST	SETTL.
0.45	–	0.44	0.46	C	1.20	P	–	0.01	–	0.01
0.39	–	0.38	0.40	C	1.26	P	–	0.02	–	0.01
0.35	–	0.34	0.36	C	1.30	P	–	0.02	–	0.01
0.26	–	0.25	0.27	C	1.40	P	–	0.02	–	0.01
0.17	0.16	0.15	0.17	C	1.51	P	0.01	0.03	–	0.02
0.10	–	0.08	0.10	C	1.60	P	0.04	0.05	–	0.04
0.05	0.04	0.04	0.05	C	1.70	P	0.09	0.10	–	0.09
0.03	0.02	0.01	0.03	C	1.77	P	0.14	0.15	0.14	0.14
0.01	–	–	0.02	C	1.90	P	–	0.27	–	0.26
0.01	–	–	0.01	C	2.02	P	–	0.39	–	0.37
0.01	–	–	0.01	C	2.27	P	–	0.65	–	0.62

There are three boxes in Table 22.1. The first relates to the option contract and it can be seen that Air France-KLM's option ticker is AF2, is denominated in euros and is of European type (that is, it can be exercised only on the expiration date). Each option contract relates to purchasing or selling 100 shares. On 26 May 2023, there were 83,825 contracts outstanding.

The second box relates to the underlying asset, which is Air France-KLM equity. This is traded on Euronext Paris and is denominated in euros. There were 1,695,923 shares traded in the equity and the last transaction price was €1.64 on 26 May 2023 at 10:52, which was the time the information was recorded. Other price information, such as high and low price, is also presented.

The final box provides information on individual call and put contracts. 'Settl.' is the previous day's settlement price.

22.6 Option Combinations

Puts and calls can serve as building blocks for more complex option contracts. Figure 22.4, for example, illustrates the payoff from buying a put option on a share and simultaneously buying the share.

Figure 22.4 Payoff to the Combination of Buying a Put and Buying the Underlying Equity

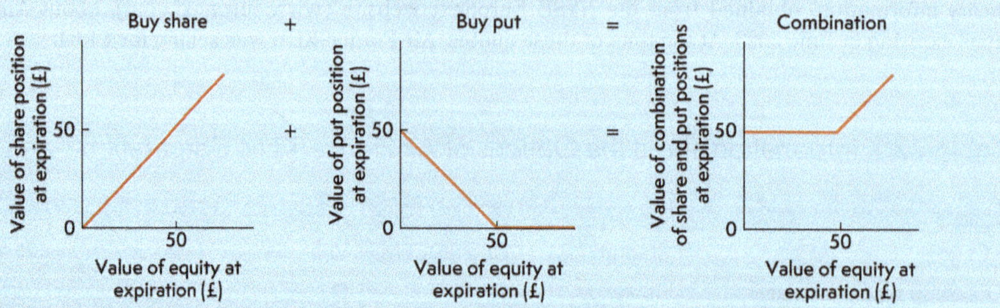

If the share price is higher than the exercise price, the put option is worthless, and the value of the combined position is equal to the value of the equity. If, instead, the exercise price is higher than the share price, the decline in the value of the shares will be exactly offset by the rise in the value of the put.

The strategy of buying a put and buying the underlying share is called a *protective* put. It is as if we are buying insurance for the share. The share can always be sold at the exercise price, regardless of how far the market price of the share falls.

Note that the combination of buying a put and buying the underlying share has the same *shape* in Figure 22.4 as the call purchase in Figure 22.1. To pursue this point, let us consider the graph for buying a call, which is shown at the far left of Figure 22.5. This graph is the same as Figure 22.1, except that the exercise price is £50 here. Now, let us try the strategy of:

- (Leg A) Buying a call
- (Leg B) Buying a risk-free, zero coupon bond (i.e. a T-bill) with a face value of £50 that matures on the same day that the option expires.

Figure 22.5 Payoff to the Combination of Buying a Call and Buying a Zero Coupon Bond

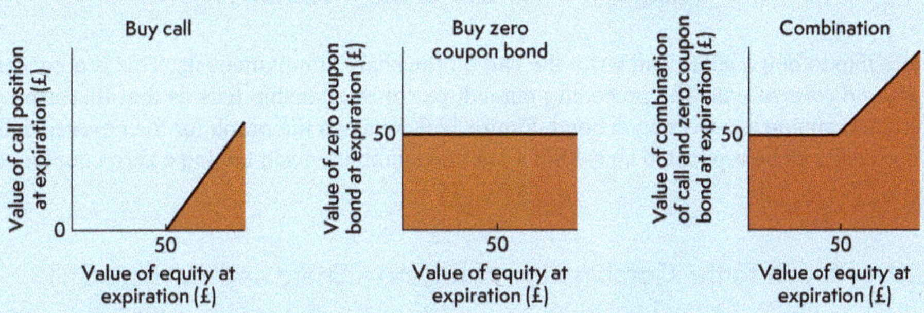

The graph of buying a call and buying a zero coupon bond is the same as the graph of buying a put and buying the share in Figure 22.4

We have drawn the graph of leg A of this strategy at the far left of Figure 22.5, but what does the graph of leg B look like? It looks like the middle graph of the figure. That is, anyone buying this zero coupon bond will be guaranteed to receive £50, regardless of the price of the share at expiration.

What does the graph of *simultaneously* buying both leg A and leg B of this strategy look like? It resembles the far right of Figure 22.5. That is, the investor receives a guaranteed £50 from the bond, regardless of what happens to the share price. In addition, the investor receives a payoff from the call of £1 for every £1 that the share price rises above the exercise price of £50.

The far right graph of Figure 22.5 looks *exactly* like the far right graph of Figure 22.4. Thus, an investor gets the same payoff from the strategy of Figure 22.4 and the strategy of Figure 22.5, regardless of what happens to the price of the underlying equity. In other words, the investor gets the same payoff from:

1 Buying a put and buying the underlying share
2 Buying a call and buying a risk-free, zero coupon bond.

If investors have the same payoffs from the two strategies, the two strategies must have the same cost. Otherwise, all investors will choose the strategy with the lower cost and avoid the strategy with the higher cost. This leads to the following interesting result:

Equation 22.1

$$\text{Price of underlying equity} + \text{Price of put} = \text{Price of call} + \text{Present value of exercise price}$$

$$\text{Cost of first strategy} = \text{Cost of second strategy}$$

This relationship is known as put-call parity and is one of the most fundamental relationships concerning options. It says that there are two ways of buying a protective put. You can buy a put and buy the underlying equity simultaneously. Here, your total cost is the share price of the underlying equity plus the price of the put. Or you can buy the call and buy a zero coupon bond. Here, your total cost is the price of the call plus the price of the zero coupon bond. The price of the zero coupon bond is equal to the present value of the exercise price – that is, the present value of £50 in our example.

Equation 22.1 is a precise relationship. It holds only if the put and the call have both the same exercise price and the same expiration date. In addition, the maturity date of the zero coupon bond must be the same as the expiration date of the options.

To see how fundamental put-call parity is, let us rearrange the formula, yielding:

$$\text{Price of underlying equity} = \text{Price of call} - \text{Price of put} + \text{Present value of exercise price}$$

This relationship now states that you can replicate the purchase of a share of equity by buying a call, selling a put and buying a zero coupon bond. (Note that, because a minus sign comes before 'Price of put', the put is sold, not bought.) Investors in this three-legged strategy are said to have purchased a *synthetic* share.

Let us do one more transformation . . .

Covered call strategy

$$\text{Price of underlying equity} - \text{Price of call} = \text{Price of put} + \text{Present value of exercise price}$$

Many investors like to buy a share and write the call on the share simultaneously. This is a conservative strategy known as *selling a covered call.* The preceding put-call parity relationship tells us that this strategy is equivalent to selling a put and buying a zero coupon bond. Figure 22.6 develops the graph for the covered call. You can verify that the covered call can be replicated by selling a put and simultaneously buying a zero coupon bond.

Figure 22.6 Payoff to the Combination of Buying a Share and Selling a Call

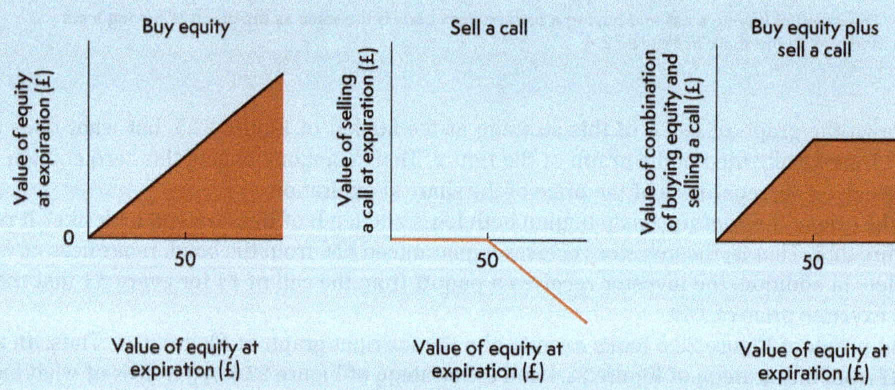

Of course, there are other ways of rearranging the basic put-call relationship. For each rearrangement, the strategy on the left side is equivalent to the strategy on the right side. The beauty of put-call parity is that it shows how any strategy in options can be achieved in two different ways.

To test your understanding of put-call parity, suppose Nokia shares are selling for €10.95. A three-month call option with a €10.95 strike price goes for €0.35. The risk-free rate is 0.5 per cent per month. What is the value of a three-month put option with a €10.95 strike price?

We can rearrange the put-call parity relationship to solve for the price of the put as follows:

$$\text{Price of put} = \text{Price of underlying equity} + \text{Price of call} + \text{Present value of strike price}$$

$$= €10.95 + €0.35 + 10.95/1.005^3$$

$$= €0.1873$$

As shown, the value of the put is €0.1873.

Example 22.3

A Synthetic T-Bill

Suppose shares of Kassam plc are selling for £110. A call option on Kassam with one year to maturity and a £110 strike price sells for £15. A put with the same terms sells for £5. What is the risk-free rate?

To answer, we need to use put-call parity to determine the price of a risk-free, zero coupon bond:

Price of underlying share + Price of put − Price of call = Present value of the exercise price

Plugging in the numbers, we get:

£110 + £5 − £15 = £100

Because the present value of the £110 strike price is £100, the implied risk-free rate is 10 per cent.

22.7 Valuing Options

In Section 22.6 we determined what options are worth on the expiration date. Now we wish to determine the value of options when you buy them well before expiration.[4] We begin by considering the lower and upper bounds on the value of a call.

Bounding the Value of a Call

Lower Bound

Consider an American call that is in the money prior to expiration. Assume that the share price is £60 and the exercise price is £50. In this case, the option cannot sell below £10. To see this, note the following simple strategy if the option sells at, say, £9:

Date	Transaction	£
Today	(1) Buy call.	−9
Today	(2) Exercise call – that is, buy underlying share at exercise price.	−50
Today	(3) Sell share at current market price.	+60
Arbitrage profit		+1

The type of profit that is described in this transaction is an *arbitrage* profit. Arbitrage profits come from transactions that have no risk or cost and cannot occur regularly in normal, well-functioning financial markets. The excess demand for these options would quickly force the option price up to at least £10 (= £60 − £50).

Of course, the price of the option is likely to be above £10. Investors will rationally pay more than £10 because of the possibility that the share will rise above £60 before expiration. Suppose, say, that the call actually sells for £12. In this case, we say that the *intrinsic value* of the option is £10, meaning it must always be worth at least this much. The remaining £12 − £10 = £2 is sometimes called the *time premium,* and it represents the extra amount that investors are willing to pay because of the possibility that the share price will rise before the option expires.

Upper Bound

Is there an upper boundary for the option price as well? It turns out that the upper boundary is the price of the underlying share. That is, an option to buy equity cannot have a greater value than the equity itself. A call option can be used to buy equity with a payment of the exercise price. It would be foolish to buy equity this way if the shares could be purchased directly at a lower price. The upper and lower bounds are represented in Figure 22.7.

The Factors Determining Call Option Values

The previous discussion indicated that the price of a call option must fall somewhere in the shaded region of Figure 22.7. We will now determine more precisely where in the shaded region it should be. The factors that determine a call's value can be broken into two sets. The first set contains the features of the option contract.

The two basic contractual features are the exercise price and the expiration date. The second set of factors affecting the call price concerns characteristics of the equity and the market.

Figure 22.7 The Upper and Lower Boundaries of Call Option Values

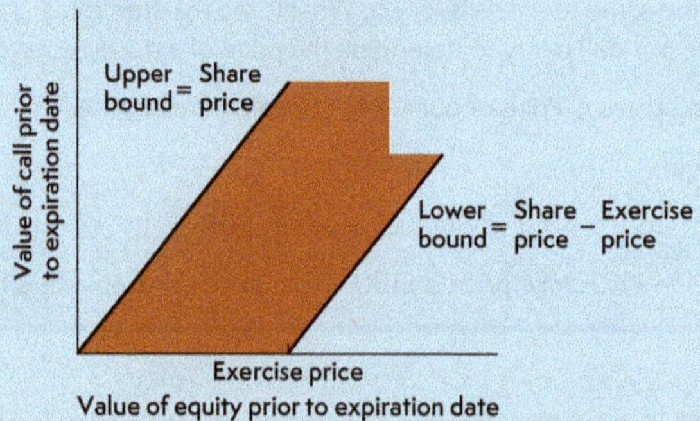

Value of the call must lie in the shaded region

Exercise Price

An increase in the exercise price reduces the value of the call. Imagine, for instance, that there are two calls on a share selling at £60. The first call has an exercise price of £50 and the second one has an exercise price of £40. Which call would you rather have? Clearly, you would rather have the call with an exercise price of £40 because that one is £20 (= £60 − £40) in the money. In other words, the call with an exercise price of £40 should sell for more than an otherwise identical call with an exercise price of £50.

Expiration Date

The value of an American call option must be at least as great as the value of an otherwise identical option with a shorter term to expiration. Consider two American calls: one has a maturity of nine months and the other expires in six months. Obviously, the nine-month call has the same rights as the six-month call, and it also has an additional three months within which these rights can be exercised. It cannot be worth less and will generally be more valuable.[5]

Share Price

Other things being equal, the higher the share price, the more valuable the call option will be. For example, if a share is worth £80, a call with an exercise price of £100 is not worth very much. If the share soars to £120, the call becomes much more valuable.

Now consider Figure 22.8, which shows the relationship between the call price and the share price prior to expiration. The curve indicates that the call price increases as the share price increases. Furthermore, it can be shown that the relationship is represented not by a straight line but by a *convex* curve. That is, the increase in the call price for a given change in the share price is greater when the share price is high than when the share price is low.

Figure 22.8 Value of an American Call as a Function of Share Price

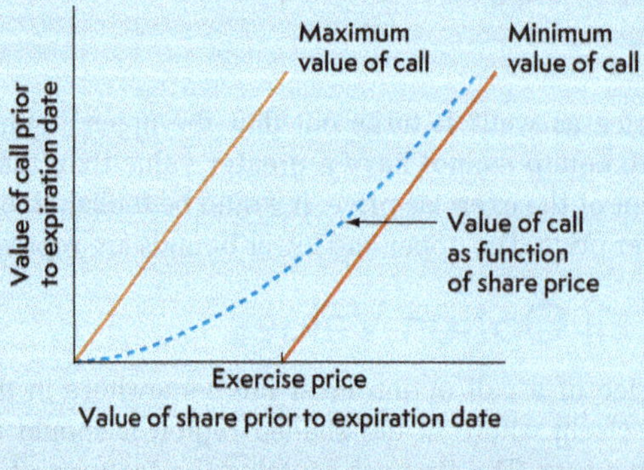

The call price is positively related to the share price. In addition, the change in the call price for a given change in the share price is greater when the share price is high than when it is low.

There are two special points on the curve in Figure 22.8:

1 *The equity is worthless.* The call must be worthless if the underlying equity is worthless. That is, if the equity has no chance of attaining any value, it is not worthwhile to pay the exercise price to obtain the share.

2 *The share price is very high relative to the exercise price.* In this situation, the owner of the call knows that she will end up exercising the call. She can view herself as the owner of the share now, with one difference: she must pay the exercise price at expiration.

Thus, the value of her position – that is, the value of the call – is:

$$\text{Share price} - \text{Present value of exercise price}$$

These two points on the curve are summarized in the bottom half of Table 22.2.

Table 22.2 Factors Affecting American Option Values

Increase in	Call Option*	Put Option*
Value of underlying asset (share price)	+	–
Exercise price	–	+
Share price volatility	+	+
Interest rate	+	–
Time to expiration	+	+

In addition to the preceding, we have presented the following four relationships for American calls:

1. The call price can never be greater than the share price (*upper bound*).
2. The call price can never be less than either zero or the difference between the share price and the exercise price (*lower bound*).
3. The call is worth zero if the underlying equity is worth zero.
4. When the share price is much greater than the exercise price, the call price tends towards the difference between the share price and the present value of the exercise price.

* The signs (+, –) indicate the effect of the variables on the value of the option. For example, the two + s for share volatility indicate that an increase in volatility will increase both the value of a call and the value of a put.

The Key Factor: The Variability of the Underlying Asset

The greater the variability of the underlying asset, the more valuable the call option will be. Consider the following example. Suppose that, just before the call expires, the share price will be either £100 with probability 0.5, or £80 with probability 0.5. What will be the value of a call with an exercise price of £110? Clearly, it will be worthless because no matter what happens to the equity, the share price will always be below the exercise price.

What happens if the share price is more variable? Suppose we add £20 to the best case and take £20 away from the worst case. Now the equity has a one-half chance of being worth £60 and a one-half chance of being worth £120. We have spread the share returns, but of course the expected value of the share has stayed the same:

$$(1/2 \times £80)+(1/2 \times £100)= £90 = (1/2 \times £60)+(1/2 \times £120)$$

Notice that the call option has value now because there is a one-half chance that the share price will be £120, or £10 above the exercise price of £110. This illustrates an important point. There is a fundamental distinction between holding an option on an underlying asset and holding the underlying asset. If investors in the marketplace are risk-averse, a rise in the variability of the equity will decrease its market value. However, the holder of a call receives payoffs from the positive tail of the probability distribution. As a consequence, a rise in the variability in the underlying equity increases the market value of the call.

This result can also be seen from Figure 22.9. Consider two shares, A and B, each of which is normally distributed. For each security, the figure illustrates the probability of different share prices on the expiration date. As can be seen from the figures, share B has more volatility than does share A. This means that share B has a higher probability of both abnormally high returns and abnormally low returns. Let us assume that options on each of the two securities have the same exercise price. To option holders, a return much below average on share B is no worse than a return only moderately below average on share A. In either situation, the option expires out of the money. However, to option holders, a return much above average on share B is better than a return only moderately above average on share A. Because a call's price at the expiration date is the difference between the share price and the exercise price, the value of the call on B at expiration will be higher in this case.

Figure 22.9 Distribution of Equity Price at Expiration for Both Security A and Security B. Options on the Two Securities Have the Same Exercise Price

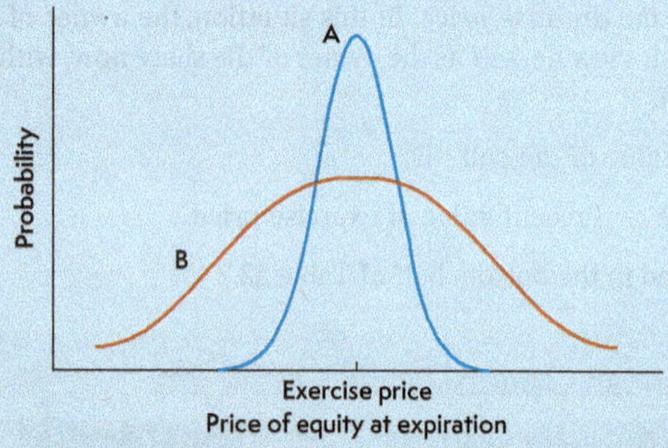

The call on share B is worth more than the call on share A because share B is more volatile. At expiration, a call that is deep in the money is more valuable than a call that is only slightly in the money. However, at expiration, a call way out of the money is worth zero, just as is a call only slightly out of the money.

The Interest Rate

Call prices are also a function of the level of interest rates. Buyers of calls do not pay the exercise price until they exercise the option, if they do so at all. The ability to delay payment is more valuable when interest rates are high and less valuable when interest rates are low. Thus, the value of a call is positively related to interest rates.

A Quick Discussion of Factors Determining Put Option Values

Given our extended discussion of the factors influencing a call's value, we can examine the effect of these factors on puts very easily. Table 22.2 summarized the five factors influencing the prices of both American calls and American puts. The effect of three factors on puts are the opposite of the effect of these three factors on calls:

1. The put's market value *decreases* as the share price increases because puts are in the money when the equity sells below the exercise price.
2. The value of a put with a high exercise price is *greater* than the value of an otherwise identical put with a low exercise price for the reason given in (1).
3. A high interest rate *adversely* affects the value of a put. The ability to sell a share at a fixed exercise price at some time in the future is worth less if the present value of the exercise price is reduced by a high interest rate.

The effect of the other two factors on puts is the same as the effect of these factors on calls:

4. The value of an American put with a distant expiration date is greater than an otherwise identical put with an earlier expiration.[6] The longer time to maturity gives the put holder more flexibility, just as it did in the case of a call.
5. Volatility of the underlying share price increases the value of the put. The reasoning is analogous to that for a call. At expiration, a put that is way in the money is more valuable than a put only slightly in the money. However, at expiration, a put way out of the money is worth zero, just as is a put only slightly out of the money.

22.8 An Option Pricing Formula

We have explained *qualitatively* that the value of a call option is a function of five variables:

1. The current price of the underlying asset, which for equity options is the share price
2. The exercise price
3. The time to expiration date
4. The variance of the underlying asset
5. The risk-free interest rate.

It is time to replace the qualitative model with a precise option valuation model. The model we choose is the famous Black-Scholes option pricing model. You can put numbers into the Black-Scholes model and get values back.

Chapter 6 Page 147

The Black-Scholes model is represented by a rather imposing formula. A derivation of the formula is simply not possible in this textbook, as many students will be happy to learn. However, some appreciation for the achievement as well as some intuitive understanding is in order.

In the early chapters of this book, we showed how to discount capital budgeting projects using the net present value formula (see Chapter 6, Section 6.1). We also used this approach to value shares and bonds. Why, students sometimes ask, can't the same NPV formula be used to value puts and calls? This is a good question: the earliest attempts at valuing options used NPV. Unfortunately, the attempts were not successful because no one could determine the appropriate discount rate. An option is generally riskier than the underlying share, but no one knew exactly how much riskier.

Black and Scholes attacked the problem by pointing out that a strategy of borrowing to finance an equity purchase duplicates the risk of a call. Then, knowing the price of an equity already, we can determine the price of a call such that its return is identical to that of the share-with-borrowing alternative.

We illustrate the intuition behind the Black-Scholes approach by considering a simple example where a combination of a call and an equity eliminates all risk. This example works because we let the future share price be one of only *two* values. Hence, the example is called a *two-state* or *binomial option pricing model*. By eliminating the possibility that the share price can take on other values, we are able to duplicate the call exactly.

A Two-state Option Model

Consider the following example. Suppose the current market price of a share is £50 and the share price will be either £60 or £40 at the end of the year. Further, imagine a call option on this share with a one-year expiration date and a £50 exercise price. Investors can borrow at 10 per cent. Our goal is to determine the value of the call.

To value the call correctly, we need to examine two strategies. The first is to simply buy the call. The second is to:

1. Buy one-half of a share of equity
2. Borrow £18.18, implying a payment of principal and interest at the end of the year of £20 (= £18.18 × 1.10).

As you will see shortly, the cash flows from the second strategy match the cash flows from buying a call. (A little later, we will show how we came up with the exact fraction of a share of equity to buy and the exact borrowing amount.) Because the cash flows match, we say that we are *duplicating* the call with the second strategy.

At the end of the year, the future payoffs are set out as follows:

	Future Payoffs	
Initial Transactions	**If Share Price is £60**	**If Share Price is £40**
1 Buy a call	**£60 − £50 = £10**	£ 0
2 Buy ½ share of equity	**1/2 × £60 = £30**	**1/2 × £40 = £20**
Borrow £18.18 at 10%	**−(£18.18 × 1.10) = −£20**	− £20
Total from equity and borrowing strategy	£ 10	£ 0

Note that the future payoff structure of the 'buy-a-call' strategy is duplicated by the strategy of 'buy a share and borrow'. That is, under either strategy an investor would end up with £10 if the share price rose and £0 if the share price fell. Thus these two strategies are equivalent as far as traders are concerned.

If two strategies always have the same cash flows at the end of the year, how must their initial costs be related? The two strategies must have the *same* initial cost. Otherwise, there will be an arbitrage possibility. We can easily calculate this cost for our strategy of buying share and borrowing:

Buy ½ share of equity	½ × £50 = £25.00
Borrow £18.18	− 18.18
	£ 6.82

Because the call option provides the same payoffs at expiration as does the strategy of buying equity and borrowing, the call must be priced at £6.82. This is the value of the call option in a market without arbitrage profits.

We left two issues unexplained in the preceding example.

Determining the Delta

How did we know to buy one-half share of equity in the duplicating strategy? Actually, the answer is easier than it might at first appear. The call price at the end of the year will be either £10 or £0, whereas the share price will be either £60 or £40. Thus, the call price has a potential swing of £10 (= £10 − £0) next period, whereas the share price has a potential swing of £20 (= £60 − £40). We can write this in terms of the following ratio:

$$\text{Delta} = \frac{\text{Swing of call}}{\text{Swing of equity}} = \frac{£10 - £0}{£60 - £40} = \frac{1}{2}$$

As indicated, this ratio is called the *delta* of the call. In words, a £1 swing in the share price gives rise to a £1/2 swing in the price of the call. Because we are trying to duplicate the call with the equity, it seems sensible to buy one-half share of equity instead of buying one call. In other words, the risk of buying one-half share of equity should be the same as the risk of buying one call.

Determining the Amount of Borrowing

How did we know how much to borrow? Buying one-half share of equity brings us either £30 or £20 at expiration, which is exactly £20 more than the payoffs of £10 and £0, respectively, from the call. To duplicate the call through purchase of equity, we should also borrow enough money so that we have to pay back exactly £20 of interest and principal. This amount of borrowing is merely the present value of £20, which is £18.18 (= £20/1.10).

Now that we know how to determine both the delta and the borrowing, we can write the value of the call as follows:

Equation 22.2

$$\begin{array}{ccccccc} \text{Value of call} & = & \text{Share price} & \times & \text{Delta} & - & \text{Amount borrowed} \\ £6.82 & = & £50 & \times & 1/2 & - & £18.18 \end{array}$$

We will find this intuition useful in explaining the Black-Scholes model.

Risk-neutral Valuation

Before leaving this simple example, we should comment on a remarkable feature. We found the exact value of the option without even knowing the probability that the equity would go up or down! If an optimist thought the probability of an up move was high and a pessimist thought it was low, they would still agree on the option value. How can that be? The answer is that the current £50 share price already balances the views of the optimists and the pessimists. The option reflects that balance because its value depends on the share price.

This insight provides us with another approach to valuing the call. If we do not need the probabilities of the two states to value the call, perhaps we can select *any* probabilities we want and still come up with the right answer. Suppose we selected probabilities such that the return on the equity is equal to the risk-free rate of 10 per cent. We know that the equity return, given a rise, is 20 per cent (= £60/£50 − 1) and the equity return, given a fall, is –20 per cent (= £40/£50 − 1). Thus, we can solve for the probability of a rise necessary to achieve an expected return of 10 per cent as follows:

$$10\% = \text{Probability of a rise} \times 20\% + (1 - \text{Probability of a rise}) \times -20\%$$

Solving this formula, we find that the probability of a rise is 3/4 and the probability of a fall is 1/4. If we apply these probabilities to the call, we can value it as:

$$\text{Value of call} = \frac{\frac{3}{4} \times £10 + \frac{1}{4} \times £0}{1.10} = £6.82$$

which is the same value we got from the duplicating approach.

Why did we select probabilities such that the expected return on the equity is 10 per cent? We wanted to work with the special case where investors are *risk-neutral*. This case occurs when the expected return on *any* asset (including both the share and the call) is equal to the risk-free rate. In other words, this case occurs when investors demand no additional compensation beyond the risk-free rate, regardless of the risk of the asset in question.

What would have happened if we had assumed that the expected return on a share of equity was greater than the risk-free rate? The value of the call would still be £6.82. However, the calculations would be difficult. For example, if we assumed that the expected return on the equity was, say, 11 per cent, we would have had to derive the expected return on the call. Although the expected return on the call would be higher than 11 per cent, it would take a lot of work to determine the expected return precisely. Why do any more work than you have to? Because we cannot think of any good reason, we (and most other financial economists) choose to assume risk neutrality.

Thus, the preceding material allows us to value a call in the following two ways:

1 Determine the cost of a strategy duplicating the call. This strategy involves an investment in a fractional share of equity financed by partial borrowing.

2 Calculate the probabilities of a rise and a fall under the assumption of risk neutrality. Use these probabilities, in conjunction with the risk-free rate, to discount the payoffs of the call at expiration.

Real World Insight 22.1

Adidas Call Option Valuation

Assume the Adidas share price is €2.25 (this is equal to the actual share price of Adidas at the time of writing) and investors can borrow at 5 per cent. There is an at-the-money call option with the same strike price and one year to expiry. In that time, the Adidas share price can either increase to €2.50 or fall to €2.00.

Step 1: Calculate Delta

The call price at the end of the year can be either €0.25 or €0, a swing of €0.25, and the Adidas share price swing will be €0.50. We can now calculate delta:

$$\text{Delta} = \frac{\text{Swing of call}}{\text{Swing of equity}} = \frac{€0.25}{€0.50} = 0.5$$

Step 2: Determine Borrowing

Since delta is 0.5, if we buy 0.5 of Adidas equity, it will be worth either €1.25 or €1.00 at expiry. This is exactly €1.00 more than the call option payoffs in either state. To duplicate the call we must borrow a sum to pay back €1.00 in one year. This is done as follows:

$$\text{Borrowing} = \frac{€1.00}{1.05} = €0.9524$$

Step 3: Calculate Call Option Value

$$\begin{aligned} \text{Call value} &= \text{Share price} \times \text{Delta} - \text{Amount borrowed} \\ €0.1726 &= €2.25 \times 0.5 - €0.9524 \end{aligned}$$

The call value is €0.1726.

The value of the call can also be calculated using risk-neutral probabilities. We know that the Adidas price can go up by 11.11 per cent (€2.50/€2.25 – 1) or fall by 11.11 per cent (€2.00/€2.25 – 1).

Step 1: Calculate the Probability of a Rise

$$5\% = p \times 11.11\% + (1 - p) \times -11.11\%$$

Solving for p gives a probability of a rise as 0.7250.

Step 2: Calculate Call Option Value

$$\text{Call value} = \frac{0.7250 \times €0.25 + 0.2750 \times €0}{1.05} = €0.1726$$

Again, the value of the Adidas call option is €0.1726.

The Black-Scholes Model

The preceding example illustrates the duplicating strategy. Unfortunately, a strategy such as this will not work in the real world over, say, a one-year time frame because there are many more than two possibilities for next year's share price. However, the number of possibilities is reduced as the period is shortened. Is there a time period over which the share price can have only two outcomes? Academics argue that the assumption that there are only two possibilities for the share price over the next infinitesimal instant is quite plausible.[7]

In our opinion, the fundamental insight of Black and Scholes is to shorten the time period. They show that a specific combination of equity and borrowing can indeed duplicate a call over an infinitesimal time horizon. Because the share price will change over the first instant, another combination of equity and borrowing is needed to duplicate the call over the second instant, and so on. By adjusting the combination from moment to moment, they can continually duplicate the call. It may boggle the mind that a formula can (1) determine the duplicating combination at any moment, and (2) value the option based on this duplicating strategy. Suffice to say that their dynamic strategy allows them to value a call in the real world, just as we showed how to value the call in the two-state model.

This is the basic intuition behind the Black-Scholes (BS) model. Because the actual derivation of their formula is, alas, far beyond the scope of this text, we simply present the formula itself:

Black-Scholes model

$$C = S\mathrm{N}(d_1) - Ee^{-Rt}\mathrm{N}(d_2)$$

where

$$d_1 = \left[\ln(S/E) + (R + \sigma^2/2)t\right] / \sqrt{\sigma^2 t}$$

$$d_2 = d_1 - \sqrt{\sigma^2 t}$$

This formula for the value of a call, C, is one of the most complex in finance. However, it involves only five parameters:

1 S = Current share price
2 E = Exercise price of call
3 R = Annual risk-free rate of return, continuously compounded
4 σ^2 = Variance (per year) of the continuous share price return
5 t = Time (in years) to expiration date.

In addition, there is this statistical concept:

$\mathrm{N}(d)$ = Probability that a standardized, normally distributed, random variable will be less than or equal to d.

Rather than discuss the formula in its algebraic state, we illustrate it with an example.

Example 22.4

Black-Scholes

Consider Private Equipment Company (PEC). On 4 October of year 0, the PEC 21 April call option (exercise price = £49) had a closing value of £4. The equity itself was selling at £50. On 4 October, the option had 199 days to expiration (maturity date = 21 April, year 1). The annual risk-free interest rate, continuously compounded, was 7 per cent.

This information determines three variables directly:

1 The share price, S, is £50.
2 The exercise price, E, is £49.
3 The risk-free rate, R, is 0.07.

In addition, the time to maturity, t, can be calculated quickly: the formula calls for t to be expressed in *years*.

4 We express the 199-day interval in years as $t = 199/365$.

In the real world, an option trader would know S and E exactly. Traders generally view government Treasury bills as riskless, so a current quote from newspapers, such as the *Financial Times* or a similar source, would be obtained for the interest rate. The trader would also know (or could count) the number of days to expiration exactly. Thus, the fraction of a year to expiration, t, could be calculated quickly.

The problem comes in determining the variance of the underlying equity's return. The formula calls for the variance between the purchase date of 4 October and the expiration date. Unfortunately, this represents the future, so the correct value for variance is not available. Instead, traders frequently estimate variance from past data, just as we calculated variance in Section 9.5. In addition, some traders may use intuition to adjust their estimate. For instance, if anticipation of an upcoming event is likely to increase the volatility of the share price, the trader might adjust her estimate of variance upwards to reflect this.

The preceding discussion was intended merely to mention the difficulties in variance estimation, not to present a solution. For our purposes, we assume that a trader has come up with an estimate of variance:

5 The variance of Private Equipment Corporation has been estimated to be 0.09 per year.

Using these five parameters, we calculate the Black-Scholes value of the PEC option in three steps:

Step 1: Calculate d_1 and d_2

These values can be determined by a straightforward, albeit tedious, insertion of our parameters into the basic formula. We have:

$$d_1 = \left[\ln\left(\frac{S}{E}\right) + (R + \sigma^2/2)t\right] / \sqrt{\sigma^2 t}$$

$$= \left[\ln\left(\frac{50}{49}\right) + \left(0.07 + 0.09/2\right) \times \frac{199}{365}\right] / \sqrt{0.09 \times \frac{199}{365}}$$

$$= [0.0202 + 0.0627]/0.2215 = 0.3742$$

$$d_2 = d_1 - \sqrt{\sigma^2 t}$$

$$= 0.1527$$

Step 2: Calculate N (d_1) and N (d_2)

We can best understand the values N(d_1) and N(d_2) by examining Figure 22.10. The figure shows the normal distribution with an expected value of 0 and a standard deviation of 1. This is frequently called the **standardized normal distribution.** We mentioned in an earlier chapter that the probability that a drawing from this distribution will be between −1 and +1 (within one standard deviation of its mean, in other words) is 68.26 per cent.

Figure 22.10 Graph of Cumulative Probability

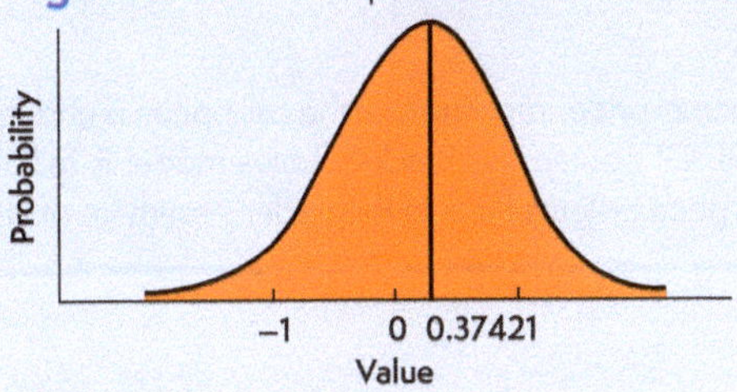

Now let us ask a different question. What is the probability that a drawing from the standardized normal distribution will be *below* a particular value? For example, the probability that a drawing will be below 0 is clearly 50 per cent because the normal distribution is symmetric. Using statistical terminology, we say that the **cumulative probability** of 0 is 50 per cent. Statisticians also say that N(0) = 50 per cent. It turns out that:

$$N(d_1) = N(0.3742) = 0.6459$$

$$N(d_2) = N(0.1527) = 0.5607$$

The first value means that there is a 64.59 per cent probability that a drawing from the standardized normal distribution will be below 0.3742. The second value means that there is a 56.07 per cent probability that a drawing from the standardized normal distribution will be below 0.1527. More generally, N(d) is the probability that a drawing from the standardized normal distribution will be below d. In other words, N(d) is the cumulative probability of d. Note that d_1 and d_2 in our example are slightly above zero, so N(d_1) and N(d_2) are slightly greater than 0.50.

Perhaps the easiest way to determine N(d_1) and N(d_2) is from the EXCEL function NORMSDIST. In our example, NORMSDIST(0.3742) and NORMSDIST(0.1527) are 0.6459 and 0.5607, respectively.

We can also determine the cumulative probability from Table 22.3. For instance, consider d = 0.37. This can be found in the table as 0.3 on the vertical and 0.07 on the horizontal. The value in the table for d = 0.37 is 0.1443. This value is *not* the cumulative probability of 0.37. We must first make an adjustment to determine cumulative probability. That is:

$$N(0.37) = 0.50 + 0.1443 = 0.6443$$

$$N(-0.37) = 0.50 - 0.1443 = 0.3557$$

Unfortunately, our table handles only two significant digits, whereas our value of 0.3742 has four significant digits. Hence we must interpolate to find N(0.3742). Because N(0.37)= 0.6443 and N(0.38)= 0.6480, the difference between the two values is 0.0037(= 0.6480 – 0.6443). Since 0.3742 is 42 per cent of the way between 0.37 and 0.38, we interpolate as:[8]

$$N(0.3742) = 0.6443 + 0.42 \times 0.0037 = 0.6459$$

Table 22.3 Cumulative Probabilities of the Standard Normal Distribution Function

d	0.00	0.01	0.02	0.03	0.04	0.05	0.06	0.07	0.08	0.09
0.0	0.0000	0.0040	0.0080	0.0120	0.0160	0.0199	0.0239	0.0279	0.0319	0.0359
0.1	0.0398	0.0438	0.0478	0.517	0.0557	0.0596	0.0636	0.0675	0.0714	0.0753
0.2	0.0793	0.0832	0.0871	0.0910	0.0948	0.0987	0.1026	0.1064	0.1103	0.1141
0.3	0.1179	0.1217	0.1255	0.123	0.1331	0.1368	0.1406	0.1443	0.1480	0.1517
0.4	0.1554	0.1591	0.1628	0.1664	0.1700	0.1736	0.1772	0.1808	0.1844	0.1879
0.5	0.1915	0.1950	0.1985	0.2019	0.2054	0.2088	0.2123	0.2157	0.2190	0.2224

N(*d*) represents areas under the standard normal distribution function. Suppose that $d_1 = 0.24$. The table implies a cumulative probability of 0.5000 + 0.0948 = 0.5948. If d_1 is equal to 0.2452, we must estimate the probability by interpolating between N(0.25) and N(0.24).

Step 3: Calculate C

We have:

$$\begin{aligned} C &= S \times [N(d_1)] - E \times e^{-Rt}[N(d_2)] \\ &= 50 \times [N(d_1)] - 49 \times e^{-0.07 \times (199/365)} \times [N(d_2)] \\ &= (50 \times 0.6459) - (49 \times 0.9626 \times 0.5607) \\ &= 32.295 - 26.447 \\ &= 5.85 \end{aligned}$$

The estimated price of £5.85 is greater than the £4 actual price, implying that the call option is underpriced. A trader believing in the Black-Scholes model would buy a call. Of course the Black-Scholes model is fallible. Perhaps the disparity between the model's estimate and the market price reflects error in the trader's estimate of variance.

The previous example stressed the calculations involved in using the Black-Scholes formula. Is there any intuition behind the formula? Yes, and that intuition follows from the share purchase and borrowing strategy in our binomial example. The first line of the Black-Scholes equation is:

$$C = S \times N(d_1) - Ee^{-Rt}N(d_2)$$

which is exactly analogous to Equation 22.2:

Equation 22.2 Value of call = Share price × Delta – Amount borrowed

We presented this equation in the binomial example. It turns out that $N(d_1)$ is the delta in the Black-Scholes model. $N(d_1)$ is 0.6459 in the previous example. In addition, $Ee^{Rt}N(d_2)$ is the amount that an investor must borrow to duplicate a call. In the previous example, this value is £26.45(= £49 × 0.9626 × 0.5607). Thus, the model tells us that we can duplicate the call of the preceding example by both:

1 Buying 0.6459 share of equity
2 Borrowing £26.45.

It is no exaggeration to say that the Black-Scholes formula is among the most important contributions in finance. It allows anyone to calculate the value of an option given a few parameters. The attraction of the formula is that four of the parameters are observable: the current share price, *S*; the exercise price, *E*; the interest rate, *R*; and the time to expiration date, *t*. Only one of the parameters must be estimated: the variance of return, σ^2.

To see how truly attractive this formula is, note what parameters are not needed. First, the investor's risk aversion does not affect value. The formula can be used by anyone, regardless of willingness to bear risk. Second, it does not depend on the expected return on the equity! Investors with different assessments of the equity's expected return will nevertheless agree on the call price. As in the two-state example, this is because the call depends on the share price, and that price already balances investors' divergent views.

Black-Scholes with Dividends

Chapter 18
Page 478

The Black-Scholes model assumes that a company does not pay dividends. What happens when dividends are paid? Assume that a firm pays a regular dividend with a constant continuous dividend yield, q. From Chapter 18, we showed that dividends cause share prices to fall by the same amount as the dividend to reflect cash leaving the company. So if a share price grows from S to S_t when paying dividends, it will have to grow to $S_t e^{qt}$ if it does not pay any dividends. This is because the equity will have a higher growth rate because it isn't paying out any cash to shareholders.

An alternative way to express this argument is that we can say that the share price will grow from S to S_t when dividends are paid and Se^{-qt} to S_t if no dividends are paid. In the second formulation, we are anchoring time at t, the exercise date.

All this complexity simply means that we substitute S for Se^{-qt} in the standard Black-Scholes formula. The revised formula is:

$$C = Se^{-qt}\mathrm{N}(d_1) - Ee^{-Rt}\mathrm{N}(d_2)$$

$$d_1 = \left[\ln\left(\frac{Se^{-qt}}{E}\right) + \left(R + \frac{\sigma^2}{2}\right)t\right] / \sqrt{\sigma^2 t} = \left[\ln\left(\frac{S}{E}\right) + \left(R - q + \frac{\sigma^2}{2}\right)t\right] / \sqrt{\sigma^2 t}$$

$$d_2 = d_1 - \sqrt{\sigma^2 t}$$

Sustainability in Action 22.1

Managing Energy Price Risk

When renewable energy companies plan new large-scale investments, they need to forecast energy prices for at least five years. However, volatility in electricity, oil and gas prices can have a massive impact on the risk of these investments. One way to reduce investment risk is to anchor future prices so that risk is associated with the general investment without being exacerbated by temporary fluctuations in energy prices. This is what many oil companies have done in response to the massive drop in energy prices since 2022.

Figure 22.11 Electricity Prices, 2021-2023

Source: Ofgem, Office for Gas and Electricity Markets, UK government.

The question that is being asked is whether we will see a return to the exceptionally high electricity, oil and gas prices over the next few years. Electricity call options give companies that need electricity the right to buy it at a set price by a certain date and electricity put options give companies that sell electricity the right to sell it at a set price by a certain date.

22.9 The 'Greeks'

In the previous section, we introduced delta, which is the change in the option price with respect to a change in the value of the underlying asset. This measure of risk is one of four in option pricing that is important to corporate finance practitioners.

Table 22.2 presented the main factors that influence the price of an option. These are the value of the underlying asset (the share price), the exercise price, volatility in the value of the underlying asset, the interest rate and time to expiry. While we know that the exercise price will not change during the lifetime of the option, it is inevitable that the other factors will vary to some extent during this period.

The 'Greeks' measure the rate of change in the value of a call or put with respect to these major factors. Fortunately for you, their derivation and calculation (except for delta) are beyond the scope of this book. However, it is important that the reader is aware of the Greeks and what they represent.

Delta measures the rate of change in the value of an option with respect to a change in the underlying equity's share price. The delta for call options will always be between 0 and 1, and for put options it will always be between 0 and –1. Thus, if a delta is 0.8, this means that the call will increase in value by €0.80 for every €1.00 increase in the underlying equity's share price. Since put option values fall when the value of the underlying equity goes up, the delta of put options will be negative.

Gamma measures the rate of change in delta with respect to a change in the value of the underlying share price. Since delta is central to the valuation of options, it is also important to understand how delta behaves during the lifetime of an option. Consider a call option that has a gamma of 0.05 and a delta of 0.8. If the underlying share price increases in value by €1.00, the delta of the option will grow by 0.05 to 0.85. Similarly, if the underlying share price falls by €1.00, the delta of the option will drop by 0.05 to 0.75.

Gamma has several important characteristics:

- Gamma is very small when options are deep out of the money (that is, when the share price is low relative to the exercise price for call options or when the share price is high relative to the exercise price for put options).
- Gamma is very small when options are deep in the money (that is, when the share price is high relative to the exercise price for call options or when the share price is low relative to the exercise price for put options).
- Gamma is at its highest when options are at the money (that is when the share price is equal to the exercise price of the option).
- Gamma is positive when you hold the option (that is, you are long in the option) and negative when you have written the option (that is, you are short in the option).

Theta measures the rate of change in the value of an option with respect to the change in time to maturity of the option. An option will necessarily lose value as the exercise date gets closer and, as a result, theta is always negative. Options lose value faster the closer they are to expiry.

Finally, vega measures the rate of change in an option's value with respect to changes in its implied volatility. Implied volatility can be calculated using the Black-Scholes option-pricing model when both the underlying share price and option value are available. It is useful as a measure of expected volatility during the remaining life of an option. Many traders take the market's estimate of an option value to be the correct estimate and use this to calculate the volatility of the asset. Call and put options increase in value when volatility increases and, as a result, vega will always be positive.

22.10 Shares and Bonds as Options

The previous material in this chapter described, explained and valued publicly traded options. This is important material to any finance student because much trading occurs in these listed options. However, the study of options has another purpose for the student of corporate finance.

You may have heard the one-liner about the elderly gentleman who was surprised to learn that he had been speaking prose all of his life. The same can be said about the corporate finance student and options. Although options were formally defined for the first time in this chapter, many corporate policies discussed earlier in the text were actually options in disguise. Though it is beyond the scope of this chapter to recast all of corporate finance in terms of options, the rest of the chapter considers three examples of implicit options:

1. Shares and bonds as options
2. Capital structure decisions as options
3. Capital budgeting decisions as options.

We begin by illustrating the implicit options in shares and bonds.

Example 22.5

Shares and Bonds as Options

A British firm, Jenkins Brothers Ice Creams, has been awarded the contract for football-related ice cream packaging at the 2022 World Cup in Qatar. Because it is unlikely that there will be much need for football-related ice cream after the World Cup, the enterprise will disband afterwards. The firm has issued debt to help finance this venture. Interest and principal due on the debt next year will be £800, at which time the debt will be paid off in full. The firm's cash flows next year are forecast as follows:

	Jenkins Brothers Cash Flow Schedule			
	Very Successful World Cup (£)	Moderately Successful World Cup (£)	Moderately Unsuccessful World Cup (£)	Outright Failure (£)
Cash flow before interest and principal	1,000	850	700	550
Interest and principal	−800	−800	−700	−550
Cash flow to shareholders	200	50	0	0

As can be seen, there are four equally likely scenarios. If either of the first two scenarios occurs, the bondholders will be paid in full. The extra cash flow goes to the shareholders. However, if either of the last two scenarios occurs, the bondholders will not be paid in full. Instead, they will receive the firm's entire cash flow, leaving the shareholders with nothing.

This example is similar to the bankruptcy examples presented in Sections 19.1 and 19.2 in our chapter about capital structure. Our new insight is that the relationship between the equity and the firm can be expressed in terms of options. We consider call options first because the intuition is easier. The put option scenario is treated next.

The Firm Expressed in Terms of Call Options

The Shareholders

We now show that equity can be viewed as a call option on the firm. To illustrate this, Figure 22.12 graphs the cash flow to the shareholders as a function of the cash flow to the firm. The shareholders receive nothing if the firm's cash flows are less than £800; here all of the cash flows go to the bondholders. However, the shareholders earn a pound for every pound that the firm receives above £800. The graph looks exactly like the call option graphs that we considered earlier in this chapter.

Figure 22.12 Cash Flow to Shareholders of Jenkins Brothers Ice Creams as a Function of Cash Flow of Firm

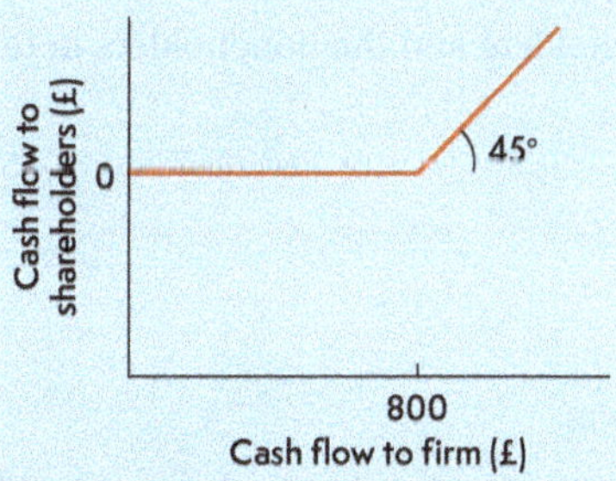

The shareholders can be viewed as having a call option on the firm. If the cash flows of the firm exceed £800, the shareholders pay £800 in order to receive the firm's cash flows. If the cash flows of the firm are less than £800, the shareholders do not exercise their option. They walk away from the firm, receiving nothing.

But what is the underlying asset upon which the equity is a call option? The underlying asset is the firm itself. That is, we can view the *bondholders* as owning the firm. However, the shareholders have a call option on the firm with an exercise price of £800.

If the firm's cash flow is above £800, the shareholders would choose to exercise this option. In other words, they would buy the firm from the bondholders for £800. Their net cash flow is the difference between the firm's cash flow and their £800 payment. This would be £200 (= £1,000 – £800) if the World Cup is very successful and £50 (= £850 – £800) if the World Cup is moderately successful.

Should the value of the firm's cash flows be less than £800, the shareholders would not choose to exercise their option. Instead, they would walk away from the firm, as any call option holder would do. The bondholders would then receive the firm's entire cash flow.

This view of the firm is a novel one, and students are frequently bothered by it on first exposure. However, we encourage students to keep looking at the firm in this way until the view becomes second nature to them.

The Bondholders

What about the bondholders? Our earlier cash flow schedule showed that they would get the entire cash flow of the firm if the firm generates less cash than £800. Should the firm earn more than £800, the bondholders would receive only £800. That is, they are entitled only to interest and principal. This schedule is graphed in Figure 22.13.

Figure 22.13 Cash Flow to Bondholders of Jenkins Brothers Ice Creams as a Function of Cash Flow of Firm

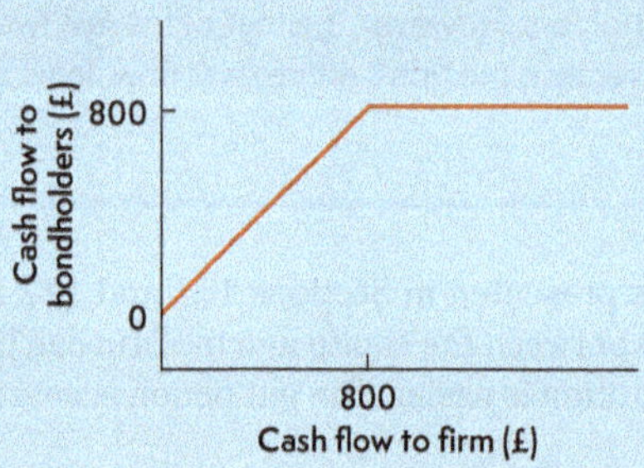

The bondholders can be viewed as owning the firm but writing a call option on the firm to the shareholders as well. If the cash flows of the firm exceed £800, the call is exercised against the bondholders. The bondholders give up the firm and receive £800. If the cash flows are less than £800, the call expires. The bondholders receive the cash flows of the firm in this case.

In keeping with our view that the shareholders have a call option on the firm, what does the bondholders' position consist of? The bondholders' position can be described by two claims:

1 They own the firm.
2 They have written a call on the firm with an exercise price of £800.

As we mentioned before, the shareholders walk away from the firm if cash flows are less than £800. Thus, the bondholders retain ownership in this case. However, if the cash flows are greater than £800, the shareholders exercise their option. They call the equity away from the bondholders for £800.

The Firm Expressed in Terms of Put Options

The preceding analysis expresses the positions of the shareholders and the bondholders in terms of call options. We can now express the situation in terms of put options.

The Shareholders

The shareholders' position can be expressed by three claims:

1 They own the firm.
2 They owe £800 in interest and principal to the bondholders.

If the debt were risk-free, these two claims would fully describe the shareholders' situation. However, because of the possibility of default, we have a third claim as well:

3 The shareholders own a put option on the firm with an exercise price of £800. The group of bondholders is the seller of the put.

Now consider two possibilities.

Cash Flow is Less than £800

Because the put has an exercise price of £800, the put is in the money. The shareholders 'put' – that is, sell – the firm to the bondholders. Normally, the holder of a put receives the exercise price when the asset is sold. However, the shareholders already owe £800 to the bondholders. Thus, the debt of £800 is simply cancelled – and no money changes hands – when the equity is delivered to the bondholders. Because the shareholders give up the equity in exchange for extinguishing the debt, the shareholders end up with nothing if the cash flow is below £800.

Cash Flow is Greater than £800

Because the put is out of the money here, the shareholders do not exercise. Thus, the shareholders retain ownership of the firm but pay £800 to the bondholders as interest and principal.

The Bondholders

The bondholders' position can be described by two claims:

1. The bondholders are owed £800.
2. They have sold a put option on the firm to the shareholders with an exercise price of £800.

Cash Flow is Less than £800

As mentioned before, the shareholders will exercise the put in this case. This means that the bondholders are obligated to pay £800 for the firm. Because they are owed £800, the two obligations offset each other. Thus, the bondholders simply end up with the firm in this case.

Cash Flow is Greater than £800

Here, the shareholders do not exercise the put. Thus, the bondholders merely receive the £800 that is due them.

Expressing the bondholders' position in this way is illuminating. With a riskless default-free bond, the bondholders are owed £800. Thus, we can express the risky bond in terms of a riskless bond and a put:

$$\text{Value of risky bond} = \text{Value of default-free bond} - \text{Value of put option}$$

That is, the value of the risky bond is the value of the default-free bond less the value of the shareholders' option to sell the company for £800.

A Resolution of the Two Views

We have argued that the positions of the shareholders and the bondholders can be viewed either in terms of calls or in terms of puts. These two viewpoints are summarized in Table 22.4.

Table 22.4 Positions of Shareholders and Bondholders in Jenkins Brothers Ice Creams in Terms of Calls and Puts

Shareholders	Bondholders
Positions viewed in terms of call options	
1 Shareholders own a call on the firm with an exercise price of £800.	1 Bondholders own the firm. 2 Bondholders have sold a call on the firm to the shareholders.
Positions viewed in terms of put options	
1 Shareholders own the firm. 2 Shareholders owe £800 in interest and principal to bondholders. 3 Shareholders own a put option on the firm with an exercise price of £800.	1 Bondholders are owed £800 in interest and principal. 2 Bondholders have sold a put on the firm to the shareholders.

We have found from experience that it is generally harder for students to think of the firm in terms of puts than in terms of calls. Thus, it would be helpful if there were a way to show that the two viewpoints are equivalent. Fortunately there is *put-call parity*. In an earlier section, we presented the put-call parity relationship as Equation 22.1, which we now repeat:

Equation 22.1

$$\text{Price of underlying equity} + \text{Price of put} = \text{Price of call} + \text{Present value of exercise price}$$

Using the results of this section, Equation 22.1 can be rewritten like this:

Equation 22.3

$$\text{Value of call on firm} - \text{Value of firm} = \text{Value of put on firm} - \text{Value of default-free bond}$$

$$\text{Shareholders' position in terms of call options} = \text{Shareholders' position in terms of put options}$$

Going from Equation 22.1 to Equation 22.2 involves a few steps. First, we treat the firm, not the equity, as the underlying asset in this section. (In keeping with common convention, we refer to the *value* of the firm and the *price* of the equity.) Second, the exercise price is now £800, the principal and interest on the firm's debt. Taking the present value of this amount at the riskless rate yields the value of a default-free bond. Third, the order of the terms in Equation 22.1 is rearranged in Equation 22.2.

Note that the left side of Equation 22.2 is the shareholders' position in terms of call options, as shown in Table 22.3. The right side of Equation 22.2 is the shareholders' position in terms of put options, as shown in the same table. Thus, put-call parity shows that viewing the shareholders' position in terms of call options is equivalent to viewing the shareholders' position in terms of put options.

Equation 22.3b

$$\text{Value of firm} - \text{Value of call on firm} = \text{Value of default-free bond} - \text{Value of put on firm}$$

$$\text{Bondholders' position in terms of call options} = \text{Boldholders' position in terms of put options}$$

The left side of Equation 22.2b is the bondholders' position in terms of call options, as shown in Table 22.4. (The minus sign on this side of the equation indicates that the bondholders are *writing* a call.) The right side of the equation is the bondholders' position in terms of put options, as shown in Table 22.4. Thus, put-call parity shows that viewing the bondholders' position in terms of call options is equivalent to viewing the bondholders' position in terms of put options.

A Note about Loan Guarantees

In the Jenkins Brothers example given earlier, the bondholders bore the risk of default. Of course, bondholders generally ask for an interest rate that is high enough to compensate them for bearing risk. When firms experience financial distress, they can no longer attract new debt at moderate interest rates. Thus, firms experiencing distress have frequently sought loan guarantees from the government. Our framework can be used to understand these guarantees.

If the firm defaults on a guaranteed loan, the government must make up the difference. In other words, a government guarantee converts a risky bond into a riskless bond. What is the value of this guarantee?

Recall that with option pricing:

$$\text{Value of default-free bond} = \text{Value of risky bond} + \text{Value of put firm}$$

This equation shows that the government is assuming an obligation that has a cost equal to the value of a put option.

This analysis differs from that of either politicians or company spokespeople. They generally say that the guarantee will cost the taxpayer nothing because the guarantee enables the firm to attract debt, thereby staying solvent. However, it should be pointed out that, although solvency may be a strong possibility, it is never a certainty. Thus, when the guarantee is made, the government's obligation has a cost in terms of present value. To say that a government guarantee costs the government nothing is like saying a put on the equity of Apple plc has no value because the equity is *likely* to rise in price.

Several governments (such as those of Britain, France, Germany and the USA) used loan guarantees to help firms get through the major recession that began in 2008. Under the guarantees, if a company defaulted on new loans, the lenders could obtain the full value of their claims from the company's government. From the lender's point of view, the loans became as risk-free as Treasury bonds. Loan guarantees enable firms to borrow cash to get through a difficult time.

Who Benefits from a Typical Loan Guarantee?

- If existing risky bonds are guaranteed, all gains accrue to the existing bondholders. The shareholders gain nothing because the limited liability of corporations absolves the shareholders of any obligation in bankruptcy.
- If new debt is issued and guaranteed, the new debtholders do not gain. Rather, in a competitive market, they must accept a low interest rate because of the debt's low risk. The shareholders gain here because they are able to issue debt at a low interest rate. In addition, some of the gains accrue to the old bondholders because the firm's value is greater than would otherwise be true. Therefore, if shareholders want all the gains from loan guarantees, they should renegotiate or retire existing bonds before the guarantee is in place.
- Obviously, employees of distressed firms benefit because otherwise the firm may go into bankruptcy if new funding is not provided from lenders. In addition, employees of firms that are suppliers and customers of distressed firms would also benefit. This was the main rationale underlying the government rescue packages of 2008 and 2009.

Sustainability in Action 22.2

Climate Derivatives

Climate derivatives are financial instruments that can be used to hedge against the financial risks associated with climate change, such as extreme weather events, natural disasters, or changes in temperature or precipitation. Also known as weather derivatives, they are similar to insurance contracts, but are based on specific weather variables or indices.

An example of a climate derivative is a temperature swap, which involves two parties exchanging fixed and floating payments based on the difference between the actual and expected temperature over a certain period of time. For instance, a utility company that relies on natural gas for heating may enter into a temperature swap with a financial institution to hedge against the risk of warmer-than-expected winters, which would reduce the demand for gas and lower its revenues. The utility company would pay a fixed amount to the financial institution and receive a floating amount that increases when the temperature is higher than a predetermined level. Conversely, the financial institution would pay a floating amount to the utility company and receive a fixed amount that increases when the temperature is lower than a predetermined level.

Another example of a climate derivative is a rainfall option, which gives the buyer the right, but not the obligation, to receive a payment if the rainfall in a certain location falls below or exceeds a specified threshold during a certain period of time. For example, an agricultural producer that depends on rainfall for irrigation may buy a rainfall option from an insurance company to hedge against the risk of drought, which would reduce its crop yield and income. The agricultural producer would pay a premium to the insurance company and receive a payout if the rainfall is lower than a predetermined level. Conversely, the insurance company would receive the premium and pay out if the rainfall is higher than a predetermined level.

Climate derivatives are useful for various sectors and industries that are exposed to climate-related risks, such as agriculture, energy, tourism, transportation, construction and retail. By using climate derivatives, these sectors and industries can reduce their uncertainty and volatility in cash flows, and improve their planning and budgeting.

Summary and Conclusions

This chapter serves as an introduction to options.

1. The most familiar options are puts and calls. These options give the holder the right to sell or buy shares of equity at a given exercise price. American options can be exercised any time up to and including the expiration date. European options can be exercised only on the expiration date.
2. We showed that a strategy of buying a share and buying a put is equivalent to a strategy of buying a call and buying a zero coupon bond. From this, the put-call parity relationship was established:

$$\text{Value of stock} + \text{Value of put} - \text{Value of call} = \text{Present value of exercise price}$$

3 The value of an option depends on five factors:

(a) The price of the underlying asset
(b) The exercise price
(c) The expiration date
(d) The variability of the underlying asset
(e) The interest rate on risk-free bonds.

The Black-Scholes model can determine the intrinsic price of an option from these five factors.

4 The 'Greeks' (delta, gamma, theta and vega) measure different aspects of the risk of options.

5 Much of corporate financial theory can be presented in terms of options. In this chapter, we pointed out that:

(a) Equity can be represented as a call option on the firm.
(b) Shareholders enhance the value of their call by increasing the risk of their firm.

Questions and Problems

McGraw Hill connect

CONCEPT

1 **Options** Many laypeople find the whole concept of options difficult to understand. Use a non-financial example to explain how options work and why they are so important for flexible decision-making. What are the types of option contracts corporations can buy? Why would a corporation buy these options? Explain.

2 **Differences between American and European Options** What is the difference between an American and European option? Is an American call option on a dividend-paying stock always worth at least as much as its intrinsic value? How about for a European call option? Explain.

3 **American Versus European Options** Why is it that an American option is always worth the same as a European option? If it were not, what strategy could an arbitrageur use to profit?

4 **Options and Asset Values** Suppose that sustainable green bond yields unexpectedly rise. Ceteris paribus, what would happen to the value of call options and put options?

5 **Option Quotes** Normally the settlement price falls as the strike price increases for call options. Conversely, the settlement price generally increases as the strike price gets higher for put options. Explain why, using Table 22.1 as an example.

6 **Option Combinations** Why would a corporation wish to combine put and call options on a commodity? Provide an example of a case where this might happen.

7 **Valuing Options** Review the factors that affect the value of call and put options. Do you think options on sustainable firms are likely to have different value drivers? Explain.

8 **Option Pricing** Why can't you just value an option using discounted cash flows, as in net present value?

9 **The Greeks** What are the Greeks? Why are they important to a corporation? Do you think they are more or less important in firms that pursue sustainable development goals? Explain.

10 **Shares and Bonds as Options** Show how a share of equity can be viewed as an option. Why is this perspective helpful?

11 **Options and Corporate Decisions** In many countries, governments have encouraged bank mergers to reduce their risk. Use option analysis to show why this may be bad news for the bank's shareholders. Does this mean that you should not buy the shares of a newly merged bank? Explain.

REGULAR

12 **Option Pricing: Pirelli & C. SpA** The Pirelli & C. SpA share price is €8.895. A call option with an exercise price of €9 sells for €0.35 and a put option with the same exercise price sells for €0.65. Does this make sense? Explain.

13 **Two-state Option Pricing Model** T-bills currently yield 2.1 per cent and the Man Group plc share price is £0.97. There is no possibility that the equity will be worth less than £0.50 per share in one year.

(a) What is the value of a call option with a £0.97 exercise price? What is the intrinsic value?

(b) What is the value of a call option with a £0.70 exercise price? What is the intrinsic value?

(c) What is the value of a put option with a £1.10 exercise price? What is the intrinsic value?

14 **Understanding Option Quotes** Use the option quote information from Euronext Liffe shown here for Xstrata plc to answer the questions that follow. The equity is selling for £11.025.

Calls									Puts					
Settl.	O.I.	Day Vol.	Last	Bid	Ask		Strike		Bid	Ask	Last	Day Vol.	O.I.	Settl.
463.00	–	–	–	431.50	490.00	C	6.40	P	–	5.50	–	–	62	0.50
423.00	558	–	–	391.50	450.00	C	6.80	P	–	6.00	–	–	781	0.50
383.00	35	–	–	352.50	410.00	C	7.20	P	–	6.50	–	–	1,276	1.00
343.00	27	–	–	312.50	370.00	C	7.60	P	–	5.50	–	–	47	2.50
303.00	419	–	–	272.00	330.50	C	8.00	P	0.50	7.00	–	–	641	3.50
263.50	88	–	–	233.50	291.50	C	8.40	P	2.50	8.50	–	–	135	5.50
225.50	583	–	–	208.00	238.00	C	8.80	P	7.00	12.50	–	–	944	9.50
188.50	16	–	–	171.00	201.00	C	9.20	P	12.50	17.50	–	–	1,339	14.50
153.50	149	–	–	144.00	159.00	C	9.60	P	20.00	22.50	–	–	1,017	21.00
122.00	2,620	–	–	112.00	127.00	C	10.00	P	30.00	33.50	–	–	1,830	31.00
80.50	154	–	–	76.00	82.00	C	10.60	P	50.50	55.00	49.00	15	1,095	51.00
58.50	699	–	–	55.00	60.00	C	11.00	P	69.00	74.50	66.00	15	4,477	69.50
38.00	4,742	20	43.50	34.50	39.00	C	11.50	P	97.50	104.00	–	–	1,729	99.00
22.50	3,537	47	21.00	20.00	23.50	C	12.00	P	130.00	142.50	127.00	3	3,038	134.00
8.00	2,456	–	–	5.50	9.50	C	13.00	P	205.00	235.00	205.00	5	973	219.00
1.50	1,679	–	–	–	5.00	C	14.00	P	285.50	345.00	–	–	454	313.00
0.00	140	–	–	–	3.50	C	15.00	P	384.00	443.00	–	–	8	412.00
0.00	116	–	–	–	5.00	C	16.00	P	484.00	543.50	–	–	22	512.00

(a) Are the call options in the money? What is the intrinsic value of an Xstrata plc call option?

(b) Are the put options in the money? What is the intrinsic value of an Xstrata plc put option?

(c) Looking at the quotes on their own, do you think that the market expects the price of Xstrata to increase or decrease during the period of the option? What range of prices are anticipated? Look at the share price history for Xstrata on Yahoo! Finance and find out what actually happened. Who made a profit from their trading – the call or put holders?

15 **Calculating Payoffs** Use the option quote information on Unilever NV from Euronext below to answer the questions that follow. Assume that 100 shares make 1 contract.

UNDERLYING

Name	Unilever PLC	ISIN	GB00B10RZP78		Market	Euronext Amsterdam	
Currency	EUR	Best Bid	47.76	26 May 23 11:05	Best Ask	47.77	26 May 23 11:05
Time	CET	Last	47.77	26 May 23 11:04	Last change	−0.28%	
Volume	189,718	High	47.99		Low	47.63	

Expiry

Jun 2023 × | Select all | Compact | All strikes | SUBMIT

JUNE 2023 PRICES - 26/05/23

SETTL.	LAST	BID	ASK		STRIKE		BID	ASK	LAST	SETTL.
5.99	-	5.85	6.00	C	42.00	P	0.04	0.08	-	0.02
4.06	-	3.90	4.01	C	44.00	P	0.08	0.12	-	0.10
3.14	-	2.95	3.04	C	45.00	P	0.12	0.16	0.12	0.15
2.24	-	2.04	2.13	C	46.00	P	0.20	0.24	0.23	0.24
1.41	1.33	1.24	1.31	C	47.00	P	0.39	0.41	0.39	0.41
0.74	0.62	0.62	0.67	C	48.00	P	0.74	0.81	0.85	0.74
0.31	0.24	0.24	0.28	C	49.00	P	1.38	1.45	1.50	1.33
0.10	0.09	0.06	0.09	C	50.00	P	2.21	2.31	2.26	2.13
0.03	-	0.02	0.05	C	51.00	P	3.19	3.29	-	3.10
0.01	-	-	0.04	C	52.00	P	-	4.29	-	4.10
0.01	-	-	0.04	C	53.00	P	-	5.30	-	5.10

(a) Suppose you buy 20 contracts of the June €51.00 call option. How much will you pay, ignoring commissions?

(b) In part (a), suppose that Unilever is selling for €52.50 per share on the expiration date. How much is your options investment worth? What if the terminal share price is €50.50? Explain.

(c) Suppose you buy 10 contracts of the June €51 put option. What is your maximum gain? On the expiration date, Unilever is selling for €48 per share. How much is your options investment worth? What is your net gain?

(d) In part (c), suppose you sell 10 of the June €51 put contracts. What is your net gain or loss if Unilever is selling for €48 at expiration? For €54? What is the break-even price – that is, the terminal share price that results in a zero profit?

16 **Two-state Option Pricing Model** The share price of ABC plc will be either £2 or £1.5 at the end of the year. Call options are available with one year to expiration. UK government bond yields are currently at 3 per cent.

(a) Suppose the current share price of ABC plc is £1.74. What is the value of the call option if the exercise price is £1.75 per share?

(b) Suppose the exercise price is £1.9 in part (a). What is the value of the call option now?

17 **Two-state Option Pricing Model: National Bank of Greece** The price of National Bank of Greece shares will be either €1.74 or €1.43 at the end of the year. Call options are available with one year to expiration. T-bills currently yield 7 per cent.

(a) Suppose the current price of National Bank of Greece shares is €1.68. What is the value of the call option if the exercise price is €1.50 per share?

(b) Suppose the exercise price is €1.68 in part (a). What is the value of the call option now?

18 **Put-Call Parity: BP plc** BP plc shares are currently selling for £4.29 per share. A put option with an exercise price of £4.40 sells for £0.25 and expires in three months. If the risk-free rate of interest is 2.6 per cent per year, compounded continuously, what is the price of a call option with the same exercise price?

19 **Put-Call Parity: Alcatel-Lucent** Alcatel-Lucent has a put option and a call option with an exercise price of €1 and three months to expiration, sell for €0.28 and €0.11, respectively. If the risk-free rate is 2.5 per cent per year, compounded continuously, what is the current share price?

20 **Put-Call Parity: Arcellormittal** Arcellormittal call and put options with an exercise price of €17 expire in four months and sell for €2.07 and €2.03, respectively. If the equity is currently priced at €17.03, what is the annual continuously compounded rate of interest?

21 **Black-Scholes and Real Options** Coal mining is becoming more popular because of the demand for energy in Asia. Assume that you have the rights to a coal mine and the most recent valuation of the mine was £6.7 million. Because of increasing demand from Asia, the price of similar mines has grown by 15 per cent per annum, with an annual standard deviation of 20 per cent. A buyer has recently approached you and wants an option to buy the mine in the next 12 months for £7 million. The risk-free rate of interest is 3 per cent per year, compounded continuously. How much should you charge for the option?

22 **Black-Scholes and Asset Value** In the previous problem, suppose you wanted the option to sell the mine to the buyer in one year. Assuming all the facts are the same, describe the transaction that would occur today. What is the price of the transaction today?

23 **Black-Scholes Valuation** The spot price of XYZ plc is 394.5p, with a standard deviation of 20 per cent. A call option on the stock expires in 219 days; it has a strike price of 400p, with a quoted price of 18p. The risk-free rate is 1 per cent.

(a) Find the Black-Scholes value of the call.

(b) Why does the Black-Scholes value not match the quoted price of the call?

24 **Black-Scholes: Xstrata** Xstrata plc is currently priced at £10.52. A call option with an expiration of six months has an exercise price of £9.00. The risk-free rate is 3 per cent per year, compounded continuously, and the standard deviation of the equity's return is infinitely large. What is the price of the call option?

25 **Equity as an Option** Shire plc has a zero coupon bond issue outstanding with £12 billion face value that matures in five years. The current market value of the firm's assets is £20 billion. The standard deviation of the return on the firm's assets is 23 per cent per year, and the annual risk-free rate is 3 per cent per year, compounded continuously. Based on the Black-Scholes model, what is the market value of the firm's equity and debt?

26 **Equity as an Option and Stakeholders** Suppose Shire plc (see the previous problem) is considering two mutually exclusive investments. Project A has an NPV of £700 million and project B has an NPV of £1.2 billion. As the result of taking project A, the standard deviation of the return on the firm's assets will increase to 55 per cent per year. If project B is taken, the standard deviation will fall to 19 per cent per year.

(a) What is the value of the firm's equity and debt if project A is undertaken? If project B is undertaken?

(b) Which project would the shareholders prefer? Can you reconcile your answer with the NPV rule?

(c) Suppose the shareholders and bondholders are in fact the same group of investors. Would this affect your answer to (b)?

(d) What does this problem suggest to you about shareholder incentives?

27 **Mergers and Equity as an Option** Suppose Shire plc (see Problem 25) decides to reorient its operations and, as a result, the return on assets now has a standard deviation of 30 per cent per year.

(a) What is the value of Shire plc equity now? The value of debt?

(b) What was the gain or loss for shareholders? For bondholders?

(c) What happened to shareholder value here?

28 **Equity as an Option and NPV** A company has a single zero coupon bond outstanding that matures in 10 years with a face value of £30 million. The current value of the company's assets is £22 million and the standard deviation of the return on the firm's assets is 39 per cent per year. The risk-free rate is 6 per cent per year, compounded continuously.

(a) What is the current market value of the company's equity?

(b) What is the current market value of the company's debt?

(c) What is the company's continuously compounded cost of debt?

(d) The company has a new project available. The project has an NPV of £750,000. If the company undertakes the project, what will be the new market value of equity? Assume volatility is unchanged.

(e) Assuming the company undertakes the new project and does not borrow any additional funds, what is the new continuously compounded cost of debt? What is happening here?

29 **Synthetic Call Options** Ken is interested in buying a European call option written on Southeastern Airlines plc, a non-dividend-paying equity, with a strike price of £110 and one year until expiration. Currently, Southeastern's equity sells for £100 per share. In one year Ken knows that Southeastern's shares will be trading at either £125 per share or £80 per share. Ken is able to borrow and lend at the risk-free EAR of 2.5 per cent.

(a) What should the call option sell for today?

(b) If no options currently trade on the equity, is there a way to create a synthetic call option with identical payoffs to the call option just described? If there is, how would you do it?

(c) How much does the synthetic call option cost? Is this greater than, less than or equal to what the actual call option costs? Does this make sense?

30 **Two-state Option Pricing Model: Maverick Manufacturing** Maverick Manufacturing plc must purchase gold in three months for use in its operations. Maverick's management has estimated that if the price of gold were to rise above $875 per ounce, the firm would go bankrupt. The current price of gold is $850 per ounce. The firm's chief financial officer believes that the price of gold will either rise to $900 per ounce or fall to $825 per ounce over the next three months. Management wishes to eliminate any risk of the firm going bankrupt. Maverick can borrow and lend at the risk-free APR of 16.99 per cent.

(a) Should the company buy a call option or a put option on gold? To avoid bankruptcy, what strike price and time to expiration would the company like this option to have?

(b) How much should such an option sell for in the open market?

(c) If no options currently trade on gold, is there a way for the company to create a synthetic option with identical payoffs to the option just described? If there is, how would the firm do it?

(d) How much does the synthetic option cost? Is this greater than, less than or equal to what the actual option costs? Does this make sense?

31 **Black-Scholes and Collar Cost** An investor is said to take a position in a 'collar' if she buys the asset, buys an out-of-the-money put option on the asset and sells an out-of-the-money call option on the asset. The two options should have the same time to expiration. Suppose Marie wishes to purchase a collar on Zurich Re, a non-dividend-paying equity, with six months until expiration. She would like the put to have a strike price of 50 Swiss francs (SFr) and the call to have a strike price of SFr120. The current price of Zurich Re's equity is SFr80 per share. Marie can borrow and lend at the continuously compounded risk-free rate of 10 per cent per annum, and the annual standard deviation of the equity's return is 50 per cent. Use the Black-Scholes model to calculate the total cost of the collar that Marie is interested in buying. What is the effect of the collar?

CHALLENGE

32 **Debt Valuation and Time to Maturity** McLemore Industries has a zero coupon bond issue that matures in two years with a face value of £30,000. The current value of the company's assets is £13,000, and the standard deviation of the return on assets is 60 per cent per year.

(a) Assume the risk-free rate is 5 per cent per year, compounded continuously. What is the value of a risk-free bond with the same face value and maturity as the company's bond?

(b) What price would the bondholders have to pay for a put option on the firm's assets with a strike price equal to the face value of the debt?

(c) Using the answers from (a) and (b), what is the value of the firm's debt? What is the continuously compounded yield on the company's debt?

(d) From an examination of the value of the assets of McLemore Industries, and the fact that the debt must be repaid in two years, it seems likely that the company will default on its debt. Management has approached bondholders and proposed a plan whereby the company would repay the same face value of debt, but the repayment would not occur for five years. What is the value of the debt under the proposed plan? What is the new continuously compounded yield on the debt? Explain why this occurs.

33 **Debt Valuation and Asset Variance** Brozik plc has a zero coupon bond that matures in five years with a face value of £60,000. The current value of the company's assets is £57,000 and the standard deviation of its return on assets is 50 per cent per year. The risk-free rate is 6 per cent per year, compounded continuously.

(a) What is the value of a risk-free bond with the same face value and maturity as the current bond?

(b) What is the value of a put option on the firm's assets with a strike price equal to the face value of the debt?

(c) Using the answers from (a) and (b), what is the value of the firm's debt? What is the continuously compounded yield on the company's debt?

(d) Assume the company can restructure its assets so that the standard deviation of its return on assets increases to 60 per cent per year. What happens to the value of the debt? What is the new continuously compounded yield on the debt? Reconcile your answers in (c) and (d).

(e) What happens to bondholders if the company restructures its assets? What happens to shareholders? How does this create an agency problem?

34 **Two-state Option Pricing and Corporate Valuation** Strudler Property plc, a construction firm financed by both debt and equity, is undertaking a new project. If the project is successful, the value of the firm in one year will be £500 million, but if the project is a failure the firm will be worth only £320 million. The current value of Strudler is £400 million, a figure that includes the prospects for the new project. Strudler has outstanding zero coupon bonds due in one year with a face value of £380 million. Treasury bills that mature in one year yield 7 per cent EAR. Strudler pays no dividends.

(a) Use the two-state option pricing model to find the current value of Strudler's debt and equity.

(b) Suppose Strudler has 500,000 shares of equity outstanding. What is the price per share of the firm's equity?

(c) Compare the market value of Strudler's debt to the present value of an equal amount of debt that is riskless with one year until maturity. Is the firm's debt worth more than, less than or the same as the riskless debt? Does this make sense? What factors might cause these two values to be different?

(d) Suppose that, in place of the preceding project, Strudler's management decides to undertake a project that is even more risky. The value of the firm will either increase to £800 million or decrease to £200 million by the end of the year. Surprisingly, management concludes that the value of the firm today will remain at exactly £400 million if this risky project is substituted for the less risky one. Use the two-state option pricing model to determine the value of the firm's debt and equity if the firm plans on undertaking this new project. Which project do bondholders prefer?

35 **Black-Scholes and Dividends** In addition to the five factors discussed in the chapter, dividends also affect the price of an option. The Black-Scholes option pricing model with dividends is:

$$C = S \times e^{-dt} \times N(d_1) - E \times e^{-Rt} \times N(d_2)$$
$$d_1 = [\ln(S/E) + (R - d + \sigma^2/2) \times t]/(\sigma \times \sqrt{t})$$
$$d_2 = d_1 - \sigma \times \sqrt{t}$$

All of the variables are the same as the Black-Scholes model without dividends except for the variable *d*, which is the continuously compounded dividend yield on the share.

(a) What effect do you think the dividend yield will have on the price of a call option? Explain.

(b) Genmab A/S is currently priced at 2.26 Danish Kroner (DKr) per share, the standard deviation of its return is 50 per cent per year, and the risk-free rate is 5 per cent per year compounded continuously. What is the price of a call option with a strike price of DKr2.00 and a maturity of six months if the share has a dividend yield of 2 per cent per year?

36 **Put-Call Parity and Dividends** The put-call parity condition is altered when dividends are paid. The dividend adjusted put-call parity formula is:

$$S \times e^{-dt} + P = E \times e^{-Rt} + C$$

where *d* is again the continuously compounded dividend yield.

(a) What effect do you think the dividend yield will have on the price of a put option? Explain.

(b) From the previous question, what is the price of a call option with a strike price of DKr2.00 and a maturity of six months if the share has a dividend yield of 2 per cent per year? What is the price of a put option with the same strike price and time to expiration as the call option?

37 **Put Delta** In the chapter, we noted that the delta for a put option is $N(d_1) - 1$. Is this the same thing as $-N(-d_1)$? (*Hint:* Yes, but why?)

38 **Black-Scholes Put Pricing Model** Use the Black-Scholes model for pricing a call, put-call parity and the previous question to show that the Black-Scholes model for directly pricing a put can be written as follows:

$$P = E \times e^{-Rt} \times N(-d_2) - S \times N(-d_1)$$

39 **Black-Scholes Paradox** An equity is currently priced at £50. The share will never pay a dividend. The risk-free rate is 12 per cent per year, compounded continuously and the standard deviation of the share's return is 60 per cent. A European call option on the share has a strike price of £100 and no expiration date, meaning that it has an infinite life. Based on Black-Scholes, what is the value of the call option? Do you see a paradox here? Do you see a way out of the paradox?

40 **Delta** You purchase one call and sell one put with the same strike price and expiration date. What is the delta of your portfolio? Why?

Exam Question (45 minutes)

A developer has just acquired 60 acres of property in Ngorongoro to develop a safari wildlife centre. The safari centre will also include a hotel development. In order to generate operating capital, the developer is selling rights. The rights give the holder of the contract the right to purchase a lodge in the hotel development for a fixed price. Each lodge is half an acre. The agreements expire six months after they are signed.

The developer is offering the following inducement. A potential lodge owner can purchase the lodge for TSh25 million at the end of six months if the lodge owner enters into the contract this week. The purchase price for a lodge increases to TSh40 million on all contracts signed after this week.

1 Describe and explain the type of option being sold by the developer. **(15 marks)**

2 Describe and explain the position held by the potential lodge owner as an option. **(15 marks)**

3 Discuss the risks associated with this transaction to both the developer and the lodge owner. **(15 marks)**

4 Suppose we purchased a right on one of the lodges during the inducement period, and it has just been discovered that a very rare type of lion has been discovered close to the lodge. Explain what you think will happen to the value of the right that you own. Is this contract in the money? Explain. **(15 marks)**

5 Suppose that the developer was selling two contracts. One contract permits you to purchase a lodge any time during the six-month period and the other allows you to purchase the lodge only at the end of six months. Which of the two contracts is worth more? Explain. **(15 marks)**

6 To reduce your cash outflows shortly before it became public knowledge that the rare lions live near the lodge, you sign a contract with a colleague. This contract gives you the right to sell the lodge at any time in the next six months to your friend for TSh35 million. Describe your position and that of your friend. **(15 marks)**

7 Describe the potential obligations associated with the options involving the developer and the two friends. Use diagrams to illustrate your answer. **(10 marks)**

Total: 100 Marks

Mini Case

Clissold Industries Options

You are currently working for Clissold Industries. The company, which went public five years ago, engages in the design, production and distribution of lighting equipment and speciality products worldwide. Because of recent events, Mal Clissold, the company president, is concerned about the company's risk, so he asks for your input.

In your discussion with Mal, you explain that the CAPM proposes that the market risk of the company's equity is the determinant of its expected return. Even though Mal agrees with this, he argues that his portfolio consists entirely of Clissold Industry shares and options, so he is concerned with the total risk, or standard deviation, of the company's equity. Furthermore, even though he has calculated the standard deviation of the company's equity for the past five years, he would like an estimate of the share's volatility moving forward.

Mal states that you can find the estimated volatility of the share for future periods by calculating the implied standard deviation of option contracts on the company equity. When you examine the factors that affect the price of an option, all of the factors except the standard deviation of the shares are directly observable in the market. You can also observe the option price as well. Mal states that because you can observe all of the option factors except the standard deviation, you can simply solve the Black-Scholes model and find the implied standard deviation.

Strike Price (£)	Option Price (£)
30	23.00
40	16.05
50	9.75
55	7.95

To help you find the implied standard deviation of the company's equity, Mal has provided you with the following option prices on four call options that expire in six months. The risk-free rate is 6 per cent, and the current share price is £50.

1 How many different volatilities would you expect to see for the equity?

2 Unfortunately, solving for the implied standard deviation is not as easy as Mal suggests. In fact, there is no direct solution for the standard deviation of the equity even if we have all other variables for the Black-Scholes model. Mal would still like you to estimate the implied standard deviation of the share. To do this, set up a spreadsheet using the Solver function in Excel to calculate the implied volatilities for each of the options.

3 Are all of the implied volatilities for the options the same? (*Hint:* No.) What are the possible reasons that can cause different volatilities for these options?

4 After you discuss the importance of volatility on option prices, your boss mentions that he has heard of the FTSE 100 Volatility Index (VFTSE) on Euronext. What is the VFTSE and what does it represent?

5 Look for current option quotes for the FTSE 100 Volatility Index on Euronext. To find these, search on the Euronext website for the ISIN: QS0011052162. What does the implied volatility of a VFTSE option represent?

Practical Case Study

Vodafone Group Option Pricing

In this practical case study, you will use real data to value Vodafone options.

1 Visit the Eurex options page for Vodafone (https://www.eurex.com/ex-en/markets/equ/opt/Vodafone-Group-952440). You should see a screen similar to the following:

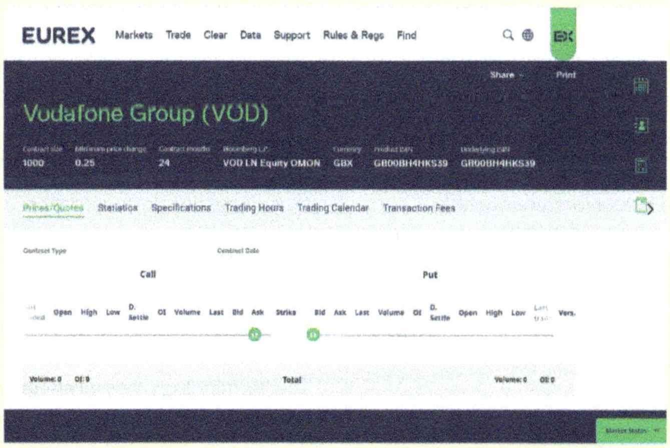

2 Using the information in Sections 22.7 and 22.8, find data on the current Vodafone share price, volatility, interest rate, dividend yield and time to maturity of the underlying assets and the contracts.
3 Using the data you have collected, value a Vodafone option contract using the binomial model and the Black-Scholes model.
4 Compare the results of the different methods and explain the reasons for any discrepancies or similarities.
5 How do your estimated prices compare to the market price on Eurex?
6 Which method for valuing options do you prefer. Why?

Relevant Accounting Standards

IAS 39 *Financial Instruments: Recognition and Measurement* and IFRS 7 *Financial Instruments: Disclosure* are exceptionally important for options. Since the potential exposure to losses from options can be significant, it is important their impact is reflected in a firm's accounting statements. Visit the IASPlus website (www.iasplus.com) for more information.

Reference

Hull, J.C. (2012) *Options, Futures and Other Derivatives*, 8th edn. Upper Saddle River, NJ: Prentice Hall.

Additional Reading

A very rich empirical and theoretical research field considers option pricing dynamics. The reference list below focuses on options as they relate to corporate finance.

1 Amram, M., F. Li and C.A. Perkins (2006) 'How Kimberly-Clark Uses Real Options', *Journal of Applied Corporate Finance*, Vol. 18, No. 2, 40–47.
2 Chi, T., J. Li, L.G. Trigeorgis and A.E. Tsekrekos (2019) 'Real Options Theory in International Business', *Journal of International Business Studies*, Vol. 50, No. 4, 525–553.
3 Giaccotto, C., G.M. Goldberg and S.P. Hegde (2007) 'The Value of Embedded Real Options: Evidence from Consumer Automobile Lease Contracts', *Journal of Finance*, Vol. 62, No. 1, 411–445.
4 Granadier, S.R. and A. Malenko (2011) 'Real Options Signaling Games with Applications to Corporate Finance', *Review of Financial Studies*, Vol. 24, No. 2, 3993–4036.
5 Ioulianou, S., M.J. Leiblein and L. Trigeorgis (2018) 'The Impact of Real Options Awareness on Downside Risk in Multinational Firms', *Academy of Management Proceedings*, Vol. 2018, No. 1, 12170. Briarcliff Manor, NY 10510: Academy of Management.
6 Lambrecht, B.M. and G. Pawlina (2010) 'Corporate Finance and the (In)efficient Exercise of Real Options', *Multinational Finance Journal*, Vol. 14, No. 1/2, 129–156.
7 McDonald, R.L. (2006) 'The Role of Real Options in Capital Budgeting: Theory and Practice', *Journal of Applied Corporate Finance*, Vol. 18, No. 2, 28–39.
8 Trigeorgis, L. and J.J. Reuer (2017) 'Real Options Theory in Strategic Management', *Strategic Management Journal*, Vol. 38, No. 1, 42–63.

Endnotes

1 We use *buyer*, *owner* and *holder* interchangeably.
2 This example assumes that the call lets the holder purchase one share at £7.00. In reality, one call option contract would let the holder purchase 100 shares. The profit would then equal £100 [= (£8.00 – £7.00) × 100].
3 Actually, because of differing exercise prices, the two graphs are not quite mirror images of each other.
4 Our discussion in this section is of American options because they are more commonly traded in the real world. As necessary, we will indicate differences for European options. American options are differentiated from European options through their ability to be exercised at any time before the expiration date. The terminology has nothing to do with where the options are traded.

5 This relationship need not hold for a European call option. Consider a firm with two otherwise identical European call options, one expiring at the end of May and the other expiring a few months later. Further assume that a *huge* dividend is paid in early June. If the first call is exercised at the end of May, its holder will receive the underlying share. If he does not sell the share, he will receive the large dividend shortly thereafter. However, the holder of the second call will receive the share through exercise after the dividend is paid. Because the market knows that the holder of this option will miss the dividend, the value of the second call option could be less than the value of the first.

6 Though this result must hold in the case of an American put, it need not hold for a European put.

7 A full treatment of this assumption can be found in Hull (2012).

8 This method is called *linear interpolation*. It is only one of a number of possible methods of interpolation.

Chapter 23

Options and Corporate Finance: Extensions and Applications

Learning Objectives

After reading this chapter you should be able to:

LO1 Explain the concept and implications of executive share options in the context of corporate finance.

LO2 Evaluate the process and criteria for valuing a start-up, including factors influencing valuation and methods used.

LO3 Appreciate the role of options in capital budgeting.

LO4 Assess the strategic considerations and financial impacts of shutdown and reopening decisions.

In recent years, many companies have exchanged their employee share options for restricted stock units (RSUs). An RSU is a share of equity that cannot be sold or exchanged until it is vested. The vesting period can vary but is usually between three and five years. When an RSU vests, the employee receives a full share of equity. The biggest advantage of RSUs for employees is that they receive the equity no matter what the share price. In comparison, with employee share options the employee may receive nothing.

The reason for this change in policy was that most executive share options were worthless as a result of the major market falls in the immediate aftermath of the global financial crisis. The main purpose of executive share options is that they reward employees for good performance and loyalty to their company. If the options are worth nothing, there is no financial reason why the best executives should stay in a company if their services are demanded elsewhere. Restricted stock units are therefore better in a down market because executives always receive something for their efforts.

Source: loft39studio/123RF

Key Notations

C	Value of a call option
P	Value of a put option
S	Current share price
E	Exercise price of option
R	Annual risk-free rate of return, continuously compounded
σ^2	Variance (per year) of the continuous share price return
t	Time (in years) to expiration date
$\mathrm{N}(d)$	Probability that a standardized, normally distributed, random variable will be less than or equal to d

$$d_1 = [\mathrm{In}(S/E) + (R + \sigma^2/2)t] / \sqrt{\sigma^2 t}$$

$$d_2 = d_1 - \sqrt{\sigma^2 t}$$

23.1 Executive Share Options

Why Options?

Executive compensation (see Chapter 2, Section 2.2 for more on executive compensation) is usually made up of base salary plus some or all of the following elements:

- Base salary
- Annual bonuses
- Long-term incentives, such as retirement contributions, options and restricted stock units.

Chapter 2 Page 24

When stock markets are on an upward trajectory, the final component of compensation, options, is by far the most significant part of total compensation for many top executives. In many parts of Europe, full disclosure of executive pay is not yet standard practice. However, this has not stopped politicians and the media from criticizing the total compensation of executives, whose share options are a major component of their total remuneration. Figure 23.1 presents a breakdown of chief executive pay in Europe in 2015–2017. Bonuses represent any payments paid for performance during the year, and LTI is long-term incentives, which include executive share options.

Figure 23.1 Total Direct Compensation at CEO level

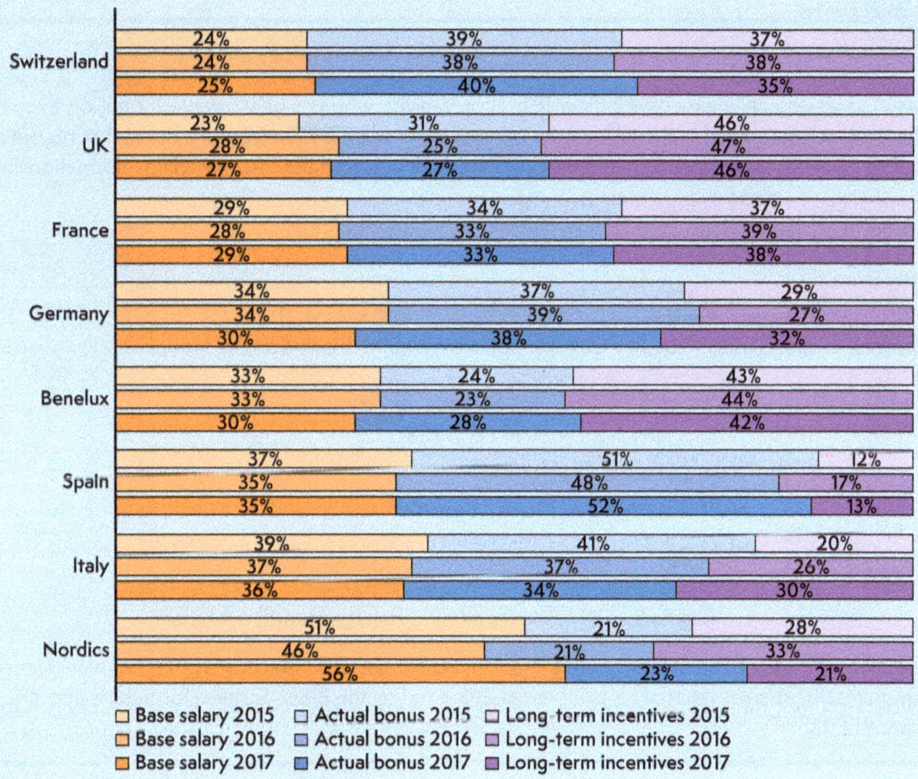

Source: Towers Watson, 'CEO Pay Landscape in Europe's Top 100 Companies' report, Autumn 2018.

As can be seen, long-term incentives, such as executive share options, have been prevalent in European countries, particularly in Benelux, France, the UK and Switzerland. Some of the reasons given for using executive share options were these:

- Options align executives' interests to those of the shareholders. By aligning interests, executives are more likely to make decisions for the benefit of the shareholders.

- Options allow the company to lower the executives' base pay. This removes pressures on morale caused by disparities between the salaries of executives and those of other employees.
- Options put an executive's pay at risk, rather than guaranteeing it regardless of the performance of the firm.

At the same time, there are significant criticisms of executive share options. The most notable criticism is that share options encourage managers to take on more risky projects to increase the size of their remuneration. Given the role of executive compensation in the banking sector and the perverse incentives to maximize bank share price at the expense of bank risk, regulators across the world have moved to limit top executive pay. However, as it stands, regulators have been successful only in constraining executive pay and not reducing it.

Valuing Executive Compensation

In this section, we value executive share options. Not surprisingly, the complexity of the total compensation package often makes valuation a difficult task. The economic value of the options depends on factors such as the volatility of the underlying equity and the exact terms of the option grant.

Only a few countries fully disclose the details of executive pay, and in Example 23.1 we will estimate the economic value of the options held by the chief executive of a hypothetical company. Example 23.1 is necessarily simplistic, but it serves to illustrate the way we can value executive share options. Simple matters such as requiring the executive to hold the option for a fixed period – the freeze-out period – before exercising, can significantly diminish the value of a standard option.

Example 23.1

Executive Options

Consider Ray Davies, the chief executive officer (CEO) of Vankins, who has been granted 2 million executive share options. The average share price at the time of the options grant was €39.71. We will assume that his options are at the money. The risk-free rate is 5 per cent and the options expire in five years. The preceding information implies that:

- The share price (S) of €39.71 equals the exercise price (E).
- The risk-free rate $R = 0.05$.
- The time interval $t = 5$.

In addition, the variance of Vankins is estimated to be $(0.2168)^2 = 0.0470$.

This information allows us to value Ray Davies's options using the Black-Scholes model:

$$C = SN(d_1) - E\,e^{-Rt}N(d_2)$$

$$d_1 = [(R + 1/2\sigma^2)t]/\sqrt{\sigma^2 t} = 0.758$$

$$d_2 = d_1 - \sqrt{\sigma^2 t} = 0.273$$

$$N(d_1) = 0.776$$

$$N(d_2) = 0.608$$

$$e^{-0.05\times 5} = 0.7788$$

$$C = €39.71 \times 0.776 - €39.71 \times (0.778 \times 0.608) = €12.03$$

Thus the value of a call option on one share of Vankins equity is €12.03. Because Mr Davies was granted options on 2 million shares, the market value of his options, as estimated by the Black-Scholes formula, is about €24 million (= 2 million × €12.03).

Equally important, the Black-Scholes formula has to be modified if the equity pays dividends and is no longer applicable if the volatility of the equity is changing randomly over time. Intuitively, a call option on a dividend-paying equity is worth less than a call on an equity that pays no dividends: all other things being equal, the dividends will lower the share price. Nevertheless, let us see what we can do.

The value of the options we computed in Example 23.1 would be the economic value of the options if they were to trade in the market. The real question is this: whose value are we talking about? Are these the costs of the options to the company? Are they the values of the options to the executives?

The total value of €24 million for Ray Davies's options in Example 23.1 is the amount that the options would trade at in the financial markets, and that traders and investors would be willing to pay for them.[1] If Vankins was very large, it would not be unreasonable to view this as the cost of granting the options to the CEO, Ray Davies. Of course, in return, the company would expect Mr Davies to improve the value of the company to its shareholders by more than this amount. As we have seen, perhaps the primary purpose of options is to align the interests of management with those of the shareholders of the firm. Under no circumstances, though, is the €24 million necessarily a fair measure of what the options are worth to Mr Davies.

As an illustration, suppose that the CEO of London Convers plc has options on 1 million shares with an exercise price of €30 per share, and the current share price of London Convers is €50. If the options were exercised today, they would be worth €20 million (an underestimation of their market value). Suppose that the CEO owns €5 million in company equity and has €5 million in other assets. The CEO has an undiversified personal portfolio. By the standards of modern portfolio theory, having 25/30, or about 83 per cent, of your wealth in one equity and its options is unnecessarily risky.

Although the CEO is wealthy by most standards, shifts in share price impact the CEO's economic well-being. If the price drops from €50 per share to €30 per share, the current exercise value of the options on 1 million shares drops from €20 million down to zero. Ignoring the fact that if the options had more time to mature they might not lose all of this value, we nevertheless have a rather startling decline in the CEO's net worth from about €30 million to €8 million (€5 million in other assets plus equity that is now worth €3 million). But that is the purpose of giving the options and the equity holdings to the CEO – namely, to make the CEO's fortunes rise and fall with those of the company. It is why the company requires the executive to hold the options for at least a freeze-out period rather than letting the executive sell them to realize their value.

The implication is that, when options are a large portion of an executive's net worth, the total value of the position to the executive is less than market value. As a purely financial matter, an executive might be happier with €5 million in cash rather than €20 million in options. At least the executive could then diversify his personal portfolio. The recent shift from executive share options to restricted stock units suggests that, in practice, the effective minimum value of executive share options is not zero. If companies systematically respond to deep out-of-the-money options by converting them to RSUs, the firms are exercising another option: to exchange the share option for an RSU. As with any option, this has value to the holder, in this case the senior executive.

23.2 Investment in Real Projects and Options

Chapter 8 Page 207

In Chapter 8, we considered projects where forecasts for future cash flows were made at date 0. The expected cash flow in each future period was discounted at an appropriate risky rate, yielding an NPV calculation. For independent projects, a positive NPV meant acceptance and a negative NPV meant rejection. This approach treated risk through the discount rate.

We later considered decision tree analysis, an approach that handles risk in a more sophisticated way. We pointed out that the firm will make investment and operating decisions on a project over its entire life. We value a project today, assuming that future decisions will be optimal. However, we do not yet know what these decisions will be because much information remains to be discovered. The firm's ability to delay its investment and operating decisions until the release of information is an option. We now illustrate this option through an example.

Example 23.2

Options and Sustainable Investments

Consider a hypothetical scenario involving GreenEnergy plc, an international renewable energy company. It is considering purchasing a sustainable farm in the Trondheim Valley, northern Norway. The current owner is asking for a price of £10,000 (equivalent in Norwegian Kroner) and is keen to sell immediately. The initial investment in infrastructure and equipment is estimated to be £500,000.

GreenEnergy expects to produce 10,000 tons of sustainable produce per year for many decades. Given the far-off and uncertain termination date, the company treats the anticipated revenue from the farm as a perpetuity. The selling price of the sustainable produce is £50 per ton, and the cost of sustainable farming practices is £46 per ton, yielding a net profit margin of £4 per ton.

With the expectation of price increases matching the inflation rate, GreenEnergy predicts a consistent £4 cash flow per ton in real terms. The applicable real discount rate is 10 per cent. GreenEnergy also has tax credits from less profitable years, meaning it won't need to pay taxes on any profits from this sustainable farm. Given these conditions, should GreenEnergy make the purchase?

The NPV of the farm to GreenEnergy is:

$$-£110{,}000 = -£10{,}000 - £500{,}000 + \frac{£4 \times 10{,}000}{0.10}$$

According to this analysis, GreenEnergy should not purchase the land.

Though this method employs standard capital budgeting techniques covered in various finance resources, it may not be fully applicable here. To illustrate this, consider the insights provided by Professor Amjad Al-Farsi, a consultant to GreenEnergy plc. He concurs with the assumption that the price of sustainable produce will rise at the rate of inflation. However, he highlights that the next year is particularly uncertain for sustainable produce prices.

On one side, new regulations could push sustainable produce prices up to £65 per ton in real terms for many years ahead. Conversely, a prolonged economic slowdown might lower demand for premium sustainable products. In this case, Professor Al-Farsi suggests that sustainable produce prices may drop to £35 per ton in real terms for a considerable duration. Complete information on both these scenarios will become clear in exactly one year.

Should prices rise to £65 a ton, the NPV of the project would be:

$$£1{,}390{,}000 = -£10{,}000 - £500{,}000 + \frac{(£65 - £46) \times 10{,}000}{0.10}$$

However, should prices fall to £35 a ton, the NPV of the farm will be even more negative than it is today.

Professor Al-Farsi proposes two recommendations to GreenEnergy's board. He suggests:

1 The land should be acquired.
2 The decision to invest in the farming infrastructure should be deferred until more information about the new regulations and the economic downturn is known.

Al-Farsi begins his explanation to the board by presupposing that the land purchase has already been made, suggesting that under this scenario, the decision to invest should be postponed. He then examines his initial suggestion that the land purchase should be undertaken. This approach of examining the second decision (investment) after assuming that the first decision (to buy the farm) has been made was also used in our earlier presentation on decision trees.

If we follow Al-Farsi's analysis, we assume the land has already been purchased. Should the company immediately invest in farming infrastructure? If the investment is made immediately, the NPV is –£110,000. However, if the investment decision is deferred until new data are available in a year, the optimal decision can be made then.

If sustainable produce prices drop to £35 per ton, GreenEnergy should abandon the project, incurring only the initial £10,000 land purchase cost. If prices rise to £65 per ton, the investment should be made. Al-Farsi emphasizes that, by deferring the decision, the £500,000 investment is only made if prices rise, hence avoiding this cost if prices fall.

Regarding the initial decision, if we already know that deferring the investment decision until new information emerges is optimal, should the land be purchased at all? While we can't precisely predict the likelihood of a price increase, Al-Farsi remains confident that the land purchase is worthwhile. The project's NPV at £65 per ton price is £1,390,000, while the land cost is only £10,000. Al-Farsi acknowledges that a price rise is possible but not certain. Nonetheless, he maintains that the potential high return justifies the risk.

Professor Al-Farsi highlights that, by postponing the investment decision, GreenEnergy will commit the £500,000 infrastructure cost only if sustainable produce prices increase. Therefore, by deferring, the company saves £500,000 if the prices drop. Al-Farsi concludes that, once the land is acquired, the decision to invest in infrastructure should be delayed.

Should the land have been purchased in the first place? We now know that, if the land has been purchased, it is optimal to defer the investment decision until further information is available. Given that we know this optimal decision concerning the investment decision, should the land be purchased in the first place? Without knowing the exact probability that sustainable food prices will rise, Professor Al-Farsi is nevertheless confident that the land should be purchased.

The project's NPV at a sustainable produce price of £65 per ton is £1,390,000, while the land purchase cost is a mere £10,000. Al-Farsi believes that a price increase is plausible, albeit not certain. Nevertheless, he contends that the potential for high returns outweighs the risk.

This example presents an approach that is similar to our decision tree analysis in Section 8.4. Our purpose in this section is to discuss this type of decision in an option framework. When GreenEnergy purchases the land, it is actually purchasing a call option. That is, once the land has been purchased, the firm has an option to buy a sustainable farm at an exercise price of £500,000. As it turns out, one should generally not exercise a call option immediately. In this case, the firm should delay exercise until relevant information concerning the sustainable produce prices is released.

This section points out a serious deficiency in classical capital budgeting: net present value calculations typically ignore the flexibility that real-world firms have. In our example, the standard techniques generated a negative NPV for the land purchase. Yet, by allowing the firm the option to change its investment policy according to new information, the land purchase can easily be justified.

We encourage the reader to look for hidden options in projects. Because options are beneficial, managers are short-changing their firm's projects if capital budgeting calculations ignore flexibility.

23.3 Valuing a Start-up

Ralph Simmons was not your typical master's student. Since childhood, he had one ambition: to open a restaurant that sold wild boar meat. He went to business school because he realized that, although he knew 101 ways to cook wild boars, he did not have the business skills necessary to run a restaurant. He was extremely focused, with each course at graduate school being important to him only to the extent that it could further his dream.

While taking his school's course in entrepreneurship, he began to develop a business plan for his restaurant, which he now called Wild Boar for Everyone. He thought about marketing; he thought about raising capital; he thought about dealing with future employees. He even devoted a great deal of time to designing the physical layout of the restaurant. Against the professor's advice in his entrepreneurship class, he designed the restaurant in the shape of a wild boar, where the front door went through the animal's mouth. Of course, his business plan would not be complete without financial projections. After much thought, he came up with the projections shown in Table 23.1.

Table 23.1 Financial Projections for Wild Boar for Everyone

	Year 1 (£)	Year 2 (£)	Year 3 (£)	Year 4 (£)	All Future Years (£)
(1) Sales	300,000	600,000	900,000	1,000,000	1,000,000
(2) Cash flows from operations	−100,000	−50,000	75,000	250,000	250,000
(3) Increase in working capital	50,000	20,000	10,000	10,000	0
(4) Net cash flows [(2) − (3)]	−150,000	−70,000	65,000	240,000	250,000
Present value of net cash flows in years 1–4 (discounted at 20%)			−20,255		
Present value of terminal value			$\frac{£250{,}000}{0.20} \times \frac{1}{(1.20)^4} = £602{,}816$		
Present value of restaurant			£602,812 − £20,255 = £582,561		
Less cost of building			−£700,000		
Net present value of restaurant			−£117,439		

Table 23.1 starts with sales projections, which rise from £300,000 in the first year to a steady state of £1 million a year. Cash flows from operations are shown in the next line, although we leave out the intermediate calculations needed to move from line (1) to line (2). After subtracting working capital, the table shows net cash flows in line (4). Net cash flows are negative initially, which is quite common in start-ups, but they become positive by year 3. However, the rest of the table presents the unfortunate truth. The cash flows from the restaurant yield a present value of £582,561, assuming a discount rate of 20 per cent. Unfortunately, the cost of the building is greater, at £700,000, implying a negative net present value of −£117,439.

The projections indicate that Ralph's lifelong dream may not come to pass. He cannot expect to raise the capital needed to open his restaurant; and if he did obtain the funding, the restaurant would be likely to go under anyway. Ralph checked and rechecked the numbers, hoping in vain to discover either a numerical error or a cost-saving omission that would move his venture from the red to the black. In fact, he saw that, if anything, his forecasts were generous: a 20 per cent discount rate and an infinitely lived building are on the optimistic side.

It was not until Ralph took a course in corporate strategy that he saw the hidden value in his venture. In that course, his instructor repeatedly stated the importance of positioning a firm to take advantage of new opportunities. Although Ralph did not see the connection at first, he finally realized the implications for Wild Boar for Everyone. His financial projections were based on expectations. There was a 50 per cent probability that wild boar meat would be more popular than he thought, in which case actual cash flows would exceed projections. And there was a 50 per cent probability that the meat would be less popular, in which case the actual flows would fall short of projections.

If the restaurant did poorly, it would probably fold in a few years because he would not want to keep losing money for ever. However, if the restaurant did well, he would be in a position to expand. With wild boar meat being popular in one locale, it would probably prove popular in other locales as well. Thus, he recognized two options: the option to abandon under bad conditions and the option to expand under good conditions. Although both options can be valued according to the principles of the previous chapter, we focus on the option to expand because it is probably much more valuable.

Ralph reasoned that, as much as he personally liked wild boar meat, consumer resistance in some regions of the United Kingdom would doom Wild Boar for Everyone. So he developed a strategy of catering only to those regions where wild boar meat is somewhat popular already. He forecast that, although he could expand quickly if the first restaurant proved successful, the market would limit him to 30 additional restaurants.

Ralph believes that this expansion will occur about four years from now. He believes that he will need three years of operating the first restaurant to (1) get the initial restaurant running smoothly, and (2) have enough information to place an accurate value on the restaurant. If the first restaurant is successful enough, he will need another year to obtain outside capital. Thus, he will be ready to build the 30 additional units around the fourth year.

Ralph will value his enterprise, including the option to expand, according to the Black-Scholes model. From Table 23.1 we see that each unit costs £700,000, implying a total cost over the 30 additional units of £21,000,000 (= 30 × £700,000). The present value of the cash inflows from these 30 units is £17,476,830 (= 30 × £582,561), according to the table. However, because the expansion will occur around the fourth year, this present value calculation is provided from the point of view of four years in the future. The present value as of today is £8,428,255 [= £17,476,830/$(1.20)^4$], assuming a discount rate of 20 per cent per year. Thus, Ralph views his potential restaurant business as an option, where the exercise price is £21,000,000 and the value of the underlying asset is £8,428,255. The option is currently out of the money, a result that follows from the negative value of a typical restaurant, as calculated in Table 23.1. Of course, Ralph is hoping that the option will move into the money within four years.

Ralph needs three additional parameters to use the Black-Scholes model: R, the continuously compounded interest rate; t, the time to maturity; and σ, the standard deviation of the underlying asset. Ralph uses the yield on a four-year zero coupon bond, which is 3.5 per cent, as the estimate of the interest rate. The time to maturity is four years. The estimate of standard deviation is a little trickier because there is no historical data on wild boar restaurants. Ralph finds that the average annual standard deviation of the returns on publicly traded restaurants is 0.35. Because Wild Boar for Everyone is a new venture, he reasons that the risk here would be somewhat greater. He finds that the average annual standard deviation for restaurants that have gone public in the last few years is 0.45. Ralph's restaurant is newer still, so he uses a standard deviation of 0.50.

There is now enough data to value Ralph's venture. The value according to the Black-Scholes model is £1,455,196. The actual calculations are shown in Example 23.3. Of course, Ralph must start his pilot restaurant before he can take advantage of this option. Thus, the net value of the call option plus the negative present value of the pilot restaurant is £1,337,757 (= £1,455,196 – £117,439). Because this value is large and positive, Ralph decides to stay with his dream of Wild Boar for Everyone. He knows that the probability that the restaurant will fail is greater than 50 per cent. Nevertheless, the option to expand is important enough that his restaurant business has value. And if he needs outside capital, he probably can attract the necessary investors.

This finding leads to the appearance of a paradox. If Ralph approaches investors to invest in a single restaurant with no possibility of expansion, he will probably not be able to attract capital. After all, Table 23.1 shows a net present value of –£117,439. However, if Ralph thinks bigger, he is likely to be able to attract all the capital he needs. But this is really not a paradox at all. By thinking bigger, Ralph is offering investors the option – not the obligation – to expand.

The example we have chosen may seem frivolous, and certainly we added offbeat characteristics for interest. However, if you think that business situations involving options are unusual or unimportant, let us state emphatically that nothing is further from the truth. The notion of embedded options is at the heart of business. There are two possible outcomes for virtually every business idea. On the one hand, the business may fail, in which case the managers will probably try to shut it down in the most cost-efficient way. On the other hand, the business may prosper, in which case the managers will try to expand. Thus, virtually every business has both the option to abandon and the option to expand. You may have read pundits claiming that the net present value approach to capital budgeting is wrong or incomplete. Although criticism of this type frequently irritates the finance establishment, the pundits definitely have a point. If virtually all projects have embedded options, only an approach such as the one we have outlined can be appropriate. Ignoring the options is likely to lead to serious undervaluation.

Example 23.3

Valuing a Start-up Firm (Wild Boar for Everyone) as an Option

1 The value of a single restaurant is negative, as indicated by the net present value calculation in Table 23.1 of −£117,439. Thus, the restaurant would not be funded if there was no possibility of expansion.

2 If the pilot restaurant is successful, Ralph Simmons plans to create 30 additional restaurants around year 4. This leads to the following observations:

(a) The total cost of 30 units is £21,000,000 (= 30 × £700,000).

(b) The present value of future cash flows as of year 4 is £17,476,830 (= 30 × £582,561).

(c) The present value of these cash flows today is £8,428,255 [= £17,476,830/(1.20)[4]].

Here we assume that cash flows from the project are discounted at 20 per cent per annum.

Thus, the business is essentially a call option, where the exercise price is £21,000,000 and the underlying asset is worth £8,428,255.

3 Ralph Simmons estimates the standard deviation of the annual return on Wild Boar for Everyone's equity to be 0.50.

Parameters of the Black-Scholes model:

$$S(\text{share price}) = £8{,}428{,}255$$
$$E(\text{exercise price}) = £21{,}000{,}000$$
$$t(\text{time to maturity}) = 4 \text{ years}$$
$$\sigma(\text{standard deviation}) = 0.50$$
$$R(\text{standard compounded interest rate}) = 3.5\%$$

Calculation from the Black-Scholes model:

$$C = SN(d_1) - Ee^{-Rt}N(d_2)$$
$$d_1 = \left[\ln(S/E) + (R + 1/2\sigma^2)t\right]/\sqrt{\sigma^2 t}$$
$$d_2 = d_1 - \sqrt{\sigma^2 t}$$
$$d_1 = \left[\ln\frac{8{,}428{,}255}{21{,}000{,}000} + \left(0.035 + \frac{1}{2}\left(0.50\right)^2\right)4\right]/\sqrt{(0.50)^2 4} = -0.27293$$
$$d_2 = -0.27293 - \sqrt{(0.50)^2\,4} = -1.27293$$
$$N(d_1) = N(-0.27293) = 0.3936$$
$$N(d_2) = N(-1.27293) = 0.1020$$
$$C = £8{,}428{,}555 \times 0.3936 - €21{,}000{,}000 \times e^{-0.035\times 4} \times 0.1020$$
$$= £1{,}455{,}196$$

The value of the business including the cost of the pilot restaurant is £1,337,757 (= £1,455,196 − £117,439).

23.4 More about the Binomial Model

Earlier in this chapter, we examined three applications of options: executive compensation, options to abandon or expand, and the start-up decision. In two cases we valued the option using the Black-Scholes model. Although this model is justifiably well known, it is not the only approach to option valuation. As mentioned in the previous chapter (see **Chapter 22**, Section 22.8), the two-state or binomial model is an alternative and – in some situations – a superior approach to valuation. The rest of this chapter examines two applications of the binomial model.

Chapter 22 Page 602

Heating Oil

Two-date Example

Consider Anthony Meyer, a typical heating oil distributor, whose business consists of buying heating oil at the wholesale level and reselling it to homeowners at a somewhat higher price. Most of his revenue comes from sales during the winter. Today, 1 September, heating oil sells for €2.00 per litre. Of course, this price is not fixed. Rather, oil prices will vary from 1 September until 1 December, the time when his customers will probably make their big winter purchases of heating oil. Let us simplify the situation by assuming that Mr Meyer believes that oil prices will be at either €2.74 or €1.46 on 1 December. Figure 23.2 portrays this possible price movement. This potential price range represents a great deal of uncertainty because Mr Meyer has no idea which of the two possible prices will actually occur. However, this price variability does not translate into that much risk because he can pass price changes on to his customers. That is, he will charge his customers more if he ends up paying €2.74 per litre than if he ends up paying €1.46 per litre.

Figure 23.2 Movement of Heating Oil Prices from 1 September to 1 December in a Two-date Example

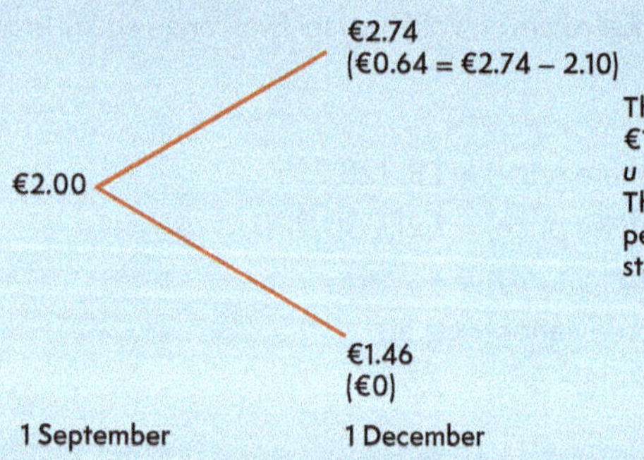

The price of heating oil on 1 December will be either €2.74 or €1.46. Because the price on 1 September is €2.00, we say that u = 1.37 (= €2.74/€2.00) and d = 0.73 (= €1.46/€2.00). The loss per litre to Mr Meyer (or, equivalently, the gain per litre to CECO) of €0.64 in the up state or €0 in the down state is shown in parentheses.

Of course, Mr Meyer is avoiding risk by passing on that risk to his customers. His customers accept the risk, perhaps because they are each too small to negotiate a better deal. This is not the case with CECO, a large electric utility in his area. CECO approaches Mr Meyer with the following proposition. The utility would like to be able to buy *up to* 6 million litres of oil from him at €2.10 per litre on 1 December.

Although this arrangement represents a lot of oil, both Mr Meyer and CECO know that Mr Meyer can expect to lose money on it. If prices rise to €2.74 per litre, the utility will happily buy all 6 million litres at only €2.10 per litre, clearly creating a loss for the distributor. However, if oil prices decline to €1.46 per litre, the utility will not buy any oil. After all, why should CECO pay €2.10 per litre to Mr Meyer when the utility can buy all the oil it wants at €1.46 per litre in the open market? In other words, CECO is asking for a *call option* on heating oil. To compensate Mr Meyer for the risk of loss, the two parties agree that CECO will pay him €1,000,000 up front for the right to buy up to 6 million litres of oil at €2.10 per litre.

Is this a fair deal? Although small distributors may evaluate a deal like this by gut feel, we can evaluate it more quantitatively by using the binomial model described in the previous chapter. In that chapter, we pointed out that option problems can be handled most easily by assuming *risk-neutral pricing*. In this approach, we first note that oil will either rise 37 per cent (= €2.74/€2.00 – 1) or fall –27 per cent (= €1.46/€2.00 – 1) from 1 September to

1 December. We can think of these two numbers as the possible returns on heating oil. In addition, we introduce two new terms, u and d. We define u as $1 + 0.37 = 1.37$ and d as $1 - 0.27 = 0.73$.[2] Using the methodology of the previous chapter, we value the contract in the following two steps.

Step 1: Determining the Risk-neutral Probabilities

We determine the probability of a price rise such that the expected return on oil exactly equals the risk-free rate. Assuming an 8 per cent annual interest rate, which implies a 2 per cent rate over the next three months, we can solve for the probability of a rise as follows:[3]

$$2\% = \text{Probability of rise} \times 0.37 + (1 - \text{Probability of rise}) \times (-0.27)$$

Solving this equation, we find that the probability of a rise is approximately 45 per cent, implying that the probability of a fall is 55 per cent. In other words, if the probability of a price rise is 45 per cent, the expected return on heating oil is 2 per cent. In accordance with what we said in the previous chapter, these are the probabilities that are consistent with a world of risk neutrality. That is, under risk neutrality, the expected return on any asset would equal the riskless rate of interest. No one would demand an expected return above this riskless rate, because risk-neutral individuals do not need to be compensated for bearing risk.

Step 2: Valuing the Contract

If the price of oil rises to €2.74 on 1 December, CECO will want to buy oil from Mr Meyer at €2.10 per litre. Mr Meyer will lose €0.64 per litre because he buys oil in the open market at €2.74 per litre, only to resell it to CECO at €2.10 per litre. This loss of €0.64 is shown in parentheses in Figure 23.2. Conversely, if the market price of heating oil falls to €1.46 per litre, CECO will not buy any oil from Mr Meyer. That is, CECO would not want to pay €2.10 per litre to him when the utility could buy heating oil in the open market at €1.46 per litre. Thus, we can say that Mr Meyer neither gains nor loses if the price drops to €1.46. The gain or loss of zero is placed in parentheses under the price of €1.46 in Figure 23.2. In addition, as mentioned earlier, Mr Meyer receives €1,000,000 up front.

Given these numbers, the value of the contract to Mr Meyer can be calculated as:

Equation 23.1

$$\underbrace{[0.45 \times (€2.10 - €2.74) \times 6 \text{ million} + 0.55 \times 0]/1.02}_{\text{Value of the call option}} + €1{,}000{,}000{,}000 = -€694{,}118$$

As in the previous chapter, we are valuing an option using risk-neutral pricing. The cash flows of −€0.64 (= €2.10 − €2.74) and €0 per litre are multiplied by their risk-neutral probabilities. The entire first term in Equation 23.1 is then discounted at €1.02 because the cash flows in that term occur on 1 December. The €1,000,000 is not discounted because Mr Meyer receives it today, 1 September. Because the present value of the contract is negative, Mr Meyer would be wise to reject the contract.

As stated before, the distributor has sold a call option to CECO. The first term in the preceding equation, which equals −€1,694,118, can be viewed as the value of this call option. It is a negative number because the equation looks at the option from Mr Meyer's point of view. Therefore, the value of the call option would be +€1,694,118 to CECO. On a per-litre basis, the value of the option to CECO is:

Equation 23.2

$$[0.45(€2.74 - €2.10) + 0.55 \times 0]/1.02 = €0.282$$

Equation 23.2 shows that CECO will gain €0.64 (= €2.74 − €2.10) per litre in the up state because CECO can buy heating oil worth €2.74 for only €2.10 under the contract. By contrast, the contract is worth nothing to CECO in the down state because the utility will not pay €2.10 for oil selling for only €1.46 in the open market. Using risk-neutral pricing, the formula tells us that the value of the call option on one litre of heating oil is €0.282.

Three-date Example

Although the preceding example captures a number of aspects of the real world, it has one deficiency. It assumes that the price of heating oil can take on only two values on 1 December. This is clearly not plausible: oil can take on essentially any value in reality. Although this deficiency seems glaring at first glance, it is easily correctable. All we have to do is to introduce more intervals over the three-month period of our example.

For example, consider Figure 23.3, which shows the price movement of heating oil over two intervals of 1½ months each.[4] As shown in the figure, the price will be either €2.50 or €1.60 on 15 October. We refer to

€2.50 as the price in the *up state* and €1.60 as the price in the *down state*. Thus, heating oil has returns of 25 per cent (= €2.50/€2.00) and –20 per cent (= €1.60/€2) in the two states.

We assume the same variability as we move forward from 15 October to 1 December. That is, given a price of €2.50 on 15 October, the price on 1 December will be either €3.12 (= €2.50 × 1.25) or €2 (= €2.50 × 0.80). Similarly, given a price of €1.60 on 15 October, the price on 1 December will be either €2 (= €1.60 × 1.25) or €1.28 (= €1.60 × 0.80). This assumption of constant variability is quite plausible because the rate of new information impacting heating oil (or most commodities or assets) is likely to be similar from month to month.

Figure 23.3 Movement of Heating Oil Prices in a Three-date Model

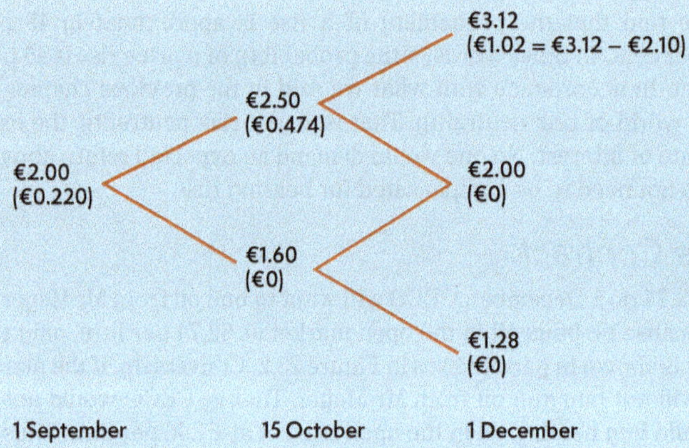

The figure shows the prices of a litre of heating oil on three dates, given $u = 1.25$ and $d = 0.80$. There are three possible prices for heating oil on 1 December. For each one of these three prices, we calculate the price on 1 December of a call option on a litre of heating oil with an exercise price of €2.10. These numbers are in parentheses. Call prices at earlier dates are determined by the binomial model and are also shown in parentheses.

Note that there are three possible prices on 1 December, but there are two possible prices on 15 October. Also, note there are two paths to a price of €2 on 1 December. The price could rise to €2.50 on 15 October before falling back down to €2 on 1 December. Alternatively, the price could fall to €1.60 on 15 October before going back up to €2 on 1 December. In other words, the model has symmetry, where an up movement followed by a down movement yields the same price on 1 December as a down movement followed by an up movement.

How do we value CECO's option in this three-date example? We employ the same procedure that we used in the two-date example, although we now need an extra step because of the extra date.

Step 1: Determining the Risk-neutral Probabilities

As we did in the two-date example, we determine what the probability of a price rise would be such that the expected return on heating oil exactly equals the riskless rate. However, in this case, we work with an interval of 1½ months. Assuming an 8 per cent annual rate of interest, which implies a 1 per cent rate over a 1½ month interval,[5] we can solve for the probability of a rise like this:

$$1\% = \text{Probability of a rise} \times 0.25 + (1 - \text{Probability of a rise}) \times (-0.20)$$

Solving the equation, we find that the probability of a rise here is 47 per cent, implying that the probability of a fall is 53 per cent. In other words, if the probability of a rise is 47 per cent, the expected return on heating oil is 1 per cent per each 1½-month interval. Again these probabilities are determined under the assumption of risk-neutral pricing.

Note that the probabilities of 47 per cent and 53 per cent hold for both the interval from 1 September to 15 October and the interval from 15 October to 1 December. This is the case because the return in the up state is 25 per cent and the return in the down state is –20 per cent for each of the two intervals. Thus, the preceding equation must apply to each of the intervals separately.

Step 2: Valuing the Option as of 15 October

As indicated in Figure 23.3, the option to CECO will be worth €1.02 per litre on 1 December if the price of heating oil has risen to €3.12 on that date. That is, CECO can buy oil from Mr Meyer at €2.10 when it would otherwise have to pay €3.12 in the open market. However, the option will be worthless on 1 December if the price of a litre of heating oil is either €2 or €1.28 on that date. Here the option is out of the money because the exercise price of €2.10 is above either €2 or €1.28.

Using these option prices on 1 December, we can calculate the value of the call option on 15 October. If the price of a litre of heating oil is €2.50 on 15 October, Figure 23.3 shows us that the call option will be worth either €1.02 or €0 on 1 December. Thus if the price of heating oil is €2.50 on 15 October, the value of the option on one litre of heating oil at that time is:

$$[0.47 \times €1.02 + 0.53 \times 0]/1.01 = €0.474$$

Here we are valuing an option using the same risk-neutral pricing approach that we used in the earlier two-date example. This value of €0.474 is shown in parentheses in Figure 23.3.

We also want to value the option on 15 October if the price at that time is €1.60. However, the value here is clearly zero, as indicated by this calculation:

$$[0.47 \times €0 + 0.53 \times €0]/1.01 = 0$$

This is obvious once we look at Figure 23.3. We see from the figure that the call must end up out of the money on 1 December if the price of heating oil is €1.60 on 15 October. Thus, the call must have zero value on 15 October if the price of heating oil is €1.60 on that date.

Step 3: Valuing the Option on 1 September

In the previous step, we saw that the price of the call on 15 October would be €0.474 if the price of a litre of heating oil were €2.50 on that date. Similarly, the price of the option on 15 October would be €0 if oil were selling at €1.60 on that date. From these values, we can calculate the call option value on 1 September:

$$[0.47 \times €0.474 + 0.53 \times €0]/1.01 = €0.220$$

Notice that this calculation is completely analogous to the calculation of the option value in the previous step, as well as the calculation of the option value in the two-date example that we presented earlier. In other words, the same approach applies regardless of the number of intervals used. As we will see later, we can move to many intervals, which produces greater realism, yet still maintains the same basic methodology.

The previous calculation has given us the value to CECO of its option on one litre of heating oil. Now we are ready to calculate the value of the contract to Mr Meyer. Given the calculations from the previous equation, the contract's value can be written as:

$$-€0.220 \times 6{,}000{,}000 + €1{,}000{,}000 = -€320{,}000$$

That is, Mr Meyer is giving away an option worth €0.220 for each of the 6 million litres of heating oil. In return, he is receiving only €1,000,000 up front. On balance, he is losing €320,000. Of course, the value of the contract to CECO is the opposite, so the value to this utility is €320,000.

Extension to Many Dates

We have looked at the contract between CECO and Mr Meyer using both a two-date example and a three-date example. The three-date case is more realistic because more possibilities for price movements are allowed here. However, why stop at just three dates? Moving to four dates, five dates, 50 dates, 500 dates, and so on, should give us ever more realism. Note that, as we move to more dates, we are merely shortening the interval between dates without increasing the overall time period of three months (1 September to 1 December).

Imagine, for instance, a model with 90 dates over the three months. Here each interval is approximately one day long because there are about 90 days in a three-month period. The assumption of two possible outcomes in the binomial model is more plausible over a one-day interval than it is over a 1½-month interval, let alone a three-month interval. Of course, we could probably achieve greater realism still by going to an interval of, say, one hour or one minute.

How do we adjust the binomial model to accommodate increases in the number of intervals? It turns out that two simple formulas relate u and d to the standard deviation of the return of the underlying asset:[6]

$$u = e^{\sigma/\sqrt{n}} \text{ and } d = 1/u$$

where σ is the standard deviation of the annualized return on the underlying asset (heating oil, in this case) and n is the number of intervals over a year.

When we created the heating oil example, we assumed that the annualized standard deviation of the return on heating oil was 0.63 (or, equivalently, 63 per cent). Because there are four quarters in a year, $u = e^{0.63/\sqrt{4}} = 1.37$ and $d = 1/1.37 = 0.73$, as shown in the two-date example of Figure 23.2. In the three-date example of Figure 23.3, where each interval is 1½ months long, $u = e^{0.63/\sqrt{8}} = 1.25$ and $d = 1/1.25 = 0.80$. Thus the binomial model can be applied in practice if the standard deviation of the return of the underlying asset can be estimated.

We stated earlier that the value of the call option on a litre of heating oil was estimated to be €0.282 in the two-date model and €0.220 in the three-date model. How does the value of the option change as we increase the number of intervals while keeping the time period constant at three months (from 1 September to 1 December)? We have calculated the value of the call for various time intervals in Table 23.2.[7] The realism increases with the number of intervals because the restriction of only two possible outcomes is more plausible over a short interval than over a long one. Thus, the value of the call when the number of intervals is 99 or infinity is likely to be more realistic than this value when the number of intervals is, say, 1 or 2.

Table 23.2 Value of a Call on One Litre of Heating Oil

Number of Intervals*	Call Value (€)
1	0.282
2	0.220
3	0.244
4	0.232
6	0.228
10	0.228
20	0.228
30	0.228
40	0.228
50	0.226
99	0.226
Black-Scholes infinity	0.226

Note: *The number of intervals is always one less than the number of dates.
In this example, the value of the call according to the binomial model varies as the number of intervals increases. However, the value of the call converges rapidly to the Black-Scholes value. Thus the binomial model, even with only a few intervals, appears to be a good approximation to Black-Scholes.

However, a very interesting phenomenon can be observed from Table 23.2. Although the value of the call changes as the number of intervals increases, convergence occurs quite rapidly. The call's value with six intervals is almost identical to the value with 99 intervals. Thus, a small number of intervals appears serviceable for the binomial model. Six intervals in a three-month period implies that each interval is two weeks long. Of course the assumption that heating oil can take on only one of two prices in two weeks is simply not realistic. The paradox is that this unrealistic assumption still produces a realistic call price.

What happens when the number of intervals goes to infinity, implying that the length of the interval goes to zero? It can be proved mathematically that we end up with the value of the Black-Scholes model. This value is also presented in Table 23.2. Thus, we can argue that the Black-Scholes model is the best approach to value the heating oil option. It is also quite easy to apply. We can use a calculator to value options with Black-Scholes, whereas we must generally use a computer program for the binomial model. However, as shown in Table 23.2, the values from the binomial model, even with relatively few intervals, are quite close to the Black-Scholes value. Thus, although Black-Scholes may save us time, it does not materially affect our estimate of value.

At this point it seems as if the Black-Scholes model is preferable to the binomial model. Who would not want to save time and still get a slightly more accurate value? However, such is not always the case. There are plenty of situations where the binomial model is preferred to the Black-Scholes model. One such situation is presented in Section 23.5.

23.5 Shutdown and Reopening Decisions

Some of the earliest and most important examples of special options have occurred in the natural resources and mining industries.

Valuing a Palladium Mine

Norilsk Nickel JSC is the world's largest nickel and palladium producer, with mines in Russia, Botswana and South Africa. Its annual production of palladium makes up 41 per cent of the world's global production of the metal. The book value of Norilsk Nickel is just under €3 billion but the market value is more than 10 times this amount. What could possibly explain why a company has such a high market to book ratio? The answer lies in the options that Norilsk Nickel implicitly owns in the form of its nickel and palladium mines.

Every mine and oil well costs money to extract the underlying resource. Conditions vary from mine to mine and in a large percentage of locations the cost of extraction can be greater than the current price of the metal. When it costs more to extract a resource than the revenues it can generate in the open market, a company will choose to close the mine until such time as it is profitable to resume operations. This is when the price per unit of ore is higher than the extraction cost per unit.

Consider a single hypothetical mine. Assume the current price of palladium is about €320 per ounce, and the cost of extraction and processing at the mine is about €350 per ounce. Norilsk Nickel would keep this mine closed. Every ounce of palladium extracted costs €350 and can be sold for only €320, for a loss of €30 per ounce. Presumably, if the price of palladium were to rise, the mine could be opened. It costs €2 million to open the mine; when it is opened, production is 50,000 ounces per year. Geologists believe that the amount of palladium in the mine is essentially unlimited, and Norilsk Nickel has the right to mine it for the next 100 years.

Under the terms of its lease, Norilsk Nickel cannot stockpile palladium and must, each year, sell all the palladium it mines. Closing the mine, which costs €1 million, requires equipment to be mothballed and some environmental precautions to be put in place. We will refer to the €2 million required to open the mine as the entry fee or investment and the €1 million to close it as the closing or abandonment cost. (We cannot avoid the abandonment cost by simply keeping the mine open and not operating.)

From a financial perspective, the mine is really just a package of options on the price of palladium. The basic option is a call on the price of palladium where the exercise price is the €350 extraction cost. The option is complicated by having an exercise fee of €2 million – the opening cost – whenever it is exercised and a closing fee of €1 million when it is abandoned. It is also complicated by the fact that it is a perpetual option with no final maturity.

The Abandonment and Opening Decisions

Before valuing the option implicit in the mine, it is useful to see what we can say by just applying common sense. To begin with, the mine should be opened only when the price of palladium is sufficiently above the extraction cost of €350 per ounce. Because it costs €2 million to open the mine, the mine should not be opened whenever the price of palladium is only slightly above €350. At a palladium price of, say, €350.10, the mine would not be opened because the 10-cent profit per ounce translates into €5,000 per year (= 50,000 ounces × €0.10/ounce). This would not begin to cover the €2 million opening costs. More significantly, though, the mine probably would not be opened if the price rose to €360 per ounce, even though a €10 profit per ounce – €500,000 per year – would pay the €2 million opening costs at any reasonable discount rate.

The reason is that here, as in all option problems, volatility (in this case the volatility of palladium) plays a significant role. Because the palladium price is volatile, the price has to rise sufficiently above €350 per ounce to make it worth opening the mine. If the price at which the mine is opened is too close to the extraction price of €350 per ounce, say at €360 per ounce, we would open the mine every time the price went above €360. Unfortunately, we would then find ourselves operating at a loss or facing a closing decision whenever palladium fell by €10 per ounce (or only 3 per cent) to €350.

The estimated volatility of the return on palladium is about 15 per cent per year. This means that a single annual standard deviation movement in the palladium price is 15 per cent of €320, or €48 per year. Surely with this amount of random movement in the palladium price, a threshold of, say, €352 is much too low at which to open the mine. A similar logic applies to the closing decision. If the mine is open, we will clearly keep it open as long as the palladium price is above the extraction cost of €350 per ounce because we are profiting on every ounce of palladium mined. But we also will not close the mine down simply because the palladium price drops below €350 per ounce. We will tolerate a running loss because palladium may later rise back above €350. If we closed the mine, we would pay the €1 million abandonment cost, only to pay another €2 million to reopen the mine if the price rose again.

To summarize, if the mine is currently closed, then it will be opened – at a cost of €2 million – whenever the price of palladium rises *sufficiently* above the extraction cost of €350 per ounce. If the mine is currently operating, then it will be closed down – at a cost of €1 million – whenever the price of palladium falls *sufficiently* below the extraction cost of €350 per ounce. Norilsk Nickel's problem is to find these two threshold prices at which it opens a closed mine and closes an open mine. We call these prices p_{open} and p_{close}, respectively, where:

$$p_{open} > €350/\text{ounce} > p_{close}$$

In other words, Norilsk Nickel will open the mine if the palladium price option is sufficiently in the money and will close it when the option is sufficiently out of the money.

We know that, the more volatile the palladium price, the further away p_{open} and p_{close} will be from €350 per ounce. We also know that the greater the cost of opening the mine, the higher p_{open} will be; and the greater the cost of abandoning the mine, the lower will be p_{close}. Interestingly, we should also expect that p_{open} will be higher if the abandonment cost is increased. After all, if it costs more to abandon the mine, Norilsk Nickel will need to be more assured that the price will stay above the extraction cost when it decides to open the mine. Otherwise, the company will face a costly choice between abandonment and operating at a loss if the price falls below €350 per ounce. Similarly, raising the cost of opening the mine will make Norilsk Nickel more reluctant to close an open mine. As a result, p_{close} will be lower.

The preceding arguments have enabled us to reduce the problem of valuing the mine to two stages. First, we have to determine the threshold prices, p_{open} and p_{close}. Second, given the best choices for these thresholds, we must determine the value of a palladium option that is exercised for a cost of €2 million when the palladium price rises above p_{open} and is shut down for a cost of €1 million whenever the palladium price is below p_{close}.

When the mine is open – that is, when the option is exercised – the annual cash flow is equal to the difference between the palladium price and the extraction cost of €350 per ounce times 50,000 ounces. When the mine is shut down, it generates no cash flow.

The diagram in Figure 23.4 describes the decisions available at each point in time:

Figure 23.4 Decision Analysis of Mine Operation

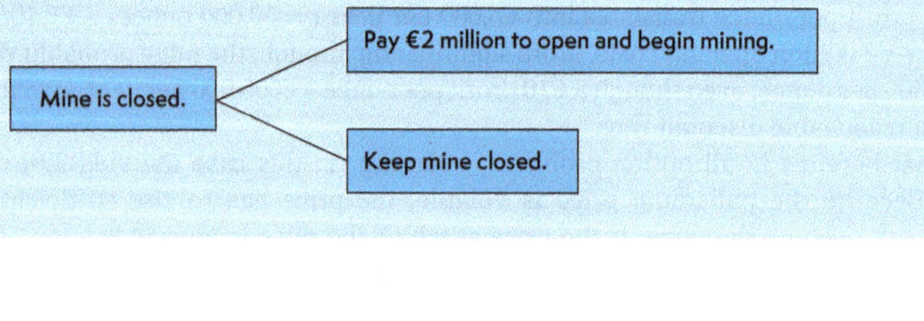

How do we determine the critical values for p_{open} and p_{close} and then the value of the mine? It is possible to get a good approximation by using the tools we have currently developed.

How to Value a Mine: Binomial Option Pricing Model and Monte Carlo Simulation

Here is what has to be done both to determine p_{open} and p_{close} and to value the mine.

Step 1

Find the risk-free interest rate and the volatility. We assume a semi-annual interest rate of 3.4 per cent and a volatility of 15 per cent per year for palladium.

Step 2

Construct a binomial tree and fill it in with palladium prices. Suppose, for instance, that we set the steps of the tree six months apart. If the annual volatility is 15 per cent, u is equal to $e^{0.15\sqrt{2}}$, which is approximately equal to 1.11. The other parameter, d, is 0.90 (= 1/1.11). Figure 23.5 illustrates the tree. Starting at the current price of €320, the first 11 per cent increase takes the price to €355 in six months. The first 10 per cent decrease takes the price to €288. Subsequent steps are up 11 per cent or down 10 per cent from the previous price. The tree extends for the 100-year life of the lease or 200 six-month steps.

Figure 23.5 A Binomial Tree for Palladium Prices

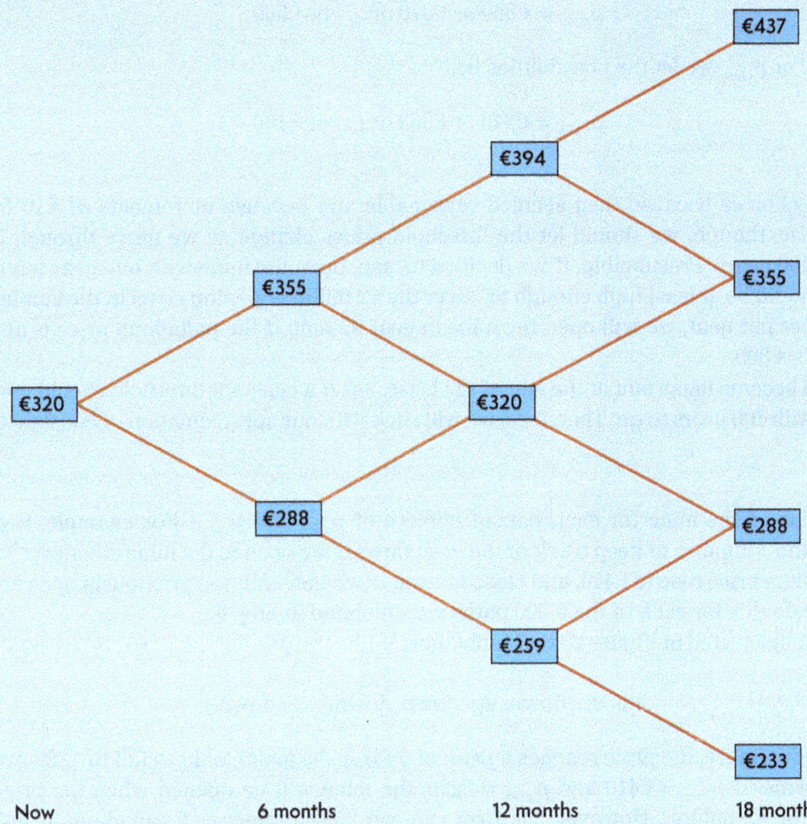

Steps of the binomial tree are 6 months apart. For each step, u is equal to 1.11 and d is equal to 0.90.

Using our analysis from the previous section, we now compute the risk-adjusted probabilities for each step. Given a semi-annual interest rate of 3.4 per cent, we have:

$$3.4\% = \text{Probability of a rise} \times 0.11 + (1 - \text{Probability of a rise}) \times -0.10$$

Solving this equation gives us 0.64 for the probability of a rise, implying that the probability of a fall is 0.36. These probabilities are the same for each six-month interval. In other words, if the probability of a rise is 0.64, the expected return on palladium is 3.4 per cent per each six-month interval. These probabilities are determined under the assumption of risk-neutral pricing. In other words, if investors are risk-neutral, they will be satisfied with an expected return equal to the risk-free rate because the extra risk of palladium will not concern them.

Step 3

Now we turn the computer on and let it simulate, say, 5,000 possible paths through the tree. At each node, the computer has a 0.64 probability of picking an 'up' movement in the price and a corresponding 0.36 probability of picking a 'down' movement in the price. A typical path might be represented by whether the price rose or fell each six-month period over the next 100 years; it would be a list like:

up, up, down, up, down, down, . . ., down

where the first 'up' means the price rose from €320 to €355 in the first six months, the next 'up' means it again went up in the second half of the year from €355 to €394, and so on, ending with a down move in the last half of year 100.

With 5,000 such paths we will have a good sample of all the future possibilities for movement in the palladium price.

Step 4

Next we consider possible choices for the threshold prices, p_{open} and p_{close}. For p_{open}, we let the possibilities be:

$$p_{open} = €360 \text{ or } €370 \text{ or} \ldots \text{or } €500$$

a total of 15 values. For p_{close} we let the possibilities be:

$$p_{close} = €340 \text{ or } €330 \text{ or} \ldots \text{or } €100$$

a total of 25 values.

We picked these choices because they seemed reasonable and because increments of €10 for each seemed sensible. To be precise, though, we should let the threshold prices change as we move through the tree and get closer to the end of 100 years. Presumably, if we decided to, say, open the mine with one year left on the lease, the price of palladium should be at least high enough to cover the €2 million opening costs in the coming year. Because we mine 50,000 ounces per year, we will open the mine in year 99 only if the palladium price is at least €40 above the extraction cost, or €390.

Although this will become important at the end of the lease, using a constant threshold should not have too big an impact on the value with 100 years to go. Therefore, we will stick with our approximation of constant threshold prices.

Step 5

We calculate the value of the mine for each pair of choices of p_{open} and p_{close}. For example, if p_{open} = €410 and p_{close} = €290, we use the computer to keep track of the cash flows if we opened the mine whenever it was previously closed and the palladium price rose to €410, and closed the mine whenever it was previously open and the palladium price fell to €290. We do this for each of the 5,000 paths we simulated in Step 4.

Consider the path illustrated in Figure 23.6, for instance:

up, up, down, up, down, down, . . . , down

As can be seen from the figure, the price reaches a peak of €437 in 2½ years, only to fall to €288 over the following four six-month intervals. If p_{open} = €410 and p_{close} = €290, the mine will be opened when the price reaches €437, necessitating a cost of €2 million. However, the firm can sell 25,000 ounces of palladium at €437 at that time, producing a cash flow of €2.175 million [= 25,000 × (€437 – €350)]. When the price falls to €394 six months later, the firm sells another 25,000 ounces, yielding a cash flow of €1.1 million [= 25,000 × (€394 – €350)]. The price continues to fall, reaching €320 a year later. Here, the firm experiences a cash outflow because production costs are €350 per ounce. Next, the price falls to €288. Because this price is below p_{close} of €290, the mine is closed at a cost of €1 million. Of course, the price of palladium will fluctuate in further years, leading to the possibility of future mine openings and closings.

This path is just a possibility. It may or may not occur in any simulation of 5,000 paths. For each of the 5,000 paths that the computer simulated, we have a sequence of semi-annual cash flows using a p_{open} of €410 and a p_{close} of €290. We calculate the present value of each of these cash flows, discounting at the interest rate of 3.4 per cent. Summing across all the cash flows, we have the present value of the palladium mine for one path.

We then take the average present value of the palladium mine across all the 5,000 simulated paths. This number is the expected value of the mine from following a policy of opening the mine whenever the palladium price hits €410 and closing it at a price of €290.

Figure 23.6 A Possible Path for the Price of Palladium

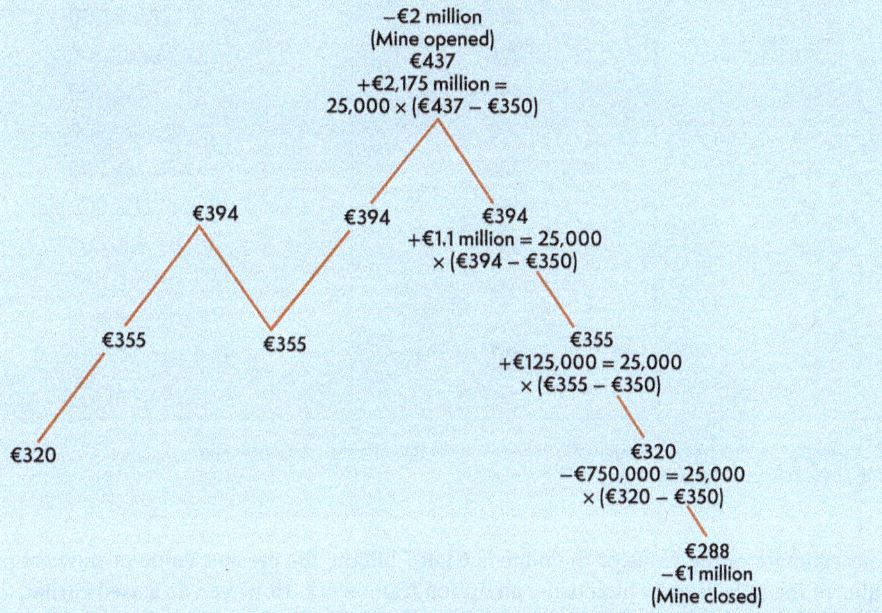

Imagine that this path is one of the 5,000 simulated price paths for palladium. Because p_{open} = €410 and p_{close} = €290, the mine is opened when the price reaches €437. The mine is closed when the price reaches €288.

Step 6

The final step is to compare the different expected discounted cash flows from Step 5 for the range of possible choices for p_{open} and p_{close} and to pick the highest one. This is the best estimate of the expected value of the mine. The values for p_{close} and p_{open} corresponding to this estimate are the points at which to open a closed mine and to shut an open one.

As mentioned in Step 3, there are 15 different values for p_{open} and 25 different values for p_{close}, implying 375 (= 15 × 25) different pairs. Consider Table 23.3, which shows the present values associated with the 20 best pairs. The table indicates that the best pair is p_{open} = €400 and p_{close} = €140, with a present value of €1.467 billion. This number represents the average present value across 5,000 simulations, all assuming the preceding values of p_{open} and p_{close}. The next best pair is p_{open} = €460 and p_{close} = €300, with a present value of €1.459 billion. The third best pair has a somewhat lower present value, and so on.

Table 23.3 Valuation of Palladium Mine for the 20 Best Choices of p_{open} and p_{close}

p_{open} (€)	p_{close} (€)	Estimated Value of Palladium Mine (€)
400	140	1,466,720,900
460	300	1,459,406,200
380	290	1,457,838,700
370	100	1,455,131,900
360	190	1,449,708,200
420	150	1,448,711,400
430	340	1,448,450,200
430	110	1,445,396,500
470	200	1,435,687,400

p_{open} (€)	p_{close} (€)	Estimated Value of Palladium Mine (€)
500	320	1,427,512,000
410	290	1,426,483,500
420	290	1,423,865,300
400	160	1,423,061,900
360	320	1,420,748,700
360	180	1,419,112,000
380	280	1,417,405,400
450	310	1,416,238,000
450	280	1,409,709,800
440	220	1,408,269,100
440	240	1,403,398,100

Note: For our simulation, Norilsk Nickel opens the mine whenever the palladium price rises above p_{open} and closes the mine whenever the palladium price falls below p_{close}.

Of course, our estimate of the value of the mine is €1.467 billion, the present value of the best pair of choices. Note that the value of the mine is quite high using an option framework. However, as stated earlier, the mine would appear worthless if a regular discounted cash flow approach were used. This occurs because the initial palladium price of €320 is below the extraction cost of €350.

This example is not easy, either in concepts or in implementation. However, the extra work involved in mastering this example is worth it because the example illustrates the type of modelling that actually occurs in corporate finance departments in the real world.

Furthermore, the example illustrates the benefits of the binomial approach. We merely calculate the cash flows associated with each of a number of simulations, discount the cash flows from each simulation and average present values across the simulations. Because the Black-Scholes model is not amenable to simulations, it cannot be used for this type of problem. In addition, there are a number of other situations where the binomial model is more appropriate than the Black-Scholes model. It is well known, for example, that the Black-Scholes model cannot properly handle options with dividend payments prior to the expiration date. This model also does not adequately handle the valuation of an American put. By contrast, the binomial model can easily handle both of these situations.

Thus, any student of corporate finance should be well versed in both models. The Black-Scholes model should be used whenever appropriate because it is simpler to use than is the binomial model. However, for the more complex situations where the Black-Scholes model breaks down, the binomial model becomes a necessary tool.

23.6 Options and Capital Budgeting

We now consider two issues regarding capital budgeting. What we will show is that, for a leveraged firm, the shareholders might prefer a lower NPV project to a higher one. We then show that they might even prefer a *negative* NPV project to a positive NPV project.

As usual, we will illustrate these points first with an example. Here is the basic background information for the firm:

Market value of assets	£20 million
Face value of pure discount debt	£40 million
Debt maturity	5 years
Asset return standard deviation	50%

The risk-free rate is 4 per cent. As we have now done several times, we can calculate equity and debt values:

	£
Market value of equity	5.724 million
Market value of debt	14.276 million

This firm has a fairly high degree of leverage: the debt–equity ratio based on market values is £14.276/£5.724 = 2.5, or 250 per cent. This is high, but not unheard of. Notice also that the option here is out of the money; as a result, the delta is 0.546.

The firm has two mutually exclusive investments under consideration. The projects affect both the market value of the firm's assets and the firm's asset return standard deviation as follows:

	Project A	Project B
NPV	£4	£2
Market value of firm's assets (£20 + NPV)	£24	£22
Firm's asset return standard deviation	40%	60%

Which project is better? It is obvious that project A has the higher NPV, but by now you are wary of the change in the firm's asset return standard deviation. One project reduces it; the other increases it. To see which project the shareholders like better, we have to go through our by now familiar calculations:

	Project A (£)	Project B (£)
Market value of equity	5.938	8.730
Market value of debt	18.062	13.270

There is a dramatic difference between the two projects. Project A benefits both the shareholders and the bondholders, but most of the gain goes to the bondholders. Project B has a huge impact on the value of the equity, plus it reduces the value of the debt. Clearly the shareholders prefer B.

What are the implications of our analysis? Basically, we have discovered two things. First, when the equity has a delta significantly smaller than 1.0, any value created will go partially to bondholders. Second, shareholders have a strong incentive to increase the variance of the return on the firm's assets. More specifically, shareholders will have a strong preference for variance-increasing projects as opposed to variance-decreasing ones, even if that means a lower NPV.

Let us do one final example. Here is a different set of numbers:

Market value of assets	£20 million
Face value of pure discount debt	£100 million
Debt maturity	5 years
Asset return standard deviation	50%

The risk-free rate is 4 per cent, so the equity and debt values are these:

	£
Market value of equity	2 million
Market value of debt	18 million

Notice that the change from our previous example is that the face value of the debt is now £100 million, so the option is far out of the money. The delta is only 0.24, so most of any value created will go to the bondholders.

The firm has an investment under consideration that must be taken now or never. The project affects both the market value of the firm's assets and the firm's asset return standard deviation as follows:

Project NPV	– £1 million
Market value of firm's assets (£20 million + NPV)	£19 million
Firm's asset return standard deviation	70%

Thus, the project has a negative NPV, but it increases the standard deviation of the firm's return on assets. If the firm takes the project, here is the result:

	£
Market value of equity	4.821 million
Market value of debt	14.179 million

This project more than doubles the value of the equity! Shareholders have a strong incentive to increase volatility, particularly when the option is far out of the money. What is happening is that the shareholders have relatively little to lose because bankruptcy is the likely outcome. As a result, there is a strong incentive to go for a long shot, even if that long shot has a negative NPV. It is a bit like using your very last euro on a lottery ticket. It is a bad investment, but there are not a lot of other options!

Sustainability in Action 23.1

Sustainable Investment at Microsoft

Microsoft has made headlines with its commitment to sustainability. Its innovative 'Carbon Negative' pledge promises to remove more carbon than it emits by 2030. Furthermore, it aims to remove all the carbon it has historically released by 2050. To meet these goals, Microsoft is investing in a variety of sustainability projects, illustrating the use of real options in practice.

A notable example is its investment in Climeworks (www.climeworks.com), a company that captures carbon directly from the air. This commitment can be viewed as a real option – an investment with a significant up-front cost but a range of possible future benefits. If Climeworks' technology proves viable and cost-effective, Microsoft will be well positioned to benefit. It may allow it to offset its carbon emissions more efficiently, or possibly even profit from selling captured carbon.

Microsoft's commitment to renewable energy is another example. It has invested in wind and solar projects and is using green power purchasing agreements (PPAs) to finance these investments. These PPAs can also be seen as real options. If renewable energy prices fall, Microsoft will be able to buy electricity at a lower cost. If prices rise, it will still be protected by the PPA price.

Summary and Conclusions

Real options, which are pervasive in business, are not captured by net present value analysis. Chapter 8 valued real options via decision trees. Given the work on options in Chapter 22, we are now able to value real options according to the Black-Scholes model and the binomial model.

In this chapter, we described six different types of options:

1. Executive share options, which are technically not real options
2. The option to expand and abandon operations
3. The embedded option in a start-up company
4. The option in simple business contracts
5. The option to shut down and reopen a project
6. Options and capital budgeting.

We tried to keep the presentation simple and straightforward from a mathematical point of view. The binomial approach to option pricing in Chapter 22 was extended to many periods. This adjustment brings us closer to the real world because the assumption of only two prices at the end of an interval is more plausible when the interval is short.

Questions and Problems

CONCEPT

1 **Executive Share Options** Why do companies issue options to executives if they cost the company more than they are worth to the executive? Why not just give cash and split the difference? Wouldn't that make both the company and the executive better off?

2 **Real Options** What are the two options that many businesses have? Why does a traditional NPV analysis tend to underestimate the value of an investment opportunity? Explain.

3 **Valuing a Start-up** Given that anything is possible in the future, why can't an entrepreneur who is seeking funding choose assumptions that make a start-up look good when it isn't? Is this more a danger with real option analysis than with normal capital budgeting analysis?

4 **The Binomial Model** Why is the binomial model more appropriate for real option analysis than Black-Scholes?

5 **Executive Stock Options** Do you think that executive stock options motivate executives to act in the best interests of the company? Explain.

REGULAR

6 **Stock Option Exercises and Share Prices** The stock price of ABC plc is currently at £30, and the company has 2 million shares outstanding. The company's CEO exercises 200,000 stock options with a strike price of £20. What will happen to the share price of ABC plc?

7 **Real Options** Utility companies often face a decision to build new plants that burn coal, oil or both. If the prices of both coal and gas are highly volatile, how valuable is the decision to build a plant that can burn either coal or oil? What happens to the value of this option as the correlation between coal and oil prices increases?

8 **Real Options and Sustainability** As a corporation committed to sustainable development, your company seeks to align its business strategies with the United Nations Sustainable Development Goals (SDGs), particularly SDG3: Good Health and Well-being. This goal focuses on ensuring healthy lives and promoting well-being for all ages. Within this context, your company possesses a vacant plot in a suburban locale.

In relation to pursuing SDG3, what potential advantages might your company gain by delaying the development of the vacant suburban plot? What real options relating to SDG3 exist and how do you think you could value these?

9 **Real Options and Spare Capacity** Ventiora SpA has a disused warehouse it is holding until land prices increase before selling to potential buyers. In option terminology, what type of option(s) does the company have on the warehouse?

10 **Real Options and Capital Budgeting** Most companies use traditional capital budgeting techniques, such as payback period and net present value. Why do you think this is the case? How would you justify the use of real option methodology to a reluctant chief executive?

11 **Insurance as an Option** Insurance, whether purchased by a corporation or an individual, is in essence an option. What type of option is an insurance policy?

12 **Real Options and Competition** How would the analysis of real options change if a company has competitors?

13 **Employee Share Options** Kevin Swinson is the finance director of Mountainbrook Trading plc. The board of directors has just granted Mr Swinson 30,000 at-the-money European call options on the company's equity, which is currently trading at £30 per share. The equity pays no dividends. The options will expire in four years, and the standard deviation of the returns on the shares is 55 per cent. Treasury bills that mature in four years currently yield a continuously compounded interest rate of 3 per cent.

(a) Use the Black-Scholes model to calculate the value of the share options.

(b) You are Mr Swinson's financial adviser. He must choose between the previously mentioned share option package and an immediate £500,000 bonus. If he is risk-neutral, which would you recommend?

(c) How would your answer to (b) change if Mr Swinson were risk-loving and he could not sell the options prior to expiration?

14 **Employee Share Options** Joseph-Benoit Suvee has just been named the new chief executive officer of BluBell Fitness NV. In addition to an annual salary of €400,000, his three-year contract states that his compensation will include 10,000 at-the-money European call options on the company's shares that expire in three years. The current share price is €40 per share, and the standard deviation of the returns on the firm's equity is 68 per cent.

The company does not pay a dividend. Treasury bills that mature in three years yield a continuously compounded interest rate of 5 per cent. Assume that Mr Suvee's annual salary payments occur at the end of the year and that these cash flows should be discounted at a rate of 9 per cent. Using the Black-Scholes model to calculate the value of the share options, determine the total value of the compensation package on the date the contract is signed.

15 **Binomial Model** Gasworks AG has been approached to sell up to 5 million litres of gasoline in three months at a price of €1.85 per litre. Gasoline is currently selling on the wholesale market at €1.65 per litre and has a standard deviation of 46 per cent. If the risk-free rate is 6 per cent per year, what is the value of this option?

16 **Real Options: Two-state Valuation** Webber plc is an international conglomerate with a real estate division that owns the right to erect an office building on a parcel of land on the outskirts of Leeds over the next year. This building would cost £10.5 million to construct. Due to low demand for office space in the area, such a building is worth approximately £10 million today. If demand increases, the building would be worth £12.5 million a year from today. If demand decreases, the same office building would be worth only £8 million in a year. The company can borrow and lend at the risk-free rate of 2.5 per cent effective annual rate. A local competitor in the real estate business has recently offered £750,000 for the right to build an office building on the land. Should the company accept this offer? Use a two-state model to value the real option.

17 **Real Options: Option to Buy** You run a global education company committed to quality education. Your company's mission is to ensure inclusive and equitable quality education and promote lifelong learning opportunities for all. In this context, your company is involved in providing educational resources and infrastructure to communities in need. Your firm has been given the option to purchase four new mobile libraries at a price of $2.25 million per unit from one supplier. This offer is only valid for the next two months. Concurrently, you are in negotiation with another provider for similar mobile libraries, but the purchase price has not yet been finalized. Your financial team believes there's a 75 per cent chance you can purchase the libraries from the second provider for $2 million each. However, if negotiations are unsuccessful, the only alternative deal available would be at $3.5 million per unit. The negotiations are expected to conclude in two months, and the outcome is uncertain until then. Your company can borrow or lend at 4 per cent per annum. What is the value of the option to buy the mobile libraries at $2.25 million per unit?

18 **Real Options: Bid Price** Jet Black is an international conglomerate with a petroleum division and is currently competing in an auction to win the right to drill for crude oil on a large piece of land in one year. The current market price of crude oil is $55 per barrel, and the land is believed to contain 125,000 barrels of oil. If found, the oil would cost $10 million to extract. Treasury bills that mature in one year yield a continuously compounded interest rate of 6.5 per cent, and the standard deviation of the returns on the price of crude oil is 50 per cent. Use the Black-Scholes model to calculate the maximum bid that the company should be willing to make at the auction.

19 **Real Options and Leases** Sardano and Sons is a large publicly held company that is considering leasing a warehouse. One of the company's divisions specializes in manufacturing steel and this particular warehouse is the only facility in the area that suits the firm's operations. The current price of steel is £3,600 per ton. If the price of steel falls over the next six months, the company will purchase 400 tons of steel and produce 4,800 steel rods. Each steel rod will cost £120 to manufacture and the company plans to sell the rods for £360 each. It will take only a matter of days to produce and sell the steel rods. If the price of steel rises or remains the same, it will not be profitable to undertake the project, and the company will allow the lease to expire without producing any steel rods. Treasury bills that mature in six months yield a continuously compounded interest rate of 4.5 per cent, and the standard deviation of the returns on steel is 45 per cent. Use the Black-Scholes model to determine the maximum amount that the company should be willing to pay for the lease.

20 **Real Options: Option to Abandon** Mouillez Pour L'été SA (MPLE) manufactures filters for swimming pools. The company is deciding whether to implement a new technology in its pool filters. One year from now the company will know whether the new technology is accepted in the market. If the demand for the new filters is high, the present value of the cash flows in one year will be €10 million. Conversely, if the demand is low, the value of the cash flows in one year will be €6 million. The value of the project today under these assumptions is €9.1 million and the risk-free rate is 6 per cent. Suppose that, in one year, if the demand for the new technology is low, the company can sell the technology for €7 million. What is the value of the option to abandon?

CHALLENGE

21 **Binomial Model** There is an American put option on an equity that expires in two months. The share price is €13.20 and the standard deviation of the share price returns is 35 per cent. The option has a strike price of €14.00 and the risk-free interest rate is a 3.5 per cent annual percentage rate. What is the price of the put option today using one-month steps? (*Hint:* How will you find the value of the option if it can be exercised early? When would you exercise the option early?)

22 **Real Options** You are in discussions to purchase an option on an office building with a strike price of £47 million. The building is currently valued at £45 million. The option will allow you to purchase the building either six months from today or one year from today. Six months from today, accrued rent payments from the building in the amount of £500,000 will be made to the owners. If you exercise the option in six months, you will receive the accrued rent payments; otherwise, the payment will be made to the current owners. A second accrued rent payment of £500,000 will be paid one year from today with the same payment terms. The standard deviation of the value of the building is 25 per cent, and the risk-free rate is an 8 per cent annual percentage rate. What is the price of the option today using six-month steps? (*Hint:* The value of the building in six months will be reduced by the accrued rent payment if you do not exercise the option at that time.)

23 **Water Resource Management and Sanitation Infrastructure** Fan and Zhu (2010) propose a real options framework to value oil exploration projects in the presence of three sources of uncertainty: the overseas investment environment, the exchange rate and the oil price. How can the real options framework be adapted and applied to investment evaluations in water resource management and sanitation infrastructure projects? Explain how the real options methodology can aid in investment evaluation for these types of projects.

24 **Downsizing and Shared Services** With increased globalization, many firms have chosen to share services or facilities with another firm in different countries. An example is the joint venture by Fiat and Chrysler to share their manufacturing facilities in Europe and North America. Explain how the real options approach can be used to assess the value of this type of investment decision.

25 **Electrical Interconnectors** In the electricity industry, interconnectors give the owner the option to transmit electricity to one of two locations. Show, using your own example, how real option analysis can be used to value an electrical interconnector.

26 **Research and Development** You have recently been employed as a finance consultant to a growing company, R&D Industries, which consistently develops successful products. After a meeting with the company's management, you estimate that the company produces, on average, two new product proposals every three years. The company's management informs you that the investment opportunities the company produces typically have an initial investment requirement of £10 million and return annual cash flows of £1 million in perpetuity. After conducting a scenario analysis, you estimate that these cash flows could grow at one of three possible rates, which have an equal probability of occurring: –3 per cent, 0 per cent and 3 per cent. The company's management tells you that the projects are 'take it or leave it' opportunities. In other words, the company does not have the option to wait to invest under more favourable circumstances.

(a) If the company's cost of capital is 12 per cent, what is the present value of the company's future growth opportunities under each scenario?

(b) Which projects would be accepted or rejected?

Exam Question (45 minutes)

1 Your firm is considering a bid for a financially distressed football club that is in administration. The administrators have said you must pay an exclusivity fee of £500,000 to develop the bid further, show the seriousness of your bid and present your commitment to resolving the issue. There are three potential bidders and the exclusivity fee will guarantee you a period of one month in which you will be sole bidder. Since the club is in administration, your investment will be used to pay off all the outstanding creditors of the club, who are owed a total of £134 million. Your plan is to enter into a company voluntary agreement (CVA) with the creditors where they will receive £0.06 for every £1 of debt and you have estimated that there is a 50 per cent probability that they will accept. If this were to happen, you estimate the NPV of the bid is £3 million. However, if they do not accept the CVA, the bid will not go ahead and your exclusivity fee will be lost. Your company can borrow and lend at the risk-free rate of 6 per cent per annum. Is it worthwhile for you to pay the exclusivity fee? Explain. **(40 marks)**

2 What are the benefits of real option methodology over traditional methods? Why, in your opinion, do many firms not use real options to value investments? Explain. **(30 marks)**

3 In real options analysis, why is the binomial model preferred to Black-Scholes? Explain your answer, using a quantitative example. **(30 marks)**

Total: 100 Marks

Mini Case

Exotic Cuisines Employee Share Options

As a new university graduate, you have taken a management position with Exotic Cuisines plc, a restaurant chain that went public just last year. The company's restaurants specialize in exotic main dishes, using ingredients such as wild boar, crocodile and pheasant. A concern you had going in was that the restaurant business is very risky. However, after some due diligence, you discovered a common misperception about the restaurant industry. It is widely thought that 90 per cent of new restaurants close within three years; however, recent evidence suggests the failure rate is closer to 60 per cent over three years. So it is a risky business, although not as risky as you originally thought.

During your interview process, one of the benefits mentioned was employee share options. Upon signing your employment contract, you received options with a strike price of £50 for 10,000 shares of company equity. As is fairly common, your share options have a three-year vesting period and a 10-year expiration, meaning that you cannot exercise the options for three years and you lose them if you leave before they vest. After the three-year vesting period, you can exercise the options at any time. Thus, the employee share options are European (and subject to forfeit) for the first three years and American afterwards. Of course, you cannot sell the options, nor can you enter into any sort of hedging agreement. If you leave the company after the options vest, you must exercise within 90 days or forfeit.

Exotic Cuisines equity is currently trading at £24.38 per share, a slight increase from the initial offering price last year. There are no market-traded options on the company's equity. Because the company has been traded for only about a year, you are reluctant to use the historical returns to estimate the standard deviation of the equity's return. However, you have estimated that the average annual standard deviation for restaurant company shares is about 55 per cent. Because Exotic Cuisines is a newer restaurant chain, you decide to use a 60 per cent standard deviation in your calculations. The company is relatively young, and you expect that all earnings will be reinvested back into the company for the near future. Therefore, you expect no dividends will be paid for at least the next 10 years. A three-year Treasury note currently has a yield of 3.8 per cent and a 10-year Treasury note has a yield of 4.4 per cent.

1. You are trying to value your options. What minimum value would you assign? What is the maximum value you would assign?
2. Suppose that, in three years, the company's equity is trading at £60. At that time should you keep the options or exercise them immediately? What are some of the important determinants in making such a decision?
3. Your options, like most employee share options, are not transferable or tradable. Does this have a significant effect on the value of the options? Why?
4. Why do you suppose employee share options usually have a vesting provision? Why must they be exercised shortly after you depart the company even after they vest?
5. As we have seen, much of the volatility in a company's share price is due to systematic or market-wide risks. Such risks are beyond the control of a company and its employees. What are the implications for employee share options? In light of your answer, can you recommend an improvement over traditional employee share options?

Practical Case Study

Consider the cement example from Chapter 8. What are the real options that exist for the project? How would you incorporate these into your consultancy work? What would be the process you would follow to arrive at future decisions and what would be the main inputs into your analysis?

Relevant Accounting Standards

The important standard for executive share options is IFRS 2 *Share-based Payment.* Although not directly linked to real option analysis, there is an accounting standard for exploration and mining activities. This is IFRS 6 *Exploration for and Evaluation of Mineral Resources.* Visit the IASPlus website (www.iasplus.com) for more information.

References

Fan, Y. and L. Zhu (2010) 'A Real Options Based Study on Overseas Oil Investment and its Application in China's Overseas Oil Investment', *Energy Economics*, Vol. 32, 627–637.

Hull, J.C. (2012) *Options, Futures, and Other Derivatives*, 8th edn. Upper Saddle River, NJ: Prentice Hall.

Additional Reading

This chapter focuses on practical applications of real option analysis and, consequently, the reading list reflects this. The references are categorized into executive compensation research (which should also be read in conjunction with material in Chapter 2) and other research related to the application of real option analysis.

Executive Compensation

1 Babenko, L. (2009) 'Share Repurchases and Pay-Performance Sensitivity of Employee Compensation Contracts', *Journal of Finance*, Vol. 64, No. 1, 117–150. **USA.**

2 Brockman, P., X. Martin and E. Unlu (2010) 'Executive Compensation and the Maturity Structure of Corporate Debt', *Journal of Finance*, Vol. 65, No. 3, 1123–1161.

3 Burns, N. and S. Kedia (2006) 'The Impact of Performance-based Compensation on Misreporting', *Journal of Financial Economics*, Vol. 79, No. 1, 35–57. **USA.**

4 Burns, N., B.C. McTier and K. Minnick (2015) 'Equity-incentive Compensation and Payout Policy in Europe', *Journal of Corporate Finance*, Vol. 30, 85–97.

5 Bolton, P., H. Mehran and J. Shapiro (2015) 'Executive Compensation and Risk Taking', *Review of Finance*, Vol. 19, No. 6, 2139–2181.

6 Chhaochharia, V. and Y. Grinstein (2009) 'CEO Compensation and Board Structure', *Journal of Finance*, Vol. 64, No. 1, 231–261. **USA.**

7 Coles, J.L., N.D. Daniel and L. Naveen (2006) 'Managerial Incentives and Risk Taking', *Journal of Financial Economics*, Vol. 80, No. 2, 431–468. **USA.**

8 Cvitanic, J., Z. Wiener and F. Zapatero (2008) 'Analytic Pricing of Employee Stock Options', *Review of Financial Studies*, Vol. 21, No. 2, 683–724. **USA.**

9 De Cesari, A. and N. Ozkan (2015) 'Executive Incentives and Payout Policy: Empirical Evidence from Europe', *Journal of Banking & Finance*, Vol. 55, 70–91.

10 Edmans, A., X. Gabaix and D. Jenter (2017) 'Executive Compensation: A Survey of Theory and Evidence', *Handbook of the Economics of Corporate Governance* (Vol. 1, pp. 383–539). North-Holland.

11 Efendi, J., A. Srivastava and E.P. Swanson (2007) 'Why Do Corporate Managers Misstate Financial Statements? The Role of Option Compensation and Other Factors', *Journal of Financial Economics*, Vol. 85, No. 3, 667–708. **USA.**

12 Frydman, C. and R.E. Saks (2010) 'Executive Compensation: A New View from a Long-term Perspective, 1930–2005', *Review of Financial Studies*, Vol. 23, No. 5, 2099–2138.

13 Graham, J.R., S. Li and J. Qiu (2012) 'Managerial Attributes and Executive Compensation', *Review of Financial Studies*, Vol. 25, No. 1, 144–186.

14 Gregoric, A., S. Polanec and S. Slapnicar (2010) 'Pay Me Right: Reference Values and Executive Compensation', *European Financial Management*, Vol. 16, No. 5, 778–804. **Europe.**

15 Kato, H.K., M. Lemmon, M. Luo and J. Schalheim (2005) 'An Empirical Examination of the Costs and Benefits of Executive Stock Options: Evidence from Japan', *Journal of Financial Economics*, Vol. 78, No. 2, 435–461. **Japan.**

16 Klein, D. (2018) 'Executive Turnover and the Valuation of Stock Options', *Journal of Corporate Finance*, Vol. 48, 76–93.

17 Narayanan, M.P. and H.N. Seyhun (2008) 'The Dating Game: Do Managers Designate Option Grant Dates to Increase the Compensation?', *Review of Financial Studies*, Vol. 21, No. 5, 1907–1945. **USA.**

Other Relevant Research

18 Ang, A. and N.P.B. Bollen (2010) 'Locked Up by a Lockup: Valuing Liquidity as a Real Option', *Financial Management*, Vol. 39, No. 3, 1069–1096.

19 Fan, Y. and L. Zhu (2010) 'A Real Options Based Model and its Application to China's Overseas Oil Investment Decisions', *Energy Economics*, Vol. 32, No. 3, 627–637. **China.**

20 Hackbarth, D. and E. Morellec (2008) 'Stock Returns in Mergers and Acquisitions', *Journal of Finance*, Vol. 63, No. 3, 1213–1252. **USA.**

21 Hillier, D. and A. Marshall (1998) 'A Model of Complex Equity Funding for Contingent Acquisitions – A Case Study of Non-interest Bearing Convertible Unsecured Loan Stock', *Journal of Corporate Finance*, Vol. 4, No. 2, 133–152. **UK.**

22 Su, N., R. Akkiraju, N. Nayak and R. Goodwin (2009) 'Shared Services Transformation: Conceptualization and Valuation from the Perspective of Real Options', *Decision Sciences*, Vol. 40, No. 3, 381–402.

Endnotes

1 We ignore warrant dilution in this example. See Chapter 24 for a discussion of warrant dilution.

2 As we will see later, here *u* and *d* are consistent with a standard deviation of the annual return on heating oil of 0.63.

3 For simplicity, we ignore both storage costs and a convenience yield.

4 Though it is not apparent at first glance, we will see later that the price movement in Figure 23.3 is consistent with the price movement in Figure 23.2.

5 For simplicity, we ignore interest compounding.

6 See Hull (2012) for a derivation of these formulas.

7 In this discussion we have used both *intervals* and *dates*. To keep the terminology straight, remember that the number of intervals is always one less than the number of dates. For example, if a model has two dates, it has only one interval.

Chapter 24
Warrants and Convertibles

Learning Objectives

After reading this chapter you should be able to:

LO1 Define key terms related to warrants and convertible bonds.

LO2 Explain the difference between warrants and call options.

LO3 Apply the Black-Scholes Model to calculate the theoretical price of a warrant.

LO4 Evaluate the value of convertible bonds by examining the bond's terms, the underlying stock's price, volatility and other relevant factors.

LO5 Justify the reasons for issuing warrants and convertible bonds from the perspective of a company's management.

Source: Andrii Yalanskyi/123RF

In the past few years, there has been a major paradigm shift in the way in which corporate finance is practised. We have come through a sustained period of deregulation and globalization in the world's markets. Financial innovation and the introduction of new securities have been commonplace as a result of the free markets that have spread throughout the world. However, things are very much different going into the second decade of the twenty-first century.

The financial world has seen a glut of corporate insolvencies. Governments of the major developed economies have all reduced interest rates to near zero and pumped cash into their ailing firms. Whole industries have effectively been nationalized and purchased by governments. Corporate strategies that were successful because of the availability of cheap debt are no longer possible. Finally, financial instruments that may have been viable and popular in a vibrant economy have become obsolete.

Convertible bonds are part of many companies' capital structure. They allow bondholders to convert the debt instruments into equity during a specified window in the future. The conversion feature is an embedded option that holders will exercise if the convertible is in the money. At the turn of the century, these became exceptionally popular investment targets of hedge funds that looked for a quick return from conversion and although we have seen much market volatility in recent times, convertible bonds are more popular than ever.

Warrants are similar to standard call options, except that the company must issue new shares if the holder chooses to exercise them. Because of changes in the global financial environment they have become less popular. However, they are present in the financial structure of many companies and tend to be issued in conjunction with standard bond issues.

This chapter is concerned with valuing the option embedded in these financial instruments.

Key Notations

#	Number of shares outstanding	σ^2	Variance (per year) of the continuous share price return
#w	Number of warrants	t	Time (in years) to expiration date
c_w	Value of a call option written on the equity of a firm *without* warrants	N(d)	Probability that a standardized, normally distributed, random variable will be less than or equal to d
S	Current share price		
E	Exercise price of option		
R	Annual risk-free rate of return, continuously compounded		$d_1 = [\ln(S/E) + (R + \sigma^2/2)t]/\sqrt{\sigma^2 t}$ $d_2 = d_1 - \sqrt{\sigma^2 t}$

24.1 Warrants

Warrants are securities that give holders the right, but not the obligation, to buy shares of equity directly from a company at a fixed price for a given period. Each warrant specifies the number of shares of equity that the holder can buy, the exercise price and the expiration date.

From the preceding description of warrants, it is clear that they are similar to call options. The differences in contractual features between warrants and the call options that trade on Euronext Liffe are small. For example, warrants have longer maturity periods. Some warrants are actually perpetual, meaning that they never expire.

Warrants are referred to as *equity kickers* because they are usually issued in combination with privately placed bonds.[1] In most cases, warrants are attached to the bonds when issued. The loan agreement will state whether the warrants are detachable from the bond – that is, whether they can be sold separately. Usually, the warrant can be detached immediately.

In the past few years, only a very few corporations have issued warrants and these have largely been in the United States. In recent times, governments purchased warrants from banks that needed financial assistance, and in the Greek sovereign debt bailout, bondholders received GDP-linked warrants that pay off if the Greek economy beats growth expectations.[2]

To illustrate warrants, we will focus on a hypothetical example of a firm, Hellas Shipping, which has issued warrants. Each warrant gives the holder the right to purchase one share of equity at an exercise price of €19.32 and the warrants expire in four years. The share price of Hellas Shipping is €17.57 and the price of a warrant is €4.05.

The relationship between the value of Hellas Shipping's warrants and its share price can be viewed as similar to the relationship between a call option and the share price, described in Section 22.7. Figure 24.1 depicts this relationship. The lower limit on the value of the warrants is zero if Hellas Shipping's share price is below €19.32 per share. If the price of Hellas Shipping's equity rises above €19.32 per share, the lower limit is the share price minus €19.32. The upper limit is the share price of Hellas Shipping. A warrant to buy one share of equity cannot sell at a price above the price of the underlying shares.

The price of Hellas Shipping's warrants was higher than the lower limit. The height of the warrant price above the lower limit will depend on the following:

- The variance of Hellas Shipping's share price returns
- The time to expiration date
- The risk-free rate of interest
- The share price of Hellas Shipping
- The exercise price
- Cash dividends.

With the exception of cash dividends, these are the same factors that determine the value of a call option.[3]

Warrants can also have unusual features. For example, when the French specialist metals group Carbone Lorraine was unable to raise financing for solar power acquisitions, it entered into a financing deal with

Figure 24.1 Relationship Between Warrant Value and Equity Value for Hellas Shipping

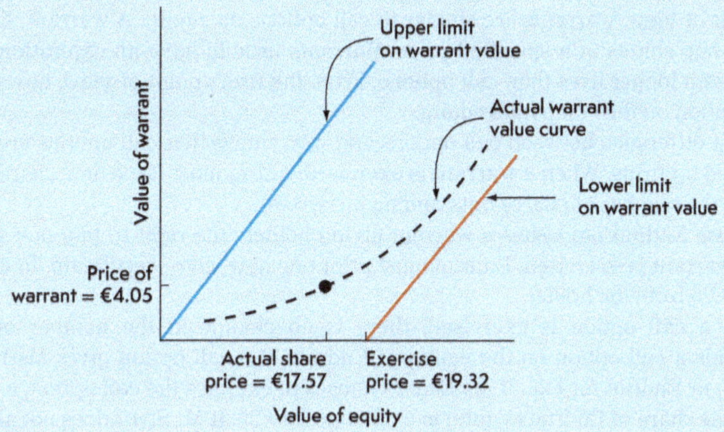

Société Générale. Under the deal, Carbone Lorraine issued convertible warrants to SocGen that allowed the French bank to buy up to 17.5 per cent of Carbone Lorraine's equity at a 10 per cent discount whenever the metals company needed funds. This innovative financing deal was a warrant, where the decision to exercise was with the issuer and not the holder. In effect, it mimicked an equity-linked credit line that bypassed the credit squeeze in the markets at the time.

Real World Insight 24.1

Windtree Therapeutics, Inc.

In the excerpt below, you can see the way in which a warrant issue is presented to potential investors. Notice how the wording uses legal terminology. This is because the press release must be no different from what is written in more detail in the legal prospectus. All of the information in the press release is enough to fully understand how the issue is structured and the impact of the issue on existing shareholders.

(*Excerpts from a Windtree Therapeutics, Inc. press release, 20 January 2023*)

Windtree Therapeutics, Inc. (NASDAQ: WINT) ('Windtree' or the 'Company') today announced it has entered into warrant inducement offer letters (the 'Inducement Offer Letters') to raise approximately $1.0 million in gross proceeds from the exercise of warrants to purchase 4,808,595 shares of the Company's common stock, par value $0.001 per share ('Common Stock'), in the aggregate.

Pursuant to the Inducement Offer Letters, the Company agreed to reduce the exercise price of certain of its previously issued warrants to $0.20 per share of Common Stock underlying such warrants. The warrants so amended include (i) warrants issued in December 2019 to purchase 78,643 shares of Common Stock (prior exercise price: $12.09 per share), (ii) warrants issued in May 2020 to purchase 279,889 shares of Common Stock (prior exercise price: $7.975 per share); and (iii) warrants issued in March 2021 to purchase 4,450,063 shares of Common Stock (prior exercise price: $3.60 per share) (collectively, the 'Warrants').

Concurrently with the reduction in exercise prices of the Warrants, the investors party to the Inducement Offer Letters agreed to exercise their Warrants at the reduced exercise price (collectively, the 'Warrant Exercise'). In addition, the Company agreed to issue to such investors new warrants to purchase 9,617,190 shares of Common Stock in the aggregate at an exercise price of $0.2152 per share (the 'New Warrants'). The New Warrants will be exercisable six months from the date of issuance and will expire five years from their initial exercise date.

The exercise of the Warrants is expected to result in gross proceeds to the Company of approximately $1.0 million, before deducting fees and expenses.

24.2 The Difference between Warrants and Call Options

From the holder's point of view, warrants are similar to call options on equity. A warrant, like a call option, gives its holder the right to buy shares at a specified price. Warrants usually have an expiration date, though in most cases they are issued with longer lives than call options. From the firm's point of view, however, a warrant is very different from a call option on the company's equity.

The most important difference between call options and warrants is that call options are issued by individuals and warrants are issued by firms. When a warrant is exercised, a firm must issue new shares of equity. Each time a warrant is exercised the number of shares outstanding increases.

To illustrate, suppose Endrun Ltd issues a warrant giving holders the right to buy one share of equity at €25. Further, suppose the warrant is exercised. Endrun must print one new share certificate. In exchange for the share certificate, it receives €25 from the holder.

In contrast, when a call option is exercised, there is no change in the number of shares outstanding. Suppose Ms Eager holds a call option on the equity of Endrun. The call option gives Ms Eager the right to buy one share of the equity of Endrun for €25. If Ms Eager chooses to exercise the call option, a seller, say Mr Swift, is obligated to give her one share of Endrun's equity in exchange for €25. If Mr Swift does not already own a share, he must enter the stock market and buy one. The call option is a side bet between buyers and sellers on the value of Endrun shares. When a call option is exercised, one investor gains and the other loses. The total number of shares outstanding of the Endrun Company remains constant, and no new funds are made available to the company.

Warrants also affect accounting numbers. Warrants and (as we shall see) convertible bonds cause the number of shares to increase. This causes the firm's net income to be spread over more shares, thereby decreasing earnings per share. Firms with significant amounts of warrants and convertible issues must report earnings on a primary basis and a fully diluted basis.

24.3 Warrant Pricing and the Black-Scholes Model

Chapter 22 Page 602

We now wish to express the gains from exercising a call and a warrant in more general terms (reread Section 22.8 for the Black-Scholes model). The gain on a call can be written like this:

Gain from exercising a single call

Equation 24.1

$$\underbrace{\frac{\text{Firm's value net of debt}}{\#}}_{\text{(Value of a share of equity)}} - \text{Exercise price}$$

We define the *firm's value net of debt* to be the total firm value less the value of the debt. The # stands for the number of shares outstanding. The ratio on the left is the value of a share of equity. The gain on a warrant can be written as follows:

Gain from exercising a single warrant

Equation 24.2

$$\underbrace{\frac{\text{Firm's value net of debt} + \text{Exercise price} \times \#_w}{\# + \#_w}}_{\text{(Value of a share of equity after warrant is exercised)}} - \text{Exercise price}$$

The numerator of the left term is the firm's value net of debt *after* the warrant is exercised. It is the sum of the firm's value net of debt *prior* to the warrant's exercise plus the proceeds the firm receives from the exercise. The proceeds equal the product of the exercise price multiplied by the number of warrants. The number of warrants appears as $\#_w$. (Our analysis uses the plausible assumption that all warrants in the money will be exercised.) The denominator, $\# + \#_w$, is the number of shares outstanding *after* the exercise of the warrants. The ratio on the left is the value of a share of equity after exercise. By rearranging terms, we can rewrite Equation 24.2 as follows.[4]

Gain from exercising a single warrant

Equation 24.3

$$\frac{\#_w}{\# + \#_w} \times \underbrace{\left(\frac{\text{Firm's value net of debt}}{\#} - \text{Exercise price}\right)}_{\text{(Gain from a call on a firm with no warrants)}}$$

Formula 24.3 relates the gain on a warrant to the gain on a call. Note that the term within parentheses is Equation 24.1. Thus, the gain from exercising a warrant is a proportion of the gain from exercising a call in a firm without warrants. The proportion $\#/(\# + \#_w)$ is the ratio of the number of shares in the firm without warrants to the number of shares after all the warrants have been exercised. This ratio must always be less than 1. Thus, the gain on a warrant must be less than the gain on an identical call in a firm without warrants.

The preceding implies that we can value a warrant using the Black-Scholes model, adjusted for the dilution effect:

Equation 24.4

$$w = \frac{1}{\left(1 + \frac{\#_w}{\#}\right)} c_w$$

where c_w is the value of a call option written on the equity of a firm *without* warrants.[5]

Example 24.1

Warrant Valuation

Veld NV is planning to issue 10,000 warrants that, when exercised, can be converted on a one-for-one basis. The proceeds of the warrant issuance will be distributed to the existing shareholders. Besides this dividend, the company is not planning to pay out any other cash dividend during the lifetime of the warrants. The company currently has 50,000 shares outstanding. If the share price of Veld NV is €2.50 and the exercise price of the warrants is €2.30, what is the value of the warrant today? The continuously compounded annual risk-free rate of interest is 7 per cent, the variance of returns of Veld NV is 0.09 and the time to expiry is one year.

Step 1. First we need to calculate the value of a comparable call option on the firm's equity. This is done by simply plugging the relevant values into the Black-Scholes Option Pricing Formula (see Chapter 22).

Step 1a. Calculate d_1 and d_2.

$$\begin{aligned}
d_1 &= \left[\ln\left(\frac{S}{E}\right) + (R + \sigma^2/2)t\right] / \sqrt{\sigma^2 t} \\
&= \left[\ln\left(\frac{€2.50}{€2.50}\right) + (0.07 + 0.09/2)1\right] / \sqrt{0.09} \\
&= [0.0834 + 0.115]/0.3 \;=\; 0.6613 \\
d_2 &= d_1 - \sqrt{\sigma^2 t} \\
&= 0.3613
\end{aligned}$$

Step 1b. Calculate $N(d_1)$ and $N(d_2)$ using a spreadsheet or tables.

$$N(d_1) = N(0.6613) = 0.7458$$
$$N(d_2) = N(0.3613) = 0.6411$$

Step 1c. Calculate c_w.

$$\begin{aligned}
c_w &= S \times [N(d_1)] - E_e^{-Rt} \times [N(d_2)] \\
&= €2.50 \times [N(d_1)] - €2.30 \times e^{-0.07} \times N(d_2) \\
&= (€2.50 \times 0.7458) - (€2.30 \times 0.9324 \times 0.6411) \\
&= €1.8645 - €1.3749 \\
&= €0.49
\end{aligned}$$

Step 2. The value of the Veld NV warrant is thus:

$$\begin{aligned}
W &= \frac{1}{\left(1 + \frac{\#_w}{\#}\right)} c_w = \frac{1}{\left(1 + \frac{10{,}000}{50{,}000}\right)} €0.49 \\
&= 0.8333(€0.49) \\
&= €0.4083
\end{aligned}$$

24.4 Convertible Bonds

A convertible bond is similar to a bond with warrants. The most important difference is that a bond with warrants can be separated into distinct securities and a convertible bond cannot. A convertible bond gives the holder the right to exchange it for a given number of shares any time up to and including the maturity date of the bond.

Preference shares can frequently be converted into equity. A convertible preference share is the same as a convertible bond except that it has an infinite maturity date.

Real World Insight 24.2

Convertibles

In 2019, Uber Technologies, Inc. paid $3.1 billion for its Middle Eastern counterpart, Careem, to strengthen the company's global dominance in taxi-like services.

The deal consisted of $1.4 billion in cash and $1.7 billion in convertible bonds for a 100 per cent ownership stake.

The notes will be convertible into Uber shares at a price equal to $55 apiece, Uber says, marking a nearly 13 per cent increase over Uber's share price in its last financing round, led by SoftBank Group Corp. more than a year ago.

Bond traders speak of the conversion price of the bond, which is equal to the share price at which the bond can be converted into equity. The conversion price of the Uber bond was $55, which represented a conversion premium of 13 per cent over the price the last time Uber went for new financing. The premium reflects the fact that the conversion option in Uber convertible bonds was *out of the money*. This conversion premium is typical, if slightly low.

The number of shares received for each bond is called the conversion ratio. At the time of writing, details of the conversion ratio were not available. However, assume the face value of each Uber bond was $5,500 and since the conversion price is $55, 100 shares (=5,500/55) would be received for each bond.

Convertibles are almost always protected against stock splits and share dividends. If Uber's equity had been split two for one, the conversion ratio would have increased from 100 to 200.

Conversion ratio, conversion price and conversion premium are well-known terms in the real world. For that reason alone, the student should master the concepts. However, conversion price and conversion premium implicitly assume that the bond is selling at par. If the bond is selling at another price, the terms have little meaning. By contrast, conversion ratio can have a meaningful interpretation regardless of the price of the bond.

24.5 The Value of Convertible Bonds

Chapter 5 Page 116

The value of a convertible bond can be described in terms of three components: straight bond value (see Chapter 5, Sections 5.1–5.3), conversion value and option value. We examine these three components next.

Straight Bond Value

The straight bond value is what the convertible bonds would sell for if they could not be converted into equity. It will depend on the general level of interest rates and on the default risk. Consider a convertible bond issued by a hypothetical firm, Cold Dawn plc. On 1 November 2020, Cold Dawn plc raised £300 million by issuing 6.75 per cent convertible subordinated debentures due in 2036. It planned to use the proceeds to invest in new plant and equipment. Like typical debentures, they had a sinking fund and were callable. Cold Dawn's bonds differed from other debentures in their convertible feature: each bond was convertible into 2,353 shares of Cold Dawn equity any time before maturity. When Cold Dawn issued its convertible bonds, its share price was £22.625. The conversion price of £42.50 (=£100,000/2,353) was 88 per cent higher than the actual equity price. Suppose that straight debentures issued by Cold Dawn plc had been rated A, and A-rated bonds were priced to yield 4 per cent per six months on 1 November 2020. The straight bond value of Cold Dawn convertible bonds can be determined by discounting the £3,375 semi-annual coupon payment and principal amount at 4 per cent:

$$\text{Straight bond} = \sum_{t=1}^{32} \frac{£3{,}375}{1.04^t} + \frac{£100{,}000}{(1.04)^{32}}$$
$$= £3{,}375 \times A_{0.04}^{32} + \frac{£100{,}000}{(1.04)^{32}}$$
$$= £60{,}323 + £28{,}506$$
$$= £88{,}829$$

The straight bond value of a convertible bond is a minimum value. The price of Cold Dawn's convertible could not have gone lower than the straight bond value.

Figure 24.2 illustrates the relationship between straight bond value and share price. In Figure 24.2 we have been somewhat dramatic and implicitly assumed that the convertible bond is default free. In this case, the straight bond value does not depend on the share price, so it is graphed as a straight line.

Figure 24.2 Minimum Value of a Convertible Bond Versus the Value of the Equity for a Given Interest Rate

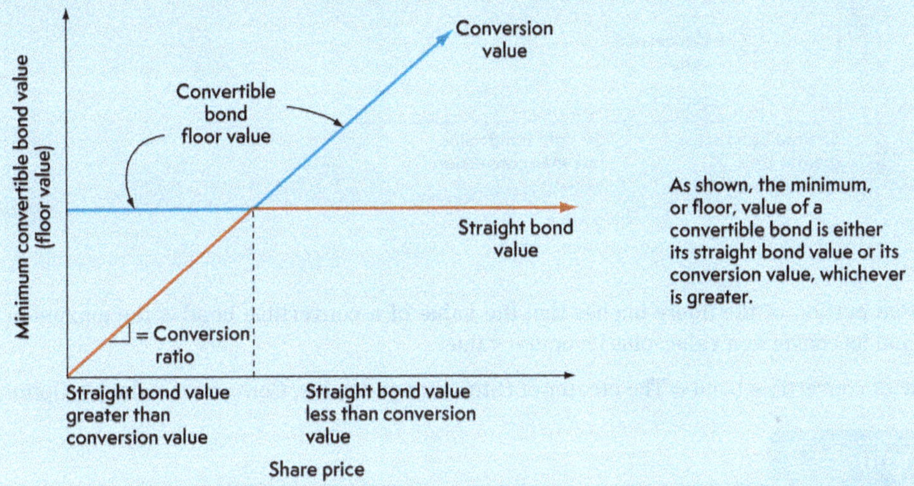

Conversion Value

The value of convertible bonds depends on conversion value. Conversion value is what the bonds would be worth if they were immediately converted into equity at current prices. Typically, we compute conversion value by multiplying the number of shares of equity that will be received when the bond is converted by the current price of the equity.

On 1 November 2020, each Cold Dawn convertible bond could have been converted into 2,353 shares of Cold Dawn equity. Cold Dawn shares were selling for £22.625. Thus, the conversion value was 2,353 × £22.625 = £53,237. A convertible cannot sell for less than its conversion value. Arbitrage prevents this from happening. If Cold Dawn's convertible sold for less than £53,237, investors would have bought the bonds and converted them into equity and sold the shares. The profit would have been the difference between the value of the shares sold and the bond's conversion value.

Thus, convertible bonds have two minimum values: the straight bond value and the conversion value. The conversion value is determined by the value of the firm's underlying equity. This is illustrated in Figure 24.2. As the value of equity rises and falls, the conversion price rises and falls with it. When the value of Cold Dawn's equity increased by £1, the conversion value of its convertible bonds increased by £2,353.

Option Value

The value of a convertible bond will generally exceed both the straight bond value and the conversion value.[6] This occurs because holders of convertibles need not convert immediately. Instead, by waiting they can take advantage of whichever is greater in the future: the straight bond value or the conversion value. This option to wait has value, and it raises the value over both the straight bond value and the conversion value.

When the value of the firm is low, the value of convertible bonds is most significantly influenced by their underlying value as straight debt. However, when the value of the firm is very high, the value of convertible bonds is mostly determined by their underlying conversion value. This is illustrated in Figure 24.3.

Figure 24.3 Value of a Convertible Bond versus the Value of the Equity for a Given Interest Rate

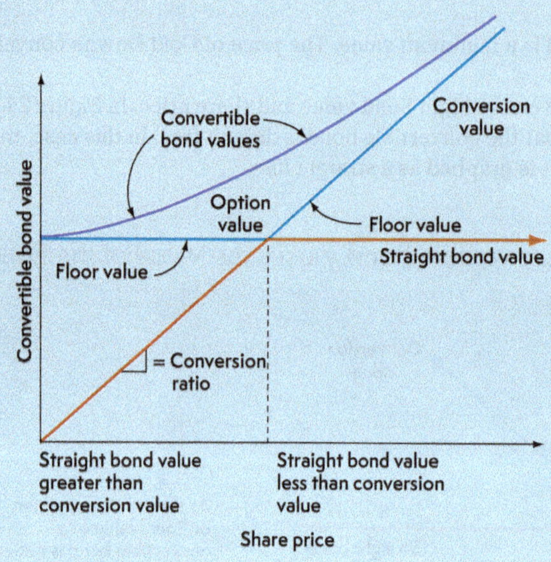

As shown, the value of a convertible bond is the sum of its floor value and its option value.

The bottom portion of the figure implies that the value of a convertible bond is the maximum of its straight bond value and its conversion value, plus its option value:

Value of convertible bond = The greater of (Straight bond value, Conversion value) + Option value

Example 24.2

Conversion

Suppose Avaya plc has outstanding 1,000 shares of equity and 100 bonds. Each bond has a face value of £100,000 at maturity. They are discount bonds and pay no coupons. At maturity each bond can be converted into 10 shares of newly issued equity.

What circumstances will make it advantageous for the holders of Avaya convertible bonds to convert to equity at maturity?

If the holders of the convertible bonds convert, they will receive 100 × 10 = 1,000 shares of equity. Because there were already 1,000 shares, the total number of shares outstanding becomes 2,000 upon conversion. Thus, converting bondholders own 50 per cent of the value of the firm, *V*. If they do not convert, they will receive £10,000,000 or *V*, whichever is less. The choice for the holders of the Avaya bonds is obvious. They should convert if 50 per cent of *V* is greater than £10,000,000. This will be true whenever *V* is greater than £20,000,000. This is illustrated as follows:

Payoff to Convertible Bondholders and Shareholders of Avaya plc

	(1) $V \leq$ £10,000,000	(2) £10,000,000 $< V \leq$ £20,000,000	(3) $V >$ £20,000,000
Decision:	Bondholders will not convert	Bondholders will not convert	Bondholders will convert
Convertible bondholders	V	£10,000,000	$0.5V$
Shareholders	0	V − £10,000,000	$0.5V$

Real World Insight 24.3

HSBC CoCos

The multinational bank, HSBC, has $2.25 billion of bonds that convert into shares if the bank's risk rises above a certain level. The contingent convertible bonds, or 'CoCos', have an annual coupon of 6.375 per cent, which will be converted into equity if the bank's regulatory capital falls below a specified benchmark. CoCos are becoming more popular because of regulatory requirements that banks keep below a certain level of risk. If a bank becomes financially risky, CoCos convert into equity and their financial leverage risk is subsequently lowered.

24.6 Reasons for Issuing Warrants and Convertibles

Probably there is no other area of corporate finance where real-world practitioners disagree as they do on the reasons for issuing convertible debt. To separate fact from fantasy, we present a rather structured argument. We first compare convertible debt with straight debt. Then we compare convertible debt with equity. For each comparison, we ask in which situations is the firm better off with convertible debt and in which it is worse off.

Convertible Debt versus Straight Debt

Convertible debt pays a lower interest rate than does otherwise identical straight debt. For example, if the interest rate is 10 per cent on straight debt, the interest rate on convertible debt might be 9 per cent. Investors will accept a lower interest rate on a convertible because of the potential gain from conversion.

Imagine a firm that seriously considers both convertible debt and straight debt finally deciding to issue convertibles. When would this decision have benefited the firm and when would it have hurt the firm? We consider two situations.

The Share Price Later Rises so that Conversion is Indicated

The firm clearly likes to see the share price rise. However, it would have benefited even more had it previously issued straight debt instead of a convertible. Although the firm paid out a lower interest rate than it would have with straight debt, it was obligated to sell the convertible holders a chunk of the equity at a below-market price.

The Share Price Later Falls or Does Not Rise Enough to Justify Conversion

The firm hates to see the share price fall. However, as long as the share price does fall, the firm is glad that it had previously issued convertible debt instead of straight debt. This is because the interest rate on convertible debt is lower. Because conversion does not take place, our comparison of interest rates is all that is needed.

Summary

Compared to straight debt, the firm is worse off having issued convertible debt if the underlying equity subsequently does well. The firm is better off having issued convertible debt if the underlying equity subsequently does poorly. In an efficient market, we cannot predict future share prices. Thus, we cannot argue that convertibles either dominate or are dominated by straight debt.

Convertible Debt versus Equity

Next, imagine a firm that seriously considers both convertible debt and equity but finally decides to issue convertibles. When would this decision benefit the firm and when would it hurt the firm? We consider our two situations.

The Share Price Later Rises so that Conversion is Indicated

The firm is better off having previously issued a convertible instead of equity. To see this, consider the Cold Dawn case. The firm could have issued equity for £22. Instead, by issuing a convertible, the firm effectively received £42.50 for a share upon conversion.

The Share Price Later Falls or Does Not Rise Enough to Justify Conversion

No firm wants to see its share price fall. However, given that the price did fall, the firm would have been better off if it had previously issued equity instead of a convertible. The firm would have benefited by issuing equity above its later market price. That is, the firm would have received more than the subsequent worth of the equity. However, the drop in share price did not affect the value of the convertible much because the straight bond value serves as a floor.

Summary

Compared with equity, the firm is better off having issued convertible debt if the underlying equity subsequently does well. The firm is worse off having issued convertible debt if the underlying equity subsequently does poorly. We cannot predict future share prices in an efficient market. Thus, we cannot argue that issuing convertibles is better or worse than issuing equity. The preceding analysis is summarized in Table 24.1.

Table 24.1 The Case For and Against Convertible Bonds (CBs)

	If Firm Subsequently Does Poorly	If Firm Subsequently Prospers
Convertible bonds (CBs)	No conversion because of low share price.	Conversion because of high share price.
Compared to: Straight bonds	CBs provide cheap financing because coupon rate is lower.	CBs provide expensive financing because bonds are converted, which dilutes existing equity.
Equity	CBs provide expensive financing because firm could have issued equity at high prices.	CBs provide cheap financing because firm issues equity at high prices when bonds are converted.

Modigliani–Miller (MM) pointed out that, abstracting from taxes and bankruptcy costs, the firm is indifferent to whether it issues equity or issues debt. The MM relationship is a quite general one. Their pedagogy could be adjusted to show that the firm is indifferent to whether it issues convertibles or issues other instruments. To save space (and the patience of students) we have omitted a full-blown proof of MM in a world with convertibles. However, our results are perfectly consistent with MM. Now we turn to the real-world view of convertibles.

The 'Free Lunch' Story

The preceding discussion suggests that issuing a convertible bond is no better and no worse than issuing other instruments. Unfortunately, many corporate executives fall into the trap of arguing that issuing convertible debt is actually better than issuing alternative instruments. This is a free lunch type of explanation, of which we are quite critical.

Example 24.3

Are Convertibles Always Better?

The share price of RW SE is €20. Suppose this company can issue subordinated debentures at 10 per cent. It can also issue convertible bonds at 6 per cent with a conversion value of €800. The conversion value means that the holders can convert a convertible bond into 40 (= €800/€20) shares of equity.

A company treasurer who believes in free lunches might argue that convertible bonds should be issued because they represent a cheaper source of financing than either subordinated bonds or equity. The treasurer will point out that, if the company does poorly and the price does not rise above €20, the convertible bondholders will not convert the bonds into equity. In this case the company will have obtained debt financing at below-market rates by attaching worthless equity kickers. On the other hand, if the firm does well and the price of its equity rises to €25 or above, convertible holders will convert. The company will issue 40 shares. The company will receive a bond with face value of €1,000 in exchange for issuing 40 shares of equity, implying a conversion price of €25. The company will have issued equity at €25 per share, or 20 per cent above the €20 equity price prevailing when the convertible bonds were issued. This enables it to lower its cost of equity capital. Thus, the treasurer happily points out, regardless of whether the company does well or poorly, convertible bonds are the cheapest form of financing.

Although this argument may sound quite plausible at first, there is a flaw. The treasurer is comparing convertible financing *with straight debt* when the share price subsequently falls. However, the treasurer compares convertible financing *with equity* when the share price subsequently rises. This is an unfair mixing of comparisons. By contrast, our analysis of Table 24.1 was fair because we examined both share price increases and decreases when comparing a convertible with each alternative instrument. We found that no single alternative dominated convertible bonds in *both* up and down markets.

The 'Expensive Lunch' Story

Suppose we stand the treasurer's argument on its head by comparing (1) convertible financing with straight debt when share prices rise, and (2) convertible financing with equity when share prices fall.

From Table 24.1, we see that convertible debt is more expensive than straight debt when share prices subsequently rise. The firm's obligation to sell convertible holders a chunk of equity at a below-market price more than offsets the lower interest rate on a convertible.

Also from Table 24.1, we see that convertible debt is more expensive than equity when share prices subsequently fall. Had the firm issued equity, it would have received a price higher than its subsequent worth. Therefore, the expensive lunch story implies that convertible debt is an inferior form of financing. Of course, we dismiss both the free lunch and the expensive lunch arguments.

A Reconciliation

In an efficient financial market there is neither a free lunch nor an expensive lunch. Convertible bonds can be neither cheaper nor more expensive than other instruments. A convertible bond is a package of straight debt and an option to buy equity. The difference between the market value of a convertible bond and the value of a straight bond is the price investors pay for the call option feature. In an efficient market, this is a fair price.

In general, if a company prospers, issuing convertible bonds will turn out to be worse than issuing straight bonds and better than issuing equity. In contrast, if a company does poorly, convertible bonds will turn out to be better than issuing straight bonds and worse than issuing equity.

24.7 Why Are Warrants and Convertibles Issued?

From studies it is known that firms that issue convertible bonds are different from other firms. Here are some of the differences:

- The bond ratings of firms using convertibles are lower than those of other firms.[7]
- Convertibles tend to be used by smaller firms with high growth rates and more financial leverage.[8]
- Convertibles are usually subordinated and unsecured.

The kind of company that uses convertibles provides clues to why they are issued. Here are some explanations that make sense.

Sustainability Objectives

Convertible bonds can play a unique role in sustainable firms for several reasons.

Linking conversion terms to sustainability goals: Companies can tie the conversion terms of a bond to their sustainability targets. For example, a bond could be structured so that the conversion ratio (i.e. the number of shares into which the bond can be converted) improves if the company hits certain environmental, social or governance (ESG) metrics. This provides a financial incentive for the firm to achieve its sustainability goals.

Attracting sustainable investors: Convertible bonds can be particularly attractive to sustainable investors. These investors look for investments that align with their values, and a convertible bond issued by a company committed to sustainability fits the bill. Furthermore, the potential for equity-like returns from the conversion feature can help to offset the perceived risk coming from investing in sustainability-focused companies, which may be operating in newer, less proven markets.

Green convertible bonds: A relatively new development in the sustainable finance space is the issuance of green convertible bonds. These are convertible bonds where the proceeds are specifically used to finance green projects. These bonds provide investors with not only the potential upside from the conversion feature but also the knowledge that their money is being used to support environmentally friendly initiatives.

Matching Cash Flows

If financing is costly, it makes sense to issue securities whose cash flows match those of the firm. A young, risky and (it hopes) growing firm might prefer to issue convertibles or bonds with warrants because these will have lower initial interest costs. When the firm is successful, the convertibles (or warrants) will be converted. This causes expensive dilution, but it occurs when the firm can most afford it.

Risk Synergy

Another argument for convertible bonds and bonds with warrants is that they are useful when it is very costly to assess the risk of the issuing company. Suppose you are evaluating a new product by a start-up company. The new product is a genetically engineered virus that may increase the yields of corn crops in northern climates. It may also cause cancer. This type of product is difficult to value properly. Thus, the risk of the company is very hard to determine: it may be high or it may be low. If you could be sure the risk of the company was high you would price the bonds for a high yield, say 15 per cent. If it was low you would price them at a lower yield, say 10 per cent.

Convertible bonds and bonds with warrants can protect somewhat against mistakes of risk evaluation. Convertible bonds and bonds with warrants have two components: straight bonds and call options on the company's underlying equity. If the company turns out to be a low-risk company, the straight bond component will have high value and the call option will have low value. However, if the company turns out to be a high-risk company, the straight bond component will have low value and the call option will have high value. This is illustrated in Table 24.2.

Table 24.2 A Hypothetical Case of the Yields on Convertible Bonds*

	Firm Risk	
Bond Yield	**Low (%)**	**High (%)**
Straight bond yield	10	15
Convertible bond yield	6	7

Note:* The yields on straight bonds reflect the risk of default. The yields on convertibles are not sensitive to default risk.

However, although risk has effects on value that cancel one another out in convertibles and bonds with warrants, the market and the buyer nevertheless must make an assessment of the firm's potential to value securities, and it is not clear that the effort involved is that much less than is required for a straight bond.

Agency Costs

Convertible bonds can resolve agency problems associated with raising money. In a previous chapter (Section 22.10) we showed that straight bonds are like risk-free bonds minus a put option on the assets of the firm. This creates an incentive for creditors to force the firm into low-risk activities. In contrast, holders of equity have incentives to adopt high-risk projects. High-risk projects with negative NPV transfer wealth from bondholders to shareholders. If these conflicts cannot be resolved, the firm may be forced to pass up profitable investment opportunities. However, because convertible bonds have an equity component, less expropriation of wealth can occur when convertible debt is issued instead of straight debt.[9] In other words, convertible bonds mitigate agency costs. One implication is that convertible bonds have less restrictive debt covenants than do straight bonds in the real world. Casual empirical evidence seems to bear this out.

Backdoor Equity

A popular theory of convertibles views them as backdoor equity.[10] The basic story is that young, small, high-growth firms cannot usually issue debt on reasonable terms due to high financial distress costs. However, the owners may be unwilling to issue equity if current share prices are too low.

Lewis et al. (1998) examine the risk shifting and backdoor equity theories of convertible bond debt. They find evidence for both theories.

The European Puzzle

Until very recently, there has been no research on convertible bond issuance in Europe. However, two recent papers that have explored this issue provide additional insights into why European managers issue convertibles. Bancel and Mittoo (2004) and Dutordoir and Van de Gucht (2009) both ask the question 'Why do European firms issue convertible debt instead of straight debt or equity?' Surprisingly, their findings differ somewhat from the established view of convertible issuance that has been propagated by US researchers.

Bancel and Mittoo (2004) surveyed 229 firms in 16 European countries that issued convertible bonds. This sample represented 295 convertible bond issues amounting to a total of €97,933 million. Only 29 firms responded to the sample and most of these were French. Normally, such a small sample would be problematic but given that this was the first study of its type, we can be forgiving. They found that there was no one reason why firms opt for convertibles over other forms of financing. French respondents argued that the liquidity of the convertibles market was a strong motivator for issuing convertibles. Clearly, this appears to be consistent with the situation in financial markets as we move into the second decade of the twenty-first century. In addition, firms whose equity appears to be overvalued opt for convertibles to avoid the share price falling because of equity dilution.

Dutordoir and Van de Gucht (2009) act as an interesting counterpoint to the work of Bancel and Mittoo and earlier US research. Using a much larger sample of security issues, they find that European issuers of convertible bonds are actually large companies with low financing costs. This is the opposite to US convertible issuers who tend to be small and highly levered. Again, unlike the US, convertible bonds in Europe are rarely callable and only 27 per cent have been converted into equity. In Europe, it appears that convertible bonds are not used as backdoor equity but instead as 'sweetened debt', to reduce financing costs of raising debt.

The findings of Dutordoir and Van de Gucht (2009) raise important questions about the motivation for European firms that issue convertible bonds. Given that issuers tend to be large, financially healthy and mature, the explanations relating to financing costs that have been proposed do not appear to explain the reality in Europe. A possible reason may simply be due to market timing, as argued by Baker and Wurgler (2002) and discussed in an earlier chapter. The contrast in findings between the USA and Europe highlight the need to recognize differences in environment, culture and motivations of corporate managers in these two very heterogeneous regions.

Finally, Dong et al. (2018) asked top executives from Australia, Canada, the UK and the USA why their firms issued convertible bonds. Although the findings were not conclusive, most support was given to the 'risk synergy' rationale. The executives also stated that they issued convertible bonds because debt was too costly or covenant-heavy and their share price was too low.

Who Buys Convertible Bonds?

Because of their hybrid debt and equity characteristics, convertible bonds attract two main types of investor. Originally, financial institutions bought convertibles because they provided exposure to upside share price growth and limited downside credit risk. However, a new type of investor, hedge funds, now comprises a major part of the convertible market. Hedge funds buy the convertible bond and short the equity of the issue to take advantage of any undervaluation in the convertible bond price. Unfortunately, this can lead to falls in the share price of the convertible issuing firm because of the short-selling activity.[11]

Sustainability in Action 24.1

Schneider Electric's Sustainability-linked Convertible Bond (SLCB)

Schneider Electric, a French multinational specializing in digital automation and energy management, issued the world's first sustainability-linked convertible bond (SLCB) in 2020 to further its sustainability objectives. The €650m issue was linked to three key performance indicators (KPIs): CO_2 emission reduction, the proportion of women in management positions, and the number of underprivileged people the company trains in energy management programmes.

Schneider's management chose to opt for the equity-linked structure rather than a straight bond because they believed the company's share price is positively related to the achievement of these KPIs. The conversion component embedded these KPIs to the value obtained by investors from the bond.

Source: www.IFRE.com

24.8 Conversion Policy

There is one aspect of convertible bonds that we have omitted so far. Firms are sometimes granted a call option on the bond. It should be noted that, in the USA, call features are significantly more common than in Europe. The typical arrangements for calling a convertible bond are simple. When the bond is called, the holder has about 30 days to choose between the following:

- Converting the bond to equity at the conversion ratio
- Surrendering the bond and receiving the call price in cash.

What should bondholders do? It should be obvious that if the conversion value of the bond is greater than the call price, conversion is better than surrender; and if the conversion value is less than the call price, surrender is better than conversion. If the conversion value is greater than the call price, the call is said to force conversion.

What should financial managers do? Calling the bonds does not change the value of the firm as a whole. However, an optimal call policy can benefit the shareholders at the expense of the bondholders. Because we are speaking about dividing a pie of fixed size, the optimal call policy is simple: do whatever the bondholders do not want you to do.

Bondholders would love the shareholders to call the bonds when the bonds' market value is below the call price. Shareholders would be giving bondholders extra value. Alternatively, should the value of the bonds rise above the call price, the bondholders would love the shareholders not to call the bonds because bondholders would be allowed to hold on to a valuable asset.

There is only one policy left. This is the policy that maximizes shareholder value and minimizes bondholder value:

Call the bond when its value is equal to the call price.

It is a puzzle that firms do not always call convertible bonds when the conversion value reaches the call price. Ingersoll (1977) examined the call policies of 124 firms between 1968 and 1975.[12] In most cases he found that the company waited to call the bonds until the conversion value was much higher than the call price. The median company waited until the conversion value of its bonds was 44 per cent higher than the call price. This is not even close to our optimal strategy. Why?

One reason is that if firms attempt to implement the optimal strategy, it may not be truly optimal. Recall that bondholders have 30 days to decide whether to convert bonds to equity or to surrender bonds for the call price in cash. In 30 days the share price could drop, forcing the conversion value below the call price. If so, the convertible is 'out of the money' and the firm is giving away money. The firm would be giving up cash for equity worth much less. Because of this possibility, firms in the real world usually wait until the conversion value is substantially above the call price before they trigger the call.[13] This is sensible.

Summary and Conclusions

1. A warrant gives the holder the right to buy shares of equity at an exercise price for a given period. Typically, warrants are issued in a package with privately placed bonds. Afterwards, they may become detached and trade separately.
2. A convertible bond is a combination of a straight bond and a call option. The holder can give up the bond in exchange for shares.
3. Convertible bonds and warrants are like call options. However, there are some important differences:
   (a) Warrants and convertible securities are issued by corporations. Call options are traded between individual investors.
      (i) Warrants are usually issued privately and are combined with a bond. In most cases, the warrants can be detached immediately after the issue. In some cases, warrants are issued with preference shares, with equity or in executive compensation programmes.
      (ii) Convertibles are usually bonds that can be converted into equity.
      (iii) Call options are sold separately by individual investors (called *writers* of call options).

(b) Warrants and call options are exercised for cash. The holder of a warrant gives the company cash and receives new shares of the company's equity. The holder of a call option gives another individual cash in exchange for shares. When someone converts a bond, it is exchanged for equity. As a consequence, bonds with warrants and convertible bonds have different effects on corporate cash flow and capital structure.

(c) Warrants and convertibles cause dilution to the existing shareholders. When warrants are exercised and convertible bonds converted, the company must issue new shares of equity. The percentage ownership of the existing shareholders will decline. New shares are not issued when call options are exercised.

4 Many arguments, both plausible and implausible, are given for issuing convertible bonds and bonds with warrants. One plausible rationale for such bonds has to do with risk. Convertibles and bonds with warrants are associated with risky companies. Lenders can do several things to protect themselves from high-risk companies:

(a) They can require high yields.

(b) They can lend less, or not at all, to firms whose risk is difficult to assess.

(c) They can impose severe restrictions on such debt.

Another useful way to protect against risk is to issue bonds with equity kickers. This gives the lenders the chance to benefit from risks, and reduces the conflicts between bondholders and shareholders concerning risk.

5 One puzzle particularly vexes financial researchers: convertible bonds may have call provisions. Companies appear to delay calling convertibles until the conversion value greatly exceeds the call price. From the shareholders' standpoint, the optimal call policy would be to call the convertibles when the conversion value equals the call price.

Questions and Problems

Mc Graw Hill connect

CONCEPT

1 **Warrants** What are warrants? Why are warrants sometimes referred to as equity kickers? What does this mean?

2 **Warrants and Options** What is the primary difference between a warrant and a traded call option? Why is the dilution factor important in warrant pricing?

3 **Warrants: Advantages and Disadvantages** What are the advantages and disadvantages of issuing warrants?

4 **Convertible Bonds** What is a convertible bond? What are the key features of such a security?

5 **Reasons for Issuing Warrants and Convertibles** Why do firms issue convertibles? What impact do convertibles have on firms with target debt to equity ratios? Discuss convertible bonds in the context of the trade-off, pecking order and market timing theories of capital structure.

6 **Reasons for Buying Convertible Bonds** Why might an investor buy a convertible security?

7 **Conversion Policy** Why will convertible bonds not be voluntarily converted to equity before expiration? When and why should a firm force conversion of convertibles?

REGULAR

8 **Warrants: Price Bounds** Explain the following limits on the prices of warrants:

(a) If the share price is below the exercise price of the warrant, the lower bound on the price of a warrant is zero.

(b) If the share price is above the exercise price of the warrant, the lower bound on the price of a warrant is the difference between the share price and the exercise price.

(c) An upper bound on the price of any warrant is the current value of the firm's equity.

9 **Convertible Bonds and Equity Volatility** Assume that Barclays plc has just issued a callable convertible bond. You are concerned that the share price of Barclays is going to become more volatile over the next year. Should you buy the bond? Explain.

10 **Convertible Bond Value** Using the same bond as in the previous problem, assume that you believe interest rates are going to increase. What do you think will happen to the value of the bond? What if the bond were a putable convertible bond? Explain.

11 **Dilution** What is dilution, and why does it occur when warrants are exercised?

12 **Warrants and Convertibles** What is wrong with the simple view that it is cheaper to issue a bond with a warrant or a convertible feature because the required coupon is lower?

13 **Warrants and Convertibles: Financing Issues** You are employed as a financial consultant to a company that has undergone severe financial distress over the last number of years. Lacking in internal financing resources, the company tells you that it must go to the market to obtain funds, and has suggested issuing a convertible bond with a warrant attached to it. What are your thoughts on this?

14 **Convertible Bonds and Sustainability** Schneider Electric (see this chapter's Sustainability in Action) issued the world's first sustainability-linked convertible bond (SLCB) as part of its sustainability objectives. The issue was linked to three key performance indicators (KPIs): CO_2 emission reduction, the proportion of women in management positions, and the number of underprivileged people the company trains in energy management programmes.

(a) Discuss how convertible bonds can be used as a tool for companies to meet their sustainability objectives.

(b) Explain the benefits and potential challenges a company like Schneider Electric might face in linking the performance of a convertible bond to sustainability KPIs.

(c) If Schneider Electric does not meet its KPIs, what impact might this have on the company's share price and the value of the convertible bond?

(d) How might the issue of SLCBs influence the broader market for sustainability-linked financial instruments?

15 **Warrant Valuation** A warrant with five months until expiration entitles its owner to buy 100 shares of the issuing firm's equity for an exercise price of €23 per share. If the current market price of the equity is €10 per share, will the warrant be worthless?

16 **Convertible Bonds** Why do you think executives believe the risk synergy rationale for issuing convertibles and not the other explanations? Explain.

17 **Conversion Price** A convertible bond with a face value of €1,000 has a conversion ratio of 16:4. What is the conversion price?

18 **Conversion Ratio** A convertible bond with a face value of SKr10,000 has a conversion price of SKr356. What is the conversion ratio of the bond?

19 **Conversion Value** A convertible bond has a conversion ratio of 100. If the shares are currently priced at £9.20, what is the conversion value of the bond?

20 **Conversion Premium** Citic Securities recently issued bonds with a face value of 100,000 renminbi and conversion ratio of 420. If the share price at the bond issue was 124 renminbi, what was the conversion premium?

21 **Convertible Bonds: Hannon Home Products** Hannon Home Products recently issued £43,000,000 worth of 8 per cent convertible debentures. Each convertible bond has a face value of £100,000. Each convertible bond can be converted into 2,425 shares of equity any time before maturity. The share price is £31.25, and the market value of each bond is £118,000.

(a) What is the conversion ratio?

(b) What is the conversion price?

(c) What is the conversion premium?

(d) What is the conversion value?

(e) If the stock price increases by £2, what is the new conversion value?

22 **Warrants and Sustainability** A sustainable investment fund has been established to support companies that contribute towards UN Sustainable Development Goal SDG1: No Poverty. A firm which is focused on poverty alleviation in rural Sweden has issued a warrant giving its owner the right to purchase three shares of equity at an exercise price of 64 Swedish krona per share. The current market price of the equity is 69 Swedish krona. The warrant is intended to attract impact investors interested in both financial return and contributing to SDG1. What is the minimum value of this sustainability-focused warrant? Why would the warrant attract impact investors?

23 **Convertible Bond Value and Conversion** An analyst has recently informed you that, at the issuance of a company's convertible bonds, one of the two following sets of relationships existed:

	Scenario A (€)	Scenario B (€)
Face value of bond	1,000	1,000
Straight value of convertible bond	900	950
Market value of convertible bond	1,000	900

Assume the bonds are available for immediate conversion. Which of the two scenarios do you believe is more likely? Why?

24 **Convertible Bond Value** Tvep plc issued convertible bonds with a conversion price of £20. The bonds are available for immediate conversion. The current price of the company's equity is £18 per share. The current market price of the convertible bonds is £990. The convertible bonds' straight value is not known.

(a) What is the minimum price for the convertible bonds?

(b) Explain the difference between the current market price of each convertible bond and the value of the equity into which it can immediately be converted.

25 **Callable Convertible Bonds** You own a callable, convertible bond with a conversion ratio of 500. The equity is currently selling for £22 per share. The issuer of the bond has announced a call at a call price of 105 on a face value of £100. What are your options here? What should you do?

26 **Warrant Value: UK Agritech Solutions** UK Agritech Solutions has five-year warrants that currently trade in the open market. Each warrant gives its owner the right to purchase one share of equity for an exercise price of £45.

(a) Suppose the equity is currently trading for £43 per share. What is the lower limit on the price of the warrant? What is the upper limit?

(b) Suppose the equity is currently trading for £50 per share. What is the lower limit on the price of the warrant? What is the upper limit?

27 **Convertible Bonds: Trichet SA** Trichet SA has just issued a 30-year callable, convertible bond with a coupon rate of 7 per cent annual coupon payments. The bond has a conversion price of €125. The company's equity is selling for €32 per share. The owner of the bond will be forced to convert if the bond's conversion value is ever greater than or equal to €1,100. The required return on an otherwise identical non-convertible bond is 12 per cent.

(a) What is the minimum value of the bond?

(b) If the share price were to grow by 15 per cent per year for ever, how long would it take for the bond's conversion value to exceed €1,100?

28 **Convertible Bonds: Isner Construction** Rob Stevens is the chief executive officer of Isner Construction plc and owns 500,000 shares. The company currently has 4 million shares and convertible bonds with a face value of £20 million outstanding. The convertible bonds have a conversion price of £20, and the equity is currently selling for £25.

(a) What percentage of the firm's equity does Mr Stevens own?

(b) If the company decides to call the convertible bonds and force conversion, what percentage of the firm's equity will Mr Stevens own? He does not own any convertible bonds.

29 **Warrants Issues** Survivor NV, an all-equity firm, has three shares outstanding. Yesterday, the firm's assets consisted of 5 ounces of platinum, currently worth €1,000 per ounce. Today, the company issued Ms Wu a warrant for its fair value of €1,000. The warrant gives Ms Wu the right to buy a single share of the firm's equity for €2,100 and can be exercised only on its expiration date one year from today. The firm used the proceeds from the issuance to immediately purchase an additional ounce of platinum.

(a) What was the price of a single share of equity *before* the warrant was issued?

(b) What was the price of a single share of equity immediately *after* the warrant was issued?

(c) Suppose platinum is selling for €1,100 per ounce on the warrant's expiration date in one year. What will be the value of a single share of equity on the warrant's expiration date?

30 **Warrants Exercise and Share Prices** The capital structure of Ricketti Enterprises plc consists of 10 million shares of equity and 1 million warrants. Each warrant gives its owner the right to purchase one share of equity for an exercise price of £15. The current share price is £17, and each warrant is worth £3. What is the new share price if all warrant holders decide to exercise today?

CHALLENGE

31 **Convertible Calculations** You have been hired to value a new 25-year callable, convertible bond. The bond has a 6.80 per cent coupon rate, payable annually. The conversion price is £150, and the equity currently sells for £44.75. The stock price is expected to grow at 12 per cent per year. The bond is callable at £1,200 but based on prior experience it will not be called unless the conversion value is £1,300. The required return on this bond is 10 per cent. What value would you assign to this bond?

32 **Warrant Value with Black-Scholes Model** Superior Clamps AB has a capital structure consisting of 4 million shares of equity and 500,000 warrants. Each warrant gives its owner the right to purchase one share of newly issued equity for an exercise price of €20. The warrants are European and will expire one year from today. The market value of the company's assets is €88 million, and the annual variance of the returns on the firm's assets is 0.04. Treasury bills that mature in one year yield a continuously compounded interest rate of 7 per cent. The company does not pay a dividend. Use the Black-Scholes model to determine the value of a single warrant.

33 **Warrant Value: Omega Airlines** Omega Airlines' capital structure consists of 1.5 million shares of equity and zero coupon bonds with a face value of $10 million that mature in six months. The firm just announced that it will issue warrants with an exercise price of $95 and six months until expiration to raise the funds to pay off its maturing debt. Each warrant can be exercised only at expiration and gives its owner the right to buy a single newly issued share of equity. The firm will place the proceeds from the warrant issue immediately into Treasury bills.

The market value balance sheet shows that the firm will have assets worth $160 million after the announcement. The company does not pay dividends. The standard deviation of the returns on the firm's assets is 65 per cent, and Treasury bills with a six-month maturity yield 6 per cent. How many warrants must the company issue today to be able to use the proceeds from the sale to pay off the firm's debt obligation in six months?

Exam Question (45 minutes)

1 You have been hired to value a new 10-year callable, convertible bond. The bond has a 5.6 per cent coupon rate, payable annually. The conversion price is £150 and the equity currently sells for £44.75. The share price is expected to grow at 8 per cent per year. The bond is callable at £1,100 but based on prior experience it will not be called unless the conversion value is £1,200. The required return on this bond is 6 per cent. What value would you assign to this bond? **(30 marks)**

2 Your firm has 3 million shares of equity and 100,000 warrants. Each warrant gives its owner the right to purchase one share of newly issued equity for an exercise price of €15. The warrants are European and will expire one year from today. The market value of the company's assets is €60 million and the annual standard deviation of the returns on the firm's assets is 24 per cent. Treasury bills that mature in one year yield a continuously compounded interest rate of 2 per cent. The company does not pay a dividend. Use the Black-Scholes model to determine the value of a single warrant. **(30 marks)**

3 Review the reasons given for why firms issue convertible bonds. Which one do you think is the most valid? Explain. **(40 marks)**

Total: 100 Marks

Mini Case

S&S Air's Convertible Bond

Kartner Meister was recently hired by S&S Air AB to assist the company with its short-term financial planning and to evaluate the company's performance. Kartner graduated from university five years ago with a finance degree. He has been employed in the finance department of a major German company since then.

S&S Air was founded 10 years ago by two friends, Stephan Lochner and Hans Multscher. The company has manufactured and sold light airplanes over this period, and the company's products have received excellent reviews for safety and reliability. The company has a niche market in that it sells primarily to individuals who own and fly their own airplanes. The company has two models: the Birdie, which sells for €53,000, and the Eagle, which sells for €78,000.

S&S Air is not publicly traded, but the company needs new funds for investment opportunities. In consultation with Conrad Witz of underwriter Koerbecke and Pleydenwurff, Kartner decided that a convertible bond issue with a 20-year maturity is the way to go. He met with the owners, Stephan and Hans, and presented his analysis of the convertible bond issue. Because the company is not publicly traded, Kartner looked at comparable publicly traded companies and determined that the average PE ratio for the industry is 12.5. Earnings per share for the company are €1.60. With this in mind, Kartner concluded that the conversion price should be €25 per share.

Several days later Stephan, Hans and Kartner met again to discuss the potential bond issue. Both Hans and Stephan have researched convertible bonds and have questions for Kartner. Hans begins by asking Kartner if the convertible bond issue will have a lower coupon rate than a comparable bond without a conversion feature. Kartner replies that to sell the bond at par value, the convertible bond issue would require a 6 per cent coupon rate with a conversion value of €800, while a plain vanilla bond would have a 7 per cent coupon rate. Hans nods in agreement, and he explains that the convertible bonds are a win-win form of financing. He states that if the value of the company equity does not rise above the conversion price, the company has issued debt at a cost below the market rate (6 per cent instead of 7 per cent). If the company's equity does rise to the conversion value, the company has effectively issued shares at above the current value.

Stephan immediately disagrees, arguing that convertible bonds are a no-win form of financing. He argues that, if the value of the company equity rises to €25, the company is forced to sell shares at the conversion price. This means the new shareholders (those who bought the convertible bonds) benefit from a bargain price. Put another way, if the company prospers, it would have been better to have issued straight debt so that the gains would not be shared.

Kartner has gone back to Conrad for help. As Conrad's assistant, you have been asked to prepare another memo answering the following questions:

1. Why do you think Kartner is suggesting a conversion price of €25? Given that the company is not publicly traded, does it even make sense to talk about a conversion price?
2. What is the floor value of the S&S Air convertible bond?
3. What is the conversion ratio of the bond?
4. What is the conversion premium of the bond?
5. What is the value of the option?
6. Is there anything wrong with Hans's argument that it is cheaper to issue a bond with a convertible feature because the required coupon is lower?
7. Is there anything wrong with Stephan's argument that a convertible bond is a bad idea because it allows new shareholders to participate in gains made by the company?
8. How can you reconcile the arguments made by Hans and Stephan?
9. During the debate, a question comes up concerning whether the bonds should have an ordinary (not make-whole) call feature. Kartner confuses everybody by stating, 'The call feature lets S&S Air force conversion, thereby minimizing the problem Stephan has identified.' What is he talking about? Is he making sense?

Practical Case Study

Download the financial accounts of 10 companies and look for any issues of warrants or convertibles. You may find examples of bonds that have conversion options or warrant-like properties. Are convertibles an important part of your firms' capital structures? Write a brief report on the use of convertibles and warrants for your sample of firms.

Relevant Accounting Standards

The most important accounting standard for warrants and convertibles is IAS 39 *Financial Instruments: Recognition and Measurement.* IAS 39 provides definitions for different types of financial securities, and states how the different components of a security should be valued and presented in a firm's financial accounts. Visit the IASPlus website (www.iasplus.com) for more information.

References

Altintig, Z.A. and A.W. Butler (2005) 'Are They Still Called Late? The Effect of Notice Period on Calls of Convertible Bonds', *Journal of Corporate Finance*, Vol. 11, 337–350.

Asquith, P. (1995) 'Convertible Bonds Are Not Called Late', *Journal of Finance*, Vol. 50, 1275–1289.

Baker, M. and J. Wurgler (2002) 'Market Timing and Capital Structure', *Journal of Finance*, Vol. 57, No. 1, 1–32.

Bancel, F. and Mittoo, U.R. (2004) 'Why Do European Firms Issue Corporate Debt?', *European Financial Management*, Vol. 10, 339–373.

Barnea, A., R.A. Haugen and L. Senbet (1985) *Agency Problems and Financial Contracting*, Prentice Hall Foundations of Science Series. New York: Prentice Hall.

Brigham, E.F. (1966) 'An Analysis of Convertible Debentures', *Journal of Finance*, Vol. 21, 35–54.

Choi, D., M. Getmansky, B. Henderson and H. Tookes (2010) 'Convertible Bond Arbitrageurs as Suppliers of Capital', *Review of Financial Studies*, Vol. 23, 2492–2522.

Dong, M., M. Dutordoir and C. Veld (2018) 'Why Do Firms Issue Convertible Bonds?', *Critical Finance Review*, Vol. 7, No. 1, 111–164.

Duca, E., M. Dutordoir, C. Veld and P. Verwijmeren (2012) 'Why Are Convertible Bond Announcements Associated with Increasingly Negative Issuer Stock Returns? An Arbitrage-based Explanation', *Journal of Banking and Finance*, Vol. 36, No. 11, 2884–2899.

Dutordoir, M. and L. Van de Gucht (2009) 'Why Do Western European Firms Issue Convertibles Instead of Straight Debt or Equity?', *European Financial Management*, Vol. 15, No. 3, 563–583.

Ederington, L.H., G.L. Caton and C.J. Campbell (1997) 'To Call or Not to Call Convertible Debt', *Financial Management*, Vol. 26, No. 1, 26–31.

Harris, M. and A. Raviv (1985) 'A Sequential Signalling Model of Convertible Debt Policy', *Journal of Finance*, Vol. 40, 1263–1281.

Ingersoll, J. (1977) 'An Examination of Corporate Call Policies on Convertible Bonds', *Journal of Finance*, Vol. 32, 463–478.

Lewis, C.M. and P. Verwijmeren (2011) 'Convertible Security Design and Contract Innovation', *Journal of Corporate Finance*, Vol. 17, 809–831.

Lewis, C.M., R.J. Rogalski and J.K. Seward (1998) 'Understanding the Design of Convertible Debt', *Journal of Applied Corporate Finance*, Vol. 11, No. 1, 45–53.

Mazzeo, M.A. and W.T. Moore (1992) 'Liquidity Costs and Stock Price Response to Convertible Security Calls', *Journal of Business*, Vol. 65, 353–369.

Mikkelson, W.H. (1981) 'Convertible Calls and Security Returns', *Journal of Financial Economics*, Vol. 9, 237–264.

Schulz, G.U. and S. Trautmann (1994) 'Robustness of Option-like Warrant Valuation', *Journal of Banking and Finance*, Vol. 18, No. 5, 841–859.

Singh, A.K., A.R. Cowan and N. Nayar (1991) 'Underwritten Calls of Convertible Bonds', *Journal of Financial Economics*, Vol. 29, 173–196.

Stein, J. (1992) 'Convertible Bonds as Backdoor Equity Financing', *Journal of Financial Economics*, Vol. 32, 3–21.

Ter Horst, J. and C. Veld (2008) 'An Empirical Analysis of the Pricing of Bank Issued Options Versus Options Exchange Options', *European Financial Management*, Vol. 14, No. 2, 288–314.

Additional Reading

Much of the recent research in this area has already been discussed in the main text. The following papers will add to your understanding. In 2014, the *Journal of Corporate Finance* issued a full special issue on convertible bonds, edited by Craig Lewis and Chris Veld. The issue (Volume 24) contained a number of papers on the area and should be read first if you are wanting to get an up-to-date insight into convertible bond financing. In particular, the following paper gives a review of research in this area to date:

Dutordoir, M., C. Lewis, J. Seward and C. Veld (2014) 'What We Do and Do Not Know about Convertible Bond Financing', *Journal of Corporate Finance*, Vol. 24, 3–20.

Other interesting papers include:

1 Agarwal, V., W.H. Fung, Y.C. Loon and N.Y. Naik (2011) 'Risk and Return in Convertible Arbitrage: Evidence from the Convertible Bond Market', *Journal of Empirical Finance*, Vol. 18, No. 2, 175–194.

2 Batten, J.A., K.L.H. Khaw and M.R. Young (2018) 'Pricing Convertible Bonds', *Journal of Banking & Finance*, Vol. 92, 216–236.

3 Choi, D., M. Getmansky and H. Tookes (2009) 'Convertible Bond Arbitrage, Liquidity Externalities, and Stock Prices', *Journal of Financial Economics*, Vol. 91, No. 2, 227–251. **USA.**

4 Choi, D., M. Getmansky, B. Henderson and H. Tookes (2010) 'Convertible Bond Arbitrageurs as Suppliers of Capital', *Review of Financial Studies*, Vol. 23, No. 6, 2492–2522.

5 Dong, M., M. Dutordoir and C. Veld (2019) 'How Can We Improve Inferences from Surveys? A New Look at the Convertible Debt Questions from the Graham and Harvey Survey Data', *Journal of*

International Financial Markets, Institutions and Money, Vol. 61, 213–222.

6 Finnerty, J.D. (2015) 'Valuing Convertible Bonds and the Option to Exchange Bonds for Stock', *Journal of Corporate Finance*, Vol. 31, 91–115.

7 Gajewski, J.-F., E. Ginglinger and M. Lasfer (2007) 'Why Do Companies Include Warrants in Seasoned Equity Offerings?', *Journal of Corporate Finance*, Vol. 13, No. 1, 25–42. **France.**

8 Gillet, R. and H. De La Bruslerie (2010) 'The Consequences of Issuing Convertible Bonds: Dilution and/or Financial Restructuring', *European Financial Management*, Vol. 16, No. 4, 552–584. **France.**

9 Grundy, B.D. and P. Verwijmeren (2016) 'Disappearing Call Delay and Dividend-Protected Convertible Bonds', *Journal of Finance*, Vol. 71, No. 1, 195–224.

10 Jarrow, R.A. and S. Trautmann (2011) 'A Reduced-form Model for Warrant Valuation', *Financial Review*, Vol. 46, No. 3, 413–425.

11 Krishnaswami, S. and D. Yaman (2008) 'The Role of Convertible Bonds in Alleviating Contracting Costs', *Quarterly Review of Economics and Finance*, Vol. 48, No. 4, 792–816.

12 Li, W. H., S.G. Rhee and C.H.H. Shen (2018) 'CEO Inside Debt and Convertible Bonds', *Journal of Business Finance & Accounting*, Vol. 45, No. 1–2), 232–249.

13 Loncarski, I., J. Ter Horst and C. Veld (2009) 'The Rise and Demise of the Convertible Arbitrage Strategy', *Financial Analysts Journal*, Vol. 65, 35–50.

14 Rastad, M. (2016) 'Capital Structure Pre-balancing: Evidence from Convertible Bonds', *Journal of Corporate Finance*, Vol. 41, 43–65.

15 Zabolotnyuk, Y., R. Jones and C. Veld (2010) 'An Empirical Comparison of Convertible Bond Valuation Models', *Financial Management*, Vol. 39, No. 2, 675–706.

16 Zeidler, F., M. Mietzner and D. Schiereck (2012) 'Risk Dynamics Surrounding the Issuance of Convertible Bonds', *Journal of Corporate Finance*, Vol. 18, No. 2, 273–290.

Endnotes

1 Warrants are also issued with publicly distributed bonds and new issues of equity.

2 At the turn of the twenty-first century many banks began issuing options on other companies under the name 'call warrants'. These are not warrants in the real sense because the companies on which the call warrants are written do not issue new equity in response to an exercise of the call warrants. In this chapter, we will not consider the valuation of these call warrants. See Ter Horst and Veld (2008) for more information on call warrants.

3 Just like call options, warrants are protected against stock splits and stock dividends but not against cash dividends. The latter generally does not cause a problem for the valuation of call options, since these only have short maturities and therefore a relatively small amount of dividends are paid during their lifetime. Given that warrants generally have maturities of several years, the effect of cash dividends can be significant.

4 To derive Formula 24.3, we separate 'Exercise price' in Equation 24.2. This yields

$$\frac{\text{Firm's value net of debt}}{\# + \#_w} - \frac{\#}{\# + \#_w} \times \text{Exercise price}$$

By rearranging terms, we can obtain Formula 24.3.

5 Equation 24.4 is not exactly correct. After a warrant is issued, the share price and volatility of returns will change to reflect the warrant's existence. However, Schulz and Trautmann (1994) report that Equation 24.4 performs just as well as more complex valuation models, except when the warrant is deep out of the money.

6 The most plausible exception is when conversion would provide the investor with a dividend much greater than the interest available prior to conversion. The optimal strategy here could very well be to convert immediately, implying that the market value of the bond would exactly equal the conversion value. Other exceptions occur when the firm is in default or the bondholders are forced to convert.

7 Brigham (1966).

8 Mikkelson (1981).

9 Barnea et al. (1985), Chapter VI.

10 Stein (1992). See also Lewis et al. (1998), and Lewis and Verwijmeren (2011).

11 See Duca et al. (2012) and Choi et al. (2010).

12 See also Harris and Raviv (1985). Harris and Raviv describe a signal equilibrium that is consistent with Ingersoll's result. They show that managers with favourable information will delay calls to avoid depressing stock prices.

13 See Altintig and Butler (2005) and Asquith (1995). On the other hand, the stock market usually reacts negatively to the announcement of a call. For example, see Singh et al. (1991), and Mazzeo and Moore (1992). Ederington et al. (1997) tested various theories about when it is optimal to call convertibles. They found evidence consistent with the preceding 30-day 'safety margin' theory. They also found that calls of in-the-money convertibles are highly unlikely if dividends to be received (after conversion) exceed the company's interest payment.

Chapter 25
Financial Risk Management with Derivatives

Learning Objectives

After reading this chapter you should be able to:

LO1 Explain the basic characteristics and purposes of derivatives, including forward contracts, futures contracts, interest rate derivatives and swap contracts.

LO2 Apply the concept of hedging to design strategies for mitigating financial risks.

LO3 Analyse and evaluate the risk/return trade-offs of various derivatives strategies.

Anyone studying corporate finance must be familiar with the principles of financial risk management. Many students think that only financial institutions use derivatives such as futures and swaps. However, every company that does business overseas, sources raw materials from other countries, borrows or lends money, or buys commodities today for delivery in the future will use risk-management techniques to manage risk and optimize its business.

For example, automobile exporters, such as BMW and Renault, are regularly faced with uncertainty regarding the value of currencies. Since automobiles are manufactured in one country and exported to the rest of the world, currency depreciation or appreciation can be a major issue. The same concerns are had by firms in many industries, and the current economic environment, with so much volatility and uncertainty, means that companies must prioritize risk management. This chapter will review some of the methods open to exporters and importers to manage their financial risk.

Source: Nataliya Hora/Shutterstock

Key Notations

P	Price
R	Discount rate; yield to maturity

25.1 Derivatives, Hedging and Risk

Chapter 22 Page 602

The name *derivatives* is self-explanatory. A derivative is a financial instrument whose payoffs and values are derived from, or depend on, something else. Often, we speak of the thing that the derivative depends on as the *primitive* or the *underlying*. In Chapter 22, for example, we studied how options work. An option is a derivative. The value of a call option depends on the value of the underlying equity on which it is written. Actually, call options are quite complicated examples of derivatives. The vast majority of derivatives are simpler than call options. Most derivatives are forward or futures agreements, or what are called *swaps*, and we will study each of these in some detail.

Why do firms use derivatives? The answer is that derivatives are tools for changing the firm's risk exposure. Someone once said that derivatives are to finance what scalpels are to surgery. By using derivatives, the firm can cut away unwanted portions of risk exposure and even transform the exposures into quite different forms. However, scalpels can also be exceptionally dangerous in the hands of the unskilled or unethical!

A central point in finance is that risk is undesirable. In Chapters 9 and 10, about risk and return, we pointed out that individuals would choose risky securities only if the expected return compensated for the risk. Similarly, a firm will accept a project with high risk only if the return on the project compensates for this risk. Not surprisingly, then, firms are usually looking for ways to reduce their risk. When the firm reduces its risk exposure with the use of derivatives, it is said to be **hedging**. Hedging offsets the firm's risk, such as the risk in a project, by one or more transactions in the financial markets.

Derivatives can also be used to merely change or even increase the firm's risk exposure. When this occurs, the firm is speculating on the movement of some economic variables – those that underlie the derivative. For instance, if a derivative is purchased that will rise in value if interest rates rise, and if the firm has no offsetting exposure to interest rate changes, then the firm is speculating that interest rates will rise and give it a profit on its derivatives position. Using derivatives to translate an opinion about whether interest rates or some other economic variable will rise or fall is the opposite of hedging – it is risk enhancing. Speculating on your views on the economy and using derivatives to profit if that view turns out to be correct is not necessarily wrong, but the speculator should always remember that sharp tools cut deep: if the opinions on which the derivatives position is based turn out to be incorrect, then the consequences can prove costly. Efficient market theory teaches how difficult it is to predict what markets will do. Most of the disastrous experiences with derivatives have occurred not from their use as instruments for hedging and offsetting risk, but rather from speculation.

Real World Insight 25.1

Virgin Atlantic

The origin of Virgin Atlantic offers an intuitive and simple example of the importance of risk management in company operations. In 1984, Richard Branson was stranded in Puerto Rico trying to get to the British Virgin Islands. Because there weren't enough passengers, the airline he was due to fly on cancelled the flight.

Taking matters into his own hands, Branson hired his own smaller plane and approached each passenger offering one-way tickets for $39 to the British Virgin Islands. When he had enough takers, he arranged the flight himself!

Shortly after this event, Branson called Boeing and leased new 747s to fly select routes under a new company, Virgin Atlantic. The key to the deal was that if Virgin Atlantic wasn't a success, he could return the planes to Boeing at no loss.

Branson effectively hedged against downside risk while exposing the company to upside risk. Where Virgin Atlantic managed this risk through business operations, many companies can replicate the asymmetric risk-reward pattern through using financial derivatives.

25.2 Forward Contracts

We can begin our discussion of hedging by considering forward contracts. You have probably been dealing in forward contracts your whole life without knowing it. Suppose you walk into a bookstore on, say, 1 February to buy the bestseller, *Corporate Finance for Chefs*. The cashier tells you the book is currently sold out, but he takes your phone number, saying he will reorder it for you. He says the book will cost £10.00. If you agree on 1 February to pick up and pay £10.00 for the book when called, you and the cashier have engaged in a **forward contract**. That is, you have agreed both to pay for the book and to pick it up when the bookstore notifies you. Because you are agreeing to buy the book at a later date, you are *buying* a forward contract on 1 February. In commodity parlance, you will be taking delivery when you pick up the book. The book is called the deliverable instrument.

The cashier, acting on behalf of the bookstore, is selling a forward contract. (Alternatively, we say that he is writing a forward contract.) The bookstore has agreed to turn the book over to you at the predetermined price of £10.00 as soon as the book arrives. The act of turning the book over to you is called making delivery. Table 25.1 illustrates the book purchase. Note that the agreement takes place on 1 February. The price is set and the conditions for sale are set at that time. In this case, the sale will occur when the book arrives. In other cases, an exact date of sale would be given. However, *no* cash changes hands on 1 February; cash changes hands only when the book arrives.

Table 25.1 Illustration of Book Purchase as a Forward Contract

1 February	Date When Book Arrives
Buyer	
Buyer agrees to: 1. Pay the purchase price of £10.00. 2. Receive book when book arrives.	**Buyer** 1. Pays purchase price of £10.00. 2. Receives book.
Seller	
Seller agrees to: 1. Give up book when book arrives. 2. Accept payment of £10.00 when book arrives.	**Seller** 1. Gives up book. 2. Accepts payment of £10.00.

Note: Cash does not change hands on 1 February. Cash changes hands when the book arrives.

Though forward contracts may have seemed exotic to you before you began this chapter, you can see that they are quite commonplace. Dealings in your personal life probably have involved forward contracts. Similarly, forward contracts occur all the time in business. Every time a firm orders an item that cannot be delivered immediately, a forward contract takes place. Sometimes, particularly when the order is small, an oral agreement will suffice. Other times, particularly when the order is larger, a written agreement is necessary.

Note that a forward contract is not an option. Both the buyer and the seller are obligated to perform under the terms of the contract. Conversely, the buyer of an option *chooses* whether to exercise the option.

A forward contract should be contrasted with a cash transaction – that is, a transaction where exchange is immediate. Had the book been on the bookstore's shelf, your purchase of it would constitute a cash transaction.

In Islamic financing, the equivalent hedge transaction is called a *bai salam*. The difference between a *bai salam* and a forward contract is that money is transferred today in a *bai salam* but is transferred at a future date with a forward contract. See Chapter 30 for more information on the *bai salam*.

25.3 Futures Contracts

A variant of the forward contract takes place on financial exchanges. Contracts on exchanges are usually called **futures contracts**. There are a number of futures exchanges around the world, and more are being established. The big three futures exchanges are the Chicago Mercantile Exchange, the Intercontinental Exchange and Eurex. While trading on these exchanges spans whole geographic regions, there are many exchanges, such as Nasdaq, National Stock Exchange of India, BM&FBOVESPA (Brazil), the Moscow Exchange (Russia) and the Shanghai Futures Exchange (China).

Table 25.2 gives the specification for cocoa futures contracts from ICE, the Intercontinental Exchange. Note that the contracts are for delivery of 10 tonnes of cocoa and are quoted in dollars per tonne. The contracts are traded in New York, London and Singapore. If the futures contract is held until expiry, the cocoa will actually be delivered to a warehouse in the USA. Almost always, however, the futures trader will take an opposite position on the futures to cancel it out. For instance, a trader who is long in the futures and will buy the cocoa could take an opposite position to sell the cocoa, thereby closing out the contract.

Table 25.2 Cocoa Futures Contract Specification

Description	The cocoa contract is the world benchmark for the global cocoa market. The contract prices the physical delivery of exchange-grade product from a variety of African, Asian, and Central and South American origins to any of five US delivery ports.
Symbol	CC
Contract size	10 metric tonnes
Price quotation	$/metric tonnes
Contract listing	March, May, July, September, December
Minimum price movement	$1.00/metric tonnes, equivalent to $10.00 per contract
Settlement	Physical delivery
Daily price limit	None
Deliverable growths	The growth of any country or clime, including new or yet unknown growths. Growths are divided into three classifications. Group A-Deliverable at a premium of $160/ton (including main crops of Ghana, Lomé, Nigeria, Côte d'Ivoire and Sierra Leone). Group B-Deliverable at a premium of $80/ton (includes Bahia, Arriba, Venezuela, Sanchez, among others). Group C-Deliverable at par (includes Haiti, Malaysia and all others). Commencing with the July expiry, the growths of Peru and Colombia will be included in Group B.
Delivery points	At licensed warehouses in the Port of New York District, Delaware River Port District, Port of Hampton Roads, Port of Albany or Port of Baltimore.

In Table 25.3, the price and volumes of hypothetical cocoa futures contracts are provided. The price of cocoa for delivery in the future is expected to steadily fall and then rise over the next year. The price of a July 2024 cocoa futures contract, for example, was $2,409, falling to $2,413 for a March 2025 contract, and $2,426 for a July 2025 contract.

Table 25.3 Cocoa Futures Price and Volume Data

Month	July 2024	September 2024	December 2024	March 2025	May 2025	July 2025	September 2025
Price	2,409	2,418	2,416	2,413	2,417	2,426	2,417
Volume	20,502	6,566	4,031	752	213	164	123

For the cocoa contract with a July 2024 maturity, the first number in the row is the *last price* ($2,409), and it is essentially the most recent transaction price in the cocoa contract. The final price of the day is known as the *settlement price* and for the purposes of marking to market, this is the figure used. The volume of 20,502 contracts represents the number of cocoa contracts traded that day. Notice that the futures volume falls as the length of the contract grows. This is because most of the hedging requirements are for the next few months after the quote.

Though we are discussing a futures contract, let us work with a forward contract first. Suppose you wrote a *forward* contract for September coffee at $2,418. From our discussion of forward contracts, this would mean that you would agree to turn over 10 tonnes of cocoa beans for $2,418 per tonne on some specified date in the month of September.

A futures contract differs somewhat from a forward contract. First, the seller can choose to deliver the cocoa on any day during the delivery month – that is, the month of September. This gives the seller leeway that he would not have with a forward contract. When the seller decides to deliver, he notifies the exchange clearinghouse that he wants to do so. The clearinghouse then notifies an individual who bought a September cocoa contract that she must stand ready to accept delivery within the next few days. Though each exchange selects the buyer in a different way, the buyer is generally chosen in a random fashion. Because there are so many buyers at any one time, the buyer selected by the clearinghouse to take delivery almost certainly did not originally buy the contract from the seller now making delivery.

Second, futures contracts are traded on an exchange, whereas forward contracts are generally traded off an exchange. Because of this, there is generally a liquid market in futures contracts. A buyer can net out her futures position with a sale. A seller can net out his futures position with a purchase. If a buyer of a futures contract does not subsequently sell her contract, she must take delivery.

Third, and most important, the prices of futures contracts are marked to the market daily. That is, suppose the price falls to $2,415 on Monday's close. Because all buyers lost $30 per contract on that day, they each must turn over the $30 per contract to their brokers within 24 hours, who subsequently remit the proceeds to the clearinghouse. All sellers gained $30 per contract on that day, so they each receive $30 per contract from their brokers. Their brokers are subsequently compensated by the clearinghouse. Because there is a buyer for every seller, the clearinghouse must break even every day.

Now suppose that the price rises to $2,421 on the close of the following Tuesday. Each buyer receives $60 ($24,210–$24,150) per contract, and each seller must pay $60 per contract. Finally, suppose that on Tuesday a seller notifies his broker of his intention to deliver.[1] The delivery price will be $2,421, which is Tuesday's close.

There are clearly many cash flows in futures contracts. However, after all the dust settles, the *net price* to the buyer must be the price at which she bought originally. That is, an individual buying at Friday's closing price of $2,418 and being called to take delivery on Tuesday pays $30 per contract on Monday, receives $60 per contract on Tuesday, and takes delivery at $2,421. Her net outflow per 10 tonnes is −$24,180 (= −$30 + $60 − $24,210), or $2,418 per tonne, which is the price at which she contracted on Friday. (Our analysis ignores the time value of money.) Conversely, an individual selling at Friday's closing price of $2,418 and notifying his broker concerning delivery the following Tuesday receives $30 per contract on Monday, pays $60 per contract on Tuesday and makes delivery at $2,421. His net inflow per contract is −$24,180 (= −$30 + $60 − $24,210) or $2,418 per tonne, which is the price at which he contracted on Friday. These details are presented in the box below.

Illustration of Example Involving Marking to Market in Futures Contracts

Both buyer and seller originally transact at Friday's closing price. Delivery takes place at Tuesday's closing price.*

	Friday 13 April	Monday 16 April	Tuesday 17 April	Delivery (notification given by seller on Tuesday)
Closing price	$2,418	$2,415	$2,421	
Buyer	Buyer purchases futures contract for 10 tonnes at closing price of $2,418/tonne.	Buyer must pay $30 per contract to clearinghouse within one business day.	Buyer receives $60 per contract from clearinghouse within one business day.	Buyer pays $24,210 per contract and receives cocoa within one business day.
Buyer's net payment of −$24,180 (= −$30 + $60 − $24,210) is the same as if buyer purchased a forward contract for $2,418 per tonne.				
Seller	Seller sells futures contract for 10 tonnes at closing price of $2,418/tonne.	Seller receives $30 per contract from clearinghouse within one business day.	Seller pays $60 per contract to clearinghouse within one business day.	Seller receives $24,210 per contract and delivers cocoa within one business day.
Seller's net receipts of $24,180 (= $30 − $60 + $24,210) are the same as if seller sold a forward contract for $2,418 per tonne.				

Note: * For simplicity, we assume that buyer and seller both (1) initially transact at the same time, and (2) meet in the delivery process. This is actually very unlikely to occur in the real world because the clearinghouse assigns the buyer to take delivery in a random manner.

For simplicity, we assumed that the buyer and seller who initially transact on Friday's close meet in the delivery process. The point in the example is that the buyer's net payment of $24,180 per contract is the same as if she purchased a forward contract for $24,180. Similarly, the seller's net receipt of $24,180 per contract is the same as if he sold a forward contract for $24,180. The only difference is the timing of the cash flows. The buyer of a forward contract knows that he will make a single payment of $24,180 on the expiration date. He will not need to worry about any other cash flows in the interim. Conversely, though the cash flows to the buyer of a futures contract will net to exactly $24,180 as well, the pattern of cash flows is not known ahead of time.

The mark-to-the-market provision on futures contracts has two related effects. The first concerns differences in net present value. For example, a large price drop immediately following the purchase means an immediate payout for the buyer of a futures contract. Though the net outflow of $24,180 is still the same as under a forward contract, the present value of the cash outflows is greater to the buyer of a futures contract. Of course, the present value of the cash outflows is less to the buyer of a futures contract if a price rise follows purchase.[2] Though this effect could be substantial in certain theoretical circumstances, it appears to be of quite limited importance in the real world.[3]

Second, the firm must have extra liquidity to handle a sudden outflow prior to expiration. This added risk may make the futures contract less attractive.

Students frequently ask, 'Why in the world would managers of the commodity exchanges ruin perfectly good contracts with these bizarre mark-to-the-market provisions?' Actually, the reason is a very good one. Consider the forward contract of Table 25.1 concerning the bookstore. Suppose the public quickly loses interest in *Corporate Finance for Chefs*. By the time the bookstore calls the buyer, other stores may have dropped the price of the book to £6.00. Because the forward contract was for £10.00, the buyer has an incentive not to take delivery on the forward contract. Conversely, should the book become a hot item selling at £15.00, the bookstore may simply not call the buyer.

Mark-to-the-market provisions minimize the chance of default on a futures contract. If the price rises, the seller has an incentive to default on a forward contract. However, after paying the clearinghouse, the seller of a futures contract has little reason to default. If the price falls, the same argument can be made for the buyer. Because changes in the value of the underlying asset are recognized daily, there is no accumulation of loss and the incentive to default is reduced.

Because of this default issue, forward contracts generally involve individuals and institutions who know and can trust one another. However, lawyers earn a handsome living writing supposedly airtight forward contracts, even among friends. The genius of the mark-to-the-market system is that it can prevent default where it is most likely to occur – among investors who do not know one another.

25.4 Hedging

Now that we have determined how futures contracts work, let us talk about hedging. There are two types of hedge, long and short. We discuss the short hedge first.

Example 25.1

Futures Hedging

In March, Simon Agyei-Ampomah, a Ghanaian farmer, anticipates a harvest of 5,000 tonnes of cocoa at the end of September. He has two alternatives.

1 *Write futures contracts against his anticipated harvest.* From the example in the previous section, the September cocoa contract is trading at $24,180/per contract (10 tonnes) on 13 April. He executes the following transaction:

Date of transaction	Transaction	Price per 10 tonnes
13 April	Write 500 September futures contracts	$24,180

He notes that transportation costs to the designated delivery point in London are $100 per 10 tonnes. Thus, his net price per contract is $24,080 = $24,180 – $100.

2 *Harvest the cocoa without writing a futures contract.* Alternatively, Mr Agyei-Ampomah could harvest the cocoa without the benefit of a futures contract. The risk would be quite great here because no one knows what the cash price in September will be. If prices rise, he will profit. Conversely, he will lose if prices fall.

We say that strategy 2 is an unhedged position because there is no attempt to use the futures markets to reduce risk. Conversely, strategy 1 involves a hedge. That is, a position in the futures market offsets the risk of a position in the physical – that is, in the actual – commodity.

Though hedging may seem quite sensible to you, it should be mentioned that not everyone hedges. Mr Agyei-Ampomah might reject hedging for at least two reasons.

First, he may simply be uninformed about hedging. We have found that not everyone in business understands the hedging concept. Many executives have told us that they do not want to use futures markets for hedging their inventories because the risks are too great. However, we disagree. While there are large price fluctuations in these markets, hedging actually reduces the risk that an individual holding inventory bears.

Second, Mr Agyei-Ampomah may have special insight or private information that commodity prices will rise. He would not be wise to lock in a price of $2,418 if he expects the cash price in September to be well above this price.

The hedge of strategy 1 is called a short hedge because Mr Agyei-Ampomah reduces his risk by *selling* a futures contract. The short hedge is very common in business. It occurs whenever someone either anticipates receiving inventory or is holding inventory. Mr Agyei-Ampomah is anticipating the harvest of cocoa. A manufacturer of soybean meal and oil may hold large quantities of raw soybeans that are already paid for. However, the prices to be received for meal and oil are not known because no one knows what the market prices will be when the meal and oil are produced. The manufacturer may write futures contracts in meal and oil to lock in sales prices. An oil company may hold large inventories of petroleum to be processed into heating oil. The firm could sell futures contracts in heating oil to lock in the sales price. A mortgage banker may assemble mortgages slowly before selling them in bulk to a financial institution. Movements of interest rates affect the value of the mortgages while they are in inventory. The mortgage banker could sell Treasury bond futures contracts to offset this interest rate risk. (This last example is treated in Section 25.5.)

Example 25.2

More Hedging

On 1 April, Maan Chemical agreed to sell petrochemicals (in US dollars) to the Dutch government in the future. The delivery dates and prices have been determined. Because oil is a basic ingredient of the production process, Maan Chemical will need to have large quantities of oil on hand. The firm can get the oil in one of two ways:

1 *Buy the oil as the firm needs it.* This is an unhedged position because, as of 1 April, the firm does not know the prices it will later have to pay for the oil. Oil is quite a volatile commodity, so Maan Chemical is bearing a good bit of risk. The key to this risk bearing is that the sales price to the Dutch government has already been fixed. Thus, Maan Chemical cannot pass on increased costs to the consumer.

2 *Buy futures contracts.*[4] The firm can buy futures contracts with expiration months corresponding to the dates the firm needs inventory. The futures contracts lock in the purchase price to Maan Chemical. Because there is a crude oil futures contract for every month, selecting the correct futures contract is not difficult. Many other commodities have only five contracts per year, frequently necessitating buying contracts one month away from the month of production.

As mentioned earlier, Maan Chemical is interested in hedging the risk of fluctuating oil prices because it cannot pass any cost increases on to the consumer. Suppose, alternatively, that Maan Chemical was not selling petrochemicals on fixed contract to the Dutch government. Instead, imagine that the petrochemicals were to be sold to private industry at currently prevailing prices. The price of petrochemicals should move directly with oil prices because oil is a major component of petrochemicals. Because cost increases are likely to be passed on to the consumer, Maan Chemical would probably not want to hedge in this case. Instead, the firm is likely to choose strategy 1, buying the oil as it is needed. If oil prices increase between 1 April and 1 September, Maan Chemical will, of course, find that its inputs have become quite costly. However, in a competitive market, its revenues are likely to rise as well.

Strategy 2 is called a long hedge because one *purchases* a futures contract to reduce risk. In other words, one takes a long position in the futures market. In general, a firm institutes a long hedge when it is committed to a fixed sales price. One class of situations involves actual written contracts with customers, such as Maan Chemical had with the Dutch government. Alternatively, a firm may find that it cannot easily pass on costs to consumers or does not want to pass on these costs.

25.5 Interest Rate Derivatives

In this section, we consider interest rate derivatives. Our examples deal with futures contracts on Treasury bonds because of their high popularity. We first price Treasury bonds and Treasury bond forward contracts. Differences between futures and forward contracts are explored. Hedging examples are provided next.

Pricing of Treasury Bonds

As mentioned earlier in the text, a Treasury bond pays semi-annual interest over its life. In addition, the face value of the bond is paid at maturity. Consider a 20-year, 8 per cent coupon bond that was issued on 1 March. The first payment is to occur in six months – that is, on 1 September. The value of the bond can be determined as follows:

Pricing of Treasury bond

Equation 25.1

$$P_{\text{TB}} = \frac{€40}{1+R_1} + \frac{€40}{(1+R_2)^2} + \frac{€40}{(1+R_3)^3} + \ldots + \frac{€40}{(1+R_{39})^{39}} + \frac{€1{,}040}{(1+R_{40})^{40}}$$

Because an 8 per cent coupon bond pays interest of €80 a year, the semi-annual coupon is €40. The principal and semi-annual coupons are both paid at maturity. As we mentioned in Chapter 5, the price of the Treasury bond, PTB, is determined by discounting each payment on a bond at the appropriate spot rate. Because the payments are semi-annual, each spot rate is expressed in semi-annual terms. That is, imagine a horizontal term structure where the effective annual yield is 12 per cent for all maturities. Because each spot rate, R, is expressed in semi-annual terms, each spot rate is $\sqrt{1.12} - 1 = 5.83$. Coupon payments occur every six months, so there are 40 spot rates over the 20-year period.

Interest Rate Forward Contracts

Now imagine a *forward* contract where, on 1 March, you agree to buy a new 20-year, 8 per cent coupon Treasury bond in six months (on 1 September). As with typical forward contracts, you will pay for the bond on 1 September, not 1 March. The cash flows from both the Treasury bond issued on 1 March and the forward contract that you purchase on 1 March are presented in Figure 25.1. The cash flows on the Treasury bond begin exactly six months earlier than do the cash flows on the forward contract. The Treasury bond is purchased with cash on 1 March (date 0). The first coupon payment occurs on 1 September (date 1). The last coupon payment occurs at date 40, along with the face value of €1,000. The forward contract compels you to pay $P_{\text{FORW.CONT.}}$, the price of the forward contract, on 1 September (date 1). You receive a new Treasury bond at that time. The first coupon payment you receive from the bond occurs on 1 March of the following year (date 2). The last coupon payment occurs at date 41, along with the face value of €1,000.

Figure 25.1 Cash Flows for Both a Treasury Bond and a Forward Contract on a Treasury Bond

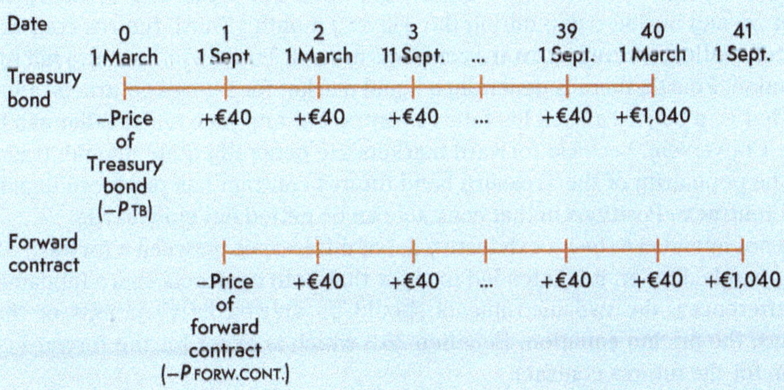

Given the 40 spot rates, Equation 25.1 showed how to price a Treasury bond. How do we price the forward contract on a Treasury bond? Just as we saw in Section 5.2 that net present value analysis can be used to price bonds, we will now show that net present value analysis can be used to price forward contracts. Given the cash flows for the forward contract in Figure 25.1, the price of the forward contract must satisfy the following equation:

Equation 25.2

$$\frac{P_{\text{FORW.CONT.}}}{1+R_1} = \frac{€40}{(1+R_2)^2} + \frac{€40}{(1+R_3)^3} + \frac{€40}{(1+R_4)^4} + \ldots + \frac{€40}{(1+R_{40})^{40}} + \frac{€1,040}{(1+R_{41})^{41}}$$

The right side of Equation 25.2 discounts all the cash flows from the delivery instrument (the Treasury bond issued on 1 September) back to date 0 (1 March). Because the first cash flow occurs at date 2 (March 1 of the subsequent year), it is discounted by $1/(1+R_2)^2$. The last cash flow of €1,040 occurs at date 41, so it is discounted by $1/(1+R_{41})^{41}$. The left side represents the cost of the forward contract as of date 0. Because the actual out-payment occurs at date 1, it is discounted by $1/(1+R_1)$.

Students often ask, 'Why are we discounting everything back to date 0 when we are actually paying for the forward contract on 1 September?' The answer is simply that we apply the same techniques to Equation 25.2 that we apply to all capital budgeting problems: we want to put everything in today's (date 0's) euros. Given that the spot rates are known in the marketplace, traders should have no more trouble pricing a forward contract by Equation 25.2 than they would have pricing a Treasury bond by Equation 25.1.

Forward contracts are similar to the underlying bonds themselves. If the entire term structure of interest rates unexpectedly shifts upwards on 2 March, the Treasury bond issued the previous day should fall in value. This can be seen from Equation 25.1. A rise in each of the spot rates lowers the present value of each of the coupon payments. Hence, the value of the bond must fall. Conversely, a fall in the term structure of interest rates increases the value of the bond.

The same relationship holds with forward contracts, as we can see by rewriting Equation 25.2 like this:

Equation 25.3

$$P_{\text{FORW.CONT.}} = \frac{€40\times(1+R_1)}{(1+R_2)^2} + \frac{€40\times(1+R_1)}{(1+R_3)^3} + \frac{€40\times(1+R_1)}{(1+R_4)^4} + \ldots + \frac{€40\times(1+R_1)}{(1+R_{40})^{40}} + \frac{€1,040\times(1+R_1)}{(1+R_{41})^{41}}$$

We went from Equation 25.2 to 25.3 by multiplying both the left and the right sides by $(1+R_1)$. If the entire term structure of interest rates unexpectedly shifts upwards on 2 March, the *first* term on the right side of Equation 25.3 should fall in value.[5] That is, both R_1 and R_2 will rise an equal amount. However, R_1 enters as a *squared* term, $1/(1+R_2)^2$, so an increase in R_2 more than offsets the increase in R_1. As we move further to the right, an increase in any spot rate, R_i, more than offsets an increase in R_1. Here R_i enters as the ith power, $1/(1+R_i)^i$. Thus, as long as the entire term structure shifts upwards an equal amount on 2 March, the value of a forward contract must fall on that date. Conversely, as long as the entire term structure shifts downwards an equal amount on 2 March, the value of a forward contract must rise.

Interest Rate Futures Contracts

The previous discussion concerned a forward contract in Treasury bonds – that is, a forward contract where the deliverable instrument is a Treasury bond. What about a futures contract on a Treasury bond?[6] We mentioned earlier that futures contracts and forward contracts are quite similar, though there are a few differences between the two. First, futures contracts are generally traded on exchanges, whereas forward contracts are not traded on an exchange. Second, futures contracts generally allow the seller a period of time in which to deliver, whereas forward contracts generally call for delivery on a particular day. The seller of a Treasury bond futures contract can choose to deliver on any business day during the delivery month.[7] Third, futures contracts are subject to the mark-to-the-market convention, whereas forward contracts are not. Traders in Treasury bill futures contracts must adhere to this convention. Fourth, there is generally a liquid market for futures contracts, allowing contracts to be quickly netted out. That is, a buyer can sell his futures contract at any time and a seller can buy back her futures contract at any time. Conversely, because forward markets are generally quite illiquid, traders cannot easily net out their positions. The popularity of the Treasury bond futures contract has produced liquidity even higher than that on other futures contracts. Positions in that contract can be netted out quite easily.

This discussion is not intended to be an exhaustive list of differences between a forward contract and a futures contract on Treasury bonds. Rather, it is intended to show that both contracts share fundamental characteristics. Though there are differences, the two instruments should be viewed as variations of the same species, not different species. Thus, the pricing equation, Equation 25.3 which is exact for the forward contract, should be a decent approximation for the futures contract.

Hedging in Interest Rate Futures

Now that we have the basic institutional details under our belts, we are ready for examples of hedging using either futures contracts or forward contracts on Treasury bonds. Because the T-bond futures contract is extremely popular, whereas the forward contract is traded sporadically, our examples use the futures contract.

Example 25.3

Interest Rate Hedging

Erik Werenskiold owns a mortgage banking company. On 1 March he made a commitment to lend a total of €1 million to various homeowners on 1 May. The loans are 20-year mortgages carrying a 12 per cent coupon, the going interest rate on mortgages at the time. Thus, the mortgages are made at par. Though homeowners would not use the term, we could say that he is buying a *forward contract* on a mortgage. That is, he agrees on 1 March to give €1 million to his borrowers on 1 May in exchange for principal and interest from them every month for the next 20 years.

Like many mortgage bankers, he has no intention of paying the €1 million out of his own pocket. Rather, he intends to sell the mortgages to an insurance company. Thus, the insurance company will actually lend the funds, and will receive principal and interest over the next 20 years. Mr Werenskiold does not currently have an insurance company in mind. He plans to visit the mortgage departments of insurance companies over the next 60 days to sell the mortgages to one or many of them. He sets 30 April as a deadline for making the sale because the borrowers expect the funds on the following day.

Suppose Mr Werenskiold sells the mortgages to Superbe Insurance on 15 April. What price will Superbe pay for the bonds?

You may think the insurance company will obviously pay €1 million for the loans. However, suppose interest rates have risen above 12 per cent by 15 April. The insurance company will buy the mortgage at a discount. Suppose, say, that the insurance company agrees to pay only €940,000 for the mortgages. Because the mortgage banker agreed to lend a full €1 million to the borrowers, the mortgage banker must come up with the additional €60,000 (= €1 million – €940,000) out of his own pocket.

Alternatively, suppose interest rates fall below 12 per cent by 15 April. The mortgages can be sold at a premium under this scenario. If the insurance company buys the mortgages at €1.05 million, the mortgage banker will have made an unexpected profit of €50,000 (= €1.05 million – €1 million).

Because Erik Werenskiold is unable to forecast interest rates, this risk is something that he would like to avoid. The risk is summarized in Table 25.4.

Table 25.4 Effects of Changing Interest Rates on Erik Werenskiold, Mortgage Banker

	Mortgage Interest Rate on 15 April	
	Above 12%	**Below 12%**
Sale price to Superbe Insurance	Below €1 million (we assume €940,000).	Above €1 million (we assume €1.05 million).
Effect on mortgage banker	He loses because he must lend the full €1 million to borrowers.	He gains because he lends only €1 million to borrowers.
Euro gain or loss	Loss of €60,000 (= €1 million – 940,000).	Gain of €50,000 (= €1.05 million – €1 million).

Note: The interest rate on 1 March, the date when the loan agreement was made with the borrowers, was 12 per cent. The mortgages were sold to Superbe Insurance on 15 April.

Seeing the interest rate risk, students at this point may ask, 'What does the mortgage banker get out of this loan to offset his risk bearing?' Mr Werenskiold wants to sell the mortgages to the insurance company so that he can get two fees. The first is an *origination fee,* which is paid to the mortgage banker by the insurance company on 15 April – that is, on the date the loan is sold. An industry standard in certain locales is 1 per cent of the value of the loan, which is €10,000 (= 1% × €1 million). In addition, Mr Werenskiold will act as a collection agent for the insurance company. For this service he will receive a small portion of the outstanding balance of the loan each month. For example, if he is paid 0.03 per cent of the loan each month, he will receive €300 (= 0.03% × €1 million) in the first month. As the outstanding balance of the loan declines, he will receive less.

Though Mr Werenskiold will earn profitable fees on the loan, he bears interest rate risk. He loses money if interest rates rise after 1 March, and he profits if interest rates fall after 1 March. To hedge this risk, he writes June Treasury bond futures contracts on 1 March. As with mortgages, Treasury bond futures contracts fall in value if interest rates rise. Because he *writes* the contract, he makes money on these contracts if they fall in value. Therefore, with an interest rate rise, the loss he endures in the mortgages is offset by the gain he earns in the futures market. Conversely, Treasury bond futures contracts rise in value if interest rates fall. Because he writes the contracts, he suffers losses on them when rates fall. With an interest rate fall, the profit he makes on the mortgages is offset by the loss he suffers in the futures markets.

The details of this hedging transaction are presented in Table 25.5. The column on the left is labelled 'Cash Markets' because the deal in the mortgage market is transacted off an exchange. The column on the right shows the offsetting transactions in the futures market. Consider the first row. The mortgage banker enters into a forward contract on 1 March. He simultaneously writes Treasury bond futures contracts. Ten contracts are written because the deliverable instrument on each contract is €100,000 of Treasury bonds. The total is €2 million (= 10 × €100,000), which is equal to the value of the mortgages. Mr Werenskiold would prefer to write May Treasury bond futures contracts. Here, Treasury bonds would be delivered on the futures contract during the same month that the loan is funded. Because there is no May T-bond futures contract, Mr Werenskiold achieves the closest match through a June contract.

Table 25.5 Illustration of Hedging Strategy for Erik Werenskiold, Mortgage Banker

	Cash Markets	Futures
1 March	Mortgage banker makes forward contracts to lend €1 million at 12 per cent for 20 years. The loans are to be funded on 1 May. No cash changes hands on 1 March.	Mortgage banker writes 10 June Treasury bond futures contracts.
15 April	Loans are sold to Superbe Insurance. Mortgage banker will receive sale price from Superbe on the 1 May funding date.	Mortgage banker buys back all the futures contracts.
If interest rates rise:	Loans are sold at a price below €1 million. Mortgage banker loses because he receives less than the €1 million he must give to borrowers.	Each futures contract is bought back at a price below the sales price, resulting in *profit*. Mortgage banker's profit in futures market offsets loss in cash market.
If interest rates fall:	Loans are sold at a price above €1 million. Mortgage banker gains because he receives more than the €1 million he must give to borrowers.	Each futures contract is bought back at a price above the sales price, resulting in loss. Mortgage banker's loss in futures market offsets gain in cash market.

If held to maturity, the June contract would obligate the mortgage banker to deliver Treasury bonds in June. Interest rate risk ends in the cash market when the loans are sold. Interest rate risk must be terminated in the futures market at that time. Thus, Mr Werenskiold nets out his position in the futures contract as soon as the loan is sold to Superbe Insurance.

As our example shows, risk is clearly reduced via an offsetting transaction in the futures market. However, is risk totally eliminated? Risk would be totally eliminated if losses in the cash markets were *exactly* offset by gains in the futures markets, and vice versa. This is unlikely to happen because mortgages and Treasury bonds are not identical instruments. First, mortgages may have different maturities from Treasury bonds. Second, Treasury bonds have a different payment stream from mortgages. The principal is paid only at maturity on T-bonds, whereas principal is paid every month on mortgages. Because mortgages pay principal continuously, these instruments have a shorter *effective* time to maturity than do Treasury bonds of equal maturity.[8] Third, mortgages have default risk whereas Treasury bonds do not. The term structure applicable to instruments with default risk may change even when the term structure for risk-free assets remains constant. Fourth, mortgages may be paid off early and hence have a shorter *expected maturity* than Treasury bonds of equal maturity.

Because mortgages and Treasury bonds are not identical instruments, they are not identically affected by interest rates. If Treasury bonds are less volatile than mortgages, financial consultants may advise Mr Werenskiold to write more than 10 T-bond futures contracts. Conversely, if these bonds are more volatile, the consultant may state that fewer than 10 futures contracts are indicated. An optimal ratio of futures to mortgages will reduce risk as much as possible. However, because the price movements of mortgages and Treasury bonds are not *perfectly correlated*, Mr Werenskiold's hedging strategy cannot eliminate all risk.

The preceding strategy is called a *short hedge* because Mr Werenskiold sells futures contracts to reduce risk. Though it involves an interest rate futures contract, this short hedge is analogous to short hedges in agricultural and metallurgical futures contracts. We argued at the beginning of this chapter that individuals and firms institute short hedges to offset inventory price fluctuation. Once Mr Werenskiold makes a contract to lend money to borrowers, the mortgages effectively become his inventory. He writes a futures contract to offset the price fluctuation of his inventory.

We now consider an example where a mortgage banker institutes a long hedge.

Example 25.4

Short versus Long Hedging

Margaret Boswell is another mortgage banker. Her firm faces problems similar to those facing Mr Werenskiold's firm. However, she tackles the problems through the use of advance commitments, a strategy that is the opposite of Mr Werenskiold's. That is, she promises to deliver loans to a financial institution *before* she lines up borrowers. On 1 March her firm agreed to sell mortgages to No-State Insurance. The agreement specifies that she must turn over 12 per cent coupon mortgages with a face value of €1 million to No-State by 1 May. No-State is buying the mortgages at par, implying that it will pay Ms Boswell €1 million on 1 May. As of 1 March, Ms Boswell had not signed up any borrowers. Over the next two months, she will seek out individuals who want mortgages beginning 1 May.

As with Mr Werenskiold, changing interest rates will affect Ms Boswell. If interest rates fall before she signs up a borrower, the borrower will demand a premium on a 12 per cent coupon loan. That is, the borrower will receive more than par on 1 May.[9] Because Ms Boswell receives par from the insurance company, she must make up the difference.

Conversely, if interest rates rise, a 12 per cent coupon loan will be made at a discount. That is, the borrower will receive less than par on 1 May. Because Ms Boswell receives par from the insurance company, the difference is pure profit to her.

The details are provided in Table 25.6. As did Mr Werenskiold, Ms Boswell finds the risk burdensome. Therefore, she offsets her advance commitment with a transaction in the futures markets. Because she *loses* in the cash market when interest rates fall, she *buys* futures contracts to reduce the risk. When interest rates fall, the value of her futures contracts increases. The gain in the futures market offsets the loss in the cash market. Conversely, she gains in the cash markets when interest rates rise. The value of her futures contracts decreases when interest rates rise, offsetting her gain.

Table 25.6 Illustration of Advance Commitment for Margaret Boswell, Mortgage Banker

	Cash Markets	Futures
1 March	Mortgage banker makes a forward contract (advance commitment) to deliver €1 million of mortgages to No-State Insurance. The insurance company will pay par to Ms Boswell for the loans on 1 May. The borrowers are to receive their funding from the mortgage banker on 1 May. The mortgages are to be 12 per cent coupon loans for 20 years.	Mortgage banker buys 10 June Treasury bond futures contracts.
15 April	Mortgage banker signs up borrowers to 12 per cent coupon, 20-year mortgages. She promises that the borrowers will receive funds on 1 May.	Mortgage banker sells all futures contracts.
If interest rates rise:	Mortgage banker issues mortgages to borrowers at a discount. Mortgage banker gains because she receives par from the insurance company.	Futures contracts are sold at a price below purchase price, resulting in loss. Mortgage banker's loss in futures market offsets gain in cash market.
If interest rates fall:	Loans to borrowers are issued at a premium. Mortgage banker loses because she receives only par from insurance company.	Futures contracts are sold at a price above purchase price, resulting in gain. Mortgage banker's gain in futures market offsets loss in cash market.

We call this a *long hedge* because Ms Boswell offsets risk in the cash markets by buying a futures contract. Though it involves an interest rate futures contract, this long hedge is analogous to long hedges in agricultural and metallurgical futures contracts. We argued at the beginning of this chapter that individuals and firms institute long hedges when their finished goods are to be sold at a fixed price. Once Ms Boswell makes the advance commitment with No-State Insurance, she has fixed her sales price. She buys a futures contract to offset the price fluctuation of her raw materials – that is, her mortgages.

25.6 Duration Hedging

Section 25.5 concerned the risk of interest rate changes. We now want to explore this risk in a more precise manner. In particular, we want to show that the concept of duration is a prime determinant of interest rate risk. We begin by considering the effect of interest rate movements on bond prices.

The Case of Zero Coupon Bonds

Imagine a world where the interest rate is 10 per cent across all maturities. A one-year pure discount bond pays €110 at maturity. A five-year pure discount bond pays €161.05 at maturity. Both of these bonds are worth €100, as given by the following:

Value of one-year pure discount bond

$$€100 = \frac{€110}{1.10}$$

Value of five-year pure discount bond

$$€100 = \frac{€161.05}{(1.10)^5}$$

Which bond will change more when interest rates move? To find out, we calculate the value of these bonds when interest rates are either 8 or 12 per cent. The results are presented in Table 25.7. As can be seen, the five-year bond has greater price swings than does the one-year bond. That is, both bonds are worth €100 when interest rates are 10 per cent. The five-year bond is worth more than the one-year bond when interest rates are 8 per cent and worth less than the one-year bond when interest rates are 12 per cent. We state that the five-year bond is subject to more price volatility. This point, which was mentioned in passing in an earlier section of the chapter, is not difficult to understand. The interest rate term in the denominator, 1+R, is taken to the fifth power for a five-year bond and only to the first power for the one-year bond. Thus, the effect of a changing interest rate is magnified for the five-year bond. The general rule is this:

The percentage price changes in long-term pure discount bonds are greater than the percentage price changes in short-term pure discount bonds.

Table 25.7 Value of a Pure Discount Bond as a Function of Interest Rate

Interest Rate (%)	One-year Pure Discount Bond	Five-year Pure Discount Bond
8	$€101.85 = \frac{€110}{1.08}$	$€109.61 = \frac{€161.05}{(1.08)^5}$
10	$€100.00 = \frac{€110}{1.10}$	$€100.00 = \frac{€161.05}{(1.10)^5}$
12	$€98.21 = \frac{€110}{1.12}$	$€91.38 = \frac{€161.05}{(1.12)^5}$

Note: For a given interest rate change, a five-year pure discount bond fluctuates more in price than does a one-year pure discount bond.

The Case of Two Bonds with the Same Maturity but with Different Coupons

The previous example concerned pure discount bonds of different maturities. We now want to see the effect of different coupons on price volatility. To abstract from the effect of differing maturities, we consider two bonds with the same maturity but with different coupons.

Consider a five-year, 10 per cent coupon bond and a five-year, 1 per cent coupon bond. When interest rates are 10 per cent, the bonds are priced like this:

Value of five-year, 10 per cent coupon bond

$$€100 = \frac{€10}{1.10} + \frac{€10}{(1.10)^2} + \frac{€10}{(1.10)^3} + \frac{€10}{(1.10)^4} + \frac{€110}{(1.10)^5}$$

Value of five-year, 1 per cent coupon bond

$$€65.88 = \frac{€1}{1.10} + \frac{€1}{(1.10)^2} + \frac{€1}{(1.10)^3} + \frac{€1}{(1.10)^4} + \frac{€101}{(1.10)^5}$$

Which bond will change more in *percentage terms* if interest rates change?[10] To find out, we first calculate the value of these bonds when interest rates are either 8 or 12 per cent. The results are presented in Table 25.8. As we would expect, the 10 per cent coupon bond always sells for more than the 1 per cent coupon bond. Also as we would expect, each bond is worth more when the interest rate is 8 per cent than when the interest rate is 12 per cent.

Table 25.8 Value of Coupon Bonds at Different Interest Rates

Interest Rate (%)	Value
5-year, 10% coupon bond	
8	$€107.99 = \frac{€10}{1.18} + \frac{€10}{(1.08)^2} + \frac{€10}{(1.08)^3} + \frac{€10}{(1.08)^4} + \frac{€110}{(1.08)^5}$
10	$€100.00 = \frac{€10}{1.10} + \frac{€10}{(1.10)^2} + \frac{€10}{(1.10)^3} + \frac{€10}{(1.10)^4} + \frac{€110}{(1.10)^5}$
12	$€92.79 = \frac{€10}{1.12} + \frac{€10}{(1.12)^2} + \frac{€10}{(1.12)^3} + \frac{€10}{(1.12)^4} + \frac{€110}{(1.12)^5}$
5-year, 1% coupon bond	
8	$€72.05 = \frac{€1}{1.08} + \frac{€1}{(1.08)^2} + \frac{€1}{(1.08)^3} + \frac{€1}{(1.08)^4} + \frac{€101}{(1.08)^5}$
10	$€65.35 = \frac{€1}{1.10} + \frac{€1}{(1.10)^2} + \frac{€1}{(1.10)^3} + \frac{€1}{(1.10)^4} + \frac{€101}{(1.10)^5}$
12	$€60.35 = \frac{€1}{1.12} + \frac{€1}{(1.12)^2} + \frac{€1}{(1.12)^3} + \frac{€1}{(1.12)^4} + \frac{€101}{(1.12)^5}$

We calculate percentage price changes for both bonds as the interest rate changes from 10 to 8 per cent and from 10 to 12 per cent:

	10% Coupon Bond	1% Coupon Bond
Interest rate changes from 10% to 8%:	$7.99\% = \frac{€107.99}{€100} - 1$	$9.37\% = \frac{€72.05}{€65.88} - 1$
Interest rate changes from 10% to 12%:	$-7.21\% = \frac{€92.79}{€100} - 1$	$-8.39\% = \frac{€60.35}{€65.88} - 1$

As we can see, the 1 per cent coupon bond has a greater percentage price increase than does the 10 per cent coupon bond when the interest rate falls. Similarly, the 1 per cent coupon bond has a greater percentage price decrease than does the 10 per cent coupon bond when the interest rate rises. Thus, we say that the percentage price changes on the 1 per cent coupon bond are greater than are the percentage price changes on the 10 per cent coupon bond.

Duration

The question, of course, is 'Why?' We can answer this question only after we have explored a concept called duration. We begin by noticing that any coupon bond is actually a combination of pure discount bonds. For example, the five-year, 10 per cent coupon bond is made up of five pure discount bonds:

1 A pure discount bond paying €10 at the end of year 1
2 A pure discount bond paying €10 at the end of year 2
3 A pure discount bond paying €10 at the end of year 3
4 A pure discount bond paying €10 at the end of year 4
5 A pure discount bond paying €110 at the end of year 5.

Similarly, the five-year, 1 per cent coupon bond is made up of five pure discount bonds. Because the price volatility of a pure discount bond is determined by its maturity, we would like to determine the average maturity of the five pure discount bonds that make up a five-year coupon bond. This leads us to the concept of duration.

We calculate average maturity in three steps. For the 10 per cent coupon bond, we have these:

1 *Calculate present value of each payment.* We do this as follows:

Year	Payment (€)	Present Value of Payment by Discounting at 10% (€)
1	10	9.091
2	10	8.264
3	10	7.513
4	10	6.830
5	110	68.302
		100.00

2 *Express the present value of each payment in relative terms.* We calculate the relative value of a single payment as the ratio of the present value of the payment to the value of the bond. The value of the bond is €100. We obtain these values:

Year	Payment (€)	Present Value of Payment (€)	Relative value = $\frac{\text{Present value of payment}}{\text{Value of bond}}$
1	10	9.091	9.091/100=0.09091
2	10	8.264	0.08264
3	10	7.513	0.07513
4	10	6.830	0.06830
5	110	68.302	0.68302
		100.00	1.0

The bulk of the relative value, 68.302 per cent, occurs at year 5 because the principal is paid back at that time.

3 *Weight the maturity of each payment by its relative value:*

$$4.169 \text{ year} = 1 \text{ year} \times 0.09091 + 2 \text{ year} \times 0.08264 + 3 \text{ year} \times 0.07513$$
$$+4 \text{ year} \times 0.6830 + 5 \text{ year} \times 0.68302$$

There are many ways to calculate the average maturity of a bond. We have calculated it by weighting the maturity of each payment by the payment's present value. We find that the *effective* maturity of the bond is 4.1699 years. *Duration* is a commonly used word for effective maturity. Thus, the bond's duration is 4.1699 years. Note that duration is expressed in units of time.[11]

Because the five-year, 10 per cent coupon bond has a duration of 4.1699 years, its percentage price fluctuations should be the same as those of a zero coupon bond with a duration of 4.1699 years.[12] It turns out that the five-year, 1 per cent coupon bond has a duration of 4.8742 years. Because the 1 per cent coupon bond has a higher duration than the 10 per cent bond, the 1 per cent coupon bond should be subject to greater price fluctuations. This is exactly what we found earlier. In general we say the following:

The percentage price changes of a bond with high duration are greater than the percentage price changes of a bond with low duration.

A final question: Why *does* the 1 per cent bond have a greater duration than the 10 per cent bond, even though they both have the same five-year maturity? As mentioned earlier, duration is an average of the maturity of the bond's cash flows, weighted by the present value of each cash flow. The 1 per cent coupon bond receives only €1 in each of the first four years. Thus the weights applied to years 1 through 4 in the duration formula will be low. Conversely, the 10 per cent coupon bond receives €10 in each of the first four years. The weights applied to years 1 through 4 in the duration formula will be higher.

Matching Liabilities with Assets

In Section 25.3, we argued that firms can hedge risk by trading in futures. Because some firms are subject to interest rate risk, we showed how they can hedge with interest rate futures contracts. Firms may also hedge interest rate risk by matching liabilities with assets. This ability to hedge follows from our discussion of duration.

Example 25.5

Using Duration

The Bank of Amsterdam has the following market value balance sheet:

BANK OF AMSTERDAM Market Value Balance Sheet		
	Market Value (€)	**Duration**
Assets		
Overnight money	35 million	0
Accounts receivable-backed loans	500 million	3 months
Inventory loans	275 million	6 months
Industrial loans	40 million	2 years
Mortgages	150 million	14.8 years
	1,000 million	
Liabilities and Owners' Equity		
Chequing and savings accounts	400 million	0
Certificates of deposit	300 million	1 year
Long-term financing	200 million	10 years
Equity	100 million	
	1,000 million	

The bank has €1,000 million of assets and €900 million of liabilities. Its equity is the difference between the two: €100 million (= €1,000 million − €900 million). Both the market value and the duration of each individual item are provided in the balance sheet. Both overnight money and chequing and savings accounts have a duration of zero. This is because the interest paid on these instruments adjusts immediately to changing interest rates in the economy.

The bank's managers think that interest rates are likely to move quickly in the coming months. Because they do not know the direction of the movement, they are worried that their bank is vulnerable to changing rates. They call in a consultant, Jan Mandyn, to determine a hedging strategy.

Mr Mandyn first calculates the duration of the assets and the duration of the liabilities:[13]

Duration of assets

Equation 25.4

$$2.56 \text{ years} = 0 \text{ year} \times \frac{€500 \text{ million}}{€1{,}000 \text{ million}} + ¼ \text{ year} \times \frac{€500 \text{ million}}{€1{,}000 \text{ million}} + ½ \text{ year} \times \frac{€275 \text{ million}}{€1{,}000 \text{ million}} + 2 \text{ years} \times \frac{€40 \text{ millon}}{€1{,}000 \text{ million}} + 14.8 \text{ years} \times \frac{€150 \text{ million}}{€1{,}000 \text{ million}}$$

Duration of liabilities

Equation 25.5

$$2.56 \text{ years} = 0 \text{ year} \times \frac{€400 \text{ million}}{€900 \text{ million}} + 1 \text{ year} \times \frac{€300 \text{ million}}{€900 \text{ million}} + 10 \text{ years} \times \frac{€200 \text{ million}}{€900 \text{ million}}$$

The duration of the assets, 2.56 years, equals the duration of the liabilities. Because of this, Mr Mandyn argues that the firm is immune to interest rate risk.

Just to be on the safe side, the bank calls in a second consultant, Gabrielle Aertsen. Ms Aertsen argues that it is incorrect to simply match durations because assets total €1,000 million and liabilities total only €900 million. If both assets and liabilities have the same duration, the price change on a *euro* of assets should be equal to the price change on a euro of liabilities. However, the *total* price change will be greater for assets than for liabilities because there are more assets than liabilities in this bank. The firm will be immune from interest rate risk only when the duration of the liabilities is greater than the duration of the assets. Ms Aertsen states that the following relationship must hold if the bank is to be immunized – that is, immune to interest rate risk:

Equation 25.6 Duration of assets × Market value of assets = Duration of liabilities × Market value of liabilities

She says that the bank should not *equate* the duration of the liabilities with the duration of the assets. Rather, using Equation 25.6, the bank should match the duration of the liabilities to the duration of the assets. She suggests two ways to achieve this match.

1 *Increase the duration of the liabilities without changing the duration of the assets.* Ms Aertsen argues that the duration of the liabilities could be increased to:

$$\text{Duration of assets} \times \frac{\text{Market value of assets}}{\text{Market value of liabilities}} = 2.56 \text{ years} \times \frac{€1{,}000 \text{ million}}{€900 \text{ million}} = 2.84 \text{ years}$$

Equation 25.5 then becomes:

$$2.56 \times €1 \text{ billion} = 2.56 \times €900 \text{ million}$$

2 *Decrease the duration of the assets without changing the duration of the liabilities.* Alternatively, Ms Aertsen points out that the duration of the assets could be decreased to:

$$\text{Duration of liabilities} \times \frac{\text{Market value of liabilities}}{\text{Market value of assets}} = 2.56 \text{ years} \times \frac{€900 \text{ million}}{€1{,}000 \text{ million}} = 2.30 \text{ years}$$

Duration and the accompanying immunization strategies are useful in other areas of finance. For instance, many firms establish pension funds to meet obligations to retirees. If the assets of a pension fund are invested in bonds and other fixed-income securities, the duration of the assets can be computed. Similarly, the firm views the obligations to retirees as analogous to interest payments on debt. The duration of these liabilities can be calculated as well. The manager of a pension fund would commonly choose pension assets so that the duration of the assets is matched with the duration of the liabilities. In this way, changing interest rates would not affect the net worth of the pension fund.

Life insurance companies receiving premiums today are legally obligated to provide death benefits in the future. Actuaries view these future benefits as analogous to interest and principal payments of fixed-income securities. The duration of these expected benefits can be calculated. Insurance firms frequently invest in bonds where the duration of the bonds is matched to the duration of the future death benefits.

The business of a leasing company is quite simple. The firm issues debt to purchase assets, which are then leased. The lease payments have a duration, as does the debt. Leasing companies frequently structure debt financing so that the duration of the debt matches the duration of the lease. If a firm did not do this, the market value of its equity could be eliminated by a quick change in interest rates.

25.7 Swaps Contracts

Swaps are close cousins to forwards and futures contracts, and are arrangements between two counterparties to exchange cash flows over time. There is enormous flexibility in the forms that swaps can take, but the two basic types are interest rate swaps and currency swaps. Often these are combined when interest received in one currency is swapped for interest in another currency.

Companies will undertake a swap if they have a cash flow stream in one form and wish to convert it into another form. With interest rate swaps, the company will want to convert fixed rate coupon payments to floating rate payments (or vice versa). With currency swaps, the company will want to convert a cash flow stream it pays or receives in one currency for another. The reasons for seeking a swap can be strategic, to minimize risk or to simply save cash.

Interest Rate Swaps

Like other derivatives, swaps are tools firms use to change their risk exposures and balance sheets. Consider a firm that has an obligation to repay a 10-year loan for €100 million of principal and an annual 9 per cent coupon rate. Ignoring the possibility of calling the loan, the firm expects to pay coupons of €9 million every year for 10 years and a balloon payment of €100 million at the end of the loan. Suppose the firm is uncomfortable with having this obligation on its books. Perhaps the firm is a cyclical business where revenues vary and may fall to a point where it would be difficult to make the debt payment.

Suppose, too, the firm earns a lot of its revenue from financing the purchase of its products. For instance, a manufacturer may offer trade credit through a leasing or credit subsidiary. Usually, these short-term loans are financed at a premium over the prevailing short-term rate of interest. This means the firm's revenues move up and down with interest rates, while its costs are relatively fixed.

The firm may find it more attractive to match the variable revenues with variable costs to minimize its risk. When interest rates rise, the firm would pay more on the loan, but it would also be making more on its product financing. An interest rate swap is ideal in this situation.

Of course, the firm could also just go into the capital markets and borrow €100 million at a variable interest rate and then use the proceeds to retire its outstanding fixed-rate loan. Although this is possible, it is generally quite expensive, requiring underwriting a new loan and buying back the existing loan. The ease of entering a swap is its inherent advantage.

In this specific example, the swap would exchange the firm's fixed obligation for an agreement to pay a floating rate. Every year it would agree to pay a coupon based on the prevailing interest rate in exchange for an agreement from a counterparty to pay the firm's fixed coupon.

In years past, a common reference point for floating-rate commitments was LIBOR, which stands for the London Interbank Offered Rate, which is the rate most international banks charge one another for sterling and US dollar loans in the London market. However, because of a manipulation scandal involving several multinational banks, the use of LIBOR was discontinued in 2021. The replacement reference point for floating-rate commitments is now the ICE Bank Yield Index and based on unsecured bank debt over one-, three- and six-month periods in the currency of choice. This is administered by the Intercontinental Exchange, but other benchmarks may also be created in the future.

If we assume our firm must pay a bond with a floating rate benchmark (FRB) plus 50 basis points, then in a swap it would be exchanging its fixed 9 per cent obligation for the obligation to pay the prevailing FRB plus 50 basis points. Table 25.9 displays how the cash flows on this swap would work. In the table, we have assumed the FRB starts at 8 per cent, rises for three years to 11 per cent and then drops to 7 per cent. As the table illustrates, the firm would owe a coupon of 8.5% × €100 million = €8.5 million in year 1, €9.5 million in year 2, €10.5 million in year 3 and €11.5 million in year 4. The precipitous drop to 7 per cent lowers the annual payments to €7.5 million thereafter. In return, the firm receives the fixed payment of €9 million each year.

Rather than swapping the full payments, the cash flows would be netted so only the difference would be paid. For example, the firm owes €8.5 million and is owed by its counterparty, who is paying fixed, €9 million. Hence, net, the firm would receive a payment of €0.5 million. Because the firm has to pay its lender €9 million but gets a net payment from the swap of €0.5 million, it really pays out only the difference, or €8.5 million. In each year, then, the firm would effectively pay only FRB plus 50 basis points.

Table 25.9 Fixed for Floating Swap: Cash Flows (€ million)

	Coupons									
Year	1	2	3	4	5	6	7	8	9	10
Swap										
Fixed obligation	9	9	9	9	9	9	9	9	9	9
FRB floating	−8.5	−9.5	−10.5	−11.5	−7.5	−7.5	−7.5	−7.5	−7.5	−7.5
Original loan										
Fixed obligation	−9	−9	−9	−9	−9	−9	−9	−9	−9	109
Net effect	−8.5	−9.5	−10.5	−11.5	−7.5	−7.5	−7.5	−7.5	−7.5	−107.5

Notice, too, that the entire transaction can be carried out without any need to change the terms of the original loan. In effect, by swapping, the firm has found a counterparty that is willing to pay its fixed obligation in return for the firm paying a floating obligation.

Currency Swaps

FX stands for foreign exchange, and currency swaps are sometimes called FX swaps. Currency swaps are swaps of obligations to pay cash flows in one currency for obligations to pay in another currency.

Currency swaps arise as a natural vehicle for hedging the risk in international trade. Consider the problem of BMW, for instance, which sells a broad range of its product line in the US market. Every year the firm can count on receiving revenue from the United States in dollars. We will study international finance in Chapter 30, but for now we can just observe that, because exchange rates fluctuate, this subjects the firm to considerable risk.

If BMW produces its products in Germany and exports them to the United States, then the firm has to pay its workers and its suppliers in euros. But it is receiving some of its revenues in dollars. The €/$ exchange rate changes over time. As the dollar rises in value, the US revenues are worth more euros, but as it falls they decline. Suppose the firm can count on selling $100 million of automobiles each year in the United States. If the exchange rate is $2 for each €, then the firm will receive €50 million, but if the exchange rate were to rise to $3 for each €, the firm would receive only €33.333 million for its $100 million. Naturally, the firm would like to protect itself against these currency swings.

To do so BMW can enter a currency swap. We will learn more about exactly what the terms of such a swap might be, but for now we can assume the swap is for five years at a fixed term of $100 million for €50 million each year. Now, no matter what happens to the exchange rate between the dollar and the euro over the next five years, as long as BMW makes $100 million each year from the sale of its automobiles, it will swap this for €50 million each year.

We have not addressed the question of how the market sets prices for swaps – either interest rate swaps or currency swaps. In the fixed for floating example and in the currency swap, we just quoted some terms. We will not go into great detail on exactly how it is done, but we can stress the most important points.

Swaps, like forwards and futures, are essentially zero-sum transactions, which is to say that in both cases the market sets prices at a fair level, and neither party has any substantial bargain or loss at the moment the deal is struck. In the currency swap, for instance, the swap rate is some average of the market expectation of what the exchange rate will be over the life of the swap. In the interest rate swap, the rates are set as the fair floating and fixed rates for the creditor, taking into account the creditworthiness of the counterparties. We can actually price swaps fairly once we know how to price forward contracts. In our interest rate swap example, the firm swapped FRB plus 50 basis points for a 9 per cent fixed rate, all on a principal amount of €100 million. This is equivalent to a series of forward contracts extending over the life of the swap. In year 1, for instance, having made the swap, the firm is in the same position that it would be if it had sold a forward contract entitling the buyer to receive FRB plus 50 basis points on €100 million in return for a fixed payment of €9 million (9 per cent of €100 million). Similarly, the currency swap can also be viewed as a series of forward contracts.

Exotics

Up to now, we have dealt with the meat and potatoes of the derivatives markets: swaps, options, forwards and futures. Exotics are the complicated blends of these that often produce surprising results for buyers.

One of the more interesting types of exotics is called an *inverse floater*. In our fixed for floating swap, the floating payments fluctuated with an FRB. An inverse floater is one that fluctuates inversely with some FRB. The floater might, say, pay an interest rate of 20 per cent minus FRB. If FRB is 9 per cent, then the inverse pays 11 per cent, and if FRB rises to 12 per cent, the payments on the inverse would fall to 8 per cent. Clearly, the buyer of an inverse profits if interest rates fall.

Both floaters and inverse floaters have a supercharged version called *superfloaters* and *superinverses* that fluctuate more than one for one with movements in interest rates. As an example of a superinverse floater, consider a floater that pays an interest rate of 30 per cent minus *twice* FRB. When the FRB is 10 per cent, the inverse pays

$$30 - 2 \times 10\% = 30\% - 20\% = 10\%$$

And if the FRB falls by 3 per cent to 7 per cent, then the return on the inverse rises by 6 per cent from 10 per cent to 16 per cent:

$$30 - 2 \times 7\% = 30\% - 14\% = 16\%$$

Sometimes derivatives are combined with options to bound the impact of interest rates. The most important of these instruments are called *caps* and *floors*. A cap is so named because it puts an upper limit, or cap, on the impact of a rise in interest rates. A floor, conversely, provides a floor below which the interest rate impact is insulated.

To illustrate the impact of these, consider a firm that is borrowing short term and is concerned that interest rates might rise. Using a floating rate benchmark (FRB), the firm might purchase a 7 per cent cap. The cap pays the firm the difference between the FRB and 7 per cent on some principal amount, provided the FRB is greater than 7 per cent. As long as the FRB is below 7 per cent, the holder of the cap receives no payments.

By purchasing the cap the firm has assured itself that, even if interest rates rise above 7 per cent, it will not have to pay more than a 7 per cent rate. Suppose that interest rates rise to 9 per cent. While the firm is borrowing short term and paying 9 per cent rates, this is offset by the cap, which is paying the firm the difference between 9 per cent and the 7 per cent limit. For any FRB rate above 7 per cent, the firm receives the difference between FRB and 7 per cent and, as a consequence, it has capped its cost of borrowing at 7 per cent.

On the other side, consider a financial firm that is in the business of lending short term and is concerned that interest rates – and consequently its revenues – might fall. The firm could purchase a floor to protect itself from such declines. If the limit on the floor is 7 per cent, then the floor pays the difference between 7 per cent and FRB whenever the FRB is below 7 per cent, and nothing if the FRB is above 7 per cent. Thus, if interest rates were to fall to, say, 5 per cent while the firm is receiving only 5 per cent from its lending activities, the floor is paying it the difference between 7 per cent and 5 per cent, or an additional 2 per cent. By purchasing the floor, the firm has assured itself of receiving no less than 7 per cent from the combination of the floor and its lending activities.

We have only scratched the surface of what is available in the world of derivatives. Derivatives are designed to meet marketplace needs, and the only binding limitation is the human imagination. Nowhere should the buyer's warning *caveat emptor* be taken more seriously than in the derivatives markets, and this is especially true for the exotics. If swaps are the meat and potatoes of the derivatives markets, then caps and floors are the meat and potatoes of the exotics. As we have seen, they have obvious value as hedging instruments, but much attention has been focused on truly exotic derivatives, some of which appear to have arisen more as the residuals that were left over from more straightforward deals. We will not examine these in any detail, but suffice to say that some of these are so volatile and unpredictable that market participants have dubbed them 'toxic waste'.

Real World Insight 25.2

Airlines: The Risks of Hedging

Although hedging is designed to reduce downside risk, there is still risk. Take the airline sector during Covid as an example. Several European airlines, including Lufthansa, IAG, Ryanair and Air France, showed significant losses from oil hedging contracts, amounting to over $4 billion. IAG, the parent company of British Airways, was most affected, with losses exceeding $2 billion, while Lufthansa lost almost $1.4 billion. This was due to unexpected price fluctuations brought about by the Covid-19 pandemic.

To manage how much they are affected by oil price fluctuations, airlines purchase fuel at low prices on the futures market with long-term contracts of up to 24 months ahead. They then agree with insurers on a price range for the rest of the fuel they will need that year, with the insurers covering the difference in price should the cost of fuel exceed that threshold.

Travel restrictions due to the Covid-19 pandemic led to a drastic fall in demand and traffic, making it the worst year in aviation history. This unexpected downturn affected the effectiveness of their hedging strategies, leading to significant losses reported in their financial accounts.

25.8 Financial Risk Management in Practice

Because the true extent of derivatives does not usually appear in financial statements, it is much more difficult to observe the use of derivatives by firms compared to, say, bank debt. Much of our knowledge of corporate derivative use comes from academic surveys. Most surveys report that the use of derivatives appears to vary widely among large publicly traded firms. Large firms are far more likely to use derivatives than are small firms. Table 25.10 shows the percentage of firms across the world that use derivatives, where it can be seen that foreign currency and interest rate derivatives are most popular.

The prevailing view is that derivatives can be very helpful in reducing the variability of firm cash flows, which, in turn, reduces the various costs associated with financial distress. Therefore, it is somewhat puzzling that large firms use derivatives more often than small firms – because large firms tend to have less cash flow variability than small firms. Also some surveys report that firms occasionally use derivatives when they want to speculate about future prices and not just to hedge risks. However, most of the evidence is consistent with the theory that derivatives are most frequently used by firms where financial distress costs are high and access to the capital markets is constrained. Finally, because derivatives hedge distress risk, firms who hedge have lower costs of equity and higher values.[14]

Sustainability in Action 25.1

Sustainability-linked Hedging with Enel and Primetals Technologies

Italian Electricity and Gas supplier, Enel, has made significant strides in sustainability by linking key performance indicators to financial securities. In 2019, Enel issued its first sustainability-linked bond, and now approximately half of the company's total debt is dedicated to sustainable finance. Enel's Head of Treasury, Fabio Casinelli, explained that the company's approach integrates business strategy and finance, delivering on both energy and finance transitions, as promised in COP26 commitments made in Glasgow.

Primetals Technologies, a subsidiary of Mitsubishi Heavy Industries, is another example of a company using sustainability-linked hedging. Primetals has committed to an ESG-aligned foreign exchange hedging programme to showcase its contribution to the green transition in the steel industry. The structure of these programmes can vary as companies have different instruments and needs. For instance, Enel updates its Sustainability Performance Targets annually and receives a premium from counterparties under its sustainability-linked foreign exchange agreements when it meets its ESG goals. Conversely, Primetals' foreign exchange options programme requires a pre-defined penalty in the form of a donation if the company fails to meet its targets.

Source: www.flow.db.com (2022) 'How ESG-linked FX Hedging Works'

Table 25.10 Derivative Use Around the World

	Number of Firms	% Firms Using Derivatives	Hedging Intensity	FX General	FX Forward	FX Swap	FX Option	Interest Rate General	Interest Rate Forward	Interest Rate Swap	Interest Rate Option	Commodity Price General	Commodity Price Futures	Commodity Price Swaps	Commodity Price Options
Austria	41	56.1	1.3	56.1	43.9	17.1	22	22	0	17.1	7.3	7.3	2.4	4.9	2.4
Belgium	60	50	0.8	36.7	26.7	8.3	6.7	23.3	0	21.7	3.3	3.3	0	1.7	0
China	32	12.5	0.2	6.3	6.3	3.1	0	3.1	0	3.1	0	3.1	3.1	0	0
Denmark	80	87.5	1.5	80	72.5	12.5	18.8	26.3	1.3	21.3	6.3	5	1.3	2.5	1.3
Finland	100	64	1.7	58	45	18	27	37	9	29	17	8	3	1	3
France	159	66	1.6	52.8	37.1	22.6	25.8	44.7	1.9	38.4	15.1	3.8	1.3	1.3	0.6
Germany	395	47.1	1	39	27.3	10.6	12.4	24.1	1.8	17.7	9.4	4.8	1.8	0.5	0.5
Greece	19	21.1	0.5	21.1	10.5	5.3	5.3	10.5	0	10.5	0	5.3	5.3	0	0
India	40	70	0.9	62.5	60	7.5	0	12.5	0	12.5	0	5	2.5	0	0
Ireland	47	85.1	1.9	70.2	61.7	27.7	8.5	53.2	4.3	46.8	8.5	14.9	2.1	6.4	4.3
Italy	93	61.3	1	38.7	29	16.1	3.2	33.3	3.2	23.7	3.2	2.2	1.1	2.2	0
Malaysia	289	20.1	0.2	16.3	12.5	1.4	0.7	4.2	0	3.8	1	1	0.7	0	0
Netherlands	131	56.5	1.2	48.1	38.9	18.3	12.2	33.6	1.5	27.5	9.2	4.6	0.8	0.8	0.8
Norway	85	67.1	1.4	56.5	48.2	17.6	17.6	29.4	2.4	24.7	5.9	8.2	2.4	0	3.5
Poland	11	45.5	1.1	36.4	18.2	18.2	27.3	18.2	9.1	9.1	9.1	9.1	0	0	0
Singapore	219	55.3	0.8	50.7	42.5	5.9	3.7	11.4	0.5	9.6	1.8	2.3	0	1.8	0
South Africa	55	89.1	1.7	89.1	87.3	9.1	14.5	38.2	0	32.7	5.5	14.5	5.5	0	1.8
Spain	29	62.1	1.5	37.9	27.6	10.3	10.3	37.9	3.4	34.5	13.8	20.7	6.9	6.9	6.9
Sweden	135	63.7	0.9	45.2	35.6	7.4	8.1	13.3	2.2	9.6	2.2	4.4	0.7	0.7	1.5
Switzerland	119	77.3	1.6	68.1	61.3	14.3	23.5	42.9	3.4	35.3	7.6	5.9	0.8	0.8	0.8
UK	860	64.4	1.3	55	49.4	17.1	7.8	36.5	0.6	32.1	10.8	3.7	1.5	1.4	0.7
USA	2076	65.1	1.2	37.8	30.9	6.4	7.5	40.4	0.7	36	6.8	16.1	6	5.2	3.3
Europe	2421	61.5	1.3	51.1	42.3	15.3	12.5	32.3	1.8	26.9	9.2	5	1.6	1.4	1
All firms	6896	60.5	1.2	45.5	37.9	11.2	9.8	33.1	1.1	29.1	7.4	9.8	3	2.9	2.3

Note: Hedging intensity is the number of instruments used by an average firm.
Source: Adapted from Bartram (2019), Table A-2.

Summary and Conclusions

1. Firms hedge to reduce risk. This chapter described a number of hedging strategies.
2. A forward contract is an agreement by two parties to sell an item for cash at a later date. The price is set at the time the agreement is signed. However, cash changes hands on the date of delivery. Forward contracts are generally not traded on organized exchanges.
3. Futures contracts are also agreements for future delivery. They have certain advantages, such as liquidity, that forward contracts do not. An unusual feature of futures contracts is the mark-to-the-market convention. If the price of a futures contract falls on a particular day, every buyer of the contract must pay money to the clearinghouse. Every seller of the contract receives money from the clearinghouse. Everything is reversed if the price rises. The mark-to-the-market convention prevents defaults on futures contracts.
4. We divided hedges into two types: short hedges and long hedges. An individual or firm that sells a futures contract to reduce risk is instituting a short hedge. Short hedges are generally appropriate for holders of inventory. An individual or firm that buys a futures contract to reduce risk is instituting a long hedge. Long hedges are typically used by firms with contracts to sell finished goods at a fixed price.
5. An interest rate futures contract employs a bond as the deliverable instrument. Because of their popularity, we worked with Treasury bond futures contracts. We showed that Treasury bond futures contracts can be priced using the same type of net present value analysis that is used to price Treasury bonds themselves.
6. Many firms face interest rate risk. They can reduce this risk by hedging with interest rate futures contracts. As with other commodities, a short hedge involves the sale of a futures contract. Firms that are committed to buying mortgages or other bonds are likely to institute short hedges. A long hedge involves the purchase of a futures contract. Firms that have agreed to sell mortgages or other bonds at a fixed price are likely to institute long hedges.
7. Duration measures the average maturity of all the cash flows in a bond. Bonds with high duration have high price variability. Firms frequently try to match the duration of their assets with the duration of their liabilities.
8. Swaps are agreements to exchange cash flows over time. The first major type is an interest rate swap in which one pattern of coupon payments, say fixed payments, is exchanged for another, say coupons that float with a floating rate benchmark. The second major type is a currency swap, in which an agreement is struck to swap payments denominated in one currency for payments in another currency over time.

Questions and Problems

CONCEPT

1. **Derivatives: Hedging and Risk** Discuss the differences between hedging and speculation with derivatives. Many corporations' risk management divisions earn significant profits each year. What does this say about derivative use in large corporations?
2. **Forward Contracts** Explain what is meant by a forward contract. Use a non-financial example to illustrate how a forward contract works. What are the advantages and disadvantages of forward contracts?
3. **Futures Contracts** What is a futures contract? What are the advantages and disadvantages of futures contracts?
4. **Interest Rate Futures Contracts** Explain how interest rates can be hedged by futures contracts. Provide an example of how you could use one to hedge against an increase in interest rates.
5. **Duration Hedging** What is duration and how can it be used to hedge against interest rate changes? Use an example to illustrate your answer.
6. **Swaps** Explain why a swap is effectively a series of forward contracts. Suppose a firm enters a swap agreement with a swap dealer. Describe the nature of the default risk faced by both parties.
7. **Financial Risk Management** Using Table 25.10, discuss the main concerns of corporations when using derivatives to manage risk.

REGULAR

8 **Hedging** Provide an overview of the empirical determinants of hedging. If you were the corporate treasurer for a company, would you recommend hedging as a risk management strategy? Explain.

9 **Hedging Strategies** If a firm is buying futures contracts on lumber as a hedging strategy, what must be true about the firm's exposure to lumber prices? If a firm is writing call options on cocoa futures as a hedging strategy, what must be true about the firm's exposure to cocoa prices?

10 **Hedging Strategies and Currency Risk** What are the three strategies a firm has at its disposal to deal with currency risk? What are the advantages and disadvantages of each? Explain.

11 **Hedging Risks** Vestas Wind Systems A/S, the Danish wind energy company, would like to consider hedging the risk of its operations. What are the main risks the company faces and how would it hedge these risks? Provide at least two reasons why it probably will not be possible to achieve a completely flat risk profile with respect to the identified risks.

12 **Sources of Risk** A company produces an energy-intensive product and uses natural gas as the energy source. The competition primarily uses oil. Explain why this company is exposed to fluctuations in both oil and natural gas prices.

13 **Hedging Commodities** If a textile manufacturer wanted to hedge against adverse movements in cotton prices, it could buy cotton futures contracts or buy call options on cotton futures contracts. What would be the pros and cons of the two approaches?

14 **Option** Explain why a put option on a bond is conceptually the same as a call option on interest rates.

15 **Hedging Interest Rates** A company has a large bond issue maturing in one year. When it matures, the company will float a new issue. Current interest rates are attractive, and the company is concerned that rates next year will be higher. What are some hedging strategies that the company might use in this case?

16 **Working with Swaps** Suppose a firm enters a fixed for floating interest rate swap with a swap dealer. Using an example and a diagram, illustrate the cash flows that will occur as a result of the swap. Why would a swap be preferable to other derivative transactions?

17 **Transactions versus Economic Exposure** What is the difference between transactions and economic exposure? Which can be hedged more easily? Why?

18 **Hedging Exchange Rate Risk** If a Dutch company exports its goods to the UK, how would it use a futures contract on sterling to hedge its exchange rate risk? Would it buy or sell sterling futures? Does the way the exchange rate is quoted in the futures contract matter?

19 **Hedging and Effective Exchange Rates** You are the finance director of a British company that is expecting a payment in euros of €200 million at the end of September and wish to hedge against currency risk. However, the nearest maturity date for a euro futures contract is 13 December and it is now 29 January. The face value of one euro futures contract is €100,000. The spot rate today is £0.9/€ and the futures rate is £0.85/€.

(a) Estimate the number of futures contracts required.

(b) Assume that, at the end of September, the spot rate turns out to be £0.95/€ and a futures contract taken out at the end of September to expire on 13 December is quoted at £0.92/€. Estimate the total gain or loss earned by your company.

(c) Estimate the effective exchange rate received by your company.

20 **Swaps: Syco SA** Syco SA, a distributor of food and food-related products, has announced it has signed an interest rate swap. The interest rate swap effectively converts the company's €100 million, 4.6 per cent interest rate bonds for a variable rate payment, which is the six-month FRB minus 0.52 per cent. Why would Syco use a swap agreement? In other words, why didn't Syco just go ahead and issue floating-rate bonds because the net effect of issuing fixed-rate bonds and then doing a swap is to create a variable rate bond?

21 **Interest Swaps** Consider two firms, Larss plc and Sousa plc. Larss plc has a better credit rating and can borrow cheaper than Sousa plc in both fixed and floating rate markets. Specifically, Larss pays 6.35 per cent fixed and FRB plus 0.5 per cent floating. Sousa plc pays 9.85 per cent fixed and FRB plus 1.5 per cent floating.

(a) If Larss plc prefers to borrow floating and Sousa plc prefers to borrow fixed, determine the spread differential that they will split if they do a swap with each other.

(b) Construct a swap in which both Larss plc and Sousa plc can exploit Sousa plc's comparative advantage. Your answer should include a swap diagram and a description of the cash flows transferred as a result of the swap.

(c) Describe what is meant by a currency swap and the conditions under which a company may wish to undertake this type of transaction.

22 Personal Hedging Strategies Suntharee Lhaopadchan is a Thai student who is planning a one-year stay in the United Kingdom. She expects to arrive in the UK in eight months. She is worried about depreciation in the Thai baht relative to the British pound over the next eight months and wishes to take a position in foreign exchange futures to hedge this risk. What should Miss Lhaopadchan's hedging position be? Assume the exchange rate between the baht and sterling is quoted as baht/pound.

23 Future Quotes: Cocoa Suppose you purchase a September cocoa futures contract on 16 May, at the last price of the day. What will your profit or loss be if the cocoa prices turn out to be $3,000 per metric ton at expiration? (Refer to Table 25.3 to help answer this question.)

24 Futures Quotes: Gold Suppose you sell five May gold futures contracts on 16 April, at the last price of the day at $1,648.6 per ounce. What will your profit or loss be if gold prices turn out to be $1,500 per ounce at expiration and $1,300 per ounce at expiration? Assume each contract is for 100 ounces.

25 Put and Call Payoffs Suppose a financial manager buys call options on 35,000 barrels of oil with the same exercise price of £120 per barrel. She simultaneously sells a put option on 35,000 barrels of oil with the same exercise price of £120 per barrel. Consider her gains and losses if oil prices are £115, £120, £125, £130 and £135. What do you notice about the payoff profile?

26 Marking to Market You are long 10 gold futures contracts, established at an initial settle price of €1,000 per ounce, where each contract represents 100 ounces. Over the subsequent four trading days, gold settles at €1,003, €1,009, €1,012 and €1,004, respectively. Compute the cash flows at the end of each trading day, and compute your total profit or loss at the end of the trading period.

27 Floating Rate Agreement Quotes Rock Spring plc decides it wants to borrow capital for a six-month period in two three-month instalments. The company can borrow at FRB + 2 per cent. FRB rates today are 4 per cent. However, because the firm must agree the contract in advance and pay later, it will be exposed to the risk of interest rates over the next three months, since the level of its second interest payment will not be established until the end of the first period. In order to manage this risk, the firm decides to acquire a floating rate agreement from an investment bank. The company receives the following floating rate agreement quotes:

Period	Dealer 1	Dealer 2
3 vs. 6	1.8–1.85%	1.9–1.95%
3 vs. 6	1.7–1.86%	1–1.82%
6 vs. 9	2–2.3%	2.1–2.5%
6 vs. 9	3–3.5%	2.9–3.3%
9 vs. 12	3.2–3.9%	3–3.7%
9 vs. 12	3.7–4%	3.8–4.2%

Which quote should the firm use to hedge its exposure and at what interest rate?

28 Duration What is the duration of a bond with four years to maturity and a coupon of 9 per cent paid annually if the bond sells at par?

29 Duration of Assets and Liabilities Pillow Private Bank has the following market value balance sheet:

Asset or Liability	Market Value (in £ billions)	Duration (in years)
Government deposits	28	0
Trade receivables	580	1.20
Short-term loans	390	2.65
Long-term loans	84	7.25
Mortgages	315	16.25
Liabilities		
Chequing and savings deposits	520	0
Certificates of deposit	340	2.60
Long-term financing	260	17.80
Equity	277	N/A

(a) What is the duration of the assets?

(b) What is the duration of the liabilities?

(c) Is the bank immune from interest rate risk?

30 Hedging with Futures: Cocoa Suppose today is 16 April, your firm produces chocolate and needs 75,000 tonnes of cocoa in July for an upcoming promotion. You would like to lock in your costs today because you are concerned that cocoa prices might go up between now and June. The closing price for July futures is £1,468 per tonne of cocoa.

(a) How could you use cocoa futures contracts to hedge your risk exposure?

(b) Suppose cocoa prices are £1,500 per contract in July. What is the profit or loss on your futures position? Explain how your futures position has eliminated your exposure to price risk in the cocoa market.

31 Interest Rate Swaps ABC Company and XYZ Company need to raise funds to pay for capital improvements at their manufacturing plants. ABC Company is a well-established firm with an excellent credit rating in the debt market; it can borrow funds either at 11 per cent fixed rate or at FRB + 1 per cent floating rate. XYZ Company is a fledgling start-up firm without a strong credit history. It can borrow funds either at 10 per cent fixed rate or at FRB + 3 per cent floating rate.

(a) Is there an opportunity here for ABC and XYZ to benefit by means of an interest rate swap?

(b) Suppose you have just been hired at a bank that acts as a dealer in the swaps market and your boss has shown you the borrowing rate information for your clients ABC and XYZ. Describe how you could bring these two companies together in an interest rate swap that would make both firms better off while netting your bank a 2.0 per cent profit.

32 Duration of Personal Liabilities Per and Birthe Clausen have a son who will begin university three years from today. Expenses of €30,000 will need to be paid at the beginning of each of the four years that their son plans to attend university. What is the duration of this liability to the couple if they can borrow and lend at the market interest rate of 10 per cent?

33 Bond Duration What is the duration of a bond with two years to maturity if the bond has a coupon rate of 8 per cent paid semi-annually and the market interest rate is 7 per cent?

CHALLENGE

34 Forward Pricing: Theory The forward price (F) of a contract on an asset with neither carrying costs nor convenience yield is the current spot price of the asset (S_0) multiplied by 1 plus the appropriate interest rate between the initiation of the contract and the delivery date of the asset. Derive this relationship by comparing the cash flows that result from the following two strategies:

Strategy 1: Buy silver on the spot market today and hold it for one year. (*Hint:* Do not use any of your own money to purchase the silver.)

Strategy 2: Take on a long position in a silver forward contract for delivery in one year. Assume that silver is an asset with neither carrying costs nor convenience yield.

35 Forward Pricing and Spot Rate Movement You enter into a forward contract to buy a 10-year, zero coupon bond that will be issued in one year. The face value of the bond is £100,000, and the one-year and 11-year spot interest rates are 5 per cent and 9 per cent, respectively.

(a) What is the forward price of your contract?

(b) Suppose both the one-year and 11-year spot rates unexpectedly shift downwards by 2 per cent. What is the new price of the forward contract?

36 Forward Pricing and Interest Rate Movement This morning you agreed to buy a one-year Treasury bond in six months. The bond has a face value of £100,000. Use the spot interest rates listed in the table below to answer the questions that follow.

Time (Months)	EAR (%)
6	7.42
12	8.02
18	8.79
24	9.43

(a) What is the forward price of this contract?

(b) Suppose that, shortly after you purchased the forward contract, all rates increased by 30 basis points. For example, the six-month rate increased from 7.42 per cent to 7.72 per cent. What is the price of a forward contract otherwise identical to yours given these changes?

37 **Financial Engineering** Suppose there were call options and forward contracts available on coal but no put options. Show how a financial engineer could synthesize a put option using the available contracts. What does your answer tell you about the general relationship between puts, calls and forwards?

Exam Question (45 minutes)

Malaika plc, a British company, is planning to make a payment in euros of €150 million at the end of September. However, the nearest maturity date for a euro futures contract is at 13 December and it is now 29 January. The face value of one euro futures contract is €250,000. The spot rate today is €1.49/£ and the futures rate is €1.45/£.

1 Estimate the number of futures contracts required. **(25 marks)**

2 Assume that, at the end of September, the spot rate turns out to be €1.55/£ and a futures contract taken out at the end of September to expire on 13 December is quoted at €1.50/£. Estimate the total gain or loss earned by Malaika plc. **(25 marks)**

3 Review the primary differences between hedging with futures and hedging with forwards. **(25 marks)**

4 Explain what is meant by a currency option. Provide a worked example of a currency option strategy and the reasons for its use. Explain why currency put options are not necessarily a bearish investment. **(25 marks)**

Total: 100 Marks

Mini Case

McAfee Mortgages Ltd

Jennifer McAfee recently received her university master's degree and has decided to enter the mortgage brokerage business. Rather than work for someone else, she has decided to open her own shop. Her cousin Finn has approached her about a mortgage for a house he is building. The house will be completed in three months and he will need the mortgage at that time. Finn wants a 25-year, fixed-rate mortgage for the amount of £500,000, with monthly payments.

Jennifer has agreed to lend Finn the money in three months at the current market rate of 8 per cent. Because Jennifer is just starting out, she does not have £500,000 available for the loan, so she approaches Ian MacDuff, the president of IM Insurance, about purchasing the mortgage from her in three months. Ian has agreed to purchase the mortgage in three months, but he is unwilling to set a price on the mortgage. Instead, he has agreed in writing to purchase the mortgage at the market rate in three months. There are Treasury bond futures contracts available for delivery in three months. A Treasury bond contract is for £100,000 in face value of Treasury bonds.

1 What is the monthly mortgage payment on Finn's mortgage?

2 What is the most significant risk Jennifer faces in this deal?

3 How can Jennifer hedge this risk?

4 Suppose that, in the next three months, the market rate of interest rises to 9 per cent.
   (a) How much will Ian be willing to pay for the mortgage?
   (b) What will happen to the value of Treasury bond futures contracts? Will the long or short position increase in value?

5 Suppose that, in the next three months, the market rate of interest falls to 7 per cent.
   (a) How much will Ian be willing to pay for the mortgage?
   (b) What will happen to the value of T-bond futures contracts? Will the long or short position increase in value?

6 Are there any possible risks Jennifer faces in using Treasury bond futures contracts to hedge her interest rate risk?

Practical Case Study

Every company that uses international accounting standards must have a statement on its hedging activity. Download the financial accounts of a company from your country. Read through the risk section and write a report on its hedging activity, if any.

Relevant Accounting Standards

The derivative positions held by all companies that follow IFRS must be reported at fair value. Guidance is contained in IAS 39 *Financial Instruments: Recognition and Measurement*. You should also be familiar with IFRS 7 *Financial Instruments: Disclosures*. Visit the IASPlus website for more information (www.iasplus.com).

References

Aretz, K. and S.M. Bartram (2010) 'Corporate Hedging and Shareholder Value', *Journal of Financial Research*, Vol. 33, No. 4, 317–371.

Bartram, S.M. (2019) 'Corporate Hedging and Speculation with Derivatives', *Journal of Corporate Finance*, Vol. 57, 9–34.

Cox, J.C., J.E. Ingersoll and S.A. Ross (1981) 'The Relationship between Forward and Future Prices', *Journal of Financial Economics*, Vol. 9, 321–346.

Gay, G.D., C.-M. Lin and S.D. Smith (2011) 'Corporate Derivatives Use and the Cost of Equity', *Journal of Banking and Finance*, Vol. 35, No. 6, 1491–1506.

Additional Reading

With the exception of Gates and Nantes (2006), and Nocco and Stulz (2006), the papers listed below relate to corporate hedging activity. Gates and Nantes, and Nocco and Stulz provide interesting reviews of enterprise risk management, which integrates all the disparate risks a company faces into one cohesive policy.

Corporate Hedging

1 Aretz, K., and S.M. Bartram (2010) 'Corporate Hedging and Shareholder Value', *Journal of Financial Research*, Vol. 33, No. 4, 317–371.

2 Bartram, S.M., G.W. Brown and F.R. Fehle (2009) 'International Evidence on Financial Derivatives Usage', *Financial Management*, Vol. 38, No. 1, 185–206.

3 Campello, M., C. Lin, Y. Ma and H. Zou (2011) 'The Real and Financial Implications of Corporate Hedging', *Journal of Finance*, Vol. 66, No. 5, 1615–1647.

4 Clark, E. and A. Judge (2009) 'Foreign Currency Derivatives versus Foreign Currency Debt and the Hedging Premium', *European Financial Management*, Vol. 15, No. 3, 606–642. **UK.**

5 Faulkender, M. (2005) 'Hedging or Market Timing? Selecting the Interest Rate Exposure of Corporate Debt', *Journal of Finance*, Vol. 60, No. 2, 931–962. **USA.**

6 Graham, J.R. and D.A. Rogers (2002) 'Do Firms Hedge in Response to Tax Incentives?', *Journal of Finance*, Vol. 57, No. 2, 815–839. **USA.**

7 Guay, W. and S.P. Kothari (2003) 'How Much Do Firms Hedge with Derivatives?', *Journal of Financial Economics*, Vol. 70, No. 3, 423–461. **USA.**

8 Haushalter, G.D. (2000) 'Financing Policy, Basis Risk, and Corporate Hedging: Evidence from Oil and Gas Producers', *Journal of Finance*, Vol. 55, No. 1, 107–152. **USA.**

9 Jin, Y. and P. Jorion (2006) 'Firm Value and Hedging: Evidence from US Oil and Gas Producers', *Journal of Finance*, Vol. 61, No. 2, 893–929. **USA.**

10 Kamiya, S., J.K. Kang, J. Kim, A. Milidonis and R.M. Stulz (2021) 'Risk Management, Firm Reputation, and the Impact of Successful Cyberattacks on Target Firms', *Journal of Financial Economics*, Vol. 139, No. 3, 719–749.

11 Lel, U. (2012) 'Currency Hedging and Corporate Governance: A Cross-country Analysis', *Journal of Corporate Finance*, Vol. 18, No. 2, 221–237. **International.**

12 Marshall, A. (2000) 'Foreign Exchange Risk Management in UK, USA, and Asia Pacific Multinational Companies', *Journal of Multinational Financial Management*, Vol. 10, No. 2, 185–211. **International.**

13 Opie, W. and S.J. Riddiough (2020) 'Global Currency Hedging with Common Risk Factors', *Financial Economics*, Vol. 136, No. 3, 780–805.

Enterprise Risk Management

14 Gates, S. and A. Nantes (2006) 'Incorporating Strategic Risk into Enterprise Risk Management: A Survey of Current Corporate Practice', *Journal of Applied Corporate Finance*, Vol. 18, No. 4, 81–90. **USA.**

15 Nocco, B.W. and R.M. Stulz (2006) 'Enterprise Risk Management: Theory and Practice', *Journal of Applied Corporate Finance*, Vol. 18, No. 4, 8–20.

Endnotes

1 He will deliver on Thursday, two days later.

2 The direction is reversed for the seller of a futures contract. However, the general point that the net present value of cash flows may differ between forward and futures contracts holds for sellers as well.

3 See Cox et al. (1981).

4 Alternatively, the firm could buy the oil on 1 April and store it. This would eliminate the risk of price movements because the firm's oil costs would be fixed upon the immediate purchase. However, this strategy would be inferior to strategy 2 in the common case where the difference between the futures contract quoted on 1 April and the 1 April cash price is less than the storage costs.

5 We are assuming that each spot rate shifts by the same amount. For example, suppose that on 1 March $R_1 = 5\%$, $R_2 = 5.4\%$ and $R_3 = 5.8\%$. Assuming that all rates increase by 1/2 per cent on 2 March, R_1 becomes 5.5 per cent (0.5% + 1/2%), R_2 becomes 5.9 per cent and R_3 becomes 6.3 per cent.

6 Futures contracts on bonds are also called *interest rate futures contracts.*

7 Delivery occurs two days after the seller notifies the clearinghouse of her intention to deliver.

8 Alternatively, we can say that mortgages have shorter duration than do Treasury bonds of equal maturity. A precise definition of duration is provided later in this chapter.

9 Alternatively, the mortgage would still be at par if a coupon rate below 12 per cent were used. However, this is not done because the insurance company wants to buy only 12 per cent mortgages.

10 The bonds are at different prices initially. Thus, we are concerned with percentage price changes, not absolute price changes.

11 The mathematical formula for duration is:

$$\text{Duration} = \frac{PV(C_1) + PV(C_2)^2 + \ldots + PV(C_T)^T}{PV}$$

and

$$PV = PV(C_1) + PV(C_2) + \ldots + PV(C_T)$$

$$PV(C_T) = \frac{C_T}{(1+R)^T}$$

where C_T is the cash to be received in time T and R is the current discount rate.

Also note that in our numerical example, we discounted each payment by the interest rate of 10 per cent. This was done because we wanted to calculate the duration of the bond before a change in the interest rate occurred. After a change in the rate to, say, 8 or 12 per cent, all three of our steps would need to reflect the new interest rate. In other words, the duration of a bond is a function of the current interest rate.

12 Actually, this relationship exactly holds only in the case of a one-time shift in a flat yield curve, where the change in the spot rate is identical for all maturities.

13 Note that the duration of a group of items is an average of the duration of the individual items, weighted by the market value of each item. This is a simplifying step that greatly increases duration's practicality.

14 See Aretz and Bartram (2010), and Gay et al. (2011).

PART 7

Financial Planning and Short-term Finance

More and more companies are coming to view short-term financial planning to be just as important to firm welfare as long-term investment appraisal. Traditionally, firms raised capital for strategic investments through retained earnings or new bond/equity financing. However, with many at debt capacity and reluctant to dilute ownership, short-term planning has gained prominence. Enhancing cash management, implementing inventory control and adhering to optimal trade credit policies can significantly influence cash generation.

Part 7 consists of two chapters. In Chapter 26, we look at short-term financial planning and inventory control. Cash management and trade credit are covered in Chapter 27. By the end of this part of the book, you will have a much better understanding of the issues involved in controlling short-term capital, and releasing cash from a firm's operations via cash, working capital and trade credit management.

Chapter 26
Short-term Finance and Planning

Learning Objectives

After reading this chapter you should be able to:

LO1 Explain the concept of cash and net working capital in corporate finance, and understand their roles in the financial health of a company.

LO2 Illustrate how cash is defined in terms of other elements within a company's financial structure.

LO3 Investigate the concepts of the operating cycle and the cash cycle, and analyse how these cycles affect a company's short-term financing needs and strategies.

Recent technological and digital advancements have revolutionized the way corporations operate. Thanks to smartphones and cloud-based phone applications, executives can make informed decisions from anywhere at any time. Artificial intelligence (AI) and big data have transformed manufacturing, leading to the emergence of fully automated factories that are not only more efficient, with superior quality control, but also promote environmental sustainability.

Source: bygermina/Shutterstock

The adoption of AI has more than doubled since 2017, with 50 per cent of organizations implementing it in at least one business function as of 2022. AI capabilities such as natural-language generation and computer vision have also doubled, from 1.9 in 2018 to 3.8 in 2022. Investment in AI has increased accordingly, with more than half of respondents in a McKinsey survey on 'The State of AI in 2022' from AI-using organizations allocating more than 5 per cent of their digital budgets to AI.

The AI market was valued at $428 billion in 2022 and is projected to reach $2.93 trillion by 2030, with applications in all business segments, including mobile phone payment systems, asset and inventory management, product tracking, logistics and passports. The use of digital technologies enables more efficient management of short-term assets such as inventory. This efficiency can positively impact a company's profitability and the value that investors attribute to it. Moreover, approximately 43 per cent of companies that have adopted AI are integrating it into their sustainability efforts, with 40 per cent actively seeking ways to reduce the environmental impact of their AI use. This focus on sustainability underscores the role of AI as a key driver of environmentally conscious corporate operations.

AI will greatly impact short-term financial planning, and this concerns everyone in business.

26.1 Tracing Cash and Net Working Capital

In this section, we trace the components of cash and net working capital as they change from one year to the next. Our goal is to describe the short-term operating activities of the firm, and their impact on cash and working capital.

Current assets are cash and other assets that are expected to be converted to cash within the year. They are normally presented in the balance sheet in order of their accounting liquidity – the ease with which they can be converted to cash at a fair price and the time it takes to do so. Table 26.1 gives the current assets and current liabilities of global mining firm Antofagasta plc for 2018. The items found in the current assets section of the Antofagasta balance sheet include inventories, trade debtors, bank and other deposits, and short-term investments for sale within one year.

Table 26.1 Current Assets and Liabilities of Antofagasta plc for Year Ending 2018

Current Assets	$ millions	Current Liabilities	$ millions
Inventories	576.3	Trade creditors	608.3
Trade debtors	873.5	Short-term loans and overdrafts	646.0
Cash and cash equivalents	1,034.4	Corporation tax	52.8
Derivatives	0.8	**Current liabilities**	**1,307.1**
Current tax assets	90.7		
Liquid investments	863.2		
Current assets	**3,438.9**		

Analogous to their investment in current assets, firms use several kinds of short-term debt, called current liabilities. Current liabilities are obligations that are expected to require cash payment within one year or within the operating cycle, whichever is shorter.[1] The items found as *current liabilities* are trade creditors, short-term loans or overdrafts, and accrued expenses to be paid off within one year.

26.2 Defining Cash in Terms of Other Elements

Now we will define cash in terms of the other elements of the *statement of financial position,* or *balance sheet.* The balance sheet equation is:

Equation 26.1

$$\text{Net working capital} + \text{Non-current assets} = \text{Non-current liabilities} + \text{Equity}$$

Net working capital is cash plus the other elements of net working capital:

Equation 26.2

$$\text{Net working capital} = \text{Cash} + \text{Other current assets} = \text{Current liabilities}$$

Substituting Equation 26.2 into 26.1 yields:

Equation 26.3

$$\text{Cash} + \text{Other current assets} - \text{Current liabilities} = \text{Non-current liabilities} + \text{Equity} - \text{Non-current assets}$$

and rearranging, we find that:

Equation 26.4

$$\text{Cash} + \text{Non-current liabilities} + \text{Equity} = \text{Net working capital (excluding cash)} - \text{Non-current assets}$$

The natural interpretation of Equation 26.4 is that increasing non-current liabilities and equity, and decreasing non-current assets and net working capital (excluding cash) will increase cash to the firm.

The Sources and Uses of Cash

We first introduced the statement of cash flows in Chapter 3. This is the accounting statement that describes the sources and uses of cash. In this section we look at where cash comes from and how it is used. From the right side of Equation 26.4 we can see that an increase in non-current liabilities or equity leads to an increase in cash.

Moreover, a decrease in net working capital or non-current assets leads to an increase in cash. In addition, the sum of net income and depreciation increases cash, whereas dividend payments decrease cash. This reasoning allows an accountant to create a statement of cash flows, which shows all the transactions that affect a firm's cash position.

Let us trace the hypothetical changes in cash for Antofagasta. From the firm's statement of cash flows (Table 26.2), we find that Antofagasta generated cash as follows:

- Generated cash flow of $1,310.8 million from operations.
- Reduced net financing by $934.1 million.

Antofagasta plc used cash for the following reasons:

- Paid off existing borrowings of $733.8 million.
- Invested $872.9 million in non-current assets such as land and machinery.
- Paid dividends of $587 million.

This example illustrates the difference between a firm's cash level on the statement of financial position and its cash flows from operations.

Table 26.2 Sources and Uses of Cash in Antofagasta plc

	$ millions
Net cash inflow from operating activities	1,310.8
Net cash flow from investing activities	−399.8
Equity dividends paid	−587.0
Proceeds from new borrowings	420.0
Repayments of borrowings and other obligations	−733.8
Repayment of obligations under finance leases	−33.3
Net cash flow	**−23.1**

26.3 The Operating Cycle and the Cash Cycle

Short-term finance is concerned with the firm's short-term operating activities. A typical manufacturing firm's short-term operating activities consist of a sequence of events and decisions:

Events	Decisions
1 Buying raw materials	1 How much inventory to order?
2 Paying cash for purchases	2 To borrow or draw down cash balance?
3 Manufacturing the product	3 What choice of production technology?
4 Selling the product	4 To offer cash terms or credit terms to customers?
5 Collecting cash	5 How to collect cash?

These activities create patterns of cash inflows and cash outflows that are both unsynchronized and uncertain. They are unsynchronized because the payment of cash for raw materials does not happen at the same time as the receipt of cash from selling the product. They are uncertain because future sales and costs are not known with certainty.

Figure 26.1 depicts the short-term operating activities and cash flows for a typical manufacturing firm along the cash flow timeline. The operating cycle is the interval between the arrival of inventory stock and the date when cash is collected from receivables.

Figure 26.1 Cash Flow Timeline and the Short-term Operating Activities of a Typical Manufacturing Firm

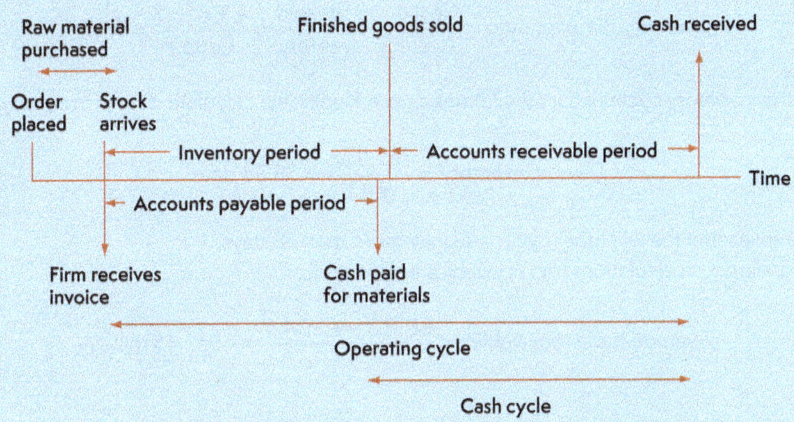

The *operating cycle* is the period from the arrival of stock until the receipt of cash. (Sometimes the operating cycle is defined to include the time from placement of the order until arrival of the stock.) The *cash cycle* begins when cash is paid for materials, and ends when cash is collected from receivables.

The cash cycle begins when cash is paid for materials and ends when cash is collected from receivables. The cash flow timeline consists of an operating cycle and a cash cycle. The need for short-term financial decision-making is suggested by the gap between cash inflows and outflows. This is related to the lengths of the operating cycle and the accounts or trades payable period. This gap can be filled either by borrowing or by holding a liquidity reserve for marketable securities. The gap can be shortened by changing the inventory, receivable and payable periods. Now we take a closer look at the operating cycle.

The length of the operating cycle is equal to the sum of the lengths of the inventory and accounts receivable periods. The inventory period is the length of time required to order raw materials, and produce and sell a product. The accounts receivable period is the length of time required to collect cash receipts.

The cash cycle is the time between cash disbursement and cash collection. It can be thought of as the operating cycle less the accounts payable period:

$$\text{Cash cycle} = \text{Operating cycle} - \text{Accounts payable period}$$

The accounts payable period is the length of time the firm is able to delay payment on the purchase of various resources, such as labour and raw materials.

In practice, the inventory period, the accounts receivable period and the accounts payable period are measured by days in inventory, days in receivables and days in payables, respectively. In Example 26.1 we illustrate how the operating cycle and the cash cycle can be measured.

Example 26.1

Cash Cycle

In this example, we will determine the operating cycle and the cash cycle for Sackowoe NV after calculating the appropriate ratios for inventory, receivables and payables. Consider inventory first. The inventory levels for the firm this year and last were €369.3 million and €402.1 million, respectively. The average inventory is:

$$\text{Average inventory} = \frac{€369.3 + €402.1}{2} = €385.7\text{ million}$$

We next calculate the inventory turnover ratio. The cost of goods sold for Sackowoe this year was €3,650.7 million.

$$\text{Inventory turnover ratio} = \frac{\text{Cost of goods sold}}{\text{Average inventory}} = \frac{€3,650.7}{€385.7} = 9.47$$

This implies that the inventory cycle occurs 9.47 times a year. Finally, we calculate days in inventory:

$$\text{Days in inventory} = \frac{365 \text{ days}}{9.47} = 38.54 \text{ days}$$

Our calculation implies that the inventory cycle is slightly more than 38 days.

We perform analogous calculations for receivables and payables:[2]

$$\text{Average trade receivables} = \frac{€810.3 + €904.6}{2} = €857.45 \text{ million}$$

$$\text{Average receivables turnover} = \frac{\text{Credit sales}}{\text{Average trade receivables}} \frac{€5,290.4}{€857.45} = 6.17$$

$$\text{Days in receivables} = \frac{365}{6.17} = 59.16 \text{ days}$$

$$\text{Average trade payables} = \frac{€793.8 + €776.6}{2} = €785.2 \text{ million}$$

$$\text{Trade payables deferral period} = \frac{\text{Cost of goods sold}}{\text{Average trade payables}} = \frac{€3,650.7}{€785.2} = 4.65$$

$$\text{Days in payables} = \frac{365}{4.65} = 78.49 \text{ days}$$

The preceding calculations allow us to determine both the operating cycle and the cash cycle:

$$\begin{aligned}\text{Operating cycle} &= \text{Days in inventory} + \text{Days in receivables} \\ &= 38.54 \text{ days} + 59.16 \text{ days} = 97.70 \text{ days} \\ \text{Cash cycle} &= \text{Operating cycle} + \text{Days in payables} \\ &= 97.70 \text{ days} - 78.49 \text{ days} = 19.21 \text{ days}\end{aligned}$$

The cash cycle is longer in some industries than others because of different products and industry practices. Table 26.3 illustrates this point by comparing the current assets and current liabilities for four different companies. Of the four, Walmart has the highest level of inventories. Does this mean Walmart is less efficient? Probably not; instead, it is likely that the relatively high inventory levels are consistent with the industry. Walmart needs a higher level of inventory to satisfy customers who walk into its stores. In contrast, Dell makes products to order, so its inventory levels are lower. What might seem surprising is Boeing's relatively low level of inventory, especially given that much of its inventory consists of aircraft under construction. However, notice that the current assets for Boeing are only 37 per cent of total assets, implying that fixed assets are large, as you would expect from such a capital-intensive company – plus Boeing has been aggressive in recent years in reducing its inventory. In contrast, Amazon's fixed assets are small relative to its current assets, which again is what we would expect given the nature of its business.

Table 26.3 Current Assets and Current Liabilities as a Percentage of Total Assets for Selected Companies

	Amazon (%)	Boeing (%)	Dell (%)	Walmart (%)
Cash and near cash	27.41	11.04	30.47	4.56
Marketable securities	26.70	0.94	8.72	0.00
Accounts receivable	9.82	8.17	17.69	1.43
Inventories	15.31	12.42	2.49	24.49
Other current assets	0.00	4.49	17.24	1.53
Total current assets	79.25	37.07	76.62	32.02
Accounts payable	52.19	27.23	42.58	29.20
Short-term borrowings	0.00	3.20	3.20	6.47
Other short-term liabilities	0.00	4.32	0.00	0.00
Current liabilities	52.19	34.75	68.92	35.67

26.4 Some Aspects of Short-term Financial Policy

The policy a firm adopts for short-term finance will be composed of at least two elements:

1 *The size of the firm's investment in current assets:* This is usually measured relative to the firm's level of total operating revenues. A flexible or accommodative short-term financial policy would maintain a high ratio of current assets to sales. A restrictive short-term financial policy would entail a low ratio of current assets to sales.

2 *The financing of current assets:* This is measured as the proportion of short-term debt to long-term debt. A restrictive short-term financial policy means a high proportion of short-term debt relative to long-term financing, and a flexible policy means less short-term debt and more long-term debt.

The Size of the Firm's Investment in Current Assets

Flexible short-term financial policies include:

- Keeping large balances of cash and marketable securities
- Making large investments in inventory
- Granting liberal credit terms, which results in a high level of accounts receivable.

Restrictive short-term financial policies are:

- Keeping low cash balances and no investment in marketable securities
- Making small investments in inventory
- Allowing no credit sales and no accounts receivable.

Determining the optimal investment level in short-term assets requires an identification of the different costs of alternative short-term financing policies. The objective is to trade off the cost of restrictive policies against those of the flexible ones to arrive at the best compromise.

Current asset holdings are highest with a flexible short-term financial policy and lowest with a restrictive policy. Thus, flexible short-term financial policies are costly in that they require higher cash outflows to finance cash and marketable securities, inventory and accounts receivable. However, future cash inflows are highest with a flexible policy. Sales are stimulated by the use of a credit policy that provides liberal financing to customers. A large amount of inventory on hand ('on the shelf') provides a quick delivery service to customers and increases in sales.[3] In addition, the firm can probably charge higher prices for the quick delivery service and the liberal credit terms of flexible policies. A flexible policy also may result in fewer production stoppages because of inventory shortages.[4]

Managing current assets can be thought of as involving a trade-off between costs that rise with the level of investment and costs that fall with the level of investment. Costs that rise with the level of investment in current assets are called carrying costs. Costs that fall with increases in the level of investment in current assets are called **shortage costs**.

Carrying costs are generally of two types. First, because the rate of return on current assets is low compared with that of other assets, there is an opportunity cost. Second, there is the cost of maintaining the economic value of the item. The cost of warehousing inventory belongs here, for example.

Determinants of Corporate Liquid Asset Holdings

Firms with high holdings of liquid assets will have:	Firms with low holdings of liquid assets will have:
High-growth opportunities	Low-growth opportunities
High-risk investments	Low-risk investments
Small firms	Large firms
Low-credit firms	High-credit firms

Firms will hold more liquid assets (i.e. cash and marketable securities) to ensure that they can continue investing when cash flow is low relative to positive NPV investment opportunities. Firms that have good access to capital markets will hold less liquid assets.

Source: Opler et al. (1999).

Shortage costs are incurred when the investment in current assets is low. If a firm runs out of cash, it will be forced to sell marketable securities. If a firm runs out of cash and cannot readily sell marketable securities, it may need to borrow or default on an obligation. (This general situation is called *cash-out.*) If a firm has no inventory (a *stockout*) or if it cannot extend credit to its customers, it will lose customers.

There are two kinds of shortage costs:

1 *Trading or order costs:* Order costs are the costs of placing an order for more cash (*brokerage costs*) or more inventory (*production set-up costs*).

2 *Costs related to safety reserves:* These are costs of lost sales, lost customer goodwill and disruption of production schedules.

Figure 26.2 illustrates the basic nature of carrying costs. The total costs of investing in current assets are determined by adding the carrying costs and the shortage costs. The minimum point on the total cost curve (CA*) reflects the optimal balance of current assets. The curve is generally quite flat at the optimum, and it is difficult, if not impossible, to find the precise optimal balance of shortage and carrying costs. Usually, we are content with a choice near the optimum.

Figure 26.2 Carrying Costs and Shortage Costs

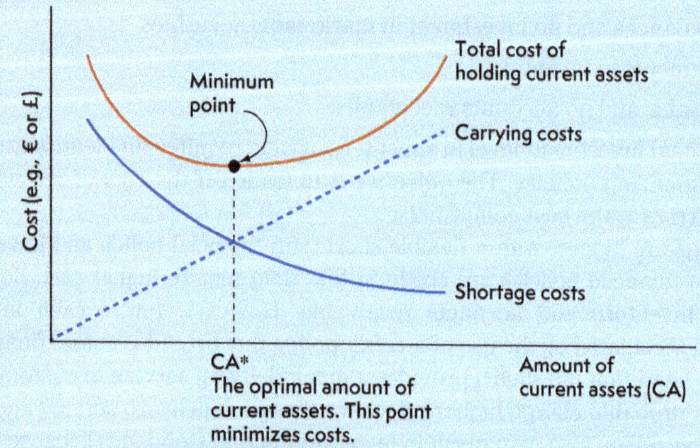

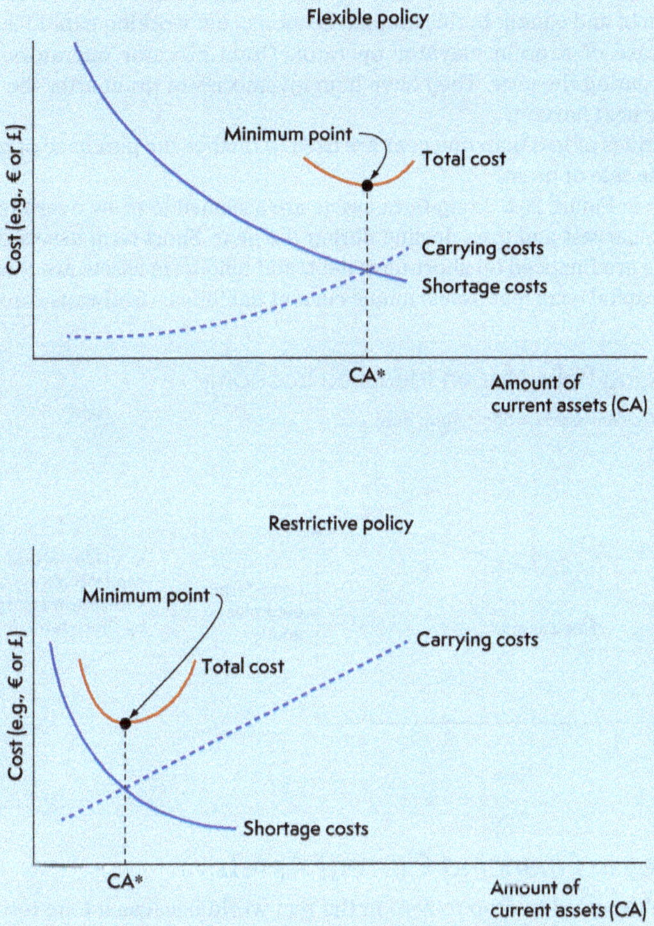

Carrying costs increase with the level of investment in current assets. They include both opportunity costs and the costs of maintaining the asset's economic value. *Shortage costs* decrease with increases in the level of investment in current assets. They include trading costs and the costs of running out of the current asset (for example, being short of cash).

If carrying costs are low or shortage costs are high, the optimal policy calls for substantial current assets. In other words, the optimal policy is a flexible one. This is illustrated in the second graph of Figure 26.2.

If carrying costs are high or shortage costs are low, the optimal policy is a restrictive one. That is, the optimal policy calls for modest current assets. This is illustrated in the third graph of Figure 26.2.

Opler et al. (1999) examine the determinants of holdings of cash and marketable securities by publicly traded firms. They find evidence that firms behave according to the static trade-off model described earlier. Their study focuses only on liquid assets (i.e. cash and market securities), so that carrying costs are the opportunity costs of holding liquid assets and shortage costs are the risks of not having cash when investment opportunities are good. In a study of UK firms, Gogineni et al. (2012) find similar results and that private firms have lower cash holdings when their size is large, and there is high net working capital and leverage. Cash is higher when dividends are large, capital expenditure is high and cash flow is more volatile.

Alternative Financing Policies for Current Assets

In the previous section, we examined the level of investment in current assets. Now we turn to the level of current liabilities, assuming the investment in current assets is optimal.

An Ideal Model

In an ideal economy, short-term assets can always be financed with short-term debt, and long-term assets can be financed with long-term debt and equity. In this utopian economy, net working capital is always zero.

Imagine the simple case of a grain elevator operator. Grain elevator operators buy crops after harvest, store them and sell them during the year. They have high inventories of grain after the harvest and end with low inventories just before the next harvest.

Bank loans with maturities of less than one year are used to finance the purchase of grain. These loans are paid with the proceeds from the sale of grain.

The situation is shown in Figure 26.3. Long-term assets are assumed to grow over time, whereas current assets increase at the end of the harvest and then decline during the year. Short-term assets end at zero just before the next harvest. These assets are financed by short-term debt, and long-term assets are financed with long-term debt and equity. Net working capital – current assets minus current liabilities – is always zero.

Figure 26.3 Financing Policy for an Idealized Economy

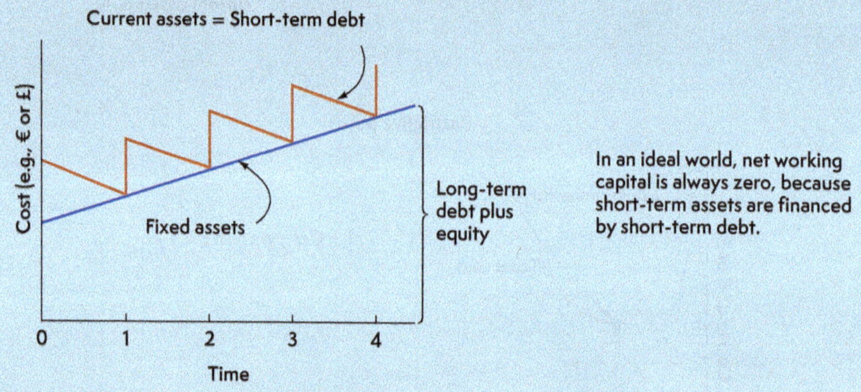

Different Strategies in Financing Current Assets

Current assets cannot be expected to drop to zero in the real world because a long-term rising level of sales will result in some permanent investment in current assets. A growing firm can be thought of as having a permanent requirement for both current assets and long-term assets. This total asset requirement will exhibit balances over time, reflecting (1) a secular growth trend, (2) a seasonal variation around the trend, and (3) unpredictable day-to-day and month-to-month fluctuations. This is depicted in Figure 26.4. (We have not tried to show the unpredictable day-to-day and month-to-month variations in the total asset requirement.)

Figure 26.4 The Total Asset Requirement over Time

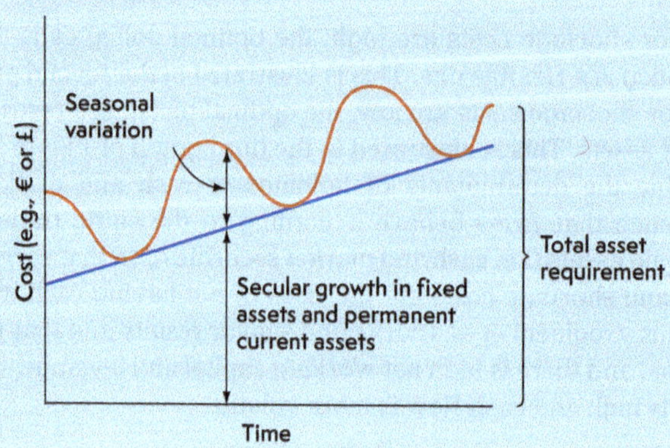

Now let us look at how this asset requirement is financed. First, consider the strategy (strategy F in Figure 26.5) where long-term financing covers more than the total asset requirement, even at seasonal peaks. The firm will have excess cash available for investment in marketable securities when the total asset requirement falls from peaks. Because this approach implies chronic short-term cash surpluses and a large investment in net working capital, it is considered a flexible strategy.

Figure 26.5 Alternative Asset Financing Policies

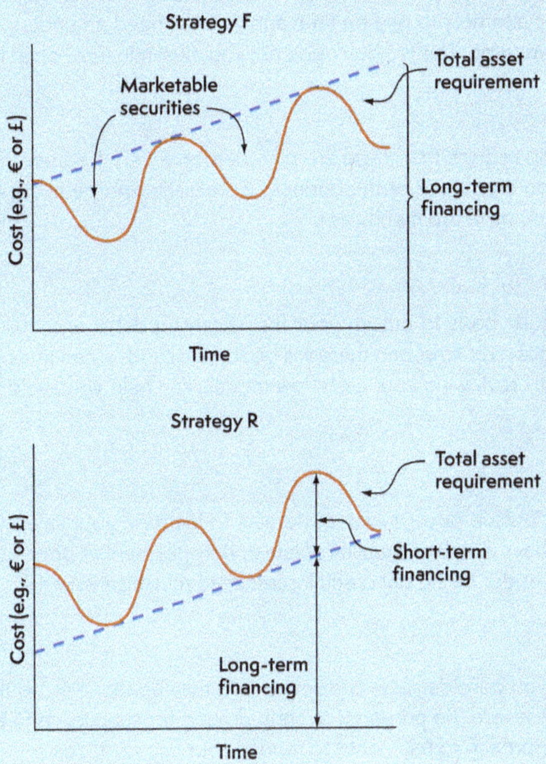

Strategy F always implies a short-term cash surplus and a large investment in cash and marketable securities. Strategy R uses long-term financing for secular asset requirements only, and short-term borrowing for seasonal variations.

When long-term financing does not cover the total asset requirement, the firm must borrow short term to make up the deficit. This restrictive strategy is labelled strategy R in Figure 26.5.

Which Is Best?

There is no definitive answer as to the most appropriate amount of short-term borrowing. Several considerations must be included in a proper analysis:

- *Cash reserves:* The flexible financing strategy implies surplus cash and little short-term borrowing. This strategy reduces the probability that a firm will experience financial distress. Firms may not need to worry as much about meeting recurring short-term obligations. However, investments in cash and marketable securities are zero net present value investments at best.
- *Maturity hedging:* Most firms finance inventories with short-term bank loans and fixed assets with long-term financing. Firms tend to avoid financing long-lived assets with short-term borrowing. This type of maturity mismatching would necessitate frequent financing and is inherently risky because short-term interest rates are more volatile than longer rates. This type of activity was precisely the reason why many banks found themselves in difficulty during the global credit crunch of 2007 and 2008. Banks financed long-term assets (loans and mortgages granted to borrowers) by short-term borrowing. In some cases, this borrowing had just a 30-day maturity. Northern Rock plc, for instance – the British bank that requested emergency central bank funding in September 2007 – funded its loans and mortgages by 61 per cent short-term borrowing and 39 per cent deposits just before it made the request to the Bank of England. Because of the collapse in credit, the funding base of Northern Rock collapsed.
- *Term structure:* Short-term interest rates are normally lower than long-term interest rates. This implies that, on average, it is more costly to rely on long-term borrowing than on short-term borrowing.

Real World Insight 26.1

Practical Advice in Managing Cash Flow

Avoid Downside Risk

Cash flow is the oil that makes the corporate engine run and you must always ensure enough cash is available to pay suppliers on time. This means pushing your own customers to pay on time and you will need an understanding of the impact of late or non-payment for your firm over time. This is a downside risk you must minimize on a daily basis.

Plan Ahead

Become very familiar with cash flow forecasts and require that these are provided on a very frequent basis – for instance, every day, week or month, depending on the nature of the business. Forecasting properly allows you to anticipate cash flow shortfalls and periods when you have too much cash.

Continually Review your Short-term Financial Policy

Review your short-term financial policy on a regular basis to ensure your firm is paying debts and collecting on outstanding credit efficiently. The economy changes over time, and there will be some periods when firms are doing well and others when cash flow is tight. Periodically reviewing your cash flow models can help you avoid structural difficulties in the future.

Avoid Bad Customers

While new customers are always attractive, don't pursue poor-quality customers to increase your sales. Carry out your own credit checks and avoid customers who have a high probability of late or non-payment. A poor-quality sale now is likely to lead to acute pain in the future. Consider taking out credit insurance to minimize your risk.

Seek Out Good Suppliers

Suppliers will look on your firm in the same way you consider new customers. You may appear risky to them, and payment terms on your purchases could be quite severe. Be prepared to shop around for suppliers and negotiate credit terms on all purchases. Be flexible in your approach to payments, to reduce your financing costs.

Incentivize Early Payment

Be creative in the payment terms you offer your customers. Discounts for early payments may be more effective in bringing in cash than going for the full price repaid over a longer period. Likewise, explore opportunities to minimize costs for your own credit purchases.

Be Ethical

Just as you expect to be paid on time and as promised, do the same with your own suppliers. Ethical business practices will enhance your trust over the longer term and your good reputation will allow you to renegotiate credit terms with your long-term suppliers.

26.5 Cash Budgeting

The cash budget is a primary tool of short-term financial planning. It allows the financial manager to identify short-term financial needs (and opportunities). It will tell the manager the required borrowing for the short term. It is the way of identifying the cash flow gap in the cash flow timeline. The idea of the cash budget is simple: it records estimates of cash receipts and disbursements. We illustrate cash budgeting in Example 26.2.

Example 26.2

Cash Collections

All of Fun Toys' cash inflows come from the sale of toys. Cash budgeting for Fun Toys starts with a sales forecast for the next year, by quarter:

	First Quarter	Second Quarter	Third Quarter	Fourth Quarter
Sales (€ millions)	100	200	150	100

Fun Toys' fiscal year starts on 1 July. Fun Toys' sales are seasonal and are usually very high in the second quarter due to holiday sales. But Fun Toys sells to department stores on credit, and sales do not generate cash immediately. Instead, cash comes later from collections on accounts receivable. Fun Toys has a 90-day collection period, and 100 per cent of sales are collected in the following quarter. In other words:

$$\text{Collections} = \text{Last quarter's sales}$$

This relationship implies that:

Equation 26.5 $$\text{Accounts receivable at end of last quarter} = \text{Last quarter's sales}$$

We assume that sales in the fourth quarter of the previous fiscal year were €100 million. From Equation 26.5 we know that accounts receivable at the end of the fourth quarter of the previous fiscal year were €100 million, and collections in the first quarter of the current fiscal year are €100 million.

The first-quarter sales of the current fiscal year of €100 million are added to the accounts receivable, but €100 million of collections are subtracted. Therefore, Fun Toys ended the first quarter with accounts receivable of €100 million. The basic relation is:

$$\text{Ending accounts receivable} = \text{Starting accounts receivable} + \text{Sales} - \text{Collections}$$

Table 26.4 shows cash collections for Fun Toys for the next four quarters. Though collections are the only source of cash here, this need not always be the case. Other sources of cash could include sales of assets, investment income and long-term financing.

Table 26.4 Sources of Cash (€ millions)

	First Quarter	Second Quarter	Third Quarter	Fourth Quarter
Sales	100	200	150	100
Cash collections	100	100	200	150
Starting receivables	100	100	200	150
Ending receivables	100	200	150	100

Cash Outflow

Next, we consider cash disbursements. These can be put into four basic categories, as shown in Table 26.5.

1 *Payments of accounts payable:* These are payments for goods or services, such as raw materials. These payments will generally be made after purchases. Purchases will depend on the sales forecast. In the case of Fun Toys, assume that:

$$\text{Payments} = \text{Last quarter's purchases}$$

$$\text{Purchases} = 1/2 \text{ next quarter's sales forecast}$$

2 *Wages, taxes and other expenses:* This category includes all other normal costs of doing business that require actual expenditures. Depreciation, for instance, is often thought of as a normal cost of business but requires no cash outflow.

3 *Capital expenditures:* These are payments of cash for long-lived assets. Fun Toys plans a major capital expenditure in the fourth quarter.

4 *Long-term financing:* This category includes interest and principal payments on long-term outstanding debt and dividend payments to shareholders.

The total forecast outflow appears in the last line of Table 26.5.

Table 26.5 Disbursement of Cash (€ millions)

	First Quarter	Second Quarter	Third Quarter	Fourth Quarter
Sales	100	200	150	100
Purchases	100	75	50	50
Uses of cash				
Payments of accounts payable	50	100	75	50
Wages, taxes and other expenses	20	40	30	20
Capital expenditures	0	0	0	100
Long-term financing expenses	10	10	10	10
Total uses of cash	80	150	115	180

The Cash Balance

The net cash balance appears in Table 26.6, and a large net cash outflow is forecast in the second quarter. This large outflow is not caused by an inability to earn a profit. Rather, it results from delayed collections on sales. This results in a cumulative cash shortfall of €30 million in the second quarter.

Table 26.6 The Cash Balance (€ millions)

	First Quarter	Second Quarter	Third Quarter	Fourth Quarter
Total cash receipts	100	100	200	150
Total cash disbursements	80	150	115	180
Net cash flow	20	(50)	85	(30)
Cumulative excess cash balance	20	(30)	55	25
Minimum cash balance	5	5	5	5
Cumulative finance surplus (deficit)				
Requirement	15	(35)	50	20

Fun Toys had established a minimum operating cash balance equal to €5 million to facilitate transactions, protect against unexpected contingencies and maintain compensating balances at its banks. This means that it has a cash shortfall in the second quarter equal to €35 million.

26.6 The Short-term Financial Plan

Fun Toys has a short-term financing problem. It cannot meet the forecast cash outflows in the second quarter from internal sources. Its financing options include (1) unsecured bank borrowing, (2) secured borrowing and (3) other sources.

Unsecured Loans

The most common way to finance a temporary cash deficit is to arrange a short-term unsecured bank loan. Firms that use short-term bank loans usually ask their bank for either a non-committed or a committed *line of credit*. A *non-committed* line is an informal arrangement that allows firms to borrow up to a previously specified limit without going through the normal paperwork. The interest rate on the line of credit is usually set equal to the bank's prime lending rate plus an additional percentage.

Committed lines of credit are formal legal arrangements and usually involve a commitment fee paid by the firm to the bank (usually the fee is approximately 0.25 per cent of the total committed funds per year). For larger firms, the interest rate is often tied to a floating interest rate benchmark or to the bank's cost of funds, rather than the benchmark rate. Mid-sized and smaller firms often are required to keep compensating balances in the bank.

Compensating balances are deposits a firm keeps with the bank in low-interest or non-interest-bearing accounts. Compensating balances are commonly in the order of 2 to 5 per cent of the amount used. By leaving these funds with the bank without receiving interest, the firm increases the effective interest earned by the bank on the line of credit. For example, if a firm borrowing £100,000 must keep £5,000 as a compensating balance, the firm effectively receives only £95,000. A stated interest rate of 10 per cent implies yearly interest payments of £10,000 (=£100,000 × 0.10). The effective interest rate is 10.53 per cent (=£10,000/£95,000).

Secured Loans

Banks and other finance companies often require *security* for a loan. Security for short-term loans usually consists of accounts receivable or inventories.

Under accounts receivable financing, receivables are either *assigned* or *factored*. Under assignment, the lender not only has a lien on the receivables but also has recourse to the borrower. Factoring involves the sale of accounts receivable. The purchaser, who is called a *factor*, must then collect on the receivables. The factor assumes the full risk of default on bad accounts.

As the name implies, an inventory loan uses inventory as collateral. Some common types of inventory loans are:

- *Blanket inventory lien:* The blanket inventory lien gives the lender a lien against all the borrower's inventories.
- *Trust receipt:* Under this arrangement the borrower holds the inventory in trust for the lender. The document acknowledging the loan is called the trust receipt. Proceeds from the sale of inventory are remitted immediately to the lender.
- *Field warehouse financing:* In field warehouse financing, a public warehouse company supervises the inventory for the lender.

Other Sources

A variety of other sources of short-term funds are employed by corporations. The most important of these is the issuance of commercial paper and financing through banker's acceptances. Commercial paper consists of short-term notes issued by large, highly rated firms. Typically these notes are of short maturity, ranging up to 270 days (beyond that limit the firm will normally be required to file a registration statement with the appropriate stock exchange). Because the firm issues these directly and because it usually backs the issue with a special bank line of credit, the rate the firm obtains is often significantly below the rate the bank would charge it for a direct loan.

A banker's acceptance is an agreement by a bank to pay a sum of money. These agreements typically arise when a seller sends a bill or draft to a customer. The customer's bank *accepts* this bill and notes the acceptance on it, which makes it an obligation of the bank. In this way, a firm that is buying something from a supplier can effectively arrange for the bank to pay the outstanding bill. Of course, the bank charges the customer a fee for this service.

Summary and Conclusions

1 This chapter introduced the management of short-term finance. Short-term finance involves short-lived assets and liabilities. We traced and examined the short-term sources and uses of cash as they appear on the firm's financial statements. We saw how current assets and current liabilities arise in the short-term operating activities and the cash cycle of the firm. From an accounting perspective, short-term finance involves net working capital.

2 Managing short-term cash flows involves the minimization of costs. The two major costs are carrying costs (the interest and related costs incurred by over-investing in short-term assets such as cash) and shortage costs (the cost of running out of short-term assets). The objective of managing short-term finance and short-term financial planning is to find the optimal trade-off between these costs.

3 In an ideal economy, a firm could perfectly predict its short-term uses and sources of cash, and net working capital could be kept at zero. In the real world, net working capital provides a buffer that lets the firm meet its ongoing obligations. The financial manager seeks the optimal level of each of the current assets.

4 The financial manager can use the cash budget to identify short-term financial needs. The cash budget tells the manager what borrowing is required or what lending will be possible in the short term. The firm has a number of possible ways of acquiring funds to meet short-term shortfalls, including unsecured and secured loans.

Questions and Problems

CONCEPT

1 **Net Working Capital** What is short-term financial planning? Why is short-term financial planning crucial to a company? Provide an example of a company that has either undergone an insolvency event or is in financial distress due to poor short-term financial planning.

2 **Cash** Review the different ways in which cash can increase or decrease in a firm. Use the accounting equation to support your answer. What are some of the characteristics of a firm with a long operating cycle? Similarly, what are some of the characteristics of a firm with a long cash cycle?

3 **Short-term Financing Needs** Will firms that pursue sustainable development goals have different short-term financing needs than other companies? Explain, using an example of a company from your country.

4 **Short-term Financial Policy** Your friend has recently started up a new ice-cream shop business but is worried about the seasonality of cash flows the business will face. This is because the demand for ice cream will most likely be higher in summer than in other seasons, particularly winter. He asks you for help on how he should manage this risk. What would your advice be?

5 **Financing Strategies** Give an overview of different working capital financing strategies. What are the advantages and disadvantages of each?

6 **The Short-term Financial Plan** Explain what is meant by cash budgeting. Review the various ways a firm can finance a short-term cash deficit and the various financing policies to manage current assets.

REGULAR

7 **Sources and Uses** For the last year, you have gathered the following information about Rock Spring plc:

(a) The company undertook a £200 million share buyback programme.

(b) £300 million was invested in property, plant and equipment.

(c) Deferred revenue increased by £400 million.

(d) Corporation tax payments were £500 million.

(e) Staff redundancy payments of £50 million were made.

Label each as a source or use of cash and describe its effect on the firm's cash balance.

8 **Short-term Financial Management** A bank has recently installed a new contactless payment system for rural communities in Malawi. Describe the effect this is likely to have on the company's short-term financial management.

9 **Operating and Cash Cycle Length** You have just been appointed financial manager of a food processing and manufacturing firm. The production engineer has said that the cash cycle of your firm should always be longer than its operating cycle. Do you agree with this? Explain why, or why not.

10 **Shortage Costs** Assume you work for Evraz plc, the coal and iron ore miner. What would be the costs of shortages in such a firm? Explain using examples.

11 **Reasons for Net Working Capital** Why is net working capital always zero in an ideal economy, but positive in the real economy? Does this introduce any risks to a company?

Use the following information to answer Problems 12–15.

In the last year, Education Empowerment SA, a firm actively pursuing Sustainable Development Goal 4 (SDG4), which aims to ensure inclusive and equitable quality education and promote lifelong learning opportunities for all, has shortened its bill payment period to 40 days from the previous 82 days. The company's rationale for this change is to 'be socially progressive and fair to its suppliers'. This change in payment policy applies to all of the company's 10,000 suppliers, ranging from educational content creators to digital platform providers. Education Empowerment SA believes that this strategic financial management decision will allow it to better allocate resources towards initiatives that further enhance access to quality education and contribute towards the achievement of SDG4.

12 **Operating and Cash Cycles** What impact did this change in payables policy have on Education Empowerment's operating cycle? Its cash cycle?

13 **Operating and Cash Cycles: Suppliers** What impact do you think the policy change had on Education Empowerment's suppliers?

14 **Corporate Ethics** Is it ethical for large firms to unilaterally lengthen their payable periods, particularly when dealing with smaller suppliers? Is an 82-day payables period necessarily bad? Explain.

15 **Payables Period** Why do you think Education Empowerment really reduced its payables period? Is its explanation that this would 'be socially progressive and fair to its suppliers' sensible? Will there be any direct or indirect cash benefits to Education Empowerment from the change in payables period? Explain.

16 **Accounts Receivable** You are the owner of a professional basketball team with €3.5 million in the bank and a monthly cost base of around €1 million. Worried about potentially running out of cash during the playing season, you have asked supporters to pay for season tickets up front and in full. The basketball season starts four months from now. Do you think this is a wise strategy? Explain.

17 **Changes in the Cash Account** Indicate the impact of the following corporate actions on cash, using the letter *I* for an increase, *D* for a decrease or *N* when no change occurs.

(a) A dividend is paid with funds received from a sale of debt.
(b) Property is purchased and paid for with short-term debt.
(c) Inventory is bought on credit.
(d) A short-term bank loan is repaid.
(e) Next year's taxes are prepaid.
(f) Preference shares are redeemed.
(g) Sales are made on credit.
(h) Interest on long-term debt is paid.
(i) Payments for previous sales are collected.
(j) The trade payables balance is reduced.
(k) A dividend is paid.
(l) Production supplies are purchased and paid with a short-term note.
(m) Utility bills are paid.
(n) Cash is paid for raw materials purchased for inventory.
(o) Marketable securities are sold.

18 **Cash Equation** IFU Live plc has total non-current assets of £4,938 million. Non-current liabilities are £1,038 million. Current assets, other than cash, are £2,098 million. Current liabilities are £1,161 million. Total equity is worth £7,176 million. How much cash does the company have?

19 **Changes in the Operating Cycle** Indicate the effect that the following will have on the operating cycle. Use the letter *I* to indicate an increase, the letter *D* for a decrease and the letter *N* for no change.

(a) Receivables average goes up.
(b) Credit repayment times for customers are increased.
(c) Inventory turnover goes from 3 times to 6 times.
(d) Payables turnover goes from 6 times to 11 times.

(e) Receivables turnover goes from 7 times to 9 times.

(f) Payments to suppliers are accelerated.

20 **Changes in Cycles** Indicate the impact of the following on the cash and operating cycles, respectively. Use the letter *I* to indicate an increase, the letter *D* for a decrease and the letter *N* for no change.

(a) The terms of cash discounts offered to customers are made less favourable.

(b) The cash discounts offered by suppliers are increased, thus payments are made earlier.

(c) An increased number of customers begin to pay in cash instead of with credit.

(d) Fewer raw materials than usual are purchased.

(e) A greater percentage of raw material purchases are purchased on credit.

(f) More finished goods are produced for inventory instead of for order.

21 **Calculating Cash Collections** Assume that Next plc has projected the following quarterly sales amounts for the coming year:

	Q1	Q2	Q3	Q4
Sales	£824m	£920m	£620m	£1,600m

(a) Trade receivables at the beginning of the year are £145 million. Next plc has a 10-day collection period. Calculate cash collections in each of the four quarters by completing the following:

	Q1	Q2	Q3	Q4
Beginning receivables				
Sales				
Cash collections				
Ending receivables				

(b) Rework (a) assuming a collection period of 20 days.

(c) Rework (a) assuming a collection period of 30 days.

22 **Calculating Cycles** Consider the following financial statement information for Bulldog Ice plc. Calculate the operating and cash cycles. How do you interpret your answer?

Item	Beginning (£)		Ending (£)
Inventory	8,413		10,158
Accounts receivable	5,108		5,439
Accounts payable	6,927		7,625
Net sales		67,312	
Cost of goods sold		52,827	

23 **Calculating Payments: Lewellen Products** Lewellen Products has projected the following sales for the coming year:

	Q1	Q2	Q3	Q4
Sales (£)	540	630	710	785

Sales in the year following this one are projected to be 15 per cent greater in each quarter.

(a) Calculate payments to suppliers assuming that Lewellen places orders during each quarter equal to 30 per cent of projected sales for the next quarter. Assume that the company pays immediately. What is the payables period in this case?

	Q1	Q2	Q3	Q4
Payment of accounts (£)				

(b) Rework (a) assuming a 90-day payables period.

	Q1	Q2	Q3	Q4
Payment of accounts (£)				

(c) Rework (a) assuming a 60-day payables period.

	Q1	Q2	Q3	Q4
Payment of accounts (£)				

24 Calculating Payments: Marshall plc Marshall plc's purchases from suppliers in a quarter are equal to 75 per cent of the next quarter's forecast sales. The payables period is 60 days. Wages, taxes and other expenses are 20 per cent of sales, and interest and dividends are £60 per quarter. No capital expenditures are planned.

Here are the projected quarterly sales:

	Q1	Q2	Q3	Q4
Sales (£)	750	920	890	790

Sales for the first quarter of the following year are projected at £970. Calculate the company's cash outlays by completing the following:

	Q1	Q2	Q3	Q4
Payment of accounts				
Wages, taxes, other expenses				
Long-term financing expenses (interest and dividends)				
Total				

25 Calculating Cash Collections The following is the sales budget for Freezing Snow plc for the first quarter of the year:

	January	February	March
Sales budget (£)	150,000	173,000	194,000

Credit sales are collected as follows:

- 65 per cent in the month of the sale
- 20 per cent in the month after the sale
- 15 per cent in the second month after the sale.

The accounts receivable balance at the end of the previous quarter was £57,000 (£41,000 of which was uncollected December sales).

(a) Compute the sales for November.

(b) Compute the sales for December.

(c) Compute the cash collections from sales for each month from January to March.

CHALLENGE

26 Calculating the Cash Budget Here are some important figures from the budget of Sagmo AB for the first quarter of the year:

	January (NKr)	February (NKr)	March (NKr)
Credit sales	380,000	396,000	438,000
Credit purchases	147,000	175,500	200,500
Cash disbursements			
Wages, taxes and expenses	39,750	48,210	50,300
Interest	11,400	11,400	11,400
Equipment purchases	83,000	91,000	0

The company predicts that 5 per cent of its credit sales will never be collected, 35 per cent of its sales will be collected in the month of the sale and the remaining 60 per cent will be collected in the following month. Credit purchases will be paid in the month following the purchase.

In December of the previous year, credit sales were NKr210,000, and credit purchases were NKr156,000. Using this information, complete the following cash budget:

	January (NKr)	February (NKr)	March (NKr)
Beginning cash balance	280,000		
Cash receipts			
Cash collections from credit sales			
Total cash available			
Cash disbursements			
Purchases			
Wages, taxes and expenses			
Interest			
Equipment purchases			
Total cash disbursements			
Ending cash balance			

27 Sources and Uses: Balance Sheet Refer to the balance sheet of a hypothetical firm below. Determine whether each item is a source or a use of cash, and the amount:

CONSOLIDATED BALANCE SHEET as at 31 December (€ millions)		
	This Year	Last Year
Intangible assets	2,322	2,316
Property, plant and equipment	40,549	39,810
Environmental rehabilitation trusts	360	379
Investments in associates	5,240	4,900
Financial asset investments	2,896	3,220
Trade and other receivables	437	321
Deferred tax assets	530	389
Other financial assets (derivatives)	668	465
Other non-current assets	138	178
Total non-current assets	**53,140**	**51,978**
Inventories	3,517	3,604
Trade and other receivables	3,674	3,731
Current tax assets	207	235
Other financial assets (derivatives)	172	377
Cash and cash equivalents	11,732	6,401
Total current assets	**19,302**	**14,348**
Assets classified as held for sale	–	330
Total assets	**72,442**	**66,656**
Trade and other payables	(5,098)	(4,950)
Short-term borrowings	(1,018)	(1,535)
Provisions for liabilities and charges	(372)	(446)
Current tax liabilities	(1,528)	(871)
Other financial liabilities (derivatives)	(162)	(80)

CONSOLIDATED BALANCE SHEET as at 31 December (€ millions)		
	This Year	Last Year
Total current liabilities	**(8,178)**	**(7,882)**
Medium- and long-term borrowings	(11,855)	(11,904)
Retirement benefit obligations	(639)	(591)
Deferred tax liabilities	(5,730)	(5,641)
Other financial liabilities (derivatives)	(950)	(755)
Provisions for liabilities and charges	(1,830)	(1,666)
Other non-current liabilities	(71)	(104)
Total non-current liabilities	**(21,075)**	**(20,661)**
Liabilities directly associated with assets classified as held for sale	–	(142)
Total liabilities	**(29,253)**	**(28,685)**
Net assets	**43,189**	**37,971**
Equity		
Called-up share capital	738	738
Share premium account	2,714	2,713
Other reserves	283	3,642
Retained earnings	35,357	27,146
Equity attributable to equity shareholders of the company	**39,092**	**34,239**
Non-controlling interests	4,097	3,732
Total equity	**43,189**	**37,971**

28 Cash Budgeting The sales budget for your company in the coming year is based on a 20 per cent quarterly growth rate with the first-quarter sales projection at £100 million. In addition to this basic trend, the seasonal adjustments for the four quarters are 0, –£10, –£5 and £15 million, respectively. Generally, 50 per cent of the sales can be collected within the quarter and 45 per cent in the following quarter; the rest of sales are bad debt. The bad debts are written off in the second quarter after the sales are made. The beginning accounts payable balance is £81 million. Assuming all sales are on credit, compute the cash collections from sales for each quarter.

29 Calculating the Cash Budget Wildcat SA has estimated sales (in millions) for the next four quarters as follows:

	Q1	Q2	Q3	Q4
Sales (€m)	230	195	270	290

Sales for the first quarter of the year after this one are projected at €250 million. Accounts receivable at the beginning of the year were €79 million. Wildcat has a 45-day collection period.

Wildcat's purchases from suppliers in a quarter are equal to 45 per cent of the next quarter's forecast sales, and suppliers are normally paid in 36 days. Wages, taxes and other expenses run at about 30 per cent of sales. Interest and dividends are €15 million per quarter.

Wildcat plans a major capital outlay in the second quarter, of €90 million. Finally, the company started the year with a €73 million cash balance and wishes to maintain a €30 million minimum balance.

(a) Complete a cash budget for Wildcat by filling in the following:

WILDCAT SA Cash Budget (€m)				
	Q1	Q2	Q3	Q4
Beginning cash balance	73			
Net cash inflow				
Ending cash balance				
Minimum cash balance	30			
Cumulative surplus (deficit)				

(b) Assume that Wildcat can borrow any needed funds on a short-term basis at a rate of 3 per cent per quarter, and can invest any excess funds in short-term marketable securities at a rate of 2 per cent per quarter. Prepare a short-term financial plan by filling in the following schedule. What is the net cash cost (total interest paid minus total investment income earned) for the year?

WILDCAT SA Short-term Financial Plan (€m)				
	Q1	Q2	Q3	Q4
Beginning cash balance	73			
Net cash inflow				
New short-term investments				
Income from short-term investments				
Short-term investments sold				
New short-term borrowing				
Interest on short-term borrowing				
Short-term borrowing repaid				
Ending cash balance				
Minimum cash balance	30			
Cumulative surplus (deficit)				
Beginning short-term investments				
Ending short-term investments				
Beginning short-term debt				
Ending short-term debt				

30 **Cash Management Policy** Rework Problem 29 assuming the following:

(a) Wildcat maintains a minimum cash balance of €30 million.

(b) Wildcat maintains a minimum cash balance of €10 million.

Based on your answers in (a) and (b), do you think the firm can boost its profit by changing its cash management policy? Should other factors be considered as well? Explain.

31 **Short-term Finance Policy** Renault SA and Peugeot SA are competing automobile manufacturing firms. Download their annual financial accounts for the most recent period from each company's website.

(a) How are the current assets of each firm financed?

(b) Which firm has the larger investment in current assets? Why?

(c) Which firm is more likely to incur carrying costs, and which is more likely to incur shortage costs? Why?

Exam Question (45 minutes)

1 Consider the following financial statement information for Orologio SpA. Calculate the operating and cash cycles. How do you interpret your answer? **(40 marks)**

Item	Beginning (€)		Ending (€)
Inventory	44,234		34,048
Accounts receivable	43,211		35,532
Accounts payable	35,603		53,503
Net sales		360,302	
Cost of goods sold		120,400	

2 You have been hired by a manufacturing firm that is currently experiencing significant levels of financial distress. The managers have asked you to find ways in which the company can increase its cash levels so as to improve liquidity. Write a report to the managers, using figures to illustrate your answer, on how they can achieve this most efficiently. **(60 marks)**

Total Marks: 100

Mini Case

Wolgemut Manufacturing Working Capital Management

You have recently been hired by Wolgemut Manufacturing to work in its established treasury department. Wolgemut Manufacturing is a small company that produces highly customized cardboard boxes in a variety of sizes for different purchasers. Adam Wolgemut, the owner of the company, works primarily in the sales and production areas of the company. Currently, the company basically puts all receivables in one pile and all payables in another, and a part-time accountant periodically comes in and attacks the piles. Because of this disorganized system, the finance area needs work, and that is what you have been brought in to do.

The company currently has a cash balance of €115,000, and it plans to purchase new machinery in the third quarter at a cost of €200,000. The purchase of the machinery will be made with cash because of the discount offered for a cash purchase. Adam wants to maintain a minimum cash balance of €90,000 to guard against unforeseen contingencies. All of Wolgemut's sales to customers and purchases from suppliers are made with credit, and no discounts are offered or taken.

The company had the following sales each quarter of the year just ended:

	Q1	Q2	Q3	Q4
Gross sales (€)	565,000	585,000	628,000	545,000

After some research and discussions with customers, you are projecting that sales will be 8 per cent higher in each quarter next year. Sales for the first quarter of the following year are also expected to grow at 8 per cent. You calculate that Wolgemut currently has an accounts receivable period of 57 days and an accounts receivable balance of €426,000. However, 10 per cent of the accounts receivable balance is from a company that has just entered bankruptcy, and it is likely that this portion will never be collected.

You have also calculated that Wolgemut typically orders supplies each quarter to the amount of 50 per cent of the next quarter's projected gross sales, and suppliers are paid in 53 days on average. Wages, taxes and other costs run at about 25 per cent of gross sales. The company has a quarterly interest payment of €120,000 on its long-term debt. Finally, the company uses a local bank for its short-term financial needs. It currently pays 1.2 per cent per quarter on all short-term borrowing and maintains a money market account that pays 0.5 per cent per quarter on all short-term deposits.

Adam has asked you to prepare a cash budget and short-term financial plan for the company under the current policies. He has also asked you to prepare additional plans based on changes in several inputs.

1 Use the numbers given to complete the cash budget and short-term financial plan.

2 Rework the cash budget and short-term financial plan assuming Wolgemut changes to a minimum cash balance of €70,000.

3 Rework the sales budget assuming an 11 per cent growth rate in sales and a 5 per cent growth rate in sales. Assume a €90,000 target cash balance.

4 Assuming the company maintains its target cash balance at €90,000, what sales growth rate would result in a zero need for short-term financing? To answer this question, you may need to set up a spreadsheet and use the 'Solver' function.

Practical Case Study

1 **Cash and Operating Cycles** Find the most recent financial statements for two companies from your country. Calculate the cash and operating cycle for each company for the most recent year. Are the numbers similar for these companies? Why, or why not?

2 **Cash and Operating Cycles** Download the most recent quarterly financial statements for another company from your country. Calculate the operating and cash cycle for the firm over each of the last four quarters. Comment on any changes in the operating or cash cycle over this period.

Relevant Accounting Standards

The relevant accounting standards are those that apply to the presentation of financial statements and cash flow. These are IAS 1 *Presentation of Financial Statements* and IAS 7 *Statement of Cash Flows.*

References

Gogineni, S., S. Linn and P. Yadav (2012) 'Evidence on the Determinants of Cash Holdings By Private and Public Companies', Working Paper.

Opler, T., L. Pinkowitz, R. Stulz and R. Williamson (1999) 'The Determinants and Implication of Corporate Cash Holdings', *Journal of Financial Economics,* Vol. 52, No. 1, 3–46.

Additional Reading

The literature on cash holdings has exploded in recent years and the papers below give a flavour of the work in this area.

1 Bigelli, M. and J. Sánchez-Vidal (2012) 'Cash Holdings in Private Firms', *Journal of Banking and Finance,* Vol. 36, No. 1, 26–35.

2 Brown, J.R. and B.C. Petersen (2011) 'Cash Holdings and R&D Smoothing', *Journal of Corporate Finance,* Vol. 17, No. 3, 694–709.

3 Denis, D.J. and V. Sinilkov (2010) 'Financial Constraints, Investment, and the Value of Cash Holdings', *Review of Financial Studies,* Vol. 23, No. 1, 247–269.

4 Duchin, R. (2010) 'Cash Holdings and Corporate Diversification', *Journal of Finance,* Vol. 65, No. 3, 955–992.

5 Fresard, L. (2010) 'Financial Strength and Product Market Behavior: The Real Effects of Corporate Cash Holdings', *Journal of Finance,* Vol. 65, No. 3, 1097–1122.

6 Hanlon, M., E.L. Maydew and D. Saavedra (2017) 'The Taxman Cometh: Does Tax Uncertainty Affect Corporate Cash Holdings?', *Review of Accounting Studies,* Vol. 22, No. 3, 1198–1228.

7 Klasa, S., W.F. Maxwell and H. Ortiz-Molina (2009) 'The Strategic Use of Corporate Cash Holdings in Collective Bargaining with Labor Unions', *Journal of Financial Economics,* Vol. 92, No. 3, 421–442.

8 Lins, K.V., H. Servaes and P. Tufano (2010) 'What Drives Corporate Liquidity? An International Survey of Cash Holdings and Lines of Credit', *Journal of Financial Economics,* Vol. 98, No. 1, 160–176.

9 Palazzo, B. (2012) 'Cash Holdings, Risk and Expected Returns', *Journal of Financial Economics,* Vol. 104, No. 1, 162–185.

10 Paul, S. and C. Guermat (2010) 'Trade Credit as Short-term Finance, in the UK', *Accounting and Finance,* Working Paper.

11 Schauten, M.B.J., D. van Dijk and P. van der Waal (2013) 'Corporate Governance and the Value of Excess Cash Holdings of Large European Firms', *European Financial Management,* Vol. 19, No. 5, 991–1016.

12 Yun, H. (2009) 'The Choice of Corporate Liquidity and Corporate Governance', *Review of Financial Studies,* Vol. 22, No. 4, 1447–1475.

Endnotes

1 As we will learn in this chapter, the operating cycle begins when inventory is received and ends when cash is collected from the sale of inventory.

2 We assume Sackowoe makes no cash sales.

3 This is true of some types of finished goods.

4 This is true of inventory of raw material but not of finished goods.

Chapter 27
Short-term Capital Management

Learning Objectives

After reading this chapter you should be able to:

LO1 Explain the reasons for holding cash, and the trade-off between liquidity and profitability.

LO2 Apply the Baumol model and the Miller–Orr model to determine the target cash balance for a firm.

LO3 Calculate the cash conversion cycle and the net operating cycle for a firm, and identify ways to improve them.

LO4 Describe the terms of sale and how they affect the cash flow and profitability of a firm.

LO5 Determine the optimal credit policy for a firm.

Even if a firm is growing and has excellent performance, if it runs out of cash or does not manage its short-term capital properly it cannot survive. In any sale, one of the most important decisions made by the seller is whether to grant credit and, if credit is granted, the terms of the credit sale. As with many other decisions, there is variation from company to company, but credit policies tend to be similar within industries.

One way to examine a company's credit policy is to look at the days' sales in receivables, or the length of time from the sale until the company is paid. The receivables period for a typical firm in Europe is about 55 days, or a little under two months. For some firms, the period is much shorter. For British retailer Sainsbury's, for instance, it is about eight days and for Tesco about eleven. Although both firms have operations in several industries, neither routinely grants credit to its customers and so these numbers come as no surprise. In contrast, in the mining sector, credit periods are longer. Antofagasta, for example, has an average credit period of about 73 days.

In this chapter, we examine cash management and the various issues a firm must consider. We also examine how a firm sets its credit policy, including when to grant credit and for how long. Taken together, cash and credit policy represent the firm's short-term capital management.

Source: gonewiththewind/123RF

Key Notations

C	Cash balance
C^*	Optimal cash balance
R	Opportunity cost of holding cash
F	Fixed cost of selling securities to replenish cash
T	Total amount of new cash needed for transaction purposes over the relevant planning period
TC	Total cost of cash-balance policy
$U; L$	upper (U) and lower (L) control limits
Z	Target cash balance
Z^*	Optimal target cash balance
P_0	Price per unit received at time 0
C_0	Cost per unit paid at time 0
Q_0	Quantity sold at time 0
NCF	Net cash flow
h	Probability that customers will pay outstanding credit

27.1 Reasons for Holding Cash

Chapter 26 Page 715

The term *cash* is a surprisingly imprecise concept. The economic definition of cash includes currency, savings account deposits at banks and undeposited cheques. However, financial managers often use the term *cash* to include short-term marketable securities. Short-term marketable securities are frequently referred to as *cash equivalents*, and include Treasury bills, certificates of deposit and repurchase agreements. The balance sheet item 'cash' usually includes cash equivalents.

Chapter 26 discussed the management of net working capital. Net working capital includes both cash and cash equivalents. This chapter is concerned with cash, not net working capital, and it focuses on the narrow economic definition of cash.

The basic elements of net working capital management, such as carrying costs, shortage costs and opportunity costs, are relevant for cash management. However, cash management is more concerned with how to minimize cash balances by collecting and disbursing cash effectively.

There are two primary reasons for holding cash. First, cash is needed to satisfy the transactions motive. Transaction-related needs come from normal disbursement and collection activities of the firm. The disbursement of cash includes the payment of wages and salaries, trade debts, taxes and dividends. Cash is collected from sales from operations, sales of assets and new financing. The cash inflows (*collections*) and outflows (*disbursements*) are not perfectly synchronized, and some level of cash holdings is necessary as a buffer. If the firm maintains too small a cash balance, it may run out of cash. If so, it must sell marketable securities or borrow. Selling marketable securities and borrowing involve *trading costs.*

Another reason to hold cash is for compensating balances. Cash balances are kept at banks to compensate for banking services rendered to the firm. The cash balance for most firms can be thought of as consisting of transaction balances and compensating balances. However, it would not be correct for a firm to add the amount of cash required to satisfy its transaction needs to the amount of cash needed to satisfy its compensatory balances to produce a target cash balance. The same cash can be used to satisfy both requirements.

The cost of holding cash is, of course, the opportunity cost of lost interest. To determine the target cash balance, the firm must weigh the benefits of holding cash against the costs. It is generally a good idea for firms to figure out first how much cash to hold to satisfy transaction needs. Next, the firm must consider compensating balance requirements, which will impose a lower limit on the level of the firm's cash holdings. Because compensating balances merely provide a lower limit, we ignore compensating balances for the following discussion of the target cash balance.

Table 27.1 presents average statistics on general cash holdings of firms across the world. There is clearly significant variation across countries, with firms in some countries having very low average cash balances and others holding cash in excess of 10 per cent of their total assets. For example, Indian firms hold only 6.6 per cent of their assets in cash compared to Chinese firms, which hold 17.7 per cent of their assets in cash.

Table 27.1 Average Corporate Cash Holdings by Country

		Market-to-book ratio		Cash holdings	
Country	Number of Items	Mean	Median	Mean	Median
Austria	96	0.855	0.761	0.105	0.074
Belgium	126	0.938	0.779	0.115	0.074
China	639	1.218	1.040	0.177	0.149
Czechia	16	0.570	0.481	0.072	0.047
Denmark	130	1.035	0.839	0.119	0.081
Finland	155	0.989	0.839	0.102	0.067
France	832	0.951	0.759	0.119	0.088
Germany	708	0.948	0.777	0.104	0.061
Greece	235	0.971	0.837	0.072	0.042
India	635	1.245	0.856	0.066	0.031
Ireland	61	1.207	0.993	0.145	0.096
Italy	275	0.880	0.713	0.117	0.083
Malaysia	807	0.912	0.739	0.107	0.072
Netherlands	215	1.060	0.868	0.092	0.051
Norway	182	1.047	0.875	0.131	0.102
Poland	152	1.161	0.905	0.091	0.062
Russia	61	1.206	0.996	0.076	0.062
Singapore	525	0.930	0.773	0.155	0.121
South Africa	297	1.048	0.899	0.115	0.090
Spain	149	0.987	0.837	0.078	0.048
Sweden	323	1.131	0.897	0.116	0.081
Switzerland	217	1.087	0.869	0.135	0.107
UK	1727	1.154	0.942	0.109	0.073
USA	3372	1.416	1.132	0.121	0.063

The table shows the number of firms per country, the mean and median market-to-book ratio (the sum of the year-end market capitalization and the book value of debt, divided by total assets), and the mean and median cash holdings (cash and short-term investments divided by total assets).

Source: Adapted from Kyröläinen et al. (2013), Table 1, Panel B.

27.2 Determining the Target Cash Balance

The **target cash balance** involves a trade-off between the opportunity costs of holding too much cash and the trading costs of holding too little. Figure 27.1 presents the problem graphically. If a firm tries to keep its cash holdings too low, it will find itself selling marketable securities (and perhaps later buying marketable securities to replace those sold) more frequently than if the cash balance were higher. Thus, trading costs will tend to fall as the cash balance becomes larger. In contrast, the opportunity costs of holding cash rise as the cash holdings rise. At point C^* in Figure 27.1, the sum of both costs, depicted as the total cost curve, is at a minimum. This is the target or optimal cash balance.

Figure 27.1 Cost of Holding Cash

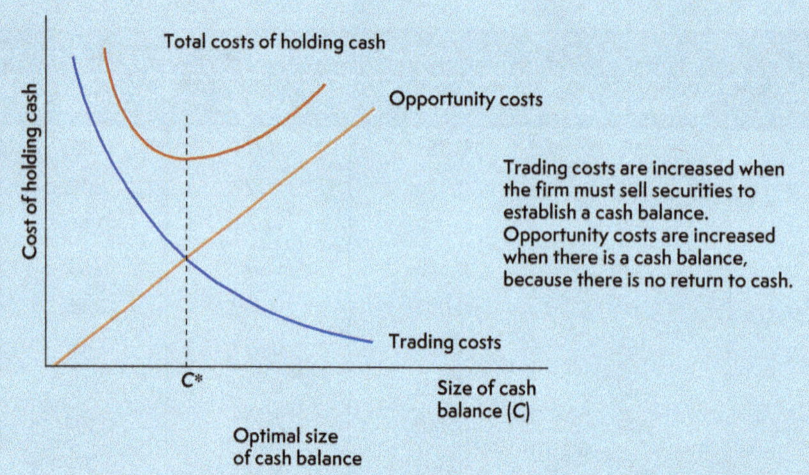

The Baumol Model

William Baumol (1952) was the first to provide a formal model of cash management incorporating opportunity costs and trading costs. His model can be used to establish the target cash balance.

Suppose Golden Socks plc began week 0 with a cash balance of C = £1.2 million, and outflows exceed inflows by £600,000 per week. Its cash balance will drop to zero at the end of week 2, and its average cash balance will be $C/2$ = £1.2 million/2 = £600,000 over the two-week period. At the end of week 2, Golden Socks must replace its cash either by selling marketable securities or by borrowing. Figure 27.2 shows this situation.

Figure 27.2 Cash Balances for Golden Socks plc

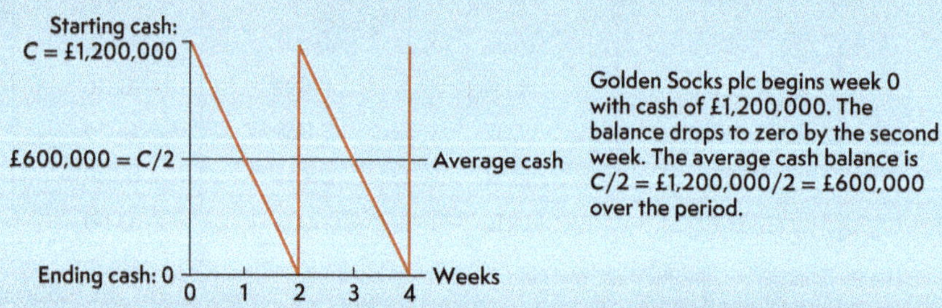

If C were set higher, say at £2.4 million, cash would last four weeks before the firm would need to sell marketable securities, but the firm's average cash balance would increase to £1.2 million (from £600,000). If C were set at £600,000, cash would run out in one week and the firm would need to replenish cash more frequently, but its average cash balance would fall from £600,000 to £300,000.

Because transaction costs must be incurred whenever cash is replenished (for example, the brokerage costs of selling marketable securities), establishing large initial cash balances will lower the trading costs connected with cash management. However, the larger the average cash balance, the greater the opportunity cost (the return that could have been earned on marketable securities).

To solve this problem, Golden Socks needs to know the following three things:

1 The fixed cost of selling securities to replenish cash (F)

2 The total amount of new cash needed for transaction purposes over the relevant planning period – say, one year (T)

3 The opportunity cost of holding cash; this is the interest rate on marketable securities (R).

With this information, Golden Socks can determine the total costs of any particular cash-balance policy. It can then determine the optimal cash-balance policy.

The Opportunity Costs

The total opportunity costs of cash balances, in monetary terms, must be equal to the average cash balance multiplied by the interest rate:

$$\text{Opportunity costs (£)} = (C/2) \times R$$

The opportunity costs of various alternatives are given here:

Initial Cash Balance C(£)	Average Cash Balance C/2 (£)	Opportunity Costs (R = 0.10) (C/2) × R (£)
4,800,000	2,400,000	240,000
2,400,000	1,200,000	120,000
1,200,000	600,000	60,000
600,000	300,000	30,000
300,000	150,000	15,000

The Trading Costs

We can determine total trading costs by calculating the number of times that Golden Socks must sell marketable securities during the year. The total amount of cash disbursement during the year is £600,000 × 52 weeks = £31.2 million. If the initial cash balance is set at £1.2 million, Golden Socks will sell £1.2 million of marketable securities every two weeks. Thus, trading costs are given by:

$$\frac{\text{£31.2 million}}{\text{£1.2 million}} \times F = 26F$$

The general formula is:

$$\text{Trading costs £} = (T/C) \times F$$

A schedule of alternative trading costs follows:

Total Disbursements During Relevant Period *T*(£)	Initial Cash Balance C(£)	Trading Costs (*F* = £1,000) (*T*/*C*) × *F*(£)
31,200,000	4,800,000	6,500
31,200,000	2,400,000	13,000
31,200,000	1,200,000	26,000
31,200,000	600,000	52,000
31,200,000	300,000	104,000

The Total Cost

The total cost of cash balances consists of the opportunity costs plus the trading costs:

$$\begin{aligned}\text{Total cost} &= \text{Opportunity costs} + \text{Trading costs}\\ &= (C/2) \times R + (T/C) \times F\end{aligned}$$

Cash Balance (£)	Total Cost (£)	=	Opportunity Costs (£)	+	Trading Costs (£)
4,800,000	246,500		240,000		6,500
2,400,000	133,000		120,000		13,000
1,200,000	86,000		60,000		26,000
600,000	82,000		30,000		52,000
300,000	119,000		15,000		104,000

The Solution

We can see from the preceding schedule that a £600,000 cash balance results in the lowest total cost of the possibilities presented: £82,000. But what about £700,000 or £500,000, or other possibilities? To determine minimum total costs precisely, Golden Socks must equate the marginal reduction in trading costs as balances rise with the marginal increase in opportunity costs associated with cash balance increases. The target cash balance should be the point where the two offset each other. This can be calculated with either numerical iteration or calculus. We will use calculus, but if you are unfamiliar with such an analysis you can skip to the solution.

Recall that the total cost equation is:

$$\text{Total costs } (TC) = (C/2) \times R + (T/C) \times F$$

If we differentiate the TC equation with respect to the cash balance and set the derivative equal to zero, we will find:

$$\frac{dTC}{dC} = \frac{R}{2} - \frac{TF}{C^2} = 0$$

We obtain the solution for the general cash balance, C^*, by solving this equation for C:

$$\frac{R}{2} = \frac{TF}{C^2}$$

$$C^* = \sqrt{2TF/R}$$

If F = £1,000, T = £31,200,000 and R = 0.10, then C^* = £789,936.71. Given the value of C^*, opportunity costs are:

$$(C^*/2) \times R = \frac{£789{,}936.71}{2} \times 0.10 = £39{,}496.84$$

Trading costs are:

$$(TC^*) \times F = \frac{£31{,}200{,}000}{£789{,}936.71} \times 1{,}000 = \$39{,}496.84$$

Hence, total costs are:

$$£39{,}496.84 + £39{,}496.84 = £78{,}993.68$$

Limitations

The Baumol model represents an important contribution to cash management. The limitations of the model include the following:

- *The model assumes the firm has a constant disbursement rate.* In practice, disbursements can be only partially managed because due dates differ and costs cannot be predicted with certainty.
- *The model assumes there are no cash receipts during the projected period.* In fact, most firms experience both cash inflows and outflows daily.
- *No safety stock is allowed.* Firms will probably want to hold a safety stock of cash designed to reduce the possibility of a cash shortage or *cash-out*. However, to the extent that firms can sell marketable securities or borrow in a few hours, the need for a safety stock is minimal.

The Baumol model is possibly the simplest and most stripped-down sensible model for determining the optimal cash position. Its chief weakness is that it assumes discrete, certain cash flows. We next discuss a model designed to deal with uncertainty.

The Miller–Orr Model

Merton Miller and Daniel Orr (1966) developed a cash balance model to deal with cash inflows and outflows that fluctuate randomly from day to day. In the Miller–Orr model, both cash inflows and cash outflows are included. The model assumes that the distribution of daily net cash flows (cash inflow minus cash outflow) is normally distributed. On each day the net cash flow could be the expected value or some higher or lower value. We will assume that the expected net cash flow is zero.

Figure 27.3 shows how the Miller–Orr model works. The model operates in terms of upper (U) and lower (L) control limits and a target cash balance (Z). The firm allows its cash balance to wander randomly within the lower and upper limits. As long as the cash balance is between U and L, the firm makes no transaction. When the cash balance reaches U, such as at point X, the firm buys $U - Z$ units (e.g. euros or pounds) of marketable securities.

Figure 27.3 The Miller–Orr Model

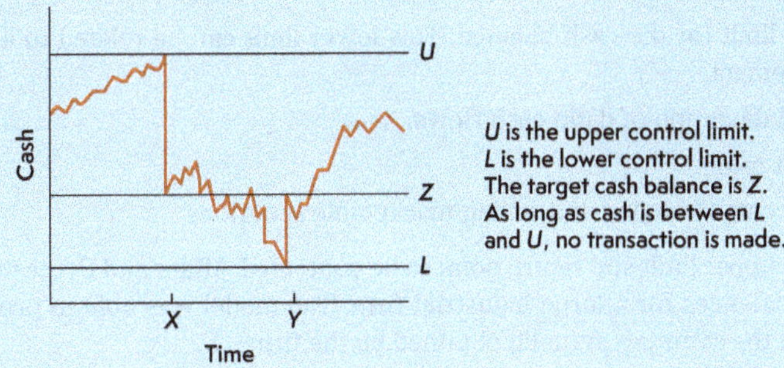

This action will decrease the cash balance to Z. In the same way, when cash balances fall to L, such as at point Y (the lower limit), the firm should sell $Z - L$ securities and increase the cash balance to Z. In both situations, cash balances return to Z. Management sets the lower limit, L, depending on how much risk of a cash shortfall the firm is willing to tolerate.

Like the Baumol model, the Miller–Orr model depends on trading costs and opportunity costs. The cost per transaction of buying and selling marketable securities, F, is assumed to be fixed. The percentage opportunity cost per period of holding cash, R, is the daily interest rate on marketable securities. Unlike in the Baumol model, the number of transactions per period is a random variable that varies from period to period, depending on the pattern of cash inflows and outflows.

As a consequence, trading costs per period depend on the expected number of transactions in marketable securities during the period. Similarly, the opportunity costs of holding cash are a function of the expected cash balance per period.

Given L, which is set by the firm, the Miller–Orr model solves for the target cash balance, Z, and the upper limit, U. Expected total costs of the cash balance return policy (Z, U) are equal to the sum of expected transaction costs and expected opportunity costs. The values of Z (the return cash point) and U (the upper limit) that minimize the expected total cost have been determined by Miller and Orr:

$$Z^* = \sqrt[3]{3F\sigma^2/(4R)} + L$$
$$U^* = 3Z^* - 2L$$

Here * denotes optimal values, and σ^2 is the variance of net daily cash flows.

The average cash balance in the Miller–Orr model is:

$$\text{Average cash balance} = \frac{4Z - L}{3}$$

Example 27.1

Miller–Orr

To clarify the Miller–Orr model, suppose F = £1,000, the interest rate is 10 per cent annually and the standard deviation of daily net cash flows is £2,000. The daily opportunity cost, R, is:

$$(1 + R)^{365} - 1 = 0.10$$
$$1 + R = \sqrt[365]{1.10} = 1.000261$$
$$R = 0.000261$$

The variance of daily net cash flows is:

$$\sigma^2 = (2{,}000)^2 = 4{,}000{,}000$$

Let us assume that $L = 0$:

$$Z^* = \sqrt[3]{(3 \times £1{,}000 \times 4{,}000{,}000)/(4 \times 0.000261) + 0}$$
$$= \sqrt[3]{(£11{,}493{,}900{,}000{,}000)} = £22{,}568$$
$$U^* = 3 \times £22{,}568 = £67{,}704$$
$$\text{Average cash balance} = \frac{4 \times £22{,}568}{3} = £30{,}091$$

Implications of the Miller–Orr Model

To use the Miller–Orr model, the manager must do four things:

1. Set the lower control limit for the cash balance. This lower limit can be related to a minimum safety margin decided on by management.
2. Estimate the standard deviation of daily cash flows.
3. Determine the interest rate.
4. Estimate the trading costs of buying and selling marketable securities.

These four steps allow the upper limit and return point to be computed. Miller and Orr tested their model using nine months of data for cash balances for a large industrial firm. The model was able to produce average daily cash balances much lower than the averages actually obtained by the firm.

The Miller–Orr model clarifies the issues of cash management. First, the model shows that the best return point, Z^*, is positively related to trading costs, F, and negatively related to R. This finding is consistent with and analogous to the Baumol model. Second, the Miller–Orr model shows that the best return point and the average cash balance are positively related to the variability of cash flows. That is, firms whose cash flows are subject to greater uncertainty should maintain a larger average cash balance.

Other Factors Influencing the Target Cash Balance

Borrowing

In our previous examples, the firm obtained cash by selling marketable securities. Another alternative is to borrow cash. Borrowing introduces additional considerations to cash management:

- Borrowing is likely to be more expensive than selling marketable securities because the interest rate is likely to be higher.
- The need to borrow will depend on management's desire to hold low cash balances. A firm is more likely to need to borrow to cover an unexpected cash outflow with greater cash flow variability and lower investment in marketable securities.

Compensating Balance

The costs of trading securities are well below the lost income from holding cash for large firms. Consider a firm faced with either selling £2 million of Treasury bills to replenish cash or leaving the money idle overnight. The daily opportunity cost of £2 million at a 10 per cent annual interest rate is 0.10/365 = 0.027 per cent per day. The daily return earned on £2 million is 0.00027 × £2 million = £540. The cost of selling £2 million of Treasury bills is much less than £540. As a consequence, a large firm will buy and sell securities many times a day before it will leave substantial amounts idle overnight.

However, most large firms hold more cash than cash balance models imply, suggesting that managers disagree with this logic. Here are some possible reasons:

- Firms have cash in the bank as a compensating balance in payment for banking services.
- Large corporations have thousands of accounts with several dozen banks. Sometimes it makes more sense to leave cash alone than to manage each account daily.

27.3 Managing the Collection and Disbursement of Cash

A firm's cash balance as reported in its financial statements (*book cash* or *ledger cash*) is not the same thing as the balance shown in its bank account (*bank cash* or *collected bank cash*). The difference between bank cash and book cash is called **float** and represents the net effect of transactions in the process of collection. Twenty years ago, float was a major consideration for companies because of the widespread use of cheques. However, with the universal adoption of new technologies and the Revised Payment Services Directive introduced throughout the European Union in 2018, cash float is much less of a pressing concern. This is because the time between payment and receipt of cash, especially within the European Union, has shortened substantially.

Electronic data interchange (EDI) is a general term that refers to direct electronic information exchange between all types of businesses. One important use of EDI – often called financial EDI, or FEDI – is to electronically transfer financial information and funds between parties, thereby eliminating paper invoices, paper cheques, mailing and handling. For example, it is possible to arrange to have your account directly debited each month to pay many types of bills, and corporations now routinely pay directly into employee accounts.

More generally, EDI allows a seller to send a bill electronically to a buyer, thereby avoiding the mail. The buyer can then authorize payment, which also occurs electronically. Its bank then transfers the funds to the seller's account at a different bank. The net effect is that the length of time required to initiate and complete a business transaction is shortened considerably, and much of what we normally think of as float is sharply reduced or eliminated. As the use of FEDI increases (which it will), float management will evolve to focus much more on issues surrounding computerized information exchange and fund transfers.

The Single Euro Payments Area (SEPA) is a European initiative to reduce payment times across most countries in Europe. The SEPA aims to harmonize payments across Europe by treating the different countries within the region as a single area. This has already resulted in significant reductions in business transaction times.

27.4 Investing Idle Cash

If a firm has a temporary cash surplus, it can invest in short-term marketable securities. The market for short-term financial assets is called the *money market*. The maturity of short-term financial assets that trade in the money market is one year or less.

Most large firms manage their own short-term financial assets, transacting through banks and dealers. Some large firms and many small firms use money market funds. These are funds that invest in short-term financial assets for a management fee. The management fee is compensation for the professional expertise and diversification provided by the fund manager. Among the many money market mutual funds, some specialize in corporate customers. Banks also offer *sweep accounts*, where the bank takes all excess available funds at the close of each business day and invests them for the firm.

Firms have temporary cash surpluses for these reasons: to help finance seasonal or cyclical activities of the firm, to help finance planned expenditures of the firm and to provide for unanticipated contingencies.

Sustainability in Action 27.1

Citi's Contribution to Sustainability

At COP26 in Glasgow, global financial institutions made a commitment to play their part in creating a new sustainable world. As part of their own corporate initiatives, the global banking institution, Citi, introduced a new sustainable time deposit solution designed to assist institutional clients in aligning their cash management strategies with their sustainability goals.

Funds deposited into sustainable time deposits are used to finance or refinance assets in a portfolio of eligible green and social finance projects. The projects eligible for these funds range from renewable energy and energy efficiency projects to water quality and conservation projects, with a special focus on social projects that expand financial inclusion for women and traditionally under-represented communities.

'Finance and treasury teams are playing an increasingly strategic role in helping their firms to support their sustainability and environmental, social and governance (ESG) goals,' said Stephen Randall, Global Head of Liquidity Management Services, Treasury and Trade Solutions, Citi. 'Our new sustainable time deposit solution reflects Citi's commitment to providing tools that help our clients reach their goals with their own organizations and their communities.' Citi press release (5 April 2023)

Source: Citi Group Press Release

Seasonal or Cyclical Activities

Some firms have a predictable cash flow pattern. They have surplus cash flows during part of the year and deficit cash flows the rest of the year. For instance, many retailers have a seasonal cash flow pattern influenced by holiday (especially Christmas) sales. Such a firm may buy marketable securities when surplus cash flows occur and sell marketable securities when deficits occur. Of course bank loans are another short-term financing device. Figure 27.4 illustrates the use of bank loans and marketable securities to meet temporary financing needs.

Figure 27.4 Seasonal Cash Demands

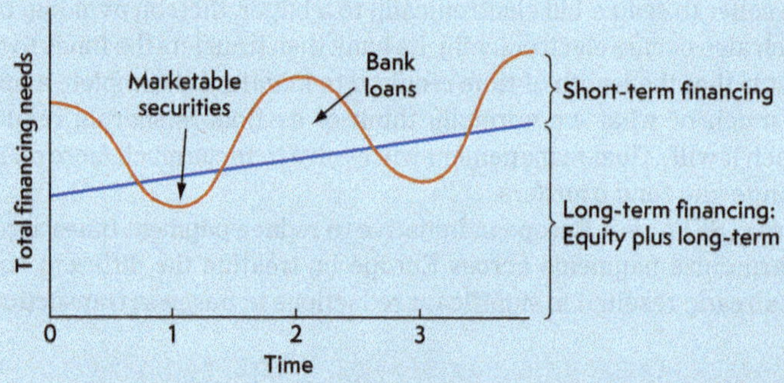

Time 1: A surplus cash flow exists. Seasonal demand for investing is low. The surplus cash flow is invested in short-term marketable securities.

Time 2: A deficit cash flow exists. Seasonal demand for investing is high. The financial deficit is financed by selling marketable securities, and by bank borrowing.

Planned Expenditures

Firms frequently accumulate temporary investments in marketable securities to provide the cash for a plant construction programme, dividend payment and other large expenditures. Thus, firms may issue bonds and shares before the cash is needed, investing the proceeds in short-term marketable securities and then selling the securities to finance the expenditures.

The important characteristics of short-term marketable securities are their maturity, default risk, marketability and taxability.

Maturity

Maturity refers to the time period over which interest and principal payments are made. For a given change in the level of interest rates, the prices of longer-maturity securities will change more than those for shorter-maturity securities. As a consequence, firms that invest in long-maturity securities are accepting greater risk than those that invest in securities with short-term maturities. This type of risk is usually called *interest rate risk*. Most firms limit their investments in marketable securities to those maturing in fewer than 90 days. Of course, the expected return on securities with short-term maturities is usually less than the expected return on securities with longer maturities.

Default Risk

Chapter 20 Page 548

Default risk refers to the probability that interest or principal will not be paid on the due date and in the promised amount. In Chapter 20, Section 20.5, we observed that various financial reporting agencies, such as Moody's and Standard & Poor's, compile and publish ratings of various corporate and public securities. These ratings are connected to default risk. Of course, some securities have negligible default risk, such as Treasury bills. Given the purposes of investing idle corporate cash, firms typically avoid investing in marketable securities with significant default risk.

Marketability

Marketability refers to how easy it is to convert an asset to cash. Sometimes marketability is referred to as *liquidity*. It has two characteristics:

1. *No price pressure effect:* If an asset can be sold in large amounts without changing the market price, it is marketable. Price pressure effects are those that come about when the price of an asset must be lowered to facilitate the sale.
2. *Time:* If an asset can be sold quickly at the existing market price, it is marketable. In contrast, a Renoir painting or antique desk appraised at €1 million is likely to sell for much less if the owner must sell at short notice.

In general, marketability is the ability to sell an asset for its face market value quickly and in large amounts. The most marketable of all securities are Treasury bills of developed countries.

Taxability

Several kinds of securities have varying degrees of tax exemption. The interest on the bonds of governments tends to be exempt from taxes. Pre-tax expected returns on government bonds must be lower than on similar taxable investments and therefore are more attractive to corporations in high marginal tax brackets.

The market price of securities will reflect the total demand and supply of tax influences. The position of the firm may be different from that of the market.

Different Types of Money Market Securities

Money market securities are generally highly marketable and short term. They usually have low risk of default. They are issued by governments (e.g., Treasury bills), domestic and foreign banks (e.g., certificates of deposit) and business corporations (e.g., commercial paper).

Treasury bills are obligations of the government that mature in 90, 180, 270 or 360 days. They are pure discount securities. The 90-day and 180-day bills will be sold by auction every week, and 270-day and 360-day bills will be sold at longer intervals, such as every month.

Treasury notes and bonds have original maturities of more than one year. They are interest-bearing securities. The interest may be exempt from state and local taxes.

Commercial paper refers to short-term securities issued by finance companies, banks and corporations. Commercial paper typically is unsecured. Maturities range from a few weeks to 270 days. There is no active secondary market in commercial paper. As a consequence, their marketability is low. (However, firms that issue commercial paper will directly repurchase before maturity.) The default risk of commercial paper depends on the financial strength of the issuer. Moody's and Standard & Poor's publish quality ratings for commercial paper.

Certificates of deposit (CDs) are short-term loans to commercial banks. There are active markets in CDs of 3-month, 6-month, 9-month and 12-month maturities.

Repurchase agreements are sales of government securities (such as Treasury bills) by a bank or securities dealer with an agreement to repurchase. An investor typically buys some Treasury securities from a bond dealer and simultaneously agrees to sell them back at a later date at a specified higher price. Repurchase agreements are usually very short term – overnight to a few days.

Eurodollar CDs are deposits of cash with foreign banks.

Banker's acceptances are time drafts (orders to pay) issued by a business firm (usually an importer) that have been accepted by a bank that guarantees payment.

Real World Insight 27.1

Genpact

This Real World Insight comes from a case study undertaken by the consultancy firm Genpact, which helped a major multinational client to improve its cash management.

Genpact's client was an industrial manufacturer that was grappling with delayed payments and high costs to serve each customer. The main reason was its traditional approach to debtor collections, which was built on monetary thresholds and limited data, and failed to consider evolving payment patterns or customer behaviours. As a result, the firm was increasingly experiencing ageing invoices, dwindling cash flow and bad debt.

Genpact helped the company implement a revamp of its collections processes and introduced a predictive model for better customer collections. Drawing from a large database that included information on customer payment track record, payment terms and products purchased, Genpact was able to identify key factors leading to payment delays by analysing more than 10,000 active customer accounts for delinquency figures and invoice volumes. With these insights, it built a predictive model that used advanced analytics and artificial intelligence to forecast which customers were likely to pay late, early or on time.

Within six months, the manufacturing company had slashed delinquent invoices by more than 40 per cent, increased collections productivity and anticipated an annual cash flow improvement of more than $50 million. A low-touch strategy for reliable payers was implemented, and the predictive model was accurate 85 per cent of the time with on-time payments.

Source: Genpact (2021).

27.5 Terms of Sale

The *terms of sale* refer to the period for which credit is granted, the cash discount and the type of credit instrument. Suppose, say, a customer is granted credit with terms of 2/10, net 30. This means that the customer has 30 days from the **invoice** date within which to pay. In addition, a cash discount of 2 per cent from the stated sales price is to be given if payment is made in 10 days. If the stated terms are net 60, the customer has 60 days from the invoice date to pay and no discount is offered for early payment.

When sales are seasonal, a firm might use seasonal dating. O.M. Scott and Sons is a manufacturer of lawn and garden products with a seasonal dating policy that is tied to the growing season. Payments for winter shipments of fertilizer might be due in the spring or summer. A firm offering 3/10, net 60, 1 May dating, is making the effective invoice date 1 May. The stated amount must be paid on 30 June, regardless of when the sale is made. The cash discount of 3 per cent can be taken until 10 May.

A trade or account receivable is created when credit is granted; a trade or account payable is created when a firm receives credit. These accounts are illustrated in Figure 27.5. The term 'trade credit' refers to credit granted to other firms.

Figure 27.5 Trade Credit

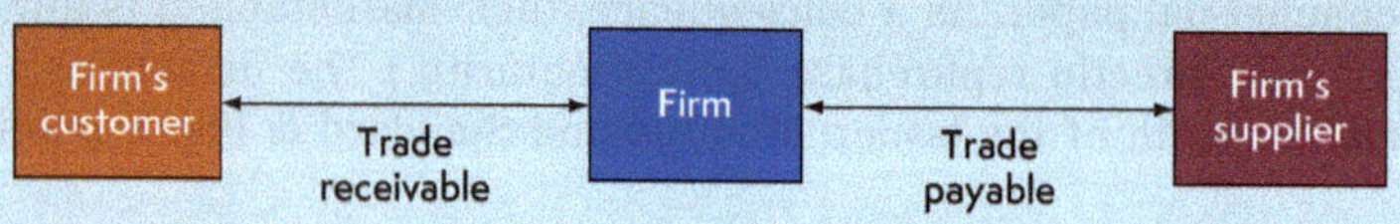

Trade credit extended to a customer by a firm appears as a trade receivable.
Trade credit extended by the firm's supplier to the firm appears as a trade payable.

Credit Period

Credit periods vary between different industries. A jewellery store, for example, may sell diamond engagement rings for 5/30, net 4 months. A food wholesaler, selling fresh fruit and produce, might use net 7. Generally, a firm must consider three factors in setting a credit period:

1. *The probability that the customer will not pay:* A firm whose customers are in high-risk businesses may find itself offering restrictive credit terms.
2. *The size of the account:* If the account is small, the credit period will be shorter. Small accounts are more costly to manage, and small customers are less important.
3. *The extent to which the goods are perishable:* If the collateral values of the goods are low and cannot be sustained for long periods, less credit will be granted.

Lengthening the credit period effectively reduces the price paid by the customer. Generally, this increases sales. Figure 27.6 illustrates the cash flows from granting credit.

Figure 27.6 The Cash Flows of Granting Credit

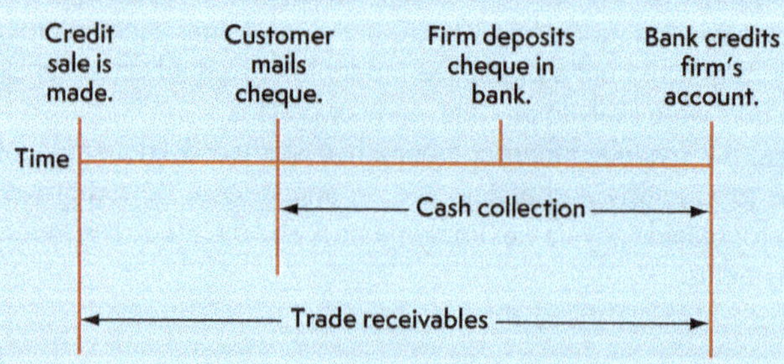

Example 27.2

Credit Policy

Edward Manalt, the chief financial officer of Ruptbank, is considering the request of the company's largest customer, who wants to take a 3 per cent discount for payment within 20 days on a £10,000 purchase. In other words, he intends to pay £9,700 [= £10,000 × (1 − 0.03)]. Normally, this customer pays in 30 days with no discount. The cost of debt capital for Ruptbank is 10 per cent. Edward has worked out the cash flow implications illustrated in Figure 27.7. He has calculated the present value of the two proposals:

Figure 27.7 Cash Flows for Different Credit

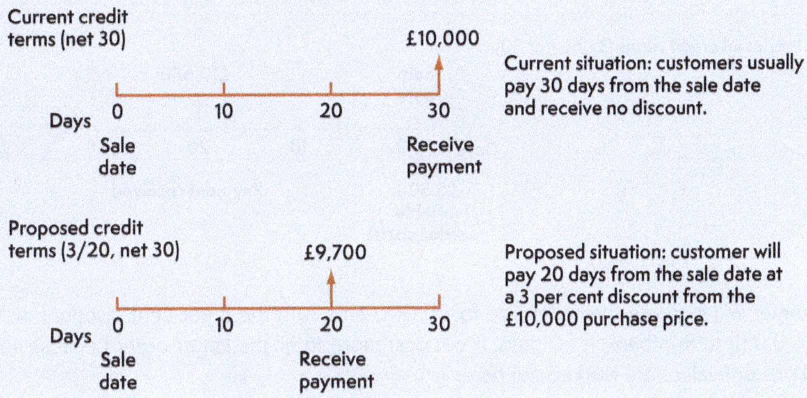

Current policy:

$$PV = \frac{£10,000}{1 + (0.1 \times 30/365)} = £9,918.48$$

Proposed policy:

$$PV = \frac{£9,700}{1 + (0.1 \times 20/365)} = £9,647.14$$

His calculation shows that granting the discount would cost Ruptbank £271.34 (= £9,918.48 − £9,647.14) in present value. Consequently, Ruptbank is better off with the current credit arrangement.

Cash Discounts

Cash discounts are often part of the terms of sale. One reason they are offered is to speed up the collection of receivables. The firm must trade this off against the cost of the discount.

In Example 27.2 we implicitly assumed that granting credit had no side effects. However, the decision to grant credit may generate higher sales and involve a different cost structure. Example 27.3 illustrates the impact of changes in the level of sales and costs in the credit decision.

Example 27.3

More Credit Policy

Suppose that Ruptbank has variable costs of £0.50 per £1 of sales. If offered a discount of 3 per cent, customers will increase their order size by 10 per cent. This new information is shown in Figure 27.8.

Figure 27.8 Cash Flows for Different Credit Terms: The Impact of New Sales and Costs

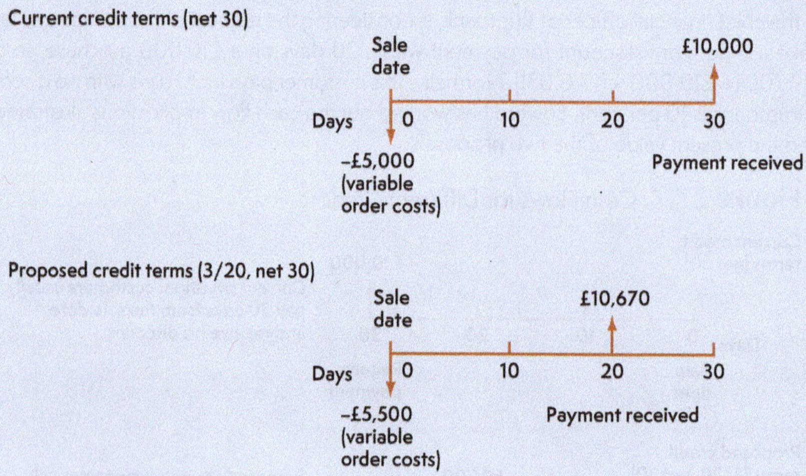

That is, the customer will increase the order size to £11,000 and, with the 3 per cent discount, will remit £10,670 [= £11,000 × (1 – 0.03)] to Ruptbank in 20 days. It will cost more to fill the larger order because variable costs are £5,500. The net present values are worked out here:

Current policy:

$$NPV = -\pounds 5{,}000 + \frac{\pounds 10{,}000}{1 + (0.1 \times 30/365)} = \pounds 4{,}918.48$$

Proposed policy:

$$NPV = -\pounds 5{,}500 + \frac{\pounds 10{,}670}{1 + (0.1 \times 20/365)} = \pounds 5{,}111.85$$

Now it is clear that the firm is better off with the proposed credit policy. This increase is the net effect of several different factors, including the larger initial costs, the earlier receipt of the cash inflows, the increased sales level and the discount.

Credit Instruments

Most credit is offered on *open account*. This means that the only formal **credit instrument** is the invoice, which is sent with the shipment of goods, and which the customer signs as evidence that the goods have been received. Afterwards, the firm and its customers record the exchange on their accounting books.

At times, the firm may require that the customer sign a *promissory note*, or IOU. This is used when the order is large and when the firm anticipates a problem in collections. Promissory notes can eliminate controversies later about the existence of a credit agreement.

One problem with promissory notes is that they are signed after delivery of the goods. One way to obtain a credit commitment from a customer before the goods are delivered is through the use of a *commercial draft*. The selling firm typically writes a commercial draft calling for the customer to pay a specific amount by a specified date. The draft is then sent to the customer's bank with the shipping invoices. The bank has the buyer sign the draft before turning over the invoices. The goods can then be shipped to the buyer. If immediate payment is required, it is called a *sight draft*. Here, funds must be turned over to the bank before the goods are shipped.

Frequently, even a signed draft is not enough for the seller. In this case she might demand that the banker pay for the goods and collect the money from the customer. When the banker agrees to do so in writing, the document is called a *banker's acceptance*. That is, the banker *accepts* responsibility for payment. Because banks generally are well-known and well-respected institutions, the banker's acceptance becomes a liquid instrument. In other words, the seller can then sell (*discount*) the banker's acceptance in the secondary market.

A firm can also use a *conditional sales contract* as a credit instrument. This is an arrangement where the firm retains legal ownership of the goods until the customer has completed payment. Conditional sales contracts usually are paid off in instalments and have interest costs built into them.

27.6 The Decision to Grant Credit: Risk and Information

Locust Industries has been in existence for two years. It is one of several successful firms that develop computer programs. The present financial managers have set out two alternative credit strategies: the firm can offer credit or the firm can refuse credit.

Suppose Locust has determined that if it offers no credit to its customers, it can sell its existing computer software for €50 per program. It estimates that the costs to produce a typical computer program are €20 per program.

The alternative is to offer credit. In this case, customers of Locust will pay one period later. With some probability, Locust has determined that if it offers credit, it can charge higher prices and expect higher sales.

Strategy 1: Refuse Credit

If Locust refuses to grant credit, cash flows will not be delayed, and period 0 net cash flows, *NCF*, will be:

$$P_0 Q_0 - C_0 Q_0 = NCF$$

The subscripts denote the time when the cash flows are incurred, where P_0 is the price per unit received at time 0, C_0 is the cost per unit paid at time 0 and Q_0 is the quantity sold at time 0.

The net cash flows at period 1 are zero, and the net present value to Locust of refusing credit will simply be the period 0 net cash flow:

$$NPV = NCF$$

For example, if credit is not granted and $Q_0 = 100$, the *NPV* can be calculated as:

$$(€50 \times 100) - (€20 \times 100) = €3,000$$

Strategy 2: Offer Credit

Alternatively, let us assume that Locust grants credit to all customers for one period. The factors that influence the decision are listed here:

	Strategy 1 Refuse Credit	Strategy 2 Offer Credit
Price per unit	$P_0 = €50$	$P'_0 = €50$
Quantity sold	$Q_0 = 100$	$Q'_0 = 200$
Cost per unit	$C_0 = €20$	$C'_0 = €25$
Probability of payment	$h = 1$	$h = 0.90$
Credit period	0	1 period
Discount rate	0	$R_B = 0.01$

The prime (′) denotes the variables under the second strategy. If the firm offers credit and the new customers pay, the firm will receive revenues of $P'_0 Q'_0$ one period hence, but its costs, $C'_0 Q'_0$, are incurred in period 0. If new customers do not pay, the firm incurs costs $C'_0 Q'_0$ and receives no revenues. The probability that customers will pay, *h*, is 0.90 in the example. Quantity sold is higher with credit because new customers are attracted. The cost per unit is also higher with credit because of the costs of operating a credit policy.

The expected cash flows for each policy are set out as follows:

	Expected Cash Flows	
	Time 0	Time 1
Refuse credit	$P_0Q_0 - C_0Q_0$	0
Offer credit	$-C_0'Q_0'$	$h \times P_0'Q_0'$

Note that granting credit produces delayed expected cash inflows equal to $h \times P_0'Q_0'$. The costs are incurred immediately and require no discounting. The net present value if credit is offered is:

$$\text{NPV (offer)} = \frac{h \times P_0'Q_0'}{1+R_B} - C_0'Q_0'$$
$$= \frac{0.9 \times \text{€}50 \times 200}{1.01} = \text{€}5{,}000 = \text{€}3{,}910.89$$

Locust's decision should be to adopt the proposed credit policy. The NPV of granting credit is higher than that of refusing credit. This decision is very sensitive to the probability of payment. If it turns out that the probability of payment is 81 per cent, Locust Industries is indifferent to whether it grants credit or not. In this case, the NPV of granting credit is €3,000, which we previously found to be the NPV of not granting credit:

$$\text{€}3{,}000 = h \times \frac{\text{€}50 \times 200}{1.01} - \text{€}5{,}000$$
$$\text{€}8{,}000 = h \times \frac{\text{€}50 \times 200}{1.01}$$
$$h = 80.8\%$$

The decision to grant credit depends on four factors:

1 The delayed revenues from granting credit, $P_0'Q_0'$
2 The immediate costs of granting credit, $C_0'Q_0'$
3 The probability of payment, h
4 The appropriate required rate of return for delayed cash flows, R_B.

The Value of New Information about Credit Risk

Obtaining a better estimate of the probability that a customer will default can lead to a better decision. How can a firm determine when to acquire new information about the creditworthiness of its customers?

It may be sensible for Locust to determine which of its customers are most likely not to pay. The overall probability of non-payment is 10 per cent. But credit checks by an independent firm show that 90 per cent of Locust's customers (computer stores) have been profitable over the last five years and that these customers have never defaulted on payments. The less profitable customers are much more likely to default. In fact, 100 per cent of the less profitable customers have defaulted on previous obligations.

Locust would like to avoid offering credit to the deadbeats. Consider its projected number of customers per year of $Q_0' = 200$ if credit is granted. Of these customers, 180 have been profitable over the last five years and have never defaulted on past obligations. The remaining 20 have not been profitable. Locust expects that all of these less profitable customers will default. This information is set out here:

Type of Customer	Number	Probability of Non-payment (%)	Expected Number of Defaults
Profitable	180	0	0
Less profitable	20	100	20
Total customers	200	10	20

The NPV of granting credit to the customers who default is:

$$\frac{hP_0'Q_0'}{1+R_B} - C_0'Q_0' = \frac{0 \times \text{€}50 \times 20}{1.01} - \text{€}25 \times 20 = -\text{€}500$$

This is the cost of providing them with the software. If Locust can identify these customers without cost, it will certainly deny them credit.

In fact, it actually costs Locust €3 per customer to figure out whether a customer has been profitable over the last five years. The expected payoff of the credit check on its 200 customers is then:

$$\text{Gain from not extending credit } €500 - \text{Cost of credit checks } €3 \times 200 = -€100$$

For Locust, credit is not worth checking. It would need to pay €600 to avoid a €500 loss.

Future Sales

Up to this point, Locust has not considered the possibility that offering credit will permanently increase the level of sales in future periods (beyond next month). In addition, payment and non-payment patterns in the current period will provide credit information that is useful for the next period. These two factors should be analysed.

In the case of Locust, there is a 90 per cent probability that the customer will pay in period 1. But, if payment is made, there will be another sale in period 2. The probability that the customer will pay in period 2, if the customer has paid in period 1, is 100 per cent. Locust can refuse to offer credit in period 2 to customers who have refused to pay in period 1. This is diagrammed in Figure 27.9.

Figure 27.9 Future Sales and the Credit Decision

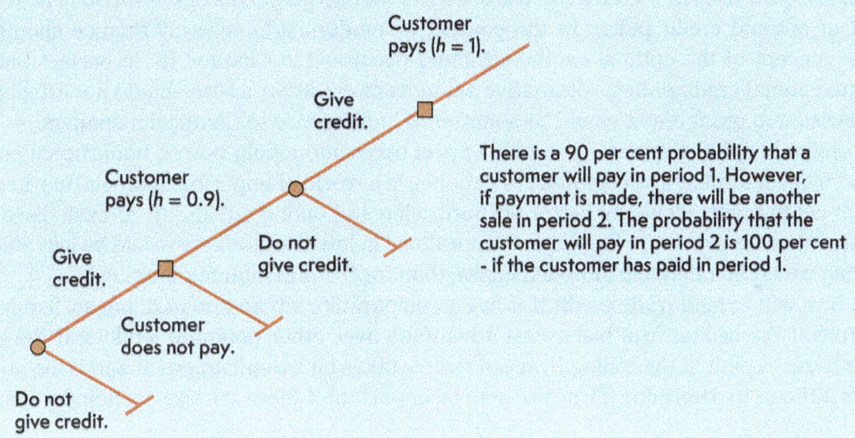

27.7 Optimal Credit Policy

So far, we have discussed how to compute net present value for two alternative credit policies. However, we have not discussed the optimal amount of credit. At the optimal amount of credit, the incremental cash flows from increased sales are exactly equal to the carrying costs from the increase in accounts receivable.

Consider a firm that does not currently grant credit. This firm has no bad debts, no credit department and relatively few customers. Now consider another firm that grants credit. This firm has lots of customers, a credit department and a bad debt expense account.

It is useful to think of the decision to grant credit in terms of carrying costs and opportunity costs:

- *Carrying costs* are the costs associated with granting credit and making an investment in receivables. Carrying costs include the delay in receiving cash, the losses from bad debts and the costs of managing credit.
- *Opportunity costs* are the lost sales from refusing to offer credit. These costs drop as credit is granted.

We represent these costs in Figure 27.10.

Figure 27.10 The Costs of Granting Credit

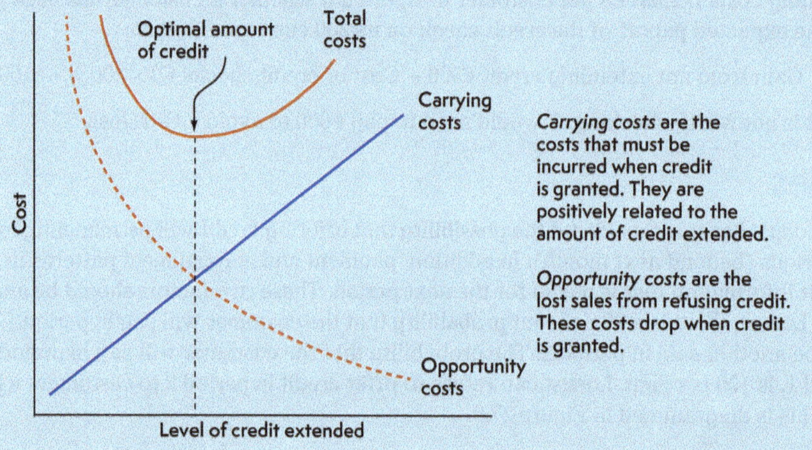

The sum of the carrying costs and the opportunity costs of a particular credit policy is called the *total credit cost curve*. A point is identified as the minimum of the total credit cost curve. If the firm extends more credit than the minimum, the additional net cash flow from new customers will not cover the carrying costs of this investment in receivables.

The concept of optimal credit policy in the context of modern principles of finance should be somewhat analogous to the concept of the optimal capital structure discussed in Chapter 18. In perfect financial markets, there should be no optimal credit policy. Alternative amounts of credit for a firm should not affect the value of the firm. Thus, the decision to grant credit would be a matter of indifference to financial managers.

Just as with optimal capital structure, we could expect taxes, monopoly power, bankruptcy costs and agency costs to be important in determining an optimal credit policy in a world of imperfect financial markets. For example, customers in high tax brackets would be better off borrowing and taking advantage of cash discounts offered by firms than would customers in low tax brackets. Corporations in low tax brackets would be less able to offer credit because borrowing would be relatively more expensive than for firms in high tax brackets.

In general, a firm will extend trade credit if it has a comparative advantage in doing so. Trade credit is likely to be advantageous if the selling firm has a cost advantage over other potential lenders, if the selling firm has monopoly power it can exploit, if the selling firm can reduce taxes by extending credit and if the product quality of the selling firm is difficult to determine. Firm size may be important if there are size economies in managing credit.

The Decision to Grant Credit

Trade credit is more likely to be granted by the selling firm if:

1 *The selling firm has a cost advantage over other lenders.*

Example: York Manufacturing Ltd produces widgets. In a default, it is easier for York Manufacturing Ltd to repossess widgets and resell them than for a finance company to arrange for it with no experience in selling widgets.

2 *The selling firm can engage in price discrimination.*

Example: National Motors can offer below-market interest rates to lower-income customers who must finance a large portion of the purchase price of cars. Higher-income customers pay the list price and do not generally finance a large part of the purchase.

3 *The selling firm can obtain favourable tax treatment.*

Example: A.B. Production offers long-term credit to its best customers. This form of financing may qualify as an instalment plan and allow A.B. Production to book profits of the sale over the life of the loan. This may save taxes because the present value of the tax payments will be lower if spread over time.

4 *The selling firm has no established reputation for quality products or services.*

Example: Advanced Micro Instruments (AMI) manufactures sophisticated measurement instruments for controlling electrical systems on commercial aeroplanes. The firm was founded by two engineering graduates from the University of Amsterdam in 2005. It became a public firm in 2013. To hedge their bets, aircraft manufacturers will ask for credit from AMI. It is very difficult for customers of AMI to assess the quality of its instruments until the instruments have been in place for some time.

5 *The selling firm perceives a long-term strategic relationship.*

Example: Food.com is a fast-growing, cash-constrained internet food distributor. It is currently not profitable. Fantastic Food will grant Food.com credit for food purchased because Food.com will generate profits in the future.

6 *The selling firm has more differentiated products.*

Example: TUI, the holiday firm, has gradually concentrated more and more on differentiated and unusual holiday destinations and themes. Because of their distinctiveness, demand directly related to the holiday characteristics is high and customers can deal only with TUI for specific holidays. This makes it easier to provide credit to customers.

Source: Long et al. (1993); Mian and Smith (1994); Deloof and Jegers (1996); Petersen and Rajan (1997); Giannetti et al. (2011).

The optimal credit policy depends on characteristics of particular firms. Assuming that the firm has more flexibility in its credit policy than in the prices it charges, firms with excess capacity, low variable operating costs, high tax brackets and repeat customers should extend credit more liberally than others.

27.8 Credit Analysis

When granting credit, a firm tries to distinguish between *customers* who will pay and customers who will not pay. There are a number of sources of information for determining creditworthiness.

Credit Information

Information commonly used to assess creditworthiness includes the following:

- *Financial statements:* A firm can ask a customer to supply financial statements. Rules of thumb based on calculated financial ratios can be used.
- *Credit reports on customer's payment history with other firms:* Many organizations sell information on the credit strength of business firms. Firms such as Experian, Equifax and Dun & Bradstreet provide subscribers with credit reports on individual firms.
- *Banks:* Banks will generally provide some assistance to their business customers in acquiring information on the creditworthiness of other firms.
- *The customer's payment history with the firm:* The most obvious way to obtain an estimate of a customer's probability of non-payment is whether he or she has paid previous bills.

Credit Scoring

Once the information has been gathered, the firm faces the hard choice of either granting or refusing credit. Many firms use the traditional and subjective guidelines referred to as the 'five Cs of credit':

1. *Character:* The customer's willingness to meet credit obligations.
2. *Capacity:* The customer's ability to meet credit obligations out of operating cash flows.
3. *Capital:* The customer's financial reserves.
4. *Collateral:* A pledged asset in the case of default.
5. *Conditions:* General economic conditions.

Conversely, firms such as credit card issuers have developed elaborate statistical models (called credit scoring models) for determining the probability of default. Usually, all relevant and observable characteristics of a large pool of customers are studied to find their historic relation to default. Because these models determine who is and who is not creditworthy, not surprisingly they have been the subject of government regulation.

27.9 Collection Policy

Collection refers to obtaining payment of past-due accounts. The credit manager keeps a record of payment experiences with each customer.

Average Collection Period

Paragon Vinyl Records sells 100,000 vintage record players a year at €300 each. All sales are for credit with terms of 2/20, net 60.

Suppose that 80 per cent of Paragon's customers take the discounts and pay on day 20; the rest pay on day 60. The average collection period (ACP) measures the average amount of time required to collect a trade or account receivable. The ACP for Paragon is 28 days:

$$0.8 \times 20 \text{ days} + 0.2 \times 60 \text{ days} = 28 \text{ days}$$

(The average collection period is frequently referred to as *days' sales outstanding* or *days in receivables*.)

Of course, this is an idealized example where customers pay on either one of two dates. In reality, payments arrive in a random fashion, so the average collection period must be calculated differently.

To determine the ACP in the real world, firms first calculate average daily sales. The average daily sales (ADS) equal annual sales divided by 365. The ADS of Paragon are:

$$\text{Average daily sales} = \frac{€300 \times 100{,}000}{365 \text{ days}} = €82{,}192$$

If receivables today are €2,301,376, the average collection period is:

$$\begin{aligned}\text{Average collection period} &= \frac{\text{Accounts receivable}}{\text{Average daily sales}}\\ &= \frac{€2{,}301{,}376}{€82{,}192}\\ &= 28 \text{ days}\end{aligned}$$

In practice, firms observe sales and receivables daily. Consequently, an average collection period can be computed and compared to the stated credit terms. For instance, suppose Paragon had computed its ACP at 40 days for several weeks, versus its credit terms of 2/20, net 60. With a 40-day ACP, some customers are paying later than usual. Some accounts may be overdue.

However, firms with seasonal sales will often find the *calculated* ACP changing during the year, making the ACP a somewhat flawed tool. This occurs because receivables are low before the selling season and high after the season. Thus, firms may keep track of seasonal movement in the ACP over past years. In this way, they can compare the ACP for today's date with the average ACP for that date in previous years. To supplement the information in the ACP, the credit manager may make up an accounts receivable ageing schedule.

Ageing Schedule

The **ageing schedule** tabulates receivables by age of account. In the following schedule, 75 per cent of the accounts are on time, but a significant number are more than 60 days past due. This signifies that some customers are in arrears.

Age of Account	Percentage of Total Value of Accounts Receivable
0–20 days	50
21–60 days	25
61–80 days	20
Over 80 days	5
	100

The ageing schedule changes during the year. Comparatively, the ACP is a somewhat flawed tool because it gives only the yearly average. Some firms have refined it so that they can examine how it changes with peaks and valleys in their sales. Similarly, the ageing schedule is often augmented by the payments pattern. The *payments pattern* describes the lagged collection pattern of receivables. Like a mortality table that describes the probability that a 23 year old will live to be 24, the payments pattern describes the probability that a 67-day-old account will still be unpaid when it is 68 days old.

Collection Effort

The firm usually employs the following procedures for customers that are overdue:

1. Send a delinquency letter informing the customer of the past-due status of the account.
2. Make a telephone call to the customer.
3. Employ a collection agency.
4. Take legal action against the customer.

At times, a firm may refuse to grant additional credit to customers until arrears are paid. This may antagonize a normally good customer, and points to a potential conflict of interest between the collections department and the sales department.

Factoring

Factoring refers to the sale of a firm's trade receivables to a financial institution known as a *factor*. The firm and the factor agree on the basic credit terms for each customer. The customer sends payment directly to the factor, and the factor bears the risk of non-paying customers. The factor buys the receivables at a discount, which usually ranges from 0.35 to 4 per cent of the value of the invoice amount. The average discount throughout the economy is probably about 1 per cent.

One point should be stressed. We have presented the elements of credit policy as though they were somewhat independent of one another. In fact, they are closely interrelated. The optimal credit policy, for example, is not independent of collection and monitoring policies. A tighter collection policy can reduce the probability of default, and this, in turn, can raise the NPV of a more liberal credit policy.

27.10 How to Finance Trade Credit

In addition to the unsecured debt instruments described earlier in this chapter, there are three general ways of financing accounting receivables: secured debt, a captive finance company and securitization.

Use of secured debt is usually referred to as asset-based receivables financing. This is the predominant form of receivables financing. Many lenders will not lend without security to firms with substantive uncertainty or little equity. With secured debt, if the borrower gets into financial difficulty, the lender can repossess the asset and sell it for its fair market value.

Many large firms with good credit ratings use captive finance companies. The captive finance companies are subsidiaries of the parent firm. This is similar to the use of secured debt because the creditors of the captive finance company have a claim on its assets and, as a consequence, the accounts receivable of the parent firm. A captive finance company is attractive if economies of scale are important and if an independent subsidiary with limited liability is warranted.

Securitization occurs when the selling firm sells its accounts receivable to a financial institution. The financial institution pools the receivables with other receivables and issues securities to finance items.

Summary and Conclusions

The chapter discussed how firms manage cash.

1 A firm holds cash to conduct transactions and to compensate banks for the various services they render.

2 The optimal amount of cash for a firm to hold depends on the opportunity cost of holding cash and the uncertainty of future cash inflows and outflows. The Baumol model and the Miller–Orr model are two transaction models that provide rough guidelines for determining the optimal cash position.

3 Because of seasonal and cyclical activities, to help finance planned expenditures, or as a reserve for unanticipated needs, firms temporarily find themselves with cash surpluses. The money market offers a variety of possible vehicles for parking this idle cash.

4 The components of a firm's credit policy are the terms of sale, the credit analysis and the collection policy.

5 The terms of sale describe the amount and period of time for which credit is granted and the type of credit instrument.

6 The decision to grant credit is a straightforward NPV decision that can be improved by additional information about customer payment characteristics. Additional information about the customer's probability of defaulting is valuable, but this value must be traded off against the expense of acquiring the information.

7 The optimal amount of credit the firm offers is a function of the competitive conditions in which it finds itself. These conditions will determine the carrying costs associated with granting credit and the opportunity costs of the lost sales from refusing to offer credit. The optimal credit policy minimizes the sum of these two costs.

8 We have seen that knowledge of the probability that customers will default is valuable. To enhance its ability to assess customers' default probability, a firm can score credit. This relates the default probability to observable characteristics of customers.

9 The collection policy is the method of dealing with past-due accounts. The first step is to analyse the average collection period and to prepare an ageing schedule that relates the age of accounts to the proportion of the accounts receivable they represent. The next step is to decide on the collection method and to evaluate the possibility of factoring – that is, selling the overdue accounts.

Questions and Problems

McGraw Hill connect

CONCEPT

1 **Reasons for Holding Cash** Why do firms hold cash? What are the consequences of holding too little cash? Is it possible for a firm to have too much cash? Why would shareholders care if a firm accumulates large amounts of cash? Explain.

2 **Determining the Target Cash Balance** Show, using both the Baumol model and the Miller–Orr model, how a firm can determine its optimal cash balance. What are the advantages and disadvantages of each?

3 **Investing Idle Cash** What options are available to a firm if it believes it has too much cash? How about too little?

4 **Terms of the Sale** Explain what is meant by the credit terms of a sale. Provide an example of a typical trade credit agreement.

5 **Establishing a Credit Policy** What steps are involved in establishing a credit policy?

6 **Optimal Credit Policy** Is it possible to have an optimal credit policy? In this context, discuss the total credit curve and its impact on a firm's approach to trade credit.

7 **Credit Analysis** What are the 'five Cs' of credit? Give an example of what happens when one of the five Cs is not met. Are there any other factors a firm should consider?

8 **Collection Policy** How can a firm use an ageing schedule of payments to maximize its total collection of outstanding debtors?

REGULAR

9 **Opportunity versus Trading Costs** Konyagi plc has an average daily cash balance of £10,500. Total cash needed for the year is £65,000. The interest rate is 3 per cent, and replenishing the cash costs €17 each time. What are the opportunity cost of holding cash, the trading cost and the total cost? What do you think of Konyagi's strategy?

10 **Costs and the Baumol Model** EmpowerHer Ltd requires €54,000 in cash annually for various needs and payments. It keeps some securities as a backup and sells €20,000 worth of them when cash is low. The cash is then transferred to its account. The interest rate on the securities is 3 per cent per year and each sale costs €100.

(a) What is the opportunity cost under the current policy? The trading cost? With no additional calculations, would you say that EmpowerHer keeps too much or too little cash? Explain.

(b) What is the target cash balance derived using the Baumol model?

11 **NPV and Reducing Float** Starthub Ltd has an agreement with its bank whereby the bank handles Rm500 million in collections a day and requires a Rm40,000,000 compensating balance. Starthub is contemplating cancelling the agreement and dividing its Malaysian activities so that two other banks will handle its business. Banks *A* and *B* will each handle Rm200 million of collections a day, and each requires a compensating balance of Rm12 million. Starthub's financial manager expects that collections will be accelerated by one day if the Malaysian activities are divided between two banks. Should the company proceed with the new system? What will be the annual net savings? Assume that the T-bill rate is 2 per cent annually.

12 **Determining Optimal Cash Balances** TByrne Ltd is currently holding €700,000 in cash. It projects that over the next year its cash outflows will exceed cash inflows by €360,000 per month. How much of the current cash holding should be retained, and how much should be used to increase the company's holdings of marketable securities? Each time these securities are bought or sold through a broker, the company pays a fee of €500. The annual interest rate on money market securities is 6.5 per cent. After the initial investment of excess cash, how many times during the next 12 months will securities be sold? Use the Baumol model.

13 **Using Miller–Orr** SlapShot plc has a fixed cost associated with buying and selling marketable securities of £100. The interest rate is currently 0.021 per cent per day, and the firm has estimated that the standard deviation of its daily net cash flows is £75. Management has set a lower limit of £1,100 on cash holdings. Calculate the target cash balance and upper limit using the Miller–Orr model, and describe how the system will work.

14 **Using Baumol** Grampian plc has a weekly cash requirement of £60,000. The cost of selling marketable securities to raise cash is £50. The interest rate is 7 per cent per annum. Determine the optimal order quantity and the optimal order period.

15 **Cash Discounts** You place an order for 200 units of inventory at a unit price of £95. The supplier offers terms of 2/10, net 30.

(a) How long do you have to pay before the account is overdue? If you take the full period, how much should you remit?

(b) What is the discount being offered? How quickly must you pay to get the discount? If you take the discount, how much should you remit?

(c) If you do not take the discount, how much interest are you paying implicitly? How many days' credit are you receiving?

16 **ACP and Accounts Receivable** Dalglish plc sells earnings forecasts for British securities. Its credit terms are 2/10, net 30. Based on experience, 65 per cent of all customers will take the discount.

(a) What is the average collection period for Dalglish?

(b) If Dalglish sells 1,200 forecasts every month at a price of £2,200 each, what is its average balance sheet amount in accounts receivable?

17 **Terms of Sale** A firm offers terms of 2/9, net 40. What effective annual interest rate does the firm earn when a customer does not take the discount? Without doing any calculations, explain what will happen to this effective rate if:

(a) The discount is changed to 3 per cent

(b) The credit period is increased to 60 days

(c) The discount period is increased to 15 days.

18 **ACP and Receivables Turnover** Water Wise BV takes 52 days on average to collect cash from its customers. It has €46,000 invested in receivables on an average day. How much are its credit sales in a year? How many times does it turn over its receivables?

19 **Early Payment Discount** XYZ plc has recently won a very large order to supply a retail chain, called TT Ltd, with items over the next two years. The size of any order may vary considerably and XYZ is obliged to deliver within two days of an order being placed. This will mean that XYZ has to invest heavily in stocks. TT Ltd also usually requires 90 days' credit from any of its suppliers. XYZ is considering either debt factoring, loan financing or offering TT Ltd a 3 per cent discount to settle within 10 days, in order to meet its operational requirements. Calculate whether it is better for XYZ to offer the discount to get payment within 10 days or to finance its operational requirements via a loan. XYZ's bank charges 12 per cent per annum for a loan.

20 Size of Accounts Receivable Baker Ginger Ltd sells on credit terms of net 25. Its accounts are, on average, nine days past due. If annual credit sales are £8 million, what is the company's balance sheet amount in accounts receivable?

21 Evaluating Credit Policy Air Spares is a wholesaler that stocks engine components and test equipment for the commercial aircraft industry. A new customer has placed an order for eight high-bypass turbine engines, which increase fuel economy. The variable cost is €1.5 million per unit and the credit price is €1.8 million each. Credit is extended for one period and, based on historical experience, payment for about 1 out of every 200 such orders is never collected. The required return is 2.5 per cent per period.

(a) Assuming that this is a one-time order, should it be filled? The customer will not buy if credit is not extended.

(b) What is the break-even probability of default in part (a)?

(c) Suppose that customers who do not default become repeat customers and place the same order every period for ever. Further, assume that repeat customers never default. Should the order be filled? What is the break-even probability of default?

(d) Describe in general terms why credit terms will be more liberal when repeat orders are a possibility.

22 Credit Policy Evaluation Champions SA is considering a change in its cash-only sales policy. The new terms of sale would be net one month. Based on the following information, determine if Champions should proceed. Describe the build-up of receivables in this case. The required return is 1.5 per cent per month.

	Current Policy	New Policy
Price per unit	€800	€800
Cost per unit	€475	€475
Unit sales per month	1,130	1,195

23 Evaluating Credit Policy: Bruce Jacks plc Bruce Jacks plc is in the process of considering a change in its terms of sale. The current policy is cash only; the new policy will involve one period's credit. Sales are 70,000 units per period at a price of £530 per unit. If credit is offered, the new price will be £552. Unit sales are not expected to change, and all customers are expected to take the credit. Bruce Jacks estimates that 2 per cent of credit sales will be uncollectible. If the required return is 2 per cent per period, is the change a good idea?

24 Credit Policy Evaluation: Clapton Erich GmbH Clapton Erich GmbH sells 3,000 pairs of running shoes per month at a cash price of €90 per pair. The firm is considering a new policy that involves 30 days' credit and an increase in price to €91.84 per pair on credit sales. The cash price will remain at €90, and the new policy is not expected to affect the quantity sold. The discount period will be 10 days. The required return is 1 per cent per month.

(a) How would the new credit terms be quoted?

(b) What is the investment in receivables required under the new policy?

(c) Explain why the variable cost of manufacturing the shoes is not relevant here.

(d) If the default rate is anticipated to be 10 per cent, should the switch be made? What is the break-even credit price? The break-even cash discount?

25 Factoring The factoring department of Inter Scandinavian Bank (ISB) is processing 100,000 invoices per year, with an average invoice value of €1,500. ISB buys the accounts receivable at 3.5 per cent off the invoice value. Currently 2.5 per cent of the accounts receivable turns out to be bad debt. The annual operating expense of this department is €400,000. What are the EBIT for the factoring department of ISB?

26 Factoring Receivables Your firm has an average collection period of 34 days. Current practice is to factor all receivables immediately at a 2 per cent discount. What is the effective cost of borrowing in this case? Assume that default is extremely unlikely.

27 Credit Analysis: Silicon Wafers plc Silicon Wafers plc (SW) is debating whether to extend credit to a particular customer. SW's products, primarily used in the manufacture of semiconductors, currently sell for £1,850 per unit. The variable cost is £1,200 per unit. The order under consideration is for 12 units today; payment is promised in 30 days.

(a) If there is a 20 per cent chance of default, should SW fill the order? The required return is 2 per cent per month. This is a one-time sale, and the customer will not buy if credit is not extended.

(b) What is the break-even probability in part (a)?

(c) This part is a little harder. In general terms, how do you think your answer to part (a) will be affected if the customer will purchase the merchandise for cash if the credit is refused? The cash price is £1,700 per unit.

28 Credit Analysis Decisions Consider the following information about two alternative credit strategies:

	Refuse Credit	Grant Credit
Price per unit	£51	£55
Cost per unit	£29	£31
Quantity sold per quarter	3,300	3,500
Probability of payment	1.0	0.90

The higher cost per unit reflects the expense associated with credit orders, and the higher price per unit reflects the existence of a cash discount. The credit period will be 90 days, and the cost of debt is 0.75 per cent per month.

(a) Based on this information, should credit be granted?

(b) In part (a), what does the credit price per unit have to be to break even?

(c) In part (a), suppose we can obtain a credit report for £2 per customer. Assuming that each customer buys one unit and that the credit report correctly identifies all customers who will not pay, should credit be extended?

29 NPV of Credit Policy Switch Suppose a corporation currently sells Q units per month for a cash-only price of P. Under a new credit policy that allows one month's credit, the quantity sold will be Q' and the price per unit will be P''. Defaults will be π per cent of credit sales. The variable cost is ν per unit and is not expected to change. The percentage of customers who will take the credit is α, and the required return is R per month. What is the NPV of the decision to switch? Interpret the various parts of your answer.

30 Credit Policy The Wiggins Bicycle Shop has decided to offer credit to its customers during the spring selling season. Sales are expected to be 400 bicycles. The average cost to the shop of a bicycle is £280. The owner knows that only 97 per cent of the customers will be able to make their payments. To identify the remaining 3 per cent, she is considering subscribing to a credit agency. The initial charge for this service is £500, with an additional charge of £4 per individual report. Should she subscribe to the agency?

31 Credit Policy Evaluation Dschungel AG is considering a change in its cash-only policy. The new terms would be net one period. Based on the following information, determine if Dschungel should proceed. The required return is 3 per cent per period.

	Current Policy	New Policy
Price per unit	€75	€80
Cost per unit	€43	€43
Unit sales per month	3,200	3,500

CHALLENGE

32 Baumol Model Solaris plc, a renewable energy company, has an optimal cash balance of £10 million, according to its CFO, Rajesh Patel, who used the Baumol model. The annual interest rate on securities that can be sold to raise cash is 5.8 per cent. The fixed cost of each sale is £5,000. The Baumol model fits well with Solaris's cash flow pattern. What can you deduce about Solaris's average cash disbursement per week?

33 Miller–Orr Model Gold Star Ltd and Silver Star Ltd both manage their cash flows according to the Miller–Orr model. Gold Star's daily cash flow is controlled between £95,000 and £205,000, whereas Silver Star's daily cash flow is controlled between £120,000 and £230,000. The annual interest rates Gold Star and Silver Star can get are 5.8 per cent and 6.1 per cent, respectively, and the costs per transaction of trading securities are £2,800 and £2,500, respectively.

(a) What are their respective target cash balances?

(b) Which firm's daily cash flow is more volatile?

34 Credit Policy: Netal Ltd Netal Ltd has annual sales of 50 million rand, all of which are on credit. The current collection period is 45 days and the credit terms are net 30. The company is considering offering terms of 2/10, net 30. It anticipates that 70 per cent of its customers will take advantage of the discount. The new policy will reduce the collection period to 28 days. The appropriate interest rate is 6 per cent. Should the new credit policy be adopted? How does the level of credit sales affect this decision?

Exam Question (45 minutes)

1 León Dung SA, a large fertilizer distributor based in the north of Spain, is planning to speed up collections from its customers located in the Castilla y León region. A Valladolid-area bank will provide this service for an annual fee of €25,000 plus 10 cents per transaction. The estimated reduction in collection and processing time is one day. If the average customer payment in this region is €5,500, how many customers each day, on average, are needed to make the system profitable for León Dung? Treasury bills are currently yielding 5 per cent per year. **(40 marks)**

2 Based on the Miller–Orr model, describe what will happen to the lower limit, the upper limit and the spread (the distance between the two) if the variation in net cash flow grows. Give an intuitive explanation for why this happens. What happens if the variance drops to zero? **(30 marks)**

3 Given an annual interest rate of 4 per cent, a fixed order cost of €10 and total cash needed of €5,000, calculate the target cash balance using the Baumol model. How do you interpret your answer? **(30 marks)**

Total Marks: 100

Mini Case

Credit Policy at Schwarzwald AG

Dagmar Bamberger, the president of Schwarzwald AG, has been exploring ways of improving the company's financial performance. Schwarzwald manufactures and sells office equipment to retailers. The company's growth has been relatively slow in recent years, but with an expansion in the economy it appears that sales may increase more quickly in the future. Dagmar has asked Johann Rüstow, the company's treasurer, to examine Schwarzwald's credit policy to see if a different credit policy can help increase profitability.

The company currently has a policy of net 30. As with any credit sales, default rates are always of concern. Because of Schwarzwald's screening and collection process, the default rate on credit is currently only 1.5 per cent. Johann has examined the company's credit policy in relation to other vendors and has determined that three options are available.

The first is to relax the company's decision on when to grant credit. The second is to increase the credit period to net 45, and the third is a combination of the relaxed credit policy and the extension of the credit period to net 45. On the positive side, each of the three policies under consideration would increase sales. However, the three policies have the drawbacks that default rates would increase, the administrative costs of managing the firm's receivables would increase and the receivables period would increase. The credit policy change would impact all four of these variables to different degrees. Johann has prepared the following table outlining the effect on each of these variables:

	Annual Sales (€ millions)	Default Rate (% of Sales)	Administrative Costs (% of Sales)	Receivables Period (Days)
Current policy	120	1.5	2.1	38
Option 1	140	2.4	3.1	41
Option 2	137	1.7	2.3	51
Option 3	150	2.1	2.9	49

Schwarzwald's variable costs of production are 45 per cent of sales, and the relevant interest rate is a 6 per cent effective annual rate. Which credit policy should the company use? Also, notice that in option 3 the default rate and administrative costs are below those in option 2. Is this plausible? Why, or why not?

Practical Case Study

BP plc

For this practical case study, you will study BP plc's short-term capital management using publicly available data. Using the firm's most recent financial accounts and annual report (to find these, visit www.bp.com), collect data on BP's cash flows, accounts receivable, inventory, accounts payable and short-term financing sources for the past year.

1 From the company's annual accounts, calculate financial ratios relating to its operating efficiency (see Section 3.7).
2 What can you say about how BP handles its short-term cash management?
3 Comment on BP's trade credit policy. How does BP manage its accounts receivables and payables? What are the trade-offs of BP's strategy?
4 Use financial ratios to provide insight into how BP manages its inventory.
5 How does BP measure and monitor its working capital performance? What are some of the key indicators and benchmarks that it uses? You will need to use the notes to the annual report to answer this question.
6 How does BP compare with its competitors in terms of operating efficiency?
7 Do you think BP's sustainable finance practices impact the firm's short-term capital management?

References

Baumol, W.S. (1952) 'The Transactions Demand for Cash: An Inventory Theoretic Approach', *Quarterly Journal of Economics*, Vol. 66, No. 4, 545–556.

Deloof, M. and M. Jegers (1996) 'Trade Credit, Product Quality, and Intragroup Trade: Some European Evidence', *Financial Management*, Vol. 25, No. 3, 33–43.

Genpact (2021) 'Engineering a New Approach to Cash Management', https://website-files. genpact. com/downloadable-content/downloads/insight/engineering-a-new-approach-to-cash-management. pdf.

Giannetti, M., M. Burkart and T. Ellingsen (2011) 'What You Sell is What You Lend? Explaining Trade Credit Contracts', *Review of Financial Studies*, Vol. 24, No. 4, 1261–1298.

Kyröläinen, P., I. Tan and P. Karjalainen (2013) 'How Creditor Rights Affect the Value of Cash: A Cross-country Study', *Journal of Corporate Finance*, Vol. 22, 278–298.

Long, M., I.B. Malitz and S.A. Ravid (1993) 'Trade Credit, Quality Guarantees, and Product Marketability', *Financial Management*, Vol. 22, No. 4, 117–127.

Mian, S.I. and C.W. Smith (1994) 'Extending Trade Credit and Financing Receivables', *Journal of Applied Corporate Finance*, Vol. 7, No. 1, 75–84.

Miller, M.H. and D. Orr (1966) 'A Model of the Demand for Money by Firms', *Quarterly Journal of Economics*, Vol. 80, 413–435.

Petersen, M.A. and R.G. Rajan (1997) 'Trade Credit: Theories and Evidence', *Review of Financial Studies*, Vol. 10, No. 3, 661–691.

Additional Reading

Many papers on cash holdings are presented in Chapter 26. The following papers also consider the cash management function in firms. In addition, recent important papers on trade credit are presented.

1 Aktas, N., E. Croci and D. Petmezas (2015) 'Is Working Capital Management Value-enhancing? Evidence from Firm Performance and Investments', *Journal of Corporate Finance*, Vol. 30, 98–113.

2 Albuquerque, R., T. Ramadorai and S.W. Watugala (2015) 'Trade Credit and Cross-country Predictable Firm Returns', *Journal of Financial Economics*, Vol. 115, No. 3, 592–613.

3 Almeida, H., M. Campello and M.S. Weisbach (2004) 'The Cash Flow Sensitivity of Cash', *Journal of Finance*, Vol. 59, No. 4, 1777–1804. **USA.**

4 Amess, K., S. Banerji and A. Lampousis (2015) 'Corporate Cash Coldings: Causes and Consequences', *International Review of Financial Analysis*, Vol. 42, 421–433.

5 Atanasova, C. (2007) 'Access to Institutional Finance and the Use of Trade Credit', *Financial Management*, Vol. 36, No. 1, 49–67. **UK.**

6 Bates, T.W., K.M. Kahle and R.M. Stulz (2009) 'Why Do US Firms Hold so Much More Cash than They Used To?', *Journal of Finance*, Vol. 64, No. 5, 1985–2021. **USA.**

7 Bougheas, S., S. Mateut and P. Mizen (2009) 'Corporate Trade Credit and Inventories: New Evidence of a Trade-off from Accounts Payable and Receivable', *Journal of Banking and Finance*, Vol. 33, No. 2, 300–307.

8 Carbo-Valverde, S., F. Rodriguez-Fernandez and G.F. Udell (2016) 'Trade Credit, the Financial Crisis, and SME Access to Finance', *Journal of Money, Credit and Banking*, Vol. 48, No. 1, 113–143.

9 Chen, R.R., S. El Ghoul, O. Guedhami and R. Nash (2018) 'State Ownership and Corporate Cash Holdings', *Journal of Financial and Quantitative Analysis*, Vol. 53, No. 5, 2293–2334.

10 Cunat, V. (2007) 'Trade Credit: Suppliers as Debt Collectors and Insurance Providers', *Review of Financial Studies*, Vol. 20, No. 2, 491–527. **UK.**

11 Dittmar, A. and J. Mahrt-Smith (2007) 'Corporate Governance and the Value of Cash Holdings', *Journal of Financial Economics*, Vol. 83, No. 3, 599–634. **USA.**

12 Durán, R.F., M.B. Lozano and S. Yaman (2016) 'Is Family Control Relevant for Corporate Cash Holding Policy?', *Journal of Business Finance & Accounting*, Vol. 43, No. 9–10, 1325–1360.

13 El Ghoul, S. and X. Zheng (2016) 'Trade Credit Provision and National Culture', *Journal of Corporate Finance*, Vol. 41, 475–501.

14 Fabbri, D. and A.M.C. Menichini (2010) 'Trade Credit, Collateral Liquidation, and Borrowing Constraints', *Journal of Financial Economics*, Vol. 96, No. 3, 413–432.

15 Foley, C.F., J.C. Hartzell, S. Titman and G. Twite (2007) 'Why Do Firms Hold so Much Cash? A Tax Based Explanation', *Journal of Financial Economics*, Vol. 86, No. 4, 579–607. **USA.**

16 Gao, H., J. Harford and K. Li (2013) 'Determinants of Corporate Cash Policy: Insights from Private Firms', *Journal of Financial Economics*, Vol. 109, No. 3, 623–639.

17 Garcia-Teruel, P.J. and P. Martinez-Solano (2009) 'A Dynamic Approach to Accounts Receivable: A Study of Spanish SMEs', *European Financial Management*, Vol. 16, No. 3, 400–421. **Spain.**

18 Giannetti, M., M. Burkart and T. Ellingsen (2011) 'What You Sell is What You Lend? Explaining Trade Credit Contracts', *Review of Financial Studies*, Vol. 24, No. 4, 1261–1298.

19 Harford, J., S. Klasa and W.F. Maxwell (2014) 'Refinancing Risk and Cash Holdings', *Journal of Finance*, Vol. 69, No. 3, 975–1012.

20 Howorth, C. and B. Reber (2003) 'Habitual Late Payment of Trade Credit: An Empirical Examination of UK Small Firms', *Managerial and Decision Economics*, Vol. 24, Nos. 6 and 7, 471–482. **UK.**

21 Kalcheva, I. and K.V. Lins (2007) 'International Evidence on Cash Holdings and Expected Managerial Agency Problems', *Review of Financial Studies*, Vol. 20, No. 4, 1087–1112. **International.**

22 Klapper, L.F., L. Laeven and R. Rajan (2012) 'Trade Credit Contracts', *Review of Financial Studies*, Vol. 25, No. 3, 838–886.

23 Klasa, S., W.F. Maxwell and H. Ortiz-Molina (2009) 'The Strategic Use of Corporate Cash Holdings in Collective Bargaining with Labor Unions', *Journal of Financial Economics*, Vol. 92, 421–442. **USA.**

24 Love, I., L.A. Preve and V. Sarria-Allende (2007) 'Trade Credit and Bank Credit: Evidence from Recent Financial Crises', *Journal of Financial Economics*, Vol. 83, No. 2, 453–469. **International.**

25 Pinkowitz, L., R. Stulz and R. Williamson (2007) 'Cash Holdings, Dividend Policy, and Corporate Governance: A Cross-country Analysis', *Journal of Applied Corporate Finance*, Vol. 19, No. 1, 81–87. **International.**

26 Qiu, J. and C. Wan (2015) 'Technology Spillovers and Corporate Cash Holdings', *Journal of Financial Economics*, Vol. 115, No. 3, 558–573.

27 Sufi, A. (2009) 'Bank Lines of Credit in Corporate Finance: An Empirical Analysis', *Review of Financial Studies*, Vol. 22, No. 3, 1057–1088. **UK.**

28 Wilner, B.S. (2000) 'The Exploitation of Relationships in Financial Distress: The Case of Trade Credit', *Journal of Finance*, Vol. 55, No. 1, 153–178. **USA.**

PART 8

Special Topics

Part 8 covers three topics in corporate finance: mergers and acquisitions, financial distress, and international corporate finance. Chapter 28 explains why firms combine with others and how it affects their value. Chapter 29 explores the causes of and solutions for financial distress, and how to detect it. Chapter 30 discusses the challenges and opportunities of doing business internationally, and how to adapt capital budgeting methods for international projects.

Chapter 28
Mergers and Acquisitions

Learning Objectives

After reading this chapter you should be able to:

LO1 Define the basic forms of acquisition, and explain the difference between friendly and hostile takeovers.

LO2 Analyse the sources and effects of synergy in mergers and acquisitions.

LO3 Evaluate the NPV of a merger using appropriate valuation methods.

LO4 Identify and critique the defensive tactics used by target firms to resist takeovers.

The \$19.4 billion acquisition of WhatsApp by Facebook (now Meta) is just one of many corporate restructurings, mergers and acquisitions that have taken place over the past few years. Facebook had just gone through its own \$16 billion initial public offering and WhatsApp was the first major investment since the company became public. Analysts were perplexed as to why Facebook had paid so much money to a firm that had made only \$300 million in revenues, virtually no profit and employed 55 people. It should also be noted that \$19.4 billion was more than twice the gross revenues Facebook earned, and larger than the annual GDPs of Honduras, Iceland or Nepal! Without a doubt, the purchase price was eye-watering and the valuation multiple was enormous. Whereas very successful technology companies like Alphabet (Google's holding company) and Apple are priced at 28 and 18 times earnings, respectively, Facebook priced WhatsApp at 66 times gross revenues and an almost infinite valuation multiple against net income.

Source: Diego Thomazini/Shutterstock

A number of reasons have been put forward for the acquisition. First, Meta wished to create a social media conglomerate that spans all areas of the internet world. A second is that Meta plans to dominate mobile internet, and WhatsApp was one of the most successful companies in that sector. An interesting perspective is that WhatsApp provides Meta with a very strong presence in the developing world, where Meta has not had as much success as it has had in Europe and the United States. Finally, WhatsApp provides Meta with a huge database of conversations that will allow it to exploit big data and AI opportunities that present themselves to the combined firm.

How do companies like Meta determine whether an acquisition or merger is a good idea? This chapter explores the reasons why corporate restructurings, such as acquisitions, should take place. Just as important, it also presents reasons why they should not.

Key Notation

V	Value of a firm

28.1 The Basic Forms of Acquisition

Acquisitions follow one of three basic forms: (1) merger or consolidation; (2) acquisition of shares; and (3) acquisition of assets.

Merger or Consolidation

A **merger** refers to the absorption of one firm by another. The acquiring firm retains its name and identity, and it acquires all of the assets and liabilities of the acquired firm. After a merger, the acquired firm ceases to exist as a separate business entity.

A **consolidation** is the same as a merger except that an entirely new firm is created. In a consolidation both the acquiring firm and the acquired firm terminate their previous legal existence and become part of the new firm.

Example 28.1

Merger Basics

Suppose firm A acquires firm B in a merger. Further, suppose firm B's shareholders are given one share of firm A's equity in exchange for two shares of firm B's equity. From a legal standpoint, firm A's shareholders are not directly affected by the merger. However, firm B's shares cease to exist. In a consolidation, the shareholders of firm A and firm B exchange their shares for shares of a new firm (e.g. firm AB).

Because of the similarities between mergers and consolidations, we shall refer to both types of reorganization as mergers. Here are two important points about mergers and consolidations:

1. A merger is legally straightforward and does not cost as much as other forms of acquisition. It avoids the necessity of transferring the title of each individual asset of the acquired firm to the acquiring firm.
2. The shareholders of each firm must approve a merger.[1] Typically, votes of the owners of two-thirds of the shares are required for approval. In addition, shareholders of the acquired firm have *appraisal rights*. This means that they can demand that the acquiring firm purchase their shares at a fair value. Often the acquiring firm and the dissenting shareholders of the acquired firm cannot agree on a fair value, which results in expensive legal proceedings.

Acquisition of Shares

A second way to acquire another firm is to purchase the firm's voting shares in exchange for cash, or shares of equity and other securities. This process may start as a private offer from the management of one firm to another. At some point, the offer is taken directly to the selling firm's shareholders, often by a tender offer. A **tender offer** is a public offer to buy shares of a target firm. It is made by one firm directly to the shareholders of another firm. The offer is communicated to the target firm's shareholders by public announcements such as newspaper advertisements. Sometimes a general mailing is used in a tender offer. However, a general mailing is difficult because the names and addresses of the shareholders of record are not usually available.

The following factors are involved in choosing between an acquisition of shares and a merger:

- In an acquisition of shares, shareholder meetings need not be held and a vote is not required. If the shareholders of the target firm do not like the offer, they are not required to accept it and need not tender their shares.
- In an acquisition of shares, the bidding firm can deal directly with the shareholders of a target firm via a tender offer. The target firm's management and board of directors are bypassed.
- Target managers often resist acquisition. In such cases, acquisition of shares circumvents the target firm's management. Resistance by the target firm's management often makes the cost of acquisition by shares higher than the cost by merger.
- Frequently a minority of shareholders will hold out in a tender offer, and thus the target firm cannot be completely absorbed.
- Complete absorption of one firm by another requires a merger. Many acquisitions of shares end with a formal merger.

Acquisition of Assets

One firm can acquire another by buying all of its assets. The selling firm does not necessarily vanish, because its 'shell' can be retained. A formal vote of the target shareholders is required in an acquisition of assets. An advantage here is that although the acquirer is often left with minority shareholders in an acquisition of shares, this does not happen in an acquisition of assets. Minority shareholders often present problems, such as holdouts. However, asset acquisition involves transferring title to individual assets, which can be costly.

A Classification Scheme

Financial analysts have typically classified acquisitions into three types:

1 *Horizontal acquisition:* Here, both the acquirer and acquired are in the same industry. Examples include Facebook and Instagram, Disney and Pixar (the makers of the *Toy Story* franchise), Ladbrokes and Coral, and Lloyds TSB and HBOS. All of these mergers increased the power and influence of the merged entities in each sector.

2 *Vertical acquisition:* A vertical acquisition involves firms at different steps of the production process. There are two types of vertical integration. A forward vertical acquisition is when a company at one stage of the supply chain buys another company further down the supply chain. A backward vertical acquisition is the opposite, and a firm later in the supply chain buys a firm further up the supply chain. The acquisition of Thomson Holidays by the travel conglomerate TUI Group would be a vertical acquisition. Another example is Tesco's purchase of Booker plc.

3 *Conglomerate acquisition:* The acquiring firm and the acquired firm are not related to each other. Amazon's purchase of Whole Foods, LVMH and Tiffany, and Berkshire Hathaway's acquisitions across several industries are examples of conglomerate acquisitions.

A Note about Takeovers

Takeover is a general and imprecise term referring to the transfer of control of a firm from one group of shareholders to another.[2] A firm that has decided to take over another firm is usually referred to as the bidder. The bidder offers to pay cash or securities to obtain the equity or assets of another company. If the offer is accepted, the target firm will give up control over its equity or assets to the bidder in exchange for *consideration* (i.e. its equity, its debt or cash).

Takeovers can occur by acquisition, proxy contests and going-private transactions. Thus, takeovers encompass a broader set of activities than acquisitions, as depicted in Figure 28.1.

Figure 28.1 Varieties of Takeover

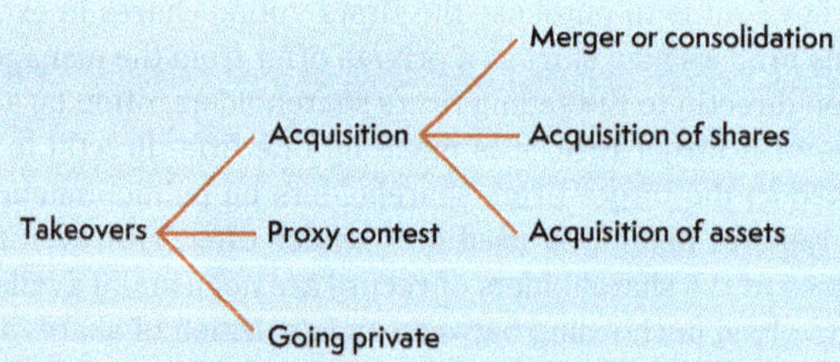

If a takeover is achieved by acquisition, it will be by merger, tender offer for shares of equity, or purchase of assets. In mergers and tender offers, the acquiring firm buys the voting ordinary shares of the acquired firm.

Proxy contests can result in takeovers as well. Proxy contests occur when a group of shareholders attempts to gain seats on the board of directors. A *proxy* is written authorization for one shareholder to vote for another shareholder. In a proxy contest, an insurgent group of shareholders solicits proxies from other shareholders.

In *going-private transactions,* a small group of investors purchases all the equity shares of a public firm. The group usually includes members of incumbent management and some outside investors. The shares of the firm are delisted from the stock exchange and can no longer be purchased in the open market.

28.2 Synergy

Section 28.1 discussed the basic forms of acquisition. We now examine why firms are acquired. (Although the previous section pointed out that acquisitions and mergers have different definitions, these differences will be unimportant in this and many of the following sections. Thus, unless otherwise stated, we will refer to acquisitions and mergers synonymously.)

Much of our thinking here can be organized around the following four questions:

1 Is there a rational reason for mergers? Yes – in a word, *synergy*.

Suppose firm A is contemplating acquiring firm B. The value of firm A is V_A and the value of firm B is V_B. (It is reasonable to assume that, for public companies, V_A and V_B can be determined by observing the market prices of the outstanding securities.) The difference between the value of the combined firm (V_{AB}) and the sum of the values of the firms as separate entities is the synergy from the acquisition:

$$\text{Synergy} = V_{AB} - (V_A + V_B)$$

In words, synergy occurs if the value of the combined firm after the merger is greater than the sum of the value of the acquiring firm and the value of the acquired firm before the merger.

2 Where does this magic force, synergy, come from?

Chapter 7 Page 178
Chapter 8 Page 207

Increases in cash flow create value (see Chapters 7 and 8 for more information). We define ΔCF_t as the difference between the cash flows at date t of the combined firm and the sum of the cash flows of the two separate firms. From the chapters about capital budgeting, we know that the cash flow in any period t can be written as:

$$\Delta CF_t = \Delta Rev_t - \Delta Costs_t - \Delta Taxes_t - \Delta Capital\ requirements_t$$

where ΔRev_t is the incremental revenue of the acquisition, $\Delta Costs_t$ is the incremental costs of the acquisition, $\Delta Taxes_t$ is the incremental acquisition taxes, and $\Delta Capital\ Requirements_t$ is the incremental new investment required in working capital and fixed assets.

It follows from our classification of incremental cash flows that the possible sources of synergy fall into four basic categories: revenue enhancement, cost reduction, lower taxes and lower capital requirements. Improvements in at least one of these four categories create synergy. Each of these categories will be discussed in detail in Section 28.4.

In addition, reasons are often provided for mergers where improvements are not expected in any of these four categories. These 'bad' reasons for mergers will be discussed in Section 28.5.

3 How are these synergistic gains shared?

In general, the acquiring firm pays a premium for the acquired, or target, firm. If, for example, the equity of the target is selling for €50, the acquirer might need to pay €60 a share, implying a premium of €10, or 20 per cent. The gain to the target in this example is €10. Suppose that the synergy from the merger is €30. The gain to the acquiring firm, or bidder, would be €20 (= €30 – €10). The bidder would actually lose if the synergy were less than the premium of €10. A more detailed treatment of these gains or losses will be provided in Section 28.7.

4 Are there other motives for a merger besides synergy? Yes.

As we have said, synergy is a source of benefit to shareholders. However, the *managers* are likely to view a potential merger differently. Even if the synergy from the merger is less than the premium paid to the target, the managers of the acquiring firm may still benefit. For instance, the revenues of the combined firm after the merger will almost certainly be greater than the revenues of the bidder before the merger. The managers may receive higher compensation once they are managing a larger firm. Even beyond the increase in compensation, managers generally experience greater prestige and power when managing a larger firm. Conversely, the managers of the target could lose their jobs after the acquisition and they might very well oppose the takeover even if their shareholders would benefit from the premium. These issues will be discussed in more detail in Section 28.10.

28.3 Intangibles

A specific challenge in valuing many companies is dealing with intangible assets, such as intellectual property, brand values, patents, trademarks, data and customer relationships. These assets are often not reflected on the statement of financial position but can have significant value for the acquirer. For instance, Amazon's brand value was estimated at $705 billion in 2022, while its book value was only $146 billion. Intangible assets can also be a source of competitive advantage and synergies for companies that merge or acquire other firms.

There are several ways to value intangible assets in an acquisition, but they are heavily based on assumptions and values can vary widely depending on the approach used. In this section, we will consider four ways to value intangibles.

Multiperiod Excess Earnings

The multiperiod excess earnings method values intangibles by estimating the revenues generated by the intangible asset and subtracting the costs of maintaining it.

Assume, say, that the Coca-Cola brand name generates $12 billion of annual revenue for 20 years, with a 50 per cent profit margin. The company also has tangible assets worth $50 billion and a discount rate of 10 per cent. The value of the brand name to Coca-Cola using the multiperiod excess earnings method would be:

Step 1: Calculate the earnings the intangible asset will make for Coca-Cola each year. This is called the *earnings attributable to the intangible asset:* $12 billion × 50% = $6 billion.

Step 2: Calculate how much Coca-Cola needs to spend on other assets that support the brand name, like buildings, machines or inventory. This is called the *contributory asset charge:* $50 billion × 10% = $5 billion.

Step 3: Calculate how much extra money the brand name makes for Coca-Cola after paying for all other assets. This is known as the annual *excess earnings* of the Coca-Cola brand name: $6 billion – $5 billion = $1 billion.

Step 4: Calculate the present value of the excess earnings over 20 years:

$$\text{PV} = C\left[\frac{1}{r} - \frac{1}{r(1+r)^t}\right] = 1\left[\frac{1}{0.1} - \frac{1}{0.1(1.1^{20})}\right] = \$8.51 \text{ billion}$$

The value of the Coca-Cola brand name using the multiperiod excess earnings method is $8.51 billion.

Relief from Royalties

The relief from royalties method estimates the value of an intangible asset by calculating how much it would cost to license it from a third party. To illustrate this method, consider the Covid-19 vaccine patent owned by firms like Pfizer and AstraZeneca. Assume that the AstraZeneca Covid-19 vaccine generates £5 billion of annual revenue for 10 years, with a royalty rate of 10 per cent and a discount rate of 8 per cent.

Step 1: Calculate the annual revenues the intangible asset will generate for AstraZeneca each year. This is called the *royalty base.* For AstraZeneca, we know this is £5 billion per annum.

Step 2: Calculate the percentage of the revenue AstraZeneca would have to pay to a third party to use the Covid-19 patent. This is called the *royalty rate.* For this example, we assume a royalty rate of 10 per cent.

Step 3: Multiply the royalty base by the royalty rate to get the annual royalty payment for the patent: £5 billion × 10% = £500 million.

Step 4: Calculate the present value of the royalty payments over all the years that the intangible asset lasts:

$$\text{PV} = C\left[\frac{1}{r} - \frac{1}{r(1+r)^t}\right] = 500\left[\frac{1}{0.08} - \frac{1}{0.08(1.08^{10})}\right] = £3{,}355 \text{ million}$$

The value of the Covid-19 patent to AstraZeneca is £3,355 million.

Differential Value Method

This is possibly the simplest approach to valuing intangibles. To find the value of an intangible, you find the value of a company with the intangible asset and compare it to a peer firm without the asset. The difference is the intangible asset value. You can also use this method with price multiples.

Assume, for instance, that L'Oréal's brand name generates €30 billion in revenues, resulting in a net income contribution of €4 billion. The average price–earnings ratio for European cosmetics companies is 25. The value of L'Oréal's brand name using this method would be calculated as follows:

Step 1: Find a similar cosmetics firm that does not have a brand name and estimate its value using the price–earnings ratio. For example, suppose there is a brandless generic cosmetics company with €2 billion in annual earnings. Its value using the price–earnings ratio would be €2 billion × 25 = €50 billion.

Step 2: Find the value of L'Oréal: €4 billion × 25 = €100 billion.

Step 3: Subtract the value of the generic business from the value of the business with the brand name: €100 billion – €50 billion = €50 billion.

The value of L'Oréal's brand name using this method is, therefore, €50 billion, which means that L'Oréal's brand adds €50 billion to its value compared with a similar business without a brand name.

When valuing intangible assets in mergers and acquisitions, you must identify which intangible assets are to be acquired and how they contribute to the value of the combined entity. This means you should consider any synergies generated between the merging firms just as with tangible assets.

28.4 Sources of Synergy

In this section, we discuss several sources of synergy.

Revenue Enhancement

A combined firm may generate greater revenues than two separate firms. Increased revenues can come from marketing gains, strategic benefits and market power.

Marketing Gains

It is frequently claimed that, due to improved marketing, mergers and acquisitions can increase operating revenues. Improvements can be made in the following areas:

- Previously ineffective media programming and advertising efforts
- A weak existing distribution network
- An unbalanced product mix.

Strategic Benefits

Some acquisitions promise a *strategic* benefit, which is more like an option than a standard investment opportunity. Imagine, for instance, that a sewing machine company acquires a computer company. The firm will be well positioned if technological advances allow computer-driven sewing machines in the future.

Michael Porter (1998) has used the word *beachhead* to denote the strategic benefits of entering a new industry. He uses the example of Procter & Gamble's acquisition of the Charmin Paper Company as a beachhead that allowed Procter & Gamble to develop a highly interrelated cluster of paper products – disposable nappies, paper towels, feminine hygiene products and bathroom tissue.

Market or Monopoly Power

One firm may acquire another to reduce competition. If so, prices can be increased, generating monopoly profits. However, mergers that reduce competition do not benefit society, and government regulators may challenge them.

Sustainability

Synergies can be gained using sustainability to expand into new markets or segments, enhancing customer loyalty and retention, and attracting new investors or partners. For example, an acquisition of a company with a strong social impact brand can boost the reputation and sales of the acquirer in the growing market of socially conscious consumers. A high-performance ESG culture can also transfer best practices and values to the acquirer or target and create a more motivated and productive workforce.

Cost Reduction

A combined firm may operate more efficiently than two separate firms. This is the primary reason for many mergers and acquisitions. A merger can increase operating efficiency in the following ways.

Economies of Scale

An economy of scale means that the average cost of production falls as the level of production increases. Figure 28.2 illustrates the relation between cost per unit and size for a typical firm. As can be seen, average cost first falls and then rises. In other words, the firm experiences economies of scale until optimal firm size is reached. Diseconomies of scale arise after that.

Figure 28.2 Economies of Scale and the Optimal Size of the Firm

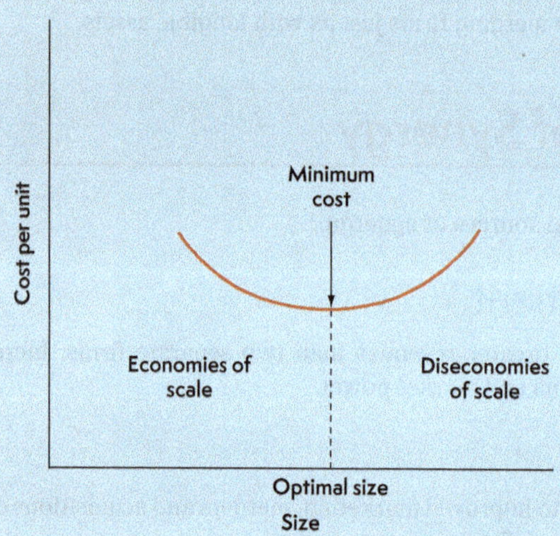

Though the precise nature of economies of scale is not known, it is one obvious benefit of horizontal mergers. The phrase *spreading overhead* is frequently used in connection with economies of scale. This refers to sharing central facilities such as corporate headquarters, top management and computer systems.

Economies of Vertical Integration

Operating economies can be gained from vertical combinations as well as from horizontal combinations. The main purpose of vertical acquisitions is to make coordination of closely related operating activities easier. This is probably why most forest product firms that cut timber also own sawmills and hauling equipment. Costco opening its own chicken farms is another example of vertical integration. Costco had faced a number of supply chain issues with the largest poultry providers and its chosen response was to open its own farms. Similarly, Starbucks purchased Chinese farms so that it could produce its own coffee beans rather than buying them in the market. Economies from vertical integration probably also explain why most airline companies own aeroplanes. They also may explain why some airline companies have purchased hotels and car rental companies.

Technology Transfer

Technology transfer is another reason for a merger. An automobile manufacturer might well acquire an aircraft company if aerospace technology can improve automotive quality. This technology transfer was the motivation behind the acquisition of Nokia devices and services by Microsoft.

Complementary Resources

Some firms acquire others to improve usage of existing resources. A ski equipment store merging with a tennis equipment store will smooth sales over both the winter and summer seasons, thereby making better use of store capacity.

Elimination of Inefficient Management

A change in management can often increase firm value. Some managers overspend on perquisites and pet projects, making these firms ripe for takeover. Alternatively, incumbent managers may not understand changing market conditions or new technology, making it difficult for them to abandon old strategies. Although the board of directors should replace these managers, the board is often unable to act independently. Thus, a merger may be needed to make the necessary replacements.

Mergers and acquisitions can be viewed as part of the labour market for top management. This is known as the market for corporate control, in which alternative management teams compete for the rights to manage corporate activities.

Tax Gains

Tax reduction may be a powerful incentive for some acquisitions. This reduction can come from:

- The use of tax losses
- The use of unused debt capacity
- The use of surplus funds
- Tax differentials across countries.

One of the biggest reasons for cross-border mergers in recent years has been an activity called *tax inversion*. This happens when the country in which a firm is domiciled has a very high corporate tax rate. In a tax inversion, a firm will merge with or acquire a competitor in a low tax regime and transfer its headquarters to the low tax country to minimize tax payments.

Tax inversion is suspected to be the main motivation for many US cross-border mergers and acquisitions, such as Medtronic (USA) and Covidien (Ireland); AbbVie (USA) and Shire (Ireland);[3] and Burger King (USA) and Tim Hortons (Canada). As you would expect, the US government has actively tried to disincentivize this type of tax arbitrage via a number of new tax code changes and regulations. Ireland is the most common destination for US and UK tax inversions because the differential in corporate tax rates between Ireland and both the USA and the UK is so large.

There are four types of tax inversion:

1. A naked inversion. This is also known as redomiciling. With a naked inversion, a company in a high tax domicile creates a subsidiary in the low tax domicile. The parent and subsidiary exchange each other's equity to such an extent that the subsidiary becomes the parent and the former parent becomes the foreign subsidiary.
2. A company in a low tax domicile acquires a firm in a high tax domicile.
3. A company in a high tax domicile acquires a firm in a low tax domicile and the acquired firm becomes the parent.
4. A hybrid inversion. A firm in a high tax domicile transfers a large part of its intellectual property rights to a low tax domicile.

Net Operating Losses

A firm with a profitable division and an unprofitable one will have a low tax bill because the loss in one division offsets the income in the other. However, if the two divisions are actually separate companies, the profitable firm will not be able to use the losses of the unprofitable one to offset its income. Thus, in the right circumstances, a merger can lower taxes.

Consider Table 28.1, which shows pre-tax income, taxes and after-tax income for firms A and B. Firm A earns €200 in state 1 but loses money in state 2. The firm pays taxes in state 1 but is not entitled to a tax rebate in state 2. Conversely, firm B turns a profit in state 2 but not in state 1. This firm pays taxes only in state 2. The table shows that the combined tax bill of the two separate firms is always €68, regardless of which state occurs.

However, the last two columns of the table show that, after a merger, the combined firm will pay only €34 in taxes. Taxes drop after the merger because a loss in one division offsets the gain in the other.

The message of this example is that firms need taxable profits to take advantage of potential losses. These losses are often referred to as *net operating losses,* or NOL for short. Mergers can sometimes bring losses and profits together. However, there are two qualifications to the previous example:

1. Many country tax laws permit firms that experience alternating periods of profits and losses to equalize their taxes by carry-back and carry-forward provisions. A firm that has been profitable but has a loss in the current

Table 28.1 Tax Effect of Merger of Firms A and B

	Before Merger				Before Merger	
	Firm A		Firm B		Firm AB	
	If State 1	If State 2	If State 1	If State 2	If State 1	If State 2
Taxable income (€)	200	−100	−100	200	100	100
Taxes (€)	68	0	0	68	34	34
Net income (€)	132	−100	−100	132	66	66

Note: Neither firm will be able to deduct its losses prior to the merger. The merger allows the losses from A to offset the taxable profits from B, and vice versa.

year, for example, may be able to get refunds of income taxes paid in *three previous years* and can carry the loss *forward for 15 years*. Thus, a merger to exploit unused tax shields must offer tax savings over and above what can be accomplished by firms via carryovers.[4]

2 Tax authorities in many countries are likely to disallow an acquisition if its principal purpose is to avoid the payment of taxes.

Sustainability

Mergers and acquisitions can also benefit from improvements in sustainability by improving resource efficiency, reducing waste and emissions, optimizing supply chains, and lowering regulatory and legal risks. A merger between two companies with complementary renewable energy portfolios, for instance, can reduce their dependence on fossil fuels and lower their carbon taxes.

Debt Capacity

There are at least two cases where mergers allow for increased debt and a larger tax shield. In the first case, the target has too little debt, and the acquirer can infuse the target with the missing debt. In the second case, both target and acquirer have optimal debt levels. A merger leads to risk reduction, generating greater debt capacity and a larger tax shield. We treat each case in turn.

Case 1: Unused Debt Capacity

Chapter 16
Page 433

In Chapter 16, we pointed out that every firm has a certain amount of debt capacity. This debt capacity is beneficial because greater debt leads to a greater tax shield. More formally, every firm can borrow a certain amount before the marginal costs of financial distress equal the marginal tax shield. This debt capacity is a function of many factors, perhaps the most important being the risk of the firm. Firms with high risk generally cannot borrow as much as firms with low risk. For example, a utility or a supermarket, both firms with low risk, can have a higher debt-to-value ratio than can a technology firm.

Some firms, for whatever reason, have less debt than is optimal. Perhaps the managers are risk averse, or perhaps they simply do not know how to assess debt capacity properly. Is it bad for a firm to have too little debt? The answer is yes. As we have said, the optimal level of debt occurs when the marginal cost of financial distress equals the marginal tax shield. Too little debt reduces firm value.

This is where mergers come in. A firm with little or no debt is an inviting target. An acquirer could raise the target's debt level after the merger to create a bigger tax shield.

Case 2: Increased Debt Capacity

Chapter 10
Page 260

Let us move back to the principles of modern portfolio theory, as presented in Chapter 10. Consider two equities in different industries, where both equities have the same risk or standard deviation. A portfolio of these two equities has lower risk than that of either equity separately. In other words, the two-equity portfolio is somewhat diversified, whereas each equity by itself is completely undiversified.[5]

Now, rather than considering an individual buying both equities, consider a merger between the two underlying firms. Because the risk of the combined firm is less than that of either one separately, banks should be willing to lend more money to the combined firm than the total of what they would lend to the two firms separately. In other words, the risk reduction that the merger generates leads to greater debt capacity.

Imagine, say, that each firm can borrow €100 on its own before the merger. Perhaps the combined firm after the merger will be able to borrow €250. Debt capacity has increased by €50(= €250 – €200).

Remember that debt generates a tax shield. If debt rises after the merger, taxes will fall. That is, simply because of the greater interest payments after the merger, the tax bill of the combined firm should be less than the sum of the tax bills of the two separate firms before the merger. In other words, the increased debt capacity from a merger can reduce taxes.

To summarize, we first considered the case where the target had too little leverage. The acquirer could infuse the target with more debt, generating a greater tax shield. Next, we considered the case where both target and acquirer began with optimal debt levels. A merger leads to more debt even here. That is, the risk reduction from the merger creates greater debt capacity and thus a greater tax shield.

Surplus Funds

Another quirk in the tax laws involves surplus funds. Consider a firm that has *free cash flow*. That is, it has cash flow available after payment of all taxes and after all positive net present value projects have been funded. In this situation, aside from purchasing securities, the firm can either pay dividends or buy back shares.

We have already seen in our previous discussion of dividend policy that an extra dividend will increase the income tax paid by some investors. Investors pay lower taxes in a share repurchase.[6] However, a share repurchase is not normally a legal option if the sole purpose is to avoid taxes on dividends.

Instead, the firm might make acquisitions with its excess funds. Here, the shareholders of the acquiring firm avoid the taxes they would have paid on a dividend.[7]

Reduced Capital Requirements

Earlier in this chapter, we stated that due to economies of scale, mergers can reduce operating costs. It follows that mergers can reduce capital requirements as well. Accountants typically divide capital into two components: fixed capital and working capital.

When two firms merge, the managers are likely to find that they have duplicate facilities. For instance, if both firms had their own headquarters, all executives in the merged firm could be moved to one headquarters building, allowing the other headquarters to be sold. Some plants might be redundant as well. Or two merging firms in the same industry might consolidate their research and development, permitting some R&D facilities to be sold.

The same goes for working capital. The inventory-to-sale ratio and the cash-to-sales ratio often decrease as firm size increases. A merger permits these economies of scale to be realized, allowing a reduction in working capital.

28.5 Two 'Bad' Reasons for Mergers

Earnings Growth

An acquisition can create the appearance of earnings growth, perhaps fooling investors into thinking that the firm is worth more than it really is. Let us consider two companies, Global Resources and Regional Enterprises, as depicted in the first two columns of Table 28.2. As can be seen, earnings per share are €1 for both companies. However, Global sells for €25 per share, implying a price–earnings (PE) ratio of 25 (= 25/1). By contrast, Regional sells for €10, implying a PE ratio of 10. This means that an investor in Global pays €25 to get €1 in earnings, whereas an investor in Regional receives the same €1 in earnings on only a €10 investment. Are investors getting a better deal with Regional? Not necessarily. Perhaps Global's earnings are expected to grow faster than are Regional's. If this is the case, an investor in Global will expect to receive high earnings in later years, making up for low earnings in the short term. In fact, Chapter 5 argues that the primary determinant of a firm's PE ratio is the market's expectation of the firm's growth rate in earnings.

Chapter 5
Page 116

Now let us imagine that Global acquires Regional, with the merger creating no value. If the market is smart, it will realize that the combined firm is worth the sum of the values of the separate firms. In this case, the market value of the combined firm will be €3,500, which is equal to the sum of the values of the separate firms before the merger.

At these values, Global will acquire Regional by exchanging 40 of its shares for 100 shares of Regional, so that Global will have 140 shares outstanding after the merger.[8] Global's share price remains at €25 (= €3,500/140). With 140 shares

Table 28.2 Financial Positions of Global Resources and Regional Enterprises

	Global Resources Before Merger	Regional Enterprises Before Merger	Global Resources After Merger	
			The Market is 'Smart'	The Market is 'Fooled'
Earnings per share (€)	1.00	1.00	1.43	1.43
Price per share (€)	25.00	10.00	25.00	35.71
Price–earnings ratio	25	10	17.5	25
Number of shares	100	100	140	140
Total earnings (€)	100	100	200	200
Total value (€)	2,500	1,000	3,500	5,000

Note: Exchange ratio: 1 share in Global for 2.5 shares in Regional.

outstanding and €200 of earnings after the merger, Global earns €1.43 (= €200/140) per share after the merger. Its PE ratio becomes 17.5 (= 25/1.43), a drop from 25 before the merger. This scenario is represented by the third column of Table 28.2. Why has the PE dropped? The combined firm's PE will be an average of Global's high PE and Regional's low PE before the merger. This is common sense once you think about it. Global's PE should drop when it takes on a new division with low growth.

Let us now consider the possibility that the market is fooled. As we just said, the acquisition enables Global to increase its earnings per share from €1 to €1.43. If the market is fooled, it might mistake the 43 per cent increase in earnings per share for true growth. In this case, the price–earnings ratio of Global may not fall after the merger. Suppose the price–earnings ratio of Global remains at 25. The total value of the combined firm will increase to €5,000 (= 25 × €200), and the share price of Global will increase to €35.71 (= €5,000/140). This is reflected in the last column of the table.

This is earnings growth magic. Can we expect this magic to work in the real world? Managers of a previous generation certainly thought so, with firms such as LTV Industries, ITT and Litton Industries all trying to play the PE-multiple game in the 1960s. However, in hindsight it looks as if they played the game without much success. These operators have all dropped out, with few, if any, replacements. It appears that the market is too smart to be fooled this easily.

Diversification

Diversification is frequently cited as a reason for two firms to merge. Is diversification a good reason to merge? It might seem so. After all, in Section 10.6, we spent a lot of time explaining why diversification is valuable for investors in their own portfolios because of the elimination of unsystematic risk.

To investigate this issue, let us consider two companies, Sunshine Swimwear (SS) and Polar Winterwear (PW). For obvious reasons both companies have highly seasonal cash flows, and in their respective off-seasons both companies worry about cash flow. If the two companies were to merge, the combined company would have a much more stable cash flow. In other words, a merger would diversify away some of the seasonal variation and, in fact, would make bankruptcy much less likely.

Notice that the operations of the two firms are very different, so the proposed merger is a purely 'financial' merger. This means that there are no 'synergies' or other value-creating possibilities except, possibly, gains from risk reduction. Here is some pre-merger information:

	Sunshine Swimwear	Polar Winterwear
Market value of assets	€30 million	€10 million
Face value of pure discount debt	€12 million	€4 million
Debt maturity	3 years	3 years
Asset return standard deviation	50%	60%

The risk-free rate, continuously compounded, is 5 per cent. Given this, we can view the equity in each firm as a call option and calculate the following using Black–Scholes (see Section 22.10) to determine equity values (check these for practice):

	Sunshine Swimwear (€)	Polar Winterwear (€)
Market value of equity	20.394 million	6.992 million
Market value of debt	9.606 million	3.008 million

If you check these, you may get slightly different answers if you use Table 22.3 (we used a spreadsheet). Notice that we calculated the market value of debt using the market value balance sheet identity.

After the merger, the combined firm's assets will simply be the sum of the pre-merger values, €30 + €10 = €40, because no value was created or destroyed. Similarly, the total face value of the debt is now €16 million. However, we will assume that the combined firm's asset return standard deviation is 40 per cent. This is lower than for either of the two individual firms because of the diversification effect.

So, what is the impact of this merger? To find out, we compute the post-merger value of the equity. Based on our discussion, here is the relevant information:

	Combined Firm
Market value of assets	€40 million
Face value of pure discount debt	€16 million
Debt maturity	3 years
Asset return standard deviation	40%

Once again, we can calculate equity and debt values:

	Combined Firm (€)
Market value of equity	26.602 million
Market value of debt	13.398 million

What we notice is that this merger is a terrible idea, at least for the shareholders! Before the merger, the equity in the two separate firms was worth a total of €20.394 + €6.992 = €27.386 million compared to only €26.602 million post-merger; so the merger destroyed €27.386 – €26.602 = €0.784 million.

Where did €0.784 million in equity go? It went to the bondholders. Their bonds were worth €9.606 + €3.008 = €12.614 million before the merger and €13.398 million after – a gain of exactly €0.784 million. Thus this merger neither created nor destroyed value, but shifted it from the shareholders to the bondholders.

Our example shows that pure financial mergers are a bad idea, and it also shows why. The diversification works in the sense that it reduces the volatility of the firm's return on assets. This risk reduction benefits the bondholders by making default less likely. This is sometimes called the 'coinsurance' effect. Essentially, by merging, the firms insure each other's bonds. The bonds are thus less risky and they rise in value. If the bonds increase in value, and there is no net increase in asset values, then the equity must decrease in value. Thus, pure financial mergers are good for creditors but not for shareholders.

Another way to see this is that because the equity is a call option, a reduction in return variance on the underlying asset has to reduce its value. The reduction in value in the case of a purely financial merger has an interesting interpretation. The merger makes default (and thus bankruptcy) *less* likely to happen. That is obviously a good thing from a bondholder's perspective, but why is it a bad thing from a shareholder's perspective? The answer is simple: the right to go bankrupt is a valuable shareholder option. A purely financial merger reduces the value of that option.

Real World Insight 28.1

Valuing Technology Firms

In recent years, the most prominent companies to have listed on the stock market have been technology firms. The social media platform Reddit, for example, is expected to IPO late in 2023 or early 2024, followed by the satellite internet provider Starlink-2025. In 2022, the autonomous driving company Mobileye raised $861 million, and if we go further back, we can also include Netscape, Yahoo!, Alphabet, Amazon, eBay, Facebook, LinkedIn, Twitter, Alibaba, Snap, Uber, Slack, Palantir, Netflix and Airbnb among those companies.

Valuing tech companies is similar to valuing any type of business. The characteristics of every valuation are the same in that future cash flows and company risk have to be estimated. The difference for technology firms is that information regarding future cash flows is difficult to forecast, and corporate risk is a challenge to calculate because technology firms rarely have peer companies to compare against.

Another issue for technology firms is that valuation metrics are not as closely linked to profits, cash or sales as is the case when valuing other firms. Relevant metrics for technology firms include the number of users, the number of players of a game or even the number of followers of the company on social media.

Bitcoin exchanges and other cryptocurrencies add a further dimension to valuation because of the lack of information regarding the underlying corporate fundamentals.

A key factor in tech company valuation is subscriber or user growth. The more users, the larger the customer population and the more likely it is that cash will be generated from the users through subscriptions or payments. Forecasting subscriber growth is therefore fundamental to any valuation. This is the greatest challenge facing valuation efforts because past subscriber growth does not necessarily translate into future subscriber growth.

Many technology firms use advertising revenues to drive profits, and so, in addition to subscriber growth, analysts must also forecast advertising demand and the effectiveness of advertising on technology platforms. Arguably, X (previously Twitter) and WhatsApp have been unsuccessful in converting users into revenue because the platforms have been ineffective in leveraging their popularity for revenue generation.

Techniques such as sensitivity analysis, scenario analysis and simulation (see Chapter 8) are regularly used in valuing technology firms because they capture the inherent uncertainty in the company operations today and in the future. Sensitivity analysis and Monte Carlo simulation allow modelling of the company's fundamentals, and scenario analysis can assess the impact of external events, such as new government regulation. Real option valuation permits the assessment of opportunities that arise from using the core technology in other industries or geographical locations. Common examples include scale-up, diversification and abandonment opportunities.

Diversification is often mentioned as a benefit of one firm acquiring another. However, we argue that diversification, by itself, cannot produce increases in value. To see this, recall that a business's variability of return can be separated into two parts: (1) what is specific to the business and called *unsystematic*, and (2) what is *systematic* because it is common to all businesses.

Systematic variability cannot be eliminated by diversification, so mergers will not eliminate this risk at all. By contrast, unsystematic risk can be diversified away through mergers. However, the investor does not need widely diversified companies such as Unilever to eliminate unsystematic risk. Shareholders can diversify more easily than corporations by simply purchasing equity in different corporations. Instead of Air France and KLM merging to form Air France-KLM, say, the shareholders of Air France could have purchased shares in KLM if they believed there would be diversification gains from doing so. Thus, diversification through merger may not benefit shareholders.[9]

Diversification can produce gains to the acquiring firm only if one of two things is true:

1 Diversification decreases the unsystematic variability at a lower cost than by investors' adjustments to personal portfolios. This seems very unlikely.
2 Diversification reduces risk and thereby increases debt capacity. This possibility was mentioned in Section 28.4.

28.6 A Cost to Shareholders from Reduction in Risk

In Section 28.5, we used option pricing theory to show that pure financial mergers are bad for shareholders. In this section, we will explore this idea from an alternative perspective and show that the diversification effects of mergers can benefit bondholders at the expense of shareholders.

The Base Case

Consider an example where firm A acquires firm B. Section I of Table 28.3 shows the net present values of firm A and firm B prior to the merger in the two possible states of the economy. Because the probability of each state is 0.50, the market value of each firm is the average of its values in the two states. For example, the market value of firm A is:

$$0.5 \times €80 + 0.5 \times €20 = €50$$

Now imagine that the merger of the two firms generates no synergy. The combined firm AB will have a market value of €75 (= €50 + €25), the sum of the values of firm A and firm B. Further, imagine that the shareholders of firm B receive equity in AB equal to firm B's standalone market value of €25. In other words, firm B receives no premium. Because the value of AB is €75, the shareholders of firm A have a value of €50 (= €75 – €25) after the merger – just what they had before the merger. Thus, the shareholders of both firms A and B are indifferent to the merger.

Table 28.3 Equity-swap Mergers

	NPV		
	State 1	State 2	Market Value
Probability	0.5	0.5	
I. Base case (no debt in either firm's capital structure)			
Values before merger:			
Firm A	€80	€20	€50
Firm B	10	40	25
Values after merger:*			
Firm AB	€90	€60	€75
II. Debt with face value of €30 in firm A's capital structure			
Debt with face value of €15 in firm B's capital structure			
Values before merger:			
Firm A	€80	€20	€50
Debt	30	20	25
Equity	50	0	25
Firm B	€10	€40	€25
Debt	10	15	12.50
Equity	0	25	12.50
Values after merger:†			
Firm AB	€90	€60	€75
Debt	45	45	45
Equity	45	15	30

Note: Values of both firm A's debt and firm B's debt rise after the merger. Values of both firm A's equity and firm B's equity fall after the merger.

* Shareholders in firm A receive €50 of equity in firm AB. Shareholders in firm B receive €25 of equity in firm AB. Thus shareholders in both firms are indifferent to the merger.

† Shareholders in firm A receive equity in firm AB worth €20. Shareholders in firm B receive equity in firm AB worth €10. Gains and losses from merger are:

Loss to equityholders in firm A: €20 – €25 = –€5

Loss to equityholders in firm B: €10 – €12.50 = –€2.50

Combined gain to bondholders in both firms: €45 – €37.50 = €7.50

Both Firms Have Debt

Alternatively, imagine that firm A has debt with a face value of €30 in its capital structure, as shown in section II of Table 28.3. Without a merger, firm A will default on its debt in state 2 because the value of firm A in this state is €20, less than the face value of the debt of €30. As a consequence, firm A cannot pay the full value of the debt claim; the bondholders receive only €20 in this state. The creditors take the possibility of default into account, valuing the debt at €25(= 0.5 × €30 + 0.5 × €20).

Firm B's debt has a face value of €15. Firm B will default in state 1 because the value of the firm in this state is €10, less than the face value of the debt of €15. The value of firm B's debt is €12.50(= 0.5 × €10 + 0.5 × €15). It follows that the sum of the value of firm A's debt and the value of firm B's debt is €37.50(= €25 + €12.50).

Now let us see what happens after the merger. Firm AB is worth €90 in state 1 and €60 in state 2, implying a market value of €75 (= 0.5 × €90 + 0.5 × €60). The face value of the debt in the combined firm is €45 (= €30 + €15). Because the value of the firm is greater than €45 in either state, the bondholders always get paid in full. Thus, the value of the debt is its face value of €45. This value is €7.50 greater than the sum of the values of the two debts before the merger, which we just found to be €37.50. Therefore, the merger benefits the bondholders.

What about the shareholders? Because the equity of firm A was worth €25 and the equity of firm B was worth €12.50 before the merger, let us assume that firm AB issues two shares to firm A's shareholders for every share issued to firm B's shareholders. Firm AB's equity is €30, so firm A's shareholders get shares worth €20 and firm B's shareholders get shares worth €10. Firm A's shareholders lose €5 (= €20 – €25) from the merger. Similarly, firm B's shareholders lose €2.50 (= €10 – €12.50). The total loss to the shareholders of both firms is €7.50, exactly the gain to the bondholders from the merger.

There are a lot of numbers in this example. The point is that the bondholders gain €7.50 and the shareholders lose €7.50 from the merger. Why does this transfer of value occur? To see what is going on, notice that, when the two firms are separate, firm B does not guarantee firm A's debt. That is, if firm A defaults on its debt, firm B does not help the bondholders of firm A. However, after the merger the bondholders can draw on the cash flows from both A and B. When one of the divisions of the combined firm fails, creditors can be paid from the profits of the other division. This mutual guarantee, which is called the *coinsurance effect*, makes the debt less risky and more valuable than before.

There is no net benefit to the firm as a whole. The bondholders gain the coinsurance effect and the shareholders lose the coinsurance effect. Three general conclusions emerge from the preceding analysis:

1 Mergers usually help bondholders. The size of the gain to bondholders depends on the reduction in the probability of bankruptcy after the combination. That is, the less risky the combined firm is, the greater are the gains to bondholders.
2 Shareholders of the acquiring firm are hurt by the amount that bondholders gain.
3 Conclusion 2 applies to mergers without synergy. In practice, much depends on the size of the synergy.

How Can Shareholders Reduce Their Losses From the Coinsurance Effect?

The coinsurance effect raises bondholder values and lowers shareholder values. However, there are at least two ways in which shareholders can reduce or eliminate the coinsurance effect. First, the shareholders in firm A could retire its debt *before* the merger announcement date and reissue an equal amount of debt after the merger. Because debt is retired at the low pre-merger price, this type of refinancing transaction can neutralize the coinsurance effect to the bondholders.

Also, note that the debt capacity of the combined firm is likely to increase because the acquisition reduces the probability of financial distress. Thus, the shareholders' second alternative is simply to issue more debt after the merger. An increase in debt following the merger will have two effects, even without the prior action of debt retirement. The interest tax shield from new corporate debt raises firm value, as discussed in Section 28.4 of this chapter. In addition, an increase in debt after the merger raises the probability of financial distress, thereby reducing or eliminating the bondholders' gain from the coinsurance effect.

Some Final Thoughts on the Coinsurance Effect

The coinsurance effect arises only if organizational restructuring has no impact on the systematic risk of a company. Diversification reduces unsystematic risk, but since systematic risk is the only important risk to investors there is no overall value impact to the firm. However, Hann et al. (2013) argue that corporate diversification may allow a firm to (a) avoid financial distress costs; (b) reduce the cost of raising external finance; or (c) retain important stakeholders such as suppliers, customers or employees. If this is the case, the coinsurance effect will reduce a firm's systematic risk and therefore lower its cost of capital. Hann and colleagues test this hypothesis and find it to be true. Specifically, diversified firms have a significantly lower cost of capital than comparable portfolios of stand-alone firms, and this will have clear value implications for the diversified firm.

So, is the coinsurance effect a real issue or do other factors drive mergers and acquisitions from a diversification motive, as Hann and colleagues suggest? Time will tell. Certainly, many believe that the coinsurance effect means diversification motives for mergers and acquisitions are bad. However, if there are strategic justifications to diversify, then coinsurance will actually enhance firm value.

28.7 The NPV of a Merger

Firms typically use NPV analysis when making acquisitions. The analysis is relatively straightforward when the consideration is cash. The analysis becomes more complex when the consideration is equity.

Cash

Suppose firm A and firm B have values as separate entities of €500 and €100, respectively. They are both all-equity firms. If firm A acquires firm B, the merged firm AB will have a combined value of €700 due to synergies of €100. The board of firm B has indicated that it will sell firm B if it is offered €150 in cash.

Should firm A acquire firm B? Assuming that firm A finances the acquisition out of its own retained earnings, its value after the acquisition is:[10]

$$\begin{aligned}\text{Value of firm A after the acquisition} &= \text{Value of combined firm} - \text{Cash paid}\\ &= €700 - €150\\ &= €550\end{aligned}$$

Because firm A was worth €500 prior to the acquisition, the NPV to firm A's equityholders is:

Equation 28.1

$$€50 = €550 - €500$$

Assuming that there are 25 shares in firm A, each share of the firm is worth €20 (= €500/25) prior to the merger and €22 (= €550/25) after the merger. These calculations are displayed in the first and third columns of Table 28.4. Looking at the rise in equity price, we conclude that firm A should make the acquisition.

Table 28.4 Cost of Acquisition: Cash versus Equity

	Before Acquisition		After Acquisition: Firm A		
	(1)	(2)	(3)	(4)	(5)
	Firm A	Firm B	Cash*	Equity† Exchange Ratio (0.75:1)	Equity† Exchange Ratio (0.6819:1)
Market value (VA, VB) (€)	500	100	550	700	700
Number of shares	25	10	25	32.5	31.819
Price per share (€)	20	10	22	21.54	22

*Value of firm A after acquisition: cash

$$\begin{aligned}V_A &= V_{AB} - \text{cash}\\ €550 &= €700 - €150\end{aligned}$$

†Value of firm A after acquisition: equity

$$\begin{aligned}V_A &= V_{AB}\\ €700 &= €700\end{aligned}$$

We spoke earlier of both the synergy and the premium of a merger. We can also value the NPV of a merger to the acquirer:

$$\text{NPV of a merger to acquirer} = \text{Synergy} - \text{Premium}$$

Because the value of the combined firm is €700 and the pre-merger values of A and B were €500 and €100, respectively, the synergy is €100 [= €700 − (€500 + €100)]. The premium is €50(= €150 − €100). Thus, the NPV of the merger to the acquirer is:

$$\text{NPV of merger to firm A} = €100 - €50 = €50$$

One caveat is in order. This textbook has consistently argued that the market value of a firm is the best estimate of its true value. However, we must adjust our analysis when discussing mergers. If the true price of firm A *without the merger* is €500, the market value of firm A may actually be above €500 when merger negotiations take place.

This happens because the market price reflects the possibility that the merger will occur. For example, if the probability is 60 per cent that the merger will take place, the market price of firm A will be:

$$€530 = \begin{matrix} \text{Market value of firm A with merger} & \times & \text{Probability of merger} & + & \text{Market value of firm A without merger} & \times & \text{Probability of no merger} \\ €550 & \times & 0.60 & + & €500 & \times & 0.40 \end{matrix}$$

The managers would underestimate the NPV from the merger in Equation 28.1 if the market price of firm A is used. Thus, managers face the difficult task of valuing their own firm without the acquisition.

Equity

Of course, firm A could purchase firm B with equity instead of cash. Unfortunately, the analysis is not as straightforward here. To handle this scenario, we need to know how many shares are outstanding in firm B. We assume that there are 10 shares outstanding, as indicated in column 2 of Table 28.4.

Suppose firm A exchanges 7.5 of its shares for the entire 10 shares of firm B. We call this an exchange ratio of 0.75:1. The value of each share of firm A's equity before the acquisition is €20. Because 7.5 × €20 = €150, this exchange *appears* to be the equivalent of purchasing firm B in cash for €150.

This is incorrect: the true cost to firm A is greater than €150. To see this, note that firm A has 32.5 (= 25 + 7.5) shares outstanding after the merger. Firm B shareholders own 23 per cent (= 7.5/32.5) of the combined firm. Their holdings are valued at €161 (= 23 per cent × €700). Because these shareholders receive equity in firm A worth €161, the cost of the merger to firm A's shareholders must be €161, not €150.

This result is shown in column 4 of Table 28.4. The value of each share of firm A's equity after an equity-for-equity transaction is only €21.54 (= €700/32.5). We found out earlier that the value of each share is €22 after a cash-for-equity transaction. The difference is that the cost of the equity-for-equity transaction to firm A is higher.

This non-intuitive result occurs because the exchange ratio of 7.5 shares of firm A for 10 shares of firm B was based on the *pre-merger* prices of the two firms. However, because the equity of firm A rises after the merger, firm B equityholders receive more than €150 in firm A equity.

What should the exchange ratio be so that firm B equityholders receive only €150 of firm A's equity? We begin by defining α, the proportion of the shares in the combined firm that firm B's shareholders own. Because the combined firm's value is €700, the value of firm B shareholders after the merger is:

Value of firm B shareholders after merger

$$\alpha \times €700$$

Setting α × €700 = €150, we find that α = 21.43 per cent. In other words, firm B's shareholders will receive equity worth €150 if they receive 21.43 per cent of the firm after merger.

Now we determine the number of shares issued to firm B's shareholders. The proportion, α, that firm B's shareholders have in the combined firm can be expressed as follows:

$$\alpha = \frac{\text{New shares issued}}{\text{Old shares + New shares issued}} = \frac{\text{New shares issued}}{25 + \text{New shares issued}}$$

Plugging our value of α into the equation yields:

$$0.2143 = \frac{\text{New shares issued}}{25 + \text{New shares issued}}$$

Solving for the unknown, we have:

$$\text{New shares} = 6.819 \text{ shares}$$

Total shares outstanding after the merger are 31.819 (= 25 + 6.819). Because 6.819 shares of firm A are exchanged for 10 shares of firm B, the exchange ratio is 0.6819:1.

Results at the exchange ratio of 0.6819:1 are displayed in column 5 of Table 28.4. Because there are now 31.819 shares, each share of equity is worth €22 (= €700/31.819), exactly what it is worth in the equity-for-cash transaction. Thus, given that the board of firm B will sell its firm for €150, this is the fair exchange ratio, not the ratio of 0.75:1 mentioned earlier.

Cash versus Equity

In this section, we have examined both cash deals and equity-for-equity deals. Our analysis leads to the following question: When do bidders want to pay with cash and when do they want to pay with equity? There is no easy formula: the decision hinges on a few variables, with perhaps the most important being the price of the bidder's equity.

In the example of Table 28.4, firm A's market price per share prior to the merger was €20. Let us now assume that, at the time, firm A's managers believed the 'true' price was €15. In other words, the managers believed that their equity was overvalued. Is it likely for managers to have a different view from that of the market? Yes – managers often have more information than does the market. After all, managers deal with customers, suppliers and employees daily, and are likely to obtain private information.

Now imagine that firm A's managers are considering acquiring firm B with either cash or equity. The overvaluation would have no impact on the merger terms in a cash deal; firm B would still receive €150 in cash. However, the overvaluation would have a big impact on a share-for-share deal. Although firm B receives €150 worth of A's equity as calculated at market prices, firm A's managers know that the true value of the equity is less than €150.

How should firm A pay for the acquisition? Clearly, firm A has an incentive to pay with equity because it would end up giving away less than €150 of value. This conclusion might seem rather cynical because firm A is, in some sense, trying to cheat firm B's shareholders. However, both theory and empirical evidence suggest that firms are more likely to acquire with equity when their own equities are overvalued.[11]

The story is not quite that simple. Just as the managers of firm A think strategically, firm B's managers are likely to think that way as well. Suppose that, in the merger negotiations, firm A's managers push for a share-for-share deal. This might tip off firm B's managers that firm A is overpriced. Perhaps firm B's managers will ask for better terms than firm A is currently offering. Alternatively, firm B may resolve to accept cash or not to sell at all. And just as firm B learns from the negotiations, the market learns also. Empirical evidence shows that the acquirer's equity price generally falls upon the announcement of an equity-for-equity deal.[12]

28.8 Valuation of Mergers in Practice

Section 28.7 provided the tools of merger valuation. However, in practice, the approach to valuation is significantly more complex and subjective. Mergers and acquisitions have two distinct differences from the typical investment project that a firm will undertake. First, the size of a merger will be significantly larger, which means that the risks of mis-evaluation are substantially higher. If an acquiring firm arrives at the wrong value of a target, it may destroy both companies. A good example of this is the Royal Bank of Scotland acquisition of Dutch bank ABN AMRO in 2007, when the Royal Bank of Scotland (with Fortis Bank and Banco Santander) bought ABN AMRO for €49 billion. The acquisition took place just before the collapse in bank valuations because of the global credit crunch. Two years later, in 2009, the Royal Bank of Scotland revalued the acquisition and reported a resultant €28 billion loss. The bank was subsequently bailed out by the British government and most of the directors lost their jobs.

The second difference is that if the target company is listed on a stock exchange, the share price can be used as an indicator of the value of the target's equity. While this makes things intuitively easier, because of the run-up in target valuations when takeover bids are rumoured, share price valuations may be too high if the current share price is used. As Section 28.6 shows, this may lead to the wrong bid price being tabled.

When considering a potential target for acquisition or merger, both firms should evaluate a variety of scenarios and consider the various embedded options that exist in most firms (see Chapter 8). We suggest that acquiring firms take the following steps to evaluate prospective targets.

Chapter 8 Page 207

Stage 1: Value the Target as a Stand-alone Firm

The first stage in the valuation process is to consider the target as a stand-alone entity. This is the base case valuation upon which the merger can be assessed. To value a company requires estimates of future cash flows and the appropriate rates for discounting the cash flows. The initial valuation should then be compared to the current share price of the target to form an initial opinion of the merger.

Stage 2: Calibrate the Valuation

It is very unlikely that your initial valuation of the target firm will be equal to its share price, and any differential in valuations needs to be explained. As mentioned in Section 28.7, share prices may also reflect takeover probabilities and potential takeover premiums. In addition, the share price may not incorporate private information that has been gained as a result of your in-depth analysis. Private information, for example, could be provided by the management of the target firm if the merger is friendly and fully supported by the target's board. Alternatively, new information may have been discovered in the course of your investigations. Because the effort in this phase is so great and the analysis so extensive, it is possible that your valuation may be better than the share price of the market. This is especially true if the target firm is listed on a small exchange or emerging market where valuations may not be so accurate.

If you do not have more information than the market and there is still a difference between your valuation and the share price, it is highly probable that your valuation is incorrect. In other words, your estimates of future cash flows and discount rates will differ from those of the market. At this point, it is strongly recommended that you revisit your assumptions to see if anything can be improved. It is imperative that you get your assumptions right because they are the building blocks for the rest of your analysis.

Stage 3: Value the Synergies

Whereas stages 1 and 2 focus on your initial valuation of the target, stage 3 concerns your assessment of the benefits of a possible merger or acquisition. To do this, you must value the synergies associated with combining the target and the acquirer. In the same way as you initially valued the target firm, you value synergies by estimating the cash flows generated by the synergies along with the appropriate discount rates. Some synergies are easier to predict while others are considerably more difficult. Synergies that come from tax savings or reductions in fixed costs, say, are easier to predict than increased sales or reductions in variable costs.

The future cash flows and the discount rates used in the base case valuation are likely to be used in valuing risky synergies. You may believe, for instance, that the proposed merger will lead to a 10 per cent increase in the target's cash flows in the five years after the merger. Valuing this synergy will require both the pre-acquisition discount rate and the cash flows of the target. In addition, valuing synergies may also require an estimate of the acquiring firm's cost of capital and expected cash flows. Hence, the acquiring firm will want to use the procedures outlined in stages 1 and 2 to value its own equity, and calibrate its cost of capital and cash flows.

When synergies are valued, it is important to discount cash flows arising from the synergy using the weighted average of both firms' cost of capital. For example, as a result of the declining population in Japan and an increasingly competitive global whisky industry, Suntory (the Japanese alcoholic spirits firm) acquired the US whisky firm Beam Inc. Assume that, as a result of the acquisition, both companies would increase their pre-tax profits by 10 per cent per year. Given that the gain in each year is proportional to the pre-acquisition cash flows of both firms, the appropriate discount rate would be an equally weighted average of the two firms' costs of capital.

The Suntory–Beam example illustrates a case where synergies affect both parties to the merger equally. However, this will not always be the case. If the acquisition was expected to result in a proportional increase in Suntory's profits but not Beam's, then you would use Suntory's cost of capital to value the synergy.

Chapter 8 Page 207

Chapter 22 Page 603

If the major gain from the acquisition is Suntory's penetration of the Americas, there will be many strategic options open to the company once it starts operations. Consequently, it might be better to consider valuing the synergy as a strategic option, using the real options methodology in Chapters 8 and 22 instead of the risk-adjusted discount rate method. When a firm expands into a new market, it has the option to expand further if prospects turn out to be more favourable than originally anticipated and to exit if the situation turns out to be unfavourable. In these situations, an investment may be substantially undervalued when such options are ignored.

Stage 4: Value the Merger

The final part of the analysis is to add the base case valuation of the target to the value of the synergies from the merger or acquisition. The rule of thumb is that the merger or acquisition should go ahead if the costs of the merger, which include the bid premium as well as all transaction costs, are lower than the combined value of the merger.

28.9 Friendly versus Hostile Takeovers

Mergers are generally initiated by the acquiring, not the acquired, firm. Thus, the acquirer must decide to purchase another firm, select the tactics to effectuate the merger, determine the highest price it is willing to pay, set an initial bid price and make contact with the target firm. Often the CEO of the acquiring firm simply calls on the CEO of the target and proposes a merger. Should the target be receptive, a merger eventually occurs. Of course, there may be many meetings, with negotiations over price, terms of payment and other parameters. The target's board of directors generally has to approve the acquisition. Sometimes the bidder's board must also give its approval. Finally, an affirmative vote by the shareholders is needed. But when all is said and done, an acquisition that proceeds in this way is viewed as *friendly*.

Of course, not all acquisitions are friendly. The target's management may resist the merger, in which case the acquirer must decide whether to pursue the merger and, if so, what tactics to use. Facing resistance, the acquirer may begin by purchasing some of the target's equity in secret. This position is often called a *toehold*. Regulation in almost every country requires that an institution or individual disclose their holding in a company once a specific percentage ownership threshold is passed. In the UK, for example, an acquiring company must disclose any holdings above 3 per cent and provide detailed information, including its intentions and its position in the target. Secrecy ends at this point because the acquirer must state that it plans to acquire the target. The price of the target's shares will probably rise after the disclosure, with the new equity price reflecting the possibility that the target will be bought out at a premium.

Although the acquirer may continue to purchase shares in the open market, an acquisition is unlikely to be effectuated in this manner. Rather, the acquirer is more likely at some point to make a *tender offer* (an offer made directly to the shareholders to buy shares at a premium above the current market price). The tender offer may specify that the acquirer will purchase all shares that are tendered – that is, turned in to the acquirer. Alternatively, the offer may state that the acquirer will purchase all shares up to, say, 50 per cent of the number of shares outstanding. If more shares are tendered, prorating will occur. For instance, if in an extreme case all the shares are tendered, each shareholder will be allowed to sell one share for every two shares tendered. The acquirer may also say that it will accept the tendered shares only if a minimum number of shares have been tendered.

National regulators normally require that tender offers be held open for a minimum period. This delay gives the target time to respond. As an example, the target may want to notify its shareholders not to tender their shares. It may release statements to the press criticizing the offer. The target may also encourage other firms to enter the bidding process.

At some point, the tender offer ends, at which time the acquirer finds out how many shares have been tendered. The acquirer does not necessarily need 100 per cent of the shares to obtain control of the target. In some companies, a holding of 20 per cent or so may be enough for control. In others, the percentage needed for control is much higher. *Control* is a vague term, but you might think of it operationally as control over the board of directors. Shareholders elect members of the board, who, in turn, appoint managers. If the acquirer receives enough equity to elect a majority of the board members, these members can appoint the managers the acquirer wants. And effective control can often be achieved with less than a majority. As long as some of the original board members vote with the acquirer, a few new board members can gain the acquirer a working majority.

Sometimes, once the acquirer gets working control, it proposes a merger to obtain the few remaining shares that it does not already own. The transaction is now friendly because the board of directors will approve it. Mergers of this type are often called *clean-up* mergers.

A tender offer is not the only way to gain control of a *hostile* target. Alternatively, the acquirer may continue to buy more shares in the open market until control is achieved. This strategy, often called a *street sweep*, is used infrequently, perhaps because of the difficulty of buying enough shares to obtain control. Also, as mentioned, tender offers often allow the acquirer to return the tendered shares if fewer shares than the desired number are tendered. By contrast, shares purchased in the open market cannot be returned.

Another means to obtain control is a *proxy fight* – a procedure involving corporate voting. Elections for seats on the board of directors are generally held at the annual shareholders' meeting, perhaps four to five months after the end of the firm's fiscal year. After purchasing shares in the target company, the acquirer nominates a slate of candidates to run against the current directors. The acquirer generally hires a proxy solicitor, who contacts shareholders prior to the shareholders' meeting, making a pitch for the insurgent slate. Should the acquirer's candidates win a majority of seats on the board, the acquirer will control the firm. And, as with tender offers, effective control can often be achieved with less than a majority. The acquirer may just want to change a few specific policies of the firm, such as the firm's capital budgeting programme or its diversification plan. Or it may simply want to replace management. If some of the original board members are sympathetic to the acquirer's plans, a few new board members can give the acquirer a working majority.

Whereas mergers end up with the acquirer owning all of the target's equity, the victor in a proxy fight does not gain additional shares. The reward to the proxy victor is share price appreciation if the victor's policies prove effective. In fact, just the threat of a proxy fight may raise the share price because management may improve operations to head off the fight.

28.10 Defensive Tactics

Target firm managers frequently resist takeover attempts. Actions to defeat a takeover may benefit the target shareholders if the bidding firm raises its offer price or another firm makes a bid. Alternatively, resistance may simply reflect self-interest at the shareholders' expense. That is, the target managers might fight a takeover to preserve their jobs. Sometimes management resists while simultaneously improving corporate policies. Shareholders can benefit in this case, even if the takeover fails.

In this section, we describe various ways in which target managers resist takeovers. A company is said to be 'in play' if one or more suitors are currently interested in acquiring it. It is useful to separate defensive tactics before a company is in play (known as shark repellants) from tactics after the company is in play.

Deterring Takeovers before Being in Play

Corporate Charters

The corporate charter refers to the articles of incorporation and corporate bylaws governing a firm. Among other provisions, the charter establishes conditions allowing a takeover. Firms frequently amend charters to make acquisitions more difficult. As examples, consider the following two amendments:

1. *Classified or staggered board:* In an unclassified board of directors, shareholders elect all of the directors each year. In a staggered board, only a fraction of the board is elected each year, with terms running for multiple years. For example, one-third of the board might stand for election each year, with terms running for three years. Staggered boards increase the time an acquirer needs to obtain a majority of seats on the board. In the previous example, the acquirer can gain control of only one-third of the seats in the first year after acquisition. Another year must pass before the acquirer is able to control two-thirds of the seats. Therefore, the acquirer may not be able to change management as quickly as it would like. However, some argue that staggered boards are not necessarily effective because the old directors often choose to vote with the acquirer.
2. *Supermajority provisions:* Corporate charters determine the percentage of voting shares needed to approve important transactions such as mergers. A supermajority provision in the charter means that this percentage is above 50 per cent. Two-thirds majorities are common, though the number can be much higher. A supermajority provision clearly increases the difficulty of acquisition in the face of hostile management. Many charters with supermajority provisions have what is known as a *board out* clause as well. Here supermajority does not apply if the board of directors approves the merger. This clause makes sure that the provision hinders only hostile takeovers.

Golden Parachutes

This colourful term refers to generous severance packages provided to management in the event of a takeover. The argument is that golden parachutes will deter takeovers by raising the cost of acquisition. However, some authorities point out that the deterrence effect is likely to be unimportant because a severance package, even a generous one, is probably a small part of the cost of acquiring a firm. In addition, some argue that golden parachutes actually *increase* the probability of a takeover. The reasoning here is that management has a natural tendency to resist any takeover because of the possibility of job loss. A large severance package softens the blow of takeover, reducing management's inclination to resist.

Golden parachutes are very controversial in economic downturns as there is nothing the media likes more than to splash an incredibly generous severance package all over the front pages when a company is in financial distress. This has been the case in recent years when many outgoing executives received massive criticism for their golden parachute deals. A good example concerns the former chief executive of British American Tobacco, Nicandro Durante, who received at least €7.5 million in 2019 as a golden parachute after the market value of the firm had fallen by almost €60 billion.

Sustainability in Action 28.1

Brookfield Infrastructure's Acquisition of Inter Pipeline

In October 2021, global energy infrastructure firm Inter Pipeline unsuccessfully fought a hostile takeover bid from Brookfield Infrastructure Partners.

Inter Pipeline exercised a number of defensive tactics to make the takeover less attractive to Brookfield Infrastructure. These included:

- *Seeking a white knight:* Months earlier, Inter Pipeline had entered into an agreement with Pembina Pipeline Corporation, a similar firm in the same industry, to merge. Pembina offered to pay 0.5 of its own shares for each Inter Pipeline share. Brookfield countered this tactic by submitting a higher bid, which made the Pembina offer unattractive to Inter Pipeline's shareholders.
- *Invoking its corporate purpose:* Inter Pipeline stated that its merger with Pembina would establish a top-tier energy infrastructure company, committed to providing long-term benefits to its shareholders, customers, employees and communities. The company emphasized its devotion towards addressing ESG challenges, including decreasing greenhouse gas emissions, financing renewable energy initiatives and promoting indigenous involvement.

Despite these defensive tactics, Brookfield did not give up on its takeover attempt. It raised its offer for Inter Pipeline several times, reaching C$8.58 billion in cash and shares. It also launched a legal challenge against the Pembina merger agreement, alleging that it was unfair and coercive to Inter Pipeline's shareholders.

In October 2021, Brookfield's perseverance succeeded and the company won its bid. In November 2021, Brookfield's management took Inter Pipeline private and delisted its shares. Inter Pipeline still exists and you can find out what happened to the company at its website.

Source: www.interpipeline.com

Shareholder Rights Plans

A shareholder rights plan (or poison pill) is a sophisticated defensive tactic that is common in the USA but illegal in Europe without shareholder approval. In the event of a hostile bid, a poison pill allows the target firm to issue new shares to every shareholder *except the bidder* at a deep discount.

Perhaps the example of pizza company Papa John's will illustrate the general idea. In 2019, Papa John's introduced a poison pill provision stating that, once a bidder acquired 15 per cent or more of Papa John's shares without the approval of directors, all shareholders except the acquirer could buy new shares from the corporation at a massively discounted price. Dilution of this magnitude causes some critics to argue that poison pills are insurmountable.

Since poison pills are illegal or actively discouraged in many countries, this has led to greater frequency of hostile takeovers, especially by hedge funds looking to quickly take over a company and sell it on at a profit. Outlawing poison pills has also led to some criticism because acquiring firms can quickly take control of a target firm before other, possibly better, bids can be prepared by other firms.

Deterring a Takeover after the Company is in Play

Greenmail and Standstill Agreements

Managers may arrange a *targeted repurchase* to forestall a takeover attempt. In a targeted repurchase, a firm buys back its own equity from a potential bidder, usually at a substantial premium, with the proviso that the seller promises not to acquire the company for a specified period. Critics of such payments label them *greenmail*.

A *standstill agreement* occurs when the acquirer, for a fee, agrees to limit its holdings in the target. As part of the agreement, the acquirer often promises to offer the target a right of first refusal in the event that the acquirer sells its shares. This promise prevents the block of shares from falling into the hands of another would-be acquirer.

Greenmail has been a colourful part of the financial lexicon since its first application in the late 1970s. Since then, pundits have commented numerous times on either its ethical or unethical nature. Greenmail is predominantly a strategy undertaken by US firms and is not common in the rest of the world.

White Knight and White Squire

A firm facing an unfriendly merger offer might arrange to be acquired by a friendly suitor, commonly referred to as a *white knight.* The white knight might be favoured simply because it is willing to pay a higher purchase price. Alternatively, it might promise not to lay off employees, fire managers or sell off divisions.

Management instead may wish to avoid any acquisition at all. A third party, termed a *white squire,* might be invited to make a significant investment in the firm, under the condition that it vote with management and does not purchase additional shares. White squires are generally offered shares at favourable prices. Billionaire investor Warren Buffett has acted as a white squire to many firms, including Champion International and Gillette.

Recapitalizations and Repurchases

Target management will often issue debt to pay out a dividend – a transaction called a *leveraged recapitalization.* A *share repurchase,* where debt is issued to buy back shares, is a similar transaction. The two transactions fend off takeovers in a number of ways. First, the equity price may rise, perhaps because of the increased tax shield from greater debt. A rise in share price makes the acquisition less attractive to the bidder. However, the price will rise only if the firm's debt level before the recapitalization was below the optimum, so a levered recapitalization is not recommended for every target. Consultants point out that firms with low debt but with stable cash flows are ideal candidates for 'recaps'. Second, as part of the recapitalization, management may issue new securities that give management greater voting control than it had before the recap. The increase in control makes a hostile takeover more difficult. Third, firms with a lot of cash are often seen as attractive targets. As part of the recap, the target may use this cash to pay a dividend or buy back equity, reducing the firm's appeal as a takeover candidate.

Exclusionary Self-tenders

An *exclusionary self-tender* is the opposite of a targeted repurchase. Here, the firm makes a tender offer for a given amount of its own equity while excluding targeted shareholders.

In a particularly celebrated case, Unocal, a large integrated oil firm, made a tender offer for 29 per cent of its shares while excluding its largest shareholder, Mesa Partners II (led by T. Boone Pickens). Unocal's self-tender was for \$72 per share, which was \$16 over the prevailing market price. It was designed to defeat Mesa's attempted takeover of Unocal by transferring wealth, in effect, from Mesa to Unocal's other equityholders. This type of activity is almost non-existent in most countries outside of the United States because of the existence of pre-emptive rights. A notable example is Barclays Bank plc and Unicredit Bank, which attempted in 2008 to bypass the pre-emptive rights of existing shareholders in order to raise cash quickly. Not surprisingly, the management of both companies came under intense pressure from institutional shareholders to change their decisions.

Asset Restructurings

In addition to altering capital structure, firms may sell off existing assets or buy new ones to avoid takeover. Targets generally sell, or divest, assets for two reasons. First, a target firm may have assembled a hodgepodge of assets in different lines of business, with the various segments fitting together poorly. Value might be increased by placing these divisions into separate firms. Academics often emphasize the concept of *corporate focus.* The idea here is that firms function best by focusing on those few businesses that they really know. A rise in equity price following a divestiture will reduce the target's appeal to a bidder.

The second reason is that a bidder might be interested in a specific division of the target. The target can reduce the bidder's interest by selling off this division. Although the strategy may fend off a merger, it can hurt the target's shareholders if the division is worth more to the target than to the division's buyer. Authorities frequently talk of selling off the *crown jewels* or pursuing a *scorched earth policy.*

While some targets divest existing assets, others buy new ones. Two reasons are generally given here. First, the bidder may like the target as is. The addition of an unrelated business makes the target less appealing to the acquirer. However, a bidder can always sell off the new business, so the purchase is probably not a strong defence. Second, antitrust legislation is designed to prohibit mergers that reduce competition. Antitrust law is enforced at both country and regional levels. For example, in the UK, mergers are governed by the Takeover Panel (UK regulator) and the European Commission (Europe). A target may purchase a company, knowing that this new division will pose antitrust problems for the bidder. However, this strategy might not be effective because, in its filings with the respective regulatory authorities, the bidder can state its intention to sell off the unrelated business.

Do Defensive Tactics Defer Takeovers?

There is very little consensus on this question, probably because of the differences in merger and acquisition environments. Takeovers initiated in 2014 would be very different from those in 2024. The industries, countries and sizes in 2024 are unlikely to be like those 10 years earlier.

In a recent study, Karpoff et al. (2022) considered 24 different takeover provisions and found that only four had a consistent negative impact on takeover likelihood, whereas one was positively related to the chances a company could be acquired. The four most effective defences were:

1 Directors' duties provisions (the ability of target company directors to flatly reject a takeover attempt as long as a justification is given).
2 Fair price provisions (the acquirer must pay a fair price for all classes of a target's shares, ensuring the rights of minority shareholders)
3 Supermajority vote requirements (see earlier in this section), and
4 Unequal voting rights (see Chapter 2).

The only defence strategy that appeared to increase the likelihood of a takeover was the golden parachute.

28.11 The Diary of a Takeover: Takeda and Shire plc

In March 2018, global pharmaceuticals firm Takeda announced it was considering a potential bid for London Stock Exchange-listed Irish pharmaceutical firm Shire plc. This was the start of a rollercoaster 10-month period for Takeda and Shire that involved shareholder revolts, share price collapses and the downgrading of Takeda's creditworthiness.

With so many bad events, it is surprising the takeover was successful at all. Many bidding companies would probably have backed off long before the actual completion in January 2019. Let's take a look at the main events that unfolded over the next few months.

28 March 2018: Takeda Announces Bid Intention

Over the previous few days, rumours spread across the financial markets that Takeda was interested in buying Shire. As you can see from the price indices (Figure 28.3) of each company, this started to have an impact on 25 March.

Figure 28.3 Shire and Takeda Price Indices 1–29 March 2018

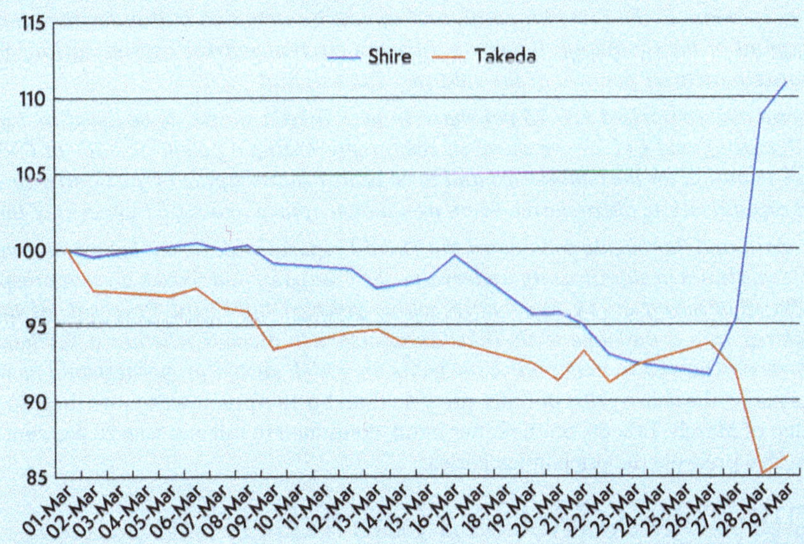

Note: Prices are converted into indices with a base date of 1 March 2018 to show the relative performance of each firm's shares over the acquisition period.

Takeda's announcement stated:

A potential transaction with Shire presents an opportunity to advance Takeda's stated Vision 2025, build on its current strong momentum, and create a truly global, value-based Japanese biopharmaceutical leader. In particular, a transaction with Shire would:

- *strengthen Takeda's core therapeutic areas of oncology, GI and neuroscience*
- *accelerate Takeda's vision to be a leader in specialized medicines that are transformative to patients through the addition of Shire's leading global rare disease franchise*
- *further enhance Takeda's robust R&D strategy, concentrating on key therapeutic areas*
- *reinforce a strong and large-molecule focused late-stage pipeline within Takeda's core therapeutic areas to complement Takeda's own pipeline and discovery capabilities*
- *balance Takeda's geographic focus to align with the market opportunity in the US*
- *drive financial value from a strong combined financial profile.*

The statement also said the company hadn't actually spoken to Shire about a bid, and the bid was at a preliminary and exploratory stage. Clearly, the announcement wasn't what Takeda expected: its shares tumbled on the announcement. In contrast, Shire's share price rocketed by more than 20 per cent.

19 April 2018: Shire Rejects a Third Bid from Takeda

Following the initial announcement Takeda made three bids to the Shire board, all of which were rejected. Another pharmaceutical giant, Alergen, also announced it was interested in buying Shire. Similar to Takeda, Alergen's price fell on the announcement and, as a result, it pulled back its interest.

Shire issued its own press release:

The First Proposal comprised €28 per share in new Takeda shares, to be listed in Japan and in the US through an ADR listing, and €16 per share in cash, representing a potential value of €44 per share and approximately €41 billion for the total issued and to be issued share capital of the Company. Based on Takeda's current market capitalisation, Shire shareholders would own approximately 50 per cent of the enlarged Takeda.

Following a thorough review of the First Proposal with its advisers and a Board meeting on 8 April 2018, the Board unanimously rejected the First Proposal, concluding that it significantly undervalued the Company, its growth prospects and pipeline.

The Board has since received two further proposals:

- *the Second Proposal comprised €28.75 per share in new Takeda shares, to be listed in Japan and in the US through an ADR listing, and €16.75 per share in cash, representing a potential value of €45.50 per share, only a marginal increase to the First Proposal, and approximately €43 billion for the total issued and to be issued share capital of the Company. Based on Takeda's current market capitalisation, Shire shareholders would own approximately 51 per cent of the enlarged Takeda; and*
- *the Third Proposal also comprised €28.75 per share in new Takeda shares, to be listed in Japan and in the US through an ADR listing, and €17.75 per share in cash, representing a potential value of €46.50 per share and approximately €44 billion for the total issued and to be issued share capital of the Company. Based on Takeda's current market capitalisation, Shire shareholders would own approximately 51 per cent of the enlarged Takeda.*

The Board met again and thoroughly considered the Third Proposal with its advisers and unanimously rejected it, concluding that it continues to significantly undervalue the Company and Shire's growth prospects and pipeline.

Following the Board meeting on 14 April 2018 which rejected the Third Proposal, at the Board's request Shire's advisers entered into a dialogue with Takeda's advisers to discuss whether a further, more attractive, proposal may be forthcoming and to understand the basis on which such a proposal would be made.

As each bid was made, the share price of Shire grew so that, by 19 April, it was more than 20 per cent above its price at the beginning of March. Takeda, on the other hand, continued to fall and was 20 per cent below its starting March price. Figure 28.4 presents the price index series.

20 April 2018: Takeda Makes a Fourth Bid

Takeda returned to the table the next day with a fourth, improved, bid. This time the terms were €26 in new Takeda stock and €21 in cash, which took the total bid value to over €19 billion. Significantly, Shire announced that it was 'considering its position', signalling that the deal was coming close to being agreed.

Figure 28.4 Shire and Takeda Price Indices 3–27 April 2018

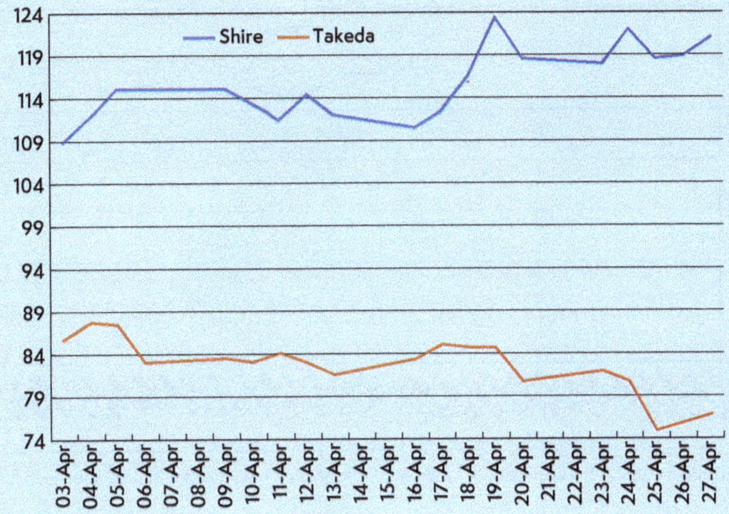

Note: Prices are converted into indices with a base date of 1 March 2018 to show the relative performance of each firm's shares over the acquisition period.

As can be seen from the price graph in Figure 28.4, both companies' share prices fell. The Shire price fall was because Alergen pulled out of the bid process on the same day, which meant that it was unlikely a bid contest would occur. Takeda's price drop was because the bid was looking more likely and concerns were raised about the amount of debt the company was taking on to fund the bid, with some analysts arguing that Takeda was becoming too indebted.

25 April 2018: Shire Accepts a Further Revised Bid

Between 20 and 25 April, both companies continued to negotiate over the terms of the bid before arriving at a final deal: Takeda would pay €27.26 in Takeda stock and €21.75 in cash, valuing Shire at approximately €46 billion.

The market responded savagely, with a 7 per cent fall in Takeda's share price, taking it to a 17-month low.

June 2018: Takeda Shareholders in Revolt

Once the bid was accepted by Shire, Takeda had to persuade its own shareholders to accept the deal. The task wasn't going smoothly and, on 5 June, a group of 130 anonymous founding shareholders and ex-employees released a statement saying:

We are not opposed to acquisitions. We fully realise that Takeda needs to strengthen its pipeline but we want [Takeda] to protect Takeda's 230-year tradition and manage the company in a sustainable and stable manner . . . You are plunging headlong into a massive financial commitment that could threaten the very future of the company. The members of our group fear for the future of our beloved Takeda.

Although the 130 shareholders held a little over 1 per cent of the company, their opposition captured the media's attention in Japan. To successfully get the bid accepted by Takeda's shareholders, at least 67 per cent of shareholders had to agree at a special meeting. For the meeting itself to be quorate, 33 per cent of the company's total votes had to be represented.

The meeting took place on 28 June, and around 90 per cent of Takeda's shareholders supported the firm's proposal to buy Shire.

Over May and June, the Shire share price continued to trend up and ended June over 30 per above its value on 1 March. Takeda was unable to regain its value over the same period. However, after the bid was formally authorized by Takeda's shareholders, both companies' share prices jumped on the announcement as uncertainty regarding the deal was eroded. Figure 28.5 presents the price trend over the period.

Figure 28.5 Shire and Takeda Price Indices 1 May–28 June 2018

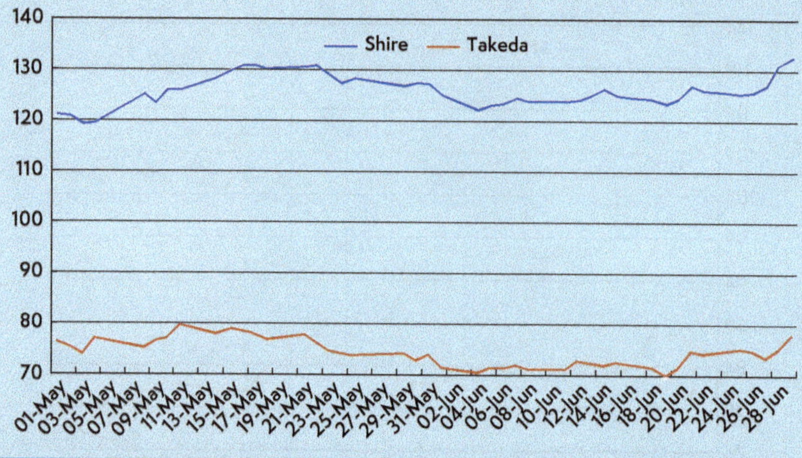

Note: Prices are converted into indices with a base date of 1 March 2018 to show the relative performance of each firm's shares over the acquisition period.

July 2018 to January 2019: Takeda Completes Purchase of Shire

Between July 2018 and January 2019, Takeda went through the actual process of delivering the acquisition of Shire. Acquisitions are an expensive activity and the €46 billion acquisition cost more than $1 billion in lawyer and investment banking fees.

In documents disclosed by the company, the costs were detailed: $648 million to be paid to investment advisers and underwriters for the acquisition; $105 million to be paid to lawyers; $26 million to accountants; $10 million to public relations advisers; and $156.7 million in other costs and expenses.

Looking at the remaining share price movements for both companies before the acquisition, it is clear that Takeda's value did not improve over the intervening months. Shire shareholders, on the other hand, did exceptionally well, with a 45 per cent premium on the March 2018 share price. Unfortunately, Takeda shares were trading at a 40 per cent discount on their March 2018 price.

Figure 28.6 presents the detailed price series between July 2018 and January 2019, and Figure 28.7 presents the full evolution of Shire and Takeda share prices over the course of the acquisition.

Figure 28.6 Shire and Takeda Price Indices 1 July 2018–10 January 2019

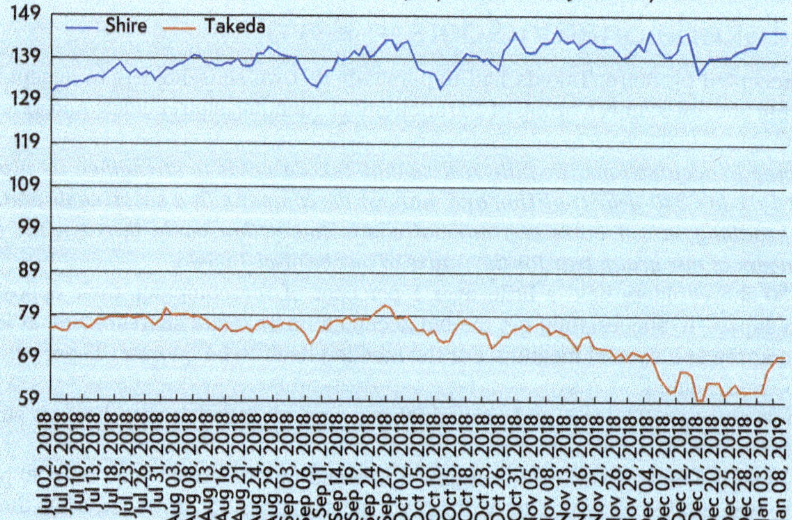

Note: Prices are converted into indices with a base date of 1 March 2018 to show the relative performance of each firm's shares over the acquisition period.

Figure 28.7 Shire and Takeda Share Price Indices, 1 March 2018–10 January 2019

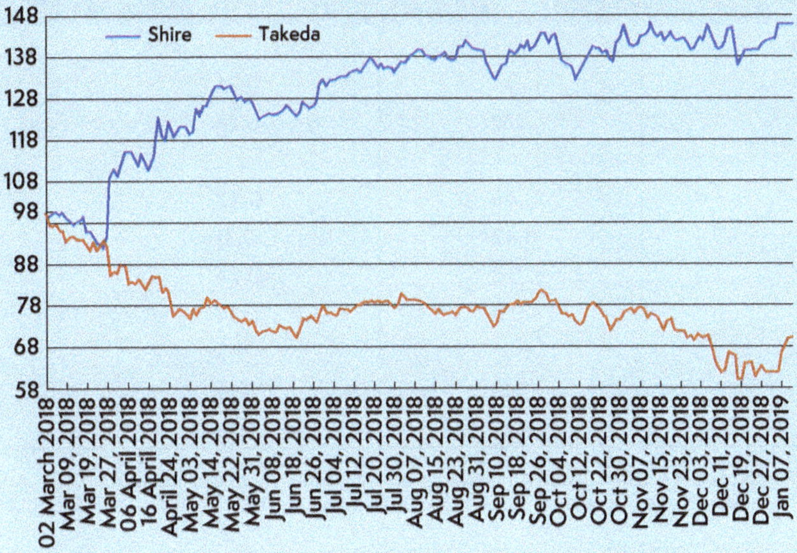

Note: Prices are converted into indices with a base date of 1 March 2018 to show the relative performance of each firm's shares over the acquisition period.

28.12 Do Mergers Add Value?

In Section 28.2, we stated that synergy occurs if the value of the combined firm after the merger is greater than the sum of the value of the acquiring firm and the value of the acquired firm before the merger. Section 28.4 provided a number of sources of synergy in mergers, implying that mergers *can* create value. We now want to know whether mergers actually create value in practice. This is an empirical question and must be answered by empirical evidence.

There are a number of ways to measure value creation, but many academics favour *event studies*. These studies estimate abnormal equity returns on, and around, the merger announcement date. An *abnormal return* is usually defined as the difference between an actual equity return and the return on a market index or control group of equities. This control group is used to net out the effect of market-wide or industry-wide influences.

Consider Table 28.5, where abnormal returns around the announcement days of European mergers are presented. The average cumulative abnormal percentage return (CAR) across all mergers between 2003 and 2017 is 0.46 per cent. This number strips out all the Carhart (1997) risk factors. Because 0.46 is positive, the market believes mergers on average create value. The median abnormal returns are also positive and the percentage of positive CARs in the sample is greater than 50 per cent, providing further support for the hypothesis that mergers are value-creating. Many other academic studies have provided similar results. Thus, it appears from Table 28.5 that the synergies we mentioned in Section 28.4 show up in the real world.

The analysis presented in Table 28.5 considers the effect of mergers on shareholders. It does not consider the effect of mergers on the whole firm, that is equity and debt. Recall from Section 28.6 that mergers may transfer value from equityholders to debtholders because of the reduction in risk of the combined company. Doukas and Kan (2006) show this to be the case for cross-border mergers involving US firms, and find that overall firm value is not reduced from this activity. If we are to consider the announcement returns of bidder and target bonds, we can understand the disaggregated effect of a merger. Given that Doukas and Kan report no change in the value of the combined firm, and Tampakoudis et al. (2018) find positive announcement period abnormal returns, we would then expect announcement period abnormal returns to be negative for bondholders. This prediction is supported by Renneboog et al. (2017) for a sample of bidder and target bonds in cross-border M&As. The bonds of bidding firms experienced a mean cumulative abnormal return in the 10-day window around a merger announcement of −0.049 per cent, whereas the target firm bondholders earned a 0.258 per cent positive cumulative abnormal return.

Table 28.5 Abnormal Returns from European Mergers, 2003–2017

Event Windows	Mean (%)	Median (%)	Positive CARs (%)
Pre-announcement			
(−20,0)	0.3	0.24	49
(−5,0)	0.21	−0.29	53
Announcement			
(−1,1)	**0.46**	**0.42**	57
(0,1)	**0.42**	**0.31**	56
(−5,5)	0.3	−0.24	53
(−20,20)	−0.11	0.36	52
Post-announcement			
(0,20)	−0.18	0.16	51
(0,5)	0.32	0.18	52

Source: Adapted from Tampakoudis et al. (2018), Table IV. This table presents abnormal returns from the results of the event study for a sample of 349 deals made among the 28 European member countries (plus Norway and Switzerland) between 2003 and 2017. Bold figures are statistically significant.

Most research on mergers and acquisitions has focused on US firms. This is largely because the activity has not been particularly common elsewhere. For example, in Europe, merger activity grew significantly only after the introduction of the euro. The exception to this is the UK, where mergers have been commonplace and come in waves, in a similar way to the USA. Figure 28.8 presents the total volume and number of European mergers over time. The number of mergers has grown slowly since the financial crisis, and, although there was a small dip in 2020 during the Covid crisis, total values have stayed high.

Figure 28.8 Volume (€ billions) and Number of European Mergers and Acquisitions by Year

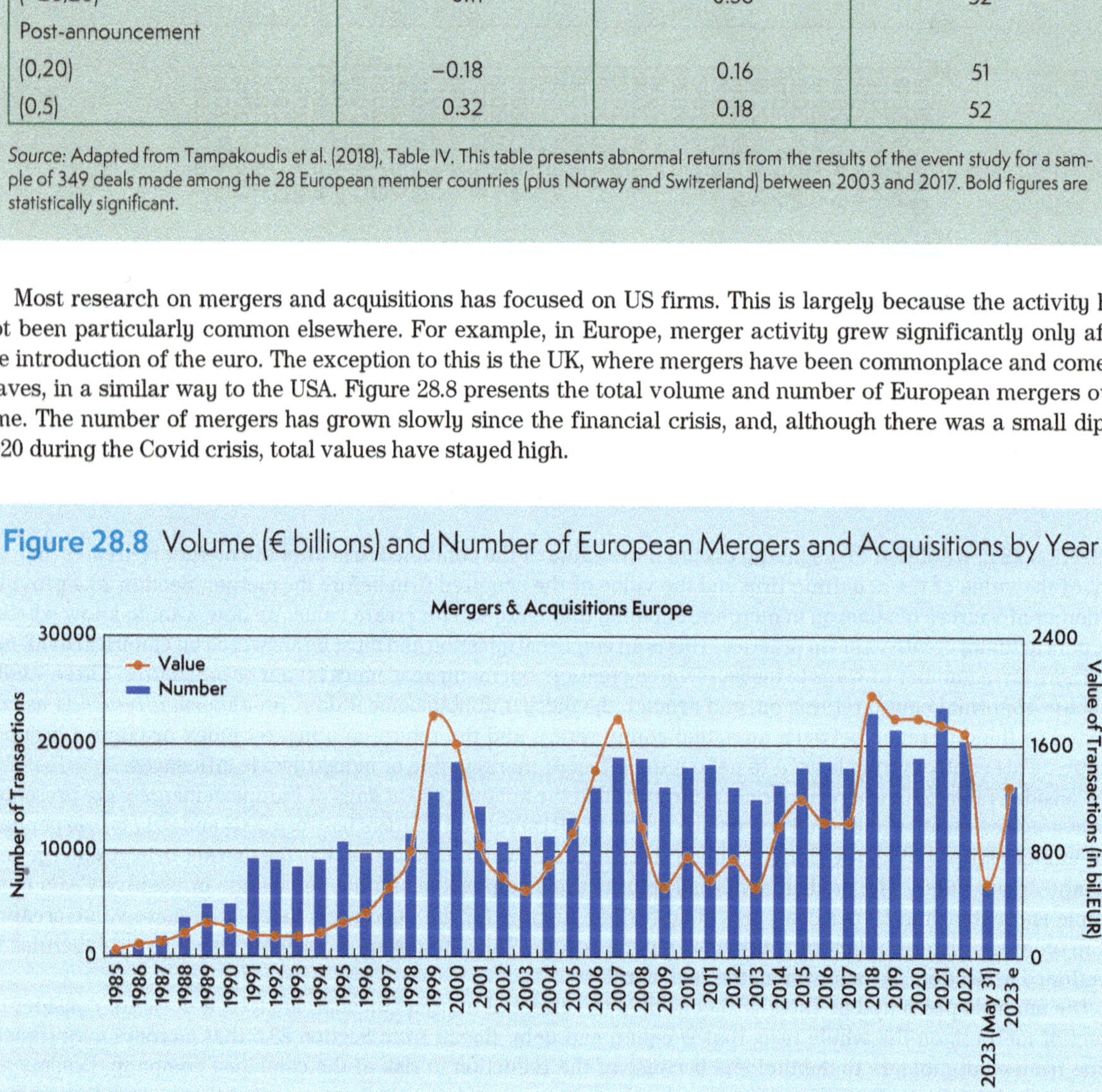

Source: Institute of Mergers, Acquisitions and Alliances.

When one considers the value benefits of mergers and acquisitions, it is important to remember that every country has a different regulatory and legal framework for dealing with acquisitions. In some places, foreign ownership is allowed only up to a certain prespecified percentage of shares. This can significantly affect the success of merger bids.

Europe is particularly interesting because, although it operates under a cohesive regulation system, corporate cultures are very different across the area. Campa and Hernando (2004) show that differences in the institutional environment can affect the benefits of mergers and acquisitions. They found that European mergers in regulated industries or those that were under government control were significantly less successful than in unregulated industries. Renneboog et al. (2017) reported that bidder and target bonds had significantly high cumulative abnormal announcement returns when the target or bidder were in a country with stronger creditor rights.

The results in a table such as Table 28.5 should have important implications for public policy because regulators are always wondering whether mergers are to be encouraged or discouraged.

Jarrad Harford, Mark Humphery-Jenner and Ronan Powell (2012) investigated how entrenched managers destroy value from their acquisition decisions. They found that poor managers avoided private targets, overpaid for firms and chose companies with poor synergy opportunities.

It is important to remember that mergers and acquisitions are often driven by different agendas. For example, the mergers and acquisitions of recent times have been in response to the consolidation needs following the financial crisis – in particular, economies of scale and risk reduction. If you go back further in time, mergers and acquisitions were largely a result of growth into new markets and exploitation of different synergies. Naturally, the performance of mergers in recent times will be different from earlier periods because of their different strategic objectives.

Before we move on, some final thoughts are in order. Readers may bother that abnormal returns are taken only around the time of the acquisition, well before all of the acquisition's impact is revealed. Academics look at long-term returns but they have a special fondness for short-term returns. If markets are efficient, the short-term return provides an unbiased estimate of the total effect of the merger. Long-term returns, while capturing more information about a merger, also reflect the impact of many unrelated events.

For example, Lee et al. (2018) found that value can be created from mergers where both bidder and target have similar human capital. The results are particularly strong when the two companies are in different industries or product markets. Lee and colleagues find that this may be the result of more flexibility in reorganizing workforces after a successful transaction, with reduced labour costs the result. Gokkaya et al. (2023) report that firms with specialized M&A staff have much stronger acquisition performance than firms without comparable staffing.

Target Companies

The Takeda–Shire case study in Section 28.11 illustrates the level of risk involved for bidders who must pay a premium for a target firm. The Shire plc share price returns were strongly positive and this tends to be replicated across many more acquisition examples. Academic research and received practical wisdom show that acquisitions undoubtedly benefit the target's equityholders. Consider Table 28.6, which shows the median merger *premium* over different periods in the United States.

Table 28.6 Takeover Premiums of Successful European Acquisitions

	Mean (%)	Median (%)	Minimum (%)	Maximum (%)
Initial premium	38.19	30.78	−71.93	259.43
Final premium	39.53	32.95	−72.63	266.67

Source: Adapted from Bessler and Schneck (2015), Table 2. Data are for 1,187 European acquisitions between 1990 and 2010.

The premium is the percentage difference between the acquisition price per share and the target's pre-acquisition share price. The average initial premium is just under 40 per cent, and the final premium is not significantly different. Considering the range of premiums is very insightful and captures significant variance over the sample of 1,187 acquisitions. For example, a target company selling at €100 per share before the acquisition that is later acquired for €139.53 per share generates a premium of 39.53 per cent. The results are similar in individual countries and, in the UK, the average premium is 45 per cent.[13]

Table 28.6 shows that some acquisitions have negative premiums, which means that target shareholders must believe that although they will lose in the short term, the longer-term benefits will still lead to positive returns.

Though other studies may provide different estimates of the average premium, all studies show positive premiums. Thus, we can conclude that mergers benefit the target shareholders. This conclusion leads to at least two implications. First, we should be somewhat sceptical of target managers who resist takeovers. These managers may claim that the target's share price does not reflect the true value of the company. Or they may say that resistance will induce the bidder to raise its offer. These arguments could be true in certain situations, but they may also provide cover for managers who are simply scared of losing their jobs after acquisition. Second, the premium creates a hurdle for the acquiring company. Even in a merger with true synergies, the acquiring shareholders will lose if the premium exceeds the value of these synergies.

The Managers versus the Shareholders

Managers of Bidding Firms

The preceding discussion was presented from the shareholders' point of view. Because, in theory, shareholders pay the salaries of managers, we might think that managers would look at things from the shareholders' point of view. However, it is important to realize that individual shareholders have little influence with managers. The typical shareholder, for instance, is simply not in a position to pick up the phone and give the managers a piece of her mind. It is true that the shareholders elect the board of directors, which monitors the managers. However, an elected director has little contact with individual shareholders.

Thus, it is fair to ask whether managers are held fully accountable for their actions. This question is at the heart of what economists call *agency theory*. Researchers in this area often argue that managers work less hard, get paid more and make worse business decisions than they would if shareholders had more control over them. And there is a special place in agency theory for mergers. Managers frequently receive bonuses for acquiring other companies. In addition, their pay is often positively related to the size of their firm. Finally, managers' prestige is also tied to firm size. Because firm size increases with acquisitions, managers are disposed to look favourably on acquisitions, perhaps even those with negative NPV.

A fascinating study[14] compared companies where managers received a lot of options on their own company's equity as part of their compensation package with companies where the managers did not. Because option values rise and fall in tandem with the firm's equity price, managers receiving options have an incentive to forgo mergers with negative NPVs. The paper reported that the acquisitions by firms where managers receive lots of options (termed *equity-based compensation* in the paper) create more value than the acquisitions by firms where managers receive few or no options.

Agency theory may also explain why the biggest merger failures have involved large firms. Managers owning a small fraction of their firm's equity have less incentive to behave responsibly because the great majority of any losses are borne by other shareholders. Managers of large firms are likely to have a smaller percentage interest in their firm's equity than are managers of small firms (a large percentage of a large firm is too costly to acquire). Thus, the merger failures of large acquirers may be due to the small percentage ownership of the managers.

Section 16.6 discussed the free cash flow hypothesis. The idea here is that managers can spend only what they have. Managers of firms with low cash flow are likely to run out of cash before they run out of good (positive NPV) investments. Conversely, managers of firms with high cash flow are likely to have cash on hand even after all the good investments are taken. Managers are rewarded for growth, so managers with cash flow above that needed for good projects have an incentive to spend the remainder on bad (negative NPV) projects. A paper tested this conjecture, finding that 'cash-rich firms are more likely than other firms to attempt acquisitions. . . . cash-rich bidders destroy seven cents in value for every dollar of cash reserves held. . . . consistent with the equity return evidence, mergers in which the bidder is cash-rich are followed by abnormal declines in operating performance'.[15]

The previous discussion has considered the possibility that some managers were knaves – more interested in their own welfare than in the welfare of their shareholders. However, one paper entertained the idea that other managers were more fools than knaves. Malmendier and Tate (2008) classified certain CEOs as overconfident, either because they refused to exercise equity options on their own company's equity when it was rational to do so, or because the press portrayed them as confident or optimistic. The authors find that these overconfident managers are more likely to make acquisitions than are other managers. In addition, the equity market reacts more negatively to announcements of acquisitions when the acquiring CEO is overconfident.

Schmidt (2015) considered the effect of friendly boards in acquisitions, where friendliness is the existence of social ties between CEOs and board members in bidder and target firms. Schmidt reported that board friendliness was associated with higher bidder announcement returns when there were synergistic benefits from the social relationships. In contrast there were lower announcement returns when the synergistic benefits were lacking.

Managers of Target Firms

Our discussion has focused on the managers of acquiring firms, finding that these managers sometimes make more acquisitions than they should. However, that is only half the story. Shareholders of target firms may have just as hard a time controlling their managers. While there are many ways that managers of target firms can put themselves ahead of their shareholders, two seem to stand out. First, we said earlier that because premiums are positive, takeovers are beneficial to the target's shareholders. However, if managers may be fired after their firms are acquired, they may resist these takeovers.[16] Tactics employed to resist takeover, generally called defensive tactics, were discussed in Section 28.10. Second, managers who cannot avoid takeover may bargain with the bidder, getting a good deal for themselves at the expense of their shareholders.

Consider Wulf's (2004) fascinating work on *mergers of equals* (MOEs). Some deals are announced as MOEs, primarily because both firms have equal ownership in and equal representation on the board of directors of the merged entity. AOL and Time Warner, Daimler-Benz and Chrysler, Morgan Stanley and Dean Witter, and Fleet Financial Group and BankBoston are generally held out as examples of MOEs. Nevertheless, authorities point out that in any deal one firm is typically 'more equal' than the other. That is, the target and the bidder can usually be distinguished in practice. For example, Daimler-Benz is commonly classified as the bidder and Chrysler as the target in their merger.

Wulf finds that targets get a lower percentage of the merger gains, as measured by abnormal returns around the announcement date, in MOEs than in other mergers. And the percentage of the gains going to the target is negatively related to the representation of the target's officers and directors on the postmerger board. These and other findings lead Wulf to conclude, 'they [the findings of the paper] suggest that CEOs trade power for premium in MOE transactions'.

28.13 Accounting and Tax Considerations

Many mergers involve companies in two different countries, which presents difficulties in assessing the value of acquisitions. This is because accounting and tax rules can be very different across countries. In recent years, there has been a concerted effort by accounting standard setters and regulatory authorities to streamline the administrative and bureaucratic challenges that face merging firms. In the subsequent discussion, we will try to be as generic as possible about the accounting and tax considerations without losing the necessary important detail. However, given the heterogeneity of regulations across countries, it is impossible to be specific about every regulation in place regarding mergers.

In Europe and many other countries (but not the USA), International Financial Reporting Standards govern the way that companies account for transactions. To improve the efficiency of the accounting treatment of cross-border mergers, the International Accounting Standards Board (IASB) and the US Financial Accounting Standards Board (FASB) have been working together to converge the standards of both systems. This is an ongoing project and developments will continue in the future.

In a similar way that the accounting treatment of mergers and acquisitions is converging to one basic standard across the world, governments have also attempted to integrate country-level tax laws. The taxation of mergers and acquisitions across national borders can be extremely complex and prohibitive in cost, and this deters many corporations from pursuing cross-border mergers. Each national tax system is different but in recent years there have been a number of treaties to smooth out these differences.

28.14 Going Private and Leveraged Buyouts

Going-private transactions and leveraged buyouts have much in common with mergers, and it is worthwhile to discuss them in this chapter. A publicly traded firm *goes private* when a private group, usually composed of existing management, purchases its equity. As a consequence, the firm's equity is taken off the market (if it is an exchange-traded equity, it is delisted) and is no longer traded. Thus, in going-private transactions, shareholders of publicly held firms are forced to accept cash for their shares.

Going-private transactions are frequently *leveraged buyouts* (LBOs). In a leveraged buyout the cash offer price is financed with large amounts of debt. Part of the appeal of LBOs is that the arrangement calls for little equity capital. This equity capital is generally supplied by a small group of investors, some of whom are likely to be managers of the firm being purchased.

The selling shareholders are invariably paid a premium above market price in an LBO, just as in a merger. As with a merger, the acquirer profits only if the synergy created is greater than the premium. Synergy is quite plausible in a merger of *two* firms, and we delineated a number of types of synergy in Section 28.4. However, it is more difficult to explain synergy in an LBO because only *one* firm is involved.

Two reasons are generally given for value creation in an LBO. First, the extra debt provides a tax deduction, which, as earlier chapters suggested, leads to an increase in firm value. Most LBOs are of firms with stable earnings and with low to moderate debt. The LBO may simply increase the firm's debt to its optimum level.

The second source of value comes from increased efficiency and is often explained in terms of 'the carrot and the stick'. Managers become owners under an LBO, giving them an incentive to work hard. This incentive is commonly referred to as the carrot. Interest payments from the high level of debt constitute the stick. Large interest payments can easily turn a firm that is profitable before an LBO into one that is unprofitable after the LBO. Management must make changes, either through revenue increases or cost reductions, to keep the firm in the black. Agency theory, a topic mentioned earlier in this chapter, suggests that managers can be wasteful with a large free cash flow. Interest payments reduce this cash flow, forcing managers to curb the waste.

Though it is easy to measure the additional tax shields from an LBO, it is difficult to measure the gains from increased efficiency. Nevertheless, this increased efficiency is considered at least as important as the tax shield in explaining the LBO phenomenon.

Academic research suggests that LBOs have, on average, created value. First, premiums are positive, as they are with mergers, implying that selling shareholders benefit. Second, studies indicate that LBOs that eventually go public generate high returns for the management group. Finally, other studies show that operating performance increases after the LBO. However, we cannot be completely confident of value creation because researchers have difficulty obtaining data about LBOs that do not go public. If these LBOs generally destroy value, the sample of firms going public would be a biased one.

Regardless of the average performance of firms undertaking an LBO, we can be sure of one thing: because of the great leverage involved, the risk is huge. On the one hand, LBOs have created many large fortunes. On the other, a number of bankruptcies and near-bankruptcies have occurred as well.

28.15 Divestitures

This chapter has primarily been concerned with acquisitions, but it is also worthwhile to consider their opposite – divestitures. Divestitures come in a number of different varieties, the most important of which we discuss here.

Sale

The most basic type of divestiture is the *sale* of a division, business unit, segment or set of assets to another company. The buyer generally, but not always, pays in cash. A number of reasons are provided for sales. First, in Section 28.10 we considered asset sales as a defence against hostile takeovers. It was pointed out in that section that sales often improve corporate focus, leading to greater overall value for the seller. This same rationale applies when the selling company is not in play. Second, asset sales provide needed cash to liquidity-poor firms. Third, it is often argued that the paucity of data about individual business segments makes large, diversified firms hard to value. Investors may discount the firm's overall value because of this lack of transparency. Sell-offs streamline a firm, making it easier to value. However, this argument is inconsistent with market efficiency because it implies that large, diversified firms sell below their true value. Fourth, firms may simply want to sell unprofitable divisions. However, unprofitable divisions are likely to have low values to everyone. A division should be sold only if its value is greater to the buyer than to the seller.

There has been a fair amount of research on sell-offs, with academics reaching two conclusions. First, event studies show that returns on the seller's equity are positive around the time of the announcement of sale, suggesting that sell-offs create value to the seller. Second, acquisitions are often sold off down the road. For example, Kaplan and Weisbach (1992) found that more than 40 per cent of acquisitions were later divested, a result that does not reflect well on mergers. The average time between acquisition and divestiture was about seven years.

Spin-off

In a spin-off a parent firm turns a division into a separate entity and distributes shares in this entity to the parent's shareholders. Spin-offs differ from sales in at least two ways. First, the parent firm receives no cash from a spin-off: shares are sent free of charge to the shareholders. Second, the initial shareholders of the spun-off division are the same as the parent's shareholders. By contrast, the buyer in a sell-off is most likely another firm. However, because the shares of the division are publicly traded after the spin-off, the identities of the shareholders will change over time.

At least four reasons are generally given for a spin-off. First, as with a sell-off, a spin-off may increase corporate focus. Second, because the spun-off division is now publicly traded, stock exchange regulators require additional information to be disseminated – so investors may find it easier to value the parent and subsidiary after the spin-off. Third, corporations often compensate executives with shares of equity in addition to cash. The equity acts as an incentive: good performance from managers leads to share price increases. However, prior to the spin-off, executives can receive equity only in the parent company. If the division is small relative to the entire firm, price movement in the parent's equity will be less related to the performance of the manager's division than to the performance of the rest of the firm. Thus, divisional managers may see little relation between their effort and equity appreciation. However, after the spin-off, the manager can be given equity in the subsidiary. The manager's effort should directly impact price movement in the subsidiary's equity. Fourth, the tax consequences from a spin-off are generally better than from a sale because the parent receives no cash from a spin-off.

Carve-out

In a carve-out, the firm turns a division into a separate entity and then sells shares in the division to the public. Generally the parent retains a large interest in the division. This transaction is similar to a spin-off, and the first three benefits listed for a spin-off apply to a carve-out as well. However, the big difference is that the firm receives cash from a carve-out but not from a spin-off. The receipt of cash can be both good and bad. On the one hand, many firms need cash. Michaely and Shaw (1995) find that large, profitable firms are more likely to use carve-outs, whereas small, unprofitable firms are more likely to use spin-offs. One interpretation is that firms generally prefer the cash that comes with a carve-out. However, small and unprofitable firms have trouble issuing equity. They must resort to a spin-off, where equity in the subsidiary is merely given to their own equityholders.

Unfortunately, there is also a dark side to cash, as developed in the free cash flow hypothesis. That is, firms with cash exceeding that needed for profitable capital budgeting projects may spend it on unprofitable ones. Allen and McConnell (1998) find that the equity market reacts positively to announcements of carve-outs if the cash is used to reduce debt. The market reacts neutrally if the cash is used for investment projects.

Summary and Conclusions

1 One firm can acquire another in several different ways. The three legal forms of acquisition are merger and consolidation, acquisition of equity, and acquisition of assets. Mergers and consolidations are the least costly from a legal standpoint, but they require a vote of approval by the shareholders. Acquisition by equity does not require a shareholder vote and is usually done via a tender offer. However, it is difficult to obtain 100 per cent control with a tender offer. Acquisition of assets is comparatively costly because it requires more difficult transfer of asset ownership.

2 The synergy from an acquisition is defined as the value of the combined firm (V_{AB}) less the value of the two firms as separate entities (V_A and V_B):

$$\text{Synergy} = V_{AB} - (V_A + V_B)$$

The shareholders of the acquiring firm will gain if the synergy from the merger is greater than the premium.

3 The possible benefits of an acquisition come from the following:

(a) Revenue enhancement

(b) Cost reduction

(c) Lower taxes

(d) Reduced capital requirements.

4 Shareholders may not benefit from a merger that is done only to achieve diversification or earnings growth. And the reduction in risk from a merger may actually help bondholders and hurt shareholders.

5 A merger is said to be friendly when the managers of the target support it. A merger is said to be hostile when the target managers do not support it. Some of the most colourful language of finance stems from defensive tactics in hostile takeover battles. *Poison pills, golden parachutes, crown jewels* and *greenmail* are terms that describe various anti-takeover tactics.

6 The empirical research on mergers and acquisitions is extensive. On average, the shareholders of acquired firms fare very well. The effect of mergers on acquiring shareholders is less clear.

7 In a *going-private* transaction, a buyout group, usually including the firm's management, buys all the shares of the other equityholders. The equity is no longer publicly traded. A *leveraged buyout* is a going-private transaction financed by extensive leverage.

Questions and Problems

CONCEPT

1 **The Basic Forms of Acquisitions** Describe the three main types of acquisition and provide a real-life example of each. Which type of merger do you think creates more value for shareholders? Explain.

2 **Synergy** Explain the concept of synergy and provide examples of sources of synergy. Where does synergy come from? Is it possible that a merged company will not benefit from synergies? Discuss.

3 **M&A Waves** Why do you think that M&A activity often clusters in time, causing M&A waves? What M&A waves can you identify from history? Are there any factors that you think are uniquely favourable to M&A activity today? Explain.

4 **Bad Reasons for Mergers**

(a) Many explanations and justifications are made by acquiring (and sometimes target) managers for a merger. Review these justifications and discuss whether they are good or bad for shareholders.

(b) An argument has been made that financial mergers are bad for shareholders because bondholders benefit from the reduction in risk. However, are there situations where a financial merger can be good for shareholders?

5 **Method of Payment in M&As** Outline the two broad methods of payment in M&A transactions. What might determine the method of payment, and what impact does this have on both the acquiring and the target firm?

6 **NPV of a Merger** Describe the main uncertainties that are involved in a merger analysis. Are mergers an ideal activity in which to use real option valuation? Discuss some of the ways in which a real option analysis could be used to value a merger.

7 **Merger Valuation in Practice** Discuss the main steps that are involved in a merger analysis.

8 **Friendly versus Hostile Takeovers** What types of actions might the management of a firm take to fight a hostile acquisition bid from an unwanted suitor? How do the target firm shareholders benefit from the defensive tactics of their management team? How are the target firm shareholders harmed by such actions? Explain.

9 **Defensive Tactics** Review the various tactics that a target firm's management may use when trying to deter a hostile takeover attempt. For each tactic, provide a balanced discussion of whether it is good or bad for the target's shareholders.

10 **The Diary of a Takeover** Compare and contrast a successful merger or acquisition with a failed one. What were the factors that contributed to the success and failure of the deals? Which defensive tactics appear to be most successful in stopping a takeover? Which appear to be the least successful?

11 **Managerial Motives for Takeovers** Outline the managerial motives for takeovers.

12 **Accounting for Mergers and Takeovers** Explain the acquisition method of accounting for mergers and acquisitions. What effect does expensing merger costs have on the viability of a potential merger or acquisition?

13 **Divestitures** Why would a firm wish to sell off its assets? If the sold divisions are so bad, why are buyers found for them?

REGULAR

14 **Merger Drivers** Indicate whether you think the following claims regarding takeovers are true or false. In each case, provide a brief explanation for your answer.

(a) By merging competitors, takeovers have created monopolies that will raise product prices, reduce production and harm consumers.

(b) Managers act in their own interests at times and in reality may not be answerable to shareholders. Takeovers may reflect runaway management.

(c) In an efficient market, takeovers would not occur because market prices would reflect the true value of corporations. Thus, bidding firms would not be justified in paying premiums above market prices for target firms.

(d) Traders and institutional investors, having extremely short time horizons, are influenced by their perceptions of what other market traders will be thinking of equity prospects and do not value takeovers based on fundamental factors. Thus, they will sell shares in target firms despite the true value of the firms.

(e) Mergers are a way of avoiding taxes because they allow the acquiring firm to write up the value of the assets of the acquired firm.

(f) Acquisitions analysis frequently focuses on the total value of the firms involved. An acquisition, however, will usually affect relative values of equities and bonds, as well as their total value.

15 **Merger Rationale** During the financial crisis that engulfed most of Europe, two large banks, Lloyds TSB Group and HBOS, merged in order to diversify risk. Is this a good or bad idea? Explain.

16 **Corporate Split** In 2019, the African conglomerate, Naspers Ltd, announced that it planned to spin off a new company that included its tech investments, ranging from food delivery to auction platforms for second-hand goods. What is the benefit of a spin-off of this type for a conglomerate? Why would another company buy the assets?

17 **Shareholder Rights Plans**

Shareholder rights plans are a common defensive tactic used by target companies to deter hostile takeovers.

(a) Evaluate the advantages and disadvantages of shareholder rights plans for equityholders, using relevant examples and evidence from academic literature and industry practice.

(b) Explain how acquiring firms can overcome or circumvent shareholder rights plans, using relevant examples and evidence from academic literature and industry practice.

(c) Analyse the impact of the legal uncertainty of shareholder rights plans in Europe on the frequency and outcome of hostile takeovers, using relevant examples and evidence from academic literature and industry practice.

18 **Merger and Taxes** Many commentators have argued that differences in tax regulations, especially regarding mergers and acquisitions, have reduced the viability of this corporate activity. Do you agree with this? Explain.

19 **Economies of Scale** Iberdrola, the Spanish electricity giant, has in recent years pursued an aggressive acquisition strategy throughout the world. Companies that have been acquired by the firm include Scottish Power (UK, 2006), Energy East (USA, 2008), Elektro (Brazil, 2011) and UIL Holdings (2015), to form Avangrid. During peak times each firm operates at 100 per cent capacity and, during off-peak times, the average usage of electricity amounts to about 60 per cent of total capacity per firm. The peak periods begin at 9.00 a.m. and 5.00 p.m. local time and last about 45 minutes. Explain why Iberdrola's acquisition strategy may make sense.

20 **Bid Offer Strategies** In 2019, GuestReady, a company that helps Airbnb hosts manage their properties, purchased the France- and Portugal-based rival BnbLord outright. Both companies provide services such as cleaning, laundry, check-in/check-out services, listing generation, price management and other services. Why do you think GuestReady was interested in buying BnbLord? What other strategies could it have followed?

21 **Bid Offer Exchange Ratios** Falcon plc and Thor plc have entered into a stock swap merger agreement whereby Falcon will pay a 30 per cent premium over Thor's pre-merger price of €30. If Falcon's pre-merger price was €40, what exchange ratio will Falcon need to offer?

22 **Calculating Synergy** Assume that ABC plc is planning to offer €30 billion cash for all of the equity in XYZ plc. Based on recent market information, XYZ is worth €20 billion as an independent operation. If the merger makes economic sense for ABC, what is the minimum estimated value of the synergistic benefits from the merger?

23 **Balance Sheets for Mergers: Pre- and Post-merger** Consider the following pre-merger information about firms X and Y:

	Firm X	Firm Y
Total earnings (€)	74,000	35,000
Shares outstanding	21,000	10,000
Per share values:		
Market (€)	25	28
Book (€)	20	7

Assume that firm X acquires firm Y by paying cash for all the shares outstanding at a merger premium of €5 per share. Assuming that neither firm has any debt before or after the merger, calculate the total assets of the combined firm.

24 **Balance Sheets for Mergers: Greenify and Sustaina Merger**

Greenify is a company that provides eco-friendly products and services, such as reusable packaging, organic food, and renewable energy solutions. Sustaina helps other businesses and organizations improve their environmental and social performance, such as reducing their carbon footprint, enhancing their diversity and inclusion, and supporting their local communities. Greenify wishes to buy Sustaina to expand its market share and customer base in the sustainability sector. By acquiring Sustaina, Greenify plans to leverage its expertise and network to offer more comprehensive and customized solutions to its clients, as well as cross-sell its products and services to Sustaina's clients. Greenify also plans to benefit from Sustaina's reputation and brand recognition as a leader in sustainability consulting and certification, and achieve synergies and cost savings by integrating Sustaina's operations and resources with its own.

Assume that the following balance sheets are stated at book value. Construct a post-merger balance sheet assuming that Greenify purchases Sustaina, and both sets of accounts are presented according to International Financial Reporting Standards.

Greenify Statement of Financial Position			
	(€m)		(€m)
Current assets	19,000	Current liabilities	12,100
Non-current assets	32,000	Non-current liabilities	16,900
		Equity	12,000
Total	41,000	Total	41,000

Sustaina Statement of Financial Position			
	(€m)		(€m)
Current assets	6,400	Current liabilities	1,600
Non-current assets	2,600	Non-current liabilities	2,900
		Equity	4,500
Total	9,000	Total	9,000

The fair market value of Sustaina's non-current assets is €10,000 million versus the €2,600 million book value shown. Greenify pays €18,000 million for Sustaina and raises the needed funds through an issue of long-term debt. Construct the post-merger balance sheet.

25 **Balance Sheets for Mergers: Silver Enterprises** Silver Enterprises has acquired All Gold Mining in a merger transaction. Construct the balance sheet for the new corporation. The following balance sheets represent the pre-merger book values for both firms.

SILVER ENTERPRISES			
	(€)		(€)
Current assets	6,600	Current liabilities	4,800
Goodwill	800	Non-current liabilities	5,900
Net non-current assets	7,900	Equity	4,600
Total	15,300	Total	15,300

ALL GOLD MINING			
	(€)		(€)
Current assets	1,100	Current liabilities	900
Goodwill	350	Non-current liabilities	0
Non-current assets	2,800	Equity	3,350
Total	4,250	Total	4,250

The market value of All Gold Mining's non-current assets (excluding goodwill) is €5,800; the market values for current assets and goodwill are the same as the book values. Assume that Silver Enterprises issued €8,400 in new long-term debt to finance the acquisition.

26 **Cash versus Equity Payment** Fresnillo plc, the silver and gold mining firm, is analysing the possible acquisition of Weir Group plc, the Scottish-based engineering firm. Assume both firms have no debt. Fresnillo believes the acquisition will increase its total after-tax annual cash flows by €183 million indefinitely. The current market value of Weir Group is €1.3 billion and that of Fresnillo is €2.9 billion. The appropriate discount rate for the incremental cash flows is 12 per cent. Fresnillo is trying to decide whether it should offer 50 per cent of its equity or €1.6 billion in cash to Weir Group's shareholders.

(a) What is the cost of each alternative?

(b) What is the NPV of each alternative?

(c) Which alternative should Fresnillo choose?

27 **EPS, PE and Mergers** The shareholders of Flannery SA have voted in favour of a buyout offer from Stultz plc. Information about each firm is given here:

	Flannery	Stultz
Price–earnings ratio	5.25	21
Shares outstanding	60,000	180,000
Earnings	€300,000	€675,000

Flannery's shareholders will receive one share of Stultz equity for every three shares they hold in Flannery.

(a) What will the EPS of Stultz be after the merger? What will the PE ratio be if the NPV of the acquisition is zero?

(b) What must Stultz feel is the value of the synergy between these two firms? Explain how your answer can be reconciled with the decision to go ahead with the takeover.

28 **Merger Rationale: GEUK** Green Energy UK (GEUK) is a public utility that provides renewable electricity to the whole Yorkshire region. Recent events at its Windmill Farm have been discouraging. Several shareholders have expressed concern over last year's financial statements:

Income Statement Last Year (in € millions)		Balance Sheet End of Year (in € millions)	
Revenue	110	Assets	400
Fuel	50	Debt	100
Other expenses	30	Equity	100
Interest	30		
Net income	0		

Recently, a group of wealthy individuals has offered to purchase half of GEUK's assets at fair market price. Management recommends that this offer be accepted because 'We believe our expertise in green energy can be better exploited by GEUK if we sell our wind power generation and transmission assets and enter the solar power business. Although solar power is a riskier business than providing wind electricity as a public utility, it is also potentially very profitable.'

Should the management approve this transaction? Why, or why not?

29 **Comparing Cash to Equity Payments** Consider the following pre-merger information about a bidding firm (firm B) and a target firm (firm T). Assume that both firms have no debt outstanding.

	Firm B	Firm T
Shares outstanding	1,500	900
Price per share	€34	€24

Firm B has estimated that the value of the synergistic benefits from acquiring firm T is €3,000.

(a) If firm T is willing to be acquired for €27 per share in cash, what is the NPV of the merger?

(b) What will the price per share of the merged firm be assuming the conditions in (a)?

(c) In part (a), what is the merger premium?

(d) Suppose firm T is agreeable to a merger by an exchange of equity. If B offers three of its shares for every one of T's shares, what will the price per share of the merged firm be?

(e) What is the NPV of the merger assuming the conditions in (d)?

30 **Cash versus Equity as Payment** In the previous problem, are the shareholders of firm T better off with the cash offer or the equity offer? At what exchange ratio of B shares to T shares would the shareholders in T be indifferent between the two offers?

31 **Effects of an Equity Exchange** Consider the following pre-merger information about firms A and B:

	Firm A	Firm B
Total earnings (DKr)	900	600
Shares outstanding	550	220
Price per share (DKr)	40	15

Assume that firm A acquires firm B via an exchange of equity at a price of DKr20 for each share of B's equity. Both A and B have no debt outstanding.

(a) What will the earnings per share (EPS) of firm A be after the merger?

(b) What will firm A's price per share be after the merger if the market incorrectly analyses this reported earnings growth (that is, the price–earnings ratio does not change)?

(c) What will the price–earnings ratio of the post-merger firm be if the market correctly analyses the transaction?

(d) If there are no synergy gains, what will the share price of A be after the merger? What will the price–earnings ratio be? What does your answer for the share price tell you about the amount A bid for B? Was it too high? Too low? Explain.

32 **Merger NPV and Synergies** Show that the NPV of a merger can be expressed as the value of the synergistic benefits, ΔV, less the merger premium.

33 **Merger NPV: Tazza and Bichiery** Tazza is analysing the possible acquisition of Bichiery. Neither firm has debt. The forecasts of Tazza show that the purchases would increase its annual after-tax cash flow by €1.3 million indefinitely. The current market value of Bichiery is €500 million. The current market value of Tazza is €1.5 billion. The appropriate discount rate for the incremental cash flows is 8 per cent. Tazza is trying to decide whether it would offer 40 per cent of its equity or €600 million in cash to Bichiery.

(a) What is the synergy from the merger?

(b) What is the value of Bichiery to Tazza?

(c) What is the cost to Tazza of the share offer?

(d) What is the NPV to Tazza of each alternative?

(e) What alternative should Tazza use?

34 **Merger NPV: Farrods and Redridge** Farrods plc has a market value of €800 million and 35 million shares outstanding. Redridge department store has a market value of €300 million and 25 million shares outstanding. Farrods is contemplating acquiring Redridge. Farrods' CFO concludes that the combined firm with synergy will be worth €1.5 billion, and Redridge can be acquired at a premium of €200 million.

(a) If Farrods offers 20 million shares of its equity in exchange for the 25 million shares of Redridge, what will the equity price of Farrods be after the acquisition?

(b) What exchange ratio between the two equities would make the value of an equity offer equivalent to a cash offer of €350 million?

35 **Mergers and Shareholder Value** Gentley plc and Rolls Manufacturing are considering a merger. The possible states of the economy and each company's value in that state are shown here:

State	Probability	Gentley	Rolls
Boom	0.45	€300,000	€260,000
Recession	0.55	€110,000	€80,000

Gentley currently has a bond issue outstanding with a face value of €140,000. Rolls is an all equity company.

(a) What is the value of each company before the merger?

(b) What are the values of each company's debt and equity before the merger?

(c) If the companies continue to operate separately, what are the total value of the companies, the total value of the equity and the total value of the debt?

(d) What would be the value of the merged company? What would be the value of the merged company's debt and equity?

(e) Is there a transfer of wealth in this case? Why?

(f) Suppose that the face value of Gentley's debt was €100,000. Would this affect the transfer of wealth?

CHALLENGE

36 Calculating NPV Plant AG is considering making an offer to purchase Palmer AG. Plant's vice president of finance has collected the following information:

	Plant	Palmer
Price–earnings ratio	12.5	9
Shares outstanding	1,000,000	550,000
Earnings	€2,000,000	€580,000
Dividends	€600,000	€290,000

Plant also knows that securities analysts expect the earnings and dividends of Palmer to grow at a constant rate of 5 per cent each year. Plant management believes that the acquisition of Palmer will provide the firm with some economies of scale that will increase this growth rate to 7 per cent per year.

(a) What is the value of Palmer to Plant?

(b) What would Plant's gain be from this acquisition?

(c) If Plant were to offer €18 in cash for each share of Palmer, what would the NPV of the acquisition be?

(d) What is the most Plant should be willing to pay in cash per share for the equity of Palmer?

(e) If Plant were to offer 100,000 of its shares in exchange for the outstanding equity of Palmer, what would the NPV be?

(f) Should the acquisition be attempted? If so, should it be as in (c) or as in (e)?

(g) Plant's outside financial consultants think that the 7 per cent growth rate is too optimistic and a 6 per cent rate is more realistic. How does this change your previous answers?

37 Mergers: Bondholder and Shareholder Value The Chocolate Ice Cream Company and the Vanilla Ice Cream Company have agreed to merge and form Fudge Swirl Consolidated. Both companies are exactly alike except that they are located in different towns. The end-of-period value of each firm is determined by the weather, as shown below. There will be no synergy to the merger.

State	Probability	Value (€)
Rainy	0.1	100,000
Warm	0.4	200,000
Hot	0.5	400,000

The weather conditions in each town are independent of those in the other. Furthermore, each company has an outstanding debt claim of €200,000. Assume that no premiums are paid in the merger.

(a) What are the possible values of the combined company?

(b) What are the possible values of end-of-period debt values and equity values after the merger?

(c) Show that the bondholders are better off and the equityholders are worse off in the combined firm than they would have been had the firms remained separate.

Exam Question (45 minutes)

1 Linfrae plc is a computer software development firm. It is considering a hostile takeover of Jaffikake plc, a software distribution firm. Linfrae has been advised by its investment bankers that a combined development and distribution firm would lead to annual cost savings of €7 million for the foreseeable future (in perpetuity). Both firms are financed entirely by equity. Linfrae has 29 million shares outstanding at a price of €4.70 each, whereas Jaffikake has 10 million shares outstanding at a price of €10.07 each. The investment bank that is advising Linfrae suggests that an initial bid with a premium of 33 per cent would be sufficiently high as to persuade Jaffikake's shareholders to sell their holdings to Linfrae. Linfrae has enough cash reserves to fund the takeover bid. If the cost of capital of the combined firm is 20 per cent, evaluate the proposed takeover from the perspective of Linfrae's shareholders. **(30 marks)**

2 It has been proposed that Linfrae plc should bid for Jaffikake using equity instead of cash. Linfrae's investment bankers advise Linfrae to offer three shares of Linfrae for every one share of Jaffikake. What is the percentage premium offered to Jaffikake's shareholders? Evaluate the takeover from the perspective of Linfrae's shareholders. **(30 marks)**

3 Explain what is meant by vertical, horizontal and conglomerate mergers. Review the motives for undertaking each type of merger and provide real examples of each case. **(40 marks)**

Total Marks: 100

Mini Case

The Birdie Golf–Hybrid Golf Merger

Birdie Golf has been in merger talks with Hybrid Golf Company for the past six months. After several rounds of negotiations, the offer under discussion is a cash offer of €550 million for Hybrid Golf. Both companies have niche markets in the golf club industry, and the companies believe a merger will result in significant synergies due to economies of scale in manufacturing and marketing, as well as significant savings in general and administrative expenses.

Bryce Bichon, the financial officer for Birdie, has been instrumental in the merger negotiations. Bryce has prepared the following pro forma financial statements for Hybrid Golf assuming the merger takes place. The financial statements include all synergistic benefits from the merger.

	2024 (€)	2025 (€)	2026 (€)	2027 (€)	2028 (€)
Sales	800,000,000	900,000,000	1,000,000,000	1,125,000,000	1,250,000,000
Production costs	562,000,000	630,000,000	700,000,000	790,000,000	875,000,000
Depreciation	75,000,000	80,000,000	82,000,000	83,000,000	83,000,000
Other expenses	80,000,000	90,000,000	100,000,000	113,000,000	125,000,000
EBIT	83,000,000	100,000,000	118,000,000	139,000,000	167,000,000
Interest	19,000,000	22,000,000	24,000,000	25,000,000	27,000,000
Taxable income	64,000,000	78,000,000	94,000,000	114,000,000	140,000,000
Taxes (40%)	25,600,000	31,200,000	37,600,000	45,600,000	56,000,000
Net income	38,400,000	46,800,000	56,400,000	68,400,000	84,000,000

Bryce is also aware that the Hybrid Golf division will require investments each year for continuing operations, along with sources of financing. The following table outlines the required investments and sources of financing.

	2024 (€)	2025 (€)	2026 (€)	2027 (€)	2028 (€)
Investments:					
Net working capital	20,000,000	25,000,000	25,000,000	30,000,000	30,000,000
Non-current assets	15,000,000	25,000,000	18,000,000	12,000,000	7,000,000
Total	35,000,000	50,000,000	43,000,000	42,000,000	37,000,000
Sources of financing:					
New debt	35,000,000	16,000,000	16,000,000	15,000,000	12,000,000
Profit retention	0	34,000,000	27,000,000	27,000,000	25,000,000
Total	35,000,000	50,000,000	43,000,000	42,000,000	37,000,000

The management of Birdie Golf feels that the capital structure at Hybrid Golf is not optimal. If the merger takes place, Hybrid Golf will immediately increase its leverage with a €110 million debt issue, which would be followed by a €150 million dividend payment to Birdie Golf. This will increase Hybrid's debt-to-equity ratio from 0.50 to 1.00. Birdie Golf will also be able to use a €25 million tax loss carry-forward in 2022 and 2023 from Hybrid Golf's previous operations. The total value of Hybrid Golf is expected to be €900 million in five years, and the company will have €300 million in debt at that time.

Equity in Birdie Golf currently sells for €94 per share, and the company has 18 million shares of equity outstanding. Hybrid Golf has 8 million shares of equity outstanding. Both companies can borrow at an 8 per cent interest rate. The risk-free rate is 6 per cent and the expected return on the market is 13 per cent. Bryce believes the current cost of capital for Birdie Golf is 11 per cent. The beta for Hybrid Golf equity at its current capital structure is 1.30.

Bryce has asked you to analyse the financial aspects of the potential merger. Specifically, he has asked you to answer the following questions.

1 Suppose Hybrid shareholders will agree to a merger price of €68.75 per share. Should Birdie proceed with the merger?

2 What is the highest price per share that Birdie should be willing to pay for Hybrid?

3 Suppose Birdie is unwilling to pay cash for the merger but will consider an equity exchange. What exchange ratio would make the merger terms equivalent to the original merger price of €68.75 per share?

4 What is the highest exchange ratio Birdie would be willing to pay and still undertake the merger?

Practical Case Study

The HBOS–Lloyds TSB merger was one of the biggest in European banking history. Both banks had been hit hard by the global banking crisis in 2008 and the British government strongly encouraged them to merge in order to be safe enough to ride out the forthcoming recession. Both companies argued that there would be cost savings and the merger would be good for both sets of shareholders. In a similar manner, Dresdner Bank was taken over by Commerzbank in May 2009. Look at Commerzbank's share price history since then.

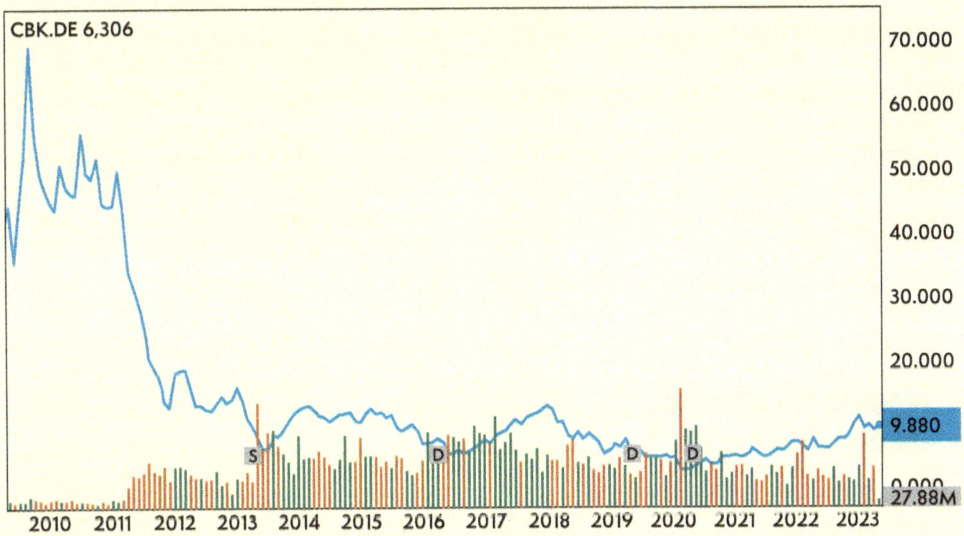

The long-term banking environment has changed significantly. Carry out your own research into either merger and use the merger techniques in this chapter to ascertain, from an *ex ante* perspective, whether the merger was good over the long term for the acquirer and target shareholders. Write a brief report on your analysis.

Relevant Accounting Standards

The main accounting standard for mergers and acquisitions is IFRS 3 *Business Combinations.* For restructuring activities, the relevant standard is IAS 37 *Provisions, Contingent Liabilities, and Contingent Assets.*

References

Allen, J. and J. McConnell (1998) 'Equity Carve-outs and Managerial Discretion', *Journal of Finance*, Vol. 53, 163–186.

Andrade, G., M. Mitchell and E. Stafford (2001) 'New Evidence and Perspectives on Mergers', *Journal of Economic Perspectives*, Vol. 15, No. 2, 103–120.

Antoniou, A., P. Arbour and H. Zhang (2008) 'How Much is too Much? Are Merger Premiums too High?', *European Financial Management*, Vol. 14, No. 2, 268–287.

Bessler, W. and C. Schneck (2015) 'Excess Premium Offers and Bidder Success in European Takeovers', *Eurasian Economic Review*, Vol. 5, No. 1, 23–62.

Campa, J.M. and I. Hernando (2004) 'Shareholder Value Creation in European M&As', *European Financial Management*, Vol. 10, 47–81.

Carhart, M.M. (1997) 'On Persistence in Mutual Fund Performance', *Journal of Finance*, Vol. 52, No. 1, 57–82.

Datta, S., M. Iskandar-Datta and K. Raman (2001) 'Executive Compensation and Corporate Acquisition Decisions', *Journal of Finance*, Vol. 56, 2299–2336.

Doukas, J. and O.B. Kan (2006) 'Does Global Diversification Destroy Firm Value?', *Journal of International Business Studies*, Vol. 37, 352–371.

Gokkaya, S., X. Liu and R.M. Stulz (2023) 'Do Firms with Specialized M&A Staff Make Better Acquisitions?', *Journal of Financial Economics*, Vol. 147, No. 1, 75–105.

Hann, R.N., M. Ogneva and O. Ozbas (2013) 'Corporate Diversification and the Cost of Capital', *Journal of Finance*, Vol. 68, No. 5, 1961–1999.

Harford, J. (1999) 'Corporate Cash Reserves and Acquisitions', *Journal of Finance*, Vol. 54, 1969–1997.

Harford, J., M. Humphery-Jenner and R. Powell (2012) 'The Sources of Value Destruction in Acquisitions by Entrenched Managers', *Journal of Financial Economics*, Vol. 106, No. 2, 247–261.

Heron, R. and E. Lie (2002) 'Operating Performance and the Method of Payment in Takeovers', *Journal of Financial and Quantitative Analysis*, Vol. 37, 137–155.

Kaplan, S. and M. Weisbach (1992) 'The Success of Acquisitions: Evidence from Divestitures', *Journal of Finance*, Vol. 47, 107–138.

Karpoff, J.M., R. Schonlau and E. Wehrly (2022) 'Which Antitakeover Provisions Deter Takeovers?', *Journal of Corporate Finance*, Vol. 75, 102218.

Lee, K.H., D.C. Mauer and E.Q. Xu (2018) 'Human Capital Relatedness and Mergers and Acquisitions', *Journal of Financial Economics*, Vol. 129, No. 1, 111–135.

Malmendier, U. and G. Tate (2008) 'Who Makes Acquisitions? CEO Overconfidence and the Market's Reaction', *Journal of Financial Economics*, Vol. 89, 20–43.

Michaely, R. and W. Shaw (1995) 'The Choice of Going Public: Spinoffs vs. Carveouts', *Financial Management*, Vol. 24, No. 3, 5–21.

Myers, S. and N. Majluf (1984) 'Corporate Financing and Investment Decisions When Firms Have Information that Investors Do Not Have', *Journal of Financial Economics*, Vol. 13, No. 2, 187–221.

Porter, M. (1998) *Competitive Advantage*. New York: Free Press.

Renneboog, L., P.G. Szilagyi and C. Vansteenkiste (2017) 'Creditor Rights, Claims Enforcement, and Bond Performance in Mergers and Acquisitions', *Journal of International Business Studies*, Vol. 48, No. 2, 174–194.

Schmidt, B. (2015) 'Costs and Benefits of Friendly Boards during Mergers and Acquisitions', *Journal of Financial Economics*, Vol. 117, No. 2, 424–447.

Tampakoudis, I., M. Nerantzidis, D. Soubeniotis and A. Soutsas (2018) 'The Effect of Corporate Governance Mechanisms on European Mergers and Acquisitions', *Corporate Governance: The International Journal of Business in Society*, Vol. 18, No. 5, 965–986.

Wulf, J. (2004) 'Do CEOs in Mergers Trade Power for Premium? Evidence from "Mergers of Equals"', *Journal of Law, Economics, and Organization*, Vol. 20, 60–101.

Additional Reading

As the size of this chapter attests, the study of mergers, acquisitions and corporate restructuring is huge. Below is a list of recent papers in the area. Naturally, the categorization of papers is not mutually exclusive and papers do overlap categories. However, hopefully the groupings will aid the reading effort.

The Merger, Acquisition and Corporate Restructuring Process

1 Aktas, N., A. Baros and E. Croci (2022) 'Corporate Divestitures Around Acquisitions', *Journal of Corporate Finance*, Vol. 73, 102189.

2 Aktas, N., E. De Bodt and R. Roll (2013a) 'Learning from Repetitive Acquisitions: Evidence from the Time between Deals', *Journal of Financial Economics*, Vol. 108, No. 1, 99–117.

3 Aktas, N., E. De Bodt and R. Roll (2013b) 'MicroHoo: Deal Failure, Industry Rivalry, and Sources of Overbidding', *Journal of Corporate Finance*, Vol. 19, 20–35.

4 Alexandridis, G., D. Petmezas and N.G. Travlos (2010) 'Gains from Mergers and Acquisitions Around the World: New Evidence', *Financial Management*, Vol. 39, No. 4, 1671–1695.

5 Anderson, C.W., J. Huang and G. Torna (2017) 'Can Investors Anticipate Post-IPO Mergers and Acquisitions?', *Journal of Corporate Finance,* Vol. 45, 496–521.

6 Antoniou, A., P. Arbour and H. Zhao (2008) 'How Much is too Much: Are Merger Premiums too High?', *European Financial Management,* Vol. 14, No. 2, 268–287. **UK.**

7 Arikan, A.M. and R.M. Stulz (2016) 'Corporate Acquisitions, Diversification, and the Firm's Life Cycle', *Journal of Finance,* Vol. 71 No. 1, 139–194.

8 Baker, M., X. Pan and J. Wurgler (2012) 'The Effect of Reference Point Prices on Mergers and Acquisitions', *Journal of Financial Economics,* Vol. 106, No. 1, 49–71.

9 Becht, M., A. Polo and S. Rossi (2016) 'Does Mandatory Shareholder Voting Prevent Bad Acquisitions?', *Review of Financial Studies,* Vol. 29, No. 11, 3035–3067.

10 Bereskin, F., S.K. Byun, M.S. Officer and J.M. Oh (2018) 'The Effect of Cultural Similarity on Mergers and Acquisitions: Evidence from Corporate Social Responsibility', *Journal of Financial and Quantitative Analysis,* Vol. 53, No. 5, 1995–2039.

11 Betton, S., B.E. Eckbo and K.S. Thorburn (2009) 'Merger Negotiations and the Toehold Puzzle', *Journal of Financial Economics,* Vol. 91, No. 2, 158–178. **USA.**

12 Bonaime, A., H. Gulen and M. Ion (2018) 'Does Policy Uncertainty Affect Mergers and Acquisitions?', *Journal of Financial Economics,* Vol. 129, No. 3, 531–558.

13 Boone, A.L. and J.H. Mulherin (2007) 'How Are Firms Sold?', *Journal of Finance,* Vol. 62, No. 2, 847–875. **USA.**

14 Bouwman, C., K. Fuller and A. Nain (2009) 'Market Valuation and Acquisition Quality: Empirical Evidence', *Review of Financial Studies,* Vol. 22, No. 2, 633–679. **USA.**

15 Boyson, N.M., N. Gantchev and A. Shivdasani (2017) 'Activism Mergers', *Journal of Financial Economics,* Vol. 126, No. 1, 54–73.

16 Burkart, M. and S. Lee (2022) 'Activism and Takeovers', *Review of Financial Studies,* Vol. 35, No. 4, 1868–1896.

17 Danbolt, J., A. Siganos and E. Vagenas-Nanos (2015) 'Investor Sentiment and Bidder Announcement Abnormal Returns', *Journal of Corporate Finance,* Vol. 33, 164–179.

18 Deng, X., J.K. Kang and B.S. Low (2013) 'Corporate Social Responsibility and Stakeholder Value Maximization: Evidence from Mergers', *Journal of Financial Economics,* Vol. 110, No. 1, 87–109.

19 Dhaliwal, D.S., P.T. Lamoreaux, L.P. Litov and J.B. Neyland (2016) 'Shared Auditors in Mergers and Acquisitions', *Journal of Accounting and Economics,* Vol. 61, No. 1, 49–76.

20 Di Giuli, A. (2013) 'The Effect of Stock Misvaluation and Investment Opportunities on the Method of Payment in Mergers', *Journal of Corporate Finance,* Vol. 21, 196–215.

21 Dittmann, I., E. Maug and C. Schneider (2008) 'How Preussag Became TUI: A Clinical Study of Institutional Blockholders and Restructuring in Europe', *Financial Management,* Vol. 37, No. 3, 571–598. **Germany.**

22 Duchin, R. and B. Schmidt (2013) 'Riding the Merger Wave: Uncertainty, Reduced Monitoring, and Bad Acquisitions', *Journal of Financial Economics,* Vol. 107, No. 1, 69–88.

23 Eckbo, B.E. (2009) 'Bidding Strategies and Takeover Premiums: A Review', *Journal of Corporate Finance,* Vol. 15, No. 1, 10–29. **International.**

24 Edmans, A., I. Goldstein and W. Jiang (2012) 'The Real Effects of Financial Markets: The Impact of Prices on Takeovers', *Journal of Finance,* Vol. 67, No. 3, 933–971.

25 Ekkayokkaya, M., P. Holmes and K. Paudyal (2009) 'The Euro and the Changing Face of European Banking: Evidence from Mergers and Acquisitions', *European Financial Management,* Vol. 15, No. 2, 451–476. **Europe.**

26 El-Khatib, R., K. Fogel and T. Jandik (2015) 'CEO Network Centrality and Merger Performance', *Journal of Financial Economics,* Vol. 116, No. 2, 349–382.

27 Erel, I., R.C. Liao and M.S. Weisbach (2012) 'Determinants of Cross-border Mergers and Acquisitions', *Journal of Finance,* Vol. 67, No. 3, 1045–1082.

28 Erel, I., Y. Jang and M.S. Weisbach (2015) 'Do Acquisitions Relieve Target Firms' Financial Constraints?', *Journal of Finance,* Vol. 70, No. 1, 289–328.

29 Faccio, M. and R. Masulis (2005) 'The Choice of Payment Method in European Mergers and Acquisitions', *Journal of Finance,* Vol. 60, No. 3, 1345–1388. **Europe.**

30 Fairhurst, D.D. and D.T. Greene (2022) 'Too Much of a Good Thing? Corporate Social Responsibility and the Takeover Market', *Journal of Corporate Finance,* Vol. 73, 102172.

31 Ferreira, M.A., M. Massa and P. Matos (2010) 'Shareholders at the Gate? Institutional Investors and Cross-border Mergers and Acquisitions', *Review of Financial Studies,* Vol. 23, No. 2, 601–644.

32 Field, L.C. and A. Mkrtchyan (2017) 'The Effect of Director Experience on Acquisition Performance', *Journal of Financial Economics,* Vol. 123, No. 3, 488–511.

33 Fu, F., L. Lin and M.S. Officer (2013) 'Acquisitions Driven by Stock Overvaluation: Are They Good Deals?', *Journal of Financial Economics,* Vol. 109, No. 1, 24–39.

34 Hann, R.N., M. Ogneva and O. Ozbas (2013) 'Corporate Diversification and the Cost of Capital', *Journal of Finance,* Vol. 68, No. 5, 1961–1999.

35 Harford, J. (2005) 'What Drives Merger Waves?', *Journal of Financial Economics,* Vol. 77, No. 3, 529–560. **USA.**

36 Hoberg, G. and G. Phillips (2010) 'Product Market Synergies and Competition in Mergers and Acquisitions: A Text-based Analysis', *Review of Financial Studies,* Vol. 23, No. 10, 3773–3811.

37 Hodgkinson, L. and G.H. Partington (2008) 'The Motivation for Takeovers in the UK', *Journal of Business Finance and Accounting,* Vol. 35, Nos. 1 and 2, 102–126. **UK.**

38 Holmen, M. and J. Knopf (2004) 'Minority Shareholder Protection and Private Benefits of Control for Swedish Mergers', *Journal of Financial and Quantitative Analysis,* Vol. 39, 167–191.

39 Humphery-Jenner, M., Z. Sautner and J.A. Suchard (2017) 'Cross-border Mergers and Acquisitions: The Role of Private Equity Firms', *Strategic Management Journal,* Vol. 38, No. 8, 1688–1700.

40 John, K., A. Knyazeva and D. Knyazeva (2015) 'Employee Rights and Acquisitions', *Journal of Financial Economics,* Vol. 118, No. 1, 49–69.

41 Kisgen, D.J., J. Qian and W. Song (2009) 'Are Fairness Opinions Fair? The Case of Mergers and Acquisitions', *Journal of Financial Economics,* Vol. 91, No. 2, 179–207.

42 Laeven, L. and R. Levine (2007) 'Is There a Diversification Discount in Financial Conglomerates?', *Journal of Financial Economics,* Vol. 85, No. 2, 331–367. **USA.**

43 Lambrecht, B.M. and S.C. Myers (2007) 'A Theory of Takeovers and Disinvestment', *Journal of Finance,* Vol. 62, No. 2, 809–845. **Theoretical paper.**

44 Lebedev, S., M.W. Peng, E. Xie and C.E. Stevens (2015) 'Mergers and Acquisitions In and Out of Emerging Economies', *Journal of World Business,* Vol. 50, No. 4, 651–662.

45 Li, K., B. Qiu and R. Shen (2018) 'Organization Capital and Mergers and Acquisitions', *Journal of Financial and Quantitative Analysis,* Vol. 53, No. 4, 1871–1909.

46 Luo, Y. (2005) 'Do Insiders Learn from Outsiders? Evidence from Mergers and Acqusitions', *Journal of Finance,* Vol. 60, No. 3, 1951–1982. **USA.**

47 Ma, Q., D.A. Whidbee and W. Zhang (2019) 'Acquirer Reference Prices and Acquisition Performance', *Journal of Financial Economics,* Vol. 132, No. 1, 175–199.

48 Maksimovic, V. and G. Phillips (2008) 'The Industry Life Cycle, Acquisitions and Investment: Does Firm Organisation Matter?', *Journal of Finance,* Vol. 62, No. 2, 673–708. **USA.**

49 Martynova, M. and L. Renneboog (2008) 'A Century of Corporate Takeovers: What Have We Learned and Where Do We Stand?', *Journal of Banking and Finance,* Vol. 32, No. 10, 2148–2177.

50 Martynova, M. and L. Renneboog (2009) 'What Determines the Financing Decision in Corporate Takeovers: Cost of Capital, Agency Problems, or the Means of Payment?', *Journal of Corporate Finance,* Vol. 15, No. 3, 290–315. **Europe.**

51 Nguyen, N.H. and H.V. Phan (2017) 'Policy Uncertainty and Mergers and Acquisitions', *Journal of Financial and Quantitative Analysis,* Vol. 52, No. 2, 613–644.

52 Offenberg, D. and C. Pirinsky (2015) 'How do Acquirers Choose between Mergers and Tender Offers?', *Journal of Financial Economics,* Vol. 116, No. 2, 331–348.

53 Rhodes-Kropf, M., D.T. Robinson and S. Viswanathan (2005) 'Valuation Waves and Merger Activity: The Empirical Evidence', *Journal of Financial Economics,* Vol. 77, No. 3, 561–603. **USA.**

54 Rossi, S., and P.F. Volpin (2005) 'Cross-country Determinants of Mergers and Acquisitions', *Journal of Financial Economics,* Vol. 74, No. 2, 277–304. **International.**

55 Serdar Dinc, I. and I. Erel (2013) 'Economic Nationalism in Mergers and Acquisitions', *Journal of Finance,* Vol. 68, No. 6, 2471–2514.

56 Veld, C. and Y.V. Veld-Merkoulova (2004) 'Do Spin-offs Really Create Value? The European Case', *Journal of Banking and Finance,* Vol. 28, No. 5, 1111–1135. **Europe.**

57 Wright, M., L. Renneboog, T. Simons and L. Scholes (2006) 'Leveraged Buyouts in the UK and Continental Europe: Retrospect and Prospect', *Journal of Applied Corporate Finance,* Vol. 18, No. 3, 38–55. **Europe.**

Pre-restructuring

58 Anton, M., J. Azar, M. Gine and L.X. Lin (2022) 'Beyond the Target: M&A Decisions and Rival Ownership', *Journal of Financial Economics,* Vol. 144, No. 1, 44–66.

59 Atanassov, J. and E.H. Kim (2009) 'Labor and Corporate Governance: International Evidence from Restructuring Decisions', *Journal of Finance,* Vol. 64, No. 1, 341–374.

60 Botsari, A. and G. Meeks (2008) 'Do Acquirers Manage Earnings Prior to a Share for Share Bid?', *Journal of Business Finance and Accounting,* Vol. 35, Nos. 5 and 6, 633–670. **UK.**

61 Dong, M., D. Hirshleifer, S. Richardson and S.H. Teoh (2006) 'Does Investor Mis-valuation Drive the Takeover Market?', *Journal of Finance,* Vol. 61, No. 2, 725–762. **USA.**

62 Field, L.C. and J.M. Karpoff (2002) 'Takeover Defenses of IPO Firms', *Journal of Finance,* Vol. 57, No. 5, 1857–1889. **USA.**

63 Huang, Q., F. Jiang, E. Lie and K. Yang (2014) 'The Role of Investment Banker Directors in M&A', *Journal of Financial Economics,* Vol. 112, No. 2, 269–286.

64 Jenkinson, T. and H. Jones (2004) 'Bids and Allocations in European IPO Bookbuilding', *Journal of Finance,* Vol. 59, No. 5, 2309–2338. **Europe.**

65 Kisgen, D.J., J. Qian and W. Song (2009) 'Are Fairness Opinions Fair? The Case of Mergers and Acquisitions', *Journal of Financial Economics*, Vol. 91, No. 2, 179–207. **USA.**

66 Liu, B. and J.J. McConnell (2013) 'The Role of the Media in Corporate Governance: Do the Media Influence Managers' Capital Allocation Decisions?' *Journal of Financial Economics*, Vol. 110, No. 1, 1–17.

67 Tsang, A., N. Yang and L. Zheng (2021) 'Cross-listings, Antitakeover Defenses, and the Insulation Hypothesis, Journal of Financial Economics, Vol. 145, No. 1, 259–276.

68 Veld, C. and Y.V. Veld-Merkoulova (2008) 'An Empirical Analysis of the Stockholder–Bondholder Conflict in Corporate Spin-offs', *Financial Management*, Vol. 37, No. 1, 103–124. **USA.**

Post-restructuring

69 Alexandridis, G., K.P. Fuller, L. Terhaar and N.G. Travlos (2013) 'Deal Size, Acquisition Premia and Shareholder Gains', *Journal of Corporate Finance*, Vol. 20, 1–13.

70 Boguth, O., R. Duchin and M. Simutin, M. (2022) 'Dissecting Conglomerate Valuations', *Journal of Finance*, Vol. 77, No. 2, 1097–1131.

71 Custódio, C. and D. Metzger (2013) 'How Do CEOs Matter? The Effect of Industry Expertise on Acquisition Returns', *Review of Financial Studies*, Vol. 26, No. 8, 2008–2047.

72 Devos, E., P. Kadapakkam and S. Krishnamurthy (2009) 'How do Mergers Create Value? A Comparison of Taxes, Market Power, and Efficiency Improvements as Explanations for Synergies', *Review of Financial Studies*, Vol. 22, No. 3, 1179–1211. **USA.**

73 Draper, P. and K. Paudyal (2008) 'Information Asymmetry and Bidders' Gains', *Journal of Business Finance and Accounting*, Vol. 35, Nos. 3 and 4, 376–405. **UK.**

74 Hagendorff, J., M. Collins and K. Keasey (2008) 'Investor Protection and the Value Effects of Bank Merger Announcements in Europe and the US', *Journal of Banking and Finance*, Vol. 32, No. 7, 1333–1348. **Europe.**

75 Harford, J. and R.J. Schonlau (2013) 'Does the Director Labor Market Offer Ex Post Settling-up for CEOs? The Case of Acquisitions', *Journal of Financial Economics*, Vol. 110, No. 1, 18–36.

76 Harford, J., M. Humphery-Jenner and R. Powell (2012) 'The Sources of Value Destruction in Acquisitions by Entrenched Managers', *Journal of Financial Economics*, Vol. 106, No. 2, 247–261.

77 Li, X. (2013) 'Productivity, Restructuring, and the Gains from Takeovers', *Journal of Financial Economics*, Vol. 109, No. 1, 250–271.

78 Masulis, R.W., C. Wang and F. Xie (2007) 'Corporate Governance and Acquirer Returns', *Journal of Finance*, Vol. 62, No. 4, 1851–1889. **USA.**

79 Moeller, S.B., F.P. Schlingemann and R.M. Stulz (2005) 'Wealth Destruction on a Massive Scale? A Study of Acquiring-firm Returns in the Recent Merger Wave', *Journal of Finance*, Vol. 60, No. 2, 757–782. **USA.**

80 Paul, D.L. (2007) 'Board Composition and Corrective Action: Evidence from Corporate Responses to Bad Acquisition Bids', *Journal of Financial and Quantitative Analysis*, Vol. 42, No. 3, 759–78. **USA.**

81 Rajan, R., H. Servaes and L. Zingales (2000) 'The Cost of Diversity: The Diversification Discount and Inefficient Investment', *Journal of Finance*, Vol. 55, No. 1, 35–80. **USA.**

82 Renneboog, L. and P.G. Szilagyi (2008) 'Corporate Structuring and Bondholder Wealth', *European Financial Management*, Vol. 14, No. 4, 792–819.

83 Santalo, J. and M. Becerra (2008) 'Competition from Specialized Firms and the Diversification–Performance Linkage', *Journal of Finance*, Vol. 62, No. 2, 851–883. **USA.**

84 Sheen, A. (2014) 'The Real Product Market Impact of Mergers', *Journal of Finance*, Vol. 69, 2651–2688.

85 Wang, C. and F. Xie (2009) 'Corporate Governance Transfer and Synergistic Gains from Mergers and Acquisitions', *Review of Financial Studies*, Vol. 22, No. 2, 829–858. **USA.**

Endnotes

1 Mergers between corporations require compliance with government laws. In virtually all countries, the shareholders of each corporation must give their assent.

2 *Control* can usually be defined as having a majority vote on the board of directors.

3 The AbbVie–Shire merger ultimately failed.

4 Every country's tax system is different and almost always complex. The best place to find up-to-date information is by visiting the website of the country's tax authority. A good site with summary information on many countries' tax systems is www.worldwide-tax.com.

5 Although diversification is most easily explained by considering equities in different industries, the key is

really that the returns on the two equities are less than perfectly correlated – a relationship that should occur even for equities in the same industry.

6 A dividend is taxable to all tax-paying recipients. A repurchase creates a tax liability only for those who choose to sell (and do so at a profit).

7 The situation is actually a little more complex: the target's shareholders must pay taxes on their capital gains. These shareholders are likely to demand a premium from the acquirer to offset this tax.

8 This ratio implies a fair exchange because a share of Regional is selling for 40 per cent (= €10/€25) of the price of a share of Global.

9 In fact, a number of scholars have argued that diversification can *reduce* firm value by weakening corporate focus, a point to be developed in Section 28.5.

10 The analysis will be essentially the same if new equity is issued. However, the analysis will differ if new debt is issued to fund the acquisition because of the tax shield to debt. An adjusted present value (APV) approach would be necessary here.

11 The basic theoretical ideas are presented in Myers and Majluf (1984).

12 See, for example, Andrade et al. (2001) and Heron and Lie (2002).

13 Antoniou et al. (2008).

14 Datta et al. (2001).

15 From Harford (1999), p. 1969.

16 However, as stated earlier, managers may resist takeovers to raise the offer price, not to prevent the merger.

Chapter 29
Financial Distress

Learning Objectives

After reading this chapter you should be able to:

LO1 Define financial distress and explain its causes and consequences for firms and stakeholders.

LO2 Evaluate the different stages and outcomes of financial distress, such as default, renegotiation, foreclosure and liquidation.

LO3 Discuss the advantages and disadvantages of private workouts versus bankruptcy as a way of resolving financial distress.

LO4 Apply the *Z*-score model to assess the likelihood of financial distress for a given firm based on its financial ratios.

The global economy is in a constant state of flux. What may seem like a sure thing today can quickly turn into a major risk factor tomorrow. The oil and gas industry is a prime example of this, as it has caused many companies to become financially distressed. In 2020, the price of liquid natural gas was at a steady 55p/Thm, causing firms to develop their energy-based business models around this price. However, after the lifting of Covid restrictions and the start of the Ukraine–Russia war, natural gas prices spiked to £8.80, causing significant financial stress worldwide. Companies that relied on energy as a major cost found themselves in financial difficulty, and some even went into liquidation as a result.

Source: Wantanee Chantasilp/123RF

A firm that does not generate enough cash flow to make a contractually required payment, such as an interest payment, will experience financial distress. A firm that defaults on a required payment may be forced to liquidate its assets. More often, a defaulting firm will reorganize its financial structure. Financial restructuring involves replacing old financial claims with new ones, and takes place with private workouts or legal bankruptcy. Private workouts are voluntary arrangements to restructure a company's debt, such as postponing a payment or reducing the size of the payment. If a private workout is not possible, formal bankruptcy is usually required.

Key Notation

Z	Altman's *Z*-score

29.1 What is Financial Distress?

Financial distress is surprisingly hard to define precisely. This is true partly because of the variety of events befalling firms under financial distress. The list of events is almost endless, but here are some examples:

- Dividend reductions
- Plant closures
- Losses
- Layoffs
- CEO resignation
- Plummeting share prices.

Financial distress is a situation where a firm's operating cash flows are not sufficient to satisfy current obligations (such as outstanding trade credit or interest expenses) and the firm is forced to take corrective action[1] (Chapter 19 discusses the costs of financial distress from taking on too much debt). Financial distress may lead a firm to default on a contract, and it may involve financial restructuring between the firm, its creditors and its equity investors. Usually the firm is forced to take actions that it would not have taken if it had sufficient cash flow.

Our definition of financial distress can be expanded somewhat by linking it to insolvency. Insolvency is defined in *Black's Law Dictionary* as:[2]

Inability to pay one's debts; lack of means of paying one's debts. Such a condition of a woman's (or man's) assets and liability that the former made immediately available would be insufficient to discharge the latter.

This definition has two general themes: value and flows.[3] These two ways of thinking about insolvency are depicted in Figure 29.1. Value-based insolvency occurs when a firm has negative net worth, so the value of assets

Figure 29.1 Insolvency

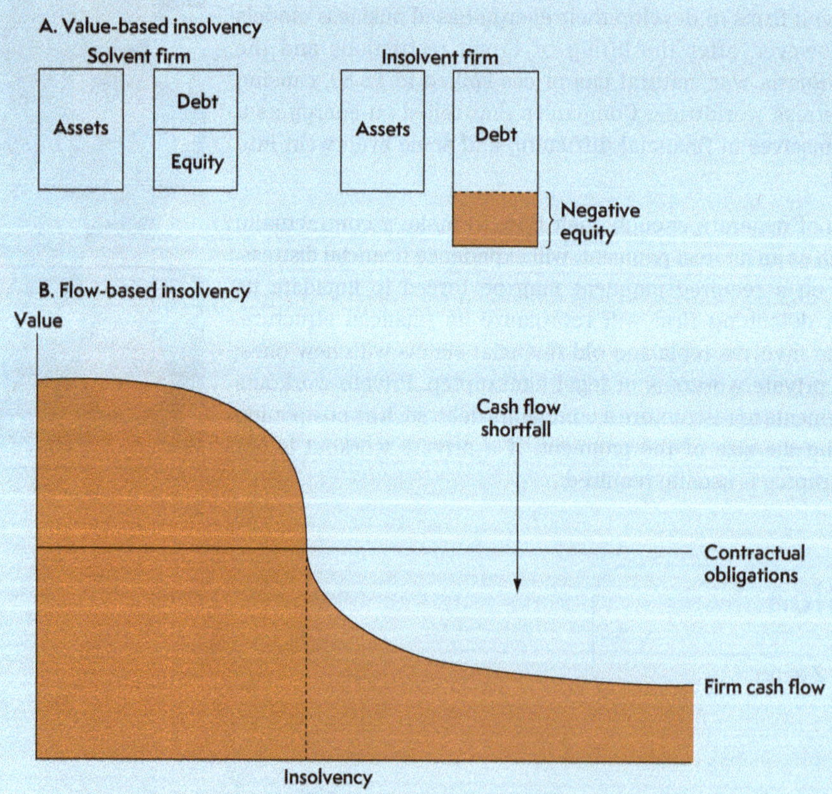

Value-based insolvency occurs when the value of the assets of a firm is less than the value of the debts. This implies negative equity. Flow-based insolvency occurs when firm cash flows are insufficient to cover contractually required payments.

Table 29.1 Large European Corporate Bankruptcies Since 2014

Company	Industry
NMC Health plc	Healthcare
Wirecard AG	Fintech
Thomas Cook Group	Travel
Carillion	Construction
Steinhoff International Holdings	Retail
Abengoa	Energy
Debenhams plc	Retail
Flybe Group plc	Aviation
Arcadia Group Ltd	Retail/fashion
Greensill Capital (UK) Ltd	Finance/supply chain management

is less than the value of its debts. Flow-based insolvency occurs when operating cash flow is insufficient to meet current obligations. Flow-based insolvency refers to the inability to pay one's debts.

Table 29.1 presents some high-profile insolvencies that have occurred since 2014, but every year around 150,000 companies become insolvent in Europe. The reasons are many but can mainly be linked to three areas:

1 The economic or industry environment
2. The company's business model
3 Cash flow issues.

Table 29.2 presents the time series of insolvencies for selected countries. While most countries experienced fewer insolvencies over time, there are some notable exceptions, not least the United Kingdom. The year 2022 was the first for companies to emerge from Covid restrictions amid exceptionally high inflation and energy prices. Many companies could not survive in this harsh economic environment. For example, in the UK, which was also suffering because of Brexit frictions, insolvencies jumped 55 per cent between 2021 and 2022. A similar picture emerged for Belgium, France, Ireland, Norway, Spain and Switzerland.

Table 29.2 Corporate Insolvencies in Selected Countries

	2022	2021	2020	2019	2018
Austria	4,913	3,076	3,106	5,235	5,224
Belgium	9,260	6,533	7,203	10,598	9,878
Denmark	7,818	8,339	5,614	8,474	7,155
Finland	2,656	2,473	2,135	2,597	2,534
France	41,215	27,470	31,036	51,201	53,887
Germany	14,660	14,130	16,040	18,830	19,410
Greece	46	108	102	107	84
Ireland	500	401	575	568	767
Italy	7,164	9,017	7,650	11,161	11,259
Luxembourg	1,054	1,199	1,199	1,263	1,195
Netherlands	1,854	1,536	2,703	3,209	3,145
Norway	3,040	2,688	4,100	5,013	5,010
Portugal	3,869	4,770	5,000	5,071	5,888
Spain	4,755	4,098	4,097	4,464	4,131
Sweden	7,266	6,901	7,695	7,776	7,599
Switzerland	6,799	5,127	4,893	6,009	6,878
UK	23,104	14,820	13,298	18,256	18,733
Total	**139,973**	**112,686**	**116,446**	**159,832**	**162,777**

Source: Corporate Insolvencies in Europe, 2022, Creditreform.

29.2 What Happens in Financial Distress?

There are many responses to financial distress that a firm can make. These include one or more of the following turnaround strategies:

- Asset expansion policies
- Operational contraction policies
- Financial policies
- External control activity
- Changes in managerial control
- Wind up company.

Asset Expansion Policies

If a firm finds itself in difficulty, it may try to reduce the risk of its operations by increasing the size of its business or assets. Asset expansion policies include the full acquisition of another firm, a partial acquisition, setting up a new joint venture, increasing capital expenditure, higher levels of production, or expansion of existing facilities.

With the collapse in the oil price from $100, many oil-producing and exploration firms sought potential targets to merge with so as to reduce their financial distress risk. This led to a wave of merger and acquisition deals in the sector in Europe and across the world. The largest such merger attempt was between Royal Dutch Shell and BG Group to create one of the largest oil firms in the world.

Operational Contraction Policies

Chapter 28 Page 767

The opposite of expansion is contraction and many firms choose to focus on their most profitable businesses during a downturn. Operational contraction policies include asset sales, spin-offs and divestitures (see Chapter 28). Plants may also be closed, production can be cut and employees made redundant. Redundancies are politically very sensitive and many countries have very strong trade unions that can dramatically constrain the flexibility of firms when dealing with their own workforces. Staying with the energy theme, because of sustained low oil and gas prices, the oil industry underwent a significant contraction of operations, including the cancellation of strategic investments and large-scale redundancy programmes of specialized staff.

Financial Policies

Financially distressed firms will definitely face some type of cash liquidity problem. Several remedies are available. One is that the company can reduce its annual dividend. Another option is to restructure its existing debt facilities so that less interest is paid. The equity and debt markets may also be tapped to raise further funding.

Real World Insight 29.1

The Collapse of Flybe Group plc

Flybe Group plc was a British airline that had provided regional flights across the UK and Europe since 1979. It was the largest independent regional airline in Europe and carried approximately 8 million passengers annually.

Unfortunately, in 2023, Flybe went into administration due to several factors that contributed to the company's decline. These factors included:

- Currency fluctuations and a rise in fuel costs, which reduced Flybe's profit margins
- A drop in passenger demand due to Brexit uncertainty and increased competition from low-cost carriers
- A decrease in revenue due to the impact of the Covid-19 pandemic on the travel industry and reduced demand for flights.

Flybe attempted to secure a rescue deal from the UK government, but negotiations failed, and the airline first ceased trading and entered administration on 5 March 2020, putting around 2,400 jobs at risk.

The Covid-19 crisis was a significant contributing factor to Flybe's collapse, making it the first major UK airline to suffer during the pandemic.

After Flybe's collapse, its brand and intellectual property were sold to Thyme Opco Ltd, a former shareholder of the airline, which relaunched the company as a smaller regional carrier in 2021. However, despite this attempt at a rescue, the company could not find a viable way to continue operating and went into administration again in 2023, with no one able to save the struggling firm this time.

External Control Activity

External control activity means that the firm has been taken over or an outside investor takes a significant stake in the firm. A change in external control means that one or more major shareholders sell their shares to another investor with a larger capital base and greater access to capital.

Changes in Managerial Control

The ultimate penalty for poor performance is losing your job, and many firms opt to remove their chairman, chief executive or other directors when they are in financial distress. This will normally go hand in hand with other forms of restructuring.

Wind Up Company

The final, and least desirable, strategy a financially distressed firm will follow is to wind up its operations and go into some form of bankruptcy. Bankruptcy laws differ on a country-by-country basis and, even within the United Kingdom, bankruptcy law differs in Scotland from the rest of the country. Bankruptcy may not always end in the disappearance of a company, and firms may be split, sold to a new buyer or restructured.

Figure 29.2 shows how large public firms will normally move through financial distress. Approximately half of financial restructurings are done via private workouts. Most large public firms (approximately 70 per cent) that file for bankruptcy are able to reorganize and continue to do business.[4]

Figure 29.2 What Happens in Financial Distress

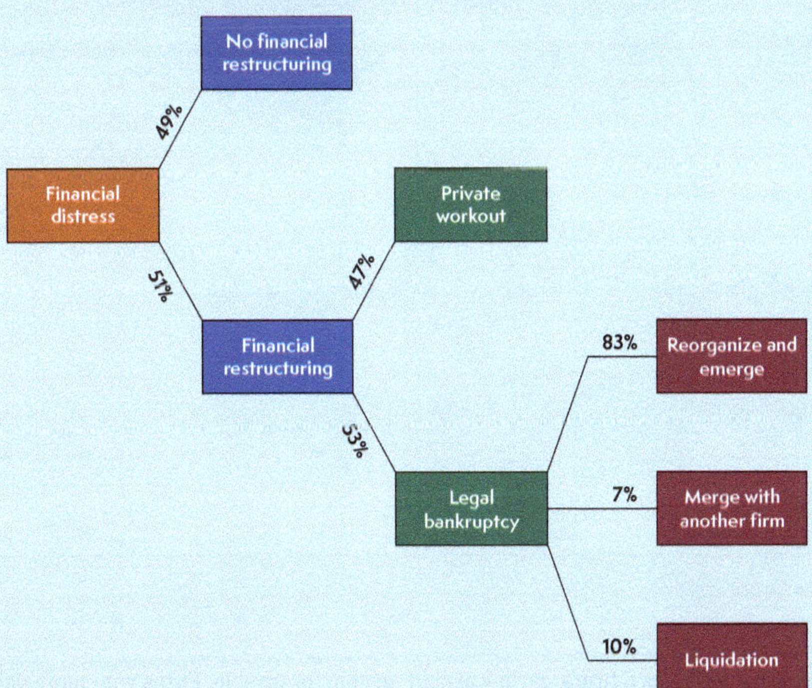

Source: Wruck (1990), Figure 2. See also Gilson et al. (1990) and Weiss (1990).

Firms in Europe follow a very similar process when they are financially distressed. For example, Table 29.3 presents the turnaround strategies of British firms that faced financial distress. The majority of firms reduced their scope of operations and underwent some form of financial restructuring.

Table 29.3 Turnaround Strategies of Financially Distressed UK Firms

Reported Action	Percentage of Firms
Asset expansion policies	
Full acquisition	32.46
Partial acquisition	4.55
Joint venture	8.44
Increase investment expenditures	0.65
Increase output/expand production facilities	2.60
Total	48.70
Asset contraction policies	
Asset sale/spin-off/divestiture	29.87
Plant closure	1.30
Withdrawal from line of business	7.14
Unspecified cost-cutting programme	16.23
Cut in employment	13.64
Total	68.18
Financial policies	
Cut dividend	45.45
Debt restructuring/renegotiation	1.95
Issue debt	4.55
Rights issue	3.90
Placing	6.49
Total	62.34
External control activity	
Non-financial block purchase	0.65
Negotiations	4.55
Unsuccessful offer	0
Total	5.20
Change in managerial control	
CEO turnover	20.78
Forced CEO turnover	8.44
Total	29.22

Source: Hillier and McColgan (2007).

Financial distress can serve as a firm's 'early warning' system for trouble. Firms with more debt will experience financial distress earlier than firms with less debt, and will have more time for private workouts and reorganization. Firms with low leverage will experience financial distress later and, in many instances, be forced to liquidate.

29.3 Bankruptcy, Liquidation and Reorganization

Firms that cannot, or choose not to, make contractually required payments to creditors have two basic options: liquidation or reorganization.

Liquidation means termination of the firm as a going concern; it involves selling the assets of the firm for salvage value. The proceeds, net of transactions costs, are distributed to creditors in order of established priority.

Reorganization is the option of keeping the firm as a going concern; it sometimes involves issuing new securities to replace old securities.

Liquidation and formal reorganization may be done by bankruptcy. *Bankruptcy* is a legal proceeding and can be done voluntarily, with the corporation filing the petition, or involuntarily, with the creditors filing the petition.

Bankruptcy Law

Bankruptcy law across the world is converging to a similar process. However, there are important country-level differences. The UK introduced the Corporate Insolvency and Governance Act in 2020, and the European Union has its 'Regulation on Insolvency Proceedings', which is followed by all EU countries, with the exception of Denmark. This was updated in 2015 to accommodate new thinking on financial distress and recovery. Since bankruptcy law is very similar across Europe, the regulations facing British bankruptcy will be discussed in detail here, followed by an overview of the salient differences in other countries.

Financially distressed firms in the UK can voluntarily or compulsorily be dissolved or liquidated. Liquidation means the firm's assets are sold to allow payment of the outstanding liabilities of the firm. However, this is the very last and least desirable option, and it will be considered only when all other strategies have been exhausted. An alternative is to appoint an administrator, who will attempt to restructure the firm's outstanding claims, introduce a viable business model or look for a potential buyer. It is important to note that when a firm is in administration, it will continue business until a solution (which may be liquidation) is found.

The UK Corporate Insolvency and Governance Act (2020) introduced a new opportunity for firms in financial distress by including a moratorium giving financially distressed firms protection from creditor action. This allows firms to devise a restructuring plan with limited interference from creditors. Additionally, the law prohibits suppliers from halting or threatening to stop the provision of goods or services through termination clauses.

Liquidation

For a firm to be liquidated or made insolvent, a creditor, the directors or the shareholders must petition a court for a winding-up order. If a judge decides there is a case for liquidation, an official receiver will be appointed who liquidates the assets of the firm and distributes the proceeds to all creditors. Normally, creditors will not be paid all that they are due because of direct bankruptcy costs from legal and administration fees.

Priority of Claims

Once a corporation is determined to be bankrupt, liquidation takes place. The distribution of the proceeds of the liquidation occurs according to the following general priority:

1. Administration expenses associated with liquidating the bankrupt's assets
2. Unsecured claims arising after the filing of an involuntary bankruptcy petition
3. Wages, salaries and commissions
4. Contributions to employee benefit plans arising within a set period before the filing date
5. Consumer claims
6. Tax claims
7. Secured and unsecured creditors' claims
8. Preference shareholder claims
9. Ordinary shareholder claims.

The priority rule in liquidation is known as the absolute priority rule (APR).

One qualification to this list concerns secured creditors. Liens on property are outside APR ordering. However, if the secured property is liquidated and provides cash insufficient to cover the amount owed them, the secured creditors join with unsecured creditors in dividing the remaining liquidating value. In contrast, if the secured property is liquidated for proceeds greater than the secured claim, the net proceeds are used to pay unsecured creditors and others.

Example 29.1

APR

The B.O. Deodorant Company is to be liquidated. Its liquidating value is £2.7 million. Bonds worth £1.5 million are secured by a mortgage on the B.O. Deodorant Company corporate headquarters building, which is sold for £1 million; £200,000 is used to cover administrative costs and other claims (including unpaid wages, pension benefits, consumer claims and taxes). After paying £200,000 to the administrative priority claims, the amount available to pay secured and unsecured creditors is £2.5 million. This is less than the amount of unpaid debt of £4 million.

Under APR, all creditors must be paid before shareholders, and the mortgage bondholders have first claim on the £1 million obtained from the sale of the headquarters building.

The trustee has proposed the following distribution:

Type of Claim		Prior Claim (£)	Cash Received Under Liquidation (£)
Bonds (secured by mortgage)		1,500,000	1,500,000
Subordinated debentures		2,500,000	1,000,000
Ordinary shareholders		10,000,000	0
Total		14,000,000	2,500,000
Calculation of the Distribution			
Cash received from sale of assets available for distribution			2,500,000
Cash paid to secured bondholders on sale of mortgaged property			1,000,000
Available to bond and debenture holders			1,500,000
Total claims remaining (£4,000,000 less payment of £1,000,000 on secured bonds)			3,000,000
Distribution of remaining £1,500,000 to cover total remaining claims of £3,000,000			
		Claim on Liquidation	
Type of Claim Remaining		**Proceeds (£)**	**Cash Received (£)**
Bonds		500,000	500,000
Debentures		2,500,000	1,000,000
Total		3,000,000	1,500,000

Administration

When a company enters administration, the administrator will attempt to restructure the company's liabilities, look for a buyer or break up the company into viable parts. Possible strategies also include exchanging debt for equity, which allows the financially distressed firm to dispense with paying interest on debt and at the same time gives the creditor a stake in the company should it recover.

The legal agreement that details how the firm's liabilities are to be restructured is known as a company voluntary agreement (CVA). If creditors reject the CVA or the company does not submit a CVA to the court, the judge can give the corporation an extension during which it must come up with an acceptable plan or ask the creditors to come up with their own reorganization plan. In most cases, at least one extension is granted. Under UK bankruptcy law, a CVA will be accepted if at least 75 per cent of the company's claimholders, including shareholders, vote in favour of it. Once accepted, the agreement is legally binding.

In Scotland, bankruptcy law is slightly more complex. In addition to administration and insolvency procedures, firms may also go into receivership. This is also a characteristic of bankruptcy law in England and Wales for firms that have outstanding securities issued before 2003. The differences between administration and receivership are important. When in administration, the financially distressed firm is legally protected from its creditors while a CVA is prepared. An insolvency practitioner, such as an accounting firm, is normally appointed to run the business while the agreement is being drawn up. A firm will go into receivership if its creditors do not believe that the company can recover and repay its liabilities. A receiver – again normally an accounting firm – will thus be appointed to sell the assets of the firm so that the creditors can be paid.

Example 29.2

Suppose B.O. Deodorant Co. decides to go into administration and reorganize. Generally, senior claims are honoured in full before various other claims receive anything. Assume that the 'going concern' value of B.O. Deodorant Co. is £3 million and that its statement of financial position is as shown:

	£
Assets	3,000,000
Liabilities	
Mortgage bonds	1,500,000
Subordinated debentures	2,500,000
Shareholders' equity	−1,000,000

The firm has proposed the following reorganization plan:

Old Security	Old Claim (£)	New Claim with Reorganization Plan (£)
Mortgage bonds	1,500,000	1,500,000
Subordinated debentures	2,500,000	1,500,000

and a distribution of new securities under a new claim with this reorganization plan:

Old Security	Received under Proposed Reorganization Plan
Mortgage bonds	£1,000,000 in 9% senior debentures
	£500,000 in 11% subordinated debentures
Debentures	£1,000,000 in 8% preference shares
	£500,000 in ordinary shares

However, it will be difficult for the firm to convince secured creditors (mortgage bonds) to accept unsecured debentures of equal face value. In addition, the corporation may wish to allow the old shareholders to retain some participation in the firm. Needless to say, this would be a violation of the absolute priority rule, and the holders of the debentures would not be happy.

Bankruptcy in Other Countries

Bankruptcy procedures in most countries follow the same model as that in the United Kingdom. In the United States, financially distressed firms may file for US Chapter 11 bankruptcy (equivalent to administration) or Chapter 7 bankruptcy (equivalent to liquidation). All other aspects of the system are practically the same.

Countries in the European Union follow the 2015 amended version of 'Regulation on Insolvency Proceedings'. Some country-level differences do exist, however. France has two types of bankruptcy proceedings and these were updated in 2015. The first stage involves out-of-court hearings. These are voluntary and designed to facilitate a resolution of the financial distress by working out a solution that suits the company and its major creditors. If the hearings cannot resolve the situation, a petition will be made to a commercial court to restructure the company's liabilities, organize a sale of assets or liquidate the firm.

South Africa follows a similar system to other countries; there is no administration process. Thus, creditors, shareholders or the company itself will go directly to the South African High Court to request that the firm be placed in liquidation. The process is then worked through the system, and restructuring or winding up may be an outcome of this process.

In Their Own Words

Edward I. Altman* on Corporate Financial Distress and Bankruptcy

Corporate distress and bankruptcy is no longer a niche area of corporate evolution. The average company is far riskier today than it was just two decades ago, and the roles of the bankruptcy courts and restructuring specialists have never been more important. Financial distress of private and public entities throughout the world is a frequent occurrence, with important implications for their many stakeholders. While the role of corporate bankruptcy laws is clear – either to provide a legal procedure that permits firms, which have temporary liquidity problems, to restructure and emerge successfully as continuing entities, or to provide an orderly process to liquidate assets for the benefit of creditors before asset values are dissipated – bankruptcy laws differ markedly from country to country. The differences, however, are shrinking as a number of countries are adopting changes in their bankruptcy codes to become closer to the US Chapter 11 process.

It is generally agreed that the US Chapter 11 provisions under the Bankruptcy Code of 2005 provide the most protection for bankrupt firms' assets and result in a greater likelihood of successful reorganization than is found in other countries where liquidation and sale of the assets for the benefit of creditors is more likely to be the result. But the US code's process can be lengthy (averaging more than a year, except where a sufficient number of creditors agree in advance via a prepackaged Chapter 11) and expensive, and the reorganized entity is not always successful in avoiding subsequent distress. If the reorganization is not successful, then liquidation under Chapter 7 usually ensues.

The bankruptcy process in the industrialized world outside the United States strongly favours senior creditors, who obtain control of the firm and seek to enforce greater adherence to debt contracts. The UK process, for example, is speedy and less costly, but the reduced costs can result in undesirable liquidations, unemployment and underinvestment. The new bankruptcy code in Germany attempts to reduce the considerable power of secured creditors, but it is still closer to the UK system, and the changes in Italy and China are as yet untested. Changes to the Insolvency Act in India represent a case where the new regime is having a measurable impact.

Regardless of the location, one of the objectives of bankruptcy and other distressed workout arrangements is that creditors and other suppliers of capital clearly know their rights and expected recoveries in the event of a distressed situation. When these are not transparent and/or are based on outdated processes, with arbitrary and possibly corrupt outcomes, then the entire economic system suffers and growth is inhibited. Such is the case in several emerging market countries. Revision of these outdated systems should be a priority.

**Edward I. Altman is Max L. Heine Professor of Finance, NYU Stern School of Business. He is widely recognized as a world expert on bankruptcy and credit analysis, as well as the distressed debt and high-yield bond markets.*

29.4 Private Workout or Bankruptcy: Which is Best?

A firm that defaults on its debt payments will need to restructure its financial claims. The firm will have two choices: formal bankruptcy or private workout. Section 29.3 described two types of formal bankruptcy: bankruptcy liquidation and bankruptcy reorganization. This section compares private workouts with bankruptcy reorganizations. Both types of financial restructuring involve exchanging new financial claims for old financial claims. Usually senior debt is replaced with junior debt and debt is replaced with equity. Much recent academic research has described what happens in private workouts and formal bankruptcies.[5]

- Historically, half of financial restructurings have been private, but recently formal bankruptcy has dominated.
- Firms that emerge from private workouts experience share price increases that are much greater than those for firms emerging from formal bankruptcies.
- The direct costs of private workouts are much less than the costs of formal bankruptcies.
- Top management usually loses pay and sometimes jobs in both private workouts and formal bankruptcies.

These facts, when taken together, seem to suggest that a private workout is much better than a formal bankruptcy. We then ask: Why do firms ever use formal bankruptcies to restructure?

The Marginal Firm

For the average firm, a formal bankruptcy is more costly than a private workout, but for some firms formal bankruptcy is better. Formal bankruptcy allows firms to issue debt that is senior to all previously incurred debt. This new debt is 'debtor in possession' (DIP) debt. For firms that need a temporary injection of cash, DIP debt makes bankruptcy reorganization an attractive alternative to a private workout. There are some tax advantages to bankruptcy. Firms do not lose tax carry-forwards in bankruptcy, and the tax treatment of the cancellation of indebtedness is better in bankruptcy. Also, interest on pre-bankruptcy unsecured debt stops accruing in formal bankruptcy.

Holdouts

Bankruptcy is usually better for equity investors than it is for the creditors. Using DIP debt and stopping pre-bankruptcy interest on unsecured debt helps the shareholders and hurts the creditors. As a consequence, equity investors can usually hold out for a better deal in bankruptcy. The absolute priority rule, which favours creditors over equity investors, is usually violated in formal bankruptcies. One study found that in 81 per cent of recent bankruptcies the equity investor obtained some compensation.[6] When a firm is in administration, the creditors are often forced to give up some of their seniority rights to get management and the equity investors to agree to a deal.

Complexity

A firm with a complicated capital structure will have more trouble putting together a private workout. Firms with secured creditors and trade creditors will usually use formal bankruptcy because it is too hard to reach an agreement with many different types of creditors.

Lack of Information

There is an inherent conflict of interest between equity investors and creditors, and this conflict is accentuated when both have incomplete information about the circumstances of financial distress. When a firm initially experiences a cash flow shortfall, it may not know whether the shortfall is permanent or temporary. If the shortfall is permanent, creditors will push for a formal reorganization or liquidation. However, if the cash flow shortfall is temporary, formal reorganization or liquidation may not be necessary. Equity investors will push for this viewpoint. This conflict of interest cannot easily be resolved.

These last two points are especially important. They suggest that financial distress will be more expensive (cheaper) if complexity is high (low) and information is incomplete (complete). Complexity and lack of information make cheap workouts less likely.

Institutional Factors

Most research on corporate bankruptcies has looked at single countries, such as the United States and United Kingdom. However, an examination of only one country can mask the effect of important institutional factors that relate to the legal and corporate system. Davydenko and Franks (2008) look at the French, German and British systems of bankruptcy, and investigate whether their country-specific regulations impact upon the likelihood of firms going into and surviving formal administration.

Davydenko and Franks found that banks required higher levels of collateral when lending to French companies, to offset the lower likelihood of receiving outstanding debts in the event of a default. Moreover, recovery rates (i.e. the percentage of outstanding debts that are received by creditors) are significantly higher in the United Kingdom (92 per cent) than in Germany (67 per cent) or France (56 per cent). Interestingly, British firms are more likely to survive administration because their creditors, normally banks, are more likely to work with the financially distressed company to see it through the administration period.

Sustainability in Action 29.1

The Fall of Abraaj Group: How a Sustainability Champion Collapsed

The Abraaj Group, formerly the biggest private equity firm in emerging markets, prided itself on its dedication to sustainable investing. Established in 2002, the Dubai-based company had a global presence and specialized in impact investing, concentrating on industries such as healthcare, education, energy and climate change. Abraaj invested in more than 30 sectors, with a goal of achieving positive social and environmental outcomes as well as financial returns.

However, in 2018, allegations of financial misconduct surfaced, putting Abraaj's reputation under scrutiny. The company was accused of misusing investor funds, leading to a significant loss of confidence among its investors, including high-profile organizations such as the Bill & Melinda Gates Foundation. The scandal resulted in the firm's collapse and tarnished its sustainability credentials.

Despite its commitment to socially responsible investments, Abraaj failed to adhere to the fundamental principles of transparency, accountability and good governance, which are critical to sustainable business practices. The mishandling of funds, particularly those allotted to its healthcare fund, stood in stark contrast to its sustainability commitments, highlighting the significance of robust financial management and operational integrity in sustainable investing.

29.5 Predicting Financial Distress: The Z-score Model

Many potential lenders use credit scoring models to assess the creditworthiness of prospective borrowers. The general idea is to find statistical factors that enable the lenders to discriminate between good and bad credit risks. To put it more precisely, lenders want to identify attributes of the borrower that can be used to predict default or bankruptcy.

Edward Altman (1993) has developed a model using financial statement ratios and multiple discriminant analyses to predict bankruptcy for publicly traded manufacturing firms. The resultant model for US companies is of the form:

$$\begin{aligned} Z = 3.3\frac{\text{EBIT}}{\text{Total assets}} &+ 1.2\frac{\text{Net working capital}}{\text{Total assets}} \\ &+ 1.0\frac{\text{Sales}}{\text{Total assets}} + \frac{\text{Market value of equity}}{\text{Book value of debt}} \\ &+ 1.4\frac{\text{Accumulated retained earnings}}{\text{Total assets}} \end{aligned}$$

where Z is an index of bankruptcy.

A score of Z less than 2.675 indicates that a firm has a 95 per cent chance of becoming bankrupt within one year. However, Altman's results show that, in practice, scores between 1.81 and 2.99 should be thought of as a grey area. In actual use, bankruptcy would be predicted if $Z \leq 1.81$ and non-bankruptcy if $Z \geq 2.99$. Altman shows that bankrupt firms and non-bankrupt firms have very different financial profiles one year before bankruptcy. These different financial profits are the key intuition behind the Z-score model and are depicted in Table 29.4.

Table 29.4 Financial Statement Ratios One Year Before Bankruptcy: Manufacturing Firms

	Bankrupt Firms (%)	Non-bankrupt Firms (%)
$\frac{\text{Net working capital}}{\text{Total assets}}$	−6.1	41.4
$\frac{\text{Accumulated retained earnings}}{\text{Total assets}}$	−62.6	35.5
$\frac{\text{EBIT}}{\text{Total assets}}$	−31.8	15.4
$\frac{\text{Market value of equity}}{\text{Total liabilities}}$	40.1	247.7
$\frac{\text{Sales}}{\text{Total assets}}$	150	190

Source: Altman (1993), Table 3.1, p. 109.

Altman's original Z-score model requires a firm to have publicly traded equity and be a manufacturer. He uses a revised model to make it applicable for private firms and non-manufacturers. The resulting model for non-manufacturing and emerging market firms is this:

$$Z = 6.56\frac{\text{Net working capital}}{\text{Total assets}} + 3.26\frac{\text{Accumulated retained earnings}}{\text{Total assets}} + 6.72\frac{\text{EBIT}}{\text{Total assets}} + 1.05\frac{\text{Book value of equity}}{\text{Total liabilities}}$$

where $Z < 1.1$ indicates a bankruptcy prediction, $1.1 \geq Z \leq 2.60$ indicates a grey area and $Z > 2.60$ indicates no bankruptcy.

The resulting model for private firms is given below:

$$Z = 0.717\frac{\text{Net working capital}}{\text{Total assets}} + 0.847\frac{\text{Accumulated retained earnings}}{\text{Total assets}} + 3.10\frac{\text{EBIT}}{\text{Total assets}} + 0.420\frac{\text{Book value of equity}}{\text{Total liabilities}} + 0.998\frac{\text{Sales}}{\text{Total assets}}$$

where $Z < 1.23$ indicates a bankruptcy prediction, $1.23 \geq Z \leq 2.90$ indicates a grey area and $Z > 2.90$ indicates no bankruptcy.

Real World Insight 29.2

Carillion plc

In 2018, the UK's largest ever trading liquidation took place with the multinational facilities management and construction firm, Carillion. Carillion was a London Stock Exchange listed firm with more than 40,000 employees worldwide. When it was liquidated it owed nearly £7 billion.

Could we have predicted Carillion's demise using Altman's Z-score? Recall that the threshold for financial distress for a listed company is $Z < 1.81$.

	2017	2016	2015	2014	2013	2012
Z-score	1.20	1.35	1.64	1.46	1.53	1.59

In each of the six years before the collapse of Carillion, its Z-score was in the red territory and should have raised concerns among investors. Decomposing the final Z-score of 1.20 into its component parts gives more insight into the problems facing Carillion.

Net Working Capital/Total Assets	Accumulated Retained Earnings/ Total Assets	EBIT/ Total Assets	Market Value of Equity/Total Liabilities	Sales/ Total Assets
1.18%	2.09%	4.67%	1.72%	99.14%

$$Z = 1.2 \times 0.0118 + 1.4 \times 0.0209 + 3.3 \times 0.0467 + 0.6 \times 0.0172 + 1.0 \times 0.9914 = 1.20$$

Carillion had better ratios than other bankrupt firms for net working capital, retained earnings and EBIT. However, its equity market value/total liabilities and sales/total assets ratios were substantially lower than those of other bankrupt firms. A comparison of Carillion with non-bankrupt firms shows that all five ratios were significantly worse for Carillion.

An alert reader will wonder why US Z-score coefficients can be used for a firm that is based in Europe or another country. This would be a very good observation. In practice, banks use a variety of proprietary prediction models when assessing the creditworthiness of potential borrowers, and Altman's Z-score model is just one of these. Another approach is to use neural networks to predict failure in borrowers. Recognizing this criticism, Altman et al. (2017) examined the performance of the original model across 31 European and three non-European countries, and found that, in general, the Altman Z-score model performed reasonably well for most countries.

Irrespective of the model used, good-quality data on credit defaults is required in order to calibrate the coefficients. The coefficients in any model will clearly be a function of the borrower and lender demographics, institutional factors and the quality of data that the analyst has in their possession. In practice, each country will have its own set of important variables and coefficients. All Altman's model does is provide a prediction of failure, which is not a perfect prediction of the future. As a general indicator, the US coefficients can be used to provide some insight on the bankruptcy risk of corporations in other countries. Only, do not take the outcome as particularly precise.

Summary and Conclusions

This chapter examined what happens when firms experience financial distress.

1 Financial distress is a situation where a firm's operating cash flow is not sufficient to cover contractual obligations. Financially distressed firms are often forced to take corrective action and undergo financial restructuring. Financial restructuring involves exchanging new financial claims for old ones.

2 Financial restructuring can be accomplished with a private workout or formal bankruptcy. Financial restructuring can involve liquidation or reorganization. However, liquidation is not common.

3 Corporate bankruptcy involves liquidation or reorganization. An essential feature of bankruptcy codes is the absolute priority rule. The absolute priority rule states that senior creditors are paid in full before junior creditors receive anything. However, in practice the absolute priority rule is often violated.

Questions and Problems

connect

CONCEPT

1 **Financial Distress** Define financial distress using the value-based and flow-based approaches. Do you think these are appropriate definitions for financial distress? Explain.

2 **What Happens in Financial Distress?** Review the turnaround strategies that firms can follow when in financial distress. Which do you think are most effective? Why?

3 **Bankruptcy Liquidation and Administration** What is the difference between administration and reorganization? What are some benefits of financial distress?

4 **Private Workouts and Bankruptcy** Do you think country-level institutional factors affect the turnaround strategies that financially distressed firms may adopt? What is the trade-off for policymakers between debtor-friendly and creditor-friendly bankruptcy law? Explain.

5 **Predicting Financial Distress** Review the variables and decision rule in Altman's *Z*-score model. Why do you think these variables are important in predicting financial distress? Is Altman's *Z*-score successful in correctly categorizing distressed and non-distressed firms? How do you think Altman's *Z*-score should be adapted for firms pursuing long-term sustainability goals? Should it be adapted at all?

REGULAR

6 **Financial Distress** What do you think are the main causes of financial distress? Explain your answer using a case study firm of your choice.

7 **APR and DIP Loans** What is the absolute priority rule? What are DIP loans? Where do DIP loans fall in the APR?

8 **Costs of Bankruptcy** What are the costs to a company of financial distress? Discuss your answer using a case study company of your choice.

9 **Bankruptcy Ethics: Pre-pack Arrangements** Firms that are in financial distress can use 'pre-pack' arrangements, where the financially distressed firm sells its assets and then immediately declares that it wishes to stop trading. This action transfers the assets to a completely new firm but without the debts of the old firm. Is this an ethical tactic?

10 **Bankruptcy Ethics: Labour Costs** Several firms have entered bankruptcy, or threatened to enter bankruptcy, at least in part, as a means of reducing labour costs. Whether this move is ethical, or proper, is hotly debated. Is this an ethical use of bankruptcy?

11 **Bankruptcy versus Private Workouts** Empirical evidence has shown that private workouts are faster and more cost-effective than a Chapter 11 bankruptcy procedure. Yet, according to Wruck (1990), more than half of financial restructurings in the United States occur in Chapter 11 rather than through a private workout. Why do you think this is?

12 **Administration: Liquidating Value** When Beacon Computers entered insolvency, it had the following balance sheet information:

Liquidating Value (£)		Claims (£)	
		Trade credit	3,000
		Secured mortgage notes	6,000
		Senior debentures	5,000
		Junior debentures	9,000
Total assets	15,500	Book equity	−7,500

Assuming there are no legal fees associated with the bankruptcy, as trustee what distribution of liquidating value do you propose?

13 **Administration and Reorganization** When Masters Printing filed for bankruptcy, it entered administration. Key information is shown below. As trustee what reorganization plan would you accept?

Assets (£)		Claims (£)	
		Mortgage bonds	10,000
		Senior debentures	6,000
		Junior debentures	4,000
Going concern value	15,000	Book equity	−5,000

Refer to Real World Insight 29.2 for Problems 14 to 17.

14 **Insolvency** Look at Carillion's *Z*-scores. If you were chief financial officer of Carillion what would you view as being the most important issue for the future viability of the company? Develop a turnaround plan and justify your proposal. Refer to Real World Insight 29.2 in your answer.

15 ***Z*-score Models** An analyst may argue that Carillion was a special case because so much of its business was with the British government. Given its importance to UK industry, the ratios should not have been taken literally because it was 'too big to fail'. Critically assess this argument, and discuss why you think it may or may not be valid. Which variables do you perceive to be most important for Carillion? Which do you think are less relevant? Explain your answer. Refer to Real World Insight 29.2 in your answer.

16 **Negative Equity** Four of the *Z*-score variables were negative for Carillion. Does this explain why few people anticipated the insolvency event? Explain. Why do you think Carillion wasn't considered a risk in the years prior to the bankruptcy? Refer to Real World Insight 29.2 in your answer.

17 **Net Working Capital** One year after the death of Carillion, its erstwhile competitors had the following *Z*-scores. What does this say about the health of Carillion's industry?

- K.H. Group Holdings Ltd: 4.40
- Dekpol SA: 1.77
- Doosan Engineering & Construction Co Ltd: −0.45
- Projektengagemang Sweden AB: 0.90
- AJ Lucas Group Ltd: −0.63
- Arkil Holding A/S: 2.86
- Malton Bhd: 1.24
- Tekmar Group plc: 0.45
- Yau Lee Holdings Ltd: 1.78

18 **Turnaround Strategies** Firms that are in financial distress sometimes increase the size of their assets. Explain why firms would pursue such a strategy instead of a more standard cost-cutting approach.

CHALLENGE

19 **Altman's *Z*-score** In 2023, Apple Inc. had the following data. Calculate its Altman *Z*-score. What can you say about the health of Apple?

- Total assets: $352,755 million
- Current assets: $135,405 million
- Current liabilities: $153,982 million
- Retained earnings: –$3,068 million
- Earnings before taxes: $119,103 million
- Interest expense: –$2,931 million
- Revenue: $394,328 million
- Market value of equity: $2.84 trillion
- Book value of liabilities: $302,083 million

20 **Private Equity** Many publicly traded financially distressed firms are purchased by private equity funds and delisted from the stock exchange. Several years later they are brought back to the exchange for a new share listing. Why do you think private equity firms delist financially distressed firms? Why do they bring them back to market?

Exam Question (45 minutes)

A listed company in which you have invested a lot of your personal wealth has just filed for insolvency. Using Altman's *Z*-score analysis, would you have been able to predict its financial distress? What is your interpretation of the results? Are there any figures that would have given you cause for concern? Explain. **(100 marks)**

	2024 £000	2023 £000	2022 £000	2021 £000	2020 £000
Fixed assets	322,644	344,870	350,614	303,533	203,628
Current assets	349,696	310,489	377,044	336,785	161,131
Current liabilities	320,069	289,848	397,075	370,244	175,526
Long-term liabilities	25,277	33,956	40,175	66,152	31,897
Book value of equity	326,994	331,555	290,408	203,922	157,336
Market value of equity	26,059	243,222	368,308	441,275	868,652
Retained earnings	156,714	164,426	130,472	61,276	23,852
Sales	1,625,034	1,772,358	1,971,905	1,491,914	801,306
EBIT	28,850	89,128	128,345	76,703	33,212

Total Marks: 100

Mini Case

HealingTech plc

In 2024, the wearable technology firm HealingTech plc applied to go into administration. The decision was made when the company realized its cash balance of £16.6 million could not meet its liabilities of £29.7 million. The firm's key statistics, income statement and balance sheet for a number of years are given below.

Key statistics:

	31/03/2023 £000	31/03/2022 £000	31/03/2021 £000	31/03/2020 £0001	31/03/2019 £000
Turnover	13,665	11,420	5,809	4,187	1,914
Profit (loss) before taxation	–520	2,396	421	887	–476
Net tangible assets (liab.)	8,114	8,454	2,208	3,824	1,317
Shareholders' funds	8,450	6,866	2,440	2,186	1,626
Profit margin	–3.81	20.98	7.25	21.18	–24.89
Return on shareholders' funds	–6.15	34.90	17.25	40.58	–29.29
Return on capital employed	–6.13	27.65	17.25	21.85	–29.29
Liquidity ratio (x)	1.20	1.26	1.06	1.15	1.06
Gearing (%)	82.97	140.64	363.40	210.75	77.85
Number of employees	44	26	18	15	14

Income statement:

	31/3/2023	31/3/2022	31/3/2021	31/3/2020
Turnover	13,665	11,420	5,809	4,187
Cost of sales	–3,997	–3,279	–2,443	–736
Gross profit	9,668	8,141	3,366	3,451
Administration expenses	–10,553	–5,770	–2,990	–2,632
Other operating income	382	54		
Operating profit	–504	2,425	376	820
Total other income and interest received	33	29	110	113
Profit (loss) before interest paid	–471	2,454	486	933
Interest received	33	29		
Interest paid	–49	–58	–65	–46
Net interest	–16	–29	–65	–46
Profit (loss) before tax	–520	2,396	421	887
Taxation	104	–670	–153	–337
Profit (loss) for period	–416	1,726	268	550

Balance sheet:

Fixed Assets	**2023**	**2022**	**2021**	**2020**
Tangible assets	1,270	734	254	189
Intangible assets	372	212	232	236
Investments		27	364	489
Fixed assets	3,653	2,956	2,495	2,433
Current Assets				
Trade debtors	2,318	4,139	2,389	2,254
Bank and deposits	27,371	23,260	16,567	16,572
Other debtors	8,944	0	0	365
Prepayments	1,589	1,289		
Deferred taxation	133			

Fixed Assets	**2023**	**2022**	**2021**	**2020**
Investments	7,238	3,953	5,176	
Current assets	40,356	36,816	26,674	24,367
Current Liabilities				
Trade creditors	−20,588	−14,207	−12,802	−12,067
Short-term loans and overdrafts	−6,974	−7,856	−8,867	−2,733
Corporation tax	0	−333	−28	−29
Accruals	−869	−569	−336	−245
Other current liabilities	−5,079	−6,157	−3,051	−6,147
Current liabilities	−33,511	−29,123	−25,083	−21,221
Total assets	41,997	37,789	27,523	25,281
Long-term Liabilities				
Long-term debt		−1,800		−1,700
Provisions for other liabilities	−37			−174
Long-term liabilities	−37	−1,800		−1,874
Shareholders' Funds				
Issued capital	8,012	6,012	3,312	3,312
Profit (loss) account	319	735	−991	−1,258
Other reserves	118	118	118	132
Shareholders' funds	8,450	6,866	2,440	2,186

1 Assume that you had taken over the financial manager's role in 2020. Would you have predicted that HealingTech plc would be in financial distress within a year? Explain.

2 Assume now that you are in 2023 and the company has experienced a torrid year. What is the *Z*-score for the firm? Does this give you any insight into the risk or insolvency status of the firm?

3 Now that you know HealingTech is in financial distress, what are the different turnaround strategies you would follow? What do you think is most appropriate in this particular case? Explain.

Practical Case Study

It is not difficult to find firms that are in financial distress. Download the financial accounts for five firms in your country that have performed poorly over the past year. Carry out a *Z*-score analysis for these companies. Now download the financial accounts for five firms that performed strongly in the past year and carry out a similar analysis. Are the *Z*-scores for the poor performance sample different from those of the good performance sample? Write a report on your analysis.

Relevant Accounting Standards

Many financially distressed firms choose to restructure their assets and sell off poorly performing divisions. An important standard in this regard is IAS 37 *Provisions, Contingent Liabilities and Contingent Assets.* If firms wish to sell off divisions or non-current assets, they should also be familiar with IFRS 5 *Non-current Assets Held for Sale and Discontinued Operations.*

References

Altman, E. (1993) *Corporate Financial Distress: A Complete Guide to Predicting, Avoiding, and Dealing with Bankruptcy*, 2nd edn. New York: John Wiley & Sons.

Altman, E.I., M. Iwanicz-Drozdowska, E.K. Laitinen and A. Suvas (2017) 'Financial Distress Prediction in an International Context: A Review and Empirical Analysis of Altman's Z-score Model', *Journal of International Financial Management & Accounting*, Vol. 28, No. 2, 131–171.

Beranek, W., R. Boehmer and B. Smith (1996) 'Much Ado about Nothing: Absolute Priority Deviations in Chapter 11', *Financial Management*, Vol. 25, No. 3, 102–109.

Davydenko, S.A. and J. Franks (2008) 'Do Bankruptcy Codes Matter? A Study of Defaults in France, Germany and the UK', *Journal of Finance*, Vol. 63, 565–609.

Gilson, S. (1991) 'Managing Default: Some Evidence on How Firms Choose between Workouts and Bankruptcy', *Journal of Applied Corporate Finance*, Vol. 4, No. 2, 62–70.

Gilson, S.C., J. Kose and L.N.P. Lang (1990) 'Troubled Debt Restructuring: An Empirical Study of Private Reorganization of Firms in Defaults', *Journal of Financial Economics*, Vol. 27, 315–353.

Hillier, D. and P. McColgan (2007) 'Managerial Discipline and Firm Responses to a Decline in Operating Performance', Working Paper.

Weiss, L.A. (1990) 'Bankruptcy Resolution: Direct Costs and Violation of Priority and Claims', *Journal of Financial Economics*, Vol. 27, 285–314.

Wruck, K. (1990) 'Financial Distress: Reorganization and Organization Efficiency', *Journal of Financial Economics*, Vol. 27, No. 2, 419–444.

Additional Reading

Financial distress is another topic that has taken on a new lease of life in recent years because of the unprecedented events in the world economy. The literature can be separated into factors that influence financial distress and turnaround strategies once a company is in trouble.

A good review paper is:

Cole, R., S. Johan and D. Schweizer (2021) 'Corporate Failures: Declines, Collapses, and Scandals', *Journal of Corporate Finance*, Vol. 67, 101872.

Other areas of research are given below.

Predictors of Distress

1 Acharya, V.V., S.T. Bharath and A. Srinivasan (2007) 'Does Industry-wide Distress Affect Defaulted Firms? Evidence from Credit Recoveries', *Journal of Financial Economics*, Vol. 85, No. 3, 787–821. **USA.**

2 Agarwal, V. and R. Taffler (2008) 'Comparing the Performance of Market-based and Accounting-based Bankruptcy Prediction Models', *Journal of Banking and Finance*, Vol. 32, No. 8, 1541–1551. **UK.**

3 Almamy, J., J. Aston and L.N. Ngwa (2016) 'An Evaluation of Altman's Z-score Using Cash Flow Ratio to Predict Corporate Failure Amid the Recent Financial Crisis: Evidence from the UK', *Journal of Corporate Finance*, Vol. 36, 278–285.

4 Braun, M. and B. Larrain (2005) 'Finance and the Business Cycle: International, Inter-Industry Evidence', *Journal of Finance*, Vol. 60, No. 3, 1097–1127. **International.**

5 Campbell, J.Y., J. Hilscher and J. Szilagyi (2008) 'In Search of Distress Risk', *Journal of Finance*, Vol. 63, No. 6, 2899–2939. **USA.**

6 Garlappi, L. and H. Yan (2011) 'Financial Distress and the Cross-section of Equity Returns', *Journal of Finance*, Vol. 66, No. 3, 789–822.

7 Greenwood, R., S.G. Hanson, A. Shleifer and J.A. Sørensen (2022) 'Predictable Financial Crises', *Journal of Finance*, Vol. 77, No. 2, 863–921.

8 Koh, S., R.B. Durand, L. Dai and M. Chang (2015) 'Financial Distress: Lifecycle and Corporate Restructuring', *Journal of Corporate Finance*, Vol. 33, 19–33.

9 Liang, D., C.C. Lu, C.F. Tsai and G.A. Shih (2016) 'Financial Ratios and Corporate Governance Indicators in Bankruptcy Prediction: A Comprehensive Study', *European Journal of Operational Research*, Vol. 252, No. 2, 561–572.

10 Megginson, W.L., A. Meles, G. Sampagnaro and V. Verdoliva (2019) 'Financial Distress Risk in Initial Public Offerings: How Much Do Venture Capitalists Matter?', *Journal of Corporate Finance*, Vol. 59, December, 10–30.

11 Richardson, G., R. Lanis and G. Taylor (2015) 'Financial Distress, Outside Directors and Corporate Tax Aggressiveness Spanning the Global Financial Crisis: An Empirical Analysis', *Journal of Banking & Finance*, Vol. 52, 112–129.

12 Yang, L. (2008) 'The Real Determinants of Asset Sales', *Journal of Finance*, Vol. 63, No. 5, 2231–2262. **USA.**

Turnaround Strategies and the Bankruptcy Process

13 Abebe, M.A. and C. Tangpong (2018) 'Founder-CEOs and Corporate Turnaround Among Declining Firms', *Corporate Governance: An International Review*, Vol. 26,No. 1, 45–57.

14 Amankwah-Amoah, J. (2016) 'An Integrative Process Model Of Organisational Failure', *Journal of Business Research*, Vol. 69, No. 9, 3388–3397.

15 Ang, J., A. De Jong and M. Van der Poel (2014) 'Does Familiarity with Business Segments Affect CEOs'

Divestment Decisions?', *Journal of Corporate Finance*, Vol. 29, 58–74.

16 Bates, T.W. (2005) 'Asset Sales, Investment Opportunities, and the Use of Proceeds', *Journal of Finance*, Vol. 60, No. 1, 105–135. **USA.**

17 Bernstein, S., E. Colonnelli and B. Iverson (2019) 'Asset Allocation in Bankruptcy', *Journal of Finance*, Vol. 74, No. 1, 5–53.

18 Bris, A., I. Welch and N. Zhu (2006) 'The Costs of Bankruptcy: Chapter 7 Liquidation versus Chapter 11 Reorganization', *Journal of Finance*, Vol. 61, No. 3, 1253–1303. **USA.**

19 Brown, D.T., B.A. Ciochetti and T.J. Riddiough (2006) 'Theory and Evidence on the Resolution of Financial Distress', *Review of Financial Studies*, Vol. 19, No. 4, 1357–1397. **USA.**

20 Davydenko, S.A. and J.R. Franks (2008) 'Do Bankruptcy Codes Matter? A Study of Defaults in France, Germany and the UK', *Journal of Finance*, Vol. 62, No. 2, 565–608. **Europe.**

21 Eckbo, B.E. and K. Thorburn (2009) 'Creditor Financing and Overbidding in Bankruptcy Auctions: Theory and Tests', *Journal of Corporate Finance*, Vol. 15, No. 1, 10–29. **Sweden.**

22 Eisdorfer, A. (2008) 'Empirical Evidence of Risk Shifting in Financially Distressed Firms', *Journal of Finance*, Vol. 62, No. 2, 609–637. **USA.**

23 Faccio, M., R.W. Masulis and J.J. McConnell (2006) 'Political Connections and Corporate Bailouts', *Journal of Finance*, Vol. 16, No. 6, 2597–2635. **International.**

24 Hillier, D., A. Marshall, P. McColgan and S. Werema (2007) 'Employee Layoffs, Shareholder Wealth and Firm Performance: Evidence from the UK', *Journal of Business Finance and Accounting*, Vol. 34, Nos. 3 and 4, 467–494. **UK.**

25 Jostarndt, P. and Z. Sautner (2008) 'Financial Distress, Corporate Control, and Management Turnover', *Journal of Banking and Finance*, Vol. 32, No. 10, 2188–2204. **Germany.**

26 Koh, S., R.B. Durand, L. Dai and M. Chang (2015) 'Financial Distress: Lifecycle and Corporate Restructuring', *Journal of Corporate Finance*, Vol. 33, 19–33.

27 Lee, E. and S. Lin (2008) 'Corporate Sell-offs in the UK: Use of Proceeds, Financial Distress and the Long-run Impact on Shareholder Wealth', *European Financial Management*, Vol. 14, No. 2, 222–242. **UK.**

28 Molina, C.A. and L.A. Preve (2009) 'Trade Receivables Policy of Distressed Firms and its Effect on the Costs of Financial Distress', *Financial Management*, Vol. 38, No. 2, 663–686.

29 Zhang, E.Q. (2022) 'Why are Distressed Firms Acquisitive?', *Journal of Corporate Finance*, Vol. 72, 102126.

Other Relevant Research

30 Davydenko, S.A., I.A. Strebulaev and X. Zhao (2012) 'A Market-based Study of the Cost of Default', *Review of Financial Studies*, Vol. 25, No. 10, 2959–2999.

31 Gennaioli, N. and S. Rossi (2013) 'Contractual Resolutions of Financial Distress', *Review of Financial Studies*, Vol. 26, No. 3, 602–634.

32 Jenter, D. and K. Lewellen (2021) 'Performance-induced CEO Turnover', *Review of Financial Studies*, Vol. 34, No. 2, 569–617.

33 Ongena, S., D.C. Smith and D. Michalsen (2003) 'Firms and Their Distressed Banks: Lessons from the Norwegian Banking Crisis', *Journal of Financial Research*, Vol. 67, No. 1, 81–112. **Norway.**

Endnotes

1 This definition is close to the one used by Wruck (1990), p. 425.

2 *Black's Law Dictionary*, 10th edn (St Paul, MN: West Publishing Company).

3 Edward Altman (1993) was one of the first to distinguish between stock-based insolvency and flow-based insolvency.

4 However, only fewer than 20 per cent of all firms (public or private) going through a bankruptcy are successfully reorganized.

5 For example, see Gilson (1991) and Gilson et al. (1990).

6 Weiss (1990). However, Beranek et al. (1996) find that 33.8 per cent of bankruptcy reorganizations leave shareholders with nothing.

Chapter 30
International Corporate Finance

Learning Objectives

After reading this chapter you should be able to:

LO1 Explain the key terms and concepts related to international corporate finance and foreign exchange markets.

LO2 Apply the theories of purchasing power parity, interest rate parity and the international Fisher effect to estimate and compare exchange rates and interest rates across countries.

LO3 Evaluate the profitability and feasibility of foreign investment projects using international capital budgeting techniques and accounting for foreign currency exposure.

LO4 Identify and manage the different types of exchange rate risk and political risk faced by multinational corporations operating in global markets.

LO5 Compare the main features and characteristics of long-term Islamic financing instruments and their implications for international corporate finance.

Relatively few large companies operate in a single country. As a financial manager in a corporation, even if your sales are not overseas, it is very likely that your competitors or suppliers are from overseas. In most industries, raw materials and components are sourced and imported from overseas, and many services and products are sold to different countries. Internet companies have no borders and services can be bought and sold from across the world.

An analysis of import and export revenue for the United Kingdom shows that most of the UK's export revenue comes from the United States, Germany and France. Similarly, the United Kingdom's main import partners are Germany, China and the United States. Table 30.1 presents the main import and export partners for other selected countries.

Key Notations

P	Price
S_0	Spot exchange rate
$E(S_t)$	Expected exchange rate in t periods
h_{HC}	Inflation rate in the home currency
h_{FC}	Foreign country inflation rate
F_t	Forward exchange rate for settlement at time t
R_{HC}	Home currency nominal risk-free interest rate
R_{FC}	Foreign country nominal risk-free interest rate

Source: Sven Hansche/123RF

Table 30.1 Main Import and Export Partners of Selected Countries

Country	Top 3 Export Partners	Top 3 Import Partners
Austria	Germany, Italy, USA	Germany, Italy, China
Bahrain	Saudi Arabia, UAE, USA	China, Saudi Arabia, UAE
Belgium	Germany, France, Netherlands	Netherlands, Germany, France
China	USA, Hong Kong, Japan	South Korea, Japan, USA
Denmark	Germany, Sweden, USA	Germany, Sweden, Netherlands
European Union	USA, China, UK	China, UK, USA
Finland	Germany, Sweden, USA	Germany, Russia, Sweden
France	Germany, Spain, USA	Germany, China, Belgium
Germany	USA, France, China	China, Netherlands, France
Greece	Italy, Germany, Turkey	Germany, Italy, China
India	USA, UAE, China	China, USA, UAE
Ireland	USA, UK, Belgium	UK, USA, Germany
Italy	Germany, France, USA	Germany, France, China
Malaysia	Singapore, China, USA	China, Singapore, USA
Netherlands	Germany, Belgium, USA	Germany, China, Belgium
Norway	UK, Germany, Sweden	Sweden, Germany, China
Oman	China, UAE, India	UAE, China, India
Russia (pre-Ukraine War)	China, Netherlands, Germany	China, Germany, Belarus
Saudi Arabia	China, Japan, India	China, USA, UAE
Singapore	China, Hong Kong, Malaysia	China, Malaysia, USA
South Africa	China, USA, Germany	China, Germany, USA
Spain	France, Germany, Portugal	Germany, France, China
Sweden	Germany, Norway, USA	Germany, Netherlands, China
Switzerland	Germany, USA, China	Germany, USA, Italy
UAE	India, China, Japan	China, India, USA
UK	USA, Germany, France	Germany, China, USA
USA	Canada, Mexico, China	China, Mexico, Canada

Source: World Bank, World Integrated Trade Solution, wits.worldbank.org

Changes in the behaviour of countries because of the global Covid pandemic, the Russian invasion of Ukraine and the ongoing effects of the 2016 Brexit vote will have undoubtedly impacted the figures. The UK's main exports are manufactured goods, fuels, chemicals, food, beverages and tobacco. Its main imports are manufactured goods, machinery, fuels and foodstuffs.

Currency fluctuations will clearly have an impact on firms. If the euro strengthens against the British pound, for example, British exports become cheaper in Europe. Similarly, raw materials sourced from Europe will become more expensive and British corporations will look elsewhere for cheaper inputs. One of the reasons why European Monetary Union was introduced was because countries in the Eurozone trade heavily with one another. With a single currency, the risk of fluctuations is eradicated. In this chapter, we explore the roles played by currencies and exchange rates, along with a number of other key topics in international corporate finance.

Corporations with significant foreign operations are often called *international corporations* or *multinationals*. Such corporations must consider many financial factors that do not directly affect purely domestic firms.

These include foreign exchange rates, differing interest rates from country to country, different – and possibly more complex – accounting methods for foreign operations, foreign tax rates and foreign government intervention.

The basic principles of corporate finance still apply to international corporations; like domestic companies, these firms seek to invest in projects that create more value for the shareholders than they cost, and to arrange financing that raises cash at the lowest possible cost. In other words, the net present value (NPV) principle holds for both foreign and domestic operations, although it is usually more complicated to apply the NPV rule to foreign investments.

One of the most significant complications of international finance is foreign exchange. The foreign exchange markets provide important information and opportunities for an international corporation when it undertakes capital budgeting and financing decisions. As we will discuss, international exchange rates, interest rates and inflation rates are closely related. We will spend much of this chapter exploring the connection between these financial variables.

We will not have much to say here about the role of cultural and social differences in international business. Neither will we be discussing the implications of differing political and economic systems. These factors are of great importance to international businesses, but it would take another book to do them justice. Consequently we will focus only on some purely financial considerations in international finance and some key aspects of foreign exchange markets.

30.1 Terminology

A common buzzword for the student of business finance is *globalization*. The first step in learning about the globalization of financial markets is to conquer the new vocabulary. As with any specialized field, international finance is rich in jargon. Accordingly, we get started on the subject with a highly eclectic vocabulary exercise.

The terms that follow are presented alphabetically, and they are not all of equal importance. We choose these particular terms because they appear frequently in the financial press or because they illustrate the colourful nature of the language of international finance.

1. An **American depositary receipt (ADR)** is a security issued in the United States that represents shares of a foreign equity, allowing that equity to be traded in the United States. Foreign companies use ADRs, which are issued in US dollars, to expand the pool of potential US investors. ADRs are available in two forms for a large and growing number of foreign companies: company sponsored, which are listed on an exchange, and unsponsored, which usually are held by the investment bank that makes a market in the ADR. Both forms are available to individual investors, but only company-sponsored issues are quoted daily in newspapers. A global depositary receipt (GDR) is an equivalent security denominated in sterling or euros, and issued and traded in financial centres such as London or Frankfurt.
2. The **cross-rate** is the implicit exchange rate between two currencies (usually an emerging or transitional economy) when both are quoted in some third currency, usually the US dollar, euro or British pound.
3. A **Eurobond** is a bond issued in multiple countries but denominated in a single currency, usually the issuer's home currency. Such bonds have become an important way to raise capital for many international companies and governments. Eurobonds are issued outside the restrictions that apply to domestic offerings, and are syndicated and traded mostly from London. Trading can and does take place anywhere there are buyers and sellers.
4. **Eurocurrency** is money deposited in a financial centre outside of the country whose currency is involved. For instance, Eurodollars – the most widely used Eurocurrency – are US dollars deposited in banks outside the US banking system. Eurosterling and euroyen are British and Japanese equivalents.
5. **Foreign bonds**, unlike Eurobonds, are issued in a single country and are usually denominated in that country's currency. Often, the country in which these bonds are issued will draw distinctions between them and bonds issued by domestic issuers – including different tax laws, restrictions on the amount issued, and tougher disclosure rules.

   Foreign bonds often are nicknamed for the country where they are issued: Yankee bonds (United States), Samurai bonds (Japan), Rembrandt bonds (the Netherlands), Panda bonds (China) and Bulldog bonds (UK). Partly because of tougher regulations and disclosure requirements, the foreign bond market hasn't grown in past years with the vigour of the Eurobond market.

30.2 Foreign Exchange Markets and Exchange Rates

The **foreign exchange market** is undoubtedly the world's largest financial market. It is the market where one country's currency is traded for another's. Most of the trading takes place in a few currencies: the US dollar ($), the British pound sterling (£), the Japanese yen (¥) and the euro (€). Table 30.2 lists some of the more common currencies and their symbols.

Table 30.2 International Currency Symbols

Country	Currency	Symbol
China	Renminbi	¥
Denmark	Danish krone	DKr
Eurozone	Euro	€
India	Indian rupee	₹
Japan	Yen	¥
Norway	Norwegian krone	NKr
Saudi Arabia	Saudi riyal	SR
South Africa	Rand	R
Sweden	Swedish krona	SKr
Switzerland	Swiss franc	SFr
UK	Pound sterling	£
USA	Dollar	$

The foreign exchange market is an over-the-counter market, so there is no single location where traders get together. Instead, market participants are located in the major commercial and investment banks around the world. They communicate using computers, telephones and other telecommunications devices. As an example, one communications network for foreign transactions is maintained by the Society for Worldwide Interbank Financial Telecommunication (SWIFT), a Belgian not-for-profit cooperative. Using data transmission lines, a bank in Berlin can send messages to a bank in London via SWIFT regional processing centres.

The many different types of participants in the foreign exchange market include the following:

- Importers who pay for goods using foreign currencies
- Exporters who receive foreign currency and may want to convert to the domestic currency
- Portfolio managers who buy or sell foreign equities and bonds
- Foreign exchange brokers who match buy and sell orders
- Traders who 'make a market' in foreign currencies
- Speculators who try to profit from changes in exchange rates.

In 2022, as a result of its invasion of Ukraine, Russia was excluded from SWIFT. In response, Russia and China have been promoting their own systems (the System for Transfer of Financial Messages, SPFS, and the Cross-Border Interbank Payments System, CIPS, respectively).

Exchange Rates

An **exchange rate** is simply the price of one country's currency expressed in terms of another country's currency. In practice, almost all trading of currencies takes place in terms of the US dollar, yen, sterling or euro.

Exchange Rate Quotations

Table 30.3 reproduces an excerpt of exchange rate quotations as they appeared in the *Financial Times* on 13 June 2023. The four main columns give the number of units of foreign currency it takes to buy one pound, dollar, euro and yen (× 100), respectively. Because this is the price in foreign currency with respect to pounds, dollars, euros

Table 30.3 Exchange Rate Quotations

		POUND		DOLLAR		EURO		YEN (x100)	
Jun 13	Currency	Closing Mid	Day's Change	Closing Mid	Day's Change	Closing Mid	Day's Change	Closing Mid	Day's Change
Pakistan	(Pak Rupee)	362.3919	2.8418	287.5000	0.0900	310.5724	1.6789	205.6289	-0.2154
Panama	(Balboa)	1.2605	0.0095	1.0000	-	1.0803	0.0055	0.7152	-0.0010
Papua New Guinea	(Kina)	4.4680	0.0280	3.5447	-0.0045	3.8291	0.0147	2.5352	-0.0067
Paraguay	(Guarani)	9125.1700	38.8701	7239.3600	-23.8600	7820.3326	14.1933	5177.8135	-24.1345
Peru	(New Sol)	4.5892	0.0129	3.6408	-0.0173	3.9330	0.0014	2.6040	-0.0159
Philippines	(Peso)	70.5328	0.4142	55.9565	-0.0935	60.4471	0.2074	40.0218	-0.1214
Pitcairn Is	(Sterling £)	1.0000	-	0.7933	-0.0060	0.8570	-0.0021	0.5674	-0.0051
Poland	(Zloty)	5.2297	0.0584	4.1489	0.0152	4.4819	0.0392	2.9675	0.0068
Portugal	(Euro)	1.1669	0.0029	0.9257	-0.0047	1.0000	-	0.6621	-0.0043
Puerto Rico	(US $)	1.2605	0.0095	1.0000	-	1.0803	0.0055	0.7152	-0.0010
Qatar	(Riyal)	4.5882	0.0346	3.6400	-	3.9321	0.0200	2.6034	-0.0035
Reunion Is de la	(Euro)	1.1669	0.0029	0.9257	-0.0047	1.0000	-	0.6621	-0.0043
Romania	(New Leu)	5.7902	0.0212	4.5936	-0.0179	4.9622	0.0060	3.2855	-0.0173
Russia	(Rouble)	105.8515	1.6119	83.9763	0.6513	90.7155	1.1621	60.0624	0.3847
Rwanda	(Fr)	1431.8577	10.4080	1135.9500	-0.3000	1227.1122	5.9288	812.4665	-1.3205
St Christopher	(E Carib $)	3.4033	0.0256	2.7000	-	2.9167	0.0149	1.9311	-0.0026
St Helena	(£)	1.0000	-	0.7933	-0.0060	0.8570	-0.0021	0.5674	-0.0051
St Lucia	(E Carib $)	3.4033	0.0256	2.7000	-	2.9167	0.0149	1.9311	-0.0026
St Pierre & Miquelon	(Euro)	1.1669	0.0029	0.9257	-0.0047	1.0000	-	0.6621	-0.0043
St Vincent	(E Carib $)	3.4033	0.0256	2.7000	-	2.9167	0.0149	1.9311	-0.0026
San Marino	(Euro)	1.1669	0.0029	0.9257	-0.0047	1.0000	-	0.6621	-0.0043
Sao Tome	(Dobra)	28.6121	0.1519	22.6992	-0.0508	24.5208	0.0703	16.2351	-0.0585
Saudi Arabia	(Riyal)	4.7270	0.0356	3.7501	-	4.0511	0.0206	2.6822	-0.0036
Senegal	(CFA Fr)	765.4059	1.8769	607.2271	-3.1074	655.9582	0.0019	434.3075	-2.8166
Serbia	(Dinar)	136.8014	0.3422	108.5300	-0.5500	117.2397	0.0061	77.6240	-0.4995
Seychelles	(Rupee)	17.5901	0.0886	13.9549	-0.0350	15.0748	0.0391	9.9810	-0.0387
Sierra Leone	(Leone)	17499.8031	131.7870	13883.2800	-	14997.4504	76.3977	9929.7501	-13.5123
Singapore	($)	1.6901	0.0087	1.3408	-0.0033	1.4484	0.0039	0.9590	-0.0036
Slovakia	(Euro)	1.1669	0.0029	0.9257	-0.0047	1.0000	-	0.6621	-0.0043
Slovenia	(Euro)	1.1669	0.0029	0.9257	-0.0047	1.0000	-	0.6621	-0.0043
Solomon Is	($)	10.5304	0.0793	8.3542	-	9.0247	0.0460	5.9752	-0.0081
Somali Rep	(Shilling)	716.5906	9.7752	568.5000	3.5000	614.1232	6.8902	406.6087	1.9534
South Africa	(Rand)	23.3806	0.1636	18.5488	-0.0100	20.0373	0.0913	13.2666	-0.0252
Spain	(Euro)	1.1669	0.0029	0.9257	-0.0047	1.0000	-	0.6621	-0.0043
Spanish Ports N Af	(Euro)	1.1669	0.0029	0.9257	-0.0047	1.0000	-	0.6621	-0.0043
Sri Lanka	(Rupee)	386.7951	11.0382	306.8600	6.4950	331.4861	8.6692	219.4757	4.3531
Sudan Rep	(£)	757.5567	9.4582	601.0000	3.0000	649.2314	6.5316	429.8537	1.5637
Surinam	(Dollar)	47.8647	0.3955	37.9730	0.0280	41.0204	0.2391	27.1595	-0.0169
Swaziland	(Lilangeni)	23.3806	0.1636	18.5488	-0.0100	20.0373	0.0913	13.2666	-0.0252
Sweden	(Krona)	13.4929	-0.0327	10.7045	-0.1074	11.5635	-0.0565	7.6562	-0.0873
Switzerland	(Fr)	1.1413	0.0037	0.9054	-0.0039	0.9781	0.0008	0.6476	-0.0037
Taiwan	($)	38.7217	0.2466	30.7195	-0.0360	33.1848	0.1304	21.9715	-0.0557
Tanzania	(Shilling)	3006.2774	22.6403	2385.0000	-	2576.4012	13.1248	1705.8256	-2.3213
Thailand	(Baht)	43.5501	0.2654	34.5500	-0.0500	37.3227	0.1364	24.7112	-0.0694
Togo Rep	(CFA Fr)	765.4059	1.8769	607.2271	-3.1074	655.9582	0.0019	434.3075	-2.8166
Tonga Is	(Pa'anga)	2.9554	0.0216	2.3447	-0.0006	2.5328	0.0123	1.6770	0.0027
Trinidad & Tobago	($)	8.4964	0.0727	6.7405	0.0069	7.2814	0.0446	4.8210	-0.0016
Tunisia	(Dinar)	3.9049	0.0148	3.0979	-0.0117	3.3465	0.0045	2.2157	-0.0114
Turkey	(New Lira)	29.7971	0.2016	23.6393	-0.0183	25.5363	0.1105	16.9075	-0.0361
Turkmenistan	(New Manat)	4.4117	0.2084	3.5000	0.1400	3.7809	0.1697	2.5033	0.0969
Turks & Caicos	(US$)	1.2605	0.0095	1.0000	-	1.0803	0.0055	0.7152	-0.0010
Tuvalu	(Australian$)	1.8564	0.0028	1.4728	-0.0090	1.5909	-0.0015	1.0534	-0.0078
Uganda	(New Shilling)	4691.5582	30.3271	3722.0000	-4.0000	4020.6986	16.1831	2662.0892	-6.4874
Ukraine	(Hryvnia)	46.5280	0.5599	36.9125	0.1675	39.8748	0.3832	26.4010	0.0840
UAE	(Dirham)	4.6296	0.0348	3.6729	-0.0001	3.9676	0.0202	2.6269	-0.0036
United Kingdom	(£)	1.0000		0.7933	-0.0060	0.8570	-0.0021	0.5674	-0.0051
United States	($)	1.2605	0.0095	1.0000	-	1.0803	0.0055	0.7152	-0.0010
Uruguay	(Peso Uruguay)	48.7149	0.2374	38.6475	-0.1035	41.7490	0.1014	27.6419	-0.1117
Uzbekistan	(Sum)	14451.6815	137.1951	11465.0900	22.6700	12385.1893	87.4563	8200.1860	5.0777
Vanuatu	(Vatu)	150.4210	1.5582	119.3350	0.3400	128.9119	1.0221	85.3521	0.1274
Vatican	(Euro)	1.1669	0.0029	0.9257	-0.0047	1.0000	-	0.6621	-0.0043
Venezuela	(Bolivar Fuerte)	1.0000	-	1.0000	-	1.0000	-	1.0000	-
Vietnam	(Dong)	29614.7126	241.1335	23494.5000	14.5000	25380.0021	144.8738	16803.9911	-12.4817
Virgin Is British	(US $)	1.2605	0.0095	1.0000	-	1.0803	0.0055	0.7152	-0.0010
Virgin Is US	(US $)	1.2605	0.0095	1.0000	-	1.0803	0.0055	0.7152	-0.0010
Western Samoa	(Tala)	3.4449	0.0269	2.7330	0.0008	2.9523	0.0158	1.9547	-0.0021
Yemen Rep of	(Rial)	315.2810	2.2493	250.1250	-0.1000	270.1980	1.2690	178.8971	-0.3151
Zambia	(Kwacha)	23.8548	-0.6335	18.9250	-0.6500	20.4438	-0.5944	13.5357	-0.4840
Zimbabwe	($)	456.1726	3.4354	361.9000	-	390.9432	1.9916	258.8420	-0.3522
SDR	(SDR)	0.9452	0.0052	0.7499	-0.0015	0.8100	0.0025	0.5363	-0.0018

or yen, it is called an *indirect* quote. The Thai baht (Bt), for instance, is quoted at 43.5501 against the pound, which means that you can buy one British pound with 43.5501 Thai baht.

If you were a Thai person and the quote was Bt43.5501/£, the quote would be a *direct* quote because it is in the home currency (baht) with respect to the foreign currency (£).

Example 30.1

Rand for Euros

Suppose you have £1,000. Based on the rates in Table 30.3, how many South African rand can you get? Alternatively, if a Porsche costs €100,000, how many pounds will you need to buy it?

The exchange rate in terms of rand per pound is 23.3806. Your £1,000 will thus get you:

£1,000 × 23.3806 rand per £1 = 23,380.60 rand

Because the exchange rate in terms of pound per euro is 0.8570, you will need:

€100,000 × £0.8570 per € = £85,700

Cross-rates and Triangle Arbitrage

The *Financial Times* quotes exchange rates in terms of the British pounds, US dollars, euros and Japanese yen. Using any of these currencies as the common denominator in quoting exchange rates greatly reduces the number of possible cross-currency quotes. For example, with five major currencies, there would potentially be 10 exchange rates instead of just 4.[1] Also, the fact that the one currency (pound, dollar, euro or yen) is used throughout cuts down on inconsistencies in the exchange rate quotations.

Earlier, we defined the cross-rate as the exchange rate for a foreign currency expressed in terms of another foreign currency. Suppose, say, we observe the following for the Russian rouble and the Bahraini dinar:

Russian rouble per €1 = 45.8022
Bahraini dinar per €1 = 0.4831

Suppose the cross-rate is quoted as:

Dinar per rouble = 0.01

What do you think?

The cross-rate here is inconsistent with the exchange rates. To see this, suppose you have €100. If you convert this to Russian roubles, you will receive:

€100 × 45.8022 roubles/€ = 4,580.22 roubles

If you convert this to dinar at the cross-rate, you will have:

4,580.22 roubles × 0.01 per rouble = 45.8022 dinars

However, if you just convert your euros to dinar without going through Russian roubles, you will have:

€100 × 0.4831 dinars per €1 = 48.31 dinars

What we see is that the dinar has two prices, 0.4831 dinar per €1 and 0.4580 dinar per €1, with the price we pay depending on how we get the dinar.

To make money, we want to buy low and sell high. The important thing to note is that dinar are cheaper if you buy them with euros because you get 0.4831 dinar instead of just 0.4580 dinar. You should proceed as follows:

1 Buy 48.31 dinar for €100.
2 Use the 48.31 dinar to buy Russian roubles at the cross-rate. Because it takes 0.01 dinar to buy a Russian rouble, you will receive 48.31 dinar/0.01 roubles = 4,831 roubles.
3 Use the 4,831 roubles to buy euros. Because the exchange rate is 45.8022 roubles per euro, you receive 4,831 roubles/45.8022 = €105.48, for a round-trip profit of €5.48.
4 Repeat steps 1 through 3 *ad infinitum*.

This particular activity is called *triangle arbitrage* because the arbitrage involves moving through three different exchange rates:

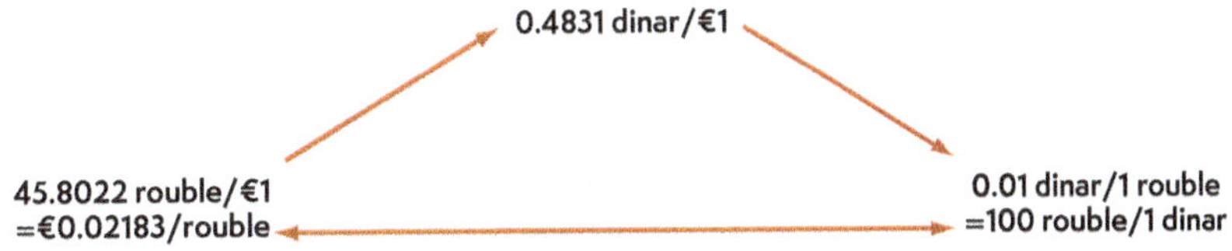

To prevent such opportunities, it is not difficult to see that because a euro will buy you either 45.8022 Russian roubles or 0.4831 Bahraini dinar, the cross-rate must be:

$$(€1/0.4831 \text{ dinar})/(45.8022 \text{ rouble}/€1) = 0.0105 \text{ dinar/rouble}$$

That is, the cross-rate must be 0.0105 Bahraini dinar per 1 Russian rouble. If it were anything else, there would be a triangle arbitrage opportunity.

Example 30.2

Shedding Some Pounds

According to Table 30.3, the exchange rates for the British pound against the euro and dollar are:

€/£ = 1.1669
$/£ = 1.2605

The cross-rate is $1.0802/€. Show that the exchange rates are consistent.

Types of Transaction

There are two basic types of trade in the foreign exchange market: spot trades and forward trades. A **spot trade** is an agreement to exchange currency 'on the spot', which actually means that the transaction will be completed or settled within two business days. The exchange rate on a spot trade is called the **spot exchange rate**. Implicitly, all of the exchange rates and transactions we have discussed so far have referred to the spot market.

A **forward trade** is an agreement to exchange currency at some time in the future. The exchange rate that will be used is agreed upon today and is called the **forward exchange rate**. A forward trade will normally be settled some time in the next 12 months.

Table 30.4 presents forward quotes on the €/£ rate for a range of currencies as recorded on 14 June 2023. The spot €/£ exchange rate, for example, is €1.0816/£ and the one-year forward exchange rate is €1.1103/£. This means that you can buy a pound today for €1.0816, or you can agree to take delivery of a pound in one year and pay €1.1103 at that time.

Notice that the British pound is more expensive in the forward market (€1.1103 versus 1.0816). Because the British pound is more expensive in the future than it is today, it is said to be selling at a *premium* relative to the euro. For the same reason, the euro is said to be selling at a *discount* relative to the British pound.

Table 30.4 €/£ Forward Rates, 14 June 2023

Term	Forward Rate	Term	Forward Rate
Tomorrow	1.0813	5 Month	1.0900
1 Week	1.9816	6 Month	1.0917
2 Week	1.0821	7 Month	1.0942
3 Week	1.0826	8 Month	1.0957
1 Month	1.0831	9 Month	1.0971
2 Month	1.0849	10 Month	1.0986
3 Month	1.0868	11 Month	1.0999
4 Month	1.0884	1 Year	1.1013

Source: Data adapted from real time €/£ forward rates feed, 14 June 2023.

Why does the forward market exist? One answer is that it allows businesses and individuals to lock in a future exchange rate today, thereby eliminating any risk from unfavourable shifts in the exchange rate.

Example 30.3

Looking Forward

Suppose you are a British business expecting to receive €1 million in three months, and you agree to a forward trade to exchange your euros for pounds. Based on Tables 30.3 and 30.4, how many pounds will you get in three months? Is the euro selling at a discount or a premium relative to the pound?

In Table 30.3, the spot exchange rate in terms of pounds per euro is £0.8570 = €1. If the three-month forward rate is €1.0868/£, this means that you can get £0.9201 (= 1/1.0868) for every euro. If you expect €1 million in three months, then you will get €1 million × 0.9201 per pound = £920,100. Because it is more expensive to buy a pound in the forward market than in the spot market (£0.8570 versus £0.9201), the euro is said to be selling at a discount relative to the pound.

As we mentioned earlier, it is standard practice around the world (with a few exceptions) to quote exchange rates in terms of the pound, dollar, euro and yen. This means that rates are quoted as the amount of currency per pound, dollar, euro or yen. For the remainder of this chapter, we will stick with this form. Things can get extremely confusing if you forget this. Thus, when we say things like 'the exchange rate is expected to rise', it is important to remember that we are talking about the exchange rate quoted as units of foreign currency per dollar, euro or yen.

30.3 Purchasing Power Parity

Now that we have discussed what exchange rate quotations mean, we can address an obvious question: What determines the level of the spot exchange rate? In addition, because we know that exchange rates change through time, we can ask the related question: What determines the rate of change in exchange rates? At least part of the answer in both cases goes by the name of **purchasing power parity (PPP)**, the idea that the exchange rate adjusts to keep purchasing power constant among currencies. As we discuss next, there are two forms of PPP: *absolute* and *relative*.

Absolute Purchasing Power Parity

The basic idea behind *absolute purchasing power parity* is that a commodity costs the same regardless of which currency is used to purchase it or where it is selling. This is a very straightforward concept. If a beer costs NKr50 in Oslo, and the exchange rate is NKr10 per pound, then a beer costs NKr50/10 = £5 in London. In other words, absolute PPP says that £1 or €1 will buy you the same number of, say, cheeseburgers anywhere in the world.

More formally, let S_0 be the spot exchange rate between the euro and the dollar today (time 0), and we are quoting exchange rates as the amount of foreign currency per euro. Let P_{US} and P_{Euro} be the current US and euro prices, respectively, on a particular commodity – say, apples. Absolute PPP simply says that:

$$P_{US} = S_0 \times P_{Euro}$$

This tells us that the US price for something is equal to the euro price for that same something multiplied by the exchange rate.

The rationale behind PPP is similar to that behind triangle arbitrage. If PPP did not hold, arbitrage would be possible (in principle) if apples were moved from one country to another. For instance, suppose apples are selling in Milan for €2 per bushel, whereas in New York the price is $3 per bushel. Absolute PPP implies that:

$$P_{US} = S_0 \times P_{Euro}$$
$$\$3 = S_0 \times €2$$
$$S_0 = \$3/€2 + \$1.50/€$$

That is, the implied spot exchange rate is $1.50 per euro. Equivalently, a dollar is worth €1/$1.5 = €0.667/$.

Suppose instead that the actual exchange rate is $1.2815/€. Starting with €2, a trader could buy a bushel of apples in Madrid, ship it to New York and sell it there for $3. Our trader could then convert the $3 into euros at the prevailing exchange rate, S_0 = $1.2815/€, yielding a total of $3/€1.2815 = €2.34. The round-trip gain would be 34 cents.

Because of this profit potential, forces are set in motion to change the exchange rate and/or the price of apples. In our example, apples would begin moving from Madrid to New York. The reduced supply of apples in Madrid would raise the price of apples there, and the increased supply in the USA would lower the price of apples in New York.

In addition to moving apples around, apple traders would be busily converting dollars back into euros to buy more apples. This activity would increase the supply of dollars and simultaneously increase the demand for euros. We would expect the value of a dollar to fall. This means that the euro would be getting more valuable, so it would take more dollars to buy one euro. Because the exchange rate is quoted as dollars per euro, we would expect the exchange rate to rise from \$1.2815/£.

For absolute PPP to hold absolutely, several things must be true:

- The transaction costs of trading apples – shipping, insurance, spoilage, and so on – must be zero.
- There must be no barriers to trading apples – no tariffs, taxes or other political barriers.
- Finally, an apple in New York must be identical to an apple in Madrid. It will not do for you to send red apples to Madrid if the Spanish eat only green apples.

Given the fact that the transaction costs are not zero and that the other conditions are rarely met exactly, it is not surprising that absolute PPP is really applicable only to traded goods, and then only to very uniform ones.

For this reason, absolute PPP does not imply that a Mercedes costs the same as a Ford or that a nuclear power plant in France costs the same as one in New York. In the case of the cars, they are not identical. In the case of the power plants, even if they were identical, they are expensive and would be very difficult to ship. On the other hand, we would be very surprised to see a significant violation of absolute PPP for gold.

Violations of purchasing power parity are actually sought out by corporations. For example, in 2017, Apple built a \$1.3 billion data centre in Iowa, USA. At the same time, the company was investing in other locations, including China, Denmark, Ireland and Nevada. In all cases, low electricity costs and generous tax incentives were the attraction (data centres are very energy-intensive). Meanwhile, the company had several plants in California that were facing higher electricity prices and stricter environmental regulations.

Another example is IKEA, the Swedish furniture retailer, which has been accused of exploiting the differences in price levels between countries to avoid taxes. The company has constructed a network of subsidiaries and franchises in different countries to direct profits and reduce its tax burden.

One of the more famous violations of absolute PPP is the Big Mac Index constructed by *The Economist*. To construct the index, prices for a Big Mac in different countries are gathered from McDonald's. Below you will find the January 2023 Big Mac index from www.economist.com. (We will leave it to you to find the most recent index.)

2023 Big Mac Index

Country	Big Mac Price in Local Currency	Local Currency/US\$ Exchange Rate	Big Mac Price in Dollars	Implied PPP of Dollar	Under (-)/over (+) Valuation Against the Dollar (%)
United Arab Emirates	18.0	3.7	4.9	3.5	−4.8
Bahrain	1.6	0.4	4.2	0.3	−17.6
Switzerland	6.5	1.0	6.7	1.3	30.3
China	24.0	6.7	3.6	4.7	−30.9
Euro area	4.7	1.0	4.8	0.9	−7.5
Britain	3.7	0.8	4.4	0.7	−13.8
India	191.0	80.0	2.4	37.1	−53.6
Jordan	2.3	0.7	3.2	0.4	37.1
Malaysia	10.9	4.5	2.4	2.1	−52.4
Norway	62.0	9.9	6.3	12.0	21.6
Oman	1.4	0.4	3.7	0.3	−28.4
Poland	16.7	4.6	3.6	3.2	−30.3
Saudi Arabia	17.0	3.8	4.5	3.3	−12.1
Singapore	5.9	1.4	4.2	1.1	−17.7
Sweden	57.0	10.2	5.6	11.1	8.5
United States	5.2	1.0	5.2	1.0	0.0
South Africa	39.9	17.0	2.3	7.7	−54.5

Source: The Economist (2023).

As you can see from the index, absolute PPP does not seem to hold, at least for the Big Mac. In fact, in very few currencies surveyed by *The Economist* is the exchange rate within 20 per cent of that predicted by absolute PPP. The largest disparity is in South Africa, where the currency is apparently undervalued by about 54.5 per cent. And many currencies are 'incorrectly' priced by more than 25 per cent. Why?

There are several reasons. First, a Big Mac is not really transportable. Yes, you can load a ship with Big Macs and send it to Switzerland where the currency is supposedly overvalued by more than 30 per cent. But do you really think people would buy your Big Macs? Probably not. Even though it is relatively easy to transport a Big Mac, it would be relatively expensive, and the hamburger would suffer in quality along the way.

If you bought Big Macs wholesale in South Africa and transported them to Switzerland, the price differential is so large you might actually make some money!

Having examined the Big Mac, we can say that absolute PPP should hold more closely for more easily transportable items. For instance, there are many companies with equity listed on exchanges in more than one country. If you examine the share prices on the two stock exchanges you will find that the price of the shares is almost exactly what absolute PPP would predict. The reason is that a share of equity in a particular company is (usually) the same wherever you buy it and whatever currency you use.

Relative Purchasing Power Parity

As a practical matter, a relative version of purchasing power parity has evolved. ***Relative purchasing power parity*** does not tell us what determines the absolute level of the exchange rate. Instead, it tells us what determines the *change* in the exchange rate over time.

The Basic Idea

Suppose the British pound–US dollar exchange rate is currently S_0 = \$1.30. Further suppose that the inflation rate in the USA is predicted to be 10 per cent over the coming year, and (for the moment) the inflation rate in the United Kingdom is predicted to be zero. What do you think the exchange rate will be in a year?

If you think about it, you see that a pound currently costs \$1.30 in the USA. With 10 per cent inflation, we expect prices in the USA to generally rise by 10 per cent. So we expect that the price of a pound will go up by 10 per cent, and the exchange rate should rise to \$1.30 × 1.1 = \$1.43.

If the inflation rate in the United Kingdom is not zero, then we need to worry about the *relative* inflation rates in the two countries. Suppose, say, the UK inflation rate is predicted to be 4 per cent. Relative to prices in the United Kingdom, prices in the United States are rising at a rate of 10 per cent – 4 per cent = 6 per cent per year. So we expect the price of the pound to rise by 6 per cent, and the predicted exchange rate is \$1.30 × 1.06 = \$1.378.

The Result

In general, relative PPP says that the change in the exchange rate is determined by the difference in the inflation rates of the two countries. To be more specific, we will use the following notation:

- S_0 = Current (time 0) spot exchange rate (foreign currency per home currency).
- $E(S_t)$ = Expected exchange rate in t periods.
- h_{HC} = Inflation rate in the home currency.
- h_{FC} = Foreign country inflation rate.

Based on our discussion just preceding, relative PPP says that the expected percentage change in the exchange rate over the next year, $[E(S_1) - S_0]/S_0$, is:

Equation 30.1
$$[E(S_1) - S_0]/S_0 = h_{FC} - h_{HC}$$

In words, relative PPP simply says that the expected percentage change in the exchange rate is equal to the difference in inflation rates. If we rearrange this slightly, we get:

Equation 30.2
$$E(S_1) = S_0 \times [1 + (h_{FC} - h_{HC})]$$

This result makes a certain amount of sense, but care must be used in quoting the exchange rate.

In our example involving the United States and United Kingdom, relative PPP tells us that the exchange rate will rise by $h_{FC} - h_{HC} = 10\% - 4\% = 6\%$ per year. Assuming the difference in inflation rates does not change, the expected exchange rate in two years, $E(S_2)$, will therefore be:

$$\begin{aligned} E(S_2) &= E(S_1) \times (1 + 0.06) \\ &= 1.378 \times 1.06 \\ &= 1.461 \end{aligned}$$

Notice that we could have written this as:

$$\begin{aligned} E(S_2) &= 1.378 \times 1.06 \\ &= 1.30 \times (1.06 \times 1.06) \\ &= 1.30 \times 1.06^2 \end{aligned}$$

In general, relative PPP says that the expected exchange rate at some time in the future, $E(S_t)$, is:

Equation 30.3

$$E(S_t) = S_0 \times [1 + (h_{FC} - h_{HC})]^t$$

As we will see, this is a very useful relationship.

Because we do not really expect absolute PPP to hold for most goods, we will focus on relative PPP in the following discussion. Henceforth, when we refer to PPP without further qualification, we mean relative PPP.

Example 30.4

It Is All Relative

From Table 30.3, the Turkish lira–euro exchange rate is 25.5363 lira per euro. The inflation rate in Turkey over the next three years will run at 43 per cent per year (2023 forecast), whereas the Eurozone inflation rate will be 6 per cent. Based on relative PPP, what will the exchange rate be in three years?

Because the Eurozone inflation rate is lower, we expect that a euro will become more valuable. The exchange rate change will be 43 per cent –6 per cent = 37 per cent per year. Over three years the exchange rate will rise to:

$$\begin{aligned} E(S_3) &= S_0 \times [1 + (h_{FC} - h_{HC})]^3 \\ &= 25.5363 \times [1 + (0.37)]^3 \\ &= 65.6628 \end{aligned}$$

Currency Appreciation and Depreciation

We frequently hear things like 'the euro strengthened (or weakened) in financial markets today' or 'the euro is expected to appreciate (or depreciate) relative to the pound'. When we say that the euro strengthens or appreciates, we mean that the value of a euro rises, so it takes more foreign currency to buy a euro.

What happens to the exchange rates as currencies fluctuate in value depends on how exchange rates are quoted. Because we are quoting them as units of foreign currency per home currency, the exchange rate moves in the same direction as the value of the home currency: it rises as the home currency strengthens, and it falls as the home currency weakens.

Relative PPP tells us that the exchange rate will rise if the home currency inflation rate is lower than the foreign country's inflation rate. This happens because the foreign currency depreciates in value and therefore weakens relative to the home currency.

30.4 Interest Rate Parity, Unbiased Forward Rates and the International Fisher Effect

The next issue we need to address is the relationship between spot exchange rates, forward exchange rates and interest rates. To get started, we need some additional notation:

- F_t = Forward exchange rate for settlement at time t
- R_{HC} = Home currency nominal risk-free interest rate
- R_{FC} = Foreign country nominal risk-free interest rate

As before, we will use S_0 to stand for the spot exchange rate. You can take the home currency nominal risk-free rate, R_{HC}, to be the home country T-bill rate.

Covered Interest Arbitrage

Assume we observe the following information about the British pound and the US dollar in the market:

- $S_0 = \$1.6117$
- $F_1 = \$1.6064$
- $R_{HC} = 2.13\%$
- $R_{FC} = 0.27\%$

where R_{FC} is the nominal risk-free rate in the United States. The period is one year, so F_1 is the 360-day forward rate.

Do you see an arbitrage opportunity here? Suppose you have £10,000 to invest, and you want a riskless investment. One option you have is to invest the £10,000 in a riskless UK investment such as a 360-day T-bill. If you do this, then in one period your £1 will be worth:

$$\begin{aligned}\text{£ value in 1 period} &= \text{£}1 \times (1 + R_{HC}) \\ &= \text{£}10{,}213\end{aligned}$$

Alternatively, you can invest in the US risk-free investment. To do this, you need to convert your £10,000 to US dollars and simultaneously execute a forward trade to convert dollars back to pounds in one year. The necessary steps would be as follows:

1. Convert your £10,000 to £10,000 × S_0 = \$16,117.
2. At the same time, enter into a forward agreement to convert US dollars back to pounds in one year. Because the forward rate is \$1.6064, you will get £1 for every \$1.6064 that you have in one year.
3. Invest your \$16,117 in the United States at R_{FC}. In one year, you will have:

$$\begin{aligned}\$\text{ value in 1 year} &= \$16{,}117 \times (1 + R_{FC}) \\ &= \$16{,}117 \times 1.0027 \\ &= \$16{,}161\end{aligned}$$

4. Convert your \$16,161 back to pounds at the agreed-upon rate of \$1.6064 = £1. You end up with:

$$\begin{aligned}\text{£ value in 1 year} &= \$16{,}161/1.6064 \\ &= \text{£}10{,}060\end{aligned}$$

Notice that the value in one year resulting from this strategy can be written as:

$$\begin{aligned}\text{£ value in 1 year} &= \text{€}10{,}000 \times S_0 \times (1 + R_{FC})/F_1 \\ &= \text{£}10{,}000 \times 1.6117 \times 1.0027/1.6064 \\ &\ \text{£}10{,}060\end{aligned}$$

The return on this investment is apparently 0.60 per cent. This is lower than the 2.13 per cent we get from investing in the United Kingdom. Because both investments are risk-free, there is an arbitrage opportunity.

To exploit the difference in interest rates, you need to borrow, say, \$10 million at the lower US rate and invest it at the higher British rate. What is the round-trip profit from doing this? To find out, we can work through the steps outlined previously:

1. Convert the \$10 million at \$1.6117/£ to get £6,204,629.
2. Agree to exchange dollars for pounds in one year at \$1.6064 to the pound.
3. Invest the £6,204,629 for one year at R_{UK} = 2.13 per cent. You end up with £6,336,787.
4. Convert the £6,336,787 back to dollars to fulfil the forward contract. You receive £6,336,787 × \$1.6064/£ = \$10,179,415.
5. Repay the loan with interest. You owe \$10 million plus 0.27 per cent interest, for a total of \$10,027,000. You have \$10,179,415, so your round-trip profit is a risk-free \$152,415.

The activity that we have illustrated here goes by the name of *covered interest arbitrage*. The term *covered* refers to the fact that we are covered in the event of a change in the exchange rate because we lock in the forward exchange rate today.

Interest Rate Parity

If we assume that significant covered interest arbitrage opportunities do not exist, then there must be some relationship between spot exchange rates, forward exchange rates and relative interest rates. To see what this relationship is, note that, in general, strategy 1 from the preceding discussion, investing in a riskless home currency investment, gives us $1 + R_{HC}$ for every unit of home currency we invest. Strategy 2, investing in a foreign risk-free investment, gives us $S_0 \times (1 + R_{FC})/F_1$ for every unit of home currency we invest. Because these have to be equal to prevent arbitrage, it must be the case that:

$$1 + R_{FC} = S_0 \times (1 + R_{FC})/F_1$$

Rearranging this a bit gets us the famous **interest rate parity (IRP)** condition:

Equation 30.4

$$F_1/S_0 = (1 + R_{FC})/(1 + R_{HC})$$

There is a very useful approximation for IRP that illustrates clearly what is going on and is not difficult to remember. If we define the percentage forward premium or discount as $(F_1 - S_0)/S_0$, then IRP says that this percentage premium or discount is *approximately* equal to the difference in interest rates:

Equation 30.5

$$(F_1 - S_0)/S_0 = R_{FC} - R_{HC}$$

Loosely, what IRP says is that any difference in interest rates between two countries for some period is just offset by the change in the relative value of the currencies, thereby eliminating any arbitrage possibilities. Notice that we could also write:

Equation 30.6

$$F_1 = S_0 \times [1 + (R_{FC} - R_{HC})]$$

In general, if we have t periods instead of just one, the IRP approximation is written like this:

Equation 30.7

$$F_t = S_0 \times [1 + (R_{FC} - R_{HC})]^t$$

Example 30.5

Parity Check

Suppose the exchange rate for the South African rand, S_0, is currently R10.2992 = €1. If the interest rate in the Eurozone is $R_{Euro} = 2.12$ per cent and the interest rate in South Africa is $R_{SA} = 10.95$ per cent, then what must the forward rate be to prevent covered interest arbitrage?

From IRP, we have:

$$\begin{aligned} F_1 &= S_0 \times [1 + (R_{SA} - R_{Euro})] \\ &= \text{R}10.2992 \times [1 + (0.1095 - 0.0212)] \\ &= \text{R}10.2992 \times 1.0883 \\ &= \text{R}11.2086 \end{aligned}$$

Notice that the rand will sell at a discount relative to the euro. Why?

Forward Rates and Future Spot Rates

In addition to PPP and IRP, there is one more basic relationship we need to discuss. What is the connection between the forward rate and the expected future spot rate? The **unbiased forward rates (UFR)** condition says that the forward rate, F_1, is equal to the *expected* future spot rate, $E(S_1)$:

$$F_1 = E(S_1)$$

With t periods, UFR would be written as:

$$F_t = E(S_t)$$

Loosely, the UFR condition says that, on average, the forward exchange rate is equal to the future spot exchange rate.

If we ignore risk, then the UFR condition should hold. Suppose the forward rate for the South African rand is consistently lower than the future spot rate by, say, 10 rand. This means that anyone who wanted to convert euros to rand in the future would consistently get more rand by not agreeing to a forward exchange. The forward rate would have to rise to get anyone interested in a forward exchange.

Similarly, if the forward rate were consistently higher than the future spot rate, then anyone who wanted to convert rand to euros would get more euros per rand by not agreeing to a forward trade. The forward exchange rate would have to fall to attract such traders.

For these reasons, the forward and actual future spot rates should be equal to each other on average. What the future spot rate will actually be is uncertain, of course. The UFR condition may not hold if traders are willing to pay a premium to avoid this uncertainty. If the condition does hold, then the one year forward rate that we see today should be an unbiased predictor of what the exchange rate will actually be in one year.

Putting It All Together

We have developed three relationships – PPP, IRP and UFR – that describe the interactions between key financial variables such as interest rates, exchange rates and inflation rates. We now explore the implications of these relationships as a group.

Uncovered Interest Parity

To start, it is useful to collect our international financial market relationships in one place:

$$\text{PPP}: \ \text{E}(S_1) = S_0 \times [1 + (h_{\text{FC}} - h_{\text{HC}})]$$
$$\text{IRP}: \ F_1 = S_0 \times [1 + (R_{\text{FC}} - R_{\text{HC}})]$$
$$\text{UFR}: F_1 = \text{E}(S_1)$$

We begin by combining UFR and IRP. Because we know that $F_1 = \text{E}(S_1)$ from the UFR condition, we can substitute $\text{E}(S_1)$ for F_1 in IRP. The result is:

Equation 30.8

$$\text{UIP}: \text{E}(S_1) = S_0 \times [1 + (R_{FC} - R_{HC})]$$

This important relationship is called **uncovered interest parity (UIP)**, and it will play a key role in the international capital budgeting discussion that follows. With *t* periods, UIP becomes:

Equation 30.9

$$\text{E}(S_t) = S_0 \times [1 + (R_{\text{FC}} - R_{\text{HC}})]^t$$

The International Fisher Effect

Next we compare PPP and UIP. Both of them have $\text{E}(S_1)$ on the left side, so their right sides must be equal. We thus have:

$$S_0 \times [1 + (h_{\text{FC}} - h_{\text{CH}})] = S_0 \times [1 + (R_{\text{FC}} - R_{\text{CH}})]$$
$$h_{\text{FC}} - h_{\text{HC}} = R_{\text{FC}} - R_{\text{HC}}$$

This tells us that the difference in returns between the home country and a foreign country is just equal to the difference in inflation rates. Rearranging this slightly gives us the **international Fisher effect (IFE)**:

Equation 30.10

$$\text{IFE}: R_{\text{HC}} - h_{\text{HC}} = R_{\text{FC}} - h_{\text{FC}}$$

The IFE says that *real* rates are equal across countries. The conclusion that real returns are equal across countries is really basic economics. If real returns were higher in, say, Britain than in the Eurozone, money would flow out of Eurozone financial markets and into British markets. Asset prices in Britain would rise and their returns would fall. At the same time, asset prices in Europe would fall and their returns would rise. This process acts to equalize real returns.

Having said all this, we need to note a couple of things. First, we have not explicitly dealt with risk in our discussion. We might reach a different conclusion about real returns once we do, particularly if people in different countries have different tastes and attitudes towards risk. Second, there are many barriers to the movement of money and capital around the world. Real returns might be different in two different countries for long periods if money cannot move freely between them.

Despite these problems, we expect that capital markets will become increasingly internationalized. As this occurs, any differences in real rates will probably diminish. The laws of economics have little respect for national boundaries.

30.5 International Capital Budgeting

Chapter 7 Page 178

International capital budgeting involves the estimation of the cash flows associated with a potential foreign investment, but it also incorporates additional complexities such as exchange rate fluctuations, political risk, tax considerations and other variables unique to international business environments.

Differences between International and Domestic Capital Budgeting

Domestic and international capital budgeting are similar in many ways, and the fundamental concepts of capital budgeting apply to both. However, there are additional factors that a manager must consider when undertaking international capital budgeting because of the different environments in which decisions are being made.

The most important considerations are:

- *Exchange rate risk:* Because foreign investments are in a different currency, the investing company takes on exchange rate risk due to fluctuations in exchange rates over time. An understanding of the international parity conditions is essential to investment appraisal in foreign countries and international capital budgeting.
- *Political and country risk:* When considering international capital budgeting, it's important to carefully assess the potential political risks involved. These risks can arise from a range of factors, such as shifts in government leadership, the possibility of assets being expropriated or nationalized, civil unrest, and changes in laws or policies that could negatively impact the company's operations. Taking these factors into account can help businesses make informed decisions when it comes to investing in foreign markets.
- *Different tax systems:* Differences in tax systems can significantly impact the profitability of international investments and firms must be aware of the tax regimes in every country in which they operate.
- *Cost of capital:* The discount rate to apply to an investment appraisal will vary depending on the country in which the project is operating. This is because risk-free rates and market risk premiums will be dependent on the host country of the investment. Foreign investments may also be subject to withholding taxes on dividends and interest payments, which will increase the cost of capital of the project.
- *Cultural and social factors:* These factors can have a significant impact on the success of an international investment. Understanding local business customs, financing models, consumer behaviours and social norms is necessary for international capital budgeting decisions. For example in many parts of the world, companies follow a form of Islamic business, which restricts the industry sectors that are permitted for investment as well as the financing to fund it.

Fundamentals of International Capital Budgeting

We'll now illustrate international capital budgeting decisions using a simple example: Kihlstrom Equipment, a US-based international company that is evaluating an overseas investment. Kihlstrom's exports of drill bits have increased to such a degree that it is considering building a distribution centre in France. The project will cost €2 million to launch. The cash flows are expected to be €0.9 million a year for the next three years.

The current spot exchange rate for euros is €0.5/\$. Recall that this is euros per dollar, so a euro is worth \$1/0.5 = \$2. The risk-free rate in the United States is 5 per cent, and the risk-free rate in France is 7 per cent. Note that the exchange rate and the two interest rates are observed in financial markets, not estimated. Kihlstrom's required return on dollar investments of this sort is 10 per cent.

Should Kihlstrom take this investment? As always, the answer depends on the NPV; but how do we calculate the net present value of this project in US dollars? There are two basic methods:

1. *The home currency approach:* Convert all the euro cash flows into dollars, and then discount at 10 per cent to find the NPV in dollars. Notice that for this approach we have to come up with the future exchange rates to convert the future projected euro cash flows into dollars.
2. *The foreign currency approach:* Determine the required return on euro investments and then discount the euro cash flows to find the NPV in euros. Then convert this euro NPV to a dollar NPV. This approach requires us to somehow convert the 10 per cent dollar required return to the equivalent euro required return.

Chapter 6 Page 147

The difference between these two approaches is primarily a matter of when we convert from euros to dollars. In the first case, we convert before estimating the NPV. In the second case, we convert after estimating NPV (NPV is discussed in detail in Chapter 6).

It might appear that the second approach is superior because for it we have to come up with only one number, the euro discount rate. Furthermore, because the first approach requires us to forecast future exchange rates, it probably seems that there is greater room for error with this approach. As we illustrate next, however, based on our previous results, the two approaches are really the same.

Method 1: The Home Currency Approach

To convert the project future cash flows into dollars, we will invoke the uncovered interest parity, or UIP, relation to come up with the projected exchange rates. Remember that the euro is the foreign currency in this example. Based on our earlier discussion, the expected exchange rate at time t, $E(S_t)$, is:

$$E(S_t) = S_0 \times [1 + (R_€ - R_{US})]^t$$

where $R_€$ stands for the nominal risk-free rate in France. Because $R_€$ is 7 per cent, R_{US} is 5 per cent and the current exchange rate (S_0) is €0.5:

$$\begin{aligned} E(S_t) &= 0.5 \times [1 + (0.07 - 0.05)]^t \\ &= 0.5 \times 1.02^t \end{aligned}$$

The projected exchange rates for the drill bit project are thus as shown here:

Year	Expected Exchange Rate
1	$€0.5 \times 1.02^1 = €0.5100$
2	$€0.5 \times 1.02^2 = €0.5202$
3	$€0.5 \times 1.02^3 = €0.5306$

Using these exchange rates, along with the current exchange rate, we can convert all of the euro cash flows to dollars (note that all of the cash flows in this example are in millions):

Year	(1) Cash Flow in €m	(2) Expected Exchange Rate	(3) Cash Flow in $m (1)/(2)
0	−2.0	0.5000	−4.00 ×
1	0.9	0.5100	1.76
2	0.9	0.5202	1.73
3	0.9	0.5306	1.70

To finish off, we calculate the NPV in the ordinary way:

$$\begin{aligned} NPV &= -\$4 + \$1.76/1.10 + \$1.73/1.10^2 + \$1.70/1.10^3 \\ &= \$0.3 \text{ million} \end{aligned}$$

So, the project appears to be profitable.

Method 2: The Foreign Currency Approach

Kihlstrom requires a nominal return of 10 per cent on the dollar-denominated cash flows. We need to convert this to a rate suitable for euro-denominated cash flows. Based on the international Fisher effect, we know that the difference in the nominal rates is:

$$\begin{aligned} R_€ - R_{US} &= h_€ - h_{US} \\ &= 7\% - 5\% = 2\% \end{aligned}$$

The appropriate discount rate for estimating the euro cash flows from the drill bit project is approximately equal to 10 per cent plus an extra 2 per cent to compensate for the greater euro inflation rate.

If we calculate the NPV of the euro cash flows at this rate, we get:

$$\begin{aligned} NPV &= -€2 + €0.9/1.12 + €0.9/1.12^2 + €0.9/1.12^3 \\ &= €0.16 \text{ million} \end{aligned}$$

The NPV of this project is €0.16 million. Taking this project makes us €0.16 million richer today. What is this in dollars? Because the exchange rate today is €0.5, the dollar NPV of the project is:

$$NPV\$ = NPV_€/S_0 = €0.16/0.5 = \$0.3 \text{ million}$$

This is the same dollar NPV that we calculated previously.

The important thing to recognize from our example is that the two capital budgeting procedures are actually the same and will always give the same answer. In this second approach, the fact that we are implicitly forecasting exchange rates is simply hidden. Even so, the foreign currency approach is computationally a little easier.

Unremitted Cash Flows

The previous example assumed that all after-tax cash flows from the foreign investment could be remitted to (paid out to) the parent firm. Actually, substantial differences can exist between the cash flows generated by a foreign project and the amount that can be remitted, or 'repatriated', to the parent firm.

A foreign subsidiary can remit funds to a parent in many forms, including the following:

- Dividends
- Management fees for central services
- Royalties on the use of trade names and patents.

However cash flows are repatriated, international firms must pay special attention to remittances because there may be current and future controls on them. Many governments are sensitive to the charge of being exploited by foreign national firms. In such cases, governments are tempted to limit the ability of international firms to remit cash flows. Funds that cannot currently be remitted are sometimes said to be *blocked*.

30.6 Exchange Rate Risk

Exchange rate risk is the natural consequence of international operations in a world where relative currency values move up and down. Managing exchange rate risk is an important part of international finance. As we discuss next, there are three different types of exchange rate risk or exposure: short-term exposure, long-term exposure and translation exposure.

Short-term Exposure

The day-to-day fluctuations in exchange rates create short-term risks for international firms. Most such firms have contractual agreements to buy and sell goods in the near future at set prices. When different currencies are involved, such transactions have an extra element of risk.

Imagine, say, that you are importing imitation pasta from Italy and reselling it in the United Kingdom under the Impasta brand name. Your largest customer has ordered 10,000 cases of Impasta. You place the order with your supplier today, but you will not pay until the goods arrive in 60 days. Your selling price is £6 per case. Your cost is €8.40 per case, and the exchange rate is currently €1.50, so it takes 1.50 euros to buy £1.

At the current exchange rate, your cost in pounds of filling the order is €8.40/1.5 = £5.60 per case, so your pre-tax profit on the order is 10,000 × (\$6 – 5.60) = \$4,000. However, the exchange rate in 60 days will probably be different, so your profit will depend on what the future exchange rate turns out to be.

For example, if the rate goes to €1.60, your cost is €8.40/1.60 = £5.25 per case. Your profit goes to £7,500. If the exchange rate goes to, say, €1.40, then your cost is €8.40/1.40 = £6, and your profit is zero.

The short-term exposure in our example can be reduced or eliminated in several ways. The most obvious of these is to enter into a forward exchange agreement to lock in an exchange rate. Suppose, for example, the 60-day forward rate is €1.58. What will be your profit if you hedge? What profit should you expect if you do not hedge?

If you hedge, you lock in an exchange rate of €1.58. Your cost in pounds will thus be €8.40/1.58 = £5.32 per case, so your profit will be 10,000 × (£6 – 5.32) = £6,800. If you do not hedge, then, assuming that the forward rate is an unbiased predictor (in other words, assuming the UFR condition holds), you should expect that the exchange rate will actually be €1.58 in 60 days. You should expect to make £6,800.

Alternatively, if this strategy is not feasible, you could simply borrow the pounds today, convert them into euros, and invest the euros for 60 days to earn some interest. Based on IRP, this amounts to entering into a forward contract.

Long-term Exposure

In the long term, the value of a foreign operation can fluctuate because of unanticipated changes in relative economic conditions. Imagine, say, that we own a labour-intensive assembly operation located in another country to take advantage of lower wages. Through time, unexpected changes in economic conditions can raise the foreign wage levels to the point where the cost advantage is eliminated or even becomes negative.

Hedging long-term exposure is more difficult than hedging short-term risks. For one thing, organized forward markets do not exist for such long-term needs. Instead, the primary option that firms have is to try to match up foreign currency inflows and outflows. The same thing goes for matching foreign currency-denominated assets and liabilities. A firm that sells in a foreign country, for example, might try to concentrate its raw material purchases and labour expense in that country. That way, the home currency values of its revenues and costs will move up and down together. Probably the best examples of this type of hedging are the so-called transplant auto manufacturers such as BMW, Honda, Mercedes and Toyota, which now build a substantial portion of the cars they sell in the United States at plants located in the United States, thereby obtaining some degree of immunization against exchange rate movements. This has also become a viable strategy in an era of increasing trade barriers between the world's major economies.

The German firm BMW, for instance, produces 350,000 cars in South Carolina, USA, and exports about 230,000 of them. The costs of manufacturing the cars are paid mostly in dollars, and when BMW exports the cars to Europe it receives euros. When the dollar weakens, these vehicles become more profitable for BMW. At the same time, BMW exports about 217,000 cars to the United States each year. The costs of manufacturing these imported cars are mostly in euros, so they become less profitable when the dollar weakens. Taken together, these gains and losses tend to offset each other and give BMW a natural hedge.

Similarly, a firm can reduce its long-term exchange rate risk by borrowing in the foreign country. Fluctuations in the value of the foreign subsidiary's assets will then be at least partially offset by changes in the value of the liabilities.

Translation Exposure

When a British company calculates its accounting net income and EPS for some period, it must translate everything into pounds. Similarly, a Eurozone firm must translate all overseas income into euros. This can create some problems for accountants when there are significant foreign operations. In particular, two issues arise:

1. What is the appropriate exchange rate to use for translating each account in the statement of financial position?
2. How should accounting gains and losses from foreign currency translation be handled?

To illustrate the accounting problem, suppose we started a small foreign subsidiary in Lilliputia a year ago. The local currency is the gulliver, abbreviated GL. At the beginning of the year, the exchange rate was GL2 = €1, and the statement of financial position for gulliver looked like this:

	GL		GL
Assets	1,000	Liabilities	500
		Equity	500

At 2 gullivers to the euro, the beginning statement of financial position in euros was as follows:

	€		€
Assets	500	Liabilities	250
		Equity	250

Lilliputia is a quiet place, and nothing at all actually happened during the year. As a result, net income was zero (before consideration of exchange rate changes). However, the exchange rate did change to 4 gullivers = €1 purely because the Lilliputian inflation rate is much higher than the Eurozone inflation rate.

Because nothing happened, the ending statement in financial position in gullivers is the same as the beginning one. However, if we convert it to euros at the new exchange rate, we get these figures:

	€		€
Assets	250	Liabilities	125
		Equity	125

Notice that the value of the equity has gone down by €125, even though net income was exactly zero. Despite the fact that absolutely nothing happened, there is a €125 accounting loss. How to handle this €125 loss has been a controversial accounting question.

The current approach to handling translation gains and losses is based on rules set out in the International Accounting Standards Board (IASB) *International Accounting Standard 21* (IAS 21). For the most part, IAS 21 requires that all assets and liabilities be translated from the subsidiary's currency into the parent's currency using the exchange rate that currently prevails. Income and expenses are treated differently and these are translated at the exchange rate that prevails at the time of the transaction or at the average rate for the period when this is a reasonable approximation.

Managing Exchange Rate Risk

For a large multinational firm, the management of exchange rate risk is complicated by the fact that there can be many different currencies involved in many different subsidiaries. It is likely that a change in some exchange rate will benefit some subsidiaries and hurt others. The net effect on the overall firm depends on its net exposure.

For example, suppose a firm has two divisions. Division A buys goods in Italy for euros and sells them in Britain for pounds. Division B buys goods in Britain for pounds and sells them in Italy for euros. If these two divisions are of roughly equal size in terms of their inflows and outflows, then the overall firm obviously has little exchange rate risk.

In our example, the firm's net position in pounds (the amount coming in less the amount going out) is small, so the exchange rate risk is small. However, if one division, acting on its own, were to start hedging its exchange rate risk, then the overall firm's exchange rate risk would go up. The moral of the story is that multinational firms have to be conscious of the overall position that the firm has in a foreign currency. For this reason, management of exchange rate risk is probably best handled on a centralized basis.

30.7 Political Risk

One final element of risk in international investing is **political risk** – that is, changes in value that arise as a consequence of political actions. This is not a problem faced exclusively by international firms. For instance, changes in British tax laws and regulations may benefit some British firms and hurt others, so political risk exists nationally as well as internationally.

Some countries have more political risk than others, however. When firms have operations in these riskier countries, the extra political risk may lead the firms to require higher returns on overseas investments to compensate for the possibility that funds may be blocked, critical operations interrupted and contracts abrogated. In the most extreme case, the possibility of outright confiscation may be a concern in countries with relatively unstable political environments.

Political risk also depends on the nature of the business: some businesses are less likely to be confiscated because they are not particularly valuable in the hands of a different owner. An assembly operation supplying subcomponents that only the parent company uses would not be an attractive takeover target, for example. Similarly, a manufacturing operation that requires the use of specialized components from the parent is of little value without the parent company's cooperation.

Natural resource developments, such as copper mining or oil drilling, are just the opposite. Once the operation is in place, much of the value is in the commodity. The political risk for such investments is much higher for this reason. Also, the issue of exploitation is more pronounced with such investments, again increasing the political risk.

Chapter 2 Page 24

Corruption is a very big issue in many countries and the payment of kickbacks, or 'business facilitation fees', is the norm in many areas. Government officials, petty bureaucrats and cumbersome administrative regulations can significantly restrict the efficiency of international operations.

Many organizations present rankings of political risk in countries and it is paramount that these are considered before any foreign direct investment takes place. *Transparency International*'s 'perceptions of corruption' ranking is an example of such an assessment and is presented in Figure 2.3 of Chapter 2.

Political risk can be hedged in several ways, particularly when confiscation or nationalization is a concern. The use of local financing, perhaps from the government of the foreign country in question, reduces the possible loss because the company can refuse to pay the debt in the event of unfavourable political activities. Based on our discussion in this section, structuring the operation in such a way that it requires significant parent company involvement to function is another way to reduce political risk.

Real World Insight 30.1

Doing Bitcoin Business in Venezuela

(Excerpt from 'The bitcoin bubble, Venezuela, and political risk', GlobalRiskInsights.com, 22 December 2017)

Venezuelans are not newcomers to cryptocurrencies. The country has one of the highest concentrations of bitcoin miners in the world thanks to electricity subsidies that render the power-crunching practice widely affordable. Yet electricity is perhaps one of the few things Venezuelans are able to afford in a country grappling with widespread food and medicine shortages.

Venezuelans are living though the worst hyperinflation since post-WWI Germany. A third of all Venezuelans reported an average of 8 kg in weight loss due to rising food prices. The International Monetary Fund further estimates the inflation rate will reach 2,3000 per cent alongside a 12 per cent contraction in gross domestic product.

Adding to hyperinflation and food shortages is the overall scarcity of cash in the country. Hence, even when accounting for recent volatility in bitcoin and its many offshoots, it is not difficult to understand why Venezuelans are trading Bolivars for bitcoin.

Cryptocurrencies are widely available to anyone with a smartphone, unwound from central banks, which regulate the overall availability of cash. They also allow remittances to bypass state-mandated transfer and convertibility laws that might either prohibit the transfer, or set a conversion rate that would discourage remittances. Bitcoin likewise trades in public spaces: anyone can readily see what a bitcoin is worth at any point in time (this particular feature resonates in Venezuela where it is illegal to publish the free-market value of the Bolivar).

If cryptocurrencies have a lot to offer average Venezuelans, they are also, and for different reasons, appealing to authoritarian regimes.

President Nicolás Maduro announced early December 2017 his intent to launch an oil-backed cryptocurrency called the 'Petro'. He made no effort to hide the fact that the Petro would circumvent US financial sanctions on Venezuelan government officials and the country's debt issuance.

Indeed, the Petro could theoretically help President Maduro get around current and future sanctions because it provides an alternative path for sending money. This doesn't mean global oil and commodity contracts will be based on the Petro anytime soon, but President Maduro's desire to avoid dollar transactions is not new, and other countries such as Russia and China share his view.

Moreover, the reason it probably won't be the Petro reflects another form of political risk, in that the Petro will likely be a hotbed of corruption. Part of what makes mainstream investors wary of bitcoin is its perceived vulnerability to corruption inside the community, and to cyberattacks that would compromise its value.

Be it the Petro or any other cryptocurrency, the rise of peer-to-peer currencies will have an indelible effect on country risk at transaction level. Exchange rates, interest rates and rollover risks are all likely to be affected. International monetary regulations will now have to factor in a currency outside a state's financial policy, or a central bank without a chairperson. The true scale of these risks is hard to assess at present: bitcoin is unprecedented.

30.8 Long-term Islamic Financing

In recent years, many countries have developed financial instruments and business practices that reflect the religious values of Islam. This is known as Islamic financing, with the main characteristic being that interest of any kind is not allowed to be charged on financial securities. The United Kingdom is at the forefront of Islamic financing in Western Europe, followed by Switzerland, France and Luxembourg. In the Middle East, Bahrain is the Islamic financing centre and Malaysia is the main country in South East Asia. Islamic financing need not be confined only to Muslims, and in Malaysia, for example, nearly a quarter of all users of Islamic products are non-Muslims.

Not having interest-bearing securities presents a number of challenges to firms wishing to raise financing for investment projects. In response, banks have created a number of innovative instruments and financing methods that are consistent with Islamic or Shariah principles and have debt-like characteristics. The most common of these involve elements of profit-sharing, known as *mudharabah*, joint ventures (*musharakah*), leasing (*ijarah*) and compensation for facilitating the financing activity (*murabahah*). Islamic securities that can be traded on exchanges are known as *sukuk*.

Types of Islamic Financing Methods

An Advanced Payment Sale

A *bai salam* is a contract where two parties trade today in return for a good to be delivered at some specified date in the future. The transfer of cash must be made today, and the quality and quantity of the good must be specified at the time of the trade. One of the requirements of *bai salam* is that there can be no uncertainty in the quality or quantity of a good or commodity. Therefore, raw agricultural produce is not allowed to be traded in this way because flooding or an earthquake may result in loss of quality or quantity.

Example 30.6

Bai Salam

Shukran plc is undertaking a new warehouse expansion and has commissioned a company, Temsaah Ltd, to build it on the site of an existing warehouse. The warehouse with full facilities will take one year to build and the price of the new warehouse will be £3,000,000 in one year. In a *bai salam* sale, Shukran may pay £2.7 million today for the warehouse (fully specified at the time of the contract) to be ready for use exactly one year from the date of the trade.

Stated Cost Plus Profit

Murabahah is one of the most common forms of Islamic financing contracts. In this transaction, the seller of a commodity expressly states the cost that has been incurred in producing, manufacturing or buying a commodity or asset. A pre-agreed markup or profit margin is then applied to the cost in order to find the price of the trade. Clearly, a *murabahah* contract requires the seller to be honest about the base cost of the commodity. *Murabahah* is used for the financing of asset purchases and property investments. So that there is no doubt that it was the underlying asset that has been traded (to avoid accusations of interest payments in another form), the seller of the commodity or asset must be the owner before selling it. As in other Islamic financing contracts, a seller may consult the debt markets to ascertain competitive markup rates.

In a *murabahah* sale, the purchaser may pay the stated amount in fixed instalments. When only one payment in the future is made, this is known as a *bai' bithaman ajil* contract.

Example 30.7

Murabahah

Shukran plc is undertaking a new warehouse expansion and has commissioned a company, Temsaah Ltd, to build It on the site of an existing warehouse. Temsaah needs cash equalling the construction costs of £2.7 million today to finance the building of the warehouse. Unfortunately, Shukran does not have the funds in place. The CEO of Shukran goes to Bahrain Bank and enters into a *murabahah* transaction.

Bahrain Bank agrees to pay £2.7 million today to Temsaah and notifies Shukran's CEO of the cost. Given market conditions, with comparable loans currently at 10 per cent, the manager of Bahrain Bank enters into an agreement with the CEO of Shukran to charge a markup of £270,000 on the building, to be paid in one year. This markup of 10 per cent makes the *murabahah* contract competitive with Western financing deals.

In this transaction, Bahrain Bank owns the warehouse until the date of the trade. In one year, Bahrain Bank sells the warehouse for £2,970,000 (£2,700,000 cost plus £270,000 markup) and the transfer of title deeds to Shukran takes place at that date. As you will have noticed, this transaction is actually a *bai' bithaman ajil* contract, which is a subtype of *murabahah* financing.

Goodwill Loan

Perhaps unique to the global financial markets, a *qard hassan* is a loan without any interest. The lender will provide the borrower with funds and, at some point in the future, these will be paid back to the bank. The borrower may, at his own discretion, repay an extra amount to compensate the lender for supplying the funds. A *qard hassan* is normally very small, say £2,000, and is given to pay for school education, medical fees or some other socially improving purpose.

Hire Purchase

Hire purchase agreements originally came from the United Kingdom and are most commonly used in the automobile industry. In a Western hire purchase agreement, the buyer of an asset puts down an initial deposit on the price of an asset and agrees to hire or rent it for a set period. When the sum of the rental payments reaches a certain amount, the buyer may purchase the asset outright for a pre-agreed price and take ownership.

With a little modification, hire purchase agreements are ideal instruments for Islamic financing. In an *ijarah thumma al bai'* contract, the buyer agrees to first lease or rent the asset for a certain period. When this period has expired, the buyer may purchase the asset for a specific price that is agreed at the very beginning of the contract.

Example 30.8

Using Western Loans to Determine Payments in an *Ijarah Thumma Al Bai'*

Shufaa Al Beity wishes to purchase a car whose sale price is €25,000. Unfortunately, she is a student and cannot afford to part with that amount of money today. She decides to enter into an *ijarah thumma al bai'* contract to buy the car over five years in monthly instalments. How much would she pay?

To determine a set of monthly payments that is competitive with other Western lenders, an Islamic bank would study the range of Western loans that are on offer today. Assume that most banks are giving personal loans with an APR of 10 per cent. This is the effective interest rate on car loans for €25,000 over five years and equates to a rate of 0.7974 per cent per month (work it out yourself!). Using the standard annuity formula, the monthly payment on a loan of €25,000 paid over 60 monthly instalments at a rate of 0.7974 per cent per month is:

$$C = \frac{€25{,}000}{A_{0.007974}^{60}} = \frac{€25{,}000}{47.5385} = €525.89$$

The total payments that Shufaa will need to make if she takes out a Western loan is 60 × €525.89 = €31,553.37. For an Islamic bank to be competitive with its Western counterpart, the total amount paid in an *ijarah thumma al bai'* must be equal to or less than €31,553.37.

Shufaa can only afford a monthly payment of €500, so she enters into an *ijarah thumma al bai'* contract where the Islamic bank buys the car from the car dealer for €25,000. It then leases the car to Shufaa for a monthly payment of €500 a month for 60 months. At the end of the term of the *ijarah thumma al bai'* she will have paid a total of €30,000. To be competitive with Western loans, the final payment must be less than or equal to €31,553.37 – €30,000 = €1,553.37.

Joint Venture

A *musharakah* is a contract between two parties to invest in a joint venture and share in any profit or losses that may arise from the investment. Companies that require partial funding for an investment can go to an Islamic bank, enter into a *musharakah* agreement and raise the required funds.

This type of financing is an important alternative to standard bank loans and illustrates the cooperative nature of the Islamic approach to doing business. In each transaction, the supplier and demander of funds directly bear the cash flow risk of the underlying investment.

Leasing

Leasing, or *ijarah*, is a form of financing that is available to companies. With a lease, the lessee pays rent for an asset for a period of time from the lessor. In this type of contract, the payments are for the use of the asset. Lease financing is covered in more detail in Chapter 17.

Profit Sharing

In a *mudharabah* contract, a businessman uses the funds of a bank or lender to invest in a project. The two parties share the profits of the business according to predetermined ratios. In this transaction, the lender bears the financial risk of the investment but gains from the specialized skills of the entrepreneur. Both parties benefit financially from the joint investment through the contribution of different skills or assets.

Safekeeping

Like Western banks, Islamic banks require deposits to fund their activities. A company or individual may lodge funds at an Islamic bank and is able to draw those funds at any time from the bank. In some situations, the bank may give the depositor a *hibah*, which is a small sum of money to compensate the depositor for leaving the funds with the Islamic bank. This is known as *wadiah*. Although this could be seen as an interest payment by another name, because the *hibah* payment is not contractual it is not viewed as such under Shariah law.

Sale and Buyback

With a *bai' al-inah* agreement, a company buys an asset from a seller and agrees to pay for it at some point in the future. The seller immediately buys the asset back at a discount.

Example 30.9

Bai' Al-inah

Shukran plc needs £2,700,000 to undertake a new warehouse expansion. It approaches an Islamic bank, which agrees to participate in a *bai' al-inah* agreement. In this transaction, the bank sells a building today to Shukran for £3,000,000 to be paid in one year. Immediately, the bank buys the building back for £2,700,000 today. In this transaction, Shukran now has £2,700,000 but must pay £3,000,000 to the bank in one year. This is very similar to a one-year loan, but the crucial thing is that a real asset and not money is driving the payments. This is acceptable under Islamic law.

Sustainability in Action 30.1

Biotrend's Alternative Energy *Sukuk*

In April 2023, Turkish firm Biotrend Cevre ve Enerji Yatirimlari (Biotrend), an alternative energy production company, issued its debut *sukuk* – a three-month TRY60 million ($2.83 million) sustainability facility. The *sukuk* was to finance Biotrend's sustainable investments, including energy efficiency, the circular economy and renewable energy, with operations in 11 cities across Turkey. The company also invests in integrated solid waste management, recovered heat, and carbon certification and trading.

The Biotrend *sukuk* is not just an example of sustainable investment but also illustrates the flexibility and potential of Islamic finance structures in supporting sustainability goals. The use of the *sukuk* model, a form of Islamic bond discussed in Section 16.6, aligns with the principles of risk sharing, asset backing and the prohibition of interest (*riba*), making it a suitable tool for financing sustainable projects.

Source: Islamic Sustainable Finance and Investment

Summary and Conclusions

The international firm has a more complicated life than the purely domestic firm. Management must understand the connection between interest rates, foreign currency exchange rates and inflation, and it must become aware of many different financial market regulations and tax systems. This chapter is intended to be a concise introduction to some of the financial issues that come up in international investing.

Our coverage has been necessarily brief. The main topics we discussed are as follows:

1 *Some basic vocabulary:* We briefly defined some exotic terms in international finance.

2 *The basic mechanics of exchange rate quotations:* We discussed the spot and forward markets, and how exchange rates are interpreted.

3 *The fundamental relationships between international financial variables:*

(a) Absolute and relative purchasing power parity (PPP)

(b) Interest rate parity (IRP)

(c) Unbiased forward rates (UFR).

Absolute purchasing power parity states that a currency, such as the euro, should have the same purchasing power in each country. This means that an orange costs the same whether you buy it in Brussels or in Oslo.

Relative purchasing power parity means that the expected percentage change in exchange rates between the currencies of two countries is equal to the difference in their inflation rates.

Interest rate parity implies that the percentage difference between the forward exchange rate and the spot exchange rate is equal to the interest rate differential. We showed how covered interest arbitrage forces this relationship to hold.

The unbiased forward rates condition indicates that the current forward rate is a good predictor of the future spot exchange rate.

4 *International capital budgeting:* We showed that the basic foreign exchange relationships imply two other conditions:

(a) Uncovered interest parity

(b) The international Fisher effect.

By invoking these two conditions, we learned how to estimate NPVs in foreign currencies and how to convert foreign currencies into the home currency to estimate NPV in the usual way.

5 *Exchange rate and political risk:* We described the various types of exchange rate risk, and discussed some common approaches to managing the effect of fluctuating exchange rates on the cash flows and value of the international firm. We also discussed political risk and some ways of managing exposure to it.

6 In many parts of the world where the Muslim faith is common, standard investment instruments that involve interest payments are not acceptable. In response, Islamic financing has developed to counter the problems associated with raising capital for firms wishing to adhere to Islamic principles.

Questions and Problems

CONCEPT

1 **Terminology** Explain the difference between a domestic bond, a foreign bond and a Eurobond, and give an example of each.

2 **Foreign Exchange Markets and Exchange Rates** What is meant by triangular arbitrage? Is this likely to occur in real life? Explain.

3 **Purchasing Power Parity** Do you think purchasing power parity exists in the world economies? As country barriers fall, is purchasing power parity likely to become more prevalent? Does the empirical evidence support the PPP theory? Discuss.

4 **Interest Rate Parity, Unbiased Forward Rates and the International Fisher Effect** Review the international parity conditions. Which ones do you think are likely to exist and which are less likely to be valid? During a global recession, do you think they are less or more likely to be valid? Explain.

5 **International Capital Budgeting** Should international capital budgeting projects be assessed from the perspective of a multinational's subsidiary or from that of the parent company? Are there any circumstances under which this would change? Explain.

6 **Exchange Rate Risk** In 2016 the British pound depreciated by approximately 20 per cent as a result of the British vote to leave the EU. In your opinion, did the depreciation in sterling damage the UK economy? Are exchange rate movements necessarily good or bad for a country? Explain.

7 **Political Risk** Why is country risk analysis important? Can multinationals reduce their exposure to country risk? As a result of Brexit, many companies announced contingency plans to move their headquarters elsewhere in Europe. Why do you think they did this? Explain.

8 **Islamic Financing** Explain what is meant by Islamic financing. What are the different types of securities that are used in this sector? In this context, explain what is meant by a *sukuk*. Construct a practical example of a *sukuk* and explain the issues that arise in its use.

REGULAR

9 **Spot and Forward Rates** Suppose the exchange rate for the Australian dollar is quoted as A$3/£ in the spot market and A$4/£ in the 90-day forward market.

(a) Is the British pound selling at a premium or a discount relative to the Australian dollar?

(b) Does the financial market expect the Australian dollar to weaken relative to the pound? Explain.

(c) What do you suspect is true about relative economic conditions in the United Kingdom and Australia?

10 **Purchasing Power Parity and Inflation Differentials** Suppose the rate of inflation in the Eurozone will run about 3 per cent higher than the UK inflation rate over the next several years. All other things being the same, what will happen to the euro versus pound exchange rate? What relationship are you relying on in answering?

11 **Exchange Rates** The exchange rate for the Australian dollar is currently A$0.9641/US$. This exchange rate is expected to rise by 10 per cent over the next year.

(a) Is the Australian dollar expected to get stronger or weaker?

(b) What do you think about the relative inflation rates in the USA and Australia?

(c) What do you think about the relative nominal interest rates in the USA and Australia? Relative real rates?

12 **Bulldog Bonds** Which of the following most accurately describes a Bulldog bond?

(a) A bond issued by Vodafone in Frankfurt with the interest payable in British pounds.

(b) A bond issued by Vodafone in Frankfurt with the interest payable in euros.

(c) A bond issued by BMW in Germany with the interest payable in British pounds.

(d) A bond issued by BMW in London with the interest payable in British pounds.

(e) A bond issued by BMW worldwide with the interest payable in British pounds.

13 **International Risks** At one point, Duracell International confirmed that it was planning to open battery manufacturing plants in China and India. Manufacturing in these countries allows Duracell to avoid import duties of between 30 and 35 per cent that have made alkaline batteries prohibitively expensive for some consumers. What additional advantages might Duracell see in this proposal? What are some of the risks to Duracell?

14 **Islamic Financing and Leasing** Explain why leasing is consistent with Islamic financing principles. Explain what is meant by a *musharakah* transaction in Islamic finance. Give an example to illustrate your answer.

15 **Multinational Corporations** Given that many multinationals have much greater sales outside their domestic markets than within them, what is the particular relevance of their domestic currency?

16 **Exchange Rate Movements** Are the following statements true or false? Explain why.

(a) If the central bank decreases interest rates in the United Kingdom, but holds them constant in the United States, then we would expect the pound to depreciate relative to the dollar.

(b) Suppose you are a German machine tool exporter and you invoice all of your sales in foreign currency. Further suppose that there are higher inflation rates in Germany relative to those in other countries, then you should use the forward markets to protect yourself against future losses resulting from the deterioration in the value of the euro.

(c) The 2016 Brexit vote was widely anticipated to result in a vote to remain in the EU. Instead, the British public voted to leave. Against this backdrop, we should expect the pound to depreciate relative to the euro.

17 **Exchange Rate Movement Impacts** Some countries encourage movements in their exchange rate relative to those of some other countries as a short-term means of addressing foreign trade imbalances. For each of the following scenarios, evaluate the impact the announcement would have on a Danish importer and a Danish exporter doing business with the foreign country.

(a) Officials in the Danish government announce that they are comfortable with a rising krone relative to the euro.

(b) The Bank of England announces that it feels the krone has been driven too low by currency speculators relative to the British pound.

(c) The European Central Bank announces that it will print billions of new euros and inject them into the economy in an effort to reduce the country's unemployment rate.

18 **International Capital Market Relationships** We discussed five international capital market relationships: relative PPP, IRP, UFR, UIP and the international Fisher effect. Which of these would you expect to hold most closely? Which do you think would be most likely to be violated?

19 **Exporting and Exchange Rate Risk** If you are an exporter who must make payments in foreign currency three months after receiving each shipment and you predict that the domestic currency will appreciate in value over this period, is there any value in hedging your currency exposure?

20 **Domestic versus Foreign Investments** Suppose it is your task to evaluate two different investments in new subsidiaries for your company, one in your own country and the other in a foreign country. You calculate the cash flows of both projects to be identical after exchange rate differences. Under what circumstances might you choose to invest in the foreign subsidiary? Give an example of a country where certain factors might influence you to alter this decision and invest at home.

21 **FX Risk** What are the types of foreign exchange risk a multinational faces? How do these risks arise? Explain.

22 **International Borrowing** If a South African firm raises funds for a foreign subsidiary, what are the disadvantages to borrowing in South Africa? How would you overcome them?

23 **International Investment** If financial markets are perfectly competitive and the Eurodollar rate is above that offered in the US loan market, you would immediately want to borrow money in the United States and invest it in Eurodollars. True or false? Explain.

24 **Eurobonds** Explain motives companies might have for raising money on the international bond markets.

25 **Using Exchange Rates** Take another look at Table 30.3 to answer the following questions.

(a) If you have €100, how many British pounds can you get?

(b) How much is one pound worth against the euro?

(c) If you have £5 million, how many euros do you have?

(d) Which is worth more, a Trinidad and Tobago dollar or a Singapore dollar?

(e) Which is worth more, a Pakistani rupee or a Sri Lankan rupee?

(f) How many Swiss francs can you get for a Swedish krona? What do you call this rate?

(g) Per unit, what is the most valuable currency of those listed? The least valuable?

26 **Using the Cross-rate** Use the information in Table 30.3 to answer the following questions.

(a) Which would you rather have, €100 or £100? Why?

(b) Which would you rather have, 100 Swiss francs (SFr) or 100 Swedish krona (SKr)? Why?

(c) What is the cross-rate for Swiss francs in terms of Swedish krona? For Swedish krona in terms of Swiss francs?

27 **Forward Exchange Rates** Use the information in Table 30.3 to answer the following questions.

(a) If the three-month forward rate for the US dollar per euro is F90 = \$1.3215 (per €), is the dollar selling at a premium or a discount? Explain.

(b) If the three-month forward rate for British pounds in euros per pound is F90 = €1.2198, is the euro selling at a premium or a discount? Explain.

28 **Using Spot and Forward Exchange Rates** Suppose the spot exchange rate for the South African rand is R15/£ and the six-month forward rate is R16/£.

(a) Which is worth more, the British pound or the South African rand?

(b) Assuming absolute PPP holds, what is the cost in the United Kingdom of a Castle beer if the price in South Africa is R20? Why might the beer actually sell at a different price in the UK?

(c) Is the British pound selling at a premium or a discount relative to the South African rand?

(d) Which currency is expected to appreciate in value?

(e) Which country do you think has higher interest rates – the United Kingdom or South Africa? Explain.

29 **Cross-rates and Arbitrage** Use Table 30.3 to answer the following questions.

(a) What is the cross-rate in terms of Rwandan franc per Thai baht?

(b) Suppose the cross-rate is 12 Rwandan franc = 1 Thai baht. Is there an arbitrage opportunity here? If there is, explain how to take advantage of the mispricing.

30 **Interest Rate Parity Use Table 30.3** to answer the following question. Suppose interest rate parity holds and the current annual risk-free rate in the Eurozone is 3.8 per cent. Assume the UK one-year forward rate is £0.8251. What must the annual risk-free rate be in the UK?

31 **Interest Rates and Arbitrage** The treasurer of a major British firm has £30 million to invest for three months. The annual interest rate in the United Kingdom is 0.45 per cent per month. The interest rate in the Eurozone is 0.6 per cent per month. The spot exchange rate is €1.12/£ and the three-month forward rate is €1.15/£. Ignoring transaction costs, in which country would the treasurer want to invest the company's funds? Why?

32 **Inflation and Exchange Rates** Suppose the current exchange rate for the Polish zloty is Z5.1134/£. The expected exchange rate in three years is Z5.2/£. What is the difference in the annual inflation rates for the United Kingdom and Poland over this period? Assume that the anticipated rate is constant for both countries. What relationship are you relying on in answering?

33 **Exchange Rate Risk: Break-even Exchange Rates** Suppose your company, which is based in Nantes, France, imports computer motherboards from Singapore. The exchange rate is given in Table 30.3. You have just placed an order for 30,000 motherboards at a cost to you of 158.5 Singapore dollars each. You will pay for the shipment when it arrives in 90 days. You can sell the motherboards for €100 each. Calculate your profit if the exchange rate goes up or down by 10 per cent over the next 90 days. What is the break-even exchange rate? What percentage rise or fall does this represent in terms of the Singapore dollar versus the euro?

34 **Exchange Rates and Arbitrage** Suppose the spot and six-month forward rates on the Swedish krona are SKr10.7917/£ and SKr12.00/£, respectively. The annual risk-free rate in the United Kingdom is 2.5 per cent and the annual risk-free rate in Sweden is 1.13 per cent.

(a) Is there an arbitrage opportunity here? If so, how would you exploit it?

(b) What must the six-month forward rate be to prevent arbitrage?

35 **The International Fisher Effect** You observe that the inflation rate in the United Kingdom is 3.5 per cent per year and that T-bills currently yield 3.9 per cent annually. What do you estimate the inflation rate to be in:

(a) Australia, if short-term Australian government securities yield 5 per cent per year?

(b) Canada, if short-term Canadian government securities yield 7 per cent per year?

(c) Taiwan, if short-term Taiwanese government securities yield 10 per cent per year?

36 **Spot versus Forward Rates** Suppose the spot and three-month forward rates for the Indian rupee are R68.81/€ and R61.8/€, respectively.

(a) Is the rupee expected to get stronger or weaker?

(b) What would you estimate is the difference between the inflation rates of the Eurozone and India?

37 **Expected Spot Rates** Suppose the spot exchange rate for the Tanzanian shilling is TSh2500/£. The inflation rate in the United Kingdom is 3.5 per cent and it is 8.6 per cent in Tanzania. What do you predict the exchange rate will be in one year? In two years? In five years? What relationship are you using?

38 **Forward Rates** The spot rate of foreign exchange between the United States and the United Kingdom is $1.6117/£. If the interest rate in the United States is 13 per cent and it is 8 per cent in the United Kingdom, what would you expect the one-year forward rate to be if no immediate arbitrage opportunities existed?

39 **Capital Budgeting: ABS Equipment** Dutch firm ABS Equipment has an investment opportunity in the United Kingdom. The project costs £12 million and is expected to produce cash flows of £2.7 million in year 1, £3.5 million in year 2 and £3.3 million in year 3. The current spot exchange rate is €1.12/£ and the current risk-free rate in the Eurozone is 2.12 per cent, compared to that in the United Kingdom of 2.13 per cent. The appropriate discount rate for the project is estimated to be 13 per cent, the Eurozone cost of capital for the company. In addition, the subsidiary can be sold at the end of three years for an estimated £7.4 million. What is the NPV of the project?

40 **Islamic Financing Strategies** You plan to raise funds through following Islamic principles. You require funding today of 3 billion Bahrain dinars and would like to pay it back in equal amounts over 10 years in monthly instalments. How would you do this?

41 **Foreign Direct Investment Evaluation** As a German company, you are evaluating a proposed expansion of an existing subsidiary located in Switzerland. The cost of the expansion would be SFr27.0 million. The cash flows from the project would be SFr7.5 million per year for the next five years. The euro required return is 13 per cent per year, and the current exchange rate is SFr1.48/€. The going rate on EURIBOR is 8 per cent per year. It is 7 per cent per year on Swiss francs.

(a) What do you project will happen to exchange rates over the next four years?

(b) Based on your answer in (a), convert the projected franc flows into euro cash flows and calculate the NPV.

(c) What is the required return on franc cash flows? Based on your answer, calculate the NPV in francs and then convert to euros.

CHALLENGE

42 **Murabahah** You manage an Islamic financing division and have been approached by a company for funding of 6 billion Bahrain dinars. The company wishes to pay the funding back in equal instalments over 10 years through Islamic principles. Western banks quote comparable interest-paying loans of 8 per cent. Construct a *murabahah* contract that makes you competitive with your Western counterparts.

43 **Ijarah Thumma Al Bai'** You run an Islamic financing division and have been approached by a customer for a 40,000 Bahrain dinar *ijarah thumma al bai'* financing deal. The customer wishes to pay a maximum of 1,000 Bahrain dinars per month over five years. Comparable loans in Western banks are quoted at 12 per cent interest. Construct a financing deal for your customer.

44 **Bai' Al-inah** You run an Islamic financing bank and have been approached by a company to construct a sale and buyback financing deal. The firm requires financing of £8 billion and wishes to pay back the financing over seven years. Comparable Western loans quote 7 per cent interest for financing of this type. Construct a *bai' al-inah* contract for your customer.

45 **Using the Exact International Fisher Effect** From our discussion of the Fisher effect in this chapter, we know that the actual relationship between a nominal rate, R, a real rate, r, and an inflation rate, h, can be written as follows:

$$1 + r = (1 + R)/(1 + h)$$

This is the *domestic* Fisher effect.

(a) What is the non-approximate form of the international Fisher effect?
(b) Based on your answer in (a), what is the exact form for UIP? (*Hint:* Recall the exact form of IRP and use UFR.)
(c) What is the exact form for relative PPP? (*Hint:* Combine your previous two answers.)
(d) Recalculate the NPV for the Kihlstrom drill bit project (discussed in Section 30.5) using the exact forms for the UIP and the international Fisher effect. Verify that you get precisely the same answer either way.

Exam Question (45 minutes)

On 14 June 2023, the €/$ exchange rate was €0.85/$ compared to €0.86/$ exactly one year before. On the same day, the £/$ exchange rate was £0.79/$ compared with £0.82/$ one year earlier.

1 Calculate the percentage appreciation of the euro against the dollar over the previous year. Calculate the percentage appreciation of sterling against the dollar over the previous year. **(20 marks)**
2 Calculate the percentage appreciation or depreciation of sterling against the euro over the previous year. Calculate the percentage appreciation or depreciation of the euro against sterling over the previous year. **(20 marks)**
3 Does the percentage appreciation or depreciation of sterling in (1) equal the euro depreciation or appreciation in (2) multiplied by negative one? Explain your answer. **(20 marks)**
4 Review the international parity conditions. Do you believe they work? Explain. **(40 marks)**

Total Marks: 100

Mini Case

West Coast Yachts

The Islamic Bank of Britain (IBB) released a new product in 2024 called a Home Purchase Plan (HPP). This product allows individuals to invest over the long term in a mortgage-equivalent financing deal.

According to ITS publicity materials, the Home Purchase Plan consists of two components:

(a) *Co-ownership agreement:* IBB will agree to sell its share of the property to you at an agreed monthly amount over a fixed period (known as the term). Your share in the property increases with every monthly payment made towards acquiring IBB's share in the property.

(b) *Lease agreement:* IBB will then agree to lease its share in the property to you, for which you will pay a monthly rent.

Your monthly HPP payment is therefore made up of two elements: an acquisition payment and a rental payment. As you make your monthly payments, your share in the property increases as IBB's share gets smaller, and although your monthly payments remain constant (subject to quarterly reviews) the rental payment element will decrease while your acquisition payment element increases. Rent is reviewed every three months, in March, June, September and December. The rent rate may increase, decrease or stay the same at each rent review.

1 Explain this product in terms of a normal mortgage. Assume the interest rate for similar risk mortgages is 4.19 per cent.
2 Construct a Home Purchase Plan so that it has the exact same cash flows as a normal mortgage. Is this possible? Explain.

Practical Case Study

Search online for the price of a specific model of car (your choice) that is sold in the United Kingdom, Ireland, France, Italy, Spain and Germany. Does absolute purchasing power parity hold?

Relevant Accounting Standards

When investing or doing business overseas, companies need to be sure of the accounting standards to which the target country adheres. Although more than 100 countries follow International Accounting Standards, many do not, including the United States. Foreign currency earnings need to be translated according to IAS 21 *The Effects of Changes in Foreign Exchange Rates*. Further, if a company is carrying out business in countries with a hyperinflationary environment (examples are Zimbabwe, Angola and Myanmar) it may have to adhere to IAS 29 *Financial Reporting in Hyperinflationary Economies*. Sometimes overseas investments are in the form of joint ventures. If this is the case, IAS 31 *Interests in Joint Ventures* is also important.

Additional Reading

1 Bekaert, G., C.R. Harvey, C.T. Lundblad and S. Siegel (2013) 'The European Union, the Euro, and Equity Market Integration', *Journal of Financial Economics*, Vol. 109, No. 3, 583–603.
2 Bekaert, G., C.R. Harvey, C.T. Lundblad and S. Siegel (2014) 'Political Risk Spreads', *Journal of International Business Studies*, Vol. 45, No. 4, 471–493.
3 Brennan, M.J. and Y. Xia (2006) 'International Capital Markets and Foreign Exchange Risk', *Review of Financial Studies*, Vol. 19, No. 3, 753–795. **International.**
4 Rime, D., A. Schrimpf and O. Syrstad (2022) 'Covered Interest Parity Arbitrage', *Review of Financial Studies*, Vol. 35, No. 11, 5185–5227.
5 Xu, J. (2012) 'Profitability and Capital Structure: Evidence from Import Penetration', *Journal of Financial Economics*, Vol. 106, No. 2, 427–446.

Very few papers exist that examine international capital budgeting in any detail. However, there are a couple:

6 Greene, W.H., A.S. Hornstein and L.J. White (2009) 'Multinationals Do it Better: Evidence on the Efficiency of Corporations' Capital Budgeting', *Journal of Empirical Finance*, Vol. 16, No. 5, 703–720.
7 Holmén, M. and B. Pramborg (2009) 'Capital Budgeting and Political Risk: Empirical Evidence', *Journal of International Financial Management and Accounting*, Vol. 20, No. 2, 105–134.

Endnote

1 There are four exchange rates instead of five because one exchange rate would involve the exchange of a currency for itself. More generally, it might seem that there should be 25 exchange rates with five currencies. There are 25 different combinations, but, of these, 5 involve the exchange of a currency for itself. Of the remaining 20, half are redundant because they are just the reciprocals of another exchange rate. Of the remaining 10, 6 can be eliminated by using a common denominator.

Table of Equations

Chapter 3

Equation 3.1

$$\text{Current ratio} = \frac{\text{Current assets}}{\text{Current liabilities}}$$

Equation 3.2

$$\text{Quick ratio} = \frac{\text{Current assets} - \text{Inventory}}{\text{Current liabilities}}$$

Equation 3.3

$$\text{Cash ratio} = \frac{\text{Cash and cash equivalents}}{\text{Current liabilities}}$$

Equation 3.4

$$\begin{aligned}\text{Total debt ratio} &= \frac{\text{Total assets} - \text{Total equity}}{\text{Total assets}}\\ &= \frac{£20{,}258 - 4{,}023}{£20{,}258} = 0.8014 \text{ times}\end{aligned}$$

Equation 3.5

$$\begin{aligned}\text{Debt} - \text{equity ratio} &= \text{Total debt/Total equity}\\ &= £0.8014/£0.1986 = 4.036 \text{ times}\end{aligned}$$

Equation 3.6

$$\begin{aligned}\text{Equity multiplier} &= \text{Total assets/Total equity} = £1/£0.1986 = 5.036 \text{ times}\\ &= (\text{Total equity} + \text{Total debt})/\text{Total equity}\\ &= 1 + (\text{Debt/equity ratio}) = 5.036 \text{ times}\end{aligned}$$

Equation 3.7

$$\text{Times interest earnest earned ratio} = \frac{\text{Profit before and taxes}}{\text{Interest}} = \frac{£1{,}222}{£140} = 8.73 \text{ times}$$

Equation 3.8

$$\begin{aligned}\text{Cash coverage ratio} &= \frac{\text{EBIT} + \text{Depreciation}}{\text{Interest}}\\ &= \frac{£704 + 550}{£285} = 4.34 \text{ times}\end{aligned}$$

Equation 3.9

$$\text{Inventory turnover} = \frac{\text{Cost of goods sold}}{\text{Inventory}}$$

Equation 3.10

$$\begin{aligned}\text{Days' sales in inventory} &= \frac{365 \text{ days}}{\text{Inventory turnover}}\\ &= \frac{365}{42.12} = 8.66 \text{ days}\end{aligned}$$

Equation 3.11

$$\text{Receivables turnover} = \frac{\text{Revenues}}{\text{Trade receivables}}$$
$$= \frac{£15{,}321}{4{,}524} = 3.39 \text{ times}$$

Equation 3.12

$$\text{Days' sales in receivable} = \frac{365 \text{ days}}{\text{Receivable turnover}}$$
$$= \frac{365}{3.39} = 107.78 \text{ days}$$

Equation 3.13

$$\text{Total asset turnover} = \frac{\text{Revenues}}{\text{Total assets}}$$
$$= \frac{£15{,}321}{£20{,}258} = 0.76 \text{ times}$$

Equation 3.14

$$\text{Profit margin} = \frac{\text{Net income}}{\text{Revenues}}$$
$$= \frac{£238}{£15{,}321} = 1.55\%$$

Equation 3.15

$$\text{Return on assets} = \frac{\text{Net income}}{\text{Total assets}}$$
$$= \frac{£238}{£20{,}258} = 1.17\%$$

Equation 3.16

$$\text{Return on equity} = \frac{\text{Net income}}{\text{Total assets}}$$
$$= \frac{£238}{£4{,}023} = 5.92\%$$

Equation 3.17

$$\text{EPS} = \frac{\text{Net income}}{\text{Share outstanding}} = \frac{£238}{5{,}667} = £0.042$$

Equation 3.18

$$\text{PE ratio} = \frac{\text{Price per share}}{\text{Earning per share}}$$
$$= \frac{£1.3655}{£0.042} = 32.51 \text{ times}$$

Equation 3.19

$$\text{Market-to-book ratio} = \frac{\text{Market value per share}}{\text{Book value per share}}$$
$$= \frac{£1.3655}{£4{,}023/5{,}667} = 1.92 \text{ time}$$

Equation 3.20

$$\text{ROE} = \underbrace{\frac{\text{Net income}}{\text{Sales}} \times \frac{\text{Sales}}{\text{Assets}}}_{\text{Return on assets}} \times \frac{\text{Assets}}{\text{Total equity}}$$
$$= \text{Profit margin} \times \text{Total asset turnover} \times \text{Equity multiplier}$$

Chapter 4

Equation 4.1
$$PV = \frac{C_1}{1+r}$$

Equation 4.2
$$NPV = -\text{Cost} + PV$$

Equation 4.3
$$FV = C_0 \times (1+r)^{\mathrm{T}}$$

Equation 4.4
$$PV = \frac{C_T}{(1+r)^T}$$

Equation 4.5
$$NPV = -C_0 + \frac{C_1}{1+r} + \frac{C_2}{(1+r)^2} + \cdots + \frac{C_2}{(1+r)^T}$$
$$= -C_0 + \sum_{t=1}^{T} \frac{C_t}{(1+r)^t}$$

Equation 4.6
$$C_0 \left(1 + \frac{r}{m}\right)^m$$

Equation 4.7
$$\left(1 + \frac{r}{m}\right)^m - 1$$

Equation 4.8
$$FV = C_0 \left(1 + \frac{r}{m}\right)^{mT}$$

Equation 4.9
$$PV = C_0 + \frac{C_1}{1+\text{APR}} + \frac{C_2}{(1+\text{APR})^2} + \cdots + \frac{C_T}{(1+\text{APR})^T}$$
$$= C_0 + \sum_{i=1}^{T} \frac{C_t}{(1+\text{APR})^i}$$

Equation 4.10
$$C_0 \times e^{rT}$$

Equation 4.11
$$PV = \frac{C}{r}$$

Equation 4.12
$$PV = \frac{C}{1+r} + \frac{C}{(1+r)^2} + \frac{C}{(1+r)^3} + \cdots$$
$$= \frac{C}{r}$$

Equation 4.13
$$PV = \frac{C}{r-g}$$

Equation 4.14
$$PV = \frac{C}{r}$$

Equation 4.15
$$PV = \frac{C}{r}\left[\frac{1}{(1+r)^T}\right]$$

Equation 4.16
$$PV = C\left[\frac{1 - \frac{1}{r(1+r)^T}}{r}\right]$$

Equation 4.17

$$FV = C\left[\frac{(1+r)^T}{r} - \frac{1}{r}\right] = C\left[\frac{(1+r)^T - 1}{r}\right]$$

Equation 4.18

$$PV = C\left[\frac{1}{r-g} - \frac{1}{r-g} \times \left(\frac{1+g}{1+r}\right)^T\right] = C\left[\frac{1 - \left(\frac{1+g}{1+r}\right)^T}{r-g}\right]$$

Chapter 5

Equation 5.1

$$P_0 = \frac{Div}{1+R} + \frac{P1}{1+R}$$

Equation 5.2

$$P_1 = \frac{Div_2}{1+R} + \frac{P_2}{1+R}$$

Equation 5.3

$$\begin{aligned} P_0 &= \frac{1}{1+R}\left[Div_1 + \left(\frac{Div_{2+P_2}}{1+R}\right)\right] \\ &= \frac{Div_1}{1+R} + \frac{Div_2}{(1+R)^2} + \frac{P_2}{(1+R)^2} \end{aligned}$$

Equation 5.4

$$P_0 = \frac{Div_1}{1+R} + \frac{Div_1}{(1+R)^2} + \frac{Div_3}{(1+R)^3} + \cdots = \sum_{t=1}^{\infty} \frac{Div_t}{(1+R)^t}$$

Equation 5.5

$$\text{Earnings next year} = \text{Earnings this year} + \underbrace{\text{Retained earnings this year} \times \text{Return on retained earnings}}_{\text{Increase in earnings}}$$

Equation 5.6

$$\frac{\text{Earnings next year}}{\text{Earnings this year}} = \frac{\text{Earnings this year}}{\text{Earnings this year}} + \left(\frac{\text{Retained earnings this year}}{\text{Earnings this year}}\right) \times \text{Return on retained earnings}$$

Equation 5.7

$$1 + g = 1 + (\text{Retention ratio} \times \text{Return on retained earnings})$$

Equation 5.8

$$g = \text{Retention ratio} \times \text{Return on retained earnings}$$

Equation 5.9

$$\begin{aligned} R - g &= Div_1/P_0 \\ R &= Div_1/P_0 + g \end{aligned}$$

Equation 5.10

$$\frac{EPS}{R} + NPVGO$$

Equation 5.11

$$-€1{,}000{,}000 + \frac{€210{,}000}{0.1} = €1{,}100{,}000$$

Equation 5.12

$$-€6 = \frac{€1.20}{0.16} = €1.50$$

Equation 5.13 $$-€6.72 = \frac{€1.344}{€0.16} = €1.68$$

Equation 5.14 $$-€7.5264 = \frac{€1.5053}{0.16} = €1.882$$

Equation 5.15 $$\frac{€1.50}{1.16} + \frac{€1.68}{(1.16)^2} + \frac{€1.882}{(1.16)^3} + \cdots$$

Equation 5.16 $$\text{FCFF} = \text{Cash flow from operations} + \text{Cash flow from investing activities}$$

Equation 5.17 $$\begin{aligned}\text{FCFF} &= \text{Cash flow from operations} + \text{Cash flow from investing activities}\\ &\quad + \text{Net interest payment} \times (1 - \text{Tax rate})\end{aligned}$$

Chapter 6

Equation 6.1 $$£0.94 = -£100 + \frac{£100}{1.06}$$

Equation 6.2 $$(£500{,}000 + 400{,}000 + 300{,}000 + 200{,}000 + 100{,}000 + 0)/6 = £250{,}000$$

Chapter 7

Equation 7.1 $$\text{Real interest rate} = \frac{1 + \text{Nominal interest rate}}{1 + \text{Inflation rate}} - 1$$

Equation 7.2 $$\text{Real interest rate} \cong \text{Nominal interest rate} - \text{Inflation rate}$$

Equation 7.3 $$\begin{aligned}\text{OCR} &= \text{Net income} + \text{Depreciation}\\ &= £144 + 600 = £744\end{aligned}$$

Equation 7.4 $$\begin{aligned}\text{OCF} &= \text{Sales} - \text{Costs} - \text{Taxes}\\ &= £1{,}500 - 700 - 56 = £744\end{aligned}$$

Equation 7.5 $$\text{OCF} = (\text{Sales} - \text{Costs}) \times (1 - t_c) + \text{Depreciation} \times t_c$$

Chapter 8

Equation 8.1 $$\begin{matrix}\text{Number of grills sold}\\ \text{by entire industry}\end{matrix} \times \begin{matrix}\text{Market share of BBs}\\ \text{hydrogen grill (in per cent)}\end{matrix} \times \begin{matrix}\text{Price per}\\ \text{hydrogen grill}\end{matrix}$$

Equation 8.2 $$\begin{matrix}\text{Next year's price}\\ \text{per hydrogen grill}\end{matrix} = \begin{matrix}€190 + €11 \times \text{Industry wide unit sales}\\ \text{(in millions)} + /-€3\end{matrix}$$

Equation 8.3 $$0.02 = 0.02 \times 0.20 \times 0.50$$

Equation 8.4 $$50\% \times £18 \text{ million} + 50\%\,(-£22 \text{ million}) = £2 \text{ million}$$

Chapter 9

Equation 9.1 $$\text{Geometric average return} = [(1+R_1)\times(1+R_2)\times\cdots\times(1+R_T)]^{1/T} - 1$$

Equation 9.2 $$R(T) = \frac{T-1}{N-1}\times \text{Geometric average} + \frac{N-T}{N-1}\times \text{Arithmetic average}$$

Chapter 10

Equation 10.1 $$(R_{\text{At}} - \overline{R}_{\text{A}})\times(R_{\text{Bt}} - \overline{R}_{\text{B}})$$

Equation 10.2 $$\sigma_{\text{A,B}} = \text{Corr}\,(R_{\text{A}},R_{\text{B}}) = \frac{\text{Cov}\,(R_{\text{A}},R_{\text{B}})}{\sigma_{\text{A}}\times\sigma_{\text{B}}} = \frac{-0.004875}{0.2586\times 0.1150} = -0.1639$$

Equation 10.3 $$\text{Expected return on portfolio} = X_{\text{A}}\overline{R}_{\text{A}} + X_{\text{A}}\overline{R}_{\text{B}} = \overline{R}_p$$

Equation 10.4 $$\text{Var (portfolio)} = X^2_{\text{Super}}\sigma^2_{\text{Super}} + 2X_{\text{Super}}X_{\text{Super}}\sigma_{\text{Super, Slow}} + X^2_{\text{Super}}\sigma^2_{\text{Super}}$$

Equation 10.5 $$\sigma_p = \text{SD (potfolio)} = \sqrt{\text{Var (portfolio)}} = \sqrt{0.023851}$$
$$= 0.1544 = 15.44\%$$

Equation 10.6 $$\text{Weight average of standard deviations} = X_{\text{Super}}\sigma_{\text{Super}} + X_{\text{Slow}}\sigma_{\text{Slow}}$$
$$0.2012 = 0.6\times 0.2586 + 0.4\times 0.115$$

Equation 10.7 $$S_{\text{Super, Slow}} = \rho_{\text{Super, Slow}}\sigma_{\text{Super}_{\text{Slow}}}$$

Equation 10.8 $$= X^2_{\text{Super}}\sigma^2_{\text{Super}} + 2X_{\text{Super}}X_{\text{Slow}}\rho_{\text{Super, Slow}}\sigma_{\text{Super}} + X^2_{\text{Super}}\sigma^2_{\text{Super}}$$
$$0.023851 = 0.36\times 0.066875 + 2\times 0.6\times 0.4\times(-0.1639)$$
$$\times 0.2586\times 0.115 + 0.16\times 0.013225$$

Equation 10.9 $$\text{Standard deviation of portfolio's return} = \sqrt{0.040466} = 0.2012 = 20.12\%$$

Equation 10.10

$$\text{Variance of portfolio} = \underbrace{N}_{\text{Number of diagonal terms}} \times \underbrace{\left[\frac{1}{N^2}\right]\overline{\text{var}}}_{\text{Each diagonal term}} + \underbrace{N(N-1)}_{\text{Number of off-diagonal terms}} \times \underbrace{\left[\frac{1}{N^2}\right]\overline{\text{cov}}}_{\text{Each off-diagonal term}}$$
$$= \left[\frac{1}{N}\right]\overline{\text{var}} + \left[\frac{N^2-N}{N^{22}}\right]\overline{\text{cov}}$$
$$= \left[\frac{1}{N}\right]\overline{\text{var}} + \left[\frac{N^2-N}{N^2}\right]\overline{\text{cov}}$$

Equation 10.11 $$\text{Variance of portfolio (when } N\rightarrow\infty) = \overline{\text{cov}}$$

Equation 10.12

$$\text{Expected return on portfolio composed of one riskless and one risky asset} = 0.114 = (0.35 \times 0.14) + (0.65 \times 0.10)$$

Equation 10.13

$$\text{Variance of portolio composed of one riskless and one risky asset} = X^2_{\text{Merville}}\,\sigma^2_{\text{Merville}} = (0.35)^2 \times (0.20)^2 = 0.0049$$

Equation 10.14

$$\text{Standard deviation of portolio composed of one riskless and one risky asset} = X_{\text{Merville}}\,\sigma_{\text{Merville}} = 0.35 \times 0.20 = 0.07$$

Equation 10.15

$$\beta_i = \frac{\text{Cov}(R_i, R_M)}{\sigma^2(R_M)}$$

Equation 10.16

$$\sum_{i=1}^{N} X_i \beta_i = 1$$

Equation 10.17

$$\underset{\substack{\text{Expected}\\ \text{return}\\ \text{on a security}}}{E[R_i]} = \underset{\substack{\text{Risk-free}\\ \text{rate}}}{R_F} + \underset{\substack{\text{Beta of}\\ \text{the}\\ \text{security}}}{\beta} \times \underset{\substack{\text{Difference between}\\ \text{expected return on market}\\ \text{and risk-free rate}}}{(E[R_M] - R_F)}$$

Equation 10.18a

$$15.0\% = 3\% + 1.5 \times 8.0\%$$

Equation 10.18b

$$8.6\% = 3\% + 0.7 \times 8.0\%$$

Equation 10.19

$$11.8\% = 0.5 \times 15.0\% + 0.5 \times 8.6\%$$

Equation 10.20

$$11.8\% = 3\% + 1.1 \times 8.0\%$$

Equation 10.21

$$\underset{\substack{\text{Expected}\\ \text{return}\\ \text{on a secuity}}}{\overline{R}} = \underset{\substack{\text{Risk-free}\\ \text{rate}}}{R_F} + \underset{\substack{\text{Consumption}\\ \text{beta of the}\\ \text{security}}}{\beta_c} \times \underset{\substack{\text{Difference between}\\ \text{expected return on market}\\ \text{and risk-free rate}}}{(\overline{R}_M - R_F)}$$

Chapter 11

Equation 11.1

$$R_i = E(R_i) + \beta_i F + \varepsilon_i$$

Equation 11.2

$$R_P = X_1 R_1 + X_2 R_2 + X_3 R_3 + \cdots + X_N R_N$$

Equation 11.3

$$R_p = X_1 \underset{\text{(Return on equity 1)}}{[E(R_1) + \beta_1 F_1 + \varepsilon_1]} + X_2 \underset{\text{(Return on equity 2)}}{[E(R_2) + \beta_2 F_2 + \varepsilon_2]} + X_3 \underset{\text{(Return on equity 3)}}{[E(R_3) + \beta_3 F_3 + \varepsilon_3]} + \cdots + X_N \underset{\text{(Return on equity N)}}{[E(R_N) + \beta_N F_N + \varepsilon_N]}$$

Equation 11.4

$$R_p = X_1 E(R_1) + X_2 E(R_2) + X_3 E(R_3) + \cdots + X_N E(R_N)$$

Equation 11.4′

$$R_P = \underset{\substack{\text{From}\\ \text{row 1 of}\\ \text{Equation 11.4}}}{\overset{10\%}{\updownarrow}} + \underset{\substack{\text{From}\\ \text{row 1 of}\\ \text{Equation 11.4}}}{\overset{F}{\updownarrow}} + \underbrace{\left(\frac{1}{N}\varepsilon_1 + \frac{1}{N}\varepsilon_2 + \frac{1}{N}\varepsilon_3 + \cdots + \frac{1}{N}\varepsilon_N\right)}_{\text{From row 3 of Equation 11.4}}$$

Equation 11.4″

$$R_P = 10\% + F$$

Equation 11.5

$$E(R) = R_F + \beta\left[E(R_p) - R_F\right]$$

Equation 11.6

$$R - r_f = E(R) + \beta[E(R_M) - r_F] + \gamma HML + \delta SMB + \eta RMW + \theta CMA + \varepsilon$$

Chapter 12

Equation 12.1

$$R_E = R_F + \beta \times (R_M - R_F)$$

Equation 12.2

$$\beta_{\text{Asset}} = \frac{E}{D+E} \times \beta_{\text{Equity}} + \frac{D}{D+E} \times \beta_{\text{Debt}}$$

Equation 12.3

$$\beta_{\text{Asset}} = \frac{E}{D+E} \times \beta_{\text{Equity}}$$

Equation 12.4

$$\text{Average cost of capital} = \left(\frac{E}{D+E}\right) \times R_E + \left(\frac{D}{D+E}\right) \times R_D \times (1 - t_c)$$

Chapter 13

Equation 13.1

$$P_t = P_{t-1} + \textit{Expected return} + \textit{Random error}_t$$

Chapter 17

Equation 17.1

$$NPV = €10{,}000 - €2{,}155 - €2{,}072 - €1{,}995 - €1{,}923 - €1{,}855$$
$$= €0$$

Chapter 18

Equation 18.1

$$V = D + E$$

Equation 18.2

$$R_{WACC} = \frac{E}{D+E} \times R_E + \frac{D}{D+E} \times R_D$$

Equation 18.3

$$R_F = R_A + \frac{D}{E}(R_A - R_D)$$

Equation 18.4

$$\underbrace{t_c}_{\text{Corporate tax rate}} \times \underbrace{R_D \times D}_{\text{Interest paid}}$$

Equation 18.5

$$V_L = \frac{\text{EBIT} \times (1 - t_c)}{R_A} + \frac{t_c R_D D}{R_D} = V_U + t_c D$$

Equation 18.6

$$R_E = R_A + \frac{D}{E} \times (1 - t_c) \times (R_A - R_D)$$

Equation 18.7

$$(1 - t_c) \times (1 - t_E) = 1 - t_D$$

Chapter 20

Equation 20.1

$$\text{NPV(loan)} = +\text{Amount borrowed} - \begin{matrix}\text{Present value}\\ \text{of after-tax}\\ \text{interest payments}\end{matrix} - \begin{matrix}\text{Present value}\\ \text{of loan}\\ \text{repayments}\end{matrix}$$

Equation 20.1′

$$£804{,}105 = +£7{,}575{,}758 - \frac{£545{,}455}{0.10} \times \left[1 - \left(\frac{1}{1.10}\right)^5\right] - \frac{£7{,}575{,}758}{(1.10)^5}$$

Equation 20.1″

$$£1{,}205{,}470 = +£7{,}500{,}000 - \frac{£432{,}000}{0.10} \times [1 - (11.10)^5] - \frac{£7{,}500{,}000}{(1.10)^5}$$

Equation 20.2

$$\text{APV} = \text{All-equity value} - \text{Flotation costs of dept} + \text{NPV (loan)}$$

Equation 20.2′

$$£768{,}749 = £21{,}642 - £59{,}998 + £804{,}105$$

Equation 20.2″

$$£1{,}227{,}112 = £21{,}642 - £0 + £1{,}205{,}470$$

Equation 20.3

$$\beta_{\text{Equity}} = \beta_{\text{Asset}} \left(1 + \frac{\text{Dept}}{\text{Equity}}\right)$$

Equation 20.4

$$\beta_{\text{Equity}} = \left[1 + \frac{(1 - t_C)\,\text{Dept}}{\text{Equity}}\right] \beta_{\text{Unlevered firm}}$$

Equation 20.5

$$\frac{\text{Equity}}{\text{Equity} + (1 - t_C) \times \text{Dept}} \times \beta_{\text{Equity}} = \beta_{\text{Unlevered firm}}$$

$$\frac{\$200 \text{ million}}{\$200 \text{ million} + (1 - 0.28) \times \$100 \text{ million}} \times 2 = 1.47$$

Chapter 21

Equation 21.1

$$£10 + \frac{£10}{1.1} = £19.09$$

Equation 21.2

$$£11 + \frac{£8.90}{1.1} = £19.09$$

Equation 21.3
$$\$850 \times (1.072)^5 = \$1{,}203.35$$

Equation 21.4
$$\$1{,}402.55 \times (1 - 0.15) = \$1{,}192.17$$

Equation 21.5
$$\text{Cash flow} = \text{Capital expenditures} + \text{Dividends}$$

Equation 21.6
$$\text{Dividend change} \equiv Div_1 - Div_0 = s \times (tEPS_1 - Div_0)$$

Chapter 22

Equation 22.1
$$\begin{matrix}\text{Price of underlying} \\ \text{equity}\end{matrix} + \begin{matrix}\text{Price of} \\ \text{put}\end{matrix} = \begin{matrix}\text{Price of} \\ \text{call}\end{matrix} + \begin{matrix}\text{Present value of} \\ \text{exercise price}\end{matrix}$$

Equation 22.2
$$\begin{matrix}\text{Value of call} & = & \text{Share price} & \times & \text{Delta} & - & \text{Amount borrowed} \\ \pounds 6.82 & = & \pounds 50 & \times & 1/2 & - & \pounds 18.18\end{matrix}$$

Equation 22.3
$$\begin{matrix}\text{Value of call} \\ \text{on firm}\end{matrix} - \begin{matrix}\text{Value of} \\ \text{firm}\end{matrix} = \begin{matrix}\text{Value of put} \\ \text{on firm}\end{matrix} - \begin{matrix}\text{Value of} \\ \text{default-free bond}\end{matrix}$$

Equation 22.3b
$$\begin{matrix}\text{Value of} \\ \text{firm}\end{matrix} - \begin{matrix}\text{Value of call} \\ \text{on firm}\end{matrix} = \begin{matrix}\text{Value of} \\ \text{default-free bond}\end{matrix} - \begin{matrix}\text{Value of put} \\ \text{on firm}\end{matrix}$$

Chapter 23

Equation 23.1
$$\underbrace{[0.45 \times (\$2.10 - \$2.74) \times 6 \text{ million} + 0.55 \times 0]/1.02 + \$1{,}000{,}000{,}000 = -\$694{,}118}_{\text{Value of the call option}}$$

Equation 23.2
$$[0.45(\$2.74 - \$2.10) + 0.55 \times 0]/1.02 = \$0.282$$

Chapter 24

Equation 24.1
$$\underbrace{\frac{\text{Firm's value net of debt}}{\#}}_{\text{(Value of a share of equity)}} - \text{Exercise price}$$

Equation 24.2
$$\underbrace{\frac{\text{Firm's value net of debt} + \text{Exercise price} \times \#_\omega}{\# + \#_\omega}}_{\text{(Value of a share of equity after warrant is exercised)}} - \text{Exercise price}$$

Equation 24.3
$$\frac{\#_\omega}{\# + \#_\omega} \times \underbrace{\left(\frac{\text{Firm's value net of dept}}{\#} - \text{Exercise price}\right)}_{\text{(Gain from a call on a firm with no warrants)}}$$

Equation 24.4
$$\omega = \frac{1}{\left(1 + \frac{\#_\omega}{\#}\right)} c_\omega$$

Chapter 25

Equation 25.1

$$P_{\text{TB}} = \frac{€40}{1+R_1} + \frac{€40}{(1+R_2)^2} + \frac{€40}{(1+R_3)^3} + \cdots + \frac{€40}{(1+R_{39})^{39}} + \frac{€1{,}040}{(1+R_{40})^{40}}$$

Equation 25.2

$$\frac{P_{\text{FORW.CONT}}}{1+R_1} = \frac{€40}{1+R_2} + \frac{€40}{(1+R_3)^2} + \frac{€40}{(1+R_4)^3} + \cdots + \frac{€40}{(1+R_{40})^{40}} + \frac{€1{,}040}{(1+R_{41})^{41}}$$

Equation 25.3

$$P_{\text{FORW.CONT}} = \frac{€40 \times (1+R_1)}{(1+R_2)^2} + \frac{€40 \times (1+R_1)}{(1+R_3)^3} + \frac{€40 \times (1+R_1)}{(1+R_4)^4} + \cdots + \frac{€40 \times (1+R_1)}{(1+R_{40})^{40}} + \frac{€1{,}040 \times (1+R_1)}{(1+R_{41})^{41}}$$

Equation 25.4

$$2.56 \text{ years} = 0 \text{ year} \times \frac{€500 \text{ million}}{€1{,}000 \text{ million}} + 1/4 \text{ year} \times \frac{€500 \text{ million}}{€1{,}000 \text{ million}} + 1/2 \text{ year} \times \frac{€275 \text{ million}}{€1{,}000 \text{ million}} + 2 \text{ year} \times \frac{€40 \text{ million}}{€1{,}000 \text{ million}} + 14.8 \text{ year} + \frac{€150 \text{ million}}{€1{,}000 \text{ million}}$$

Equation 25.5

$$2.56 \text{ years} = 0 \text{ year} \times \frac{€400 \text{ million}}{€900 \text{ million}} + 1 \text{ year} \times \frac{€300 \text{ million}}{€900 \text{ million}} + 10 \text{ years} \times \frac{€200 \text{ million}}{€900 \text{ million}}$$

Equation 25.6

Duration of assets × Market value of assets = Duration of liabilities × Market of liabilities

Chapter 26

Equation 26.1

Net working capital + Non-current assets = Non-current liabilities + Equity

Equation 26.2

Net working capital = Cash + Other current assets = Current liabilities

Equation 26.3

Cash + Other current assets − Current liability = Non-current liabilities + Equity − Non-current assets

Equation 26.4

Cash + Non-current liabilities + Equity = Net working capital (excluding cash) − Non-current assets

Equation 26.5

Accounts receivable at end of last quarter = Last quarter's sales

Chapter 28

Equation 28.1

£50 = £550 − £500

Chapter 30

Equation 30.1	$[E(S_1) - S_0]/S_0 = h_{FC} - h_{HC}$
Equation 30.2	$E(S_1) = S_0 \times [1 + (h_{FC} - h_{HC})]$
Equation 30.3	$E(S_t) = S_0 \times [1 + (h_{FC} - h_{HC})]^t$
Equation 30.4	$F_1/S_0 = (1 + R_{FC})/(1 + R_{HC})$
Equation 30.5	$(F_1 - S_0)/S_0 = R_{FC} - R_{HC}$
Equation 30.6	$F_1 = S_0 \times [1 + (R_{FC} - R_{HC})]$
Equation 30.7	$F_t = S_0 \times [1 + (R_{FC} - R_{HC})]^t$
Equation 30.8	$\text{UIP} : \text{E}(S_1) = S_0 \times [1 + (R_{FC} - R_{HC})]$
Equation 30.9	$\text{E}(S_t) = S_0 \times [1 + (R_{FC} - R_{HC})]^t$
Equation 30.10	$\text{IFE}: R_{HC} - h_{HC} = R_{FC} - h_{FC}$

Glossary

A

Ageing Schedule A compilation of trade receivables by the age of each account.

American depositary receipt (ADR) A security issued in the United States representing shares of a foreign equity, and allowing that equity to be traded in the United States.

Annual Percentage Rate (APR) The harmonized interest rate that expresses the total cost of borrowing or investing as a percentage interest rate.

Annuity A level stream of cash flows for a fixed period of time.

Arithmetic Average Return The return earned in an average year over a multi-year period.

Average Accounting Return (AAR) An investment's average net income divided by its average book value.

B

Balance Sheet Under International Financial Reporting Standards, a firm's balance sheet is also known as the statement of financial position.

Beta Coefficient The amount of systematic risk present in a particular risky asset relative to that in an average risky asset.

Bubble A situation where observed prices soar far higher than fundamentals and rational analysis would suggest.

C

Call Option An option that gives the owner the right, but not the obligation, to buy an asset.

Call Premium The amount by which the call price exceeds the par value of a bond.

Capital Asset Pricing Model (CAPM) The equation of the SML showing the relationship between expected return and beta.

Capital Budgeting The process of planning and managing a firm's long-term investments.

Capital Gains Yield The dividend growth rate, or the rate at which the value of an investment grows.

Capital Rationing The situation that exists if a firm has positive-NPV projects but cannot find the necessary financing.

Capital Structure The mixture of long-term debt and equity maintained by a firm.

Cash Discount A discount given to induce prompt payment. Also, *sales discount.*

Competitive Offer Where underwriters compete with one another and bid to lead the issue offer.

Compound Interest Interest earned on both the initial principal and the interest reinvested from prior periods.

Compound Value Also known as future value, the amount an investment is worth after one or more periods.

Compounding The process of accumulating interest on an investment over time to earn more interest.

Consolidation A consolidation is the same as a merger except that an entirely new firm is created, with both the acquiring firm and the acquired firm terminating their previous legal existence and become part of the new firm.

Corporation A business created as a distinct legal entity composed of one or more individuals or entities.

Coupon The stated interest payment made on a bond.

Credit Instrument The evidence of indebtedness.

Credit Period The length of time for which credit is granted.

Cross-rate The implicit exchange rate between two currencies quoted in some third currency.

D

Depreciation Tax Shield The tax saving that results from the depreciation deduction, calculated as depreciation multiplied by the corporate tax rate.

Discounting Calculating the present value of some future amount.

Diversifiable Risk A risk that affects at most a small number of assets. Also, *unique* or *unsystematic risk.*

Dividend Information Content Effect The market's reaction to a change in corporate dividend payout.

Dividend Yield An equity's expected cash dividend divided by its current price.

Dividend A payment made out of a firm's earnings to its owners, in the form of either cash or stock.

Dutch Auction Underwriting The type of underwriting in which the offer price is set based on competitive bidding by investors. Also known as a *uniform.*

E

Effective Annual Rate (EAR) The interest rate expressed as if it were compounded once per year.

Efficient Market Hypothesis (EMH) The hypothesis that actual capital markets are efficient.

Erosion The cash flows of a new project that come at the expense of a firm's existing projects.

Eurobond International bond issued in multiple countries but denominated in a single currency (usually the issuer's currency).

Eurocurrency Money deposited in a financial centre outside the country whose currency is involved.

Exchange Rate Risk The risk related to having international operations in a world where relative currency values vary.

Exchange Rate The price of one country's currency expressed in terms of another country's currency.

F

Face Value The principal amount of a bond that is repaid at the end of the term. Also called *par value.*

Fixed Costs Costs that do not change when the quantity of output changes during a particular time period.

Float The difference between book cash and bank cash, representing the net effect of transactions in the process of collection.

Foreign Bonds International bonds issued in a single country, usually denominated in that country's currency.

Foreign Exchange Market The market in which one country's currency is traded for another's.

Forward Contract A legally binding agreement between two parties calling for the sale of an asset or product in the future at a price agreed on today.

Forward Exchange Rate The agreed-upon exchange rate to be used in a forward trade.

Forward Trade An agreement to exchange currency at some time in the future.

Future Value (FV) Also known as compound value, the amount an investment is worth after one or more periods.

Futures Contract A forward contract with the feature that gains and losses are realized each day rather than only on the settlement date.

G

General Cash Offer An issue of securities offered for sale to the general public on a cash basis.

Geometric Average Return The average compound return earned per year over a multi-year period.

Green Shoe Provision A contract provision giving the underwriter the option to purchase additional shares from the issuer at the offering price. Also called the *overallotment option.*

H

Hedging Reducing a firm's exposure to price or rate fluctuations. Also, *immunization.*

Homemade Dividend Policy The tailored dividend policy created by individual investors who undo corporate dividend policy by reinvesting dividends or selling shares of equity.

I

income statement Financial statement summarizing a firm's performance over a period of time.

Initial Public Offering (IPO) A company's first equity issue made available to the public. Also called an *unseasoned new issue.*

Interest Rate Parity (IRP) The condition stating that the interest rate differential between two countries is equal to the percentage difference between the forward exchange rate and the spot exchange rate.

Internal Rate of Return (IRR) The discount rate that makes the NPV of an investment zero.

International Financial Reporting Standards (IFRS) Accounting standards issued by the IFRS Foundation and the International Accounting Standards Board (IASB) to provide a common global language so that company accounts are understandable and comparable.

International Fisher Effect (IFE) The theory that real interest rates are equal across countries.

Invoice A bill for goods or services provided by the seller to the purchaser.

M

Market Risk A risk that influences a large number of assets. Also, *systematic risk.*

Maturity Date (Maturity) The specified date on which the principal amount of a bond is paid.

Merger The complete absorption of one company by another, wherein the acquiring firm retains its identity and the acquired firm ceases to exist as a separate entity.

MM Proposition I The proposition that the value of the firm is independent of the firm's capital structure.

MM Proposition II The proposition that a firm's cost of equity capital is a positive linear function of the firm's capital structure.

Monte Carlo Simulation A combination of scenario and sensitivity analysis.

Mutually Exclusive Investments A situation in which taking one investment prevents the taking of another.

N

Net Present Value (NPV) The difference between an investment's market value and its cost.

Net Working Capital Current assets minus current liabilities.

Non-cash Items Expenses charged against revenues that do not directly affect cash flow, such as depreciation.

Normal Distribution A symmetric, bell-shaped frequency distribution that is completely defined by its mean and standard deviation.

O

Opportunity Cost The most valuable alternative that is given up if a particular investment is undertaken.

Option A contract that gives its owner the right to buy or sell some asset at a fixed price on or before a given date.

P

Par Value The principal amount of a bond that is repaid at the end of the term. Also called *face value*.

Partnership A business formed by two or more individuals or entities.

Perpetuity An annuity in which the cash flows continue for ever.

Portfolio A group of assets such as equities and bonds held by an investor.

Preference Shares Equity with dividend priority over ordinary shares, normally with a fixed dividend rate, sometimes without voting rights.

Present Value (PV) The current value of future cash flows discounted at the appropriate discount rate.

Private Placement Loan (usually long term) provided directly by a limited number of investors.

Profitability Index (PI) The present value of an investment's future cash flows divided by its initial cost. Also called the *benefit–cost ratio*.

Protective Covenant A part of the indenture limiting certain actions that might be taken during the term of the loan, usually to protect the lender's interest.

Purchasing Power Parity (PPP) The idea that the exchange rate adjusts to keep purchasing power constant among currencies.

Put Option An option that gives the owner the right, but not the obligation, to sell an asset.

R

Real Option An option that involves real assets as opposed to financial assets such as shares of equity.

Regular Cash Dividend A cash payment made by a firm to its owners in the normal course of business, usually paid four times a year.

Risk Premium The excess return required from an investment in a risky asset over that required from a risk-free investment.

S

Scenario Analysis The determination of what happens to NPV estimates when we ask what-if questions.

Seasoned Issue A new equity issue of securities by a company that has previously issued securities to the public.

Security Market Line (SML) A positively sloped straight line displaying the relationship between expected return and beta.

Sensitivity Analysis Investigation of what happens to NPV when only one variable is changed.

Shortage Costs The costs associated with holding too little cash. Also, *cash shortage costs*.

Simple Interest Interest earned only on the original principal amount invested.

Sole Proprietorship A business owned by a single individual.

Spot Exchange Rate The exchange rate on a spot trade.

Spot Trade An agreement to trade currencies based on the exchange rate today for settlement within two business days.

Standard Deviation The positive square root of the variance.

Statement of Financial Position (Balance Sheet) Financial statement showing a firm's accounting value on a particular date.

Statement of Profit and Loss Financial statement summarizing a firm's performance over a period of time.

Stock Dividend A payment made by a firm to its owners in the form of equity, diluting the value of each share outstanding.

Stock Split An increase in a firm's shares outstanding without any change in owners' equity.

Sunk Cost A cost that has already been incurred and cannot be removed, and which therefore should not be considered in an investment decision.

Swaps Agreements to exchange two securities or currencies.

Synergy The positive incremental net gain associated with the combination of two firms through a merger or acquisition.

Systematic Risk A risk that influences a large number of assets. Also, *market risk*.

T

Target Cash Balance A firm's desired cash level as determined by the trade-off between carrying costs and shortage costs.

Tender Offer A public offer by one firm to directly buy the shares of another firm.

U

Unbiased Forward Rates (UFR) The condition stating that the current forward rate is an unbiased predictor of the future spot exchange rate.

Uncovered Interest Parity (UIP) The condition stating that the expected percentage change in the exchange rate is equal to the difference in interest rates.

Underwriting Syndicate A group of underwriters formed to share the risk and to help sell an issue.

Unique Risk A risk that affects at most a small number of assets. Also, *diversifiable* or *unsystematic risk*.

Unsystematic Risk A risk that affects at most a small number of assets. Also, *unique* or *asset-specific risk*.

V

Variable Costs Costs that change when the quantity of output changes.

Variance The average squared difference between the actual return and the average return.

W

Weighted Average Cost of Capital (WACC) The weighted average of the cost of equity and the after-tax cost of debt.

Y

Yield to Maturity (YTM) The rate required in the market on a bond.

Index

A

B

C

D

E

F

G

H

I

J

K

L

M

N

P

Q

R

S

W